THE HINDU WORLD

THE HINDU WORLD

AN ENCYCLOPEDIC SURVEY OF HINDUISM

by

BENJAMIN WALKER

VOLUME II M–Z

FREDERICK A. PRAEGER, *Publishers*

New York · Washington

BOOKS THAT MATTER

Published in the United States of America in 1968
by Frederick A. Praeger, Inc., Publishers
111 Fourth Avenue, New York, N.Y. 10003

Library of Congress Catalog Card Number: 68–26182

Printed in Great Britain

CONTENTS

VOLUME II M–Z

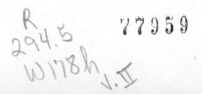

VOLUME II

MADHVA (1197–1280), philosopher-founder of dualism, also called Ānanda-tīrtha, was a Kanarese brāhmin born in a village near Uḍipi, about sixty miles north of Mangalore. A prodigy of learning he was said to have mastered the Vedas and Vedāṅgas before the age of five. While still a boy he once disappeared from home and was eventually found after four days in the temple teaching both gods and men how to worship Vishṇu. As he grew up he became convinced of the error of Vedāntic monism and resolved to show up its folly and falsity. He took leave of his parents, much to their disappointment as he was their only child, and became a wandering preacher.

Touring South India Madhva visited Trivandrum, and the stronghold of Vedānta, Śriṅgeri, where Śaṅkara had established a *maṭh* or monastery four centuries earlier. At Rāmeśvaram he had a series of discourses with the Vedāntists and wrote his well-known commentary on the *Bhagavad-gītā* and the *Vedānta-sūtra*. Proceeding to the north he visited Banāras and on the way performed many miracles, such as multiplying loaves to meet the needs of his followers, walking on water, and stilling the angry waves of the stormy sea. He spoke of giving out the 'good news', and 'fishing for men'.

Always a great controversialist, he studied Persian in order to make his arguments against the Muslims more effective, and ably defended his theses against the mullas. He finally settled down at Uḍipi his birthplace where he founded the Mādhva sect. Although he wrote in Sanskrit he inspired many Kanarese religious works. Members of the sect still exist in large numbers in the Kanarese districts of Bombay, in Mysore and the west coast of India.

Madhva was a strenuous opponent of Śaṅkara's advaita, non-dualistic philosophy. In his system, referred to as *dvaita,* or dualism, Brahma or God is supreme, and the cause of the world, yet is essentially different from the *jīva,* or the human soul. Both have a real and eternally distinct essence. This distinction between Brahma and jīva is fundamental, and it is a fallacy to think that they are different in the world of *saṁsāra* (birth-and-death) but identical when the jīva is freed. Though absolutely dependent on Brahma, the jīva is an active and responsible agent, albeit imperfect.

The Mādhvas worship Vishṇu though some do not exclude Śiva. Vāyu the son of Vishṇu helps mankind to gain the saving knowledge and obtain release. By his followers Madhva is regarded as a reincarnation of Vāyu, born for the purpose of destroying the pernicious doctrines of advaita. Like

Rāmānuja, Madhva adopted the practice of branding the shoulder with a hot metal bearing the arms of Vishṇu. He prohibited bloody sacrifices. In the temples of the sect figures of dough are offered instead of sheep, and the employment of temple prostitutes is not permitted. In most respects however the sect has relapsed into the usual forms of Hindu worship.

Madhva is one of the few important Hindu thinkers who believed in eternal damnation. According to him those in hell, like those eternally liberated, are not subject to birth and rebirth. Ordinary men, however, continue the cycle of birth and rebirth. The doctrines of the exclusive mediatorship of Vāyu, son of Vishṇu, the miracles associated with Madhva's name, and the missionary zeal of the Mādhvas strongly suggest Christian influence.

Books

I. Aiyar, C. N. K. *Sri Madhwa and Madhwaism*, Madras, 1936.
II. Bhandarkar, R. G. *Vaisnavism, Saivism & Minor Religious Systems*, Strassburg, 1913.
III. Padmanabhacharya, S. *Life & Teachings of Sri Madhva*, Madras, 1913.
IV. Singh, Pritam. *Saints & Sages of India*, New Delhi, 1948.

MADRA (or Madraka), an ancient Śaka tribe, not mentioned in the early Vedic records, but known to have occupied the north-western regions of India, from Kashmīr eastwards towards the Chenāb, from about the fifth century BC. Modern Siālkoṭ derives its name from their ancient capital, Śākala or 'Śaka Town'. Founded probably as a result of a Scythian incursion before the time of Alexander, it was described as a city of great beauty and considerable size in the time of Menander the Bactrian Greek king, who made it his capital.

In the Purāṇas the Madras are classed with the Gandhārans, Yavanas and other barbarian, outcaste tribes. They earned notoriety as an outlandish people with wicked customs. The *Mahābhārata* refers to them as 'befouled and untutored' people, who drink heavily, eat cow's flesh, sing unrhymed rubbish, make water standing like camels and cattle, dance unclothed and follow their lusts openly with whoever is at hand.

On the other hand the Brāhmaṇas state that learned members of the Madra tribe were exponents of Vedic lore and that the sages of northern India repaired to the Madra country to study the Vedas. Owing to the beauty of their women many Indian princes of Kāśī, Kaliṅga, Vaṅga and other principalities sought brides from among the Madras. Sāvitrī* was a Madra princess, and so was Mādrī*, second wife of Pāṇḍu. Mādrī's brother Śalya, first a friend of the Pāṇḍavas, went over to the Kaurava side during the Mahābhārata war, and acted as the charioteer of Karṇa in the great battle of Kurukshetra, and on Karṇa's death succeeded him as commander-in-chief of the army on the last day of the battle. He was slain by Yudhishṭhira, the eldest Pāṇḍava prince.

Like their neighbours the Kāmbojas, the Madra people migrated through the Gangetic plain towards Bengal, and we find them in the ninth century as allies of the Pāla* kings of Bengal (I, p. 59).

Books

I. Law, B. C. *Tribes in Ancient India*, Poona, 1943.
II. Raychaudhuri, H. *Political History of Ancient India*, Calcutta, 6th Ed., 1953.
III. Tarn, W. W. *The Greeks in Bactria and India*, London, 1938.

MAGA, the name of an ancient sun-worshipping people associated with Śakadvīpa of Vedic legend, who were ruled by a class of hierophants. Many theories have been advanced to account for their origin and their association with India. It appears that they were an integral part of the indigenous population of Elam. The Elamites belong to that category of unidentifiable peoples that includes the Mycenaeans, Pelasgians, Phrygians, Etruscans and others, although these were not necessarily related stocks. Authorities claim variously that the Maga were of Akkadian, Mongolian or even Negro origin. Elam, of which Susa was the capital, already had an advanced culture in 4500 BC, cultivated grains, domesticated animals, had a hieroglyphic writing, and used the *chakra* symbol.

Their religious leaders were the sorcerer-priests known as the magi, from which the word *magic* is derived. They were near enough to Babylon for the great Nebuchadnezzar to consult their 'magicians' to interpret his mysterious dreams. Sometimes identified with the Chaldeans they were perhaps related to the Sumerian people upon the ruins of whose kingdom the First Babylonian Empire was reared. Aristotle's statement that the magi were even more ancient than the Egyptians would not appear to be quite devoid of plausibility.

The Maga religion was associated with the raising of megalithic monuments, the practice of sorcery, the reading and interpretation of celestial signs, the adoration of the serpent and the sun, the worship of fire, and devotion to the Mother Goddess. Orgiastic rites and sexual mutilation were linked with this religion and it may have influenced both the libidinous cults and the ascetic systems of the Ancient Middle East and Indus Valley India.

The magi possessed a deep knowledge of the black arts combined with a natural predilection for witchcraft and sorcery, which helped them to secure high priestly offices not only under the Babylonians and Assyrians, but under the Medes and Persians, the kings of ancient India, and later still under the Parthian and Scythian rulers.

The first Aryan migration to the south Iranian plateau dislodged some of the magian tribes who moved eastwards along the coast through Gedrosia into India. Their appearance on the Indian scene preceded the Aryan invasion, so they must have witnessed the Indus Valley civilization at its zenith. Here also their superior knowledge of architecture, astrology, medicine and the black arts, enabled them to secure positions of influence, and, known as the maya or maga they formed the new priestly aristocracy of the various Indian tribes against whom the Aryans had to contend when they entered the Indian plains. According to Professor Ghose there is a close connection between the magi and the pre-Vedic Indian priestly hierarchy. Scholars have also found some resemblance between the Indus Valley and Elamite scripts, and Professor J. N. Banerjea declares, 'The Magas of India are the same as the Magi, the priestly class of ancient Iran' (VII, p. 72).

References to the Magas occur in the *Rāmāyaṇa*, the *Mahābhārata* and the Purāṇas. Those passages in the *Mahābhārata* that attribute the erection, by magic power, of mighty buildings of stone and great moated palaces with arches and roofs supported by a thousand columns to the giants Dānava Maya and Asura Maya, are believed by Spooner to refer to the magi. In several Sanskrit texts Maya is the name of an *asura*, a skilled artificer, magician and teacher of astronomy. The *Rāmāyaṇa* speaks of the architect named Maya who built Laṅkā (in Ceylon), the greatest metropolis of the epic period. This Maya also built ingenious mechanical devices for the defence of the island which were a source of profound astonishment to the invaders pursuing Rāvaṇa. These references, says Raghavan, 'gain some significance when we bear in mind the relation of Maya with the Asuras, and of the Asuras with Iran and the Near West, and the continuous contact which ancient India had with these neighbouring and cognate civilizations in the West' (VIII, p. 5).

So abundant are the allusions to the magi in Indian tradition that Max Müller believed that they were originally from India. He said, 'It can be proved, even by geographical evidence, that Zoroastrians had settled in India before they immigrated to Persia' (IV, p. 2). We are not aware of these proofs, but the testimony of magian presence must have been strong to have influenced the opinion of so eminent an authority. Clearchus of Soli, Aristotle's pupil, considered the Indian gymnosophists (yogis) to be the descendants of the magi. There is an ancient account which relates how Śāmba, a son of Kṛishṇa, constructed a temple to Sūrya the sun god on the banks of the Chenāb, and how he brought over to India certain Maga priests from Śakadvīpa in Persia. These Magas were the descendants of Jarasasta (Zarathustra, or Zoroaster) son of the sun god, who united with the daughter of a priest of the sun and became the progenitor of all the Magas.

The route of the magian migration into India has been only tentatively traced. They presumably came by way of the Indus valley for here they left some evidence of their culture, if their affinity with the Vrātyas* be accepted. Bhandarkar says, 'It seems that the Vrātya cult, which afterwards developed into Śaivism originally came to the Indus valley with the migration of the Magadhas from outside India' (I, p. 48). The designation Magadha is of some significance, for it would suggest that the Magas settled down in southern Bihar in the region known after them as Magadha, which also became the chief focus of Vrātya culture. The same line of migration from the north-west through the Gangetic plain to Bengal was followed by several other tribes such as the Kāmboja, Madra, and Ambashṭha peoples.

The earliest known cultural centres of ancient India were located in the Indus Valley and the lower Gangetic plain, and in both places the religious and cultural evolution seems to have run along similar lines. Their art was strikingly similar. Modern archaeologists who have studied the Indus Valley toys find them 'exactly similar to those still made in Bengal today', and Coomaraswamy believed that 'the folk arts that survive in Bengal are directly descended from the Indus Valley' (VI, p. 10).

The Magas brought with them to Magadha strange customs and new religious and social practices that stamped them as a class apart. In Bengal they became adepts in astrology, in Bihār in medicine, both sciences closely associated with them. Oldenberg held that Magadha was the abode of the first Aryan immigrants, i.e. pioneers in advance of the general body of Aryans, and as such looked down upon by their later brethren. Powerful hierophants, they were subsequently classed as Maga-Brāhmins and accepted as a sect of the twice-born who had been rendered outcaste by default, through neglect of the Vedic religious ceremonial and observance of unorthodox rites.

Adoration of the sun in its form of fire was the chief feature of magi worship. But besides the sun, other heavenly bodies also received their homage, notably Saturn, and the earliest fire-temples built by the magians in India were dedicated to this planet or to the sun. The tradition of magians building temples dedicated to the sun and heavenly bodies survived in India till comparatively recent times, and frequently some evidence is still found to be preserved of these ancient associations. The walls of the eleventh century sun-temple of Modera have representations of the sun god with Central Asian boots and a belt. An inscription dated the twelfth century AD found near Gaya mentions magian or Persian priests who constructed sun temples in India. It is indeed of some interest to remark how many sacred cities of the Hindus are Zoroastrian or Maga foundations, among them Mathurā, Dvārakā, Gaya and Konārak (*see* towns). The possible influence of Zoroastrianism* on Buddha's life and teachings has been pointed out by scholars, and although the evidence does not warrant any specific conclusions along this line, it still seems to merit further enquiry.

Against the background of such information as has been gleaned through the study of comparative cultures the Magas loom as a shadowy but distinct entity. Who they were, and the precise nature of their contribution to Indian civilization is still unknown. Little can be said about them and that too with considerable caution.

Books

I. Bhandarkar, D. R. *Some Aspects of Ancient Indian Culture*, Madras, 1940.
II. Durant, W. *The Story of Civilization*, New York, 1935.
III. Ghose, N. *The Aryan Trail in Iran and India*, Calcutta, 1937.
IV. Hodivala, S. K. *Parsis of Ancient India*, Bombay, 1920.
V. Mansouri, S. M. *Art-Culture of India & Egypt*, Calcutta, 1959.
VI. Mookerjee, A. *Folk Art of Bengal*, Calcutta, 1946.
VII. Morgan, K. W. (Ed.) *The Religion of the Hindus*, New York, 1953.
VIII. Raghavan, V. *Yantras, of Mechanical Contrivances in Ancient India*, Bangalore, 1952.
IX. Samaddar, J. N. *The Glories of Magadha*, Patna, 1925.
X. Vidyarthi, L. P. *The Sacred Complex in Hindu Gaya*, Bombay, 1961.

MAGADHA, one of the earliest historical kingdoms of northern India whose story can be dated with some degree of certainty. The name Magadha is believed to be connected with the Maga* people, and the inhabitants are sometimes associated with the Vrātyas, and also frequently identified with the non-Aryan Kīkata of the *Ṛig-veda*. Magadha was known for the grace and beauty of its women, and for the sweetness of its singers. At the same time it was a region execrated for its racial impurity, and was always regarded as beyond the pale of Aryan civilization. References to the inhabitants in the

Āraṇyakas and Upanishads are invariably derogatory. Only degraded brāhmins lived there, and immigration to that area was forbidden on pain of penance, a prohibition which was observed by certain brāhmins till quite recently.

By the sixth century BC Magadha ranked with the leading *mahājanapadas** or early autonomous states mentioned in the Buddhist and Jain chronicles. Its first capital, Rājagṛiha (or Girivraja), between Paṭṇa and Gaya became in epic times the capital of Jarāsandha, later the scene of the first great Buddhist Council in 483 BC. Girdled by seven hills, this fortified town had immensely strong walls of cyclopean proportions constructed with undressed stone blocks between three and four feet in length.

Much uncertainty surrounds the dynasties ruling Magadha at the beginning of the historical period, since the genealogies given in the Buddhist *Mahāvaṁsa*, the Purāṇas, the Jain records and Aśvaghosha and other authorities vary considerably both in chronological dating and dynastic succession.

The earliest dynasty seems to have been the **BĀRHADRATHA,** of which virtually nothing is known except that the last king of the line, **Ripuñjaya,** was killed by his minister who established the **HARYAṄKA** dynasty of the Great Nāgas, which rose to prominence under **Bimbisāra** (*c.* ?554 BC), founder of Magadha's greatness. Bimbisāra had five hundred wives, and furthered his territorial ambitions by his matrimonial alliances. According to Buddhist tradition Bimbisāra was slowly starved to death or poisoned by **Ajātaśatru** (*c.* 485 BC) his son by a Lichchhavi princess, at the instigation of Devadatta, Buddha's wicked cousin. Having accomplished this act of parricide Ajātaśatru ascended the throne, but unable to find peace he later confessed his crime to Buddha. In an ensuing conflict he worsted Prasenajit of Kosala, Bimbisāra's brother-in-law, and annexed some of his territory. He also founded the fortress of Pāṭaliputra*, which his son and successor **Udāyi** (*c.* 450 BC) made the capital of Magadha.

The next dynasty, that of the **ŚAIŚUNĀGA** (*c.* 430–364 BC) or Lesser Nāgas, a subsidiary branch of the Great Nāgas, was founded by **Śiśunāga** or Susunāga (*c.* 430 BC) son of a Lichchhavi prince and a courtesan. Śiśunāga's son **Kākavarṇa** (*c.* 390 BC) 'black-skinned', also called Kālāśoka, succeeded him, and is described as 'good to his subjects, a hater of brāhmins, and a great non-believer', though a staunch Buddhist. The second Buddhist Council of Vaiśālī (*c.* 390 BC) was held during his reign, if not directly under his auspices.

Jain and Buddhist records relate that the queen of the last Śaiśunāga monarch became enamoured of a śūdra barber named Mahāpadma Nanda who was able with her collusion to kill the king, and establish the **NANDA*** dynasty (364–322 BC) whose kings were on the throne of Magadha when Alexander invaded India.

The last member of the unpopular Nanda line died in 322 BC at the hands of Chandragupta Maurya, founder of the **MAURYA*** dynasty (322–183 BC), whose most famous member was Aśoka*. A brāhminical reaction set in as soon as the strong paternal hand of Aśoka was removed on his death in 232 BC, and by the middle of the second century BC the kingdom bordered on chaos. In 183 BC the downfall of the last of the Mauryas, the Buddhist Bṛihadratha was engineered by the brāhmin coterie who found an instrument for their designs in the commander-in-chief Pushyamitra; he slew the king and ascended the throne as the first of the Hindu **ŚUṄGA*** dynasty (*c.* 183–72 BC) of Magadha. There followed ten Śuṅga kings, the last of whom was so dissolute a character that he aroused universal hostility and the brāhmins conspired to murder him.

Vasudeva, the minister of the last Śuṅga, who successfully led the conspiracy, was crowned king of the new **KĀṆVA** line (72–28 BC). The Kāṇvas, established by treachery and violence, lasted for less than half a century, and like the Śuṅgas failed to fulfil the aspirations of their indefatigable brāhmin sponsors. The fourth and last Kāṇva was slain by the Āndhra ruler of the Sātavāhana dynasty in an attack on Pāṭaliputra in 28 BC.

Magadha, however, continued to exercise great intellectual influence because it remained the heart of Buddhist cultural activity. The Hindu princes of northern India had to wait for more than three centuries before they could make their next effective bid for supremacy, for by this time the Dravidians ruled the south, and the Greek, Mongolian and Persian kings dominated the north and north-west of India.

At the beginning of the fourth century Magadha once more rose to political importance under the Imperial Guptas, after whom it passed to Harsha when his power overshadowed the remnants of the declining Gupta empire. After Harsha's death its destiny was linked with the dynasties of Kanauj and Bengal until it fell to the Muslims.

Books

I. Samaddar, J. N. *The Glories of Magadha*, Patna, 1925.
II. Sinha, B. P. *The Decline of the Kingdom of Magadha*, Patna, 1954. (*See also* under History.)

MĀGHA (AD ?700–900?) Sanskrit poet, the grandson of a minister to a king of northern India. In the twenty cantos of his masterpiece, the *mahākāvya*, *Śiśupālavadha*, he relates with extraordinary metrical invention and wonderful command of the 'ornaments of style', the episode from the *Mahābhārata* of the slaying (vadha) of Śiśupāla king of Chedi by Kṛishṇa because he had so reviled the god.

Like other writers of great *kāvyas*, Māgha introduces with supreme dexterity all manner of verbal tricks into his writing. A canto read backwards is identical with the preceding canto read in the ordinary way; some lines have two meanings, according to the way in which the compound words are divided; there are stanzas which look like geometrical figures, or a lotus vase, or a crescent moon; lines in which only two or three consonants are used.

Māgha was another of the host of Sanskrit bards of the technique of love, who fulsomely described the female form and the delights of sex. Like Kālidāsa, Māgha is also a poet's poet, and many Sanskrit writers were nurtured on the study of 'Māgha and Megha', the latter referring to Kālidāsa's *Meghadūta*.

One legend although anachronistic is worth recounting. As the great rival of Kālidāsa, Māgha was once invited to Ujjain by King Vikramāditya, to compete for the laureate with Kālidāsa. The latter, aware of Māgha's reputation went to the frontiers of the kingdom to meet him and begged him to display his art for the benefit of the villagers gathered to receive him. Māgha courteously complied, giving a wonderful display of his graceful and sophisticated art, but was met with silence by the unappreciative yokels. Kālidāsa then recited a simple piece and met with resounding applause. The bewildered Māgha concluded that the court of Vikramāditya must consist of persons of low critical faculties, and when he appeared before the scintillating court a week later, he recited only simple unadorned poetry, while Kālidāsa now employed all the resources of his genius and so won the prize. Kālidāsa then came forward with his prize and presented it to his rival, confessing that he had won it by a ruse, and that Māgha's mastery in the domain of poetry was unsurpassed. But Māgha graciously returned the prize saying it was indeed Kālidāsa's since he knew his audience and had aptly recited pieces suited to their understanding, whereas he himself had utterly misjudged his hearers on both occasions and had therefore been a blunderer, lacking in true poetic perception.

Books

I. Kak, R., and H. Sastri (Ed.). *Magha's Sisupalabadha*, Srinagar, 1935. (*See also under* Sanskrit.)

MAHĀBHĀRATA, one of the two great epic poems of the Hindus, the other being the *Rāmāyaṇa*. Probably the longest of all the world's epics, the *Mahābhārata* is a vast anthological miscellany of pre-Aryan and Aryan material. It is believed to have started as a short ballad in prose and verse first composed in Prākṛit, with some early additional material also in Prākṛit. The language in which it is now preserved is something between Vedic and Classical Sanskrit. The Mahābhārata tells the story of the descendants of Bharata, the eponymous founder of the great Indian families of yore, reaching its climax in the war of succession between the Kauravas and Pāṇḍavas. The chief protagonists, long deemed to be of 'pure Aryan descent', are now believed to have been 'mixed Aryans', if not entirely non-Aryan.

The original Prākṛit ballad was at some later date elaborated into a larger work in Sanskrit consisting of 8,000 ślokas, which is taken by some scholars to be the original length of the Sanskrit epic. According to legend its author was the sage Vyāsa, who composed it in 24,000 verses, although another tradition has it that Vyāsa only arranged the material, which was considerably more voluminous. He was assisted in his task by the sage Paila, who had previously helped him in compiling the Vedas. Vyāsa dictated the poem to Gaṇeśa the elephant god, and then taught it to one of his pupils. This pupil, Vaiśampāyana, himself the guru of Yājñavalkya and teacher of the Black *Yajur-veda*, recited the epic for the first time during the intervals of the great ceremonial sacrifice of Janamejaya, grandson of Abhimanyu*. In the present text Vaiśampāyana is the speaker. In another legend a *sauti* or bardic sage (*sūta*=bard) named Ugraśravas, son of Lomaharshaṇa, first recited the epic before an assembly of sages at the twelve-year sacrifice of

Śaunaka son of Gṛitsamada* in the forest of Nimisha (or Naimisha) near the Gūmtī river.

At present the *Mahābhārata* consists of 110,000 couplets, or 220,000 lines, in 18 *parvans* or sections, plus a nineteenth parvan, the *Harivaṁśa* supplement, which makes this megatome the largest such compendium in the world. This means that the work has expanded to many times its original size, much of it being the result of brāhminical accretions.

The doctrines and beliefs as revealed in the *Mahābhārata* are not coherent, and in fact are often flagrantly contradictory, and an examination of the metre, style and structure, shows that it is not an integrated whole, but has been subjected to extensive revision and modification and has received considerable increment from diverse sources. A host of poets and editors, partisans of different sects and propagators of new doctrines have through the ages added to the material, and tampered with the fabric of the story. There is a theory that at some stage in its development the epic may have been re-written by a Pāṇḍava partisan, making the Kauravas, who were the original heroes, into the villains. Some time between 200 BC and AD 200, Kṛishṇa was made the chief deity of the epic.

The 'story' itself occupies only about one fourth of the poem. The rest is episodical, comprising cosmology, theogony, statecraft, the science of war, ethics, legendary history, mythology, fairy tales, and several digressions and philosophical interludes, of which the best known is the *Bhagavadgītā*. The most notable divagations are the result of brāhminical redactions of the text, where the religious and priestly interest is made to overshadow the heroic, and the legends narrated are distorted to suit brāhminical bias in support of brāhmin supremacy.

The date of the great battle of Kurukshetra*, around which the whole epic is woven, has been tentatively fixed between 850 BC and 650 BC. This episode follows the events of the Rāmāyaṇa by about two centuries. Both the Vedas and the Buddhist *Tripiṭakas* are silent about the battle; it is not mentioned in any Sanskrit work till the end of the Brāhmaṇa period, and then only in the later sūtras. Of the epic itself there is no evidence before about 200 BC, and it appears that neither Patañjali nor Pāṇini knew of it in its developed form.

Although many of the stories and legends relate to an extremely early period and reflect conditions and beliefs of pre-Vedic, aboriginal India, many others are comparatively modern. Scholars have traced several chronological layers in the work. From the use of Greek words it is clear that certain portions were written after the Greek invasion. Again, since the Roman denarius is mentioned in the first and last books, these must have come after the importation of Roman coins. Sidhanta says, 'The last book, the introduction to the first book, and the thirteenth book in its present form, must have been added about AD 200–400'. Parts certainly date even as late as AD 500, when the epic was still growing with additions of Purāṇic material.

There is no universally recognized standard text of the *Mahābhārata*. The recensions as they exist today vary not only in their North and South Indian versions, but in many differing and contrary renderings of identical incidents. The manuscripts of each recension themselves vary considerably. Apart from certain important outside editions like the Nepalese, there are about one thousand three hundred manuscripts of the *Mahābhārata* and the *Harivaṁśa* preserved in the Devanāgarī and other Indian scripts. The earliest extant manuscript belongs to the fifteen century AD.

The eighteen books of the *Mahābhārata* are:

1. *Ādi-parva*, 'first section', tells of the birth of the two sons of Vichitravīrya: Dhṛitarāshṭra and Pāṇḍu, and their upbringing by Bhīshma*; their marriage and the birth of their children, the Kaurava* and Pāṇḍava* princes; the training of the princes at Hastināpura by Droṇa*; the growing enmity of the Pāṇḍavas and Kauravas; the great tournament and the quarrel between Arjuna and Karṇa*; the first exile of the Pāṇḍavas and the attempt to kill them through the agent Purochana*; the slaying of Hiḍimba, Vaka and other *rākshasas* by Bhīma*; the sojourn in Drupada's* capital, and the winning of Draupadi*; the return of the Pāṇḍavas from exile; the division of the kingdom, with Indraprastha going to the Pāṇḍavas; the exile and return of Arjuna*; Yudhishṭhira's* *rājasūya* sacrifice; the killing of Jarāsandha* by Bhīma; the slaying of Śiśupāla* by Kṛishṇa.

2. *Sabhā-parva*, 'assembly section'; the assembly of the princes at Hastin-āpura; Yudhishṭhira's game of dice with Śakuni*, and the loss of the kingdom; the second exile of the Pāṇḍavas.

3. *Vana-parva*, 'forest section'; the Pāṇḍavas in Kāmyaka forest; the adventures of Arjuna; the capture of Duryodhana* by the *gandharvas* and his rescue by the Pāṇḍavas; the abduction of Draupadī by Jayadratha* and the latter's defeat. This section of the epic contains extraneous episodes which are variously introduced. Thus while Yudhishṭhira broods over his sufferings the sage Bṛihadaśva consoles him by narrating the story of Nala* and Damayantī; similarly, the sage Mārkaṇḍeya tells him the story of Rāma (this outline of the *Rāmāyana* is called the *Rāmopākhyāna*), and the tale of Sāvitrī* and Satyavān; and of Pramadvara and Ruru (although the latter episode is sometimes found in the Ādi-parva, or first section of the epic). Also related in this book is the story of Śivi (*see* Uśīnara), and the episode of the *Kirāt-ārjunīya*.

4. *Virāṭa-parva*, 'Virāṭa section'; the thirteenth year of the Pāṇḍava exile, while they serve king Virāṭa* in disguise.

5. *Udyoga-parva*, 'effort section'; the preparations of the Pāṇḍavas and Kauravas for war. Kṛishṇa and Balarāma* decide not to fight; the mustering of the armies at Kurukshetra*.

6. *Bhīshma-parva*, 'Bhīshma book'; a description of the battlefield of Kurukshetra; the doubts of Arjuna; the teaching of the *Bhagavadgītā*'*; the battles fought with Bhīshma in command of the Kaurava army, until he falls under Arjuna's arrows.

7. *Droṇa-parva*, 'Droṇa section'; the war during Droṇa's command of the Kaurava forces until his death at the hands of Dhṛishṭadyumna, son of Drupada.

8. *Karṇa-parva*, 'Karṇa-section'; Karṇa's command of the Kauravas, till his death at the hands of Arjuna.

9. *Śalya-parva*, 'Śalya section'; Śalya's command; Duryodhana's mortal wound; only three Kauravas left alive.

10. *Sauptika-parva*, 'nocturnal book'; the night attack by the three surviving Kauravas on the Pāṇḍava camp. The death of Duryodhana.
11. *Strī-parva*, 'the section of the Women'; the lament of Queen Gāndhārī and the other women over the slain heroes.
12. *Śānti-parva*, 'peace-section'. The coronation of Yudhishṭhira at Hastinā-pura, followed by Bhīshma's long discourse on politics and kingship, delivered in order to assuage the grief of Yudhishṭhira. This parva contains a portion called the *Nārāyaṇīya* which is one of the sources of the Vaishṇava tradition.
13. *Anuśāsana-parva*, 'precept book'. Bhīshma's discourses continued on the duties of kings, liberality and fasting; at the end of his long discourse Bhīshma dies. The section is a fairly late addition.
14. *Aśvamedhika-parva*, 'aśvamedha section'; Yudhishṭhira's horse sacrifice in token of his sovereignty; the further adventures of Arjuna. Also a portion called *Anugītā*, another source of the Vaishṇava tradition.
15. *Āśrama-parva*, 'hermitage book'; the retirement of Dhṛitarāshṭra and Gāndhārī, and Kuntī, mother of the Pāṇḍavas to a hermitage in the woods; the great forest fire in which they were all burned to death.
16. *Mausala-parva*, 'club section'; the death of Kṛishṇa and Balarāma; the submersion of Dvārakā under the sea; the mutual extermination of the Yādavas in a series of fights with clubs (*musala*).
17. *Mahāprasthānika-parva*, 'great sojourn section'; Yudhishṭhira's renunciation of the throne; his departure with his brothers to the Himālayas on the way to Indra's heaven on Mount Meru.
18. *Svargārohaṇa-parva*, 'heaven-ascent book'; admission to heaven of Yudhishṭhira with his brothers and their wife Draupadī.
19. *Harivaṁśa*, a poem of 16,375 verses, which forms an appendix (*khila*) to the *Mahābhārata*, but does not strictly belong to the epic. It is of a much later date, definitely post-Christian, and bears evidence of having been written in South India. The book is a loose collection of Purāṇic tales; a jumble of texts which does not bear the mark of authorship by one person. It consists of an introduction, detailing the story of creation, the establishment of patriarchal and dynastic lines on earth, and the genealogy (*vaṁśa*) of Hari (Vishṇu), whence its name. This is followed by an account of the birth and youthful adventures of Kṛishṇa. The last part relates to the future of the world, the corruptions of the present Kali age, and the pogressive degeneration of mankind at the end of this period.

Books

I. Dutt, M. N. (Tr.) *The Mahabharata*, Calcutta, 1895–1905.
II. Dutt, R. *The Mahabharata*, London, 1929.
III. Ganguly, K. M. (Tr.) *The Mahabharata*, Calcutta, New Ed. 1926–32.
IV. Held, G. J. *The Mahabharata, An Ethnological Study*, London, 1935.
V. Hopkins, E. W. *The Great Epic of India*, 2nd Ed., New York, 1920.
VI. Krishnacharya, T. R. *et al. Mahabharata*, 6 Vols., Bombay, 1906.
VII. Roy, P. C. (Tr.) *The Mahabharata*, 11 Vols., Calcutta, 1883.
VIII. Rajagopalachari, C. *The Mahabharata*, Bombay, 1954.
IX. Sidhanta, N. K. *The Heroic Age of India*, London, 1929.

MAHĀJANAPADA, 'great community'; the large aggregates of peoples or tribes which constituted the kingdoms, principalities and republican states of ancient India. The term is specifically applied to the first historical states that emerged after the Epic period. The earliest mahājanapadas, called *Gaṇa* in the *Mahābhārata* and *Saṅgha* in Pāṇini, are those of the seventh century BC in northern India and parts of the Deccan. Buddhist records speak of sixteen mahājanapadas, but several others are mentioned in Jain accounts, in Pāṇini, Kauṭilya and Megasthenes.

Chief among the mahājanapadas were: **Aṅga,** ancient name of modern east Bihār, embracing some of the Bāleya* kingdoms; **Aśmaka** (or Assaka) on the Godāverī, with capital at Potana (Paiṭhān), though sometimes identified with a place between Śūrasena and Avanti, or on the Indus; **Avanti** in modern Mālwā, with capital at Ujjain*; in Buddha's time it was ruled by the Pradyota dynasty (*c.* 550 BC); **Chedi,** with capital at Śuktimatī, between the Jamnā and Narmadā; in epic times its kings were Uparichara and Śiśupāla; **Gandhāra***, the home of several immigrant non-Ayran and mixed tribes; its chief town of Takshaśilā (Taxila) was one of the most famous educational centres of ancient India; **Kāśī,** founded by a grandson of Purūravas; its capital Vārāṇasī, modern Banāras*, is the most sacred city of the Hindus; **Kāmboja*** in south-west Kashmīr, founded by a non-Aryan tribe of probably Perso-Mongolian stock; **Kośala** (or Kosala) in modern Oudh, with capital at Ayodhyā* ruled by the Solar kings, including Rāma; in Buddha's time it was ruled over by Prasenajit; **Kuru,** founded by one of Bharata's* descendants, covered the modern district of Thānesar, Delhi and Meerut; **Lichchhavi***, famous republican state with capital at Vaiśālī in northern Bihār; **Madra***, principality of a Śaka tribe of that name with capital at Śākala, modern Siālkoṭ; **Magadha*** in modern south Bihār; in Buddha's time it was ruled by the Haryaṅka dynasty; **Mālava,** named after a republican tribe of Scythian origin who lived between the Rāvi and the Chenāb (*see* Ujjain); **Malla,** principality of the Malla tribe, in the region of Gorakhpur in the Himālayan foothills; the Malla are supposed to be descendants of the Vrātyas*; they are sometimes identified with the Mālava; **Matsya** in the area of modern Jaipur in epic times it was ruled by Virāṭa*; **Pañchāla,** in the Panjāb, founded by one of the descendants of Purañjaya; in epic times it was ruled over by Drupada* (Northern Pañchāla) and by Droṇa (Southern Pañchāla); **Śākya***, republican state of probably Mongolian origin, with capital at Kapilavastu near the birthplace of Buddha; **Śūrasena,** of which Mathurā* was capital; it is said to derive its name from Asura-sena (Asura General) indicating its non-Aryan affinities; **Vajji** (or Vṛiji), a confederacy of republican states in north Bihār of which the Lichchhavi* was one; **Vatsa,** with capital at Kauśāmbī at the confluence of the Ganges and Jamnā, near modern Allāhābād; in Buddha's time it was ruled by Udayana (550 BC); **Videha** in modern north Bihār, with capital at Mithilā; its most famous ruler was Janaka*; **Yaudheya,** which in historical times was instrumental in ending the Kushān* power in India.

Books

See under History.

MAHĀVĪRA (?599–467? BC), title of the twenty-fourth *tīrthaṅkara** of the Jains, and the Jina of the present age. He was born Vardhamāna, the second son of a nobleman of Vaiśāli, the capital of Videha (modern Bihār). His father Siddhārtha, a prince of the Jñātṛika clan, was a follower of Pārśva, the twenty-third tīrthaṅkara. His mother Triśalā was the sister of the governor of Vaiśāli and related to the ruling Lichchhavi house of Videha. Legend relates that during her pregnancy she had dreams portending the birth of a hero. The boy Vardhamāna was therefore trained to be a warrior and in due time married Yaśodā, a lady of noble birth, by whom he had one daughter, Aṇojjā.

In his thirtieth year his parents ended their lives, according to the teaching of their sect, by voluntary starvation. His elder brother Nandivardhana succeeded to the principality, while Vardhamāna renounced the world and became an ascetic. He was borne from home in a palanquin to the shade of an aśoka tree where he divested himself of his ornaments and fine raiment, and plucked out his hair. From then on, for thirteen years, till the age of forty-three, he lived a life of extreme self-mortification. He discarded all clothing for he considered nudity essential to true asceticism and allowed vermin to infest his body since killing was contrary to the precepts of his faith.

At the end of this period while he was in the sunny field of a householder named Samaga near an old Hindu temple, under a *śāla* tree on the banks of the river Ṛijupālika, squatting in deep meditation, with heels joined, knees high, and head low between them, he achieved the state called *nirvāṇa* (cessation) or *kaivalya* (isolation). He was acclaimed as a tīrthaṅkara (ford-finder), *kaivalin* (supreme omniscient), *jina* (conqueror), and *arhat* (Blessed One), and one of the great spiritual teachers who are ordained to appear at regular intervals to enlighten mankind. He was thenceforth known as Mahāvīra, 'Great Hero'.

Early in his career, while at Nālandā, he came into contact with Gośāla, founder of the Ājīvikas*. The two ascetics lived together for six years, when, following a bitter quarrel, they separated. In a final encounter Gośāla cursed Mahāvīra, but the curse redounded upon Gośāla and he himself died. A few days later Mahāvīra was taken ill, as a consequence of the curse, but made a quick recovery, 'after eating the flesh of a cockerel killed by a cat'. Mahāvīra had eleven disciples known as *gaṇadhara*, 'multitude-grippers'.

Unlike Buddha, Mahāvīra did not preach to the masses, but his teachings gained considerable influence with kings and intellectuals, and spread mostly to the west and south of India. To the four vows of Pārśva he added a fifth, that of *aparigraha* (non-ownership) and is said to have introduced the practice of confession into Jainism. Mahāvīra founded a celibate clergy and an order of nuns. He died aged seventy-two, at Pāvapuri in the Paṭṇa district.

Books

I. Jacobi, H. 'On Mahavira and His Predecessors'. *Indian Antiquary*, Bombay, IX, 1880, 158–83.
II. Jain, S. K. *The Life of Mahavira*, 1913.
(*See also under* Tīrthaṅkara and Jain.)

MAHĀYĀNA, a divergent form of Buddhism, somewhat removed from the teachings of Gautama Buddha, which evolved from an esoteric interpretation of the fundamental Buddhist concepts. The term Mahāyāna means 'Greater Vehicle' (i.e. of Salvation), in contradistinction to Hīnayāna, the 'Lesser Vehicle' of orthodox Buddhism. Mahāyāna has its origins in the schismatics who broke from the orthodox Buddhists during the Second Buddhist Council held at Vaiśālī, formed their own great assembly (*mahāsaṅgha*), and put forth their first doctrinal shoots in the teachings of the Mahāsaṅghika sect, which received a great impetus under Kanishka's patronage (see Buddhist history).

From the beginning Mahāyāna showed abundant vitality and is believed to have borrowed in good measure from the gnostic and esoteric sects of Persia and Egypt, and rapidly moved further and further from the strict interpretation of Buddha's teachings. It made Buddha divine, surrounded him with angels and spiritual beings, and formulated an elaborate ceremonial for Buddhist worship. In the various countries of its adoption, Kashmīr, Nepāl, Tibet, China, Korea, and Japan, Java and Sumatra, it adapted itself to the religious susceptibilities of the people, and syncretized with the native faiths.

Mahāyāna Buddhists hold that the wisdom of Buddha was delivered in a two-fold way. One, designed for the uninitiated, was the Doctrine of the Eye and Ear, embodying the external forms and interpretations; the other, for the elect, was the Doctrine of the Heart, embodying the secret wisdom that is transcendent to the things of this world. A favourite story tells how Buddha once took up a handful of *siṁsapa* leaves from the forest floor and explained to his disciples that as the leaves in his hand were less than the leaves in all the forest around him, so was the proportion of truths revealed by him, to those not revealed. Mahāyāna only 'picks up a few more leaves', and enlarges on the recorded revelation of Buddha.

Mahāyāna accepted several basic tenets of Hīnayāna but added a number of its own, and there were soon points of difference between the two, which may be broadly indicated as follows: (*a*) Hīnayāna held firm to the letter of Buddha's teachings, Mahāyāna to the spirit; (*b*) Hīnayāna developed with the Saṅgha (Order, or Church) as the centre, Mahāyāna with the individual; (*c*) Hīnayāna scriptures are written mainly in Pāli and are founded on the Tripiṭaka; Mahāyāna scriptures, written in Sanskrit, are the Sūtras; (*d*) Hīnayāna believes in salvation by works, that each man must work out his own salvation; Mahāyāna in salvation by faith; (*e*) Hīnayāna developed around the acts of Buddha, Mahāyāna around the symbolism of his life and personality; (*f*) Hīnayāna stressed righteous action and the law of karma; Mahāyāna held that over and above the law of karma was the law of *karuṇā* or compassion; (*g*) the Hīnayāna ideal is the *arhat*, who strives after his own redemption; Mahāyāna upholds the ideal of the *bodhisattva* or saviour, who is concerned with the salvation of others.

But it is in the Buddha concept that the two schools differ most widely. Hīnayāna regards Buddha as a man, albeit of extraordinary intuition and profound knowledge, but nothing more than a man, and reveres but does not worship him. Mahāyāna conceives of Buddha as a transcendent Being, a form of Logos, with idealized and divine qualities such as Mahākaruṇā (great compassion) and Mahāprajñā (great wisdom), loving all, understanding all, and saving all.

Buddha was also said to have three bodies, which were aspected forms of the Enlightened One on progressively higher planes. This *trikāya* (three-bodies) doctrine arose about the third century AD, and assumed a metaphysical and cosmological significance. The three bodies were: (1) *nirmāṇa-kāya*, 'formed body', which was the ordinary human aspect of Buddha, the aspect of the man Śākyamuni as he walked the earth; (2) *saṁbhoga-kāya*, 'bliss body', the saviour ideal or bodhisattva, i.e. the highest aspect of the manifested Buddha; (3) *dharma-kāya*, 'law body', the highest unmanifest form of Buddha, the essence of wisdom and compassion; as such he is Śūnya, the Void, Reality itself, and identical with Tathatā or the Absolute.

Apart from the trikāya, or aspects of Buddha in three planes, Buddha is also manifested in a multitude of different forms, though no clear distinction exists between some of these forms, and the terms used for them are sometimes interchanged. The following are a few of the Buddha manifestations or aspects: *Ādi-Buddha*, 'First Buddha', the primordial wisdom, a Buddha conceived like the Logos of St John's gospel; he is the first cause and eternal deity. *Bodhisattva** a saviour Buddha; more commonly the term denotes a being in whom the spirit of Buddha is active, and who, having achieved salvation, returns to the world to lead others to salvation. *Tathāgata*, one who has 'thus come'; the wholly and fully enlightened Buddha, who has reached a state of absoluteness. *Dhyāni-Buddha*, 'meditation Buddha'; the primordial Ādi-Buddha who operates in the manifested world through seven (five revealed and two unrevealed) Dhyāni Buddhas. The five revealed Dhyāni Buddhas are often confused with the Bodhisattvas; *Pratyeka-Buddha*, 'individualistic Buddha'; who is somewhat below a fully-developed Buddha. The Pratyeka-Buddha is an independent or 'private' Buddha, who, having acquired enlightenment by his own efforts, takes his reward and enters into bliss. He is likened to the Hīnayāna arhat, and represents a stage below the Bodhisattva. *Buddhatā*, 'Buddhaness', the divine Buddha-fragment that resides in all human beings like a tiny seed. Man possesses Buddhatā like one who has a jewel but does not know it. Because of this divine element all men will ultimately attain enlightenment and be saved.

Several other important concepts were elaborated in the course of its evolution by Mahāyāna Buddhism. The idea of *śūnya** was one of its fundamental notions; that voidness was all, and that in its ultimate dynamic sense, the Void was the true reality. The doctrine of śūnyavāda, based on this premise was expounded by Nāgārjuna. No less important was the notion of *tathatā*, 'thusness' (also translated thatness, or suchness), which is the state of the Absolute, beyond multiplicity. A realization that śūnya (emptiness) is really tathatā (the Absolute) brings man to the supreme spiritual experience of *nirvāṇa* (*see* Trance). Another category was that of *vijñāna* or consciousness, signifying that Mind is the fundamental reality. First set forth by the philosopher Aśvaghosha*, the principles of vijñāna were further expanded in the vijñānavāda doctrine of Vasubandhu. Underlying all things is the ālaya-vijñāna, 'abiding consciousness', a permanent substratum of awareness which remains through all the changes of individual consciousness. If there were no individuals to experience consciousness, ālaya-vijñāna would still abide.

There was a strong current in Mahāyāna Buddhism towards vāmāchāra or left-hand forms, which found expression in the theories of Asaṅga* and in chīnāchāra methods, and were further elaborated in a synthesis with the sex mysticism of tantrism*, and included *vajrayāna*, *kālachakra*, and other sexualized interpretations of Buddhist categories.

Books

I. Lamotte, É. *Samdhinirmochana-Sutra*; *L'Explication des Mystères*, Paris, 1935.
II. McGovern, W. *Introduction to Mahayana Buddhism*, London, 1922.
III. Obermiller, E. *History of Buddhism*, 2 parts, Heidelberg, 1931 and 1932.
IV. Suzuki, B. L. *Mahayana Buddhism*, 1938.
V. Suzuki, D. T. *Outlines of Mahayana Buddhism*, Chicago, 1908.

MAHĪDĀSA, a *ṛishi* poet and philosopher of formidable intellect, was the son of the sage Viśāla, by one of his many wives, a śūdra slave girl named Itarā. During a family sacrifice the brāhmin father gave instruction on the ritual to the sons born of his brāhmin wives, and ignored the son born of his śūdra wife. When the child told his mother about this discrimination she replied, 'Son, we are śūdras, the children of Mahī, the Earth. We have no friends but the Earth'. She then called upon the Earth who came and took the child to the chthonian kingdom where she taught him for twelve years. His great devotion to his Earth mother earned him the epithet, 'Mahīdāsa', Slave of the Earth. The *Chhāndogya Upanishad* refers to his exceptional longevity of one hundred and sixteen years, resulting from his great spiritual powers.

After his real mother Itarā, Mahīdāsa was known as Aitareya, and as such gained immortality by composing three great works, the Brāhmāṇa, Āraṇyaka, and Upanishad, which bear this name. They are among the most ancient treatises of their kind. An interesting feature of the *Aitareya Brāhmaṇa* is that it speaks of god as the supreme artist and states that the arts of this world derive their inspiration from the art of the Divine. It lays stress on aesthetic creation and says that as a means of worship art is not inferior to sacrifice.

The *Aitareya Brāhmaṇa* relates an incident connected with another śūdra ṛishi, named *Kavasha*, who was the son of Ilūsha by a *dāsa* or slave girl. While certain brāhmins were engaged in a sacrifice on the banks of the river Sarasvatī, Kavasha tried to approach the scene but was driven off because he was the son of a slave. He thereupon retired to the wilderness and the waters of the Sarasvatī left their bed and swirled around his feet. The brāhmins seeing the miracle recognized him as specially favoured by the gods, and extolling his spiritual strength and learning paid him reverential homage. Kavasha (also known by his patronymic, Ailūsha), lived in the reign of Sudāsa, and was the author of several hymns in the tenth book of the *Ṛig-veda*. He was drowned in the Battle of the Ten Kings.

Books

See under Mythology, Upanishads, and Philosophy.

MAITRAKA (AD 450–775), a dynasty of Saurāshṭra and eastern Kāṭhiāwār founded by the Mihira, an immigrant Gujar tribe who were originally worshippers of the Persian sun-god Mithra, whence their name. The Maitrakas claimed descent from Kuśa son of Rāma, and were classed with the Solar line of Rājput kings. A divergent branch of the Mihira may have given their name to the Marāṭhas*. There were about twenty rulers in the Maitraka dynasty, a few of them Śaivites but the majority Buddhists and Jains.

The founder of the line, **Bhaṭārka** (*c.* AD 450), once a feudatory of the Guptas, fixed his capital at Valabhī, an ancient town known in Buddha's day, and in the fifth century still an important Buddhist centre, and also the site of a famous Jain council held there about AD 455. Subsequently a Buddhist monastic establishment, the Valabhī university, was founded in this city by **Duḍḍā,** grand-daughter of Bhaṭārka, and for over two hundred years remained the foremost educational* centre of western India, specializing in higher studies in logic, astronomy and law.

The early history of the Maitrakas is linked with that of the Chālukyas and with Harsha. **Dhruvabhaṭa** (*c.* 641) was once defeated by Harsha, but later married Harsha's daughter and attended the imperial court as a subordinate ally of the great emperor. Dhruvabhaṭa was the patron of the poet Bhartṛihari, and gave liberal endowments to both Jain and Buddhist foundations. When Hiuen-Tsang visited Valabhī in AD 639 the university was almost as big as Nālandā.

In 775 a Hindu merchant on promise of a rich reward advised the Arabs of Sind on the best strategic means of taking the well-fortified Valabhī. A Muslim naval expedition (Valabhī was then a port) attacked and destroyed the city, reducing it to rubble. The attackers killed the ruler and put an end to the Maitraka line. Not a single trace of the great university now exists.

Books

See under History and Education.

MALAYĀLAM, a Dravidian language related to Tamil, and greatly modified by Sanskrit, spoken by about eight million people in Kerala*, i.e. Malabār, Cochin and Travancore. Unlike the early literature of most other Indian languages, early Malayāli writing is more secular than religious. The few extant inscriptions relate to kingly activities and the early *champūs* (mixed prose and verse compositions) deal with such topics as the troubles of the householder and the lives of courtesans. The wealth of medieval ballads, folk-songs and proverbs, which are only now being collected, are full of interest, where they are not 'retouched' by modern patriotic hands.

Sanskrit influence gained ascendancy from tht fifteenth century onwards, and a spate of translations from the Epics, Purāṇas, and other classics, for long overshadowed the indigenous muse. This preoccupation with Sanskrit resulted in a form of writing called *maṇi-pravālam* (pearl-coral) i.e. Malayālam-Sanskrit, where the two languages are welded together in the same text.

Malayāli words thus employed are declined and conjugated as in Sanskrit, producing a clumsy and uncouth effect. The Sanskrit *kāvya* style became fashionable, especially the *saṁdeśa* (message-bearing) kāvya, modelled on Kālidāsa's *Meghadūta*, which gave Malayālam poets ample scope for describing their enchanting palm-dotted country. Songs and poems on the Kṛishṇa theme were also turned out in abundance, most of them appallingly deficient in poetic quality, but a few showing great skill. One such is a *gātha* (song-story) in about fifty episodes attributed to **Cherusseri** (*c.* AD 1570), although even this work, full of poetic beauty and literary charm, contains 'portions not quite fit to be read in public' (II, p. 210).

The greatest Malayāli writer was the śūdra **Elutaccan** (or Ezhuttachan) (*c.* 1650), whose *Rāmāyaṇa* earned him the title of the 'Tulsīdās of Malayālam'. He also wrote a notable version of the *Bhāgavata Purāṇa* and a shortened version of the *Mahābhārata*. He was responsible for popularizing the *kili-pāṭṭu* (parrot-song) style of writing, in which the stories are related on some pretext or other in the traditional manner by a parrot, although a swan, goose or even a bee are often used instead. Various metres are employed for the narrative verse, usually woven around Purāṇic episodes, philosophical themes and local legends.

The eighteenth century saw the development of what is known as *aṭṭha-kathā*, the literature of the kathākali* dance-drama. This ranged from verse commentaries sung or recited by a small chorus standing behind the main actors, to the full-length kathākali plays. Kathākali writing is amazingly rich and varied, and frequently of high quality, and most Malayālam writers of any distinction did not consider their work complete until they had tried their hand at this genre. Most kathākali stories are taken from the *Rāmāyaṇa*, the *Mahābhārata* (the episode of Nala and Damayantī is very popular) and the Purāṇas.

The best known Malayālam writer of the eighteenth century, **Kunchan-nambiār** (fl. 1740) created several new literary modes and brought into vogue a form of narrative poetry called *tullal*, which accompanied the dance of certain outcaste and untouchable communities. His verse is full of humour and social satire, and snipes at all classes, but is universally popular with all communities in Malabār.

Christian missionaries established themselves in Kerala during the first half of the nineteenth century, and in their wake came the printing press, along with grammars, dictionaries and textbooks, that revolutionized the country's educational system. That the keen Malayāli mind benefited from this bounty is witnessed by the fact that today, due largely to Christian incentive and enterprise, Kerala has a higher standard of education than any other state in India. At first there was a reaction against all 'native' forms among the more progressive writers, but wiser councils prevailed and poets and dramatists have turned back to their own sources for inspiration. The distaste that had been created for the 'baseness and bestiality' (I, p. 218) of Sanskrit inspiration, however, was more enduring; the Malayāli's strong critical sense rejected the erotic extravagances and artificialities provided by Sanskrit examples, and a healthy forceful approach to literature took its place. Modern writing is still formative and experimental, much of the best work being done by historians and critics, whose sober judgment and broad outlook makes the Malayāli contribution to Indian thought among the most notable in modern times.

Books

I. Gokak, V. K. *Literature in Modern Indian Languages,* New Delhi, 1957.
II. Nagendra, Dr. (Ed.) *Indian Literature,* Agra, 1959.

MAN OF THE WORLD. The term *nāyaka,* 'leader', in army* parlance a captain, is applied in Sanskrit literature to the chief male character or protagonist of a story or drama*, and suggests the 'ideal man'. This beau ideal was a character like Kṛishṇa, and even more so, Arjuna, a combination of warrior, scholar and lover.

In erotics* the term referred to the 'compleat lover', of whom the model was king Udayana*. The man generally successful with women is wealthy, young, handsome, generous, daring, luxury-loving, versed in the arts, and boasts a reputation with the fair sex.

The *kāmaśāstras* and other works on erotics divide men (and women, for which see strītantra) into three or four sexual types, namely: (1) *śaśa,* 'hare', graceful, slender, round-faced, large-eyed, with fine soft hair, small slender member, and quick in reaching sexual culmination. He is generous, God-fearing, and the best mate for a woman of the *padminī* type; (2) *mṛiga,* 'buck', tall, handsome, with a commanding personality, ready for war. He has a long neck, restless attractive eyes, medium member, and is quick in consummation; a fit mate for padminī or *chitrinī*; (3) *vṛishabha,* 'bull', tall, well-built, rough, quick-tempered, fond of eating and the pleasures of the flesh. Long slender member, very quick culmination. It is difficult to find a suitable mate for him, as he is selfish, cruel, sadistic and unfaithful. The best choice for him is the *śaṅkhinī*; (4) *aśva,* 'horse', heavily built, ugly, broad-chested, not tall; has a long, heavy member, slow culmination. Suited for chitrinī and *hastinī*. He is the only type who can give satisfaction to the śaṅkhinī, although he does not care for her.

By the fifth century AD the ideal hero had become the *nāgaraka,* a 'town' man, or man of the world, a cultured degenerate and dandy whose portrait is set forth in Vātsyāyana's work, and further embellished by other writers on erotics. He is described as handsome in appearance, with a full-lipped, fleshy, moon-shaped or egg-shaped face, arching eyebrows, large heavy-lidded eyes; of medium height, broad shouldered, long armed, 'lion waisted', with firm legs and slender liṅga, slow to arouse and quick to culminate. In love he concentrates on the preliminary love-play before the sexual act. He is rich, leisured, elegant, fond of soft couches, spiced foods, bright colours. He is supposed to be accomplished in the sixty-four auxiliary arts and skills* as an aid to the supreme art of the bedchamber.

He spends a great deal of time attending to his person, and every detail of his toilet is discussed. The regimen referred to as the *dina-kārya* (daily practice) covers the ablutionary and hygienic routines which he is obliged to perform daily, weekly or at regular intervals. He cleans his teeth with a fresh nīm stick; scrapes his tongue with a flat metal tongue-scraper. He evacuates every day; anoints his body every other day; discharges his seminal fluid at least every third day; shaves his beard every fourth day; pares his nails every fifth day; and shaves his whole body every tenth day; has an emetic every twelfth day; a laxative every thirtieth day; and venesection after every six months.

Before anointing his body he bathes in hot water into which aromatic twigs and leaves are dropped. He then applies various ointments and oils to his person, paying special attention to the soles of his feet and his genitals; he uses perfumed unguent for his chest and armpits; massages his hair with perfumed pomades of three varieties. He then applies salves and collyrium to his eyes and red paint to his lips. His dress is colourful, even gaudy, and he wears a garland of jasmine blossoms round his neck. 'Wearing garlands, ornaments and jewels, strengthens the vital power and wards off evil spirits', and the man of the world is adorned accordingly. The final touch is given by a bright red or yellow flower which he fastens to his outer garment. Thus scented, groomed and garlanded he ventures out for his social and amorous adventures.

Books

See under Kāmaśāstra.

MĀNASĀRA (AD ?500–700?) 'building summary', a treatise of unknown authorship on the subject of all types of constructions. The work, divided into seventy chapters, may be said to deal with 'architecture' in a very broad sense. It gives elaborate details on the structural and sculptural dimensions of practically every constructed thing, from the nest of a bird to the palace of a king, from the representation of an insect to the idols of gods and goddesses. It discusses the site of buildings; the method of orientation; sacrificial inauguration; plans for the layout and building of towns, villages, roads, bridges, gardens, ponds, temples, assembly halls, hospitals, cremation grounds, cemeteries. It describes the ceremonies of house-warming, and first entry; specifies the correct proportions of the liṅga or emblem of Śiva; the proportions of the image in relation to the building, of the liṅga to the size of the door; gives instructions on the chiselling of the eye of an image; the setting of precious stones in different parts of the image, and a hundred other recondite particulars on similar lines.

The *Mānasāra* first came to be known a little over a century ago, through an essay on architecture by a Madrās judge. The exact date of the work is a matter of speculation, the latest limit being fixed at about AD 700, although it may have been composed about a century or two before that date.

It was in all probability the work of a practising architect whose knowledge of the niceties of language was limited, for it is written in a style that has been branded as 'barbarous Sanskrit', full of defects in grammar, metre and rhetoric.

The *Mānasāra* mentions thirty-two preceding authorities, including Viśvakarman the divine architect, Manu and lawgiver, Tvashṭṛi the heavenly artificer, the god Indra, and also Maya, the latter probably indicative of Persian influence on the work. Roman inspiration is clearly discernible, especially that of the Roman architect and military engineer Vitruvius (15 BC). In the opinion of A. B. Keith, 'The striking similarities between the prescriptions of the *Mānasāra* and Vitruvius are unquestionably established.'

Books

I. Acharya, P. K. *Architecture of Manasara,* 1934.
II. Acharya, P. K. *Illustrations of Architectural and Sculptural Objects Described in Manasara,* 1934.
III. Acharya, P. K. *Indian Architecture According to Manasara,* Oxford, 1921.
IV. Dandekar, R. N. (Ed.) *Silver Jubilee Volume of the Bhandarkar Oriental Research Institute, 1917–1942,* Poona, 1943.
V. Keith, A. B. *A History of Sanskrit Literature,* Oxford, 1928.

MAṆḌALA, 'circle', a symbolical diagram usually bounded by a circle, within which squares, traingles, labyrinthine patterns, floral, crystalline, stellar and other designs are engraved on metal, stone, wood, bone, skin, paper or other material. Those who have the necessary powers of concentration frequently build up *maṇḍalas* mentally. There are many elaborations not only within but also around the simple maṇḍala pattern, and these have been endlessly explained by various scholars of Hindu and Buddhist philosophy, and in more recent times adopted by psychologists of the Jungian school to symbolize the structure of the deep psyche.

The maṇḍala is held to be a potent centre of psychic energy, a consecrated enclosed space separated from the profane by barricades of magical figures and by 'guardians' of the doors. The various marked spaces within the maṇḍala represent the heavenly or terrestrial abodes of deities, such as paradise, temples, palaces and altars, and contain their images or emblems. In demonology the spaces are reserved for the grim lords of the nether regions.

During the inscribing of the maṇḍala special rites are performed and *mantras* (spells) intoned. When it is completed the gods or demons are invoked by further rites and incantations and are then believed to appear and occupy the place in the diagram assigned to them.

In Tantrism the maṇḍala is often a more specialized figure referred to as a *yantra,* 'instrument' or 'engine', which is widely used in worship. Each god or goddess worshipped has a yantra of their own and the designs are full of symbolism. The triangle pointing down represents the yoni; the triangle pointing up, i.e. standing on its base, is the liṅga; two superimposed triangles, like the Seal of David, symbolize the union of yoni and liṅga. More triangles form the lotus, and so on. The central point is called the *bindu**, 'drop', and represents the focal area of psychic power. Although drawn flat a yantra represents a three dimensional figure.

The most potent of all yantras, called the *śrīyantra,* is very elaborate, with four 'directions', symbols for the male and female organs, sanctuaries for the deities and guardians of the entrances, the whole being enclosed within lotus petals framed by a wavy line called the *śiśiratā,* 'shivery'. The general concept of the śrīyantra, as in fact of all maṇḍala patterns, is believed to be basically sexual. Says Chattopadhyaya, 'A tantrika when he really confides in you, will frankly confess that these diagrams are but representations of the female organ, and competent scholars have repeatedly noted this point'. The śrīyantra, according to Bhandarkar, is a picture of the female organ drawn in the centre of a circle of nine such organs.

Maṇḍalas are often used for decorative and protective purposes, and are marked on floors as colourful raṅgoli designs during the Dīvālī festival. They are also traced in red with the juice of certain plants on the palms and feet of women.

Books

I. Bhandarkar, R. G. *Vaisnavism, Saivism and Minor Religious Systems*, Strassburg, 1913.

II. Chattopadhyaya, D. *Lokayata: A Study of Ancient Indian Materialism*, New Delhi, 1959.

III. Jung, C. G. 'On Mandala Symbolism', in *Archetypes and the Collective Unconscious*, E. T., London, 1959.

IV. Tucci, G. *The Theory and Practice of the Mandala*, London, 1961.

MĀNDHĀTṚI, author of a hymn in the *Ṛig-veda*, was the son of *Yuvanāśva*, a descendant of the Solar king Purañjaya*. The Harivaṁśa states that he was born in the natural manner from his mother Gaurī, but the Purāṇas relate otherwise. According to the Purāṇas, Yuvanāśva had no son, so the ṛishis, led by the sage Bhṛigu, instituted a rite to secure progeny for him. They placed upon the altar a vessel of water which they had magically endowed with great potency, and which they intended to give to his queen to drink. Yuvanāśva awoke at night feeling very thirsty, and inadvertently drank the water himself, and after one hundred years a child came forth from his right side. Indra gave the miraculous infant his finger to suckle, saying, *Māṁ dhātā*, (he shall suckle me), and from these words the boy's name was derived.

When Māndhātṛi grew up he married Bindumatī daughter of the Yādava king Śaśabindu of Ayodhyā, and became the father of three sons and fifty beautiful daughters. One day an old, emaciated sage named Saubhari came to Māndhātṛi and asked for one of his daughters in marriage. Unwilling to give any of his daughters to an old man and yet afraid to refuse, the father answered that the choice should be left to the girls. The sage assumed a youthful and handsome appearance and was immediately selected by them all, and in the end took them all. He had Viśvakarman the celestial architect build separate palaces for each of his fifty brides, split himself into fifty vigorous husbands, and enjoyed and satisfied them all, each believing that he was devoted to her and her alone. By his wives he had a hundred and fifty sons, but his happiness was marred by the fact that his hopes and ambitions for them kept increasing and became a source of distraction to him. He accordingly abandoned his children, retired to the forest with his fifty wives and devoted himself to penance to the end of his days.

Māndhātṛi's three elder sons were Ambarīsha (who appears in the legend of Śunaḥśephas*), Purukutsa, and Muchukunda. Purukutsa succeeded his father on the throne, and it was while he ruled that the god Vishṇu entered into his person when he wanted to destroy the sixty million Mauneya. These creatures, related to and sometimes identified with the Gandharvas were the sons of the sage Kaśyapa and dwelt beneath the earth. They had overpowered the Nāga people, seized their domains and plundered their wealth. The Nāgas fled, and the Nāga princess Narmadā appealed to Vishṇu for help. In the person of Purukutsa, Vishṇu annihilated the Mauneya. In token of their gratitude the Nāgas gave him the princess Narmadā for a wife. Purukutsa and Narmadā became the parents of Trasadasyu, author of several Vedic hymns.

Muchukunda, the third son of Māndhātṛi, rendered valuable assistance to the gods in their struggle against the demon asuras, and was in fact, the celestial general before the birth of Kārttikeya. As a reward for his services he asked for and obtained the boon of long uninterrupted sleep to enable him to rest after his exertions. It was ordained that whosoever disturbed him would be consumed by fire that would flash forth from his eyes. By a stratagem Kṛishṇa lured the formidable chieftain Kālayavana to the cave where Muchukunda slept and so brought about his death (*see* Gārgya). Muchukunda was privileged to enter the celestial regions and here he was further rewarded, but was also rebuked by Kubera for putting too much faith in priests, ritualism and sacrifice.

Books
See under Mythology.

MANGO TRICK. What is known as the mango trick consists of making a small mango tree sprout from a seed buried in the ground, and bear fruit, all within the space of about half an hour. The conjurer takes a dry mango stone, buries it in the presence of his audience in a little hole he digs in the earth. He then fills the hole with earth and covers the spot with a piece of cloth. He intones some mantras over it, and after a few minutes removes the cloth, to reveal a young shoot with two mango leaves emerging from the ground. He covers the young shoot and mutters more mantras, in this fashion repeating the process at intervals, until there is a sapling a foot or two high with a cluster of genuine fruit on it.

The mango trick has never been authentically photographed. Descriptions of it vary, and of course numerous frauds have been exposed. But there are genuine reports of its occurrence by reputable witnesses, whose only explanation, even after they have tasted the fruit of the young mango tree, is that, where it is not due to legerdemain, it is the result of mass hypnosis and delusion.

Some however prefer to attribute it to black magic and the intervention of diabolical agencies. The French traveller, Jean Baptiste Tavernier (1605–89) who was the first European to record this trick, says that the conjurer he saw placed a small block of wood on the ground which he then covered with a piece of cloth. From his point of vantage Tavernier observed the magician cutting the flesh of his arm and anointing the wooden block with his blood; by this means the tree was supposedly given power for its miraculous growth.

Such accounts of magical phenomena given by early travellers and alleged witnesses are now discounted as relics of a more credulous age. Like the rope* trick, the mango trick is hardly heard of today, and is relegated to the realm of fantasy, except among a small coterie who continue to set store by it to prove the potency of Hindu occultism*.

Books

See under Occultism.

MĀṆIKKAVĀŚAGAR (fl. A D 980) (*māṇikka-vāśagar*, 'ruby-worded') Śaiva mystic and Tamil poet, was born of brāhmin parents near Madura and rose to the position of chief minister to the king of Madura. According to legend he was sent by his sovereign to a neighbouring country to purchase horses for the royal stables. Passing through a village on his way he suddenly saw a glorious company of saints seated in reverent meditation around a personage of divine bearing and glowing countenance. He had always sought a guru, and thinking this to be a heaven-sent opportunity he immediately exchanged his state robes for the garb of an ascetic, distributed to the poor the money he had been given to buy the horses, and settled down in the circle of disciples. In a little while the illustrious personage, who was none other than Śiva himself, disappeared along with his adoring assembly, and Māṇikkavāśagar was left all alone in what was in reality a deserted place populated by jackals.

He had now to reckon with the king of Madura who had entrusted him with the duty of buying the horses. In his perplexity he prayed to Śiva to relieve him from a predicament that was actually his doing, and the deity turned the jackals into handsome steeds, which the poet then led to the delighted king. The joy of the monarch was short lived for at night the horses reverted to their jackal form. The king realized that his minister was spiritually blest, and that his interest did not lie in matters of state, and accordingly released him from his office, leaving him free to devote himself to Śiva. The poet was once asked to explain one of his hymns; in reply he pointed to an image of Śiva and then disappeared in a flash of light, never to be seen again.

Māṇikkavāśagar's most famous work is the *Tiruvāśagam*, 'Blest Utterance', which reveals his piety and poetic excellence. It has been the inspiration of all later devotional poetry in Tamil, and the book itself receives the homage of worshippers. His lyrics, which might be compared to the Psalms, are committed to memory and sung throughout the Tamil country. The Tamils say, 'He whose heart is not melted by the *Tiruvāśagam* must have a heart of stone'. The influence of the *Bhagavadgītā* is discernible in his writings, but Śiva takes the place of Kṛishṇa. Śiva the supreme deity assumed human form and dwelt among men, opening the way of salvation to all classes so that the soul of man might dwell in the presence of the everlasting and ever-present Lord.

Books

I. Pope, G. U. *The Tiruvasagam*, Oxford, 1900.
(*See also under* Śaivism, Tamil.)

MANTRA, a word of Persian origin. In Vedic literature the Mantras are those portions that consist of the metrical psalms of praise, as distinct from the liturgical prose portions of the Brāhmaṇas*. They constitute the main body of the Vedic *saṁhitā*, or collection, and are the most ancient part of the sacred writings, although some of the Mantras represent a later stage of development, and their language as a whole is not homogeneous.

In course of time the term mantra came to be applied to any sacred verse from the Scriptures, to spells, cryptic syllables, and 'words of power', based on the magical properties believed to be inherent in sound*. The mantra in this sense has been defined as a thought movement, or an articulated astral potency. The Tantriks often refer to their 'rememberable' mantras as *dhāriṇī* (or dhāraṇī), which are longer than *bīja* mantras (*see* mystic syllables).

An important branch of Hindu esoteric study is concerned with mantras, known variously as *mantra-yāna* (mantra-path), *mantra-marga* (mantra-way), *mantra-vidyā* (mantra-knowledge), *mantra-śāstra* (mantra-learning). A branch of yoga called *mantra-yoga* is exclusively devoted to this study. It consists of sixteen stages, mostly variations of yoga disciplines, with particular stress on the repetition of magical syllables.

Mantras were sometimes revealed to the *ṛishis* by direct inspiration, but many were composed by them after long meditation on the mysteries of sound, by means of which they were able to reduce voluminous doctrines to small compass. Many powerful mantras are ostensibly without meaning, and are quite beyond the comprehension of ordinary men, but in fact carry a profound and subtle significance, containing as they do the concentrated essence of much hidden wisdom (*see* secrecy). According to certain Buddhist teachings meditation on 'meaningless' mantras can lead to a realization of the meaninglessness of all manifestation, and so to a true realization of Śūnya (the Void).

Every Hindu ritual has its own prescribed formulas and words of power appropriate for the occasion, and great stress is laid on the proper recitation of mantras, for much of the efficacy of a rite depends on their correct use. A mantra incorrectly enunciated, uttered at an inappropriate time, or by the wrong person, or with misplaced intent, can it is said, have disastrous consequences. The good or evil effects of a mantra are felt either immediately or after an interval of time; the repercussions may be carried over into the next world, or even into the next incarnation.

The results produced by mantras are varied. Some bring mystic trance and some enlightenment. One class, called *kavacha*, 'armour' mantras, protect one from spiritual harm and contamination, or guard one against the weapons used by malignant powers; another class, called *astra*, 'missile' mantras, send forth psychic arrows at evil beings; another, called *vidyut*, 'lightning', flash forth and destroy. In short, there is nothing beyond the power of a mantra, and all the siddhis* 'are at the command of the yogi who can master the mantra'. Mantras are of course used for many prosaic purposes: there is one mantra which can cause a woman to go through the experience of physical union and orgasm, and Arthur Avalon (Sir John Woodroffe) refers to a yogi who lit a sacrificial fire simply by uttering a certain magical formula.

Generally, mantras are of no practical value if read from a book, but they acquire great power if they are learned through the living voice of a guru (preceptor). Initiation into the arcana of an esoteric group is often performed by the guru intoning a mantra into the ear of the *chela* (pupil). A mantra of this kind is a vibratory talisman of cultic lore and power, and it communicates in a flash all the secret wisdom of the order to the new initiate. These mantras are therefore not to be repeated aloud for it is sufficient to hear or even overhear them to acquire their benefits. There is a story told of an unlettered carpenter who while repairing a brāhmin's house overheard a mantra of initiation being repeated to a pupil, and who received full enlightenment as though he had studied the doctrine himself.

Mantras are variously and arbitrarily classified as male and female, sun and moon, sleeping and waking, and so on. But the generally accepted division is under two broad headings as follows: (1) **Kaṇṭhika,** 'throated', or mantras given expression to by the voice. These include (*a*) *vāchika*, 'spoken' or uttered aloud: sacrificial mantras, prayers and invocations to the deity fall into this category; (*b*) *bhramara*, 'humming', the method generally used for japa or repetition*; (*c*) *janāntikā* (lit. 'people nearby'), whispered or spoken in a low voice, so as not to be overheard; (*d*) *karṇika*, whispered into the 'ear'; a special class of initiatory mantra, conveyed to the pupil by this means directly.

(2) **Ajapa,** 'non-uttered', mantras which are not spoken but repeated internally. These are subdivided into: (*a*) *upāṁśu*, 'silent', i.e. mantras which may be visualized in their Sanskrit form and consciously repeated without vocalization. The silent prayer is such a mantra; (*b*) *mānasa*, 'mental' mantras, which are meditated upon. This class also includes a large number of very secret mantras devised by ṛishis for their own use, which are never transmitted to another person and thus never brought to light. They may be recovered from the *ākāśa* or ether by adepts during trance.

Besides the verses taken from the Vedas, such as the most famous of all mantras, the *Gāyatrī**, the *mahākārika* or great maxims (*see* sayings) of the Upanishads are extensively used as mantras. Also commonly used is the *mātṛikā*, 'mother', the title given to the fifty letters of the Sanskrit alphabet as the source of all wisdom. The alphabet is repeated in various ways, e.g. each part of the body is assigned to one letter, and the hand is placed there as the letter is uttered, to spread the blessings of the mantra to all parts of the body. Sometimes the alphabet is written in the form of a diagram and used as a talisman or static mantra.

Unlimited powers are said to reside in the shorter mantras, especially the mystic* syllables known as the *bījākshara* (monosyllabic) mantras, and great benefits accrue from their repetition. The true bījākshara ends in an *anusvāra* (*ṁ*), and the most powerful of all is the sound *Oṁ*. There are, however, many other classes of short mantras. Many of the exclamations and ejaculations used during the sacrificial ceremonies have passed into the mantra class, such as: *svasti*, 'fortune'; *svadhā*, 'oblation'; *svāhā*, 'offering'; *vashaṭ*, 'bravo'; *śaṁ yoḥ*, 'all hail' or 'blessings'. The mantra *phaṭ*, 'crack', is used by Buddhists as a weapon for driving off obstructing spirits, the fingers being snapped around the head the while; it forms part of the death rite and is uttered at the moment of the soul's departure from the body.

Other mantras are: *ojaḥ sahaḥ saha ojaḥ*, 'might, power, power, might'; *bhūr bhuvaḥ svaḥ*, three words which are given the title of *vyā hṛiti*, 'concealed utterance', and according to the legend they were milked from the Vedas by the god Prajāpati; they are said to represent the three worlds (heaven, atmosphere, earth), the three Vedas (*Ṛig, Yajur, Sāma*); this mantra is uttered before the *Gāyatrī* mantra. The phrase *oṁ tat sat*, 'Oṁ That Reality', found in the *Bhagavadgītā* is very commonly used as a mantra by Hindus.

The principal mantra of the Buddhists is *oṁ maṇi padme huṁ*, 'Oṁ Jewel Lotus Huṁ', and is subject to many interpretations: e.g. 'Oṁ (here one should inhale) Jewel (male) in the Lotus (Female), Huṁ (here exhale)'; or 'Oṁ, the Jewel of the Doctrine in the Lotus of the World. Amen'. Among Tantriks it is subjected to further recondite interpretations. The mantra *oṁ aḥ huṁ* is used by both Hindus and Buddhists, and is said to mean, 'Creation, Preservation, Destruction', 'Silence, Sound, Meaning', 'Male, Female, Male-Female', and so on.

Mantras are also formed from the names of deities, and are often called from the number of syllables they contain: *pañchākshara*, 'five-syllabled' e.g. *nāma śivāya* (Name of Śiva); or *shaḍakshara*, 'six-syllabled' e.g. oṁ maṇi padme huṁ, mentioned above; or *dvādaśākshara*, 'twelve-syllabled' e.g. the Vaishṇavite *oṁ namo bhagavate vāsudevāya*, 'Oṁ, Salutation to the Worshipful Lord Vishṇu'.

Calling out the name of one's deity is held to be amongst the most powerful of mantras. Divine names are often used for *japa* or repetition; thus a Śaivite will recite the 1,008 chief names of his god in the belief that such repetition will procure the god's blessings. There is a legend told about *Ajāmila*, a brāhmin of Kanauj who, deserted by his parents, married a slave girl and had children by her. This disregard of his caste might have had serious consequences in his next life, but the story goes that when he was dying he called aloud the name of his son Nārāyaṇa, whom he loved dearly. This is also the name of the god Vishṇu, and for uttering the deity's name Ajāmila's death was postponed and he was assured of salvation.

Books

I. Das, M. K. *The Mysteries of Sabda*, 1919.
II. Dhole, R. M. *Mantrik Powers*, 1907.
III. Sivananda, Swami, *Japa Yoga: A Comprehensive Treatise on Mantrasastra*, 1952.

MANU (?600 BC–AD 300?), called the Lawgiver, the supposed author of a famous code of Hindu law and jurisprudence. Nothing but the name connects him with Manu Svāyaṁbhuva* of mythology, and little is actually known about him. He probably belonged to the kshattriya or princely caste and was the compiler of legal doctrines long antecedent to him, the name Manu having been affixed to the code in order to elevate its sanctity and strengthen its authority. Some scholars hold that the Code represents a metrical version of the traditional ordinances of a class of brāhmins called Mānava, who were followers of the Black *Yajur-veda*.

The Code of Manu is known variously as the *Manu-Smṛiti*, the *Mānava-*

dharmaśāstra, or the *Manu-saṁhitā*. The remote antiquity assigned by paṇḍits to the present text is extremely doubtful; from references in the tenth chapter to the Yavanas (Greeks), Śakas (Scythians) and Pahlavas (Persians) the lower date-limit of its composition is conclusively fixed between AD 100 to 300. But according to orthodox Hindu tradition the Code dates from immemorial antiquity; it was dictated by Manu Svāyaṁbhuva to the sage Bhṛigu in 100,000 verses; this was reduced to 12,000 by the sage Nārada; to 8,000 verses by the sage Mārkaṇḍeya; and to 4,000 verses by Sumati. Today it consists of 2,685 verses, divided into twelve books.

The Code is fundamentally a handbook of Hindu jurisprudence, the first systematic treatment of Hindu Law, and the precursor of all other dharmaśāstras or brāhminical legal manuals. Brāhmins regard it as the most important work after the Vedas and Śrautasūtras. The Code lays down social, moral and ethical precepts for the guidance of the people and formulates rules for the observance of rites and ceremonies. It is held to be absolutely binding on Hindus. A famous Vedic verse declares, 'All that Manu said is medicine', a reference to the mythological Manu, although taken as applying to the Manu of the Code. In later manuals an injunction preceded by 'manur abravīt' (thus spake Manu), carried the weight of law. A smṛiti (law manual) opposed to Manu was not approved.

Book I of Manu's Code is cosmological in content and gives a semi-philosophical account of creation; Book II gives the sources of law, and describes the first of the *āśramas* (stages of life) i.e. that of a *brahmachāri* or student, and summarizes his duties; Book III describes the life of the second of the āśramas, the *gṛihastha* or householder, with reference to his marriage, daily rites, funeral offerings. Book IV treats of the various occupations and general rules of life for the householder; Book V lays down rules concerning women, and dietary obligations such as lawful and forbidden foods; Book VI gives rules about the next two stages of life, namely *vānaprastha* and *sannyāsin*; Book VII discusses the sources of law, general political maxims and the duties of kings. Among other things the Code advocates sowing dissension among enemies, fomenting intrigues in the courts of neighbouring kings and the employment of spies; Book VIII relates to civil and criminal law, procedure, evidence, debts, ownership; Book IX relates to domestic law, the rules governing women (generally to their detriment), husbands, and marriage; parents and children, inheritance, deaths, funerals; Book X is about the origin, development and rules of caste; also rules for vaiśyas, śūdras and mixed castes, and caste occupations; Book XI deals with the general laws of morality, the nature of good and evil; gifts and sacrifices; the *pātakas* or sins; penance and expiation for sins, particularly sins against caste; Book XII describes the future consequences of good and bad action, the nature of the soul, the path of liberation and the means of attaining release, the doctrine of transmigration.

The chief design of the Code seems to have been to give divine sanction to the institution of caste, to make caste supreme in India and the brāhmins supreme among the castes. Says Manu, 'When a brāhmin is born he springs to light above the world; he is the chief of all creatures, entitled by eminence of birth to the wealth of the world'.

The position assigned to brāhmins in the laws of Manu was not that which they held in early Indo-Aryan society, but what they claimed for themselves by the early centuries of the Christian era. The fixing of caste in the strait-jacket of Manu's dispensation at this particular juncture of history, when the claims of the high born and pure in blood had ceased to have any genuine validity in areas exposed to ten centuries of miscegenation* with foreign barbarians*, was a futile undertaking, since it was already too late to legislate about it. Manu's brāhmins* were a creation which emerged in opposition to the Eurasian and other hybrid peoples who had been flooding India for a thousand years. It was the wishful thought that assumed the semblance of reality through the need for self-preservation.

Although held in great reverence by brāhmins, the *Manu-smṛiti* is today execrated by the lower castes, who regard it virtually as a blueprint of brāhmin domination, a flagrant piece of brāhminical imposture, which they make a point of publicly burning at their processions.

Books

I. Aiyangar, K. V. R. *Aspects of the Social and Political System of Manusmriti*, Lucknow, 1949.
II. Bühler, G. (Ed.) *The Laws of Manu*, Oxford, 1886.
III. Burnell, A. C. *Ordinances of Manu*, London, 1884.
IV. Jha, G. (Tr. & Ed.) *Manu-smrīti*, Calcutta, 1920–26.
V. Jayaswal, K. P. *Manu & Yajnavalkya*, Calcutta, 1930.
VI. Jolly, J. E. *Manava-dharmasastra*, 1887.
VII. Jones, M. C. (Tr.) *Manusmriti*, 1908.
VIII. Hopkins, E. W. *Manu*, 1884.

MANU, from *man*, think; the title given to certain semi-divine beings who in Hindu mythology are called patriarchs, progenitors of mankind, and rulers of the earth. Each Manu holds sway over an aeon* or period of time, called a *manvantara* (Manu-antara, 'Manu-period'). The number and duration of the manvantaras are discrepantly given. It is sometimes said that each succeeding manvantara is progressively shorter than the preceding, and that each ends in a deluge. In one version each of the fourteen Manus presides over a fourteenth part of a *kalpa* (a day-and-night of Brahmā); in a second version each rules over seventy-one *yugas*; in another each rules over a *mahāyuga*, or 4,320,000 years. Still another version has it that the first Manu presided over the first yuga; the second and third ruled over the second yuga; the fourth, fifth and sixth over the third yuga; the seventh, Manu Vaivasvata, and the remaining lesser Manus preside over the last and present Kali Yuga.

The fourteen Manus generally named are: (1) Svāyaṁbhuva*, often identified with Manu* the lawgiver; (2) Svārochisha, son of Ākūti the daughter of Svāyaṁbhuva; (3) Uttama (or Auttami); (4) Tāmasa and (5) Raivata, sons of Priyavrata, who was the son of Svāyaṁbhuva; (6) Chākshusha, grandson of Dhruva*; (7) Vaivasvata*, the Hindu Noah, descendant of Chākshusha, and Manu of the present age; (8) Sāvarṇa (or Sāvarṇi), son of Vivasvat and Chhāyā.

The next six Manus all take their name from Sāvarṇa, the eighth Manu. Little is known of them except that they represent a later addition to the original list, and may have belonged to a single dynastic line of ṛishi kings. They are: (9) Daksha-sāvarṇa, a son of Daksha; (10) Brahmā-sāvarṇa, a son of Brahmā; (11) Dharma-sāvarṇa, a son of Dharma; (12) Rudra-sāvarṇa, a son of Rudra; (13) Rauchya, a son of Ruchi, and (14) Bhautya, a prince of the *bhūta* (ghosts).

Books

See under Mythology.

MARĀṬHA, a people of partly non-Aryan stock, and predominantly śūdra by caste. They are thought to be primarily derived from the *pañchama* tribe of the Mahār (not to be confused with the śūdra Mahār caste) who were among the original inhabitants of Western India, and are still regarded as authorities on village boundaries. From earliest times up to the historical period this aboriginal strain received admixtures from the Scythians and the Huns (the name Marāṭha may preserve the name of the Ephthalite Mihira tribe) who settled in their territory (*rāshṭra*) and were spoken of variously as Rāshṭrika, Mahārāshṭrika, and later as Marāṭha. Their land, Mahārāshṭra, is interpreted as either Great (Mahā) realm, or the realm of the Mahārs.

Basically the Marāṭhas were of hardy peasant stock, possessed of great piety, and produced many bhakta saints. The religious movement which sprang up with their ascendancy from the fourteenth century on was remarkable for its democracy: it numbered the lowest castes amongst its leaders, made a determined stand against the pretensions of the brāhmin priesthood, and expressed its devotion in hymns written not in Sanskrit but in the vernacular, Marāṭhi.

But in keeping with the regrettable complex that infected all those who came under the brāhminical sphere of influence, the Marāṭhas began to claim a higher caste than their origins warranted. Some scholars concede that they might have been of Rājput stock, but this opinion is disputable. The Holkar (Marāṭha chiefs of Indore) who came from the banks of the river Hol near Poona, were of the *ḍhāngar* or shepherd caste, although they claimed a higher status. The house of Sindhia of Gwālior was of low-caste origin, whose scions proved outstanding soldiers and rose in rank to become slipper-bearers of the Peshwās. Dr Ambedkar mentions a famous case that came up before the High Court of Madras in 1924 where it was 'conclusively proved' in the course of a judgment covering over two hundred pages that the Marāṭhas were not kshattriyas as they claimed to be, but śūdras.

There were indeed well-known classes of brāhmins among the Marāṭhas too, although the antecedents of these clerics leave much room for doubt as to their initial status, since they also appear to have been of non-Aryan derivation. Chief of the Mahārāshṭrian brāhmins are the Chitpāvan, distinguished for their shrewdness and intelligence, and, by Indian standards, for their fair complexion. Their patron hero is Paraśurāma*, who, according to the legend, after his contest with the kshattriyas took up his abode on the Koṅkaṇ coast. Here he had a quarrel with certain brāhmins and to spite them went to the sea-shore and finding fourteen funeral piles (*chitā*, cf. chaitya) with the remains of the bodies that had been cremated he resuscitated them, and converted them into brāhmins. This story, like the legend connected with the creation of the Rājputs, strongly suggests a late and outcaste, probably foreign, origin of the Chitpāvans. Many famous leaders of Mahārāshṭra in cultural and political life have been Chitpāvans, such as Rānaḍe, Gokhale, Tilak, Paranjpe, and Rājwāḍe.

The hardy Marāṭha mercenaries were widely employed by Muslim sultāns of the Deccan, and they grew in wealth and power in the service of these princes. The strategy of guerilla warfare in particular, they acquired from a great master of that art, Malik 'Ambar, the Abyssinian minister of the Ahmadnagar sultān. One such Marāṭha mercenary was Shāhjī, who faithfully served several Muslim princes. His son ŚIVĀJĪ* (1627–1680) rose to become the greatest of the Marāṭhas, who led the struggle against the tyranny of Aurangzeb, and laid the foundations of an independent Marāṭha empire.

On Śivājī's death a civil war broke out between his two contending sons. The victor, **Śambhūjī** (d. 1689), addicted to wine and women, proved an arrogant and cruel ruler, till a group of leading brāhmins arranged for his capture by the Moghuls. He was surprised one day by his Moghul enemies during a raid on a pleasure resort where he was engaged in a debauch. He was taken to Aurangzeb, publicly degraded, tortured and executed with barbarous cruelty. His son **Shahu,** later known as Śivājī II, received his education at the Delhi court.

Strife, discord, intrigue and treachery seemed to plague the destinies of the Marāṭhas thereafter. Their history, for all their widespread conquests, is sordid and inglorious, with hardly a bright patch in the telling. For some time a queen, **Tārābāi** (1700–1708) ruled the kingdom, and filled it with violence. **Śivāji II** (1708–1748) who had been brought up in the effeminate atmosphere of the Moghul court was unfit to rule, and the brahmin Peshwā, or Peshwār (the title is Persian) the Prime Minister took over control of state affairs. From this time on the Peshwāship became hereditary. The rulers gradually faded into the background, and became known as the Rājas of Sātārā, and the country was governed by the autocratic Peshwās.

The Marāṭha empire grew steadily as the Moghul power declined, and in 1714 only seven years after the death of Aurangzeb, the Marāṭhas made a treaty with the Emperor of Delhi by which they were recognized as 'co-partners in the revenues of the Imperial provinces'. In a short time they were in virtual control of the north-eastern territories of the Moghul Empire, besides the huge area already under their direct domination. To the Marāṭhas therefore fell the task of defending the subcontinent from its age-long enemies —invaders from the north-west.

The last of the great battles that took place in India before the Europeans arrived on the scene was the Third Battle of Pānipat, fought on January 13, 1761, between Ahmad Shāh Durrānī, an Afghan invader, and the Marāṭhas. Marāṭha success would have meant the establishment of a Hindu empire at Delhi after more than five centuries of Muslim rule. The whole of northern India seemed to be aware of the issues that hung in the balance. As the Marāṭha troops marched northwards reinforcements poured in from every side. 'The expedition', says Rawlinson, 'assumed the character of a national crusade.'

The Marāṭhas were nominally headed by the Peshwā's young son, but in fact commanded by Bhao Sāheb, the cousin of the Peshwā. The commanders and nobles went to battle in resplendent dress, accompanied by their harems and bands of musicians. When two veteran Marāṭha generals, Holkar and Sindhia, advised the Peshwā's cousin to put aside these trappings and fight in the traditional Marāṭha fashion in which they had achieved glory and renown, the haughty brāhmin dismissed them saying that he would not listen to 'the chatter of goatherds', referring to the lowly birth of Holkar.

Ranged against the Marāṭhas were the fierce mountain troopers of Afghanistan, led by a master strategist. The battle ended in tragic disaster, with a staggering number of Marāṭha casualties: 28,000 killed in battle; 50,000 slain in flight; 22,000 taken captive; 50,000 horse and 200,000 draught cattle captured. Every Marāṭha family lost one or more of its members in that catastrophic fight. And amazement was mingled with their grief at the thought that the invincible Marāṭha hosts had been so devastatingly shattered by a handful of barbarians from the outer hills. The Peshwā himself, who had lost both his son and his cousin, was given the news as he advanced to Pānipat with a relief force. Returning to his capital, the grief-stricken and humiliated Peshwā 'turned his face to the wall and died.'

That the Marāṭhas were able seemingly to recover in a comparatively short time from this shattering blow, was due less to their vitality than to the deplorable state of affairs in India at the time, for at this particular juncture there was not a single organized Hindu kingdom that could take their place. India was at this stage in sore need of efficient leadership. In fact with the Muslims at the end of their tether, the Marāṭhas were not only Hinduism's but India's last hope before the Europeans. Unfortunately, these critical days found them wanting, and the cause of their inadequacy before the challenge is to be traced once more to caste.

The family of the Peshwās who had assumed control of the Marāṭha imperial system and corrupted the straightforward nationalism of Śivājī, were of foreign stock; Persian, according to V. K. Rajwade. It was only a matter of time for the post of peshwāship assumed by them to be made hereditary. It was only a matter of a little more time for the local brāhmins to turn on the 'foreign' Peshwā brāhmins, and for all these brāhmins to start quarrelling among themselves on points of seniority, prestige and protocol. In the words of Sir Jadunath Sarkar, 'The head of the state, though a brāhmin, was despised by his other brāhmin servants, because the first Peshwā's great-grandfather's great-grandfather had once been lower in society than the Desh brāhmins' great-grandfather's great-grandfather'. Both Justice M. G. Ranade and Jadunath Sarkar, experts in the Marāṭha period, emphasized the part played by caste in the disintegration and fall of the Marāṭha empire.

Śivājī had welded the Marāṭhas into a disciplined and martial nation. With his death the main inspiration perished and the nation deteriorated rapidly. The strict discipline and code of honour and decency maintained by Śivājī disappeared with his exit. In fact except for his magnetic and magnanimous personality, and the devotional hymns of Marāṭha saints, there is hardly anything in Marāṭha history of which the nation may be proud.

Wherever the Marāṭhas now went they left a long trail of desolation. Contemporary records speak of them as slayers of children, murderers of pregnant women, robbers of the poor, abductors of chaste women, and generations after their decline their name was still being used as a bogey with which mothers hushed their children. They rode rough-shod over small, helpless communities, oppressing and ravaging vast areas. By every known device of treachery, cruelty and guile they reduced to abject docility the once powerful indigenous race of the Gonds, in the Central Provinces, numbering over three million.

From Rājputāna to Orissa, and from the Koṅkaṇ Coast to Bengal the Marāṭhas despoiled what they touched. 'Other Indian rulers', says Rawlinson, 'took a great pride in settling the country they conquered, building roads, resthouses and temples and digging wells. The Marāṭhas did nothing of the kind. Like a swarm of locusts they swept upon a district when the crops were ripe and demanded blackmail. If this were not forthcoming the village headman was tortured. If this, too, proved unsuccessful, the village was plundered and fired and the crops destroyed'. Lord Macaulay in his inimitable concrete style has summed up the effects of Marāṭha attempts at empire building, 'Wherever their kettle-drums were heard, the peasant threw his bag of rice over his shoulder, hid his small savings in his girdle, and fled with his wife and children to the mountains or the jungles to the milder neighbourhood of the hyaena and the tiger'.

As for the finer side of life, the Marāṭhas, so far as history records, were innocent of any appreciation of the gentle arts that are the concomitants of civilization. During the decline of the Moghuls they stabled their horses in the imperial palaces, broke up and carried off whatever was valuable, stripped the silver ornaments from the ceilings in the palaces of Delhi, and turned the Tāj Mahal into a dwelling place. In the words of Sir Jadunath Sarkar, 'The period of Marāṭha ascendancy has not left India richer by a single grand building, or beautiful picture, or finely written manuscript'.

Books

I. Ambedkar, B. R. *Who Were the Sudras?* Bombay, 1946.
II. Duff, J. C. G. *History of the Mahrattas*, London, 1921.
III. Rawlinson, H. G. *India, A Short Cultural History*, London, 1952.
IV. Sardesai, G. S. *New History of the Marathas*, 3 vols., Bombay, 1948.
V. Sen, S. *The Administrative System of the Marathas*, 1923.
VI. Sharma, S. R. *Maratha History Re-examined*, Bombay, 1948.
VII. Telang, K. T. *Rise of Maratha Power*, Bombay, 1961.

MARĀṬHI, a modern Indo-Aryan language spoken in Mahārāshṭra and parts of Central India, Koṅkaṇ and Kanara. It bears many traces of Austric and Pre-Dravidian borrowings, and, through the Central Asian nomads, of many Chinese words, for, says Gune, 'our contact with China is age old'. Also buried in its remote past is evidence of contact with the Jews, as a result of which several Hebrew words found their way into Marāṭhi. Dravidian and Sanskrit words were incorporated by the thousand.

Marāṭhi evolved from the medieval *apabhraṁśa* called Mahārāshṭri, some forms of which are preserved in Sanskrit plays, where they are used by women, bards and inferior characters. Hāla's* *Sattasai* is a classic of Mahārāshṭri prākṛit. Early variants of the language were also employed in a large number of Jain works, and in several important epigraphic inscriptions between the tenth and thirteen centuries.

Marāṭhi literature received the patronage of the Yādava rulers (*see* Chālukyas), but it also led to a heavy infusion of Sanskrit words and forms from which the language has never been able to recover. At the same time outside the courtly circles native Marāṭhi acquired considerable vitality from the songs of sectarian devotees. They generally used popular rhymed metres, unlike the quantitative and syllabic metres of Sanskrit. Such were the works of *Mukundrāj* (fl. A D 1190) whose patron was Jaitrapāl a petty chief of Berār and who belonged to one of the reformist cults of the day. He wrote his masterpiece, *Vivekasindhu*, at the age of sixty, with the object, he claimed, of bringing the substance of the Vedas within the reach of all.

Another fresh stream of Marāṭhi poetry is found in the works of the *Mānbhāv* (or Mahānu-bhāva) sect, founded in A D 1263, whose contribution to the development of Marāṭhi prose and verse has only recently been brought to notice, since many of their teachings were enshrined in hitherto secret texts. In a vigorous reaction against the decadence and corruption of the paṇḍits, the followers rejected the śruti and avoided the temples. They eschewed Sanskrit in favour of simple and chaste Marāṭhi to express their devotion to god, especially Kṛishṇa and Dattātreya, and their love of nature and man. The sect, which included women, broke the barriers of caste and the pretensions of orthodoxy, thus preparing the way for the great writers whose devotional songs, called *abhaṅga*, are the chief glory of Marāṭhi literature.

These writers include *Jñānadeva** (1275–1296) who reputedly taught a buffalo to recite the Vedas in order to confound the orthodox; *Nāmdev** (1270–1350) a low-caste tailor who became a saint; *Ekanātha** (fl. 1560) whose devotional verses were written to bring salvation to śūdras and outcastes; *Tukārām** (1607–1649) the son of a poor grocer, and one of the most popular poets of Mahārāshṭra; and Rāmdās, the favourite of Śivājī.

Rāmdās (1608–1681), poet and saint, was the son of a brāhmin of Nāsik. Legend relates that his conversion took place during his marriage. When the priest uttered the word '*svadhan*' (Be constant), the young man interpreted it as a divine command to serve God, and fled from the room. Leaving his parents' home he began his wanderings as a devotee of Rāma. He gathered a following, established *maṭhs* (monasteries), rebuilt dilapidated temples, and wrote several works designed to bring about a spiritual rebirth. Śivājī fell under his influence and bestowed his kingdom on the saint who returned the gift after one day. The principal work of this Vaishṇava poet is the *Dāsbodh*, dealing with religious duties. Rāmdās died at Parāli at the age of seventy-three.

The influence of Islam on the writings of these Mahārāshṭrian saints has frequently been noted. By the seventeenth century Marāṭhi was so full of Persian words that brāhmin paṇḍits induced Śivājī to sponsor the compilation of a lexicon of Sanskrit equivalents for Persian terms (II, p. 332).

Thus, with the establishment of Muslim power, and later with the advent of the Europeans, many fundamental changes were wrought in Marāṭhi literature. Three names may be mentioned as illustrative of this period and tendency. First is the English missionary, Father Thomas Stephens who came to India in 1549. He wrote a Marāṭhi and Koṅkaṇi grammar, and the Koṅkaṇi classic *Krishṭa-Purāṇa* in 1614, relating the events of the Old and New Testaments. He acquired a mastery of the language rare in foreigners because he not only learnt it, but loved it. 'Like a jewel among pebbles,' he wrote, 'like a sapphire among jewels is the excellence of the Marāṭhi tongue.' The second name is that of *Mukteśvar* (fl. 1580), grandson of Ekanātha, who retold the two great epics in a contemporary setting, adapting the exploits of the Pāṇḍavas to include the heroic Marāṭha battles against the Muslims and the English. Only five *parvas* of his *Mahābhārata* are now extant; the others were destroyed since it was feared that the excellent Marāṭhi version might eclipse the Sanskrit original of Vyāsa himself. The third name is that of *Shaikh Muhammad* (fl. 1590), who is placed among the Marāṭhi saints and regarded as an incarnation of Kabīr. He wrote on Hindu themes and was one of several Muslim writers who were collectively responsible for a voluminous literature in Marāṭhi (III, p. 115). Muslim writers introduced a new style of historical prose writing known, by an inversion of the Persian *khabar*, as *bakhar*, in which several romantic chronicles were written, beginning from about 1720.

The eighteenth century also saw the development of two other important poetical forms in Marāṭhi: the *powaḍa* or heroic ballad, based largely on the life and exploits of Śivājī and other popular heroes, and sung to the accompaniment of a hand-drum and a one-stringed instrument; and the *lavani* or love lyric. Two names stand out at this time. The first is *Moropant* (fl. 1770) who enjoyed the patronage of an influential family related to the Peshwārs. He was a learned purāṇik by profession who read out passages from the Purāṇas in the temple, and commented on them. He was besides well-versed in Sanskrit classics. But to his credit he wrote his best works in Marāṭhi and staunchly defended it against Sanskrit. He rendered the *Mahābhārata*, the *Rāmāyaṇa* and *Bhāgavata Purāṇa* into Marāṭhi in the āryā metre. The other name is that of *Rāmjośi* (1762–1812), whose erotic hymns were very popular though bordering on the indecent.

By the time the British took over Mahārāshṭra in the beginning of the nineteenth century, 'society had disintegrated, traditions were lost, and all the currents of literature dried up' (VII, p. 254). The revival of Marāṭhi life and letters was due largely to the inspiration and example of English administrators and Christian missionaries, whose impact is seen in Marāṭhi word borrowings from Portuguese, French, Dutch and English.

The resurgence of Marāṭhi literature followed the pattern of other Indian vernaculars when confronted with the same influences. Marāṭhi grammars, dictionaries, translations from the Bible and the Western classics into simple, understandable Marāṭhi, all helped to clear the turbid and sluggish stream of its accumulated debris and set the currents moving again.

The infatuation with the West found its most fervent exponent in Bābā *Padamañji* (fl. 1830) author of the first Marāṭhi social novel, who wrote in a hybrid anglicized style, wholly condemning orthodox Hindu society and suggesting its remoulding on Western patterns. Others were not such enthusiastic supporters of the West, but could not quite withstand the pressure of European influence being felt on all sides. Marāṭhi prose, drama, poetry, and even philosophy, continued to receive inspiration from western sources for more than half a century, before the native genius asserted itself again.

The leader of this reaction was Chiplunkar (fl. 1850), one of the pioneers of modern Marāṭhi prose, whose vitriolic style and learned invective did much to stem the tide and turn Marāṭhi back to the Sanskrit fountainhead. Under his leadership many brilliant writers were converted into partisans and nationalists, and the talents of others diverted to the churning out of religious works on Sanskrit models.

In between were men like Agarkar (fl. 1870), who for all his sobriety wrote eloquently on social themes, fearlessly attacked untouchability and the degradation of contemporary Indian womanhood, and agitated for the spread of education, dress reform and even birth control.

The social and reformist zeal, often tending to pomposity and bombast reached its culmination in the great Marāṭhi trio: Justice Mahādeo Govind Rānaḍe (1842–1901), a pillar of the Prārthanā* Samāj; Gopāl Kṛishṇa Gokhale (1866–1915), and the revolutionary 'Lokmanya' Bāl Gaṅgādhar Tilak (1856–1920). Men of powerful intellect and incisive style, they were the last of the Reformation.

With Indian independence the ringing tones of Tilak do not find an echo in the market place, and the writer seeks in vain for new themes demanding utterance. Everywhere, it seems, it is being better said, and he can do worse than take his subjects from the drying fount of Sanskrit. Those who do not look back, turn their gaze once more to the West, and it is difficult for the critic to discern any pattern emerging from the confusion that arises from Kṛishṇa's escapades and the Purāṇic play married to D. H. Lawrence and Tennessee Williams.

Books

I. Abbott, J. E. *The Poet Saints of Maharashtra*, Poona, 1926–34.
II. Dandekar, R. N. (Ed.) *Silver Jubilee Volume of the Bhandarkar Oriental Research Institute, 1917–1942*, Poona, 1943.
III. Gokak, V. K. *Literature in Modern Indian Languages*, New Delhi, 1957.
IV. Gune, P. D. *An Introduction to Comparative Philology*, 2nd Ed., Poona, 1950.
V. Macnicol, N. *Psalms of the Marathi Saints*, London, 1919.
VI. Nadkarni, M. K. *A Short History of Marathi Literature*, Baroda, 1921.
VII. Nagendra, Dr. (Ed.) *Indian Literature*, Agra, 1959.
VIII. Ranade, R. D. *Mysticism in Maharashtra*, Poona, 1925.

MĀRGA, 'path', the road, way, or steps leading to a particular goal, such as salvation, bliss, knowledge, pleasure. The term is also used as an equivalent of method, or means, for reaching certain ends, generally in consonance with dharma. It is commonly suffixed to an operative word which serves to indicate the object or goal aimed at (see list below). Several suffixes are used in the same sense: *mārga*, 'way', e.g. *pushṭi-mārga*, 'grace-way'; *pada*, 'step', e.g. *jñāna-pada*, 'knowledge-path'; *yāna*, 'vehicle', e.g. Mahāyāna, 'Great Vehicle'; *yoga*, 'yoke' e.g. *bhakti-yoga*, 'faith-union'; *vāda*, 'thesis', e.g. *guru-vāda*, the doctrines of the guru or teacher (the follower of a vāda is called a vādin); *āchāra*, 'rule' e.g. Chīnāchāra, the Chinese method (*see* tantrism), or Āryāchārā, the Aryan way i.e. the way of the ancient Aryans, a healthy, naturalistic, god-fearing attitude; or *vāmāchāra* (*see* Hinduism); *upāya*, 'means', usually in the sense of stratagems, techniques, or expedients.

The means of attaining the end one has in view are many and varied, and they form an integral part of the various cults, creeds, sects and systems that abound in Hinduism. It is recognized that men differ, and have different *adhikāra* or competency, and not any path chosen at random is suited to all. Each path-seeker is entitled to a specific grade of work suited to his capacity (*see* svabhāva). Saving knowledge comes by progressive revelation, every man being in a different *bhūmikā*, 'stage', or degree of advancement. It is unwise to force a man along a path to which he is not suited, or to divulge things too subtle to the unsubtle lest they become confused.

With the aid of the suffixes named above the list of *mārgas* can be endlessly compounded depending on the goal in view and the means used for attaining them. These means may include: *bhoga* (enjoyment and pleasure), *dhyāna* (meditation*), *laya* (stimulation of the chakras*); *mantra** (incantations and spells); *tapas* (asceticism*); *yajña* (sacrifice*); *upāsana* (meditation, worship*, prayer); *rasavāda*, (alchemy* and drugs); *dharma* (duties), and so on.

The following are the chief mārgas mentioned in the texts dealing with Hindu religion and philosophy: *karma-mārga* (or karma-yoga), the method of good works, and doing one's duty without fear of consequences or thought of reward and punishment; it often implies ritualism, sacrifice and asceticism; *kriyā-marga*, 'action-way', refers specifically to devotion as expressed in ritual, the making of idols, and the building and consecration of temples; it sometimes implies magical operations; *akriyā-vāda*, 'nonaction-method', cultivation of the passive virtues; the path of neutrality or indifference to action, good or bad (*see* Pūraṇa under Ājīvika); *jñāna-mārga*, the way of right knowledge, e.g. Vedānta*; *tarka-vāda*, salvation through reasoning and discussion; according to Nyāya* philosophy, logic and debate are among the paths that lead to liberation; *bhakti-mārga*, the way of faith; love, adoration and devotion to the deity (*see* bhakti); *pushṭi-mārga*, 'efflorescence-path', i.e. the way of salvation that lies not in man's endeavour, but in the blossoming of God's grace (*see* Vallabha); *īśvara-vāda*, 'god-way', salvation through worship of a personal deity such as Vishṇu, Śiva, Kṛishṇa; *syād-vāda*, the 'perhaps way'; based on the belief that things are perhaps so, or perhaps not so (*see* Jainism); *śūnya-vāda*, 'nothingness-way', based on the Mahāyāna* doctrine that all is śūnya, void and nothingness; *deha-vāda*, 'body-way' through cultivation of the powers of the body (*see* physical culture); *śava-vāda*, 'cadaver-way', meditation on the dead in graveyards and cremation grounds as a reminder of the transience of things (*see* necrophilia).

It is generally recognized that no single mārga can be all-sufficient, and that a blending of two or more is essential; one should, for instance, balance faith with works, devotion with ritual, meditation with practice. This is exemplified in the story of two rival cousins, Keśidhvaja, who was endowed with profound meditative powers, and Khāṇḍikya, who was an expert in religious rites. They came to understand that each needed the knowledge that the other had in order to attain salvation, so Keśidhvaja learnt the intricacies of ritual to expiate the sin of killing a cow, while Khāṇḍikya was initiated into the mysteries of yogic meditation.

Books

See under Philosophy.

MARĪCHI, a prajāpati and brahmaṛishi, was the chief of the Maruts or storm gods, and father of the mage Kaśyapa. In some legends he is described as a strict celibate, but in others he is the progenitor of the Solar dynasty of kings, of whom Rāma was the greatest.

One day certain courtesans of the country of Aṅga were discussing their various conquests, and one of them, the beautiful *Kāmamañjarī* (passion-blossom), gave a boastful account of her many triumphs. Her companions taunted her saying that she spoke as though she had seduced no other than Marīchi himself, a sage known for his aversion to women. Kāmamañjarī replied that this would not be such a difficult task and wagered to do it. She dressed herself in humble garb, appeared before the sage and begged him to accept her as his disciple. The sage was on the point of driving her off, when a party of women, as pre-arranged by Kāmamañjarī, came to the hermitage, and one of them said that the girl was her daughter and had been brought up in the family profession of courtesan. As such it was her duty to be a courtesan and not an anchorite and spend her time, as she was in the habit of doing, singing the praises of Marīchi. The girl herself sidled up to the sage and took up the theme, pleading her cause with great eloquence, paying tribute to his wisdom, and so flattered his vanity that he accepted her.

The 'mother' and companions departed from the scene, and the courtesan and her victim were left alone together. It was a simple matter now for the experienced and ravishing courtesan to seduce the poor mahāṛishi, and he was soon so far gone in his infatuation that he went before the king of Aṅga and publicly proclaimed his love for her.

Books

See under Mythology.

MARRIAGE. According to tradition the once universally prevalent custom of indiscriminate sexual union was stopped by the sage Śvetaketu, son of Uddālaka*, who established the custom of the permanent monandrous union. Marriage, known in Sanskrit as *vivāha,* is one of the major *saṁskāras* or sacraments* of the Hindus, and the only one permitted to *śūdras* and lower castes. It is binding not only in this life but in the life hereafter. Manu declared that for a woman marriage was 'for all time, irrevocable, and indissoluble'. Divorce and remarriage were absolutely forbidden. As a result of Hindu reformist movements widows are now permitted to remarry, and by the Hindu Marriage Act of 1955 divorce is also possible.

The main purpose of marriage is to produce male offspring, and the legitimate opportunities that marriage provides for *ratī* or sexual pleasure are only meant to serve this end. Males alone can properly perform the domestic sacrifices to please the gods, and the funerary rites for the well being of the ancestors, and through males alone can the family line be perpetuated.

The age of the partners was set by convention, the age of thirteen for the girl and sixteen for the boy being regarded as the best. But already in the Vedic period an earlier marriage for girls began to gain approval, and it became obligatory to have the girl married before she attained puberty. This age was lowered still further in the brāhminical period, resulting in the abuse of child-marriage*.

In early times the girl was examined before marriage by the female relatives of the groom to confirm that she was a potential *strī* or woman, that she had no physical defects, and was otherwise eligible*. Sometimes the girl was picked by lot, and many kinds of such lots were devised in various parts of India to help decision in this matter. In one, four round balls were made of earth taken from four places: from a sacrificial altar, from a field, from a lump of cowdung, and from a cemetery, and the girl was asked to choose one. If she pointed to any of the first three she would be accepted, but was rejected if she picked the last. In most cases the outcome was prearranged, the inauspicious ball being made blacker than the others. The ceremony of *varaṇa*, 'choosing', next took place, when the suitor, after the girl had been seen and finally selected by the parents, came to the girl's house, or she to his, and he had an opportunity of seeing her and formally choosing her, and she him. This mutual introduction was often attended by a small ceremony, at which the important matter of the dowry* was also settled.

An astrologer had by this time already made up and studied the horoscopes of the prospective bride and groom to ensure that the stars offered no insurmountable obstacle to their union. He now decided on the proper moment for the marriage, and the date and time for the ceremony was fixed accordingly. Generally the northern course of the sun, and the *śukla-paksha* or the bright half of the lunar month is considered the best for marriage.

Many forms of marriage were practised among the Hindus, of which eight were traditionally recognized, and of which only two or three survive today. Of these eight forms, named below, four (the *gāndharva*, *āsura*, *paiśācha* and *rākshasa*) are non-Aryan, and one (*rākshasa*) probably Dravidian. The eight forms are (1) *paiśācha*, called after the savage Piśācha* tribe, was marriage by rape, where the girl was carried off by force, or under false pretext, or ravished while she was asleep, intoxicated or unconscious, or against her will. An example is found in the legend of Aniruddha and Ushā. Although this form was universally condemned, the maxim of *factum valet* was recognized and the girl's marriage was accepted as having been accomplished to confer on her the legal status of a wife; (2) *rākshasa*, named after the ogres of Hindu mythology, was the 'heroic' marriage, where a woman, carried off as a prize of war, was married without the consent of her father, usually by her captor. It was a custom permitted to kshattriyas and therefore called the *kshātra* form. In the marriage songs of Gujarāt and Uttar Pradesh which are sung today when the bride departs for her new home, the groom is compared to a robber and is showered with abuse; in some places a mock chase and fight are enacted. Examples of the rākshasa form are seen in the case of Arjuna and Subhadrā, and Kṛishṇa and Rukmiṇī; the most famous historical instance was the abduction by Pṛithvirāj of Saṁyogitā the princess of Kanauj; (3) *gāndharva*, named after the Gandharvas, is 'the marriage of a desiring woman with a desiring man'. This is the romantic type of union, springing from affection and love, and may be consummated without any nuptial rites. When accompanied by rites it ranks with the highest forms of marriage. An example is seen in the marriage of Dushyanta and Śakuntalā. The gāndharva union forms the basis of many romantic tales. A variation of the gāndharva was the *svayaṁvara** now obsolete, where the bride herself chooses her husband from a number of assembled suitors. Another kind of marriage also based on desire is the *śaiva*, which is to this day performed in secret among certain śākta worshippers, joining man and woman for a short period. For instance, it will permit the members of a circle to have sexual union during the *chakrapūjā**. It is not, of course, legally recognized outside the circle, and is valid only for the duration of the ceremony; (4) *āsura*, named after the Asuras, is marriage by sale of the bride. The bride's price, called the *śulka* (hence the āsura marriage was often called *śaulka*) did not go to the father but to the bride herself. In medieval Sanskrit literature the term śulka applied to the price paid to a courtesan for her services. The āsura marriage was condemned by Manu and the lawbooks as immoral since it encouraged the marketing of daughters, and was thus only open to vaiśyas and śūdras. An inverse form of this marriage is almost universal today, for a high price is paid, not for the bride but for the bridegroom (*see* dowry). The marriage of Pāṇḍu and Mādrī is an example of the āsura form. A heavy bride price was paid to the guardians of Kaikeyī and Gāndhārī when they were married; (5) *prājāpatya*, a vaguely defined form of marriage, whose chief feature appears to be that its conditions were fixed, and the father gave away the daughter on the distinct understanding that husband and wife should perform their civil and religious duties together. It was named after Prajāpati and is now obsolete; (6) *ārsha*, 'ṛishi-like', current only among priestly families, where the father of the bride received a pair of kine for the purpose of sacrifice or for facilitating the performance of sacrifices requiring cow's milk. It is a relic of the bride price and is now obsolete. An example is found in the marriage of Agastya and Lopāmudrā; (7) *daiva*, 'divine', the giving of a girl, 'duly decked with ornaments', to a priest as a gift or as a sacrificial fee. The presentation of a daughter to a ṛishi. Also obsolete, it is exemplified in the marriage of Chyavana to Sukanyā; (8) *brāhmya*, 'brāhmin-like', formerly open only to brāhmins, but now adopted even by śūdras. It is 'the gift of a daughter properly bedecked and ornamented, and with a suitable dowry to a brāhmin'. It forms the basis of the regular Hindu marriage, arranged by the parents, attended by religious ceremonies. In its purest form it is free from coercion and physical desire, but a suitable dowry is obligatory. Examples are found in the marriage of Śiva and Pārvatī and of Vasishṭha and Arundhatī.

The formal marriage rite itself varies considerably, depending on caste, sectarian belief and local custom, and it is impossible to give a comprehensive description of a ceremony that would be universally followed in India. The features mentioned below are common to many forms, and all have been practised at one time or another in different communities.

A short invocatory *śrāddha* sacrifice is offered to the manes for blessings at the commencement of the marriage preparations. This is done separately by the father of the bride and of the bridegroom. The place where the nuptial sacrifice is to be performed is freshly daubed with cowdung and marked with auspicious lines. A fire is then set up and the articles and implements required are arranged in their proper order; a millstone and a waterpot are placed to the west and north of the fire.

On the day fixed for the marriage the prospective bride has to perform various ablutionary rites. Her female helpers for this occasion all have to be 'unwidowed women who have borne a male child'. The body of the bride is dusted with powdered turmeric in a rite called *gātra-haridrā*, 'body-turmericking', in order to 'generate sexual desire'. She then has a special hygienic bath after which her body is anointed with fragrant oils. Among certain classes the girl's genitals are daubed with honey before the marriage ceremony to impart fecundity and sweetness (VI, p. 266). In the past the cloth with which her body was dried used to be taken to the woods and fastened to a tree to make her fruitful. The girl's temples and forehead are painted with floral designs, her cheeks rouged with saffron, and colour applied to her lips, and collyrium to her eyes to make them appear larger. A woollen thread dyed yellow is fastened around the girl's wrist by her mother. This *kautuka* or nuptial cord is removed on the third day after the consummation of the marriage.

The bridegroom in the meantime is also prepared by dusting with turmeric and a 'lust-bestowing bath'. He is anointed with cosmetic oils, and his neck, arms, wrist, head and ears adorned with jewels. Prayers are offered to the god of love: 'Your name is Love, but your real appellation is Lust. Let your intoxication bring bride and groom together in the fire of sexual desire.' The bridegroom's party consisting of his male relatives and friends, proceeds to the bride's house, the bridegroom garlanded with flowers, usually riding a caparisoned horse, with attendants holding a ceremonial umbrella and a fly whisk, preceded by a band of musicians. At the gate of the bride's house, which has been suitably decorated with arches of greenery, flowers and coloured lights, the bride's father receives him.

The following ceremonies are now observed, sometimes lasting for several hours: (*a*) *arghya*, 'respectfulness', or showing hospitality. Says one Hindu authority, 'The marriage ceremony entails the worship of the bridegroom in the pūjā fashion by the father of the bride' (V, p. 182). The father of the bride receives the groom with due honour and presents him with perfumed water and *madhuparka* (honey-mixture), a drink of honey and curds. In ancient times the arghya was not complete without sacrificing a cow in honour of the guest, but such a sacrifice is now obsolete; (*b*) *kanyā-dāna*, 'virgin-giving', or the formal gift of the daughter to the groom. At this stage, in some communities, a yoke is placed lightly on the girl's neck by the groom, symbolizing his authority over her; a gold chain is placed on the yoke for luck and prosperity, and bangles are put on the girl's wrist; (*c*) *maṅgalāshṭa*, 'eight blessings'; here the couple seated on the ground face each other and a sheet of silk is suspended in front of them while the priests invoke the blessings. In South India a little golden or gold-coloured ornament on a gold chain, known as the *tāli* is tied around the bride's neck, a relic of an ancient devadāsī rite. Other symbolic gifts of rice, coconuts, seeds and so on are also presented to the couple, making eight gifts in all; (*d*) *kaṇṭhibadala*, 'necklet-exchange'; here the young couple exchange their necklets, which are often made of beads; this rite is found among the Vaishṇavas of Bengal and among some other sects, with whom it constitutes the high point of the marriage proceedings; (*e*) *pāṇi-grahaṇa*, 'hand-grasping', or the acceptance of the bride, symbolized by the man taking hold of the girl's hand over the sacred fire. The groom says, 'I seize thy hand that I may gain fortune; this am I, thou art that; I am the words thou the melody; I the seed thou the bearer; the heaven I, the earth thou'. During this part of the ceremony the ends of the nuptial garments of the bride and groom are tied together; (*f*) *aśmārohaṇa*, 'stone-mounting'. The bride resting her hands on the shoulders of the bridegroom treads on a millstone with her right foot and is enjoined to be faithful and steadfast like the stone; to be untiring in domestic duties, obedient to the commands of her husband, determined and devoted in all she does. The *Atharva-veda* prescribes that the stone should be set up on a mound of cow-dung; (*g*) then follows the *homa* sacrifice at the nuptial fire, with oblations of *ājya* or clarified butter, while the couple hold hands. Sometimes at this stage the husband tells his bride: 'First Soma had thee for his bride; then the gandharva Viśvāvasu took thee; Agni was thy third husband; thy fourth husband am I, born of man'. After further oblations he adds, 'O my bride, be thou pleasant to the members of my family and to the cattle we possess'; give birth to heroic children; never miscarry and never have an empty lap; (*h*) *agni-pradakshiṇā*, 'fire-circumambulation'; the bride is led around the nuptial fire in a clockwise direction. An offering of fried grains is then made by the wife, the husband saying, 'May this woman, strewing grains, bring bliss to her husband'. After that the groom unties the two locks of the girl's hair, 'releasing her from the fetters of her virgin state'. As a token of his responsibility for maintaining her through life he gives her two pieces of raiment, one for the upper part of her body and one for the lower; (*i*) *sapta-padī*, 'seven-steps'. Here the bride and groom together take seven steps before the fire, each step representing a particular blessing, namely, food, strength, wealth, happiness, progeny, cattle, devotion. The priest sprinkles the couple with holy water. The marriage is complete and irrevocable with the taking of the seventh step. The man now places his hand over his wife's heart and says, 'Into my heart will I take thy heart; thy mind shall follow my mind'. Finally the forehead of the bride is marked with red lead, and water is sprinkled on the heads of the couple.

The married partners are now conducted to their new home, which is usually with the groom's family. The bride must enter the house without touching the threshold. The groom shows her around and displays certain auspicious objects. Other sacrifices are offered, after which a little boy, 'having an auspicious name', is placed on the lap of the bride and mantras chanted to ensure that the bride will in due course give birth to a male child. The boy is then given fruits and made to rise. The groom now removes the girdle from the bride's waist.

In olden times and even now among certain orthodox families the marriage was not consummated* on the wedding night, but on the fourth or sometimes the tenth night, by which time the evil eye is removed from the bridal scene, and the dangers of deflowering a virgin* mitigated.

At any time during the marriage a special rite called *garbhādhāna* (*see* pregnancy) could be performed in order to secure progeny.

Books

I. Banerjee, G. *The Hindu Law of Marriage & Stridhana*, Calcutta, 5th Ed., 1923.
II. Kapadia, K. M. *Marriage & Family in India*, Bombay, 1955.
III. Kearns, J. F. *Marriage Ceremonies of the Hindus of South India*, Madras, 1868.
IV. Mace, D. & V. *Marriage East and West*, London, 1960.
V. Morgan, K. W. (Ed.) *The Religion of the Hindus*, New York, 1953.
VI. Neumann, E. *The Great Mother*, New York, 1955.
VII. Pandey, R. B. *Hindu Samskaras*, Banaras, 1949.
VIII. Sastri, A. M. *The Vedic Law of Marriage*, Mysore, 1908.
IX. Thomas, P. *Women and Marriage in India*, London, 1939.
X. Tripathi, G. M. *Marriage Forms under Ancient Hindu Law*, Bombay, 1906.

MARUTTA, a mythological king of the Solar dynasty, descended from Manu Vaivasvata, famed for a sacrifice of unparalleled magnificence he performed in honour of the gods, the like of which had never been seen before and has never been seen since. All the implements and utensils were of gold. Only the highest brāhmins were allowed to officiate. Only the costliest ingredients were used. The wind gods were the guards of the sacrificial arena, and all the deities of heaven were invited to witness and participate. Indra became intoxicated with the heady libations of Soma and the other deities were transported with joy at the lavishness of the offerings. Even the brāhmins could not contain their astonishment at the liberality of the dakshiṇā or gifts bestowed on them. For the excellence of his performance the chief officiating priest, *Saṁvarta*, was translated to heaven, and Marutta at his own request was allowed to lay aside his crown and retire to the forest to meditate.

Marutta's son (or grandson) *Dama* succeeded to the throne and won his bride Sumanā from a number of contending rivals. One of them, *Vapushmat*, in revenge went to the forest where the aged Marutta lived in retirement and murdered him. Dama in a rage slew Vapushmat and would have drunk his blood had not the gods restrained him. At the funeral rites he offered to the manes of his father an oblation of the blood and part of the flesh of Vapushmat, and with the rest of the flesh fed the brāhmins. These brāhmins were said to have been of *rākshasa* (ogre) descent, to account for their partaking of a cannibal meal.

Books

See under Mythology.

MATAṄGA, 'elephant', a pseudo-brāhmin aspirant to brāhminhood whose story is told in the *Mahābhārata*. He once most cruelly beat a young donkey, and the mother of the animal to console her offspring said that since the man beating him was only a chaṇḍāla (untouchable caste) nothing better could be expected of him. Mataṅga turned to the mother donkey for an explanation, for he claimed to be a brāhmin and not a chaṇḍāla. The mother donkey then disclosed the fact that Mataṅga's mother in a state of intoxication had once sought the arms of a low-born barber and that he was the offspring of that reprehensible union.

Stung to the quick Mataṅga embarked upon a course of austerities to obtain from the gods his promotion to brāhminical status. First for a period of ten, then a hundred, and then a thousand years he remained wrapt in meditation, abstaining from food and sexual intercourse, but Indra, although greatly perturbed, would not relent. Then for another hundred years he stood balanced upon the big toe of one foot to conjure up occult power in order to coerce the now frightened gods. By now reduced to a living skeleton Mataṅga almost fell and, to avert the disaster of his possible curse, Indra rushed forward to support him, but still refused to change his caste. At the request of the persevering saint the god agreed to give him the power of flight and of changing his shape at will, and assured him that he would receive all the honour due to him, but declared that it was impossible for him to become a brāhmin. The *Rāmāyaṇa* relates that during their exile Rāma and Sītā visited the chaṇḍāla sage in his retreat near Ṛishyamūka mountain in the Deccan.

Books

See under Mythology.

MATHEMATICS. The oldest works on Indian mathematics are the *Śulva-sūtra* (?400 BC–AD 200?) or 'cord verses', which are supplements to the *Kalpa* or ritual canon. They deal with the construction of *vedis* or altars and sacrificial places, by stretching cords between stakes. They are not primarily mathematical, but consist of rules ancillary to religious ritual. The formulae of the Śulva-sūtras are of an empirical nature and not the result of a systematic theory of geometry. The many points of resemblance between the geometrical portions of these sūtras and the work of the Greeks, prompted Cantor and Weber to say that the Śulva-sūtras were influenced by the Alexandrian school.

Between the earliest of the Śulva-sūtras and the first of the later mathematicians there is a blank in Indian mathematical theory of nearly a thousand years, and there is no connection between the methods of the Śulva-sūtras and subsequent mathematical speculation, which completely ignored them. The span of nine centuries that separates these sūtras from the first great name in Indian mathematics is mainly characterized by the introduction of astronomical and mathematical ideas from the West.

Āryabhaṭa (AD 476–520) is the first great landmark in the history of Indian mathematics. His treatise on the subject is the earliest Hindu work on pure mathematics, and consists of thirty-three couplets of bare rules so condensed as to be nearly impossible to interpret. Little is known about his life except that he was born in Pāṭaliputra and that his ideas were bitterly opposed by the orthodox. He explained the causes of the solar and lunar eclipse; gave a rule for the solution of simple indeterminate equations, and also an accurate determination of the value of *pi*, i.e. the relation of the circumference of a circle to its diameter, but curiously enough never utilized this value, nor was it used by any mathematician in India before the twelfth century, and no Indian writer quotes Āryabhaṭa as having recorded this value. Nevertheless, Āryabhaṭa did give a definite direction to Indian mathematics, and subsequent Indian works on the subject dealt with the same topics, employed the same methods and even carried over the same errors. There is another mathematician and astronomer of a later date also called Āryabhaṭa, but distinguished by the title of '*Laghu Āryabhaṭa*' (Āryabhaṭa the Less).

To the period immediately preceding and following Āryabhaṭa belong the Siddhānta or scientific treatises on astronomy*. These treatises include the *Pañcha-siddhāntikā* and other works of the astronomer **Varāhamihira***, (d. 587) all of which show indisputable evidence of influences from Greece, Alexandria, Rome and Persia. Among the mathematical terms adopted from Greek at this time were *kendra* or centre (from Greek *kentron*); *trikoṇa* or triangle (Gk. *trigonon*) and *koṇa* or angle (Gk. *gonia*). To this period also belongs one of the most significant of human inventions, the zero. From some source, still disputed, the mathematicians evolved a numerical* system of nine digits and a zero, with a place notation for tens, hundreds, thousands, and so on.

Brahmagupta (598–660) of Ujjain was the next great name in the history of Hindu mathematics. He attacked his predecessor Āryabhaṭa in most offensive terms, although it was his own fate to be dubbed a 'blundering devil' by Bhāskara five hundred years later. Brahmagupta's work, the *Brahma-siddhānta*, composed at the time of the decline of the Alexandrian school, 'is almost what one might expect to find in the period of decay of Alexandria'. It contains one or two gems, but it is not a scientific exposition of its subject, and the material is obviously taken from Western sources. Some of Brahmagupta's theorems and rules could not be appreciated by his successors, and by the time of Bhāskara they had ceased to be understood. There was never at any time an established mathematical tradition in India, and after Bhāskara no Indian mathematical work of value is known. Says Dr Winter, 'Hindu mathematics has from time to time shown brilliant flashes of intuition by isolated geniuses, only to fail through lack of systematic development by their successors'.

The great Muslim traveller and historian, Muhammad al-Bīrūnī, who visited India in the tenth century cogently expressed the degeneration of Indian science of his day: 'In former times the Hindus used to acknowledge that the progress of science due to the Greeks was much more important than that which is due to themselves.' He himself found little trace of any mathematical or astronomical tradition, only a pitiful conceit in their own ancient heritage, combined with a profound ignorance of these same ancient achievements. He was unable to find a scholar who could explain to him the principles of Indian mathematics. Even the paṇḍits whom he met and consulted had ceased to understand the significance of the earlier theories. He writes,

'You mostly find the so-called scientific theorems of the Hindus in a state of utter confusion, devoid of any logical order. Since they cannot raise themselves to the methods of strictly scientific deduction I began to show them the elements on which the science rests'.

It should be mentioned that this Perso-Arab scholar was one of the greatest minds produced by the Islamic world, perhaps the most learned scholar of his age, an astronomer and mathematician of the highest order, equally at home in Greek and Sanskrit as in his own Arabic, who spent many years in India and quoted from more than thirty Sanskrit works.

In Brahmagupta's wake the following Indian mathematicians and astronomers also distinguished themselves in sundry ways: **Lalla** (*c.* AD 748) wrote a slender treatise on mathematical theory; **Mahāvīra** (*c.* AD 850) wrote an elementary work on mathematics, and in another later work discussed quadratic equations; MAÑJULA (*c.* 932) and ŚRĪDHARA (*c.* 1028) also made small contributions to the subject.

Valuable information on Hindu mathematics is found in the *Bakhshāli Manuscript* written in old Śārada characters on seventy folios of birch bark discovered in north-west India in 1881. Some authorities date it about AD 300, but more moderate opinion assigns it to about AD 1100. In this manuscript a small cross (like a plus sign) is used to represent the negative quality; and the zero is represented by a dot.

Bhāskara (1114–1160) sometimes referred to as Bhāskara II to distinguish him from an earlier mathematician of lesser renown, is the last notable name in Indian mathematics and astronomy. He is the author of the *Bīja-gaṇita*, a work on mathematics; the *Siddhānta-Śiromaṇi*, on astronomy; and the *Līlāvatī*, on algebra. In this latter work he presents his algebraical and arithmetical theorems in the form of problems set to a beautiful maiden, in terms chosen from bees and flowers. Bhāskara teaches nothing new and is completely dependent on Brahmagupta. Much disputable credit has been given to him for his work, and it is claimed that he anticipated many mathematical theories. But it is difficult to agree that his formula for the calculation of a table of sines implies his use of the principles of the Differential Calculus, or to find, as Seal does, that he anticipated the computation of the size of the hydrogen atom.

Books

I. Clark, W. E. *The Aryabhatiya of Aryabhata*, Chicago, 1930.
II. Colebrooke, H. T. *Algebra, with Arithmetic and Mensuration from the Sanskrit of Brahmagupta and Bhaskara*, London, 1817.
III. Datta, B. *The Science of Sulba*, Calcutta, 1932.
IV. Datta, B., & Singh, A. N. *History of Hindu Mathematics*, Lahore, 1935.
V. Kaye, G. R. 'Ancient Hindu Spherical Astronomy', *Journal of the Asiatic Society of Bengal*, No. 15, 1919.
VI. Kaye, G. R. *The Bakhshali Manuscript*, Calcutta, 2 vols., 1927.

VII. Kaye, G. R. 'Indian Mathematics', *Isis*, 6, 2, 1919.
VIII. Kaye, G. R. *Indian Mathematics*, Calcutta, 1915.
IX. Seal, B. N. *The Positive Sciences of the Ancient Hindus*, London, 1915.
X. Sengupta, P. C. 'Aryabhata', *Calcutta University Journal of Letters*, Vol. XVIII, pp. 9–15.
XI. Smith D. E. 'The Geometry of the Hindus', *Isis*, 1, 2, 1913.
XII. Winter, H. J. J. *Eastern Science*, London, 1952.

MATHURĀ (modern Mattra or Muttra), a town on the Jamnā, fifty miles south east of Delhi, was an ancient seat of Maga* worship originally called Mayatār or Mahetār. It was known to legend as the capital of the **Śūrasena** tribal kingdom, the name of which has been derived from Asura-sena (Asura-general). This personage, of probably Maga ancestry figures in legend as the asura* king Madhu, after whom Mathurā is named. For some time Mathurā was the capital of the mythological Yādava line, and the Śūrasenas claimed descent from Yadu, but they are not mentioned in Vedic literature and were undoubtedly of non-Aryan antecedents. In epic times the Śūrasenas sided with Duryodhana in the battle of Kurukshetra.

The Buddhists who consistently took over sites already hallowed by prehistoric, especially Maga cults, claimed Mathurā as their own. It became a great Buddhist stronghold, and the *Lalitavistara* recounts a legend in which this city is one of the places suggested by the gods as a suitable birthplace for Buddha. In Buddha's time the king of Mathurā was related to the ruler of Avanti, a great cosmopolitan centre further south-west.

Megasthenes (*c.* 295 BC) mentioned Mathurā as a centre for the worship of Heracles by the 'Indian tribe of the Sourasenoi', and this Heracles is variously identified with Buddha, with one of the Jain *tīrthaṅkaras*, or with Kṛishṇa. Just as Buddhists took over Maga sites, so Hindus took over Buddhist sites, and Mathurā in due time became one of the sacred cities of the Hindus. It was associated with the tyrant Kaṁsa and was famous as the birthplace of Kṛishṇa. Both the town and the countryside around it are rich in associations with the youthful deity. Here is the tank in which his baby linen was washed, the churn from which he would steal the butter he loved so much, and the fields in which he sported with the *gopīs*. In Hindu legend Kṛishṇa (or Vishṇu) slew the Śūrasena king Madhu (above).

Following the Bactrian Greek incursions Mathurā fell to the Bactrian kings, and became part of the dominions of Menander (170 BC). The last Indo-Greek king to rule in Mathurā was Strato I (75 BC), whose sovereignty in that area alternated with that of the Parthians and the Śaka Satraps. The latter made Mathurā one of their chief administrative towns; and from them it passed, after a brief Hindu interregnum, to the Kushāns. It became the centre of Kushān power and was adorned by them with many fine monuments. When the Chinese pilgrim Fa-hien (*c.* AD 410) visited the city in the reign of the Guptas, it contained twenty monasteries, mainly Hīnayāna, and three thousand monks, but other sects flourished as well. For five centuries thereafter its destiny was linked with that of the various principalities that rose and fell in northern India.

In AD 1017 Mahmud of Ghazni pillaged and destroyed the town. According to his own account it had over one thousand religious edifices, the greater number of them in marble. One temple, dedicated to Kṛishṇa contained five images of red gold, each one fifteen feet high, studded with rubies, sapphires and pearls. The precious stones and gold, estimated today at five million pounds were carried off, the temple 'burnt with naphtha and fire' and levelled to the ground. It was rebuilt, and again sacked by the Lodis; and in 1668 Aurangzeb demolished all the chief temples of the city, including the ancient Keśava Deo temple of special sacrosanctity, which had originally been the site of a Buddhist *vihāra*, and before that of a Maga fire altar. On its site he built a mosque.

Lying athwart the path of conquering invaders, Mathurā was from time immemorial a crossroads of the peoples of many nations. It was situated at the trijunction of the great subcontinental trade routes, between the northern cultural centre of Gandhāra, the eastern imperial metropolis of Pāṭaliputra, and the western port of Broach, and thus constituted a natural clearing house for new ideas and art forms. It was a city of many different religions, Zoroastrian, Greek, Gnostic, Buddhist, Śaivite and Jain. The Bhāgavata cult was born here. For centuries it continued to be fed from several cultural streams and it never lost its cosmopolitan and heterogeneous character. There can be little doubt of the influence of foreign elements on the development not only of Vaishṇavism and Kṛishṇaism, but also in the artistic and architectural traditions of this area.

Scholars have traced elements of Mathurā art to Persia, the Middle East and Central Asia, notably through the Kushān kings. Greece and Rome made substantial contributions which came mainly by way of Gandhāra*, but also to some extent by the sea via Broach. The actual presence of foreign artists is supported by the earliest surviving example of Indian portrait sculpture, namely, the headless figure of Kanishka, which is believed to be the work of Scythian craftsmen in India, as are also the life-size portrait statues of the other Śaka and Kushān kings.

In general early Mathurā art shows unmistakable signs of eclecticism, and the unassimilated motifs of its borrowings are everywhere evident. Corinthian columns, the acanthus and vine leaf from the Hellenistic world; motifs from Assyria, side by side with the Indian lotus and palmette. The Bacchanalian scenes in relief, the statues with Western subjects, the stylized folds in the sculptured drapery show Roman influence. This again came through the Kushāns, for Mathurā is the chief find spot of Kushān sculpture.

With the aid of such diverse material the artists of Mathurā, during the period AD 150–300, evolved an art form that acquired characteristically Indian features, and the city grew into one of the foremost centres of indigenous art, which expressed itself in Mahāyāna, Jain and Hindu work. The early sculpture* was done on Buddhist sites and it was at Mathurā that the Buddha image, first created and perfected in Gandhāra was given its Indian features and turned out on a large scale. The commercialized Mathurā workshops were soon supplying Buddhist markets in India and even Central Asia with their work.

The indiscriminate production of cheap Buddhas was controlled under the Guptas, and the standard of the Buddha image improved and finally Indianized. Both artistically and culturally Mathurā reached its zenith and found its fulfilment in the reign of the Imperial Guptas.

Books

I. Cole, H. H. *Ancient Buildings in Muttra and Agra*, 2 vols., 1869–73.
II. Growse, F. S. *Mathura*, 3rd Ed., 1883.
III. Lal, Kanwar. *Holy Cities of India*, Delhi, 1961.
IV. Majumdar, R. C. (Ed.) *The Age of Imperial Unity*, Bombay, 1951.
V. Smith, V. A. *The Jaina Stupa and Other Antiquities of Mathura*, Allahabad, 1901.
VI. Winstedt, R. (Ed.) *Indian Art*, London, 1947.

MATRIARCHY. There have always been communities in India throughout her history, where the woman has played the predominant role in society and where in the religious systems the goddess rather than the god has been given first place. Among the Śāktas for instance the female divinity takes precedence over the male, and in the dual form of divine names the goddess is always named first, e.g. Lakshmī-Nārāyaṇ, Gaurī-Śaṅkar, Rādhā-Kṛishṇa.

The several legends of *strīrājya**, or states ruled by women, whatever their historicity, suggest that the fact of political government by women was not beyond probability. The rule of queens in ancient times, especially in South India would confirm that tradition. Even in northern India the role of women in society indicated that they did not always hold a subordinate position. Among the Śakas, Kushāns, Pahlavas and other peoples of Central Asian origin, descent was often traced through the female line.

This matrilineal system is also part of ancient Indian usage, and many tribes were named after women. Such were the Kādraveya, descendants of Kadrū; the Vinateya of Vinatā; the Daitya of Diti; the Dānavas of Danu. The custom of taking names after the mother might indicate that the father was unknown, as in the case of the ṛishi Satyakāma. In some circumstances it may point to the superior pedigree of the maternal line which would cause it to be preserved, as among certain Rājputs*. More often it points to a matriarchal society.

The social organization of the Khāsi of Assam is said to be one of the most perfect examples of a matriarchal institution. The mother is the head of the family, the main bond of union, the owner of the property, and through her alone is inheritance transmitted. Another modern example are the Nāirs* of South India, where the members of a family consist of the women, their children, their brothers and maternal uncles; and daughters but not sons transmit the rights of inheritance to their children. Relationship and descent are traced through women.

Closely linked with matriarchy is the system of polyandry, which permits a woman to have more than one husband at the same time. This custom of sharing a common wife by two or more husbands, who may or may not be brothers, prevailed among all classes in ancient India; it was common among the non-Aryans, particularly the Austrics, and was found among brāhmins and *ṛishis* (IV, p. 44). The verses of the *Atharva-veda* saying that a woman can marry even after having ten husbands cannot but refer to polyandry.

Similarly, mythology speaks of the common wife of the Maruts and of the Aśvins.

Many scions of the ancient ṛishi clans were said to be 'born of two fathers', or 'the sons of many fathers', and there are a number of references in Vedic literature to women with several husbands, or to a maiden being 'given unto husbands'. A passage in the *Āpastamba* seems to refer to the practice of marrying a girl to the male members of a whole family. The Vedic ṛishi Prachetas had ten sons who married a common wife Mārishā daughter of Kaṇḍu. The beautiful Gautamī married seven ṛishis whom she served as a common wife. The fish-woman Satyavatī had two children by one of her husbands, Śāntanu, and by another husband bore the renowned sage Vyāsa. Jaṭilā the virtuous daughter of a Vedic ṛishi was, according to the *Mahābhārata*, the wife of seven learned brāhmins. So also Vārkshī, daughter of a sage, who in the *Mahābhārata* was the wife of ten brothers.

There is a story in the Purāṇas of the beautiful Mādhavī who was jointly queen to three contemporary and neighbouring kings, and bore sons to three different families, after which she bore a son to the sage Viśvāmitra. Not content with this performance she held a *svayaṁvara* and selected as her husband the king Haryaśva with whom she went into exile (*see* Gālava). The *Kunāla Jātaka* relates that the princess Kaṇhā selected five husbands at her svayaṁvara and married them all. Sarkar deems it not unlikely that in the original tradition Sītā was the common wife of Rāma and Lakshmaṇa (V, p. 151).

The most conspicuous instance of this type of polyandry is of course the marriage of the five Pāṇḍava brothers to the peerless Draupadī. The origin of the five Pāṇḍavas is itself a mystery since their father Pāṇḍu was precluded by a curse from intercourse with his wives. Kuntī, one of his wives, knew several 'husbands', and had a son born to her even before her marriage. The polyandry of the Pāṇḍavas surprised Drupada who questioned Yudhishṭhira about the strange custom, 'contrary to precept and morals', and Yudhishṭhira replied, 'It is beyond our power to discover the origin of this practice. We only follow the old and righteous path taken by our ancestors' (VI, p. 97).

Today polyandry is prevalent among communities like the Nāirs, and such tribes as the Todas*, and in other small communities. Dr R. C. Majumdar says, 'The custom of several brothers marrying only one woman is even today more common in India than is generally believed, not only among non-Aryans, but also among brāhmins' (III, p. 558).

Books

I. Briffault, R. *The Mothers*, 2nd Ed., London, 1952.
II. Ehrenfels, O. R. *Mother Right in India*, Hyderabad, 1941.
III. Majumdar, R. C. (Ed.) *The Age of Imperial Unity*, Bombay, 1951.
IV. Raychaudhuri, H. *Materials for the Study of the Early History of The Vaishvana Sect*, Calcutta, 1936.
V. Sarkar, S. C. *Some Aspects of the Earliest Social History of India*, London, 1928.
VI. Visvanatha, S. V. *Racial Synthesis in Hindu Culture*, London, 1928.

MATSYENDRA (fl. AD 980) or Matsyendranāth, the first human guru to whom the esoteric doctrines of the Nātha* sect were communicated. He was so called because he received the secret teachings while in the form of a fish. The nature of the doctrine was such that it was not possible for more than one being at a time to comprehend it. Once Śiva was telling his wife Pārvatī about its deeper mysteries as they both sat by the sea. Pārvatī found it boring and fell asleep, but Matsyendra who happened to be swimming nearby overheard the discourse and became enlightened. Matsyendra had a great weakness for women, and in popular terms this was expressed by saying that he was fond of eating the entrails of fish. The word for fish intestines in Tibetan is *luipa*, hence Matsyendra is also known as **Luipā.** Another of his names is **Mīnanāth,** 'fish-lord'.

Matsyendra is said to have sojourned for many years in the *strīrājya**, or female kingdom, of **Uḍḍiyāna.** This strange realm has never yet been identified; its location has been given by various authorities as the Swat valley in north-west India; in Orissa; in Nepāl; or in Assam. Legend has it that it was founded in a remote locality during the seventh century AD for the express purpose of perpetuating a secret cult in which women played an important part. The cult received a great fillip during the reign of Indrabhūti (*c.* AD 790) the reputed author of the *Jñāna-siddhi* and other works on sex-magic, tantrism, yab-yum techniques, *kāya-sādhanā* and yoga. Both sexes joined in homosexual and heterosexual rites, including bestiality and other perversions. The moving spirit of the cult was Indrabhūti's gifted daughter Lakshmīṅkarā, who has been compared to Eleanor of Aquitaine. The Court of Love she established was notorious for the employment of women in tantrik sex magic.

Attached to the court of one of Indrabhūti's descendants was Matsyendra, who acquired his powers through left-hand occultism practised there. It is said that he was so enchanted with life in this kingdom of women that he refused to leave, and was only rescued through the determined efforts of his pupil, the renowned Gorakhnāth*.

Books

See under Nātha and Gorakhnāth.

MAURYA (320–183 BC), the greatest dynastic line of ancient India, founded by Chandragupta Maurya. There is still much uncertainty concerning the origin of the name. It has been connected with Chandragupta's śūdra mother, Murā; or with the Śākya principality of Chandragupta's putative father, where the *mayūra* or peacock abounded; others link it with Mayara, a variant derivative of the Maga* people who were believed to have settled in Magadha. Spooner connects it with the Avestan town of Mouru, which also appears in Achaemenian inscriptions. In one of the Purāṇas Mayūra is the name of a class of asuras. Other historians consider it to be of Śākya origin, and generally hold that the Mauryas were a Himālayan tribe of Mongolian stock who claimed kshattriya status.

Chandragupta Maurya (320–297 BC) was a warrior of low caste, the illegitimate son of Murā, a queen or concubine of the Nanda ruler of Magadha. He became commander-in-chief of the Nanda army, tried to wrest the throne from the king, was frustrated and had to flee. He met Alexander the Great and made a close study of his military methods and, according to some authorities, sought to induce the Macedonian to conquer Magadha (I, p. 59). He remained in exile till the death of Alexander, then returned to Magadha, where he fomented a popular uprising against the Nandas and in 322 BC usurped the throne of Magadha after slaying Dhana Nanda. He then set out on a career of conquest with a large army of mercenaries, took Taxila and the Panjāb, and in the course of his victorious progress repulsed the advance of Seleucus, the greatest of Alexander's generals, bringing 'under the umbrella of his sovereignty' an empire extending from Afghanistan to Bengal.

Among those who helped Chandragupta in his struggle against the Nandas, were the Śakas (Scythians), Yavanas (Greeks), and Parasīkas (Persians); and on the side of the Nanda kings we again find the mercenary Yavanas (Greeks), and also the Chīnas (Chinese) and Hunas (Huns), which shows the extent of India's alliances.

Like most Indian civilization during its finest periods, the Mauryan age welcomed new ideas from abroad, and created with the foreign material a fresh synthesis of wonder and delight. Chandragupta had contacts with Greece, received a Greek embassy headed by Megasthenes at his court, and married the daughter of Seleucus. He had a bodyguard of foreign, probably Greek, women, who kept watch over the palace and protected the king when he went out. The bazaars of Pāṭaliputra teemed with a cosmopolitan crowd of merchants from various parts of Asia, Greece, Egypt and the Middle East. Imports included among other things, horses from Arabia and silks from China. In his advance westward Chandragupta occupied territories which had been under Persian rule, and which were ripe for the transmission of Persian ideas, and through Persia, of Greek ideas. In these parts a Persian script was officially employed for the vernaculars. All these conditions operated forcefully on the empire of the young śūdra prince who adapted some of the features of the alien cultures for his own government.

Chandragupta organized his army and judicial system on the Persian model and introduced important innovations on Greek lines. His Great Royal Highway, the precursor of the Grand Trunk Road, was a remarkable piece of work, conceived in imitation of the highway that linked Susa to Sardis. He made Pāṭaliputra* his capital a thing of beauty, as we know from descriptions of it preserved in contemporary Greek records. The identification of his name with the Sandracottus of Greek chronicles represents a landmark in Indian chronology.

He organized his vast empire on the Persian model, splitting it up into manageable units after the manner of the Achaemenian satrapies. The best known of the satraps or viceroys was *Pushyamitra*, who administered the distant province of Kāṭhiāwār. He carried through a great irrigation project forming the Sudarśana Lake near Girnār by damming up a river with great walls of masonry, this being one of the most notable examples of irrigation in ancient India.

The organizing genius behind Chandragupta's government was the mysterious personality of Kauṭilya*, under whom the Mauryan empire became virtually a police state, but also a model of efficiency. Descriptions in the *Arthaśāstra,* a book on politics attributed to Kauṭilya, of the palace that the king is advised to build, with its 'delusive chambers' (*mohanagṛiha*), its secret passages built into walls; its underground chambers and concealed doors, its exits in hollowed pillars, and its whole structure so conceived with mechanical contrivances 'that it may be caused to collapse when necessary', all suggest that the king lived in constant danger. Chandragupta had many enemies and it was said that he never slept for two successive nights in the same bedroom in order to defeat any plots by treacherous servants. As his beginning, so his end is obscure. One tradition has it that during a famine he abdicated his throne and for twelve years lived the life of a Jain* ascetic. He then starved himself to death.

Chandragupta's son, **Bindusāra** (297–273 BC) succeeded him and conquered the Deccan as far as the latitude of modern Madrās. He maintained cordial relations with the Greeks, whom he greatly admired. The Greek envoy, Deimachus, residing at his court, was a close friend, and there was a considerable Greek colony in the capital. He remained a staunch ally of the Seleucids throughout his reign, even aiding them in their foreign wars, as when he reinforced the armies of the Macedonians by providing them with elephants in their war against Persia. Bindusāra was sufficiently appreciative of Greek achievements in the sphere of thought to request Antiochus Soter, son and successor of Seleucus, to send him 'a real Greek philosopher' for whom he was willing to pay a high price.

Bindusāra's son **Aśoka*** (273–232 BC) was one of the greatest kings of India, and one of the most remarkable rulers the world has known. He was also the last of the great Mauryas; under his successors the break-up of the empire began its relentless course.

The last king of the Maurya dynasty was the Buddhist **Bṛihadratha** (d. 183 BC) who lost some of his northwestern territories to the Bactrian Greeks under Demetrius or Apollodotus. He was slain in full view of his own army by his commander-in-chief Pushyamitra who then ascended the throne as the first king of the Śuṅga* dynasty.

Books

I. Majumdar, R. C. (Ed.) *The Age of Imperial Unity*, Bombay, 1951.
II. Mookerji, R. K. *Chandragupta Maurya & His Times*, Madras, 1943.
III. Raychaudhuri, H. *Political History of Ancient India*, Calcutta, 6th Ed., 1953.
IV. Sastri, K. A. N. *The Mauryas and Satavahanas*, London, 1959.
V. Sastri, K. A. N. *The Age of the Nandas & Mauryas*, Banaras, 1952.

MĀYĀ. The term occurs in the *Ṛig-veda* in the sense of magical power, such as the power of a deity or demon to change shape or to create illusory effects by supernatural means. In the Upanishads it stands for false knowledge, or the negative principle, which ascribes to the manifestations of the manifold universe an identity and distinctiveness apart from and independent of the one true reality which is Brahma.

According to advaita doctrine there is but one reality, Brahma. The phenomenal world of nature and the identities of all beings have no real existence, but are illusive, the result of *māyā*. It is the temporal, negative, deceptive veil of creation, the obscuring force of nature (*see* Śaṅkara) and the result of *avidyā* or ignorance.

The world, according to another interpretation of the subject, is the sportive diversion (*vilāsa*) or play (*līlā*) of Brahma. It is the expression of his whimsical urge to become many (*see* God). In created beings māyā causes a state of *moha* (or mohana), 'delusion', in which consciousness of the ultimate reality is lost, and bewildered men believe in the reality of the manifest world presented to their senses. It is a cosmic delusion which draws a veil across men's perception, leading them to error and to infatuation with the world and the flesh, obscuring from the mind the vision of their true destiny. The veil of māyā is rent when it is realized that Brahma alone is real. He who has this knowledge attains *moksha* or salvation.

Some systems of philosophy such as Kashmīr Śaivism have tried to explain the operation of māyā. It is shown that in the phenomenal or manifest world the absolute and transcendental *tattva*, or essence, of Brahma is contracted and distorted by what is called *kañchuka*. A kañchuka is a 'restraining' vestment, like the husk that envelops the seed, and is thus the limitation imposed on creation and all created things by the very process of their coming into existence. Mind and matter are subject to this limitation. So the Eternality of Brahma is limited by the kañchuka of *kāla* or time and results in mortality. The Omnipresence of Brahma is limited by the kañchuka of *dik* or space, and results in the illusion of individuality. The Completeness of Brahma is limited by the kañchuka of *rāga* or desire, leading to action and consequent suffering. The Omniscience of Brahma is limited by *vijña* or learning, resulting in limited knowledge which is ignorance. The Omnipotence of Brahma is limited by the kañchuka of *niyati* or fatality, resulting in dependence on things, and causing to sprout forth the seeds of its own destruction.

Many tales are told of great sages who have tried to grasp the significance of māyā. Best known is the one about the *ṛishi* Nārada who implored Vishṇu to give him some understanding of this profound mystery. Vishṇu asked the sage first to fetch some water from a nearby pool. On his way Nārada had many adventures, fell in love with a young woman, married her and had several children. His children grew up and had children of their own, and they in turn had children, and these again had children. Nārada was thus blessed with seeing many generations of his descendants. Then a series of misfortunes befell him. His house burned down, his children perished one by one. The last survivor, his grandson's great-grandson, fell into a pool and was drowning, and Nārada put his hand into the water to save him and found that he had only just dipped his jar into the pool to fetch water for Vishṇu who was still standing beside him. All his experiences had been but the result of māyā. So also is all life and all experience, merely māyā.

Books

I. Devanandam, P. D. *The Concept of Maya*, London, 1950.
II. Shastri, P. B. *The Doctrine of Maya*, London, 1911.

MECHANICS. In India, as in other parts of the ancient world, the people were familiar with the elementary principles of mechanics, which were applied to operate the water pulley, to help the oil presser, to lift weights and measure commodities. The more intricate operations of this branch of science were unknown to India until her contact with the exponents of the Alexandrian school during the early centuries of this era.

Apart from the figurative references to flying ships and aerial palaces in Vedic literature, and the fabulous tales of Purāṇic lore, which speak of machines moved by will-power, mystic syllables and black magic, there are also more modest references in Sanskrit literature to the application of mechanical principles for operating ingenious contraptions of all kinds, known as *yantra*, 'engines', which were employed in warfare or architecture, or used for recreation and pleasure.

It is interesting to note that the authors of most of these inventions were spoken of as Greeks. Yavana (Greek) carpenters, metal-workers and artisans serving under Indian rulers produced many mechanical devices, and the association of this type of skilled craft with the Yavanas was so well known that we find it mentioned not only in Sanskrit literature of the north, but in Tamil writings of South India as well.

The first inventor in this field in the ancient world was probably Archytas (*c.* 340 BC) a Greek philosopher of Tarentum, who reputedly constructed some kind of flying machine set in motion by 'hidden and enclosed air'. One section of the book on architecture by Vitruvius (*c.* 15 BC) the Roman architect, is wholly devoted to mechanical inventions, and as the influence of Vitruvius on Indian architectural theory is fairly well established, the portions of his book dealing with mechanisms may also be regarded as having left their mark on Indian works on the subject. Hero of Alexandria (*c.* AD 100) another fabricator of mechanical engines wrote treatises on the subject which have also influenced Indian applied science (II, p. 212).

Many of the inventions described by these writers correspond in essential detail with descriptions of Indian contrivances given by Sanskrit writers. A number of automatic toys and gadgets are referred to in Somadeva's* collection of tales, the *Kathā-sarit-sāgara*, including mechanical birds that sing, statues that pour out libations, an elephant machine large enough to carry eight men, a robot door-keeper as good as a living sentinel, a mechanical soldier which can fight, revolving machines that play music, and the like, and Sanskrit writers attribute these and other inventions to the Greeks.

One type of yantra in particular has invariably been associated with the Greeks, and that curiously is the so-called flying machine, although what this strange device actually was is not known. There is a fanciful reference to an aerial car called *Pushpaka*, belonging to Kubera*, which one scholar rashly declares 'was clearly an aeroplane' (I, p. 84); and also occasional mention of the *vimāna* or celestial chariot of the gods, and the *vyomaga*, 'sky-moving', or aerial vehicle. One such flying machine looked like a great bird with outspread wings, and was moved by 'mercury heated over a small fire in the interior; the heated mercury set in motion the wings'. Its flight was guided by a mechanical man. It was made chiefly of wood, but iron, copper and lead were also employed in its construction. It could leave the ground, carrying several persons, cruise thousands of miles in any direction, and the sound of its movement through the sky could be heard like a faint rumble from the ground.

References to the Yavanas building flying machines for Indian kings are found in several Sanskrit books. In Bāṇa's *Harshacharita* (*c.* AD 650) we read of a vehicle that could fly and that carried away a king, as having been built by a Yavana (III, p. 14). Daṇḍin in his *Avantisundarī* (*c.* AD 600) and Budhasvāmin (*c.* AD 800) in his version of the *Bṛihatkathā*, both refer to the great skill of the Yavanas in building aerial vehicles, a point which is also repeatedly mentioned in Bhoja's *Samarańgana-sūtradhāra* (*c.* AD 1085).

The construction of these mythical aerial conveyances represented the acme of scientific achievement, and was thought to be an art of such extreme complexity that its principles could not be understood by non-Yavanas (III, p. 15). There is nothing to suggest that such flying machines ever had any existence outside legend, but that the Greeks were credited with their invention indicates the high esteem in which they were held. Even higher tribute was paid to Greek intelligence by Sanskrit writers, one of whom confesses that the Yavanas are worthy of being honoured like ṛishis and gods.

Books

I. Acharya, P. K. *Glories of India*, Allahabad, n.d.
II. Banerjee, G. N. *Hellenism in Ancient India*, Calcutta, 1919.
III. Raghavan, V. *Yantras or Mechanical Contrivances in Ancient India*, Bangalore, 1952.

MEDICINE. The ingredients used in the preparation of āyurvedic medicines covered well-nigh every natural substance available. The materia medica of the Hindus classifies hundreds of items of all kinds, and a thorough mastery of *dravya-vidyā*, 'substance knowledge', or an acquaintance with the general properties and specific action of medicinal substances, was considered indispensable for the proper functioning of a good physician.

These were first classified under animal, plant or mineral headings as follows: (*a*) *animal substances*: milk and its products, honey, flesh, bones, bile, fat (especially of the bear, alligator, ass), marrow, blood; hair, nails, claws, hoofs, horns, gallstones (the *gorochanā* or gallstones of the cow were esteemed for their therapeutic properties); urine, faeces and semen, especially of the elephant, horse, ass, sheep, and goat. Also mentioned among medicinal ingredients in the *Atharva-veda* are rotten fish, dog-flesh, animal saliva, pulverized shells, teeth scourings, feathers, insects, frogs and lice; (*b*) *plant substances*: fruit, flowers, seeds, buds, sap, herbs, leaves, thorns, bark, root, pith, sprouts, cinders of vegetable matter. Great care was taken in the gathering of plants. The land in which they grew had to be free from holes and burrows; not sandy, not mouldy, neither stony nor undulating. The plant, says the āyurveda text, must not be cut by a weapon of war, withered by frost, dried by the sun, rotted by water, or contaminated by insects; it must be plucked by a pious man while facing northward; (*c*) *mineral substances* included gold, silver, rocks, stones, salt. Mercury played a major part in alchemical remedies, as well as mica, sulphur, acids and ochre.

Āyurveda also classified substances according to their *rasa* or taste, since each taste is believed to have its own properties which produce definite effects. Thus, sweet (*madhura*) increases phlegm, chyle, flesh; appeases thirst and hunger; causes flatulence, worms and goitre; acid (*amla*) increases salivation and appetite; improves the digestion; causes heartburn; salt (*lavaṇa*) purifies the blood and stimulates digestion, but in excess gives headache, causes convulsions; pungent (*kaṭu*) provokes the appetite, lessens corpulence, purifies the blood, clears the head; bitter (*tikta*) stimulates the appetite, clears the complexion, reduces the heat of the body; astringent (*kashāya*) augments the action of any of the above if taken with it.

Anything taken internally both in sickness and in health was regarded as falling into the category of food (*āhāra*), medicine (*aushadha*), antidote (*agada*), elixir (*rasāyana*), and aphrodisiac (*vājīkaraṇa*).

Another scheme of classification followed certain fixed dichotomies, namely: hot* (*ushṇa*) or cold (*śīta*); heavy (*guru*) or light (*laghu*); sticky (*snigdha*) or dry (*rūksha*); energizing (*tīkshṇa*) or sluggish (*manda*); stationary (*sthira*) or fluid (*sara*); soft (*mṛidu*) or hard (*kaṭina*); clear (*viśada*) or slimy (*pichchhila*); smooth (*ślakshṇa*) or rough (*khara*); coarse (*sthūla*) or subtle (*sūkshma*); dense (*sāndra*) or liquid (*drava*).

Medicines were further considered from the point of view of their action (*karma*); potency (*śakti*); strength (*vīrya*); place of operation (*ādhi-kāraṇa*); time (*kāla*) of operation; mode (*upāya*) of operation; the maturing or ripening (*vipāka*) of the action; and their fruit or result (*phala*). There was besides an unknown, and inconceivable (*achintya*) manner in which a medicine operates, which is referred to as *prabhāva*, 'supernatural' or effulgent power. This is found in amulets, in unpleasant medicines with nasty ingredients prepared to drive away the seed of the disease, and in secret remedies compounded under certain astrological signs.

The study of medicines frequently assumed greater importance than the study of the disease. If the symptoms were prominent a medicine was prescribed for the symptoms, leaving the disease otherwise severely alone. Thus if a patient complained of excessive sweating he was given one of the 'sweat-suppressing' remedies, and if he had fever he was given a 'fever-losing' drug. For a combination of symptoms a polypharmaceutical syrup or bolus was prescribed. Already in the time of Charaka medicines were divided into fifty classes, and by what may be called the middle period of Hindu medicine the categories of drugs went into hundreds.

The chief types of drugs considered in terms of their effects are as follows: *brimhaṇīya* (fattening) or weight increasing; those producing the reverse effect are known as *lekhanīya* (attenuating), which reduce weight and size; *dīpanīya* (inflaming) or those which promote digestion and increase the appetite; the *rochaka* (stimulating) medicines, also increase the appetite, and are in addition stomachics, strengthening the action of the stomach; *svedanīya* (sweat-inducing), sudorific or diaphoretic medicines; the *sveda-nigrahaṇa* (sweat-suppressing) drugs produce the opposite effect; *mutra-virechanīya* (urine-inducing), diuretics to promote urine; *mutra-nigrahaṇa* (urine-suppressing); *ṛitu-vardhanīya* (menses-augmenting) a medicine that promotes or restores menses that have stopped i.e. an emmenagogue; its opposite is the *ṛitu-nigrahaṇa*, which inhibits the flow; *chardanīya* (vomit-causing), an emetic; its opposite is *vama-nigrahaṇa* (vomit-suppressing).

Other classes include: *bhedanīya* (splitting) which promotes excretions of all kinds; *saṁdhānīya* (coalescing), which accelerates the joining of fractured bones; *virechanīya* (opening), an aperient or laxative; *kashāya* (styptic), an astringent; *gvara-hara* (fever-losing), a febrifuge, or antipyretic; *kṛimi-ghna* (worm-killing), a vermifuge or anti-helminthic; *srāvaṇīya* (shedding), an abortifacient, causing abortion or miscarriage; *nidrā-kāraka* (sleep-making), a soporific; *pūti-ghna* (sepsis-killing), an antiseptic; *ākshepa-hara* (convulsion-losing), an anti-spasmodic; *stambha-hara* (paralysis-losing) an anti-paralysant; *vāta-ghna* (wind-killing) a carminative, to relieve flatulence; *nasya* (nasal), a sternutatory, to induce sneezing; *śula-ghna* (pain-killing) a sedative or analgesic; *snehopaga* (*sneha-upaga*, smoothness-producing), an emollient, used in poultices and fomentations.

There were many remedies of a general nature. The *jīvanīya* (life-giving) medicines or medicinal foods, which were calculated to prolong life; some of these were meant to prevent the effects of old age; others were meant to give one a feeling of well-being; *balya* (invigorating) were energizing medicines, to increase strength and vitality; others again were stimulating, tonic, restorative and analeptic.

There were medicines to improve the complexion, the hair and the voice; to promote cheerfulness, to remove phlegm, to promote the secretion of milk in mothers; to relieve hiccups, quench thirst, relieve body heat, remove cold from the bones, banish fatigue. There were medicines to increase nose discharge and to lessen it; to produce loose motions or constipate one; to change the texture and colour of faeces.

A special section was devoted in many texts to matters appertaining to sexual faculties. This was generally dealt with under the head of *vājīkaraṇa* (*see* virility), which prescribed drugs and methods for increasing virile power, and for improving the quality of the seminal fluid, as also for curing sterility.

Medicines were used in several forms such as *chūrṇa* or powders (prepared by pounding dried ingredients in a mortar), pastes (by grinding fresh ingredients on a stone and muller and adding some liquid), decoctions (extraction by boiling), infusions (steeping in hot or cold water or milk), emulsions (by mixing in oils), extracts (by various processes), or as pills, or boluses; or in the pure state.

Books

I. Ainslie, A. *Materia Medica of Hindustan*, 1826.
II. Basu, K. C. *Official Indigenous Drugs of India*, 1902.
III. Chakravarty, C. *A Comparative Study of Hindu Materia Medica*, 1929.
IV. Dutt, U. C. *The Materia Medica of the Hindus*, Calcutta, 1877.
V. Sastri, B. *The Medical Lore of the Ancient Hindus*, 1901.
VI. Srivastava, G. P. *History of Indian Pharmacy*, Calcutta, 2nd Ed., 1954.

MEDITATION is one of the chief aims of yogic mental exercises. The term *manaskāra*, 'mind-work', is applied to all mental operations specifically undertaken to increase the powers of the mind, improve the memory, help concentration, and develop the capacity for one-pointedness. Reading, reciting, memorizing, and other disciplines assist manaskāra; in later stages *āsanas, mantras, paramudrās* are combined with special manaskāra exercises for higher spiritual experience.

The enemies of all mental work are sloth (*tandrā*), lust (*kāmarāgo*), obstinacy (*abhiniveśa*), apathy (*styāna*) or the lack of disposition to work, doubt (*saṁśaya*) and so on. Having resolved to study and assumed the correct attitude towards it, one must practice assiduously. The essential requirements of manaskāra include: *abhyāsa*, persistence, practice, application; *niśchaya*, determination or resolve; *samādhāna*, single-mindedness or convergence of attention; *viveka*, sifting, discrimination, discernment; *saṁkalpa*, 'together doing', a gathering together of the faculties in order to achieve the end one has in view; *vichāra*, reflection or serious thought, careful and deliberate cogitation; *saṁyama*, 'together going', a mobilization of all the mental faculties; *ekāgratā*, one-pointedness, or exclusive attention to the subject of one's thoughts.

To develop concentration a practitioner may choose any one of the **trāṭaka,** 'fixing' techniques which are widely used in Hindu occult practice. Trāṭaka is usually performed by gazing fixedly at a small object, or focusing one's mind's eye on a certain point. These points of concentration are known as *lakshya*, 'marks', and different goals are achieved by concentrating on different lakshya. Five or six bodily lakshya are especially favoured, e.g. the crown of the head; the point just above the junction of the eyebrows; the tip of the nose; the navel; the tip of the erect phallus; the perineum, the space between the genitals and the rectum. While the eyes are thus fixed the 'diffused attention is gathered together' and, by the process of 'single pointedness' (*ekāgratā*) centred on the subject of contemplation.

Several methods of trāṭaka are employed, each regarded as proper for a particular purpose: (*a*) staring at a minute object, such as a mustard seed or a speck on a white wall, without blinking, until the tears come to the eyes. This is called *vaishṇavi-mudrā* by Vaishṇavites, and *śāṁbhavī-mudrā* (Śiva-gesture) by Śaivites, since the method was used by these gods for their meditations. It is described as being most effective with the mind concentrated on the energy 'moving in the void', for by means of it some of the energy is absorbed by the practitioner; (*b*) turning the eyeballs upwards and attempting to look at a spot between the brows, with eyes either shut or open. This is called *chāchari*, and is a good means of concentration preparatory to projecting one's thoughts towards another person; (*c*) fixing the eyes on a distant object like a cloud or mountain peak, until all surrounding objects disappear. It is useful in directing the thoughts outwards after chāchari; (*d*) fixing the eyes on the sun and letting its rays 'stream inwards' to illumine and warm the subtle inner channels; (*e*) fixing the eyes on the *nāsikāgra*, 'nose-tip', and concentrating on the sahasrāra. Called the *agochari* it is a method of inducing samādhi (trance) and may be done with eyes open or shut. The *Bhagavadgītā* recommends sitting still, gazing at the tip of the nose, and meditating on Kṛishṇa, for the attainment of peace culminating in deliverance; (*f*) mentally focusing the eyes on certain letters of the Sanskrit alphabet, or gazing at a sacred picture, a *maṇḍala* (occult diagram), an image, the flame of a lamp, or some bright shining thing; (*g*) fixing the eyes on the tip of one's erect member or on the female yoni, and focusing the thoughts on Kāma god of lust. This is one of the secret forms of trantrik concentration which is meant to draw down the sexual powers of the deity.

It is to be borne in mind that like other psycho-physiological practices trāṭaka can be injurious, because although it assists concentration it is not, in Buddhist phraseology, always 'right concentration', and can lead to dangerous paths. According to the textbooks trāṭaka even in its simple form will enable a person 'to see through all substances and to know what is happening in different places'. The practice is extremely ancient in India, and evidence of its use can be found in an Indus Valley statuette (*c.* 1500 BC) representing a man with half-closed lids, looking at the tip of his nose. He is probably a hierophant, as the trefoil pattern of his robe suggests a priestly office.

It is understood that the ultimate purpose of all serious manaskāra operations is the attainment of the trance* state of samādhi, and the development of the powers of concentration are only minor exercises leading up to the three pre-samādhi stages of yoga known as *pratyāhāra, dhāraṇā* and *dhyāna.*

Pratyāhāra, 'withholding', is a higher meditative technique which consists of withdrawing the senses (*indriya*) from outward distraction and turning the mind inwards. The commonest method of doing this is the actual physical closing of the organs of sense, as in the *shaṇmukhi-mudrā* (*see* orifices); another involves fixing the gaze on the tip of the nose or between the brows or on a bright object, as in trāṭaka. Other methods require mastery of the techniques of prāṇayāma and the āsanas, mantras and paramudrās. But the highest form of pratyāhāra is the power of enlightened discernment which deprives the senses of their natural 'lust' for external satisfaction. Only such discernment, and control of the passions can 'stop the traffic of the senses' and cause the mental faculties to become 'like a lamp in a windless place' and prepare the aspirant for samādhi.

After pratyāhāra comes **dhāraṇā** (*dhar*, 'hold') or concentration. The texts define it: 'To hold the mind motionless, that is dhāraṇā'. This stage is regarded as the beginning of the actual meditative process, and without dhāraṇā no higher spiritual experience is held to be possible. The ideal state is for the mind to be blank, but so blank that it is not even aware of its own blankness.

This stage is followed by **dhyāna,** 'meditation', intellectual contemplation or ecstatic musing on a single subject or on spiritual realities. It is the last of the possible mental processes and stands on the threshold of samādhi. In the early stages of dhyāna a deity or one's guru are meditated upon; later the mind is centred on 'the point where the unmanifest becomes manifest'. The step beyond is samādhi, which is no longer on the mental plane, and is thus beyond the operations of manaskāra.

Books

See under Psychology and Yoga.

MENSTRUATION, known by a number of terms, but commonly referred to as *rajas*, was early recognized as the physiological manifestation of a girl's maturity or ability to bear children. Vātsyāyana speaks of it as 'that illness that comes without being called, cannot be concealed, cannot be revealed, and yet is always present'. In an Āyurvedic text it is said that rajas starts at the age of thirteen, lasts till the age of forty-eight, occurs once every 'moon' and continues for three days.

A woman in her periods is *aśaucha*, 'unclean', and the degrees of her impurity for the three days are described as follows: on the first day it is as if she were an untouchable pariah, on the second day as if she had killed a brāhmin; on the third day she is in a state intermediate between the first two. During her monthly 'uncleanliness' a woman is isolated, either in a separate part of the house, or in a separate house altogether, with no communication with the outside world, so that she might not contaminate anyone by her presence, speech or look. Several women in a similar condition may be placed together but must not talk.

Among the primitive Urāli, a jungle tribe of Trichinopoly and Madura, women are isolated in special shelters constructed on trees about fifty feet above the ground, and instructions are shouted to them from a distance. In northern Bengal as soon as a woman's period begins she goes with all haste to a special rush hut standing in the fields. Among many communities e.g. the Nāirs, when a man builds a house there is always a room set aside for the sequestration of women during menses, the puerperium and childbirth. In Travancore the queens had a palace of their own for these occasions (IV, p. 606).

During her periods a woman had to sit completely idle and observe the following precautions and prohibitions: (1) she remained strictly continent; for a woman even to desire a man at this time was a heinous sin. According to Manu cohabitation at such a time destroyed a man's brain, energy, eyesight and manhood; (2) she was to avoid sleeping by day; (3) she could not touch a child in case her touch should blight the child; (4) she was to refrain from weeping, loud laughter, and even speech; or the hearing of harsh sounds; (5) she was not to run, ride, or indulge in violent physical exertion in any form; (6) she could not rinse her mouth, bathe, wash, anoint her body with oil, comb her hair, use cosmetics and collyrium or pare her nails; (7) she was not allowed to cook since what she touched was not fit to be eaten; a spare diet was sent to her; (8) she was not allowed to think of the gods. The *Mahābhārata* and the Manusmṛiti prohibit a menstruating woman from even looking at the image of a deity; (9) she had scrupulously to observe the rule of remaining indoors, preferably in a dark room. Strong sunlight it was believed could fertilize a woman at this time.

On the fourth day after its commencement the flow should have stopped. The woman could now purify herself with ablutions, first using cowdung and water; then using saffron and washing again. Returning home she had to drink *pañchagavya*, a mixture of the five products of a cow. The rajas period is intimately linked with erotic desire in women. It is often called *śoṇita*, 'crimson', suggesting both the colour of blood and increased desire, and its onset marks a time of heightened passion. Marital relations could be resumed on the fourth day, and on the seventh day, i.e. three days after the cessation of the flow, the woman was permitted to enter a temple.

The period immediately following rajas is known as *ṛitu*, the 'right' season for sexual union, because it is favourable for conception. Strictly ṛitu is the period from the fourth day onwards till the twelfth day (the eleventh is inauspicious), during which a woman can receive the male seed and bear fruit. It is considered a crime to let it pass wasted, and intercourse was obligatory during this period. Ṛitu is thought to be a thing of extreme malignancy which can only be neutralized by marital relations. A husband's virility is increased by intercourse with his wife in ṛitu, but it causes a blight if not allayed. The auspicious red dot (*see* caste mark) worn on the forehead by a married woman is a sign of *saubhāgya*, or blessedness in a married woman; it is said to be the outward token of her utilized ṛitu, signifying that her husband is alive. Tantrik literature goes into great detail regarding the psychic potencies of the ṛitu and sets forth precise methods of using these for magical ends.

Virgins who have reached puberty and widows before the menopause place in jeopardy the household where they dwell. The lawgivers declared that it was a grave sin for a girl to have her first period while she was yet in her father's care, for the terrible force of the first ṛitu drew down certain calamity on all the household and caused the ancestors to suffer great torment. It was particularly necessary that the first ṛitu should be 'utilized', and it became binding on a man to get his daughter married before she reached puberty. The lawgivers condemned to hell the parents in whose house the first ṛitu of a girl was wasted for want of a husband for her. This was one of the underlying causes of the institution of child* marriage.

So seriously was the 'waste' of the ṛitu regarded, that an adult woman who had no husband could ask anyone she wished to satisfy her sexual urge at that time, and it was the man's religious duty to do so. From the *Mahābhārata* and Purāṇas it is seen that women took full advantage of this liberty (II, p. 314). To illustrate, the *Mahābhārata* relates that when the sage Dhaumya was away from his hermitage, one of his wives was in ṛitu, and his co-wives asked Uttaṅka, a pupil of Dhaumya (*see* Uddālaka) to ensure that it did not pass away fruitlessly (V, p. 5).

In certain places the images of goddesses are believed to have the 'monthly sickness' like ordinary mortals. In Travancore a public ceremony is performed about eight to ten times a year in the temples of the patron goddess. It is a purification ceremony in connection with her rajas. A cloth wrapped around the image is found to be discoloured with red, and the image is removed to a separate shed. The cloth is sent to the women of the village for examination, and is then washed by a washerwoman and never used again by the goddess. There is a great demand among the people for these cloths which are kept as holy relics (I, p. 435). A caste in South India, the Pokunātivaru, claim to have their origin from such a cloth thrown away by the goddess Pārvatī (III, p. 136). In Chuṅganur much importance is attached to the rajas of the goddess Pārvatī, and a similar ritual is kept up in Kāmākhyā in Assam, for the goddess there.

Books

I. Briffault, R. *The Mothers*, 2nd Ed., London, 1952, Vol. II.
II. Chakraberty, C. *The Cultural History of the Hindus*, Calcutta, n.d.
III. Dare, Paul. *Indian Underworld*, London, 1938.
IV. Dingwall, E. J. (Ed.) *Woman: An Historical & Anthropological Compendium*, London, 1935, Vol. I.
V. Upadhyaya, S. C. (Ed.) *Kamasutra of Vatsyayana*, Bombay, 1961.

MESOPOTAMIA, like Egypt, was in close contact with India for many centuries. The Dravidians themselves are believed to have been a Sumerian people who had migrated from the Euphrates valley and settled in India in prehistoric times. They may have come both by the land route via the south Persian littoral as well as the sea route via the Persian Gulf and, being a riverine people, colonized the Indus Valley first, introducing into the primitive Indian communal settlements a knowledge of architecture and irrigation, the use of iron, the idea of civic organization, and the other arts and activities associated with these. It is not improbable that later immigrants from Mesopotamia also settled in India from time to time. Some authorities identify the Kassites who in the eighteenth century BC invaded Babylonia, with the Keśins who not long after settled in India under their own ruler.

At all events contact between the two countries was closely maintained for several centuries. Mohenjodaro seals and other objects of art from the Indus Valley have been discovered at Kish, Ur, Lagash, and other Mesopotamian sites. What is probably Indian teak was found in the ruins of the Chaldean city of Ur, and in the palace of Nebuchadnezzar III. The library of Assurbanipal contains ideographs for Indian cotton, and in the time of Buddha Indian traders took the first peacock by sea to Babylon.

The Babylonians on their part visited Indian ports with their merchandise, and as the demand for their products increased they established themselves inland. Among their varied commodities were slaves and virgins for the harems of kings and nobles. In all likelihood there was a Babylonian colony on the border of India during the Greek period, for Strabo relates that the followers of Alexander found a Babylonian trade emporium at Taxila, which included a slave and marriage market.

Assyria followed in the wake of Babylon, and left a few faintly discernible marks on Indian history. D. R. Bhandarkar and A. P. Banerji-Sastri suggest that the Asuras of the *Ṛig-veda* were Assyrians who had settled in Magadha in pre-Vedic times and established an independent kingdom. Indeed, as another authority points out, 'the similarity of the name Ahura (Asura in Vedic) and Ashur, the eponymous god of Assyria, is striking' (VIII, p. 122). Arrian states that Indians living between the Indus and modern Kabul were in his time subject to the Assyrians. There is also the now discredited legend told by Ctesias and repeated by Diodorus Siculus that Semiramis, the mythical queen of Nineveh had once invaded India (IX, p. 8).

The assertion of paramountcy, known in Hindu polity as *digvijaya*, or the conquest of contiguous areas, in which Indian rulers indulged from earliest times, was originally termed *asura-vijaya*, or demon's conquest, in the

Arthaśāstra. Says Raychaudhuri, 'The name may have been derived from the Assyrians, the ruthlessness of whose warfare is well known' (X, p. 537).

Assyria's interest in India, like Babylon's, was commercial rather than imperial, and the quinqueremes of Nineveh returned from Indian ports laden, not with the spoils of war but with many bartered cargoes rich and strange. They brought spices, precious stones, cotton fabrics, exotic fruits, plants and animals. On the obelisk of Shalmaneser III are engraved some of the creatures purchased from the lands of the east: Bactrian camels, Indian elephants, and apes from the Vindhyan hills.

From the civilization that flourished in the valley of the Tigris and Euphrates came several of the legends that are now part of Hindu mythology, and many words and concepts that are now regarded as part of Hinduism. Professor Dasgupta believes that the early materialistic philosophy of India was of foreign origin, subsequently modified in India, and that 'probably the Lokāyata doctrines had their beginnings in the preceding Sumerian civilization'. The famous Creation hymn that was later added to the tenth book of the *Ṛig-veda* bears traces of having been derived from a common source with the story of Creation as found in the first chapter of Genesis; its Sumerian origin, through the Dravidians, is considered probable. The story of the Flood and of the Ark which carried Manu with the seven wise men and all kinds of seeds, is an obvious variant of the Babylonian tradition of the Deluge and the epic of Gilgamesh. The general concept of *vāhanas*, or gods using men and animals as mounts, may similarly be of Mesopotamian origin.

Hindu astrology, as in fact all astrology, was deeply influenced by the Chaldeans, the greatest mathematicians and astrologers of antiquity. It is to the Chaldeans that the Hindu science of celestial divination owes the system of the *nakshatras*, the traditional division of the sky into twenty-four sections, and the week into seven days named after the sun, moon and five planets, as also the art of prognostication by the disposition of the constellations.

The *Atharva-veda* contains many curious terms and notions, that are attributed to pre-Aryan and Mesopotamian influences. The magical lore of this work is believed to be of Chaldean origin (II, p. 30), although doubtless Maga influences are also present. A number of hymns in this Veda bristle with foreign words (*urukrama, urugāya, urukshaya, urvaśī, urugūla, tābuva*), which scholars like B. G. Tilak and others, believed were of Chaldean derivation. Taimāta of the *Atharva-veda* is equated with Tiamat, the sea-dragon who in the Babylonian creation story opposed Bel Marduk; Apsu of the Babylonians with Āpas (waters) of the Vedas. Urugūla in the *Atharva-veda* is said to correspond to the Babylonian goddess Gula, wife of Marduk, chief deity of Babylon. Vilagi, the serpent in the *Atharva-veda* is a god of the same name in Akkadian myth. Helavo of the Brāhmaṇas was the battlecry of the Asuras and is related to the Semitic Illu, or God, whose name the Asuras invoked when they went forth to give battle to the enemy. Parallels are traced between the ziggurat, the stepped-pyramid of the Euphrates plain, and the *śikhara* of South Indian temples. The custom of urn-burial found in scattered sites in India is also thought to have been taken from Babylonian practice.

To Lydia, further north, the world owes that useful commodity, coined money; and to Assyria, through Indian sources, the English-speaking world probably owes its name, 'cash'. Kārshāpaṇa, a small silver coin of the Jākata period, was named after the Sanskrit word paṇa, prefixed by the foreign word, karsha. This prefix, according to one school of philologists, is traceable to the Assyrian word, *karshu,* meaning berry (used in barter); it is found in Koṅkaṇi as kaśu, was later merged with the Portuguese caixa, and passed into English currency, as cash.

Books

I. Agrawala, V. S. 'Ancient Contacts Between India and the Middle East', *Hindustan Times Weekly,* New Delhi, May 6, 1951.

II. Bhandarkar, D. R. *Some Aspects of Ancient Indian Culture,* Madras, 1940.

III. Dasgupta, S. N. *A History of Indian Philosophy,* Vol. III, Cambridge, 1922.

IV. Fabri, C. L. 'Mesopotamian & Early Indian Art Comparisons', *Oriental Studies of the Musée Guimet,* Paris, 1923.

V. Jairazbhoy, R. A. *Foreign Influences in Ancient India,* Bombay, 1963.

VI. Kennedy, J. 'Early Commerce of India with Babylon', *Journal of the Royal Asiatic Society,* London, 1898, pp. 241 ff.

VII. Leemans, W. F. *Foreign Trade in the Old Babylonian Period,* Leiden, 1960.

VIII. Masson-Oursel, P., *et al. Ancient India and Indian Civilization,* London, 1934.

IX. Rawlinson, H. G. *Intercourse Between India & The Western World,* Cambridge, 1916.

X. Raychaudhuri, H. *Political History of Ancient India,* Calcutta, 6th Ed., 1953.

METALS. Ancient India shared with many other cultures the knowledge of the mining and working of metals (*loha* or *dhātu*). The Indus Valley people worked metallic copper and were familiar with gold, silver, bronze and lead. By 1500 BC tin was known, and by 900 BC iron. Steel came into use about 500 BC and brass followed a few centuries later. A comprehensive account of ores, metals and minerals with their extraction and working is found in the *Arthaśāstra* and in the early works on Āyurveda such as those of Charaka and Suśruta. *Loha-śāstra,* 'metallurgy', was one of the basic crafts of Indian culture.

Of the principal metals, eight, known as the *ashṭa-dhātu,* 'eight metals', were believed to be of supreme importance. The lists vary as usual, although gold, silver, copper and bronze figure in all. Gold (*suvarṇa* or *svarṇa*), the perfection of metals, was called a fragment of the sun. The word is said to be derived either from *su-varṇa,* 'beautiful colour', or *sva-arṇa,* 'self-surging', or *svarṇa,* 'heavenly'. Gold, rustless, stainless, pure, was the deity of metals, and was always found in abundance in India. India paid her tribute to Darius of Persia in gold dust, all other vassal states paying in silver. Herodotus tells of the Indian custom of employing 'gold-digging ants' to obtain the precious commodity, a phrase which continues to puzzle posterity. The horns of the ants mentioned by Pliny may refer to the pickaxes of the miners which in

Ladakh and Tibet were made of the horns of wild sheep mounted on wooden handles. Another suggested interpretation is that they were dogs. It is known that the gold diggers of north-west India and Central Asia up to the Gobi desert used watch-dogs to guard their camps, and these dogs may have been referred to by a word which also meant 'ants'.

Silver, or *rūpya*, 'of good appearance', was regarded as a fragment of the moon. Amulets of this metal were believed to soothe fevers, cool the brain, draw down potent influences from the region of the moon. Small quantities of silver were often added to baser metals in the manufacture of receptacles, utensils, bells, and ornaments in order to lend them sanctity.

The term *loha*, applied to iron, is also used for metals generally. The most famous example of all artifacts made of iron by the Indians is the Iron Pillar of Meharaulī, near the Kutb Minār, Delhi. It was erected by the Śaka king Chandravarman (*c.* AD 325), and some authorities hold that Mathurā was probably the original site of this pillar and that it may have been the work of foreign metallurgists. The pillar is twenty-three feet high and consists of a single shaft of almost pure, malleable, rustless iron, six tons in weight, welded to a tapering cylinder. After 1500 years it still shows no signs of rusting. Writing in 1811, Ball says, 'It is not many years since the production of such a pillar would have been an impossibility in the largest foundries in the world, and even now there are comparatively few where a similar mass of metal could be turned out'. Dr Ray accepting the conclusion of researchers believes that the low humidity of Delhi is one of the factors in the preservation of the iron pillar, and concludes, 'This should lay to rest all speculations, and eliminate all hypotheses, regarding the alleged intrinsic superiority of the iron of the Delhi Pillar, so far as its corrosion resistance is concerned'. The fact remains that it is one of the most extraordinary productions of metallurgical art.

Steel or *sāraloha* ('fine-iron') began to be used in India by about 500 BC. It was of excellent quality and in time became known throughout the ancient and medieval world. The art of tempering steel to which the medieval world owed the so-called Damascus sword, was perfected in India. But whether in such processes as Varāhamihira's lay the secret of hardening steel is questionable: 'Plunge the steel red hot into a solution of plantain ashes in whey'; or 'Apply to the steel the juice of the arka plant, the glue from the horn of a sheep the dung of a pigeon and mouse. Then make the steel thus treated red hot, and finally sprinkle with horse milk, blood, fat or bile.'

Copper (*tāmra*) was believed to have magical properties since it had its own inner glow. It was used in the rites of the Mother Goddess (*see* Kāmarūpa). Bronze, an alloy of copper and tin, was also widely used for ceremonial purposes. There is no specific word for bronze, but the term *pañcha-lauha*, 'five-irons', covered the alloys related to bronze. Brass and copper were often classified with the bronzes and these metals, either alone or together, or combined with tin (*trapu*), zinc (*vaṅgaja*) and lead (*sīsaka*) with a little gold and silver added for good fortune were frequently used for statuary work.

Brass (*rīti*) seems to have first been introduced to north India through Chinese trade. It was regarded as a 'shinable' metal which reflects light from outside but does not have its own glow as copper does. Its primary significance is for the ear, as it has qualities of resonance, and is said to be self-sounding. It is widely used for ceremonial utensils. Related to it is the brass bell-metal (*kāṁsya*).

Books

I. Ball, V. *Economic Geology of India*, 1881.

II. Banerjee, M. N. 'Iron and Steel in the Rigvedic Age', *Indian Historical Quarterly*, Calcutta, V, 3 (1929), 432–40.

III. Banerjee, M. N. 'On Metals and Metallurgy in Ancient India', *Indian Historical Quarterly*, III, 1 (1927), 121–33 & III, 4 (1927), 793–802.

IV. Britton, S. C. 'Iron in Ancient India', *Nature*, August 18, 1934.

V. Neogi, P. 'Copper in Ancient India'. *Bulletin of the Indian Association for the Cultivation of Science*, Calcutta, 1918.

VI. Ray, P. (Ed.) *History of Chemistry in Ancient and Medieval India*, Calcutta, 1956.

VII. Smith, V. A. 'The Iron Pillar of Delhi', *Journal of the Royal Asiatic Society*, 1897, 1–18.

METEOROLOGY. The study of the weather, climate and seasonal atmospheric changes, was known in Sanskrit as *ākāśa-vidyā*, 'atmosphere lore'. A great deal of information on this branch of knowledge lies buried in books on astronomy and astrology, but there is also an extraordinarily rich tradition of folk lore on the same subject.

The mythological origin of atmospheric phenomena and natural convulsions is everywhere taken for granted: earthquakes result from the yawning, twisting and trembling of the cosmological creatures that support the earth; eclipses are caused by Rāhu* devouring the sun. But parallel with these there is much sound information based on actual observation and deduction.

The months of the year and the *nakshatras* of the moon are allotted specific potencies, and the behaviour of men on earth is largely conditioned by the position of the heavenly bodies. A study of these also helps in prognosticating the kind of weather that will prevail in a particular season or year. The month of *Pausha* (December–January) is believed to be a miniature index on the state of the weather during the forthcoming twelve months, every two and a half days reflecting the conditions of one month of the ensuing year.

The control of weather was early related to ritual acts. Songs to the Rain God, ceremonial spinning, dances in the nude (*see* Rājbansi dance*) and union with a celibate (*see* Ṛishyaśṛiṅga) were believed to bring down rain. Weather was predicted by various kinds of natural phenomena: from the colour of sunrise and sunset; the presence of clouds and their types (twenty-three kinds of clouds and cloud movements were distinguished); the strength of winds (flags were used as wind indicators); the halo around the moon; the haze of the atmosphere; the behaviour of animals, birds and insects; the condition of trees, plants and flowers.

There was believed to be an intimate connection between natural phenomena and the lives of great men, and the great events of human history. The birth of holy men is presaged by the appearance of stars, by the general air of expectation that infuses animals and in fact all nature. Great and bloody battles are accompanied by darkness, earthquake and thunder, and preternatural rumblings in the bowels of the earth. The night-time and graveyard animals show signs of excitement: thus owls are heard hooting, and jackals howl incessantly. Ominous sounds are heard all around, which actually emanate from ghouls who impatiently await their feast of flesh and blood.

Books

I. Gupta, S. Sen. *Rain in Indian Life and Lore,* Calcutta, 1963.
II. Sen, A. K. *Weather Science in Ancient India,* 1911.

MICROCOSM. The concept of man as a microcosm reflecting the greater cosmos was as fully developed in India as in Ancient Greece. Much of Hindu mysticism is based on the belief that every individual is a *sūkshma-jagat,* 'minute world'. It is held that whatever exists in the universe exists in the human body, which is indeed a true microcosm. One can develop one's potentiality by controlling the natural forces around one, but the signal triumph for man is the understanding and control of the forces within, since in these inner forces are comprehended all the powers and potencies of the cosmic plenum.

Man is Brahma, spirit, soul, sky, cloud, the elements, and all matter of which the animal, vegetable and mineral worlds are fashioned. All truth is within; all states of heaven and hell; the universe with all its objects and localities; space with all its dimensions; time in all its divisions and subdivisions. The complete wheel of duration, continuity and eternity (*kāla-chakra,* 'time-wheel') is within the compass of man's existence.

Furthermore, in man are found all the contradictions and conflicts of the universe. These opposites may be perceived in the dual nature of human sexuality, since every individual is both male and female (*see* androgyny) and within himself can achieve fulfilment. This is reflected in the whole notion of gender* that infuses much of tantrik and esoteric Hinduism. The resolution or fusion of this male-female polarity into a single non-dual unity is the object of much speculation and practice. The Upanishads compare men and women to the sacrificial ground and declare that through the union of man and woman great sacrifices can be performed. Man's speech is the fuel, his breath the smoke, the tongue the flames, his eyes the coals, the ear the spark, his fluid the oblation, the vulva the altar and *maithuna* the sacrifice.

The basic idea underlying the concept of the microcosm is that the universe and the human body are composed of identical material, operate on the same principles and in the same manner. If one can develop and express the forces lying dormant within one, one can master the world. In meditation* the *lakshya* or points of concentration are believed to be heavenly spheres and the abode of the deities, and the various *vyoman,* or 'firmaments' are all located in the body. A further elaboration of this idea is found in the precise analogies drawn between the cosmological spheres and the centres of the subtle and gross bodies. Mount Meru is the *merudaṇḍa* (*see* Chakra); the Ganges is equated with the *iḍā* and the Jamnā with the *piṅgalā* (*see* nāḍi); Prayāga is in the *brahmarandhra*; the Sarasvatī is the *sushumṇā*; Kailāsa the *sahasrāra*. The earth is present in the bones; the waters in the bodily fluids; the atmosphere in the vital airs; fire in the power of the *mūlādhāra*; the *prāṇa* in the air we breathe. The erogenous zones are the crosspoints in the great roadways of the cosmos.

If the Ganges is within the body, then clearly pilgrimages are unnecessary. From this follows the notion that all forms and trappings of religion, the scriptures, the temples and priests, the sacraments and ceremonies, are all superfluous, since the Ganges, Banāras, Kailāsa, temples, shrines and so on, are within oneself.

This doctrine was open to grave abuse. From it stemmed the philosophy of *dehavāda*, the 'body-way' of salvation, or ultimate realization through perfection of the body and physical culture*, which accounts for that peculiar feature basic to much of Hinduism, namely, anthropolatry, or the worship of man. It leads beyond the search for god within man, and seeks means to draw down and incorporate god in one's own person, as in *nyāsa*; identifies god and man, and in certain rites presumes that man can receive worship from the gods themselves. (II, p. 210.)

Books

I. Biswas, A. K. *The Heavenly & Bodily Spheres in Hinduism*, 1902.
II. Eliade, M. *Yoga, Immortality & Freedom*, New York, 1958.

MILINDAPAÑHO, 'The Questions of Milinda', a Pāli masterpiece, dated between 150 BC and AD 100 by an author or authors unknown. Written in the form of a dialogue between the Bactrian Greek king Menander (Pāli: Milinda) and the Buddhist sage Nāgasena, it sets forth the arguments by which the sage wins over the Greek monarch to the Buddhist faith. The story opens with a description of the king in his capital at Śākala (Siālkoṭ) where he meets certain brāhmin sages and in argument soon reduces them to silence. Menander expresses his disappointment: 'India is empty. People here can only prate!' The king is advised to meet one more sage before giving up; he is the Buddhist Nāgasena who happens to be passing through the capital. In the long discussion that follows the king is convinced and converted to Buddhism.

Much doubt has been cast on the historical basis of this story. The work is thoroughly Hellenistic in character and tone and was probably originally written in Greek and translated into Pāli. The author of the first part of the book was well acquainted with the Greek classics and was quite at home in the current Hellenistic Greek of his day. Rhys Davids calls the *Milindapañho* 'the only prose work composed in ancient India which would be considered from the modern point of view, a successful work of art'. Louis Finot observed that the restraint, vitality and freshness of the dialogue resembled the Socratic dialogue rather than anything Indian. The ideal city pictured in the second part of the book is the only Utopia in Indian literature, and suggests the author's familiarity with the *Republic* of Plato. It seemed, as Tarn says, that 'at some time or other the author had read Greek literature or breathed Greek air'.

In a list of people quoted in the text the order is given as Yonakas (Greeks), kshattriyas, brāhmins and householders, and it is not likely that anyone but a Greek would have put the Greeks at the head of the list. The term '*Yonaka*' is not the usual Sanskrit word (which is *Yavana*), nor is it the Pāli word (which is *Yona*). Yonaka is in fact taken from the current Hellenistic Greek of the time, and bodily carried into the Pāli translation.

Further mystery is added to the subject by the fact that in its important details this Indian masterpiece lacks verisimilitude to Indian conditions, and it is therefore better referred to a Greek or Hellenized author. Again, the second part is not only of a later date than the first part but is also by a different hand. And Nāgasena, the sage of the book, is not known to be a historical personage at all. His antecedents have been thoroughly investigated and he has been found to be a fictional character. He had such an extraordinary memory that he got by heart the whole Buddhist canon after hearing it recited once, and mastered its meaning at the second recital. As for Menander becoming a Buddhist and entering the Order, Tarn says, 'it may be dismissed at once'.

Books

I. Davids, C. A. F. *The Milinda Questions*, London, 1930.
II. Davids, T. W. Rhys (Ed.) *The Questions of King Milinda*, 2 vols, Oxford, 1890–94.
III. Dutt, S. *The Buddha and Five After-Centuries*, London, 1957.
IV. Horner, I. B. *Milinda's Questions*, 2 vols., London, 1964.
V. Tarn, W. W. *The Greeks in Bactria and India*, London, 1938.
VI. Trenckner, V. (Ed.) *The Milindapanho*, London (reprinted), 1962.

MĪMĀṀSĀ (from *man*, 'think'), one of the six orthodox systems of Hindu philosophy, founded by **Jaimini** (*c.* 200 BC). He was a pupil of Bādarāyaṇa, and was also said to have helped Vyāsa to arrange the Veda, and to have founded an Upanishadic school.

Strictly the term Mīmāṁsā is applied to the investigation of the Vedic texts, and in philosophy to a system of Vedic interpretation, especially of the Brāhmaṇas and Mantras, with the object of correctly performing the Vedic rituals and ceremonies. Renou called it 'the jurisprudence of the ritual act'. Jaimini in his text, the *Mīmāṁsā-sūtra* (present version *c.* AD 200–450) reduced the traditional interpretations to writing.

Mīmāṁsā accepts the philosophical tenets of the other orthodox schools, but holds that knowledge alone cannot give salvation, for the soul must fulfil itself through action or religious ritual. Ceremonial, rather than philosophy, is emphasized. Belief in the existence of God was not incumbent on the *mīmāṁsaka* or follower of the Mīmāṁsā system. Without right action, or dharma, knowledge is fruitless and true happiness unattainable. Right action confers merit and yields benefits by generating an 'invisible effect', for it is the means of planting the seeds that fructify in the next life. A sacrificial act of apparently only ceremonial value brings forth rewards that are manifested in the future.

There is an elaborate epistemology in Mīmāṁsā. Jaimini believed in the self-inherent authority of the Vedas which he regarded as being above and independent of any authority; independent even of divine revelation. Verbal testimony or *śabda* (*see* Sound) was regarded as the only means by which knowledge could be obtained. For this reason it became necessary to perfect a system of scriptural interpretation, and Mīmāṁsā therefore lays down rules for resolving and explaining the obscure or doubtful passages and discrepancies in the Vedic texts, and ways of discussing and refuting wrong views, and presents a clear cut method of interpretation. The contents of the Vedas are exhaustively classified, elaborated and interpreted as injunctions (*vidhi*), prohibitions (*nishedha*), and so on (*see* Law). The grammatical rules and literary devices employed in Vedic ritual are examined, analysed and likewise interpreted. Correct performance, correct enunciation, stress on accents, are all emphasized in Mīmāṁsā.

The Mīmāṁsā system of philosophy is also known as the *Pūrva-mīmāṁsā* (early Mīmāṁsā) to distinguish it from the *Uttara-mīmāṁsā* (later Mīmāṁsā) or the Vedānta system. It is also known as *Karma-mīmāṁsā* since it stresses action or ritual; and *Vākya-śāstra* or the study of words.

Books

I. Keith, A. B. *Karma Mimamsa*, Calcutta, 1921.
II. Sandal, M. L. *Introduction to the Mimamsa Sutras of Jaimini*, Allahabad, 1925.
III. Sastri, P. *Introduction to Purva Mimamsa*, Banaras, 1924.
IV. Thadani, N. V. *Mimamsa. The Secret of the Sacred Books of the Hindus*, Delhi, 1952.

MĪNĀKSHĪ (*mīna-akshī*, 'fish-eye'), tutelary goddess of South India, whose origins are obscured by later Śaivite legends, which attempted to absorb her into the cycle of myths connected with the gods of the north. She is generally regarded as the daughter of Kubera*, but there are many other legends about her birth.

It is said that Indra, while wandering about trying to atone for the sin of having killed Vṛitra, who was a brāhmin, accidentally brushed against an upright stone and felt the burden of his guilt slip off his conscience. Realizing that this must be a true liṅga of Śiva he gathered some golden lilies from a nearby pond and worshipped the stone. He was observed by a merchant who whispered the secret to his private deity, Kulaśekhara. Kulaśekhara thereupon worshipped the liṅga himself, and ordered that homage should henceforth be paid to Śiva.

Kulaśekhara's son Malayodhvaja being without issue performed a sacrifice to obtain a son, but instead of a son got a daughter. The child was very beautiful and had elongated fish-shaped eyes, whence her name, Mīnākshī, but she also had a fish-like odour from her body and possessed three breasts. She became a great warrior and made many conquests, until Śiva appeared to her in the form of Sundareśvar (Beauty-Lord) and she immediately became maidenly and shy, her fish odour vanished and her third breast disappeared, all signifying that Śiva was her lord.

Historically, Mīnākshī may have been a princess of an early Pāṇḍyan dynasty, whose patron deity was Kulaśekhara. Being defeated by a Śaivite ruler she may have married him and a Śaivite form of worship prevailed in the kingdom thereafter. Her son was Ugra.

According to the traditional account, the goddess Mīnākshī agreed to marry Śiva and the solemnities were arranged. But the maternal uncle (or brother) did not appear in time and the auspicious moment passed, so that the nuptials had to be put off till the following year. The great festival of Madura is still annually celebrated in the sumptuous temple of Mīnākshī. Each spring Mīnākshī's maternal uncle is summoned from his home in a neighbouring village to solemnize the marriage. Before the actual marriage an inauspicious sneeze from his cortège compels them to postpone the ceremony for twelve months. The divine couple reside in separate temples as though the union of the Mother Goddess Mīnākshī and the god Śiva still awaits its consummation.

Books

I. Elmore, W. T. *Dravidian Gods in Modern Hinduism*, Madras, 1925.
II. Godbole, R. K. *The of Gods Maharashtra*, Poona, 1912.
III. Shiner, R. *The Lesser of Gods Hinduism*, 1928.
IV. Whitehead, H. *The Village Gods of South India*, London, 2nd Ed., 1921.

MINERALS are spoken of in Sanskrit as *khānija*, 'pit-born', since they come from the bowels of the earth. That minerals are not inanimate is eloquently set forth in Jain philosophy which emphasises that everything has a soul and even so-called unliving matter is endowed with a soul of sorts. This soul becomes enlivened by contact with man and is easily coloured by his passion. If greed is associated with a gem it acquires a malignant force that in due time attaches to it and causes sorrow and suffering to those who come in contact with it. If even a simple pebble found in the river bed is regarded with faith and tended with devotion it brings peace and blessing.

Certain minerals have their own potency, just as different animals have their own nature and different men their own character. These traits can best be utilized if one knows their excellences. The virtues and defects of all metals* should similarly be understood so that no man in ignorance might, for instance, use gold in a case when its sovereign qualities are of no avail, or even run contrary to the end intended. So also with the more powerful congealed energies that lie in gems.

The lesser elements of the mineral world were also thought to have specific virtues, and in sculpture, in metallurgy, in alchemy, and āyurveda, the study of minerals became of great practical importance. The *śilpa-śāstras* or craftsmen's manuals of the medieval period show that considerable attention was paid by artisans to the materials used by them, and the merits of different raw materials for sculptural work are discussed. Mud (*paṅka*) and plaster (*lepa*) were considered pure but primitive, and the powers that were made to inhere in idols fashioned of these substances were easily dissipated. Clay (*mṛittikā*) preferably baked in the sun or furnace was an advance on these. In a few cases a clay idol was deemed better than one of stone for its moulding required the use of the hands and the hands were thoroughly immersed in the substance from which the idol was formed. Some idols had to be made of clay for they were meant to be used for a single brief occasion and were broken up or dissolved in water afterwards. Stone (*prastara*) was a noble medium for the artist, and marble (*pāshāṇa*) better still, but the best of all materials was metal* (*dhātu*). Among the metals gold and silver of course stood supreme, but there was a particular merit attached to brass and bronze. Often copper, tin, zinc, and lead, mixed with a little gold or silver for good fortune, was the prescribed material for auspicious statues.

An appreciation of the virtues inherent in stone (*śilā*) makes such practices as litholatria or stone-worship intelligible. This type of worship is widespread in Hinduism. Any elongated or holed rock formation shaped by nature, is taken to be endowed with the virtues of the liṅga of Śiva or the yoni of Pārvatī. Holed stones and liṅga-shaped stones are found in the Indus Valley; and the ancient mystic stone, the *āmalaka* is a feature of Hindu columns* and temples. Its origin is obscure but it appears to have been a holed stone first called *amaraśilā*, 'immortality stone'. In association with tree worship it was called āmalaśilā or āmalaka from the fruit of the sacred āmalaka (myrobalan) tree.

Certain stones were believed to symbolize particular deities. Thus, the stone of Vishṇu was the *śālagrāma*, the fossilized ammonite found in the bed of the Gaṇḍakī river, which resulted from the deity's passion for the beautiful woman Vṛindā*. Śiva's stone, the *bāṇaliṅga*, was a kind of pebble found in the bed of the Narmadā river (hence also called the *narmadeśvara*), which received the devotion of the Liṅgāyat* sect. The stone of Devī was the *svarṇarekhā*, 'gold-streaked', found in southern India. The stone of Sūrya was the *sūryakānta*, 'sunstone', or the *sphaṭika*, crystal, or any other bright transparent stone. Gaṇeśa's symbol was the *svarṇabhadra*, ('gold-auspicious') a red stone found in the bed of the Son river near Arrali.

In ancient times it was thought that stones could be magically endowed with the life-energy of a man by special ceremonies, and thus be made to contain the soul-force of that person. In southern India it was customary to install a stone, called the *vīrakkal*, in honour of a great king or hero. A stone was chosen, bathed in holy water, sometimes shaped or carved to represent the hero, suitably inscribed, and at an auspicious hour fixed firmly into the ground. Such hero-stones were believed to emanate great virtues and to inspire heroic deeds, and became objects of veneration.

Another life-endowed stone, dedicated to snake-deities by women desiring children, is the *nāgakal*, generally consisting of a stone slab with pictures of the snake deity cut out on it in relief. Such stones are placed in a pond for six months to imbue them with the life-giving power of the watery element, and then consecrated to the snake deities, and set up as votive tablets in temple courtyards, at the entrance of villages, near ponds, and under trees.

Books

See under Gems.

MĪRĀBAI (?1450–1547?) Hindi poetess and mystic. There is much uncertainty about the details of her life, and a large apocryphal literature has been woven around her name. She was said to have been a Rājput princess of Chitor (sometimes identified with Jhālī, queen of Chitor) and to have married the Rānā of Udaipur. Having already surrendered her life to the god Kṛishṇa in maidenly ardour, she could not give her complete devotion to her wifely duties, and so incurred the displeasure of her husband and his family. Their resentment was increased when she became the disciple of the *chamār* (low-caste) saint, Raidās*. She composed and sang hymns of praise in honour of Kṛishṇa, and was found during most of the day and night before the image of her deity in his form as Giridhāri. A legend has it that the emperor Akbar and his musician Tānsen disguised as mendicants went to the temple where she worshipped in order to witness her devotions. Her dancing and singing so captivated the Muslim emperor that he fell at her feet and gave an offering for Kṛishṇa. The story reached the ears of her husband and his persecution of her increased. Then Kṛishṇa appeared to her and commanded her to leave her mortal husband and seek her divine spouse. She spent her last days in the orchards and bowers of Vṛindāvana, worshipping the image of Kṛishṇa with such fervour that the idol came to life and ordered her to follow. A fissure opened in the earth and Mīrā and her divinity disappeared into it.

Mīrābai wrote in the Brāj dialect of Western Hindi, and her devotional lyrics, mainly about Kṛishṇa, are simple and naïve but full of restrained feeling. She was contemptuous of Śaivite ascetics, of excessive ritualism and the pretensions of caste. 'If living on water lead to heaven, fish and turtles would go to paradise before men. If feeding on leaves and nuts were acts of virtue goats and monkeys would attain liberation.' Her spiritual inspiration is felt in Rājputāna and Gujarāt to this day.

Books

I. Lal, G. B. *The Songs of Mirabai*, 1921.
II. Singh, Pritam. *Saints & Sages of India*, New Delhi, 1948.
III. Vaswani, T. L. *Saint Mira*, Poona, 1957.

MISCEGENATION. The still widely held notions that the Indian castes and peoples have, as a result of the social system of the *varṇas*, preserved their original strains; that the brāhmin is of 'pure blood', a descendant of the highest class of the Aryan immigrants; that the kshattriya is a scion of the knightly families of yore; the vaiśyas are the generations of the simple peasants of the Aryan highlands; all these are among the fondest illusions of students of Indian sociology. The truth is far removed from these conceptions, and the so-called historical tradition that insists on these features of India's caste origins is a myth which was long regarded as authentic, and provided for the most regressive pattern of thinking in India.

Anyone who has attempted to sort out the pedigrees of the great dynastic families of Ancient India will have discovered that, apart from the difficulty of reconciling the conflicting versions given in the available sources, all the tribes, both Aryan and non-Aryan are related from an early stage in their history by ties of blood through a steady process of intermarriage. This development is reflected in their pantheons, for the Aryan deities began to contract matrimonial alliances with the goddesses of the native people soon after their arrival in the Indian plains. Indeed, one hymn in the *Atharva-veda* has been interpreted as referring to the seduction of Indra himself by an *asura* woman.

The early priests, like the early kings, sprang from the union of aboriginal ṛishi and royal families with the priestly and princely families of the Aryan settlers. Nishāda and other non-Ayran rulers of the lowest caste thus rose to become kshattriya kings. The whole fabric of Indian genealogies is shot through with the most variegated alliances of the Aryans and other invaders with indigneous and aboriginal tribes.

There are numerous recorded instances of native rulers and chieftains of local tribes being accepted as Aryans, like the Dāsa chief Balbutha, who is mentioned in the *Ṛig-veda* as having adopted the Aryan culture and patronized brāhmins; and evidence is available in ancient Sanskrit literature of gipsy bands and wandering tribes straying into Vedic encampments and being admitted into the Ayran fold after the performance of purificatory rites. Says A. D. Pusalker, 'The brāhmin missionaries who accompanied the kshattriya conquerors paved the way for social and cultural contact by allowing high-born Aryans to marry with non-Aryans'.

Many prominent Ṛig-vedic Aryans were the sons of slave mothers. K. M. Sen observes, 'It is significant to note that many of the best known and most admired characters in Hindu literature were half-castes'. Honoured Vedic personages like Auśija, Kavasha and Vatsa were the sons of *dāsa* (slave) or śūdra (low-caste) women. S. K. Chatterji believes that 'Kṛishṇa was at least a half-caste'. Sūta and Vidura were śūdras; and Vasishṭha and Agastya were born of a prostitute. There is a verse in the *Mahābhārata* which says, 'Vyāsa was born of a fisherwoman and Parāśara of a chaṇḍāla woman. Many others who were originally not twice born, became brāhmins'.

The *Ṛig-veda* laments the prevalence of marriages between 'black' and 'white' and the fact that Aryans have been made out of Dāsas; and there is one anguished cry, almost moving in its utter futility, 'O Indra, find out who is an Aryan and who is a Dāsa and separate them'. The Aryans were at length obliged to bow to the inevitable. Old racial prejudices lingered awhile, but after the first antipathy and xenophobia were overcome, the indigenous inhabitants were slowly accepted as Aryans if they fulfilled certain basic religious requirements. Speaking of this period Havell says, 'It is probable that the Aryans were always numerically a very minute fraction of the people of India; and even among those who called themselves Aryans there were many of mixed blood'.

The convention of tracing a person's descent and preserving genealogical trees showing his pure lineage from Vedic and Epic heroes is a medieval expedient, first propagated by the brāhmins after the miscegenation of Aryan with non-Aryan had become universal and complete. The ancestors of the great Hindu dynasties do not shine as exemplars of racial purity or religious orthodoxy. All the great families of ancient India were of mixed origin, brāhmin as well as kshattriya, whatever they might have been before the Aryan advent. This needs reiteration since there are large numbers of educated Hindus who are carried away by sentimental attachment to the heroic names of the legendary past, and like to think of them as 'pure kshattriyas in shining armour', of uncontaminated lineage and mighty prowess, united with pure virgins of like unimpeachable descent. But it must be emphasized: pure families and pure castes are pure fiction.

If the lineage of any noble or priestly line, kshattriya or brāhmin, king or ṛishi, be examined, it will be found that the 'contamination' of Aryan purity began quite early in the family history. Even by the Vedic period the Aryans were already 'tainted' by low-caste marriages and their pedigrees confused by ties with families of low birth, alliances with dynastic houses that were aboriginal, or union with maidens who bore every trace of indigenousness. Non-Ayran women were frequently mentioned as the brides of Aryan heroes. It is also generally agreed that all the nymphs, apsarās*, forest maidens and earth-women, referred to in the sacred books, are indigenous, including the 'furrow-born' Sītā. The device of using sylphs, undines, dryads and fairies is employed in mythologies throughout the world to indicate this kind of 'native' liaison. The later lawgivers recognized the kinship of such females and expressly forbade an Aryan from marrying a woman with a name* suggesting her native birth.

With the *mélange* of peoples growing progressively more mixed it is not surprising that the *Mahābhārata* declares in plain terms, 'In all the varṇas (castes) and in all the āśramas (brāhminical hermitages) one finds the existence of dasyus (outcastes)'. And from the mouth of Yudhishṭhira himself we learn, 'Caste is at present (i.e. in Epic times) indistinguishable, in consequence of the great mixture of races, which has been very great indeed'. The Pauravas, Bhāratas, Pañchālas, Kauravas, Purus, Yadus, Turvasus, Āyus, Druhyus, to name but a few, were all impure. Those paragons of Aryan chivalry, the Pāṇḍavas, were perhaps the most 'tainted' with non-Aryan alliances and the most thoroughly mixed.

By the first half of the fifth century BC we find northern India divided into a number of independent kingdoms and republics, variously named in the Buddhist and Jain records and in the Purāṇas. Some of the older traditional names persist, but several new names appear. The *smṛitis* (*c.* 200 BC) class most of these states as definitely beyond the pale of Aryan civilization and dub most of their inhabitants as outcastes. These regions comprise, be it noted, practically every area in which 'pure' Aryans once flourished and performed their deeds of mickle might that are immortalized in the Epics.

At some time or other practically every important Aryan tribe or the region occupied by them, from Kirāta (Assam) to Kāmboja (Afghanistan) was stigmatized as impure, mixed and outcaste. In the *Mahābhārata* we are told, 'The eastern people are noted for their śūdra habits; the Deccanis for their irreligiousness, the Vālhīkas of the north-west for their thievish habits, the Panjābis for their lack of refinement, and the Saurāshṭras for their mixture of castes'. In the beginning of the historical period we find the classification extended according to the prejudice of the particular authority. As each lawgiver gives his own list of outcaste and undesirable tribes and areas, and as many of these lists differ, the combined catalogue embraces practically the whole of the Indian subcontinent. Thus we find condemned and unfit for Aryan habitation the regions of Avanti (Mālwā), Aṅga (West Bengal), Magadha (Bihār), Saurāshṭra (Kāṭhiāwār), Sind and Sauvīra (Lower and Middle Indus). So also it was decreed that whoever shall visit the countries of the Aratta, Kāraskara, Puṇḍra, Kaliṅga, Vaṅga or Praṇūna, shall offer a sacrifice to purify himself. Baudhāyana and Āpastamba, both of whom belonged to the South, nevertheless condemned Dakshiṇāpatha (the whole of the Deccan) as the home of unclean people. In fact the regions south of the Vindhyas were regarded as beyond the pale to begin with, and utterly beneath contempt. The rulers of South India did sometimes contract matrimonial alliances with 'Aryan' princesses, but since the children of such unions were held by all lawgivers without exception to be even more degraded than those relegated to the outer dark in their schedule of casteless peoples, these scions can hardly be invoked as genuine instances of Aryan monarchs. The lawgiver Hārīta says, 'From a śūdra womb, brāhmins, kshattriyas and vaiśyas can never be born'.

The process of miscegenation received a further impetus during the Greek and barbarian periods. There can be little doubt that Alexander's greatest general, Seleucus Nikator, continued the racial policy of his great predecessor, for the wonderful period of peaceful relations that existed between the Greeks and Indians during the Maurya reign, was probably the result of a far closer liaison than is apparent from the history books. According to recent theory the *epigamia* of the treaty between Seleucus and Chandragupta meant a grant to the Greeks of the right to marry into the kshattriya 'colour', i.e. the Indian king formally recognized them as kshattriyas.

On the strength of the matrominial alliance between the Mauryas and the Seleucids, the suggestion has been put forward of the possible Greek origin of Bindusāra and Aśoka; and the likelihood of Greek-Indian intermarriage down the line among the Macedonian soldiers and local women is not at all remote. Many Greeks settled down in India, and must have had Indian wives, as they did not at first bring their own women with them. Tarn thinks that the Euthydemids actually put into practice the dream of Alexander of uniting East and West, and their success can be measured by the remarkable assimilation of the Greeks with the Indians. The Bactrian Greeks as a whole were so completely intermixed that they have been called 'the Goanese of antiquity'. The complete absorption of the Greeks was merely a matter of time; they became first Eurasians, and finally Indians.

Miscegenation, especially among the princely and patrician families in India was assisted by the beauty of the Greek people, and the great partiality of those who could afford to buy and maintain them, for the women of the Greek race. Chandragupta married a Greek princess belonging to the family of Seleucus, and Greek women were brought to north and west India for centuries, to fill the steady demand for them.

Confirmation is found in Poseidonius who, writing at the end of the second century BC, speaks of the shipment of Greek singing girls and flute-girls to India. Eudoxus (d. 117 BC) who once employed a rescued Indian to guide him to India, seeing that there was a flourishing market for European women, started out with an expedition from Cadiz with a cargo of Spanish dancing beauties. Among the items listed by the author of the 'Periplus' (AD 80) for which there was a ready market at Barygaza, were 'good-looking virgins for concubines and choice girls for the royal harems', and the way it is put suggests that there was a 'standing order' for this commodity.

The flourishing western seaports of India which received Greek trading vessels in large numbers were cosmopolitan towns, thoroughly permeated with Grecian customs, filled with a predominantly Grecian or Hellenized population. The great slave-markets in the interior were largely recruited from here. Both in Bhāsa (fl. AD 350) who writes as a contemporary, and in Kālidāsa's day, almost two centuries later, the kings in the plays are represented accompanied by Yavana female bodyguards. It is beyond dispute that a tradition that could last so long, showing the presence of Greek slaves in the royal household, was very well established. It is curious to note also that the women of Saurāshṭra (Kāṭhiāwār and Gujarāt) long after the Greeks had vanished from the scene, continued to use the Greek form of salutation.

How many Greek, Persian, Parthian, Chinese, Śaka, Kushān and other foreign names lie concealed in the ponderous syllabary of Sanskrit, who can tell? We know too little about those great Indians of antiquity who added to the immense treasury of Sanskrit literature and philosophy to be dogmatic about their origins. There is seldom any preserved record of any authenticity about them, except a vague semi-mythical sentimental tradition. And there was always a strong tendency on the part of those who recorded or retailed their legends to merge them with their own common background or to erase all evidence of their true identity if it went contrary to their own caste preconceptions. Names do not necessarily indicate origins, for foreign names were frequently corrupted almost beyond recognition by the linguistic and orthographical peculiarities of Sanskrit. This is found to be a universal phenomenon. The Indian Chandra becomes Chan-ti-an in Chinese; and in Greek Chandragupta becomes Sandrocottus; Plato lives in Arabic as Aflatoon; the Graecized Persepolis becomes Parsapuri in Sanskrit. And, to bring it down to more recent times with a droll example, Siraj-ud-Dowlah becomes, for the British Tommy, Sir Roger Dowler.

If we cannot tell a person's origin from his name, or from the language in which he wrote, still less can we deduce anything from his religion, for with his conversion to Hinduism or Buddhism, the alien assumed a native name and became a thoroughgoing Indian. Chinese, Korean, Japanese and Central Asian Buddhists assumed Indian names on changing their religion. Many donors whose lavish bequests are recorded in Buddhist caves and on pillars of that period, bear such Indian names as Dharma, Indrāgnidatta, Vishṇudatta, Chitra, Chandra, Siṁhādhaya, Dhammadeva, Timitra, Thavaraputra and Damachika, and yet they were not Indians, but Bactrian, Śaka, and Kushān converts to Buddhism, as can often be found from the inscriptions. The donor who raised the famous votive pillar in Besnagar to the god Vāsudeva was not an Indian, but Heliodorus, a Greek convert to Hinduism, and one of the rare devotees whose original Greek name survives.

This was only one aspect of the gradual Indianization of foreign immigrants which was further promoted by the conversion or the patronage of their leaders. Just as the deadly Mongol became Muslim, and the wild Norseman became Christian, so the terrible Śakas, Kushāns and Huns became Buddhists and Hindus. Having accepted the Indian religion they worshipped the Indian gods, visited the sacred places, observed the ritual ceremonies, gave donations to the priests, adopted the court ceremonials of the country, married into Indian families, and claimed descent from the ancient mythological dynasties. Most of the great medieval kingdoms which came into prominence during the Śaka period were foreign, where they were not śūdra. After their naturalization or elevation to high caste status the new converts became more Indian than the Indians themselves. Indeed, as Dr Kalidas Nag reminds us, they 'emerged as champions of Indian culture'. This assimilation of large foreign elements into the Hindu and Buddhist fold, is one of the most noteworthy phenomena of early and medieval Indian history.

The Bactrian king Menander and the Kushān Kadphises I were both said to be Buddhists. Kadphises II was ostensibly a devotee of Śiva, but cared for none of the innumerable cults that flourished in his domain. Kanishka was a great patron of Buddhism and built a monastery at Peshāwar that was famous throughout the Buddhist world as a seat of Buddhist learning. Among the Śakas, Nahapāna endowed villages to brāhmins and undertook pilgrimages to Hindu holy places. He married an Indian wife. His Śaka son-in-law Ṛishabhadatta (or Ushavadatta) also granted villages to brāhmins, provided them with the means of marriage and annually feasted them. He also made arrangements for the livelihood and maintenance of Buddhist monks. Rudradāman the Śaka satrap, adopted Hinduism wholeheartedly, wrote in Sanskrit, patronized the brāhmins and was responsible for the first official inscription written wholly in Sanskrit. His successors also took Hindu names, many assuming kshattriya name-endings like varman, datta, daman, sena and siṁha.

The absorption of aliens, an ever-present feature of Indian history, has at certain times been particularly pronounced, but rarely more so than during the Muhammadan period. The sudden influx of the followers of Islam, coming as they did from widespread areas and belonging to many races, and their conquest of the country, led not only to a wide-scale conversion of the local inhabitants, but also to another fruitful term of contact, assimilation and miscegenation, perhaps more striking and extensive than any in the past.

The multiracial elements of which the invading armies were composed, Arabs, Afghans, Turks, Persians, Mongols, Egyptians, Abyssinians, Moors and others, did not as a rule bring their wives with them, and when they settled down in India the majority of them chose native women as wives, handmaidens and concubines. During the Turko-Afghan period female slaves were brought from Turkestan, Persia and even China. Georgian women, reputed to be among the most beautiful in the world, were widely sought for the harems of the rich and the noble, and in the later Moghul period many Armenians and some European and Eurasian women were also to be found in the seraglios of Muslim rulers because of their fair skin, since Muslim nobles were desirous of perpetuating the 'Moghul complexion' for their descendants. Among the local women the Kashmīris were the most favoured, for the same reason.

All the peoples who accepted the new democratic faith of Islam, irrespective of their caste, were able to intermarry, a process which began soon after the arrival of the Muhammadans. From the seventh century onwards, Arab and Persian traders who had settled in large numbers in Malabār and the west coast, took as their legal wives the women of the country, and founded important dynastic families. Such were the Newāyats of the Koṅkaṇ, the Labbes of Cape Comorin, the Ravuttans of Madura and Trichinopoly, and the Dudekulas of Pennukoṇḍa, all of whom are of mixed Arab, Persian and Indian descent. Many Muslim communities of the north-west also trace their ancestry to the conquerors. Among them are the Kasbatis of Ahmadabād, descendants of the Khorasani soldiers, who defeated their forefathers in battle.

Under the Moghuls, at whose court the foreign elements predominated, the newer arrivals for long endeavoured to maintain their ascendency over the 'Hindustānis', a term which embraced the India-born Muslims of Rājput, Marāṭha or other native descent. But in the long run even these foreign factions, calling themselves the 'Turāni' and 'Irāni' parties, comprising Persians, Afghans, Arabs, Abyssinians, Tartars and Turks, were likewise gradually assimilated.

If the process of miscegenation among the lower ranks of the nobility was sometimes fraught with strife, it was achieved quite painlessly in the higher social levels, for practically every important dynasty became mixed within one or two generations. The Pathān Khiljis, the Turki Tughluqs, the Arab Sayyids, the Afghan Lodis, the Georgian Bijapuris, all made dynastic alliances with converted Hindu royal houses. Even Moghul intermixture began early in their rule. No one who is remotely conversant with Indian history need be reminded of Akbar's tolerance in matters of race. He himself married Hindu women, and his successor Jahāngīr, was the son of a Rājput princess. Jahāngīr's son, Shāh Jahān, himself had a Rājput mother.

The final phase of miscegenation came with the advent of British, French, Dutch and Danish colonials, many of whom married Indian women. The Portuguese encouraged mixed marriages as a matter of political expediency. Albuquerque (1453–1515) urged his soldiers to take Indian wives, a policy which left a fruitful legacy in the community of the Goans.

The history of the half-caste communities of India in the seventeenth and eighteenth centuries forms part of the colourful pageant of the growth and consolidation of Empire. The first stage in their evolution was what might be termed a newer version of the Marriage of Europe and Asia by which Alexander the Great dreamed of uniting all mankind. The counterparts of Alexander's Macedonians were those swashbuckling freebooters from all parts of Europe who came to India to shake the seemingly inexhaustable pagoda tree. They married Indians and left many notable descendants.

The Eurasian community in India represents only one facet of a process much more widespread than is at first apparent. Many Indians owe their mixed heritage to European mothers, and thus do not figure in Eurasian statistics at all, although marriages between Indian men and European and Eurasian women have been going on for centuries and continue to this day; today more than ever before. As Cedric Dover points out, 'The Indian nobility from Akbar downwards have shown a preference for European and Eurasian wives. In India some of the best Indian families are really Eurasian, and they are being extended every day.'

Books

I. Ambedkar, B. R. *Who Were the Sudras?*, Bombay, 1946.
II. Bhandarkar, D. R. *Some Aspects of Ancient Indian Culture*, Madras, 1940.
III. Chand, Tara. *The Influence of Islam on Indian Culture*, Allahabad, 1936.
IV. Dover, Cedric, *Half-Caste*, London, 1937.
V. Garratt, G. T. (Ed.) *The Legacy of India*, Oxford, 1937.
VI. Havell, E. B. *The History of Aryan Rule in India*, London, n.d.
VII. Majumdar, R. C. (Ed.) *The Vedic Age*, London, 1951.
VIII. Mookerji, R. K. *Hindu Civilisation*, Bombay, 2nd Ed., 1950.
IX. Nag, Kalidas. 'Spread of Indian Culture in Asian Countries', *Foreign Review*, New Delhi, July 1950.
X. Rawlinson, H. G. *Intercourse Between India and the Western World*, Cambridge, 1916.
XI. Sarkar, S. C. *Some Aspects of the Earliest Social History of India*, London, 1928.
XII. Sarkar, B. K. 'Varnashrama Dharma & Race Fusion in Ancient India', *Modern Review*, 1917, pp. 211 ff.
XIII. Sen, K. M. *Hinduism*, Penguin Books, 1961.
XIV. Tarn, W. W. *The Greeks in Bactria & India*, London, 1938.
XV. Vaidya, C. V. *Epic India*, Bombay, 1907.
XVI. Visvanatha, S. V. *Racial Synthesis in Hindu Culture*, London, 1928.

MONGOLIANS. The influence of the Mongolians in India has been extensive and deep, although its significance has been consistently understated. They have been responsible for the racial make-up of important indigenous communities, altering the facial appearance and cranial shape of the inhabitants from Kashmīr to Kāmarūpa (Assam). They have played a major part in the evolution of Indian history, and have contributed much to the development of Indian thought and religion. Ancient Mongolian tribes gave India a number of her earliest languages belonging to the Muṇḍa (Chota Nāgpur), Mon-Khmer (Assam), Austronesian (Central India) and Tibeto-Chinese linguistic groups.

Mongolian characteristics are found in some of the skulls and terracotta figurines unearthed at Mohenjodaro. Prehistoric Deccan India was the dispersion area of certain Oceanic Mongols like the Malays. There is a tradition that an ancient branch of the Yueh-chi, a yellow race, emigrated to India from the Central Asian plateau long before the Aryan settlers.

Mongolian tribes on her north-western borders were India's neighbours from ancient times, and played a conspicuous part in Indian affairs until well into the historical period. For centuries they alternated with the Aryans in invading the Indian peninsula: Iranians, Macedonians, Śakas, Bactrian Greeks, Kushāns, Huns, Pahlavas, Afghans, Turks and Mongols.

The Vedas, Epics and Purāṇas preserve the names and customs of several tribes which ethnologists have identified as belonging to the Mongolian race. These peoples who were either partly or wholly of Mongolian stock founded some of the leading dynasties of the epic and post-epic period. Such were the Ābhīras, Ambashṭhas, Gandhāras, Ikshvākus, Kāmbojas, Kekayas, Kirātas, Lichchhavis, Madras, Mallas, Nāgas, Pāṇḍavas, Piśāchas, Puṇḍras, Śākyas, Śibis, Uśīnaras, Videhas, Vṛijjis and Yaudheyas.

To a lesser extent Mongolian influences also infiltrated into India through the length of the Himālayan foothills. The region of Mahāchīna in Indian geography, although incorrectly believed to refer to China, relates specifically to Tibet and Nepāl. Mahāchīna was regarded as one of the zones of India, and to this region sixty-four out of the one hundred and ninety-two Tantras are assigned. Much of tantrism and esoteric Mahāyāna evolved here. A huge fund of tradition associated with Vedānta, Buddha, Aśoka, Kanishka and other kings, saints and mystics, lost in India, is still preserved in Tibet and Nepāl. Further east, the region of Kāmarūpa (Assam) retains traditions of Mongolian provenance. The north-east, no less than the north-west, was a recruiting ground for vast numbers of Mongolian peoples coming to India. Assam was believed by Vincent Smith to have been 'a gate through which successive hordes of immigrants from the great hive of the Mongolian race in Western China have poured into India'.

Judged from a study of its origins, growth and decline in India, and its rapid development and universal influence in the Mongolian world, it would appear that Buddhism did not find a milieu favourable for its evolution in the country of its origin, but that it evoked a special response in the Mongolian mind. In fact it is not unlikely that Buddha himself was of Mongolian descent. His mother, Māyā, belonged to the Lichchhavi tribe, and his father was the chieftain of the Śākya clan, both these racial stocks being Mongolian or partly Mongolian in origin.

Buddha's teaching was strongly contra-caste, anti-brāhmin and anti-Vedic, and thus opposed to the traditional teachings of the *sanātana dharma*, the ancient religion, and hence in many ways alien to the spirit of Hinduism. Although Buddhism survived in India for several centuries, and transformed the face of Hinduism, it seems to have appealed with particular force to the religious complex fundamental to the Mongolian race, and its true development and final fruition were achieved among the Mongolian peoples.

Books

I. Chatterji, S. K. *Kirata-Jana-Kirti: The Indo-Mongolians: Their Contribution to the History & Culture of India*, Calcutta, 1951.

II. Sen, S. *The Mongolian Influence in India*, 1921.

(*See also under* History.)

MOUNTAINS and mountain ranges share with other natural objects the reverence of the Hindu people. They are the abode of the gods, auspicious sites for meditation, consecrated by countless legends, and the scene of deeds both heroic and divine. All mountains were once winged and flew about freely and often upset the balance of the earth. Indra cut off their wings and arranged them in fixed positions in order to steady the land. Mountains are therefore spoken of as *achala*, 'immoveable'.

There are said to be seven principal ranges of mountains, known as the *kula-parvata*, 'family ranges', which are frequently mentioned in the Purāṇas but are not consistently identified. The chief ranges are:

HIMĀLAYA (*hima-ālaya*, 'snow-abode') the mightiest range of them all, which plays a conspicuous part in Indian history, mythology, religion, art and literature. Kālidāsa refers to the Himālayas as the measuring rod of the universe and the dear calf of mother earth. Legends of Vishṇu, Brahmā, Śiva and many lesser gods have a Himālayan setting. Śiva is Girīśa, Lord of the Hills, and among his consorts is Pārvatī or Haimavatī, daughter of the eternal mountains. In Indian legendary every *ṛishi* or yogi credited with universal knowledge or divine power has a contemplative retreat in the Himālayas.

PAŚCHIMĀCHALA (*paśchima-achala*, 'western mountain') a fabulous range of mountains behind which the sun is supposed to set. Some identify it with the Aravalli range, and others with the Kirthār and Sulaiman ranges of Baluchistan.

PĀRIYĀTRA (or Pāripātra), thought to be the ancient name of the Aravalli range of Rājputāna. This range was once very high but was trampled down by the feet of the gods Indra and Kṛishṇa as they fought for supremacy.

VINDHYA, the range marking the division between north and south India. Legend says that it was once higher than the Himālayas, but was made to bow low by the sage Agastya*. Many strange tales are told of the beautiful nymphs who haunt the Vindhyan hills.

ṚIKSHA, the Satpura range between the Narmadā and Taptī, once the haunt of the monkey and the bear. For many aeons it was quite barren, having been cursed by a ṛishi to become ṛiksha, 'bald', because it did not offer him proper respect. Later the sage Agastya restored its mantle of green trees.

SAHYA (or Sahyadri), the Western Ghats, the abode of demons and evil spirits. During the Flood when most of the earth was submerged, and the mountain peaks of the earth was dissolved, the Sahya mountains endured the longest and were the last to succumb to the waters. Hence they were named Sahya, 'enduring'.

MALAYA, the hills of Malabār; the southern part of the Western Ghats stretching from the Nilgiris to Cape Comorin. The country of Malabār emerged from the sea when at the request of Paraśurāma* the god Varuṇa withdrew the ocean from this area to provide land for brāhmins. Paraśurāma pinched the land between thumb and fingers as it appeared from the sea and pulled it up, thus forming the Malaya hills.

MAHENDRA, 'great Indra', the Eastern Ghats, once a continuous rampart of high ranges ruled over by kings who resisted the gods for centuries. The gods hacked the hills, destroyed the summit citadels that guarded them and subdued the inhabitants. The range was also associated with Paraśurāma, and was the venue of the first Tamil* *śaṅgam*.

GANDHAMĀDANA, 'perfume of delight', the Maikala range with the hills of Gondwāna and of Chota Nāgpur. Legends telling of the gods who dwell on the hills and the sweet-scented *apsarās* who serve them abound in local lore. It was probably named from its aromatic forests.

ŚUKTIMĀN, 'twisted', situated in the east, and sometimes identified, though not very reliably, with the Gāro and Khāsi hills of Assam.

Besides the mountain ranges, there are hundreds of separate hills and peaks, which are regarded as endowed with special sacrosanctity. Some are of mythological fame, such as Kailāsa, Meru and Mandara (*see* paradise). Temples and shrines are built on the top of sacred hills and devotees make pilgrimages to them. There is hardly a prominent hill that is not associated with some tradition about the gods; and the *māhātmyas* or books written in praise of holy places are filled with such legends.

The most famous single mountain peak of the Hindus is **Kailāsa** in Tibet, described as standing behind the Himālayas. In cosmography it lies east of Mount Meru and is one of the mountains of paradise. Here Śiva and Pārvatī lie wrapt in eternal *maithuna*. Here Śiva's court of evil spirits, ghosts and goblins pay the divine pair perpetual homage even as they unite. It is also called Rajatādri, 'silver mountain', or Hemakūṭa, 'golden peak'. Kālidāsa refers to Kailāsa as a mountain formed of crystals and used as a mirror by celestial *apsarās*. Devotees regard Kailāsa as the Śivaliṅga itself. Pilgrims perform a circumambulation about this mountain, a distance of twenty-five miles, which is completed in two or three days. 'Those who cannot make the perambulation on account of physical inability may have it done through a substitute like the sheep, horse, etc.' (II, p. 148). At the foot of Kailāsa lies Lake Mānasa (Mānasarovara), where the right palm of Satī fell. It is described as 'the haunt of golden birds and the place of golden lotuses'. It is here that the wild swans migrate in the breeding season at the beginning of the monsoons. Quite close is the source of the Sutlej river. A ghāṭ named after this lake was built in modern times in Banāras around a stone said to have been brought from Mānasarovara in prehistoric days. This stone grows daily to the extent of a sesamum seed and is now four and a half feet high and fifteen feet in periphery.

Among the other better known hills are the following: **Pārasnāth,** also called Sameta-Śikhara, in the Hazāribāgh district of Bihār, about two hundred miles north-west of Calcutta, a celebrated place of Jain pilgrimage. Twenty out of the twenty-four Jain *tīrthaṅkaras* attained *nirvāṇa* here. Here also Pārśva the twenty-third tīrthaṅkara died. **Palni,** near Madura, dedicated to Kārttikeya* son of Śiva, hence also called Śivagiri. Legend has it that the sage Agastya, wishing to build a dam commanded a demon to carry two mounds of earth in a kāvaḍi or pair of baskets suspended from a bamboo pole. The demon dropped the earth at this spot and it formed the two hills of Palni. Pilgrims carry kāvaḍis filled with milk and sugar, observe the vow of fasting and silence. Women pilgrims invariably offer their hair, and huge quantities are sold to interested merchants every year. **Tirumalai,** 'holy hill', part of a small range of ten peaks, called the Śeshāchala because it undulates like a serpent. It is a site where Vishṇu stayed for some time, and the spot is marked by a temple to Veṅkaṭeśa. The town of Tirupati at the foot of the hill is a famous place of pilgrimage. **Arbuda,** 'serpent', the name of a mountain popularly known as Mount Ābū, in the Aravalli range in Rājputāna, on whose slopes stood the hermitage of the sage Vasishṭha. It was on this mountain that the agnikuṇḍa or fire-pit was built from which originated the Rājput* clans. It is regarded as sacred by the Jains, and contains the famous Dilwāra temples built by the Solaṅkis*. Two miles beyond Dilwāra lies **Achalgarh,** an ancient stronghold of the Paramāra kings, which has a number of temples, one of them containing the toe of Śiva. **Girnār,** in Junagaḍh, is another sacred hill of the Jains, dedicated to Nemi. It was a place of pilgrimage from before the time of Aśoka. One of its outcrops is a *bhairav-japa*, 'terrible leap', a rock from which devotees cast themselves, falling over one thousand feet to their death. Many famous Jain temples were built on Girnār by the Solaṅki kings. **Śatruñjaya,** once sacred to the Buddhists and associated with Nāgārjuna, is now hallowed by the Jains, and dedicated to Ṛishabha. Situated near Palitana, in Kāṭhiāwār, the hill contains more than 860 temples and 11,000 images, many dating from about A D 960 and built by the Solaṅkis. This hill is meant for the gods alone. Food cannot be cooked there and pilgrims bring food with them. All persons, pilgrims and priests must leave the holy spot on its summit before nightfall, so that the gods might meditate there undisturbed.

Books

I. Cunningham, A. *The Ancient Geography of India,* 1871.
II. Dave, J. H. *Immortal India,* Vol. IV, Bombay, 1961.

MUDRĀ, 'seal', a word of Iranian origin meaning gesture. The *mudrā* is one of the component parts of *aṅgika** or bodily position. The term is loosely used for the *paramudrās, āsanas, sthānas,* and dance positions. In tantrism the mudrā is also a special parched cereal wafer eaten during the *chakrapūjā** ritual. In recent years the term has been applied almost exclusively to the *mudrikā,* or symbolic positions of the hands, also called *hasta-mudrā,* 'hand-gesture'. Such gestures are employed in ritual, dancing and occult symbolism, and are frequently seen in sculptures. When executed with one hand they are called *asaṁyukta,* 'unconnected'; when with both hands, *saṁyukta,* 'connected'.

Hand mudrās are believed to have a religious origin. Some authorities trace it to the positions taken by the hand in the mnemo-technical finger-devices called *sāmahasta,* used by Vedic reciters to remember the accent and stress of the sacred chants; the thumb counted off the phalanges of the fingers which represented the notes, timings, and accompanying actions. They therefore served as cues to assist in remembering the order of the ceremonial. Besides, mudrās served to evoke an idea in the mind to symbolize certain powers or deities, or again to emphasize the import of the text. The sequence of such ritual hand postures may have contributed to the development of the dance mudrās.

All mudrās have traditional pictorial significance, and their interpretation is often extremely complex. The hastamudrās of classical dance have about five hundred basic meanings, although here the dancer brings into play not only the fingers and palms, but also the wrists, elbows and shoulders (*see* dance). In theory the arrangement of fingers, palms and wrists are all meaningful, but in practice no one can possibly 'read' the various meanings, even when, as in classical dancing, the performer follows a known sequence of gestures whose interpretation is familiar to the spectator. Ordinarily they become meaningful to the layman only when a particular 'phrase' is suggested by the correlative motions of the dance composition and can then be understood in the context. Thus, the hand may assume the shape of a bud, the bud will open its petals one by one, the eyes of the dancer will quicken suggestively as though fascinated by its beauty, then he will smell the perfume; then the other hand becomes a bee, circles over the flower, hovers and descends and sips the honey.

There are thirty-two major hand positions, twelve hand movements, twenty-four combined hand positions and, in theory at least, over eighty-eight million minor variations. Of these, something like eight or nine hundred are described in manuals on the subject. There are hand gestures denoting the gods, demons, ogres, the upper, middle and lower worlds, famous emperors, ṛishis, princes of renown, cities and gardens, rivers, trees, animals, serpents, insects, fish, plants, flowers (including over sixty lotus postures); disputes, the love encounter in a hundred forms, the parts of the body. Also, the various symbols of Hindu mythology, the shell, the conch, discus, thunderbolt, sun, stars, moon and half-moon; and the whole gamut of emotions, love, hate, surprise, anguish, anger, jealousy, forgiveness, and so on.

All the single-hand gestures, whether used in dancing, cult practice or sculpture, are formed around the basic positions of (*a*) the open palm, (*b*) the hollowed palm, (*c*) the hand with finger tips together, and (*d*) the closed fist. Below is a representative selection of the major mudrās, with some of their variants.

Patākā, 'flag', the open palm upright, usually facing the spectator, fingers close together and pointing upward, thumb slightly bent inwards to touch the lower side of the forefinger. In the dance this mudrā stands for assurance, meditation, a flower, cloud, forest, night, river, horse. The patākā with the ring-finger (second last) bent forward is called the *tri-patākā,* and represents coition. The tri-patākā with the tips of thumb and ring-finger touching is the *vajra-patākā,* and represents a thunderbolt, an arrow, a tree. The patākā with the ring finger and little-finger bent is the *ardha-patākā,* and signifies dagger, temple tower, horn, river bank. The patākā, with slightly hollowed palm turned upward, sometimes with the thumb stretched out at right angles to the palm is the *ardha-chandra,* signifying a spear, prayer, greeting, half-moon, battleaxe. The patākā with forefinger and ring-finger bent is the *suka-tuṇḍa,* 'parrot beak', and denotes shooting an arrow, dismissal, mystery, ferocity. The patākā with the little finger bent is the *triśula* which stands for three objects together, a leaf, desire for love's union. The patākā with the forefinger bent is the *arāla,* meaning a bird, blame, the drinking of poison. The patākā held hanging loosely, drooping down at right angles to the wrist is the *lola,* 'restless'. In the *gaja,* 'elephant' gesture, the arm is extended in front or sideways, with the hand in the lola mudrā. The patākā with the right hand raised upward as though about to strike someone is the *chapeṭādana,* 'slap-giving', and signifies strife, anger. The patākā with the hand pointing downwards, palms towards the spectator, fingers stretched and sloping downwards as if offering something is the *varada,* signifies the bestowing of gifts. In sculpture the seated figure is often shown with the varada gesture, but the fingers do not touch the ground. The patākā held upright and rigid like the sign for 'Stop', is the *abhaya,* 'fearless'. It banishes fear, gives protection, and bestows a benediction. With the abhaya mudrā Buddha reassured his frightened disciples and tamed a raging elephant charging towards them at Rājagṛiha. Buddha statues often show this mudrā.

Padma, 'lotus', or *padma-kośa,* 'lotus-bud'. The palm is gently hollowed, fingers separated and a little bent as if holding a round object. It signifies the female breast, a fruit, a bud, the hole of a snake, an egg. The padma with the forefinger and middle finger straightened out forms the *saura-padma,* or full-blown lotus, signifying the yearning for the lover, caressing the breast, the full moon. The saura-padma with the thumb straightened out is the *alapadma,* representing summer, hastening to the rendezvous, sexual bliss. The padma with the ring-finger stretched out is the *laṅgūla,* 'tail', and denotes the water lily, picking a flower, virgin experience. The padma with the fingers graspingly and passionately bent is the *saṁdaṁśa,* signifying the climax of love, the offerings of love's fruits. The padma-hand on hip, thumb pointing back is called *kaṭi,* 'hip', or kaṭi-hasta, often seen in dance poses and in statues of upright figures.

Mukula, 'bud', where the tips of the fingers and the thumb are brought together. It signifies a bud, virgin, delicacy, littleness, an offering, the yoni, the god of love, a monkey, eating, contempt. The mukula with the forefinger separated and bent to form the crest of a cock is the *tāmra-chūḍā,* 'red-crest', and besides a cock it signifies a crane, camel, calf, writing, hook and noose. The mukula with the little finger raised is the *chatura,* 'quick', which means a jackal, a cunning enemy, a pander. The mukula with the little and forefinger raised is the *siṁha-mukha,* 'lion-face', symbolizing a pearl, lion, salvation, garland. The siṁha-mukha with thumb over the bent ring and middle fingers is known in the dance mudrās as the *karaṇa-ḍamaru,* after the little drum, that is held between the raised little and forefingers. The mukula with thumb, forefinger and middle finger joined, the others outstretched, is the *haṁsa,* 'swan', and signifies tying the marriage thread, initiation, the wedding night, a drop of water, painting a picture, rubbing, holding a garland. The haṁsa with the forefinger bent so that its tip touches the first joint of the thumb is the *bhramara,* 'bee', and signifies silence, bath, parrot, sexual union. The mukula with only the tips of the thumb and ring finger touching, the little and forefinger upright and back, the middle finger straight but slightly forward is the *mayūra,* 'peacock', which signifies beak, creeper, wiping away tears, discussion. The mukula with the tips of the thumb and forefinger (or else the thumb and ring or middle finger) touching, palms outward facing the spectator, the other fingers loosely open is the *chin-mudrā,* the 'reflection' or realization pose, sometimes called the *vitarka* or discussion pose.

Mushṭi, 'fist', with thumb bent over the closed palm, indicates strength, holding a weapon, wrestling. The mushṭi with the thumb upraised is the *śikhara,* 'peak', signifying the erect phallus, husband, embracing, pillar, tooth, silence. The mushṭi with thumb and forefinger out is the *chandra-kāla* and represents Śiva, eyebrows, boar-tusks, crescent moon. The mushṭi with forefinger bent over the top of the straight thumb so that the thumb sticks out between forefinger and middle finger is the *kapittha,* 'wood-apple', and signifies Lakshmī, Sarasvatī, milking a cow, holding a veil, the end of a robe, offering incense, amorous dalliance, sexual intercourse. In the *sūchī,* 'needle' the forefinger is raised, the other fingers folded in, encircling the thumb; it denotes a circle, universe, flame, elephant tusks, one hundred, sin, city, astonishment, umbrella. The sūchī with the middle finger also upright but slightly forward to form a 'V', is the *kartari*, 'scissors', signifies separation, lightning, death, hypocrisy, opposition, disagreement. The sūchī in a menacing attitude, i.e. with the forefinger raised, the others locked up in the fist as if warning, or scolding, is the *tarjanī*, 'reviling' and denotes a threat.

Mudrikās performed with two hands are called saṁyukta hasta mudrās, and once again their combinations are endless, with hundreds of fanciful names. The best-known basic gestures involving both hands are: the *añjali*, 'salutation', the hollowed palms held together, signifying salutation*, beseeching, begging; if used in supplication it is often called *kṛitāñjala*. When the flattened palms are joined the gesture is called *saṁhatala*. In the *pushpapuṭa*, 'flower-basket', the hands are slightly curved, joined at the sides, palms up as though to receive water in them. It denotes a water or flower offering. In *kīlaka*, 'wedge' the fists are closed and little fingers intertwined, signifying the union of love, or the conversation of lovers. In the *utpala* or night lotus the palms are joined, the thumbs together, index fingers touching and slightly bent, middle fingers straight out, ring-fingers bent inwards and concealed within palms, little fingers slightly out; it signifies a temple tower, wrestling, sexual intercourse. In the *kshepaṇa*, the mudra of sprinkling, the two hands are joined palm to palm, the stretched-out fingers turned downwards as though to dip into a vessel. In the *vajra-hūṁkāra*, the wrists are crossed at the chest, palms closed and turned inwards; it signifies the dawn of enlightenment, release from the fetters of passion, the mystery of sound. More recondite is the class known as *kaśyapa* or kachchhapa, which covers a variety of joined hand-mudrās with fingers intertwining, all of them representing the liṅga within the yoni.

Books

I. Akiyama, A. *Buddhist Hand Symbols*, Yokohama, 1939.
II. Coomaraswamy, A. K. *The Mirror of Gesture*, 2nd Ed., New York, 1936.
III. Coomaraswamy, A. K. 'Mudra, Mudda,' *Journal of the American Oriental Society*, New Haven, XLVIII, 1928, 279–81.
IV. La Meri. *The Gesture of the Hindu Dance*, New York, 1941.
V. Poduval, R. V. *Kathakali & Diagrams of Hand Poses*, Trivandrum, 1930.
VI. Saunders, E. D. *Mudra. A Study of Symbolic Gesture*, New York, 1960.
VII. Shiner, L. P. *The Mudras or Hindu Body Symbols*, 1918.

MUSIC, in Hindu musical theory, is regarded as only a means to a definite emotional end. An emotional effect is said to be produced from each note singly, and from notes in succession, and the creation of a specific mood by this means is the ultimate object of all musical composition. To those brought up in the European tradition Indian music takes time to get used to. The timing is excellent, and the rhythm often reminiscent of syncopation, but the general effect is monotonous and can on occasion be nerve-racking.

Central to the idea of Indian music is the notion inherent in *śabda* or sound*. Of the manifested sounds which constitute the domain of music, the human voice is the highest form, hence intoning, chanting, the recitation of mantras, and singing*, are regarded as the most effective means of expressing sound. Next on the scale of sound comes the musical instrument*, which helps in creating the desired mood that is the purpose of all music.

The *adhyāya* or divisions under which music is considered in Sanskrit works are (1) *tāla*, time, (2) *svara*, notes, (3) *grāma*, scales, (4) *rāga*, tunes, (5) *vādya* or vāditra, musical instruments, (6) *nṛitta* or dance, (7) *gāyan*, singing, and (8) *rasa*, the emotional states.

Rhythm in music is guided by the rules governing the pattern of *tāla* (also tāl or tālam) or time*, maintained principally by hand-clapping and the use of hand drums. This tempo or rhythm is called *laya*, of which three kinds are distinguished: quick (*druta*), middling (*madhya*) and slow (*vilambita*). The beats are not equal, hence the rhythm is complex. Besides, as the music gathers momentum the time may be doubled or quadrupled.

The higher drum, usually tuned to the tonic of the musician's voice, also marks the fraction of the *mātrā*, 'measure' (*see* time) or beat, the lower drum marking the longer beats and played in the form of a staccato drone. A certain number of mātrās unite to form an *avarta*, 'not-proceeding', or bar, of specific length. Rhythm is extremely syncopated and seemingly with abrupt alterations in tempo. There is tremendous scope in the periods of the Indian time system for the exciting and suspenseful interplay between the hand drum and the solo instrument each of which makes its own variations on the basic framework, and both ending triumphantly together on the first beat of the next period, which is therefore called *sam*, 'together'. The technique requires an extraordinarily well developed sense of timing in order to beat out the intricate rhythmic pattern. When two or more of these complex patterns of cross-rhythms, each ornamented with grace notes and enlivened by syncopation are sounded at the same time, the result is a texture of extreme subtlety and power. This pattern may be said to take the place of harmony and counterpoint in European music.

The fundamental unit of music is the note or *svara*, and Indian music consists of svaras sung or played in succession according to certain rules based on euphony and consonance. Indian music is thus essentially linear or melodic, and does not exploit the rich resources of harmony, counterpoint or choral singing, Within its scope, in theory at any rate, it seems to have exhausted the possibilities of melodic line.

The number of notes used in a particular system of music constitutes its scale. The monotone (single note) and duotone (two notes) are used for the intoning of mantras. The early *sāman* chants consisted of three notes, namely, *udātta*, *anudātta* and *svarita* (*see* prosody). Melodies based on only four notes were declared by ancient authorities to be used by tribes like the Śavaras, Pulindas, Kāmbojas, Vaṅgas, Kirātas, Vālhīkas, Āndhras, Dravidians and forest peoples. A class of stage song, known as the *dhruvā*, also employs only four notes. Other melodies are pentatonic, like the *oḍava*, sexatonic like the *khāḍava*, and septatonic like the *saṁpūrṇa*.

Systems using four notes or less are spoken of as *tāna*, or tānam, i.e. thread, signifying that the mode is spun out like a single thread and cannot provide the 'texture' or warp-and-woof that make true music. Only schemes more elaborate than the tāna fall into the category of the *rāga* classical system. Improvizations of the tāna are sometimes sung, using syllables instead of words.

As in Western music, Indian music has a basic scale of eight notes, consisting of the first note or Tonic, followed by six others situated at musical intervals correlated by the laws of consonance, and an eighth note which is the Tonic again but with double its original pitch. This is known as the octave in the West, but is called the *saptak* (septet) in Sanskrit texts. The duplication of the Tonic or keynote as the eighth note, as in European music, is not part of the Indian scheme.

According to Indian musical theory the saptak has three increasing orders of pitch, called *sthāna*. These sthāna or ranges might be said to be equivalent to three octaves, and are recognized as being one in each register, first a *mandra* or low one in the breast register, then a *madhya* or middle one in the throat register, and a *tāra* or high tone in the head register. Pitch in Indian music is relative and has no connection with the notes. The identification of *Sa* (see below) with C is about fifty years old and dates from the introduction of the portable harmonium. A singer chooses his Sa according to his convenience and keeps it for the duration of the performance, irrespective of the number of rāgas he sings. The same is the case with the instrumentalists. When more than one musician performs at the same function each has his own drummer tuned to the Sa he has chosen.

The saptak then consists of seven notes or tones, and is subdivided into twelve semitones consisting of seven original (*prākṛit*), pure, natural, or normal notes called *śuddh* svaras, and five modified (*vikṛit*) notes, called *komala* or soft (i.e. flat) if lowered by half a tone, and *tīvra* (or sharp) if raised by half a tone. The komala constitute the variations of the five inner notes of the octave, the two outer ones being unchangeable.

The tonic solfa names of the śuddh notes are *Sa, Ri, Ga, Ma, Pa, Dha, Ni*, and together they are called the *sargam* (from Sa, Ri, Ga). They are popularly said to represent certain animal sounds. Music may sometimes be rendered by means of the sargam, i.e. by uttering the note-cum-name or singing out the names of the notes. Often a pattern of meaningless syllables such as *te, rā, nā* (hence called *terānā*) are sung out as a background for rāga and other music. The terānā form was reputedly introduced by Amīr Khusrau to simplify the difficult Sanskrit words originally used. The vikṛit notes fall between Sa-Ri, Ri-Ga, Ga-Ma, Pa-Dha, and Dha-Ni.

The above semitonal division is, however, not the limit of the Indian musical scale. Indian writers distinguish twenty-two sub-tones or microtones called *śruti* (from *śru*, 'hear'), audible sounds, or intervals within the saptak employed, at which every note is considered suitable for use in the system. In one scheme if the twenty-two śrutis are placed in order, then the seven śuddh notes will fall in the 4th, 7th, 9th, 13th, 17th, 20th and 22nd places. It is to be noted that the scheme based on the twelve semitones forms a separate system from the heptatonic scheme of the twenty-two śrutis. Attempts to reconcile the two systems by equivalence of vibrations per second or other mathematical means have not proved successful.

In any system of notes adopted for a particular musical scheme, the dominant note is known as the *vādī*, 'announcer', compared to a 'king' in the whole musical design; in the rāga it is often identified with the *aṁśa*. Bharata, author of the *Nāṭyaśāstra*, held that notes at a distance of nine or thirteen śruti from one another (i.e. fourths or fifths) are *saṁvādī* or consonant; the saṁvādī in relation to the vādī is compared to the 'minister';

those at a distance of two or twenty śrutis (seconds or sevenths) are *vivādī* or dissonant and are regarded as the 'enemy', and the vivādī note is therefore avoided; the remaining intervals are *anuvādī* or assonant, and are compared to the 'vassal' or servant. These terms are frequently applied to the notes of the rāga design.

Each śruti has been given a name generally indicative of the emotional effect it can produce in the mode in which it predominates. Among these effects are the energizing, dulling, tranquillizing, delightful, serene, wrathful, argumentative, loving, purifying, infatuating, amorous, ardent, serious, and so on. The notes Ri and Pa are forbidden in the early morning; the prolonged voicing of Ri may even produce fatal results, and that of Pa damages the teeth. The śrutis are never used in succession, like the semitones of the chromatic scale, but are chiefly employed in ornamentation, and to a small extent in melody.

The position, names, significance, and so on, of the śuddh notes in the semitonal subdivision may be indicated as follows:

Śruti notes	Tonic solfa names of śuddh notes	Full name of śuddh notes	Old name of notes for singing Vedic chants	Equivalent in the Western system	Number of śrutis in solfa notes	Animal sounds represented
1						
2						
3						
4	Sa	shaḍja	prathama (first)	C	4 śrutis	peacock
5						
6						
7	Ri	ṛishabha	dvitīya (second)	D	3 śrutis	cuckoo
8						
9	Ga	gāndhāra	tṛitīya (third)	E	2 śrutis	heron
10						
11						
12						
13	Ma	madhyama	chaturtha (fourth)	F	4 śrutis	goat
14						
15						
16						
17	Pa	pañchama	pañchama (fifth)	G	4 śrutis	horse
18						
19						
20	Dha	dhaivata	atisvarya (sharp-toned)	A	3 śrutis	frog
21						
22	Ni	nishāda	kṛishṭa (dragged)	B	2 śrutis	elephant

A fixed arrangement of śrutis constitutes a *grāma*, 'group' roughly translated scale. These scales are usually composed by taking any one of the śruti notes as the Tonic and selecting a saptak from the other śrutis at certain diatonic intervals fixed by the laws of consonance. Originally there were three grāmas, named after three of the śuddh notes, namely *shaḍja*, with intervals as given above; *madhyama* which does not differ much from it; and *gāndhāra* which differs considerably and is believed to be the scale used in heaven. The latter was either given up or lost by the time Bharata wrote his *Naṭyaśāstra*, and the madhyama was virtually merged with the shaḍja by the thirteenth century AD. The shaḍja is the only grāma now in use and forms the basis of both the Hindustāni (North Indian) and Karṇāṭaka (South Indian) schools of music, the madhyama being almost indistinguishable from it.

The term *mūrchhanā*, 'bubbling' is variously defined as the extensions, grades or modulations of Indian scale systems. It is used in several senses, among them, the rise and fall of the voice in song, or the rise and fall of a particular note in a specific scale of seven notes. Starting from any one of the seven notes of the saptak as the basis of a new series of a scale, the *mūrchhanās* can be sung in their natural order, diatonic order, or in meandering sequences. They are generally patterned around a specified *ārohī* (ascent) and *avarohī*, or avrohī, (descent) of musical notes. There are supposed to be twenty-one mūrchhanās or modes, seven from each of the three grāmas, but only fourteen (seven from the shaḍja and seven from the madhyama) are practicable. Ancient tradition says that the rāga is born from the mūrchhanā, which is in fact the first step in the development of the classical rāga system.

The *jāti* or modal family is an intermediate stage in the development from mūrchhanā to rāga. Out of the fourteen mūrchhanās of the two grāmas, seven assumed the status of jāti or basic mode. Each jāti has its 'pillar notes', incipient, final and melodic centre, and some additional features which stamp it as the predecessor of the rāga. The jāti is thus the original, basic scale pattern, the skeleton of the rāga system. The jāti is often referred to as the *mātṛikā*, 'maternal', because its womb forms the specific mould of the rāga.

The classification of Indian musical modes is determined by the different jātis or basic scale patterns. These are made by arranging combinations of the twelve semitones of the octave, from which again a number of parent scales are devised which are called thāṭa or mela. The term *thāṭa* or thāṭ, 'array', is used in the Northern or Hindustāni system for the categories of group notes from which distinct musical modes of similar texture can be derived. It was originally applied to the arrangement of the moveable frets of a sitār or vīna, where one setting served for several modes of a given pattern. In the Karṇāṭaka or South Indian system the concept of the thāṭa is called *mela* or melakartā, 'union-maker', which, like the thāṭa is an elaboration of the ancient arrangement of the jātis. There are seventy-two melakartās, divided into two exactly parallel groups of thirty-six each, of almost identical character. The melakartās are comprehensive, and, according to an Indian authority, 'can neither be increased nor decreased by Śiva himself'.

The thāṭa or mela (both terms are frequently used synonymously) therefore groups together in significant relationship the embryonic modes having a similar texture and construction, which form the parent stock from which the rāgas are derived. It consists of a fixed pattern from which a number of minor melodies can be devised on the basis of their unity. Most of the thāṭas and melakartās listed are purely theoretical and are never employed, and only about ten thāṭas and twenty melas are recognized or are of any practical utility. The thāṭa has the ascent and descent of notes of the regular modal form, with distinctive assonant and consonant notes, but unlike the rāga a thāṭa has no aesthetic value. 'It is not necessary', say the authorities, 'that a thāṭa should please listeners.' Musical pleasure starts with the rāga*.

Books

I. Bandopadhyaya, S. *The Music of India,* Bombay, 1945.
II. Clements, E. *Introduction to the Study of Indian Music,* London, 1913.
III. Daniélou, A. *Northern Indian Music,* 2 vols., London, 1949.
IV. Fox-Strangways, A. H. *The Music of Hindustan,* Oxford, 1914.
V. Mukerji, D. P. *The Indian Music,* Bombay, 1945.
VI. Popley, A. H. *The Music of India,* London, 1921.
VII. Rahamin, Begum Fyzee. *The Music of India,* London, 1926.
VIII. Ranade, G. H. *Hindustani Music,* Poona, 1939.
IX. Swarup, B. *Theory of Indian Music,* Allahabad, Revised Ed., 1950.
X. Wellesz, E. (Ed.) *Ancient & Oriental Music,* London, 1957.

MUSIC HISTORY. The art of music was once known only in paradise. Indra had musicians in Svarga who excelled in the various forms of this art. The *apsarās* were devoted to the dance, the kinnaras were instrumentalists, and the gandharvas* the celestial singers. A general theory of sound, with its physics and metaphysics is popularly believed to have been enshrined in a work, now lost, composed by the gandharvas and called the *Gāndharva-veda,* devoted mainly to singing*. There is no actual evidence that any such work ever existed, but it is traditionally included among the upavedas, and treated as having formed part of the *Sāma-veda.*

The elements of musical theory are first found in the Vedas, especially the *Sāma-veda,* whose chants were sung in a special manner. The ritual steps of the early priests as they performed the Vedic sacrifices are said to have been the origin of the classical dance*, and the finger devices called *sāma-hasta* used by Vedic reciters to remember the measure were the beginning of the *mudrās**, or hand gestures.

The earliest theories of Hindu music were formulated subsequent to the Greek period, and some scholars see their origins in the works of Greek writers on the subject. A very ancient tradition speaks of Dionysus as having come to India with his companions and having taught the Indians to worship the gods and himself by playing cymbals and drums; he also taught them the satyr dance which the Greeks called *kordax.* Inconclusive attempts have been made to identify this Dionysus with Manu, Śiva or Kṛishṇa. Like the Greeks, the Indians never knew harmony, their music being a succession of notes, essentially linear. And like the Phrygian, Dorian, Lydian and other modes, the Indian *rāgas* were supposed to arouse in the listener feelings of aggressiveness, tranquility, sensuousness and so forth.

Nothing can be said with any certainty regarding these influences, but it is noteworthy that though we have no record of Indian musicians visiting Greece, we do know that Greek singers and musical instruments were imported into India (I, p. 285) for centuries, and must in some measure have modified the original barbaric (III, p. 60) monotone of Indian strains. The close connection between Bharata's theories and those of Aristotle have also frequently been pointed out.

The first authorities on Hindu music were *Dattila* (AD 190) and *Kohala* (*c.* AD 280) whose writings are lost, but who are quoted by the great master *Bharata** (*c.* AD 300), who devotes the last six of the thirty-six chapters of his *Nāṭyaśāstra* to the subject of music. Bharata established the *mārga* or method, setting the basis for the classical musical pattern. He nowhere defines the rāga, and classifies melodies under the name of *jāti*. His doctrines were extensively elaborated by his imitators and commentators.

The growing complexities of Indian musical theory are well brought out in a sly humorous fashion in the seventh century collection of fables, the *Pañchatantra,* in the story about the musical ass. Inspired by the beauty of the night the ass wanted to sing, and on being implored to desist by his friend the fox, indignantly replied,

'Do you imagine I do not know how to sing? Look, I will show you. There are seven notes, three scales, twenty-one modes, forty-nine melodic improvizations, three units of time, three voice registers, six ways of singing, nine emotions, thirty-six varieties of melody, forty-eight minor melodies. Thus there are one hundred and eighty-five parts of song'.

By the eighth century a number of musical works were ascribed to the mythological ṛishi Nārada*, of which the best known were the *Nāradīya-śikshā* (eighth century), the *Saṁgītā-Makaranda* (ninth century), the *Pañchama-sāra* (fifteenth century); there are others of still later date.

The prolific Kashmīri writer on poetics*, philosophy and other subjects, **Abhinavagupta** (fl. 1000) wrote the best commentary on the *Nāṭya-śāstra,* in which he discusses the theories of dance, drama and classical music. **Mataṅga** (*c.* 1100) was the author of *Bṛihaddeśī,* a treatise on the music of ancient India, probably compiled from earlier material, some of it at least as old as the sixth century AD. Its importance lies in that it preserves the *deśī* or folk traditions of Hindu music, as sung and played by people in different parts of India, as distinct from the *mārga* or classical music treated by Bharata. Patronized by the Yādava kings of Devagiri, was **Śārṅgadeva** (*c.* 1230) author of *Saṁgīta-ratnākara* (Music Jewel-mine). It covers sundry topics like cosmogony, the human body, the stages of pregnancy, before it gets down to the subject of music. It is chiefly valuable for the abhinaya dance movements described by him. **Nandikeśvara** (*c.* 1280) authority on rāga music and expounder of the twelve-note scale, wrote the *Abhinaya-darpaṇa* (Gesture-Mirror), which describes in detail the various movements of head, face, eyes and other parts of the body, along with their significance.

By the end of the eleventh century there were several hundred distinct schools of Hindu music; one authority specifies the precise number: seven hundred and eighty-four. This would mean that teaching theories differed from place to place, based on the individual interpretations of the works of old masters. With the growing ascendency of the Muhammadans, whose rulers imported musicians from Persia, Arabia, Egypt and Turkey, to serve at their courts, the schools of Indian music fell under two broad divisions, namely, the **Hindustāni School,** which prevailed in north India and was deeply coloured by Mussulman melodies, and the **Karṇāṭaka School** of the Deccan which preserved the Hindu, largely Dravidian modes.

The full flood of Muhammadan influence on Indian music may be dated from the time of **Amīr Khusrau** (1255–1325). Born in the Panjāb of Persian parentage, he lived in Delhi through three dynasties and the reign of eleven kings, and served at the court of the Khilji monarch. Man-at-arms, courtier, linguist, historian, lexicographer, writer of Persian and Hindi* poems, Amīr Khusrau was also the most accomplished musician of his day. He noted certain defects in the Hindu rendering of the rāgas as sung and played by the greatest contemporary Hindu expert, Nāik-gopāl, and proved his point with a correct rendering. Amīr Khusrau introduced several new modes, new musical instruments including the sitār, and new techniques which wrought a profound change in subsequent musical composition.

The greatest Hindu exponent of the rāgas of his day was **Nāik-gopāl,** patronized by the Khilji kings and honoured at many Hindu courts. His encounter with the Persian Amīr Khusrau (above) in which his composition was shown to be incorrectly rendered and inelegant in conception, is regarded by some as aprocryphal. **Puraṁdaradāsa** (fl. 1555), the earliest and most celebrated of the Kanarese classical singers, and once the favourite of the Vijayanagar court, was said to have been very rich and miserly in his youth, but later gave away his entire possessions and lived as a mendicant, singing the praises of Vishṇu. He systematized Karṇāṭaka music in his masterly compositions.

The seventeenth century was prolific in outstanding musicians, of whom the most famous were: **Tansen*** (1550–1610) patronized by Akbar, and regarded by some as the greatest Indian musician of all time, and by others as having been responsible for the corruption of the classic Hindu modes; **Puṇḍarīka-viṭṭhal** (fl. 1600) of the Deccan who in his three treatises dealt mainly with north Indian music; he classified sixteen Persian melodies and related them to the Indian musical system; Govind **Dīkshitar** (1614–1640) author of *Saṁgītā Sudhā*, composed under the patronage of the Nāyyaka kings and the princes of Tanjore, and founded a famous school of music; **Rāmdās** (fl. 1660) second only to Tānsen, was the protégé of Shāh Jahān.

The Moghul emperor Aurangzeb (1659–1707) a religious puritan ceased to give royal patronage to the arts, and was especially vehement in his hatred of music. It is said that when a funeral procession was passing his palace and he enquired whose it was he was told that it was the corpse of Music, being taken for burial (referring to his having slain the Arts). Aurangzeb, not the least bit abashed said, 'Bury her deep. So deep that not a sound reaches my ears'.

The further development of music was therefore confined to South India and in this region two names stand out. **Veṅkaṭamakhin** (fl. 1680), the innovator of the *Janaka-Mela* system of rāga scales in which he attempted to reconcile the various melakartā systems. He has been called the Pāṇini of Karṇāṭaka music. South India's best known and best loved musician was the saintly **Tyāgarāja** (1767–1847) of Tanjore. His mother tongue was Tamil but he composed his songs in Telugu which he thought was more melodious and better suited to music. An ardent devotee of Rāma, most of his *kīrtans* and rāgas were in honour of that deity. He is regarded as the chief exponent of the *gāna-mārga* (song-way), i.e. salvation by means of devotional song.

Modern Indian music has not advanced much beyond the medieval rāga system, and musical theory is merely a matter of the reassessment of early works. Paṇḍit **Bhatkhaṇḍe** (d. 1940), regarded as the foremost modern scholar on the rāga, codified the material of older authorities with much learned labour.

Western music has found a firm foothold in Indian films, which often cleverly combines rāga patterns with jazz rhythms, much to the consternation of the purists.

Books

I. Banerjee, G. N. *Hellenism in Ancient India*, Calcutta, 1919.
II. Daniélou, Alain. *Northern Indian Music*, Vol. I, Calcutta, 1949.
III. Rawlinson, H. G. *Intercourse Between India and the Western World*, Cambridge, 1916.
IV. Sambamoorthy, P. *History of Indian Music*, Madras, 1960.
(*See also under* Music.)

MUSICAL INSTRUMENTS. Accomplishment in music was once considered an essential requirement of a good education. Both boys and girls of good families were taught to play and sing, and an acquaintance with music was one of the attributes of the man of the world, who was invariably a *vādana* or proficient in playing a musical instrument of some kind. Later the playing of such vulgar devices became the trade mark of the eunuch and temple prostitute, and the musical profession has only recently emerged from that odium.

The *vādya* or *vāditra*, as musical instruments are called in India, may be divided into five classes, namely: (1) *tata*, or stringed instruments played with the bow; (2) *betat*, stringed instruments played by plucking the strings; (3) *sushira*, air-blown instruments; (4) *ḍhola*, drums, and (5) *ghana*, metallic percussion instruments. A number of conventions once determined the use or prohibition of musical instruments, such as that no bells may be used in the worship of Lakshmī, nor bamboo flute in the worship of Durgā; drums should not be beaten at the moment of sunset, or conchs blown at the moment of sunrise.

TATA are stringed instruments played by drawing a bow across the strings. Principal examples of this class are: *ektāra*, a 'one-stringed', non-fretted fiddle popular with village players, religious mendicants and wandering minstrels like the Bauls; *dilruba*, a fretted instrument introduced by the Muslims, popular in Bombay and the Deccan; related to it is the *esrāj*, used in Bengal, suited to solo accompaniment; *saraṅgi*, non-fretted, with three playing and sometimes as many as twenty sympathetic strings, is the Indian equivalent of the violin. A special close-form pattern of music known as the *lahrā*, 'wave', is played on the saraṅgi; the precursor of the saraṅgi in ancient times was the *rābaṇāstrana,* said to have been invented by Rāvaṇa, king of Ceylon.

BETAT, stringed instruments played by plucking the strings with a *mizrab* or plectrum. Included in this class are: *sarod,* which comes from Persia and is now favoured in Bengal. It has four strings of steel and brass, gives a metallic sound and looks like an overgrown mandoline; *sitār,* a 'three-stringed', non-fretted instrument invented by Amīr Khusrau, which was later provided with additional strings to give it a drone effect; *tambura,* four stringed and non-fretted, is among the most popular of Indian musical instruments, and in mythology was the favourite of the sage Nārada. Its top is held over the left shoulder while playing. The tambura maintains the key note (*śruti*) and also supplies a very rich droning accompaniment; *vīna,* the Indian lute, is also the oldest of Indian musical instruments. It has seven strings and is shaped to represent the goddess Sarasvatī by reason of the curved neck and two large gourds (her breasts) and the frets along its length (her bracelets). The two gourds are the resonating chambers, one situated at the end which rests on the ground, and the other near the top which rests on the lap.

SUSHIRA, 'holed'; this class includes all air-blown instruments, of which the chief are: *kākalī,* described in the *kāvyas* as having a soft and gentle note; it was played near a sleeping mistress to test whether she was really asleep or feigning; *śṛiṅga,* made of animal horn, of which one type, the *kahala,* is mentioned in ancient texts; the *siṅgnād* is a kind of whistle made of horn, and used for cult and religious purposes by sādhus; *nāgasvara,* 'snake-note', a kind of fife, commonly used in South India; *bansri* (from Sanskrit, vaṁśa, 'reed'), a bamboo flute, of which the best known is the *muralī* or *veṇu,* the divine flute played by Kṛishṇa; *bīn,* the snake-charmer's gourd; *śaṅkha,* 'shell', the conch-shell of the large mollusc used in temple services or in battle; its sound is regarded as very auspicious; *śanai,* derived from Persia, resembles the oboe, is about twelve inches long, with seven holes, and is best suited for classical music.

ḌHOLA, includes all the *avanaddha,* 'roaring', instruments, of which there is a great variety. The skill of the Indian musician in beating out highly complex patterns on his drums is perhaps excelled only by the Negro. A characteristic of Indian drummers is that as they beat they accompany themselves by violent agitations of the head, shoulders, and arms, in peculiar convulsive movements; their eyes turn up and they reach an almost trance-like state. Chief among the drums are: *ḍamru,* or *ḍamaru,* a very small, double-sided, narrow waisted drum, first used by Śiva as an accompaniment to the tāṇḍava dance. With this drum he sets the rhythm of the universe. The drum is held in the hand, around its waist, and when it is shaken the thongs binding the tympana on either side constrict the parchment at each end and a rapid rattling sound ensues; today it is used by itinerant monkey men; *ḍholak,* a simple, cylindrical, double-headed drum, played with one hand and a stick, of which there are again many varieties. In Bengal one type called the *maḍol* is generally used by players of the depressed classes who at set intervals perform the maḍol-pūjā before their drums, offering them homage with flowers, lights and dances, as they are believed to contain a divine spirit; *mṛidaṅga*, 'clay-body', so called because it was originally made of clay; a general term for the barrel-shaped drum beaten at both ends. It is among the best accompaniments for classical music, and indispensable for the Bharata-nāṭyam dance. One variety known as *pakhwaj* was introduced by the Muslims; related to it is the popular *tabla* of Persian origin, said to be a pakhwaj divided into two and played with both hands on one end; *dundubhi*, the Indian kettle-drum, also includes a number of war and tribal drums; one variety, called *bhūmi-dundubhi*, 'earth-drum', is made by digging a hole in the ground and covering it with a piece of hide. Like it is the huge *tamak*, used for long-distance signalling and for summoning the clan in time of need; another tribal war-drum is the *muraśu*, covered with the skin of a bull that has killed a tiger; the *bherī* is a smaller drum of the same class for calling warriors to the fray; the *nakara* accompanies village dances; *dhakkā* is another of Śiva's drums. Legend has it that in order to help certain sages who were struggling to put the science of language into form, Śiva performed a dance and while in the ecstatic state produced fourteen beats on his dhakkā which he interpreted as a series of fourteen grammatical aphorisms; on these aphorisms the grammar of Pāṇini was later built; *chenda*, or chhenda, a large, loud-sounding cylindrical drum, standing upright, and beaten with sticks or the hands. Associated with it is the *muddalam* or maddalam, which is suspended by a string from the neck of the player, and beaten on both ends with the hands or with sticks. Both these drums are played during Kathākali dance dramas, which often feature a contest of skill between the two instrumentalists playing them.

GHANA, 'striking', the whole class of metallic percussion instruments, largely used in religious ceremonies and during processions. They include: *ghaṇṭā*, bells; *ghaṇṭikā*, little bells; *jhallarī*, cymbals played with two hands; *talam*, small finger cymbals played with one hand and used for marking time as in the dances of Bharata-nāṭyam; *kāṁsya* or gongs; *ghuṅgru* or *ghargharikā*, dance-bells; *nūpura* or *mañjīra*, anklets with tiny bells attached to them, worn by dancing girls; *chiṁṭa* or tongs, used by sādhus* and mendicants; *jala-taraṅg*, 'water-waves', different-sized bowls filled with water and beaten with two sticks to produce a variety of tones.

Books

I. Rajaram, S. *The Musical Instruments of the Hindu People*, 1912.

II. Rosenthal, Ethel. *The Story of Indian Music and Its Instruments*, London, 1928.

MUSLIMS. In the recurrent pattern of medieval Indian history, the chaos ensuing after the death of Harsha* was resolved once more only with the advent of a new civilization that came in the wake of Islam. The Muslim invasion brought with it not only the freshening genes of many virile races, but the explosive force of a mighty religion whose fundamental doctrines differed widely from the brāhminical creed. By AD 650, less than twenty years after the death of Muhammad in AD 632, the armies of Islam had advanced as far as Baluchistan, taking in their stride the paganized frontier towns of the land of al-Hind, or Hindustān. They engulfed the border in a matter of months and then moved on towards the heart of India. First Sind, then the Panjāb, the western Coast, the East, and finally the South. Today the subcontinent of India counts more Muslims than any other country on the earth's surface, most of them descendants of converts from Hinduism.

Islam brought a conception of life which although hard in many ways, attenuated and sparse as compared with the tropic luxury of Hinduism, severe in outlook and puritanical in thought, nevertheless profoundly modified the character of Indian religions. There is no reform movement since the advent of the Arabs but bears the stamp of Islam. How this conquest was achieved and how the revolution in thought and spirit was effected is not to be gleaned from brāhminical sources, for, says Havell, 'Brāhminical books for the most part pass over the Muhammadan invasions in silence'.

The expedition that led to the conquest of Sind consisted of a small army of six thousand men, commanded by a youth of twenty named Muhammad ibn-Kāsim. It was achieved with the assistance of Hindus themselves, opportunists and renegades who went over to the enemy. Sind was conquered in AD 712. From Sind the Muhammadans pushed inland towards Mārwār, Broach, Ujjain, Mālwā, and the territories of Cutch, Saurāshṭra, Gujarāt and Western Rājputāna. In the words of G. S. Ghurye, 'The story is uniform in this, that in spite of large numbers and great valour, every great battle ended in the utter defeat and great massacre of the Hindus'.

A new era in the Muhammadan conquest of India was opened in the beginning of the eleventh century with the periodical incursions of Mahmud of Ghazni, one of the greatest military leaders in history and, according to Gibbon, 'undoubtedly one of the greatest kings of the world'. He invaded India seventeen times, each time defeating more massive forces, and returning to Ghazni (in modern Afghanistan) with incalculable treasures, including the fabled riches of the temple of Somnāth*. In his wake came the Sultans of Ghor, also an Afghan dynasty, who captured Gwālior, Meerut, Delhi, Ranthambhor, and other key cities, more than once snatching victory from the jaws of disaster owing to the jealousies, feuds and rivalries of the Rājput and Hindu chiefs.

In 1197 a young Muslim general, Ikhtiār Khilji, son of Bakhtiār Khilji, occupied Bihār and Bengal, taking the Sena capital of Nadia one year later with a mere two hundred horsemen. His initial advance was made with only eighteen horsemen, and the people thought he was a merchant who had come to sell horses (*see* Pāla). Says Rawlinson, 'Soon after AD 1200, the whole of Northern India, except Rājputāna, Mālwā and part of Gujarāt, had been conquered, and Hindu supremacy was at an end'.

The conquest of the South was no less spectacular. In 1294 Alā-ud-dīn Khilji set out from the neighbourhood of Allāhābād, crossing the Vindhya range with eight thousand horse, on what was meant to be a minor raid. He completed the journey of five hundred miles along unknown routes through mountains and jungles without any supplies, eventually ending up by conquering Deogiri, the capital of the Yādava kingdom, the most powerful in the South. This expedition was followed in succeeding years by others, and by 1309 the Muslims had taken Dorasamudra (modern Halebīd) the Hoysaḷa capital; Madura the Pāṇḍya capital; and Warangal the Kākatīya capital; and Malik Kāfūr the Muslim general built a mosque at Cape Comorin, the southernmost tip of the subcontinent. The whole of India had fallen under the sway, and the greater part under the direct rule, of the Muslims.

Two centuries later the Moghuls had only to consolidate the work of their predecessors. The bright side of Moghul rule is seen in the reign of Akbar the Great (1556–1605), and its more sinister aspect in the reign of Aurangzeb who in the single year of 1679 reduced to rubble sixty-six temples in Amber, sixty-three in Chitor, one hundred and three at Udaipur; and in Banāras, holy city of the Hindus, razed to the ground a Hindu shrine of special sacrosanctity and built on its site a Muslim mosque.

So considerable has been the influence of Islam, that there is not an aspect of Hindu life, including its religion and domestic routine that has not been touched by it. The patronage of Muhammadan kings was not confined to those skills and studies in which Muslims alone had a controlling interest. When the old crusading zeal had cooled down they were foremost in their championship of indigenous sciences and local literature. The Moghuls in particular, at whose courts an élite of Persian, Afghan, Turkish, Egyptian and Arab scholars and artists mixed in communal intercourse, set the final seal to Islamic enterprise on the sub-continent, and with them another combination of ingredients was lowered into the melting-pot of Indian culture. 'The Empire of the Moghuls' says S. R. Sharma, 'has vanished forever, but their influence endures in a thousand different forms.' A brief survey of these forms will indicate the truth of this statement.

In painting and handicrafts the Muslim, particularly Moghul, schools evolved an exquisite Persian-Hindu style, in which the native motifs of Iran, Bactria, Asia Minor and Egypt can be discerned. Many of the artists who flourished at the Moghul courts and who have left their impress on Indian painting*, came from the Middle East and Central Asia. The Rājput, Kāṅgṛā, Himāchal and other schools of art, with their delicate touches and delightful colours, are in the main indebted to Moghul inspiration.

Muslim artists brought with them perfected techniques of enamelling and faience, and Muslim horticulturists* gave Hindu princes their first experience of the graceful Moghul gardens. Muslims were also responsible for introducing the manufacture of paper, the art of calligraphy and the making of illuminated manuscripts.

In music an entire school, known as the Northern or Hindustāni school evolved as a result of Hindu-Muslim contact. New *rāgas** were created, besides a number of refined variations on the old rāga themes, and several new musical instruments to accompany them, including the sitār. Hindustāni music and musical instruments are largely the products of Muhammadan patronage.

In architecture the Muslim bequest to India has been universally acknowledged. The passion of Islam for building was proverbial, and the monuments and mosques raised by Muslims in India are among her most treasured possessions. Hindu rulers, not insensitive to the beauty of Muslim styles, were quick to adopt them, and literally thousands of palaces, temples, tombs, cenotaphs, pavilions, and towers, throughout the length and breadth of India bear the stamp of Islamic genius. 'In fact', says Tara Chand, 'almost every building of architectural importance in modern times, except of course, those of the western styles, follows the Hindu-Muslim style.'

Muslim rulers gave their support, financial and otherwise, to scholars, poets and writers, irrespective of their religion, and Muslim courts were frequently graced by Hindu men of learning who occupied an honoured place among their Muslim colleagues. Dr J. B. Chaudhuri has shown that Sanskrit scholarship received the patronage of many Muhammadan kings who liberally subsidized translations of Sanskrit classics, and even included Sanskrit in the curriculum of Islamic institutions of learning.

Muslim interest in local vernaculars was equally impartial and generous, and often the best work in these languages was done by those who directly or indirectly benefited by their support. Muhammadan princes took a keen interest in Telugu, Tamil, Malayālam and Kanarese letters, and Muslim writers enriched the treasury of their literature with many notable works. The Muslim influence on Hindi is evident from its vocabulary, grammar, metaphor, prosody and style, and, as Dr Tara Chand points out, 'what is true of Hindi is true of Marāṭhi, Bengali, and more so of Panjābi and Sindhi'. In Bengal we find that Bengali first developed as an independent literary medium not under Hindu but under Muslim rule. The Hindu courts of Bengal gave no encouragement to their native tongue. Critical opinion holds that if Hindu kings had continued to enjoy independence, Bengali would scarcely have received royal patronage (I, p. 212).

Astronomy, a science in which Indians were believed to be supreme, received its modern impetus from the Muhammadans. From the Arabs Hindu astronomers took over a number of technical terms, the calculation of latitudes and longitudes, various items of the calendar, and a whole new branch of study, namely horoscopy. The remarkable observatories at Jaipur, Mathurā, Delhi and Banāras built by the astronomer-king Jaisingh II (1686–1743) were based on his studies of the work of Nāsir-ud-dīn of Tūs, and the astronomical tables of Ulugh Beg, Al Gurgān and others, and were directly inspired by the observatory built at Samarqand in 1425 by Ulugh Beg.

Āyurveda too was generously leavened with the medical theories of Rhazes and Avicenna. In chemistry India took over certain chemical processes, the use of metallic acids, and various chemical substances, and also those experimental techniques that grew from the pursuit of alchemy and which, through Gebir, were Islam's bequest to modern scientific research.

After little more than two centuries of rule the Moghuls, besides establishing Persian as an official language, gave northern India and much of the Deccan as well, a new popular language, namely, Hindustāni, that was being rapidly acquired by all classes except the brāhmins and stationary village folk. The Moghul way of life permeated areas outside the actual territory administered by them, influencing the administrative system, court manners, speech, food and dress of the neighbouring states, both Hindu and Muslim.

Tailored clothes, as distinct from the general one-piece garment of the

Hindus, had been introduced by the Śakas and Kushāns, but the styles underwent a radical change with the coming of the Muslims who set a new fashion in dress. The present-day Hindustāni dress, both of men and women, is basically much the same as that seen in Moghul paintings, being adapted from the fashions brought by the Arab, Turkish, and Persian nobles. The manner of wearing the turban, the knee-length buttoned-up tunic and tight-fitting trousers, even the style of trimming the beard and cultivating the mustaches, spread from the Moghul court to the populace and was adopted by both Muslims and Hindus.

Reviewing the vast area of this cultural legacy, the eminent historian Dr Tara Chand said, 'It is hardly possible to exaggerate the extent of Muslim influence over Indian life in all its departments', and indeed the catalogue is past reckoning, for Muslim ways of life and thought have penetrated into the remotest areas of Hindu culture. Its influence is found in intimate details of the domestic life of the Hindu; in the food he eats, the manner of seasoning, cooking and serving it; in his habits at home; his behaviour in society; in his domestic routine; even in religious ceremonies such as weddings and the celebration of festivals and fairs. Forms of address and salutation, social etiquette, and the courtly institutions were all touched and refined under Muslim influence. The princely arts and fashions spread from the Moghul kingdom to the Marāṭha, Rājput and Sikh principalities (I, p. 141). Further south, Bijāpur, Golkondā, Amber, Bundi, and most of the petty courts were modelled on the pattern established at Delhi.

Such was the glamour of Moghul rule that when the huge empire had crumbled it still retained its glory, and the prestige of the court endured even when its power had completely waned. The long and splendid history of Moghul rule had left too deep an impress on the Indian mind for the seal of their approval not to be eagerly sought in subsequent adventures by others. Marāṭha rulers who later became independent of the Moghuls and controlled larger areas than the emperors of Delhi, were still proud of any titles received from the Moghuls.

So widespread, so deep and so tenacious has been the influence of those spacious centuries, that northern India may be said to have been permanently Moghulized, and the rest of India indelibly stamped with the impress received from Islam.

Books

I. Chand, Tara. *The Influence of Islam on Indian Culture*, Allahabad, 1936.
II. Chaudhuri, J. B. *Muslim Patronage to Sanskrit Learning*, Calcutta, 1942.
III. Ghurye, G. S. *Caste & Race in India*, London, 1932.
IV. Jaffar, S. M. *Some Cultural Aspects of Muslim Rule in India*, Peshawar, 1939.
V. Kaumudi, S. 'Mingling of Islamic & Indigenous Traditions in Indian Music', *Roopa Lekha*, New Delhi, 1950.
VI. Majumdar, R. C. *Arab Invasion of India*, Madras, 1931.
VII. Rawlinson, H. G. *India: A Short Cultural History*, London, 1952.
VIII. Sharma, S. R. *The Mughal Empire in India*, Bombay, 1947.
IX. Thomas, F. W. *Mutual Influence of Muhammadans and Hindus in India*, 1892.

MYSTIC SYLLABLES. The most powerful class of mantras* and magical utterances is the *bījākshara*, 'seed syllable', or *bīja-mantra*, 'seed mantra'. The term bījākshara is made up of two words: bīja, meaning seed, and akshara meaning both syllable and imperishable. In general parlance the term is applied to any pithy mantra, but according to Tantriks every true bījākshara mantra must fulfil two requirements: firstly, it must consist of only one syllable, the 'seed', and secondly, it must end with an *anusvāra* to make it 'imperishable'. It is the result of a divine union, and the process of enunciating a bījākshara mantra has been described thus: 'The two lips are Śiva and Śakti; their *maithuna* (union) is the movement which results in the seed or bīja'.

The indispensable concomitant of every true bījākshara mantra, the *anusvāra*, 'overtone', is a nasalized sound of the Sanskrit alphabet. Fanciful etymology derives it from the neigh (*svara*) of a horse, it being one of the mysteries concealed in this animal by Brahmā. The anusvāra is defined as pure nasal, sounded without being modified by any stop. Actually it is only an adaptation of an unpronouncable 'vibration', which can only be employed in conjunction with a letter of the alphabet to render it capable of articulation.

In Sanskrit the anusvāra is written as a dot above the letter which it follows, and in romanized transliteration by the letter 'm', with a dot above (or below)it, thus, 'ṁ'. Often its specially sacred character is emphasized by providing it with a couch in the form of a semicircle, in which the dot is inserted, thus ँ. This dot is related to the *bindu** or drop, and is also said to be the visible form of *śūnya**, 'emptiness'. Although rendered by an 'm', the anusvāra is not a labial, and the lips do not meet to pronounce it. Thus, a rough approximation to the sound transliterated 'boṁ', would be the French word *bon*. The anusvāra, correctly intoned, is said to set up cerebral vibrations and interior echoes of irresistible potency.

The true bījākshara, or anusvāric monosyllable, is believed to bear the full potentiality of its completed significance, and contains the germ of a whole philosophy or doctrine. A huge treatise of 8,000 *ślokas* (verses) may be summarized in a few stanzas, these further reduced to a few lines, then to one line, and finally to a bījākshara. Yet the latter will contain the full power of the 8,000 ślokas, and by merely repeating the mantra one can master the entire doctrine.

A bījākshara is admirably suited for *japa* or repetition*, for it is short, easy to remember and to repeat. Properly intoned for some time it creates cerebral vibrations so that the mantra is carried on even after its audible repetition has ceased. Adepts need chant a mantra only once for its reverberations to continue for a full day or even a week. Because of the presence of the anusvāra in each of the bījāksharas, it can be directed 'between the brows', or 'the back of the head', or a spot 'above the head'; it can pile up layers of power in the cerebral centres and build up like a battery, and this power can then be projected for good or ill.

Bījāksharas are associated with particular deities, and it is imperative to know what powers a mantra possesses before uttering it since many of the mantras can have dangerous repercussions and even lead to madness. A few of the principal bījākshara mantras are given here: *aiṁ*, used for the worship of Sarasvatī; *boṁ* for Kāma; *ḍuṁ* for Durgā; *eṁ* for Yoni; *gāṁ* for Gaṇeśa; *hriṁ* for Māyā; *hūṁ* for Śiva; *klīṁ* for Kāma; *krīṁ* for Kālī; *śrīṁ* for Lakshmī; *rāṁ* for Rāma; *kroṁ* for Śiva. A deity may be worshipped with more than one bījākshara.

The most solemn of all the bījāksharas is the portentous *oṁ*, given the title of *praṇava* or uttering. The brief *Māṇḍukya Upanishad* is entirely devoted to this mystic syllable. It is compounded of three sounds, *a u m*, representing the three Vedas (*Ṛig, Yajur, Sāma*), the three worlds (heaven, atmosphere, earth), the three chief deities (Brahmā, Vishṇu, Śiva). Embracing all the secrets of the universe, which are, as it were, gathered to a point within it, it is used for invocations, affirmations, and blessings, and at the commencement and termination of prayer, meditation or work. It is said to be the mystical quintessence of the entire cosmos and is 'nothing less than the theophany itself reduced to the state of a phoneme'. It is the monarch of all sounded things, the mother of vibrations, and the key to eternal wisdom and power.

Books

See under Mantra.

MYTHOLOGY. Folk lore and myths long antedate written works among all nations. Hinduism is extremely rich in legendary tales which may be regarded as forming the bulk of Hindu literature. The mythopoeic tendency has been so strong in India that there is hardly a facet of Hindu life and culture that has not been touched by the symbolical and the imaginary. Myths enter into religion, the arts, history, philosophy, geography, science, sociology, laws, institutions and everyday life.

Indian mythology is immensely rich and varied, and there can be little doubt that a vast quantity of material relating to prehistoric beliefs and practices of profound sociological interest and value lies embedded in the Hindu myths. The main sources of this early lore are to be found in the Vedas, which enshrine much Aryan material; in the Epics, which have preserved both Aryan and local legends; and in the Purāṇas, which embody an abundance of native traditions.

Hindu mythology has been fed from countless sources. The creation myths, the stories of the kalpas and of Brahmā's cycle of days, myths concerning the Flood, the incarnations of deity, of gods and titans, of ogres and demons, of *ṛishis* and *rākshasas*, star myths and solar myths, are derived from a multitude of peoples. The notion that the huge fund of Hindu mythology was contributed to by the Aryans alone has now all but disappeared. The roots of India's legendary past lie deeper than was at first apparent. They go back to a time before the Aryans to the Dravidians, to the pre-Dravidian peoples of the Indus Valley, to the primitive Proto-Australoids and Negritos. And much is traceable to races outside India, the Egyptians, Babylonians, Jews, Phoenicians. Substantial contributions have also been made to the treasury by peoples of the post-Aryan period: the Persians, Greeks, Scythians, Chinese and Central Asians.

The significance and symbolism of Hindu and Buddhist myths constitute part of the study of mythology in general, the guiding principle of which is that primitive peoples do not just invent stories out of nothing for their own amusement or entertainment, but formulate them to account for something, to preserve a tradition, or to justify an archaic rite. Thus, the euhemeristic theory regards myths as garbled versions of real events, and holds that they have their roots in history; the deities are in fact culture heroes and kings of a remote antiquity. An extension of this theory is that a myth preserves a particular auspicious event associated with a culture hero, which is embodied in a ritual formula. The rite is thus an attenuated and stylized enactment of the myth, and symbolically embodies a reality which is to be constantly perpetuated through this rite.

Another theory is that myths are exteriorized formulations of the human psyche, and represent correspondences with the vast and dim unconscious mind, revealed in the dreams of kings, the inspirations of sages, and the drug-induced visions of hierophants, bearing a special significance to the community since they are believed to contain messages from the gods.

Others hold that the gods and other supernatural beings of ancient legend are personifications of the heavenly bodies (Sūrya is the sun, Rudra is Sagittarius, Dhruva the Pole Star); or that they represent terrestrial phenomena (Rudra is the thunder, Rahu the eclipse); or the powers of nature, especially procreation and fertility (Śakti is the force that underlies growth, Śiva the generative power, Sītā the functions of ploughing and agriculture); or again that they are idealized aspects of the human body (Brahmā personifies the Pons Varolii of the cerebro-spinal nervous system, Śiva the phallus, Durgā the devouring vulva). More extravagant still are recent hypotheses that equate the deities with chemical elements (Mitra is oxygen, Varuṇa hydrogen), or physical phenomena (Indra is electricity); and the lesser beings with pests and vermin (the rākshasa is a blood-sucking worm; *bhūta* and *preta* are poisonous germs; apsarās are malarial mosquitoes) (VII, p. 37 et seq.).

Occasionally the speculations of the mythologists presume to invade the historical field itself and find myth even in history, not always with fortunate results. Thus, there is the theory that Buddha's life is modelled on Zoroaster's*, and that his is a Maga legend. Or that Buddha represents a sun myth. Buddha's pre-enlightenment period is equated with the night, his attainment of Truth is the sunrise, the Four Truths represent the four directions, and so on. To all but the proponents of such theories, the pitfalls that lie in the path will be plainly discernible.

Books

I. Dowson, J. *Classical Dictionary of Hindu Mythology & Religion*, 3rd Ed., 1891.
II. Hopkins, E. W. *Epic Mythology*, Strassburg, 1915.
III. Kennedy, Vans. *Researches into the Nature and Affinity of Ancient & Hindu Mythology*, London, 1831.
IV. Macdonell, A. A. *Vedic Mythology*, Strassburg, 1897.
V. Mackenzie, D. A. *Indian Myth & Legend*, London, 1914.
VI. Malinowski, B. *Myth in Primitive Psychology*, London, 1936.

VII. Mehta, D. D. *Some Positive Sciences in the Vedas*, New Delhi, 1961.
VIII. Moor, E. *Hindu Pantheon*, London, 1810.
IX. Nivedita, Sister, and A. Coomaraswamy. *Myths of the Hindus and Buddhists*, New York, 1914.
X. Pargiter, F. E. *Ancient Indian Historical Tradition*, London, 1922.
XI. Pillai, G. K. *Hindu Gods & Hidden Mysteries*, Allahabad, 1958.
XII. Thomas, P. *Epics, Myths & Legends of India*, Bombay, n.d.
XIII. Vaidya, D. *Hindu Myths and Their Meaning*, 1902.
XIV. Wilkins, W. J. *Hindu Mythology, Vedic & Puranic*, 1901.
XV. Zimmor, H. *Myths & Symbols in Indian Art & Civilization* (Ed. by J. Campbell), New York, 1946.

NĀGA, a mixed Mongolian people whose original home was probably in the highlands (Sanskrit: *naga*) of Iran, which have ever been the meeting-ground for Aryan and Mongolian races. Nāgadvīpa was one of the nine geographical divisions of Bhārata-varsha or Ancient India, which formed a belt extending from Iran across Afghanistan to parts of the Panjāb.

The Nāgas were of Scythic affinities and associated with the serpent totem, of which some evidence is found in Ancient Persian and South Russian myths. Herodotus relates the story of Hercules who during his search for his lost mare, mated with Echidna, half-woman half-serpent, and left a bow for his son Scythes. Thus does Greek mythology, with instructive symbolism, explain the origin of the Scythian people.

The Nāgas were in all probability a matriarchal people, whose culture appears to have been linked, like heliolithic culture in other areas, with the worship of the sun and the serpent*, the erection of great stone monuments and the use of the gammadion symbol. The theory of their relationship with the ancient Maga people may find some confirmation in these parallels. Sun worship, ophiolatry, and the use of the swastika as a talismanic symbol (since it was supposed to be marked on the cobra's hood), and the erection of megalithic pillars, may all have been composite contributions, not necessarily attributable to any single source. But it is not improbable that the Nāgas were responsible for the introduction of some of these elements to India. Huge stone pillars were found in India from earliest historical times, and it is known that Aśoka had many of his famous inscriptions carved on previously existing monoliths.

Some authorities hold the view that the Nāgas were Tibeto-Burmese who occupied northern India before the advent of the Aryans, but this is an offshoot of the old theory connecting the Nāgas with such aboriginal tribes as the head-hunting Nāgas of Assam, so called by their Assamese neighbours because they went about nude (nagna). Whatever their subsequent admixtures it is clear that they were Mongolians, and their later contact with the Dravidians and with the primitive races of Central India is merely an indication of their widespread diffusion.

The north-western region of India, through which the Nāga migration took place, was traditionally believed to be guarded by the serpent king Nīlanāga, who appointed other subordinate serpent-princes to guard its hills and lakes. Kashmīr, which has preserved innumerable relics of her historic associations bears ample evidence, in her place-names in particular, of connection with the Nāgas.

In Indian geography the word 'nāga' appears in many place-names, of which one of the oldest was Nāgasāhvaya (later Hastināpura). The best-known of the present-day names, Nāgpur, is perhaps merely an analogous appellation given to an area where the cobra is common.

Similarly, the term 'nagara', which originally meant the imperial capital, and now means 'town' or 'locality', is still used as a suffix in the naming of new towns. Nālandā*, site of a famous Buddhist university, was also called after a Nāga, namely, Nāga Nanda, and Takshaśilā (Taxila) after the Nāga king Takshaka.

Legend speaks of the Nāgas as acquainted with many sciences, skilled in medicine and having the power to restore life to the dead. They were expert in the arts and crafts, including woodwork and sculpture, and were highly accomplished painters. Just as traditionally the earliest music was attributed to the Gandharvas, so the earliest paintings were said to be the work of Nāgas. Their mode of writing influenced the shape of the Indian scripts, a fact that is preserved in the name of the Sanskrit script, which is called *nāgarī**, from *nāga-lipi*, the writing of the Nāgas.

Several eminent saints, kings and philosophers have borne names in honour of the serpent, among them Nāgārjuna and Nāgasena. The name of Vālmīki, author of the *Rāmāyaṇa*, signifies 'anthill', favourite haunt of the cobra, which may be a patronymic indicating Nāga ancestry. The intellectual capabilities of the Nāgas were of such a high order, and so greatly did Buddha esteem them that, according to the legend, he entrusted to their keeping the most highly reverenced of the doctrines, later embodied in the Mahāyāna *Prajña-pāramitā*. This doctrine was regarded as too abstruse to be understood by Buddha's contemporaries, and only when Nāgārjuna, the later great master of Mahāyāna, appeared in this world, did the Nāgas invite him to their mysterious realm and deliver it to him.

The Nāgas are always depicted as formidable opponents in strife. They appear in the *Ṛig-veda* as enemies of Indra, and are abhorred as a serpent-worshipping non-Aryan people. Subsequent Hindu mythology is filled with references to serpent deities and snake kings of great prowess and awe-inspiring ability in war. If Kṛishṇa himself was not of Nāga descent, as some scholars suggest, the myth that makes him the brother of the fair-complexioned Balarāma, who was the reincarnation of Śesha the World Serpent, probably symbolizes an alliance between the indigenous dark-hued hero and a northern snake-worshipping king.

In Sanskrit texts the Nāgas are described as a handsome, intelligent, race. One of India's most venerable sages, the *muni* Nārada, after his visit to their north-western home, the serpent paradise, declared that it was more enchanting that Indra's heaven. Their women were of striking beauty, and Sanskrit literature describes in numerous passages the exquisite grace of the Nāga maidens. Nothing was more complimentary than to describe a woman as surpassing a Nāga maiden in comeliness.

Nāga women were therefore frequently sought as brides for the royal harems of Indian princes, both Aryan and Dravidian, since they were beautiful and cultured, and fitted easily into the ways of palace life. The marriages of Purukutsa son of Māndhāṭri of Ayodhyā, with Narmadā, a Nāga princess; of Kuśa, son of Rāma with the Nāga princess Kumudvatī; of Aśvatthāman, son of Droṇa, with a Nāga maiden; of Arjuna with Ulūpī, a Nāga princess, are conspicuous instances of such alliances.

In historical times practically every important dynasty was linked with the Nāgas. Nāga queens graced the courts of the Kadambas, Pallavas, Kārkoṭas, Cholas, Vākāṭakas, Bhāraśivas, Cheras, Bhaums, Sātavāhanas, Manipuris, Gonds, and Marāṭhas, to name but a few. The Guptas maintained friendly relations with the Nāgas, and Samudragupta's son married the Nāga princess, Kuberanāgā.

Apart from these alliances the Nāgas founded several important dynasties of their own; those in historical times included the Haryaṅka dynasty, founded by Bimbisāra of Magadha; the Śiśunāgas, also of Magadha; the Lichchhavis of the Himālayan foothills; the Bhāraśivas of the Upper Ganges region; the Nāga dynasty of Padmāvatī in Central India. There is epigraphic, numismatic and literary evidence of Nāga rule from the third century A D in Vidisā, Kāntipura and Mathurā. The Nāgas of Mathurā, after the decline of the Kushāns, rose to prominence under king Vīrasena, a great ruler whose kingdom extended over wide areas of western Uttar Pradesh. The Purāṇas state that between the Kushān occupation and the rise of the Guptas, no less than seven Nāga kings ruled at Mathurā.

The Yādavas, the tribe to which Kṛishṇa belonged, were a serpent people; so also were the Vijayanagar kings. Among others claiming descent from the Nāgas were the Nhāvi of the Deccan, the Kūr of Chota Nāgpur, and certain of the princely families of Mysore.

Books

I. Majumdar, R. C. (Ed.) *The Vedic Age*, London, 1951.
II. Majumdar, R. C. (Ed.) *The Age of Imperial Unity*, Bombay, 1951.
III. Vogel, J. P. *Indian Serpent Lore*, London, 1926.

NĀGARĪ, the 'city' cultivated script, also called *devanāgarī*, the script of the 'divine city' of the gods. Orthodox Hindus believe that Sanskrit letters are the actual eternal outlines of the sounds they represent, and that if the impression made on the ether by uttering the letters could be seen, they would be found to have the shape of the devanāgarī characters. The term *nāgarī* given to the current form of the alphabet in which Sanskrit is written today is of uncertain provenance. According to some scholars the term indicates that it owes its development to the Nāgas*, an early Mongolian people of north-western India, since the script was also called Nāgalipi, 'Naga-writing'.

Nāgarī is known to be ultimately derived from a North Semitic or Aramaic mode of writing adapted in north-western India to the phonetic needs of the Sanskrit language, in a form first known as Brāhmī (*see* script). Its present alphabetic arrangement and order belong to the second or third century A D, but the outlines are believed to be derived from an earlier variant of devanāgarī once called Harsha or Śrīharsha, which was presumed to have been current in Rājasthān, parts of Gujarāt and Uttar Pradesh. Thus, although the sacred books of the Hindus were composed and orally handed down from about the first millennium BC, the writing in which they were finally set down was devised and developed by non-Aryans, and was not perfected till the beginning of the Christian era.

The earliest extant examples of devanāgarī are found in the Ghosuṇḍi stone inscription and the Ayodhyā stone inscription of Dhanadeva, both dating from about AD 100, and both very crude and primitive. The Junagaḍh rock inscription of Rudradāman the Śaka*, belonging to the second century AD is a better specimen of the script. The first inscription wholly in nāgarī characters is dated AD 754, and the oldest manuscript written in devanāgarī belongs to the eleventh century AD.

Variants of nāgarī include Balbodh, used for Marāṭhi; Moḍī, 'twisted' for several dialects of Marāṭhi; Nandināgarī used in parts of the Deccan; Rājasthānī in Rājaputāna; Mārwāṛī in Mārwāṛ; Mahājanī in parts of northern India. Several scripts* closely related to nāgarī are also loosely covered by this term.

Devanāgarī was not at first universally employed for the writing of Sanskrit in India, each state using its own script for the purpose. Actually it was only about two hundred years ago that devanāgarī was made the pan-Indian script for Sanskrit texts (I, p. 72). The script in the meanwhile continued to evolve from the time of its so-called 'final' standardization in the seventh and eighth centuries AD and has been modified by influences as recent as the Moghul, when diacritical marks were made on existing letters for certain 'alien' but indispensable sounds like *f* and *z*. The rule for writing *o* and *au* with the radical *a* is quite modern, dating from the early eighteenth century.

Although devanāgarī is highly systematized and bears the marks of scientific and planned arrangement it is far from possessing the perfection claimed for it by enthusiasts. Briefly its shortcomings may be summarized thus:

(1) It has too many symbols. Most of the consonants have an entirely separate outline for their aspirated forms. Thus *k* and *kh* have two distinct symbols, as do *g* and *gh*, *ch* and *chh*, *j* and *jh*, and so on. A single sign for an aspirate could have done away with the need for ten letters.

(2) Like its predecessor, Aramaic, devanāgarī is not alphabetic, but semi-syllabic. The short *a* is inherent in each consonant, unless otherwise indicated by a small mark, called the *virāma* (stop) placed at the foot of the letter.

(3) In spite of its traditional claim to represent every possible sound of human speech, devanāgarī does not possess some very elementary sounds, though the recent use of diacritical marks has mitigated this defect to some extent. Thus there are no symbols for *f*, *z*, *zh*. There are no symbols for the short *o* (as in *not*), the short *e* (as in *get*), for *d* (as in *day*) although there is one for the cerebral *ḍ* and another for a soft *d* (almost as in *they*); similarly there is no symbol for *t* (as in tell). Nor is there any symbol for *a* (as in *at*). There is no way of writing the dipthongal *w* (as in *wall*) or *iu* (as in mute). The wellnigh unpronounceable vowel *ṛī* is acknowledged to be redundant.

(4) In writing, devanāgarī is cumbersome and uneconomical in time and labour and is one of the most tiring of scripts. Each letter has to be written separately, and each has a horizontal line (the *mātrā*) above it. In some cases there are as many as five breaks requiring the lifting of the pen in writing a single letter. It has been shown that the time required to write a passage in the Roman script is about 60 per cent shorter than in Devanāgarī (III).

(5) The joining of letters, both vowels and consonants to each other, involves the further use of quite new symbols or parts of symbols which are placed sometimes above, sometimes below and sometimes clinging sideways to another letter, often shorn of most of their recognizable features.

Books

I. Chatterji, S. K., *et al. The Cultural Heritage of India*, Calcutta, Vol. I (Revised Ed.), 1958.
II. Diringer, D. *The Alphabet*, London, 1949.
III. Karve, D. D. 'The Devanagari Script', *Times of India*, New Delhi, June 6, 1961.
IV. Shamasastry, R. 'A Theory of the Origin of the Devanagari Alphabet', *Indian Antiquary*, Vol. XXXV.

NĀGĀRJUNA (?AD 100–?200) Buddhist philosopher, born of South Indian brāhmin parents from Āndhra. To account for his name it is said that he was born under an *arjuna* tree (*terminalia arjuna*) and that part of his early life was spent in the land of the Nāgas*. From them he learned the secrets of alchemy*, and he was the reputed author of an alchemical treatise, *Rasaratnakāra*, which laid the foundations of this science in India. A profound metaphysician and an acute dialectician, he was eventually converted to Buddhism, and founded the Mādhyamika school of Mahāyāna. Many Buddhist sects regard Nāgārjuna as their first patriarch, Vasubandhu being the second. He was supposed to have received his doctrines from the Buddhist semi-divinities Vairochana and Vajrasattva. According to tradition Nāgārjuna ended his life by suicide.

Nāgārjuna's school of Mādhyamika has been variously labelled Relativist, Nihilist and Negativist. According to this philosophy the whole cosmic flux even considered from its 'permanent' background is an illusive reality. The elements of which phenomena are composed may be said, in accordance with commonplace 'truth', to be real, but from the vantage point of a higher truth they are seen to be a corollary of cause-and-effect, and therefore have only temporary, relative and conditional validity, lacking independent reality and self-nature (*svabhāva*). The consciousness, which is aware of this illusiveness is at the same time part of the total unreality. Man's intellect is incapable of solving any of the final problems, and attempts to do so give rise to misleading antinomies which Buddha in his day answered by silence.

Reality is the total absence of general or specific character. It is the condition of the Middle Path (whence the name of the school, Mādhyamika, 'intermediate') and cannot be explained in words and cannot be conceived by thought. It may be remotely apprehended by an Eightfold Negation thus: that there is no becoming, no not-being, no annihilation, no persistence, no unity, no diversity, no coming, no departure.

But it must be remembered that this Middle Path, as it exists at this stage, is only a relative and precarious middle, and the true and absolute middle avoids every specification, and that according to the Four Points of Dialectics we can say of no single thing whether (1) it exists (2) or not (3) or both (4) or neither. It is the total negation of entity, identity, character and self-nature. It is *nirvāṇa*; it is *śūnyatā*; the void; emptiness; devoidness (*see* śūnya).

The three chief treatises attributed to Nāgārjuna are; *Mādhyamika Śāstra*, *Dvadasa Sāstra*, and *Śata Śāstra*.

Books

I. Keith, A. B. *Buddhist Philosophy in India and Ceylon*, Oxford, 1923.
II. May, Jacques, *Candrakirti Prasannapada Madhyama Kavritti*, Paris, 1959.
III. Murti, T. R. V. *The Central Philosophy of Buddhism*, London, 1955.
IV. Ramanan, K. V. *Nagarjuna's Philosophy as Presented in the Maha-Prajnaparamita-sastra*, Tokyo, 1966.
V. Stcherbatsky, T. *The Conception of Buddhist Nirvana*, Leningrad, 1927.
VI. Tucci, G. *Pre-Dinnaga Buddhist Texts on Logic from Chinese Sources*, 1930.

NAHUSHA, son of Āyu, king of the Lunar dynasty, was a great patron of the arts, and the first man to establish a theatre on earth. By sacrifices, austerities, sacred study and meditation, he acquired sovereignty of the three worlds, but his knowledge and achievements made him arrogant. He aspired to the possession of Śachī, wife of Indra, and insulted the brāhmins. He used a thousand *ṛishis* to draw his chariot through the air and on one occasion goaded with his foot the great sage Agastya who was pulling his vehicle. Incensed the sage cried, 'Fall, thou serpent!' and instantly the mighty monarch fell from his chariot, transformed into a serpent. At the humble supplication of Nahusha, or according to another version, through the mediation of the Pāṇḍava prince, Yudhishṭhira, the term of the curse was shortened, after which Nahusha 'cast off his ugly reptile shape, became apparelled in a celestial body and ascended to heaven'.

Another story has it that Agastya was unable to cope with the tyranny of Nahusha and appealed to the sage Bhṛigu for help. In order to remain concealed from Nahusha, Bhṛigu hid in the hair of Agastya and received the kick of Nahusha. It was Bhṛigu who cursed Nahusha and turned him into a serpent. The resemblance of the king's name to nahustan, the serpent of bronze of the Old Testament, has led some scholars to believe in the Jewish* origin of this legend.

Among the son of Nahusha the most notable was Yayāti*.

Books

See under Mythology.

NĀIR (or Nāyyar) a generic name covering a number of castes of Malabār, including the Menon, Kurup, Kutti, Nambiār, Panikkar, etc. They are matriarchal, matrilineal, sometimes polyandrous, and often warrior castes. The Nāirs regard themselves as declassed kshattriyas, but are generally listed with the śūdras. The Nāir male is not entitled to the sacred thread, and in the scale of distance observances, he must stay seven feet away from a Nambūdri brāhmin.

In the Nāir social system the undivided family, called the *tharvad*, holds all property jointly. Its members consist of the women, their children, their brothers, and maternal uncles. Relationship and descent are traced through women. Sons share the annual produce as well as daughters; but only daughters and not the sons transmit the rights of inheritance to their children. The eldest woman of a tharvad is its titular head, while the eldest male, called the *kāranavan*, acts as estate manager.

The Nāir woman always lives with her own family, and the Nāir mother arranges a ceremonial marriage for her daughter before puberty. It is brief and inexpensive, requiring mainly the tying of the bridal necklace around the neck of the girl. The ceremonial bridegroom may be a complete stranger, a mere passer-by, to whom the mother gives a rupee for obliging. He has no marital rights or privileges, goes away immediately, and probably never sees the girl again. This custom gave rise to the erroneous reports of early travellers that women of this caste offered themselves to strangers.

Later the girl manages her real matrimonial affairs at her own discretion. The marriage union is called *saṁbandham,* which may be a permanent monogamous relationship, or a temporary liaison either with a man of her own caste or with the younger son of a Nambūdri brāhmin (see below). The husband does not live with his wife and only visits her at night. The woman can terminate the union whenever she chooses, but she is allowed to enter into one saṁbandham at a time only. Dissolution of the union is generally indicated by the woman intimating to her lover at any stage in the progress of the liaison, that he must cease his visits; hence the belief that a Nāir does not know who his father is. The children belong to the mother's tharvad, and the father holds no responsibility for them. His responsibilities lie towards the children of his sister or the other women of his own tharvad.

An unusual feature of social life in Malabār is the curious symbiotic relationship of some of the Nāir castes and the Nambūdris. The Nambūdri are a brāhmin caste who are said to have migrated from the north of India. Their most notable member was the philosopher Śaṅkara. The Nambūdris are the wealthiest landlords of Malabār, and are fanatical about ceremonial and personal cleanliness. Certain *pañchama** castes cannot approach closer to them than a fixed number of paces, while others dare not even look upon them.

Till recently only the eldest son of a Nambūdri was permitted to marry a girl of his own caste; he could in fact have several Nambūdri wives. A considerable number of Nambūdri women thus did not get a chance of marriage and were kept in strict seclusion, jealously guarded even from men of their own caste. When they went out of the house they hid their faces with a fan or umbrella of palmyra leaves. Since it was considered disgraceful for a woman to remain unmarried, the corpse of a Nambūdri spinster was put through the process of a marriage ceremony with religious rites, before it was cremated. Some observers record that there used to be an actual rite of congress with the corpse in order to provide the proper token of a consummated union (I, p. 16).

Since the younger sons of a Nambūdri household were not permitted to marry Nambūdri girls, a system was evolved by which they were accepted by Nāir women for temporary unions. The influence of this brāhmin caste made a saṁbandham with a Nambūdri more honourable in the eyes of a Nāir woman, than with a man of her own caste. After such a temporary though permissible lapse into impurity with a Nāir female, the Nambūdri purified himself with a ceremonial bath. The children of these unions remain Nāirs and as such are untouchable to their own brāhmin fathers.

Books

I. Dubois, Abbe. *Hindu Manners, Customs & Ceremonies,* Oxford, 3rd Ed., 1936.
II. Hutton, J. H. *Caste in India,* Bombay, 2nd Ed., 1951.
III. Mayer, A. C. *Land and Society in Malabar,* Bombay, 1952.
IV. Slater, G. *The Dravidian Element in Indian Culture,* London, 1924.

NALA, king of Nishadha, the story of whose love for Damayantī is one of the most touching in the *Mahābhārata.* He is described as brave, handsome, virtuous, skilled in arms and the management of horses, but addicted to gambling.

In the neighbouring state of Vidarbha (modern Berār) there ruled another great king named Bhīma (or Bhīmaratha), terrible in strength. Bhīma had no children, but a visiting brāhmin whom he welcomed well gave him the boon he desired, and he soon became the father of a beautiful girl, *Damayantī* (also known as Bhaimī), and three sons, Dama, Danta, and Damana.

In course of time the fame of Damayantī's beauty reached the ears of Nala, and the fame of his valour reached the maiden, and they loved each other even before they met. A swan whose life Nala had once saved acted as a go-between for the lovers. As the time of the princess's *svayaṁvara* (bride's choice) approached, the gods Indra, Agni, Varuṇa and Yama, let it be known through Nala that they would be present and that she must choose from among them. Damayantī was determined to choose only Nala, but to her dismay she found that the four gods all came to her svayaṁvara in the guise of Nala. Damayantī was soon able to distinguish her lover from the fact that he cast a shadow and that he perspired and blinked, all of which the gods do not do. She made her choice and married Nala. The couple lived happily for twelve years and had a son Indrasena and a daughter Indrasenā.

Now the demon Kali (the evil spirit of the present *Kali-yuga,* not to be confused with the goddess) and his assistant Dvāpara, were bent on Nala's downfall. Waiting for a favourable moment Kali entered the soul of Nala when he performed an unclean act (he neglected to wash his feet at the proper time) and then inspired him to gamble with his brother Pushkara. As the two brothers played Nala lost his palace, possessions, kingdom, and even his clothes, and had to go into exile. Sending their two children to her father's palace, Damayantī followed her husband into the jungle.

Here after some time Nala deserted his wife, not wishing her to share his troubles any further. Left on her own, new perils now beset her. She was rescued from the strangling coils of a huge serpent by a hunter who afterwards desired to possess her, but her curse consumed him in a flash of fire. Picked up by a merchant caravan she brought ill fortune to them and was quickly abandoned as a bringer of bad luck. At last she found herself in the kingdom of Chedi, ruled by Subāhu, where she dwelt in the palace as the companion of the princess Sunandā, who befriended her. After a time she returned to her father at Vidarbha.

Nala too was having his share of misfortune. While saving the serpent Karkoṭaka from a fire he was bitten and transformed (for his own good) into a misshapen dwarf in order to escape recognition during the period of his exile. He was told to call himself Vāhuka (or Bāhuka) a charioteer, and in this capacity he entered the service of Ṛituparṇa, son of Sarvakāma, rāja of Ayodhyā, as a trainer of horses.

Damayantī's father now sent out agents to find Nala, and they were able by the response he gave to certain verses, to discover that Nala was in Ayodhyā. Damayantī next announced that she was holding a second svayaṁvara and for this purpose Ṛituparṇa set off for Vidarbha driven by his ungainly charioteer. On the way the prince learned the art of managing horses from Nala, and in turn taught him the science of numbers, the rules of chance, and skill in dice. Damayantī's partial recognition of her husband was complete when she recognized the flavour of a dish he cooked. At the same time Nala himself miraculously recovered his true form. The couple were married a second time. A second time Nala played dice and won back his kingdom, forgave his brother and sent him home laden with gifts.

Books

See under Mythology.

NĀLANDĀ, ancient seat of Buddhist learning, situated about eleven miles north of Rājgir in Bihār. It was so called after a *nāga* or snake deity, named Nāgānanda or Nālandā, to whom a sacred tank nearby was dedicated. Originally a tiny village, the site was purchased by a group of merchants and presented to Buddha who preached the law there for three months. It was the birthplace of Sāriputta and Moggallāna, disciples of Buddha. Here also the Jain saint Mahāvīra met his rival Gośāla.

By the second century AD Nālandā was already a well established educational* centre, where Nāgārjuna* spent many years of his life. It began to grow in importance from about AD 300 and was greatly enlarged in AD 470 by one of the Gupta kings. The Chinese scholars Hiuen-Tsang (AD 635) and I-Tsing (AD 680) both studied at Nālandā for some years when they visited India. In Hiuen-Tsang's time, the entire university area was surrounded by a brick wall. Within stood a large college, numerous subsidiary halls, priest's chambers, students' hostels, observatories, and over one hundred lecture rooms. The library alone occupied three buildings. The copying of manuscripts was an important aspect of the university's work. The Chinese travellers speak with admiration of its 'richly-carved towers, the fairy-like turrets, and the carved and coloured eaves, pillars and balustrades'.

To have studied at Nālandā became a matter of great prestige, and many false claims were made by students of having studied there. Registration was therefore tightened up. Admission to the university became extremely difficult, and pupils were only enrolled after a rigid examination, conducted by the *dvārapāla* (doorkeeper), later called the *dvārapaṇḍita* (door-cleric), who was himself a master in many branches of learning, and whose business it was to put applicants through a searching test on difficult subjects like logic, grammar, philosophy and law. Only one out of five passed this entrance examination, but even so the university had a large number of students; some authorities place it at 10,000, but this is regarded as highly exaggerated, and Hiuen-Tsang's figure of 3,000 is the generally accepted one. Scholars came from China, Japan, Central Asia, Java, Tibet (Padmasambhava, *c.* AD 748, founder of Lamaism, was among them), Mongolia, Bokhara and other places, to study Buddhist law and philosophy from about 150 teachers and lecturers. No fees were charged, and clothes, food, bedding and medicine were supplied by the university. The revenue of 200 villages was earmarked for its upkeep.

The Pāla kings of Bengal took Nālandā under their patronage, though they were more interested in the nearby university of Odantapura, founded by them. Both these institutions taught philology, yoga, grammar, medicine, logic, Mahāyāna, law and philosophy, but they also specialized in astrology, occultism, alchemy and tantrism. Hīnayānists scoffed at this 'empty learning' and 'sky-flower philosophy', equating some of their teachings with the vicious doctrines of the Kāpālikas.

The huge manuscript library of Nālandā was destroyed in the tenth century by a fire started by certain *tīrthika* (i.e. non-Buddhists, variously identified as Vaishṇavite, Śaivite, or Jain monks) who had a grievance against the monastery for some past affront.

The end of Nālandā is shrouded in mystery. Odantapura, only six miles away was razed to the ground by Ikhtiār Khilji in 1198, but Nālandā was spared and continued a perilous existence with a mere scattering of teachers and students for at least forty years after. As a result of the growing Muslim menace the great university was finally left with one master and his Tibetan pupil. When an assault by three hundred Muslim raiders threatened the monastery, the student carried his aged master on his back to a nearby temple. After having searched the place the Muslims left, and master and pupil returned. A few more scholars later joined them. The last record we have of Nālandā is this feeble spark—a handful of intimidated scholars without manuscripts or material who vainly attempted to keep alive the old traditions of learning.

Books

I. Dutt, S. *Buddhist Monks & Monasteries of India*, London, 1962.
II. Ghosh, A. *A Guide to Nalanda*, 2nd Ed., 1946.
III. Sankalia, H. D. *University of Nalanda*, Bombay, 1921.
IV. Yule, R. *Nalanda, The Great Buddhist University*, 1923.

NĀMDEV (?1270–?1350) or Nāmadeva, poet and saint of Mahārāshṭra, born in Paṇḍharpur, a centre of Vishṇu worship in the Marāṭha country. He was the son of a low-caste tailor, and was brought up in his father's trade. In his youth he was reputed to be a spendthrift and a sluggard. He fell in with a gang of thieves and killed and robbed people, until he came under the influence of a saint (Jñānadeva*, according to some) who turned him from his evil life and the idolatry of his ancestral faith, to the devotion of Viṭṭhoba (Vishṇu) of Paṇḍharpur. In one story Viṭṭhoba came to him in the guise of an aged leper and was served by the young tailor with respect and reverence; Viṭṭhoba revealed himself and blessed the young man.

Nāmdev devoted the rest of his life to the worship of Vishṇu. The twelve members of his family, as well as his personal servant, Janābāi, were all poets, and according to the legend, through their combined efforts he was enabled to fulfil his vow to compose a hundred crore (one thousand million) abhaṅga or hymns. A few of Nāmdev's *abhaṅgas* survive and some are enshrined in the Sikh scriptures. His devotional writings in Marāṭhi and Hindi make him one of the earliest leaders of the Vaishṇava revival.

Nāmdev had a number of followers, mainly from the lower castes. Among them were Gorā a potter; Sāṁvatā a gardener; Chokhā a pariah; and Jogā an oilman.

Books

See under Marāṭhi and Vaishṇavism.

NAMES. The study of Hindu names is among the few neglected fields of Indological investigation, and one that holds out promise of fruitful reward to the pioneer. The convention of bestowing names in Hindu families has its roots in the remote past, and its study is inextricably confused by considerations of race and caste. The little light from the past is further obscured by the fact that indigenous names were often subjected to and corrupted by a ruthless process of Sanskritization to conform to the imaginary etymology so beloved by Hindu name-makers.

Whatever convention the pre-Ayrans may have followed in naming their children, it is now lost, and little may be gauged from the aboriginal names that survive in Sanskrit texts. But much can be learned of the general tendency among non-Aryans in an indirect way from the prohibitions imposed on Aryans in this matter, since the early Aryans could not very well adopt the practice current among their despised subjects.

Thus Vedic Aryans avoided personal names drawn from the vocabulary of divine or religious nomenclature (I, p. 182). The custom of giving names of deities may have been common among non-Aryans, if we are to judge from its prevalence in South India even to the present day (Veṅkaṭeśvara, Nīlakaṇṭha, Mahādeva, Śivaliṅga, Subrahmaṇya). The practice was adopted during the early centuries of the present era by Buddhists and kshattriyas (Buddhaghosha, Mitrasena, Mokshadeva, Dharmaraksha, Indravarman, Brahmāgupta).

The names of stars, constellations, planets, sun, moon, asterisms, were also avoided in Vedic times by the Aryans, as was the use of names taken from nature e.g. of mountains, hills, rivers, forests (I, p. 189) since nature names were current among the non-Aryans. The lawgivers, including Manu, expressly forbade the marriage of a man of the higher castes with a girl named after any of these things (III, p. 136), as it was taken to indicate aboriginal parentage. The mother-earth origin of Sītā, wife of Rāma, is confirmed by her name which means 'furrow', and is an obvious reference to her nativeness. Women with the names of rivers include Narmadā, wife of the Paurava king Purukutsa; Kāverī, wife of Jahnu; Sarasvatī, wife of Matinara; another Sarasvatī, wife of Vadhryaśva and mother of Divodāsa; Kālindī (the original name of Jamnā) wife of Purūravas; Gaṅgā, wife of Śāntanu and mother of Bhīshma.

The use of any name suggestive of servile status was discouraged for the same reason, particularly the suffix, *dāsa* (slave or helot). In the Ṛig-Vedic period 'no Aryan would ordinarily have thought of calling himself a dāsa, even of a deity' (II, p. 656) because of the contempt in which the term was held. Hence scholars are led to the conclusion that the sage Mahīdāsa and the kings Divodāsa and Sudāsa were non-Aryans since these names occur so early in the Vedic period. In the post-Vedic age, however, dāsa became a common suffix (e.g. Kālidāsa), and from the medieval period onwards the suffix 'dās' was added to many names as a generic title of humility by Vaishṇavites to suggest their complete subjection to Vishṇu (e.g. Tulsīdās, Haridās).

A still more general interdiction was laid on the bestowal of names taken from the animal kingdom, such as lion, bull, serpent, swan, fish, frog and so on; here again the lawgivers expressed their disapproval of the marriage of Aryan males with women bearing such names (III, p. 136). Animal names were a commonplace in totemic societies, which were closely linked with aboriginal social organizations, and would thus inspire the prohibition of their use by Aryans.

In course of time the Aryans themselves adopted the native convention which became quite common. The notion that the custom of deriving names from animals was 'unknown in the Vedic period' (I, p. 186), needs considerable qualification. Actually Vedic use of animal names was not at all unusual, and betokened an intimate liaison with the natives of the country. Here evidence is strongest that early Hindu philosophy, particularly that of the Upanishads, the ṛishi families, and the renowned Indian clans of yore, were all intimately connected with indigenous peoples.

Totemism was very widespread in ancient India, and as in other totemistic societies, Hindu clans and families, and even schools of Vedic study were called after some animal, plant or inanimate object with which they were held to be totemically related. The subject is still wrapped in obscurity and needs further investigation. Little more need be done here than indicate the totemic roots of a few well-known names in Hinduism.

From *aja*, 'goat' comes the name of Āja, a tribe mentioned in the *Ṛig-veda*; *aśva*, 'horse' is the root of such names as Aśvapati and Aśvatthāman, and also of Śvetāśvatara, 'white steed', the title of an Upanishad; *bharadvāja* 'skylark', is the totemic name of a celebrated *ṛishi* family; from *chhagala*, 'goat', is derived Chhāgaleya, the name of a Vedic teacher, and also of an Upanishad now extinct in its Sanskrit form; from *gotama*, 'bull' come the names of several well-known sages; and from *haya*, 'horse' are derived the names Haihaya, a tribe, and Hayagrīva, a godling; *ibha*, 'elephant' is the totem of the Ibhya, a village people mentioned in the *Chhāndogya Upanishad*; from *kauśika*, 'owl' comes Kauśītaki, the name of an Upanishad; and from *kachchhapa*, 'tortoise' comes the name of Kaśyapa, a *mahāṛishi*; *kshudraka*, a variety of gadfly gives its name to a *gaṇa*, or clan, of ancient India; *kukkura*, 'dog'* were a tribe associated with the Vṛishṇis along the Yamunā; *malava*, a white flowering plant, is said to give the name to the Mālava tribe; from *maṇḍūka*, 'frog', comes the title of the *Māṇḍūkya Upanishad*; from *mataṅga*, 'elephant', the name of a pre-Mauryan dynasty of Magadha; *matsya*, 'fish', is the name of an important tribe in Hindu mythology; and *mayūra*, 'peacock' the origin of the name of the Mauryan dynasty; from *mudgala*, a kind of fish, is derived the name of a ṛishi; *mūshika*, 'rat', may be the origin of an ancient Indian tribe known to the Greeks as the Musicani; *nāga*, 'snake' is the name of an ancient people, and is still used as a surname by Hindus of eastern India; *nakula*, 'ichneumon', was the name of a Pāṇḍava prince; from *pīpal*, a kind of fig-tree, comes the name of Pippalāda, the founder of a Vedic school; *ṛiksha*, 'bear' is the name of the ṛishi family to which Saṁvaraṇa belonged; from *śākala*, a species of snake, comes the name of Śākalya, a teacher who founded a Ṛig-vedic śākhā; from *śārdūla*, 'tiger', comes Śārdūlīya, the ṛishi after whom a now lost *Sāma-veda* śākhā was named; *śigru*, a plant, possibly the horseradish, gave the name to a people mentioned in the *Ṛig-veda*; *siṁha*, 'lion', gives its name to Sinha, and Singh; the name Hāthīsingh (elephant-lion) is used by certain classes of Panjābi Hindus; from *śukti*, 'oyster', comes the name Śuktimatī, capital of Chedi; *śunaka*, 'dog' gives the name to Śaunaka, a famous Vedic grammarian; a sage mentioned in the *Chhāndogya Upanishad* who imparted secret knowledge to a student, was called Śunaka-kāpeya, 'dog-monkey'; *tittira*, 'partridge' gives its name to the *Taittirīya Upanishad*; and *vatsa*, 'calf' to the Vatsa tribe of the Ganges-Jamnā confluence, with capital at Kauśāmbī.

Apart from the Vedic prohibitions in the matter of giving names, specific directions are also found in some of the ancient texts. Patronymics were commonly used, generally by a modification of the father's name e.g. Upagu's son was called Aupagava. Metronymics were current in matriarchal systems, but in other areas, according to Pāṇini, one's designation by one's mother's *gotra* or clan, implied that the father's name was unknown (*see* Satyakāma). The Pāṇiniean convention for the formation of names went as follows: if Garga was the father, then Gārgi was the son, Gārgya the grandson (also called vṛiddha, 'senior'), and Gārgyāyaṇa the great-grandson or descendant (also called *yuvan*, 'younger').

Sometimes an epithet was used as part of a name because of some association e.g. a man might be referred to as Bālāki, because as a child he was brought up in the company of girls (*bālā*). Gārgya his son would be referred to by his own name along with the epithet associated with his father, thus, Gārgya Bālāki, i.e. Gārgya the son of Bālāki. Sometimes the personal name was followed by the country or locality from which a man or his ancestors came e.g. Bhīma Vaidarbha or Bhīma belonging to Vidarbha. Names could also be taken from the locality of one's birth e.g. Vyāsa, compiler of the *Mahābhārata*, was born on an island (dvīpa) and was surnamed Dvaipāyana (the suffix ayana signifies 'coming from'). Also common was the use of the *viruda* or 'praise' name, often given to kings and heroes. It was not unknown in Vedic days, as can be seen by the eulogistic titles bestowed on certain kings e.g. Purañjaya, 'city-conqueror'. Vikrama and Parākrama, signifying one boldly striding or advancing, were among the royal titles used in medieval times.

A new nomenclature was introduced during the 'barbarian' period, and became fashionable among kshattriyas. Some of the more common name-endings will indicate the character of the change. *Gupta*, 'protector' was originally a śūdra or vaiśya name. *Guha*, 'secret', was an aboriginal Nishāda name. *Varma*, 'shield', was of Central Asian origin and became a cognomen for a kshattriya. *Sena*, 'warrior', was used in Bengal for the children of the concubines of brāhmins (V, p. 144) but was at this time adopted by the nobility. *Bhaṭ*, 'mercenary', became a popular name for a warrior. *Putra*, 'son', *Datta*, 'gift', *Siṁha*, 'lion', were honorific suffixes assumed by foreign princes. This convention was firmly established by the time of the great Sanskrit dramas and *kāvyas*, and even courtesans who figured in these works were frequently given names ending in dattā, senā or siddhā.

One of the Hindu *saṁskāras* or sacraments is the rite known as *nāmakaraṇa* 'name-making', performed on the tenth or twelfth day after the birth of the child. A sacrificial fire is lighted and darbha grass is laid to the west of it in a north-south direction, but with the blades of grass pointing north. The father of the child sits on the grass facing southwards, and the mother holding the child sits facing him. Both parents dress in new unwashed clothes and the child is covered with a clean piece of cloth. Prayers are said, and at the given time the mother hands the child to the father, head first so that it is passed over from south to north. A gold object, usually a ring, is placed in a brass vessel containing ghee, oblations of ghee are poured into the fire and then the golden object is taken out, washed and tied around the child's neck by the father. The father then anoints his hand with ghee, warms it over the fire, touches the child's forehead, smells the child's head as a cow would smell its calf, and pronounces a benediction. He then gives the child the name previously selected by the priest or astrologer.

The following directions were set down by the early lawgivers with regard to the naming of children: a *boy's name* should (*a*) begin with a consonant, preferably a soft consonant, (*b*) contain a semi-vowel (*y*, *r*, *l*, *v*) in the middle, (*c*) end in *s* or, (*d*) have a *visarga* (hard aspirate) or long vowel (*ā*, *ī*, *ū*) at the end, (*e*) have an even number of syllables, (*f*) contain the name of a *ṛishi* or forefather. A *girl's name* should (*a*) have an odd number of syllables, (*b*) end in *dā* or *ā* and never in *l* or *r*; (*c*) not be that of a river, animal or bird (a Vedic convention that was later stopped). In determining the eligibility* of a bride, her name was one of the factors taken into account. In addition to the above her name had to be auspicious when considered in conjunction with the groom's name, and it was essential that she should not bear the same name as the groom's mother.

To this day there is a strong element of secrecy in the bestowal of names, and many taboos in connection with addressing people are suggestive of this secrecy. The ancients regarded the name as an intimate personal possession; it was believed to have a life of its own and to be susceptible to attack by magical means. Furthermore, there was thought to be a limit in the 'personal treasury' to the 'units' of one's name, and constant use of it depleted this stock and weakened the owner. One's name is therefore not to be bandied about, and strict conventions governing modes of address are almost universally observed in India. Visitors will ask to see 'the master of the house'; a pupil will refer to 'swāmiji' or 'mahātmaji', or 'guruji'. A Hindu husband does not utter his wife's name, nor a wife her husband's, but they will either just say what they want without address, or will call out, 'O mother of Kṛishṇa', or 'Hey, Rāma's father'. Formerly during the baptismal rites a secret personal name used to be whispered into the child's ear, which would be conveyed only to the father and grandfather of the child by the officiating priest, and would thus never be known to more than three or four persons. It was the child's talismanic, and inviolable name.

The various factors that go into the composition of Hindu names may include the *gotra-nāma* or clan name, the *kula-nāma* or family name, the *pita-nāma* or father's name, and the *janma-nāma* or name given at birth. Furthermore, names may be given to indicate the caste of the individual e.g. Ayyangar, Ayyar, Iyer (from Sanskrit Ārya) for south Indian brāhmins of a certain caste; Śarma for a caste of north Indian brāhmins. They may indicate ancestral place-names e.g. Tanjavūr, 'from Tanjore'. Other names derived from places are Bhaṭnāgar, Mālavīya and Sarvepalli. In north and west India the suffix '*vālā*' is added, signifying agency, ownership or derivation. It is anglicized as 'wallah' e.g. Bombaywallah. Some names are derived from natural objects such as stones, lakes and hills. The name Nehru comes from *nahar*, 'canal', after a canal that passed by the ancestral estates of the Nehru family. Names may be taken from professions e.g. Dalāl (broker), Dhibar (fisherman), Kārmakar (blacksmith). Among Parsees the English term is sometimes used as a surname, e.g. Engineer. Honorific religious or sectarian titles are assumed by many families e.g. Goswāmi, Prabhu. Sectarian names are given on initiation, especially among sādhus and certain sects when one joins a religious order e.g. the name of Narendranāth Dutt was changed on initiation to Swāmi Vivekānanda. Relics of princely or noble ancestry may be found in many names, although these are not always genuine since families of lower castes often assume such honorifics, e.g. Mehtar (prince), Nāyak (Leader), Mālik (Lord), Roy, Rai, Ray, Rae, Rao (king), Kumār (prince), Chakravarti (sovereign).

Names are also derived from functions performed in an ancestral or priestly calling, usually in the form of a suffix e.g. Pāṭhak, 'reciter' of sacred texts. Among certain Bengali brāhmins the suffix '*upādhyāyā*' (reciter or teacher) is added to ancestral village names e.g. Mukhopādhyāya (contracted to Mukherji); Bandopādhyāya (Banerji), Chattopādhyāya (Chatterji), Gaṅgopādhyāya (Gaṅguli). The system of suffixing Chāria, Chāriar or Āchāriar, 'teacher', to ancestral place names is common in Madras e.g. Rājagopālachāriar. In the Panjāb, Uttar Pradesh and Bihār, the names Ahujā, Ojhā or Jhā meaning 'reciter' are also common.

The use of titles of respect and affection has always been widely prevalent in India. These may be a contraction of the actual name, or a diminutive form of the name. It may be the addition of the suffix *jī* (lit. soul, or life) to indicate regard and reverence as in Paṇḍitjī or Mahātmajī. It may be an *upādhi*, 'epithet' bestowed by common consent, and is a modern form of the ancient *viruda* (see above). Upādhi are seen in the honorifics bestowed on 'Mahātma' Gāndhi, 'Sardar' Paṭel. A few examples will indicate further such name formations: Lockmanya (respect-name) Balwantrao (personal name) Bālgaṅgādhar (father's name) Tilak (forefather's name); Deshbandhu (respect-name) Chittarañjan (personal name) Dās (forefather's name)s Netājī (respect-name) Subhas Chandra (personal name) Bose (forefather'; name).

Books

I. Agrawala, V. S. *India as Known to Panini*, Lucknow, 1953.
II. Dandekar, R. N. (Ed.) *Silver Jubilee Volume of the Bhandarkar Oriental Research Institute, 1917–1942*, Poona, 1943.
III. Pargiter, F. E. *Ancient Indian Historical Tradition*, London, 1922.
IV. Roy, L. M. 'The Origin of Family Names or Surnames'. *The Modern Review*, Calcutta, 1951.
V. Vidyarthi, L. P. *The Sacred Complex in Hindu Gaya*, Bombay, 1961.

NĀNAK (1469–1538) the founder of the reformist Hindu sect of the Sikhs*, was born in the village of Talwaṇḍi (since renamed Nānakāna) near Lahore, of Khatri or warrior stock. His father was a village accountant in poor circumstances. Nānak was invested with the sacred thread of the twice-born at the age of nine, and lived for some years the life of a normal Hindu boy.

From his youth he showed a religious bent of mind. He liked to converse with religious devotees, but he soon began to question the teachings of orthodox Hinduism, and spoke out against caste and the brāhmin priesthood. He learned Persian and made a profound study of the works of Persian and Muslim mystics. Early in life he came under the influence of the great religious reformer Kabīr* to whom he was indebted for some of his later doctrines.

Nānak had been married when quite young and set up in business by his father, but gave most of his earnings to the poor. He kept home until the birth of his second son, after which he took to the road as a religious mendicant. He travelled widely, visiting Ceylon, Kashmīr, Iraq, Tibet, Turkestan and Russia. He is also supposed to have gone to Mecca, but of these travels there is no evidence, and many of the accounts are obviously later inventions since the details contradict historical facts. His meeting with the emperor Bābur is not improbable.

Legend relates that at the age of thirty-five while he was in a forest, wrapt in meditation, he was carried in a vision to the gates of paradise where a hand offered him a goblet of water, and a voice commissioned him to spread the teachings of the true faith. 'Tell people to repeat my Name, and serve with almsgiving, ablution and prayer.' He devoted the remaining forty years of his life to this end. His companion in his wanderings was a former Muslim servant, *Mardāna*, who was skilled in the rebec and who accompanied his master's singing with this musical instrument. To Hindus Nānak said, 'The evil mind is the pariah's wife, and a slanderous tongue is the sweeper woman.

What does it avail to purify your heart, when these two forever sit beside you?' To Muslims he said, 'Make love your mosque, justice your Koran, and charity your creed and prayer'. He preached purity in thought, word and deed, and forbade the eating of flesh and the drinking of wine.

To his disciples Nānak was the Guru or preceptor, and he is generally referred to as Guru Nānak. His followers were called 'Sikh' which means disciple, and it is from this word that the name of the religion of the Sikhs is derived.

Shortly before his death Nānak appointed one of his disciples as his successor Guru, and this institution of Gurus was carried on until the tenth and last Guru, Gobind Singh, abolished the Guruship. The sweetness of his character and the nobility of his life have earned Guru Nānak the affection of all religious sects in India.

Books

I. Macauliffe, M. A. *The Sikh Religion*, Oxford, 1909.
II. Singh, Jogendra. *Thus Spake Nanank*, 1934.

NANDA (?364–322? BC) a dynasty of Magadha* founded by Ugrasena, better known by the title of *Mahapadma* (?364–334? BC). Few facts are known about him but he was progably of non-Aryan ancestry. Purāṇic records make him the illegitimate son of the last Śaiśunāga monarch and a śūdra woman. Curtius the ancient historian relates the Greek version that he was the śūdra barber to the royal house of Śaiśunāga, and that the queen of the last Śaiśunāga monarch became enamoured of him. Through her influence he gained the confidence of the king, whom he slew by thrusting a dagger into his throat. According to Jain historians Mahāpadma Nanda was the son of a śūdra courtesan (possibly a Greek or Persian) and a barber, and after he had murdered the king, the citizens of Pāṭaliputra presented the state elephant, the royal parasol and other insignia of kingship to him.

He founded the new Nanda dynasty and ruled with a firm hand, extending his domain and bringing about the end of the other petty kings and princes. Mahāpadma is supposed to have finally exterminated all the kshattriyas who might have survived the avenging campaigns of Paraśurāma. The Purāṇas lament that the kings of the earth after Mahāpadma would henceforth all be śūdras, since there would be no kshattriyas left when this 'second Paraśurāma' had completed his task. The extermination of the kshattriyas by Mahāpadma was quoted as late as AD 1837 in a famous case that came up before the Privy Council, as proof that there were no more representatives of this caste left on earth.

Mahāpadma has been called 'the first great historical emperor of Northern India' (I, p. 33), and is remembered in Indian tradition as one of the wealthiest rulers of all time. The Purāṇas describe him as the sole monarch of the earth, since his territory embraced what for those days were really vast realms. Included within his domains, apart from Kaliṅga and some southern territories, were most of the brāhminical and kshattriya kingdoms of ancient renown, like Pañchāla, Kāśī (Banāras), Śūrasena (Mathurā), Aśmaka, Kuru, Mithilā and Haihaya.

There are historically nine Nanda rulers in all, who were either the brothers or the sons of Mahāpadma. The last member of this unpopular line, Dhana Nanda, was slain in 322 BC by Chandragupta Maurya, who founded the Maurya* dynasty.

Books

I. Majumdar, R. C. (Ed.) *The Age of Imperial Unity*, Bombay, 1951.
II. Pradhan, S. N. *Chronology of Ancient India*, Calcutta, 1927.
III. Sastri, K. A. N. *The Age of the Nandas and Mauryas*, Banaras, 1952.

NĀRADA, a mahāṛishi to whom a few hymns of the *Ṛig-veda* are ascribed. His origin is uncertain. He is variously described as having sprung from the forehead of Brahmā; as belonging to the Kāṇva family; as the son of the mage Kaśyapa by one of Daksha's daughters. The *Mahābhārata* states that he forestalled the scheme of Daksha for re-peopling the earth, and therefore was cursed by Daksha to be reborn from the womb of a woman. He was accordingly born again of Brahmā and one of Daksha's daughters.

Like Bhṛigu, Durvāsas and other arch-ṛishis, Nārada was a master-curser. On one occasion his father, Brahmā, cursed him to lead a life of sensuality and subjection to women, and he in turn cursed Brahmā to lust after his own daughter.

In later mythology he figures in legends associated with Kṛishṇa. It was he who warned the despot Kaṁsa of his impending death at Kṛishṇa's hands, and it was his curse that brought about the destruction of Kṛishṇa's race of the Yādavas.

Nārada was renowned as a teacher, an inspirer of poets (*see* Vālmīki), counsellor of kings, messenger between gods and men; but also as a notorious mischief-maker (*see* Atri and Satyabhāmā). A great wanderer he once paid a visit to Pātāla (hell) and was delighted with what he saw there.

As the chief of the Gandharvas or heavenly musicians, he was a patron of music and the inventor of the lute (*vīna*). Several books of music are attributed to him (*see* Music History). His name is also borne by a writer of a book of law (*see* ritual canon). Nārada is known by several names, chief among them being, Deva-brahmā, chief of brāhmins; Kali-kāraka, strife-maker; Kapi-vaktra, monkey-face; Piśuna, informer.

Books

See under Mythology.

NĀRĀYAṆA, a name applied sometimes to Brahmā, Prajāpati or Purusha, but more frequently to Vishṇu and Kṛishṇa. It is derived either from *nara* (man), the original eternal man, or from *nāra* (waters), since the primeval ocean was the first *ayana* or place of motion of Brahmā*. Nārāyaṇa may have been an aboriginal deity of waters, worshipped by an ancient sea-faring people. In some early texts he is called Nara-Nārāyaṇa.

The *Śatapatha Brāhmaṇa* has a reference to a man Nārāyaṇa who offered a sacrifice lasting five nights (*pañcha-rātra*), which gave him superiority over all beings. From this incident the Pañcharātra* sect is believed to have received its name. It was perhaps at this time also and in this connection that the name became identified with Vishṇu. As Nārāyaṇa, Vishṇu is depicted reclining on the serpent Śesha and floating on the waters. The twelfth book of the *Mahābhārata* contains a portion called the Nārāyaṇīya.

In the *Mahābhārata* and other texts, Nārāyaṇa sometimes refers to an ancient *ṛishi*, the son of Dharma, whose task it was to destroy demons and asuras, or again to Kṛishṇa or Arjuna. The penances of the ṛishi Nārāyaṇa alarmed the gods, so Indra sent the most beautiful of his nymphs to distract him. Nārāyaṇa plucked a flower and placed it on his thigh and from it there sprang an exquisite nymph whose beauty far excelled the charms of Indra's *apsarā* who returned shamefacedly to heaven. Since the nymph had sprung from the thigh (*ūru*) of the sage, she was called Urvaśī*. In another legend Nārāyaṇa painted her and the painting* came to life.

The *Mahābhārata* also speaks of the white people of Śvetadvīpa*, on the northern shore of the Ocean of Milk, as being worshippers of Nārāyaṇa, a thousand-rayed man-god. According to some scholars this may be a record of an actual journey undertaken by Indian Vaishṇavites to foreign countries in the north-west of India, from where they brought back a number of legends including a Gnostic version of Christianity*, which may possibly have influenced the Kṛishṇa mythology.

In the medieval period under Muslim influence the god Nārāyaṇa because of his non-sectarian history became known as Satyapīr, composed of *satya*, 'true', and *pīr*, 'saint', and was spoken of as the One True God. This deity was a syncretic fusion of Rahim and Rāma, the Muslim and Hindu terms for deity. Still later he was called, and continues to be known as Satyā-Nārāyaṇa.

Books

See under Mythology and Vaishṇavism.

NĀSIK, near the source of the Godāverī, is one of the sacred cities of the Hindus. Situated about one hundred miles inland from the ancient port of Sopāra, not far from Bombay, it was once an important trading centre known to the Jews, Persians, Greeks and Romans, and referred to by Ptolemy as Nasika. It lay at the crossroads of the great trade routes leading to the heart of India and was the meeting place of many ancient cultures.

The whole area around Nāsik is a place of prehistoric sanctity. An ancient site of Maga worship, it was associated with Buddhism in the first centuries preceding and succeeding the beginning of the Christian era. During the period of the brāhminical revival the region became associated first with legends of Śiva and then with the story of Rāma's wanderings. Nāsik was identified with ancient Pañchāvatī (a village of this name still exists not far away) in the Daṇḍaka forest of mythological renown. It was the scene of Rāma's banishment, and of the incident where the nose (*nāsika*) of the ogress Śūrpanakhā* was cut off by Lakshmaṇa. From this episode Nāsik is said to have received its name, although some authorities hold that the ancient name became a convenient focus for this legend.

This part of India was for long occupied by foreign tribes, and one of them, the Kshaharāta, a Śaka* people, made Nāsik their capital in about AD 120. Subsequently it fell to a succession of indigenous rulers, among them the Sātavāhanas. In the third century it passed to the Ābhīras, and then became the Vākāṭaka capital; in the fourth century it was the chief centre on the western frontier of the Gupta empire; and by the seventh century was the northern capital of the Chālukya monarch Pulakeśin II (*c.* 640).

In and around Nāsik there are over a score of Buddhist, Śaivite and Vaishṇavite *vihāras*, cave* temples—and also a *chaitya*—some of which are of great importance, both architecturally and because of the valuable early Buddhist inscriptions they contain. The Buddhist caves were excavated between 100 BC and AD 175. The cave inscriptions record donations from Buddhist inhabitants of Sind, Panjāb and north-west India. Nāsik merchants themselves made generous donations to Buddhist shrines as distant as Bhārhut.

The cave known as Sītā Gumphā (Sītā's Cave) was supposed to have been Sītā's abode in exile, and it was from here that she was carried off by Rāvaṇa. An underground chamber, now blocked, is said to lead to a hill where Rāma used to sleep. Not far away is a temple dedicated to Kāla Rāma (Black Rāma) with almost one hundred arches. Also near by is the spot where Rāma used to bathe, regarded as very sacred; the ashes of dead Hindus are taken there to be washed away along with their sins.

A temple dedicated to Kāpāleśvar (Śiva as Skull Lord) is only six hundred years old. But in Sītā's Cave there is an image of Śiva six inches high which is believed to be the same image worshipped by Rāma, Sītā and Lakshmaṇa, when they took refuge in Pañchāvatī. About twenty miles south-west of Nāsik is the celebrated liṅga* of Śiva known as Tryambaka.

A *kumbha-mela** is held at Nāsik every third year. Thirteen hundred 'heraldic' brāhmin families reside in the town and it is one of the chief centres for registering the genealogies of high caste Hindu families. Record books, or *khāṭā*, of the pedigrees of such families are maintained by the pāṇḍa class of priests, and are kept up to date by correspondence or personal visits to Nāsik by the heads of families from time to time.

Books

See under Towns.

NĀSTIKA, 'denier', or one who says, 'There is not', is the name applied to a number of unorthodox sects contemporary with the most ancient Hindu philosophers. Some authorities derive nāstika theories from the people of ancient Mesopotamia, but it is clear that they had a strong indigenous background. The nāstikas denied the existence of God, the validity of the Vedas, the possibility of an afterlife, and were so called in opposition to the orthodox *āstika*, 'asserters', thinkers who believed in the ultimate realities such as God, the soul, a future life and, above all, the Vedas.

Nāstika sects existed before Buddha, as seen from references to their activities in Vedic texts, but their philosophy found its full expression between the early Epic period and the spread of Buddhism, and continued to influence unorthodox schools of Hindu thought for many centuries after. It was a movement that ran parallel with the priestly religion, being as it were a reaction against the claims of brāhminism. The names of a few nāstika philosophers, are known but little of their original work survives, and most of what we do have is gleaned from the writings of their opponents who have at best preserved a very one-sided summary of their doctrines.

There are several facets to the nāstika philosophical structure. As already indicated they were primarily *nihilists*, denying the validity of religion, revelation, moral codes, political authority or divine judgment. Such was the philosopher Bṛihaspati*, one of the founding fathers of nāstika thought. The nāstikas were *atheists*, who held that God was an invention of the priests and that such a divine being as they conjured up had no existence in reality. As such they were spoken of as *nirīśvara*, (no-God), a term that was also sometimes loosely used to include the Buddhists, Jains, and the philosophical schools of Sāṁkhya, Yoga, and Vaiśeshika.

Because they denied the authority of the Vedas, the nāstikas were also called *avaidika*, 'non-Vedists', a large category that again comprised not only the Buddhists and Jains, but the Sāṁkhya and Yoga schools of thought as well. Because of their heterodoxy Manu referred to them as *pāshaṇḍa* or heretics, who regarded the Vedas as self-contradictory, false and absurd, replete with priestly ravings (VI, p. 24) composed by lunatics and knaves, as could be plainly seen from the rites prescribed in the *aśvamedha* or horse sacrifice.

Nāstika philosophy had a strongly *individualistic* foundation, and stressed the reality of the personal and the concrete. Each thing had its *svabhāva**, 'ownness' or inherent nature, and this individual principle, and not the dictates of deity or the prescriptions of sacred books, was the sole guide to ethics and moral behaviour. Since svabhāva was all, it followed that 'effects are self-existent and are not the result of causes', just as a wood-apple tree gives forth wood-apples and not mangoes, whatever 'causes' might be brought to operate on its growth.

The outlook was therefore strongly *deterministic*, not only man but all nature being moved by natural and self-inherent principles. Hence the nāstikas were known as *dishṭika*, 'determined', or fatalists. Such was the school of Ājīvika* and his followers. The nature of anything being given, the consequences followed in a predetermined pattern, and it was vain to try to alter them or kick against the pricks.

They held that in this material world, thought itself was a material process. This latter doctrine is known as *dehātmavāda* (*deha-ātma-vāda*, 'body-soul-doctrine') or *anātmavāda* (*an-ātma-vāda*, 'non-soul-doctrine'), the denial of the separate identity of the soul, apart from the body. Because of this view the nāstikas were called *lokāyata* ('world-directed') or *materialists*. They believed in the ultimate reality of matter in its four elements of earth, air, fire and water. Ether was rejected because it could not be known by perception. This doctrine is developed in the teachings of Ajita*, the *elementalist* Parameshṭhin, and the lokāyata Bhāguri whom we know from the *Mahābhāshya* of Patañjali.

Further, the nāstikas were *sensationalists*, deeming only that knowledge to be valid, which came through the senses, and holding *darśana*, the 'viewpoint' of the sense organs, i.e. sense perception*, to be the only valid source of knowledge. The fact that there are hundreds of viewpoints depending on who views what, was basic to the philosophy of the Jains. Some authorities hold that the term darśana now used for a philosophical system was originated by the nāstikas as a metaphysical category and borrowed by the orthodox schools. Inference was rejected because it was based on presuppositions and was like thinking in a circle. Testimony was likewise counted worthless since it involved inference.

From their materialism and sensationalism came their *hedonism*, a doctrine that the value of existence, if it has any value at all, is to be judged by the norm of pleasure it brings to the individual. The purpose of life is enjoyment and the gratification of the senses, and sensual pleasure the only object of living. Such teachings are found in Javāli and Chārvāka*.

Finally, *scepticism* was a strong trait in all nāstika systems, e.g. Jayarāśi*. The validity of the primary virtues of obedience, loyalty, courage, fidelity, was questioned, since these are devices by which the weak but clever ones could impose their will and discipline on the strong but stupid. Some were *agnostics* such as Sañjaya* who claimed that we do not know and cannot know the ultimate realities. Some were *cynics* like Javāli* who flaunted the principles of morality, condemned all social codes and ridiculed religion.

Indian materialism and rationalism, as exemplified in the theories of nāstika thinkers appear to have played a great and liberating part in the development of Indian thought, a fact which has been immensely neglected by students of Hindu philosophy. Indian nonconformity is one of the finest chapters in the history of Hindu and Buddhist speculation. For centuries, in spite of the severest restrictions of a rigid orthodoxy, India continued to produce schismatics and protestants, dissenters and rebels, who shook orthodoxy to its foundations. Hinduism was never able to contain itself within the orthodox mould owing to the ceaseless attacks on the citadels of its faith from all sides by these agnostics, and it is this more than any other single factor that has contributed to the elasticity of the Hindu organism. The catholicity of Hinduism in fact comprises precisely that aspect of the religion that is most distasteful to orthodox Hindus, although their apologists sometimes speak of it as though they had a hand in the matter themselves, or as if they welcomed this latitudinarianism.

Books

I. Barua, B. M. *A History of Pre-Buddhist Indian Philosophy*, Calcutta, 1921.
II. Chattopadhyaya, D. *Lokayata: A Study of Ancient Indian Materialism*, New Delhi, 1959.
III. Law, B. C. 'Influence of the Five Heretical Teachers on Jainism and Buddhism', *Journal of the Royal Asiatic Society of Bengal*, Calcutta, n.s. XV (1919) 123–36.
IV. Law, B. C. 'A Short Account of the Wandering Teachers at the Time of Buddha', *Journal of the Royal Asiatic Society of Bengal*, Calcutta, n.s. XIV (1918), 399–406.
V. Ruben, Walter. *Geschichte der indischen Philosophie*, Berlin, 1954.
VI. Sastri, D. *A Short History of Indian Materialism, Sensationalism and Hedonism*, Calcutta, 2nd Ed., 1957.
VII. Sastri, H. P. *Lokayata*, Dacca, 1925.

NĀTHA, 'lord', the name of a yogic cult which rose to prominence in northern India, Nepāl, Bengal and Assam, from about the tenth century A D and whose saints bear the title of Nātha. The beliefs and practices of the Nātha sect overlap many areas of esoteric Hinduism, and its currents intermingle with those of Yoga, the Siddhas, the Chīnāchāra (*see* Bogar), the Śāktas and Aghorīs, and with the doctrine of *rasavāda* or alchemy*.

The Nāthas stress the culture of the body, with a view to making it perfect and immutable and thereby attaining immortality (*see* physical culture). An immense folklore has grown up around the Nāthas. They are reputed to be healers and wizards, to have complete mastery over respiration and other bodily functions, to be able to bring rain or cause drought, control wild animals, serpents, scorpions, ants and insects, ride tigers, and transform themselves into any shape at will. Legends about them tell of magic carpets, aerial cities, visits to heaven and hell, of resurrections from the dead, levitation, clairvoyance, living without food, multiplying the body, and much else. Popular tradition holds that the saints of the Nātha cult are still living in their subtle supra-material bodies in Himālayan or jungle fastnesses. The cult was severely criticized by Kabīr, Nānak and other reformers for its occult teachings.

The term *Siddha* (South Indian, Sittar) i.e. one who has 'accomplished', is often used synonymously with Nātha, but is strictly applied to a lesser category of Nātha adept. A Siddha is one who through mastery of esoteric techniques has acquired siddhi* or occult power, often of a malefic character. A seventeenth century quietist Tamil* sect, the Sittars, attempted to purify and moderate some of their doctrines. There are traditionally nine Nāthas and eighty-four Siddhas who are venerated by the followers of the sect, and several hundreds of *charyāpada*, 'ritual stanzas', relating to the Nātha teachings are extant.

The Nāthas and Siddhas make use of intoxicants and drugs, and are specialists in therapeutic alchemy, which in India was largely derived from Chinese sources. It is not known where the Nātha cult originally evolved, but in spite of the Chinese influence on the course of its development, it was clearly an offshoot of an early form of occultism widely practised in India. Its legendary founder *Ādinātha* (First Lord) is identified with Śiva by the Hindus, and with Vajrasattva by the Buddhists, which establishes its association with Tantrism. Bengal, Assam, Nepāl and Tibet are closely tied up with the early development of Nāthism, but the cult later spread all over northern India. A tradition speaks of its being practised in the semi-mythical kingdom of Uḍḍiyāna in the seventh century, and it was at the same court about a century later that the great adept *Matsyendra** (or Matsyendranāth) flourished. He was held to be the first of the human gurus to whom the doctrines were clearly expounded. Matsyendra's name is linked with that of his famous disciple *Gorakhnāth** who founded a well-known order of yogis credited with terrible powers.

The names of the remaining Nāthas and Siddhas are variously and anachronistically given; there is much discrepancy in the accounts, and Nāthas and Siddhas are frequently classified together without distinction. The most important of the adepts are: *Udenāth*, referred to as the third of the great

Nāthas, following Matsyendra and Gorakhnāth; *Nīmnāth*, probably Nemi, the twenty-second Jain *tīrthaṅkara*; *Pārasnāth*, probably Pārśva, the twenty-third Jain tīrthaṅkara; *Bhūtanāth*, 'ghost lord', probably Buddha; *Dayānāth*, 'compassionate lord', probably a form of a *bodhisattva*; *Nāgārjunanāth*, the Buddhist philosopher Nāgārjuna; *Bharatināth*, noted for his asceticism; *Ratannāth*, a contemporary of Gorakhnāth, and the subject of many miraculous tales; *Daṇḍanāth*, founder of a cult of staff-bearing yogis; *Puranbhagat* who with his half-brother *Rasālu* has inspired hundreds of miraculous tales; *Charpaṭi* (or Charpaṭināth), a rasavāda or alchemist and poet, some of whose verses in Panjābi are extant; *Gūgā* (or Gūgānāth) whose power over serpents was phenomenal; *Manikchandra*, a bania by caste, who left his wealth to join the Nāthas; *Gahininăth*, initiated by Gorakhnāth, himself initiated *Nivṛittināth* brother of the Marāṭha saint Jñānadeva at Tryambaka; *Dharamnāth*, probably the Lord Dharma of the crypto-Buddhist Dharma cult of Bengal. There is also a semi-historical Nātha of this name who (*c.* 1380) was reputed to have stood on his head in a yogic posture for twelve years at Dhinodhar in Cutch. The dented stone on which his head rested is still shown; *Chauraṅginăth*, a prince of the Pāla dynasty of Bengal, who became a pupil of Gorakhnāth. Because of his devotion to the cult his hands and feet were cut off and he was thrown into a well. Gorakhnāth kept him alive and initiated him after twelve years of discipline; *Gopichand* (*c.* 1050) also known as Jālandhar, the son of queen Maynāmatī of Comilla in East Bengal. He came under the influence of the *ḍom* (outcaste) Siddha named *Hāḍī* whose powers were such that the dead revived at his mere kick. Gopīchand accepted Hāḍī as his guru, renounced the throne and became a renowned Siddha himself.

Books

I. Briggs, G. W. *Gorakhnath and the Kanphata Yogis*, Calcutta, 1938.

II. Gopinath, K. *Some Aspects of the History and Doctrines of the Nathas*, Banaras, 1931.

III. Mallik, K. *Siddha-Siddhanta and other Works of the Natha Yogis*, Poona, 1954.

IV. Mohan Singh. *Gorakhnath and Medieval Hindu Mysticism*, Lahore, 1937.

NECROPHILIA. The term *śavavāda* (*śava-vāda*, 'corpse-way') applies to the ritual disciplines based on necrophilic beliefs common to certain Hindu and Buddhist tantrik cults, in which matters pertaining to death, corpses (śava), decay and putrefaction, are meditated upon and constitute the material of cult practice. The preferred habitat of those who follow śavavāda is the śmaśāna, the cemetery or cremation ground. Such places are believed to be the favourite haunts of Śiva and his consort Śakti. Many old Śākta temples have been built in or near cremation grounds and burial places, and many Śākta and Śaivite ascetics live in graveyards.

The subject of śavavāda meditation includes various aspects of Śiva and Śakti (generally as Kālī) in their most awe-inspiring and repulsive forms. They may be imagined as two emaciated ascetics seated amid a forest of decaying corpses and dried bones. Kālī's body is wreathed in serpents; she holds a skull in her hand and wears a garland of human heads. Jackals

(Kālī's favourite animals) and carrion birds feed on the flesh of dead men. More often Śiva himself is a putrescent corpse with the dark-hued Kālī sitting astride him. She picks off and eats pieces of the rotting flesh, and as she does so flashes of malignant power like rings of purplish light play about her head. The patterns assumed by these flashes are used by Śākta yogis in drawing the *maṇḍalas* around corpses for their rites.

According to orthodox Hindu schools, witnessing or assisting in the burning of the dead has a purifying effect on one. It helps one to realize the evanescence of life, the dangers of the ego, the need for burning away the 'actions' that fetter one to the wheel of *saṁsāra*. But for the tantrik its value lies in the powers it bestows. The extremity of asceticism is associated with the cult of the graveyard, for those who undertake to perform the rites of śavavāda rise to a plane of mental awareness that supposedly puts terrible spiritual potentialities within their grasp. To be able to override the conventional dictates of an ordered society, to turn one's back on the writings of so-called holy books, and the teachings of puling saints, to acquire the ability of overcoming the inherited revulsion of contact with the dead; these and similar acts of will power help the sādhaka (practitioner) to rise above the law, to receive incredible siddhis*, and to defy the heavens with impunity. Killing, it is said, gives one an aura of strength that radiates into the other world and brings hidden forces into operation. Soldiers, butchers and killers therefore have great occult power, even when they are totally ignorant of it and are unable to direct and use it. The power to paralyse with a glance, to cause flood or fire with a mantra, to make men do one's bidding by a mere gesture, are held up as the rewards of śavavāda. A tale in the *Kathā-sarit-sāgara* attributes the witches' power to fly through the air to the eating of human flesh. But the neophyte should beware, for not everyone has the strength to withstand the force of the powers released by these acts, and the horror and guilt felt by them drive many to insanity.

Śavavāda sects are all Śaivite, or more specifically, Śākta, and include the Aghorīs, Kālamukhas, Kāpālikas, Kaulas and others of that category. Their chief practices may be briefly summarized. Where they get a chance they slay living things, preferably by a lingering death, as by this means the flesh and bones are believed to be properly confected. Human victims are the most suitable where available. They live in graveyards and periodically perform their own symbolic funeral, burial or cremation rites. They smear their bodies with the ashes of the dead or the earth scraped off exhumed corpses. They touch, wash, clothe, and otherwise assist in the cremation of bodies, believing that contact with cadavers instils vitality in their persons. They consort with corpses, since contact of the male member with the yoni or anus of the dead is thought to be capable of charging the practitioner with occult power.

They cut off and preserve portions of any dead bodies that are unburied or that have not been wholly consumed by fire; if necessary they exhume cadavers that have been buried. They eat the putrefying flesh, cooked or raw; regarding as especially vitalizing the brain, lungs and testicles of men. They have been known to dig up and eat the recently buried corpse of a child (I, p. 71). The Aghorī sect openly practised cannibalism till the end of the nineteenth century and still do so when opportunity offers. They make drinking bowls of skulls, after having eaten the brains and fleshy portions. The skull, which they always carry with them gives the name Kāpālika* to the best-known of the śavavāda sects. They carry rosaries and wear ornaments of human bones round their necks, around their waists and suspended from their organs. Similarly they utilize the flesh and bones of other creatures such as the bat, rat, toad, cat, snake, jackal and mad dog (which they are said to tame and kill by special mantras) and carrion birds, sacrificing each animal for particular rites. They also make use of the soiled linen of an untouchable woman, the shroud of a corpse, the discarded rag of a leper, the sputum of a consumptive, the semen of an epileptic or corpse, the vomit of an old man poisoned with hemp seeds.

Śavavāda rites include gruesome practices carried out in complete solitude at dead of night in graveyards and cremation grounds, in which evil demons who are believed to haunt cemeteries and hover over corpses, are invoked. A magic maṇḍala* is drawn on the back or breast of the corpse or on the ground around it. Postures of ritual meditation are assumed and secret mantras intoned. These mantras are not in Sanskrit and in fact they seem to be a mere babble of gibberish.

In one class of rites the sādhaka sits with a skull pressed against his genitals in one of the postures known by the generic term of *muṇḍāsana* (*muṇḍa-āsana*, 'skull-seat'). In another he lies prostrate or squats upon the cadaver in the attitude called *śavāsana* (śava-āsana, 'corpse-seat') until the flesh decays and then eats the flesh (I, p. 227). In yet another he sits in the place where the funeral pyre (*chitā*) was laid, in the posture called *chitāsana*, and performs his own funeral rites. In the *nīlasādhana* (nīla-sādhana, 'black ritual') the yogi sits astride a male corpse and animates the body by occult means. Distant cries and groans are said to be heard which gradually approach and enter the body. The corpse twitches and struggles, its tongue protrudes horribly, and the yogi cuts it off for future magical use; it is said that its organ erects and that it ejaculates and the fluid is collected and used. Variations on these themes are too numerous and revolting to quote.

Books

I. Briggs, G. W. *Gorakhnath and the Kanphata Yogis*, Calcutta, 1938.
II. Woodroffe, J. *Shakti and Shakta*, 4th Ed., Madras, 1951.
See also under Occultism *and* Tantrism.

NECTAR. The drink of the gods and the elixir of immortality is known in Hindu mythology as *amṛita*, the 'immortal' draught. The term was often applied in the Vedas to the juice of the Soma plant and other ingredients of the Soma drink. The Epics and Purāṇas relate how amṛita was produced at the dawn of time, during the portentous conflict between the gods and demons.

The gods had been frequently worsted by the demons, and to make matters worse were cursed by the insulted sage Durvāsas* to become weaker still. In danger of defeat because of their dwindling powers they approached Brahmā for assistance. Brahmā turned to Vishṇu for advice, and the latter suggested that they churn the celestial ocean of milk according to his instructions, in order to procure the chalice containing the amṛita and other precious things that had been lost in the Deluge. The *asuras* (demons or titans) were called in to help in this task and were promised a share of the nectar. They came willingly, but with the secret intention of stealing the chalice of amṛita.

The mighty undertaking, known as the *samudra-mathana*, 'ocean-stirring', the Churning of the Ocean, was one of the great events in the epic struggle between the gods and demons. Vishṇu assumed one of his famous *avatāras*, that of the tortoise, **Kūrma**, and stationed himself at the bottom of the ocean, and on his back was placed the great mountain **Mandara**, which served as a churning-stick. The tortoise back of Vishṇu thus served as a base or pivot which prevented the churning-stick from sinking into the ocean bed. Around the mountain was wound the great serpent **Vāsuki** as a rope. The gods and asuras then holding the two ends of Vāsuki proceeded to churn the ocean of milk.

As they churned there first appeared on the froth-laden surface, a viscid scum of deadly poison*, which contaminated the waters and the atmosphere. This scum Śiva scooped up and swallowed. Now there slowly emerged from the depths a number of matchless treasures, known as the *chaturdaśa-ratnam*, 'fourteen jewels', most of which became the prototypes of similar things in heaven and earth. The lists in the different texts vary slightly, but generally the fourteen precious things are named as follows: (1) Chandra, the moon (*see* Soma); (2) Pārijāta, a wonderful tree which was taken by Indra and planted in his paradise; (3) Airāvata, a four-tusked elephant*, which was also taken by Indra; (4) Kāmadhenu*, the cow of plenty; (5) Madā, goddess of wine, who was taken by Varuṇa as his wife and became Varuṇī. She held in her hand a jewelled bowl filled with *surā* or wine (*see* drinks); (6) Kalpa-vṛiksha, the wish-fulfilling tree (*see* plants); (7) Rambhā, an apsarā, the prototype of all the beautiful nymphs* of Indra's heaven; (8) Uchchhaiḥ-śravas, a wonderful white horse* taken by Indra. It lived only on *paramānna* (*parama-anna*, 'supreme-food'), also called *devānna* (*deva-anna*, 'divine-food') or ambrosia; (9) Lakshmī* goddess of fortune and beauty, who was taken by Vishṇu as his wife; (10) Śaṅkha, the conch of victory, which was given to Vishṇu (*see* animals); (11) Gadā, the mace of sovereignty; and Dhanus a magic bow, both weapons* given to Vishṇu; (12) Ratna, gems*, of which many kinds emerged from the deep; (13) Dhanvantari*, physician of the gods, who bore in his hands the most precious gift of all, namely, (14) amṛita, the nectar of immortality, in a golden *kumbha* or chalice.

On the appearance of the chalice both gods and demons strove for its possession. The demons seized the kumbha first and fled with it. In the course of their flight they rested at four places leaving the precious kumbha on the ground. In other legends they did not rest but hurried on, spilling some of the nectar at these four places, which became the sites of the great *kumbha-melas* (q.v.). The asuras would have consumed the nectar had not Vishṇu assumed the guise of the beautiful damsel Mohinī (*see* Androgyny) who by a stratagem obtained the nectar from them and gave it to the gods, and after they had drunk, disappeared along with the chalice.

A connected legend tells how the fierce demon Rāhu* assumed the form of a deity and took a sip of the immortal draught and was cut in two by the flaming discus of Vishṇu. In another story the eagle Garuḍa* steals the amṛita, but Indra recovers it.

Amṛita is also called *nirjara*, 'not aging'; and pīyūsha, 'the juice'.

Books

See under Mythology.

NEGRITO, the name of a dwarfish, Negroid race from Africa, who were among the earliest inhabitants of pre-historic India. It is conjectured that they migrated there from Africa via Arabia or the Persian littoral. Remnants of them survive in many primitive South Indian tribes of Madrās and Travancore, and among the Nāga hill tribes of eastern Assam, as well as among the aborigines of the Andaman Islands.

Their culture was rudimentary; they belonged to the eolithic stage of civilization, were food-gatherers rather than food-producers, and their sociological contributions were largely absorbed by the later arrivals, particularly the Austrics and Dravidians, and most of the original traces of their influence are obliterated.

But some of their distinctive racial characteristics have endured even in areas where they have been assimilated by miscegenation, and their features can be seen in the Ajantā frescoes and in Gupta sculpture (II, p. 147).

Certain eschatological ideas of Hinduism relating to human destiny after death, and ideas about the path of the dead to paradise which is guarded by an avenging demon, are traceable to them. Certain totemistic notions connected with fish, animals and plants may also have a Negrito origin. Scholars also attribute to them the cult of the *pīpal* tree and the use of the bow and arrow (I, p. 5.)

Books

I. Dikshitar, R. *Origin and Spread of the Tamils*, Madras, 1947.
II. Majumdar, R. C. (Ed.) *The Vedic Age*, London, 1951.
(*See also under* Anārya *and* Race.)

NIMBĀRKA (?1130–?1200), a Telugu brāhmin, Vaishṇava mystic and philosopher, and founder of the Nimandi sect. He was also an astronomer and is often identified with Bhāskara. A fanciful anecdote relates that an ascetic once paid him a visit and engaged him in controversy till evening. The philosopher offered the ascetic some food but the latter had to decline since according to his belief he could not eat after the sun had set. The philosopher immediately caught the last rays (*arka*) of the declining sun and hung them upon the branches of the bitter *nimba* tree, thus arresting sunset till the meal was cooked and eaten. This incident gave him his name.

Nimbārka held that Brahma or God has an independent reality. He is absolute existence; the creator and sustainer of the universe, and possesses infinite and unlimited consciousness. The individual soul (*jīva*) of man, which possesses self-consciousness, and the inanimate world (*prakṛiti*), which lacks self-consciousness, are both created, finite, sustained by but not identical with Brahma, and have no independent existence. They are dependent realities distinct from Brahma. This philosophy is known as *dvaitādvaita* (*dvaita-advaita*), 'dualistic non-dualism'.

In Nimbārka's philosophy, *bhakti*, 'devotion' or faith is stressed above meditation; the only destiny of the finite soul is worship of the Infinite. As long as man lives in this body release is not possible. Jīvan-mukti or salvation during this life is a false hope; salvation can only come after death. There is no other way of salvation except devotion at the lotus feet of Kṛishṇa, and his consort Rādhā, who shines with incomparable beauty as she stands on the left side of her lord, adored by thousands of female companions. Kṛishṇa and Rādhā were worshipped conjointly. The poet Jayadeva* was said to have been a friend of Nimbārka.

The sect flourished in the region around Mathurā and produced a considerable literature, of which many important works were destroyed during the reign of Aurangzeb.

Books

See under Vaishṇavism.

NISHĀDA, 'squatters', a powerful, indigenous non-Ayran tribe of ancient Indian dwelling in the region of the Vindhya mountains. References to the Nishādas are found in most of the early writings. They are described as having a complexion like the colour of charred wood, with flattened features, high cheekbones, blood-red eyes, black matted hair, and dwarfish in stature. Their present descendants are perhaps to be found in the Bhils, Kols, and other aboriginal tribes of Central India, and in some of the pañchama* (outcaste) peoples. The lawgiver Manu refers to them as descendants of a brāhmin father and śūdra mother.

Mythologically their progenitor was supposed to have been a dwarf, created from the thigh of king Veṇa*. Several of this dwarf's descendants are named in legend, often bearing the royal title of 'Guha' (secret).

Some authorities draw a careful distinction between the Nishādas who were non-Aryan, and the Nishadas who, we are told, belonged in all probability to the Aryan stock, and were of a different race from the Nishādas, 'and we may conclude that they belonged to the Aryan fold'. There is, in point of fact, nothing to support this probability or to warrant this conclusion, and the main reason why the myth of their Aryanness is so sedulously fostered is that one of the most beautiful love-stories in the *Mahābhārata* is told of the Nishada prince, **Nala***. Appparently only a pure Aryan couple was believed to be capable of such sublime heights of tender devotion.

Another renowned Nishāda (Bhil) chieftain was **Ekalavya**, who was related to Kṛishṇa, but here again, in order to dissociate Kṛishṇa's family from the aboriginal Nishādas, legend has it that Ekalavya was exposed in infancy and was only reared by the Nishādas but was not a Nishāda himself. The *Mahābhārata*, however, relates that while a young man Ekalavya once went to the mighty Droṇa for instruction in archery, but Droṇa refused to teach him the art since it was a privilege reserved for the higher castes alone. The boy made a clay image of Droṇa and practiced before it as though Droṇa himself were present. His extraordinary skill soon reached the ears of Droṇa who went to the forest and questioned the boy. Ekalavya acknowledged Droṇa as his instructor whereupon Droṇa demanded as his teaching fee nothing less than the right thumb of the young outcaste, thus depriving him of the facility in the art he so loved dearly and that he had acquired as a result of his own perseverance. Some years later Ekalavya was killed by a rock hurled by Kṛishṇa while he was participating in a night attack on Kṛishṇa's kingdom of Dvārakā.

Books

See under Mythology.

NUDITY. The climate of the Indian peninsula serves to favour nudity, and nudist tribes have been in existence in India from time immemorial. But besides the nakedness imposed by climatic conditions, nudism in India often has a religious significance and is practised even in extremely cold regions.

There is a great mass of theory behind the cult of nudity. Often nakedness is merely symbolical of renunciation of the world, a negation of the common values of conventional life, and a triumph over the needs of the physical body. But there is a deeper significance than just that. Clothing, it is believed, contaminates and impairs the innate potencies of men and women. Complete nudity is regarded in some sects as most conducive to the effective operation of ceremonial worship. All the powers engendered during the ritual acts are diffused in a natural manner around the body without any impediment, and serve to augment the efficacy of the rite and give force and direction to the sacrifice. Where a covering is necessary the permissible vestment is a garment of leaves or bark, but this being sometimes impracticable, a simple unstitched cotton cloth is allowed for draping the lower part of the body. The head, torso and feet must remain uncovered.

The Indian ascetics (*see* Kalyāṇa) whom the astonished Greeks referred to as gymnosophists or 'naked philosophers' may have been any one of the several ancient sects for whom nudity was obligatory. The Jain Digambaras or 'sky-clad', as well as the Nirgrantha ascetics who take all the Jain vows, are also nudists. The Kāpālikas and other Śaivite, Śākta and Tantrik groups, often go about completely nude. Innumerable lesser sects and yogic cultists who observe nudism in private, are scattered throughout the length and breadth of India. One of the most extraordinary features of the Kumbhamela* at Allāhābād, is a procession of naked sādhus.

Sometimes a taboo is placed on male nudity, particularly in the presence of the opposite sex, for it was once commonly believed that if a woman looked upon the nakedness of a man (even if he were her husband) he would lose his virility. An old Indian legend relates how the divine nymph Urvaśī* became the wife of Purūravas on condition that she never saw him unclothed, as she would cease to love him if she did. The heavenly companions of Urvaśī resolved to secure her return to them and beguiled Purūravas into suddenly leaving his bed at night and in a flash of lightning disclosed him naked to his wife, who thereupon abandoned her husband, for she knew that he would now no longer be able to satisfy her.

Female nudity on the other hand is universally recognized as having a beneficial effect on all things. It enlivens the procreative powers of the male, stimulates nature, and pleases the gods. The sight of a beautiful nude brings good luck, and averts the evil eye, since the goddess of Fortune and Beauty resides in her body. In the past during certain festive seasons, public women in rural areas used to be unrobed and worshipped. In many tribal cults a nude goddess is given a prominent place in the pantheon. For instance, the tutelary godling* of the non-Aryan Daitya people was *Koṭṭavi* (or Koṭori), meaning 'naked woman'. Certain Tantrik sects worship nude women in rites like kumārī-pūjā and chakra-pūjā. In such cases the woman is looked upon as the incarnation of Prakṛiti, the female principle of the universe. She is regarded with profound veneration, as if one were pondering on the unfathomable mysteries of nature or the cosmic spirit. The ritual nudity of the yoginī has an intrinsically mystic significance, and *maithuna* (sexual intercourse) has no ritual value if the nudity of the woman does not suggest the revelation of a cosmic mystery to the devotee.

The term *nagna* expresses both nudeness as well as a girl growing into womanhood. It is a girl at such an age who forms the object of Tantrik devotion (*see* strīpūjā). When Kṛishṇa stole the clothes of the gopīs he made them come to him nude, to indicate that they were emancipated from the bonds of family and society.

In accordance with an age-old belief a nude female assists the operations of nature. The rain-making dance of the Rājbansi tribe of Cooch Bihār is performed in the nude, accompanied by obscene gestures and salacious language. During the rain-making rites among the kshattriya* Kāpu tribe of Madrās, a small clay image is carried from door to door by girls who sing ribald songs. Each householder pours a little water on the image, and periodically the girls lift their skirts, expose themselves, and pass water as they stand. Observers report similar practices in other parts of India.

Books

I. Crawley, E. *Dress, Drinks & Drums*, London, 1932.
II. Crooke, W. 'Nudity in India, in Custom and Ritual', *Journal of the Royal Anthropological Institute*, XLIX, 247.
III. Dare, P. *Indian Underworld*, London, 1938.

NUMBERS play an important part in Hindu occultism, and a preoccupation with numerical themes is a feature of much Hindu speculation. The esoteric significance and relationship of numbers is believed to have originated from Babylonian, Chinese, Hebrew and Greek sources. Infinities are of particular fascination and are often circumscribed in a cyclic formula such as is seen in the concept of the ages of Brahmā and the cosmic ages of the universe. The notion of *śūnya* and the almost mystical aspect of the zero were similarly prominent in Hindu and Buddhist writings. Special potencies were thought to reside in certain numbers and the branch of crypto-science now termed numerology, received much attention particularly during the middle ages. These are indicated in brief outline below.

0: zero; symbol of śūnya or nothingness which comprises all things. It is the absence of all and the presence of All.

1: the number of divinity, of the liṅga, of the sun, signifying brightness, light, unity, wisdom.

2: the number of the moon, symbolized by the eyes, nostrils, breasts, testes, the right and left sides, and by the two genders.

3: the triad, a blessed number, exemplified in the perfect triangle; it is a vision of divinity for all mankind; a father, mother and child triad.

4: a perfect number in a higher plane. 'As the cow requires four feet, so the sacrifice must have four Vedas and four priests.'

5: a symbol reducing much diversity to meaningful measure. The whole '*pañcha*' series of things e.g. *pañcha-tattva*, *pañcha-gavya*, etc. Also, the hand.

6: a lesser variant of two and three, symbolized by the six systems of philosophy.

7: the number of the planets, the seven holy ṛishis, it is a number requiring deep study.

8: a deeply mystical number; the key to the fatality behind events.

9: the triune trinity, a number of ascending wisdom, symbolized by the nine orifices of the human body.

10: the cosmic number, perfectly prefigured in the ten avatāras of Vishṇu.

11: an unlucky number, an augury of misfortune whenever it appears.

12: the highest of the lesser series of numbers, comprehending all others.

17: a mystical number of ascent and sanctification. There are 17 chariots in the *vājapeya* race and 17 steps on the yūpa.

18: a number of completeness, typified in the 18 *parvas* of the *Mahābhārata*, the 18 days of the Great Battle, the 18 *akshauhiṇīs*, or battalions, that participated in it; the 18 chapters of the *Bhagavadgītā*.

34: a composite number; it appears in the Ṛigvedic hymn, denoting the sun, moon, the five planets, and the 27 *nakshatras* or asterisms.

84: a higher synthesis of numbers consisting of the number of planets (7) multiplied by the signs of the zodiac (12). An important number for Śaivites, who often 'count' by measures of 84, e.g. 10,084.

108: another mystical number comprising the seven planets and the two phases of the moon, i.e. 9, multiplied by the 12 signs of the zodiac, and symbolizing the whole heavens. There are said to be 108 shrines of special sanctity, 108 Upanishads, 108 beads in the Śaivite rosary.

padma: one thousand billion, used to indicate the number of gold ingots that constituted the treasure of Kubera, god of wealth. No kingdom on earth can ever have more than this treasure.

parārdha: 'other half', said to be the highest number, which is the figure one followed by 17 zeros, multiplied by itself 17 times.

Books

I. Das, R. C. *Numbers in Hindu Magic & Religion*, 1913.

II. Wescott, W. *Numbers, Their Occult Power and Mystic Virtues*, 1911.

NUMERALS. The origin of our present system of numerical notation is hidden in almost impenetrable obscurity. The science of reckoning was of course known to all the great civilizations of the past. The Babylonians, for example, had an efficient system of computing that enabled them to deal in highly complex astronomical calculations, while the arithmetical system of the Mayas of Central America was, according to Lissner, 'a piece of native ingenuity which central Europe never matched' (V, p. 268).

The actual method of notation in use among the ancients varied considerably. The decimal system was known in Ancient Egypt. One stroke signified 1, two strokes 2, nine strokes 9; ten was represented by a fresh symbol, and two such symbols denoted 20, and so on up to 100 which was represented by yet another symbol. Other cultures employed the duodecimal system, reckoning by twelves (as in our reckoning of hours); still others by the vigesimal system, reckoning by twenties (as in our scores); or the sexagesimal by sixties (a system used in Babylonia and still retained in our reckoning of minutes and seconds); and some by the centesimal, or hundreds. The Greeks and Romans used letters of the alphabet as numerals, as did the Hebrews and Arabs. In Java and Sumatra 'word numerals' were widely employed; a word was used to denote a number, the word for 'eyes' expressed the number two, the word for 'teeth' the number thirty-two, and so on.

In India, no script known to contain numerals is found until the time of Aśoka (3rd century BC) in whose Kharoshṭhī inscriptions some numerals can be seen in the form of primitive vertical marks for one, two, four and five. There are also separate and independent signs for the larger figures and multiples of ten. More developed forms of these figures have been found in the inscriptions of the Śakas, Parthians and Kushāns, between the first century BC and the second century AD. The further evolution of notation was facilitated by the adoption of Brāhmī numerals, which were introduced into India from a right to left script of West Asian origin, and which are believed to be derived from the hieroglyphic-like notation of Egyptian Demotic or Hieratic. Each of them uses nineteen symbols for the numbers 1 to 100, and out of these nineteen symbols nine of the Brāhmī symbols resemble the corresponding symbol of the Demotic or Hieratic.

In Brāhmī there were separate signs for the numbers from 1 to 9, and separate single signs for 10, 20, 30, 100, 200, etc., all independent of each other. Without place-value, without a zero, and with separate signs for the multiples of ten, these Indian numerals, as Needham points out, 'were no improvement at all on the Greek and Hebrew alphabetical script' (VI, p. 12).

Through their use by Buddhist mathematicians the Brāhmī numerals came to be known in Tibet where they underwent further modification. Indeed, some authorities hold that the actual numerals were originally invented in Tibet. It was one of these adapted forms that the Arabs later took over, and it was these so-called 'Arabic' numerals that they subsequently passed on to Europe.

Two factors are fundamental to the system of numerical notation as employed throughout the world today, namely, (*a*) the place-value given to the digits and (*b*) the zero sign. Of these two factors place-value is by far the more important. According to Needham, 'The zero symbol, as part of the numerical system, never existed, and could not have come into being, without place-value' (VI, p. 12).

Place-value was known in ancient Mesopotamia, for the Babylonians had what was practically a positioning system with base 60 (sexagesimal) instead of base 10 (decimal), and the zero sign was used by the Mayas of America in the first century AD. But it was the system combining these two factors as found in India that became the source of the modern numerical script and methods of computing.

A tradition surviving from the time of the Abbasid Caliphate ascribes the invention of the zero and place-value to the Hindu people. Actually, research on the subject is by no means complete and the full story of the development of these revolutionary concepts is not yet known. Neither place-value nor the zero sign was in use or known in India before the sixth century AD (I, p. 120), whereas in China (late Chou) a place-value system, without any symbol for zero had been in existence for several centuries before it became known in India. Long before the third century AD the Chinese had developed 'a fundamental decimal place-value system' (VI, p. 12). Chinese counting boards on which their calculations were made, indicated place value by the position of the beads or counters, leaving a blank space as a sign for what was subsequently represented by the zero.

It is significant that the term later employed to convey the zero-idea in Sanskrit was the word *śūnya*, meaning emptiness, 'just as if it were describing the empty spaces on the Chinese counting boards (VI, p. 13). For this space the dot symbol was used, as is still done in the Śāradā script of Kashmīr. It is just as likely that the 'void' of Tao mysticism, no less than the 'nothingness' of Buddhist philosophy, contributed to the zero symbol.

There is nothing at present to indicate where the idea of combining the place-value with the zero was conceived. The sixth-century inscriptions in Cambodia and Sumatra (the rendezvous of the two great cultural streams of India and China), the disputable Baroḍā and Gaṅgā inscriptions, the spurious copperplates on which some records containing numbers have been preserved, have all been successively taken up and discarded as inconclusive.

No one knows who invented the system. No one knows the city or place of its discovery, least of all the nationality of its discoverer. But it is established that it began to be generally known shortly after the flood-tide of foreign occupation of north-west India between the sixth and ninth centuries AD. This region had been dominated for seven hundred years by 'barbarian'* foreigners whose sphere of contact extended as far as Alexandria.

A remarkable fact is that in South India the old Brāhmī system continued to prevail for centuries, with separate signs for 10, 20, 30, 100, 1000, etc., and the new method was not adopted until post-British times when it was introduced, through the medium of English, into the Tamil, Malayālam, Kannaḍa and Telugu areas (I, p. 120).

When the Arabs entered India they took over the Indian notation with place-value and zero. They accepted it as one of the contributions of Hindu genius. Later scholars accepted the Hindu derivation on the basis of this tradition. Only fresh critical and historical investigation on the subject, or a chance archaeological or literary 'find' will provide a solution for these interesting academic problems. Words like *hindāsa*, once thought to derive from Hind, are now known to be actually from the Persian *andāzah*, meaning measure; the term *patigaṇita*, the Hindu science of arithmetic, is known to have originated in a non-Sanskrit vernacular of northern India. And it is also clear that Arabic references to India do not necessarily indicate India proper, but the empires of the Śakas and Kushāns, as well as the territories of Central Asia, Hinterindia, Oceanic India, and often vaguely 'the East'. Although from force of habit the conventional belief still persists that the zero sign, as an integral factor of the place-value system, came from India, the fact is that no one knows where it actually originated. One thing is beyond dispute and that is that 'behind the Hindu numerals as the West subsequently knew them, there lay 2,000 years of place-value in China' (VI, p. 15).

Books

I. Chatterji, S. K. *India and China*, Calcutta, 1961.
II. Datta, B., & Singh, A. N. *History of Hindu Mathematics*, Lahore, 1935.
III. Durant, W. *The Story of Civilisation: Our Oriental Heritage*, New York, 1935.
IV. Kaye, G. R. *Indian Mathematics*, Calcutta, 1915.
V. Lissner, Ivar. *The Living Past*, London, 1957.
VI. Needham, J. *Science and Civilisation in China*, Vol. III, London, 1959.
VII. Tarn, W. W. *The Greeks in Bactria and India*, London, 1938.
VIII. Smith, D. E. and Karpinski, L. C. *The Hindu-Arabic Numerals*, Boston, 1911.
IX. Whitehead, A. N. *An Introduction to Mathematics*, Oxford, 1945.

NUMISMATICS. There is no evidence that the art of making coins in India had any indigenous tradition. It seems to have been acquired from foreigners at every important stage of its development.

Trade in ancient India was carried on by barter, and if exchange were ever required for domestic purposes, shells and seeds were used. The cowrie shell (*varāṭa* or *kākiṇī*) continued to be in use in many parts of rural India till comparatively recent times, and the names of the *guñjā* berry (*rati*), the *kaśu* berry (*karsha*), the bean (*māsha*), the hemp seed (*śāṇa*), the *paṇa* (a bundle or 'packet' of vegetables sold as a unit), which were given to later coins, preserve the elements of this primitive numismatic period.

Gold was plentiful in India and was used for higher currency; according to Herodotus the Achaemenians received their annual tribute of 360 talents from their Indian province in the form of gold dust or ingots. It was from the Achaemenians that the Indians now learnt the art of making coins from pieces of silver and copper of recognized weight and fineness. These early coins are 'punch-marked', so called because the designs are not made by a single impression covering the whole face, but by separate punchings or stampings impressed irregularly on the surface of the metal when hot.

A great deal can be learnt from the designs impressed on coins, and on the first punch-marked Mauryan coins from the third century BC onwards we find frequent representations of Persian symbols such as the sun (worshipped by the Zoroastrians and seldom appearing in Hindu symbolism), a branch or twig (untraceable in Hinduism but related to the sacred branch of haoma), a bull (Mithraic), and a *chaitya* (representing the sacred Mount Mouru of the Avesta).

These early punch-marked coins were the śatamāna, nishka, māsha (or māshaka), kārshāpaṇa (or paṇa), and ṭaṅka (this latter named after the 'mallet' with which the metal was punched), each of varying weights. The name kārshāpaṇa (the weight of a 'packet' of berries) is derived from the word karsha, 'berry', which is thought to be of Mesopotamian origin, and of which a relic survives in the Tamil word *kāśu*. In modern times it was merged with the Portuguese word *caixa*, and inherited by the English as 'cash'.

With the advent of the Greeks in India the art of coin-making took a considerable step forward, and it is only after the Greek period that we find coins and intaglio gems, beautifully designed, of chaste and elegant execution, of uniform fineness and weight, and with the names of rulers clearly marked on them.

The coins of the Bactrian Greeks were of extraordinary beauty and workmanship, those of Demetrius (*c.* 185 BC), Eucratides (*c.* 171 BC) and Antimachus (*c.* 168 BC) being amongst the finest in the world. The artistic excellence of these coins has never been surpassed in India and they set a new standard that 'revolutionized Indian numismatics' (VI, p. 57). They were of Attic quality, based on the obolos, stater and drachma, of silver and copper, and the names of some of them have passed into the Indian languages. From the Greek drachma comes the names of the Sanskrit coin, dramma, which in the Apabhraṁśa (Middle Indian) speech became *damḍī*, a coin of insignificant value. Some philologists hold that although the popular English swearword, damn, is derived from the Latin damnum, in its sense of damning someone, as 'Damn him!', it is derived from the Indian damḍī in the sense of something 'not being worth a damn', or of one 'not caring a damn', thus making it an expression of Anglo-Indian provenance not more than a century or so old.

The Indians were never able to fashion good coins, and made no attempt to perfect the art. The best products were for the most part inexpert imitations of Greek, and later, Roman, workmanship. In certain parts of the country Indian kings took the simple expedient of importing coins wholesale and sometimes restriking them.

During the following Kushān ascendency in the north-west many varieties of Roman coins came into India, and the Kushān coins of gold, silver and copper were themselves based on Roman models. The dinār came from the Roman denarius, and the name of the gold coin, *suvarṇa*, 'beautiful colour', came from the excellence of the metal used. From the fact that Kushān coins bore an image (*rūpa*) of some kind, as distinct from the plain metal pieces or indistinct designs of Indian workmanship, they were known as *rūpaka*, which by the Gupta period was applied to a particular coin, and has come down to us as the rupee.

Numismatic evidence of this period gives an inkling of the extent of trade relations between Rome and India. Huge hoards of gold have been unearthed not only in the ports and coastal areas of India, but well in the interior. These include finds of six hundred gold and one thousand one hundred silver pieces, apart from 'pots full' and 'coolie loads' of coins, mostly belonging to the reign of Augustus (31 BC–AD 14) and Tiberius (*c.* AD 15), when trade had reached its peak. Roman coins of the period after Septimius Severus (*c.* AD 122) begin to dwindle and are scarce, although there is one hoard belonging to the days of Arcadius and Honorius (AD 395), and a few scattered specimens of the later emperors of the Western and Eastern empires, including Anastasius (AD 491) and Justinian (AD 518).

There is a story, related by the traveller Cosmas Indicopleustes (sixth century AD) of a Persian and a Roman at the court of the king of Ceylon. The Persian spoke at length of the greatness of his country, and when he had done the taciturn Roman merely produced an aureus and handed it to the king for his inspection and asked him to compare it with a Persian coin. It was a conclusive argument, for the excellence of the Roman coin showed a universal superiority, a coin being a symbol of civilization, since it needs art to design it, science to manufacture it, and confidence to give it currency.

Foreign influence on Indian numismatics continued till the Guptas, who began to make coins of fine quality. But the origin of Gupta work has been placed at a time when this dynasty was in close contact with the Kushāns, 'whose eastern Panjāb coins they copied' (IV, p. 29).

The later history of Indian numismatics shows an indigenous line of development, and coins were produced in large quantities by local rulers in all parts of the country. India knew several 'golden' ages, notably during the zenith of Chola power, when no silver was used for any large transactions, the currency for this purpose being only in gold. The rich Muslim kingdoms of the Deccan often used gold currency, of which the little gold 'pagoda' (so called because a pagoda was stamped upon it) of Golkandā was the most famous. The Moghul period saw many ups and downs, but it was also in a way a 'golden' age for the European traders and officials of the time, and the prospect of 'shaking the pagoda tree' became the chief lure of the East for many of these soldiers of fortune.

Books

I. Bhandarkar, D. R. *Lectures on Ancient Indian Numismatics*, Calcutta, 1921.
II. Brown, C. J. *The Coins of India*, Calcutta, 1922.
III. Cunningham, A. *Coins of Ancient India*, London, 1891.
IV. Dandekar, R. N. *A History of the Guptas*, Poona, 1941.
V. Gardner, P. *The Coins of the Greek and Scythic Kings of Bactria and India*, London, 1886.
VI. Majumdar, R. C. (Ed.) *The Vedic Age*, London, 1951.
VII. Rapson, E. J. *Indian Coins*, Strassburg, 1897.

NYĀYA. one of the six orthodox systems of Hindu philosophy, first formulated by the philosopher **Gautama** (?450 BC–?AD 100) (or Gotama), in his *Nyāya-sūtra*. The son of a priest he was born in northern Bihār, and spent most of his life in a hermitage with his wife Ahalyā and only son. Because of his deep contemplative studies Gautama was also known as Dīrghatapas (dīrgha-tapas, 'long-penance'), and from his habit of walking with eyes downcast wrapt in deep thought, as **Akshapāda** (*aksha-pāda*, 'eye-footed'). Gautama is regarded as the father of Indian logic and the Aristotle of Hindu thought. Other famous philosophers of the Nyāya school are Vātsyāyana and Gaṅgeśa. The traditional application of the teachings of Nyāya was best preserved in Tibet, where in the great monastic universities of Lhasa the student used to devote four years to its study.

Nyāya signifies 'going into' a subject, or analysis, and is thus opposed to the Sāṁkhya* or synthetic mode of speculation. It is concerned primarily with logic*, the processes of ratiocination and the laws of thought, as well as with epistemology, and leans heavily on reasoning by analogy. It lays down the basic principles of discussion and analysis, and formulates an elaborate scheme of inference by means of the syllogism*. It exposes the stratagems of controversy, and lists the common fallacies of thought. The Nyāya system endowed Hindu philosophy with a rich vocabulary of philosophical and especially logical terms. Nyāya is also called *Tarka-vidyā*, science of reason, and *Vāda-vidyā*, science of discussion. It should be borne in mind that though primarily concerned with logical techniques, logic is but one of the subjects with which it deals.

Nyāya teaches that ignorance is the root of all suffering and rebirth, and that only complete knowledge (*jñāna*) of the true nature of things will bring *apavarga* or deliverance. Error is thus seen to be the cause of pain, and eradication of error is the goal of man. Nyāya claims to help in distinguishing the true redeeming knowledge from the false, and provides a means of acquiring this knowledge, through the processes of logical thought which is the main road to wisdom. The *naiyāyika* or follower of Nyāya, must be willing to admit as true whatever is established by reason.

Nyāya recognizes sixteen categories* which in their various relationships are employed to explain the universe. They are (1) *pramāṇa*, the means by which knowledge* is obtained; (2) *prameya*, or the object of knowledge. The other fourteen categories relate to logic and the syllogism, but have acquired in the course of time a different connotation from that given to them in the early works on the subject; (3) *saṁśaya*, doubt; (4) *prayojana*, purpose; (5) *avayava*, the members of a syllogism*; (6) *dṛishṭānta*, familiar example; (7) *siddhānta*, established tenet; (8) *tarka*, confutation; (9) *nirṇaya*, ascertainment; (10) *vāda*, discussion; (11) *jalpa*, controversy, (12) *vitaṇḍā*, cavil; (13) *hetvābhāsa*, fallacy; (14) *chhala*, equivocation; (15) *jāti*, similarity; (16) *nigraha-sthāna*, disagreement in principle.

The *Nyāya-sūtra* makes very casual reference to God, who is defined as one of a class of souls, albeit the chief of that class. The original doctrine may have been atheistic. The later theism of the Nyāya school is generally of Śaivite inspiration.

Books

I. Ballantyne, J. R. *Lectures on the Nyaya Philosophy*, Allahabad, 1849.
II. Jha, G. N. *The Nyaya-sutras of Gautama*, 3 vols., 1912.
III. Keith, A. B. *Indian Logic and Atomism: The Nyaya and Vaiseshika Systems*, Oxford, 1921.
IV. Randle, H. N. *Indian Logic in the Early Schools*, London, 1930.

NYMPHS. In Hindu mythology the celestial nymph or *apsarā* (ap-sara, wet-flow) is a personification of the mists or clouds in the form of a beauteous damsel. Apsarās play no great part in the Vedas although a few of them are mentioned. Their prototype, Rambhā, appeared at the Churning of the Ocean, but since neither gods nor *asuras* would espouse her Indra took her and her companions to his heaven, Svarga, where they became the common property of the dwellers of paradise and dispensed their delights to all. They were the female counterparts of the *gandharvas* or divine musicians.

In the Purāṇas several *gaṇas* or groups of apsarās are named and their number is variously given as a few dozen to several million. They are spoken of as *surāṅganā* (*sura-aṅganā*, 'celestial females') and *sumad-ātmajā*, 'pleasure daughters', and heavenly courtesans. Heroes who fall in battle receive their embraces as a reward. They are fond of dancing and gambling, and to those who win their grace they grant good fortune in dice and other games of chance. They are free with their favours and frequently drive men to madness and distraction with their voluptuous charms.

The gods sometimes send down apsarās to lure from their intentions such ambitious mortals and holy sages who by austerities and self-abnegation would presume to aspire to divine powers. Sometimes they voluntarily consort with men. Several epic heroes and heroines had apsarā mothers, e.g. Drupada, father of Draupadī; Droṇa the famous archer; Pṛithā, wife of Pāṇḍu and mother of Arjuna.

Chief among the apsarās are: **Rambhā,** the first among nymphs, who emerged at the Churning of the Ocean. She became the mistress of Nala-kūbara, son of Kubera, and was ravished by Rāvaṇa even though she pleaded with him saying she was the wife of another. Rambhā was sent by Indra to distract Viśvāmitra from his penances, but the sage, already regretting his amorous encounter with Menakā, another apsarā, caused Rambhā to be turned into stone, and thus she remained petrified for a thousand years. She afterwards took part in the seduction of the demon Śumbha*; **Tilottamā,** originally a brāhmin woman who once committed the offence of bathing at an improper time and was condemned to be reborn an apsarā. Tilottamā's most famous exploit was her share in the destruction of the *daitya* Śumbha and his brother; **Ghṛitāchī,** seduced the sages Vyāsa and Bharadvāja*. Through her the Paurava king Raudrāśva became the father of ten sons, and likewise through her Viśvakarman became the progenitor of many mixed castes and tribes; **Urvaśī*** tempted the gods Mitra and Varuṇa and many others, and married Purūravas; **Menakā** was sent to beguile the sage Viśvāmitra* and through him became the mother of Śakuntalā*; **Alaṁbushā** achieved the seduction of Dadhīcha son of the ṛishi Atharvan*, **Pramlochā** of the sage Kaṇḍu*, **Aśruvindumatī** of Yayāti*, and **Jānapadī** worked her wiles on the sage Śaradvant son of Gotama*.

Books

See under Mythology.

NYSA (or Nysaea), the name of an ancient tribe inhabiting the region to the north-west of India between the Kophen (Kābul) and Indus rivers. It is generally acknowledged that they were of Greek origin, although the problem of how they happened to settle in that remote area has not yet been satisfactorily resolved.

According to Greek tradition the north-west regions of India were invaded and conquered by their legendary deities Heracles and Dionysus long before Alexander. The god Dionysus (also called Nysaeus) was supposed to have taken his revelling company across Asia Minor, and even ventured as far as India, and the panthers with which he is often represented are symbolical of these eastern travels. According to Arrian the tribe of Śivi (*see* Uśīnara) were among those who claimed descent from the members of Heracles' expedition. The Scythian hill-fort of Aornus was remembered during Alexander's campaign as the strategic citadel that even Heracles had failed to take. Alexander attached the greatest importance to its capture, and Greek chronicles describe its storming and downfall at great length.

Scholars are generally agreed that the Greeks were known to India before Alexander's time. From numismatic and other evidence Bhandarkar deduces the presence of a Greek colony in an outlying district of north-western India about 550 BC (I, p. 29). The Nysaeans may have represented one such small migration, a tiny outpost of Greek people who cherished their own heritage. They called a mountain not far from their city by the name of Meros, 'thigh', in commemoration of Dionysus' birth, which may have been the origin of Mount Meru of Hindu mythology.

Nysa was one of several autonomous principalities in the north-west that Alexander found flourishing in his day, and the only one in that hostile area where he found the atmosphere conciliatory and even familiar. Arrian records that Nysa was a non-Indian oligarchic state with a governing body of three hundred members presided over by a polemarch named Acuphis. The deputation from Nysa who came to offer tribute to Alexander told him that they were the descendants of the companions of Dionysus, who founded their city, that they cultivated the ivy and the vine sacred to him, which grew nowhere else in the region, that they had Greek customs and worshipped Greek gods. The Greeks 'experienced a keen joy of recognition' and gladly accepted them as kinsmen, and the Nysaean warriors on their mountain horses willingly joined the Macedonian, and followed him to battle in the plains of the Panjāb.

Another tribe of domiciled Greeks, the **Branchidae** are also mentioned by Strabo and Plutarch as having welcomed Alexander in north-west India. They were descended from a hierophant of the temple of Apollo in Ionia, and their forefathers had surrendered the temple treasure to Xerxes when he invaded the country. Because of the odium in which their deed was held by their fellow Greeks they joined Xerxes on his return to Persia. Xerxes settled them in a small town in Sogdiana where their descendants were found by the Macedonians. They welcomed the conqueror and surrendered their city to him, but Alexander not wishing to bring upon himself the curse of Apollo by accepting their friendship sacked their city and slew all the inhabitants.

Books

I. Bhandarkar, D. R. *Carmichael Lectures*, 1921.
II. Holdich, H. *The Gates of India*, London, 1909.
III. Law, B. C. *Tribes in Ancient India*, Poona, 1943.

IV. McCrindle, J. W. *The Invasion of India by Alexander the Great*, 2nd Ed., Westminster, 1896.
V. Narain, A. K. *The Indo-Greeks*, Oxford, 1957.
VI. Tarn, W. *The Greeks in Bactria and India*, London, 1938.

OBSEQUIES. In the Sanskrit texts the term *antyeshṭi* refers to the 'final' sacrifice, the last *saṁskāra* or sacrament in the life of the Hindu, performed to give peace to the spirit of the recently departed and to enable it to join its ancestors. The lawbooks and other *smṛitis*, especially the *Garuḍa-Purāṇa*, have much to say about the *ars moriendi* and the funeral rites. There is no consistency in the ritual and in fact a great deal of confusion exists both in the lawbooks and in practice. The final rites are divided into four parts: (*a*) the ante-mortem rites over the dying, (*b*) the rites attending the disposal of the body, (*c*) the rites to help the *preta* or spirit to become a *pitṛi* or ancestor, and (*d*) the rites devoted to the pitṛi.

The antyeshṭi ceremonies thus start somewhat before the actual decease. When it is felt that the end is approaching, the dying person is carried in his cot to a clear spot on sandy soil and placed in the proximity of three fires, and sacred passages are recited until the spirit has left the body. Often the hand of the dying man is tied to the tail of a cow in the belief that his soul when released will be led to heaven; a few leaves of the sacred tulsī plant are placed in the other hand and a little *pañcha-gavya* (a mixture of the five products of the cow*) is poured into his mouth.

In some localities it is considered unlucky for a man to die in his cot, since he will be condemned to carry it about with him in the next world, so he is placed on the ground during his last moments. In Bengal, what is not very euphemistically known as 'ghāṭ-murder' sometimes takes place, when the dying man is carried to a ghāṭ or river bank, and the lower half of the cot in which he is lying is immersed in the water, so that he generally dies of exposure or is drowned by the wavelets that ripple over his face.

Early forms of body-disposal included exposure to birds and the elements, by leaving the corpse in an elevated place or by hanging it from a tree; burial in a cave; water burial by throwing the body into the sea or river; burial in the earth; and cremation. According to the *Ṛig-veda* burial in the earth was the earlier form (VII, p. 348), and a hymn in the *Ṛig-veda* describes such a burial rite, but by the middle of the Vedic period cremation became prevalent, and remains the recognized method of corpse-disposal today. Infants, yogis, sādhus, and a few others are still usually buried and not burned. Cremation is practised because it is believed that as long as the physical body exists the spirit lingers near it, and cannot get a new body until the physical body is utterly consumed.

The next stage is the cremation of the body. Here again there is no uniform procedure, and details vary greatly from place to place. The following composite picture gives particulars, of which some are not universally observed, and others now obsolete:

(*a*) sacred verses are recited to revive the corpse. When these have failed to bring it back to life, the priest by word or gesture announces death;

(*b*) professional mourners, if they are hired, gather round the deceased with

dishevelled hair, disordered garments and dust be-sprinkled bodies and set up a doleful wailing, shrieking, sobbing and beating of breasts in measured time. Formerly in some parts of India the widow used to collect and preserve her tears in a little phial;
(*c*) the corpse is washed, the hair and nails cut, and it is dressed in a new garment and adorned with jewels. The thumbs are tied together to signify that its activities are at an end; the big toes are also tied together lest the ghost should walk back to the land of the living;
(*d*) it is then laid on a bullock-cart, or carried on a stretcher on the shoulders of relatives, followed by mourners who chant aloud the sacred names of Rāma, Hari and other gods, till they reach the *śmaśāna* or cremation ground, which is generally near a ghāṭ or river bank. A piece of wood is dragged on the ground after the corpse on the way to the burial ground, to obliterate the 'tracks' made by the corpse, to prevent him from returning by the same trail to torment the living;
(*e*) arriving at the ghāṭ the attendants rest the feet of the corpse in the river and set up the pyre, wealthy mourners using sandalwood, poorer people using some cheaper fuel;
(*f*) in some cases the body is dressed at this stage and not earlier, and it is now laid upon the funeral pile, facing southwards. Some lawgivers prescribe that the corpse be disembowelled and filled with ghee (clarified butter);
(*g*) the mourners circumambulate the pile, with left side towards the corpse, a withershins direction common to most death rites the world over;
(*h*) in olden times the widow* of the deceased would now lie down beside her husband while Vedic verses were recited. Her brother-in-law or other male representative of the husband then made her rise from the pile and once again take her place among the living. The practice of burning widows (*see* suttee) may have been a perversion of this ceremony;
(*i*) a cow is sacrificed (this is seldom, if ever, done today), and the face and head of the deceased are covered with the omentum of the animal. The kidneys of the cow are placed in the hand, the other internal organs on the other parts of the body of the deceased (II, p. 447);
(*j*) in the past, if the deceased was a kshattriya (warrior) his bow used to be placed in his hand, and before the pyre was lit it was broken and thrown into the pile of wood;
(*k*) then the chief mourner placed his lips successively on the nine orifices* of the corpse, recited mantras and applied a little ghee to each part;
(*l*) the corpse is now deprived of all its jewels, and a small ball of dry cowdung is placed on its belly or breast; then the chief mourner walks around the corpse three times and pours some water on the pile of wood from an earthen vessel carried by him. This vessel he afterwards breaks on the head of the deceased. In some cases the eldest son of the deceased delivers a blow on the skull with a mallet and cracks it. He is presented with a torch which has been lit by sacred sparks from two rubbing sticks or at a sacred fire, and with this torch he sets fire to the wood;
(*m*) in accordance with the belief expressed in the *Bṛihadāraṇyaka Upanishad*, the various parts of the dead man are directed by suitable mantras to go to their appropriate places: his voice to the sky, the eyes to the sun, the vital

airs to the atmosphere, his thoughts to the moon, his ear to the heavens, his body to the earth, his ego to the ether, his hair and head to the plants and trees, his blood and seed to the waters;
(*n*) the *Atharva-Veda* mentions the custom in which women dance around the funeral pyre with their hair loosened; they beat their breasts and wail, and taking up handfuls of dust from the ground cover themselves with it;
(*o*) after the flesh has been consumed by the fire the mourning party returns home, the youngest leading and the others following in order of their age. Each person present is given seven pebbles which he drops on the way one by one with his left hand without looking back. Since spirits are notoriously poor counters and cannot resist counting, the intention is to keep them occupied each night counting the pebbles and so prevent them from returning home;
(*p*) on reaching home the mourners bathe, ceremonially purify themselves, offer libations of water and kindle a fire, reciting *mantras* the while;
(*q*) a day or two after the funeral the chief mourner returns to the pyre and ceremonially sprinkles the dead ashes with water. The unburnt bones and ashes are collected and buried in a pit or emptied into a river. Part of the ashes may later be thrown into the Ganges, especially at Hardwār, Banāras or Allāhābād. Gāndhi's ashes were thrown into the waters of all the sacred rivers of India.
(*r*) certain water plants and a female frog were sometimes left where the body had been cremated in order to appease the burnt plot of earth.

Next come the rites to help the preta. After the physical body is destroyed, the subtle body has nothing to depend on; it exists as a *preta* or spirit, and if not helped by rites becomes a *bhūta*, ghost or demon, and wanders restlessly about, or joins the demon train of Śiva. Dr Evans-Wentz quotes the case of a European planter in the jungles of India whose uneasy ghost was successfully laid to rest only by satisfying his craving for whisky. He had been addicted to it in his lifetime, and although the villagers were religiously opposed to intoxicants they purchased the liquor and poured the contents over the grave with a regular sacrificial ritual in order to appease his spirit (IV, p. xli).

This part of the antyeshṭi ceremonies is also called *preta-karma*, i.e. rites performed to give peace to or provide a body for the preta. The ultimate intention of this rite is to enable the preta to become one of the pitṛis or ancestors, and to join the other pitṛis in their heavenly abode. These rites are devoted only to the preta and are considered *amaṅgala* (inauspicious) and should not be confused with the subsequent śrāddha* ceremonies, which are *maṅgala* (auspicious).

While the rites for providing the preta with a 'body' are being carried out, the preta is fed and looked after in several curious ways. For instance, the chief mourner grows nine kinds of grain in an earthen vessel. This vessel of sprouted grain, along with another vessel of water and a dish of rice, is placed in the room of the deceased, and over them is hung a thread suspended from the ceiling. The thread serves as a means of descent for the preta to come down and refresh himself during the ten days following his demise while his new body is being formed.

The development of the preta's new body is assisted by the ceremony known as the *sapiṇḍī-karaṇa*, 'piṇḍa ritual', generally performed as follows:

(*a*) On the first day after death a round ball of rice or flour moistened with milk and water and known as the *piṇḍa* is offered to the preta. The preta feeds on this and gets the rudiments of a frame, and on subsequent days he is fed with a piṇḍa each day, and slowly acquires arms, legs, organs, and so on till the tenth day, when the piṇḍa gives him nourishment for a head, so that he now has a complete body.
(*b*) On the eleventh day four pots are filled with a mixture of sesame, perfume and water. One is for the preta, one for his dead father, one for the grandfather, and one for the great-grandfather of the preta. If the father is alive the order is stepped back one generation. The contents of the preta's water-pot is then poured into the other three.
(*c*) Four piṇḍas are also prepared for the above. The Vedic rule is that there can be 'no fourth piṇḍa', i.e. there must be piṇḍas for only three; the ball for the preta is therefore mixed with the piṇḍas of the other three, so that only three balls remain.
(*d*) Hereafter the great-grandfather of the preta is promoted and classed among the half-mythical manus, and the preta, along with his father and grandfather, is numbered among the *pitṛi*, or ancestors and is worshipped in the śrāddha ceremonies. Some authorities hold that the deceased 'moves about in the air' for one year before he is admitted to the pitṛi class.

It is to be remembered that there are endless variations of this basic ceremony depending on the sex, age, caste, of the deceased, and the relationship of the mourner and deceased and so on.

The antyeshṭi ritual can be carried out in the absence of a corpse, as in the case of a man drowned, or killed in battle, or deceased in a far country, or eaten by wild animals, and whose body is therefore not available. A man erroneously supposed to be dead, and for whom the funeral rites have been held, is treated as dead on his return, until a special resurrection and rebirth ceremony has been enacted. The person is passed between a woman's legs (his mother's, if she is still alive), washed and dressed in swaddling clothes, and nursed on milk. The other *saṁskāras* or sacraments* marking the successive stages of a Hindu child's development are also performed, although in quick succession. He is then remarried to his wife.

Books

I. Bendann, E. *Death Customs*, London, 1930.
II. Bhattacharyya, H. (Ed.) *The Cultural Heritage of India*, Calcutta, Vol. IV, 1956.
III. De, S. M. *Death Rites of the Hindus*, 1911.
IV. Evans-Wentz, W. (Ed.) *The Tibetan Book of the Dead*, Oxford, 2nd Ed., 1949.
V. Karambelkar, V. W. *The Atharvavedic Civilization*, Nagpur, 1959.
VI. Law, B. C. *The Buddhist Conception of Spirits*, 1923.
VII. Majumdar, R. C. (Ed.) *The Vedic Age*, London, 1951.

OCCULTISM. India has been famed as the land of goety and illusory wonders from the beginning of her history. The newly arrived Aryans, before they became Hindus themselves, were amazed at the sorcerous arts of the Dravidians and aborigines. In the writings of the Ancient Greeks such as the works of Hecateus of Miletus (500 BC) and Ctesias (400 BC), and in the semi-legendary lives of Alexander the Great and Apollonius of Tyana, India was described in terms of miracles and occult wonders. Muslim travellers, and later, medieval European writers, perpetuated this fabled tradition, which did not abate even after the West became more intimately acquainted with India. The fact that it persists to this day is evidence of the deep-rooted and tenacious grip it has on the imagination of mankind.

The metaphysical basis of all Hindu occultism is traceable to the Vedas, and its practical application is found in the techniques of yoga. Hindu religion and mysticism on the one hand, and Hindu occultism and magic on the other are inextricably linked in the common tenor of their beliefs, which achieved their efflorescence in yoga and tantrism. Demonology, though condemned in the early portions of the Vedas, forms a substantial part of the *Atharva-veda*, which embodies pre-Aryan belief, and this, like all primitive faiths, presupposes a world of witchcraft, black magic and diabolism.

The hierophant is a thaumaturge before he is a priest, and the powers of the sādhu, yogi, nātha, ojhā, oḍiyan, and all *jādu-wallahs* (magic-men) are in general held in great dread by the populace. Almost invariably their spells, charms and periapts are malignant and full of evil intent. Their magic is especially virulent when they work with something belonging to the victim: his bodily substance (hair, nails, excretions), symbol (footprint), shadow (they work on the string with which they have previously measured the shadow), or name (either written or intoned). Their feats of levitation, materialization and de-materialization, apports, burial alive, crossing rivers and streams in mid-air, creating the illusion of men and things, and acts of 'glamour' like the mango trick, are believed to be done, if done at all, by intermediation of demons and elemental spirits.

One branch of Āyurveda known as *bhūta-vidyā*, 'demoncraft', is devoted exclusively to the subject of diseases caused by diabolical agency. It describes how spirits are made to plague individuals at the bidding of sorcerers, causing insanity, seizure (*graha*), and similar mental disturbances. These again can only be cured by recourse to another sorcerer who by means of exorcism, propitiatory sacrifices and magic formulas, gets rid of the malady by transferring it to a tree, animal, or man, or sending it back to its originator. Curses and malefic devices are employed to eliminate a co-wife, kill a child in its mother's womb, render a woman barren or a man impotent, cripple or maim a rival, or cause death. Scattered through the texts one finds recipes for vile compounds requiring the use of snakes, scorpions, toads, bones, horn, hair, hide, teeth, shells, saliva, and human and animal excretions including urine, semen and menstrual fluid.

The paraphernalia and ritual of the Indian magician are identical with those of sorcerers the world over, and point to the common fund from which they all draw. They believe in the menace of the moonless night and the full-moon night; often wear black robes and use a *daṇḍa* or magic rod. They perform rites in or near a fissure or natural cleft in the earth and offer blood and raw meat to attract chthonic elementals; or near cemeteries with corpses and the remains of the dead to summon demons and obtain magical powers; or at crossroads, which they regard as an *axis mundi*, to attract the ghosts of felons, and evil and restless spirits. They perform human sacrifices when opportunity offers; enact the funeral rites of a living enemy in order to compass his death; make clay or wax images to torment a victim; believe in the power of the evil eye and of the curse; believe that demons can have congress with women; that evil spirits cannot cross water; that spirits cannot count; that witches can fly through the air. They believe in the baleful association of the black cat and the owl (the messenger of Nirṛiti); and the ill-starred destinies of the deformed, of the squint-eyed, and of twins.

The recognized disciplines and training methods for acquiring occult proficiency in all its branches are to be found in yoga. The practitioner of the black arts no less than the aspirant to spiritual greatness is obliged to begin with an identical meditative and physical regimen. This includes breathing techniques, bodily postures and physical exercises of a special passive and interior nature. The incautious private student proceeds along the same path and it is here that he is likely to encounter the dangers always inherent in these ancient disciplines. These dangers lie in the spiritual no less than the physical sphere.

Most yogic exercises, even the simplest, are unnatural and often definitely harmful. Their practice requires constant supervision on the part of the instructor and vigilance on the part of the pupil. The *Gheraṇḍa-Saṁhitā* warns against the possibility of disease; and the *Haṭha-Yoga-Pradīpikā* states that 'the experimenter will be killed if the exercises are not properly done'. Ernest Wood, author of several books on Yoga speaking of haṭha yoga teachings says, 'Many people have brought upon themselves incurable illness and even madness by practising them without providing the proper conditions of body and mind'. Respiratory and cardiac diseases, and ailments affecting the head, eyes, ears, nose, stomach, kidneys and genitals, are extremely common among yogis even of advanced grade. The long life and superabundant vitality of the yogi is one of the most commonplace of fictions.

Cultivation of respiratory techniques and the retention of the breath for long periods enlarges the lung cells and weakens the heart. Standing on the head (*śīrshāsana*) flushes the face, dilates the capillaries and causes premature sagging of the facial muscles. The resultant cerebral congestion can bring on distressing hallucinations. Yogic exercises in general, far from increasing sexual vigour often permanently undermine it, as many practitioners have found to their cost. Even the simple *siddhāsana* is not to be recommended as it eventually weakens the male organ. Intensive concentration and focusing the eyes on the space between the eyeballs or the tip of the nose if overdone can strain the optic nerves and muscles and in extreme cases may lead to a permanent squint. Artificial lengthening of the tongue by pulling and daily massage ('milking') can cause an impediment in speech, while cutting the frenum (the membrane under the tongue) in order that the tongue might be rolled back into the gullet to prevent the 'leakage' of vital fluids from the brain, can be futile and dangerous.

Some forms of purificatory* exercises involve the cleansing of the stomach by swallowing a long strip of cloth and then pulling it out, or swallowing large quantities of water and then regurgitating it again. These practices in the long run injure the mucus membrane, impair the secretion of the gastric juices, weaken the digestive process and lead to general debility. Cleansing the nose by drawing water alternately through each nostril until water flows out of the mouth, or passing a piece of soft string up into one nostril and through the mouth and pulling the string back and forth, can do great damage to the blood vessels of the nose and inflame the sinuses.

The association of the anal region with the higher forms of Hindu occultism is a very prominent feature in yoga training. The titillation of the anal centres as in the cleansing of the rectum with turmeric stalks; regular and prolonged concentration on the area; the contraction and dilation of the sphincter in various 'locking' exercises, tend to divert sexual feeling from the sex organs. Some forms of tantric ritual do indeed prescribe submission of the *chela* to the passive role in homosexual relations with the guru.

Most dangerous is the extension of conscious control over the functions of the autonomic nervous system, which extends to breathing, body temperature, ejaculation, pulse, circulation and digestion, and can cause serious misfunctioning of the related organs which are normally under automatic control.

Other tricks prescribed for various purposes include sitting in a bowl of water and drawing up the water through the rectum or through the penis; or inserting a metal tube up the urethral canal; or by a slow contraction making both penis and testes disappear into the cavity so that the body has the appearance of a woman's. The harmful effects of such exercises hardly need stressing.

The prominence accorded to the erotic element is another notorious feature of Indian occultism. Phallicism plays a paramount role in many tantrik practices, and the worship of, or the preoccupation with the linga and yoni, and the genital and urethral functions, are brought to practical application in cultic rites, many of which are of such extreme perversity* as to be acceptable only to psychopathic individuals.

More serious than the physical dangers are the spiritual hazards of Hindu occultism, which stem from the philosophical and religious basis of Hinduism itself, for one cannot participate in the mysteries without surrendering one's identity to the Group Mind, and yielding one's soul to the Group Soul of Hinduism. The early Aryans when they first came in contact with these archaic forms of worship condemned them without equivocation, and the passages in the *Ṛig-Veda* denouncing the theurgic practices of the aborigines leave no room for doubt that they feared and abhorred them, and kept well away from the sphere of their possible influence. Modern occultists have frequently stressed the need for great circumspection before taking up Hindu and Buddhist occult teachings.

The scriptures of Hindu thaumaturgy, where they are available for persual, have been declared to be more terrible in their implications than the worst European grimoires, for 'even their good is evil, and even their gods are demons'. The worship and propitiation of what in the other major religions would be regarded as the powers and principalities of darkness are accepted practice in many parts of India. The metaphysical rationalization by modern Hindu apologists of phallicism, necrophilia and left-hand cults as part of the basic pattern of a 'tolerant' Hindu culture, only emphasizes the fact that this ancient antinomy persists.

Most Hindu philosophy is pantheistic, and its creed is expressed in such phrases as 'I am God', or 'God and I are one'. If repeatedly intoned, as it is required to be, the resultant autohypnotically induced feeling of the identity of Creator with creature, can sometimes lead the practitioner to believe that he is above the law, and beyond good and evil. To a rational outsider it may appear as sacrilegious arrogance and in the words of one critic 'repeats the Fall'. Indeed in some esoteric schools the identification is so complete that it is believed that the gods themselves worship the operator of certain magical rites.

Students of the subject state that Indian occultism represents a potent and dangerous residue from the archaic black-magical and demonological tradition of a remote antiquity, long extinct or outgrown in other civilized countries. It has been condemned as the deformity and decay of ancient magical lore, its sources being contaminated with the satanic wisdom of the dawn of time. In the words of a Western occultist, 'The fruits of Indian wisdom cause moral degeneration and destruction of the spirit, for its roots have been poisoned by the fangs of the infernal serpent'.

Yoga can be the first step along a hazardous path whose approaches have been so vitiated by unhealthy metaphysics and perverse ritualism, that even what might appear a superficial and innocent dabbling with its appurtenances such as prāṇayāma and āsanas, can bring one into the ambit of its more sinister influence, so charged are all its symbols, through centuries of active worship, with the potencies inherent in its teachings. The groundwork for all forms of tantrism, demon-worship, psychopathic sexuality and necrophilic rites, starts from the ostensibly innocuous preparatory exercises of breath control, standing on the head and washing out the stomach. The vast majority of those who go through these disciplines do so to obtain *siddhis** or superhuman powers, and generally the reward offered to the practitioner is freedom to indulge in all the crimes and vices of body and soul and still remain free from all sin.

For non-Hindus and those who do not, theologically speaking, wish to jeopardize their spiritual welfare, Indian occultism is best studied in an armchair. It exercises a strong hypnotic fascination on most people who study it, and Western exponents often warn against succumbing to its lure. These authorities on occultism have a special word of caution for those who are brought up in the monotheistic Jewish, Christian or Islamic traditions. They point out that persons not inured to the ramifications of Hindu religion and philosophy can never be at home in the contemplation of polymorphous deities of the kind that have been unequivocally condemned in their own scriptures, and that the recitation of strange formulas in an alien tongue, and the acceptance of beliefs strongly anathematized in their own creeds, can cause a major spiritual upheaval and lead to disastrous psychic consequences.

Books

I. Carrington, H. *Hindu Magic*, London, 1909.

II. Dare, P. *Indian Underworld*, London, 1938.

III. Dracott, A. *The Voice of Mystic India*, London, 1930.
IV. Jacolliot, L. *Occult Science in India and Among the Ancients*, London, 1919.
V. Laurence, L. W. de. *The Great Book of Magical Art and East Indian Occultism and the Book of Secret Hindu Ceremonial and Talismanic Magic*, 14th Ed., Chicago, 1939.
VI. Lévi, Eliphas. *The History of Magic*, E. T., London, 1951.
VII. Long, M. A. *Hindu Occultism and Its Dangers*, 1929.
VIII. Lovett, E. *Magic in Modern India*, 1924.
IX. Oman, J. C. *The Mystics, Ascetics and Saints of India*, London, 1905.
X. Parab, B. A. *The Miraculous and Mysterious in Vedic Literature*, Bombay, 1952.
XI. Thurston, E. *Omens and Superstitions of Southern India*, London, 1912.
XII. Wood, E. *Great Systems of Yoga*, New York, 1954.
XIII. Wood, E. *The Occult Training of the Hindus*, London, 1931.
XIV. Yonge, M. T. *Pitfalls in the Path of Occult Training*, 1891.

OLISBOI. The term *apadravya*, 'bad implement', is used in Sanskrit for all forms of artificial sex-aids or olisboi. Two main categories of such implements are mentioned by Hindu writers on the *kāmaśāstra*, namely, those taking the place of the yoni, and those taking the place of the liṅga. A third category covers all methods of roughening the male member to provide maximum satisfaction to the female.

The first category included the *viyoni*, 'without-yoni', employed by men. It was usually in the shape of a female image made of wood and cloth, with a yoni-shaped aperture of fruit, vegetables and leaves. Though such devices are referred to in the books on erotics, they were probably chiefly used in fertility rites, and generally a punishment was prescribed for any man who availed himself of an idol of any kind for purposes of self-gratification.

The second category included the olisbos proper, known in Sanskrit as the *kṛitrima-liṅga*, 'artificial phallus', also known to anthropologists as the dildo, which was widely used both by men and women. In many temples a fixed stone liṅga, located in a secluded part of the temple premises served for the ritual defloration of temple girls and virgins. They were made to sit on the stone which penetrated the vagina and caused the rupture of the hymen. Barren wives also resorted to such stone liṅgas in the hope of becoming fertile. Phallic substitutes were in common use among Lesbians, the inmates of harems, and solitary women like widows who could not remarry. In such cases the aid was often a long radish, or other suitable tuber, the brinjal (egg-plant) or the banana (I, p. 316). Phalluses of candle-wax, baked clay, wood, bone or metal, were also common. It is said that the 16,000 wives of Kṛishṇa used to make 'little figures' of him to ease their passion. Recourse to such devices by men is recommended by writers on erotics even for normal occasions in order to stimulate the partner before intercourse (III, p. 124).

Another kind of *apadravya* was the artificial corrugation or abrasion of his own member by the male. In one case a phallic-shaped cast was made of gold, silver, copper, iron, zinc, lead, ivory or wood, in one piece or in two or more jointed parts, with its tip pierced with holes. This had a rough exterior and fitted the member like a glove, so that irrespective of the erection of the male, as in the case of impotence, old age or incapacity, he could completely satisfy his partner. Those who could not afford such a gadget simply used a stalk, like the bamboo, coated with oil and tied with a string around the waist.

Yet another device was the actual perforation of the phallus, and the insertion of some type of plug into the orifice. This was widely practised 'in the Southern Provinces' in Vātsyāyana's day, and was in fact 'as common as piercing the ears of children'. The method was as follows. Standing hip-deep in water one perforated the tip of the organ with a sharp thin instrument from one end to the other, allowing the blood to flow freely. The man had to have intercourse with a woman the same night to prevent the wound from closing up, and he thereafter inserted and wore a small stem or twig, progressively increasing its size to enlarge the aperture. When the perforation was large enough he fixed in pieces of metal or wood of various sizes and shapes, depending on the mood of the woman. Similar devices were commonly used in Pegu, Malaya, Bali and other parts of Hinterindia (II, p. 50).

Yet another method was that of sewing into the skin of the phallus tiny bells made of gold, silver or bronze, depending on the status of the man. This caused the member to swell, and greatly heightened the pleasure of the female. The bells were sewn to the members of young boys and were periodically changed for larger ones as they grew up. Travellers to India up to the fifteenth and sixteenth centuries observed this practice, and remarked that old women made their livelihood by the sale of such bells, which they also sewed on to their customers, often as many as a dozen or more bells per client. The jingling could be heard while walking and was regarded as extremely attractive and even honourable. Beaux without bells were not in favour with women, but those with bells were very popular (III, p. 44).

Books

I. Chakraberty, C. *The Cultural History of the Hindus*, Calcutta, n.d.
II. Dingwall, E. J. *Women: A Historical & Anthropological Compendium*, Vol. II, London, 1935.
III. Upadhyaya, S. C. (Ed.) *Kamasutra of Vatsyayana*, Bombay, 1961.

ORIFICES OF THE BODY. The term *chhidra*, 'aperture', is used in Āyurveda for the openings of the body. A more general term denoting any aperture, hole or cavity in the body, internal or external, is *kha*. Thus the opening from one internal organ into another is called a kha. In esoteric parlance the term chhidra is used specifically in the sense of a 'leaky' orifice, and applies to the external openings through which the 'wet elements' of the body are exuded. In the case of the human male the chhidra are nine in number, namely, eyes (2), mouth (1), nose (2), ears (2), anus (1), and urethra (1).

The 'leakage' of the bodily fluids in any form sets in motion all of the internal channels through which these bodily fluids run, whether veins and arteries, or the larger tubes like the intestines. So close is the connection between the chhidra and the flowing processes that the mere use of the chhidra apparatus vitiates the prescriptions of the higher occult experiences, and it therefore becomes essential to block the apertures before certain exercises are attempted. All such blocks must be effected by means of the body itself, and no apparatus or outside aid is to be employed. Various *bandhas** (locks) and *āsanas** (positions) are used for this purpose, many of them devised to close the internal passages, such as that which prevents the escape of the esoteric 'nectar' from the subtle centre of the *sahasrāra* (*see* chakra).

The outward apertures are also to be 'blinded', and this is done by assuming a *mudrā* called the *shaṇmukhi* (*shan-mukhi*, 'six-faced') mudrā which seals the nine gates. Sitting crossed legged the yogi closes his ears with his thumbs, his eyes with his index fingers, and his nostrils with the middle fingers; the ring fingers press on the upper lip and the little fingers on the lower lip. Heel pressure on the 'yoni-place' (perineum) and the contraction of the anus shut the two portals of the lower body.

It is to be noted that as the human female has one (the vagina) or three (if we include the two breasts) extra chhidra, she has no means of blocking them, and is thus naturally precluded from the practice of this Yoga and other occult exercises. Virgins before the menstrual period are however regarded by some Śākta sects as possessing only nine apertures and certain techniques may be practised with, but not by, them.

The proper performance of the shaṇmukhi mudrā is extremely difficult. It forms part of a number of paramudrās*, and results in a temporary 'cessation' of physiological and, by extension, of certain mental functions, associated with the 'absorption of the semen' (*see* bindu). At least seven years' practice of *prāṇayāma* (breath control) and fourteen years' practice in other techniques must precede the shaṇmukhi if it is to be effective. During the first seven years of practice the hands are used for shutting the ears, eyes, etc., only as part of a symbolical gesture, and in the later stages the shaṇmukhi may be performed without this formality, so that the hands are free for other purposes in the paramudrās. The higher adepts are said to be able, for instance, to seal their ears at will, without physically blocking the aural passages, so that no external sound reaches the hearing.

Books

See under Tantrism and Yoga.

ORISSA, the modern name of the territory known in ancient times as Oḍra (Oḍradeśa or Uḍra), situated north of the Mahānadi river. It was originally the home of the Śavara and other Kolarian tribes who were known to Pliny as Oretes, but the present inhabitants have a large admixture of Dravidian elements. The Aryans always regarded the Oḍra people as beyond the pale, and a visit to their country constituted a defilement that could only be cleansed by special expiatory ceremonies.

In Sanskrit texts Oḍra was often identified and confused with *Utkala*, said to be a corruption of Utkaliṅga, or the northern (ut) part of Kaliṅga, which later comprised the southern portion of Chota Nāgpur. By the fifth century it was known as *Koṅgoda*, though the Purāṇas often make a distinction between Oḍra and Koṅgoda. Koṅgoda refers in particular to the country immediately north and south of the Mahānadi delta.

The Mahānadi delta, hallowed as a place of great sacrosanctity from prehistoric times, was the centre of an early sun-worshipping, probably Maga cult, whose rites included blood sacrifices and sexual promiscuity. With the rise of Buddhism the area became a Buddhist centre and Aśoka had a rock edict carved at Dhauli in the same region about 240 BC. Much later it came to be known as a 'kshetra' (field) sacred to Hinduism, marked by such pilgrim sites as Purī, Bhuvaneśvar, and Konārak.

Oḍra formed part of the kingdom of Khāravela (183–153 BC) and its history was closely linked with that of its southern neighbour, Kaliṅga*. For a time it was ruled by the Śaka satraps who waged frequent wars with Āndhra and other contiguous states. Historical events of this period are extremely confused. There seems to have been a considerable migration of peoples from north to south, like that of the Pallavas who established their rule in the region of Kāñchi.

From the middle of the third century AD an unknown *mlechchha* (barbarian) people appear on the scene. In the context in which they are spoken of, the term implies not a low caste or indigenous people, but a non-caste foreign race, who disputed power and reigned intermittently with native kings. They were in all probability Yavanas (Greeks). By the beginning of the fourth century the native dynasty was superseded by a king named Lohabāhu (*c.* AD 310), 'Iron Arm' or 'Red Arm'. The temple archives refer to this dynasty as Yavanas (Greeks) who were related to the Kaiṅkilās*. They became Buddhists and ruled Oḍra from AD 310 to 474.

Several notable events are associated with this foreign line of kings. They were among the first to send out expeditions to colonize the Indian archipelago and Hinterindia*, and it was during their rule in AD 318 that the image of Jagannātha* first appeared at Purī. The origin of the image is not known, but it may have been an ancient idol newly installed to give sanctity to the claim to rule. A cave near Bhuvaneśvar with representations of two Yavana warriors in western armour and leggings, probably dates from this time.

For the next two hundred years, between the middle of the fourth to the middle of the sixth centuries, the history of Orissa is inextricably interwoven with that of the Guptas, with Śaśāṅka of Gauḍa, Harsha of Kanauj, the Pālas of Bengal, the Pallavas, Chālukyas and the Cholas.

The **Keśāri** (474–950) dynasty was founded by a chieftain named Jajāti (or Yayāti) (474–526) who displaced the Yavanas, forcing them to seek a new home in the Āndhra country. Jajāti celebrated his triumph with a great horse sacrifice and established his new capital, first at Jājpur (or Jājnagar) and later at Bhuvaneśvar. He also built a temple at Purī to hold the image of Jagannātha. Another Keśāri ruler, Lelatindra (617–57) raised the *vimāna* and porch of the Great Temple at Bhuvaneśvar. Hiuen-Tsang visited Orissa during his reign, when Harsha exercised suzerainty over the area. He recorded that many of the inhabitants were zealous Buddhists, and spoke of over one hundred Buddhist monasteries in the district. A Keśāri ruler named Nṛipati (920–935) or Nrup, founded the city of Cuttack (Kaṭak) which he made his capital. The Keśāri dynasty was brought to an end by the Cholas in the middle of the tenth century.

Several local families assumed prominence in the country around Purī, Bhuvaneśvar, and Konarāk, about the same period, and made important contributions to its art and architecture. These minor dynasties have yet to be sorted out and there is much uncertainty as to their dates and achievements. Foremost among them are the **Māna** (570–620) who ruled in the area around Purī; the **Śambhuyaśa** (580–603), perhaps related to the Mānas, although often in rivalry with them; the **Śailodbhava** (620–700) of Koṅgoda and Chilka. Many of their kings had names ending in *bhīta*; the **Kara** (475–940), referred to themselves as descendants of Bhūmi, 'earth', as though to suggest that they were native to the soil and took over from a foreign dynasty. The names of sixteen rulers are recorded, all ending in *kara*; the **Bhañja** (750–1000) line ruled at Khijiṅga in the Mayurbhanj district. Some of these local dynasties were probably of aboriginal Gond antecedents, as indeed the **Tuṅga** and **Śūlki** rulers were actually known to have been.

The next dynasty of importance was the **Gaṅga** (1070–1568), also referred to as the Eastern Gaṅgas of Kaliṅga and Orissa to distinguish them from the main branch known as the Western Gaṅgas of Mysore. The family were known as early as AD 500, but only came into prominence in about 1070 when Choḍagaṅga (1070–1148), also called Anantavarman, conquered part of Orissa and established a line of kings. He and his successors were notable patrons of Sanskrit and Telugu literature. In 1200 Anaṅgabhīm (1189–1223) reconstructed the temple of Purī in expiation for the sin of killing a brāhmin; and about fifty years later Narasiṁha I (1238–1264) built the Black Pagoda. There were two short interregnums in the Gaṅga rule; once when a usurper named Kapilendra (1434–1541) assassinated the Gaṅga king and seized the throne; and again when the Bhoi (1541–1559) tribe assumed power and ruled for a short spell. In 1559 Mukunda (1559–1568), a scion of the Gaṅga line displaced the Bhois and asserted his sovereignty over Orissa. Eight years later he fell to the Muslims who destroyed his capital and were incited by a Hindu renegade who accompanied the Muslim army to desecrate the sacred images of Purī.

The rulers of Orissa had a passion for architecture, and gave lavish endowments for the construction of temples, at Purī, such as the temple of Jagannātha* (*c.* 750) and Vaitāl Deul (800); at Konārak, such as the Black Pagoda;* and at Bhuvaneśvar. All these sites were already hallowed by prehistoric cults and Maga and Buddhist associations, before being taken over by the Hindus. Bhuvaneśvar was sacred to Śiva, Konārak to Sūrya, Purī to Vishṇu, and Jājpur to Pārvatī.

The town of Bhuvaneśvar ('world-lord' i.e. Śiva) was once a sacred area in a forest called Ekambara, 'one-garmented', an allusion to the naked Śiva, and possibly relating to some ancient cultic rites practised there. It is said that over 7,000 temples and shrines once encircled the sacred lake of Bhuvaneśvar. Today there exist only a few hundred in various stages of preservation, out of which about thirty are worthy of note. Chief among these temples are Paraśurāmeśvara (750); Mukteśvara (950); Liṅgarāja (1000) the finest of them all, whose soaring tower dominates the town of Bhuvaneśvar; and Rājarānī (1100).

The central feature of the Orissan deul or temple is the sanctuary tower which rises from a square base. This tower is made up of a number of broad vertical facets or *paga*, that move upwards to form a constricting 'neck', which supports a flat, circular capstone or *āmalaka*, which in turn is surmounted by the 'water-pot' finial or *kalaśa*. The tower of the *maṇḍapa* or assembly hall has a low pyramidal roof.

The sculptures that adorn the temples of Orissa rank amongst the finest in India. Sensuously modelled female figures and fine sculptures of animals such as the lion, elephant and horse, are executed with power and sensitivity. The temple carvings on the Black Pagoda* are in a class by themselves.

Books

I. Banerji, R. D. *History of Orissa*, Calcutta, 1930–31.
II. Bose, N. K. *Canons of Orissan Architecture*, Calcutta, 1932.
III. Ganguly, M. *Orissa and Her Remains—Ancient & Medieval*, Calcutta, 1912.
IV. Hunter, W. W. *Orissa*, 1893.
V. Laurie, W. F. B. *Orissa*, 1850.
VI. Mazumdar, B. C. *Orissa in the Making*, Calcutta, 1925.
VII. Mitra, R. L. *The Antiquities of Orissa*, 1880.
VIII. Panigrahi, K. C. *Archaeological Remains at Bhuvanesvar*, Calcutta, 1961.

ORIYA (Oṛiya or Oḍiya), the language spoken by about ten million people in Orissa, is derived from Eastern Māgadhī. Much of its syntax and vocabulary is of pre-Aryan origin, but it has been largely influenced by Sanskrit and its entire superstructure is Indo-Aryan.

A number of hymns, recently discovered in Nepāl, written in what some scholars consider to be proto-Oriya, would take back the beginnings of Orissan literature to the ninth century AD, but this hypothesis does not find wide support, and the language of the hymns is not generally accepted as a form of Oriya. The earliest Oriya writings are Buddhist both in authorship and inspiration; later, Śaivite and Tantrik influences can be discerned, but the more lasting impact has been that of Vaishṇavism.

The first important name in Oriya literature is that of **Sarala-dās** (fl. AD 1360), a śūdra (low-caste) agriculturist who, having heard the story of the *Mahābhārata* casually recited in the village, turned the epic into his native, untried Oriya. He gave many of its characters Oriya names and laid some of its best scenes in his own country against a simple Orissan setting. In spite of his naïvety and the ruggedness of his style, he gave the Oriya language the impetus and direction it needed.

The century after Sarala-dās is known as the Period of the Five Friends, after a group of five contemporary writers, of whom only two are worthy of note. The first is **Balarām-dās** (fl. 1450) who wrote a popular version of the *Rāmāyaṇa*, again strongly dyed with local colour; the second is **Jagannāth-dās** (fl. 1450) author of a favourite Orissan version of the *Bhāgavata Purāṇa* written, it is said, in order to enable his illiterate mother to understand the Vaishṇava classic.

On the whole the influence of Vaishṇavism began to prove a drawback, for it sapped the native vigour and gave an alien sensuousness to the Oriya muse. The impact of Jayadeva's* Sanskrit classic, *Gītā-govinda*, was particularly unfortunate in this respect, for several gifted poets squandered their talents in fruitless attempts to imitate its glowing, sensual style.

Orissan literature had so far produced its masterpieces without the patronage of the rich, but with the seventeenth century came the age of patrons, who were themselves under the influence of brāhmin paṇḍits. Literary works were written to order, and a Sanskritized style became the fashion. Translations and imitations were produced by the score, with the erotic and *kāvya* (inflated) styles predominating, and only those poets were given the prizes of their profession who could render the mannerisms of Sanskrit poetry into the Oriya medium.

The chief representative of this period was **Upendra-bhāñja** (fl. 1630) whose prodigious output, although varied and competent, was full of eroticism and overlaid with artificial descriptions of natural scenery. His style was stilted and ornamental, abounding in all the metrical and dictional vices of the Sanskrit kāvya* form at its worst. For instance, all the lines of one of his epics start with the same letter of the alphabet; three seasons of the year are described simultaneously in a single canto, and so on.

There was a natural reaction to these excesses which found particular expression in some of the heroic poetry written at this time. Worthy of note was the *Samar Taraṅga* (Waves of War), a historical poem by **Brājnāth Bādajena** (*c.* 1730) relating the Orissan resistance to the Marāṭha invasion of the state. The devotional poets also turned away from Sanskrit conceits, and the work of the Vaishṇava bhagats (devotees) highlights the new trend. Best known of the Vaishṇava poets were **Bhaktacharan** (d. 1843), a sort of Oriya Ecclesiastes, and **Gopālkṛishṇa** (d. 1862), the greatest lyric poet of Orissa.

Perhaps the most outstanding writer of this period was the blind Khond (tribal) poet **Bhīma-bhoi** (d. 1895) whose fervent monotheistic bhajans (devotional songs) are well known among the people of the rural areas of Orissa. He was an ardent Buddhist who in 1875 tried to proclaim that the god Jagannāth was actually Buddha, but was driven away by the indignant priests.

Among modern writers three names stand out: **Fakirmohan** (d. 1918), a radical reformer of very liberal views, who was also a novelist and the 'father of Oriya prose'; **Rādhānāth** (d. 1908) who might be called the national poet of Orissa; and **Madhusudhan Rao** (d. 1912) mystic poet and saint.

Oriya writing was comparatively freed from the trammels of Sanskrit by the end of the nineteenth century, only to be overwhelmed by Bengali. Recent Oriya literature suffers by comparison with its powerful neighbour whose influence constitutes a stranglehold on the exercise of the creative spirit of Orissa. Writers in Oriya, like writers in most of the regional languages of India suffer from neglect because few people outside the province know of, and fewer still care for, its literary efflorescence.

Books

I. Gokak, V. K. *Literature in Modern Indian Languages*, New Delhi, 1957.
II. Mansinha, M. *History of Oriya Literature*, New Delhi, 1962.
III. Nagendra, Dr (Ed.) *Indian Literature*, Agra, 1959.

ORNAMENTS for the body have ever been the passion of the people of India. Even when their dress* was simple, their ornaments were usually elaborate. The Hindu aesthetic* ideal, so well illustrated in the Ajantā frescoes and

South Indian sculpture of the Hoysaḷas, is intimately linked with ornamentation. 'The Indian idea', says Zimmer, 'is that only things covered with ornaments are beautiful' (V, p. 236).

Colour, brightness and design in decoration, all once had a magical purpose, and in fashioning ornaments the metals used, the stones or glass with which they were inlaid, and the pattern in which they were arranged, had to be carefully thought out. The ornaments adorning a woman's body were given special attention. Often a man's wealth was spent on his wife's ornaments, since she represented his 'bank', symbolized his fortune, and like a powerful talisman attracted auspicious forces.

Three thousand year old necklets, rings, amulets, bracelets, waistbands, nose-studs, earrings, set with precious and semi-precious stones have been found in the Indus Valley. Gold ornaments were commonly used by wealthy Vedic Aryans, whose garments were also often embroidered with gold. By the Mauryan age dress had become quite elaborate, and Megasthenes speaks of 'robes worked in gold'. The love for coloured borders and brightly hued fabrics shot through with gold embroidery has been noted by visitors from early times.

Sanskrit writers name over seven hundred kinds of ornaments for men and women, made of gold, silver (and more recently, platinum), and mixed metals, with pearls and jewels, and shaped like flowers, butterflies, fishes, birds and animals, or stars, crescents and flames.

Head ornaments included fillets and bands called *keśa-bandha*, 'hair-band', often studded with gems; these were worn by all classes. The diadem or *chuḍā-maṇi*, 'crest-jewel', and the *mukuṭa*, a tiara or crown, were the insignia of royalty and nobility. In the medieval period a plume and *sarpesh* (turban ornament), became part of the ceremonial headdress of Hindu chieftains. The forehead was adorned with a *lalāṭā*, which could be an elaborate jewelled fringe or a string of small pearls. Some of them hung low over the forehead reaching to the cheeks. The neck was adorned with a *hāra* or necklace, multiple ropes of pearls or beads, superbly worked neckbands, jewelled collars and pendants of intricate design. *Kuṇḍala* or earrings, often very large and pendulous, or following the curve of the ear, and shaped like a snake, dragon or lion, were worn by both sexes. The *nathni*, a nose-ring or stud, was probably introduced by the Muslims, but is now the most important insignia of *saubhāgya* or married bliss among orthodox Hindu women. Even the teeth were decorated with silver or gold *rekhan* or studs, fixed into the centres of the front teeth.

The *skandha-ābharaṇa*, 'shoulder-ornaments', were decorated epaulets; the *keyūra* were upper-arm bracelets in the form of plain or embossed bands clasped over the biceps, while the forearm had a band called the *valaya*. The wrist was graced with a wrist-band called the *kaṅkaṇa*, but thick bracelets often covered the whole forearm up to the elbow. Glass was made in India from early times, but the use of glass for bangles, so common today, is not referred to by Sanskrit writers till the eighth century and was due to Hunnish influence. Finger rings and thumb rings came in all shapes and sizes, and were commonly used by all.

Women also wore a *kucha-bandha*, 'breast-band' across the chest, sometimes sewn with jewels, and there were smaller ornaments for decorating the nipples. The *mekhalā* or girdle around the waist was worn by both men and women, while an ornate *udara-bandha*, 'belly-band', of embroidered cloth or light chased metal, kept the belly in position. A *kaṭi-bandha* was a hip-band with an ornamental clasp. When worn by men a finely worked metal or cloth piece hung down the front. It was sometimes as small as a leaf, but often quite long, suggesting an elaboration of the liṅga. There were other ornamental coverings for the genitals of both sexes.

The lower limbs were not left neglected; there were the *pādapatra* for the thighs; heavy silver *nūpura* for the ankles often with clusters of tiny bells attached so that a delicate tinkling is heard when the woman walks; and toe-rings or large jewelled studs for the toes.

Books

I. Aziz, Abdul. *Arms and Ornaments*, 1930.
II. Bhushan, J. B. *Indian Jewellery, Ornaments and Decorative Designs*, n.d.
III. Oved, Sah. *The Book of Necklaces*, 1953.
IV. Wheeler, M. (Ed.) *Textiles and Ornaments of India*, 1956.
V. Zimmer, H. *The Art of Indian Asia*, Vol. I, New York, 1955.

PAINTING. Primitive hunting scenes dating from the later Stone Age and resembling the paintings of Aurignacian man in Spain are found in certain caves in the Kaimur range in Central India and the Vindhya Hills. The Jogimāra caves of the Rāmgaṛh Hills in Sirguja in the Mirzāpur District of Madhya Pradesh, date from about the first century BC, and may represent the oldest fresco paintings extant in India. The work has been very clumsily restored, but the original scheme includes a series of concentric panels depicting animals, fish and human figures. These early works, however, play no part in the development of the art in the historical period.

With the exception of murals, early paintings were normally executed on wooden boards or palm leaves, and on the whole because of the impermanence of the material used, few ancient works of any consequences have survived. But there is sufficient evidence in written records to establish the fact that painting had a long tradition in India and was in fact well developed some time before the beginning of the present era.

Ancient Sanskrit and Pāli works contain many legends relating to painting. One tells the story of the king whose son dies and whom Yama, lord of the dead refuses to yield up. The god Brahmā teaches the king to paint a portrait of the dead prince, and then brings it to life. The royal painter of this 'first picture in the world', was given the name of *Nagnajit* (*nagna-jit*, 'naked victor') because he had won back a citizen from Yama's kingdom of naked ghosts. Another legend has it that the art was invented by the sage **Nārāyaṇa** who, being importuned by certain *apsarās* seeking to divert his mind from his austerities, drew a portrait of a woman more beautiful than any of them and then endowed her with life. This was the ravishing Urvaśī*, before whose beauty the apsarās fled in humiliation. The first woman painter in mythology is **Chitralekha,** whose artistic skill helped to bring together her lovesick friend Ūshā and the man she loved, Aniruddha son of Pradyumna*.

The *Rāmāyaṇa* and the Pāli canon (*c.* 300 BC) refer to the *chitraśāla* or *chitragāra*, painting halls or galleries, in the palaces of the kings of Magadha and Kosala, whose walls were decorated with coloured murals and paintings of human and animal figures and ornamental designs. The pleasure halls of the rich nobles were similarly decorated, and painting received royal and patrician patronage.

Ancient literature also speaks of religious paintings on cloth or wood depicting deities, which were worshipped, or scenes in hell to remind the worldly of what awaited them. A relic of this type of art survives in the *paṭṭa** paintings of Bengal. The *Mahāvaṁsa* (*c.* AD 470) the epic of Ceylon, describes the murals of the Ruwanweli dagoba of 150 BC. Chinese pilgrims of the fifth, sixth and seventh centuries tell of several celebrated Buddhist pictures, and the writers of the kāvyas and dramas also make frequent references to paintings.

The Tibetan historian of Buddhism, Tāranātha (*c.* AD 1600) classified the early paintings of India into three chronological schools: (1) the Deva school in vogue in Central India and Uttar Pradesh before the time of Aśoka, (2) the Yaksha school of Aśoka's time, and (3) the Nāga school of eastern India dating from about AD 300. He does not give enough details to enable us to distinguish these styles. Little in fact can be said for certain about the early period except that painting was known and practised. When actual evidence of it appears it is found to be an already advanced art, executed by artists of supreme skill.

The Indian artist (*śilpin*) was not distinguished from the artisan, and his art was listed among the nine basic crafts. Like other artists the professional painter was classed with menials. His handbooks were included among the *śilpa-śāstra*, 'artisans' manuals', an elaborate set of aesthetic laws which coordinated the art traditions of the country. Arranged in a collection of aphorisms, they were pedantic and theoretical, providing a philosophical basis for the arts but giving little practical information on the techniques, which had to be acquired by experience. Most of the śilpa-śāstras are to be dated between the fourth and tenth centuries AD, and the earlier ones owe a great deal to foreign influence.

A ninth century handbook enumerates the *shaḍaṅga*, 'six limbs' or categories of painting traditionally believed to cover all aspects of the art. These were (1) *rūpa-bheda*, 'form-distinction', which called for a knowledge of the *lakshaṇas* or characteristic marks of the thing to be represented, so that it might be distinguished from others of the same class; (2) *pramāṇam*, 'measure', a knowledge of *talamāna* or the canons* of proportion; (3) *bhāva*, 'emotion', the mood of the subject or incident depicted; (4) *lavaṇa-yojanam*, 'salt-mixing'; saltness in a person implies beauty, charm, grace, hence the infusion of grace into a painting; (5) *sadṛiśya*, 'resemblance', likeness or similitude; (6) *varṇikā-bhaṅga*, 'pigment-analysis', or knowledge of the proper distribution of colours.

Another compilation belonging to the tenth century was the *Chitra-lakshaṇa*, 'picture attributes', dealing with pictorial art in its religious aspect, i.e. the painting of images, the size of the figures of gods, kings and men, the norms of face and figure, the painting of eyes, hair, nose and so on.

The greatest masterpieces of early Indian painting are found on the walls of the **Ajantā*** caves, which consist of frescoes executed by many generations of Buddhist artists from between A D 200 to 650. Closely related to the Ajantā style are the paintings of **Sīgiriya** in Ceylon whose twenty-five graceful frescoes, dated about A D 490, represent celestial women and attendant maids going to make offerings at a Buddhist shrine. The frescoes of BĀGH* (Gwālior State) date from about A D 600, and those of SITTANAVASAL in Pudokota in South India also belong to the same period.

In these early wall paintings we already find many of the characteristics chiefly associated with the work of Indian artists: (*a*) a wonderful sense of line, (*b*) delicacy and grace of expression, (*c*) a love for vivid colouring, (*d*) conventional patterns and poses, (*e*) a lack of realism. The forms are angulated in *bhaṅgas* (*see* aṅgika), the eyes long, almond-shaped and dreamy, the women heavy-bosomed, thin-waisted and etherealized.

After the eighth century large-scale murals give place to miniatures, as exemplified in the work of the **Pāla** School of Bengal (750–1250), which represents the earliest surviving miniature paintings of India. The names of two artists are preserved: Dhīmāna and his son Bhitpālo, who were metal workers, sculptors and painters. The work of this school is rich in colour, the figures are posed in set *mudrā* attitudes, and show a masterly command of the sinuous and graceful line. At the same time it developed a curiously angular convention with a limited number of stances, necessitated by the narrow oblong strips of palm-leaf manuscripts on which the miniatures were done and which were held together by a cord passing through the leaves. The Pāla school greatly influenced the art of Nepāl and Gujarāt.

A few ceiling paintings from some Vaishṇavite temples are also extant, especially in Western India, which historically carry the tradition from this to the next phase of Indian painting, namely the **Gujarāti** School (1100–1600), which is sometimes said to be a counterpart of Pāla art. Because this school received liberal Jain patronage and its work was largely confined to illustrations of Jain palm-leaf manuscripts, it is also referred to as the Jain School.

The earlier phase of the Gujarāti School (1100–1400) is found in illustrated texts on palm leaves (vellum, being made from the skin of animals, was not used), and the later phase (*c.* 1400 onwards) on paper, cut to resemble palm strips. Some manuscripts are in the form of rolls of cloth. The miniatures were executed in the areas left blank by the scribes. The chief characteristics of this school are: (*a*) the features are angular and rendered in half-face or three-quarter profile, the further eye protruding beyond the facial outline; (*b*) the chest is so far expanded that it is sometimes difficult to distinguish man from woman; (*c*) trees and leaves are highly stylized; water is depicted by a series of crossing lines; (*d*) the colours are laid on flat, with a predominance of red and gold, with some blue; (*e*) the figures are weak, but the costumes, jewellery and ornamentation are detailed. By the end of the sixteenth century the Gujarāti School yields to the Rājput style.

The early Muslim (Arab and Afghan) conquerors tolerated but did not encourage painting. It was the Moghuls with their Persian background who gave a great fillip to the art, and Persian, Saracenic and Central Asian art styles (notably of Herat and Samarqand) merged to form the basis of the **Moghul** School. The painters of Humāyūn's (1530–1556) court were Mir

Sayyid Ali and Abdus Samad, who belonged to the school established by the Persian genius Bihzad. Their work was graceful, aristocratic and refined, and of a high intellectual quality. The Moghul miniatures, illustrated manuscripts, and calligraphy, are among the masterpieces of the world's art.

Akbar's (1556–1605) painters included the Hindu artists Basāwan and Daswānāth (the latter belonged to the *kahar* or palanquin-bearer caste, went mad and committed suicide), and Kesu, also of the same caste. These three carried on the Central Asian tradition since, as Akbar's protégés, they studied at the Indian studios of Central Asian artists. At this time too, hundreds of chronicles, illustrated epics, poems, religious books, were produced by the dozens of artists both Hindu and Muslim who received Akbar's patronage.

The classical period of Moghul art came with Jahāngīr (1605–1627) and Shāhjahān (1627–1658) whose artists brought Moghul painting to fruition, maturity and decline. At this time we find many remarkable innovations, all attributable directly to Western influences. For the first time landscape backgrounds are shown in perspective; the drapery is very Italian; sunset and cloud effects are excellently rendered and much other detail that makes for a general effect of realism. Numbers of European paintings were cleverly copied in India. Sir Thomas Roe, Ambassador of James I states that Jahāngīr took pride in the fact that Roe was hard put to it to identify European originals when placed beside their Indian copies, so faithfully had they been reproduced.

Painting by this time had become almost an industry, with a fine regard for division of labour. One artist drew the outline of men and animals; landscapists drew the background; colourists painted in the colours. Sometimes there were as many as four or five artists working on a single painting.

By the time Aurangzeb (1658–1707) ascended the throne the decline had begun to set in. Natural and courtly themes seem to have become exhausted, and harem scenes, drinking bouts, carousels, and caricatures became popular. Aurangzeb took very seriously the Islamic prohibition against drawing likenesses, which had been hitherto ignored by his predecessors. He placed a ban on portrait painting, and practically ceased to subsidize artists of any kind, except those who designed the kufic calligraphy for the Koranic inscriptions on mosques. Only the Omrah, noblemen, employed them now, but the initiative of the artist declined and he began to be held in low esteem again. He was frequently beaten when inspiration seemed to lag. Says Bernier, 'Nothing but sheer necessity of blows from a cudgel keeps him employed'.

The Moghul style had an overwhelming effect on every subsequent school of Indian painting. Muslim rulers of the Deccan, especially Golkondā and Bijāpur during the fourteenth and fifteenth centuries encouraged art and established a **Deccani** School which was influenced first by direct contact with Central Asia and Persia and later by the Moghuls. In South India Moghul influence reached as far as Mysore and Tanjore, where local schools flourished up to the middle of the nineteenth century. But the true legatees of the Moghul tradition were the artists of the Rājasthān and Himāchal principalities.

When royal support of the Moghul kings was withdrawn by Aurangzeb, who was hostile to most of the arts, the displaced artists were welcomed by the princes of Rājputāna, and under their patronage the **Rājasthāni** School (1550–1850) of painting rose and flourished. This school derived directly from the Moghul artists, and for long continued the Persian courtly tradition. The Rājputs did splendid murals, but also excelled in miniatures and portraiture. While perspective and light and shade receive greater attention, the Moghul conventions are retained; the face and feet are shown in profile, shoulders turned towards the observer, giving an archaic and two dimensional effect. The women have large 'lotus' eyes, flowing tresses, firm breasts, slender waists. There is a marked concentration on jewellery, and the drapery is formalized.

Rājput painters were masters of brilliant glowing colours, harmony and line. Their themes were both secular and religious: scenes from the life of Kṛishṇa; incidents from the Epics; domestic scenes or themes of tender eroticism; the succession of the seasons; delicate portrayals of musical modes known as *rāgmālā* (*see* rāga). In the latter half of the eighteenth century genre painting prevailed.

Another heir to the Moghul tradition was the **Himāchal** School (from the Himālayan region of north-east Panjāb), also called the Pahāṛi School (from Hindi, pahāṛ, mountain). It flourished in the eighteenth and nineteenth centuries and its chief centres were at Jammū, Basohli, Chamba, Nurpur, Kāṅgṛā, Kūlū, Sukhet, Gaṛhwāl and Maṇḍi. The rulers and chieftains of these places did much to encourage art, and gave refuge to painters whose sources of patronage with the Moghuls and Rājputs had run dry. It shows very distinctly its origins from the Moghul, Gujarāt and Rājput schools. But it had many characteristic features entirely its own, and has been described as 'archaic, spontaneous, vital, charming, lyrical and playful, and imbued with chivalrous joy and mystic rapture'.

Pure and brilliant colours are freely used, composition is simple and the themes sentimental. Rādhā and Kṛishṇa figure prominently, and love and dance are the typical motifs. There are excellent female figures and animals, and many glimpses of hill and forest, with Westernized techniques applied to foliage and landscape. A great deal of spurious art in this form continues to be turned out with cloying sweetness and 'pretty-pretty' themes, with Kṛishṇa and the *gopīs*, love-lorn maidens and forbidden trysts. North Indian painting was for long distinguished by the characteristic *qalm* (Persian: brush or pen) such as the qalm of Kāṅgṛā and the qalm of Delhi, each of which had marked features of its own, but by the end of the nineteenth century these had become barely perceptible and were all marked by the same symptoms of inspirational fatigue and artistic decay.

The modern period is characterized by a revival of old forms, not only of Ajantā and Moghul models, but also the 'bazaar' and indigenous traditions, such as the schools of Kālīghāṭ and Trichinopoly. The first of the moderns was Ravi Varma of Travancore, who painted Indian themes in a Europeanized style and achieved great popularity, but irked the more discerning who were distressed by his alien idiom and sought a true revival of the ancient forms. In the early twentieth century this movement found champions in E. B.

Havell, Principal of the Calcutta School of Art which had been founded in 1854, and its rationale in the writings of the Eurasian art critic Ananda Coomaraswamy. The chief exponents of the revival were Abanindranāth Tagore, Asit Kumār Hāldar and Nandalāl Bose, who tried to pick up the fractured pieces of the native Indian art idiom which they felt conveyed a better idea of Hindu spirituality. But the traditional formulas did not effect the expected renaissance and soon degenerated into the sentimental stereotypes and affected mannerisms of 'oriental' art.

Contemporary Indian painting is hugely indebted to the West. Even those clinging most closely to the Indian tradition find it impossible to escape. Some like Jaimini Roy (b. 1887) though inspired by indigenous folk styles, borrowed from Picasso. The greatest of the moderns, Amrita Sher Gil (1913–1941) of mixed Indian and Hungarian descent, owed much to Gaugin; Sailoz Mookerjee to Matisse; Sheila Auden (b. 1914) to Chagall; Shaivax Chavda (b. 1914) to Picasso; George Keyt the Ceylonese to Cezanne; V. S. Gaitonde to Paul Klee; Jaswant Singh to Dali. The best of them in fact swing freely from the brilliant coloration of Van Gogh and the stained glass medievalism of Rouault to the ultra-naturalism of Kandinsky, with vague reminiscences of Ajantā and the Moghul School. It is only fair to say that the great modern Indian artist has yet to be born.

Books

I. Archer, W. G. *Bazaar Painting of Calcutta*, London, 1953.
II. Bose, P. N. *Principles of Indian Silpasastra*, Lahore, 1926.
III. Brown, P. *Indian Painting*, Calcutta, 1927.
IV. Coomaraswamy, A. C. *Rajput Painting*, 1916.
V. Gray, B. *Rajput Painting*, London, 1948.
VI. Havell, E. B. *Indian Sculpture & Painting*, 2nd Ed., London, 1928.
VII. Kaul, M. *Trends in Indian Painting*, New Delhi, 1961.
VIII. Khandelvala, Karl. *Indian Sculpture & Painting*, Bombay, 1937.
IX. Kramrisch, S. *A Survey of Painting in the Deccan*, London, 1937.
X. Venkatachalam, G. *Contemporary Indian Painters*, Bombay, n.d.

PĀLA, 'protector' (AD 760–1142) a Buddhist dynasty of Bengal and Bihār, including that part of the ancient Bāleya* kingdom known as Gauḍa. The line was founded by the śūdra chieftain **Gopāla** (745–780) who, having secured the allegiance of other local rulers, restored order to the country after almost a century of anarchy and confusion following the death of the previous Gauḍa ruler Śaśāṅka (*see* Kanauj). Gopāla also founded the celebrated university of Odantapura.

The long reign of **Dharmapāla** (780–830) son of Gopāla, marks the zenith of Pāla power, for at that period the Pāla dominions stretched from the Himālayas to the Deccan, with capital at the ancient Magadha city of Pāṭaliputra. Dharmapāla's allies in his career of aggrandisement were the Madra* people of Bengal. He invaded and captured Kanauj and installed his protégé Chakrāyudha on the throne. He is remembered as the founder of the educational centre of Vikramaśilā.

His successor **Devapāla** (830–850) established the third important Pāla university of Somapura, and shifted his capital to Monghyr, from where he maintained diplomatic relations with the Śailendra kings of Sumatra. He defeated the Kāmboja people of the north-west who had encroached on his territory, and made considerable conquests south of the Vindhyas.

Devapāla's successors proved weak and ineffective against the enemies who hemmed them in from all sides, in particular the rising Pratihāras and Kāmbojas. By the tenth century the rule of the Pāla kings was temporarily cut short by the Kāmbojas who set up one of their own chieftains as king. At the same time other noble houses of Bengal also established independent principalities, chief among them being the Chandra family of east Bengal, the Kaivarta of north Bengal, and the Śūra of south-west Bengal. Several Śūras are mentioned in local literature and inscriptions, the most notable being the semi-legendary Ādiśūra.

The Kāmbojas were finally deposed by **Mahipāla** (980–1026) the ninth king of the Pāla line who, although he effectively exercised his sovereignty among the local princelings, was sorely pressed by the Cholas from the south and the Kalachuris from the west. The next notable king, **Rāmapāla** (1077–1120) founded another seat of learning, the Buddhist Jagadalla monastery. In spite of the help he received from his Rāshṭrakūṭa allies he was unable to arrest the decline of his realm, which increasingly suffered the encroachments of ambitious rulers of the south.

In the twelfth century the anti-Buddhist, probably Kanarese, Sena chieftains invaded the Pāla kingdom from the south, put an end to the Pāla line, and established the second great dynasty of Bengal, that of the **SENA** kings (1095–1199) with capital at Vijayapura in west Bengal. Their reign brought about a revival of orthodox Vaishṇavite Hinduism with propagandist force.

Ballāla Sena (d. 1178) fostered the new Kulīn aristocracy, a class of high caste brāhmins whose arrogance and polygamous* practices later became the scandal of the province. Himself a writer, Ballāla encouraged literature, and Sanskrit writers, poets and jurists received generous court patronage.

The son and successor of Ballāla, **Lakshmaṇa** Sena (1178–1199) distinguished himself both as a warrior and a patron of learning. Among the poets who flourished at his court were Jayadeva*, and Dhoyī, the latter the author of the *Pavanadūta*, which contains a description of the Sena rulers. The Sena capital was now moved to Gaur (also called Lakhnautī, i.e. Lakshmaṇavati) on the left bank of the Ganges, but the cultural capital remained at Nadia (or Navadvīpa).

It was during the reign of Lakshmaṇasena that the Senas were overthrown by the Muslims, and the story of their collapse, which meant the fall of Bengal, is one of the most extraordinary that has ever been recorded by the historians. The conquest was achieved by Ikhtiār Khilji, governor of Mirzāpur. Collecting an army of Turks and Afghans he conquered and plundered Bihār, razing many Buddhist monasteries and Hindu temples to the ground, including the above-mentioned Tantrik monasteries of Vikramaśilā and Odantapura. He then made a raid on Nadia (1199) cultural capital of the Sena kingdom. In his impetuosity he reached the city with only eighteen horsemen. The people thought he was a trader in horses and allowed him to proceed through the streets unmolested. When he arrived at the palace gates he and his men drew their swords, overpowered the guards and forced their way into the palace. Lakshmaṇa heard the uproar just as he was about to sit down to dinner. He fled through the back door and found his way to a temple where he ended his days in hiding. The rest of the town was taken and plundered when the remainder of the army arrived.

Some scraps of territory in eastern Bengal retained their independent status under Sena princes till the latter half of the thirteenth century. Nadia remained the cultural centre, being the scene of Chaitanya's* life and works, and the headquarters of a school of logic known as Navya Nyāya. The Nadia phase of Bengali culture continued well into the eighteenth century, and was superseded only by the rise of Calcutta.

The Pālas and Senas are chiefly noted for their generous patronage of art and learning. They founded four famous universities, and through their religious zeal Tantrik Hinduism spread beyond the borders of their empire to Tibet. Bengali language and literature were born and flourished under Pāla patronage, and the stone and metal sculpture of that period is well known. Bengali artists preserved and at the same time transformed the standards of the Gupta period and established patterns that inspired the work of Nepāli, Tibetan and even Javanese artists.

The luminaries of the period were Buddhist missionaries like Dharmapāla, Atīsa Dīpaṅkara, scholars like Chakrapāṇi and Saṁdhyākara, and artists like Dhīmāna and Vītapāla.

Books

I. Banerji, R. D. 'Palas of Bengal', *Memoirs of the Asiatic Society of Bengal*, Vol. 3, 1915.

II. French, J. C. *The Art of the Pala Empire of Bengal*, Oxford, 1928.

III. Kramrisch, Stella. *Pala & Sena Sculpture*, Calcutta, 1929.

IV. Majumdar, R. C. *History of Bengal*, Dacca, 1943.

PALLAVA (250–750) a dynasty of uncertain origin, which flourished in the Tamil-speaking country on the east coast of South India, between the Kistna and Penner rivers, roughly covering the area of modern Madrās state. A great pall of obscurity covers this area during the early centuries of the present era. There is evidence of large-scale tribal movements, including alien races, southwards into these territories. When the obscurity lifts again by the middle of the third century we see a new people of probably foreign origin in occupation of the region. They are the Pallavas.

Some trace the Pallava antecedents to the Nāga chieftains who were the vassals of the Sātavāhana kings of Āndhra. H. G. Rawlinson considers them to be 'intruders' in the Tamil kingdoms, while other authorities, notably P. T. Srinivas Iyengar and J. A. Allan make the Pallavas adventurers from the north-west of India. Yet others identify them with the Pahlavas or Parthians*. The Pallavas did not speak a Dravidian language, and all their records were kept in Prākṛit or Sanskrit. Classical Tamil literature of the Śaṅgam age makes no reference to them, and local tradition speaks of them as coming from the north.

The dynasty was founded by **Bappa** (d. 265), also known as Mahārāja

Bappasvāmi, in the middle of the third century AD, who rallied to his cause the Kurumba, Marava, Kalvār, Kalla and other predatory tribes and carved himself a kingdom from the Veṅgi territories of the declining Āndhras. By about AD 350 the Pallavas established themselves in the Toṇḍai district on the east coast with capital at Kāñchipuram, called Kāñchi for short. In the early part of the fifth century, a portion of their territory was annexed by the Guptas, and in the latter half of the same century they suffered increasing aggression from the Kadamba kings of Kanara. They later regained their power and before the end of the sixth century were able to defeat the Cholas.

The Pallavas were a source of considerable harassment to the Chālukyas who were their traditional enemies. **Mahendravarman I** (600–630) whose father had been the patron of the Sanskrit poet Bhāravi, gave encouragement to scholars and poets, and was himself a writer of Sanskrit farces. In the sphere of architecture he introduced the method of scooping out entire temples from the solid rock, as at Māmallapuram. At first a devout Jain he fell under the influence of a Śaivite saint, embraced Śaivism, and ended up by persecuting the Jains and destroying their monasteries and seats of learning.

His son, **Narasiṁhavarman I** (630–660), the greatest of the Pallava kings, defeated and slew the redoubtable Chālukya, Pulakeśin II in AD 640. He built the monolithic shrines known as the Seven Pagodas at Māmallapuram, and was the patron of the Sanskrit poet Daṇḍin. When Hiuen-Tsang visited the kingdom during his reign he was impressed by the splendour of Kāñchipuram which he described as a great centre of Buddhist and Jain learning.

Narasiṁhavarman II (695–722) had a peaceful reign. He is noted chiefly for the many architectural works in the Dravidian style built under his patronage, such as the Kailāsanātha temple at Kāñchi. The art of painting and poetry flourished at his court. He sent ambassadors to China and was honoured by the Chinese emperor.

In 740 the Chālukyas captured Kāñchi and from this date the Pallava prestige declined. In 780 the Rāshṭrakūṭas decisively broke their power and subjected them to Rāshṭrakūṭa rule. About AD 900 the Pallava kingdom was annexed by the Cholas, although Pallava princes continued as petty local chieftains till the thirteenth century.

The Pallavas were great patrons of religion, philosophy, Sanskrit literature, music, and the arts. They encouraged overseas ventures and colonized areas of Hinterindia in Indonesia, Kamboja, Śrīvijaya and Angkor. They were especially notable for their achievements in architecture, at places like Māmallapuram and Kāñchi.

The town of **Māmallapuram,** about forty-five miles from Kāñchipuram, is said to have been originally named either Mahābalipuram (Great Bali City), after Bali the demon king slain by Vishṇu in his dwarf incarnation, or as others contend, Mahāmallapuram (Great Wrestler City), after Mahāmalla, the title of Narasiṁhavarman I (above). Among its monuments is a unique series of little monolithic temples of granite, popularly known as the Seven Pagodas, each called, from its general outward appearance, a *ratha*, 'chariot', and each carved from a single granite boulder. None of the rathas was ever completed, and for some unknown reason the site was abandoned, perhaps because of a Chālukya invasion. The Seven Pagodas are important in the history of Indian architecture as marking the beginning of the Dravidian style. Jouveau-Dubreuil held the opinion that the Seven Pagodas were ultimately Hellenistic in origin. Another well-known structural, not sculptured, edifice, is the Shore Temple (A D 700), so called because it is situated on the extreme foreshore of the village. Also worthy of note is a fine work of Pallava sculpture executed in relief on the face of a rock, 96 feet long and 46 feet high, at Māmallapuram. Misnamed 'Arjuna's Penance', it actually depicts the Descent of the Ganges from the celestial regions to earth, in a spectacular pageant of men and beasts and various mythical beings.

The Pallava capital, **Kāñchipuram,** 'golden city', anglicized Conjeeveram, was once a great Buddhist stronghold, reputedly visited by Buddha himself, and the site of several Aśokan stūpas, now vanished. It was for a time also associated with the Jains. With the rise of sectarian Hinduism the city became one of the centres of Śaivism. It is the site of the *pṛithivī liṅga*, one of the five great liṅgas* of India. Today it is spoken of as the Banāras of South India and as one of the seven sacred cities of the Hindus, indeed the only one sacred to both Śiva and Vishṇu.

From the fourth to the ninth centuries the Pallavas made Kāñchi a celebrated centre of art and architecture. In and around the city there were, according to the chronicles, a thousand temples, and ten thousand shrines and liṅgas, built by the Pallavas, and later added to by the Vijayanagar kings.

The Pallavas were the first builders in stone in South India. Chief among the Śaivite shrines of Kāñchi is the Kailāsanātha temple (A D 710), the most important of the Pallava structures, raised on the site of what may have been a Jain shrine, some parts of which still exist. It is considered so holy that a single circumambulation of the temple is guaranteed to bring salvation to the devout. The sculptures are full of interest; there are numerous vivid portrait images of Pallava rulers and their queens. Much use is made in this and other temples in the area of rampant lions, kneeling bulls, yālis, and other animal forms, to serve as pilasters, columns and architectural supports. In and around the temple there is an elaborate system of cisterns fed from a canal, which is suggestive of snake-worship. The Vaikuṇṭha Perumāḷ temple (A D 750) ranks first among the Vishṇu shrines. Its sanctuary with tower and pillared maṇḍapa are joined to form an imposing whole. The temple of Kāmākshī dedicated to the consort of Śiva is said to contain the *samādhi* (burial place) of the sage Śaṅkara. A later Dravadian temple is that of Varadarājasvāmi, 'boon-granting-king-swāmi', an aspect of Vishṇu, where scholars discuss and study the Viśishṭādvaita system of Rāmānuja. Of still later date is the Ekambareśvara (Śiva) temple (1509), with a main tower 188 feet high, built by a Vijayanagar king.

Books

I. Coombes, J. W. *The Seven Pagodas*, 1913.
II. Gopalan, R. *History of the Pallavas of Kanchi*, Madras, 1928.
III. Heras, H. *Studies in Pallava History*, Madras, 1933.
IV. Jouveau-Dubreuil, G. *Pallava Antiquities*, Pondicherry, 1916–18.

V. Kanwar Lal. *Holy Cities of India*, Delhi, 1961.
VI. Minakshi, C. *Administrative & Social Life under the Pallavas*, Madras, 1938.
VII. Rea, A. *Pallava Architecture*, Madras, 1909.
VIII. Sircar, D. C. *The Early Pallavas*, Lahore, 1935.
IX. Srivastava, P. *The Pallavas: Their History & Architecture*, 1915.

PAÑCHAMA, 'fifth', a comprehensive term applied in recent times to all those sections of the Hindu population who do not belong to any of the four major castes. This fifth category is made up of many classes of people of diverse stock and occupation, all of whom are regarded for various reasons as being beyond the pale of Hindu society.

By extension the term includes the *mlechchha*, 'foreigner', i.e. the non-Aryan barbarian, and the alien outcaste. In general the mlechchha was never a Hindu to start with. He was one not born a Hindu, who did not know the sacred tongue, did not acknowledge brāhmin supremacy, and did not accept the Vedas. He was uncouth in behaviour, ate beef and drank liquor, and had other, in Hindu eyes, equally offensive habits. The mlechchhas included the Greeks, Scythians, Persians, Huns, and in more recent times the Muslims and Europeans. Like the other *pañchamas* the European was, and still is, regarded as an untouchable. The orthodox Hindu will not eat with him, and will as far as possible avoid his company, and if, by any chance, he is obliged to shake hands with a European, he will cleanse himself afterwards by a purificatory bath.

Many tribes were classed with the pañchamas because they belonged to aboriginal, non-Aryan stock, of Negrito, Australoid or Proto-Dravidian antecedents. Out of these many were known, after the place of their habitation, as Jungle, or Hill Tribes and Castes. They included the Andamanese of the Andaman and Nicobar Islands; the Kolarian* tribes of Central and Deccan India; the Negrito* Kādar, a non-cultivating, food-gathering forest tribe of Cochin; the Paliyan of Madura District who subsist on hunting and food-collecting; the Izhavan (or Tiyan) of Malabār, and the Shānān of the Tamil country, who are associated with coconut culture and toddy-tapping; the Vellāla, a Tamil caste of primitive agriculturists. The pañchamas also include various tribes of eastern India, like the Ābor, 'untamed' hill people of Assam; the Aṅgami and other Nāga tribes, also of Assam, several of whom are headhunters. The Khonds, a hill-tribe of Orissa who reputedly practise human sacrifice and infanticide, have been frequently studied by anthropologists. Some of the jungle castes still retain their ancient customs, such as the Baḍaga, a primitive tribe of the Nilgiris, who practise fire-walking over a pit of glowing embers in honour of their god. The marriage system of the Baiga of Central India permits the union of grandparent and grandchild; the Ernādan of the forest regions of Malabār have a custom by which a man is allowed to take his eldest daughter as his second wife. Many pañchama classes are by no means primitive, and preserve the traditions of their race and origins with great pride and efficiency. Such are the Gonds of Central India, and the Balāhi of Madhya Pradesh, who have an extraordinary bardic* tradition.

Another category included among the pañchamas are what are known as the Criminal Tribes and Castes, so called because they derive their livelihood from criminal activities. Most criminal castes are as proud of their calling as the highest craftsmen in India. Among them are the Sānsiya, a vagrant caste of Rājputāna who live by theft and robbery; the Korava, a Tamil caste of fortune-tellers, quacks and robbers, many of whom now operate as railway thieves. Some like the Lambadi offered human sacrifices, and others like the Thugs* used to practise the custom of ritual strangling.

A number of pañchama castes originated from mixed marriages, and it would seem that the relegation of half-castes to a degraded category was an attempt by the lawgivers to put a stop to a growing tendency towards mixed unions on the part of Aryans. This tendency could not be stopped, and today there are more castes in existence resulting from mixed marriages than pure castes. From early times these mixed castes were stigmatized by opprobrious names. Such were the *Nishāda** 'squatters', descended from the union of a brāhmin male and śūdra female; the *Ugra*, 'fierce', of a kshattriya male and śūdra female; *Ambashṭha*, 'water-dwelling', from a brāhmin male and vaiśya female; *Āyogava*, 'born of a buffalo', from a vaiśya father and śūdra mother, generally carpenters by profession; *Mahishya*, 'buffalo' people, of a kshattriya father and śūdra mother.

These sub-castes sprang from anuloma unions, where the woman married a man who belonged to a higher caste than she, and reprehensible as such a marriage was, it was much to be preferred to a pratiloma union, where the woman married a man of a lower caste. Passages in the ancient texts indicate that at a very early date in the career of Aryan conquest, non-Aryan men entered into matrimonial relations with Aryan women (X, p. 56); and there also seems to have been a tradition by which the family slave could lawfully marry the widow of his master. The *Yajur-veda* alludes to śūdra-Aryan alliances, and the *Atharva-veda* has a charm directed against a wife's paramour, who is a slave, 'winning her love by sheer physical strength' (IX, p. 64).

That pratiloma unions were widespread is confirmed from the existence of large classes of outcaste peoples, such as the *Pukkaśa*, 'rats', offspring of a Nishāda male and a śūdra female; the *Pulkasa*, 'hair-spread', i.e. with hair unkempt and upstanding like a savage.s, who are descendants of a śūdra male and a vaiśya female; the *Śvapāka* (or Śvapach), 'dog-cooking', descendants of a śūdra male and kshattriya female, who eat dog's flesh; the *Sopāka*, offspring of a Pulkasa and a vaiśya (or Chaṇḍāla). Lowest in the whole category of castes were the *Chaṇḍāla*, 'wild', who are the progeny of the most unspeakable form of mixed marriage, namely, of a brāhmin woman, with a śūdra or pañchama male. Many Chaṇḍālas were thus of good birth, but were unequivocally condemned, and in Sanskrit writings they stood for all that was unclean, unrighteous, irreligious, and damned in humanity.

There are still other categories, known as *antyaja*, 'lowest born', who were condemned to perform the most menial tasks that caused them to be further isolated from normal intercourse with other Hindus. Such are the *Chamār* or leather workers of North and Central India, who tan the hides of dead animals; the *mochi* or cobbler often comes from the ranks of the Chamār. The *Bhaṅgi* and *Mahār* of Uttar Pradesh, the *Chūhra* of the Panjāb, and the

Ḍheḍ of Western India, are sweepers, public scavengers, carriers of refuse and night-soil. The *Dom* are scavengers and corpse removers, who also furnish wood for burning the dead.

The *Paraiyan* are a Tamil caste of field labourers and village slaves* whose name is derived from the parai, a small drum which they used to carry when abroad, to warn wayfarers of their approach so that they might get out of the way of their polluting presence. They are scavengers, and eat meat, including the flesh of cows, dogs and monkeys. From their name is derived the English word *pariah*. The 'pariah' of South Kanara and South Malabār are the *Cheruman*.

The *Pulayan* (Pulai or Puliah) of North Malabār, Cochin and Travancore were tree-dwellers, who built shelters in the branches of trees, since they were prohibited from building dwellings for themselves on the ground, except, in rare cases, huts consisting of no more than a thatched roof supported on four bamboo poles and open on all four sides. If they ventured out at night and saw someone coming they had to cry out and move some distance off. They could approach no other caste closer than a hundred paces. Contemporary observers of the early nineteenth century state that they could be killed with impunity.

The *Koraga* are basket makers and labourers of South Kanara. Their women wear skirts made of leaves. Till the beginning of the present century one sub-caste of the Koraga had to carry a small pot suspended by a string around the neck, into which they were to spit, to avoid polluting the road. The *Ulladah* of Malabār, are so low in the caste scale that the very sight of them to a Nambūdri brāhmin is pollution. They are therefore classed with the 'unseeable' castes. The *Vannān*, an unseeable Tamil washerman caste of Tinnevelly, wash the clothes of other exterior castes. In the past they had to work between midnight and daybreak as they were not allowed to come out in the daytime, since the sight of them brought defilement.

For a number of reasons therefore, such as non-Hindu origin, non-Aryan or tribal descent, degrading occupation, or mixed marriage, a large proportion of the peoples of India were, and continue to be, regarded as outcastes. Other outcastes like the Muslim or European mlechchhas did not fall within the scope of Hindu dominance and thus remained unaffected by their peculiar prejudices, but for the Indians within the Hindu social complex the degradation had serious consequences.

In the Hindu scriptures these social groups were regarded as *avarṇa*, 'casteless'. Whatever their individual qualifications, they were held to be backward, uncultivated, and unworthy of intercourse with Aryans, and were subjected to a policy worse than apartheid. They lived in secluded areas outside the villages, well away from the habitations of caste Hindus; had no privileges, and were even denied the ordinary consolations of religion, being forbidden to read or study the sacred books, and barred from the performance of *śrāddha* rites to their own ancestors. Any contact with them was regarded as causing both physical and psychic pollution; they were therefore *untouchable*. In short, this class was denied almost every human right; those that remained for them they shared with the animals: the right to eat and propagate. According to Manu's decree,

'Their dwelling shall be outside the village, and their wealth shall be dogs and donkeys. Their dress the garments of the dead, and their food shall be eaten from broken dishes. Black iron shall be their ornaments, and they must wander from place to place' (I, p. 26).

Some classes of brāhmins, notably those of the South, were not content with untouchability, they must needs go one better with unapproachability. The *unapproachables* caused pollution by coming near a caste Hindu, and precise scales of 'distance pollution' were worked out, especially in places like Malabār (*see* caste). There was even a belief current that pollution could result if the wind blowing from the direction of an unapproachable touched one.

Left to itself the malignant growth of untouchability and unapproachability was bound to develop, as in fact it did, reaching its fulness in the form of unseeability, duly supported by the authority of a forged* text attributed to the philosopher Śaṅkara. The *unseeable* caused contamination just by being present to the sight or crossing the field of one's vision. To a limited degree unseeable castes exist in India to the present day.

Modern reform movements initiated by Muslims, Europeans and the Christian missionaries, have done much to mitigate the humiliation of these outcaste tribes. To begin with, official terminology reflected this change. They are now called *Exterior* castes since they are outside the regular cadre of castes. They are sometimes spoken of as *Depressed*, to suggest their subordination. Because of their place in the special official schedules they are called *Scheduled* castes. Gāndhi, in a further attempt to improve their status by a change of name, called them *Harijan*, 'God's Children'; while one school of Hindu thought spoke of them as *Ādivāsi* (*ādi-nivāsi*, 'original inhabitants') or those who were in India before the Aryans.

In a democratic India Hindus are becoming increasingly aware that the pañchamas, over one hundred million in number, constitute the basic population of the subcontinent, although they are carefully hidden from view when speaking of Hindu culture and Hindu civilization. But their heads are counted when it is desired to show that every eighth man on earth is a Hindu. To borrow a phrase, these unfortunates are 'included out' of the Mother Religion of Mother India.

Throughout the long history of Hinduism, the pañchamas were seldom mentioned, and if they were, it was only in order to be vilified. With salvation assured for the twice-born, who cared for the spiritual destiny of the pañchamas? They had to console themselves with the reflection that if they were very docile and accepted their lot as laid down by Manu and the lawgivers, there was a remote chance that after a long period of rebirths they might rise to a higher level in the cadre of castes. Says Ghurye, 'In plain words it was tantamount to asking them to wait for Doomsday'.

Books

I. Ambedkar, B. R. *The Untouchables*, New Delhi, 1948.
II. Briggs, G. *The Chamars*, Calcutta, 1920.
III. Ghurye, G. S. *Caste & Race in India*, London, 1932.
IV. Ghurye, G. S. *The Scheduled Tribes*, 2nd Ed., Bombay, 1959.

V. Hunt, W. S. *India's Outcastes*, London, 1929.
VI. Hutton, J. H. *Caste in India*, Bombay, 2nd Ed., 1951.
VII. Ouwerkert, L. *The Untouchables of India*, Oxford, 1945.
VIII. Stevenson, Mrs. S. *Without the Pale: The Life Story of an Outcaste*, Calcutta, 1930.
IX. Upadhyaya, B. S. *Women in Rigveda*, 2nd Ed., Banaras, 1941.
X. Visvanatha, S. V. *Racial Synthesis in Hindu Culture*, London, 1928.

PAÑCHARĀTRA, an early Vaishṇavite sect whose origins are lost in obscurity. There is great uncertainty about the name itself, which, as it stands (pañcha-rātra), signifies 'five-nights', either because a special ceremony lasting five days and nights used to be held in honour of their deity, during which the sacred scriptures of the sect were recited, or because of the five-night sacrifice performed by Nārāyaṇa. Some authorities consider it to be a corruption of pañcharatha (five vehicles), referring to the five aboriginal doctrines which were syncretized to form a single monotheistic religion dedicated to the service and worship of a deity later equated with Vishṇu. Precisely what these five ancient religions were is not certain, but those mentioned below are generally named.

(1) *Ekāntika* (eka-antika, 'one-presence') (*c.* 300 BC), so named because of its dedication to a single deity to the exclusion of all others. The deity in question may have been Kṛishṇa whose worship appears to have been established long before the coming of the Aryans, and which after the Aryan invasion remained anti-Vedic.

(2) *Bhāgavata*, perhaps named after the god Bhaga, one of the earliest deities of the bhakti* creed. The early worship of Bhaga was independent of brāhminism and also anti-Vedic. Some think it originated with the mlechchha Yādavas in the area around Mathurā which was the site of an ancient Zoroastrian fire-temple and long a centre of Magian sun-worship. The Bhāgavata religion represented a development of sun-worship. The term Bhāgavata often referred to the Vaishṇavite religion as a whole.

(3) *Nārāyaṇīya*, the worship of an ancient deity called Nārāyaṇa. The twelfth book of the *Mahābhārata* contains a portion called the Nārāyaṇīya which is one of the sources of this tradition. The tenets of the sect were divinely communicated to the half-caste ṛishi Parāśara, and were later revealed to Vidura, brother of Dhṛitarāshṭra, born of a śūdra woman. By about 200 BC the identities of Kṛishṇa, his father Vasudeva, Vishṇu and Nārāyaṇa, were frequently confused.

(4) *Vaikhānasa*, an ancient sect named after the ṛishi Vaikhanas. The members were anchorites, both male and female, who set great store on purity of conduct and dedication to the deity. By the seventh century AD, they still flourished in the Deccan as a separate sect, and their chief contribution to Vaishṇavism lay in their emphasis on worship, service and adoration of Vishṇu, and their temple architecture and iconography.

(5) *Sātvata*, named after a small non-Aryan tribe, who were non-Vedic in their worship and anti-Vedic in sentiment. They disdained the ceremonies of the twice-born, practised black-magic and sorcery, used unorthodox mantras. Their initiation included a form of ritual branding. Early classed with the

kshattriyas, they became associated with a branch of the Yādavas and in due course were converted to Vaishṇavism.

These five sects seem to have been unified in doctrine some time during the third and second centuries BC, when they were first referred to as Pañcharātras of the Vaishṇavite persuasion. They advocated monotheism, *bhakti* (devotion) and a simple form of worship, and condemned sacrifices, even those mentioned in the Vedas, shunned long austerities and penances. They believed in a Supreme Being, known variously as Nārāyaṇa, Kṛishṇa, Vasudeva, Hari, Bhagavat, Vishṇu, who is manifested in various *vyūha*, 'ranges' (*see* God).

The Pañcharātra doctrine was first systematically promulgated by *Śāṇḍilya* (AD 100) (not to be confused with the Upanishadic sage of the same name), who composed several bhakti sūtras or devotional aphorisms about the deity. The *saṁhitās* of Śāṇḍilya and his followers, known as the Pañcharātra Āgamas, embody the chief doctrines of the Vaishṇavas.

The sect acquired great popularity, and by the tenth century AD had left its mark permanently on most of the other Hindu sects. It was somewhat corrupted by Tantrik doctrines and as such was condemned by Bādarāyaṇa, Śaṅkara, Kumārila and others as non-monastic, non-Vedic and irreligious.

Books

I. De, D. L. 'Pancharatra & the Upanishads', *Indian Historical Quarterly*, IX, 3 (1933), 645–62.
II. De, S. K. 'Bhagavatism and Sun Worship', *Bulletin of the School of Oriental Studies*, London, VI, 3 (1931), 669–72.
III. Caland, W. *Vaikhanasa Smarta-Sutras & Srauta-Sutras*, Calcutta, 1927 & 1929.
IV. Cowell, E. B. (Tr.) *Sandilya-Sutras*, Calcutta, 1878.
V. Deacon, L. *Origins of the Pancharatra Sect*, 1903.
VI. Grierson, G. A. *The Narayaniya & the Bhagavatas*, Bombay, 1909.
VII. Schrader, F. *Introduction to the Pañcharatra*, Madras, 1916.

PAÑCHATANTRA (*pañcha-tantra*, 'five-books'), of unknown authorship, is one of the most famous works of the Sanskrit *kathā* (story) genre, so called because it is divided into five sections each dealing with a different subject. The stories are presented in the form of instructions given by the aged priest Vishṇuśarma to the dullard sons of a certain king. By means of the fable, cleverly weaving one tale within another, Vishṇuśarma teaches them the science of statecraft and imparts an understanding of human nature. A number of gnomic stanzas are inserted in the prose narrative, succinctly summing up the 'moral' of each tale.

In these fables human vices and foibles are exposed through the characters of animals. The beasts devote themselves to the study of the Vedas, perform religious rites, engage in disquisitions about gods, saints and heroes, and in the course of their conversation and activities show up the hypocrisy and avarice of brāhmins, the petty scheming of sycophantic courtiers, the faithlessness of women. A cynical humour is maintained throughout, and the prevailing morals are those of expediency, intrigue, flattery and hypocrisy.

The book shows traces of Buddhist and Jain influence, and may have been originally written in one of the Prākṛits, although this hypothetical Prākrit origin cannot be proved. The fact that the book is anti-brāhmin in tone, and that the camel and the desert are prominent, suggests to one authority the north-west of India as its place of origin. The collection dates from about AD 200, but only assumed its present form from about AD 600.

In these tales a leading part is played by two jackals, Karaṭaka and Damanaka, and when the work was translated in the eighth century into Pahlavi, Syriac and Arabic, the collection was known as *Kalīlah va Dimnah,* after these jackals. The extant Sanskrit versions of the *Pañchatantra* are based on translations from Pahlavi. In the Middle Ages the Persian version was translated into several European languages as 'The Fables of Bidpai' (or Pilpay), a corruption of Vidyāpati, a wise brāhmin who figures in them. The 'framework' device of weaving a tale within a tale was subsequently employed in *The Arabian Nights* and also in *The Decameron* of Boccaccio.

Books

I. Edgerton, F. (Ed.) *The Panchatantra Reconstructed,* 2 vols, New Haven, Conn., 1924.
II. Ghosal, D. *Thirty-five Stories from the Panchatantra,* Calcutta, 1925.
III. Williams, A. (Tr.) *Tales from the Panchatantra,* Oxford, 1930.

PĀṆḌAVA, the five putative children of Pāṇḍu who became the chief protagonists and heroes of the *Mahābhārata.* PĀṆḌU, 'pale', was the son of the sage Vyāsa by Ambālikā wife of Vichitravīrya. He was so named because his mother became pale with fright while being embraced by Vyāsa. Pāṇḍu was brought up by Bhīshma who acted as regent, and when the prince came of age he ascended the throne of Hastināpura.

Paṇḍu had two wives. The first, Kuntī (or Pṛithā), while still unmarried had been vouchsafed the power to summon the gods for congress with her (*see* Śūra). She called upon the sun-god and by him had a son named Karṇa*. Subsequently she married Pāṇḍu. The second wife was the dusky-complexioned Mādrī, who came from Madra having been purchased for the king by Bhīshma. She became Pāṇḍu's favourite wife.

The story goes that Pāṇḍu while out hunting shot a young antelope in the act of mating with another. The dying animal disclosed that it was in reality a *ṛishi* (sage) who had transformed himself and his wife for the purpose of experiencing the pleasures of love in animal form, and he cursed Pāṇḍu for slaying him at the sacred time of union, declaring that he himself would die during intercourse.

From that time onward Pāṇḍu lived in strict continence in the forest. At her husband's request, Kuntī had three sons through adulterous union with certain gods, but Pāṇḍu was not content with the number and pressed his wife to have more, but she protested against the suggestion. Mādrī similarly bore two children by divine agency. The three children of Kuntī were: Yudhishṭhira* son of Dharma god of justice; Bhīma* son of Vāyu god of the wind; and Arjuna* son of Indra. The two children of Mādrī were fathered by the divine twins, the Aśvins, who visited her at her bidding, after the power possessed by Kuntī had been transferred to her. The first was Nakula (the name means ichneumon) the son of the Aśvin Nāsatya, who became a great horse-tamer, married Kareṇumatī, princess of Chedi and had a son named Niramitra. The second child of Mādrī was Sahadeva, by the Aśvin Dasra, who became mighty in swordsmanship, astronomy and the raising of cattle. Sahadeva married Vijayā and had a son named Suhotra.

Pāṇḍu did all he could to avoid temptation through too close a contact with his wives, so that he might escape the doom foretold by the ṛishi, but one day he caught sight of his favourite wife Mādrī as she was returning from a bath in a forest stream.

'As he gazed on the youthful beauty and beheld her thighs like banana trunks and other areas of delight through her light garments his desire blazed forth and he could not restrain his passion and the fire that burned within him. Mādrī used all the powers she had to dissuade him, but he, his fear gone, his senses filled with uncontrollable longing, gave his life to the imperious call of love, goaded on by fate.'

Even before he could consummate the act he fell down dead.

Interrupted union was believed to be very injurious, and since Pāṇḍu's soul was now between earth and heaven, yearning for the company of his spouse to fulfil the incompleted act, Mādrī ascended the funeral pyre of her husband to join him and give herself to his embrace. On Pāṇḍu's death his blind brother Dhṛitarāshṭra ascended the throne of Hastināpura and took the five Pāṇḍava princes under his care.

The indeterminate origin of the Pāṇḍavas has made them a topic of perennial interest to scholars. The mothers of the Pāṇḍava boys were in all probability both polyandrous. Mādrī had her two sons through the heavenly Aśvins. Kuntī had her first child through the god Sūrya, and her three other children by three other 'gods'. At the first grand tournament in which the Pāṇḍavas showed their prowess, Duryodhana taunted Arjuna and his brothers that they were not the sons of Pāṇḍu but of certain amorous deities, a taunt whose implications could have been interpreted in only one way. Sidhanta remarks, 'To say that they are the offspring of the gods is, rationally speaking, to admit that their parentage is unknown' (II, p. 122).

The five Pāṇḍava brothers themselves married a single wife, Draupadī*, thus continuing a polyandrous tradition that surprised even Drupada her father. This, added to the evidence of a matrilineal order of succession in the Pāṇḍava line; their sexual freedom; their acceptance of *niyoga*; the blood-drinking of Bhīma, all suggest a probable Mongolian, Scythian or indigenous origin (I, p. 37). If the Pāṇḍavas were 'Aryan' their Aryan antecedents were considerably less in evidence than those of the Kauravas. In the courtly art of gambling they invariably lost to the more sophisticated and knightly Kauravas. On the battlefield of Kurukshetra they fell short of the Kaurava standards, and their apparent cowardice and lack of fair play aroused the censure of their own allies.

According to certain scholars there is little to justify the belief that they were even related. 'The cousinship of the Pāṇḍavas', says Sidhanta, 'was perhaps invented later on by the bards' (II, p. 122), since the traditions of the two families are divergent at many points. The contention that the

Pāṇḍavas and Kauravas belonged not only to different clans but possibly to different races, finds some small measure of support in the Epics, and forms the basis of the theory of Schroeder and Holtzmann, according to whom the original heroes of the *Mahābhārata* were not the Pāṇḍavas, but the noble Kauravas, 'and the poem had been composed by some sorrowing child of Kuruland' (II, p. 25). At some stage, it is suggested, the Epic was taken over by a Pāṇḍava partisan and the outlines of the story reversed so that in the process the Pāṇḍavas became the heroes.

Books

I. Chatterji, S. K. *Kirata-Jana-Krti: The Indo-Mongoloids, Their Contribution to the History and Culture of India*, Calcutta, 1951.

II. Sidhanta, N. K. *The Heroic Age of India*, London, 1929.

III. Sukhdev, B. K. *The Heroes of the Mahabharata*, 1932.

(*see also under* Mahābhārata and Mythology.)

PĀṆḌYA, the name of an ancient non-Aryan, Tamil kingdom at the extreme southern tip of the Indian peninsula, covering the regions of Madura, Rāmnād, Rāmeśvaram, Tuticorin and Tinnevelly. The tradition of their origin from the Epic Pāṇḍu is not regarded as acceptable by scholars.

Megasthenes notes a legend according to which Heracles placed South India under the rule of his daughter Pandaia. The Sanskrit epics speak of this region as foreign territory. In the Mauryan period the Pāṇḍya kingdom was outside the limits of Aśoka's empire, but is mentioned in one of his inscriptions. The flourishing Pāṇḍya port of Koṛkai (or Koḷkai) not far from Tuticorin was known to the Greeks and Romans*. Strabo mentions an embassy sent to Augustus Caesar about 29 BC by a king named Pandion, who was probably a Pāṇḍya ruler.

The Pāṇḍyas had by this time established themselves at Madura on the Vagai river, the scene of the Śaṅgams, renowned in Tamil* literature. They maintained constant, often hostile, intercourse with Ceylon. About 300 BC they raided the island and continued an intermittent war with the rulers for centuries after. It is recorded that as late as AD 1001 a Pāṇḍya king of Madura invaded Ceylon and sacked Anurādhapura.

Hiuen-Tsang writing in AD 640 describes the country as hot, and the inhabitants as black in colour, impetuous in disposition, greatly interested in commerce and caring little for learning. They were mainly of the Hindu and Jain persuasion.

Shortly after Hiuen-Tsang's visit a Jain Pāṇḍya king, NEDUMARĀN (AD 700) was converted to Śaivism on his marriage to a Chola princess, and started a ferocious persecution in which 8,000 Jains were slaughtered in Madura alone.

The history of the Pāṇḍyas during the first thousand years of the present era is obscure and uncertain, and for many centuries is linked with the story of Ceylon, the Pallavas, Cheras and Cholas. They supplanted the Cholas during the reign of Jatavarman (1215–1271) and emerged as the leading power in the Tamil country.

In the early years of the fourteenth century the whole Tamil area was overrun by Malik Kāfūr, the capture and sack of Madura in 1311 being facilitated by a fratricidal war raging within the kingdom, between the two Pāṇḍya princes, one of whom sought Muslim help. After a brief interval of Muslim rule the area was absorbed into the Vijayanagar empire.

At this time the **NĀYYAKA** family (1420–1736) who were feudatories under the Vijayanagar kings became almost independent as rulers of Madura, and under the parricide **Viśvanātha** (*c.* 1560) established a new dynasty. After the fall of Vijayanagar in 1565 the Hindu elements of the ruined empire were forced southwards and this greatly helped the re-emergence of Madura which saw a wonderful renaissance under the Nāyyakas.

Most famous of the Nāyyakas was **Tirumaḷai** (1623–1660) an almost legendary ruler who was a renowned builder and a patron of the arts. A monarch filled with a sense of his own dignity he once stabbed his queen in the thigh for making a rude remark; he then immortalized the incident in a statuary group which stands in one of the maṇḍapams showing her beside him, with the gash in her thigh clearly marked. Near this work is another unique group of Śiva holding up a dozen little pigs to protect them from the arrows of a Nāyyaka ruler. The legend is that the ruler shot the mother pig, so Śiva assumed the shape of the sow and suckled the piglings.

Both Pāṇḍyas and Nāyyakas made many notable contributions to art and architecture. The Pāṇḍya style of building brought into focus many of the characteristics typical of South Indian architecture. Already the early Pāṇḍya shrines bear some of the distinctive features of the later temples, seen for example in the elaborately sculptured monolithic pillars of Avadaiyar Kovil (*c.* 1280), and the gopurams of the Śaivite temple of Tinnevelly (*c.* 1300).

When the Nāyyaka dynasty of Madura assumed the mantle of the Pāṇḍya princes the country already had hundreds of ancient shrines. Some of these they now endowed with added sanctity by building massive edifices around them. Many Pāṇḍya temples are in reality elaborations around the early fanes which were preserved untouched. Subsidiary structures were built near the temple, surrounded by a series of high enclosing walls, and topped with magnificent gopurams. Long rows of columns, hundreds in number, all profusely carved, are a striking feature of Pāṇḍya architecture.

The Pāṇḍya (Nāyyaka) temples are among the most splendid in India. They include the Great Temple of Madura (1600–1650) dedicated to Mīnākshī and her consort Sundareśvar (Śiva). It was built by Tirumaḷai in honour of the goddess because she had cured him of catarrh. It ranks as the most fabulous of the South Indian temples, with long encircling walls, eleven towering gopurams (gateway towers), a famous *teppakulam* called 'The Tank of the Golden Lilies', and a hypostyle Hall of a Thousand Pillars (actually 997) nearly all of different styles. It also includes a curious building which served for exhibiting fights between wild beasts and gladiators. The palace of king Tirumaḷai represents a singular blend of architectural expression. Says Zimmer, 'The arches are Hindu in form but Muhammadan in application, while the columns that support them are Western, and the whole building is European in character' (V, p. 285).

Another famous Nāyyaka edifice is the temple of Raṅganātha in Śriraṅgam

(1620–1689) dedicated to Vishṇu and erected on the site of a prehistoric shrine. Built on an immense scale it is like a small-size town, and is the largest of the South Indian temples, with seven *prākārams* (rectangular enclosures one within the other) and twenty-one *gopurams*. Its plan is unusual inasmuch as it lies north-south instead of east-west. Among its features are a Hall of a Thousand Pillars, actually 940 granite monoliths, and a Horse Court which probably belongs to the Vijayanagar period, and has a colonnade of rearing, rampant horses, each about nine feet high.

One mile from this temple-city is the smaller Śaivite temple of Jambukeśvara on the site of a liṅga*, built on the same plan as the Raṅganātha temple, although the larger temple is said to have been built after it.

The seventeenth-century temple of Rāmeśvaram* is like most Pāṇḍya temples, remarkable for its columns, about three thousand in this temple alone.

Books

I. Iyengar, P. T. S. *History of the Tamils to 600* AD, Madras, 1929.
II. Lal, Kanwar. *Holy Cities of India*, Delhi, 1961.
III. Pillai, K. N. S. *Chronology of the Early Tamils*, Madras, 1932.
IV. Sastri, K. A. N. *The Pandyan Kingdom*, London, 1929.
V. Zimmer, H. *The Art of Indian Asia*, Vol. I, New York, 1955.

PĀṆINI (?350 BC–250 BC?) Sanskrit grammarian of uncertain origin, born in Śalātura in Gandhāra, a few miles to the north of the confluence of the Kābul and Indus rivers. Little is known about his life, though many legends are related about him. He was a descendant of one Paṇin, as his unusual name indicates, and the grandson of Devala. His mother Dākshi came from the tribe of Daksha in north-west India. Pāṇini was said to have been extremely dull as a child and was rejected by his teacher as unfit for study, but by the grace of the Lord (Śiva or Vishṇu, according to later legend) he became endowed with knowledge and continued his education at Taxila, to become one of the most renowned students of that university, and friend of one of the Nanda emperors.

His masterpiece is the *Ashṭādhyāyī*, 'eight chapters', also known as the Pāṇinīyam, which introduced, as it were, the post-Vedic age and set the linguistic standard of Classical Sanskrit, effectively stabilizing the language. It is the most notable of all works on vyākaraṇa or grammar*, although the subject itself had a long antecedent history; Pāṇini himself mentions several of his predecessors, of whom no fewer than sixty-four are known. Among those 'whose works he most probably consulted' (I, p. 341) were Śākaṭāyana and Śākalya, both of probable Śaka origin; Sphoṭāyana who may have been Persian; and Gārgya and Gālava, thought to have been Greeks. Pāṇini refers to Yavanānī, 'Greek writing' and he may have been acquainted with the work of foreign, including Greek, scholars of his day.

Pāṇini's *Ashṭādhyāyī* consists of nearly 4,000 sūtras or aphorisms, each of two or three words only. These embody grammatical rules written in a kind of shorthand or algebra-like code, employing single letters or syllables to indicate the names of cases, moods, persons and tenses, which makes his work extremely recondite and difficult to follow without intensive study and a full commentary. As a result of this systematization of the language it came to be known from Pāṇini's time as Sanskrit (*saṁskrita*, 'elaborated'), and the phrase *'iti-Pāṇini'* 'thus, according to, Pāṇini', was an authorititave preamble for centuries after.

Pāṇini recognized the root as the basic element of the word, and classified 2,000 monosyllabic roots which, with the addition of prefixes, suffixes, and inflections, were believed to provide all the words in the language. Especially difficult are Pāṇini's rules of *sandhi* (*saṁdhi*, 'combination') governing the euphonious liaison of contiguous letters, which were still further elaborated by later grammarians. It was held that every word in a sentence was affected by its neighbours, and strict rules were formulated to govern the resultant changes and help in disentangling the modified words. For example, the final 'd' or 't' before an initial 'l' becomes 'l', e.g. *tad labdham* (that is taken) becomes *tal labdham*; or the final 'k' before an initial 'm' becomes 'n', e.g. *prāk mukhaḥ* (east facing) becomes *prān-mukh*; or a visarga, the final aspirated 'h', followed by 'a' becomes 'r', e.g. *kaviḥ ayam* (this poet) becomes *kavir ayam.*

It is to be remembered that the norm laid down by Pāṇini was for the language spoken in higher circles of contemporary society, and did not necessarily conform in all respects to any extant texts. But the standard established by him permanently influenced all subsequent Sanskrit writing. Pāṇini's treatise is the earliest extant grammar in any language, the earliest scientific grammar in the world, and one of the greatest ever written.

Pāṇini is also called Śālottarīya after his place of birth; and Dāksheya after his mother. He is also known as Āhika.

Books

I. Agrawala, V. S. *India as Known to Panini*, Lucknow, 1953.

II. Faddegon, B. *Studies on Panini's Grammar*, Amsterdam, 1936.

III. Goldstücker, T. *Panini, His Place in Sanskrit*, London, 1861.

PARADISE, or heaven covers many *lokas* (regions) of the Hindu cosmological scheme. The terms generally used for paradise are *Vyoman*, the firmament or heavenly spheres, and *Anand-loka*, 'bliss region', of which seven subdivisions are traditionally recognized. Paradise is reserved for the fortunate few, and most of these are destined to return to earth after receiving their reward there. It is the realm of supernormal experience, and its importance is reckoned according to the particular deity worshipped, the heaven of Śiva being superior to the heaven of Vishṇu if one is a Śaivite, and Kṛishṇa's heaven offering the supreme bliss if one is a devotee of that god.

In Hindu cosmology all the heavens are situated in an area known as *Ilāvṛita*, 'divine enclosure'. Although said to be lying north of the Himālayas, this is an occult region beyond the ken of mortal man. It should be noted that many actual places in India bear the names of the lokas in Ilāvṛita; they are so named after their celestial prototype, in honour of a god, or in commemoration of an event associated with his visit to that place while on earth.

In the centre of the divine area, marking as it were the very centre of the whole universe stands Mount *Meru*, famous in legend and song. The origin of this name is obscure, though some scholars derive it from Mount Meros of the Greek state of Nysa* to the north-west of India, or from Mount Mouru of the Zoroastrian Avesta. Of pure gold and 160,000 leagues high, Meru towers above the heavenly lokas, and around it all the heavenly bodies revolve. It is in a sense the Olympus of the Hindus. A gigantic jambu (rose-apple) tree grows on Mount Meru and this tree overshadows the island which is the earth, and casts its protective shadow over it, whence the earth is called *Jambu-dvīpa*. The fruits of this tree are as large as elephants and when ripe they fall on the mountains and their juice forms the Jambu river whose waters confer immortality. Indian topography placed Meru in the Himālayas, near Almora, where the Ganges takes its rise. The *Mahābhārata* gives the name Meru to a mountain in Śakadvīpa, sometimes identified with a peak in the Pāmirs, which would confirm its Iranian origin. Kālidāsa makes it a dwelling of fabulous beings. Meru is also called Sumeru (beautiful form), Hemādri (golden mountain), Ratna-sānu (jewel-peak), Karṇikāchala (lotus-mountain), Amara-parvata (immortal mountain), and Deva-parvata (divine mountain).

West of Meru rises Mount *Supārśva* in whose celestial grove, called *Vaibhrāja*, the gods and goddesses disport themselves. Another spur of Meru, Mount *Mandara*, served as the churning stick when the gods churned the ocean of milk to obtain amṛita or nectar*. According to folklore a mountain of the same name in Bhāgalpur, Bengal, represents a chip of this divine peak.

Highest of all the heavenly spheres is the one called *Brahmā-loka*, the abode of Brahmā, situated either on mount Meru, or in a place 1,848 million miles above that mountain. Brahmā-loka has several regions, namely: (1) *Satya-loka*, the abode of truth, a remote and forbidding area where only truth in its absolute form can abide; and here dwells Brahmā alone, lost in eternal meditation; (2) *Tapo-loka* (or *Tapar-loka*), the abode of Virāj, an ancient deity sometimes equated with Brahmā, and of his devotees the semi-divine Vairāja, and also of certain unsurpassed ascetics, *siddhas* and *munis*; (3) *Janar-loka*, the place of final birth, i.e. from which rebirth cannot occur. It is the abode of the three Kumāras or sons of Brahmā; (4) *Mahar-loka*, the middle region, the abode of Bhṛigu and certain *prajāpatis* who are almost equal to Brahmā. Those mortals who are absolutely uncontaminated by falsehood and passion, go to Brahmā-loka, and are exempt from rebirth on earth, having escaped the cycle of saṁsāra. They live in contemplation, free from the trammels of desire, in a state of Truth-Being-Bliss. All the regions of Brahmā-loka are destroyed at the *mahāpralaya* (*see* aeon) which consumes the universe.

The second division of paradise is *Svar-loka*, 'bright-realm', where the *dhāman*, 'abodes', of the deities are located. Those mortals who are their true devotees join them after death, and live in their respective paradises until it is time for their next incarnation. These spheres are thus the heavens of the sectarian gods and beatified mortals. The whole region is situated on or around Meru, although it is sometimes described as extending 'from the sun to the pole-star'.

It is from Svar-loka that the popular Hindu conception of paradise is derived, and from descriptions of it we find that it is primarily a place of sensual pleasure. Its joys are those of the senses: music to enchant the ear, fruits, sweetmeats and ambrosial dishes to titillate the palate, delightful perfumes to soothe or stimulate as the mood desires; jewelled palaces, golden pathways, green acres, bowers of fragrant flowers, and the crowning prospect, an endless procession of ravishing *apsarās* (nymphs) to serve the desires of passion. These heavenly companions come in all shapes and varieties and know every subtle art to please and ensure the happiness of those who ascend the heavenly spheres. Of the three hundred and thirty synonymns for prostitute and courtesan in Sanskrit, scores apply to the *gopīs* and apsarās of paradise. Svar-loka is destroyed at the end of each 'week' of Brahmā.

Indra's heaven is called Indra-loka or Svar-loka, commonly known as *Svarga*, north of Mount Meru. It encompasses the region called Antarīksha, 'mid-region', that is, the firmament between earth and heaven, whose inhabitants are clouds and birds in the lower region, and, in the upper region, apsarās or nymphs and *gandharvas*, or celestial musicians. Here too dwells the gentle-eyed Kāmadhenu, the divine cow of plenty. The capital of Svarga is Amarāvatī, the site of Indra's mangificent palace, Vaijayanta. This palace holds the famous hall, Sudharmā, the unrivalled jewel among all princely courts, which for some time was used by Kṛishṇa. In the wonderful garden Nandana (also called Pārushya or Kandasāra) surrounding the palace, grow the *kalpa-vṛiksha* or wish-fulfilling trees (*see* plants), and in the centre of the garden stands the *pārijāta* tree, with bark of gold and leaves of wondrous colour. It is the delight of the apsarās, and perfumes the whole of paradise. This tree appeared in the Churning of the Ocean and was taken by Indra to heaven from where it was once stolen by Kṛishṇa for his wife Satyabhāmā. On its restoration to paradise, Andhaka the asura* attempted to carry it off but was slain by Śiva. Svarga is also called *Tridiva*, 'third (highest) heaven'; *Trivishṭapa*, 'third world'; *Ūrdhva-loka*, 'upper world'. *Amarāvatī* is also called *Devapura*, 'divine city', and *Pūsha-bhāsā*, 'sun-splendour'.

Vaikuṇṭha, the paradise of Vishṇu, is situated on the southern slopes of Mount Meru, above Kailāsa. Flowing through it is the celestial Ganges. This glorious city has buildings of jewels, roads of gold. It is often identified with Goloka, the paradise of Kṛishṇa.

Goloka (*Go-loka*, 'cow-place'), Kṛishṇa's paradise, is situated near Vaikuṇṭha. It is the celestial prototype of the earthly Gokula and Vṛindāvana, near Mathurā, and the cow-dung hill of Govardhana. It is filled with wonderful groves and bowers, and the celestial Yamunā flows through it. Devotees of Kṛishṇa are transported there after death in the form of cows, beasts, birds, and the more fortunate ones as gopas and gopīs (cowherds and milkmaids). There they join in the sensuous moonlight dances of Kṛishṇa, forever ravishing and being ravished, forever tasting boundless bliss.

Alakā, the paradise of Kubera, is the wealthiest of the celestial cities. Kubera's garden, Chaitra-ratha, so called because it is tended by the gandharva gardener Chitra-ratha is situated on Mount Mandara (see above).

Other empyrean spheres include *Kailāsa*, the mountain* paradise of Śiva; *Māruta*, the world of the Maruts, which is the particular paradise of the vaiśyas (*see* Diti); *Vaivasvatī* (or Bhāsvatī), the celestial city of Sūrya*; *Vasudhā-nagara*, 'wealth-yielding town', celestial city of Varuṇa, situated on

Mount Pushpagiri, 'flower-hill', near Meru; *Gaṇa-parvata*, the paradise of the Gaṇadevatās (*see* godlings) situated near Kailāsa; *Soma-loka*, the region of the moon and the abode of the *pitṛis* or manes.

Books

See under Mythology.

PARAMĀRA (974–1060), a line of agnikula Rājputs, who broke away from the Pratihāras of Kanauj when that empire fell into dissolution, and made themselves independent in Mālwā, with capital first at Ujjain*, and later at Dhārā (or Dhār), fifty miles south of Ujjain. Like most other Rājput dynasties that rose to power in the Middle Ages, the Paramāras were of mixed antecedents, but were invested with kshattriya status by brāhminical decree.

One of the early kings was the Śaka-descended **Muñja** (d. 994), a great patron of poets and warlike withal, whose bid for expansion was effectively halted by the Chālukya king Taila II, who took him prisoner and put him to death. His younger brother **Sindhurāja** (d. 1000) assumed the title of Navasāhasāṅka, 'the New Sāhasāṅka' i.e. Vikramāditya, and set out on a campaign of aggrandisement and revenge. His victorious career was celebrated in a panegyric by his court poet Padmagupta.

The most famous of the Paramāra kings was his son, the versatile **Bhoja** (1018–1060), the author of works on astronomy, architecture, poetry, rhetoric and philosophy, and a great builder of irrigation lakes and dams. His great lake, 250 square miles in area, was a signal achievement by any standards. He built a number of temples at Dhārā, set up a college for Sanskrit studies (now a mosque), and beautified his capital with many other fine edifices. He also strengthened the fortress town of Māṇḍu, which later became the capital of the Muslim Sultans of Mālwā. Bhoja is renowned in Hindu legend second only to the semi-mythical Vikramāditya as a great warrior, statesman, scholar, and patron of letters. He sent out an army to resist the invasion of Mahmūd of Ghazni in 1018, and was almost constantly at war with his Hindu neighbours. In spite of his excellent qualities he was in the end unsuccessful against the Chandellas, the Rāshṭrakūṭas, and the Chāhamānas, and lost Māṇḍu, Ujjain and even his capital of Dhārā to his hereditary enemies, the Chālukyas. He died of fever while his kingdom was once again being attacked by the Chālukyas.

After Bhoja's death the weakened state continued to be involved in long and tedious struggles with its neighbours and rivals, until it was finally brought to an end by Alā-ud-dīn's generals in 1305. In 1560 the region became part of the Moghul Empire.

The history of the Paramāras is one long tale of strife and bloodshed. The good work done by the rulers in encouraging architecture and the arts, and in civic works, was more than offset by the ruthless aggression and naked ambition of even the best of them. The plunder that followed in the wake of their armies went towards the building of the Paramāra temples and the construction of public works.

The Paramāras are also known as the Pramāra, Pavār, Powār, Pawār, Panwār, Ponwār, and other variations of the name.

Books

I. Ayyangar, P. T. S. *Bhoja Raja*, Madras, 1931.
II. Ganguly, D. C. *History of the Paramara Dynasty*, Dacca, 1933.
III. Yazdani, G. *Mandu, The City of Joy*, Oxford, 1929.

PARAMUDRĀ, 'supreme posture', a purposive arrangement of the limbs and organs of the human body into certain mystical poses, for obtaining the maximum concentration of psychic power. It is the ultimate expression of *aṅgika**, and calls for a combination of the *āsana** (bodily posture), *bandha** (the 'locking' of organs), *prāṇayāma** (breath control), *mudrā** (hand gestures), with accompanying *maṇḍalas** ('mystic diagrams) and *mantras** (spells). The specific object of a paramudrā is in most cases to activate the subtle centres of the body and direct the occult energies along desired channels. The paramudrās are said to be very secret techniques, which are never fully described in writing, since the details can only be communicated by word of mouth and their practise can only be undertaken with the supervision of a guru. There are eighty-eight paramudrās, each designed for a specific occult purpose, and many are named after the āsana, bandha or mudrā associated with it. The major paramudrās are briefly described below.

MAHĀMUDRĀ, 'great posture', in which the practitioner sits with the left heel pressing the yoni-place (perineum), stretches out the right leg and holds the right foot in both hands. He then closes the nine *chhidra* or orifices* of the body, sinks the chin into the breast in *jālandhara* and controls his breath. 'All the inner channels will be activated, semen will not flow, vitality will be increased, all decay destroyed.'

KHECHARĪ-MUDRĀ (*khe-charī*, 'air-moving') also called the *chācharī-mudrā* (*chā-charī*, 'void-moving'), consists of turning the tongue backwards into the gullet, thus blocking the orifices of the nasal passage that open into the mouth. This is done in order to prevent the 'celestial nectar' of the *sahasrāra* from seeping down and becoming wasted. When the tongue is in this position the 'tenth door' is sealed, and the nectar saved and absorbed by the yogi himself. While the tongue is thrust back into the throat the eyes are focused on a spot between the eyebrows (as in *trāṭaka*) and certain mantras silently meditated upon. To accomplish this mudrā a long period of preparatory work is necessary; the tongue is lengthened by cutting the fraenum and by stretching and massaging the tongue daily (this process is called *dohana*, 'milking') till it is long enough to reach the space between the eyebrows. In order to turn the tongue back into the throat it is first necessary to achieve a loosening of the soft palate. A piece of metal bent at one end is inserted into the mouth, and the palate ridge is hooked and gently drawn forward. After some weeks the membrane becomes so flexible that, according to yogic texts, it becomes possible to touch the teeth with the soft palate. The whole process combined takes many months. 'He who knows this mudrā is not afflicted with disease, death, sloth, hunger and swooning. Nor can his semen leave its place even if a woman is embraced.' During the performance of this paramudrā the yogi attains the trance* state called *unmani*.

YONI-MUDRĀ, 'vulva-posture'. In this the yogi is required to sit in siddhāsana, assume the *shaṇmukhi* mudrā and contract the yoni-place between the testes and anus. He then concentrates on Kāma, god of lust, knowing that he is beautiful like the *bandhuk* flower, and believing that he has taken up his abode in the yoni-place. This yoni-mudrā is 'a profound secret'; through it one develops great erectile and seminal power and becomes irresistibly attractive to all women. One is freed from all sin; indeed, 'one becomes sinless even if one commits a thousand murders or countless adulteries'. A variation of this is the *vajroni-mudrā* (*vajra-yoni*, 'thunderbolt-vulva') performed with the member in the thunderbolt (erect) position.

MAHĀBANDHA, 'great-knot'; here one must assume the siddhāsana position, apply the *mūlabandha*, perform four specified breathing rhythms, fill the chest with air and lock the chin in *jālandhara*. A particular mantra is recited. Its effects are similar to those of the mahāmudrā.

MAHĀVEDHA, 'great piercing', usually done after the mahābandha. In the same position, resting both hands on the ground one rises a little and gently strikes the buttocks against the ground. The air leaving the iḍā and piṅgala starts into the middle channel, 'so that iḍā, piṅgala and agni are united, the coiled energy dissolves into Kailāsa, bringing about immortality'.

VAJROLI-MUDRĀ (vajra, 'thunderbolt'), an important mudrā for controlling the sex forces of the body, is preceded by long training in *meḍhrati*, cleansing and strengthening the male member. It is performed during intercourse and is believed to be very injurious to the woman partner, who withers under the treatment. The yogi draws up the female 'seed' through his member and brings it into his own body. This process is called *sahajoli* (*sahaja*, 'co-born') and is considered 'the most secret of all the processes of earthly wisdom, capable of making the world tremble'. Care is to be taken during the act that emission of the male seed does not occur. In a variation known as *amaroli* (*amara*, 'immortal') the semen is released into the female body and is made to unite with her seed; then both fluids are drawn back into the body. 'So in the body of the yogi, the male and female seeds are united, and his body becomes like the gods. By this mudrā a man may indulge in all worldly pleasures and still attain realization.' These and other *oli* or *uli* (variously said to mean 'wise', 'secret', 'womb', 'fire', 'mighty') techniques, as they are called, require many years of practice.

VIPARITA-KARAṆĪ, 'reverse-doing', is carried out while standing on the head in combination with special locks and breathing exercises, 'which all the makers of the rules of wisdom keep secret'. It is connected with the absorption of the *bindu** or seminal fluid either direct (as in daṇḍamukhāsana) or internally, into the body, its blending with the nectar from the sahasrāra and its assimilation by the yogi. 'The person who practices this remains unharmed even at the time of universal destruction.'

BHAGĀSANA (*bhaga-āsana*, 'vulva-seat'), another secret paramudrā in which the member is 'locked' in erection for prolonged periods within the yoni of a female disciple, while certain internal esoteric acts are performed. It is supposed to confer many potent *siddhis** or supernormal powers.

There are several other paramudrās which are only briefly described in the texts, and like those mentioned above are not to be attempted except under the guidance of a guru. Such for instance is the *śakti-chālana*, 'energy-mover', which employs the expedients of stances, breathings and mantras, to awaken the *kuṇḍalinī*, and uses the energy thus generated for sinister ends. The *pari-chālana*, 'around-moving', is a variation of the last named.

There are yet other paramudrās, seldom explained in writing, which are extremely complex in execution and, to normal minds, utterly revolting in performance. Still others are only hinted at but never even named. These are concerned not only with the physical body but with the subtle, astral and even future bodies, and require the aid of demons, demonesses and elemental spirits. Wrongly done they can cause ill effects in the practitioner for several future incarnations.

Books

I. Datta, R. *Four Secret Asanas* (*with sketches*) p.p. 1911.
II. Datta, R. *Linga-bandha Practices*, p.p. 1911.
See also under Tantrism and Yoga.

PARĀŚARA, legendary author of certain hymns in the *Ṛig-Veda*, and also of a *dharma-śāstra* (law-book). He is often cited as an indisputable example of a ṛishi born of low parentage. His father Śaktri, was the son of the celebrated sage Vasishṭha, and his mother Adṛiśyantī, was a Puliah (degraded caste) woman. Adṛiśyantī was pregnant when her husband was devoured by a *rākshasa* (*see* Kalmāshapāda), and she continued to carry her child 'under her heart' for twelve years. This child, Parāśara, spent his time in the womb studying the Vedas aloud, so that those around him benefited by the magic strains which spread as he intoned the verses. When he was born he was already familiar with the sacred writings.

He grew up to become a renowned student of the scriptures and of the arts and sciences. He continued his studies as a disciple of the sage Kapila, received the *Vishṇu Purāṇa* and the Pañcharātra doctrines from the lips of Pulastya, and in turn passed them on to his pupil Maitreya. When he reached manhood and was told the circumstances of his father's death, he instituted a sacrifice for the extermination of all rākshasas, but was dissuaded from his purpose by his grandfather Vasishṭha. Left with the powerfully charged remains of the unconsumed sacrificial fire, Parāśara flung it into the Himālayas, where according to folklore it is still sometimes seen to blaze forth, consuming the mountain forests.

Parāśara had a liaison with Satyavatī* through whom he became the father of the great sage Vyāsa.

Books

See Mahābhārata *and* Mythology.

PARAŚURĀMA, the youngest son of the sage Jamadagni and his beautiful wife Reṇukā, is regarded as the sixth *avatāra* or 'descent' of Vishṇu to earth, although curiously, Paraśurāma was a worshipper of Śiva and enjoyed that god's protection. Śiva instructed him in the use of arms and gave him the *paraśu*, a magic battle-axe, in honour of which he was called Paraśu-Rāma, 'Rāma of the Axe'. In the *Rāmāyaṇa* he appears as the loser in a brief encounter with Rāma*. Aggrieved that Rāma had broken the bow of Śiva in the contest for Sītā's hand, he challenged him to a fight, but was defeated and also 'excluded from a seat in the celestial world'. In the *Mahābhārata* he trains both Karṇa and Arjuna in the use of arms, and has a duel with Bhīma in which both heroes suffer equally. Subsequently he takes part in the war council of the Kauravas. Another well-known incident of his career occurs in the *Mahābhārata* where, in obedience to his father's order, he strikes off his mother's head with his axe. At Paraśurāma's request, however, Jamadagni* restores the woman to life.

Paraśurāma's great foe was the Haihaya* king Kārtavīrya. This kshattriya monarch once visited the hermitage of Jamadagni when the sage and his sons were out, and was welcomed by the sage's wife with due hospitality. Unmindful of the respect with which he had been received, the warrior king laid waste the trees around the hermitage and then tried to lay hands on the sacred cow belonging to Jamadagni, the calf of Kāmadhenu*, which the hermit had acquired through penance. A troop of Yavanas (?Greeks), miraculously conjured up by the calf, repulsed Kārtavīrya for a time, but he returned and bore the calf away. Hearing this on his return, Paraśurāma was exceeding wroth and going in pursuit of the plundering king, cut off his thousand arms and slaughtered him like a common animal. On the advice of his father, Paraśurāma then set out on a pilgrimage to atone for the sin of killing Kārtavīrya. In his absence the sons of Kārtavīrya went to the hermitage of Jamadagni, and in retaliation slew the sage in cold blood as he sat deep in meditation.

Paraśurāma's ire now knew no bounds. While his father's body was being cremated he took a solemn bow before the gods that he would exterminate the whole race of the accursed kshattriyas. He first massacred the sons of Kārtavīrya, and then embarked upon his famous expeditions. 'Thrice seven times' did he clear the earth of the kshattriya clans, filling with their blood the great lakes of Samanta-pañchaka and Kurukshetra.

Paraśurāma begged Varuṇa to give him land that he might bestow it upon the brāhmins in expiation for his slaughter of the kshattriyas, whereupon Varuṇa, who was god of the sea, withdrew the ocean from the hills of Gokarṇa as far as Cape Comorin and presented him with the country of Malabār. In some legends Paraśurāma himself drove back the ocean and so increased the territory, and cut fissures in the Ghāṭs with blows of his axe. He also diverted the trade from the Aryan ports of the north to the Dravidian ports of the west coast. He then settled this area, known as Aparānta, 'west-end', with brāhmins from the north, and bestowed the whole territory on the mahāṛishi Kaśyapa. The entire west coast of India, from Bhṛigukachchha down to Cape Comorin still retains its olden associations with the great 'Rāma of the Axe'.

The hero finally retired to the Mahendra mountains (the Eastern Ghāṭs), where he was visited by gods and heroes, including Arjuna. He is said to be *chirañjīva* or immortal (*see* longevity), and is still alive in some cave in Central India. He is the patron deity of the Chitpāvan brāhmins. Paraśurāma's wife was Dharaṇī, 'earth', an incarnation of Lakshmī the eternal spouse of Vishṇu.

Books

See under Mythology.

PĀRŚVA (?872–?772 BC), the twenty-third Jain *tīrthankara** or patriarch of the present cycle. After nine prior existences he was born at last to the queen, Vāmādevī, wife of the kshattriya king Aśvasena of Kāśī (Banāras). One night during her pregnancy she saw a serpent by her 'side', and accordingly named her child Pārśvataḥ or Pārśva, 'flank'. In due course Pārśva married Prabhāvatī daughter of king Prasenajit. At the age of thirty Pārśva was converted to the religious life after seeing a picture of Nemi the twenty-second tīrthankara and he felt the call to become a world-enlightener. He gave away his possessions, 'assumed a state of homelessness', plucked out his hair and retired to a hermitage. Seating himself under a *dhataki* tree he acquired knowledge after eighty-three days of meditation.

He established a community of monks to propagate his doctrines, and also admitted women into an order of nuns. He laid down the four vows of *ahiṁsā* (non-injury), *sūnṛita* (truth), *asteya* (non-stealing), and *brahmacharya* (continence). Pārśva did not insist on complete nudity and hence it is thought that his followers were probably the first of the white-clad monks of Jainism, while those of Mahāvīra were the first of the nude monks.

After his emancipation Pārśva or Pārśvanātha took to wandering and teaching and numerous legends grew up around him. His symbol was the hooded serpent, and a serpent-king once held an umbrella over his head to protect him from the heat of the sun. Many incidents are related about the enmity of his brother or cousin, or in some versions of a king or sage; the struggle between them being carried over into many spheres below and above the earth, and symbolizing the struggle between the powers of good and evil. Pārśva died of voluntary starvation aged exactly one hundred years, on a hill that later came to be known as Pārasnāth. The parents of Mahāvīra* were followers of Pārśva, and scholars are inclined to think that Pārśva was the true founder of Jainism and that Mahāvīra was its propagator.

Pārśva was probably of Persian descent, as his name suggests, and certain affinities may be traced between some of the doctrines of Jainism and the teachings of Zoroaster (II, p. 152). Other common features are the scrupulous regard for all living things, the dualism between the spiritual and material, and the preference of Jains and Zoroastrians for white raiment.

Books

I. Bloomfield, M. *The Life & Stories of the Jain Saint Parsvanatha*, Baltimore, 1919.
II. Masson-Oursel, P., *et al.*, *Ancient India and Indian Civilisation*, London, 1934.

PARTHIANS. The inhabitants of Parthia, or modern Khorasan and the regions to the south-east of the Caspian Sea, were a people of mixed Persian, Bactrian and Mongolian descent, who adopted the Mazdean religion and spoke a language related to ancient Persian. They are referred to in the *Ṛig-Veda* as the Parthava, which was also the indigenous Indian name for the Parthians. In the Epics the Parthians are spoken of as the Pahlava, who were subjugated by king Sagara, who commanded them never to shave but to let their beards grow as a token of their subordination. According to Manu, the Pahlavas were kshattriyas who had become outcastes, and in later texts they are often confused with the Bactrians and Scythians.

After Alexander's death the region of Parthia fell to the Seleucids, but about 250 BC the Parthians revolted and became independent under Arsaces. By the middle of the second century BC the Parthian ruler Mithirdates I (fl. 165 BC) carried his arms up to the Indus. The Persian rulers who exercised a nominal sovereignty there were unable to maintain control over these remote territories of their empire, and appointed Parthian governors of Drangiana (East Iran) and Arachosia (Southern Afghanistan near the region of Kandahār) to guard the security of their eastern borders against Śaka encroachments. These governors frequently helped their own cause by matrimonial alliances with the Śakas, and occasionally these mixed Persian-Parthian-Bactrian-Śaka dynasties rebelled against their Persian sovereigns and ruled independently.

Thus in about 58 BC **Vonones** (58–18 BC) the viceroy of Drangiana shook off the Persian yoke and established a local Parthian dynasty of his own, with capital at Taxila (Saraikala, Sirkap, Sirsukh) and reputedly founded the Vikrama era*. He was dethroned by his step-brother **Spalirises** (18–1 BC) who succeeded him. The best known of the Indo-Parthian rulers was **Gondophernes** (AD 21–46) (Persian: Vindapharna; Syriac: Gūdnaphar), viceroy of Arachosia who defeated the ruler of the Kābul valley but was himself constantly harassed by the Kushāns. Gondophernes is associated with the Apostle, St Thomas, who visited his court and converted him to Christianity*. By the middle of the first century AD the Parthians were overthrown by the Kushāns, after having played a brief but memorable role as intermediaries between Greece, Central Asia and India.

The Pahlavas, like other foreign elements on Indian soil, soon merged with the Indians, although stray references to them continue to be made in texts and inscriptions. According to one theory they ventured as far as South India in the early centuries of the present era and by the middle of the third century had established a dynasty called after them, the Pallavas*.

Books

I. Debevoise, N. C. *A Political History of Parthia*, Chicago, 1938.
II. Rapson, E. J. 'The Scythian and Parthian Invaders'. *Cambridge History of India*, I, pp. 563–85.

PĀRVATĪ, a consort of Śiva and an aspect of his śakti or female counterpart. Like Umā, another śakti of Śiva's, she was associated with mountains and was herself a mountaineer. She was a goddess of beauty and exceedingly voluptuous to behold, and often her mere presence was sufficient to arouse the uncontrollable desire of her spouse.

The legend goes that after the tragic death of Satī*, Śiva returned to Mount Kailāsa where he sat wrapt in meditation. In the interval Satī was reborn as Pārvatī and when she came of age she desired to marry Śiva.

Accordingly she made her abode not far from the scene of Śiva's meditations, and worshipped him.

It was at this time that the demon Tāraka began his tyranny over the fourteen worlds, and it became imperative that Śiva be the father of a child, since only a son of Śiva could be expected to cope with Tāraka. The love-god Kāma was entrusted with the task of distracting Śiva, and he waited for a suitable opportunity and shot an arrow at the god just as Pārvatī was walking past. Opening his eyes and beholding the voluptuous form Śiva emitted his seed, which fell into a fire and from this was born Kārttikeya* who eventually killed Tāraka.

Another version has it that Śiva merely blasted Kāma to death with a flash of his third eye, scorned Pārvatī for her dark complexion, for she was an aboriginal deity, and resumed his meditations. Pārvatī thereupon took to asceticism to win the god's love. The white heat of her terrible penances made her glow with a fair-skinned divine beauty, and at the same time disturbed Śiva. He divined the purpose of her exertions, and in order to test her appeared before her in the guise of a dwarf, and started vilifying Śiva. Pārvatī indignantly repudiated his allegations and defended Śiva in ardent terms. The god then revealed himself and in due time married her. They had two children, the six-headed Kārttikeya, and the elephant-headed Gaṇeśa*.

Śiva was a bad provider and allowed his family to starve, while he himself indulged in opium and other drugs. The couple were engaged in endless quarrels and reconciliations, resulting in long drawn-out embraces, some of which lasted several aeons. Once they embraced so passionately that they merged into a single androgynous* being called Ardhanārī. After another protracted union the divine couple disappeared, only to become manifest as the transcendent liṅga (phallus) and yoni (vulva).

Books

See under Mythology.

PĀŚUPATA, a Śaivite sect mentioned in the *Mahābhārata,* associated in its early stages with Śiva in his aspect of 'lord of cattle'. In its subsequent evolution this term was explained in the Purāṇas as the lord (*pati*) who helps his creatures (*paśu*) to free themselves from the bondage (*pāśa*) of this world.

The sect was said to have been founded by Śiva who imparted the doctrines secretly to certain ṛishis. It was finally brought down to the level of ordinary understanding by LAKULĪŚA (*c.* AD 200) who is regarded as its original teacher. In another legend Śiva entered the corpse of an unknown person who had been left in a cemetery along with the *lakula* or club that he used to carry. The deity, embodied in the corpse, picked up the staff and set out to teach his chosen disciples the doctrines of the Pāśupata or Lakula cult. These disciples, four in number, namely, Kuśika, Gārgya, Kaurusha, and Maitreya founded sub-sects of the Pāśupata which flourished in Gujarāt and Rājputāna. The cult was known in the time of Harsha (d. AD 648) and subsequently had many branches, mostly depraved and antinomian, which led to its total condemnation by Śaṅkara and Kumārila. From the eleventh century on another branch of the Pāśupatas became prominent; they were known as the Kālamukha (black-faced) because they wore a distinguishing black mark (*tilaka*) on the forehead. They were the immediate precursors of the Kāpālikas, Kānphaṭas, Aghoris and other left-hand sects.

The theological system of the Pāśupata is *bhedābheda* (dualism-nondualism) and recognizes five categories, namely, (1) *kāraṇa*, the cause, which creates, sustains and destroys all things, (2) *kārya*, the effect, which includes knowledge, sense-organs and individual souls, (3) *yoga*, the discipline by which the individual comes to know God, (4) *vidhi*, rules or injunctions which lead to righteousness, and (5) *duḥkhānta*, the means for the cessation of misery and the attainment of final deliverance.

Its early precepts and observances included simple asceticism, a vow to give up greed and anger, to forgive, to repeat the syllable *Oṁ*, to practice meditation. Its aim was union with Śiva through meditation, mantras, and the cessation of all action, so that a state of pure feeling was attained. The Pāśupatas also employed song and dance, accompanied by loud exclamations and bull-like roars, to precipitate trance-like states.

These practices gradually degenerated, becoming more and more obscene, and the Pāśupatas and Lakulīśas acquired an evil reputation as sorcerers, perverts, drug-addicts, drunkards, left-hand occultists, murderers and even cannibals. In their rites they simulated the gestures of coition, besmeared the body with ashes from cremation grounds, ate the flesh of corpses, used human skulls as drinking bowls, practiced techniques involving the worship of the male member in its turgid state, of which the *lakula* or *daṇḍa* (club) became the symbol. The Lakulīśa images of Gujarāt show Śiva with an erect member. Strange to say, by the twelfth century the more enlightened members of the sect went in for educational activities and set up schools, but these were later found to be dens of vice and iniquity.

Books

See under Śaivism.

PĀṬALIPUTRA, the capital of ancient Magadha and once a stronghold of Magian sun-worship. In mythology the city was said to have been magically erected by the sage Kauṇḍinya at the request of Gādhī, sister of Viśvāmitra. It is believed to be the site where the *paṭa* or cloth covering the genitals of the goddess Satī* fell to earth. The name of modern Paṭṇa which is situated near Pāṭaliputra is derived from the same source. Earlier, the city had been known as Kusumadhvaja or Kusumapura, and later as Pushpapura.

It was originally a fortress founded by Ajātaśatru (*c.* 480 BC) in place of Rājagṛiha the earlier capital of Magadha*, and the site selected was at the confluence of the Ganges and the Son, although the latter river has now changed its course. During the time of Chandragupta Maurya it was a timber and brick city nine miles long, and its massive timber fortifications were pierced by sixty-four gates and crowned by five hundred and seventy towers. Its ramparts were surrounded by a moat nearly six hundred feet wide and more than thirty cubits deep. The royal Sugaṅgeya Palace was built partly of stone and partly of teak, with rich carvings, and ornamental designs in gold and silver. The magnificent pillared hall with its exquisite decorative work was an object of wonder to all people. Megasthenes, Greek envoy at Chandragupta's court, declared that the palace at 'Palibotra' was more splendid than the palaces of Susa and Ecbatana.

Aśoka, grandson of Chandragupta, was crowned at Pāṭaliputra. He built an outer wall around it, and added many remarkable monuments. In 247 BC the third great Buddhist Council was held there during Aśoka's reign. Pāṭaliputra lost its importance after Aśoka and its power declined for over five centuries, until once again it rose to brief prominence under the Guptas, after Chandragupta I married a Lichchhavi princess of Pāṭaliputra in AD 319.

About a century later the Chinese pilgrim Fa-hien visited Pāṭaliputra, but by this time it had been virtually abandoned. Wandering among the majestic ruins of the great city, now deserted and desolate, he gazed with awe upon the huge blocks of which the palaces were built, and declared that they could not possibly have been the work of mortal hands. Modern excavations on the old site, now waterlogged, indeed suggest a great city, well planned and marvellously constructed.

It is now indisputably established that the building of Pāṭaliputra owed much to the Persians. The resemblance between the palace of Chandragupta and the Achaemenian prototype was so marked that Dr Spooner called the Indian capital a 'conscious Mauryan copy of Persepolis'. The columns of the pillared hall suggest the hypostyle throne-room of Darius and Xerxes. Masons' marks found in the Mauryan palace are similar to those found in Behistun and other places in Iran, a proof that Persian architects and stone-workers were employed in the building and in the general supervision of the work. Sir John Marshall was led to the same conclusion by the strong Persepolitan influence in the Aśokan capital. The typical shining surfaces of Mauryan stonework were unknown in India before this time, and their sudden appearance in Indian architecture points conclusively to the fact that the technique was introduced by Persian stone-masons employed by Chandragupta, in imitation of Achaemenian masonry.

Books

See under Architecture and History.

PATAÑJALI (?200 BC–?AD 500), the name both of a grammarian as well as of the compiler of the earliest systematic treatise on Yoga, believed by some authorities to be one and the same person.

One Patañjali was the author of a work on prosody, and of the *Mahābhāshya* (Great Commentary) on the grammar of Pāṇini. He rejected a number of Pāṇini's sūtras (aphorisms) but defended Pāṇini against the criticisms of his annotator, Kātyāyana. Two fanciful legends account for his name. According to one he was an incarnation of the world serpent, Śesha, and received his name because he had descended (*pata*) in the shape of a small snake into the palm (*añjali*) of Pāṇini. Another account says that it was because he fell from the *añjali* (cavity) of his mother. Patañjali is also known as Gonardīya or Goṇikāputra, after his mother Goṇikā. The theory that Goṇikā is perhaps a variation of Goṇḍā, thus making his mother a member of the Goṇḍ tribe, has also been put forward.

Another Patañjali is the reputed 'founder' of Yoga* philosophy and the author of the *Yoga-sūtra*, the first systematic presentation of Yoga. It is now generally established that he was in fact the first to collate and codify the ancient beliefs and theories current among the indigenous non-Aryans of India. Most of what is known as the science of Yoga can be called an elaboration of one of his most famous verses which reads, 'Perfection proceeds from birth, drugs, spells, austerities, or concentration'. The *sūtras* of Patañjali are arranged in four books dealing with samādhi, yoga practice, psychic powers and *kaivalya* or liberation respectively. Although the first three books may belong to the second century AD, the fourth book has been assigned to the fifth century AD.

Books

I. Bhashyacharya, N. *The Age of Patanjali*, Adyar, 1889.
II. Dasgupta, S. N. *A Study of Patanjali*, Calcutta, 1920.
III. Kielhorn, F. *Katyayana & Patanjali*, Bombay, 1876.
IV. Kielhorn, F. (Ed.) *Vyakarana Mahabhashya of Patanjali*, 3 vols., Bombay, 1892.
V. Mitra, R. *Yoga Aphorisms of Patanjali*, Calcutta, 1883.
VI. Puri, B. N. *India in the Time of Patanjali*, Bombay, 1958.
VII. Stephen, D. R. *Patanjali for Western Readers*, London, 1919.

PAṬṬA, the generic name given to a primitive style of painting, once current in many parts of India. It was an ancient art related to an early funeral cult. The painting was done on a *paṭṭa* (or *paṭa*, *paṭi*, *pattra*, or *paṭṭikā*), which might be a leaf, a strip of cloth, a canvas scroll, a wooden board, stone tablet, or metal plaque.

On this material the *paṭuā* or artist would paint or engrave figures of gods and demons, *maṇḍalas*, and other magical symbols. Śaivites favoured liṅga or yoni designs, Vaishṇavites the figures of Vishṇu, Rāma or Kṛishṇa. A popular subject was a scene of punishment in the nether world, and these '*yama-paṭa*' (hell-paintings) were very colourful and at times of considerable artistic merit, exhibiting a wonderful mastery of the brush.

Such paṭṭa designs were generally carried by sādhus or itinerant showmen. When they reached a village, they announced their presence by beating their little drum, then unrolled and set up their paṭṭa scroll on a stand and gave an explanation of its contents to the village audience. A *darśan* or sight of the illustration, accompanied by appropriate *mantras* was believed to heal sickness and grant boons.

In Bengal there used to be a special class of painters called *jādu*-paṭuā (magic painters) or duāri-paṭuā. When someone died they came to the house of the bereaved with a prepared rough likeness of the head of the deceased, but with the iris of the eye still left unpainted. They told the relatives that the deceased was groping about blindly in the next world because of his unfinished eye. For a small fee the painter would perform the ceremony of *chakshu-dāna* (sight-bestowal) by intoning some mantras and painting in the iris, and thus giving sight to the deceased. The similarity of this ceremony to that of the 'Recovery of the Eye of Horus' at Egyptian funerary rites has been pointed out.

Books

I. Rai, M. N. *Two Essays on the Art of Funerary Painting in Ancient and Mediaeval Bengal,* Dacca, 1901.

II. Ray, S. K. *Prehistoric India and Ancient Egypt,* New Delhi, 1956.

PERCEPTION. The Sanskrit term for perception, *pratyaksha,* (*prati,* towards; *aksha,* eye) refers strictly, to the direct perception or knowledge that comes through the *indriya* or senses*. In its widest connotation it includes: (*a*) sense perception, or pratyaksha proper; (*b*) mental perception or the 'understanding' of the thing perceived; (*c*) self-awareness i.e. consciousness of pleasure and pain, and conscious self-awareness, called *aham̐-pratyaya;* (*d*) the perception of yogis and ṛishis, which includes paranormal cognition; and finally (*e*) divine perception or *īśvara-pratyaksha.*

Sense perception depends upon a kind of intercourse or *sannikarsha,* a dynamic communion between the sense organ and the object perceived. This intercourse is extremely tenuous and involved, and has been further refined to hair-split degrees by the Nyāya-Vaiśeshika schools of thought. It is said to include (1) *sam̐yoga,* 'unitedness', the union or contact, not necessarily physical, between sense-organ and object; (2) *samavāya,* 'inherence', the apprehension by the sense organ of the nature of the object; (3) united inherence; (4) inherent inherence; (5) united inherent inherence; and their various combinations, depending on the negation of these relationships, in order to define, for instance, the perception of the absence of sound inherent in a letter that might have been uttered had it manifested in sense-organ intercourse.

There are five stages in sense-perception, namely: (1) *darśana,* 'seeing', or the impact of the object on sense. It is simple apprehension, indistinct and indefinite; (2) *avagraha,* 'grasp' of the details of the object, e.g. white colour; a loud sound; (3) *īhā,* the 'desire' to know the particulars of the object e.g. whether the white object is a flag or a bird; (4) *avāya,* the discerning of the details e.g. ascertainment that the white colour is a heron. It involves a recognition that the object belongs to a definite class, and requires assimilation and discrimination; (5) *dhāraṇā,* 'retaining' of the impression of the perceived object, definitely ascertained.

The means by which the sense organ apprehends the object has been the subject of contention between the various schools of Hindu thought. The Sām̐khya school holds that the sense organs are *prāpyakāri,* i.e. they must be in contact with the object in order to apprehend it. Thus, the organ of touch is in actual contact with the object touched. So also with things smelled and tasted. But the Nyāya and Vaiśeshika schools hold that this does not apply to the eyes and ears, which are *aprāpyakāri,* i.e. they can apprehend their objects without coming into contact with them.

Nothing can be known without a knower, and a profounder knowledge of the knower, makes the known still better known. Self-knowledge is for this reason an important branch of Hindu psychology. This *ahaṁ-pratyaya*, 'I-notion', or self-knowledge, is analysed as an object of perception, and has been studied in its infinite diversity by every important school of Hindu, Buddhist and Jain philosophy. Among the elements of the conscious thought, 'I know the jar', there is a consciousness of 'knowing the jar', and also of the I' or 'self' knowing the jar. Now this self exists both as the *bimba*, 'orb', or pure essence in its original 'self' form, and also as the *prati-bimba*, 'reflection', the image of self as an object under analysis by the bimba. Practical methods of increasing this self-awareness and enlarging the horizon of self-knowledge, are covered by the field of Hindu meditative techniques.

A still higher form of perception is known as *yogi-pratyaksha*, after the yogi practitioners who develop their faculties in order to gain a clearer perception of reality. These supernormal degrees of perception are above the general laws of ordinary sense perception. They do not depend on the sense organs, and transcend categories of time, space and causality. Except for the Chārvākas* and other materialist schools, all systems of Hindu philosophy accept the possibility of such supernormal perception, although they differ in their accounts of it. Evidence of yogic pratyaksha is found in clairvoyance, clairaudience, hyperaesthesia of vision, hearing and touch, telepathy, and various siddhis* and feats performed or claimed by yogis.

Sometimes a distinction is made between the perception of yogis and that of the *ṛishis* (sages) of old. The latter, called *ārsha-jñāna*, 'ṛishi-knowledge', gave the ancient ṛishis a true intuitive cognition of the great cosmic laws of the universe, enabling them to see the past, present and future, and giving them power over all things. Yogic perception is achieved through meditation, while ṛishi knowledge is achieved through austerities, but actually both classes of men employed both methods. Paranormal cognition is by no means denied to ordinary men, and intuition, premonition and prevision may occasionally flash upon the humble householder, or he may be naturally endowed with siddhis (powers) such as yogis attain after decades of practice.

The highest form of perception is *īśvara-pratyaksha*, 'divine perception', or the knowledge that God has of the things in this world and all other worlds. The Hindus have ever speculated on the nature of God and on the attributes of divine knowledge, and have held that these attributes have to be grasped if one is to understand the mysteries of the universe. Part of the instantaneous 'glow' by which God knows all things (*see* psychology) may be verily reflected in man. Eusebius preserves a record of a visit of certain Indian philosophers to Athens, one of whom conversed with Socrates and asked him to explain the object of his philosophy. Socrates replied that his philosophy was an enquiry into human phenomena, and hearing this the Indian laughed exclaiming, 'How can you gain an understanding of human phenomena when you are ignorant of divine ones!'

Books

I. Bhat, V. M. *Yogic Powers and God Realisation*, Bombay, 1960.

II. Prasad, Jwala. *History of Indian Epistemology*, Delhi, 1956.

III. Thomas, F. W. 'An Indian Doctrine of Perception and Error,' *Aristotelean Society Proceedings*, 1921–22.

PERVERSIONS, or sexual expression in unusual ways, were a prominent feature of Hindu erotics, occultism and art. Deviations from normal practice were believed, apart from the physical satisfaction they might afford to some, to have a profound occult end in view. Even the milder aberrations like voyeurism and exhibitionism helped to excite the subtle centres of the body.

Erotic relations with members of the third sex (*see* androgyny), sadism in all its diversity, masochism (as in extreme asceticism), homosexuality, lesbianism, bestiality*, autoeroticism, necrophilia*, the employment of unnatural aids (olisboi*), *maukhya* (see below), and group union, are all manifestations of perverse sexuality, which at one time or another have in Hindu esoteric teachings, been attributed a spiritual significance. They are aspects of antinomianism thought to be favoured by the gods, and regarded as methods of achieving degrees of 'intensity', which not only reveal normally hidden layers of pleasure, but release a stream of vital power which if rendered to the service of the deity is returned multifold to the giver.

Sodomy, or *adhorata*, 'under-love', either between males or opposite sexes was one of the main expedients for utilizing the potencies of the rectal centre, whose animation was believed to energize the artistic, poetic and mystical faculties. Some medieval writers speak of it as quite common and do not regard it as perverse. The anus (*guda* or *pāyu*) is one of the most important chakras of the human body, and its significance is repeatedly emphasized in the tantrik texts. Concentration on the anus, the introduction of wooden plugs into the rectum during meditation, digital insertion in ano during sex-magic rites, constriction of the anal sphincter and stimulation of the region during the paramudrās as in the *aśvinī bandha**, are common yogic disciplines, based on the belief in the occult correspondence between the rectal annulus and certain higher centres of the subtle body. Śavavāda practice goes still further.

The various forms of eroticism termed maukhyā, 'oral', involve the mouth in lieu of or in addition to the sex organs. According to some of the lawgivers, oral intercourse was classed with the sin of killing a brāhmin and could not be expiated in less than one hundred incarnations, but certain Hindu writers on erotics have held that 'the mouth is pure for purposes of congress'. The commonest form known to Western sexologists as fellatio, requires the apposition of the mouth to the male organ. According to Vātsyāyana and his school, this type of intercourse prevails among the people of Lāṭa and Sindu, Sāketa and Śūrasena, and of the eastern provinces of India. Meyer, speaking of the women of Bengal says that they 'are known for beginning with their mouth the business of the vulva to excite a man's desire, owing to their excessive craving for the joys of love' (II, p. 242). This form frequently had 'specialist' practitioners, who were generally eunuchs, prostitutes or masseurs.

A great deal of sex magic is associated with the technique of oral congress, and many 'fiery' powers of great intensity are believed to be derived from its practice, particularly if done in conjunction with anal stimulation. The prototype of occult maukhya is traced to the legend which tells how Śiva's seed was received into the mouth of Agni, god of fire, then transferred to the womb of Pārvatī, thus giving birth to the great war-god Kārttikeya. Tantrik manuals cite between six to twelve stages in the procedure of maukhya. The first stages are concerned with the ritual ablution of the liṅga of the 'owner', erection by manual massage by the 'worshipper', invocation of the deity to take possession, homage by the 'worshipper'. Then comes the excitation by oral means till the conclusion is reached, followed by 'putting to bed' and the dismissal of the deity. At one of these stages the vital powers of the organ and of the activated seed are believed to become manifest and can be absorbed by a third party present during the rite. This is done by introducing the left-hand ring finger into the rectum of the 'worshipper' throughout the performance.

The second form of maukhya, known to Western sexologists as cunnilingus, requires the apposition of the mouth to the female pudendum, and was widely current among the inmates of harems (where women practised it mutually). A couple assuming opposite positions can mutually practice fellatio and cunnilingus, and the presence of a third party with finger in the female rectum completes a magical circle of great potency. The ways of absorbing the powers thus generated are seven in number and revealed only to initiates.

Vātsyāyana speaks of methods of group union in which a man may be engaged with two or more women at the same time, examples of which can be seen depicted on the walls of certain Hindu temples. In one instance a woman kisses the man's body while another has congress with him; with his two hands he manipulates the pudenda of two women and with his mouth that of a third. Coitus *in axilla* and coitus *inter mammae* were not unusual. Women of the legendary *strīrājya** or female kingdoms were said to have group congress with their own sex, and more rarely with men. Induced satyriasis in men and uteromania in women by drugs and diet preceded such rites. Such circles of sexualism were supposed to create whirlpools of occult energy from which the participants were able to draw power for themselves.

Lesbianism was very common in harems, where women employed manual or maukhya techniques. Often artificial phalluses were used to attain culmination, after which the phallus was withdrawn and sometimes worshipped. Kṛishṇa's more than sixteen thousand wives used to 'make little images' of him to ease their passion in this way. In the absence of younger men, harem women frequently had recourse to the services of the eunuch watchmen or aged guards who were posted outside the doors. The spark of old men when kindled was said to 'burn with a purplish flame', and was believed to give great beauty to women who came in contact with it and make them irresistible to men. Legends of gerontophilia (sexual attraction of the young for the aged) are not rare in Hindu mythology.

The weaknesses and preferences of the different peoples of India in love-making were frequently discussed in texts on erotics. A study of these, it is said, immediately reveals the nature of people, for they spring from deep-rooted national or regional tendencies which reflect the character of those who indulge them. Thus, the men of Sindhu (the region of the south Indus) are not regarded as sexually strong and the women cannot yield satisfaction without oral congress. The men of Lāṭa (Gujarāt), Saurāshṭra (Kāṭhiāwār) and Aparānta (north Indus) like to kiss erogenous zones like the thigh joints, navel and armpits, and the women enjoy shrieking and cooing and favour oral congress. The inhabitants of Kuru (Panjāb) prefer anal intercourse, are very vigorous but reach a quick culmination, and disappoint their women who are forced to seek satisfaction in other ways. The women of Mālwā (around Ujjain) and Ābhīra (Vindhyas) favour oral congress, and go in for sadism, but dislike nail or teeth marks. The inhabitants of Avanti (north of Narmadā) detest kissing but favour unusual postures. Those from Madhyadeśa are restrained and sexually weak and only attain culmination by anal means. The men and women of Pañchāla are experts in the art of unnatural love, and cannot attain satisfaction except by maukhya and anal means, and artificial aids. The women of Kosala (Uttar Pradesh) also like artificial aids to be used by their men who are not satisfactory lovers. The people of Gauḍa (Bihār) and Magadha (Bengal) indulge freely in maukhya. Those of Kaliṅga (South Orissa) practice perversions including bestiality and sodomy, but do not resort to olisboi. Those from Bhoja and Mahārāshṭra are passionate and enjoy a speedy and sudden union, even by manual means. The people of Āndhra are sexually weak but 'have a taste for impure things'. Long and excessive love-play is in vogue among the Drāviḍa, who employ artificial aids and favour adhorata.

Books

I. Datta, R. *Linga-bandha Practices*, 1911.
II. Meyer, J. J. *Sexual Life in Ancient India*, Vol. I, London, 1930.
III. Mukerji, R. S. *Secret Sex Rites*, p.p. 1903
IV. Upadhyaya, S. C. (Ed.) *Kamasutra of Vatsyayana*, Bombay, 1961.

PHILOLOGY. The study of language, its origin, structure and development and the principles governing its correct usage, was known in ancient India as *bhāshikā*, 'language', a term which in its original sense referred to the vernacular (non-Sanskrit) languages, but was later extended to cover the study of language in general and Sanskrit in particular.

According to Hindu tradition language originated in heaven, a gift bestowed by Brahmā first to the gods, then to the demons and finally to mankind. Its laws were laid down by ancient sages and its grammar and construction dictated by them to their disciples. Its most perfect form is Sanskrit.

In spite of its ancient history it would seem that it was not in India but in Babylonia that the earliest attempts had been made to resolve the problems of language (I, p. 6). Indian grammarians for all their linguistic speculations took no notice of any language save Sanskrit, and thus confined their study to a narrow field. Strict prohibitions were imposed by the lawgivers on the learning of any of the tongues of the lower castes, or of the *mlechchhas* (barbarians). The *Vishṇu Dharma-śāstras* say that after speaking to a barbarian or *chaṇḍāla* (outcaste) a man should clean his mouth by *āchamana* i.e. by ritually sipping and spitting out water.

Within this limitation, however, the study of philology was carried out with extraordinary perspicacity and precision. It formed an early part of those branches of post-Vedic scholarship known as the Vedāṅgas (*see* scriptures), of which four related specifically to *bhāshikā*, namely, *vyākaraṇa* or grammar, *nirukta* or etymology, *śikshā* or phonetics, and *chhandas* or metre. The significance of language in relation to religious ceremonial made the subject one of extreme importance, since this aspect of ritual was largely a matter of correct pronunciation, accentuation, metre, grammar and interpretation. In course of time a whole philosophy (Mīmāṁsā*) was evolved to clarify and set forth the rules for the correct study of the Vedic texts.

Books

I. Chakravarti, P. C. *The Linguistic Speculations of the Hindus*, Calcutta, 1933.
II. Gune, P. D. *An Introduction to Comparative Philology*, 2nd Ed., Poona, 1950.
See also under Grammar, Phonetics, Etymology, Prosody.

PHILOSOPHY in Hinduism is essentially an enquiry into Brahma. This is the orthodox view, or the view of those who accept Brahma and the Vedas and who posit that God 'is' (*asti*). These *āstikas* are to be distinguished from the *nāstikas* (see below) who deny God*, Brahma, the Vedas and much else. Most of the āstika systems are basically advaita*, 'non-dualistic' i.e. monistic, and repeatedly emphasize the identity of all things with Brahma.

The instruments of thought and the laws governing reasoning are a primary study, hence the importance of logic* and the need for mastering the syllogism*. Linked with this is the study of the origin, methods and validity of knowledge. The metaphysical categories* are considered in the course of the main enquiry, such as Cosmic Spirit (*Purusha**) and Cosmic Substance (*Prakṛiti*), including matter (*dravya*). Subsidiary enquiries cover the sphere of psychology*, the study of the soul* (*ātman*), the senses* (*indriya*), and the boundaries of man's perception*, his mental operations, techniques of meditation*, and the significance of the body*.

The concepts underlying time*, space, quality* (*guṇa*), and sound* are analyzed, as is the sphere of aesthetics*. Notions of *māyā** or illusion, *śūnya** or voidness, action (*karma**) and suffering* are treated, along with the ultimate release from suffering and the cycle (*saṁsāra*) of birth-death-rebirth, through one of the many paths (*mārga**), such as good conduct (ethics*), ritualism*, knowledge* and faith (bhakti*).

The history of Indian philosophy is sometimes said to start with the Indus Valley, and its form is said to derive from the Indus Valley religion as deduced from the evidence of the primitive seals and other artifacts. This religion seems to have centred around the worship of the Mother Goddess, of a Śiva prototype, and of animals, trees and stones. The postures of certain figures on the seals and of the statuettes, suggest yoga techniques, from which may be inferred some form of incipient Yoga philosophy. The hypothetical association of the Magas and Vrātyas with the Indus Valley people, favoured by some schools of thought, would further imply Mesopotamian or South Persian metaphysical influence, if indeed any such ever existed.

Vedic philosophy as presented in the Vedas has many facets. One, perhaps the earliest, is naturalistic and 'pagan', arising from a keen love of life unshackled by the trammels of metaphysical complexities, expressing its wonder in questions of simple puzzlement at the mysteries of the cosmos. A deeper approach is found in the Brāhmaṇas, a hieratic religious philosophy, with emphasis on ritual, dogma, and magical spells. A third and yet more fundamental approach is found in the Upanishads, where solutions are daringly attempted of many profound metaphysical problems.

Little is known of the independent philosophical schools that flourished between the later Vedic period and the rise of Buddhism. They are all lumped together as *nāstikas**, 'deniers', a term of odious connotation to the orthodox, since the nāstikas rejected the Vedas, denied the existence of Brahma, and declined to concede the claims of the brāhmin priesthood to higher knowledge or superior status. They were hard-headed materialists, sceptics, atheists and hedonists, who represented a heretical, protestant and rebellious movement in Hinduism, radically divergent from the main stream of Hindu speculation. There are a few fragmentary references to them in the writings of the orthodox scribes and in the Epics, but they are mentioned only to be condemned, and such of their doctrines as have been preserved are now regarded as grossly perverted. The history of this, perhaps the most interesting period in the whole history of Indian philosophy, has been lost through bigotry, indifference, and neglect.

The contribution of the Buddhists, and to a lesser degree the Jains, has been substantial. They were bred in the nāstika tradition but they had a nobler ethical ideal, developed a formidable armoury of metaphysical doctrine and a precise logical terminology. The highest flights of Indian speculative thought are found in Buddhism.

The greatest period of Hindu thought is contemporary with that of the finest Greek philosophy, and scholars are not wanting who have tried to prove that India owes much to Greece; some indeed have attempted to show that direct contact between the master-minds of Greece and India is indicated from a comparative study of the two systems. A legend preserved by Eusebius states that certain Indian philosophers visited Athens during the time of Socrates and conversed with the Sage. Their oriental paradoxes, it is recorded, did not impress the pioneer of clear thinking in philosophy.

Indian metaphysics intrigued the Greeks as a curiosity. When Alexander visited India a scholar of his entourage interviewed the gymnosophists and one of them, named Kalyāṇa*, accompanied Alexander to Susa where he voluntarily immolated himself on a pyre in the presence of the astonished Macedonians. In 20 BC a Buddhist monk Sarmanokhegas, a member of the Indian embassy sent to Augustus, also burnt himself to death at Athens before a mystified gathering of Greeks (*see* Romans). It is certain that these performances aroused not so much the admiration as the amazement of the rational Athenians who could only marvel that wise men should so wantonly esteem their mortality and employ so barbarous a means of self-extinguishment.

What the disciples of these immolated philosophers and other vagrant thinkers carried back to India of Greek wisdom is not recorded in Indian works. But we know from foreign sources that the fame of Greek philosophers, especially the itinerant teachers known as the Sophists, had reached India before the time of Aristotle, and persisted throughout the Mauryan age. We hear of Bindusāra writing a letter to Antiochus, son of Seleucus, asking for sweet wine and dried figs, and adding confidentially that for a real Greek philosopher 'he was willing to pay a high price'. To this request Antiochus replied, 'We shall send you the figs and wine, but in Greece the laws forbid a sophist to be sold'. No doubt a trifle like this could not deter the son of the great Chandragupta, and he must have procured his sophist anyway, for we recall a statement of Diodorus that one Iamboulos was sent to the king of Pāṭaliputra 'who had a great love for the Grecians'.

The precise nature of Greek influence on Hindu philosophy can only be a matter of conjecture at present, but that the influence prevailed and was felt in India and left its mark on Hindu thought is regarded by many scholars as beyond dispute. Ramaswami Aiyar with much justification opines, 'There is no doubt that some of the later philosophical developments of our people owe a great deal to Greek thought' (I, p. 15).

All philosophical concepts may be regarded as being conditioned by the 'sight' of the viewer or philosopher, i.e. his own personal qualifications, his point of view, and his insight. This accounts for his specific *darśana*, 'view' or doctrine. The āstikas or orthodox differ fundamentally from the nāstikas* or deniers. The latter recognize as many points of view as there are conscious beings, since each has his own *svabhāva** or uniqueness. Jains hold that there are no less than 353 points of view. Orthodox Hindus hold that only six are valid, and these form the bases of their six systems of metaphysical speculation.

The six āstika or orthodox systems of Hindu philosophy are known as the *shaḍ-darśana*, 'six views', all of which are traditionally said to be based on Vedic writings, particularly the Upanishads. All six aim at salvation, all believe in rebirth and pre-existence. In varying degrees they adhere to the rules of caste and accept the āśrama stages for caste Hindus. Their writings are set down in the *sūtra* or aphoristic style and they make use of a large body of common terms, often in varying senses. Some (Nyāya, Vaiśeshika, and probably Mīmāṁsa) were originally atheistic, but their later adherents made them theistic systems. These systems do not comprise a coherent philosophical whole, containing as they do, mutually inconsistent and exclusive notions, but it is held that they are different expressions of the same truth.

The chronological order of their evolution is uncertain, but they were formulated between the time of Buddha and Aśoka, that is some time between the sixth and third centuries BC. It is generally said that Sāṁkhya is the oldest, followed by Yoga, Mīmāṁsā, Vedānta, and then by Vaiśeshika and Nyāya. For convenience, and because it forms a logical scheme, the systems are arranged in the following order, usually in pairs: Nyāya*, founded by Gautama, and Vaiśeshika* founded by Kaṇāda; Sāṁkhya* by Kapila, and Yoga* by Patañjali*; Mīmāṁsā* by Jaimini and Vedānta* by Bādarāyaṇa.

Hindu philosophy ranks among man's earliest attempts to answer the riddle of the universe and solve the problems of human existence. But there are not a few scholars who believe that it was limited by its presuppositions and had expended itself by the third century BC, providing nothing fresh after that time. All subsequent speculation was confined to commentaries and dissertations on the Vedas and Upanishads in the light of the six systems, and represented, as it were, 'an endless threshing of old straw'. It was characterized by extreme scholasticism, elaboration, subtlety and systematization. Buddhist philosophy followed a like course. It soon found itself in the thickets of theorizing against which Buddha had expressly warned, and the finesse of its excogitations on the great negatives of *śūnya* and *nirvāṇa* furnished it with one of the most extraordinary systems of logic ever devised. Its subtleties provided a challenge to Hinduism, which sharpened its speculative weapons on the whetstone of Buddhist logic. For centuries the old antagonisms prevailed, wearing down the opponents but producing nothing fruitful and ending in an arid metaphysical region that is the despair of students. A brief chronological list of the greater Indian philosophers and their work from the beginning of the present era is given below.

The first great names after the founding of the six orthodox schools of Hindu philosophy are the two Buddhist metaphysicians, Aśvaghosha and Nāgārjuna. Aśvaghosha* (*c.* AD 120) expounded such concepts as the three bodies of Buddha, the Bodhisattva, the Ālaya-consciousness, and Salvation by faith. Nāgārjuna* (*c.* AD 150), founder of the Mādhyamika school of Mahāyāna, expressed the view that the one thing of which anything can be posited is *śūnyatā*, 'emptiness', which he raised to the position of a philosophical category. For more than three hundred years after these philosophers, a host of minor Buddhist writers were engaged in refining the concepts adumbrated by them.

The fifth century saw the four major commentaries on the orthodox Hindu systems. Vātsyāyana (AD 400) of South India, referred to as the Indian Plato, wrote the classic commentary on Gautama's work on Nyāya*. He made the syllogism the centre of logic and reduced the members of Gautama's syllogism to five, making the process less cumbersome. Praśastapāda (*c.* AD 430) wrote the best-known dissertation on Kaṇāda, with much original observation. Śābara (*c.* 450) is similarly renowned for his outstanding *bhāshya* or commentary on the *Mīmāṁsā-sūtra*. The classic *kārikā* (explanation) on the Sāṁkhya system by Īśvarakṛishṇa (*c.* 450) has been described as 'the pearl of the whole scholastic literature of India'.

The Buddhist Asaṅga* (*c.* 500) was responsible for the introduction of Tantrik concepts into Mahāyāna through his Yogāchāra system. His brother Vasubandhu founded the Vijñānavāda school, teaching how knowledge is transformed into Enlightenment. Diṅnāga (AD 530) (or Dignāga) Buddhist logician of Kāñchi, was a disciple of Vasubandhu and founder of the Svatantra-yogāchāra school and the system of medieval Indian logic which was strongly opposed to the views of Vātsyāyana. His most important treatise is lost in its original Sanskrit form and only its first chapter has been reconstructed from a Tibetan version of the work. Uddyotakara (*c.* 620) defended Vātsyāyana against the strictures of Diṅnāga, demonstrating that his method was in every way the only sure means of attaining to the truth. Dharmakīrti (*c.* 650) Buddhist logician fiercely attacked Mīmāṁsā and Nyāya. He took up the cause of Diṅnāga whose work he elaborated and explained. His works are chiefly studied in Tibet. Prabhākara (*c.* 680) wrote another commentary on Mīmāṁsā, explaining its value and condemning its detractors.

Kumārila* (*c.* 730) also wrote a famous commentary on Mīmāṁsā which was provoked by Dharmakīrti's attack on it. Both Prabhākara and Kumārila were founders of two mutually antagonistic schools. Bhāvaviveka (*c.* 770), drawing his inspiration from Diṅnāga founded a new school of Buddhist metaphysics. The Buddhist logician Dharmottara (*c.* 810) wrote a commentary on Dharmakīrti reconciling all these confusions in favour of the Buddhist point of view.

The orthodox reaction against this series of attacks by the Buddhists was once more taken up by Gauḍapāda* (*c.* 725) who started the trend of strict an unequivocal monism. He passed on his legacy to his pupil Govindapāda (fl. 800) who was himself the teacher of one of the greatest of Hindu philosophers, namely, Śaṅkara* (788–838). The latter was an uncompromising monist who took much from the Buddhists, and perhaps from the Muslims, to formulate a rigidly advaita doctrine. One of Śaṅkara's disciples was Maṇḍana (fl. 820) who had once been Śaṅkara's opponent but became his follower after being defeated in debate by him. Ānandagiri (920) in a biography of Śaṅkara called *Śaṅkaradigvijaya* or Śaṅkara's Victory details the doctrines of his master and the victorious controversies in which he was engaged.

Vasugupta* (770–830) of Kashmīr founded a system of philosophy known as Kashmīr Śaivism which had a prolific commentarial history, starting with the work of his pupil, Kallaṭabhaṭṭa (850–900) whose *Spanda-sūtra* is one of the classics of that school. Another famous teacher of the Kashmīr Śaivite school was Somānanda (860–925) whose pupil Utpala (900–950) wrote a classic treatise on Pratyabhijñā, or the 'recognition' of the identity of the individual with the Absolute.

In the meantime commentaries on the orthodox systems continued to pour forth. Vāchaspati (880) or Vāchaspati Miśra, versatile and prolific writer, wrote a commentary on Uddyotakara and works on Sāṁkhya, Yoga and Mīmāṁsā. He is the founder of one of the important Advaita schools, named after the work he wrote, the Bhāmatī. Vyomaśiva (880) wrote a commentary on Kaṇāda's system of Vaiśeshika. A century later Udayana (984) wrote an exposition on Vāchaspati and Kaṇāda. He was followed by Śrīdhara (991) and Śrīvatśa (*c.* 1100) also known as Vallabhāchārya (not to be confused with the Vedāntin Vallabha) both of whom also wrote on Kaṇāda. The finest of all 'condensations' on the Sāṁkhya system was made by Vijñānabhikshu (1550) who also wrote a treatise on the 'essence' of Yoga.

The philosopher Bhāskara (960) in his commentary on the *Brahma-sūtra*, introduced into Hinduism the first scholastic defence of *bhedābheda*, 'different non-difference', and *viśishṭādvaita*, or qualified non-dualism, holding that although Brahma as Being and Cause is one, his manifested state is multiplicity. He influenced Yādavaprakāśa (*c.* 1020) who also made a distinction between the one and unified Brahma or Absolute Being, and the First Manifestation, Īśvara, who is the Creator. Similarly the Āḻvār* theologian Yāmunāchārya (1040) drew distinctions between the omnipotent and omniscient Īśvara, the self-conscious soul, and the material world. All these threads were united in the philosophical fabric of a pupil of Yādavaprakāśa, the great Vaishṇavite* scholar Rāmānuja* (1017–1137) who was said to have 'brought the soul back to Indian philosophy'. The logical end of this tendency is found in the work of Madhva* (1197–1280) a Vaishṇavite philosopher who wrote the greatest of all expositions on the dualistic concept of God and man.

The last phase of Hindu philosophy is associated with the Nyāya school. It starts with the work of Śrīharsha (fl. 1180), grammarian, poet (he was the author of a kāvya*) logician, and sceptical Vedāntic philosopher of Bengal. He declared invalid the old Nyāya method of dealing with knowledge of the external world, since it cannot be proved whether a thing exists or not. 'Every postulate is absurd. I have no postulate to propound, since that also could be refuted. I have a private view of Brahma, the Universe and the soul, but they cannot be of interest to anyone else.'

Greatly inspired by Śrīharsha's criticism of Nyāya was the young Gaṅgeśa (*c.* 1200) who founded the Navya-nyāya (New Nyāya) school of Mithilā in Bihār. Gaṅgeśa's son Vardhamāna (1225) carried on the teachings of the New Nyāya school, which proceeded on an even course for two hundred years. In the fifteenth century the leader of the Mithilā school of Gaṅgeśa was Pakshadhara (1400–1495). He is now chiefly remembered as the teacher of the renowned Sārvabhauma* (1450–1530) who established the Navadvīpa (Nadia) school and who numbered among his pupils the Vaishṇava saint Chaitanya*, and Raghunātha (1477–1547) the greatest of all authorities on Navya-nyāya. The philosopher Annaṁbhaṭṭa (*c.* 1650) in his *Tarka-saṁgraha* expounded a synthesis of the old and new Nyāya schools.

Books

I. Aiyar, C. P. R. *Phases of Religion and Culture*, Bombay, 1949.
II. Barua, B. M. *A History of Pre-Buddhist Indian Philosophy*, Calcutta, 1921.
III. Bernard, T. *Hindu Philosophy*, London, 1947.
IV. Dasgupta, S. N. *A History of Indian Philosophy*, 4 vols., Cambridge, 1922–55.
V. Edgerton, Franklin. *The Beginnings of Indian Philosophy*, London, 1965.
VI. Friedman, David. 'Aspects of Indian Epistemology, Logic and Ontology', *Philosophia Reformata*, Vol. 20, 1955, The Hague
VII. Garbe, R. *Philosophy of Ancient India*, Chicago, 1897.
VIII. Hiriyanna, M. *Outlines of Indian Philosophy*, London, 1956.
IX. Müller, F. M. *The Six Systems of Indian Philosophy*, London, 1899.
X. Pandya, M. C. *Intelligent Man's Guide to Indian Philosophy*, 1935.
XI. Radhakrishnan, S. *Indian Philosophy*, 2 vols., London, 1948.
XII. Renou, Louis (*et al.*) *L'Inde Classique*, Paris, 1947, 1953.
XIII. Sharma, C. *A Critical Survey of Indian Philosophy*, London, 1960.
XIV. Sinha, Jadunath. *A History of Indian Philosophy*, Calcutta, 1956.
XV. Zimmer, H. R. *Philosophies of India*, London, 1951.

PHOENICIANS. It was inevitable that the greatest traders of antiquity, the Phoenicians, who sold their merchandise as far afield as Ancient Britain, should send their biremes to the thriving ports of India. According to Strabo the Phoenicians for centuries controlled the trade with India via the Persian Gulf, whose shores were once dotted with Phoenician trading posts and temples, of which relics are still extant in the Bahrain Islands.

The *Ṛig-Veda* mentions the Paṇi, a people who stole the cows of the gods and were tracked down by Indra's dog*, Saramā. They are described as malevolent guardians of treasures, unbelievers, hard bargainers, stingy with their money and possessions. The Paṇi are sometimes identified with the Parnians, Dahae, and other Iranian tribes, but more frequently with a non-Aryan trading people from beyond Babylonia.

If the identification of the Phoenicians with the Paṇi be accepted, then we must believe that they did not confine their activities to the Indian ports, but even ventured inland. The Phoenicians continued trade relations with India until well into the Greek period, followed Alexander to the Indus, established themselves in all important centres of commerce, and even founded a small Tyre in India itself.

Again, and because so many of the traces of these ancient associations have been obliterated, it is difficult to estimate the exact scale of their influence in India. But it is not improbable that ancient India owed to the Phoenicians certain elements of her script, perhaps also her calendar, her system of weights and measures, and some of the Purāṇic legends.

Books

I. Rawlinson, H. G. *Intercourse Between India and the Western World*, Cambridge, 1916.
II. Tarn, W. W. *The Greeks in Bactria and India*, London, 1938.
III. Visvanatha, S. V. *Racial Synthesis in Hindu Culture*, London, 1928.

PHONETICS, The branch of *bhāshikā* or language study concerned with pronunciation and phonetics is known as *śikshā*, 'instruction'. It is regarded as one of the principal components of Sanskrit philological* enquiry and plays a vital part in the ceremonial aspect of the Hindu religion. There are strict injunctions against the misuse of words, the employment of corrupt words, and above all the mispronunciation of words. A priest was obliged to perform an expiatory rite called *sarasvatī* if he pronounced a word wrongly, especially during a sacrifice.

It was believed that even a minute error in pronunciation could transform an ordinary verse into an *abhichāra*, a spell or enchantment. The *asuras* (aborigines) who tried to imitate the brāhmins in performing sacrifices often mispronounced words and misplaced accents. For example, in one ceremony undertaken to gain victory over the gods, they pronounced '*arayaḥ*' like '*helaya*', and so failed to obtain the benefit of the sacrifice and suffered defeat.

Another legend states that a brāhmin while petitioning the gods for the gift of immortality, accidentally stressed the wrong word and was condemned to eternal sleep. Yet another legend, in the *Śatapatha Brāhmaṇa*, tells how a demon while uttering a curse against Indra, instead of saying Indraśatru, 'enemy of Indra', with accent on śatru, laid the stress on Indra, meaning, 'who has Indra for an enemy', and was struck dead. Manu Vaivasvata mispronounced a formula and got a daughter instead of a son.

There were several important collections of phonetic rules known as *prātiśākhya*, which were peculiar to each of the *śākhās** (schools) of the Vedas.

Books
I. Allen, W. S. *Phonetics in Ancient India*, London, 1953.
II. Chakravarti, P. C. *The Linguistic Speculations of the Hindus*, Calcutta, 1933.

PHYSICAL CULTURE is one of the primary requirements of Hindu esoteric practice. One of the mārga* or 'paths' to ultimate realization is known as *dehavāda*, 'body-way', a means of salvation through *kāya-sādhana*, 'physical culture', which implies an intimate understanding of the body, its properties and processes, including its occult affinities. It is the basis of *haṭha-yoga*, and is found in most other magical cults like those of the *nāthas*, *siddhas*, *kāpālikas* and various tantrik sects.

The prime object of kāya-sādhana varies from cult to cult. In yoga its purpose is the control of the bodily apparatus, so that it does not interfere with the practitioner, and leaves his mind free from physical distractions during meditation. In a number of tantrik* cults kāya-sādhana is a means of giving the body strength and stamina to make it fit for the strains of tantrik sexual practices. In various forms of ascetic sādhuism its purpose is the subjugation of the body by penance and brahmacharya (celibacy) to bring about a concentration of psychic power for specific magical purposes, such as the attainment of siddhis* and control over demons and elemental powers. In the nātha cult its purpose is to make the body perfect and immutable, and thereby attain immortality.

A number of techniques are brought into operation in kāya-sādhana, some of which seem to have been introduced as a result of Chinese Taoist influence. They include certain interior exercises performed as in haṭha-yoga while in passive āsana* postures, combined with a rigid diet and long periods of fasting. Rhythmical and controlled breathing (*prāṇayāma*), the use of drugs and the bodily quintessences, especially of the *bindu**, are associated with tantrik rites.

The nāthas claim to have a process where, by combining some of these methods with certain other secret techniques, they cause the natural bodily functions to cease, and while in this state of suspended animation, allow the cells and tissues of any diseased or aging organ of the body to disintegrate. Then by the technique of 'reverberation' (*pratigarjana*) they set up molecular vibrations in the organism that cause the old tissues to fall away or pass out of the system, and then by another process of 'restoration' (*pratyarpaṇa*) replace them with new tissues specially purified and vitalized by means of heliotherapeutic meditation, e.g. by adoration of the sun. They are thus said to change the composition and quality of the bodily elements so that they require less and less nourishment derived from food, and subsist more and more on pure, extra-physical and occult nourishment.

Such a body, refined, purified and transfigured, is free from pain and decay; it is in effect incorruptible and deathless. According to popular tradition siddhas several centuries old are believed to exist in certain Himālayan solitudes, guiding the destinies of mankind. But they know the imperfections of the flesh and the need for final release, and do not desire to live forever, although that is within their powers. They choose a suitable time to die, and at the chosen moment depart from the earthly sphere in a celestial form, leaving behind a mere diaphanous shell that is soon dispersed by the wind.

Books

See under Tantrism and Yoga.

PHYSICIAN. The profession of physician in ancient India was one of notoriety, as befitting the operations of a wizard or witch-doctor, since medicine was at that time regarded as a handmaid of sorcery. The physician was a man of power, a *bhishaj* or 'healer', possessed of magical skill. He generally belonged to one of the mixed castes. The term *ambashṭha* applied to a practitioner of the curative arts, was also used for a person of mixed caste with brāhmin antecedents on his father's side and one of the low castes on the mother's side. Similarly the term *vaidya*, 'having knowledge', denoted a physician, and also a person of mixed caste.

The *Atharva-veda* preserves a rich tradition of 'native' Indian lore, dating from before the arrival of the Aryans on the scene. For many centuries medicine was associated with aboriginal tribal doctors who were said to have the power of restoring the dead to life. The Maga* peoples of early Indian history were always associated with such occult vocations as that of healer and astrologer. Hence the physician was also known as *chikitsaka*, or one acquainted with the 'lore'. Because of constant contact with the sick and diseased, and, in the case of surgeons*, with cadavers, the profession continued, till the beginning of the present century, to be held in abhorrence. The vaidya was unclean and in some cases almost untouchable, and after his visit the things he had touched were washed or where possible, thrown away.

A poet of the *Ṛig-Veda* says in an oft-quoted verse, 'Many are the ways of men; the craftsman after his job; the priest after his flock; the physician after the sick. I myself am a poet; my father is a leech'. Another verse in the *Ṛig-Veda* states,

'A poet who is a poet, physician and apothecary in one person travels around the country carrying with him a wooden box full of all sorts of healing herbs, and practicing his profession, not without humour, and with a frankness that deserves recognition. He does not hide the fact that it is not philanthropy that motivates his practice, but that his main inspiration is gain'.

In the early centuries of the present era, when Greeks and Persians, Bactrians and Scythians, were making their contribution to the Indian tradition, the doors to the practice of medicine were open to the lower castes and persons of foreign origin, and Suśruta (fourth century AD) admits that 'a śūdra of good family' could also be accepted as a pupil by a medical practitioner.

Charaka (second century AD) and Suśruta between them cover the main aspects of the physician's life, starting from the student leech. The choice of a proper textbook is stressed in most of the manuals (*see* handicrafts), but more important still is the right preceptor to teach one. The good guru is a man clear of all doubts about his subject; clever in his line compassionate to his patients; pure in mind and outlook; possessing all the instruments of his craft; conversant with the nature of diseases, their causes and cures. He is without malice, free from wrath, able to bear privation, and capable of imparting knowledge.

The guru for his part is to select his pupils with care. They are not to be much below or above sixteen years of age; and instruction should not last less than six years before the pupil is allowed to attend to patients without supervision. 'His eyes, mouth and nasal line should be straight; his tongue thin, red and unfurred; he must not have defective teeth, lips or limbs, nor possess a nasal voice.' He is to be from a family whose members have followed the medical profession. He should not be addicted to hunting, gambling, dieting, sleeping during the daytime, scandal-mongering, womanizing, singing, dancing, music. In disposition and character he must be equable, noble, magnanimous, free from pride, arrogance and wrath. He should be pure in behaviour, free from cupidity and laziness, possessed of a good memory, with a power of judging human nature, liberal-minded, and understanding. He must be fond of study, disposed for solitude and keeping his own counsel; clean in his habits, and patient with all.

As with other crafts, instruction was inaugurated by a consecration ceremony, during which the preceptor gave the pupil a charge and code of conduct, the exemplar of which is found in Charaka's work, and which has often been compared with the Hippocratic Oath. The pupil is enjoined to put aside lust, anger, avarice, greed, envy, egotism, rudeness, deception, sloth and immorality. He should be ritually clean, have his hair and nails cut short and clothe himself in an orange-coloured garment. He is never to entertain evil thoughts regarding the wives or daughters of his patients, nor have covetous desires regarding their goods and possessions. He is never to gossip outside about the affairs of the household into which he has been admitted as a doctor. Nothing should be said to shock the patient or his near ones, such as will cause them to despair of his life, or make him anticipate a long life of pain. He must give free treatment to brāhmins, ascetics, and devotees, but should not treat hunters, fowlers, outcastes and sinners (I, p. 32). He should avoid boasting and learn always to be humble. 'Remember', adds the guru, 'that there is no end to knowledge', and he proceeds, 'If you desire to be a successful physician, earn wealth, acquire celebrity, and win heaven hereafter, you should ever strive, whether standing or sitting, for the good of all creatures, and endeavour with your whole heart to bring about the cure of those who are ill'.

It is essential for the physician to find out whether the disease he is called upon to cure, is curable or not. Only if the disease is curable and the patient can afford the cost of treatment should the cure be undertaken (II, p. 210). Charaka is the first to warn against the treatment of incurable cases or accepting a patient for whom the signs are *ariṣhta* or unpropitious, for by taking on such a case the practitioner will only incur loss of prestige and universal censure.

The wise physician accepts a case only when the signs are propitious, and he ought therefore to be on the lookout for favourable signs, starting from the moment when the messenger comes from the patient's house and requests his attendance. It is advisable to note the hour, day and month, the lunar asterism, and make an astrological reckoning; also observe the clothing, speech, caste, sex, mental state (excitement, fright, despair) and manner of approach (running, walking, riding) of the messenger. The things seen and heard on the way to the patient's house, such as the flight of birds and the behaviour of animals, are all to be read as omens even before the physician steps across the patient's threshold. For example, it would be inauspicious if during the lunar asterism of Ārdrā the messenger were a brāhmin, a eunuch, or a woman; or if he or she came at midday or midnight, running, or riding on a buffalo, and if the physican himself were at that time asleep unclothed. Birds whose names have masculine terminations are auspicious if seen on the left of the physician flying in a south-easterly direction. Another catalogue of omens is noted during diagnosis, and thereafter throughout the course of the treatment.

After initiation the pupil shared for many years the life of his guru, becoming a member of the household, serving him and watching and assisting him at work. He helped in preparing the medicaments, became acquainted with the tools and procedures of the calling. The assistant of the physician had to be a man of excellent character. He was expected to keep the household secrets to himself, carry out the doctor's orders, work industriously and 'never be tired'. Female attendants are not mentioned, and women patients were presumably attended by female relations and not by professionals.

There is no mention of hospitals in the early texts, which probably came into existence with Aśoka (274–236 BC).

On the completion of his apprenticeship the student received a recommendation from his guru, on the strength of which the local ruler gave him permission to practise medicine. Control was very lax and there were large numbers of quacks and illiterate *vaids* who operated on the basis of a few *ślokas,* and were called by Charaka 'cheats who wander about the streets boasting in the garb of a physician'. They used all the devices known to the huckster of today, 'like nets to ensnare birds', to get the patient started on a miracle cure. Such quacks, says Suśruta deserve to be killed by the king (II, p. lii). Quacks were, and continue to be, the bane of the medical profession in India.

The height of a vaid's ambition was to be appointed royal physician. His main duty in peace time was to supervise the royal kitchen to ensure that the king was not poisoned, but during war he occupied a tent next to the king's and attended to the sovereign, the royal princes and generals.

Books

I. Jolly, J. *Hindu Medicine,* Poona, 1951.
II. Kutumbiah, P. *Ancient Indian Medicine,* Madras, 1962.

PILGRIMAGE. Visiting holy places is one of the main religious duties of the Hindu. This *yātrā,* 'going', is enjoined as a sacred commission upon all devotees desirous of pleasing the deity, accumulating religious merit, and securing bliss hereafter. The place of pilgrimage is called the *tīrtha,* which means a bathing place or a ford across a stream, and by extension, a cross-point, an *axis mundi* or sacred spot, which in itself is worthy of reverence.

There are thousands of holy places in India, to which a pilgrimage may be undertaken. Some are of special sanctity for Śaivites, and some for Vaishṇavites, or other sects, but a Hindu need not confine himself to a sectarian shrine for purposes of pilgrimage, and if a shrine devoted to another deity, or even a Muslim saint, falls on the way, he may offer homage to it without compunction.

Śaivite tīrthas are the sites where the great liṅgas* are enshrined. Śāktas proceed to the centres where fragments of Sati's* body were believed to have fallen to earth. Vaishṇavites go to places associated with Vishṇu, Kṛishṇa and Rāma. The tīrthas also include the seven holy cities of Ayodhyā, Mathurā, Gaya, Banāras, Ujjain, Hardwār, Dvārakā; the seven sacred rivers*, namely, Ganges, Jamnā, Sarasvatī, Godāverī, Narmadā, Indus, and Kāverī; sacred hills and mountains* such as Kailāsa, Pārasnāth, Girnār, Mount Ābū, Palni, and others; also holy lakes (*sarovara*) like the Bindu lake in Siddhapur (for *śrāddha** rites), the Pampā in the Karṇāṭak, the Nārāyaṇa lake in Cutch, the Mānasarovara at the foot of Mount Kailāsa, the Pushkar lake near Ajmere, sacred to Brahmā*.

Many ancient legends are connected with each tīrtha of importance telling of the gods and saints who sanctified the area or worked miracles there and who still manifest their powers in the locality. These legends are published in popular religious guidebooks known as *māhātmya*, 'region of majesty', many of the best being drawn from Purāṇic writings (*see* literary forms).

There are special hierophants who, for a fee, will assist the pilgrim at the important tīrthas. The pilgrim generally takes a purifying bath in the sacred river or lake, worships the idol or liṅga, makes a contribution towards the feeding of brāhmins or gives them presents. An important part of all pilgrimage is the rite of *pradakshiṇa* (or parikramā), i.e. circumambulation, in which the worshipper walks several times around the idol or temple in a deasil direction, i.e. with the sacred object on his right (*see* wheel). Temples, stūpas and shrines usually have special ambulatory passages called *pradakshiṇa-patha*, 'processional paths', reserved for this purpose. In some cases the pradakshiṇas may take the pilgrim many miles, as when he is circumambulating a sacred hill, river, or city. In making the Banāras pilgrimage the path is thirty-six miles in circumference around the city and its environs, and with its 'stations' it takes six days to complete. Sometimes the pradakshiṇa is still longer, as in the circumambulation of the Ganges. Thus one may start from the source of the Ganges at Gaṅgotri in the Himālayas, walk along the left bank of the river to its mouth at Sāgar or Gaṅgāsāgara on the Bay of Bengal, and then turn back and proceed up the right bank to the source. This pilgrimage may take up to six years to complete. Lesser rivers require one or two years. The merit of a pilgrimage is enhanced if the pilgrim adds difficulties to his progress, for example, if he performs the journey by hopping on one foot, or crawling, or going on his knees; or by measuring his length on the ground, i.e. lying flat, arising and walking only up to a distance equal to the length of his body, then measuring his length again, and so on. Those who die on a pilgrimage are assured a place in heaven. Today the time spent on pilgrimage has been considerably shortened by pilgrims having recourse to railway facilities, or other modern conveyances.

Books

See under Hinduism.

PIŚĀCHA, a race of people classed in the Vedas as lower than the *rākshasas* (ogres), and amongst the most vile and noxious of beings. They are described as fiends and goblins, inhabiting cemeteries, devouring corpses and causing malignant diseases. There is much uncertainty about their origin. According to the Brāhmaṇas, they were created by Brahmā together with the asuras and rākshasas from the stray drops that fell off during the creation of the gods, gandharvas and men. According to Manu they sprang from the Prajāpatis. In the Purāṇas they are the offspring of the archṛishi Kaśyapa by the hag *Krodhavaśā*. Krodhavaśā is also known as Piśāchā or Kapiśā, and her offspring the Piśācha are also called the Kāpiśeya.

Although once held to be non-Aryan aboriginals, and usually assigned a home in the Vindhya regions, they are now believed to have been of Mongolian affinity. The *Mahābhārata* refers to the northwest as their home; they are thought to have belonged to the region immediately south of the Hindu Kush and may have been Scythians. They are described as 'reddish in appearance', and as formidable opponents in war. The *Ṛig-Veda* records a prayer to Indra against them in battle.

Their language, Paiśāchi, acquired fame through Guṇāḍhya's tale, *Bṛihat-kathā*, and their piśācha form of marriage* was recognized in the later Aryan social system. Their skill in surgery was such that this science was referred to in the *Gopatha Brāhmaṇa* as the *Piśācha Veda*.

Books

See under Mythology.

PLANTS. The generic Sanskrit term for the entire plant world is *sthāvara*, 'stationary', so named by Charaka (*c*. AD 150). All herbs, plants and trees are believed to be 'fathered by heaven, mothered by earth, with roots in the primeval cosmic ocean'.

Many classifications of the plant world are found in Sanskrit writings, but the generally accepted one is taken from āyurveda, where again no consistent scheme is followed. The term *vṛiksha* was applied to trees in general, but more specifically to large trees, bearing conspicuous flowers and fruit; *vanaspati*, 'forest-lord' was the name given to certain select plants such as the *soma*; later it was applied to small fruit-bearing trees, apparently without flowers. Small trees bearing both fruit and flowers were called *vānaspatya*. The *vīrūdh* was the low shrub or herb. Herbs that had healing properties and could be used as medicine were called *oshadhī*. Creeping plants were *latā* (or *vallī*), while tubers, rhizomes, corms and bulbs, such as onions, were *kanda-śāka*, 'root-vegetables'. Lastly there were the *yavasa* or 'grasses'*.

Multifold are the blessings of the plant world. It offers shade to the way-farer, and a resting place to birds; provides fire for the sacrifices and fuel for domestic use; fruit for the hungry and perfume for the air. Trees are the natural shelter of sages, and under their peaceful and inspiring influence seekers after truth have received enlightenment: Pārśva under the *dhataki*; Mahāvīra under the *śāla*; Buddha under the *aśvattha*.

Trees provide a natural link between the chthonian world and earth, and between earth and heaven. Offerings to the gods are sometimes hung on trees to 'raise' the gift and also to receive from the trees the blessing of fertility and abundance. In ancient offerings to Rudra and other deities the sacrificial cakes were often hung on a tree.

The curative virtues of plants were known to the Indians from earliest times, and their medicinal properties were praised in numerous hymns. 'The plant which the boar knows, giving it vigour; the herb the mongoose knows, preserving it from poison; the plant the snake knows, giving it wisdom; the shrub the gandharva knows, giving him love and joy; the plant known to the birds and bees and all winged things, all these do I call to my aid.'

The practical uses of the plant world are infinite. Its flowers please the deities; its leaves give nourishment to animals; from its berries are fashioned the rosaries of the devout; its fruit and flowers provide essences and syrups; its grasses the pasture for cattle. The bitter and astringent *nīm* (margosa) twigs are used for brushing the teeth; the *meṁdī* or myrtle (*Lawsonia alba*) yields the henna dye which is used for staining the palms of the hands and soles of the feet; the *pippalī* or long pepper (*Solanum indicum*) said to have been first planted on earth by the asuras, is believed to have special tonic properties, and a course of long-peppers taken as a diet is a popular cure-all; the *palāṇḍu* or onion and the *laśuna*, garlic, are employed both for food and for medicinal purposes, and also for their aphrodisiac effect, for which latter reason they are forbidden to celibates and brāhmins. These and many others, from the *betel** vine to the *coconut**, are of great utility to mankind.

Among the grains, first place is given to *rice* (Sanskrit, *vrīhi*), which was cultivated by the Austrics, and continues to be the staple diet of most Indian peoples to this day. The Hindi word for rice, *chāwal*, is directly derived from the aboriginal Kol root, *jom*, 'eat'. Rice is not mentioned in the *Ṛig-Veda*, but by Suśruta's time (fourth century AD), thirty-nine varieties of rice were cultivated. From the Tamil word *arisi*, came the Greek *oryza*, whence the English *rice*. In Hindu rituals rice is a symbol of fertility, and grains of rice represented the sperm which makes women fruitful (III, p. 334).

Certain grains were introduced to India from outside, of which the most important seems to have been wheat. Wheat, in Sanskrit *godhūma*, from the Persian *gandam*, is not mentioned in the *Ṛig-Veda* either (VIII, p. 56), and some of the old texts refer to wheat as the food of the *mlechchhas*, i.e. foreigners. It was not considered 'pure' for religious rites until very late, and then only by a few lawgivers. Rice, barley, and sesamum are offered to the manes, but never wheat. Similarly *sorghum*, or Indian millet (Sanskrit, *jūrṇa*) is first mentioned in the medical works of Charaka (*c.* AD 150). It is also called *yāvanāla*, which suggests its introduction by the Greeks. Most of the other lentils, pulses and vetches are indigenous to the country, but one variety of chickpea (Sanskrit, *ālisaṇḍaga*; Hindi, channa) was introduced after Alexander's invasion and may have been named after him.

Among the fruits miraculous powers were ascribed to the *āmalaka*, the acid fruit of several species of the myrobalan plant growing in the mountains, of which the best known varieties are the *Phyllanthus Emblica*, and the *harītaka*, or yellow myrobalan (*Terminalia Chebula*). It was believed that those who ate the fruit in accordance with certain prescribed rites would be visited by the goddess Śrī. It played an important part in the āyurvedic *materia medica*, and figured prominently in alchemy, elixir-making, and the preparation of aphrodisiacs. A beverage made of the pulp and juice of the āmalaka reputedly enabled ṛishis to get back their youth, and live for many centuries free from disease, enjoying great strength of body and mind.

Of the roots, *turmeric* (*haridrā*) was the most important. It was known to the Austrics of pre-Aryan India, and came to be employed in hundreds of Hindu ceremonies. Besides being used as a substitute for saffron and other yellow dyes, it is believed to have magical properties. A preparation of turmeric is rubbed over the bride's body before her marriage*. Turmeric is also chewed and spat around the house to protect the home and occupants, especially infants, from evil influences. The root of the *sarpagandha*, 'snake-odour', plant, once used for insanity, was rediscovered for its valuable properties by the sixteenth-century German physician Johann Rauwolf. Its essential ingredient now known as rauwolfia is used for high blood pressure.

The *lotus* or water-lily may be regarded as the national flower of Hindu India. Brahmā springs from a mystic lotus in the navel of Vishṇu. The goddess Lakshmī and many other deities are frequently depicted sitting on a multi-petalled lotus throne. In Hindu and Buddhist symbolism the lotus represents the vulva, just as the thunderbolt represents the phallus. No other flower has such a diversity of names. The *padma* or lotus flower represents the perfection of beauty and symmetry. It is said to open only in the day and close at night, and hence is known as the day lotus. The *nalina* and the *aravinda* are also varieties of the day lotus. The *puṇḍarīka* is the white lotus; an emblem of the human heart. The *kuvalaya* is the blue lotus, which opens only at night. The same lotus in an early stage of its opening is called *utpala* (or nilotpala), and in its fully open form *kamala*. A variety of the night lotus which is white in colour is called *kumuda*.

Plants are used for a wide range of religious purposes. Some, like the *palāśa* (*butea frondosa*) are put to ceremonial use; the *khadira* (acacia) is used in the royal consecration ceremony; the *udumbara* (*ficus glomerata*) provides branches for the marriage rites; the udumbara is said to blossom only when a Buddha is born. Another variety of fig* tree, the *aśvattha* or pīpal is sacred to the Buddhists; the *dhataki* is sacred to the Jains, since Pārśva was illuminated with divine wisdom as he sat under it. The *śamī*, 'worked' (*Prosopis spicigera*, *Mimosa suma*, or *Acacia suma*) from which the *araṇī* or ceremonial firesticks used to be made (*see* fire), is so called from the labour involved in bringing forth the fire believed to be contained in it. The *dāru*, a species of pine or cedar, referred to as the *deva-dāru*, 'divine dāru', is better known in its contracted form as *deodār*. It is praised by Kālidāsa as 'the adopted child of Śiva'. From the wood of this tree the *yūpa* or Vedic sacrificial post was carved.

Certain trees and flowers are associated with particular deities: the bilva and deodār with Śiva; the tulsī with Vishṇu; the lotus with Lakshmī; mango blossoms with Kāma; the marigold with Gaṇeśa. The *bilva* (*vilva, bel, bael, Aegle Marmelos*) or wood apple has a triple leaf and is sacred to Śiva and part of him resides in its leaves. It is forbidden to break its branches and it is not to be used for firewood except by brāhmins. The bilva leaf is taboo to certain Vaishṇavites who never use it in worship. The stately *śāla* (*sāla* or *sāl*) is sacred to Vishṇu. One beam of this tree if used in the construction of a house brings blessing and peace. The tree is said to be inhabited by a spirit who brings rain if worshipped. Mahāvīra obtained enlightenment and Buddha died under the sāl tree. The *tintiḍī* or tamarind, is associated with the sect founded by Gorakhnāth and is used in the sect rites.

A very special tree is the *rudrāksha* (*Elaeocarpus Ganitrus*) whose berries are regarded as sacred and whose seeds are used by Śaivites for making rosaries. The word rudrāksha, 'Rudra's eye' refers either to the third eye of the deity Śiva (who was also known as Rudra), which sheds these seeds as tears when he contemplates the final destruction of the world; or to the urethral meatus through which the 'seed' that has accumulated through his long austerities is periodically emitted. The rudrāksha seed has a number of faces or sides, each one with a special significance. Those having one face are seldom found and only kings are said to possess them. Anyone finding such a berry will secure every wish and will have a life of power, luxury and happiness. Such one-eyed berries are often counterfeited. The two-faced seed represents the male and female principle and its possession confers Tantrik powers; three faces represent the trident, or the three worlds; four the Vedas; the five-faced berry is the commonest and is sacred to Hanumān of the *Rāmāyaṇa* or the Pāṇḍava brothers of the *Mahābhārata*, or to the five faces of Śiva; six faces represent the six systems of philosophy; seven, the seven worlds; eight, the eight-armed Kālī; nine, the nine Nāthas or adepts; ten, the ten incarnations of Vishṇu. The eleven-faceted berry, also very auspicious, is called *askanda*, 'non-spilled', and is worn for obvious reasons by celibate tantriks.

Among the trees and shrubs that figure most frequently in Hindu mythology are the sacred *nyagrodha* or *banyan* (*see* fig); the *tulsī* (*see* Vṛinda), and the unidentified *soma** plant. Some trees are said to have a *dohada* or violent desire for the touch or attention of a beautiful woman. Thus the *bakula* (*Mimusops Elengi*) bursts into bloom when sprinkled with wine from the mouth of a young woman; the *aśoka*, 'non-sorrow' (*saraca indica*), gives forth orange or scarlet blossoms when touched by the foot of a maiden. It was under this tree that Hanumān espied Sītā as she sat, a prisoner of Rāvaṇa, mourning for Rāma. Under this tree Mahāvīra renounced the world.

Among the cosmological trees mentioned in the sacred writings, the *aśvattha* or *pīpal*, which has its roots in heaven and its branches on earth, and the *jambu*, or rose-apple tree, a gigantic specimen of which overshadows the earth (*see* paradise), are the best known. Another is the *kapittha* (*kapi-stha*, 'monkey-erection'), the prototype of which stands in Indra's garden, and whose fruit gives victory, virility and courage. Its shape is likened to a closed fist with the thumb protruding through the fingers like a monkey's phallus, whence its name. Its earthly counterpart is either the wood-apple, the mango or the cashew tree.

There are also other wondrous trees in Svarga, Indra's paradise*, which are frequently mentioned in Hindu mythology. These are the *pañcha-vṛiksha*, 'five-trees', namely: (1) the *mandāra*, under whose shade all cares are forgotten, and one experiences a divine repose undisturbed by the agitations of the flesh or ecstasies of the spirit. It has crimson blossoms, and its earthly counterpart is the coral tree (*Erythrina indica*); (2) the *pārijāta*, which arose out of the Churning of the Ocean and was taken by Indra and placed in his garden. From there it was carried off by Kṛishṇa, but after Kṛishṇa's death it was once more restored to Indra's heaven (*see* Satrājita). The pārijāta and the mandāra are often identified as the same tree; (3) *saṁtānaka* (or santānaka), a magical tree of which only three specimens exist in Svarga. Chewing the leaves of this tree ensures that one has progeny and that one's line is continued forever; (4) *chandana* (or *hari-chandana*), Indra's sandalwood tree, whose rich perfume scents the whole of paradise. Indra once inadvertently permitted one of his worshippers to enter paradise for a glimpse of its beauty, but he was sent back to earth in a hurry because the stench of a mortal was so overpowering that even the chandana could not disperse or disguise it; (5) the *kalpa-vṛiksha,* also called the *kalpa-taru,* or *kalpa-druma,* all meaning 'wishing-tree', and *kalpa-vallī*, 'wishing-creeper'. During the early 'pure' ages, this tree grew on earth and men had therefore no need of property or possessions, since all they had to do was sit under the tree and wish for whatever they desired. But owing to the ambitions and evil lusts of men in the later aeons* the wishing-tree was translated to Indra's paradise.

Tree worship is very old in India, and evidence of it is found in Mohenjodaro. It was and still is popularly believed that every tree has a *vṛiksha-devatā*, 'tree-deity', a godling* who is worshipped with circumambulations, prayers and offerings of flowers, sweetmeats, cocks, goats, and in some cases, in the past, human sacrifices. Yakshas (*see* Kubera) were often associated with trees. Trees are consulted as oracles, and credited with the power to grant children, fame and wealth. They are often garlanded and festooned with lights, and even married to other trees or to women in regular nuptial ceremonies. Before cutting down a tree, prayers are addressed to the tree-spirit so that it might depart to another tree and not wreak its vengeance on the cutter. In many parts of India it is believed that trees can be made to recieve the soul-stuff of men. In ancient times a Tamil king planted and reared a special tree known as the *kāvanmaram,* which was regarded as his particular tree, and which responded to his destiny. If it started to wither the king knew his time was at hand; if a neighbouring king felled it down, it was tantamount to his being defeated in battle.

According to Hindu belief held from time immemorial, plants have a sort of stultified or dormant life, with a latent consciousness. According to Manu, 'trees and plants are conscious and feel pleasure and pain' (VII, p. 106), a fact scientifically proved by the Bengali scientist Sir Jagdish Chandra Bose in the present century.

Books

I. Agarwala, V. S. 'Kalpa-Vriksha: the Wish Fulfilling Tree', *Journal of the Indian Society,* Calcutta, 1943, XI, 1–8.

II. Dymock, W. 'The Use of Turmeric in Hindu Ceremonial', *Journal of the Anthropological Society of Bombay*, II, 1892, pp. 441 et seq.
III. Eliade, M. *Patterns in Comparative Religion*, London, 1958.
IV. Evans, A. E. *Tree and Pillar Cult*, 1880.
V. Fergusson, J. *Tree and Serpent Worship*, 2nd Ed., London, 1873.
VI. Kirtikar, K. R. 'The Use of Saffron and Turmeric in Hindu Marriage Ceremonies', *Journal of the Anthropological Society of Bombay*, IX, 1913, 439–54.
VII. Morgan, K. W. (Ed.) *The Religion of the Hindus*, New York, 1953.
VIII. Ray, J. C. *Ancient Indian Life*, Calcutta, 1948.

POETICS. The theory of poetical and imaginative writing occupies a prominent place in Sanskrit studies. It is variously termed *kāvya-śāstra*, the knowledge of the *kavi* or poet; *alaṁkāra-śāstra*, the knowledge of poetical or literary 'adornment'; *sāhitya* or rhetorical composition and the art of verse (the *Sāhitya-darpaṇa* or Mirror of Poetry is the title of a fifteenth century work on Poetics); *rasa-śāstra*, good 'taste' and discernment in art and letters. Much of poetics is devoted to this subject of rasa (*see* empathy), and the *rasika* or man of taste and culture is invariably acquainted with the art of poetical writing.

Like much other Hindu art theory, Hindu poetics suffers from over-systematization. Here too we have conflicting definitions, discrepant categorizations, and overlapping terminology. Several *alaṁkāra* (below) are named, in addition to ten *guṇa* or excellences, and thirty-six *lakshaṇa* or 'marks' i.e. characteristics of a good kāvya*, which help to please the ear, excite the fancy, evoke the proper mood or emotion, and elevate the mind.

Essentially, poetry is ruled by convention or agreement (*saṁgati*), but within the framework of the rules, the imagination (*pratibhā*) of the poet must have freedom to produce that peculiar charm (*vichchhitti*) which distinguishes true poetry from ordinary works on subjects like logic or philosophy.

One of the basic notions of poetics is that of *dhvani*, 'suggestion' or overtone, which consists in not stating everything, but leaving much to be understood. Dhvani makes use of allusion, oblique reference, suggestive and evocative terms of speech, which create in one the mood desired. It is the means whereby the unexpressed but intended is brought out by what is expressed. Dhvani is regarded by some writers as the chief element of poetry.

Other important features of a good poem are: perspicuity (*prasāda*), although this must not be overdone; sweetness (*mādhurya*), also in moderation; where necessary there should be gentleness (*sukumāratā*) to give the poem grace (*kānti*); it must possess a sequence of thought (*arthakrama*), breadth of meaning (*audārya*), and completeness of sense (*paripūrṇatā*). Sophistication and learning are added to give it elegance (*upanāgarikā*) and charm (*śobhā*) and the proper dignity or 'elevation' (*udāratva*), thus combining to produce aesthetic* pleasure.

The methods by which such aesthetic pleasure is achieved constitute the province of *alaṁkāra*, 'adornment'. The word is said to be composed of *alam-kāra*, 'enough-making', i.e. that which helps to make adequate something that lacks adornment. The term covers the whole technical apparatus of poetry, the devices of prosody*, and rhetorical embellishments, particularly *vyañjana*.

The term *vyañjana*, 'ornament' or figure of speech, covers all terminological and syntactical devices, employed to enhance the effect of expression. The chief vyañjana are as follows: *upachāra*, 'compliment', often used as a synonym for figure of speech, is a form of exaggerated flattery, and also signifies transfer of meaning; *rūpaka*, 'image' or metaphor, makes use of the image of one thing to increase the effect of another; *upamā*, 'simile' or comparison, extensively used in philosophy and other studies; *āropa* or figurative substitution; the metonymy or synecdoche; *utprekshā*, figurative 'vision', frequently used with the historic present; *sāra*, 'augmentation', a form of climax, or a stepping up from the simple to the complex; *vyāja-stuti*, 'feigned praise' of something with the purpose of bringing into view something better by contrast; *anukaraṇa*, 'imitation' or onomatopoeia, where the sound echoes the sense; in Sanskrit the aspirated consonants lend themselves to this form; *ajahala*, 'implied' or understood but not expressed, an ellipse; *anuprāsa*, 'alliteration', where the same sound is frequently repeated; *vakroti*, an oblique or indirect mode of expression; the suggestive double entendre; *yamaka*, the pun; the use of words identical in sound but different in meaning; *atiśayokti*, 'hyperbole', or poetical exaggeration; *atyukti*, hyperbole, often in a derogatory sense; *ślesha*, 'union', an effective and euphonious combination of sounds; applied generally to the pun, alliteration, onomatopoeia, and double entendre, giving a sentence several meanings.

All these factors in the writing of poetry are but tributaries that join together to produce the river of style, *rīti*, since the style in its wholeness determines the force, beauty, and flow of all writing. Many styles are defined in Sanskrit literature, although three main styles are traditionally employed, all others being variations of these three. They are: (1) *pāñchala* (named from the region of Delhi), characterized by sweetness and delicacy; the words used are soft and smooth and the reading flows like a tranquil stream; it is likened to a gentle maiden or a bashful bride; (2) *vaidarbha* (from Berār), characterized by clarity; it demands perspicacity, graceful sound and tone, elevation and beauty, apt metaphors and the avoidance of long compounds. It is likened to a woman in the bloom of her womanhood, verging on maturity; (3) *gauḍa* (from Bengal), characterized by force; it is artificial, full of long compounds and alliteration, and makes use of harsh effects, clashing sounds and bombast. It is unrefined and likened to the courtesan or harlot.

It should be noted that the theory of poetics with all its devices of style and adornment was also applied to prose writing, but remained a branch of poetics since it was from poetry that it had its source.

The History of Poetics starts with the legendary founders, Brahmā, the supreme deity, and the sage Kaśyapa. Among the early writers were Bharata* whose *Nāṭya-śāstra* is the oldest known work on poetics; and Vararuchi (*c.* AD 579) one of the 'gems' at the court of Vikramāditya*, many of whose verses are included in anthologies. Bhartṛihari* is the author of a treatise called *Vākya-padīya* which illustrates various rhetorical forms. Bhāmaha (fl. AD 680), a Buddhist writer whose *Kāvyālaṁkāra* systematically discusses poetic embellishments. His work lays stress on subject-matter and form (ornateness) to the neglect of the 'soul' of poetry. He is regarded as one of the chief founders of the alaṁkāra school, and the Chārvāka (after the agnostic) of poetics; Daṇḍin* (seventh century), author of a work entitled *Kāvyādarśa* (*kāvya-ādarśa*, 'poetry-image') or 'The Mirror of Poetry', dealing with styles of composition, ornamentation, metrical tricks and puzzles. He is a precursor of the *Rīti* (style) school, and made an important contribution to the poetic concept of guṇa, or quality, as distinct from mere expression of language, as the primary concern of poetry. Vāmana, in the latter half of the eighth century held that rīti was the soul of poetry. His contemporary Udbhaṭa (fl. AD 740) defined over forty figures of speech and made significant contributions to the alaṁkāra school of poetics. Lollaṭa (fl. AD 750) one of the earliest interpreters of the *rasa* school. His original work is lost but its content is known through the writings of Abhinava-gupta and Mammaṭa (below). The most celebrated commentator of the rasa school was *Bhaṭṭanāyaka* (AD 930) whose work is also lost. Ānanda-vardhana (fl. AD 850) the principal exponent of the *dhvani* school. His *Dhvanyāloka* was commented on by Abhinava-gupta. The *Agni-Purāṇa* (tenth century) also deals with grammar and poetics Abhinava-gupta (fl. AD 1000) a prolific writer on a number of subjects including Śaiva philosophy, aesthetics, the dance (he wrote an excellent commentary on the *Nāṭya-śāstra*), dramatics, poetics and music (*see* music history). Mammaṭa (*c.* 1100) whose *Kāvya-prakāśa* gave a comprehensive survey of all his predecessors and became the source of several later theories. Mammaṭa is also the author of a work on music.

Books

I. De, S. D. *Studies in the History of Sanskrit Poetics*, 2 vols., London, 1923–25.
II. Kane, P. V. *History of Sanskrit Poetics*, Bombay, 1923.
III. Pandey, K. C. *Abhinavagupta*, 2nd Ed., Banaras, 1962.

POISON, in Sanskrit *visha* (from *vish*, 'dirt') originated from the venomous scum that appeared on the surface of the ocean of milk when it was churned by the gods and demons to obtain the *amṛita*, or nectar* of life. It was said to have been caused either by the sweat of the demons as they laboured with the gods, or by the agony of Vishṇu in his form of Kūrma the tortoise, as the mountain Mandara, the cosmic churning stick, was being turned on his back.

The fumes of the poisonous scum were becoming a threat to the gods, so Śiva scooped it up and swallowed it. Because of the stain left by the burning liquid as it went down his throat, Śiva was thereafter known as *Nīla-kaṇṭha*, 'blue-throat'. The remainder of the scum was drunk by Vāsuki the serpent* king who had been used as the churning rope wound around the base of the mountain in the churning operation, and he bequeathed its venom as an inheritance to other serpents. The fumes were absorbed by the nearby trees and flowers, which rendered them poisonous, a property that some plants retain to this day.

In āyurveda*, the study of visha or poison, and its *agada* or antidote was an essential part of the training. A practitioner who sought the honours of appointment as Royal Physician had to be perfect in his knowledge of *Agada-tantra*, 'antidote-lore', or toxicology, since despot kings were always in danger of being done away with by poisoning. Medical manuals gave special instructions for the daily supervision of royal kitchens, prescribed various tests for ascertaining whether food prepared for the king had been poisoned, for detecting from any suspicious behaviour on the part of the cook and other servants, such as uneasiness, looks of cunning, guilt, guile or studied indifference, whether they intended mischief; and finally, tests for the diagnosis of the symptoms of poisoning and the administration of the correct antidote. The king's food was often mixed with various antidotes just in case, and he was careful to wear gems which were believed to have the property of destroying poison. During wartime it was the duty of the Royal Physician to supervise the water supply to ensure that wells and tanks were not poisoned or contaminated by secret agents of the enemy.

The study of this subject included the venom of snakes, scorpions, spiders, insects, poison arrows and spears; and exotic poisons like the terrible *halāhala*, the Sanskritized form of a Semitic word denoting a deadly poison now unknown, whose effects were painful, protracted and fatal. No less important was an understanding of the poisons generated from the embraces of the so-called poison-maidens. According to popular legend these girls, specially chosen for their beauty, were fed from infancy on the flesh of venomous reptiles and insects, and on toxic herbs and plants, so that they became immunized to their effects and their bodies became saturated with poison. They were then sent as gifts to princes who died shortly after embracing or sleeping with them.

Books

I. James, S. C. *The Use of Poisons in the Ancient East*, 1887.
II. Mather, C. *Poisons in Hindu Medicine*, 1903.
III. Penzer, N. M. *Poison Damsels and Other Essays*, London, 1952.

POLE CEREMONIES. A number of old Hindu festivals were associated with the erection of poles, which were ceremonially set up and often worshipped.

Thus the *dhvajāropaṇa* (*dhvaja-āropaṇa*, 'pole-planting') a rite of great antiquity, is reminiscent of the erection of the Maypole in Europe. It was most frequently celebrated on the first day of the light half of *Chaitra* (March–April), or the first new moon immediately preceding the *Mesha saṁkrānti* (vernal equinox). A tall slender tree was felled, its trunk smoothed, and the pole set up in the middle of the village. It was decorated with a garland of leaves and flowers, and surmounted by a flag or sometimes crowned with a large brass drinking pot or other vessel. The erection of the pole was often an elaborate state affair and good or evil omens were read into every detail of the ceremony. The pole was worshipped with offerings and dances and after four days was pulled down. If it fell to the north-east it augured well for the land. It was then rolled into a river to drift down with the stream. In private houses a small pole, a replica of the larger, was dressed in a new garment, usually a woman's bodice, and thrust out of the window. Spiced *nīm* leaves were chewed during the ceremony.

Other popular festivals such as Holi, included pole-erecting or pole-displaying ceremonies, but the most important of these was the *dhvajamaha*, 'banner festival', also called *Indra-dhvaja-pūjā* (Indra's banner worship), or *Indra-mahotsava* (Indra's festival). It is said that when the first drama depicting the Churning of the Ocean was enacted by the gods and nymphs in honour of Indra their king, the *asuras* or demons, offended at the dramatization of the incident so derogatory to their dignity, sought to disrupt the festivities, but Indra, taking up the staff of his banner beat them off. In commemoration of that event the sage Bharata* prescribed the decoration and worship of Indra's flagstaff as a preliminary to the performance of any play, and the dhvaja was displayed as an emblem of good luck at all theatrical performances. The festival may have been of Aryan origin and its association with Indra caused Kṛishṇa to object to its observance (II, p. 26). On the other hand it may have been an Aryan adaptation of a rite connected with the worship of the liṅga, observed by the indigenous pre-Aryans of ancient India.

Books

I. Gupte, B. A. *Hindu Holidays and Ceremonials*, Calcutta, 1919.
II. Ray, J. C. *Ancient Indian Life*, Calcutta, 1948.

POLITICS in its broadest sense is called *nītiśāstra*, 'welfare lore', and covers political science and economics in all their practical aspects. The term embraces the study of *nīti*, 'conduct' or political ethics; ethics and moral behaviour; administration and state welfare; *vārtta*, 'livelihood', or economics; trade and commerce; agriculture and cattle-breeding; *artha*, 'wealth' or profit; *rāja-nīti* 'king-craft' and the laws governing kingship*; *praṇayana*, 'establishing' or administration, also called *daṇḍa-nīti*, 'rod-policy', since force of coercion was an important aspect of government.

A considerable literature on nītiśāstra is to be found in Sanskrit writings. The *Mahābhārata* states that Brahmā the Creator was the author of this science, which he set forth in 100,000 stanzas, which Śiva as Viśālāksha (*viśāla-aksha*, 'large-eyed') reduced to 10,000 stanzas; Indra to 5,000; Bṛihaspati to 3,000; and Śukra to 1,000 sections. Spurious works attributed to Bṛihaspati and Śukra still exist (see below).

Vedic writings contain much material on the subject. Thus, the *Atharva-veda* gives information on kingship; the *Aitareya Brāhmaṇa* on the coronation of kings; large portions of the Vedas are devoted to ethics, worldly wisdom and the acquisition of wealth.

The outstanding work on Hindu politics is the overtly cynical *Arthaśāstra* of Kauṭilya* who was presumably the counsellor of Chandragupta Maurya, the text of which was only discovered at the beginning of this century. The twelfth book of the *Mahābhārata*, known as the *Śāntiparvan*, contains several passages on statecraft, in particular the long discourse of the dying Bhīshma on the art of kingship and government. This section of the *Mahābhārata* is a post-Christian interpolation dating from the early centuries of the present era. In the *Mahābhārata* we also have the discourse on diplomacy, kingship and statecraft delivered by Kaṇika of the line of Bharadvāja to the blind and aged Dhṛitarāshṭra, although the precepts set forth are of dubious ethical value, advocating as they do the merciless slaying of enemies; the usurpation of weak dynasties; treachery and duplicity in dealing not only with hostile rulers but also with one's allies and helpers.

The *Bārhaspatya Arthaśāstra* (*c.* AD 400) is a brief collection of aphorisms said to be a remnant of the work of Bṛihaspati's three thousand stanzas on nītiśāstra. Many of the works on the subject written from now on are presented in the form of prose narratives and beast fables, interspersed with maxims in verse illustrating some moral precept. The *Nītisāra*, 'Essence of Politics' by Kāmandaka (*c.* AD 780) contains an exhaustive list of maxims of use to all classes from princes to peasants written in the *kāvya* style. The *Nītivākyāmṛita*, 'Nectar of Aphorisms on Politics' by Somadeva (*c.* 980) a Digambara Jain writer has a higher moral tone than the general run of Hindu works. It enjoins prudence rather than cunning, recommends the ordeal instead of torture; and finds a place for the virtuous man even though he be of low caste. The great Jain writer Hemachandra (fl. 1170) wrote a work in verse entitled *Laghu-arthanīti* or 'Brief Manual of Politics', dealing mainly with war, and very moderate in tone. It condemns war for its ruthlessness and cruelty, for its use of poisons, for its taking of life. It inveighs against recourse to treachery in state diplomacy. The *Nītiśāstra*, 'Treatise on Politics' is attributed to the Vedic sage Śukra*, the tribal priest of the asuras, but actually belongs to the fourteenth century AD. It has been much revised and corrupted.

Like most of the other specialized branches of study in Sanskrit, the treatises on government were highly systematized. There were said to be seven *prakṛiti* or constituent elements of the state, forming as it were, the basis of government, namely: (1) king* or *rāja*, (2) ministers or *amātya*, (3) forts or *durgā*, (4) territory or *rāshṭra*, (5) treasury or *kośa* (*see* taxation), (6) army* or *bala*, (7) ally or *mitra*.

There were also six states or qualities (*shaḍguṇa*) of interstate relations, namely: (1) peace or *saṁdhi*, (2) strife or *vigraha* (*see* war), (3) neutrality or *āsanna*, (4) preparedness or *yāna*, (5) alliance or *samavāya*, and (6) duplicity or *dvaidhī-bhāva*, 'double-nature'.

The six thorns in the body of the state politic were (1) miracle-mongers who help in the creation of cults and subversive groups, (2) counterfeiters who undermine the finances of government, (3) highwaymen who make travel insecure, (4) quack healers who make false claims and cause distress, (5) musicians and (6) dancers who corrupt the morals of the people.

The theoretical foundation of interstate relations was the doctrine of *maṇḍala*, 'rings', detailed by Kauṭilya and other writers on politics, which sets forth a scheme by means of which the balance of power is maintained. It presupposes the existence of two large rival states located as immediate neighbours or at not too great a distance from each other. The maṇḍala doctrine ensures that each of the two rival states would not suffer at the hands of the other, while smaller adjacent states would find a means of survival.

The powers by which a state or king is surrounded in the maṇḍala scheme can be of five kinds, namely, (1) *ari*, the 'enemy' state, i.e. the first king's immediate neighbour who, being either ambitious or covetous, and hence dangerous, is his natural enemy and always *vijigīshu*, 'desirous of vanquishing'; the policy of the first king is to try to forestall him at all times; he is to be harassed in peace and attacked when he is in trouble; (2) *mitra*, 'friend', occupies an area beyond the enemy's territory and is the first state's natural ally; the term mitra also includes all states who are the friends of the friend; (3) *madhyama*, 'middling', the neutral state that sits on the fence and will turn over to either side, depending on circumstances; (4) *udāsīna*, 'indifferent', a state that does not interfere with and is not concerned with either party, being itself both internally and externally secure; (5) *arimitra*, the enemy's ally; his kingdom is beyond that of the mitra's; he is the enemy of the first king, and friend of the king's enemy.

Besides the friend, there is also the rear friend, and the ally of the rear friend; and besides the enemy and the enemy's ally, there is the enemy's ally's ally, a rear enemy, and the ally of the rear enemy, and so on. As the various 'rings' recede in distance from the first state their importance diminishes, since a state is only likely to come into conflict with its neighbours and not with its enemy's enemy thrice removed. Scholars often worked the theory to death and in their hands it became an ingenious problem in mathematics or chess. The maṇḍala doctrine often proved a temptation to Hindu rājas, particularly during the medieval period of Indian history. Two kingdoms would enter into an alliance to encircle and crush a weaker kingdom between them; that done, they became contiguous and natural 'enemies' and intrigued with other states to form dubious alliances to crush and exterminate each other.

Writers on politics took great pains to be realistic, and at times their treatises reflected a highly cynical attitude. The king was to be primarily concerned with his own welfare, since the destiny of the realm was directly linked with his. He was above the laws that govern ordinary mortals; his weapon in dealing with the weak was the daṅḍa* or rod, i.e. coercion or intimidation; and with the strong, dvaidhī-bhāva or duplicity. He must never be deceived by the false allure of peace, but be ever ready to take over a weaker state, and defend himself against a powerful foe. Neutrality was another delusion, for the truly neutral king made the most of both sides.

All government officials, but especially ministers, ambassadors and those engaged in espionage* had to be put through a fourfold test unknown to them, in order to determine their strength or weakness in respect of (1) religion: a faithful officer should be able to subordinate the interests of his religion or dharma, or even his own and his family's virtue to the service of the king, (2) wealth: he must be free from the temptations of money and never accept bribes for any work against the king's interests, (3) lust: he must be able to resist the attractions of women and the pleasures of the flesh, and (4) fear: he must be a man of courage and resource.

Relations between different states were maintained by the *dūta* or envoy, who resided at the foreign court while conducting the business on hand. Envoys were of three kinds: (1) plenipotentiaries, or those with full power to negotiate on behalf of the monarch; (2) those who could not deviate from instructions specifically given; (3) those who merely delivered a message and returned to the king with a reply. The person of the envoy was regarded as inviolate, and the slaying of an envoy was a grave insult offensive to gods and men. The *Mahābhārata* declares that a king who kills an ambassador will go to hell with all his ministers.

Diplomacy was often little more than 'the practice of deception against the enemy'. The *Mahābhārata* discloses in parts an atmosphere of pernicious intrigue, treachery, and double dealing on both sides, and much of this tradition continued to be observed during the historical period. The four modes of diplomacy were: (1) *sāma*, 'conciliation', the use of friendly and peaceful methods, e.g. negotiation; (2) *dāna*, 'giving', e.g. bribery; (3) *bheda*, 'splitting' or causing dissension; and (4) *daṇḍa*, 'rod', or the use of force, which reached its final expression in war*.

At the apex of the pyramid of government stood the king. The kingdom was divided into provinces ruled by the *adhipā* or governor; and the provinces into districts administered by the *nāgaraka* whose headquarters was the town, and whose chief function was the collection of revenue and the preservation of law and order. Police officials, secret agents and spies, troops and watchmen were stationed in all the chief towns and villages. They were oppressive in their methods and greatly feared. The *Arthaśāstra* speaks of an official called *gopā*, 'watcher', who supervised forty houses, keeping a careful record of births, deaths, income, expenditure, activities of residents and so on. Megasthenes confirms that registers were maintained and the movements of strangers carefully checked.

The suppression of crime was one of the primary duties of rulers. Prisons were often built underground in a remote part of the royal palace, and prisoners were frequently chained to the walls of their cells. The king had virtually absolute authority in the matter of imprisoning and punishing his subjects and the operations of law did not interfere with his rights in this respect, unless it touched the interests of the higher castes. Such restraints on liberty in ancient India were the inevitable corollary of a social system which was fundamentally totalitarian and bureaucratic, based on caste and privilege.

Although monarchy, sometimes absolute, was the usual form of government in ancient India, and the feudal king had wide political and administrative powers, his authority in the matter of social and customary law, was nonetheless often limited by the various autonomous associations which started at village level and controlled many aspects of civil and communal life. In some cases oligarchies approaching the republican pattern also flourished, especially during the rise of Buddhism, and several of the *mahājanapadas** mentioned in the Buddhist texts were strongly republican. Shortly before his death Buddha warned the Vṛijjis that their security depended on their maintaining their democratic traditions.

From ancient times the business of the rural communities was carried on by a *pañchāyat* or village council presided over by a committee of five (*pañcha*) which decided village disputes, points of law*, caste matters, and revenue and state affairs as they touched the village. Matters affecting a number of villages were debated and settled by a *parishad* or assembly of learned men. Three or more persons who among them knew the Vedas, Vedāṅgas, Purāṇas and Itihāsas, and were versed in logic and Vedic interpretation and etymology, could constitute a parishad. The decision of a parishad on any legal matter was called a *pārshada*. A meeting of the heads of village councils was called a *sabhā* or Council of Elders, who decided on matters of public importance. The *samiti* was a general or popular assembly, at which princes, elders and people were present. It often had a social as well as a political significance. The samiti was sometimes convened in war-time. There were various other types of assemblies convened for specific purposes, such as the *saṅgha* (*saṁgha*) or a meeting of a religious congregation, a term also applied to the whole Buddhist community of monks. The *pūga* was a meeting of a group of traders, and a *śreṇi* an assembly of workers or craftsmen, later applied to the trade guilds (*see* caste).

The evolution of political ideas and methods owed a great deal to foreign contact. The earliest system of local kingship was modified by the Persian mode of administration by satrapies which the Mauryans acquired from the Achaemenians and which enabled Chandragupta Maurya to establish the first large-scale territorial empire in Indian history. The Greeks, Parthians and Kushāns all made contributions to the development of Indian political theory, and the threads seem to have been woven together into a larger pattern by the Śakas*, whose influence on Indian administration was very substantial, and lasted till the coming of the Muslims.

The Sassanian and Egyptian modes of government which the Arabs had taken over for their far-flung empire, were in time adopted by the entire Muslim world, and were ultimately brought to India by the Muhammadans, where they gradually superseded the Śaka forms. Land-revenue systems, methods of tax assessment, the monetary system, monetary units, the functions of officials, management of the imperial treasuries, were all adapted by the Mughals to Indian conditions. The superiority of the new form of government caused it to be adopted by independent Hindu rulers, with the result that it spread over the whole of India. This was the system that was inherited by the British, and which they developed and modified to suit modern conditions, and left as part of their legacy to independent India.

Books

I. Altekar, A. S. *State & Government in Ancient India*, Banaras, 1955.
II. Bandyopadhyaya, N. C. *Development of Hindu Polity and Political Theories*, Calcutta, 1927.
III. Basu, P. C. *Indo-Aryan Polity: Rigvedic*, 2nd Ed., 1925.
IV. Coomaraswamy, A. K. *Spiritual Authority & Temporal Power in the Indian Theory of Government*, New Haven, 1942.
V. Das, S. K. *The Economic History of Ancient India*, Calcutta, 1944.
VI. Dikshitar, V. R. R. *Hindu Administrative Institutions*, Madras, 1929.
VII. Dutt, B. N. *Studies in Ancient Indian Polity*, Calcutta, 1944.
VIII. Dutt, M. N. (Tr.) *Kamandakiya Nitisara*, Calcutta, 1896.
IX. Ghoshal, U. N. *History of Hindu Political Theories*, 2nd Ed., Oxford, 1927.
X. Jayaswal, K. P. *Hindu Polity*, Calcutta, 1925.
XI. Law, N. N. *Aspects of Ancient Indian Polity*, Oxford, 1921.
XII. Prasad, B. *The State in Ancient India*, Allahabad, 1928.
XIII. Prasad, B. *Theory of Government in Ancient India*, 1927.
XIV. Saletore, B. A. *Ancient Indian Political Thought & Institutions*, London, 1963.

XV. Sarkar, B. K. *The Political Institutions and Theories of the Hindus*, Leipzig, 1922.
XVI. Sarkar, B. K. (Tr.) *Sukra Nitisara*, 2nd Ed., Allahabad, 1923.
XVII. Thomas, F. W. (Ed. & Tr.) *Barhaspatya Arthasastra*, Lahore, 1921.

POLYGAMY may assume one of two forms, (1) polygyny, where a man has more than one wife, and (2) polyandry, where a woman has more than one husband. Both of these customs had been long established in India. Polyandry, the less usual phenomenon is closely linked with the matriarchal* system and is considered under that heading. Polygyny is more popularly referred to by the general term polygamy and will be so used here.

In common with many ancient patriarchal societies, polygamy was a feature of the social system of the Aryans, who permitted a man to take several wives, and recognized concubinage. From the Aryans the custom spread to most other peoples of India, and by the Epic period was prevalent in all parts of the country, although the polyandrous system continued to prevail in certain areas of the south and east.

The morals of the epic period were lax by any standard. The heroes of those legendary days indulged in marathon sexual orgies. Kings and princes not infrequently had harems* that spread over many acres. Such were the rulers of Ayodhyā, Kāśī, Mithilā, who according to Sanskrit chronicles each had sixteen thousand women in their seraglios. Kṛishṇa, whom S. C. Sarkar calls 'the greatest polygamist of his age', had sixty thousand wives (III, p. 219). The Pāṇḍavas, besides their polyandrous tradition, were also polygamous. They and other kshattriya princes of the time spread their matrimonial nets very wide, and their women's enclosures were sometimes as populous as townships. One of them, it is said, had, besides his own women, a sufficient surplus to supply every one of the 88,000 brāhmins residing at the capital, with thirty slave-girls each.

Hindu writers of the medieval period often described the consequences of polygamous establishments on the morals of the people concerned. Vātsyāyana, for instance, declares, 'A man marries another wife because he is a fool, sensual, immoral, miserable, childless, or soulless'. He then proceeds to advise the first wife how to deal with the later wives. He advocates tact, sympathy, kindness, and freedom from jealousy. Advice to the other co-wives is in a similar idealistic vein. The result of a man taking more women into his harem than he can possibly satisfy, leads to serious immorality. Young men are introduced into harems; the inmates have relations with guards, with vendors, with servants. They resort to artificial phallic devices, practise auto-gratification and sapphism, and in some cases bestiality with specially trained monkeys and dogs (I, p. 315). Accounts of perversions, he adds, come from Vatsa, Gauḍa, Aṅga, Kaliṅga, Saurāshṭra, Sindhu, Pañchāla, Vindhya and Drāviḍa. In short, these abuses prevail all over the country.

Indian literature shows that the *droit du seigneur* was exercised by rulers of many parts of India, not only in respect of the defloration of virgins*, but also in respect of married women. The wives of the chief ministers of Vatsa (near modern Hyderābād) spent a night with the king; pretty women of Vidarbha (Berār) were put at the king's disposal for a fortnight or a month;

in the Koṅkaṇ officers sent their wives to the king; in Saurāshṭra women went to the king's palace for his pleasure. The polygamous customs of the medieval Hindu kingdoms such as Vijayanagar* were frequently described by travellers from abroad.

There were, and still are, castes in India whose members live in symbiotic relationship with each other, amounting to a virtual polygamous pattern of life. Conspicuous examples are found among the Nambūdris and the Kulīns. The *Nambūdri* brāhmins of Malabār were permitted intercourse with the women of the Nāir* caste, and although such liaisons were not legalized by marriage, the system functioned as a form of polygamy. In Bengal on the other hand, polygamous relationships received the sanctity of the marriage ceremony. They were common among certain brāhmin sub-castes, notably the *Kulīn*, 'noble', who bear such names as Banerji, Gaṅgūli, Majumdār, Chowdhri and Bhaṭṭāchārji, and the custom is called kulīnism. These kulīn brāhmins were originally from Kanauj, and migrated eastwards before the Muslim invasion; they are regarded as being purer than the other brāhmin castes of Vaṅga (Bengal). Because the kulīn male ranked high in the hierarchy of brāhmins he was in great demand as a husband, and could command a large dowry, which led to an iniquitous system of marriage. Kulīns were known to contract as many as one hundred marriages, marrying up to five girls a day, and frequently not even visiting their wives (II, p. 54). The obnoxious practice has now been stopped largely owing to the vigorous crusade by Bengali reformers.

Books

I. Chakraberty, C. *The Cultural History of the Hindus*, Calcutta, n.d.
II. Hutton, J. H. *Caste in India*, Bombay, 2nd Ed., 1951.
III. Sarkar, S. C. *Some Aspects of the Earliest Social History of India*, London, 1928.

PRABHĀVA, 'splendour', in Hindu esotericism is the supernatural power inherent in all persons and things, and operative both in this world and in the occult sphere. Normally latent, this power in certain circumstances can blaze forth and bring blessing or blight. It can be consciously projected, but may also be active in inanimate things. The *ṛishi's* wrath is a manifestation of *prabhāva*, as are the virtues inherent in medicines*. Prabhāva is particularly evident in sacrificial ceremonies, when these dormant powers are deliberately and purposefully drawn out by the ritual procedures, to serve the purpose of the rite.

The magic power of the *mantras*, the potency of the instruments and implements used, the psychic aura radiating from priests and participants are everywhere stressed in the ancient ritual manuals. Protective formulas are constantly being pronounced, and mantras of propitiation uttered before consecrated objects are touched, used, cut, or broken. If the earth has to be dug for the *vedi* or altar, if a tree has to be cut down, if a brick has to be broken in two, if barley or rice has to be pounded in a mortar, they are first propitiated, so as to minimize the destructive emanation that arises from the bruise, hurt, or touch.

If a cult object accidentally tears or breaks, psychic contamination enters, and it has to be given an antidote by means of a purifying mantra. All sacrificial offerings are believed to be highly charged with prabhāva, and before anyone else gets a share of the offering of cakes or the oblation of ghee, the priest first takes a small portion (called *prāśitra*) himself, in order to neutralize the tremendous power with which it is charged.

Some of the deities invoked also carry danger with them. Thus, if at any time during the ceremony the officiant is obliged to utter a formula referring to Rudra, the *rākshasas*, Nirṛiti, or the *manes*, he is regarded as having been contaminated by inauspicious powers, which the priest neutralizes by touching water and reciting certain mantras.

Ritual purification precedes and follows all religious rites, and several are prescribed for personal emergencies. Thus, if the *yajamāna* (sacrificer) wants to urinate during the sacrifice he must dig up a lump of earth with a horn; this represents the sacred portion of the earth, the rest of the earth being profane he is now free to urinate upon it. He does so while uttering prescribed mantras, whereby his urine itself becomes a sacrificial gift (II, p. 74). Says Hoens, 'To prevent the urinating from ill consequences, on the one hand the earth is made profane, but on the other the urinating is indicated as a libation to the divine earth' (II, p. 75).

Before a Vedic sacrifice, a rite known as *dūrohaṇa* (*see yūpa*), raises the participant spiritually to the sacred sphere, and at the end of the ceremony the reverse is performed, bringing him back to the profane world. In lesser sacrifices special verses are intoned during the important stages of the ceremony to mark the transitions back and forth from the profane to the sacred level.

The consecrated yajamāna (sacrificer) is thought to be ablaze with a psychic glow, and he must therefore avoid water. If it rains he asks the rain not to wash off his prabhāva. If he has to pass a river on his way to the sacrificial ground he throws three lumps of earth into the water to form a psychic bridge over it. During the ceremony the yajamāna is under a vow to eat only ritually pure foods and abstain from sexual intercourse. As a result of this, and further, as a result of participation in the sacred ceremonial, he is believed to become filled with power, so much so that but for the protective invocations he would be consumed and utterly destroyed. At the end of the ceremony he is released from his vow by the aid of mantras, and the glowing power is extinguished.

After the sacrifice, all the consecrated objects are cleansed by flowing water. A piece of the yūpa or sacrificial post itself is sacrificed, and the spit which has been used for the heart, buried, since both post and spit are believed to be loaded with malignant power. Special ceremonies are performed to avert evil influences and to propitiate the deities in case any cultic mistake has been inadvertently committed. A long expiatory sacrifice, the *sarasvatī*, is prescribed for the incorrect use of language during a Vedic sacrifice.

At certain stages in the sacrificial process the magical power of prabhāva was turned to divinatory ends, and omens were read in such things as the consistency of the dough, the clearness of one's reflection in the liquid ghee, the direction taken by the rising smoke, and so on.

Books

I. Das, D. K. *The Yajna, or The Sacrifice in Hinduism*, 1911.

II. Hoens, D. J. *Santi: A Contribution to Ancient Indian Religious Terminology*, Hague, 1951.

PRADYUMNA, the son of Kṛishṇa by his chief wife Rukmiṇī, was believed to be the incarnation of Kāma, god of love, reborn after being reduced to ashes by the fiery glance of Śiva.

While still an infant Pradyumna was kidnapped by the demon Śambara and thrown into the ocean where a *jhasha* fish swallowed him. A fisherman caught the fish and took it back to Śambara's house, where it was cut open and the beautiful child found inside. He was brought up in secret by Śambara's wife Māyāvatī (or Māyādevī), a reincarnation of Ratī, who fell in love with him when he grew up. When she told him how he had been carried off by Śambara the youth confronted the demon with his evil deed and killed him in a furious duel. He then married Māyādevī and flew through the air with her to the palace of his father Kṛishṇa. Pradyumna also married Prabhāvatī daughter of king Vajranābha, after he had visited her in the shape of a bee and lived in liaison with her in the garland she used to wear around her neck. He was later slain in Kṛishṇa's presence in the course of a drunken brawl.

Pradyumna had a son, Aniruddha, and a daughter, Tṛishā, by another wife, Kakudmatī daughter of Rukmin. Like his father, *Aniruddha*, 'uncontrolled', was very handsome, and many were the hearts that succumbed to his charms, including a *daitya* (demon) princess named Ūshā, daughter of the thousand-armed Bāṇa (also called Bāṇāsura or Vairochi), eldest son of Bali, who was a friend of Śiva and an enemy of Vishṇu. It is related that Ūshā fell in love with a young prince she had seen in a dream and kept pining away for want of the reality. Her friend, Chitralekhā, a nymph skilled in painting and the magic arts, drew countless pictures of men and gods to enable her to identify her dream-prince. With guidance from Ūshā she at length drew a portrait which Ūshā immediately recognized, and by means of her magic powers Chitralekhā brought Aniruddha to Ūshā.

When Bāṇa heard that his daughter was harbouring a lover in the palace he was appalled, and immediately ordered his guards to search the palace and seize the intruder. The youth was found but was able to defend himself with an iron club and slay his assailants. However, exhausted by the fight the boy was caught and 'bound in serpent bonds' by the magic spells of Bāṇa. When Kṛishṇa, Pradyumna and Balarāma came to hear of this they flew to the rescue. Bāṇa with his daitya hosts, assisted by Śiva and Skanda, god of war, went forth to meet them. Kṛishṇa with his flashing weapon set Śiva's mouth agape and was able to overpower him. Skanda was wounded by Pradyumna, and Bāṇa in a fight with Kṛishṇa had his arms cut off, but his life was spared at the intercession of Śiva. Aniruddha was released, and together with his mistress Ūshā, accompanied the rescue party when they returned to Dvārakā.

Aniruddha had a son named *Vajra* whose mother was either the daitya princes Ūshā, or Subhadrā another of his cousin-wives. Before Kṛishṇa died he made his great-grandson king of the Yādavas at Indraprastha.

Books

See under Mahābhārata and Mythology.

PRAJĀPATI, (prajā-pati, 'creation's king'). In the Vedas the term is employed as a title for some of the early gods like Purusha, Indra, Savitṛi, and Soma. But in the later texts Prajāpati is referred to as a separate deity, a supreme god, creator of heaven and earth, lord of gods and men, and is frequently identified with Brahmā. Through his daughter Ushas* goddess of the dawn he became the father of all living things.

Associated in later legend and philosophy with Prajāpati, as with Brahmā, is the deity *Ka*. The latter name is derived from the interrogative pronoun meaning 'Who?' which occurs in figurative questions in the Vedas. This word *ka* was elevated in the Brāhmaṇas to the rank of a god, and equated with Prajāpati, and in the Purāṇas Ka was given a genealogy and a wife and ranked as a Supreme Deity. The Vedic hymns in which the word occurs were called *kadvat*, 'having a kad or who?', and were regarded as especially sacred to Ka.

In the plural, the Prajāpatis denote the *mānasā-putra*, 'mental-sons', or mind-born children of Brahmā whose number and names vary greatly in the different texts. The *Mahābhārata* names twenty-one, but generally only ten Prajāpatis are recognized. They are (1) Marīchi, (2) Atri, (3) Aṅgiras, (4) Pulastya, (5) Pulaha, (6) Kratu, (7) Daksha or Prachetas, (8) Vasishṭha, (9) Bhṛigu, (10) Nārada. Some reduce the number to seven and identify them with the *saptaṛishis*. The distinction between the prajāpatis and the greater ṛishis* is not clear.

Books

See under Mythology.

PRĀKṚIT, 'natural' language, as distinct from the 'artificial' medium of Sanskrit. The term is applied to the whole family of vernacular forms of speech that developed from the Proto-Aryan* Ādibhāsha or Ādiprākṛit, influenced by the dialectical variations found in the different localities of India. These forms evolved as a result of the gradual association of the Aryans with the indigenous non-Aryan tribes. According to Keith, 'The factor of race-mixture must have played an important part in the creation of the Prākrits'.

The Prākṛits were not an offspring of Sanskrit, but grew naturally from the people, side by side with Sanskrit, which itself owed much to them. They were the vehicle of communication in everyday life, and continued to be spoken and to evolve after Sanskrit was already a dead tongue (I, p. 294). They were the direct source of the modern Indo-Aryan languages.

Prākṛit was thus a development of the non-hieratic forms of speech current in India developing parallel with the hieratic Sanskrit form in use by the priests. Some of the Prākṛits, e.g. Pāli, retained many archaic forms that are present in Vedic but which are lost in the later classical Sanskrit. Already flourishing in 500 BC the Prākṛits are chiefly known from passages in Buddhist and Jain works. It was an accepted convention of the Sanskrit stage to have kings, heroes, brāhmins, *ṛishis* and gods speak in Sanskrit, while women and menials used Prākṛit, hence many Prākṛit dialects are also preserved in the Sanskrit dramas.

There is some evidence of a vigorous secular poetic tradition in Prākṛit, contemporary with Vedic and preceding Sanskrit, and Sanskrit literature owes a great deal to the Prākṛit vernaculars. Grierson held that even the *Mahābhārata* took its first shape in early Prākṛit and was subsequently set down in Sanskrit.

A further stage in the development of the Prākṛits towards the modern Indo-Aryan languages is seen in the *Apabhraṁśa*, 'deviation', a corrupt language, spoken by the *laukika* or common people, which developed between the sixth and tenth centuries AD. By about AD 550 the Prākṛits had become decadent, and the Apabhraṁśas came into existence. Vararuchi (*c.* AD 579), the oldest Prākṛit grammarian makes no mention of Apabhraṁśa, Hemachandra (d. 1172) being the first to treat the language with the other Prākṛits. Apabhraṁśa may be roughly defined as Prākṛit with further infusions of popular (*deśī*) speech. In other words, when the Prākṛits ceased to grow as literary languages they continued to grow as vernaculars, and soon became corrupt since there was no literature to standardize them.

The development of many of the Prākṛits and the Apabhraṁśas is still not clear, but it would appear that each major Prākṛit had its own Apabhraṁśa. These latter in course of time became cultivated, assumed literary form, and by the beginning of the tenth century many of them evolved into the beginnings of the modern Indo-Aryan languages. Since so little is known about them it is customary to define each Apabhraṁśa by the same name as the Prākṛit from which it is derived.

It is to be borne in mind that as far as vocabulary is concerned, the Apabhraṁśas, from which the modern Indo-Aryan languages are derived, drew heavily on material from indigenous or *deśya* words and idioms, largely pre-Aryan and possibly containing many Prākṛit forms. Such words, taken from indigenous vernaculars, are referred to as *tadbhava*, those having a native mother-tongue as origin, as distinguished from the *tadsama*, those having a Sanskrit derivation, and identical in form and meaning in both Sanskrit and Prākṛit, e.g. *deva, kamala*. Marāṭhi, Hindi and Bengali are overloaded with tadsamas.

From the Ādiprākṛit then, three stages of evolution are to be discerned, namely: (*a*) Primary Prākṛit, which includes Avestic, Vedic and Sanskrit; (*b*) Secondary Prākṛit, or Prākṛit proper, i.e. the regional Prākṛits with their respective apabhraṁśas, and (*c*) Tertiary Prākṛit, i.e. the neo-Indoaryan languages, like Hindi, Bengali, Oṛiya, Marāṭhi. It is admitted by scholars that as far as literary evidence goes there are distinct breaks between Vedic and Classical Sanskrit; Classical Sanskrit and the Prākṛits; the Prākṛits and the Apabhraṁśas; and the Apabhraṁśas and the Neo-Indian languages. Besides the grammatical and syntactical changes, and the simplification of declensional and conjugational terminations that marked the progressive evolution of these three Prākṛitic language groups, the most important features are the phonetic and orthographic mutations that mark their development. If we take Sanskrit, Pāli and Hindi as best representing the three stages of development we find that Prākṛit proper, e.g. Pāli, shows a tendency to drop the harsh sounds of clustered consonants such as are found in Sanskrit. In Pāli these abrasive consonants become palpably softened and liquefied. The table below indicates some of these features.

Primary Prākṛit (Sanskrit)	*Secondary Prākṛit* (Pāli)	*Tertiary Prākṛit* (Hindi)	*Meaning*
adya	*ajja*	*āj*	today
bhakta	*bhatta*	*bhāt*	boiled rice
bhramara	*bhamvara*	*bhaunrā*	bee
gaura	*gora*	*gorā*	fair
hasta	*hattha*	*hāth*	hand
karṇa	*kaṇṇa*	*kān*	ear
karma	*kamma*	*kām*	work
kleśa	*kilesa*	*kleś*	pain
matsya	*machchha*	*machchhī*	fish
pṛishṭha	*piṭṭha*	*pīṭh*	back
siṁha	*sīha*	*siṁh*	lion
śushka	*sukkha*	*sūkhā*	dried
sūrya	*suriya*	*sūraj*	sun
sūtra	*sutta*	*sūt*	thread
trayodaśa	*terasa*	*terah*	thirteen
vastra	*vattha*	*bastar*	clothing
vidyut	*vijju*	*bijlī*	lightning

The names of the principal Prākṛits known to literature are given below:

Pāli, said to be the earliest of the literary Prākṛits. The name is derived from the word *palli* meaning 'village', since it was the language of the common people, or from the word *pal*, 'to preserve', because it was the medium in which the Buddhist canon was preserved. It is the sacred language of the Southern Buddhists, and the parent of Sinhalese, the present-day language of Ceylon. It has a vast literature, starting from the third century BC, which includes the *Mahāvaṁsa*, the Pāli chronicle of Ceylon, and the *Milindapañho**. Pāli continued in use for centuries, retaining its vigour long after the other Prākṛits had become obsolete. For this reason Pāli is usually considered separately from the general list of Prākṛits. It is closely related to Māgadhī.

Gāthā, a name of Ādiprākṛit origin given to the oldest part of the Zoroastrian Avesta. It is also applied to a dialect with Avestic affinities, intermediate between Sanskrit and Prākṛit, of which some specimens are preserved in the Buddhist classic *Lalitavistara*, and in certain versified portions of other Buddhist works. Indeterminately classified, Gāthā, like Pāli, is not generally placed among the Prākṛits. The term gāthā is also applied in Sanskrit writings to a religious verse or song (*see* singing) but one not taken from the Vedas; and in prosody* to a form of metre closely related to the metre called *āryā*.

Śaurasenī, the usual prose dialect of Sanskrit plays, where it is used by men of good position, but not usually the hero. The later Digambara scriptures of the Jains are written in Śaurasenī. This dialect is nearer to Sanskrit than Mahārāshṭri, and from Śaurasenī are derived Western Hindi and Panjābi. It was spoken in the region of Mathurā.

Māgadhī, spoken in Magadha or modern South Bihar, is related to Pāli. It is mainly found scattered in Sanskrit dramas where it is used by men of low rank. Medieval forms of Māgadhī were Chāṇḍālī, Śākārī, Oḍra the ancestor of Oṛiya, and Prāchyā the ancestor of Bengali and Assamese.

Ardha-māgadhī, 'semi-Magadhī', once spoken in what is modern Oudh, is intermediate between Māgadhī and Śaurasenī. The Old Jain writings are in this language. There are strong points of similarity between Old Ardhamāgadhī and the language of Aśoka's pillar inscriptions, hence the latter is also called Aśokan Māgadhī. Ardha-māgadhī is the parent of Eastern Hindi.

Mahārāshṭri or Old Marāṭhi, once spoken south of the Vindhyas, in Berar, was the ancestor of modern Marāṭhi. The later scriptures of the Śvetāmbaras, written in 'Jaina Mahārāshṭri', became important as the Prākṛit of the dramas. *Setubandham*, a kāvya by Pravarasena (*c.* AD 500) was a Mahārāshṭri work highly praised by Daṇḍin. Another famous Mahārāshṭri work was the *Sattasai* by Hāla*.

Several lesser Prākṛits are named in Sanskrit works, most of which cannot be definitely identified and few of which have left any trace in Sanskrit writings. The generic term *Vibhāshā* was applied to the lesser Prākṛits, of which the most important are: *Paiśāchi*, identified by some authorities as the language of the Ābhīras* of the north-west. It was the medium in which Guṇāḍhya* wrote his masterpiece. No known work in Paiśāchi is preserved. *Saurāshṭri*, the Prākṛit of Saurāshṭra, intermixed with Scythian dialects. Closely related to it is *Gaurjarī* or Old Gujarāti, from which modern Gujarāti Mārwāṛī, and Rājasthāni are derived. *Vrāchaḍi* is a generic term for Prākṛits of the north-western regions, from which are derived Lahndā of W. Panjāb, Sindhī and Kashmīri.

Books

I. Chakravarti, P. C. *The Linguistic Speculations of the Hindus*, 1933.
II. Geiger, W. *Pali Language and Literature*, E. T. Calcutta, 1943.
III. Grierson, G. A. *Paisacha Language*, London, 1906.
IV. Hister, G. *The Prakrit Families of Languages*, 1929.
V. Law, B. C. *History of Pali Literature*, 2 vols., London, 1933.
VI. Peters, W. *Prakrit and Babel*, 1913.

PRĀRTHANĀ SAMĀJ, 'Prayer Society', an important offshoot of the Brahmo Samāj of Rāmmohan Roy*, which was started in Bombay in 1867. Its immediate predecessor, the Paramahaṁsa Sabhā, had been founded in 1849. This latter was a secret association at whose meetings all members partook of food prepared by cooks of the lowest caste. When the fact leaked out the society broke up in confusion as most of the members were ashamed of this disclosure of their unorthodoxy.

When Keshab Chandra Sen* visited Bombay in 1865 he roused the people by his impassioned lectures, with the result that some months later a group of erstwhile members of the extinct Sabhā founded the Prārthanā Samāj, with four avowed objects: to oppose the caste system; to introduce widow re-marriage; to encourage female education; and to abolish child-marriage. Later several other reforms were added on theistic lines. The members of the

Prārthanā Samāj did not detach themselves completely from the Hindu elements, but 'paid allegiance to Hinduism with a protest'; the movement was in fact referred to as Protestant Hinduism. It gained strength in Mahārāshṭra where its members declared it to be in true line with the great theistic (Vaishṇavite) tradition of Mahārāshṭra, made famous by such popular saints as Nāmdev, Tukārām, and Rāmdās.

Among the more prominent members of the Prārthanā Samāj were R. G. Bhandārkar and M. G. Rānaḍe. Rāmkṛishṇa Gopāl **Bhandārkar** (1837–1925) was an Orientalist of profound learning and immense breadth of outlook, who was a member of many learned societies in India, England, Germany, America, Italy, Russia, France and Austria, and was noted as much for his Sanskrit studies as for his contributions to social reform. Mahādeo Govind **Rānaḍe** (1842–1901), a chitpāvan brāhmin, the son of a government clerk, was an educationist, economist, and leader of Mahārāshṭrian social reform. When a boy of twelve Rānaḍe had been married to a girl of nine. She died of tuberculosis in 1873 and Rānaḍe married again. The fact that the foremost social reformer of Western India, agitating among other things for the abolition of infant marriage, should himself have married a second time within a month after the death of his first wife, and taken as his bride a girl of eleven while he was thirty-one, created a great uproar in the reformist camps throughout the country, equal in effect to the Cooch Bihār marriage of the son of Keshab Chandra Sen*. The incident however, did not stand in the way of his career, and he rose to become Judge of the Bombay High Court, and exercised a benevolent influence on the progress of Indian social, political and religious reform.

Intimately linked with Rānaḍe were many prominent personalities of Reformation India, though they were not necessarily members of the Prārthanā Samāj. Chief among them were 'Lokmanya' Bāl Gaṅgādhar **Tilak** (1856–1920) a fanatical Hindu and an ardent nationalist, called 'the Father of Indian Unrest'; Gopāl Kṛishṇa **Gokhale** (1866–1915), Rānaḍe's disciple, a moderate and sober politician; and finally the pioneer in the field of educational and social reform for women, Paṇḍitā **Ramābāi** (fl. 1880–1900) who eventually became a Christian much to the displeasure of her compatriots. All these were chitpāvan brāhmins.

Books

I. Athalye, P. *Life of Lokmanya Tilak*, Poona, 1921.
II. Karve, R. *Ranade, Prophet of Liberated India*, Poona, 1942.
III. Kellock, M. *Ranade, Patriot and Social Servant*, Calcutta, 1926.
IV. MacNicol, N. *Pandita Ramabai*, Calcutta, 1926.
V. Sastri, S. *History of the Brahmo Samaj*, Vol. II, Calcutta, 1912.

PRATIHĀRA, or Parihāra (*c.* AD 730–1014), the name of a prominent Gurjara dynasty of agnikula Rājputs of Kanauj, also known as the Gurjara-Pratihāras. They claimed descent from the epic hero Lakshmaṇa who was the doorkeeper (*pratihāra*) of Rāma during his exile; but an earlier tradition has it that a Rāshṭrakūṭa king defeated a Gurjara chieftain and made him serve as a doorkeeper during the performance of a sacrifice.

The son of this chieftain was **Nāgabhaṭa I** (730–756) who founded the Pratihāra dynasty, with capital at Kanauj*. He rallied to his banner several allied clans from the region of Mount Ābū, assumed the leadership of the Hindu resistance to the tide of Muslim invasion, and carried his arms eastwards to Bengal, at that time under the Pālas. Towards the end of the eighth century the Pratihāras of the north, the Rāshṭrakūṭas of the Deccan, and the Pālas of Bengal, began their three-cornered struggle for supremacy in northern India.

The grand-nephew of Nāgabhaṭa, **Vatsarāja** (*c.* 780–795) made a matrimonial alliance with the dynasty of Avanti whose capital was at Ujjain. He extended his conquests as far as Bengal, but was signally defeated by the Rāshṭrakūṭa king Dhruva, and driven into the wilderness.

The Gurjara-Pratihāra empire reached its zenith under its greatest ruler **Bhoja I** (836–885), also known as Mihira Bhoja, who consolidated his position around Kanauj and exercised his sway from the Sutlej and the Himālayan foothills to the Narmadā, and from the Pāla borders to the frontiers of the Arab principalities in Sind. Another great king, **Mahendrapāla** (885–901) controlled the vast area from Magadha to Saurāshṭra, including the Panjāb, Rājputāna, Mālwā, Gujarāt, the Indo-Gangetic valley to Magadha, and southwards as far as the Vindhyas.

By about the middle of the tenth century the Pratihāra empire began to weaken under the attacks of its enemies and rivals; its feudatories broke rapidly away, and the empire disintegrated, being reduced to a small area around Kanauj.

The last ruler, **Rājyapāla** (980–1019), unable to check Mahmūd of Ghazni's advance at the frontier of his kingdom, crossed the Ganges to safety and left his capital to its fate. Mahmūd took the seven forts surrounding the city, then stormed and plundered Kanauj (1018), and swept away the last vestiges of the great imperial dynasty. It is said that, shamed by his abject surrender of Kanauj to Mahmūd, a local subordinate chieftain caught and executed the Pratihāra king.

The principalities that arose out of the ruins of the Pratihāras, included the Chandellas of Bundelkhand, the Chāhamānas of Rājputāna in the Delhi and Ajmer region; the Chaulukyas (Solaṅkis) of Gujarāt; the Paramāras (Powārs) of Mālwā; and finally the Gāhaḍavāla (1090–1193) or Gāhaṛwāra, in the region of Kanauj, with capital at Banāras, which itself fell to Muhammad of Ghor in 1193.

The Pratihāras are noteworthy for their steadfast defence of Hindu India against the Arab invaders for over two centuries; and for their patronage of learning. The dramatists Rājaśekhara and Kshemiśvara were among the many eminent writers who received court patronage. They preserved the ancient traditions of chivalry and warfare and brought a great measure of peace to a part of India constantly subjected to turmoil. The Arab merchant Sulaimān who visited Kanauj in AD 850 during the reign of Bhoja I, remarked on the tranquillity of the land, and spoke of the beautiful horses and camels and the strength of the army; and another Muslim traveller, al-Masūdī who journeyed through the kingdom in 915 made similar observations.

Books
I. Majumdar, R. C. 'The Gurjara-Pratiharas'. *Journal of the Department of Letters*, Calcutta, Vol. X, 1923.
II. Munshi, K. M. *The Imperial Gurjaras*, 2nd Ed., Bombay, 1955.
III. Puri, B. N. *The History of the Gurjara-Pratiharas*, Bombay, 1957.
IV. Ray, H. C. *Dynastic History of Northern India*, 1931.
V. Tripathi, R. S. *History of Kanauj*, 1937.

PREGNANCY, called *garbha-dhāraṇa*, 'womb-possessing' in Sanskrit, is the most blessed state of womanhood, since conception is woman's chief function, and the bearing of sons her highest honour.

The means and tests of pregnancy are given in great detail in the texts on āyurveda and other Sanskrit manuals. Conception is assured if union is performed at the right time; if the man's semen is potent (one test is that the semen sinks in water); if the woman's menstrual fluid is lac-coloured. Besides, the woman must be desirous of union, and in her ṛitu, 'season'. The period of ṛitu is generally held to be between the fourth and twelfth day (the eleventh is inauspicious) following the cessation of menstruation*.

Prior to coitus, a woman should take a ceremonial bath and immediately thereafter look upon the face of her husband, since it is said that her son will resemble the first man she sees after her bath. Conception on even days, especially the fourth, sixth and eighth days after menses, will give male children, on odd days female.

In antiquity, impregnation of the wife was sometimes attended by the sacrament of *garbhādhāna* (*garbha-ādhāna*, 'womb-placing'), in which she ceremonially 'received the seed scattered by the husband'. The rite became obsolete in the late medieval period. The desire for a child was first formally expressed to the family or other priest, and special preparations made. The wife had to take a ritual 'seed-receiving' bath, and wait in the bed-chamber for her husband. The husband first massaged his body without oil, intoning verses expressive of his fertilizing capacity: 'Let this rubbing infuse and invigorate; let it inspire the seed to go forth endowed with power to procreate a son, a noble son, a mighty son'. He then approached his wife and invited her to be ready for conception saying, 'Mount the bed and be thou the field freshly ploughed, eager for seed. Let thy womb be thirsty as for the new rain. Let the seed enter thy womb, a male one, a hero. Let him enter thy womb as an arrow from a quiver, swiftly to its mark'.

During intercourse the husband held the little finger of his wife's hand if he desired a girl (this was extremely rare), the thumb if he desired a boy, and the whole hand if he left it to the gods to decide the issue. Appropriate mantras were intoned for the purpose. Just before consummation the final spell was uttered, 'As Vishṇu has prepared thy womb, let Prajāpati pour on; let my seed be received; let Dhātṛi place the embryo in a secure place'. After the rite the husband left his wife, performed cleansing ceremonies, received the blessings of the brāhmins who waited outside the door, and then went to sleep in a separate room.

If the ceremony were performed to obtain special issue, such as a son who would successfully fight an enemy, or a child who would become famous, certain additional precautions were taken, namely, the husband would not have sexual intercourse with his wife, or with any of his other wives, or with any woman, till he was sure that the wife had become pregnant; if she failed to conceive the ceremony was repeated; if she did become pregnant he resumed intercourse with others but did not approach her till after the birth of the child.

Speculation on embryology (*garbha-śāstra*) is very prominent in the ancient medical texts, and much of it is tinged with magic and mysticism. The *Garbhopanishad* advocates meditation on the embryo as a means of preventing rebirth in a new womb. Most of the texts agree that the foetus is created, 'when the spirit, quick as the wind, and impelled by the deeds of an earlier birth', enters the body of the mother with the *vega** of the father. The seed (*bīja*) is a miniature man containing the elements of all the organs of the male, but the *kshetra* or 'field' i.e. the womb, is also of great importance in the heredity transmitted to the child.

The mother will know she is getting a son if milk appears in her right breast first; if she seems to hold the foetus on the right side of the womb; if her right eye becomes bigger; if she starts with her right foot when walking, and dreams of white lotuses and mangoes. The pains of childbirth were greatly dreaded, and women sometimes starved in the belief that this would result in a small foetus and make labour easier.

In the first month, according to early texts, the foetus has a jelly-like appearance, and from the second month it hardens; the male foetus is spherical in shape, the female elliptical. It is not certain which part of the foetus forms first, and authorities express different opinions. According to Kumārasīra the head forms first since it is the seat of the organs of sense; according to Kāṅkāyana the heart forms first, since it is the seat of consciousness; Bhadrakāpya held that the navel forms first since food is received there; according to Śaunaka the intestines, since the *vāyu* or wind has its seat there; according to Badīsa, the hands and feet, since they are the instruments of action; Dhanvantari held that all parts grow simultaneously; Suśruta and many others declared that the embryo grows by a process of stratification, i.e. in layers; according to Kāśyapa, no one knows.

It is sometimes said that premature births are fortunate, while children born after long gestation will be world-renowned. Thus Bharata was reputedly born after his mother Śakuntalā carried him in her womb for three years; while Sagara was born after being carried for eight years.

In ancient times, during the third month of a woman's pregnancy, the *puṁsavana* (*puṁ-savana*, 'male-rite') was generally performed to ensure that the child would be a male. Descriptions of this ceremony are far from consistent in the ritual texts, nor is the order of performance at all clear. After lighting a sacrificial fire with a burning stick taken from the domestic hearth, *darbha* grass is strewn to the west of the fire in a north-south direction. On this the wife is made to sit, facing east. The husband stands behind her and with his right hand first touches her right shoulder and then her navel, intoning special mantras while doing so. An arrow is held over her head and broken, and a piece of the arrow is fastened on her like an amulet.

A *nyagrodha* (banian) shoot with fruit on both sides is pounded and pressed seven times by a virgin or a brahmachāri (celibate student), and the juice extracted. This juice is ritually purchased by the sacrificer who declares, 'I am buying *soma*'. The pregnant wife lies on her back with her head on her husband's lap, while he introduces some of the juice into her right nostril by means of a smoothed splinter taken from the sacrificial post, which has been warming near the fire.

Next, the husband places a dish of water containing tortoise-gall on the lap of his wife, touches her stomach and recites more *mantras*. He then makes a further formal purchase of twenty-one items (fourteen beans and seven barley grains) from one of the attending priests. He gives his wife a barley grain declaring it to be the male organ of the future child, then places two beans on either side of the barley grain saying that these are the testicles. This is repeated seven times till all the beans and barley grains have been handed over. Another version has it that the husband gives his wife only two beans (representing the testicles), takes a barley stalk (his member) in his hand and removes the grains (semen) from it, and then hands them to his wife. The ceremony ends with the woman being garlanded, after which she bathes her genitals in fruit juice.

Another rite called *sīmanta* or *sīmantonnayana* (*sīmanta-ud-nayana*, 'parting-moisture-bringing'), which entailed the parting of a pregnant woman's hair, was performed between the fourth and eighth months in preparation for the event of birth, as a rule only during the first pregnancy. The day chosen for the ceremony should fall within the fortnight of the waxing moon, say the texts, when the moon stands in conjunction with a constellation having a masculine name; the implements used should all be of the masculine gender, to ensure the birth of a male child.

The hide of a bull, with the neck towards the east and the direction of the hair upward, is laid behind the sacrificial fire, and wife and husband squat upon it. The wife is prepared for the ceremony by having her hair loosened and anointed with fresh butter. The husband then parts her tresses either with a tuft of three stalks of *darbha* grass or *kuśa* grass, or a porcupine quill that has three white spots on it, or with a twig of the *udumbara* (fig) tree, or else with a barley stalk containing an even number of unripe grains upon it. After parting the hair he fastens the twig (or the grass) round her neck with a string of three twisted threads saying, 'Like a tree be thou rich in sap; let thy moisture flow freely'. Some authorities prescribe that the husband should tie or plait his wife's hair in a special manner.

The wife then gazes into a pot filled with water or ghee and says, 'I behold sons, cattle, long life for my husband'. She is given a dish of boiled rice to eat and water to drink. This is followed by the singing of songs in praise of kings and heroes, in order to inspire the woman to bear heroic sons. Many prohibitions were imposed on the woman at this time. 'She should not squat on ordure, nor sit on an anthill, nor sit like a cock, nor postpone the natural flow of excretion or urine.'

The whole ceremony was performed to protect the mother and expected child from the attack of malignant forces, and help the flow of natural fluids during childbirth, and to assist in the parting of the cervix to ease the passage of the child during delivery. The *sīmanta* rite is now largely obsolete, but traces of it may be discerned in some customs surviving in Mahārāshṭra and South India, such as the adorning of an expectant mother's hair with flowers, and her listening to the deeds of gods and heroes from the Epics and Purāṇas.

Particulars are also given of the most suitable place for a pregant woman to stay in during the period immediately preceding the birth of her child. The place should have a clean odour and a pleasant view. The main door should face in the right direction; the room should be spacious, free from draughts, and from attack by beasts of prey and snakes; the bedding should be kept free from fungus, lice, scorpions, insects, and mice; and sweat, worms, bugs, urine and faeces should not be allowed to accumulate. By the medieval period and for centuries after there was a great decline from even these elementary standards, and the conditions under which the Hindu woman was permitted to undergo the ritual of childbirth were terrible in the extreme. She was allotted the most dingy room as the lying-in apartment, and such bedding as could be thrown away after the event. Here she was subjected to a month-long period of pre-natal attentions such as custom and superstition demanded, and in this 'room of horrors', as Dr H. Suhrawardy called it, she gave birth to 'the helpless infant who was the hope and future of the country'.

The old texts mention another sacrament, called *Jātakarman*, 'birth-making', which took place at the onset of childbirth and before the umbilical cord was cut, and was done in this wise. When the pains commence the attendant priest goes about loosening all the knots in the house to assist by sympathetic means the loosening of the child in the womb. Hymns for easy delivery are recited, of which one from the *Atharva-veda* is preserved: 'Let the woman rightly engender; let her joints go apart; let Pūshan unclose her; let the yoni go apart; let it not adhere to the flesh, nor to the fat, nor to the marrow. Let the spotted viscid afterbirth descend for the dog to eat'. While in labour the woman holds certain herbs in her hands to ease her pain. Any unusual aspect of delivery can be rendered normal by smoking the vagina with the skin of a black serpent burnt over dried kuśa grass.

When the child emerges a rite called *āyush-yāṇi*, 'life-giving', is performed over it to enliven and strengthen it after the exertions of its birth. The child is 'cleansed with egg-kernel and rock-salt'; two stones are rubbed on the ears of the new-born; a piece of cloth moistened with butter is placed on its head, and, if a boy, a prayer is whispered into his ear that he may live a hundred years. The father touches the lips of the child with a golden spoon containing a mixture of honey and ghee to which have been added a few hairs from a black bull and 'powdered gold dust', and repeats verses for its prosperity, intelligence and long life. A gold band is tied around the child's wrist and a piece of gold put into its hand.

Five brāhmins then breathe upon the infant: one 'back-breathing' (to strengthen the body), one 'down-breathing' (to purify the winds), one, 'up-breathing' (to give him wisdom), the fourth 'out-breathing' (to remove impurities), and the fifth 'on-breathing' (to give him power). A gold object is placed on the ground, and on it an axe, and on the axe a stone. The child is placed on the stone by the father who says, 'Be firm like this stone'. The father then heats his hands over the fire and touches the child saying, 'Agni is long-lived; possess thou too the lustre of Agni'. The father then touches the earth and asks the earth's protection. There is a short verse of praise to the earth and a verse of praise to the mother.

Various rites follow for averting the evil eye. A cow is led into the delivery chamber, and its tail is waved over mother and child, and the child's face gently slapped thrice with the end of the cow's tail. At some time during the rite the umbilical cord is cut, the child is washed and given the breast of the mother with the prayer, 'May oceans full of milk, full of the immortal sap divine, abide in your breasts to strengthen your child'. While the infant is being nursed prayers are said that it may 'suck long life, suck wealth, suck strength'.

A pot of water is held over the child's head and a prayer intoned that all misfortune, all ill-luck, and the evil eye may depart, and the influence of bad men, ghosts, and demons be removed. Prayers against demons continue to be said until the sixth day, and particularly on the sixth night. This corresponds to the still extant cult of Shashṭhī, the godling* of the 'sixth' day, who desires new-born children, and has to be placated.

In ancient times, if a mother died in childbirth she was sprinkled with water mixed with cow's urine; the husband then cut open the wife and extracted the child which, if alive, was given the dead woman's breast. The husband then covered up the mother's wound, anointed it with curd and ghee, and bathed her with mud, ashes, and cow's urine. She was wrapped in new garments and cremated.

For the first ten days after childbirth both mother and child are regarded as ritually impure. After the birth ceremony the father has a purificatory bath and does not enter his wife's chamber again, which must be ritually purified after the ten-day period is over. Thereafter he may approach his wife and child again.

When a Hindu child's horoscope portended misfortune or crime, he was symbolically made to be born again as a cow. He was dressed in scarlet, tied on to the back of a new sieve (a powerful fetish), and passed between the hind legs of a cow, forward through the forelegs, and again in the reverse direction. The ordinary birth rites were then gone through and the father smelled his son as a cow would smell a calf.

Books

See under Sacraments.

PROMISCUITY was a prominent feature of the early Indian social system, as it was in many ancient societies. The sexual freedom of the native Indians was a matter of great surprise and abhorrence to the Aryan immigrants when they first came into contact with them. At the social gatherings called *samāna*, 'togethering', a sex-goddess used to be worshipped, and one of the main objectives on these occasions was the wooing of lovers with a view to matrimony. Some authorities are inclined to the opinion that this early freedom was not only typical of Kolarian or Dravidian society, but of the Aryan as well, or at any rate that the Aryans did not take long to fall in with the native ways.

From the early texts it appears that man and maid were allowed remarkable scope for lovemaking, quite inconsistent with the later orthodox conceptions of decorum that prevailed in the Middle Ages. Unrestricted love-making before marriage was fully approved in ordinary society (V, p. 92), and there were ample opportunities for pre-marital experience, both when the maiden secretly received her paramour at night in her own chamber (VI, p. 40) and at the various festivals with their suggestive songs and dances, swinging, mock-fights, tournaments, and races, all of which permitted the freest intermingling of the sexes and an advanced state of intimacy, often running into general licence and 'extremes of promiscuity' (V, p. 94). If a child was expected the matter might be settled by mutual agreement to marry. Otherwise the child was exposed and the parties were free to go their own ways. The birth and casting away of illegitimate children, and even the destruction of the foetus, are referred to in Vedic hymns (III, p. 10). Kuntī left her unwanted child on the banks of a river, and Menakā abandoned her child Śakuntalā on the edge of a forest stream. The Vedic teacher Satyakāma was the son of a promiscuous maidservant, and the sage Dīrghatamas son of Utathya encouraged his wife's wantonness.

In certain parts of India the marriage bond was unknown. The *Mahābhārata* states that in the land of the Uttarakuru and its capital of Māhishmatī the institution of marriage did not exist, and that the women of the place had the privilege of having sexual intercourse with anyone they pleased without restriction (I, p. 167). It further relates that when Pāṇḍu was precluded by a curse from having intimacy with his wife, he bade her seek another man for the sake of progeny. 'Formerly', he explained to her, 'women were not bound in fidelity to their husbands but could go about enjoying themselves as they wished, and yet they were not considered sinful. This was the practice from ancient times and received the sanction of illustrious *ṛishis* fully acquainted with the rules of morality.' According to the legend the sage Śvetaketu, when a young man, saw a brāhmin take his mother's hand and lead her away before the eyes of his father Uddālaka*. His father's explanation that this custom had prevailed 'from time immemorial' did not satisfy the youth and he later ordained that it be stopped.

But the liberties of yore were not to be so easily surrendered, and for long conjugal obligation did not necessarily exclude intimacy with suitable outsiders. The prevalence of adultery* in ancient India is attested in the early writings, while the institution of *niyoga* (*see* levirate) by which a widow was permitted to have intercourse with her husband's brother or near relation in order to secure issue for her dead husband, more often than not led to licence. In time this custom, liberally interpreted by a number of exponents, allowed a woman to seek the services of other men even when her husband was alive and when she already had children. Far from being frowned upon niyoga received the approval of society, for the woman was doing the honourable thing in making doubly sure that the line of her spouse was not discontinued for lack of progeny. The polygamous social groups which flourished in southern and eastern India, and the existence of female kingdoms known as *strīrājya** confirm the persistence of promiscuous customs in the historical period.

Unrestrained sexual liberty appears to have continued well into the Greek period, and was a source of astonishment even to the liberal-minded sons of Hellas. One Greek writer recorded that the Indians copulated openly like cattle (VII, p. 97). Nearchus stated that girls were put up as the prize of victory in a boxing match (IV, p. 74). These remarks were in all probability based on random observation or limited rural practice. Strabo reported that if a man were unable to marry off his daughter he would lead her to the market place and assemble a crowd to the sound of trumpet and drum. Then, to anyone who came forward he would first display her naked, from the rear up to the shoulders, and then from the front. If she pleased the beholder she was presented to him for marriage (II, p. 492). If true, this again would only have been a localized custom.

Another ancient writer observed that the virtue of an Indian woman could be bartered for an elephant; the woman was proud to think that the temporary use of her body was thought worthy of so magnificent a gift. And far from seeing evidence of wifely devotion in the burning of widows the hard-headed Greeks surmised that the custom was introduced as a safeguard in case wives tried to poison their husbands and elope with someone else. The thought of being burnt alive for their pains would serve as an effective deterrent to any such intention (VII, p. 103; VI, p. 94).

It would seem that till the early Middle Ages there was still great latitude for free love. Kissing and fondling were treated very lightly as is seen by references in Yājñavalkya and Mitāksharā. A man was permitted intimacy with all women, barring those who were married, girls belonging to higher castes, or with any girl against her wishes. But these reservations were obscured by the writers on erotics. The followers of the Pañchāla sexologist Bābhravya held that a woman's chastity should continue to be respected until she had been found to be intimate with five lovers, not including her husband.

Promiscuous union received its religious and mystical sanction in the Tantras, and in various left-hand and antinomian* sects, which advocate congress with another's wife, with virgins, and even one's own mother, sister and daughter.

Books

I. Chakraberty, C. *The Cultural History of the Hindus*, Calcutta, n.d.
II. Durant, W. *The Story of Civilisation: Our Oriental Heritage*, New York, 1935.
III. Madhavananda, Swami. *Great Women of India*, Almora, 1953.
IV. Rawlinson, H. G. *India: A Short Cultural History*, London, 1952.
V. Sarkar, S. C. *Some Aspects of the Earliest Social History of India*, London, 1928.
VI. Upadhya, B. S. *Women in Rigveda*, 2nd Ed., Banaras, 1941.
VII. Vaidya, C. V. *Epic India*, Bombay, 1907.

PROSODY. In the art of Sanskrit writing great attention was paid from earliest times to the study of the structure of verse and the laws governing quality, accent, and versification. The Brāhmaṇas contain discussions on metrical matters, but according to tradition the patriarch of the subject was PINGALA (*c.* 150 BC) who was believed to be the incarnation of a great serpent king.

His *Chhandaḥ-śāstra*, dealing with the *Ṛig-Veda* and *Yajur-Veda*, is a treatise on *chhandas* or metre, and gave its name to one of the six Vedāṅgas, inaugurating a considerable literature on the subject and thus becoming the starting point of prosody. In Piṅgala's work, which belongs to the *sūtra* type, we find for the first time the use of algebraic symbols. A later work on Prākṛit measures is also attributed to Piṅgala.

The *Nidāna-sūtra*, attributed to Patañjali (*c.* 150 BC) deals with the metre of the *Sāma-Veda*. Works on metre were written by or ascribed to Kālidāsa, Vararuchi, Kshemendra and Hemachandra. More than seventy other Sanskrit writers of lesser renown have also made contributions to the study of classical accents and metres.

The four Vedas and the Brāhmaṇas are marked with accents, but accents play no part in classical Sanskrit literature (II, p. 16). The three accents of the *Ṛig-Veda* are: (1) *Udātta*, raised or acute, the most important of the accents, falling midway between the other two. Comparative philology has shown that in Sanskrit it rests on the same syllable that bore it in the proto-Aryan language; in the *Ṛig-Veda* it is not marked. (2) *Anudātta*, not raised; the low-pitch accent which precedes the acute udātta. (3) *Svarita*, 'sounded' or falling accent. It usually follows the acute. Often the acute accent is not marked at all; the anudātta is indicated by a horizontal stroke below the syllable, and the svarita by a vertical stroke above the syllable. The *Sāmaveda* indicates all three accents with the numerals 1, 2, 3; the highest, the acute, being 1.

Classical Sanskrit metre is quantitative, as in Greek and Latin, based on long and short syllables, and not, as in English, on stress. The unit of quantity is the *mātrā*, which is the time* taken to pronounce a short vowel. A long vowel counts as two mātrās, and a vowel is long according to its nature or position. The final effect of a Sanskrit verse depends on the *vṛitta*, 'turn', a combination of factors including metre, accent (where it exists), number of syllables, and the rhythm of the verse ending.

The 'ideal' verse or stanza consists of four lines, like the four 'feet 'of a quadruped. Each line is called a *pāda* (lit. 'foot'), which term is not used in the same sense that foot is used in English prosody, i.e. consisting of two or three syllables. The Sanskrit pāda represents the metrical unit, and the term pāda can mean, 'foot', 'quarter', 'fourth', or simply, 'line'. Each pāda or line generally consists of from eight to twelve (sometimes even more) syllables, although a shorter or syllabic line is also employed.

There are five principal metres, namely:

(1) *Gāyatrī* (from the *Gāyatrī mantra*), a Ṛig-vedic metre consisting of three sections of eight syllables each. It is often referred to as the brāhmin metre, and was to be used by those who desired brilliance and splendour. The gāyatrī metre entirely disappeared from later Sanskrit.

(2) *Anushṭubh*, a stanza of four lines of eight syllables each. Like the gāyatrī, but with a fourth line added. It is to be used by those who desire heaven.

(3) *Śloka*, a loose measure, developed from the Vedic anushṭubh, it also consisted of four pādas of eight syllables each. Traditionally believed to have been invented by the sage Vālmīki*. Widely used for didactic and narrative

verse it is the chief epic metre. The term śloka is often used for an aphoristic couplet or proverb of any kind.

(4) *Trishṭubh,* consists of four pādas of eleven syllables each, with a caesura after the fourth or fifth syllable. This is the commonest of the Ṛig-Vedic metres. It is called the kshattriya metre, and should be used by those who desire strength, power and dominion.

(5) *Jagatī,* like the trishṭubh, consists of four pādas, but with twelve syllables per pāda. The jagatī is the vaiśya metre, and is to be used by those who desire cattle and wealth.

The commonest of the lesser metres are: *virāj,* consisting of pādas of thirteen (sometimes ten) syllables; it is to be used by those who desire abundant food; *śakvarī,* consisting of fourteen syllables to the pāda; *atiśakvarī,* fifteen syllables to the pāda; *atyashṭi,* seventeen syllables to the pāda; *atidhṛiti,* nineteen syllables to the pāda; *prakṛiti,* twenty-one syllables to the pāda; *ushṇih,* twenty-eight syllables to the pāda; it is used by those who desire life; *bṛihatī,* thirty-six syllables to the pāda; to be used by those who desire prosperity and glory. It is frequently employed in the composition of *sāmans* or Vedic chants.

In addition to these there are some metres determined not by syllables but entirely by the short vowels (mātrā) they contain, the most famous being the *āryā* metre, also called the *gāthā* (*see* Prākṛit).

Books

I. De, S. K. *Studies in the History of Sanskrit Poetics,* 2 Vols., London, 1923–25.

II. Sastri, G. *A Concise History of Classical Sanskrit Literature,* 2nd Ed., Calcutta, 1960.

PROSTITUTION. There are over three hundred and thirty synonyms for the word prostitute in Sanskrit (VI), which cover the hierarchy of this profession in all its abundant variety. They include divine women, temple girls, royal concubines, society courtesans, demi-mondes, and plain street-walkers and harlots. They are spoken of as pleasure-women and joy-girls, and are descriptively referred to by dozens of epithets like melon-breasted, mountain-bosomed, hip-shakers, rolling-buttocked, lotus-scented, and fish-fragranced. Certain categories of persons such as old women, eunuchs and catamites, were traditionally associated with sex commerce. The wives of bards, actors, dancers, singers, washermen, dyers and others were often both harlots and procuresses.

The highest class of prostitute was the *devadāsī* (deva-dāsī, god's slave), who was dedicated to the service of the deity in a Hindu temple. The *Padma Purāṇa* recommends the purchase of girls for dedication to temples, and the *Bhavishya Purāṇa* states that a suitable place in heaven is reserved for the man who dedicates a bevy of devadāsīs to a solar temple. Men frequently gave their daughters for temple service to secure spiritual blessings. Sun temples were always the haunts of prostitutes. When Hiuen-Tsang the Chinese traveller visited India in the seventh century AD he referred to the hordes of dancing girls at the notorious temple of Sūrya at Multān. When king Rājarāja built the Tanjore temple in the tenth century he provided it with four hundred dancing girls.

Among several castes in Madrās, especially in Bellary and its neighbourhood, it was customary, where there was no son in the family to perform the obsequies of the parents, to endow a daughter with masculine privileges by dedicating her to a deity. Such a woman, generally referred to as a *basavi* (or basivi) becomes the heir to her parent's property and can perform their funeral rites as if she were a son. She can marry a man of equal or higher caste and her children take her name. Her daughter usually becomes a basavi too.

Couples often dedicated their first child, if it happened to be a daughter, to a temple as a devadāsī, as a gift to the god, in the hope of getting a son. Others presented their girls to temples in fulfilment of a vow, and others again because they wished to be rid of their daughters, since unmarried females were invariably a liability to parents. Various other methods were employed for getting girls for temple service. The Abbé Dubois, writing in the eighteenth century, relates that during the festival of Veṅkaṭeśvara (Vishṇu) when the idol from the temple of Tirupati was being taken around the streets, the priests went among the populace soliciting from among the mothers and daughters present, fresh wives for the harem of the deity.

The devadāsī as a rule started her training at the age of seven or eight. She was first 'married' to the deity, and a *tāli* or marriage badge was tied around her neck in a ceremony known as the *tālikettu*; one class of dancing girl, the *pātar* (or *pātur*), went through the ceremony of being married to a *pīpal* tree. They had Kṛishṇa as their personal god and Mahādeva (Śiva) as their guardian deity. Some girls were married to an idol of Kṛishṇa and others to a dagger. After the formal marriage ceremony the girl was ritually deflowered by the temple priest, or by being made to sit astride a stone liṅga, or on the member of an ithyphallic deity representing the god Baleśvara (II, p. 312), a form of Śiva. Sometimes a privileged customer or patron was permitted the rite of defloration. He first tied the tāli around the neck of the girl to symbolize her dedication to the deity, and then had congress with her.

Thereafter the girls were trained by brāhmins (*see* livelihood) in dancing and the erotic arts, and served as temple prostitutes available to the public, their earnings being kept by the priests. The girls, and any children born to them, were unpaid attendants of the temple. Their duties included those of a general temple servant; keeping the temple clean; fanning the idol with a palm-leaf or Tibetan yak-tails; carrying the sacred lights; dancing and singing before the idol and before the public. Says Penzer, 'Most of the songs are lewd in character, usually relating to the amorous life of Kṛishṇa' (V, p. 144).

No stigma was attached to the profession of a devadāsī, and she was often envied her freedom and her prestige. Her presence at weddings was considered auspicious since, being wedded to the god, she could live free from the burden of ever becoming a widow or a *satī*. When the devadāsī grew old she was given a certificate of good conduct and was free to wander about the country making a living as best she could.

The institution of temple harlotry was prevalent in India till the end of the last century. The ancient temples were for centuries establishments of venery, and the early writers speak of the difficulty of honest pilgrims trying to perform their religious duties because of the shameless blandishments and solicitations of the temple girls. Many visited the shrines not so much to pay homage to the deity as to make use of the young women employed there (I, p. 183). The shrines of South India were particularly notorious in this respect, and the large temples such as those at Madura, Conjeeveram and Tanjore were worked like brothels. The last of the great Hindu empires, that of Vijayanagar, was so full of temple women that worship at a shrine was rendered extremely hazardous. The temple of Somnāth*, destroyed by Mahmud of Ghazni, had hundreds of devadāsīs attached to it, and till recently the temples of Viśvanātha at Banāras and of Jagannātha at Purī were renowned for the multitudes of dancing-girls who catered to the needs of the pilgrims. The practice of temple prostitution is said, though on no reliable authority, to be current still. If it exists it is entirely clandestine. The persuasion of Christian missionaries, criticism from European observers, and agitation by Hindu reformers, have put a stop to it.

It may have been from the example of temple prostitution that lay prostitution came to be exploited, both as a source of private income by individuals and of revenue by the state. One of the earliest instances is that of the sage Dīrghatamas son of Utathya* who lived on his wife's earnings. From the *Arthaśāstra* it may be seen that in Mauryan times prostitutes were a considerable source of revenue for the state, and were moreover, invaluable as spies and intelligence agents, and special arrangements were made to use them as such. They were protected by the state and their activities supervised by an official Superintendent of Prostitutes, who inspected the brothels and collected two days earnings from each prostitute every month as a tax. The device of employing harlots for espionage was continued throughout the subsequent Hindu period, reaching enormous proportions during the Vijayanagar rule. The revenue derived from the earnings of dancing girls paid for the upkeep of the entire police force of 12,000 men in Vijayanagar, and most of the information for the police was provided by these women.

Apart from devadāsīs and the state prostitutes, there were various other categories of professional 'joy-ladies'. Dattaka, the writer on kāmaśāstra, wrote a treatise on courtesans, and Vātsyāyana devoted one whole section of his classic to the subject, giving advice on the selection of the right men as patrons, on the methods of beguiling them, on the behaviour of courtesans, on ways of extracting money, on indications of love, ways of increasing love, signs of waning love, on the different types of courtesans, and so on.

Highest among this class of 'private' courtesan, was the *rāja-kanyā*, 'king's girl'. Kings and nobles made it a practice of having, in addition to their wives, a number of young women called *vilāsinī*, selected for their youth and beauty, and used only 'for purposes of enjoyment'. It is to be noted that a courtesan (not necessarily the king's mistress) had to be present with the king in certain state ceremonies (e.g. the royal consecration), and when he sat on the throne she held the royal umbrella.

Another class of courtesans was the *gaṇika*, corresponding to the hetaerae of Ancient Greece. Originally recruited from the ranks of high-class dancing girls, actresses and singers, the gaṇika were the only women in India who enjoyed the privilege of learning to read. Later other types invaded the class and the gaṇika included the married woman (given out by her husband for a fee); the dissatisfied wife; the wife of an artisan or bard; a widow (fair game for all); any married or unmarried woman with meretricious yearnings. This class was known to French travellers as *bayadère*, derived from the Portuguese word meaning 'dance', and to English writers as nautch-girls. For centuries the art of classical dancing and singing was the preserve of this class of professional dancing-girl and public entertainer, and it was they who kept its ancient traditions alive.

The gaṇika was usually restricted to one man as his mistress, or to a select clientele of a few men of the higher, richer or noble classes. Famous in Buddhist legend is the wealthy and intellectual Ambapālī, the courtesan of Vaiśālī. Buddha dined with her and one of the most beautiful poems of the Pāli canon is said to be her work. Yet another class were the religious concubines, attached not to temples but to religious mendicants, or to Tantrik and other secret cults and used only by members. Such were the women attached to the Vrātyas, Ājīvikas, Vaishṇavas (e.g. bairāgiṇī), Sahajīyās, and other sects.

Lowest in the scale were the *veśyā*, or common harlots, 'cheap as spittoons', recruited from the ranks of discarded courtesans, from widows, from barren wives.

Books

I. Altekar, A. S. *The Position of Women in Hindu Civilization*, 2nd Ed., Banaras, 1956.

II. Chakraberty, C. *The Cultural History of the Hindus*, Calcutta, 1945.

III. Dare, P. *Indian Underworld*, London, 1938.

IV. Fawcett, H. 'Basivis: Women Who Through Dedication to a Deity Assume Masculine Privileges', *Journal of the Anthropological Society of Bombay*, Vol. II, 1892, 322–45.

V. Penzer, N. M. 'Sacred Prostitution', in *Poison Damsels and Other Essays*, London, 1952.

VI. Sternbach, L. 'Vesya: Synonyms & Aphorisms', *Bharatiya Vidya*, Bombay, Vol. IX, Nos. 1 & 2, Jan. and June, 1950, 49–65.

PROTO-ARYAN LANGUAGE. The term *Ādibhāsha*, 'original language' is sometimes used for the common predecessor of those forms of Aryan speech presumed to have been current in ancient Iran and northwest India. Scholars believe that there must have existed some basic form of speech whose essential features underlay Avestic, Vedic, and cognate tongues, although they have not been able to fix the form of this hypothetical language. On a yet wider scale philologists have pointed out many structural resemblances between Avestic, Vedic, Hittite, Sanskrit, Greek and Latin, and even Old Gothic. Dr Franz Bopp observed that when he was reading Ulfilas' translation of the Bible into Old Gothic he thought he was reading Sanskrit (II, p. 6).

From the fact that these languages were spoken in widely separated areas, it would appear that they were dialectical variations of a single basic form of speech originally much more widespread than the areas in which they flourished in historical times. This hypothetical root-language has been variously referred to as Proto-Aryan, Indo-Aryan, Indo-European, or Indo-Germanic, and is thought to have been the earliest of all the 'Aryan' tongues, the *lingua franca* of a heliolithic and sometimes snake-worshipping people who were once spread over Central Asia, from the Anatolian and Iranian highlands to the fringes of the Indus Valley.

The term Ādibhāsha is applied in particular to the Persian and Indian prototype of this foundational language, if indeed any such language ever existed. It is presumed to have been a primitive form of Prākṛit*, and certainly older than either Avestic or Vedic. This Proto-Prākṛit is antecedent to any of the Prākṛits known to scholars today, and Ādibhāsha is therefore also known as Ādiprākṛit. From this basic Ādibhāsha the Avestan and Vedic dialectical variations evolved in Persia and India respectively, until their gradual crystallization for liturgical use by the Avestan and Vedic priests. It is to be remembered that the hieratic variation of Avestan and Vedic developed independently of the Prākṛit dialects spoken by the common people, which had a vigorous and quite separate life of their own.

Books

I. Chakravarti, P. C. *The Linguistic Speculations of the Hindus*, Calcutta, 1933.
II. Kephart, C. *Sanskrit Language, Its Origin, Composition and Diffusion*, Washington, D.C., 1949.
III. Mackenzie, C. *The Language of the Early Aryans*, 1891.

PSYCHOLOGY is conceived in Hinduism as literally what the Greek origin of the term implies in Western parlance, a study of the soul* or ātman. The Mind is considered both in its absolute aspect as Universal Mind or Param-ātman, and in its fragmented forms as the individual *jīvātmans* of separate created entities.

The 'Mind' of God, or divine psychology, has been the subject of profound study by Hindu metaphysicians. There are degrees of knowledge, power and perfection in this world, rising from the level of the lower animals to that attained by man. This gradation, logically pursued, leads us to the absolutely omniscient, omnipotent and perfect Being. This is God, untouched by imperfection, above the law and beyond all processes, and possessed of a unique perception* (*īśvara pratyaksha*) which brings all things to His awareness. Divine knowledge is not attenuated by cognition either simultaneous or successive; it is not based on perception by any of the senses; it is independent of memory or inference. God does not know by fragments, or by a glance here and a glance there. He knows each separate object, past and present, gross and subtle, and also all thoughts and beings, by a single all-pervasive and everlasting glow of instantaneous Knowledge that is also Will and Power.

Hindu thinkers use a bewildering vocabulary of terms for the concept of Mind. The *chitta*, 'knowing', is generally used for mind in its universal or absolute aspect. It is derived directly from the *chit*, 'illumination' of Brahma. It embraces consciousness, perception, knowledge, awareness, and intelligence in their universal and absolute sense. In Yoga philosophy, the term is used for 'mind' as understood in Western psychology, and in some schools it is used for the individual consciousness.

The first manifestation of chitta in the universe is *mahātattva*, 'great principle', also called *mahat*, which is one of the categories of Sāṁkhya* philosophy. At this stage chitta pervades all space and permeates all things; it is about to be differentiated and is likened to the swollen surface of the ocean, just before the appearance of the waves. It is the stage when the hitherto undifferentiated potentiality of Mind sets out upon a definite direction.

The term *buddhi*, 'wisdom', is used for one of the manifestations of chitta, and represents the highest state of human consciousness. It arises from the awakening of the divine intelligence within, and results in discernment, discrimination, understanding and right knowledge.

Another aspect of the individual mind is revealed in what is called *ahaṁkāra*, 'I-maker', that part that isolates and self-identifies the person as 'I'. In man it is the ego-conscious apparatus, that limits him to his environment and enables him to be aware of fragments of Truth as they reach him and are interpreted by his five senses and his reason. The ahaṁkāra is an obfuscating element in man, although essential for his daily life.

The ordinary mental equipment of the individual is called *manas* (from *man*, 'think'), the perceiving and arranging mind. In Sāṁkhya it is also used in the sense of cosmic mind, but in general it refers to the personal organ of thought, not diffused like the ātman but localized in the individual. The manas has its own illumination (*chetas*) which gives man awareness or consciousness (*chetanā*), as well as the faculties of perception (*pratyaksha*), thought (*chintā*), imagination (*kalpaṇā*) and volition (*prayatna*), and also endows him with higher sentience and intelligence (*chaitanya*). One part of the mind is inward-directed, and this *antaḥ-karaṇa*, 'inward organ' (sometimes localized in the heart) is said to be directly connected with the buddhi or spiritual discernment, and is frequently identified with man's conscience. It is then spoken of as the *antar-yāmin*, 'inner guide'.

Although the individual mind is fed from the higher levels and can have contact with the universal mind, it normally operates on the manas level. Ignorance has its flower in manas, but it may be said to be rooted in ahaṁkāra (ego), whence come the notion of individuality, the basis of *dosha* (sin) and the beginning of karma* or causality. The relationship of the individual mind with life (*jīva*) and soul (*ātman*), the various kinds of mental operations (*see* meditation), the different degrees of awareness and perception* from full waking to dreamless sleep (*see* dream), the nature of true knowledge*, all formed part of the study of Hindu psychology. The Upanishads graphically describe the relationship of the individual's bodily and mental equipment by comparison with a chariot: the soul (ātman) is the chariot rider; the body (*śarīra*) is the chariot, the mind (*manas*) is the bridle and reins, the senses (*indriya*) are the horses, matter (*dravya*) is the roadway, and the goal is quietude (*śamana*).

The infinite series of mental activities (*chitta-vṛitti*), the protean and ever-changing world of perception and thought, constitute the psychomental stream of daily life. According to Yoga philosophy this stream has its source in the *vāsana*, 'abode', a vast reservoir of psychical latencies which has been compared to the subconscious mind. The vāsana is dominated by an unquenchable 'thirst for fruit' (*phala-tṛishṇā*), i.e. a desire for expression in conscious acts, in desires and impulses, and therefore actualizes in the chitta-vṛitti, and manifests in man's attachment to the illusions (*māyā*) of the phenomenal world. The vāsana actually constitutes a part of the karmic heritage of the *liṅga-śarīra* or subtle body, and conditions a person's behaviour and thinking as expressed in his chitta-vṛitti. It is useless to attempt to change the chitta-vṛitti, since these are being recurrently fed by the vāsana.

The way of release is to eliminate the psychomental flux by various processes and techniques such as Yoga. Yoga in fact is described as chitta-vṛitti-nirodha, i.e. the inhibition (nirodha) of the activity (vṛitti) of the mind (chitta), or the control of thought. The goal of all mental and spiritual disciplines is quietude (*see* trance states), the attainment of a condition when no further contribution is made to karma, when all action is spent before it can be performed, and where one's identity is lost in the universal consciousness, and one is united to the Universal Bliss.

Books

I. Akhilananda, Swami. *Hindu Psychology: Its Meaning for the West*, London, 1948.
II. Akhilananda, Swami. *Mental Health & Hindu Psychology*, London, 1952.
III. Davids, Mrs Rhys. *The Birth of Indian Psychology and its Development in Buddhism*, London, 1936.
IV. Jacobs, H. *Western Psycho-Therapy & Hindu Sadhana*, London, 1961.
V. Saksena, S. K. *Nature of Consciousness in Hindu Philosophy*, Banaras, 1944.
VI. Vasu, S. N. *Hindu Psychology*, 1921.

PŪJĀ, 'adoration': the origin of this term is still unexplained, but is thought by some authorities to be derived from the Dravidian *pū-chey*, 'flower-action', or worship with offerings of flowers, in contradistinction to the later *homa* rite of animal* sacrifice. Others derive it from the Dravidian word *pūśu*, to anoint or smear, i.e. with sandal-wood paste or vermilion, instead of blood. Both the word and the form of the present ritual are of Dravidian origin and it is likely that the Dravidians themselves acquired the custom from their Austric predecessors, who used to daub vermilion or red sandal-paste on their sacrificial altars.

The early Aryan or Vedic form of making ritual offerings and rendering homage to the deity was the rite of homa. Of Indo-Iranian origin, homa was essentially an animal sacrifice before a fire-pit. The image and altar were anointed with the blood of the victim and a burnt-offering of the meat and fat was made to the deity. Barley, bread, milk and butter, and a spirituous drink called *soma* were also offered. The gods were believed to be especially partial to the savour of burnt animal flesh, and granted favours to those who made such offerings.

Partly under the influence of Dravidian practice and partly due to the compulsion of the Buddhist challenge of non-violence, the Vedic homa rite, spoken of as *paśu-karma*, 'animal rite', gradually underwent a change, and the old indigenous form of bloodless offerings, hitherto regarded as primitive, powerless, and alien, was adopted by the Aryans.

By the medieval period the homa rite had become a simple daily service performed by lighting a brazier and throwing in pieces of sacred wood, or pouring on oblations of ghee or melted butter, all accompanied by suitable mantras.

Today pūjā takes many forms, depending on the sect of the worshipper and the occasion of the ceremony. The term pūjā is now used generally to include most forms of ceremonial worship*, ranging from the simple daily offerings of flowers, fruit, leaves, rice, sweetmeats and water to the deity, either at home or in the temple, to the blood sacrifice of goats as in the Kālī temple in Calcutta and Durgā temple in Banāras.

Books

I. Charpentier, Jarl. 'The Meaning and Etymology of Puja', *Indian Antiquary*, Bombay, LVI (1927), 93–8, 130–35.
II. Majumdar, R. C. (Ed.) *The Vedic Age*, London, 1951.

PULASTYA, one of the Prajāpati or mind-born sons of Brahmā through whom some of the Purāṇas were communicated to mankind. In particular it was to him that Brahmā communicated the *Vishṇu Purāṇa*, and he in turn made it known to the sage Parāśara. Although regarded as one of the eight traditional founder-ṛishis of brāhmin dynastic lines, Pulastya did not produce true brāhmin stock. His offspring were the *vānaras* (monkey people), *kiṁnaras* (bird people) and *yakshas* (supernatural beings), and he is specifically named as the ancestor of all the great *rākshasas* (ogres) of mythology. He once cursed a king who refused to make way for him in a narrow forest path, and the king became a rākshasa.

Pulastya's eldest son was *Viśravas*, though according to one legend this 'son' was actually the embodiment of half of Pulastya himself. Viśravas had five chief wives through whom he produced many children famous in Hindu mythology. His first wife, the brāhminī *Iḍāviḍā* (or Ilāviḍā) was the daughter either of the sage Bharadvāja, or of Tṛiṇabindu by the nymph Alaṁbushā, and through her he became the father of the god Kubera. His second wife *Kaikasī*, daughter of the rākshasa Sumālī and his wife Ketumatī, was also known as Keśinī or Pushpotkaṭā. Through Kaikasī, Viśravas became the father of two sons, Rāvaṇa* and Kumbhakarṇa* and one daughter Kumbhīnaśī who married Madhu the asura* king of Mathurā. By his third wife *Mālinī*, Viśravas fathered Vibhīshaṇa. Vibhīshaṇa's wife Saramā showed great kindness to Sītā during her captivity in Laṅkā; and later Vibhīshaṇa opposed Rāvaṇa, joined Rāma, and on Rāma's victory was made king of Laṅkā in his half-brother's place. By a fourth wife, *Rākā*, Viśravas became the father of Śūrpanakhā, Khara and Dūshaṇa. By his fifth wife *Nikashā* he fathered the flesh-eating ghouls known as the Piśitāśana, also known after their mother as Naikusheya or Nikashātmajas.

Books

See under Mythology.

PURĀṆA, 'ancient', a class of Sanskrit writings giving a legendary account of ancient times. They are part of the *smṛiti* (non-Vedic scriptures), and follow the *itihāsa* (Epics) in point of time and importance. Much early material is no doubt embodied in the Purāṇas, but the dates of their composition are comparatively late, ranging from the sixth century AD (*Vāyu Purāṇa*) to the sixteenth century AD (*Vāmana Purāṇa*).

Vyāsa, the 'compiler' of the Vedas and *Mahābhārata*, was said to have been responsible for arranging many of the earlier Purāṇas, some of which he even wrote. According to tradition, the Purāṇas were first recited by the bard Roma-harshaṇa (or Loma-harshaṇa), and although there has been some speculation about the possible 'Roman' ancestry of the whole class of these writings, nothing can be said about it for certain. Curiously, the earliest among the extant works of the Purāṇa type is the *Yuga Purāṇa*, whose present Sanskrit text is traced back to Prākṛit and even Greek origins, and dated about 50 BC. The *Yuga Purāṇa* forms part of an astronomical* treatise known as the Gārgī Saṁhitā.

Every genuine Purāṇa is supposed to possess certain *lakshaṇa*, 'marks', or characteristics, that distinguish this class of writing from all others. There are said to be five such marks, but not every Purāṇa has them all. Each Purāṇa should contain an account of (*a*) the creation of the universe, (*b*) the genealogy of the gods and ṛishis, (*c*) the rule of the manus, (*d*) the destruction of the universe, and its re-creation, with the history of mankind, and (*e*) dynastic legends of the Solar and Lunar dynasties.

Other common features are also found in the Purāṇas: they are all pantheistic, all written in verse, all revealed by gods, *ṛishis* (sages), or supernatural beasts to various authors, and are all presented in the form of a dialogue between a questioner and an expounder. Often they are written in 'prophetic' vein, as though describing future events.

The Purāṇas have been called 'the Veda of the common folk', since they present much traditional and orthodox material through myth and legend, story and symbol. The *Padma Purāṇa* states that listening to them is equal in merit to listening to the Vedas. Collectively, they are encyclopaedic in scope and cover the arts, grammar, lexicography, agriculture, drama, poetics, architecture, sexology, poisons, precious stones, black magic, omens. The Purāṇas lay great stress on an extravagant form of *bhakti* (faith), propagating a belief in absurd miracles, and recounting legends of the gods and ṛishis that enter the realm of gross superstition. They represent a phase of Hinduism that has received the severest censure from Hindu reformers. Dayānanda*, for instance, was especially vehement against what he called 'Purāṇic religion'.

There are eighteen Purāṇas in all, varying in length and content. They often refer to several gods, but generally each Purāṇa is devoted to the praise and glorification of one deity only. Six of them relate to Vishṇu, and in them the quality* (*guṇa*) of *sattva* or purity prevails; six are devoted to Śiva, with *tamas* (gloom) prevailing; and six to Brahmā, with *rajas* (passion) prevailing. In general Vishṇu and his incarnations are prominent in most of the Purāṇas, just as Śiva is prominent in the Tantras.

In addition to the eighteen great Purāṇas, called *Mahā-purāṇas*, there are between eighteen and eighty-eight *Upa-purāṇas* (see below), which are subordinate works of no great merit or consequence. There are still other modern works allegedly telling of past time, which are also called Purāṇas. The names of the eighteen great Purāṇas are as follows:

THE SIX VISHṆU PURĀṆAS, sattvic in quality:

(1) *Vishṇu Purāṇa*, consisting of 7,000 stanzas and bearing all the 'lakshaṇa' of the true Purāṇa. Legend has it that it was first communicated by Brahmā to Ṛibhu, who revealed it to the sage Pulastya, and Pulastya passed it on to the sage Parāśara, who in turn made it known to his disciple Maitreya, and the text takes the form of a dialogue between Parāśara and Maitreya. Its basic teaching is that Vishṇu is the creator, sustainer and controller of the world; it is in him that the world exists as a harmonious system, and in truth Vishṇu is the world. This Purāṇa is the most perfect and best known of all the works of this class. It gives much valuable information about the Maurya dynasty.

(2) *Nārada Purāṇa* (or *Nāradīya Purāṇa*), of 3,000 stanzas, in which the sage Nārada describes the essential duties of man. Another related work, known as the Bṛihan, 'Great' Nāradīya, consists of 3,500 verses. These Purāṇas belong to the period after the Muhammadan conquest, and do not bear the marks of a genuine Purāṇa.

(3) *Bhāgavata Purāṇa* (or *Śrīmad Bhāgavatam*), the most celebrated of the Purāṇas, is a voluminous work of 18,000 stanzas in length, divided into twelve skandha or books. The most popular part is the tenth book, which narrates the life story of Bhāgavata or Kṛishṇa, especially of his boyhood. The *Bhāgavata Purāṇa* is written in the form of a dialogue between a sage and a king. The latter is doomed to die within a week for having unwittingly killed a holy man, and to ensure his salvation he spends the week listening to the *Bhāgavata Purāṇa*. It lays great stress on the doctrine of bhakti* or faith, and makes the love of the *gopīs* (milkmaids with whom Kṛishṇa sported), symbolic of spiritual devotion. The name of his favourite gopī, Rādhā, does not appear in this Purāṇa. Some authorities believe it was written in South India, and it was once held to be the work of the grammarian Vopadeva (*c.* AD 1250) friend of Hemādri* who flourished at the court of the rāja of Devagiri. A few authorities place it as early as AD 900. The favourite tenth book of this Purāṇa has been translated into all the Indian languages.

(4) *Garuḍa Purāṇa*, of which there are several versions, although it is doubtful if a genuine original version is in existence. It is named after Garuḍa the vulture vehicle of Vishṇu, but there is nothing in its contents to justify the name. It deals with the rites held over the dying, the death moment, the funeral ceremonies, the ritual building up of a new body for the preta or deceased, the judgment, the various after-death states till rebirth. It also deals with sun-worship and astrology and is probably Indo-Zoroastrian in origin.

(5) *Padma Purāṇa*, an extensive work, divided into six books, which tells of the time when the world was a golden lotus (*padma*), and goes on to describe the Creation, and the spheres of earth, heaven and the underworld. To this a supplementary book on Devotion has been added. The whole work dates no earlier than about AD 1100.

(6) *Varāha Purāṇa*, has about 10,000 stanzas, and is not older than AD 1000. It was revealed by Vishṇu to Varāha (the Boar).

THE SIX ŚIVA PURĀṆAS, tamasic in quality:

(1) *Matsya Purāṇa*, bears some of the marks of the genuine Purāṇa. A heterogeneous mixture, borrowing much from the Vishṇu and Padma Purāṇas, and from the *Mahābhārata*, It was related to Manu* by Vishṇu in the form of a fish (matsya). It contains some information about the Āndhra dynasty.

(2) *Kūrma Purāṇa*, dated about AD 900. Vishṇu as a tortoise (*kūrma*) explains the purpose of life. It glorifies the worship of Śiva and Durgā.

(3) *Liṅga Purāṇa*, dated about AD 700. In this work Śiva explains the meaning of virtue, wealth, pleasure and liberation, and the spiritual significance of the liṅga (phallus). It is largely ritualistic.

(4) *Vāyu Purāṇa*, the oldest of the Purāṇas dated about AD 500. It is devoted to Śiva and his many attributes, and contains material about the sacredness of Gaya*. A variation of the Vāyu, known as the *Śiva Purāṇa*, gives information about the reign of Chandragupta I.

(5) *Skanda Purāṇa* (*c.* AD 550), related by Skanda, god of war. The longest of the Purāṇas it is said to consist of over 80,000 stanzas, although it does not exist in composite form, but only in fragments. Such, for example, is the Kāśī Khaṇḍa, describing Banāras and the Śaivite temples there, and the Utkala Khaṇḍa, giving an account of Orissa.

(6) *Agni Purāṇa* (*c.* tenth century AD), also called the *Āgneya Purāṇa*, was originally communicated by Agni, god of fire, to the ṛishi Vasishṭha. It is an encyclopaedic compilation containing, besides some original material, many extracts from other works, relating to ritual worship, cosmology, dynastic chronology, the art of war, and a section on law taken from Yājñavalkya, a chapter on medicine taken from Suśruta, and selections from Piṅgala and Pāṇini on grammar, rhetoric and prosody.

THE SIX BRAHMĀ PURĀṆAS, rajasic in quality:

(1) *Brahmā Purāṇa* (*c.* AD 1300), also called the *Ādi Purāṇa* or first Purāṇa, since it generally stands first in all the lists of Purāṇas. It is also known as the *Saura Purāṇa* because it is devoted to Sūrya the sun-god. It was revealed by Brahmā to the sage Marīchi. Apart from sections devoted to the cosmologies, ritual worship, descriptions of the temples of Orissa and so on, it promulgates the worship of Kṛishṇa as Jagannātha (partly taken from the *Vishṇu Purāṇa*). The last part, known as the *Brahmottara Purāṇa* is of a later date, and celebrates the sanctity of the Balajā river.

(2) *Brahmāṇḍa Purāṇa*, expounds the magnificence of the egg (*aṇḍa*) of Brahmā, and describes the future aeons. Like the *Skanda Purāṇa* this does not exist as a composite work, but only in parts and fragments. The popular *Adhyātma Rāmāyaṇa* is one such part of this Purāṇa. The authorship of the *Adhyātma Rāmāyaṇa* is ascribed to Vyāsa, and in it Rāma is described as a saviour god and a deliverer rather than a mortal hero.

(3) *Brahmā-Vaivasvata Purāṇa* (or *Brahmā-Vaivarta*), related by Manu Sāvarṇa, son of Vivasvat, to the rishi Nārada. It is of comparatively late

date, and enjoins the worship of Kṛishṇa and Rādhā, making this couple husband and wife so that their love is not adulterous but conjugal.

(4) *Mārkaṇḍeya Purāṇa* (*c.* AD 900), quite different in tone from all the other Purāṇas. It is related by the sage Mārkaṇḍeya and is heard by certain fabulous birds who are versed in the Vedas. These birds repeat it to the sage Jaimini. It has little to do with sect, ceremonial, or worship of Brahmā as such, but is a succession of legends, secular in tone, recommending no particular doctrine, and consisting mainly of original compositions, superior to the Purāṇas in general. An episode of this Purāṇa the *Durgā Māhātmya* (variously called Devī Māhātmya, Chaṇḍipāṭha, Chaṇḍi Saptaśatī) is older in date (*c.* AD 700) than the rest. It is a poem of seven hundred verses in thirteen chapters, devoted to the glorification Śakti* as mother-goddess, who descends to earth from time to time to rid the world of demons and monsters. This section is recited at many Hindu religious functions.

(5) *Bhavishya Purāṇa*, the title, meaning 'future' Purāṇa, seems to have been arbitrarily bestowed. It is mainly a handbook of rites and ceremonies, for the greater part very unpurāṇic in character and content.

(6) *Vāmana Purāṇa* (*c.* AD 1500), contains an account of the dwarf (Vāmana) incarnation of Vishṇu. It divides its homage between Śiva and Vishṇu.

The eighteen lesser Purāṇas, called the *Upa-Purāṇas* are variously listed, but usually drawn from the following: (1) *Āditya*, (2) *Āścharya*, (3) *Auśanasa* (from Uśanas), (4) *Bhāskara* (or *Sūrya*), (5) *Devī*, (6) *Devī-Bhāgavata*, a Śaiva Purāṇa, sometimes listed with the great Purāṇas, (7) *Durvāsasa*, (8) *Kālikā* (*c.* AD 1350), a Śākta text, the source of much Tantrik material (*see* human sacrifice), (9) *Kalki*, (10) *Kapila*, (11) *Maheśvara*, (12) *Mānava*, (13) *Marīchi*, (14) *Nandikeśvara*, (15) *Nārada* or *Vṛihan*, (16) *Narasiṁha*, (17) *Parāśara*, (18) *Śāmba*, (19) *Sanathkumāra*, (20) *Śivadharma*, (21) *Sūrya* or *Bhāskara*, (22) *Sūta-saṁhitā*, a devotional Purāṇa, like the *Bhāgavata*, but devoted to Śiva, (23) *Uśanas* or *Auśanasa*, (24) *Varuṇa*, (25) *Vāya*, (26) *Vṛihan* (*see* Nārada), (27) *Yuga* (see above, and under Astronomy).

Books

I. Aiyar, K. N. S. *The Puranas in the Light of Modern Science*, Madras, 1916.
II. Burnouf, E., *et al.* (Tr.) *Bhagavata Purana*, 5 vols., Paris, 1840–98.
III. Carlile, E. S. *The Veda of the Common People*, 1899.
IV. Dikshitar, M. *Purana Index*, 3 vols., 1951–55.
V. Dutt, M. N. (Tr.) *Garuda Purana*, Calcutta, 1908.
VI. Farquhar, J. N. *Outline of the Religious Literature of India*, 1920.
VII. Majumdar, R. N. *The Major Puranas*, 1912.
VIII. Pandya, R. G. *Puranic Legends Retold*, Poona, 1921.
IX. Sanyal, J. M. (Tr.) *The Bhagavata Purana*, Calcutta, 1930–34.
X. Wilson, H. H. (Tr.) *The Vishnu Purana*, 5 vols., London, 1864–70.

PURAÑJAYA, 'city conqueror', also called Paraṁjaya, 'foe conqueror', king of Ayodhyā, was the son of Vikukshi and grandson of Ikshvāku* founder of the solar race of kings. Purañjaya earned his name after storming the cities of the hostile *daityas* (demons or aboriginals) of the west. It so happened, the *Vishṇu Purāṇa* relates, that in the Treta age the gods were once defeated in battle against the *asuras* and appealed to Vishṇu for help. He directed them to seek the assistance of Purañjaya into whose person he would place a part of his spirit. Indra assumed the form of a bull and carried Purañjaya into battle on his hump, and thus seated Purañjaya, known ever after as Kakutstha (*kakud-stha*, 'hump-stationed') defeated the demon hosts and restored the gods to their high estate.

Sixth in descent from Purañjaya was Śrāvasta who founded the city of Śrāvastī, and whose grandson Kuvalāśva (or Kuvalayāśva) was the reputed father of 21,000 children. Attended by his army of sons he marched against the great asura Dhundhu who lived in a lake of sand in the Rājputāna desert and constantly disturbed the meditations of the pious sage Uttaṅka. They unearthed the monster and destroyed him and his fiery home, but in the terrible encounter with the flame-belching demon all the sons, except three, perished. For this exploit Kuvalāśva was given the title of Dhundhu-māra, 'slayer of Dhundhu'.

Kuvalāśva's own grandson *Haryaśva* had five (*pañcha*) sons, after whom the country of Pañchāla is said to have been named. Eighth in descent from Kuvalāśva was the miraculously-born Māndhātṛi*.

Books

See under Mythology.

PURIFICATION is referred to in Sanskrit by the term *śodhana,* derived from the root *śudh,* 'pure' (cognate with the words *śuddhi,* 'purity' and *śuddha,* 'pure'), and related to the concept of *śaucha,* 'cleanliness'. The latter term signifies freedom from contamination and is one of the yama obligations of Yoga. These terms cover both social and ceremonial, as well as physical, mental and spiritual purity. Purification plays a vital part in Hindu religious observance, and the man who practices *śaucha,* the *śāstras* (scriptures) declare, 'is qualified to witness the Self'.

Purity is of several kinds, and is achieved by various means. Spiritual purity comes through observance of the yamas of yoga; study of the Vedas and śāstras; meditation on the deity; pilgimages to holy places; repetition of the names of god; *brahmacharya* (continence); *tapas* (asceticism); *ahiṁsā* (non-violence); the avoidance of foods that breed intoxication, anger, lust, and other passions; keeping the mind under full control.

Ritual purification is necessitated because of contamination from various causes, and takes a number of forms. Thus, there is the preparatory cleansing before the performance of a ritual act; there are the purificatory rites to be undergone when a person has infringed some regulation of his caste, or omitted to discharge an obligatory act, or incorrectly performed such an act, or performed an act that he should not have performed. For example, when a person makes a journey outside the borders of India (in many cases even outside the area of his own state or province), he is regarded as defiled, and a ceremony known as *prāyaś-chitta,* 'penance', takes place on his return. This rite is also performed when twins are born, since twins are regarded as unlucky; or when the upper teeth of a child appear before the lower; or when a man marries before his older brother.

There is another type of purificatory ceremony called the *vrātya-stoma,* originally a rite by which the Vrātyas* were accepted into the Hindu fold, but now used to designate any ritual ordeal by which those persons who have fallen into a degraded mode of life (e.g. by omitting to perform their religious duties, or by failing to observe the dictates of their caste), or who have been converted to other religious faiths and desire re-conversion, are cleansed of pollution and readmitted to the Hindu caste system.

There are numerous ways of performing the prāyaś-chitta, vrātya-stoma and similar ceremonies. They include rites of ceremonial ablution; drinking the *pañchagavya* or five products of the cow*; branding the body with red-hot irons; walking over live coals; burning the tongue with a piece of heated gold; crawling several times under the belly of a cow to signify a new birth, and so forth.

Yet another form of ritual purification, called *āchamana*, 'sipping', is common to all ceremonial worship. Water is taken in the hollow of the right hand and conveyed to the mouth with a prayer to one of the gods; it is then alternately squirted out or swallowed; where it is not swallowed care has to be taken to spit out the water on the left side. Those who spit out water on the right side commit a serious ritual offence and are in danger of going to hell. Āchamana is performed before prayers and worship, and also after any action which is known to cause defilement. It is believed that evil vapours always accumulate in the mouth when one thinks or does anything impure, and this renders the saliva* and the mouth unclean. Thus, one must rinse one's mouth four times after urinating, eight times after defecation, twelve times after taking food, sixteen times after sexual intercourse, and twenty-four times after attending a funeral.

In acts of worship and adoration, water is also offered for āchamana to the deity or to the guru. Since a guru's thoughts are always holy, great power resides in his mouth. Hence the water with which he laves his mouth is regarded as holy, and among the very zealous any such water is collected and drunk by his followers. After the ritual of āchamana, homage is paid to the water vessel.

Ceremonial purity is closely connected with purity of location and direction. The first is best obtained in a quiet secluded spot, under one of the sacred trees like the *banian*, *pīpal*, *aśoka*, *bilva*, or *sāl*. The ground on which one sits in such a pure location should in addition be purified by daubing with a mixture of earth and cowdung. Purity of direction is established by facing the east or north in the daytime, and only the north at night. Further purification is achieved by dispersing unclean elements with the *tālas*, the snapping of fingers in all directions and the uttering of prescribed mantras, especially the sacred syllable *Oṁ* (*see* worship).

Purity both psychical and physical can be achieved by clearing the *nāḍis* or channels* of the subtle body, and also by flushing the ducts and cavities of the body where impurities may be produced, deposited and stored. The esoteric techniques for achieving this include the intoning of *mantras*, yogic *āsanas* (e.g. standing on the head), and *prāṇayāma* or breathing exercises.

Bodily purification is of two kinds, external and internal. External purification includes washing and bathing (*see* baths), and the natural functions of urination, evacuation (*see utsarga*), and ejaculation. Such matters as paring the nails, cutting the hair, shaving the face or the whole body, are also in this category.

The eyes are cleared by staring at the sun or at a bright object so that the tears flow, as in *trāṭaka* (*see* meditation), by washing in water, and applying collyrium to the lids. The operation of cleansing the tongue is carried out by scraping it with a piece of wood or bent metal. To clear the throat the fore-finger and middle finger are vigorously rubbed back and forth along the tongue reaching far back into the throat, accompanied by hawking and choking sounds which assist in raising the accumulated phlegm which is then expectorated. The cleaning of the teeth is performed in this wise: 'Sitting without distraction, one should take a green twig, astringent or bitter to the taste, and should clean one's teeth with the prayer, "O twig, grant me strength, fame, lustre, progeny, cattle and wealth"'. A twig of the *nīm* tree is often used for the purpose.

The nose is cleared by vigorous blowing, but the importance of keeping the nasal passages clear for facilitating breathing techniques is stressed by the special yogic exercises employed for the purpose. The best known of these exercises are: (*a*) *Neti*, cleansing, in which water is drawn through each nostril alternately until it flows out of the mouth. Then a piece of soft twine is passed into one nostril and out through the mouth, and gently pulled back and forth; the process is repeated with the other nostril. (*b*) *Kapāla-bhāti*, 'skull-brightening', often classed with prāṇayāma; in this water is drawn up through the nose and expelled from the mouth; (*c*) *Vyut*, is the reverse process, when the water is taken into the mouth and then forced out through the nostrils.

Internal cleansing is accompanied by the so-called *shaṭ-karma*, 'six acts', although their precise nature is not clear, since their enumeration varies with the authorities. Often they are regarded as part of a magical regime preparatory to the practice of Yoga. They may include such exercises as *vasti*, *dhautī*, *gajakaraṇi*, *vātasāra*, *agnisāra*, and several of the *bandhas**, especially *nauli* or shaking the abdomen.

The collective term for the purificatory exercises of the stomach and intestinal tract is *sārakaraṇa* (*sāra-karaṇa*, 'energy-making'). Among them is the *vātasāra*, 'wind power', which is performed by contracting the mouth like the beak of a crow and slowly sipping air into the stomach and then expelling it by eructation. 'Vātasāra is a very secret process, destroying all diseases and increasing the gastric fire.' Another exercise is the *agnisāra*, 'fire power', pressing the navel in towards the spine one hundred or more times, and likewise expelling the air that has been swallowed the while, by eructation or crepitation. (In a variant of this air is drawn up into the rectum by breathing techniques and expelled with a violent sound.) In *gajakaraṇi* (*gaja-karaṇi*, 'elephant action'), as much tepid water as the stomach will hold is drunk and then brought up again by putting a finger into the throat. This is of course to be done on an empty stomach, and is believed to purify and strengthen that organ. In *vārisāra*, 'water power' (also called *śaṅkha-pashāli*, 'conch-act'), water is swallowed, and by a process of muscle control is allowed to pass through the digestive tract and out through the rectum in about fifteen minutes. 'Vārisāra should be kept very secret. It purifies the body and makes it luminous and resplendent.' In *vasti* (or *basti*), 'syringe', performed while sitting in a bath, the *recti abdomini* muscles are isolated as in *nauli* (see *bandha*), and a partial vacuum created in the colon, the sphincter is then opened and the water drawn up into the rectum by anal contractions, and then expelled. It is a reverse form of peristalsis and creates suctional effects in the digestive tract. Alternatively, a tube is introduced into the rectum, one end being lowered into the water, and the water then drawn up.

In the exercise called *dhautī*, 'washing' out of the stomach, a piece of damp cloth about four inches wide and twenty-two feet long is swallowed, one end being left hanging out. The abdomen is then shaken about, after which the cloth is pulled out. Or else a long pliant stalk of cane is thrust down the gullet and then drawn out. The term dhautī is often synonymously used for many other cleansing processes.

Finally, in the extremely secret, and improbable, rite of *bahish-kṛita*, 'out-taking', one has to stand navel-deep in water, then gently 'by means of ether-power', draw out the large intestine, squeeze out the contents, wash the bowels with care, and then draw it up again into the abdomen. Needless to say this feat requires practice under the vigilant supervision of an experienced guru, and takes at least eight years to accomplish. Many of these cleaning exercises precede anal-sexual techniques involving perverse* rites.

The last of the cleansing acts is the yogic technique of *meḍhrati* (*meḍhra*, 'penis') which entails the cleansing of the male member with the object of increasing its absorbing power in order to facilitate the practice of certain secret *paramudrās*. It is preceded by the gradual introduction of a thin hollow rod of lead or silver up the meḍhra, accompanied by rhythmic contractions of the anal sphincter, breathing exercises and the repetition of certain vibratory mantras. The rod is progressively inserted further and further into the urethra until after about two years practice it reaches the bladder. Air, and in advanced stages milk, is blown into the bladder. In a variation of this the guru inserts a piece of lead wire into the chela's member to a distance of 'twenty-three fingers'. In this way cleansing of the canal is accomplished, its inner linings strengthened, its movements controlled. The next step is the practice of absorbing water through the urethra. This is done by immersing the organ into a bowl of warm water and by a special process including the isolation of the *recti abdomini*, combined with a breathing routine, drawing the water up into the bladder. Great powers are believed to arise as a result of this exercise, and its mastery is essential for the performance of the *vajroli* and similar paramudrās*, involving the reabsorption of the semen.

Books

See under Tantrism and Yoga.

PUROCHANA, an emissary of the Kaurava prince Duryodhana, who himself fell a victim to the Kaurava plot to destroy the Pāṇḍava brothers. The *Mahābhārata* relates that on the division of the kingdom between the Kauravas and the Pāṇḍavas, the Kauravas were allotted the area of which Hastināpura was capital. Duryodhana contrived to send the five brothers and their mother on a pilgrimage to the city of Vāraṇāvata. Before the Pāṇḍavas actually left Hastināpura, Duryodhana despatched his agent Purochana to make ready a large house for them at Vāraṇāvata, specially built with lac, resins and other inflammable materials, and arrange for a fire to break out, in which the Pāṇḍavas were to die.

When the Pāṇḍavas arrived, Yudhishṭhira's sagacity exposed the plot, and a stranger was asked to construct an underground tunnel by which they could escape in case of need. The lac and resin palace was burned according to plan and the Pāṇḍavas escaped through the subterranean passage. On the following morning the charred bones of a Bhīl woman and her five sons who had got drunk and slept in the house, were found among the debris and the news spread abroad that the Pāṇḍavas had been burnt to death.

For Purochana's part in the nefarious plot, Bhīma barricaded his house and set fire to it, burning him as he had intended to burn the Pāṇḍavas.

Books

See Mahābhārata and Mythology.

PURŪRAVAS, the son of Ilā (hence he was also called Aila), and grandson of Chandra, the moon, was the founder of the Lunar dynasty of kings. He ruled at Pratishṭhāna on the Ganges, near modern Allāhābād*. The principal episode of his life centred around his great infatuation for the *apsarā* or nymph Urvaśī* who bore him several children.

With the help of the gandharvas Purūravas considerably increased the extent of his wealth and dominions, and his conquests gave him the right to perform a hundred horse sacrifices. He soon became intoxicated with power, declared war on the brāhmins, plundered their wealth, and robbed them of their jewels. He coveted the golden sacrificial floor of the Naimisha sages, and one day while they were performing sacrifices he came to claim it. The outraged sages slew him and installed his son Āyu in his place. Another son *Amāvasu* was made ruler of the northern territories in the mid-Gangetic Doāb, where he founded the Kanyākubja (Kanauj) dynasty.

Āyu or Āyus (see above) the eldest son of Purūravas and Urvaśī reigned at Pratishṭhāna, and married Prabhā the daughter of the *dānava* (titan) king Svarbhānu. The couple became the parents of Nahusha, the temerarious king who incurred the wrath of the ṛishi Agastya; Kshatra-vṛiddha, who founded the Kāśī dynasty; Raji, and other sons. *Raji* or Raja was himself the father of five hundred sons and a warrior of great valour. In one of the periodic wars between the gods and asuras (demons), Brahmā declared that victory would go to the side on which Raji fought. He agreed to fight on whichever side would make him their king. The *asuras* declined this but the gods accepted and Indra was obliged to surrender his throne to Raji. Indra thereafter was reduced to such a sorry condition that he had to beg for a little sacrificial butter. In the battle against the asuras the gods were victorious and Raji ruled in heaven without fear of rivalry. When he died Indra usurped the throne from Raji's descendants and became king of heaven once more.

Books

See under Mythology.

PURUSHA, 'man', a giant being, representing the original primeval male, and by extension the whole world. He was supposed to be a form of Brahmā himself, who uttered the three words that brought the universe into existence. Associated with Purusha in his masculine aspect was Virāj the primeval female (*see* Brahmā).

The *Ṛig-Veda* contains the famous reference, in the *Purusha-sūkta*, to the sacrifice of Purusha, which served as a model for all future *yajñas* or sacrifices, and to the creation of the four castes* from his severed body: the *brāhmins* from his mouth, the *rājanyas* (kshattriyas) from his arms, the *vaiśyas* from his belly, and the *śūdras* from his feet.

Purusha is the first principle in Sāṁkhya* philosophy, and in metaphysics generally he represents the eternal, uncaused and causeless Cosmic Spirit, universal soul, the animating principle of the world. As such he is the counterpart of *Prakṛiti*, 'first-maker' (also called Pradhāna, 'primary', or Avyakta, 'unmanifest') the second principle of the Sāṁkhya system, referred to as female, and symbolizing the cosmic, primordial substance, i.e. unevolved matter, or Nature before the evolution of natural things, and regarded as uncaused, eternal, indestructible, formless, all-pervasive, limitless, and as possessed of three qualities* called *guṇas*. In Vedānta it is equated with *māyā*. Prakṛiti is animated by Purusha, but all material things emanate from Prakṛiti.

Books

See under Mythology and Philosophy.

PŪSHAN (*push*, 'nourisher'), a deity of vaguely defined character, who was probably worshipped by the wandering Aryans, and is frequently addressed in the Vedas. He is the nourisher of all created things; protector and multiplier of men and cattle, often depicted as carrying an ox-goad and riding in a cart drawn by goats. Lord of the pathways and patron of travellers, his aid is sought by those who are lost, and also by those searching for lost objects; he gives assistance to the newly married, and at the marriage ceremony his name used to be invoked to bless the bride. He is sometimes called the brother of Indra and enumerated with the twelve Ādityas, and is frequently identified with the sun-god Sūrya in his genial aspect. He is also called the lover of his sister Sūryā.

Represented as toothless and struggling for speech, Pūshan feeds on a kind of gruel of ground ingredients. A Vedic legend relates that Rudra, a precursor of Śiva, being excluded from a certain sacrifice shot an arrow at the sacrificial offering, and that the portion of the offering containing the arrow-head was presented to Pūshan who broke his teeth on it. A later Purāṇic myth relates that Śiva, enraged with him for attending the sacrifice of Daksha* kicked him and broke his teeth.

Pūshan is also known as Karambhād, 'pap', because of the sloppy food he eats; Āghṛiṇi, 'radiant'; Dasra or Dasma, 'wonder-worker'.

Books

See under Mythology.

QUALITY. The term *guṇa* or quality is of very wide application, and is extensively employed in many branches of Hindu learning. Generally guṇa is used to indicate the attribute or property of a thing. Vaiśeshika philosophy lists twenty-four kinds of guṇa of which sixteen are inherent in material substances* and eight are inherent in the soul.

The sixteen guṇas inherent in substance are: (1) colour, (2) taste, (3) smell, (4) sound, (5) touch, (6) number (*saṁkhyā*), (7) extension, (8) individuality, (9) conjunction (*saṁyoga*), (10) disjunction (*vibhāga*), (11) priority, (12) posteriority, (13) weight, (14) fluidity, (15) viscidity, and (16) self-reproduction. The eight guṇas inherent in the soul are: (1) knowledge, (2) volition, (3) desire (*ichchhā*), (4) aversion, (5) pleasure, (6) pain, (7) merit, and (8) demerit.

In Sāṁkhya philosophy the term guṇa refers specifically to the three constituent principles of Prakṛiti or primordial substance, namely, *sattva*, *rajas*, and *tamas*. These three constituent principles of guṇa have been profusely elaborated in religion, philosophy, āyurveda, dramatics, poetics, science, and other branches of art and learning. J. Przyluski held that the tripartite guṇa system was inspired by early Iranian concepts.

Sattva, 'goodness', inherent in purity and brightness, is equated with reality and intelligence. It is the power that illumines and reveals all manifestations. It resides in the mind, is white in colour and generates goodness and joy, inspires noble virtues such as faith, forbearance and courage. It is the predominant quality in the *divya* or celestial world of the deva, 'deities'. The *sāttvika* type of man, in whom sattva predominates, is of medium height, slender, 'wheat-coloured', pure in mind and body, long-lived, wise, and possessed of great physical strength. Sāttvika foods are agreeable and bland, like milk, curds, ghee, wheat, and several kinds of fruit and vegetables.

Rajas, 'passion', inherent in energy, force and movement, is the power that activates and excites the other two guṇas. It resides in life, is red in colour, and produces egoism, selfishness, jealousy and ambition. It predominates in the world of the *vīra* or hero. The *rājasika* type is tall, muscular, passionate, full of physical energy. Rājasika foods are bitter, sour, saline, pungent, astringent, and include meat (but not beef), fish and poultry.

Tamas, 'darkness', inherent in mass or matter, is equated with inertia, gloom and stupor. It is illusive and results from *avidyā* or ignorance. It is the power that drives to sensual and material desires, and it tends to restrain and suppress. It resides in the body, is black in colour and engenders stupidity, laziness, fear and immorality. It is the quality that predominates in the world of the *paśu* or animal. The *tāmasika* type of man is short and corpulent, with an 'animal' nature, and is dull and slow witted. Tāmasika foods are cold, flat, putrid, stale, made up of the leavings of others. They include beef, eels, turnips, pork, spirits, dark grains (*māsha*), vegetables that have a 'head shape' (onions, garlic) or a hood (mushrooms).

The guṇas exist in all individuals in varying degrees, and owing to the attachments to them the embodied soul is bound in *prakṛiti* as a slave. If sattva is the predominating guṇa in a man he goes to the celestial realms after death, if rajas he is reborn as a man, if tamas he reincarnates as a lower animal.

Books

See under Philosophy.

RACE. The problem of the races of India is extremely confused, and no satisfactory scheme of classification has yet been devised for the various ethnic groups that constitute the population of the subcontinent. Because of the continuous miscegenation that has taken place among the peoples, classification by skin colour, height, cranial shape, hair-form, nasal index, language, place of habitation, and so forth, can only be regarded as roughly approximate. According to a recent authority, India is the area 'where the greatest mixing has occurred and which is hardest to classify' (V, p. 696).

The caste system has to some small extent helped to preserve the purity of certain groups, but their racial origins were already mixed to begin with, and it does not provide a scientifically accurate criterion for ethnic classification. The racial groups as arranged by ethnologists are therefore only broad categories, providing convenient labels for the various groups that have some common racial, linguistic or cultural background.

The main racial groups mentioned here are not mutually exclusive. The *Negritos**, were a palaeolithic people originally from Africa, who once occupied the entire peninsula. As a distinct group they are now practically extinct, having been absorbed by the succeeding invaders. Many have left their mark among the Dravidians. Their chief characteristics are woolly hair, prognathism, low stature, excessive length of arm. Some identify them with the Nishādas* of mythology. The *Austrics** or Proto-Australoids, succeeded the Negritos. They had a neolithic culture and were part of a very widespread racial family that included the Vedda of Ceylon, the Sakai of Malaya, and even the inhabitants of Easter Island. In India the Kolarian* tribes are Proto-Australoid. The Irula of the Nilgiris belong to this category. The *Dravidians** belong to the Mediterranean or Brown Race. Their chief physical characteristics are a long head, broad nose, dark complexion, short stature, wavy hair with a tendency to curl. Many are modified by Australoid influence among the lower strata, Aryan admixture among the upper castes, and Arab admixture on the west coast. The *Mongolians* constitute the Yellow Race. Their chief characteristics are a broad head, yellowish complexion, flat nose, flat face, 'oblique' eyes. They include the Kirāta of mythology, the Ghurkas and Bhutia of the Himālayas, and the Khasis and other tribes of Assam, as well as some of the most important tribes and peoples of the semi-historical and historical periods. The *Scythians* or Central Asian Mongols played a most significant part in Hindu history, and left their mark on most aspects of Indian life and culture. They include the Śakas*, Kushāns*, Huns and Gurjaras. The *Aryans** or Indo-Aryans were a tall, fair-complexioned, long-nosed race, and included such groups as the Alpinoids, Indo-Aryans, Persians, Europeans.

Books

I. Anderson, J. D. *Peoples of India*, Cambridge, 1913.
II. Campbell, G. *The Ethnology of India*, 1870.

III. Chatterjee, S. K. *Indian Synthesis and Racial and Cultural Intermixture in India*, Poona, 1953.
IV. Chaudhuri, S. B. *Ethnic Settlements in Ancient India*, Calcutta, 1955.
V. Count, E. W. *This is Race*, New York, 1950.
VI. Cox, P. *The People of West Indian Origin in India*, Calcutta, 1935.
VII. Dover, Cedric. *Half-Caste*, London, 1937.
VIII. Ghurye, G. S. *Caste & Race in India*, London, 1932.
IX. Guha, B. S. *An Outline of the Racial History of India*, Calcutta, 1937.
X. Guha, B. S. *Racial Elements in the Population*, Bombay, 1944.
XI. Holderness, T. W. *Peoples and Problems of India*, London, 1912.
XII. Majumdar, D. N. *Races & Cultures of India*, Bombay, 1958.
XIII. Majumdar, D. N. and Karve, I. *Racial Problems in Asia*, New Delhi, 1947.
XIV. Risley, H. *The People of India*, London, 1908.
XV. Shafer, R. *Ethnography of Ancient India*, Wiesbaden, 1954.

RĀGA, 'tint', the name given to a class of modal melodies which constitute the highest expression of Indian classical music. It is so named because each rāga is believed to create a specific emotional effect that 'colours' the mind of the listener and puts him into a certain mood.

Indian music lays great stress on the emotional effects that music produces, and each rāga centres on one particular emotion, which it explains and develops. Not much emotion can be conjured out of the *thāṭas* or *melas*, i.e. parent scales (*see* music), or the *jātis*, i.e. modal families; but varied series of notes within the scales, employed in certain fixed relationships, are believed to evoke a response in the listener, and these make up the rāga.

The notes of the rāga are played or sung within a rigid framework and according to fixed rules, but within this framework the use of grace notes, ornamentation, embellishments and other variations are permitted. After singing or playing an air in a rāga, the musician commonly improvizes freely for a little while and then returns to the characteristic motifs of the melody; then meanders off again in other variations and returns once more, and so on. Often the rāga drifts into a refined form of tuning of one or two strings. The performance, whatever it might be, must be within the confines of the rules governing the rāga. Several melodies can be composed on the same rāga.

A rāga may last for several hours and there are many extraordinary improvisations within the brief compass provided. It has been said that every performance is virtually a new composition, consisting of elaborations within the traditional pattern. It was inevitable that this should result in a gradual modification of the musical patterns themselves through the centuries. Since a true musical notation was never devised in India most of the music of the ancient Indians is irretrievably lost.

A rāga is a combination of notes within the thāṭa or parent scale. Only certain notes of a particular scale are used, but not less than five notes for each rāga; most rāgas are in fact pentatonic. The notes are differentiated one from another by the predominance of certain fixed notes and by the sequence of particular notes. Each rāga has the characteristic 'signature' of its class, and a conjunction of notes peculiar to itself. The relative position of its tones and semitones is always measured against certain fixed points, which determine the character of the rāga. Only a few notes have intrinsic status in the rāga, all other notes being subordinate to and only incidentally associated with the main design.

Certain points of the scale serve as a skeleton for the structure of the individual rāga. These points are: (*a*) *graha*, the incipient note, or that on which the rāga begins, (*b*) *aṁśa*, the melodic centre of the rāga, the tonic or predominant note of the piece, often identified with the vādī (*see* music), and (*c*) *nyāsa*, the final note or notes, on which a movement ends. The nyāsa should leave its effect on the mind of the hearers as long as possible and at its highest emotional pitch (cf. the cadence of Western music). The graha and the nyāsa have now almost lost their significance, but the aṁśa still retains its importance as 'the soul of the rāga'.

The classical system of rāgas, in spite of certain minor differences and refinements, 'has nothing intrinsically different from the Western modal system' (VIII, p. 28). The Indian rāga, like all modal music exists by the relation of each of the notes to the tonic. The tonic or central note must always be heard, either as a background, like a drone, or repeated at certain intervals. This predominant note is the aṁśa (see above), and around this note and its consonant or correlative, a note about a Fourth or Fifth away from it, the phrases of the song are grouped.

Before the rāga proper is played the musicians and singers execute a pure musical presentation known as an *ālāpa*, or prelude, to give performers and listeners the tonal centre of the rāga. In this prelude the salient points are established as well as the secondary features characterizing the rāga and giving it the 'colour' and atmosphere. The complete ālāpa itself may last for an hour or more, and consists of the following parts: (*a*) *asthāi* or sthāyi (in South India it is called *pallavi*), the theme or first movement which introduces the rāga; this is often repeated cyclically and is a self-contained musical unit; (*b*) *antara* (S. Ind. *anupallavi*), the second subject; (*c*) *sañcharī* (S. Ind. *charaṇam*) or development; and (*d*) *abhog* (S. Ind. *pallavi*), a coda or return to the first part. Often only the first and second movements are played as an ālāpa.

The principal rāgas are said to be six in number and are called *janaka*, 'father' rāgas. These founder rāgas were regarded as being too stern, rigid and prosaic for all purposes and were 'married', each being given five wives called *rāgiṇi*, female rāgas. Later, in order to include still more subtle and entrancing modes and variations, each rāgiṇi was given six sons called *putra*, 'son'. The family of rāgas therefore consists of 216 members, all derived from the 72 parent scales, but usually more are listed, one authority suggesting a possible 34,848 rāgas. Like the thāṭas (or melas) from which the rāgas are derived, most of the rāgas are purely of theoretical interest and are not employed, being named only to complete the classification. Even the best musicians seldom know more than ten thāṭas, twenty melas, and fifty rāgas. Some authorities hold that when the musical phrases of a rāga have a basically ascending (*ārohī*) tendency and a predominating *rasa* (mood) of wonder or anger, they are rāgas; when a descending (*avarohī*) tendency, and rasas of love and laughter they are rāgiṇis.

The classification of this large family is cumbersome and chaotic. The rāgiṇis and putras have been assigned to the janaka rāgas quite arbitrarily, and it is impossible to distinguish them as they vary not only in the different regional systems of India, but in the schools within each system, and even among the individual musicians, so that there are almost as many classifications as there are exponents.

Like modal systems elsewhere, each rāga is said to have it own 'ethos', and is believed to produce its own effect and create its own mood. Those who play, sing or listen to music at the wrong time 'court poverty and shorten life'. Each rāga is allotted an *apsarā* (nymph), and a well-played rāga is supposed to enhance the beauty of that nymph. It is said that the sage Nārada, taken to the dwellings of the apsarās of certain rāgas he had played, saw them lying wounded and hurt as a result of his unskilled playing, and forthwith resolved to master the technique of music.

Each rāga is assigned to a particular season, and a particular time of day or night, and sometimes to a particular god or sage. The artists of the north have translated the rāgas and rāgiṇis into charming miniature paintings called *rāgmālā*, 'musical rosaries', which portray gods or mortals affected by the passion the particular rāga expresses. The rāgmālā is often accompanied by an explanatory text or title.

There is no agreement about the names of the six janaka rāgas. Commonly they are said to consist of the Bhairava, Dīpaka, Śrīrāga, Megha, Mālava and Vasanta, but others are also listed, and in fact there is a bewildering variety of names and systems.

Some rāgas are named after the *śuddh* or original notes (*see* music), e.g. Shaḍjī (from *shaḍja*), Ārshabhi (from *ṛishabha*), Madhyamadī (from *madhyama*); some are named after tribes and races who presumably originated them, e.g. Śaka (from the Śakas), Turusha (from the people of Chinese Turkestan), Jonpuri (from Yavanapuri or Greek city), Pulindā (from the Pulindas), Sauvīra (from the Sauvīras), Savara (from the Śavaras), Ābhīri or Āhirī (from the Ābhīras), Gondi (from the Gonds), Gurjarī (from the Gurjaras); a number after localities in India, e.g. Saurāshṭrī (from Saurāshṭra) Baṅgālī (from Bengal), Āndhri (Āndhra), Dākshiṇātya (Deccan), Gandhāri (Gandhāra), Kāmbojī (Kāmboja), Kambāvati (Cambay), Sindhavī (Sind), Karṇāṭa (Karṇāṭaka), Gauḍī or Gaurī (Bengal); others after places outside India, e.g. Bhoṭṭa (Tibet), Yamani (Yemen, in Arabia), Niśāvar (Nishapur, in Persia), Rahāyī (Rai, in Persia), Hijeja (Hejaz, in Arabia); some have a definite Muslim origin, e.g. Huseini and Imāmi.

The effects ascribed to the rāgas also vary. Some can cure madness (e.g. the Yamani); others can cause enmity (Vārali); or bring the dead back to life (Śrīrāga); or cause rain (Megha); or start a conflagration (Dīpaka). The best known of all rāgas are listed below.

Bhairava, 'terrible'; a late summer rāga, to be sung by a male, in August and September, at dawn only. It produces a feeling of reverence, awe and terror. It is presented to the imagination as 'Śiva in ascetic aspect, with matted locks, besmeared with ashes, and adorned with skulls'. A female form of the rāga, known as Bhairavī is sung at dusk during the same season.

Bhūpālī, 'earth protectress'; a late winter rāga, producing expectancy mingled with doubt, hope tinged with uncertainty; and conceived of as 'a lady separated from her lover, wearing an ochre sari, her body pale'.

Dīpaka, 'lamp', a summer afternoon rāga, which arouses passion and produces heat. Tānsen* was said to have set the river Jamnā on fire by singing a Dīpaka. It is pictured as 'an ardent lover on his way to his mistress; he rides on an elephant in rut, his complexion vying with the pomegranate, his imagination aroused like a river in spate, accompanied by two female attendants who are also aflame with zeal'.

Hammīra (or Hamīra), acquired from the Muslims, was said to be named after the Chāhamāna monarch whose favourite melody it was. It is an evening, post-prandial raga, visualized as 'a young prince listening to music, smiling amorously at his young wife and indicating the bed'.

Hillola, 'shaking' or Hindola, 'swinging'; a spring rāga of midnight or dawn, it arouses feelings of love. It is one of the *deśī* or 'native' rāgas and associated with the Swing Festival. It is personified as 'a fawn-eyed woman moving slowly like an elephant, with heavy hips, firm breasts quivering, long plaits dangling, eyes frisky'.

Kauśika, 'pleasing', a night rāga, producing a mood of joyous abandon and gaiety. Visualized as a woman 'with breasts like full moons, with skin like the lotus petal, and bare thighs like banana trunks, who comes smiling and singing sweetly, perfumed with saffron'.

Kedāra, a night rāga, producing a mood of devotion and awe. It is pictured as 'an ascetic worshipping Śiva with hopes of success in affairs of the heart'.

Lalitā, a spring rāga of early dawn, visualized as 'a mistress who rises from her empty bed to greet the dawn, her overfull cup of love as yet untouched by her truant lover'.

Malla (also known as Mālava, Mallāra and Malhār), of western India, a morning rāga, causing rain and bringing peace and plenty. It is conceived of as 'a mature male caressing the bosom of a beautiful damsel whose lustrous cheeks reflect her swinging ear-pendants'.

Mālkos, also known as Mālkush, and by some regarded as a vulgarized form of Malla-kośika, 'treasury of the Mallas', and sometimes identified with Malla, above. It is a winter night rāga, inspiring a martial mood, and personified as 'a warrior on the eve of battle'.

Megha, 'cloud', a monsoon morning rāga, which gives a sense of peace. It is rain-producing, and there is a story of a dancing-girl whose singing of this rāga brought rain and saved the crops. It is pictured as 'a bridal couple who have come together after the guests have departed'.

Naṭa (also Naṭanārāyaṇa or Naṭṭa-nārāyaṇa), a devotional rāga of South India, inspiring fervour. Musical concerts are frequently begun with the Naṭa rāga, and end with the Surati (below). It is personified by the Dancing Vishṇu, whence its name.

Pañchama, 'fifth', an afternoon rāga of northern India, intended to arouse erotic feelings. So called because it was a fifth rāga added to the four named in one of the classical lists, namely, Naṭanārāyaṇa, Megha, Bhairava and Śrīrāga. Pictured as 'a man engaged with a maid'.

Pillu, 'faggot', a night rāga of early summer, causing soothing dreams. Visualized as 'a man and wife satiated with the feast of love, sleeping side by side'.

Pūrvi, 'eastern', also Pauravi, an evening melody of late winter, lamenting the passing day. Represented as 'a woman watching her lover flirting with a younger sweetheart'.

Śrīrāga, 'royal rāga', an afternoon rāga of autumnal twilight, associated with the harvesting season. It is a melody of love and passion and is credited with the power of bringing the dead back to life. Portrayed as 'a man and woman in the full tide of their sexual encounter'.

Surati, originating either with the Suras or gods, or in Surāt in western India, and possibly brought to India from abroad. Musical recitals and temple rituals often end with the Surati (see Naṭa, above). It is visualized as 'a man and his wife side by side enjoying repose after union'.

Toḍī, introduced by the Muhammadans, is a late spring morning rāga of love and happiness, indicative of the beauty of nature. It is personified as 'a man and his young wife looking out of a bower at the rising sun'.

Vārali, 'opposing', a rāga whose original form is generally held to be forgotten. Teachers never teach this rāga to their pupils because it is believed that relations will become strained if this is done. Pupils learn it by overhearing their masters play it. Visualized as 'a woman living alone, estranged from her spouse'.

Vasanta, 'spring', a joyous exhilarating rāga sung or played at the beginning of the spring season. Represented as 'a young woman burning with desire for dalliance, her voice like the murmur of bees, holding her lover's heart in thrall'.

Velāvalī or Belāvala, an aboriginal melody, of late autumn; thought of as 'a woman who sits in her place of tryst, anon seeing her face in the mirror, anon turning to stroke and invoke her favourite idol, the god of love'.

Vibhāsa, 'quenched blaze', a late autumn rāga, portrayed as 'a woman who sits alone, having waited all night in vain for her fickle lover; her skin is pale and she hears the crowing of the cock with deep hatred and despair'.

Yamani, an afternoon rāga of the rainy season, said to have originated in Yemen (Arabia), and believed to cure madness. It is visualized as 'a woman who turns from her faithless husband to seek a lover of her own'.

Books

I. Bandopadhyay, S. *The Origin of Raga*, Delhi, 1946.
II. Deval, K. V. *The Ragas of Hindustan*, 3 vols, 1918–23, Poona.
III. Gangoly, O. C. *Ragas & Raginis*, Bombay, 1948.
IV. Gunther, A. *The Modal System of Indian Music*, 1929.
V. Sanyal, A. N. *Ragas & Raginis*, 1959.
VI. Tagore, Sourendro. *Six Principal Ragas*, Calcutta, 1877.
VII. Venkataram, S. V. *The Meaning of the Raga*, 1926.
VIII. Wellesz, E. (Ed.) *Ancient & Oriental Music*, London, 1957.

RAGHU, king of the Solar race, was the grandson of Khaṭvāṅga (or Dilīpa) who ruled at Ayodhyā. **Khaṭvāṅga.** 'like unto whom there has never existed any mortal', helped the gods in their struggle against the demons and was given a place in the heavenly abode. On being asked to choose a divine gift, he expressed the desire to know how long he would live, and was told that he had only one hour of mortal life left. He returned to the world of men and dedicated himself to the worship of Vishṇu with whom he became united after death.

Khaṭvāṅga's grandson Raghu subdued many tribes and nations and became master of the earth. He ruled justly but with such generosity that he was reduced to poverty. The sage Kautsa paid him a visit to beg alms and Raghu's embarrassment was saved by a sudden shower of gold. This monarch was the great-grandfather of the epic hero Rāma and it was from him that Rāma received the patronymic Rāghava and the title Rāghupati, chief of the line of Raghu.

Raghu's son **Aja,** 'unborn', won as his bride the beautiful Indumatī princess of Vidarbha. The legend about their marriage tells that a *svayaṁvara* (bride's choice) was held for Indumatī to which many valiant princes were invited. Aja, while on his way to the svayaṁvara was attacked by a wild elephant and ordered it to be killed. Before the animal died a celestial *gandharva* issued from its body and explained that he had once derided a *ṛishi* and had been cursed to be imprisoned in the body of an elephant, from which only the intervention of a prince of the Solar race could release him. Out of gratitude for his liberation the gandharva gave Aja certain magical arrows and the young prince continued his journey to the scene of the contest. The princess Indumatī chose him for her husband above all the others, thus causing a great deal of heart-burning among his rivals. As the bridal party set out for Aja's palace a band of the rejected suitors attacked them, but the prince, using his magical arrows, defeated his assailants. But Aja's reign and happiness were short lived. One day, while Indumatī was asleep, a garland belonging to the sage Nārada fell on her and struck her dead. The bereaved young man was then informed that his wife was actually a nymph from heaven who had sinned through neglect and had been punished to remain on earth until struck by a garland from heaven. This was no consolation to the grief-stricken husband, who died soon after.

The child of their brief union was **Daśaratha,** 'ten-charioted'. In his youth he had accidentally killed the son of a hermit in the forest. The mourning father decreed that the crime would only be expiated when Daśaratha himself suffered the pangs of parting from his son and died of sorrow. Now Daśaratha had a daughter named Śāntā but no son from his three wives. On the advice of his chief counsellor Sumantra, Daśaratha asked the great half-caste ṛishi, Ṛishyaśṛiṅga* to perform an *aśvamedha* sacrifice to obtain issue. To this sacrifice Daśaratha invited a number of neighbouring kings. It has been pointed out that in the list of kings invited there is no mention of any rulers of the middle regions of northern India, except the indigenous king of Kāśī, and among the rest we find specifically mentioned the rulers of Videha, Aṅga, Magadha, and Kekeya, all of them regarded, even in the most latitudinarian lawbooks, as 'impure' kingdoms, inhabited by outcaste tribes. This would confirm that the genealogy of Daśaratha was unquestionably 'native' and not Aryan.

During the ceremony the god Vishṇu appeared from the sacrificial fire and gave Daśaratha a vessel of nectar for his wives. Daśaratha gave half of it to his chief wife Kausalyā, and a fourth each to the other two. As a result four children were born to his three queens as follows: **Kausalyā,** princess of

Kosala, his chief queen, gave birth to Rāma*, hero of the *Rāmāyaṇa*. There is some reason to believe that Kausalyā was probably the sister of her husband (II, p. 125). **Kaikeyī,** princess of Kekaya* gave birth to Bharata. **Sumitrā,** a śūdra princess gave birth to the twins Lakshmaṇa* and Śatrughna.

As foretold Daśaratha died of sorrow following the enforced exile of his son Rāma which had been planned by his wife Kaikeyī.

Books

I. Basu, S. N. *The Line of Raghu*, 1918.

II. Sarkar, S. C. *Some Aspects of the Earliest Social History of India*, London, 1928.

(*See also under* Mythology.)

RĀHU, a fierce four-armed, dragon-tailed *dānava* (titan), the son of Viprachitti, 'wise-thought', and Siṁhikā, daughter of the sage Daksha. Siṁhikā, sometimes referred to as a *rākshasī* (ogress), appears in the *Rāmāyaṇa* trying to seize the shadow of Hanumān and drag him into her jaws. He allows her to swallow him and then rends her body asunder. Thereafter Rāhu her son is consumed with unquenchable hatred for the powers of righteousness.

In the story of the Churning of the Ocean, Rāhu wanted to drink of the *amṛita* (nectar*) along with the gods, and assuming the guise of a deity took a sip of the immortal draught. He was seen by the sun and moon who reported the matter to Vishṇu, whereupon Vishṇu hurled his flaming discus at Rāhu cutting him into two parts, which were named Rāhu and KETU. Rāhu burns for vengeance, unceasingly traversing the heavens in his eight-horse chariot and trying to devour the sun and moon for denouncing him, and whenever he succeeds in whole or in part an eclipse of the sun or moon takes place. To this day, during an eclipse, a great din is made to drive off Rāhu; conch shells are blown, men shout loud, and women utter shrill cries.

The moon does not move exactly in the ecliptic, but in a circle slightly inclined to it. The points where this path cuts the ecliptic are called nodes. In astronomy Rāhu and Ketu are the ascending and descending nodes, and they are also identified with certain planets, comets, meteors and constellations.

Rāhu is also called Abhra-piśācha, 'sky-demon'; Bharaṇī-bhū, born of the asterism Bharaṇī; Graha, 'seizer'; Saiṁhikeya, after his mother. Ketu is also called Akacha, 'hairless'; Muṇḍa, 'bald', and Aśleshā-bhava, 'disconnected'.

Books

See under Mythology.

RAIBHYA, a ṛishi mentioned in the *Mahābhārata* as the friend of the sage Bharadvāja*. Raibhya had two sons, *Parāvasu*, who had a very beautiful wife, and *Arvāvasu*, a devout young man who was unmarried.

One of the sons of Bharadvāja, the arrogant Yavakrīta, made love to the wife of Parāvasu, who complained to his father Raibhya. The sage in his great anger resorted to the magical arts and conjured up a *rākshasa* (ogre) who slew Yavakrīta while he was serving in his father's shrine. Struck with grief at this tragedy, Bharadvāja cursed Parāvasu that he might be instrumental in the death of his own father, and then flung himself on the funeral pyre of his son and was burnt along with him.

One night as Raibhya walked in the hermitage covered with a deer-skin, his son Parāvasu mistaking him for an antelope killed him. Horrified at the enormity of his brother's act of parricide, the young Arvāvasu retired into the depths of the forest to obtain remission of his brother's sin, and Parāvasu seeing a good opportunity to shift the blame accused Arvāvasu of their father's murder. The devoted brother accepted the accusation, and redoubled his meditations. This extraordinary conduct so aroused the admiration of the gods that after suitably punishing the cowardly Parāvasu, they restored Bharadvāja, Yavakrīta and Raibhya to life.

Books

See under Mahābhārata and Mythology.

RAIDĀS (fl. 1430), also known as Ravidās or Rohidās, was a *chamār* or leather-worker by profession, who became a disciple of Rāmānanda*, and himself acquired fame as one of the greatest *bhagats* (saints) of the Vaishṇava revival. He is especially revered in northern India, and southwards as far as the Marāṭha country.

The brāhmins despised him for his lowly origins, and resented his teaching religious doctrine. A semi-legendary account of his life states that he appeased the hostility of his enemies by miraculously multiplying his form during an assembly of brāhmins and talking to each one simultaneously, presenting such convincing arguments against each of the points they raised, that they were won over.

He wrote deeply impassioned devotional verse, and left his mark on Hindi literature for the fusion of religious sentiment with the vernacular medium. More than thirty of his hymns are embodied in the sacred Guru Granth of the Sikhs. 'O God', he writes in one of them,

'If Thou art the hill I am Thy peacock; if Thou art the moon I am the *chakora* bird that lives only on moonbeams; if Thou art the lamp I am the wick. If I am not with Thee to whom shall I go? I have turned to Thee, and turning to Thee have turned from all else. There is no one like unto Thee, O God!'

Raidās had thousands of followers, including members of the highest caste. The most famous of his disciples was the great Mīrā-bāi*, a Rājput princess who became a saint.

Books

I. Singh, Pritam. *Saints & Sages of India*, New Delhi, 1948.
II. Wilson, H. H. *Sketch of the Religious Sects of the Hindus*, Calcutta, 1846.
(*See also under* Vaishṇavism.)

RĀJPUT, the name given to a large miscellaneous category of fighting races of northern India who suddenly appeared on the Indian scene in the early Middle Ages and occupied the centre of the stage for over a thousand years.

Romantic ballads and stirring tales of chivalry are sung about their heroes. They are regarded as the special champions of Hinduism and the last custodians of Hindu culture, and their name still symbolizes the finest traditions of this ancient land.

Much as their origins are obscured, the Rājputs are known to come mainly of foreign stock. They are the descendants of those Central Asian tribes who invaded northwest India just before the Gupta period in the fourth century AD up to the reign of Harsha (*c.* AD 640). They included the remote scions of the Parthians, Kushāns and Śakas, and received fresh blood from the ferocious and newly emergent Hun* tribes, who shattered the last remnants of the Imperial Guptas and overran northern India. The invaders soon settled down, intermarried with the local women, some into high-caste families, and some into the Hinduized aboriginal tribes like the Gonds, Bhārs and Kharvars.

Just as the recurrent waves of intrusive Central Asian tribes through the centuries had brought about the extinction of most of the Vedic and Epic families, and saw the emergence of new clans at the time of the *mahājana-padas**, so we find that fresh incursions of foreign hordes now put an end to the dynastic lines of the Purus, Ikshvākus, Chedis, Matsyas, Vajjis and Lichchhavis. These in turn pass away and in their place we have the Chauhāns, Solaṅkis, Gāhaṛwāras, Rāthors, Chandellas, and other clans, arising about the ninth century AD from the new Hun-Hindu liaisons, with dynasties supposedly traced back to the sun and moon.

The Rājputs claimed descent from the long-defunct Solar and Lunar kshattriya dynastic lines of ancient India. But the gulf between the kshattriyas of ancient India on the one side, who according to legend had already been 'totally exterminated' at least three times, and the Rājput clans on the other, is too wide for any validity to be accorded to their claim of belonging to the orthodox knights of the older persuasion.

There were two methods of recruiting the neo-kshattriyas into the Hindu fold, namely, by intermarriage, and by religious rites that would lend sacrosanctity to the conversion. Two suitable myths were created to circumvent the old legend that the kshattriyas were no more. In the first we are told that a certain kshattriya chieftain, hearing that a brāhmin had killed his father, proceeded, 'with eyes glowing like the sun', to extirpate the brāhmins in the course of twenty-one expeditions; a story that sounds very much like a reverse version of the Paraśurāma* legend. However, as a result of the depletion of brāhmin males, the brāhmin females had to accept kshattriya men. Thus there came into being the various ruling dynasties of Rājputs. Not only does this legend indicate one of the stages in the evolution of the Rājput clans, but it also provides proof of the process of miscegenation that had continuously been going on between invading peoples and brāhmin women.

In fact, a kshattriya-brāhmin union is not acceptable to the orthodox, and a relic of this is preserved in the popular meaning of 'Rājput'. The term means 'king's son', and was sometimes used in common parlance to denote the natural son of a king or kshattriya. The practice of calling sons after mothers, which survives among Rājputs to the present day, is not the result of a polyandrous social system, as some scholars believe, but is due to the fact that the women were of higher birth and the men 'barbarians', and the preservation of the mother's name was a link with the past, and one way of safeguarding the ancient relationship.

The other legend was that on the fire-pit of the sage Vasishṭha on Mount Ābū the gods created a new chivalric order of pure kshattriya clans to help the brāhmins in their struggle against the Buddhists and *mlechchhas*. These AGNIKULA, 'fire-race', or *agnikuṇḍa*, 'fire-pit' Rājputs, were the progenitors of the Paramāras, Chālukyas, Parihāras, Chauhāns, Pratihāras, Solaṅkis and Ponwārs.

As the Rājputs were not united in descent from a common ancestor they formed a number of distinct clans. At present they do not recognize any kshattriyas outside their own thirty-six clans, but there is no unanimity among the authorities regarding these clans either. Significantly, included in the acceptable list of clans are the Huns.

The following are the names of the chief Rājput clans who are known to have played a conspicuous part in history: *Bāghela* or Vāghela of Gujarāt; of Gurjara origin they are related to the Chālukyas, and have given their name to Bāghelkhaṇḍ; *Bhatti* or Bhattil, of Jaisalmer, founded by Jaisal (*c.* 1156) a Lunar king. The Sikh mahārāja of Paṭiāla traces his descent from Jaisal; *Bundelā*, related to the Chandella Rājputs, gave their name to Bundelkhaṇḍ; *Chāhamāna** or Chauhān, agnikula Rājputs, with capital at Ajmere. Their famous chief was Pṛithvirāj III; *Chālukya** of Gurjara descent; capitals at Aihole, Bādāmi, Veṅgi and Kalyāṇī; related to the Solaṅkis. *Chandella**, of Gond descent, settled in Bundelkhaṇḍ, with capitals at Khajurāho and Kāliñjar; *Gāhaḍavāla* of Kanauj*; the enmity of their ruler Jaichand towards the Chauhān king Pṛithvirāj, brought about the end of the Rājputs; *Guhila** of Solar origin, ruled the area of Mewār, with chief towns at Chitor and Udaipur. One of their septs was the Śiśodīya; *Jāt*, a kshattriya* tribe, sometimes classed separately from the Rājputs though of Hunnish origin; *Kachhwāha* or Kachchhapaghāta, with chief towns at Jaipur and Amber. They established a kingdom in the tenth century, resisted the Muslims, but later allied themselves with Akbar; *Maitraka** of Valabhī, which was the centre of a renowned university destroyed by the Muslims; *Paramāra**, of Mālwā, with capital at Dhārā, whose most famous king was the great Bhoja; *Pratihāra**, agnikula Rājputs of Kanauj, of Gurjara origin, who founded the Gurjara-Pratihāra Empire; *Rāthor*, Solar line of Mārwār, with capital at Jodhpur named after Rao Jodha (*c.* 1460). From the Rāthors are descended the princes of Bikaner; *Solaṅki**, of Gurjara origin with capital at Aṇahilavāḍa. They were a branch of the Chālukyas; *Tomara*, who in AD 763 founded the town that is now Delhi. They were overcome by the Chāhamānas.

The Rājput clans fostered the fighting traditions of the Huns. They were brave in battle and loved strife, and their history is one of violence and warfare; when they were not fighting the enemy they were fighting among themselves. Their long chapters of heroism are scarcely mitigated by the appalling bloodshed that resulted from their flagrant military imperialism. There was much nobility in their social customs, but there were also elements of incredible barbarism and ruthlessness, in particular in the mass suicide* of their women in the rite of jauhar when on the point of capture. It was left to a British officer, Colonel James Tod, to assemble their legends and immortalize in his *Annals and Antiquities of Rajasthān* (1829) the vivid and colourful pageant of the Rājputs in all their glory, giving their history the haze of romanticism that must ever be associated with their name.

The general pattern of the dynastic history of the Rājput clans ran on the following lines. The rise to fame of an adventurous chieftain, either of a foreign barbarian group, or an obscure non-Aryan tribe, and his acquisition and rule of extensive districts, is followed by the realization that immediate status is available to him if he accepts the aegis of the Hindu dharma. The brāhmins, only too willing in these anxious times to have such stalwarts on their side, invest the upstart with a fictitious pedigree going back to the Solar and Lunar line of antiquity, and thus securely enmesh him within the Hindu fold. The new convert emerges as an ardent defender of Hindu traditions, and religious and social customs, and fortifies his claim by having brāhmins as his spiritual guides and political advisers (II, p. iii).

These new champions of orthodoxy became more Hindu than the Hindus themselves, and were regarded as the special custodians of the ancient heritage of India. The enemies of the Hindu dharma were their enemies, and topmost in their catalogue of hatred were the Buddhists, who knew only too well the real value of their pseudo-kshattriyahood. Religious persecution was intensified. Buddhist monasteries were demolished, monks were banished and their books were burnt. Says R. C. Dutt, 'Wherever Rājputs became rulers, Buddhist edifices went down and Hindu temples arose. By the end of the tenth century Buddhism was practically stamped out in India'.

In ceremonial purity and in caste matters the Rājputs were as rigid as the most orthodox. Hence the saying, 'Twelve Rājputs have thirteen cooking-pots', which implied more than their orthodoxy. It symbolized their deplorable lack of unity, and it was this factor more than any other that made them very uncertain bulwarks against the Muhammadan invaders who were now hammering at the outer gates of Hindustān.

The Rājputs took great pride in their architectural and constructional achievements. Their irrigation canals, dams and reservoirs, attest to their skill in engineering. Rājput kings of various dynasties have from early times undertaken the construction of Hindu and Jain temples, and Rājasthān is filled with picturesque building. The earliest examples of Hindu architecture are to be found at the Chālukya capitals at Aihole and Bādāmi (fifth to eighth centuries AD); the Chandella temples at Khajurāho erected between the tenth and eleventh centuries form a landmark in the history of Hindu art. The Solaṅki rulers (eleventh–thirteenth centuries) patronized the Jains and built veritable temple cities in Western Rājputāna and Gujarāt.

The palaces and forts of the later Rājputs are of exceptional beauty, representing a combination of Hindu and Muslim styles. Even Bābur, a severe critic of most things Indian, expressed his admiration for them and described them as 'singularly beautiful'. Their forts, some of them formidable structures with frowning bastions raised on the tops of inaccessible rocks overlooking the towns, were as magnificent in their own way, as the exquisite palaces with latticed windows and pavilions built on the shores of artificially constructed lakes. Such were the forts of Chitor, Ranthambhor, Māṇḍu, Gwālior, and Jodhpur; such were the Palace of Mān Singh at Gwālior, the

Palace of the Winds at Jaipur, the beautiful rose-red buildings at Amber which 'literally glow with bright and tender colours'.

Books

I. Banerjee, A. C. *Rajput Studies*, Calcutta, 1944.
II. Goswami, A. *The Art of the Chandellas*, Calcutta, 1957.
III. Ray, H. C. *Dynastic History of North India*, 2 vols., Calcutta, 1931–36.
IV. Satyasray, R. S. *Studies in Rajput History*, 2 vols., Calcutta, 1937–38.
V. Tod, James. *Annals and Antiquities of Rajasthan*, New Ed., 1920.

RĀKSHASA, the name of a non-Aryan people sometimes identified with the Asuras*. They are the ogres and demons of Hindu mythology, and the enemies of men, just as the asuras are the enemies of the gods. They haunt cemeteries, disturb sacrifices, steal offerings, slay infants, and interrupt the devotions of holy men.

Fierce, blood-drinking, flesh-eating and man-eating, they were especially powerful during twilight and at nightfall. They could move faster than the wind and could change their shape. Many were one-eyed and had crooked, twisted limbs, and were horribly ugly to behold. They were generally represented cyclopean in size, with voices like thunder, hollow-eyed, cavern-mouthed, huge-bellied, large-organed.

Several legends describe their origin. According to some they sprang from the toe-nail of Brahmā who created them to guard (*raksh*) the primeval waters. According to others they were descended from the sage Pulastya. The Purāṇas make them descendants of *Rākshas* son of the archṛishi Kaśyapa.

In the old hymns Agni slays a number of the 'tiger-headed' rākshasas. They play a prominent part in later mythology and in the epics. The rākshasas of the *Rāmāyaṇa* are often female, those of the *Mahābhārata* male. Presumptuous mortals, *gandharvas*, and semi-divine beings often reincarnated as rākshasas. Rāvaṇa, king of the rākshasas, was one such being. Another was *Virādha* who opposed Rāma in the Daṇḍaka forest. As a result of long penances he had been granted the boon of invulnerability by Brahmā, and the arrows of Rāma and Lakshmaṇa could not injure him. So the brothers dug a pit and buried him alive. From the mound there arose a gandharva who said that he was *Tumburu*, condemned by Kubera to be reborn as a rākshasa for the sins committed by him in his past life, and Rāma had enabled him to escape from the rākshasa form.

Another rākshasa of the *Rāmāyaṇa* was *Kabandha* (or Danu), a shapeless mass of flesh, without head of neck, with a gaping maw situated in the middle of his belly, and one huge eye in his breast. He was in fact mainly a face. He tried to impede the progress of Rāma who slew him. As he lay dying he disclosed to Rāma that he was a gandharva and the son of the goddess Śrī. During a quarrel with Indra he had been struck by Indra's thunderbolt which drove his head and thighs into his body and caused his other deformities. In accordance with his wish Rāma cremated his body when he died, and from the flames a beautiful figure appeared which was the original shape of Kabandha. He counselled Rāma to seek the help of the vānara (monkey) hosts without which he could not hope to defeat Rāvaṇa.

In the *Mahābhārata* the hero Bhīma is a mighty slayer of rākshasas. He killed Vaka and Hiḍimba, and married the latter's sister, the *rakshasī* Hiḍimbā.

Associated with the rākshasas are the *Yātu* (or Yātu-dhāna), sorcerers, fiends, and demon children of Kaśyapa and Surasā. They took the form of vultures, ravens, dogs, and hoofed spirits, and devoured the remains left by the rākshasas.

Books

See under Mythology.

RĀMA, a name of unknown and contentious origin which different scholars have found reason to relate to Egypt, Judea, the Mitanni and the Assyrians. It occurs in the *Ṛig-veda* as the name of an *asura* or aboriginal king.

In Hindu mythology Rāma, or Rāmachandra, is the seventh incarnation of Vishṇu. The story of his life as a great hero, but not as a god, is briefly told in the *Rāmopākhyāna* in the *Vana-parva* section of the *Mahābhārata,* and forms the central theme of the *Rāmāyaṇa**. He is worshipped as a supreme god in the *Rāmatāpanīyopanishad,* an Upanishad of the *Atharva-veda,* and as a saviour-god in the *Adhyātma Rāmāyaṇa,* which is part of the *Brāhmaṇa Purāṇa.*

His father Daśaratha king of Ayodhyā performed a horse sacrifice to obtain issue by his three wives. In due course four children were born: Rāma (to his wife Kausalyā), Bharata (to Kaikeyī), and Lakshmaṇa and Śatrughna (to Sumitrā). From infancy Rāma showed signs of greatness. He once craved the moon and would not be satisfied with any other object until a mirror was put into his hand and he quietened down, thinking the reflection in it was the moon.

When Rāma was sixteen years old the sage Viśvāmitra sought his assistance in ridding the country between the Śarayū and the Ganges of several fierce rākshasas who were interfering with his sacrifices. Rāma slew the ogress Tārakā* and drove away her son Mārīcha. A legend in the *Raghuvaṁśa* states that Rāma, who was very conscious of caste distinctions, once came across a śūdra named *Śambūka* performing religious ceremonies, and practising penances not permitted to a man of his caste, and in a fury of indignation at the man's impudence Rāma slew him. As a modern Hindu writer, K. M. Panikkar has expressed it, the righteous Rāma killed the śūdra 'for the heinous crime of being religious'.

While yet a lad Rāma journeyed to the court of Janaka* king of Mithilā, where he learnt that Janaka's lovely daughter Sītā would be given to the man who could lift and string the wonderful bow of Śiva. One hundred and fifty servants dragged the bow out on an eight-wheeled cart, and Rāma lightly taking it up bent and strung it. He then pulled upon it and it broke with a noise so terrific that it shook the whole earth. Daśaratha was sent for, and Rāma and Sītā were married amid great rejoicing. One legend has it that Paraśurāma, the sixth incarnation of Vishṇu, and a devotee of Śiva, was outraged that Rāma had dared to break Śiva's bow, and challenged him to mortal combat. Rāma defeated him but spared his life since he was a brāhmin.

As Daśaratha advanced in years it became necessary to choose his successor and he naturally appointed Rāma, his eldest son, and the child of his chief queen. Preparations began for the coronation, but before the ceremony could take place Rāma was banished from Ayodhyā for fourteen years through the machinations of Kaikeyī, the second wife of Daśaratha, who was determined to secure the succession for her own son Bharata.

The exile of his beloved son brought on the death of Daśaratha. Bharata refused to profit by his mother's ruse to supplant his exiled brother, and followed him into the forest to persuade him to return and rule the kingdom. But Rāma declined, since he was bound by his father's promise. The attempts of the brāhmin Javāli* to make Rāma return to Ayodhyā proved equally futile. Bharata therefore returned to Ayodhyā alone, bringing with him Rāma's sandals, which he installed on the throne as a symbol of Rāma's rule, he himself merely governing as Viceregent.

Rāma's exile was shared by his wife, the devoted Sītā, and his brother Lakshmaṇa, who would not leave Rāma's side. They passed the first week of exile by the banks of the river Tamasā, a tributary of the Ganges, and then moved southwards. For ten years the exiles wandered from one hermitage to another and finally reached the Deccan where at the suggestion of the sage Agastya they took up their abode at Pañchāvatī in the Daṇḍaka forest, near the source of the Godāverī river. Here they built a hut and dwelt for some time, and here Rāma saw his devotee, the low-caste woman Śarvarī, whom he raised to high caste for her devotions (*see* caste).

The Daṇḍaka forest was the abode of many rākshasas and demons. One of them, a female named Śūrpanakhā* fell in love with Rāma who spurned her advances. Other rākshasas who came to attack him were slain by the hero, among them Virādha, Khara, and Dūshaṇa, and the female rākshasī Taṭikā. Śurpanakhā reported the whole sad story to her brother Rāvaṇa*, the great rākshasa king, and at the same time gave him such glowing accounts of Sītā's beauty that he was filled with a fierce passion for her. He formulated a plan with his minister Mārīcha, in which the latter took the form of a deer and enticed Rāma away from the hermitage. Rāma went in pursuit of the deer and killed it. The dying Mārīcha cried out for help in the voice of Rāma, and this cry was heard by Lakshmaṇa and Sītā. Sītā knew it was not the voice of her husband but Lakshmaṇa was sure it was and went out to look for him.

Seeing Sītā alone, Rāvaṇa carried her off in his aerial car Pushpaka, to his kingdom of Laṅkā (Ceylon), defeating and delivering a mortal wound to Jaṭāyu king of the vultures who came to Sītā's aid.

When the two brothers returned to the hermitage and failed to find Sītā they set off in search of her. Rāma asked all the creatures of the forest and the trees and the brooks whether they had seen her. He came upon the dying Jaṭāyu and heard the story of the abduction. Proceeding on their way the brothers were hindered by diverse demons and beasts, among them the hideous rākshasa Kabandha, whom Rāma slew. Before he died Kabandha counselled the brothers to seek the help of the *vānara** (monkey) people, without whose aid they would never be able to defeat Rāvaṇa.

The brothers sought out Sugrīva the vānara king, restored him to his kingdom, usurped by his half-brother Bālin*, after killing the usurper. Further assistance was given by Hanumān*, the vānara chieftain. Hanumān's scouts found the vulture Saṁpāti, brother of Jaṭāyu, lying with his wings scorched on a mountain top; he informed them that Sītā had been borne across the ocean towards Laṅkā. Hanumān crossed over to Laṅkā, found Sītā, and assured her that he would return with Rāma to rescue her. He then leapt over the ocean and apprised Rāma of all that had happened. Preparations were made for a great battle, during which Rāma was joined by Vibhīshaṇa, Rāvaṇa's brother, who had refused to aid Rāvaṇa in his unrighteous war.

Rāma advanced to the edge of the ocean to cross over to Laṅkā, but was unable to do so until the vānara chief Nala built a bridge across the straits, consisting of a series of huge stepping-stones set wide apart. Rāma, mounted on the back of Hanumān, and Lakshmaṇa mounted on the back of Aṅgada (son of Bālin) led the vānara hosts across the straits to Laṅkā. Assistance and advice were also brought to the enterprise by Jāmbavat king of the bears. For this service he was granted the boon of death by Vishṇu's hand alone, and the bear king lived for many years, until he was slain by Kṛishṇa (an incarnation of Vishṇu).

On the island of Laṅkā the great encounter took place, and often the tide of battle appeared to be in favour of the formidable Rāvaṇa and his rākshasa hosts, but the two brothers as often received divine assistance. At length the forces of Rāvaṇa were driven back and Rāvaṇa's ten crowns were swept off his ten heads by an arrow from Rāma's bow, and the monarch of Laṅkā had to retire in shame. As a last resort Rāvaṇa decided to awaken the mightiest of the rākshasa warriors, Kumbhakarṇa* who lay in one of his long periods of slumber. Once awake the giant caused great havoc in the ranks of Rāma; he defeated Hanumān, took Sugrīva captive to Laṅkā, and then returned to slay Rāma. But the youthful hero shot a flaming arrow at him and the titan staggered back and fell into the sea.

A nephew of Rāvaṇa's, named *Lavaṇa* who was king of Mathurā also participated in the fray. He had inherited an invincible trident which had belonged to Śiva and with this he wrought great damage amongst Rāma's hosts. But Śatrughna, twin brother of Lakshmaṇa found an opportunity when he was without his trident and cut him down. Later Śatrughna became king of Mathurā.

Meghanāda the son of Rāvaṇa decided on a stratagem. He produced an illusory figure of Sītā and slew her in full view of Rāma's army, causing consternation in the hero's camp. But the deception was detected and confidence restored. Lakshmaṇa next slew Meghanāda, and in turn lost his own life, pierced through the heart by an arrow from the hand of Meghanāda's distraught father, Rāvaṇa. Hanumān was urgently dispatched to the Himālayas to bring healing herbs for the vānara physician Sushena. With these herbs Sushena restored Lakshmaṇa to life, healed the wounds of Rāma, and restored the limbs to those of the vānara warriors who had lost them in battle.

It was now time for the final encounter between Rāma and Rāvaṇa. As Rāvaṇa went forth to do battle, his sister Śūrpanakhā stood in his way, but

Rāvaṇa thrust her aside. Slighted, she cursed him, vowing that he would never return to Laṅkā again. Rāma shot several of his miraculous arrows at Rāvaṇa but found that for every head that was destroyed another nine immediately sprouted up. Rāma had once been given a terrible Brahmā-weapon by the sage Agastya, and this weapon he now brought out to deal with his dread opponent, and as he appeared Rāma hurled the weapon at the demon king. The fiery missile cleaved the heart of Rāvaṇa, who fell with a mighty crash across the battlefield. The rākshasa hosts broke in flight and Rāma entered the enemy city in triumph and rescued Sītā. He restored order and peace and proclaimed Vibhīshaṇa king of Laṅkā.

Rāma then started on his journey home. He stopped at the island now called Rāmeśvaram* after him, and performed a ceremony of expiation for the sin of having slain Rāvaṇa who was a brāhmin. Then in order to prevent any further invasion of Laṅkā he destroyed the famous bridge with a few shots from his bow, at a place called Dhanushkoṭi, 'bow-notch'.

Since Sītā had been associated with another man, Rāma refused to have her back as his queen, and although she proved her innocence by mounting a pyre and emerging unhurt, his misgivings were not allayed. The party returned to Ayodhyā, and Rāma ascended the throne, his period of exile having expired. Rāma's reign at Ayodhyā, known as *Rāma-rājya*, is looked upon as a golden age of perfect peace and prosperity, and is proverbial for a happy and just rule.

Rāma's suspicion of Sītā continued to grow, and matters were brought to a head when he overheard a washerman using Sītā's name in connection with his adulterous wife (*see* Sītā). Unable to bear any further insinuation Rāma banished his faithful spouse who was now heavy with child. She stayed at the hermitage of the sage Vālmīki* where she gave birth to twin sons, Lava and Kuśa.

Fifteen years later Rāma performed a great *aśvamedha* ceremony, during which the wandering horse was captured by two youths from the hermitage in the forest, and Lakshmaṇa and Śatrughna were defeated. Rāma came in person to look into this strange occurrence and he recognized his own likeness in the two boys. He became reconciled to Sītā and persuaded her to return to Ayodhyā. On her return she once more declared her innocence and then asked her mother Earth to receive her back, whereupon the earth opened up and swallowed her.

Filled with remorse and unable to endure life without his wife, the grieving king resolved to follow her. His brother Lakshmaṇa had tried to save him from the fate of Time and had already departed from this earth. Disconsolate and lonely, Rāma walked into the river Śarayū, as Lakshmaṇa had done before him, and, hailed by the voice of Brahmā, he entered into the glory of Vishṇu. There, it is said, he sits with Sītā, as Lakshmī, at his side, and the two remain united forever.

The worship of Rāma is practically universal in India. His standard of conduct as compared with many heroes of Hindu mythology, is, in spite of a few blemishes, worthy of approbation. He was 'the husband of a single wife', was devoted, affectionate, and brave. His worship never degenerates into impurity and licentiousness.

Rāma was also called Rāghava, of the line of Raghu; Raghupati, chief of the race of Raghu; Rāmachandra; and also Kapiprabhu.

Books

I. Banerji, D. K. *The Life and Adventures of Rama*, 1919.
II. Sarma, D. S. *The Prince of Ayodhya*, Madras, 1946.
III. Tripati, R. S. *Rama the God-Man*, 1922.

RĀMAKṚISHṆA (1836–1886) sectarian name of Gadādhar Chattopādhyāya, a brāhmin of Bengal who was said to have been miraculously conceived, and whose life story in other respects teems with marvels. In his youth he served as a pujārī (temple-priest) in a Kālī temple at Dakshineśvar, near Calcutta, where his elder brother was chief priest.

Like Chaitanya* he was very delicately balanced emotionally, and was prone to mystic trances and ecstatic raptures from his seventh year. He was also subject to attacks of 'falling sickness' i.e. epilepsy, with coma and bodily rigidity. His moods alternated between wild exhilaration and profound depression, and twice during the latter periods he attempted suicide. In the hope of improving his health his mother arranged for him to be married. He was twenty-five years old when he married a girl of five, but the couple did not live together. He went back to his temple, she to her father's house.

For Rāmakṛishṇa the two great obstacles to *sādhanā* or achievement were lust and gold. To the end of his life he never had sexual relations with his wife, and regarded her, as he did all women, as a mother and an embodiment of Kālī. He never handled money, and the touch of gold, even during sleep, would cause convulsions and give him physical pain. In later days he could touch no metal, not even iron. He spoke of caste distinctions and concepts of social status as great evils, and in order to rid himself of caste pride and destroy any vestige of prejudice that might remain in him as a brāhmin, he did the duties of a scavenger and cleaned the temple latrines. He also ate the leaving of beggars and outcastes.

He would meditate for long hours before the Kālī idol, and came to look upon her as his mother and the mother of the universe. He imagined that the idol lived, breathed and heard and understood him. He would sing hymns, talk and pray to her till he lost all consciousness of the outer world. Often he used to weep in his fervent desire for a vision of the goddess and his behaviour led many to believe that he was a madman and a fool. One day while he was in a trance he was rewarded for his devotion. The goddess Kālī, he believed, revealed herself to him face to face, 'a limitless, infinite, effulgent ocean of spirit'. From then on the sight of her image, or the mere mention of her name, was enough to throw him into a trance. He began to neglect his temple duties and so lost his position. He retired to a neighbouring wood where for twelve years he devoted himself to prayer, meditation, and asceticism. Of this period he said that 'it was as if a great spiritual tornado raged within'.

At this time he came in contact with a *bhairavī* or mendicant nun, a devotee of Kālī, who introduced him to tantrik *sādhanās* (magical techniques) and yogic practices, and encouraged his 'madness after God'. According to Rāmakṛishṇa some of the methods were so dangerous that they could cause a devotee to sink into moral degradation, 'but the infinite grace of the Mother carried me through unscathed'.

Shortly after an itinerant monk named Totāpuri gave him instruction in advaita and Vedānta, and initiated him as a *sannyāsin*, giving him the new name of Rāmakṛishṇa, to which in later years his disciples added the title Paramahaṁsa, 'supremely holy'. He is said to have attained *samādhi* at the first attempt, and to have remained in that state for three days.

Much of the saint's biography is a supernatural romance and it is difficult to draw the line between reality and delusion. He claimed to have had visions not only of Kālī, but of Śiva, Rāma and Kṛishṇa. In order to induce a vision of Rāma he put himself in the place of the monkey general Hanumān, and 'lived on nuts and climbed trees, jumping from branch to branch' (VIII, p. 233). His first vision of Kṛishṇa came at the age of thirty-five, after he had taken to androgynous* habits, wearing women's clothes and imagining himself to be Rādhā. Convinced that all religions were one, he tried the experiment of inducing a vision of Muhammad. With this in view he underwent religious discipline under a Muslim saint, 'accepted' Islam, and adopted the dress, manner of life and religious routine of a Mussulman, and soon had a vision of a man with a long beard and serious countenance who was presumably Muhammad. In like manner he tested Christianity, read the Bible with a friend, meditated on pictures of the Madonna and Child, and was vouchsafed a vision of Jesus, during which a voice said to him, 'This is the Christ who poured out his heart's blood for the redemption of mankind'.

His conclusion was that all religions were true. 'As one and the same fish may be made to taste differently by different styles of cooking, so God may be enjoyed differently by his devotees.' He himself preferred the 'Hindu style', found particular satisfaction in his own religion, interpreting his experiences in the context of Hinduism, and he remained thereafter within the Hindu fold. Essentially a pantheist, he saw God in everything and would sometimes place flowers on his own head and worship himself, remaining entranced for hours. On other occasions he treated his wife as a goddess and worshipped her.

At the age of thirty-six Rāmakṛishṇa met the reformer Dayānanda*, but neither man made any great impression on the other. He knew the Tagore family, and was once invited to the Tagore house for lunch by Dwarkanāth Tagore who suggested that the saint should 'cover himself up a little', as he invariably wore only a loin cloth. The ascetic replied that he had no clothes and Tagore, impatient with such eccentricity cancelled the engagement. The saint also met Keshab Chandra Sen who introduced him to the world at large. The result was that the intelligentsia of Calcutta beat a path to his doorstep and many became his disciples. Chief of his disciples was Vivekānanda* whose very presence often threw Rāmakṛishṇa into one of his trances.

Rāmakṛishṇa knew neither Sanskrit nor English, and had an imperfect knowledge of Bengali, his mother tongue. He wrote nothing, disdained learning, and shunned controversy. His speech was crude and at times 'abominably filthy', but his talks and parables were often very effective and enshrined much of the ancient wisdom of India. They have been published in numerous collections.

He held that the śāstras and philosophies teach *about* God, whereas the primary and predominant need is God-realization and God-experience. This cannot be gained through knowledge, but only through intuition, love, faith and surrender. All religions are different paths to the same God. For him there was no difference between monism and dualism, between the impersonal Brahma and the personal man, and he worshipped God in any form, seeing God in all things. 'Jīva is Śiva', (all life is God), he said. To the question, 'When shall I be free?' he replied, 'When the *I* shall cease to be'.

He used to refer to the *ādeśa* (divine command) which conveyed to him the explicit injunctions of the Higher Will. He believed that we should not waste time trying to know about God, but experience God by realization. Often 'strange fits of God-consciousness came upon him', during which he claimed to be 'eternally free', and declared that he was the incarnation of God himself, in fact the same soul that had been born as Rāma, Kṛishṇa, Buddha and Christ (II, p. 57). Many miracles of prophesy, clairvoyance and healing were attributed to him.

At the age of fifty Rāmakṛishṇa developed a throat cancer. He was taken to Calcutta where he was attended by the best physicians. But little could be done for him. Towards the end he sank into a state of coma from which he never revived.

Rāmakṛishṇa's wife, Śāradā-devī (1855–1920) came to be known as a saint in her own right. She was referred to as the Holy Mother, the living embodiment of Mahāmāyā and the Great Mother; as the goddess Sarasvatī, and Kālī herself, and she is still worshipped as such by Rāmakṛishṇa's followers.

Books

I. Farquhar, J. N. *Modern Religious Movements in India*, London, 1915.
II. Griswold, H. *Insights into Modern Hinduism*, New York, 1934.
III. Madhavananda, Swami. (Ed.) *Life of Sri Ramakrishna*, Almora, 1925.
IV. Müller, Max. *Ramakrishna: His Life and Sayings*, New York, 1899.
V. Nikhilananda, Swami. *The Gospel of Sri Ramakrishna*, New York, 1942.
VI. Rolland, Romain. *The Life of Ramakrishna*, Calcutta, 1954.
VII. Saradananda, Swami. *Sri Ramakrishna: The Great Master*, Madras, 1952.
VIII. Sarma, D. S. *The Renaissance of Hinduism*, Banaras, 1944.

RĀMĀNANDA (?1360–1470?), a Vaishṇava sannyāsin, born in Allāhābād, was the onetime leader of Rāmānuja's sect, and fifth in succession after Rāmānuja. He spent many years in travelling all over India, preaching the doctrine, and finally returned to the monastery. His fellow-monks decided that during his travels it must have been impossible for him to observe that privacy in his meals which is a strict rule of the Rāmānuja sect, and accordingly allotted him a place apart to take his meals so that he might not contaminate the others. His resentment at this affront cut so deep that he retired from the society altogether and founded a new sect. His followers are called Rāmānandī.

He taught at Banāras and Āgra, always using the simple vernacular Hindi for his speeches and writings in order that his message might reach the masses. One of his hymns is included in the Guru Granth of the Sikhs. God, he declared, should be worshipped by fervent devotion (bhakti) under the name of Rāma, who alone can grant release from the evils of transmigration. He did not condemn idolatry and made no break with the Hindu pantheon, but preached faith in the one god, Rāma, and his consort Sītā. He emphasized the equality of all men in the sight of god, preached against caste, and admitted all castes, even the lowest, to his fold, declaring, 'Whoever adores God, is God's own'. In other respects his teachings were very much like Rāmānuja's. From him there went forth a great current of religious feeling which has not abated to this day.

Rāmānanda selected twelve disciples to help him in his mission. They were: (1) Anantānanda; (2) Sukha; (3) Narahari, a goldsmith; (4) Bhavānanda; (5) Sursura; (6) the wife of Sursura. These six confined their activities to humble work among the poor. The remaining six were: (7) Raidās* (fl. 1430) a low-caste leather worker; (8) Padmāvatī (fl. 1435) regarded as a saint; (9) Kabīr* (fl. 1460) the great Muslim-born reformer; (10) Dhannā (fl. 1460) a Jāt peasant who, the legend goes, worshipped a stone with such devotion that it became transfigured into Vishṇu, who thereafter tended Dhannā's cattle for him; (11) Senā (fl. 1460) a barber, renowned in the Marātha country. Many fantastic tales are told about Senā, as indeed about most of these Vaishṇava devotees. As the barber of the rāja of Bhandogaṛh, Senā was once so absorbed in discussion while cutting the rāja's hair, that the god Vishṇu took the scissors and completed the royal haircut in case Senā should accidentally snip off the king's ear. The rāja was so impressed that he became Senā's disciple and was initiated by him; (12) Pīpā (fl. 1465) a Rājput prince. Pīpā first came to Rāmānanda at such an inconvenient time that the saint peevishly said he hoped the newcomer would fall into a well. So eager was Pīpā that Rāmānanda's words might be proved true that he promptly tried to throw himself into a well and was only restrained by the other disciples. This pleased Rāmānanda who admitted the prince to his inner circle. Pīpā built a monastery at Pīpāvati near Dvārakā. According to popular myth he visited the submarine domain of Kṛishṇa where he was affectionately received by that deity. His kidnapped wife was rescued by none other than Rāma himself. On another occasion he tamed a fierce lion with a *mantra* and converted the beast to vegetarianism.

Later members of the Rāmānanda sect were the woman saint Mīrābāi* (?1450–1547) and the Hindi poets Tulsīdās* (d. 1623), Nābhāji (*c.* 1625), and Malukdās (1574–1682).

Books

See under Vaishṇavism.

RĀMĀNUJA (?1017–1137?), Tamil brāhmin philosopher, grandson of a famous Vaishṇava pontiff of South India, was born near Madrās, at that time a part of the Chola empire, and studied at Conjeeveram under the advaita* (monistic) philosopher Yādava-prakāśa. He lost his father at an early age, was unhappily married, and was miraculously saved from an attempt to drown himself. While wandering in a forest a divine manifestation was vouchsafed him, as a result of which he left his wife to become a *sannyāsin* or religious mendicant. Such was the calibre of his mind that he was believed to be a reincarnation of Lakshmaṇa or of Śesha the cosmic serpent.

He visited all the noted holy places of pilgrimage in upper India, including Dvārakā, Mathurā, Kashmīr and Badrināth, and finally settled down in Śriraṅgam in South India, where he did his life's work. It is said that he travelled from Śriraṅgam to Madura to learn a mystic secret from the famed Āḷvār* guru Yāmunāchārya, but to test him the guru made him return without the mantra. Rāmānuja was compelled to perform the difficult journey eighteen times before the mystery was disclosed to him, under a strict pledge of secrecy.

The story goes on that Rāmānuja felt so keenly the injustice of keeping divine truths from the people that he one day ascended a tower of Conjeeveram and, risking the wrath of the brāhmins and the threat of eternal damnation, communicated to the multitude of pilgrims below, belonging to all castes, and to no caste, the mystic words of the sacred Vedas. He declared that he was quite willing to suffer eternal damnation if he could save thousands from it.

He made many converts among Jains and Śaivites, but was himself ordered by the Chola king to subscribe to Śaivite doctrines. Three years before this the king had put out the eyes of Rāmānuja's maternal uncle for refusing to accept Śaivism, and fearing a similar fate Rāmānuja fled to the Kanarese country where he converted a rāja from Jainism by expelling an evil spirit that had taken possession of his daughter. On the death of his persecutor Rāmānuja returned to Śriraṅgam, where he spent the remainder of his days. There is no certainty about the date of his birth or his death. According to tradition he died at the age of one hundred and fifteen.

Rāmānuja wrote commentaries on the *Vedānta**, the *Brahma-sūtra*, and the *Bhagavadgītā*. His *Śrībhāshya*, the great 'commentary' on the *Vedāntasūtra* is the classic text for Vaishṇavas today. He made a profound study of the Tamil* Prabandham, and was greatly influenced by the Āḷvārs. The school he established was in a way antagonistic to that of the philosopher Śaṅkara*. Śaṅkara was a Śaivite and a man of intellect and reason; Rāmānuja was a Vaishṇavite and a man of intuition and faith. He wrote only in Sanskrit but the works of his followers are chiefly in Tamil.

Rāmānuja is said to have selected seventy-four disciples and missionaries to spread his teachings. Like others before and after him he was deeply shocked at the licentiousness of the religion as practiced around him, the greed of the priests, and the ignorance of the people. Although he accepted caste divisions in a limited form, he admitted śūdras and outcastes to his order; he encouraged female education and strove for the religious and social equality of men and women. With characteristic imagery he said that in religion a man should be like salt (the same within and without), like a fowl (able to pick out what is wholesome from the rubbish), and like a crane (watchful for his prey). He permitted the worship of idols as 'auspicious bodies'. The school he founded exerted a great influence on subsequent Hindu thought. A peculiarity of his sect is the scrupulous preparation and privacy of their meals, and the fact that they never allow any hair to grow on the upper lip.

Rāmānuja taught that the Supreme Deity, referred to variously as Brahmā, Īśvara or Vishṇu, existed before all worlds, and is the cause and creator of all things. He is eternally free from all imperfections, and apart from Īśvara there is nothing. A spiritual principle is the basis of all nature, and this material world is *achit*, 'unconscious', but is not an illusion since it has reality as the 'body' of Brahmā. The will of Īśvara is supreme, and nature and human souls can at no time offer him resistance. This deity is full of love and pity for mankind, and on occasions has become incarnate in various forms for the salvation of men, the fullest and most perfect incarnation being that of Rāma.

The *jīva* or individual human soul is an *aṁśa* or fragment of, but not identical with, the Supreme. Although utterly dependent on the Supreme the soul has a separate identity, and when it is finally reunited with the Supreme it will retain its own individuality and consciousness. This doctrine, namely, that both the Supreme Being as well as the individual soul possess reality gave Rāmānuja's philosophy the name of *viśishṭ-ādvaita*, 'qualified non-dualism', and by giving the human soul a distinct, if subordinate identity, he is said to have 'brought the soul back to Hindu philosophy'.

Rāmānuja taught that the individual soul is subject to ignorance and suffering, the latter being caused only partly by ignorance, but mainly by unbelief. The means of salvation (*moksha*) is not knowledge (*jñāna*) but faith (*bhakti*), or love of God. Rāmānuja's notions were closely allied to the Christian and some authorities think that they were conceived under Nestorian Christian influence. His own influence may be discerned in the works of Madhva, Vallabha, Chaitanya, Rāmānanda, Kabīr, Nānak, and the reform Brahmo movements.

Books

I. Aiyangar, S. K. *Sri Ramanujacharya*, Madras, 1925.
II. Bhandarkar, R. G. *Vaishnavism, Saivism, etc.* Strassburg, 1913.
III. Farquhar, J. *Outline of the Religious Literature of India*, London, 1920.
IV. Govindacharyasvamin, S. *A Life of Ramanuja*, Madras, 1906.
V. Kumarappa, B. *The Hindu Concept of Deity as Culminating in Ramanuja*, London, 1934.
VI. Macnicol, Nicol. *Indian Theism*, London, 1915.

RĀMĀYAṆA, 'the goings of Rāma', is one of the two great epics of India, the other being the *Mahābhārata*. It is said to have been composed by the sage Vālmīki*. The incidents related in it precede the *Mahābhārata* by about one hundred and fifty years, but the epic was compiled after the *Mahābhārata*.

The *Rāmāyaṇa* has been preserved in three main recensions; the Northern which is the oldest and purest; the Bengal which has been subject to much tampering; and the Bombay which stands midway between the other two. These recensions differ on many points, about one-third of the verses of each version being absent from the other two. The epic as it exists today is divided into seven books called *kāṇḍa*, and the whole consists of 24,000 stanzas or 96,000 lines.

The seven kāṇḍas of the Rāmāyaṇa are: (1) *Bāla-kāṇḍa*, relating the boyhood of Rāma* of the line of Raghu; (2) *Ayodhyā-kāṇḍa*, the incidents at Ayodhyā; the marriage of Rāma to Sītā* daughter of Janaka, and the banishment; (3) *Araṇya-kāṇḍa*, 'forest section', describing Rāma's life in the forest with his wife Sītā and his brother Lakshmaṇa, and the abduction of Sītā by Rāvaṇa; (4) *Kishkindhyā-kāṇḍa*, Rāma's stay at Kishkindhyā, residence of Sugrīva the *vānara* (monkey) king; (5) *Sundara-kāṇḍa*, 'beautiful section', describes the passage of Rāma to Laṅkā across the bridge constructed by the vānara hosts; (6) *Yuddha-kāṇḍa*, 'battle section', also called *Laṅkā-kāṇḍa*, describes the war with Rāvaṇa* and his death; the recovery of Sītā; the return to Ayodhyā, and the coronation of Rāma; (7) *Uttara-kāṇḍa*, 'later section'; the banishment of Sītā; the birth of her two sons; Rāma's recognition of them; reunion with Sītā; Sītā's death and translation to heaven.

There has been considerable speculation about the origin and import of this epic. The more fanciful trace it to Ancient Egypt taking as a starting point the similarities in the names of Rāma and the Egyptian god Ra. Jacobi makes Sītā a goddess of agriculture, Rāma a form of Indra, Hanumān and his companions the Maruts, and gives the whole an atmospheric allegory. Lassen interprets the epic as describing the first attempt of the Aryans to conquer South India. The similarity between the basic story of the *Rāmāyaṇa*, which is the abduction of Sītā and the war that followed, and the *Iliad*, led Weber and others to suggest Greek influence based on the legend of Helen and the Trojan War.

The general consensus of critical opinion holds that the story is of indigenous origin, and existed in ballad form in more than one version. It was first put into literary shape by Buddhists in a Prākṛit tongue, the whole composition probably consisting of 12,000 verses. Weber suggested that the epic was based on an ancient Buddhist legend of Prince Rāma, who is depicted as an ideal of Buddhist equanimity. One Jātaka (the *Daśaratha Jātarka*) relates the story, with Rāma and Sītā as brother and sister. Winternitz explains the extreme gentleness of Rāma as indicative of 'Buddhist undercurrents'.

Whatever the origin of the slender plot it was taken over by the orthodox by the first or second century AD, rewritten in Sanskrit with many pious *ślokas* added and the epic given a brāhminical tone throughout which was not characteristic of the original work. The episodical arrangement of the books preserves fragments of its original shape, but the number of books has been increased and much of the material changed under brāhmin influence. Rāma's search for Sītā is shown as a triumphal crusade of Aryan civilization; the mighty indigenous monarch Rāvaṇa is transformed into a monster; and Buddha branded as an atheist and a thief (V, p. 77). Of the seven books, the last book and parts of the first are interpolated. In these two books Rāma is spoken of as divine, although in the genuine books (II to VI) he is a mortal hero. Evidence places the oldest part of the *Rāmāyaṇa* before 350 BC; the reference in the epic to the mingled hordes of Yavanas (Greeks) and Śakas (Scythians) suggests that it received accretions in the Graeco-Scythian period, and it may have acquired its final shape by about AD 250.

Books

I. Dutt, M. N. (Tr.) *The Ramayana*, Calcutta, 1892–94.
II. Dutt, R. *The Ramayana*, London, 1926.
III. Griffith, R. T. H. (Tr.) *Valmiki Ramayana*, 5 vols., London, 1870–74.
IV. Rajagopalachari, C. *The Ramayana*, Bombay, 1956.
V. Raychaudhuri, H. *Materials for the Study of the Early History of the Vaishnava Sect*, Calcutta, 1936.
VI. Sen, M. L. (Tr.) *The Ramayana*, 3 vols., Calcutta, 1929.
VII. Shastri, H. P. *The Ramayana of Valmiki*, London, 1950.

RĀMEŚVARAM (or Rāmeśa), an island thirty-one miles long and seven miles wide, between India and Ceylon. The town of Rāmeśvaram was said to have been founded by Rāma himself, while he was preparing for his invasion of Laṅkā (Ceylon). After his successful return to Rāmeśvaram, Rāma wished to purify himself for the slaying of Rāvaṇa and his hosts. He sent Hanumān to Banāras to bring him a liṅga to worship. Hanumān was delayed so Sītā fashioned a liṅga out of sand which Rāma set up and worshipped. When Hanumān returned with the sacred Śivaliṅga he was very pained to see that a liṅga had already been installed. To console him Rāma asked Hanumān to pull up and throw away the first liṅga and set up the one he had brought. Hanumān using all his superhuman strength was unable to shift the liṅga and thereby understood that it too was a divine liṅga. The second liṅga was installed beside the first and both were worshipped.

Rāmeśvaram is regarded as a place of special sacrosanctity by Hindus. It is in fact believed that every particle of sand on the island represents the liṅga of Śiva, and it is prohibited to plough or extract oil or make pottery on the island. The present Pāṇḍya* temple of Rāmeśvaram is a Śiva shrine supposedly founded by Rāma himself, although subsequently enlarged and embellished by the rājas of Rāmnād and Kandy in the Dravidian style. It stands in an enclosure 650 feet broad and 1000 feet long, and has a gateway 100 feet high. It is massively built in parts, and stone slabs 40 feet long are used in doorways and ceilings. The corridors are each 700 feet long. Columns surround the temple and an avenue of columns leads up to it; in the interior there are long perspectives of colonnaded halls in every direction, the total length of the colonnades being nearly 4000 feet. There are about 3000 columns in all. The temple is attended by brāhmins and maintained by the revenue of seventy-two villages. The liṅgam supposed to have been placed here by Rāma is washed daily with water specially brought from the Ganges, which is afterwards sold to pilgrims.

In AD 1311 Malik Kāfūr the Muslim general constructed a mosque on the sacred soil of the island. Among the places of interest on Rāmeśvaram are two long tombs said to be those of Cain and Abel, which are looked after by the Muslim inhabitants of the place.

Books

See under Pāṇḍyas and Architecture.

RĀSHṬRAKŪṬA (750–973), a dynasty of the Western Deccan, with capital at Mānyakheṭa (modern Mālkhed in Hyderābād) who claimed descent from the Yādava chief Sātyaki, a kinsman of Kṛishṇa. Originally a class of Dravidian agriculturists, they are sometimes classed with the Telugu Reḍḍi, sometimes given a Kannaḍa origin since they used the Kannaḍa tongue, and sometimes treated as the progenitors of the Marāṭhas.

A number of minor Rāshṭrakūṭa families ruled in the Deccan from the fifth century AD. One flourished in the Sātārā region. Another ruled in the first half of the seventh century AD over a small principality with capital at Achalapura (modern Ellichpur) in Berār. This branch had once been vassals of the Chālukyas*, until **Dantidurga** (733–755) threw off the Chālukya allegiance, asserted his independence and founded the Rāshṭrakūṭa dynasty. In the course of his career he conquered the whole of Mahārāshṭra and annexed much of the territory of the Western Chālukyas. It is thought probable that he was responsible for the excavation of the Elephanta* Caves.

He was succeeded by his uncle **Kṛishṇa I** (757–783) who is best known to posterity for having patronized the construction of the famous Kailāsanātha rock temple at Ellorā*. During the remainder of the eighth century the conqueror **Dhruva** (783–790) younger son of Kṛishṇa I was engaged in a ceaseless three-cornered struggle for supremacy with the Gurjara Pratihāras in the north, and the Pālas of Bengal in the east.

The long rule of **Amoghavarsha I** (815–877), a poet-scholar and patron of Jainism, saw a further expansion and consolidation of the kingdom. The Rāshṭrakūṭas were on good terms with the Arabs of Sind, and contemporary Muslim records speak of the Rāshṭrakūṭa king as one of the four great monarchs of the world, the other three being the Caliph of Baghdad, the emperor of China, and the emperor of Byzantium.

Under Amoghavarsha's successors the Rāshṭrakūṭas ruled over Mālwā in the north, exacted tribute from the Pallavas of Kāñchi in the south, installed a scion of the Rāshṭrakūṭa royal line as viceroy in Gujarāt, obtained the submission of the Pālas of Bengal, defeated the Pratihāra king, and in AD 916 temporarily occupied the capital city of Kanauj.

The kingdom was brought to an end by the intrigues of ministers and the protracted wars against the Chālukyas. The last king was finally defeated, and his nephew who would have succeeded him turned a Jain monk and died of voluntary starvation, thus extinguishing the illustrious Rāshṭrakūṭa line. In 973 the dynasty was succeeded by the re-established Chālukya kings.

Books

I. Altekar, A. *The Rashtrakutas and Their Times*, Poona, 1934.
II. Majumdar, R. C. *Ancient India*, Banaras, 1952.

RĀVAṆA, son of Viśravas, was the mightiest and most formidable of *rākshasa* kings. In a campaign against his half-brother, Kubera, god of wealth, Rāvaṇa defeated him, captured his aerial chariot Pushpaka, and usurped his kingdom of Laṅkā. He proceeded to embellish the new capital with many watch-towers, forts, beautiful buildings, public gardens and palaces, and its citizens showed every evidence of wealth, prosperity and happiness.

Rāvaṇa, a brāhmin on his father's side, and grandson of the progenitor *ṛishi* Pulastya, was learned in Vedic ritual, and was in fact so proficient in his knowledge of the sacred books that a certain reclassification of the Yajur-vedic texts has been attributed to him. He was deeply devoted to Brahmā and his austerities were of such a high order that they shook the foundations of the three worlds. Because of this Brahmā granted him the boon of invulnerability, so that neither gods nor demons could slay him. He conquered the celestial realms and brought all the gods in chains to Laṅkā where for a time they served him: Indra became his garland-maker, Agni his cook, Brahmā his herald, Vishṇu his chamberlain, Śiva his barber, Vāyu his sweeper, Yama his washerman, Varuṇa his water-carrier, and Kubera his treasurer.

According to a Vaishṇavite version the gods appealed to Vishṇu for protection against Rāvaṇa's growing power. Vishṇu declared that although neither gods nor demons could destroy him, he would be slain because of a woman, by a god-man aided by monkeys, bears and birds. He advised the gods to descend to earth and beget sons on female animals, especially monkeys, while he himself would incarnate as Rāma and slay Rāvaṇa.

A Śaivite version relates that on a mountain side one day Rāvaṇa met the terrible dwarf Nandīśa (or Nandīśvara), a menacing aspect of Śiva, who barred his way and refused to allow him to pass, because Śiva himself was sporting with Pārvatī on the summit. In a rage Rāvaṇa encircled the mountain with his arms and lifted it up by the roots, but Śiva pressed the mountain back into place with his great toe and held fast the arms of Rāvaṇa. The demon uttered an earth-shaking cry of pain and it was from this cry (*rāva*) that he received his name. Rāvaṇa propitiated Śiva for a thousand years with lamentations and hymns until Śiva at length released him. But because he had mocked at Nandīśa's monkey face, the god decreed that Rāvaṇa and his race would be destroyed by monkey hosts.

Rāvaṇa had supernatural powers and could assume any shape he chose. He is described as possessed of ten heads, hence he is also called Daśānana (*daśa-ānana,* 'ten-faced'), symbolic of his great learning; twenty arms, suggesting his prowess, and as being of gigantic stature and fierce visage. His muscular frame bore the scars of long and fierce battles with gods and demons.

Śiva once granted him three wishes, all of which were forfeited. The first wish, for immortality, was lost when the ṛishi Nārada, the mischief-loving sage, taunted him saying that the deity had promised him an impossible thing; provoked at what he regarded as a betrayal Rāvaṇa went to Śiva to demand an explanation; he disturbed the god's meditations and the gift was withdrawn. The second wish, for the beautiful goddess Umā, he himself rejected because he was given the illusion that she had become an aged hag. The third wish was for the *ātma-liṅga,* which he inadvertently placed on the ground to answer the call of nature, and it sank into the earth at a place called Gokarṇa (*see* liṅga).

Rāvaṇa's chief wife was *Mandodarī* but he had many other wives, and an uncontrolled passion for women in general. Once in a forest he saw and desired the fair Vedavatī, daughter of the ṛishi Kuśadhvaja son of Bṛihaspati.

This maiden had been eagerly sought by many suitors, including gods, *gandharvas* and *daityas*. The daitya king had even killed her father but she refused to wed, having reserved herself as a bride for Vishṇu. Rāvaṇa now attempted to woo her, boasting that he was superior to Vishṇu; but when he gently touched her hair Vedavatī in a fury of indignation cut off her hair and in his presence leapt into a blazing fire, swearing to be reborn for his destruction. She was to be reborn as Sītā, who was the cause of his death.

But Rāvaṇa's concupiscence was insatiable. From the serpent kingdom of Bhogavatī he bore away the wife of the Nāga Vāsuki. He seduced his own brother's wife, the *apsarā** Rambhā. He even trespassed on Indra's heaven where he ravished the nymph Puñjī-kāshṭhalā, and was cursed by Brahmā to die a hideous death if he continued his offences. Rāvaṇa's next exploit was the abduction of Sītā which brought about the fulfilment of the curse.

The enmity between Rāvaṇa and Rāma was of long standing. A legend states that Rāvaṇa conquered the whole earth and brought the rulers of all the kingdoms in chains to Laṅkā. But a descendant of Ikshvāku, named Anaraṇya king of Ayodhyā refused to submit to him, whereupon Rāvaṇa threw him off his chariot and placing his heel on his neck crushed him underfoot. Anaraṇya's dying words were that he was defeated not by Rāvaṇa but by fate, and that one of his descendant's would yet destroy him. This descendant of Anaraṇya's was the epic hero Rāma.

All these curses and predictions began to see fulfilment soon after Rāvaṇa abducted Sītā. He came to know of the beauty of Sītā through his sister, the ogress Śūrpanakhā* whose glowing descriptions inflamed his desire. With the aid of his minister Mārīcha he kidnapped Sītā and bore her off to Laṅkā. It is noteworthy that throughout the period of her captivity, he made no attempt to violate her, and his treatment of her was chivalrous and considerate.

Rāma was finally able to track Sītā's seducer to his island capital, and made preparations to cross over for a final encounter. Rāvaṇa summoned a council of war and he and his son Meghanāda agreed on a plan of action. Rāvaṇa's brother *Vibhīshaṇa* (*see* Pulastya) opposed their schemes, insisting that the violation of another man's wife was sinful, and that the war they were contemplating was an unrighteous one. Vibhīshaṇa was banished and immediately crossed the channel to join forces with Rāma, while Rāvaṇa enlisted the help of another brother Kumbhakarṇa*.

In terrible battle that followed between the demon and the monkey hosts, Rāma finding that he was being beaten back by Rāvaṇa, took as a last resource the dread weapon *brahmāstra*, laid it on his bow and with a Vedic *mantra* sent it forth. The missile struck Rāvaṇa's body with the noise of a thunderclap and the mighty rākshasa fell from his chariot. The entire living world shuddered, the earth quaked and the sky became dark. As the rākshasa king lay dying Rāma came to him and begged him to enlighten him on the science of statecraft. After his death Rāvaṇa's body was burned with full brāhminical rites.

At least one caste in South India does not believe the traditional account of the victory of Rāma, but holds that Rāma was actually defeated. They periodically celebrate what they regard as the authentic if unrecorded victory of the demon king.

Meghanāda, 'cloud-roar', was the son of Rāvaṇa and Mandodarī. For his austerities he was granted the power of invisibility by Śiva. He accompanied his father during the conquest of the celestial regions, and fought with such valour that the heavenly hosts retreated at the sight of him. The gods appealed to Indra who came to deal with Meghanāda himself, but the latter overcame Indra, bound him and took him captive to Laṅkā. The deities with Brahmā at their head proceeded to Laṅkā to obtain the release of Indra. Meghanāda agreed only on condition that he be granted the gift of immortality. Brahmā bestowed on him the title of *Indrajit*, 'Indra's vanquisher', with the promise that he (meaning his name) would live as long as mankind existed. Meghanāda, now Indrajit, released Indra believing that he had indeed been made immortal. In the struggle between Rāma and Rāvaṇa, Indrajit caused much damage to Rāma's ranks. While he was engaged in a sacrifice one day he was slain and decapitated by Rāma's brother Lakshmaṇa.

Books

See under Rāmāyana and Mythology.

RECITING. The memorizing of sacred, especially Vedic texts by 'recitation' aloud is called *pāṭha*. In the study of the Vedas a special technique was evolved in order to ensure that the text was handed down in a pure form, and the sacred scriptures conserved in their original, without change. This verbal accuracy was secured by following the methods of pāṭha.

The original text as composed is first recited in the form called *saṁhitā-pāṭha*, 'text-reading', or ordinary recitation, governed by the rules of metre and rhythm, in which the words coalesce according to the rules of *saṁdhi* (euphonic combination). Then there is the *pada-pāṭha*, 'word-recital', where every word is learnt separately, without saṁdhi variations, in its unmodified and uncompounded form. In the *krama-pāṭha*, 'step-recital', every word of the pada-pāṭha is pronounced twice in a certain order. Thus, if a b c d represent the four words of a text, if would be repeated ab, bc, cd, etc. In the *jāṭa-pāṭha*, 'woven-recital', the words are arranged ab, ba, ab; bc, cb, bc; etc. In the *ghana-pāṭha*, 'compact recital', it goes ab, ba, abc, cba, aba; bc, cb, bcd, dcb, bcb; and so on. There are still other variations of an extremely complex nature which entirely conceal the text itself. Techniques for turning the code back into the comprehensible sentences were also part of the pāṭha training.

These methods of ensuring the immutable transmission of the sacred writings were actually evolved long after the Vedas had already suffered considerable change. But from the time of the adoption of the pāṭha techniques the texts were said to have come down in very nearly the same form as when first taught. There were specialist *śrotriya* or memorizers, such as the *kramaka* who learnt the text by the *krama* method, or the *padaka* who memorized it by the *pada* method and so on. The pāṭha system continues to be taught in India with all the traditional disciplines, and it has been stated that if all the copies of the Vedas were destroyed, one would still be able to recover them whole, uncorrupted and intact from the memories of the śrotriya.

Books

See under Śākhā.

REPETITION of prayers and *mantras**, known as *japa*, 'muttering', is widely practiced, in the belief that the powers inherent in them are thereby increased. The shorter mantras, especially the monosyllabic ones are meant primarily for repetition. However meaningless a formula might appear to be, enlightenment will follow its continued iteration, and power will succeed enlightenment if the mantra is repeated often enough. Japa is an essential element in many occult rituals.

The sacred manuals hold out many promises if such and such a mantra is repeated, slowly and with proper *śraddhā* (faith) and *dhāraṇa* (concentration) a certain number of times. Thus, 'if it is repeated 100,000 times a man will have the power of attracting others; if 200,000 times all persons, men and women, will give him whatever he wants; if 300,000 times all the deities of the spheres will be brought under his dominion; if 1,800,000 times he can be levitated from the ground, travel over the universe and see the pores of the earth'.

Frequently a *mālā*, 'rosary', is used for keeping count of the repetitions. The mālā may be held in the hand but can also be worn around the neck or wound around the wrist or elbow. The beads are moved each time the mantra is uttered, or after ten or a hundred repetitions. The right type of rosaries, it is believed, have the property of keeping count of, and remembering the number of repetitions, hence they are referred to as smaraṇī, 'rememberer'.

Several varieties of rosary are used. Śaivites make a mālā of the seeds of the *rudrāksha* berry consisting of 12, 18, 28, 32, 64, 84, 108 or more seeds. Vaishṇavites use other seeds, or the flat coin-shaped shell of the fossil nummulite. Other stones and fossils, such as those resembling grains of millet or rice are also used. Śaktas count on their finger-joints or use dead men's teeth.

Books

I. Manik, S. N. *The Secret of Mantra Recital*, 1911.
II. Sivananda, Svami. *Japa Yoga: A Treatise on Mantrasastra*, 1952.

ṚIG-VEDA, the most important of the four Vedas*, and regarded as *the* Veda, since the *Yajur* and *Sāma Vedas* are merely different arrangements of the Ṛig-vedic hymns for ritual purposes, while the *Atharva-veda* is an altogether later addition to the Vedic list. In all probability the *Ṛig-veda* was composed some time between 1500 BC and 900 BC and had a fixed text from about 300 BC. Some scholars date the *Ṛig-veda* earlier; Max Müller put the date at 1200 BC, Keith at 1400, Pargiter at 1500, Weber at 2000 BC. H. Jacobi after examining the Indian calendrical system and the position of certain stars and constellations as described in the old texts, placed its composition at 4000 BC. B. G. Tilak, also on astronomical evidence, placed it at 5000 BC.

There are points of similarity between the hymns of the *Ṛig-veda* and those of the *Avesta*, and some of the Ṛig-vedic legends show a resemblance to the great *Yashts* of the *Avesta*. The latter, it is to be remembered, were composed before the *Ṛig-veda*. Some authorities claim that Book VI of this Veda was composed before the Aryan tribes entered India. But generally the language of the Ṛig-vedic hymns shows a good deal of borrowing from the Prākṛit languages. It is difficult to distinguish the Indo-European from the purely Indian portions, and the Hindus themselves have long lost the tradition of its true origins. Substantial parts of it were composed by śūdras, outcastes, and even women.

The *Ṛig-veda* is a collection of miscellaneous fragments of old legends, chants and hymns, some of them of great beauty, put together comparatively late. Twenty-one recensions of the *Ṛig-veda*, representing the rituals of different schools and even different families, are known to tradition. The *Charaṇa-vyūha* (Exposition of Schools), a supplementary work of the *sūtra* period mentions five *śākhās** or branches of the *Ṛig-veda*, representing the five chief schools based on the different recensions. These were (1) the *Śākala*, the only recension that has been preserved, (2) *Vāshkala* (or *Bāshkala*), which incorporated some additional hymns, named after a non-Aryan teacher, (3) *Āśvalāyana*, which recognized as canonical the group of eleven *Vālakhilya* hymns, (4) *Śāṅkhāyana*, which also recognized the *Vālakhilya*, but not all the eleven hymns, and (5) *Māṇḍūkeya*; the recension recognized by this school is not known. Fragments of some of these recensions (e.g. the *Vāshkala*) have been inserted into the present *maṇḍalas*, but all the remainder are lost or forgotten. The canon of the *Ṛig-veda* was probably not closed till about 500 BC, and the present text fixed about 300 BC. The special hierophants of Ṛig-vedic ritual are known as the *hotri*.

The *Ṛig-veda* is divided into ten books called *maṇḍala*, 'circles', or into eight parts called *ashṭaka*, 'octaves' (or *khaṇḍa* 'trunks' i.e. divisions). These books are subdivided into *adhyāya* or chapters, and eighty-five *anuvāka*, 'sections', containing a total of 1028 *sūkta* or hymns (actually 1017 original hymns plus the 11 apocryphal Vālakhilya hymns, mentioned below, of the eighth maṇḍala), 2006 *vargas* or classes, 10,417 *ṛich* or verses, 153,826 *pada* or words, and into many thousands of *akshara* or 'imperishable' syllables.

The *Ṛig-veda* thus consists of ten books or maṇḍalas composed of hymns and psalms of praise to the gods, among them Agni, Indra, Sūrya, Dyaus, Aditi, Varuṇa, Ushas, the Aśvins, Pṛithivi, the Maruts, Rudra, Yama and Soma. There are also a number of magical hymns and poems dealing with social customs, ethical questions, riddles, MANTRAS, myths and legends. In the opinion of Prof. B. K. Ghosh, it contains a mass of dry, stereotyped hymnology, but 'of natural outpourings of the heart there is not much to be found in the *Ṛig-veda*' (VII, p. 226). The priestly prayers are not so much for spiritual enlightenment as for victory, power, wealth, food, wine and women, and according to Bhandarkar, 'are saturated with selfish sordid aims' (I, p. 21).

Maṇḍala I is an 'eclectic ceremonial liturgy, and a veritable prayer book of the ancient priests'. Traditionally ascribed to eighteen ṛishis, although sometimes the same hymns occur under different authors, and distinct fragments are put together as a single piece. Most of the hymns are simple invocations to fire, water, the sky, etc. This first book includes one unusually long hymn known as the *asyavāmīya*, which poses the earliest metaphysical and mystical questions of the Indian mind, anticipating the Upanishads. 'Who saw that First when it was born? What is the Formless that upholds the form? From the earth are breath and blood; wherefrom the Soul?'

Maṇḍalas II to VII, the 'Family Books', are credited to ṛishis of various important families such as Bhṛigu, Viśvāmitra, Gṛitsamada, Aṅgiras, Vasishṭha, Atri, Vāmadeva, Bharadvāja. Book VI contains the poetry of the period before the tribes entered the Indian subcontinent.

Maṇḍala VIII, a book of miscellaneous and supplementary hymns, mostly by members of the Kaṇva family. Following verse 48 of this maṇḍala, eleven hymns of an apocryphal character were later interpolated. These *khila* (apocrypha) are called the *Vālakhilya*, after the children of the ṛishi Kratu.

Maṇḍala IX, a unique book inasmuch as it is almost exclusively devoted to a single deity, Soma. Its arrangement is also peculiar, as the first 60 hymns are set up in the order of diminishing length; the remainder, however, show no signs of order.

Maṇḍala X, differs from the other nine in subject and language. Linguistically this tenth book belongs to a later period than the rest, and in many respects forms a transition to the other Vedas. Many of the hymns are highly philosophical, some sacerdotal and legendary, others divinatory or designed for magical purposes, including charms for averting miscarriage, curing consumption, securing the destruction of a rival, and so on. About a dozen hymns contain dialogues foreshadowing the dramatic and epic poetry of later times. There are prayers to the greater and lesser gods, to cows, rivers, dice and rain. The *Purusha Sūkta*, which makes an allusion to the distinctions of caste, is found in this maṇḍala, and so also is the famous hymn of creation, commencing with the words, 'In the beginning there was neither nought nor aught'. Also included in this Book is the hymn on the burning of a corpse which starts, 'Let the eye repair to the sun, the breath to the wind. Go thou to heaven or to earth according to thy merit'.

An interesting feature of the *Ṛig-veda* is what is known as the *saṁvāda* (conversation) hymns, about twenty in number, scattered through the various books. They have no specific ritualistic application and were either treated as ballads, or as ceremonial dramas. Many authorities trace the origin of the Indian drama to the saṁvāda hymns.

Another set of hymns, the so-called *dānastuti* (gift-praising), are panegyrics commemorating the generosity of kings and other wealthy patrons towards the priests employed by them and describing the amount and nature of the gifts. Of late date, the dānastuti hymns possess some literary merit, and are important since they furnish historical data about the families and genealogies of the composers, their patrons, and the Vedic tribes. In these hymns are to be traced the beginnings of the future epic narratives in praise of princes and heroes of battle.

Books

I. Bhandarkar, D. R. *Some Aspects of Ancient Indian Culture*, Madras, 1940
II. Griffith, R. T. H. *The Hymns of the Rig-veda*, 1889–92.
III. Griswold, H. D. *The Religion of the Rig-veda*, Oxford, 1923.
IV. Hurst, G. L. *Sacred Literature*, London, 1905.
V. Kaegi, A. *The Rigveda*, Boston, 1886.

VI. Macdonell, A. A. (Tr.) *Hymns of the Rig-veda*, London, 1922.
VII. Majumdar, R. C. (Ed.) *The Vedic Age*, London, 1951.
VIII. Müller, F. Max, and Oldenberg, H. (Tr.) *The Rigveda Hymns*, Oxford, 1891–7.
IX. Stevenson, J. (Tr.) *Samhita of the Rigveda*, 1833.
X. Tilak, B. G. *Orion: Researches into the Antiquity of the Vedas*, 1893.
XI. Tilak, B. G. *The Arctic Home of the Vedas*, Bombay, 1903.
XII. Wilson, H. H. (Tr.) *The Rigveda*, 1859.

ṚISHABHA, the first Jain *tīrthaṅkara** or saint of the present cosmic cycle, who lived for eight and a half million years. In his epoch husbands and wives were born together as twins, had sixty-four ribs each and were five hundred poles or two miles tall, and Ṛishabha himself was of like stature. The word *ṛishabha* means 'bull', hence some scholars discern a connection with the bull-worship of Mohenjodaro. According to tradition Ṛishabha bestowed on his daughter **Brāhmī** a knowledge of the eighteen chief scripts, one of which, named after her, became the origin of Sanskrit.

Ṛishabha is also known as Ādinātha, 'first lord', a great king and the son of Nābhi and Meru, and father of a hundred sons, who renounced his kingdom in favour of his eldest son Bharata to take up the life of an ascetic. A younger brother of Bharata was another renowned *jina* (saint) named Bāhubali or Gomaṭa. He is known more elaborately as **Gomaṭeśvara** and is remembered through the centuries because of his colossal image at Śravaṇa-beḷgoḷā (Beḷgoḷā of the Jains) in Mysore. This had been a famous place of Jain pilgrimage ever since the Jain pontiff Bhadrabāhu accompanied by the Mauryan king Chandragupta lived there as monks. Bhadrabāhu died at Śravaṇa-beḷgoḷā and the spot acquired great spiritual sanctity.

The image of Gomaṭeśvara was carved about AD 983 by an unknown sculptor for the Jain minister of Rājamalla, king of the Mysore branch of the Gaṅga dynasty. Hewn out of a single vertical rock it stands fifty-seven feet high and shows the saint in the *sthāna* or stance of kāyotsarga (*see* āsana). He is entirely nude, and absorbed in profound meditation; ant-hills are shown rising on either side of his feet, and creepers entwining themselves around his legs and arms, while he remains undisturbed. A temple built at the feet of the statue maintains the uninterrupted worship of the saint. Every fifteen years the statue's head is anointed and thousands of Jains flock to the shrine to witness the ceremony. A scaffolding is erected and on this the priests and their helpers take their positions and pour potfuls of milk and ghee mixed with sweets, spices and silver coins, over the saint's head. As a result of this periodical anointing the stone looks as fresh as if it were recently quarried. This statue, and those of Kārkala and Venur near Mangalore are among the few such colossal monolithic sculptures in the world.

Books

See under Jainism.

ṚISHI, sage. The origin of the term is uncertain but it is said to be derived from a word meaning 'flow', because the influence of ṛishis flowed all about them; or from a word meaning 'push', since they possessed irresistible power.

Some derive it from *ras*, 'yell', perhaps a pointer to a long-forgotten shamanistic age. In Sanskrit literature the term is applied to a sage, patriarch, celestial poet, wizard and mage, and in general a ṛishi was an elder possessed of extraordinary power and wisdom.

He lived in a forest or mountain retreat, either in solitude or with a small group consisting of members of his family and his disciples. His religious establishment was known as an *āśrama*. The larger āśramas comprised a shrine and its attached bathing-tank, the ṛishi's living quarters, kitchen, store rooms, guest houses, cowsheds, gardens and orchards.

Several kinds of ṛishis are distinguished, such as *prajāpati*, *saptaṛishi*, *siddha*, *manu*, *nātha*, *pitṛi*, and so on. These designations are sometimes used interchangeably, and a *mahāṛishi* or 'great ṛishi' may be a prajāpati, a saptaṛishi, or a brahmaṛishi. A brief definition of the chief ṛishi groups may be given:

Prajāpati, these are specifically the ten 'mind-born' sons of Brahma, most of whom are included in the lists of the saptaṛishis or brahmaṛishis.

Brahmaṛishi, the Brahma-created sages, also called *dvija-ṛishis*, 'twice-born sages'. They are the reputed founders of the orthodox brāhmin gotras. Brahmaṛishis figure prominently in the community* system of brāhmin families. There is a great deal of inconsistency about them. They are variously and confusingly listed in the Brāhmaṇas, Epics and Purāṇas, but the seven or eight traditional brahmaṛishis are generally named from among the following: Agastya, non-Aryan in name and appearances; Aṅgiras, either Persian or Dravidian; Atri, tribal priest of outcaste races; Bharadvāja; Bhṛigu, founder of the Bhārgavas; Jamadagni; Kaṇva; Kaśyapa, non-Aryan progenitor of pre-Aryan tribes; Vasishṭha; Mārichi; Pulastya; Pulaha; Kratu; Gautama.

Saptaṛishi, one of the 'seven ṛishis', also called *ṛiksha* or *chitra-śikhaṇḍin*, 'having bright crests'. They are frequently identified with the heavenly bodies and are said to represent the seven stars of the Great Bear. Their wives are identified with the stars of the Pleiades. Thus, Kaśyapa is the Pole Star; so is Dhruva; Atri is one of the stars of the Great Bear; Arundhatī, wife of the ṛishi Vasishṭha, is the morning star; Viśvāmitra who created the Southern Cross, placed his protégé Triśaṅku among the stars of this constellation; Śukra was the planet Venus. The saptaṛishis generally named are Kaśyapa, Atri, Vasishṭha, Viśvāmitra, Gotama, Jamadagni, and Bharadvāja.

Devaṛishi, 'divine ṛishi', one who has attained perfection on earth and has been exalted to a near-divine status. Ṛishis are never regarded as truly divine, however good or powerful they may be, and are therefore not worshipped. The ṛishi Mārkaṇḍeya was a devaṛishi.

Mahāṛishi, 'great sage', or *paramaṛishi*, 'supreme sage', a term sometimes used to distinguish between the ordinary ṛishi and the exalted individuals of mythological renown.

Śrutaṛishi, 'hearing sage', the name given to the sages who intuitively 'heard' the divine truths of the śruti or Vedas and then handed them down. The title is sometimes applied to the lesser ṛishis who 'heard' the great truths from the mahāṛishis.

Rājaṛishi, 'royal ṛishis', exceptional kshattriya kings of great intellectual capacity who were accorded ṛishi status. These prince-sages included Janaka, Bhaṅgāsvana, Dhruva, Gṛitsamada.

Many ṛishis are born in extraordinary circumstances, e.g. Aurva came from his mother's thigh; Bharata was carried for three years in his mother's womb; Vāmadeva* emerged from his mother's side. In origin the ṛishis came from diverse stock. Some were brāhmins, like the brahmaṛishis; some kshattriyas like the rājaṛishis; many were of pre-Aryan, native origin such as Kratu and Pulaha. *Pulaha* married Kshamā and became the father of three sons, Kardama (himself a mahāṛishi), Arvarīvat and Sahishṇu. Pulaha, though often included with the brahmaṛishis, was the ancestor of several outcaste tribes and is not regarded as having produced true brāhmin stock. In later legends he was said to have been a fly in a temple of Śiva, reborn as Pulaha. A number of other great ṛishis were of Indo–Persian origin, such as Atharvan and Aṅgiras.

Many ṛishis were authors of Vedic hymns and founders of Vedic schools. Vālmīki composed the *Rāmāyaṇa* and Vyāsa the *Mahābhārata*. Gālava, Gṛitsamada, Kuśika, Mahīdāsa, Parāśara, Uddālaka, Vāmadeva, Vasishṭha, Viśvāmitra, Yājñavalkya, Bharata, Satyakāma, Śunaḥśephas, and a host of others were composers or amanuenses of Vedic psalms.

A few ṛishis used their power for good, and their presence removed disease (*see* Śvaphalka) or drought (*see* Ṛishyaśṛiṅga). Some were associated with acts of creation, such as Viśvāmitra, Kaśyapa, Daksha, Pulastya. But as a rule the ṛishis were a thoroughly irascible lot and unrelenting in their vengeance. The ṛishi's wrath is a favourite theme in Sanskrit literature (*see* Śakuntalā). Some ṛishis were particularly notorious in this respect, like Utathya, Daksha, Nārada, Bhṛigu, Jamadagni, Raibhya, Paraśurāma, and the great 'master-curser' Durvāsas.

The gods themselves kept away from the ṛishis in case they inadvertently offended them. The fierce black-visaged ṛishi named Bhūti (like the demon Tāraka, slain by Kārttikeya*), had so violent a temper that all nature trembled in his presence. In his hermitage the wind did not dare to blow hard, the sun to shine too strong, the wind to raise any dust. Even the river trembled when he approached to bathe.

Many were the great ṛishis who were shown at some time of their existence as undergoing the most awe-inspiring austerities, such as caused consternation in heaven, and made the gods hearken to their commands, e.g. Chyavana, Jaratkāru, Śukra, Mataṅga. To stop their depredations on the celestial plane the gods employed one almost infallible device; they would send a ravishing *apsarā* (nymph*) to distract and seduce the sage (*see* Bharadvāja, Śaradvant, Kaṇḍu). Most of the sages succumbed to the temptation and the disqualifying vega* resulted (*see* Mankanaka and Vibhāṇḍaka.)

Books

See under Mythology.

ṚISHYAŚṚIṄGA, 'deer-horned', a *ṛishi* whose story is told in the Epics. He was the grandson of the sage Kaśyapa, and the son of Vibhāṇḍaka. The latter, a model of continence, once beheld the *apsarā* (nymph) Urvaśī while she was bathing in a stream and his seed fell from him. It was consumed by a gazelle who in due time bore the child Ṛishyaśṛiṅga, so named because of a small horn on his forehead. The place of his birth in Mysore was named after him Śṛiṅgagiri or Śṛiṅgeri, later the site of a monastery established by the philosopher Śaṅkara. The legend may hint at the true origin of this well-known sage who was in fact the son of Vibhāṇḍaka by a non-Aryan woman named Mṛigī, 'doe'. Brought up by his father in the forest, Ṛishyaśṛiṅga saw no woman till he was on the threshold of manhood.

Now a great drought occurred in the country of Aṅga and the ruler Lomapāda (or Romapāda) consulted his brāhmin priests for a means of ending the calamity. They advised him to send for the young Ṛishyaśṛiṅga and marry him to Śāntā, daughter of Daśaratha, whom Lomapāda had adopted as a child. They assured the king that such a measure would not fail to bring down the rain.

The fair leader of the female embassy dispatched to the forest presented herself to Ṛishyaśṛiṅga while his father was away from the hermitage. Never having seen a woman before the young man was captivated with his guest and later described 'him' to his father thus:

'He was a chaste youth, wearing tresses, and wonderfully perfumed. He had two globes beneath the neck which he said greatly oppressed him and at his suggestion I stroked and kissed them to relieve his distress. Although small waisted he had large rounded hips. He took me by the hair and set his mouth to mine and brought to my soul a shuddering delight. And when he pressed his body to mine my senses seemed as though they would leave me. He had a mollusc-like mouth near his pubic region which he explained was torn by an arrow, and at his suggestion I soothed him as he required. Now that he has gone my body burns within me.'

Thinking they were demons the father left the hermitage in search of them, and during his absence the female company returned and persuaded Ṛishyaśṛiṅga to come to Aṅga. There he was wedded to the princess Śāntā and as the marriage was being consummated dark clouds gathered and rain fell in torrents on the thirsty land.

It was this same half-caste ṛishi, Ṛishyaśṛiṅga who performed the sacrifice for Daśaratha that brought about the birth of Rāma. Among the children of Ṛishyaśṛiṅga was Alaṁbusha, a great rākshasa, who was slain by Ghaṭotkacha on the second day of the battle of Kurukshetra*.

Books

See under Mythology.

RITUAL CANON. The whole body of scriptures dealing with the religious ceremonial and practice of Hinduism is referred to by the term *kalpa*, 'usage'. It is regarded as one of the Vedāṅgas or auxiliary Vedic studies. As the Upanishads embody the speculative side, and the Brāhmaṇas the dogmatic side of the Vedas, so the kalpas form the text of the ritual side. A sacred character was never attributed to the Kalpa-sūtras (ritual texts), because they were compiled merely to meet the practical needs of everyday life. The oldest of them go back to the time of the rise of Buddhism. The kalpas include the *śrauta-sūtras* and the *smārta-sūtras*.

The *śrauta-sūtra* are so called because they are based on the śruti, especially the Brāhmaṇas. The texts deal with the ceremonials and rules for the application of *mantras* and brahminical observances in connection with Vedic sacrifice. They teach the laying of the three sacred fires, the new and full moon sacrifices, and the soma sacrifices. Their operations call for a number of professional priests and hierophants. Attached to the śrauta-sūtras are the śulva-sūtras (*see* mathematics) which give rules and measurements for the construction of fire altars and sacrificial halls and enclosures.

The *smārta-sūtra* are so called because they are founded on the *smṛiti*. When the observance of the ancient sacrifices prescribed in the śrauta-sūtras began to decline, smārta worship based on the smṛiti or law books, gained ascendency. A smārta brāhmin is generally a follower of Śaṅkara, and strictly orthodox, but in ceremonial worship practices *pañchāyatana pūjā* (*see* God). The smārta-sūtras include the following: (*a*) *gṛihya-sūtra*, or rules relating to domestic rites and the *saṁskāras** (sacraments), e.g. birth, investiture with the sacred thread, marriage, death. The gṛihya-sūtras are the most fundamental of all the texts to the unity of Hindu society, as they determine the secular life of the Hindu householder or *gṛihin*, i.e. the keeper of the *gṛihya* or domestic fire. It is the observance of this canon of domestic ritual governing birth, marriage and death that makes the orthodox Hindu what he is. Elaborations of the gṛihya-sūtra texts relating to the *śrāddha* or funeral rites grew into a separate body of writings called the *śrāddha-kalpa*; (*b*) *dharma-sūtra*, or rules relating to the samayāchāra, 'conventional duties', hence also called *sāmayāchārika-sūtra*. More commonly they are spoken of as *dharma-śāstra*, 'law-codes'. This latter term is also used collectively for the whole body of customary rules and observances governing Hindu religious and social life. Where gṛihya-sūtras have domestic importance, the dharma-sūtras cover the wider relation of man and his fellows, and man and the state. They treat of the rules of caste, and of man in his social economic and religious relationships. They are primarily rules of practical life, including the civil and religious laws that regulate Hindu society. The terms dharma-sūtra and dharma-śāstra though used in a synonymous sense are sometimes distinguished, the former referring specifically to the works of Manu, Nārada, Vishṇu and Yājñavalkya. The dharma-sūtras are in prose, whereas the dharma-śāstras are metrical versions of previously existing dharma-sūtras. These terms are also applied to the *nibandha* or commentaries (*see* law).

The lawgivers and their texts run into almost three hundred names, mostly derived from the names of the great ṛishis. The chief texts are: (1) *Āpastamba* (?500 BC–AD 200), named after a native of Āndhra, whose rules are observed mainly in Āndhra state; his sūtras are based on a Black Yajur-veda of South India; two recensions of the *Taittirīya Saṁhitā* are also ascribed to him; (2) *Baudhāyana* (?300 BC–AD 300), also probably named after a native of Āndhra. His work is not well preserved and contains much interpolated material of a later date. It represents a South Indian school of the Black Yajur-veda; (3) *Bṛihaspati* (AD 600), named after the ṛishi. It exists in fragments and is composed of many elements borrowed from other schools. It approves the practice of widow-burning; (4) Gautama (400 BC–AD 200), the most ancient of the dharma-sūtras. It is attached to the *Sāma-veda* and is also classed as a gṛihya-sūtra; (5) *Hārīta* (200 BC–AD 500), contains fragments of an old code, but is now badly corrupted; (6) *Manu**, the most famous of all the manuals on dharma-śāstra; (7) *Nārada* (AD 150–450) author of the *Nāradīya-dharma-śāstra*, a very systematic code, practically outlined, with great emphasis laid on procedure; (8) *Śaṅkha* and *Likhita* (50 BC–AD 400), authors of a joint code embodying much ancient material; (9) *Sumantu*, of comparatively late date (*c.* AD 400–600) but attributed to Sumantu of the *Atharva-veda*; (10) *Vasishṭha* (100 BC–AD 500) named after a leader of the northern school of the *Ṛig-veda* and sometimes identified with the ṛishi of that name. The text contains many interpolations; (11) *Vishṇu* (100 BC–AD 400) belongs to a Black Yajur-veda, and is followed by Vaishṇavas. It too contains passages recommending widow-burning; (12) *Yājñavalkya* (*c.* AD 400), probably from Mithilā. The work is more concise and better arranged than Manu's.

Books

I. Bühler, G. (Tr.) *The Sacred Laws of the Aryans* (*Apastamba, Gautama, Vasishtha, Baudhayana*), Oxford, 1879–82.
II. Gopal, R. *India of the Kalpasutras*, Delhi, 1959.
III. Jolly, J. (Tr.) *The Institutes of Vishnu*, Oxford, 1889.
IV. Jolly, J. (Tr.) *The Minor Lawbooks* (*Narada and Brihaspati*), Oxford, 1889.
V. Kane, P. V. *History of Dharmasastra*, Poona, 4 vols., 1930–53.
VI. Kane, P. V. *Vedic Basis of Hindu Law*, Dharwar, 1936.

RITUALISM. The Hindu religion lays great emphasis on the rite, *kriyā*, that is, the performance of a ritual action through which the forces of the spiritual world are channelled and directed. According to the Brāhmaṇas*, which first systematized the theory behind ancient ritualism, ceremonial observances control the processes of nature and even the gods. In Mīmāṁsā* philosophy which first formulated the pattern in metaphysical form, knowledge is fruitless, good deeds in vain and true happiness impossible without ritual observance.

The simple forms of ceremonial observance were codified in the Gṛihyasūtras, rules governing the Hindu *saṁskāras** or sacraments, which cover the periodical threshold rites, starting from the impregnation of the wife, the pre-natal ceremonies and the birth of the child, and going on right through the successive stages of life: the naming of the child, carrying the child out to see the sun for the first time; feeding it with boiled rice at the age of six months; tonsure or shaving of the child's head; followed by various educational* rites such as investiture with the sacred thread, the rites on completion of studies, and the sacrament of marriage. In the past various domestic rites were enjoined on the paterfamilias, and the performance of certain sacrifices* and prayers, like the *mahāyajña* and the *savana*, was made obligatory for him. On death there were obsequial* and various *śrāddha** rites. In fact practically every sociological* event was accompanied by a ritual.

Ritual is prominent in festivals* and pilgrimages, and in such seasonal functions as wheel* ceremonies, swinging* ceremonies, pole* and thread* ceremonies. Special rites are performed by sectarian Hindus on the occasion of *dīkshā* (initiation*), *abhisheka* (ritual aspersion*), and other cult rites where particular stress is laid on mystic diagrams (*maṇḍalas*) and on sound* (*śabda*), and the initiate is taught the value of the *mantra** (spell) and the virtues of repetition*. The need for secrecy* (*rahasya*) is impressed on him. Techniques of meditation* such as *trāṭaka* also have a ritual element. The hand gestures (*mudrās*), bodily stances (*aṅgika*) and postures (*āsanas*), as well as certain aspects of physical culture, all have ritual significance and are frequently accompanied by rites.

A great deal of ritualism hedged kingship*, and solemn ceremonies were held at certain times to confirm the sovereignty of the king; such were the *rājasūya*, or royal consecration, the *vājapeya* or rejuvenation ceremony, and the *aśvamedha* or ceremony of dominion.

The rites attendant on ceremonial worship*, the dedication of an idol*, the construction of temples, are all important in what is called *kriyā-mārga*, or the pathway that leads through 'works' of this kind to ultimate salvation.

Books

See Sociology, Sacraments, Sacrifice.

RIVERS. In India there exist thousands of sacred pools and streams, but the larger currents of water, the mighty rivers upon whose banks the ancient civilizations were built, receive special homage as the givers of life and fertility. These rivers are the veins and channels on the body of Mother Earth, just as the mountains are her limbs, the forests her hair, and the cities and towns scattered about the country her organs of sense. The *gairika* or red sediment carried from the hills which periodically gives certain rivers a reddish hue is regarded as her menstrual flow.

There are traditionally 'seven rivers', *sapta-sindhava,* in India, of especial sanctity, but their names are not always consistently given. To start with there is a holy triad of rivers, namely, Ganges, Jamnā and Sarasvatī, which with the Godāverī, Narmadā, Indus and Kāverī, make up the seven sacred streams. Some texts substitute the Taptī and the Kistna for the last two on the list.

All rivers except the Son, Indus, Brahmaputra, Gogrā and Sutlej, are regarded as female. The source and confluence of sacred rivers are particularly hallowed. Thus Allāhābād, situated at the confluence of the Ganges, Jamnā and Sarasvatī, is regarded as one of the most sacred spots on the earth's surface. The chief rivers are named below.

BEAS, the Ārjīkīya of the *Ṛig-veda*; the Vipāśā, 'un-noosed', of the Epics, so called because its waters untied the noose with which the sage Vasishṭha* was about to hang himself in grief over the killing of his sons by Viśvāmitra. It was known to the Greeks as the Hyphasis, from which Alexander's invasion recoiled.

BRAHMAPUTRA, the Sanskritized name for the Tibeto-Burmese Bhullambuthur, 'making a gurgling sound'. In ancient Sanskrit texts the river is called Lauhitya, and Assam through which it flows is Lohit. On its way it passed through the kingdoms of Prāgjyotisha and Kāmarūpa*, also in Assam. One of the most famous shrines on this river is the temple of Kāmākhyā, near Gauhāti. Although the largest of the Indian rivers it does not have great sacrosanctity.

CHAMBAL, a tributary of the Jamnā. Its Sanskrit name was Charmanvatī, and it was said to be so named because the hides (*charma*) of all the animals slain to feed the guests of the hospitable king Rantideva, descendant of Bharata*, were cast into this river.

CHENĀB, the Asiknī of the *Ṛig-veda*, the Akesines of Greek records; the Chandrabhāga of the Purāṇas, so named because one of its streams was the Chandra and the other the Bhāga. Many famous warrior tribes mentioned in the Vedas made their settlements along the banks of this river.

GANGES*, known throughout India by the Austric name of Gaṅgā is regarded by Hindus as the most sacred river on earth.

GODĀVERĪ, also called Godā, 'cow-giver', because the sage Gautama once revived a cow he had accidentally killed by sprinkling some of its water on the animal. The sacredness of this river, the Ganges of the Deccan, also called the Vṛiddhagaṅgā, 'descendant of the Ganges', was revealed to Rāma by the same *ṛishi*. The river is not mentioned in the Vedas. It has its source at Tryambaka near Nāsik at the site of one of the 'resplendent' liṅgas* of Śiva. Before it meets the sea the river is said to divide into seven branches, of which three have now disappeared, and bathing in the remaining four in succession assures offspring to the childless. The waters of the Godāverī are believed by the Hindus to cure leprosy and relieve indigestion.

GOGRĀ, one of the tributaries of the Ganges, called Śarayū in Sanskrit literature, was the Sarabos of Ptolemy's Geography. Śarayū is sometimes identified with the Sarju, a tributary of the Gogrā. In mythology the Śarayū issues from the left thumb of Vishṇu. On this river ancient Ayodhyā was situated. Rāma, and later Lakshamaṇa both ended their days by walking into the Śarayū. Its modern name Gogrā (Gagrā, Gharghara, Ghaggar) is believed to be derived from the sound of its waters. The river is regarded by some as a relic of the lost Sarasvatī.

INDUS, the river from whose name 'India' and 'Hindu' are derived. It was known to the Greeks as Sinthos and to the Romans as Sindus. There is another river called the Sindhu, a tributary of the Jamnā (below) with which it is often confused. At the time of the *Mahābhārata* the ruler of the Indus region was Jayadratha.

JAMNĀ, or Jumnā, the Yamunā of Sanskrit literature, also called the Triyāmā. It takes its rise in the mythical Kalinda mountains, hence the river is also called Kālindī. It is not as sacred as the Ganges. In fact, in the belief that the Jamnā is not truly wedded, many Hindus even today will not drink its unclean water. She is personified as the goddess Yamunā daughter of the sage Kalinda, who was once dragged from her bed by Balarāma*. On the banks of this river lie Delhi (as well as ancient Indraprastha), Mathurā, Brindāban, Āgra and, at the junction with the Ganges, Allāhābād. The chief tributaries of the Jamnā include the Chambal (*see* above), Sindhu (not to be confused with the Indus), Betwa (ancient Vetravatī) and Ken (ancient Śuktimatī).

JHELUM (Jhelam), the Vitastā of the Vedas; the Hydaspes of Arrian and the Greeks; it is also known as Behat. The name Vitastā is of non-Aryan origin.
KĀVERĪ (Cauvery), like the Godāverī is also known as the Southern Ganges. The glory of the Kāverī forms an inexhaustible theme of early Tamil poetry, and a device depicting the Kāverī formed the banner of the Chola king. In legend the river was contained within the kamaṇḍalu or water-pot of the sage Agastya who released its waters in response to the prayers of a deserving king.
KISTNA (Kṛishṇa) rises, along with the river Vena (Venna or Venya), in mount Sahya in the sacred Mahābaleśvar plateau. Its chief tributary is the Bhīma at whose source stands the shrine of a famous liṅga*; the river was supposed to have been created from the sweat of Śiva. On the Bhīma is situated Alāndī, associated with the Marāṭha saint Jñānadeva, and Paṇḍharpur which has the celebrated shrine of Viṭṭhoba. Another tributary of the Kistna is the Tuṅgabhadra, the Pampā of the *Rāmāyaṇa* (*see* vānara).
MAHĀNADI, 'great river', is not frequently mentioned in literature, but its banks are dotted with local shrines. Sir William Hunter says of a trip up the Mahānadi, 'Each rocky islet, or wooded crag that rises from its banks, is crowned, not, as upon the Rhine, by the castle of a noble, but by a temple to some god. Even foreigners feel that they are treading on hallowed ground'.
MAHĪ, a river of Gujarāt; the Mophis of Ptolemy, and the Mais of the Periplus. In legend she was the daughter of Mother Earth. Solemn vows are taken on the waters of this river; a pot of the water is held while the person takes the vow, and if an untruth is uttered the person, it is believed, will fall sick shortly thereafter.
NARMADĀ, the Namedos of the geographer Ptolemy, this river is not mentioned in the Vedas. It starts from the Amarakaṇṭaka hill in the eastern Vindhyas, a place favoured for religious suicide*; those who voluntarily immolate or drown themselves or fast to death at this spot obtain liberation. The waters of the river are extremely sacred. While the Yamunā purifies a person in seven days, the Sarasvatī in three days, and the Gaṅgā immediately a person dips into it, the Narmadā purifies on sight. In mythology the Narmadā is personified as a princess variously called the daughter of the mountain-ṛishi Mekalā; or of the moon; or a mind-born daughter of the Somapa pitṛis. In the Purāṇas she is a Nāga princess and wife of Puruktsa (*see* Māndhātṛi); or the wife of Duḥsaha; in the *Harivaṃśa* she is the wife of Trasadasyu. In Sanskrit literature the term *narmadā* is used for a 'pleasure-woman' or prostitute. Narmadā is also called Nerbuddā, Mekalā, Revā, Indujā, Pūrvagaṅgā, and Somodbhavā.
RĀVI, a tributary of the Indus, was the Parushṇī of the Vedas, the Irāvatī (irā, 'water') of later Sanskrit literature, the Hydraotes of Arrian, the Adris of Ptolemy, the Hyarotes of Strabo, the Marudvṛiddha of the Purāṇas.
SĀBARMATI, of Kāṭhiāwār, so named, says the *Padma Purāṇa*, because of the 'agitation' (saṁbhrama) of the sage Vasishṭha at the sight of his rival Viśvāmitra, as a result of which his piercing glance bored a hole in the earth, causing this river to spring forth. Its sacredness was revealed by Kaśyapa, and 88,000 sages have performed penances on its banks.
SARASVATĪ, commonly Sarsutī, is conspicuously mentioned in Vedic literature. It has its source in the Himālayas but after entering the plains is lost in the

sands of the desert at a place called Vināsana (though some think it survives as the Gogrā mentioned above). It is believed to rise up again from its subterranean channel and join the Ganges and Jamnā at Prayāga (Allāhābād*). Various legends explain the reason for the river's disappearance. In one, Brahmā entrusted the river with the task of depositing the refuse of the volcanic Baḍavā into the sea; in order to save the earth from its boiling waters the river carried the igneous material by an underground channel she made. Another legend has it that the river disappeared for fear of the dreaded Ābhīras*; or that the river went into the earth because she did not desire that Śiva, who had just murdered a brāhmin, should bathe and purify himself in her waters; or that for some offence the sage Utathya caused the river to be submerged. On another occasion the waters were turned into blood by the sage Viśvāmitra during his contest with Vasishṭha*.

SIPRĀ or Kshiprā, rises in the Vindhyas and falls into the Chambal. It is said to have been formed from the blood of Vishṇu and that its waters turn into milk on a certain day occurring once every twelve years. The city of Ujjain is situated on the Siprā.

SON, the Soa of Ptolemy the geographer, was known to Sanskrit literature as Sona, Sonabhadra, or Hiraṇyavaha. It starts like the Narmadā from the sacred Amarakaṇṭaka plateau, and is a tributary of the Ganges. At one time Rājagṛiha capital of Magadha stood on the Son.

SUTLEJ or Satlaj, originally known by the non-Aryan name of Śutudrī, later Sanskritized as Śatadru, 'hundred flowing'. Legend says that its deep and treacherous waters broke into a hundred shallow and harmless streams when the sage Vasishṭha attempted to drown himself there. It was the Hesydrus or the Zaradrus of the Greek records.

TĀMRAPARṆI, the Taprobane of the Greeks and Romans (who also gave the same name to Ceylon) is frequently mentioned in the Epics and Purāṇas in legends associated with the sage Agastya, and referred to in Aśoka's inscriptions and in Kālidāsa. It was once celebrated for its pearls. At the mouth of the river lay Koṛkai, ancient capital of the Pāṇḍyas*, a flourishing port which was silted up.

TAPTI, also called Tapatī or Tāpi. In some accounts it is listed as one of the seven sacred rivers of India. She is personified as the daughter of Sūrya* the sun-god and Chhāyā, 'shade'. The love of Saṁvaraṇa, descendant of Bharata* for Tapati, forms a charming episode of the *Mahābhārata*. Their child was Kuru after whom the Kauravas were named.

Books

See under Geography.

ROMANS. Unlike the Greeks, the Romans never made any territorial conquests within the boundaries of India. Their prime interest was trade and it was inevitable that as a result of their association they should leave their mark on several aspects of Indian life. The Romaka, as they were called in the *Mahābhārata*, are mentioned as coming to Yudhishṭhira with presents on the occasion of his *rājasūya* sacrifice at Indraprastha, and figure not infrequently in later literature. There is a Pāli *Piṭaka Romaka*; and a *Romaka Jātaka* which describes a Roman ascetic eating a pigeon, as compared with a Buddhist who never eats meat in any form.

The Romans came into closer contact with India in the course of their long struggle with the Parthians, and a long period of fruitful association between the two peoples ensued. Diplomatic relations were established as early as 29 BC, when a number of Indian states sent embassies to Rome at the accession of the emperor Augustus. Among them was one from a king called Poros or Pandian, who may have been a Śaka or Pāṇḍya* monarch. The embassy sailed from Barygaza carrying a letter written on parchment in Greek, and included in its retinue tigers, a partridge as big as an eagle, a gigantic python, an enormous tortoise, and an armless boy who could shoot arrows and throw darts with his feet. To complete the train of wonders from the East there was also a Buddhist monk Sarmanokhegas (?Śramaṇāchārya) who imitated the memorable Kalanos (*see* Kalyāṇa) by burning himself on a pyre at Athens. His epitaph read, 'Here rests Khegas the *jog* (*yogi*) an Indian of Barygaza who rendered himself immortal according to the custom of his country'. According to Plutarch his tomb was for a long time shown to strangers as one of the sights of Athens.

Trajan (AD 98–117) during his Parthian expedition regally entertained a group of Indian envoys, probably despatched by the Kushān king Kadphises II, giving them senators' seats at the theatre. The name Dandamis survives as that of yet another Indian who was one of an embassy to Syria to welcome the emperor Heliogabalus to the throne in AD 218. There is mention of an Indian embassy bringing presents to Constantine the Great (307–337), and another embassy sent by an Indian king to the emperor Julian in AD 361.

The old Roman map known as the Peutingerian Tables shows a Roman settlement in South India, but in fact there were many regular trading colonies of Roman merchants on both the western and eastern coasts (*see* Trade and Shipping). In Flavian times (70–135) the whole of the west coast as far down as Malabār was opened up to Roman traders. There was a Roman stadium near Nāgārjunikoṇḍa, and at Musiris there was even a Roman temple dedicated to Augustus. Ptolemy the geographer (150) writes of meeting Romans who had resided in the Madura district for many years.

Roman soldiers, like the Swiss and Hanoverians of later times, were often professional mercenaries and enlisted in the service of Pāṇḍya and other native Indian kings, a fact frequently mentioned in Tamil literature. Because of their imposing presence they, like the Greeks, were highly prized as palace guards. According to one Tamil poet these 'powerful Yavanas' and 'dumb *mlechchhas*' (foreigners) could only express themselves by gestures since they did not speak the language. Clad in full armour, huge in stature, 'their stern looks strike terror into every beholder' (V, p. 90).

Trade with the West brought a flow of luxury products from the Roman world, and ancient Tamil records confirm the Roman chronicles regarding the variety of the imports to India. They included Egyptian decorative bronze work, horses from Parthia, red-glaze pottery from Arretium in Italy, glassware from Etruria, wines, lamps, sprinklers and vases from Greece, and choice slave-girls from Asia Minor, Crete and Cyprus. Much of this merchandise, together with large quantities of gold, which Pliny estimated drained the Roman imperial treasury of over one million sterling, was given in exchange for spices and aromatic resins, such as pepper, ginger, cinnamon, cloves, cardamom, cassia, aloes, and myrrh, from Arabia and India. These were used not only for food, but also for burning at funerals, a fashionable extravagance indulged in by the wealthy Romans of the day. Nero, for instance, who did nothing by halves, burned more aromatic gums and spices at the funeral of Poppaea (AD 66) than Arabia produced in a whole year.

In the fields of Indian architecture, art, medicine, numismatics, astronomy and science, the contribution of the Greeks is universally admitted. When Greek power waned neo-Greek and Roman influences exerted their sway. Numismatic* evidence reveals the remarkably wide extent of trade between the two countries. In science too the impress of Rome is evident. Varāhamihira* speaks of Mahāpuri, 'great city', i.e. Rome, as a notable centre of learning, and repeatedly refers to Roman astronomy in his works.

The result of this association of north-western India on the one hand and the southern ports on the other, with the Romans, was a quickening of interest in Western methods and techniques. To quote an Indian authority, 'A change in the social taste and also in the attitude towards life was but inevitable' (IV, p. 528). Roman motifs were introduced, inaugurating a new development in art. Numerous group-sculptures and reliefs, the so-called Herakles and the Nemean lion, and a number of Bacchanalian scenes in Mathurā and elsewhere are, according to Dr. Ranjan Ray, 'not only Western in theme, but also seem to have been inspired by Roman aesthetic ideals and artistic treatment' (IV, p. 523).

Similarly, in the South, the rich mercantile ports of the eastern and western Deccan which sheltered Roman trading settlements, became the focal points of Roman influence. These great trading emporiums supplied the interior, and a wide area was thus culturally affected through the trade contact between the two peoples. Some authorities hold the view that both Graeco-Buddhist and Roman-Buddhist forms are discernible in the sculptures and decorative motifs of the Andhra empire, from which evolved the art styles of Kārle, Bāgh, Ajantā, Khaṇḍagiri, Udaigiri (Orissa), Amarāvatī, and Nāgārjunikoṇḍa (near Masalia) between 100 BC and AD 300.

Books

I. Banerjee, G. N. *India as Known to the Ancient World*, Calcutta, 1921.

II. Charlesworth, M. P. *Trade Routes and Commerce of the Roman Empire*, Cambridge, 1921.

III. Jairazbhoy, R. A. *Foreign Influence in Ancient India*, Bombay, 1963.

IV. Majumdar, R. C. (Ed.) *The Age of Imperial Unity*, Bombay, 1951.

V. Mookerji, R. *A History of Indian Shipping and Maritime Activity*, 2nd Ed., Calcutta, 1957.

VI. Nag, Kalidas. 'Spread of Indian Culture in Asian Countries', *Foreign Review*, New Delhi, July 1950.

VII. Rawlinson, H. G. *Intercourse Between India and the Western World*, Cambridge, 1916.

VIII. Smith, V. 'Graeco-Roman Influence on the Civilisation of Ancient India', *Journal of the Asiatic Society of Bengal*, 1889–92, LVIII, pp. 107 ff.

IX. Srinivasachar, S. 'Indo-Roman Settlements in the Deccan', *March of India,* Delhi, 1951, III, V, 50–53.
X. Warmington, E. H. *Commerce Between the Roman Empire and India,* Cambridge, 1928.

ROPE TRICK: a magical feat of ancient ancestry, said to have been performed in China, Central Asia, Batavia and other parts of the Orient, but popularly regarded as a speciality of the Hindu magician and hence known as the Indian Rope Trick. The Arab traveller Ibn Batuta (*c.* AD 1350) describes the trick as having been performed in India in his day, and later witnesses have added to the tradition.

According to the legendary account, embellished by travellers, the trick is performed in this wise: the magician throws into the air a stout rope about thirty to forty feet in length. The rope remains upright and taut, its upper end vanishing out of sight into the open sky. The magician's assistant, a boy of about twelve years, climbs up the rope and disappears, and refuses to come down when called. The enraged magician, taking a short knife between his teeth, goes up the rope after him and also disappears. In a moment piercing shrieks are heard from the boy, and bits of his dismembered body come hurtling down. The magician then descends the rope, cleans his knife and wipes his bloodstained hands with the satisfaction of work well done. Then suddenly the boy appears from among the crowd, whole and unhurt. This is the traditional trick, but as described by more recent observers the dismemberment of the boy is omitted. The magician throws up a rope which remains suspended, and a boy simply climbs up to a height of ten feet or so, after which he descends and pulls the rope down after him.

Rewards have often been offered for the performance of the rope trick but no one has yet come forward to claim them. But in defence of the magicians it has been said that they do not read the papers to learn about these offers, and in any case might not be interested either in the money, or in the publicity and ensuing fame. It does seem that several eminent Europeans have witnessed the trick, including Sir Ralph Pearson, formerly Lieutenant-Governor of the North-West Frontier Province, who declared that he and his wife saw it in 1900 (II, p. 24). Other observers claim to have photographed the performance and the plates show the boy in the act of climbing the rope, or half-way up it, but this evidence does not bear close scrutiny. Another witness took a photograph of the scene which, after it was developed, showed the rope coiled on the ground and the magician and boy standing by it; the witness swore that at the time he took the photograph he actually saw the boy climbing the rope.

Mass hypnosis may therefore be one explanation of the rope trick, although this does not explain what might have been its original significance. The philosopher Śaṅkara in the seventeenth verse of his *Vedāntasūtra* speaks of 'the illusory juggler who climbs up the rope and disappears', and his reference implies that the trick had a long antecedent history. Nor was it confined to the Orient. Nicolas Oresme (d. 1382) Bishop of Liseux who made a study of occult matters stated that he knew a man who swore that when he was a boy he had seen a juggler throw a rope up into the air, and with his wife and servant climb up the same (III, p. 454). A similar demonstration was said to have been given in the sixteenth century in Magdeburg, Germany (I, p. 125), but no details of either of these cases are now available.

Whatever its value as an illusory wonder, there can be no doubt that the rope trick, as it is traditionally believed to be performed, with its sanguinary details, is a reminiscence of an ancient initiatory rite of shamanistic origin, which preserves fragments of the symbolic ritual dismemberment of the initiate and his ascent to heaven. In a similar manner the *Śatapatha Brāhmaṇa* describes the ascent of a priest to the summit of the yūpa* or sacrificial post of the Vedic sacrificial hall. This pole, to which the animal victim was tied, had a wheel placed horizontally upon it, and on reaching the summit the priest sat on the wheel which was then slowly turned in a sun-wise direction, while the seated brāhmin intoned verses from the *Sāma-veda*. In yet another rite, that of the mysterious *dūrohaṇa,* the sacrificer climbed to the top of the *yūpa* by means of seventeen steps, and when he reached the summit declared in a loud voice that he had reached the heavens.

Books

I. Anonymous, *Mystics and Magicians of India: An Anthology*, Calcutta, 1953.
II. Dare, Paul. *Indian Underworld: Indian Saints, Sorcerers and Superstitions*, London, 1938.
III. Thorndike, L. *History of Magic and Experimental Science*, Vol. III, New York, 1934.
IV. Ghoshal, R. N. *The Magical Tricks of Hindu Itinerants*, 1919.

ROY, RĀMMOHAN (1772–1833), 'the Father of Modern India', was born in Bardwān, Bengal, of an orthodox brāhmin family. Himself a victim of the social evils of the day (having been married to two wives in his childhood) he became 'the arch between Mediaeval and Modern India', and the source and inspiration of most of the reform movements that were to revolutionize Hindu society.

In 1811 he witnessed the rite of *suttee**, the burning alive of his brother's wife on the funeral pyre of her husband. In spite of all his efforts to induce her relatives to withhold their permission for this barbarous proceeding, the unfortunate woman was forced under pressure from the brāhmins to ascend the pyre. When the flames reached her body she struggled to escape but the priests and her relatives held her down with long bamboo poles, and the loud beating of drums drowned her dying shrieks. This incident had a profound influence on his subsequent career, and among the many reforms he advocated, the abolition of suttee by Lord Bentinck may be regarded as his crowning achievement.

After a rudimentary education in a local school Rāmmohan Roy was sent to Paṭna to learn Persian (the administrative language of India at the time) and Arabic. It was while studying the Koran in the original and reading the Persian Sufi poets that he developed his hatred of idolatry. In 1804 he published a pamphlet in Persian on the subject of Deism. From Paṭna he went to Tibet for a first-hand study of Buddhism and was nearly killed for preaching against the idolatrous teachings of the lamas. He settled in

Banāras to get better acquainted with the Hindu scriptures. In 1809 he was appointed *sherishtadār* (revenue official) at Rangpur and here he began a series of evening discussions on religion with a circle of friends, which helped in clearing his mind of many vexing problems. In order to be free to devote himself to social and religious work he retired from service with the East India Company in 1814 at the age of forty-two. He proceeded to Calcutta where he published an abridgement of the Vedānta and founded the *Ātmīya Sabhā* (Friends' Association) for the dissemination of religious truth.

Although he did not subscribe to the theory of reincarnation he was impressed by the monotheistic doctrines of the Upanishads. Unlike Śaṅkara's, his concept of the Supreme was not abstract, and he laid special emphasis on the *saguṇa* or personal aspect of the deity. His was a concrete monotheism and he believed that the Supreme Reality could be realized in samādhi through worship and meditation.

A lifelong associate and admirer of Christian missionaries and their work, he published in 1820 a tract called *The Precepts of Jesus: the Guide to Peace and Happiness*, on the teachings of the four Gospels, which he regarded as 'well fitted to regulate the conduct of the human race in the discharge of their various duties to themselves and to society'. He found 'the doctrines of Christ more conducive to moral principles and better adapted for the use of rational beings than any others which have come to my knowledge'. For a time he attended Unitarian services.

In 1828 he founded the **Brāhmo Samāj,** 'Society of God', through which he hoped to transform radically the face of Hindu life and religion. Although he intended the Samāj to be a society of true worshippers of the one God of all religions, in actual practice it turned out to be a congregation of Hindu theists. No images, statues or paintings were allowed in the hall of worship. No sacrifices or oblations of any kind were permitted, and only monotheistic services, prayers and hymns were allowed. An innovation was the introduction of congregational worship. Among the prominent Hindus who joined the Brāhmo Samāj were Devendranāth Tagore*, and Keshab Chandra Sen*, and for some time the society gained strength among the intellectuals of Bengal.

In Western India a slightly modified version of the Brāhmo Samāj, known as the **Prārthanā Samāj*** was founded, and dozens of other samājes on similar lines sprang up all over the country. The parent Brāhmo Samāj in fact gave birth to a prodigious offspring with many schismatic bodies, and although it did not have a popular appeal itself, it served as a powerful lever for almost every progressive movement in Hindu society, religion and politics.

Rāmmohan Roy was well qualified both by temperament and background to start the renaissance. He was well versed in many languages; besides his own native Bengali he knew Sanskrit, Pāli, Persian, Arabic, Hebrew, Greek and English. A man of broad sympathies and tolerant outlook he was fired with crusading zeal. He fought to abolish polytheism, polygamy, idolatry, the caste system, child marriage, female backwardness, animal sacrifice, and suttee, and strove to promote monotheism and a wider system of public education. The latter, he insisted, should be conducted through the medium of English, as the Sanskrit system of education was full of vain and empty subtleties and 'best calculated to perpetuate ignorance'. He believed that 'the learning concealed under the almost impervious veil of Sanskrit is far from sufficient to reward the labour of acquiring it'.

In November 1830 he sailed for England on a mission from the Moghul Emperor who had conferred on him the title of Rāja. He was received everywhere with great cordiality, spoke before the Select Committee of the House of Commons on Indian questions, and impressed one and all with his frankness and sincerity. Jeremy Bentham hailed him as a fellow-worker in the service of humanity. Rāmmohan Roy died in Bristol in 1833 and was buried there.

Books

I. Bal, Upendranath. *Rammohan Roy*, Calcutta, 1935.
II. Carpenter, Miss M. *Last Days of Rammohan Roy*, 1866.
III. Chakravarti, S. (Ed.) *Rammohan Roy: Father of Modern India*, 1935.
IV. Collett, Sophia. *Life and Letters of Raja Rammohan Roy*, 1914.
V. Ghose, J. C. (Ed.) *Works of Rammohan Roy*, 1888.
VI. Howels, A. *The Soul of India*, 1901.
VII. Majumdar, J. *Raja Rammohan Roy and Progressive Movements*, Calcutta, 1941.
VIII. Mozumdar, P. C. *The Faith and Progress of the Brahmo Samaj*, 1901.

ROYAL CONSECRATION, or the investiture of the ruler with the right and authority to reign, is known in Sanskrit as *rājasūya* (*rāja-sūya*, 'king's libation'). The ceremony and its attendant soma* sacrifices were based on the divine prototype of the consecration of the god Varuṇa. They were long drawn out, sometimes lasting for a year, and consisted of a series of *ekāha* (one-day *soma* sacrifices) alternating with *ishṭi* (offerings of cakes and gruel) and an occasional animal sacrifice. Some authorities find here relics of a rite re-enacting the cosmic drama of death and rebirth, ascent and descent, the fertility of the world, the motion of the sun and stars, and so forth.

Among the important functionaries who assisted in the ceremonies were representatives of the kingdom and subjects, who were referred to as the *ratnin* or jewels. They included (*a*) the *purohita* or the king's domestic priest; (*b*) the *mahishī*, chief queen; (*c*) the *senāpati* or commander-in-chief of the army; (*d*) the *prāḍvivāka*, chief judicial officer of the realm; (*e*) the *sūta*, royal charioteer and bard; (*f*) the *grāmaṇī* a headman of one of the villages; (*g*) the *saṁgrahītṛi* or chief tax-collector; (*h*) representatives of the brāhmin (priestly), kshattriya (warrior), vaiśya (merchant) and śūdra (servile) castes; (*i*) a member of the *gaṇika* or prostitute class, whose presence was regarded as auspicious; she sometimes held the ceremonial umbrella over the king's head.

The king was prepared for the function by a ceremonial bath, after which he was perfumed with musk, his forehead marked with the *tilaka*, and his genitals daubed with turmeric paste. The chief feature of the consecration was the *abhisheka*, 'aspersion*, the lustration or anointing of the king by the chief priest, followed by the anointing of the delegates of the first three castes, each of whom announced to the populace, 'He, O people, is your king!' The unction was administered to the king while he stood on a tiger-skin, after which he took three strides on it, thus magically identifying himself with Vishṇu who took three strides to overcome the demon-king Bali*. Stepping off the tiger-skin he kicked a piece of lead towards a eunuch ('a long-haired person'), and a piece of copper towards a barber. He then stepped on a silver plaque and had a golden plaque placed on his head.

Facing the people he raised his arms to symbolize that he supported the kingdom, then gazed at the sun to secure part of its glory and lustre. Taking a bow and arrow in his hand he stepped in the direction of each of the cardinal points to symbolize his dominion over the four corners of the kingdom.

The unction was followed by a drive in a four-horse chariot, combined with a raid on a herd of cows, or a sham attack on a village in which he plundered its wealth. According to some commentators the king symbolically lost his virility at a certain moment of the ceremony and regained it by moving about among a herd of cows. This was in memory of the occasion when Varuṇa was supposed to have lost his virility when he was consecrated king of the gods.

The final phase was the enthronement or investiture. A canopy was erected to the east or south side of the sacrificial fire, and a place prepared for the throne upon a central elevation of earth, with four outlet gutters. The throne made of *khadira* (acacia) or *udumbara* (figtree) wood was placed upon it, and before this the king was made to stand, while the royal robes were placed about his shoulders and the rites of enthronement performed to the chanting of mantras.

After the enthronement the king played a game of dice at which he scored a prearranged victory. There followed the recitation by the brāhmin priest of the miraculous release of Śunaḥśephas* from the sacrificial post. The ministers then presented the king with auspicious gifts, foodgrains, grasses, juices, seeds, flowers and gems, symbolizing the treasures of the earth. A retinue of bards now stepped forward and read their prepared panegyrics, extolling his virtues, bravery, beauty and power. He was King of Kings, ruler of the world, slayer of foes. Finally the ratnins made a short circumambulation of the king as in homage to a deity. The king then issued a proclamation releasing all prisoners. Yoked animals were unharnessed, birds ceremonially set free from cages, doors of palaces and private houses opened, and a new era proclaimed.

The *dakshiṇa* or reward for the priests officiating at the rājasūya ceremony was fabulous, often amounting to hundreds of thousands of cows, great quantities of gold, and several villages.

Books

I. Goshal, U. N. 'The Besprinkling Ceremony of the Rajasuya', *Indian Historical Quarterly*, Calcutta, 19, 4 (1943).
II. Heesterman, J. C. *The Ancient Indian Royal Consecration.* The Hague, 1957.
See also under Kingship and Aspersion.

RUDRA, 'howler', 'roarer', 'the terrible', 'the ruddy one', was a Vedic deity of many aspects. The Brāhmaṇas relate that when Rudra was born he cried because he had been given no name, so he was named Rudra, 'weeper'. He is sometimes identified with Agni, god of fire. Depicted riding on a wild boar Rudra represented the ruthlessness of nature, the storm and the pestilential wind. But he had two sides the destructive and disease-bearing, as well as the beneficent and healing. He was the father of the minor storm gods, the Maruts and the Rudras.

In the *Bṛihadāraṇyaka Upanishad* the Rudras are the ten vital breaths (*prāṇa*), the heart (*manas*) being the eleventh. Their number is often discrepantly given as three, seven, or eleven, sometimes even more. In some legends the Rudras are the seven manifestations of the god Rudra. According to the *Vishṇu Purāṇa,* Rudra sprang from a drop of blood which fell into the fire when Brahmā once scratched himself as he wiped the perspiration from his brow with a piece of sacrificial wood. Brahmā commanded Rudra to divide himself into male and female, then to multiply into eleven beings, and of these some were black and ferocious and some white and gentle. They were (1) Mṛigavyādha, (2) Sarpa, (3) Nirṛiti (*see* godlings), (4) Ajaikapāda, (5) Ahirbudhnya, (6) Pinākin, (7) Dahana, (8) Kapālin, 'skull-holding', a name also given to Śiva, (9) Sthāṇu, (10) Bhaga and (11) Tryambaka. In other legends again the eleven Rudras are the sons of the ṛishi Kaśyapa by Surabhī.

Yet another legend relates that a brāhmin desired a son, and a youth appeared to him. When the brāhmin asked his name the youth wept and the brāhmin named him RUDRA, 'weeper'. The lad wept seven times more and was given seven more names: Bhava, Śarva, Īśāna, Paśupati, Bhīma, Ugra, Mahādeva.

Rudra's essential importance lies in the fact that in later mythology he evolved into Śiva and grew to great prominence in the Hindu pantheon. Generally the name Rudra when applied to Śiva denotes Śiva's destructive character.

Books

I. Chaudhuri, N. 'Rudra-Siva as an Agricultural Deity', *Indian Historical Quarterly*, Calcutta, XV, 2 (1939), 183–96.

II. Moore, E. *Hindu Pantheon,* London, 1810.

RUKMIṆĪ, daughter of Bhīshmaka king of the *mlechchha* (barbarian) Bhoja people in Berār, related to the Vidarbhas. She was betrothed to Śiśupāla king of Chedi, but on her wedding day as she was on her way to the nuptials she was seen by Kṛishṇa who, struck by her beauty and filled with an irresistible desire to possess her, carried her off in his chariot.

The pair were pursued by Śiśupāla and RUKMIN brother of Rukmiṇī. Rukmin hated Kṛishṇa because the latter had killed his friend Kaṁsa, and he longed to get even with him. Kṛishṇa however, defeated both his pursuers and would have slain Rukmin but for the entreaties of Rukmiṇī. It is said that Rukmin offered his services alternately to the Pāṇḍavas and the Kauravas, but both sides rejected him due to his arrogance and boastfulness. He founded the city of Bhojakaṭa in Berār (Vidarbha) and was eventually slain by Kṛishṇa's brother Balarāma.

Rukmiṇī, believed to be the incarnation of Lakshmī, became the principal wife of Kṛishṇa (in the *Bhāgavata Pvrāṇa* she is regarded as the only true wife of Kṛishṇa) and bore him ten sons and one daughter. The sons were Pradyumna*, Chārudeshṇa, Sudeshṇa, Chārudeha, Sushena, Chārugupta, Bhadrachāru, Chāruvinda, Suchāru, and Chāru. The daughter was Chārumatī. When Kṛishna died Rukmiṇī and several of his other wives died on his funeral pyre.

As the lawful wife of Kṛishṇa, Rukmiṇī is paid greater devotion than Rādhā in some parts of India, especially the Marāṭha country, where she is known as Rakhamāi (or Rakhamābāi).

Books

See under Mahābhārata and Mythology.

SACRAMENTS. The Sanskrit term *saṁskāra,* commonly translated consecration or sacrament, is applied to the ritual observed during any of the transitionary phases in the life of a Hindu. Many of the saṁskāras go back to very early times; some were probably formulated by the pre-Aryans and taken over from them by the Aryan invaders. All periods of change and transition were believed to be fraught with occult danger, and persons at the threshold of such changes were liable to attack by demons and sorcerers, or were subject to the baleful flash of the evil eye, hence it was essential to perform special rites to counteract such influences.

The number of these saṁskāras or threshold rites was at one time quite considerable. Nearly every formal observance was referred to as a saṁskāra and was attended by fire and water rituals, prayers and sacrifices, oblations, lustrations and other ceremonies, regulated by ancient taboos. Stress was laid on proper orientation, *mantras,* auspicious times and so on, many details of which were preserved in the later saṁskāras. The number of saṁskāras was gradually reduced from over 300 to about 40, then to 18 or even 10. The generally recognized sources of the saṁskāras are the Vedas, Gṛihasūtras, Dharmasūtras, the Epics, the Purāṇas and certain other smṛitis. The following are the chief Hindu sacraments or saṁskāras:

Garbhādhāna or impregnation*, the sacrament to ensure the birth of a child, especially a son.

Puṁsavana, performed during the third month of a woman's pregnancy* to ensure that the child will be a male.

Sīmanta, the parting of the hair of the expectant mother between the fourth and eighth months, symbolizing the preparation for the event of birth (*see* pregnancy).

Jātakarman, the rites associated with childbirth and delivery (*see* pregnancy).

Nāmakaraṇa, the ceremony of giving the child a name*, generally performed between the 10th to 12th day after birth.

Nish-kramaṇa, 'first outing', when the child is taken out of doors for the first time, usually during the fourth month. A square portion of the courtyard is first plastered over with cow-dung and clay and the child is carried out to the sound of conch-shells and the chanting of hymns. He is placed facing the sun and the rite is therefore sometimes called the *sūrya-darśana* or sun showing.

Anna-prāśana, 'food eating', when the child is fed with solid food for the first time. It is generally performed in the sixth month. Nowadays the food is usually rice, but in ancient times a tiny portion of the flesh of an animal, bird or fish was given.

Karṇa-vedha, 'ear boring', performed on children of both sexes to permit the wearing of rings in the ear lobes. This takes place between the tenth day and the twelvth month after birth, but is best done during the ninth month (*see* ear).

Chūḍā-karaṇa or tonsure, when the hair of a boy's head* is first shaved; the ceremony takes place between the ages of one and seven.

Several saṁskāras are associated with education*, such as *vidyārambha*, when the boy is taught the Sanskrit alphabet usually at the age of five; the *upanayana*, when he is invested with the sacred thread* at the age of eight and begins his formal education; the *vedārambha* when he starts his study of the Vedas at the age of ten; the *keśānta* when he first shaves his beard between the ages of thirteen and fifteen, symbolizing his close control of his awakening sexual life; the *samāvartana*, any time after the age of fifteen, when he returns home after the completion of his studies.

The sacrament of marriage* is known as *vivāha*, and it ends with the rite of *samāpana* or consummation*. The *antyeshṭi* or 'final' ceremonies performed after death are the last rites of the Hindu and include the obsequies* and the *śrāddha** rites.

Books

I. Deshpande, K. *The Child in Ancient India* (*The Samskaras as Observed for Children*), Poona, 1936.

II. Gopal, Ram. *India of Vedic Kalpasutras*, New Delhi, 1959.

III. Lachchhimidar, R. *Aryan Sacraments*, Delhi, 1938.

IV. Marett, R. R. *Sacraments of Simple Folk*, Oxford, 1933.

V. Pandey, R. B. *Hindu Samskaras*, Banaras, 1949.

VI. Stevenson, Mrs. S. *The Rites of the Twice-born*, Oxford, 1920.

SACRIFICE is generally referred to in Sanskrit writings by the term *yajña*, personified as Yajña, the deer-headed son of Ruchi, and husband of Dakshiṇā (see below), goddess of the rewards given to the sacrificial priests. At the great sacrifice of Daksha*, Yajña was slain by the monster Vīrabhadra, raised to the heavens by Brahmā, and transformed into the constellation Mṛigaśiras, 'deer-head'.

The divine sacrifice of Purusha*, as mentioned in the *Ṛig-veda*, was regarded as the model for all sacrifices performed by gods and men; and the sacrifice performed by Vaivasvata* after the Flood, the first ever offered by a mortal, inaugurated the rite on earth.

Sacrifice was one of the main pillars of the Vedic religious system, and descriptions of sacrificial rites constitute a substantial part of the sacred texts. A Vedic injunction makes sacrifice an essential condition of salvation: *svarga-kāmo yajeta*, 'the heaven-desiring must sacrifice'. Sacrificial ceremonies were an integral part of the Vedic way of life, and the source of the earliest hymns, the earliest poetry, and probably the earliest drama and dance.

The Brāhmaṇas in particular emphasize the importance of sacrifices which, according to them, maintain the order of the universe and give strength to the gods. The Upanishads on the other hand tend to minimize their significance. The *Muṇḍaka Upanishad* declares that sacrifices are 'unsafe boats', and that the fools who cling to them go again to old age and death. Certain passages in the Upanishads give a figurative interpretation to the sacrificial rites; man is said to send up a constant stream of sacrifice by his thoughts, speech and behaviour. He himself is the sacrifice: speech is the fuel, breath the smoke, the tongue the flames, the eyes the coals, the ears the sparks, and so on. In another esoteric interpretation the male sacrificer performs on the sacrificial ground of the woman's body a sexual rite that lends power to the universe and gives fertility to all living things.

The purpose or object for which a sacrifice is performed is called **yajñanta** (*yajña-anta*, 'sacrifice-end'). The Hindu sacrificial system covers practically every activity of life, and any event out of the ordinary can become the occasion for the performance of a religious ceremony.

Among the more significant ends of sacrifice one is to provide strength and sustenance for the gods, who are believed to consume the essence of the offering and to be sustained thereby. Says the *Vishṇu-Purāṇa*, 'By sacrifices the gods are nourished'. Sacrifices are also offered for the expiation of sin. The victim is mystically invested with the iniquities of the *yajamāna* or sacrificer, and is offered up as a ransom. Says the *Tāṇḍya Brāhmaṇa*, 'O thou limb of the victim now consigned to the fire, thou art the expiation of our sins'. Some sacrificial rites were carried out in order to propitiate gods, demons or chthonian beings. In the Nāgapañchamī performed in the month of *Śrāvaṇa* (July–August), offerings of flour or cooked food were made to serpents.

Sacrifices were performed by kings and chiefs in order to gain power and dominion, or to confirm their authority. Such were the *rājasūya* or consecration of a king, the *aśvamedha* or horse sacrifice for territorial expansion, the *rād-yajña* performed to restore a deposed king to his throne.

Many sacrifices had an evil intent. The *saṁdaṁśa* was a one-day soma rite for bewitching a king; the *vajra* (thunderbolt) a sacrifice for bewitching a whole nation. Other rites were performed to injure one's enemies, to cause abortion, to bring about sickness and death. In many of these rites the sacrificer and the priests wore a red or black jacket instead of the customary white; the sacrificial butter was made from the milk of a sick cow; and instead of edible and potable substances, things like iron nails and refuse were offered up; the mantras were full of imprecations and maleficence. An example is the *śyena*, or 'eagle' rite which was a kind of black magical *soma* sacrifice.

There are also hundreds of sacrificial rites performed at sundry times in order to mark an important event, either on an occasion of rejoicing (*nandi*) such as a marriage, the birth of a boy, the first feeding of a child, initiation; or of sorrow (*aśru*, lit. 'tears') such as death or loss; or again to mark ceremonial 'threshold' crossings (*see* sacraments); or during festivals*, or on the occasion of taking vows* (*vrata*) for the welfare of the family or for personal advancement. One such is the *putra-kāmyā* for obtaining male offspring. Sacrifices are also performed for purificatory purposes, e.g. *prāyaśchitta* and *vrātyastoma*.

Sacrificial forms vary considerably and 'there is a good deal of confusion in the treatises themselves' (I, p. 18). The chief elements of sacrifice are as follows: (*a*) every sacrifice must have a purpose or end (yajñānta) as indicated above, and this determines the mode of sacrifice, the object offered up and the season during which the rite is to be held; (*b*) all sacrifices are believed to have great prabhāva* or occult potency, and the effects of a sacrifice reverberate through this world and the next. The implements and objects used during the rite are also imbued with magical power and any remains have to be disposed of with great care; (*c*) the sacrifice is performed on behalf of the *yajamāna* (see below), the person who pays for its performance and who expects the benefit accruing from the sacrifice; (*d*) the sacrifice may be performed by the yajamāna himself, such as in the simple domestic rites where each householder acts as his own priest. Many sacrifices, and certainly all the larger ones require the services of professional hierophants* who in some cases, as in the more complex soma *sattras*, may number hundreds of priests; (*e*) the merit of a sacrifice is increased in accordance with the *dakshiṇā* or gift bestowed on the officiating priests and brāhmin guests; (*f*) prescribed rites attend each phase of the sacrifice; ceremonial baths are taken, rigid taboos observed, fasting and continence are enjoined on the participants. *Sāmans* and *stotras* (hymns) are sung and magical mantras recited in accompaniment to the ceremonial acts performed during the choice of the sacrificial ground, the construction of the sacrificial hall, the setting up of the yūpa* or post, the building of the altar*, the arranging of the sacred fires, the kindling of the fuel and the pouring of the libations; (*g*) the sacrificial implements* were rudimentary but specialized, and included a great number of cups, ladles, sieves, receptacles, bowls and sacred pots made of metal, stone, earth or wood.

The sacrifice itself can be both very simple or very complex. The lesser sacrifices are those associated with the *pūjā**, the *mahāyajña* or Five Daily Sacrifices*, and other acts of daily worship. Slightly more elaborate are those performed during the sacraments, of which several dozens are sometimes listed. A complete sacrificial course of chants and hymns, and vegetable and animal offerings, is often referred to as a *saṁsthā*, although this term is also applied to the parts or 'stations' into which the more complex soma* rites are divided. Sacrificial rites attendant on the coronation of kings or the confirmation of royal dominions, as in the aśvamedha, often lasted for many months.

Many methods for the classification of sacrifices have been used. Some are arranged according to the deity or deities to whom they are offered, e.g. Indra, Rudra, Agni (in the Agnihotri sacrifice), Soma, Varuṇa, the manes and the Maruts. Some, called *vaiśvadeva*, 'all-gods', are offered to all these deities together.

Some rites, especially those associated with the soma sacrifices, are named according to the number of days they last: *ekāha* (one day), *ahīna* (two to twelve days), and the *sattra* (more than twelve days). A number of sacrifices are named after the month or day in which they are performed, e.g. *Śrāvaṇi*, performed in the full moon of the month of *Śrāvaṇa* (July–August); *Āgrahāyaṇī* performed on the day of the full moon in the month of *Mārgaśīrsha* (November–December), when the house is thoroughly cleaned and smoked; *Chaitrī*, in the full moon of *Chaitra* (March–April); *Āsvayuji*, in the full moon of *Āśvini* (September–October).

Many sacrifices are periodical, such as those connected with the seasonal festivals* and dependent on the motion of the sun and moon. For example, the quarterly festivals called *chātur-māsya* combine the features of both the sun and moon sacrifices. These 'four-monthly' rites were offered to 'all the gods', Varuṇa, Rudra, Indra, the Maruts, the manes, etc., at the beginning of each of the three seasons, generally on the day of the full moon. The *chātur-māsya* preceding the rainy season is followed by a sort of 'retreat', when itinerant friars and mendicants stop in a village until the rains are over.

Many important sacrifices are associated with the moon, and are known by the generic name of *chandra-yajña*, 'lunar sacrifice', chief of which were the fortnightly rites called *pārvaṇa* which took place on the day of the sighting of the new moon (*darśa-yajña*), and the day of the full moon (*pūrṇamāsa-yajña*). Others were offered on various days in between, such as the *ashṭaka*, 'eighth', held on the eighth day after the full moon, and devoted to the pitṛis. Moon sacrifices are often associated with vows*, such as the observance called *chāndrāyaṇa*, 'moon's course', in which the number of morsels eaten per day is gradually reduced with the waning moon.

The offerings made to the deities are derived from plants and animals. These include grains (*anna*), wine (*soma*), *pāka* (baked or cooked food), milk (*dugdha*), 'mixed' oblations (such as *sāṁnāya*, a mixture of fresh and sour milk). *Animal sacrifices** in ancient India included the cow (e.g. *śūlagava*) and the horse (*aśvamedha*), besides lesser animals. Human sacrifice (*see*) was not unknown. One of the most important sacrificial offerings is clarified butter (*ghṛita* or ghee), often used in its liquid form (*ājya*); it is always the product of the sacred cow and it helps to keep the fire blazing. In some rites a portion of the sacrificial ghee called *prāśitra* is eaten by the priest to neutralize the prabhāva or potency of the sacrifice.

The *ish* is the simple bloodless offering of food and water made to the gods. It consists of *ishṭi*, i.e. butter, fruit and grains; the midday ishṭi, called the *pṛishṭha*, is generally accompanied by *stotra* (hymns) and *sāmans* (chants). Offerings of cakes and curds are called *kāmyeshṭi*, often made to remove bad repute from innocent persons or to move the god to grant offspring to the sacrificer. The remains of all ish oblations are called *uchchhishṭa*, and according to the *Ṛig-veda* have a terrible potency, and great care is to be taken about their handling and final disposal.

Other offerings include the *āgrayaṇa*, consisting of first-fruits and new grain; the *iḍā* or sacrificial cake; the *piṇḍa* or rice balls offered during the *śrāddha* ceremonies in honour of the deceased; the *havis* or burnt offering of ghee, grain, milk, gruel, butter or cakes. The most important of such *havir-yajña* (*havis*-offerings) are the *agnihotra* and the *agnyādheya*. The *huta* is also a simple burnt offering. Variations of huta of vague and indeterminate application are āhuta, prahuta, and so on. The *tarpaṇa* is a libation of water poured out of a vessel, or allowed to fall from the hollow of the hand, while the gods are named. Generally the water flows from the palm to the fingers, but in the *śrāddha* rites it is made to flow from the side of the palm.

The **yajamāna** is the person who institutes, arranges, pays for and obtains the blessings of a sacrificial ceremony. In early Vedic times the chieftain or king had the sole authority to perform the tribal sacrifices on behalf of the people; the brāhmin merely served as an assistant to the king during such rituals, chanting the sacred hymns, tending the sacred fire and handling the sacred implements and vessels. In the ordinary household the paterfamilias, like his counterpart in Ancient Rome, sang the simple hymns at his own hearth, said the prayers and performed the domestic rituals without priestly intervention.

Priestly ascendancy in Indian life may be directly traced to the time when sacrifices were made more and more elaborate, and the yajamāna, both royal patron and paterfamilias, receded into the background till he became merely the one who paid the cost of the sacrifices so that he might reap its spiritual benefits. The material benefits mainly accrued to the brāhmin priests.

In hieratic theory the sacrifice became supreme. Every occasion demanded a ceremony, and every ceremony necessitated the services of a brāhmin. No important function could be held without an elaborate formulary requiring mystic mantras, magic gestures, holy benedictions and sacred pots. Facing in the wrong direction, or omitting the proper emphasis in an incantation would draw down upon the errant yajamāna all the terrible maledictions of the offended deities. Prayers became a dangerous undertaking which only brāhmins could risk uttering.

The merit of the yajamāna now consisted, not in his performance of the sacrifice, from which he was virtually precluded, but in the payment of what is known as the *dakshiṇā* or gift to the priests, and the honour he received from the sacrifice was in exact proportion to the amount he paid.

The remaining duties of the yajamāna were calculated to make him a mere puppet in the ceremonies. There was a period of preparatory fasting (called *upavasatha*) on the eve of the sacrifice, and a ritual consecration (*dīkshā*) with his wife, sometimes involving the shaving of his head and beard, starting with his right whiskers. His stances, gestures, responses, ablutions, and all the details of the ritual were laid down for strict observance by the priests. His wife or wives were also kept busy with ceremonial attendance at various times.

The purpose of each sacrifice was determined by the yajamāna, though the priest could always dictate the need for one at a given time, with the result that hundreds of sacrifices came into existence. The fourteenth century compilation of Hemādri* enumerates no less than two thousand ceremonies to be performed during the year.

The fee paid to a brāhmin for the performance of a priestly office, especially a sacrifice, is called a **dakshiṇā**, 'satisfying'. In the Purāṇas Dakshiṇā is personified as the wife of Yajña, 'sacrifice'.

In early times sacrificial fees used to be paid in coconuts, rice, cloth, and, for more important occasions, a milch cow. But the decline in the role of the yajamāna made the services of the brāhmin indispensable, and his fee was raised accordingly. As the plain business of existence became hedged in by ordinances brazenly invented by the priests and requiring their offices, the dakshiṇā became more and more exorbitant. The brāhmins were partial to gifts of cows, cattle, and horses, 'but gold was particularly efficacious in moving the priest or the god' (III, p. 405). The success of the sacrifice was said to depend largely on the liberality of the reward bestowed upon the officiating paṇḍits and their growing host of retainers. Many Hindu kings emptied the public treasury in order to pay for one or other of the elaborate rites that would ensure their sovereignty, or succession to their heirs.

The giving of a dakshiṇā soon came to cover all kinds of gifts to priests, even without service, and suitable *ślokes* (verses) were composed to show that such 'pure' gifts were very auspicious indeed. The extravagance of the Hindu lawgivers in their zeal to make men give liberally to brāhmins has seldom been exceeded. It was laid down as a principle that everything in the universe belongs to the brāhmin who is entitled to it by primogeniture and divine right, so that when a brāhmin receives a gift he receives only what is his own.

According to the code of Vasishṭha, 'He who, placing on the skin of a black antelope some sesamum, gold, honey and butter, gives it to a brāhmin, removes all sin'. With solicitous regard for the welfare of the patron the lawgivers warn, 'Money should be dipped in water before being given to a brāhmin, lest the latent glory of the brāhmin's hand should burst forth and consume the donor'. The regular feasting of brāhmins and monks has always been a common practice in India, and the giving of a *bhaṇḍāra* or banquet for brāhmins is regarded as being equal in merit to serving the gods for as many years as there are brāhmins present at the feast.

Gifts of houses and land were of unequalled merit. Sometimes such gifts were expedient, since holding on to property that has been contaminated for some reason, might be a source of pollution to the owner. For instance, 'If a house be defiled by an unclean bird sitting on it, it becomes pure when presented to a brāhmin'. The *agrahāra* or land gift to brāhmins brought great blessing and wiped out all sins. Princes and nobles often bequeathed agrahāras of whole villages, with adjoining houses built for the exclusive use of brāhmins. But the most meritorious of all gifts followed the *sarva-medha*, 'universal offering', a ten-day soma sacrifice, so called because at its conclusion the yajamāna gave away all his possessions as a dakshiṇā and retired to the forest. Such a pious donor, it was said, 'will acquire all merit, his body will be a million times more radiant than the sun, and he will have a million virgins, many chariots and palanquins, and jewels beyond computation'.

Books

I. Acharya, P. K. *Glories of India on Indian Culture and Civilization*, Allahabad, n.d.

II. Das, D. K. *The Yajnas, or The Sacrifice in Hinduism*, 1911.

III. Durant, W. *The Story of Civilization: Our Oriental Heritage*, New York, 1935.

IV. Malik, P. S. *The Hindu Sacrificial System*, 1928.

V. Potdar, K. R. *Sacrifice in the Rigveda*, Bombay, 1953.

SĀDHU, one who has attained certain powers of *siddhis**. It is a generic term applied to a Hindu ascetic or wonder-worker. A common synonym for sādhu is the term *jogi,* derived from yogi, though in actual fact it is not necessary for a jogi to know anything about yoga philosophy or even practice yoga. These terms embrace hundreds of sects and sub-sects scattered throughout India, and it is these miracle-mongers, itinerants, hermits, gymnosophists, and fakirs, who have been associated in the minds of foreigners—Ancient Greeks, Romans, Persians, Muhammadans, Europeans and the modern tourists—with the Hindu religion in practice.

Sādhuism covers disciplines and beliefs going back to pre-Aryan times, and indeed much of it is pre-Aryan. Tales related about jogis, *nāthas,* siddhas and sādhus are reminiscent of legends about the ṛishis of old. They have absorbed features from the religions of the Aryans, Egyptians, Mesopotamians, Greeks, Scythians, Persians, Chinese and Tibetans, and even later creeds like Islam.

Except that sādhus are unusual and often antinomian to a marked degree, no generalizations can be made about them. They worship the greater and lesser gods of the Hindu pantheon, follow popular forms of Hindu belief, but many of their gods are perverse variants of Hindu gods, with their own secret names. Often they behave like madmen, and many of them are probably mad. Among the names they bear is the title *pāgal,* i.e. mad. They come from all the major and minor sects of Hindus, but they are mainly Śaivites, stressing *tapas* or active asceticism and often sexuality.

There are several thousand 'schools' of sādhus, each splinter sect having its own brand of votaries and ascetics. Most of these schools are locally organized. The left-hand cults in particular are strongly independent in this respect, and acknowledge no one besides the local guru. The more 'orthodox' sādhus of India accept, in theory at least, the control of an executive committee of seven leaders, presided over by a *mahā-maṇḍaleśvar,* 'great overlord'. Śaṅkara attempted to organize all the orders of sādhus under ten heads called the *daśanāmi,* 'ten names', namely, (1) *Sārasvatī,* 'pool', (2) *Purī,* 'citadel', (3) *Vana,* 'tree', (4) *Tīrtha,* 'ford', (5) *Giri,* 'hill', (6) *Parvata,* 'mountain', (7) *Bhāratī,* 'land', (8) *Araṇya,* 'forest', (9) *Āśrama,* 'hermitage', and (10) *Sagara,* 'sea'.

A sādhu is initiated at the age of twelve, but it is not at all unusual for older candidates to receive admission. During initiation the sādhu drops his own name and assumes a new one. This new name takes many forms, but in general it may be said to consist of three parts: the first is the name of a god, saint, quality, plant, animal, or a descriptive epithet; the second is the sect termination which may be Dāsa, Nātha, Ānanda, Kaṇṭhaḍ, etc.; the third is the title taken from one of the ten subdivisions given above. The salutation of sādhus on meeting or departure is *ādeśa,* 'command', i.e. be guided by the rule of the order, a term used by Hindu reformers in a different context.

The possessions of a sādhu include several of the following items: the *daṇḍa** or staff which has varied forms; the heads of some are shaped like the phallus; some like the *khaṭvāṅga* are surmounted by a skull, some topped by a trident (*triśūla*); the *āchal* or crutch is a short cross-stick used as a support for the chin or arm during meditation and on certain other ceremonial occasions. It is also used to support the body at burial. A fan of peacock feathers or palmyra leaf or animal hair for driving off evil spirits is often carried by sādhus. Other items include the *kamaṇḍalu* or ascetic's water-pot (often found associated with the god Brahmā in pictorial representations); a *kafni* or shroud; a *laṅgoṭī* or loin cloth; a *kaupina* or narrow strip of cloth hanging down from a waist-cord to conceal the genitals; a patched cloak and a skull cap (*kapāla*); the *khappar* (or kharpara) a begging bowl made of a half coconut-shell or gourd, or of brass or other metal; the *pātra* or drinking vessel, which is sometimes a human skull; the *janeo,* a sacred thread, usually of black sheep's wool, and made up of nine strands; it is worn around the neck. To the janeo is attached a ring representing the yoni, called the *pavitrī,* made from grass blades, carved horn, or sometimes metal; the *mālā* or rosary usually of rudrāksha berries; the *kaṛā,* an iron bangle worn on the wrist. The *kaṛā-liṅga* jogis wear an iron ring or chain (*śṛiṅkhala*) fastened to the male organ to show their triumph over sex. They usually go about naked.

Some sādhus are completely shaven. Some have matted or braided hair (*jaṭā*) and beard (*śmaśru*). Others cut off the *chuṭiya* or scalp-lock. Some disdain all caste marks, others make marks on their foreheads, shoulders, chest, buttocks and organs. Some smear the whole body with ashes. Some wear magical earrings (e.g. the *kānphaṭa* yogis). Sādhus may be clothed, partly clothed, or completely naked. If they wear a robe or vestment it is usually yellow, saffron, or ochre-coloured. These colours have been variously interpreted as representing blood, ripe grain, and so forth. The saffron or ochre robe was the covering of condemned criminals being led to the place of execution. The Rājput knight donned the saffron robe for a while before going out to the last battle. He was thereafter regarded as dead.

An important element in jogi ceremonial is centred around the *dhūni* or fire, made up of smouldering logs of wood in a hollow pit. Wherever the sādhu takes up his abode he lights his dhūni, and such fires are found at all important shrines and monasteries, where some have been kept burning for centuries. In British times the Forest Department of the Government kept several such shrines supplied with wood for their fires. Householders of certain sects keep a dhūni in their houses.

The embers and charcoal in the dhūni are stirred about by means of the *chiṁṭa* or fire tongs, made from a bent-over strip of metal. The chiṁṭa is also used as a magical implement, and the ends are clapped together to make a metallic clicking; the closed end is often decorated with a metal ring, which is also shaken as an accompaniment during the chanting of mantras, the singing of songs, the summoning and dismissal of godlings and demons, the pronouncement of curses, or as a purely mechanical aid to meditation. In addition to the chiṁṭa, sādhus use small musical instruments for the same purpose of musical or ritual accompaniment. These include the bell (*ghaṇṭa*), the small drum (*ḍholak*), a one-stringed instrument (*ektāra*), or the Indian violin (*saraṅgi*). A special whistle called the *siṅgnād* made of horn is also hung on a cord around the neck.

Many sādhus are anchorites, living in solitude; some are cenobites, living in monastic communities. They may or may not marry, or may be obliged to remain celibate, but are at liberty to 'communicate' with any willing woman if they wish. Widow remarriage is permitted among sādhus; in fact widows may remarry up to seven times. Widows are sometimes kept as concubines by jogis who cannot marry. Female *joginīs* are not unusual. They are generally widows or initiated wives of jogis.

Sādhus make a living in a wide variety of ways. Some by dream-interpretation, fortune-telling, palmistry, astrology (like the renowned fortune-telling jogis called Rāval, after whom the town of Rāwalpindi, now in Pakistan, is named). Some sell amulets, small stone liṅgas and yonis, śālagrāma stones, tigers' claws, bears' teeth, rhino-horn, dead men's bones, magical berries and beads. Some live by magical exorcisms and witchcraft and the casting of spells; some by singing popular, devotional, or magical songs; some by conjuring and juggling, tattooing, selling lace and string with magical properties; some by peddling herbs and primitive medicines, drugs and dyes. Many are associated with animals, and are snake-charmers and monkey-men; some lead about strange, freakish or performing animals such as cattle, donkeys, dogs, mongooses.

They are experts in making the *kavacha* or talisman, amulet, charm and counter-charm, which they confect under auspicious astrological signs by writing on metal, wood or paper the proper mantra, *maṇḍala* or symbol, for the purpose of protection, for banishing evil spirits, ensuring the presence of guardian spirits, or curing diseases. These kavachas are worn by the person, suspended around the neck for general protection, over the heart or between the buttocks for causing harm to an enemy and suspended over the organ for securing the affection of a woman.

They may or may not beg for their food. Some accept offerings only from brāhmins (and no other castes), or only from caste Hindus (not outcastes), or from Hindus (not non-Hindus), or from anyone including the lowest castes and Muslims. Some eat only with their own sect; some will only eat alone as it is considered dangerous to be watched while eating. Most have no objection to eating with anyone, including non-Hindus and outcastes. The majority also periodically have some form of sacramental meal or feast with members of their own order. Some observe the prohibitions of the orthodox in respect of the things they eat. Many eat mutton, fish and pork. Some even beef. Others do not eat fish because their semi-legendary guru was born from a fish; some eat the flesh of snakes, donkeys, lizards and other animals but not the horse. Some again, hold that red pulse (*masūr*) is taboo because it resembles drops of blood. They are commonly addicted to spirituous liquor and drugs, and many of their so-called magical feats are executed while under their influence.

A sādhu adept is supposed to know when it is time for him to die, and some have themselves buried alive. Suicide* in fact is often the preferred mode of exit from the earthly scene. They rarely practise cremation. Most sādhus and jogis are buried sitting cross-legged in the posture of meditation. The mourning period is up to twelve days. It is believed that the buried yogi is actually in an indefinite trance.

The sādhu who is also a sorcerer or black magician is greatly feared. When functioning as such the sādhu, jogi, *jādū-wāllah* (magic-man), *ojhā* and similar shamans are believed to be veritable focuses of tremendous psychic power, whose spells and curses can bring ruin, whose glances can sear and blight. They are said to have at their command all the denizens of the devil-world, evil spirits of horrible form who torment one waking or dreaming, living or dead. Reputedly the worst place for witchcraft is Malabār, where the *Oḍiyan* or black magician is a figure of dread. Oḍiyans belong to an outcaste tribe, and are fully conversant with the magical use of poppets to cause an enemy's death, with the art of sending spirits to haunt people, with the method of exorcizing troublesome and vexatious demons, and so on.

A few of the magical techniques of these black magicians may here be described very briefly. To cripple: make a set of mystical diagrams on a thin sheet of copper, bury it with incantations at a spot over which the victim is wont to pass, such as the threshold of his hut. On stepping over it the curse will pass to him; he will soon suffer excruciating pain, fall down, and remain crippled for life. To become invisible: walk at midnight around the hut of a woman in her first pregnancy at the stage of seven months, softly tinkling a special low-toned bell and chanting mantras. This puts the woman into a trance while the rest of the household are rendered insensible. The woman comes out of the hut naked and still entranced. The sorcerer rips open the abdomen and removes the foetus. From the foetus a magical oil is extracted which is used for all kinds of purposes, for example, to render one invisible, or invulnerable, for shape changing, for sexual vigour. To kill or torment: an effigy of the enemy or rival is made of clay, dough or wax, 'enlivened' by chants, and a limb or vital organ of the image pierced with a thorn or pin, or twisted and broken, to torment the living victim. His shadow may be 'measured' with a length of string, or 'nailed' down, and treated in a manner to bring torment upon the victim.

Cruelty, violence and bloodshed are in fact a feature of large areas of sādhuism. Animal sacrifices play a major part in many sorcerous undertakings, and human sacrifices are still sometimes clandestinely offered by the Nāgas of Assam, the Khonds of Orissa, and the left-hand sects of the Aghorīs, Thugs, Kāpālikas and others. Most sādhus are pacifist, but some sects, referred to by the generic term of *Sajjikā* used to carry arms and openly advocated violence. The origin of the term is obscure, and is believed to be derived from the term *sa-jyā*, 'with a bowstring', and originally referred to a phallic cult of probably tantrik affinities, signifying those who were 'armed' or prepared for battle, specifically the erotic encounter. By extension the term was applied to all armed ascetics.

Although the adoption of the profession of arms by Hindu ascetic orders remains one of the most curious phenomena of religious history it is to be remembered that the alliance of violence and piety has not been unusual in Hinduism. Several castes classified as 'Criminal' have a tradition of cult murder as part of their religious ceremonial. Cruel blood sacrifices form a part of Śākta worship in general. The Thugs* were devout men according to their own lights. The infamous *Pindāri*, ruthless marauders and dacoits (Hindi, *ḍākaiṭ*) of Central India who followed in the wake of Marāṭha depredations, linked piety with pillage and took drugs and intoxicants at religious rites, which were a mixture of Hindu and Muslim features, before setting forth on their bloody expeditions. They were finally put down by Lord Hastings in 1818.

Sajjikā cults in various guises and under various names flourished in India during the Middle Ages. By the eleventh century many Sajjikā leaders became attached to the courts of local rulers and in some cases assumed kshattriya status, constituting, as it were, a standing elite in the little principalities. In the seventeenth century several of the leading Vaishṇava *bairāgi* sects formed themselves into a powerful armed confederacy and their gangs frequented places of pilgrimage, both to protect and plunder the pilgrims.

The pacifist cult founded by Dādū* was, within a century after his death, organized into the militant sects of the 'Fighting Nāgās', so called because they were recruited from the *nagna* or naked followers of Dādū's cult. The Fighting Nāgas helped the authorities of Jaipur to collect taxes, which they did by intimidation and threat. Many also kept what might be euphemistically called 'the peace' and were amongst the most dependable mercenaries in the wars fought by Jaipur state.

The use of arms was strongly advocated, albeit for crusades and self-protection, by the tenth Guru of the Sikhs, although the founder of Sikhism was himself a gentle and saintly character, who abhorred violence.

Books

I. Anonymous. *Mystics and Magicians of India, An Anthology*, Calcutta, 1953.
II. Bharati, Agehananda. *The Ochre Robe*, London, 1961.
III. Campbell, J. *The Mystics, Ascetics and Saints of India*, London, 1903.
IV. Dare, P. *Indian Underworld. Indian Saints, Sorcerers and Superstitions*, London, 1938.
V. Datta, P. *Hindu Dharma and the Profession of Arms*, 1929.
VI. Deo, S. B. *History of Jaina Monachism*, Poona, 1956.
VII. Ghurye, G. S. *Indian Sadhus*, Bombay, 1953.
VIII. Gibier, Paul. *Spiritism and Eastern Fakirism*, 1886.
IX. Thurston, E. *Omens and Superstitions of Southern India*, London, 1912.
X. Oman, J. C. *The Brahmins, Theists and Muslims of India*, 1907.
XI. Oman, J. C. *Cults, Customs and Superstitions of India*, 1908.
XII. Oman, J. C. *The Mystics, Ascetics and Saints of India: A Study of Sadhuism*, 1905.
XIII. Orr, W. G. 'Armed Religious Ascetics in Northern India', *Bulletin of the John Rylands Library*, Manchester, April, 1940.
XIV. Somerville, A. *Crime and Religious Belief in India*, Calcutta, 1931.

SAGARA, 'empoisoned', a descendant of Hariśchandra, king of the Solar dynasty ruling at Ayodhyā. Sagara's father *Bāhu* (or Bāhuka) had been defeated by the warlike Haihaya people and had fled from Ayodhyā with his two wives, one of whom was pregnant. The other wife, out of jealousy, gave her rival poison (*gara*), with the result that the child's growth within the womb was delayed. In the meanwhile Bāhu died, and the disconsolate woman was on the point of ascending the funeral pyre of her husband when she was prevented by the sage Aurva* who predicted that she would give birth to a universal emperor. Seven years later her child was born. From the circumstance of his birth he was named Sagara, though some authorities find here a hint that the child was actually born of a Śaka (Scythian) woman, whence his name.

The sage Aurva instructed the boy in the arts and sciences, and when he grew up told him of his father's defeat by the Haihaya. He then presented the youthful prince with the weapon* called *āgneyāstra*, or 'fire missile', to use against his hereditary enemies. Armed with the magical missile Sagara went on a crusade against the Haihaya, very nearly exterminated them, and recovered his ancestral lands. During this campaign he also brought under subjection several other barbarian tribes and forced them to assume some token of their subordination: thus the Yavanas (Greeks) had to shave their heads completely, the Śakas to shave the crown of their heads; the Pāradas (?Afghans) to wear their hair long, and the Pahlavas (Parthians) to let their beards grow long.

Sagara had no children at first by his two wives, but by undergoing penances he was promised progeny. Through his first wife *Keśinī* princess of Vidarbha he became the father of *Asamanjas* (or Pañchajana), a wild and dissolute youth who later acquired fame for his valour and continued the royal line. Sagara's second wife *Sumatī*, was the daughter of the sage Kaśyapa. She was delivered of a gourd containing 60,000 seeds which Sagara placed in vessels of milk, and in time each seed became a son.

These 60,000 sons of Sagara grew up to be infamous for their impiety. During the performance of an *aśvamedha* or horse sacrifice in thanksgiving for having been granted offspring, Sagara instructed his sons by Sumatī to guard the sacrificial horse. Because of their carelessness the horse was driven off by Indra who left it to browse in Pātāla, the infernal regions. The sons repaired thither, digging their way down to the nether world, and the chasm they dug was called *sāgara*, 'ocean'. They found the horse grazing near the spot where the sage Kapila sat in meditation, and believing him to be the thief they insulted and threatened him. Enraged at being disturbed the sage turned on the presumptuous youths with his eyes ablaze and they were all reduced to ashes. The remains were found by *Anśumat* (or Anśumān), son of Asamanjas, who had been sent out to search for them. He besought Kapila to relent and restore the sons of Sagara to life, and the sage promised that Anśumat's grandson would be the means of their deliverance which would take place when the river of heaven was brought down to earth to water the ashes of the 60,000 young men. Anśumat returned with the sacrificial horse to Sagara who then completed the interrupted ceremony.

The son of Anśumat was *Dilīpa*, who once failed to give due reverence to Kāmadhenu* the wonderful cow, and she cursed him to the effect that he would have no children unless he and his wife *Sudakshiṇā* became the slaves of Kāmadhenu's daughter Nandinī for some time. The royal pair faithfully served Nandinī, and on one occasion Dilīpa even offered his own life to save the calf from the lion of Śiva. The curse was removed and the couple freed from their bondage became the parents of Bhagīratha and, in some versions, of Raghu*.

In due time *Bhagīratha* became a great sage, and sought by means of austerities to restore to life the ashes of the sons of his ancestor Sagara. His penances were such that Śiva was persuaded to allow the sacred river Ganges, which issues from the toe of Vishṇu, to descend to earth. From the divine source it descended in invisible form in a mighty rush and would have flooded the earth had not Śiva allowed it to flow through his abundant hair from which a trickle descended to the Himālayas. As the river flowed on it flooded the sacrificial ground of the sage *Jahnu*, a descendant of Purūravas, and the sage, angered by this nuisance, drank up its waters. Bhagīratha was obliged to start his penances all over again and at last Jahnu relented and allowed the river to emerge from his ear. Bhagīratha carefully led the stream over the earth and into the sea and finally to the infernal regions of Pātāla where it flowed over the ashes of the sons of Sagara. Laved by the purifying waters the souls of the 60,000 sons of Sagara were admitted to paradise.

Because of the labours of Bhagīratha the river Ganges is also called after him Bhāgīrathī. The name Bhagīratha is proverbial for persistence and determination, and the achievement of any difficult objective is referred to as the result of 'Bhagīratha prayatnam', the Labours or Perseverence of Bhagīratha.

Books

See under Mythology.

ŚAIVA SIDDHĀNTA, 'Śaiva doctrine', the name of an important school of Śaivism* which flourished in South India. Its scriptures constitute a large segment of Tamil literature written between the seventh and tenth centuries, for most of the great Tamil saints, mystics, hymnologists, and poets came under its influence. These writings combine intense devotional fervour, comparable to the Jewish Psalms and the Old Testament Prophets, with a very rarefied and abstruse metaphysics. Dr U. Pope referred to Śaiva Siddhānta as 'the most elaborate, influential and undoubtedly the most valuable of all the religions of India' (I, p. xviii).

The best-known scriptures of the Tamil Śaivites are known as the TIRUMURAI, 'canon', an anthology of hymns by the sixty-three *Nāyaṇār* or 'Teachers' arranged in eleven books. The Nāyaṇārs made no distinctions of caste, sex or creed, and their ranks included brāhmins, toddy-drawers, Vellālas, oil-sellers, kings, princesses, singers. Chief of the texts are:

(*a*) *Tirumandiram*, consisting of 3,000 stanzas written by the mystic Tirumūlar (or Mulār) (AD 600–750?); legend says that he was born in Kailāsa where he meditated for 3,000 years, composing one stanza a year until his work was completed. He then went to South India, entered the body of a deceased cowherd and wrote down his highly abstruse masterpiece. The book embodies much tantrik material.

(*b*) *Tevāram*, containing the songs of three poets, namely, Appar (fl. AD 650), a Vellāla by caste who was converted to Jainism but on being cured of an acute colic pain after praying to Śiva became a Śaivite; Saṁbandar (d. AD 660) a child prodigy who uttered hymns in praise of Śiva at the age of three, and died at the age of seventeen; and Sundarar (fl. AD 820), a twice-married Śaivite poet about whom many miraculous legends are related.

(*c*) *Tiruvāśagam*, by the poet Māṇikkavāsagar*, one of the greatest poets of Tamil.

These works, forming the bulk of the canonical literature of the Śaiva Siddhāntas, were put together in a compilation of eleven books, collectively called the Tirumuṛai, by the poet NAMBI (also called Āṇḍār Nambi) (fl. AD 1100) who for this reason is known as the Tamil Vyāsa.

A twelfth book, 'the twelfth Tirumuṛai', was added to the collection and became known as the *Periapurāṇam*. Compiled by Śekkiḷār (*c.* 1140) it contains the lives of the sixty-three Śaiva saints. A century later Meykaṇḍa (fl. 1240) a Vellāla (low caste) saint and poet composed the *Śiva-jñāna-bodham*, a semi-philosophical work of great merit and the last great classic of the Śaiva Siddhānta school. Among this saint's pupils was the brāhmin Aruḷnandi who wrote a commentary on his master's work. Aruḷnandi's disciple was Umāpati (not to be confused with the Maithili poet), and these three founded a considerable school of Śaivism.

Books

I. Paranjoti, V. *Saiva Siddhanta.* 2nd Ed., London, 1954.

II. Pillai, J. M. N. *Studies in Saiva Siddhanta*, Madras, 1911.

III. Pillai, K. S. *The Metaphysics of the Saiva Siddhanta System*, 1940.

IV. Pillai, T. G. S. *Introduction to the History of Saiva Siddhanta*, Annamalai, 1948.

V. Ponniah, V. *The Saiva Siddhanta Theory of Knowledge*, Annamalai, 1952.

ŚAIVISM, the religion devoted to the worship of Śiva and his symbols. Śaivism shares many features of the Vaishṇava cults, such as repetition of the names of the sectarian deity, obedience to the guru and so on, but there are other features that distinguish it from Vaishṇavism, which may be briefly indicated.

Unlike the Vaishṇavites, the Śaivites do not believe in the notion of incarnations and avatārs of the deity. Śaivism is most influential in the south of India; in the north it has lost its hold, even in Banāras which is a city sacred to Śiva. Śaivite cults are generally more ascetic and stern than those of the Vaishṇavites; they insist on mortification of the flesh. All the picturesque yogis and sādhus of popular conception, those with withered arms upraised, those who lie on beds of nails, are Śaivite. Perversion and depravity are also frequently encountered among Śaivite sects. The scatophilic anchorites who feed on carrion and excrement, who haunt cemeteries, cover their bodies with ashes and cowdung, the whole galaxy of Indian magicians and wonder-workers are generally Śaivite. There are of course orthodox forms of Śaivism which differ radically from these perverse orders. The veneration of the liṅga is an integral part of most Śaivite sects. It is generally worshipped in the form of a stone image, and is sometimes represented by the *daṇḍa* or staff carried by certain Śaivite orders. The rosary or necklace used by Śaivites is made of rudrāksha berries. The priests of the Śaivites are seldom brāhmins, and brāhmins as a rule regard them with disfavour. The Śaivites are strongly monotheistic, believe in the unity and immanence of god, abhor idolatry and have a deep consciousness of personal sin, declaring, 'Even my good is evil', a probable indication, according to some scholars, of Christian influence. Their literature is almost exclusively in Sanskrit and Tamil, and is much more vigorous and masculine than that of the Vaishṇavites. Śaivite scriptures are collectively referred to as the Śaivāgama (Śiva-āgama) or Śiva codex.

The origins of Śaivism have been sought outside India, and the cult was perhaps brought to India by the Maga* and Vrātya* people. There is some evidence of Śaiva worship in the Indus Valley civilization, and the seated figure with *ūrdhva-liṅga* represented on the Mohenjodaro seals, may well be the earliest image of Śiva in existence. The invading Aryans spoke contemptuously of the native *śiśna-devatās* or phallus-worshippers.

The same figure is shown surrounded by cattle, which may have been the origin of one of the titles of Śiva, namely, Paśupati, and of the subsequent deity-devotee relationship. This later philosophy posited three *padārtha* or categories, of *pati*, 'Lord', the master of the herd; *paśu*, 'herd', i.e. the soul, and *pāśa*, the bond between the two. This last is interpreted either as the bond tethering the devotee to the deity, or as the fetters of ignorance, action and illusion that bind the herd to the material world.

Chief among the early Śaivite scriptures is the *Śvetāśvatara Upanishad**, a sort of Śaivite *Bhagavadgītā*. There is also a later work known as the *Śivagītā* to which Śaivites assign a high place. Another early Śaivite scripture, the *Nānmarai*, was originally said to have been a Tamil* śaṅgam work.

By the early centuries of the present era the sect of the Pāśupata* mentioned in the *Mahābhārata* gained popularity under Lakulīśa (AD 200). This was a perverse cult, but within the next three hundred years Śaivism acquired a more acceptable tradition bequeathed by sixty-three saints called *Purātana*, 'ancient' to whom some ślokas and sayings are attributed.

By the seventh century the sect known as the Śaiva-Siddhāntas* (*c.* 600–1000) rose to prominence, and its followers were responsible for a profuse literature. Perhaps the most profound of all the Śaivāgamas are the hymns of these Śaivite saints. Their influence continued till the eleventh century.

Kashmīr Śaivism was founded by Vasugupta* (d. AD 830), and another revival, known as Liṅgāyatism* took place later under Basava. From the middle of the tenth century a branch of the Pāśupatas, known as the Kālamukha gained popularity, but incorporated many perverse features of the Śiva cult. From this grew the sects of the Kāpālikas, Kānphaṭas, and Aghorīs.

The Tamil* works of the Sittar (Siddha) saints of the seventeenth century compiled in the Śiva-vākyam show undeniable Christian influence.

Books

I. Bhandarkar, R. G. *Vaisnavism, Saivism, and Minor Religious Systems*, Strassbourg, 1913.
II. Iyer, C. V. N. *The Origin and Early History of Saivism in South India*, Calcutta, 1923.
III. Kingsbury, F., and Philips, G. E. *Hymns of the Tamil Saivite Saints*, Calcutta, 1921.
IV. Sivapadasundaram, S. *The Saiva School of Hinduism*, London, 1934.
V. Subramanian, K. R. *Origin of Saivism and Its History in the Tamil Land*, Madras, 1941.

ŚAKA. The Central Asian nomadic tribe of Scythians known to the Romans as the Sacae and to Indian historians as the Śakas came from Kashgar. In the historical period the pressure of the Yueh-chi from Central Asia displaced them, and hordes of Śakas swarmed into Persia. In the first century BC they were signally defeated by the Persian king Mithradates and the Śaka tide was diverted southwards. They overwhelmed the Greek meridarchs or governors of Bactria, where the basileus or king maintained a precarious existence, and occupied the valley of the Helmand, which to this day is known after them as Seistān, from Śakastan i.e. the land of the Śakas.

For some time they lived in close association with the Parthians from whom they received a substantial admixture of blood. Their rule in the north-western regions of India alternated with that of the Parthians, and the identity of the various rulers at this period is still a matter of dispute among scholars.

The Śakas are of legendary antiquity in India's past. They are frequently mentioned in the *Rāmāyaṇa*, and in the *Mahābhārata* they appear fighting on the side of Duryodhana. They are associated in an important myth with the sage Sagara, whose name probably preserves his Śaka ancestry. Throughout the historical period stray Śaka tribes continued to enter the subcontinent; such were the Madra, Piśācha, Ābhīra and Kekaya. Among the towns they founded was Śākala, i.e. Śāka town, also called Sagala, modern Siālkoṭ. It was once the capital of the Madra people, and (under the name of Euthydemia) became the capital of Demetrius the Bactrian* Greek king, and of Toramāna the Hun.

The Persian kings employed Śakas, as they did the Parthians, as governors of their eastern provinces, but these governors soon fought to assert their own sovereignty over the areas they governed. The early semi-autonomous Śaka viceroys first became independent under **Maues** (*c.* 20 BC–AD 22) who occupied the territories from Gandhāra to Mathurā. His co-ruler for a time and successor after his death was his son **Azes I** (5 BC–AD 30). The latter was succeeded by **Azilises** (AD 28–40) and **Azes II** (AD 39–79). These independent Śaka chieftains held sway over large parts of India and assumed the title of 'Great King of Kings'. The 'Periplus' (*c.* AD 80), and Ptolemy in his 'Geography' (AD 160) refer to the district of Scythia, with its capital of Min (unidentified) as comprising Patalene (Indus delta), Abira (the country of the Ābhīras to the west of the lower Indus) and Saurastrene (Kāṭhiāwār).

With the disintegration of the central Śaka-Kushān-Parthian authority in Afghanistan in the first century of the present era, the governors of the subordinate areas under Śaka rule in India began to reign like independent monarchs themselves. These rulers were known as the *Kshatrapa*, a word of Old Persian origin, denoting a provincial governor, from which is also derived the still more recent pseudo-Sanskrit *chhatrapati*. By the second century AD there were known to be at least five Śaka satrapies, which had been carved out of the earlier Śaka kingdom. These were at Kāpiśa in Afghanistan, Taxila in western Panjāb, Mathurā in the Jamnā valley, Nāsik (or Junnar) in the Upper Deccan, and Ujjain in Mālwā. The most powerful satrapies were those situated in western India, known as the Western Satraps, of which the Kshaharāta of Nāsik and the Kardamakas of Ujjain were the most important dynasties. These Western Satraps ruled, with occasional gaps, for three hundred years.

The **Kshaharāta** (or Ksharāta) satrapal line was founded by Bhumaka who carved out a principality on the ruins of the early Sātavāhana empire, and made his capital at Nāsik (or Junnar). The most famous of his successors was Nahapāna (fl. AD 119–125) (the name is Persian), who ruled over the northern part of Mahārāshṭra as well as Mālwā, Kāṭhiāwār and southern Rājputāna. The Kshaharātas were involved in a lengthy struggle with the Sātavāhana king Gautamīputra Sātakarṇi, who restored the fortunes of the deposed Sātavāhanas. The Nāsik satrapy passed into the hands of another Śaka dynasty, that of the Kardamakas.

The **Kardamaka** Śaka satrapy (AD 77–398), named after the Kardama river in Bactria, was founded in AD 77 by Chashṭana, the Tiastanes of Ptolemy's 'Geography'. This Śaka svāmin (lord) set up his capital at Ujjain, and established his rule over Kāṭhiāwār and Mālwā. The greatest king of this line, and one of the greatest and most versatile rulers of India was his grandson Rudradāman (AD 130–158), a patron of letters, an able administrator and a great conqueror, whose sway extended over Mālwā, Kāṭhiāwār, Saurāshṭra, Rājputāna, Kutch and the lower Indus, Gujarāt, parts of the western Vindhyas and Aravalli, and also, if his court poet is to be believed, the area of the Koṅkaṇ in the south. Arrian who resided in Barygaza in the second century AD described a Parthian, i.e. Śaka, sovereignty as extending from the Indus to the Narmadā. Rudradāman twice defeated Gautamīputra Sātakarṇi (or his son), inflicted a crushing blow to the Yaudheya (*c.* AD 145), won the hands of several princesses in *svayaṁvara* ceremonies, and gave his daughter in marriage to Pulamāyi, son of Gautamīputra Sātakarṇi.

Rudradāman is especially notable for his patronage of Sanskrit, which exercised a profound influence on the development of the language. He himself was well-versed in Sanskrit grammar, polity and logic, and was renowned for the excellence of his Sanskrit compositions in prose and verse. In his day Ujjain* became renowned as a scientific and literary centre, and one of the intellectual capitals of the world. Rudradāman has left one of the oldest and most important epigraphic* inscriptions, written in correct Sanskrit throughout, and the first official record in that language. Known as the *Girnār Praśasti* of Junagaḍh (Kāṭhiāwār), it consists of a long panegyric which records his martial exploits and his reconstruction of the great artificial Sudarśana lake at Girnār. This lake had been previously excavated under Chandragupta Maurya and improved in the time of Aśoka.

Rudradāman was succeeded by his son Dāmajada after whose death came a disastrous civil war, resulting in the Śaka territories being taken over partly by the Sātavāhanas, and partly by the Ābhīras and the Mālavas. Till the beginning of the fourth century, however, an offshoot of the Śaka line had achieved a further brief spell of power under a line of kings whose names ended in 'varma'. One of them was Chandravarma (fl. AD 325) who ruled at Pokarna in modern Udaipur state. It was this Śaka ruler who set up the famous Iron Pillar, an unequalled masterpiece of metallurgical engineering. The pillar bears a short inscription eulogizing the king for his conquest of Vaṅga. It was said to have been erected to peg down the head of a great snake, and it remained in place until the ruler of the Rājput Tomara dynasty of Delhi moved the pillar to Mehrauli, Delhi, an act which resulted in the fall of the Tomaras. The rise of Gupta power in the first half of the fourth century saw the end of the Śaka satrapies. Chandravarma himself was conquered by Samudragupta and his kingdom annexed to the Gupta empire.

There can be no doubt that the Śakas played a prominent part in Indian history. Their long and uninterrupted rule in the heart of India provided a channel for the ingress of a great flood of cultural elements from Central Asia. Sanskrit works abound with references to their appearance, dress, diet, manners and customs, all of which profoundly influenced local social customs. Their skill in metallurgy is seen in the Mehrauli Pillar, and their influence is apparent in Hindu art, in textile weaving and designs, in the ornaments of women, and is also exemplified 'in the Bengal terracottas of the seventeenth–nineteenth centuries'.

The Śakas contributed greatly to the development of Sanskrit and the nāgarī script, and have left their stamp on other Indian languages. The patois known as Sakara and Wakhan are Śaka, as is the Bundelkhand dialect of Banaphari (named after Vanashpara, one of Kanishka's governors), and traces of Śaka linguistic peculiarities are to be found in the loan words of several Indian vernaculars.

The complex administrative machinery that had evolved in India under Persian and Greek rule in Mauryan times received fresh orientation during the Śaka supremacy and left a permanent impression on Indian polity. Although the Śakas took over many aspects of the early Indian administrative system, their own system was not a replica of the Mauryan. This was not the adaptation of an existing machinery by bewildered barbarians seeking guidance in controlling territories that had been conquered by brute force. Says Raychaudhuri,

'The little that we know of the administration of the Śaka epoch leaves no room for doubt that the institutions of the age were not haphazard improvisations of military upstarts, having no relations with the past, but a highly developed and organized system—the fruit of the labours of generations of political theorists and practical statesmen'.

The Guptas, in fact, inherited not the Mauryan mode of government but the administrative system bequeathed to north-western India by the foreign Scythians and Perso-Mongolians who ruled there for five centuries.

The Scythian bureaucracy was well co-ordinated, and although there was no great cleavage with the past, there were distinct innovations, both in general and in detail. The Scythians brought with them several institutions they had acquired in the countries through which they had passed. The Persian mode of government by satraps, for instance, was expanded to cover the newer provinces taken over by the Śakas, and officials with Greek titles like *meridarch* (governor) and *strategos* (general) guided the destinies of the Śaka empire.

To the Scythians was due the notion of a more exalted type of kingship, the employment of high-sounding semi-divine honorifics for the rulers and their chief consorts, which were later adopted by medieval Indian kings.

Terms like *mahārāja* and *mahārājādhirāja* were Indian renderings of the Persian *Shahanshah* 'king of kings', popularized by foreign princes and first introduced in about 150 BC. The use of the title *svāmin* (lord) for the heir-apparent to the throne was adopted by Bharata in his *Nāṭyaśāstra* from contemporary records of the Śaka kings. The titles of most Mauryan officials were retained, but several new posts were created.

We find from epigraphic references to the vast sums of money spent by Scythian rulers on the construction and repair of tanks, wells, lakes, and other reservoirs, that they gave close attention to public works, and we know that the building of roads and rest-houses was not neglected by them either. Village administration centred around the rural assemblies and committees, 'which afforded', says Raychaudhuri, 'a field for co-operation between kings and villagers'.

Books

I. Bachhofer, L. 'On Greeks and Sakas in India', *Journal of the American Oriental Society*, 1941, pp. 223 ff.

II. Banerji, R. D. 'The Scythian Period of Indian History', *Indian Antiquary*, Bombay, 1908.

III. Basham, A. L. 'A New Study of the Saka-Kushana Period', *Bulletin of the School of Oriental and African Studies*, 1953, pp. 80 ff.

IV. Leeuw, J. E. van Lohuizen de. *The Scythian Period*, Leiden, 1949.

V. Lévi, Sylvain. 'Notes on the Indo-Scythians', *Indian Antiquary*, Bombay, Vol. II, p. 386, 1903.

VI. Majumdar, R. C. (Ed.) *An Advanced History of India*, London, 1948.

VII. Majumdar, R. C. (Ed.) *The Age of Imperial Unity*, Bombay, 1951.

VIII. Majumdar, R. C. *Ancient India*, Banaras, 1952.

IX. Marshall, J. 'Greeks and Sakas in India', *Journal of the Royal Asiatic Society*, 1947, pp. 3 ff.

X. Raychaudhuri, H. *Political History of Ancient India*, Calcutta, 6th Ed., 1953.

XI. Shrava, S. *The Sakas in India*, Lahore, 1947.

XII. Smith, V. 'The Kushan or Indo-Scythian Period of Indian History', *Journal of the Royal Asiatic Society*, London, 1903.

ŚĀKHĀ, a 'branch' or school of Vedic learning based on a particular interpretation or rendering of the Vedic text. Scholars are of the opinion that the Vedas as they exist today represent a greatly mutilated version of an original '*Ur*-veda' or parent Veda, which was corrupted in the course of transmission through the centuries beyond any hope of reconstruction.

Renou remarks that 'the changelessness of the Veda is a fiction' (IV, p. 3), for the language of the texts as they were handed down underwent continuous change, due in part to the inevitable corruption consequent on oral transmission, or to the differing traditions of tribes and families among whom the text was current, or to the bias and personal opinion of individual sages who taught and expounded the text.

Numerous schools of Vedic study existed in the ancient past before the present compilations of the texts came to be regarded as fixed, and as numerous were the variant readings promulgated by them. These schools were called *śākhās*, each school being founded on a particular version of the Vedic text, or on varying recensions of the identical text as taught by different teachers, or handed down by a particular family, or used in a particular locality; and scholars, sages and schools became famous for the text traditionally associated with them. Each Veda thus had several śākhās, and each śākhā was based on a different 'edition' of the same original *saṁhitā* or collection (just as different manuscripts of an ancient work may differ in point of grammar, spelling, omission or addition), which reflected the bias or the viewpoint of the individual śākhā, *charaṇa* (see below), *parishad*, *kula*, *gotra*, or other school of Vedic learning.

Thus the *Ṛig-veda* had 6 śākhās; the *Yajur-veda* 86 and the *Sāma-veda* over 1000. But the greater part of these is lost and a number of recensions of the saṁhitās are only known by the names of the sages or families with whom they were associated (III, p. 76). Most of the śākhās today differ only in single words or verses, rarely in whole hymns. Pronunciation and accent, however, differ widely.

The teachings of a *paramparā*, 'succession', or line of teachers who taught a particular śākhā and through whom the tradition was handed down, were called the *charaṇa*. The charaṇa was thus a school for the propagation of a given śākhā or rendering of the Vedas. Many such charaṇas still exist, named after a founder or prominent teacher. They were formed for the Vedas and Brāhmaṇas, and later for the ritual and legal books as well. Famous founders of charaṇas include Aśvala (*see* Gṛitsamada), Kauśītaka (*see* Kuśika), Lāṭyāyana (belonging to the region of Lāṭa in western India), Yājñavalkya*, Uddālaka*, Śaunaka (*see* Gṛitsamada), and Śaṅkha.

At a certain stage the need was felt for reconciling the traditions and collating the conflicting opinions, and this task was undertaken by various scholars and schools. Even in the final saṁhitās (collections) as they have come down to us we find overlapping and contradictory viewpoints with regard to the text, pronunciation and accent. Masses of material have been effaced, and much that remains is redundant, tendentious and amorphous. At a much later date attempts were made to standardize Vedic readings (*see* pāṭha), phonetics and other aspects of Vedic study. The present Vedic compilations have aptly been called 'hymn books in a revised edition'.

The oldest treatises on the grammar and phonetics pertaining to the various śākhās of the Vedas are known as the *prātiśākhya*. These phonetic handbooks have helped considerably to preserve the Vedas from greater mutilation and corruption. Present-day recitation corresponds to the rules given in the prātiśākhyas. There are four such treatises extant: one for the *Ṛig-veda*, ascribed to Śaunaka, grandson of Gṛitsamada*; two for the *Yajur-veda*, one relating to the Black *Yajur-veda* and one to the White, the latter ascribed to Kātyāyana*; and finally, one for the *Atharva-veda*, also attributed to Śaunaka. No prātiśākhya for the *Sāma-veda* is known to exist.

Books

I. Bloomfield, M., et al. *Vedic Variants*, 3 vols., Philadelphia, 1930–4.
II. Ghurye, K. G. *Preservation of Learned Tradition in India*, Bombay, 1950.
III. Mookerji, R. K. *Education in Ancient India*, London, 1947.
IV. Renou, Louis. *Religions of Ancient India*, London, 1953.

ŚAKTI, 'energy', is the term applied to the wife of a god, and signifies the power of a deity manifested in and through his consort. The deity and his wife represent the dual aspect of the divine unity, and together symbolize the power of the godhead. But in many cases the need for a consort or companion was satisfied by creating a practically inactive goddess who played no conspicuous part in the life of her spouse, and she was often named after the deity himself, thus: Agnāyī after Agni; Brahmāṇī after Brahmā; Indrāṇī (or Aindrī) after Indra; Rudrāṇī after Rudra; Vaishṇavī after Vishṇu; Varuṇī after Varuṇa; Vāyavī after Vāyu.

On the other hand, in many instances the female deity of the divine pair was regarded as the active principle of the universe, and was often conceived of as having greater importance than the male. The principle divine couples when named conjointly were therefore named with the śakti or female name first, e.g. Rādhā-Kṛishṇa, Gaurī-Śaṅkar, Sītā-Rāma, Umā-Maheśa, Lakshmī-Nārāyaṇa; and homage was paid to the female counterpart, to Rādhā rather than Kṛishṇa, Sītā rather than Rāma, Durgā rather than Śiva.

The dual characteristics of the Hindu gods, the contemplative and the active, the reigning and the conquering, the meditating and the militant, are nowhere so prominent as in Śiva and his consorts. When the śakti is referred to it is the Śakti of the god Śiva that is specifically intended. She is identified with the One, since it is believed that she combines in her person both the Universal Male and the Universal Female. The Female is the complete One and is the central object of worship.

Many Hindu cults of very ancient provenance, some incorporating features anterior even to the Aryan invasion of India have been devoted to the worship of Śakti; such are the sects of the Āsapūri, Mekhapanthī, Nāyaka, Vilana. These cults, collectively known as the ŚĀKTA cults, all conceive of the paramount diety as female, and render devotion to all that appertains to the female sex. A vast literature, known as the *Śaktāgamas* or *Tantras**, has grown out of this devotion, and Śakta worship and Tantrism are often used interchangeably.

Śakti is worshipped under different aspects. Some sects stress the maternal nature of the goddess. They venerate her as the Mother Goddess or the Great Mother, Magna Mater, 'whose slender waist, bending beneath the burden of the ripe fruit of her breasts, swells into jewelled hips, heavy with the promise of infinite maternities'. She is spoken of as Jaganmātṛi, 'world-mother', though various lesser *mātṛi*, 'mothers', are also known. The name Umā* is probably connected with ammā, a common name for the Mother Goddess among the Dravidians. She appears under dozens of names among village godlings* throughout India.

Śakti is also the personification of the tender and devoted wife, and much tantrik symbolism and worship is centred around Śakti as wife and conjugal partner of Śiva, especially as Pārvatī and Satī. Śakti also symbolizes sexual desire and sexual joy, and the Śakti-Śiva union, the union of Energy and Being, is one of the tantrik means to ultimate knowledge. The union of yoni and liṅga, which is another aspect of the Śakti cult, is the subject of wrapt meditation among its devotees.

As the female principle Śakti is worshipped in the form of a yoni* image, sometimes substituted by a naked woman, since the worship of the genitals of the living female also forms part of the Śākta cult. As the eternal virgin Śakti is represented by a young girl of about fifteen years of age, who is the object of devotion. Worship of the female aspect of the deity is also found among Vaishṇavites (e.g. Sakhībhāva) and in various androgynous* sects.

There is the Śakti of illicit love, whose worship is found in the practices associated with incest, adultery and other antinomian* relationships.

Finally, there is Śakti in her *bhairav* or 'terror' aspect, a cruel and bloodthirsty goddess without mercy. She is then the deity of a cult of death, terror, bloodshed and destruction, and is personified as Kālī, Durgā, and Bhavānī, the goddess of the thugs.

Śiva is supposed to have 1008 names, and it is said that his wife, in her many manifestations, possesses a counterpart of each of these names, besides many more of her own. Among them are the following: Ambikā, 'the Mother' (*see* Gāṇapatya); Anna-pūrṇā 'giver of nourishment'; Bhadra-kālī, 'prosperity-making'; Bhairavī, 'terror-inspiring'; Bhavānī, wife of Bhava, worshipped by the Thugs; Bhramarī, 'bee'; Bhūta-nāyakī, 'devil chieftainess'; Chāmuṇḍā, killer of the demons Chaṇḍa and Muṇḍa (*see* Śumbha); Chaṇḍā, or Chaṇḍī, 'angry' or 'fierce'; Chhinna-mastakā, having a 'severed head' (in this form she killed Niśumbha); Daśa-bhujā, 'ten-armed'; Devī, 'Goddess'; Durgā (*see* Kālī); Gaurī, 'yellow' or 'fair' signifying either the yellow harvest or the yellowish Gaura buffalo, both associated with her; Giri-jā, 'mountain-born'; Haimavatī, daughter of Himavat; Harasiddhī, patron goddess of Ujjain; Jagad-dhātṛi, 'world sustainer'; Jagan-mātṛi or Jagan-mātā, world-mother'; Kālī*, the 'black' goddess, or 'Time' the destroyer; Kāmākhyā (*see* Kāmarūpa); Kāmākshī, 'wanton-eyed', in this form she is worshipped in Assam; Kāmeśvarī, 'love-goddess'; Kāntāravvāsinī, 'forest-dwelling'; Kanyā, or Kanyā-kumārī, 'virgin' or 'youthful virgin'; Cape Comorin, the southern tip of India is named after her; Kauśikī, of the Kuśika family; Kātyāyanī, of the Kātya family; Koṭarī, 'naked'; Lalitā, 'charming'; Mahādevī, 'great goddess'; Mahākālī, 'great destroyer'; Mahāmāyā, 'great illusion'; Mahārājanī, 'great queen'; Mahāsurī, 'great assuress'; Māheśvarī, 'great goddess'; Mahishāsuranāśinī, destroyer of the buffalo-demon Mahisha (*see* Kālī); Mātṛikā, 'mother'; Mātaṅgī (*see* godlings); Mīnākshī*; Mukta-keśī, having 'dishevelled hair'; Paraprakṛitī, 'super nature'; Pārvatī*; Piṅgā, 'dark', or 'tawny'; Rajasī, 'fierce'; Rakta-dantī, 'bloody-toothed'; Rātri, goddess of 'night'; Satī*, 'virtuous'; Siṁha-vāhinī, 'lion mouthed' (*see* Kālī); Śyāmā, 'black'; Tripura-sundarī, 'three-city beauty' i.e. the beautiful one of the three worlds, heaven, earth and hell; Umā*, 'mother'; Vāgeśvarī, 'tiger goddess', a manifestation of Kālī in her tiger form; Vijayā, 'victorious'; Vindhya-vāsanī, 'dweller in the Vindhyas', worshipped near Mirzāpur where the Vindhyas approach the Ganges; it is said that the blood of the sacrifices before her image is never allowed to get dry.

Books

I. Chakravarti, P. C. *Doctrine of Sakti in Indian Literature*, Calcutta, 1940.
II. Das, S. K. *Sakti or Divine Power*, Calcutta, 1934.
III. Dasgupta, S. B. *Obscure Religious Cults*, Calcutta, 1950.

IV. Diksitar, R. *The Lalita Cult*, Madras, 1942.
V. Ghosh, A. B. *Siva & Sakti*, Rajshahi, 1935.
VI. Pal, D. N. *Siva and Sakti*, 2 vols., Calcutta, 1910.
VII. Payne, E. A. *The Saktas*, Calcutta, 1933.
VIII. Woodroffe, J. *The Serpent Power*, 5th Ed., Madras, 1953.
IX. Woodroffe, J. *Shakti and Shakta*, 4th Ed., Madras, 1951.

ŚAKUNI, son of Subala the king of Gandhāra (hence also known as Saubala), was the brother of Gāndhārī wife of Dhṛitarāshṭra. An expert dice player and a cheat, he was responsible for the exile of the Pāṇḍavas.

The *Mahābhārata* relates that a great gambling match was arranged by the Kaurava prince Duryodhana, who was filled with envy at the growing power of the Pāṇḍavas. He challenged Yudhishṭhira to a game of dice and asked his uncle Śakuni to play for him. Śakuni used loaded dice and won every throw. The result was that the Pāṇḍava prince, in spite of the entreaties of his friends to stop the game, lost all his possessions; his ornaments, gems, gold, treasury, chariots, horses, elephants, servants, his kingdom, his army, his four brothers and himself, and finally their common wife Draupadī, all of these passing to the ownership of Duryodhana.

The brother of Duryodhana, *Duḥśāsana* (*duḥ-śāsana*, 'hard to curb'), was sent to fetch the beauteous Draupadī from the palace to sweep the hall as a sign of her servitude. But the proud woman refused to come saying that Yudhishṭhira had gambled himself away, and as such was a slave and not his own master, and therefore had no right to gamble her away. But this logic did not move Duḥśāsana who caught her by the hair and dragged her from Indraprastha to the palace of Duryodhana. Here he subjected her to great humiliation and attempted to tear off her clothes in front of the assembly, but her garments were miraculously restored to save her from shame. Duryodhana then forced her to sit on his lap.

The insults were carried out in the presence of the Pāṇḍava brothers, for though Draupadī entreated her husbands to intervene they could do nothing as they were now the slaves of Duryodhana. The hero Karṇa tried to calm her and counselled her to seek a new husband from among the Kaurava princes who would cherish her and not stake her at dice and expose her to disgrace. Burning under the indignities to which they were being subjected, Bhīma's anger now broke forth and he took a terrible oath to break the thigh of Duryodhana for having forced Draupadī to sit on his lap, and then to drink the blood of Duḥśāsana in battle, an oath which received mystic ratification in the mournful howl of a jackal outside. The oath was destined to be fulfilled on the sixteenth day of the battle of Kurukshetra*.

When the aged king, the blind Dhṛitarāshṭra, was told of all that was taking place, he hastened to the scene and declared that his sons had acted wrongly, and offered Draupadī any boon to expiate the evil of his sons. She asked for freedom for her husbands and herself. The Kauravas were incensed and proposed a final throw of the dice, the loser's party paying the penalty by going into exile for twelve years, and spending one more year incognito, returning to the kingdom after thirteen years. Once more Śakuni brought forth the loaded dice and once more Yudhishṭhira lost. As the Pāṇḍava party rose to leave Draupadī unloosed her hair, and swore that she would never allow it to be tied again except by Bhīma's hands after they had been soaked in the blood of Duḥśāsana.

Books

See under Mahābhārata and Mythology.

ŚAKUNTALĀ, daughter of the sage Viśvāmitra by the nymph Menakā, who abandoned her child on the banks of a forest stream not far from the abode of the ṛishi Kaṇva. This sage found her being cared for by birds (*śakunta*) so he named her Śakuntalā, and adopted her as his own daughter. She grew up in the hermitage of the sage which was situated on the banks of the sacred stream Mālinī.

Some sixteen years later, while engaged in a chase, *Dushyanta* (or Dushmanta) a king of the Lunar race descended from Puru, caught sight of the beautiful Śakuntalā as she was watering her favourite plants in the sacred grove of Kaṇva accompanied by her handmaidens Anasūyā and Prīyamvadā. The king was stricken with love for the girl and, in the absence of Kaṇva from the hermitage, married her 'in the *gāndharva* mode', by sanction of mutual desire. After spending some time with his bride Dushyanta had to hasten back to his kingdom, but left his signet ring with her as a pledge, with the injunction that she should present it at the palace and thus gain admittance to him.

After Dushyanta rode away Śakuntalā sat dreaming of him in an arbour, and so absorbed was she in reverie that she failed to welcome the sage Durvāsas who had come on a visit to Kaṇva. In his anger at the slight the ṛishi cursed Śakuntalā, saying that the person about whom she was so lost in thought would himself lose all thought of her. Śakuntalā's companions begged for forgiveness on her behalf and the sage relenting declared that although he could not recall the curse he would mitigate it by a proviso, that if that person saw the signet ring she was wearing his remembrance of her would be restored.

On his return to the hermitage Kaṇva was informed of Śakuntalā's gāndharva marriage and her pregnancy. He gave her his blessings and sent her and her two companions to Dushyanta's capital at Gajasāhvāya. On the way they stopped to rest by a pool where Śakuntalā while washing her hands felt the ring slip off her finger and vanish in the depths. When she arrived at the palace gates and requested the guards to lead her to the king she was refused. Insisting that she was the king's wife she was confronted by the king but he denied any association with her and had her sent away. As she stood forsaken outside the palace walls her mother, the nymph Menakā, saw her and descending to earth carried her off to her own abode midway between heaven and earth. Here, three years after her marriage to Dushyanta a son was born to her whom she named Bharata*.

One day a fisherman caught the fish that had swallowed the signet ring, and seeing the royal seal upon it he immediately carried it to the king. The moment Dushyanta's eyes fell upon the ring the memory of his encounter with Śakuntalā flashed upon his mind and he lamented over his treatment of her. A country-wide search was made for her, but in vain.

Many years later Dushyanta was asked by Indra to help him in a great war against the *asuras*. The war over, Dushyanta returned homewards in Indra's chariot, traversing the broad spaces of the celestial regions. The vehicle stopped at Menakā's dwelling where the king saw his wife and child. There was a short explanation on the king's part followed by much weeping and laughter. The reunited family returned to Gajasāhvāya and lived for many years in great happiness.

The plot of Kālidāsa's masterpiece, *Śakuntalā*, is based on this story.

Books

See under Mahābhārata and Mythology.

ŚĀKYA, an ancient tribe of probable Mongolian origin, for whom Sanskrit legend claims descent from Okkāka, i.e. Ikshvāku. Buddha's father was a chieftain of the Śākya clan, which was related to the neighbouring tribes of Nepāl. In the traditional story of Buddha's birth it is said that the gods were at a loss to decide which race in India should have the honour of Buddha's early manifestation, since all the sixteen Aryan *janapadas* were tainted with one or more evil quality. It was finally decided to let Buddha be born in a clan outside the regular cadre of Aryan tribes, and the chief among these was selected, the small but highly virtuous and valiant non-monarchical clan of the Śākyas living in the region of the present Nepāl Terāi.

The capital of the Śākyas was Kapilavastu (Pāli, *Kapila-vatthu*, 'monkey-place'), which later legend connected with the sage Kapila. Their other towns had such unusual names as Sakkara (suggesting a Śaka connection), Khomadussa and Ulumpa. There is a close connection between the Śākyas of Kapilavastu and the Mongolian Śakas who occupied the north-western regions of India in historical times, and there can now be hardly any doubt that the Śākyas had a Mongolian strain in their blood. Edward Thompson conceded that 'probably the Śākyas were of partly Mongolian blood', though E. J. Thomas thought they were composed of basically Kol or Muṇḍa elements (II, p. 244).

The Śākyas followed certain non-Aryan customs, marrying not only within the same gotra, but within prohibited degrees of relationship, like the people of Tibet. For their custom of marrying their own sisters they were often the butt of their neighbour's taunts. Says R. K. Mookerji, 'They were in the outskirts of Vedic civilization' (II, p. 244).

According to Buddhist tradition a group of Śākyas founded the 'peacock town' which gave the name to the Maurya* dynasty, and Chandragupta was the son of a princess who came from this place. Buddhists hold that Buddha and Aśoka were of the same family since both belonged to the same Śākya clan (I, p. 256).

Books

I. Law, B. C. *Tribes in Ancient India*, Poona, 1943.
II. Mookerji, R. K. *Hindu Civilization*, 2nd Ed., Bombay, 1950.
III. Thompson, E. *A History of India*, London, 1927.

SALIVA. The high-caste Hindu, and to a lesser extent Hindus of lower caste as well, have a great abhorrence of saliva, although probably few nations on earth are as habituated as the Indians are to hawking and expectoration. The essential furniture of Buddhist monks mentioned in the earliest texts included 'a reclining board (i.e. a bed), a seat and a spittoon', and Hindu monastic establishments were similarly equipped.

The belief underlying the almost national habit of spitting is that sputum constitutes a form of impurity generated spontaneously within the body by evil desires and sinful thoughts, and that therefore every effort should be made to be rid of these, by periodically clearing the throat and spitting. The morning ablution in India is almost universally attended by the ritual of inserting two fingers into the mouth and rubbing the tongue as far back in the throat as possible in order to assist in the clearing of the passages. The term for sputum is *shṭhīvana*, 'ejectable', or that which should be got rid of.

Apart from the rheum in the oral and nasal passages there is a particular quality attaching to the *lālā* or the spittle of the mouth. Spittle is believed to be peculiarly susceptible to contamination by action and thoughts, and is the medium through which the vapours of the interior body are ejected. Within the cavern of the mouth all thoughts driven from the mind take shelter. Miasmic vapours and toxic liquids are constantly generated there as a result of impure thoughts. The meditations of saints and gurus* give their saliva a special virtue and disciples believe in its medicinal value and make use of it accordingly. But the saliva of ordinary mortals is poisonous. Although bodily poisons may be voided by various means, the saliva is the direct vehicle for the disposal of these subtle poisons, since it reacts most speedily to the thoughts of our minds and the designs of our hearts. The ritual rinsing of the mouth in *āchamana* is performed specifically to wash away the saliva thus produced.

This belief in the offensive nature of saliva is found reflected in a number of prejudices. Hindus have a strong aversion to wind instruments since the mouthpiece, moistened with saliva, is applied repeatedly to the lips. As a rule strict Hindus do not drink by putting the drinking vessel to their lips, but hold it high over their upturned mouth and pour the water in. They do not use forks and spoons since these are put into the mouth, and prefer not to use crockery as the plates might be contaminated with saliva. Earthen teacups are used which are thrown away after use. Metal plates and tumblers are vigorously cleaned by scrubbing with ash. Frequently the leaves of a tree (the banana leaf is the most popular) serve as plates, and food is eaten with the fingers. One of the reasons for the Hindu's repugnance to the dog is the animal's habit of licking its master.

Books

See under Sociology.

SALUTATION among Hindus was for centuries governed by the rule that the inferior must greet the superior, but the latter should not acknowledge the greeting. Thus the brāhmin would never dream of greeting a man of low caste. The *Atri-smṛiti* says, 'If a brāhmin unknowingly salute a low caste man, he should immediately bathe and get himself purified by taking clarified butter'.

Vital energy easily flows from the higher to the lower and many restrictions were devised to prevent the inadvertent dissipation of such energy. Recognition of an inferior with whom one has no immediate business is one such form of dispersal. Looking in his direction or raising a hand to him is another. Nodding the head, involving as it does the head taboo and a breach of its sanctity, was until recently never part of the act of greeting by a superior. In this respect women were treated as menials, and in Patañjali's time a man was not to bow to a woman in return.

When one was obliged to address an inferior one took a mental and physical 'attitude' (*sthāna*) of neutrality, to prevent any psychic depletion. In spite of being ignored it was the duty of the lower castes invariably to salute the higher with deference, to stand aside with hands folded and head bowed. These injunctions, still obeyed in many parts of India, account for the complete indifference with which a man will regard the salute of a menial and the abject deference with which he will greet a superior.

Modes of salutation varied for the various castes. The *Āpastamba Dharmasūtra* says, 'A brāhmin shall salute by stretching forward his right hand on a level with his ear, a kshattriya holding it level with his breast, a vaiśya on a level with his waist. A śūdra shall bend forward with joined hands held low'. Falling at the feet or stooping to touch the sandals of their superiors, and then their own forehead is a common form of greeting by menials.

The most reverential form of salutation is the *sāshṭāṅga* (*sa-ashṭa-aṅga*, 'with-eight-limbs'), so called because eight parts of the body touch the ground in token of complete submission, namely, two hands, two feet, two knees, forehead and breast. It expresses profound reverence, as that of a *chela* (pupil) before a *guru* (preceptor), or a subject before his sovereign. It is also used as a sign of deep contrition as when a man seeks readmission into his caste after he has been excommunicated.

Fear of the evil eye governs many greeting conventions, and good wishes are rarely exchanged. Whatever is declared to be good, unless it be so declared in ritual manner, attracts inauspicious elements. The general form of salutation today is the *namaskāra*, the former śūdra salute. It consists of the *añjali* (two open hands held together) accompanied by the words '*namas*' or '*namaste*'. This is an exclamation of homage meant for the deity, as the 'Good' in the English 'Good Morning' is a relic of 'God', implying, 'God be with you this morning'. The Hindu equivalent of 'It's a fine morning' would be regarded as inviting bad luck for the day. For the same reason one does not compliment another if he is looking well, in case it should tempt the evil eye. Nor does one ever enquire after the womenfolk of the other person's household as the subject is hedged in by a total taboo with its roots buried deep in occult beliefs.

Several changes in modes of salutation were introduced in imitation of Muhammadan and European custom. The Moghul practice of touching the forehead with the fingertips or placing the right hand over the breast and bowing, are forms of the salaam. Also derived from the Muslims is the custom of the close embrace. Here a person puts his arms around the other and places his head first over the other's left shoulder and then over his right shoulder, hugging him close the while. The other does likewise.

The casually raised hand, a post-European innovation, is perhaps the most common form of all salutes today. So also is the handshake, but though people in the cities and larger towns often shake hands, the practice is slow in growing. Its unpopularity stems from the fact that it involves actual contact with the body of another, and is therefore liable to cause physical, if no other, defilement.

Books

See under Sociology.

SĀMA-VEDA (*c.* 700–300 BC) (*sāman*, 'melody'), the third Veda*. Its *saṁhitā* or principal part is wholly metrical, consisting of 1549 verses, of which only 75 are not traceable to the *Ṛig-veda*. The stanzas are arranged in two books or collections of verses.

The *Sāma-veda* embodies the knowledge of melodies and chants. The *saṁhitā* of this Veda served as a textbook for the priests who officiated at the *Soma* sacrifices. It indicates the 'tunes' to which the sacred hymns are to be sung, by showing the prolongation, the repetition and interpolation of syllables required in the singing. The *Sāma-veda* also contains a detailed account of the soma rites. The hierophants* associated with the *Sāma-veda* are known as the *udgātṛi*.

Many of the invocations in the *Sāma-veda* are addressed to Soma, some to Agni and some to Indra. The mantra part of the *Sāma-veda* is poor in literary quality and historical interest, but the Brāhmaṇas belonging to it are important. Of the once numerous saṁhitās of the *Sāma-vedā* (the Purāṇas speak of a thousand) only one has reached us, in three recensions, namely: the *Kauthama*, current in Gujarāt, the *Rāṇāyanīya* which survives in Mahārāshṭra, and the *Jaiminīya* in the Karṇāṭic.

Books

I. Griffith, R. T. H. (Ed.) *The Samaveda*, Banaras, 1896.
II. Stevenson, J. *The Samaveda*, 1843.

ŚĀMBA, the son of Kṛishṇa by Jāmbavatī (although some accounts make Rukmiṇī his mother) whose vicious career was responsible for the end of his own Yādava tribe. Already early in life he displayed his evil propensities when he attended the *svayaṁvara* of Draupadī and carried off that princess. He was pursued and caught by the Kaurava prince Duryodhana and taken to Hastināpura. Balarāma, brother of Kṛishṇa, asked for his release but was refused, whereupon he thrust his ploughshare under the ramparts of the city and threatened to topple it over. The Kauravas then gave up their prisoner and Balarāma returned with him to the town of Dvārakā. There Śāmba became notorious for his drunkenness, venery, gluttony and homosexuality. He seduced the wives of others, sported openly with his companions dressed as a female, mocked the devotions of the sages Viśvāmitra, Durvāsas and Nārada. His name, as Śāmbalī, later became a synonym for eunuch.

One day his comrades dressed Śāmba up as a pregnant woman, and presenting him to the sage Durvāsas asked him to what child the woman would give birth. Seeing through the trick the holy man replied, 'To an iron rod that will destroy the whole race of Yadu'. Sure enough Śāmba in due time gave birth to an iron club which the terrified Yādavas ground to powder and threw into the sea. From the iron dust there grew hundreds of strong rushes, while one unground piece was swallowed by a fish which was sold to a hunter *Jaras* (lit. 'old age'), who fashioned the fragment into an arrow-head.

Some time later the people of the Yādava tribe got involved in an internecine dispute, and arming themselves with the sharp rush stalks that grew up out of the iron dust, fought with one another until the whole tribe was exterminated. Kṛishṇa himself, mourning on a river bank, was shot in the foot by an arrow tipped with the fatal iron head by the hunter Jaras who mistook him for a deer, and died as a result.

Śāmba, still under the curse of Durvāsas, became a leper, and was cured only after many years of fasting, penance, prayer and devotion to Sūrya*, the sun, in whose honour he built a temple on the banks of the Chandrabhāga (Chenāb).

Books

See under Mahābhārata and Mythology.

SĀṀKHYA, one of the six orthodox systems of Hindu philosophy founded by the sage KAPILA (*c.* 500 BC). He was the son of a ṛishi and acquired the rudiments of philosophy from his mother Devahutī. The latter half of his life was spent on the Sāgar Island at the mouth of the Ganges, ninety miles from what is now Calcutta. The present version of the *Sāṁkhya-sūtra*, cannot be dated earlier than AD 1400, but is said to be based on a now-lost work traditionally ascribed to Kapila himself. A few commentaries exist which belong to the fifth century AD, notably the *Sāṁkhya-kārikā* of Īśvarakṛishṇa (*c.* 450) which has been called 'the pearl of the whole scholastic literature of India'.

Sāṁkhya is the earliest of the orthodox schools of Hindu philosophy and was said to have influenced Gautama Buddha, who in turn influenced later Sāṁkhya philosophy. Both Sāṁkhya and Buddhism are based on the notion of suffering, the rejection of Vedic sacrifice, the renunciation of ascetic extravagance, indifference to theism, and belief in the constant 'becoming' of the world.

The system recognizes no personal creator such as *Īśvara*, for which reason it is referred to as *nirīśvara* or godless. It does however start with the postulate of two ultimate uncaused realities which are regarded as the first two in a series of twenty-five *tattva* or categories*, into which the process of evolution is divided. The sāṁkhya system was once believed to have been so called because of its systematic enumeration (*saṁ-khya*), 'counting together' of these twenty-five categories formulated by it, but the term is now thought to mean 'reasoning', or 'discriminating knowledge'. It is a synthetic system and is uncompromisingly dualistic.

The two ultimate realities are *Purusha** (spirit) and *Prakṛiti* (matter). Everything is held to be potential in these two. This view is called *sat-kārya-vāda* (existence-causing-ism) meaning that the effect exists in the cause, and so something cannot come out of nothing. This principle is the distinguishing feature of the Sāṁkhya system, and through this principle the material universe is traced back to its first cause. Nothing new is created; everything is but a manifestation or emanation of what has already existed. Purusha implies a plurality of selves or purushas, each following an individual career when it gets 'intertwined' with Prakṛiti. Prakṛiti is thus the seat and seed of all manifestation, and is made up of three *guṇa* or constituted principles (*see* quality), namely, *sattva* (goodness), *rajas* (passion) and *tamas* (darkness), which form a Sāṁkhya triplicity.

The remaining twenty-three *tattvas* are regarded as transformations (*vikāra*) resulting from the inter-operation of these two principles, (1) Purusha and (2) Prakṛiti. They are: (3) *mahātattva*, the Great Principle, which is the first manifestation of the universe, or the first product of Prakṛiti; it is the third category of Sāṁkhya and is also sometimes called Mahat (*see* psychology); (4) *ahaṁkāra* or self-consciousness; (5) *manas* or Mind, sometimes called Cosmic Mind; (6–10) *tanmātra* or subtle substances, five in number; (11–15) *jñānendriya*, the agents of perception, five in number; (16–20) *karmendriya*, the agents of action, five in number; (21–25) *mahābhūta*, pure elements, five in number (*see* substance).

In this scheme the subtle elements generate the function (sight, hearing, etc.); the function produces the organ (eye, ear, etc.); and the moment these are manifested the gross elements (*mahābhūta*) come into existence. These twenty-five categories or elements are variations of the structural factors of which the universe is composed. Says Kapila, 'Liberation obtained through knowledge of the twenty-five realities teaches the one truth, that neither I am, nor is aught mine, nor do I exist'.

The sāṁkhya system with yoga admixtures had a profound influence on Hindu philosophy. It has also left its mark on the lawgivers, including Manu, on the *Mahābhārata*, the Purāṇas, and the Tantras, and on most other later systems of Hindu thought and sectarian philosophy. Some of its teachings, like those of the three guṇas, have become an integral part of the Hindu tradition in religion (e.g. the *Bhagavadgītā*), literature, art, medicine and science.

Books

I. Edgerton, F. *The Beginnings of Indian Philosophy*, London, 1965.
II. Ghosh, J. *Samkhya and Modern Thought*, Calcutta, 1930.
III. Johnston, E. H. *Early Samkhya: Its Historical Development*, London, 1937.
IV. Keith, A. B. *The Samkhya System of Philosophy*, Calcutta, 1918.

SANATVA, 'ancientness', a term signifying the sacred and unique quality of something that has come down from immemorial antiquity, something that has in fact always been. The idea underlies large areas of Hinduism, and is intimately related to the notion of ultimates and absolutes that are such a feature of Hindu religion, law, social observance, life and thought.

The consuming passion for the past may be taken as a way of establishing a priority, both in time and in authority, so as to place institutions, laws and teachings beyond human jurisdiction where they are likely to be criticized. Edward Thompson mentions a 'famous Hindu judge' who approved the statement that the *Rāmāyana* was more than sixty million years old. G. R. Kaye states that the *Sūrya Siddhānta*, a mathematical work of the sixth century AD is believed by some Hindus to have been composed over two million years ago.

Sanatva is a quality that belongs to India above all other nations. Against the background of Hindu India's past history and the long centuries of foreign domination, this quality has evolved in an exaggerated way, resulting in a violent and inflamed chauvinism which finds expression in some remarkable statements by Hindu reformers. Much of this may be interpreted as a reaction to the unfavourable estimates of Hinduism voiced by Muslim and European critics past and present. The Moghul emperor Bābur, pining for his own country bewailed the shortcomings of his new homeland. 'Hindustan', he said, 'has little to recommend it. The people have neither baths nor colleges.' The Hindu patriot retrogressing in time as required by the demands of sanatva, declares that on the contrary India is the source and fountainhead of all learning. When the Europeans were still barbarians and the Muslims illiterate desert squatters, Indian civilization was the light of the world. She is a blessed region specially created in the remote mists of time when nothing else was visible upon the bosom of the deep. It was in this region alone of all mundane places that the gods deigned to dwell. It has been sanctified by primordial associations. Its rivers are sacred, its mountains the abode of divine beings.

Aldous Huxley once expressed his opinion of India in these words: 'India is depressing as no other country I have ever known. One breathes in it, not air, but dust and hopelessness'. As though anticipating him Vivekānanda, who did much to revive the Hindu's pride in India's ancientness said, 'The very dust of India is holy, the very air is holy. It is a holy land, a place of pilgrimage'. Al-Bīrūnī wrote of the inhabitants that 'They sip the urine of cows, they use turbans as trousers, they spit and blow their noses without respect for those present'. Bābur had added his own opinion, 'The people of India are not good looking, they have no idea of the pleasures of society, no polish of manner, amiability or sympathetic feeling'. Against this are quoted the ancient virtues listed in the *śāstras*, the refinement and politeness of the people. Vivekānanda said of the people, 'Of all the nations of the world the Hindus are the handsomest and finest in feature. I am not bragging nor saying anything in exaggeration, since this fact is known to all the world'. In short, Bhāratvarsha, the ancient land of India, is beyond criticism since she is in fact perfection itself. 'Mother India', Śrī Aurobindo rhapsodized, 'is not a piece of earth; she is a power, a Godhead.'

India's influence on the rest of the world is continually emphasized. For countless ages she matured under the tutelage of gods and *ṛishis*, created ceaselessly and bestowed lavishly from her inexhaustible treasuries, providing sustenance for all the regions of the earth. Says Vivekānanda, 'Study the history of the world and you will see that every high ideal you meet with anywhere had its origin in India'. From her superfluity have come the civilizations of Egypt, Mesopotamia and Greece. Her religion won over China, Japan and the whole east; her teachings influenced Judea and were re-echoed in the words of Christ and spread throughout the western world. India is the seed and the soil, the rain and the sun, and the world is nourished and vivified from the abundance she provides.

The need to go back to a time beyond human computation to a period of divine time substantiates the claim of divine origin for the Hindu revelation. The corrupted quaternity of the Vedas, fragmentary and inconsistent as they are now, is referred back to a Golden Age (*see* aeon) when the Veda was one and immaculate. Such a Veda still exists in the empyrean and is absolutely immutable. Similarly the notion of caste is traced back to a time before even the creation of man, to whom the caste system was made to apply after he had been fashioned.

Hindus refer to their religion, social customs and way of life as *sanātana dharma*, 'eternal law', implying that it has divine sanction and is perfect and unchangeable. Hinduism is 'the mother of Religions' and the fountain-head of all faiths. It had its origin in the dawn of time and its mandates cannot be shaken by the vicissitudes of history or the edicts of earthly monarchs. This results in a great deal of tinkering with texts to prove from a verse here and a word there that the ancients anticipated Darwin, Freud and Einstein. The school of Dayānanda avers that the Vedas speak of the zeppelin, radio, motorcar, and (as newer inventions are made) also of atomic power, radar and television.

Belief in the uniqueness of the sanātana dharma is said to be responsible for the extreme reluctance of Hindus in acknowledging the cultural debt they owe to outsiders, the reason being that such a confession would undermine their dharma and vitiate their claim to priority and preeminence.

That the contributions made by foreigners have been considerable no competent scholar can possibly doubt, but of evidence of such borrowings in the written texts there exists hardly any at all. The lack of the historical sense is the direct consequence of the notion of sanatva, and all Hindu records were made to conform to the pattern of its own self-sufficiency. This tendency is seen from the very dawn of Indian history. Scholars subscribe to the view that evidence of a common 'Indo-Iranian' homeland and heritage has been subjected to a process of wilful distortion and concealment by brāhmin scribes to erase from the racial memory all knowledge of the pre-Vedic past. India borrowed extensively from the Greeks, but there is hardly a passage in Sanskrit literature that unequivocally acknowledges this. The 'barbarian' debt is overwhelming, yet nothing in Sanskrit writing betrays this fact. Muslim travellers like al-Bīrūnī noted this peculiarity which was further confirmed with the advent of the Europeans. Sanskrit and vernacular histories of the Muslim and European periods where they exist at all are conspicuous for the paucity of their information and for their marked xenophobia.

The social mobility of the ancient Indians has been considerable. There are records of Indian travellers*, merchants, seamen, scholars, monks and mercenaries having been to Persia, Greece, Asia Minor, Rome, Egypt and north Africa, as well as to Central Asia, China and Japan, but all evidence of such movement is obtained from outside and not Indian sources. For example, it is known that hundreds of Indian scholars and pilgrims visited the Far East, and of them S. Dutt says, 'Not one has left a scrap of record about his journey and experiences there'. Observers and writers of the stature of Herodotus, Xenophon and Pliny are rare in any nation, and it is not surprising that India failed to produce their equal, but that not one ancient document of any value should exist of an Indian traveller to foreign climes is a remarkable phenomenon in a country as well documented from its own sources as India. There is one text that speaks of a journey of some brāhmins to Śvetadvīpa or White Island, but the account is so vague that scholars have failed to identify the place, and it is variously said to be Alexandria, Palestine, Parthia, Tibet, China, Japan and even Britain. The account is rendered practically valueless and survives as a curiosity of ancient Indian geography.

Books

I. Dubois, Abbe. *Hindu Manners, Customs & Ceremonies,* Oxford, 3rd Ed., 1936.
II. Dutt, S. *Buddhist Monks & Monasteries of India,* London, 1962.
III. Huxley, A. *Jesting Pilate,* London, 1948.
IV. Thompson, E. *A History of India,* London, 1927.
V. Vivekananda, Swami. *Complete Works,* 7 vols., Almora, 1946.

SAÑJAYA (d. 480 BC) or Sañjaya Belātthiputta, a nāstika* sceptic and agnostic thinker, who rejected the possibility of ultimate self-knowledge, and emphasized the futility and folly of attempting to gain knowledge of the beyond, or to understand the ultimate destiny of things and the mysteries of Being. The wise man, according to him, suspends judgment on all matters, since this is the only path to peace of mind. Curiosity is stilled and with curiosity, passion, and with the allaying of passion comes peace.

Sañjaya advocated the need for calmness and equanimity, which he regarded as the mark of an emancipated mind, and he confined his enquiries to the problem of attaining this mental placidity. His method of solving any problem put to him was never to admit or deny anything, nor directly to silence his questioners. That would be like trying to still a pond into which a stone had been thrown, by throwing in another stone. All perplexity about the Self, the self, and the universe, would soon wear away. To questions such as, 'Is there a future life?' 'Does God exist?' 'Are virtuous actions meritorious?' he would give the answer, 'If it were so I should say so. But I do not say so. Nor do I say otherwise. I say neither yes nor no'.

Sañjaya and his followers incurred the censure of contemporary philosophers, and were condemned by Buddha for their equivocation and for eluding the questions of honest enquirers by 'wriggling like eels'.

Books

See under Nāstika.

ŚAṄKARA (788–838), also Śaṁkara or Śaṅkarāchārya, Vedantic philosopher, was a native of Malabār, born in Kālaḍī, in what is now Travancore. His father, a Nambūdri brāhmin was very old when Śaṅkara was born. He had despaired of having any issue, and the mother claimed that she had conceived by the grace of Śiva. When Śaṅkara was still a child the old man died, and the lad was brought up by his mother, and at the age of seven was invested with the sacred thread.

Much against his will his mother arranged a marriage for him, and all his efforts to persuade her to release him from the arrangement since he wished to become a *sannyāsin* were of no avail. One day, the story goes, while mother and son were bathing in a river the boy's foot was caught by a crocodile. Thinking that his end was near he implored his mother once again to give him permission to become a sannyāsin so that he might die in peace, and the mother was obliged to accede to his request. The crocodile, it is said, was a deity in disguise who forthwith released the boy so that he might teach the truth to all the world.

On his mother's death the members of the sect to which Śaṅkara belonged as well as his own family tried to dissuade him from performing the funeral ceremonies, the former because they regarded such observances as contrary to the rules of their order, and his own clan because they thought he was illegitimate, but he insisted on going through with the last rites, and earned the displeasure of all.

Śaṅkara studied under the guru Govindapāda who was himself a pupil of the famous philosopher Gauḍapāda (fl. AD 700). The young man dedicated his life to philosophy and early acquired a reputation as a formidable opponent in debate. He once had a famous controversy with a paṇḍit named Maṇḍana (also known as Maṇḍana Miśra, Sureśvara, or Viśvarūpa), with Maṇḍana's wife acting as judge. She awarded the victor's wreath to Śaṅkara, but just as he was about to ascend the throne that would signify his superiority over all contestants, she challenged him herself. Knowing that as a sannyāsin he would be ignorant of all matters pertaining to sex, she asked the philosopher what he knew about the science of love. Śaṅkara asked for a month's respite and retired to the banks of a stream with a few trusted disciples. Telling his followers to look after his body, he left his physical frame and occupied the body of a king named Amaru just after the latter's decease. Using the king's body he made love to the royal wives and concubines, and was soon so intoxicated with the pleasures of the flesh that in three weeks he forgot all about his controversy. His disciples, fearing just such a contingency, went around singing religious songs, one of which caught the ears of the voluptuary and immediately put him to mind of his mission. He left the body of the king, assumed his own fleshly form, continued the controversy and won, making converts of both Maṇḍana and his learned wife.

In the course of his wanderings Śaṅkara met Kumārila (some legends make him Kumārila's disciple) and many other learned philosophers. He established four great maṭhs or monasteries, one each at Badrināth in the Himālayas, Purī in the east, Dvārakā in the west, and Śṛiṅgeri in the south in Mysore. These pontifical seats were to be occupied by his followers who, like Śaṅkara, sent out missionaries to propagate his teachings all over India.

Śaṅkara died in the Himālayan village of Kedārnāth at an age, variously given as fifty, or eighty-five, although one tradition, now discredited, says he died when he was only thirty-two. His death was believed to have been hastened by black magic, directed against him by an enemy. It is said that on his deathbed he craved pardon of God for three sins: for confining Him Who is without form, to stone and mortar; for describing Him, Who transcends all qualities; and for having frequented temples, since by so doing he had denied the omnipresence of His divinity.

Śaṅkara represents the highwater mark of medieval Hindu thought, although his can hardly be called an original mind. Burdened with the ontological lumber of early Hindu speculation and the prejudices of the Nambūdri brāhmins, his was fundamentally a conservative if not reactionary genius. He is the Hindu commentator par excellence, and his various commentaries, especially on the Vedānta, are standard expositions showing a mind of the keenest quality, and a critical intellect of the highest perception. His was indeed, a critical rather than a creative genius, and as such he ranks with the lawyer rather than the prophet. As it happened he founded a metaphysical theory of extreme subtlety that added an illustrious name to the long list of Indian 'armchair' philosophers which is one of the chief glories of Hinduism.

He stood for a form of extreme and uncompromising monism, but at the same time advocated idolatry and liṅga-worship, and composed hymns to Vishṇu, Sūrya, Śiva, Śakti, and Pārvatī. He was regarded as a champion of Śaivite, especially Śakti teachings, and an ardent devotee of Durgā, in whose honour he wrote many hymns. But he opposed the grosser manifestations of Śaiva and Śākta worship. He ruthlessly suppressed the unclean worship of Śiva in his dog aspect under the name of Mallāri (*see* Khaṇḍobā), and the pernicious practices of the kāpālikas*.

Śaṅkara was extremely caste conscious, a victim of his times, and was unable to rise above many of the superstitious beliefs of his age. He held that the śūdras had no right to read the Vedas, much less perform the Vedic rites. Like other brāhmin advocates of the holy life he held out little hope of salvation for those who were not twice born. Says Vivekānanda, 'Śaṅkara had no great liberality. Besides, he used to take great pride in his brāhminism'. Hinduism could hardly expect to find its Luther in Śaṅkara.

Rāmānuja, an ardent opponent of Śaṅkara writes thus of his theories: 'This entire teaching is nothing but a web of false reasoning. His understanding must have been disturbed by illusory imaginations arising from sins he had committed in his previous births. He who knows the right relation of things must reject such foolish doctrines'.

Śaṅkara's thought owed a profound debt to Buddhism and Islam. So strong is the evidence of Buddhism in his over-protestation contra-Buddha, that some critics, including Madhva, thought he was actually a *prachchhanna-Bauddha* (crypto-Buddhist), and one of the 'heirs of Buddhism'. But the fact remains that he championed brāhmin orthodoxy and gave his unmitigated opposition to the Buddhist credo. His doctrine of māyā was probably derived from the metaphysicians of the Mādhyamika school, and from Buddhism he borrowed the monastic traditions which led to the foundations of the four great maṭhs mentioned above.

Islamic influence has also been remarked upon by critics of his philosophy. His birthplace in Kālaḍī was situated in a principality whose ruler had accepted Islam, and the whole region had been exposed to many decades of Islamic influence. Like the Muhammadans Śaṅkara rests his claim to the authenticity of his doctrines on the authority of a single divinely inspired canon, the Vedas. Like them again he was unequivocal in his emphasis on extreme monism and made no compromise, in theory at least, with a division of deity in any form. 'When one connects this similarity of outlook,' says Humayun Kabir, 'with the appearance of Islam as a living force in his birthplace just before his birth, the inference that he was influenced by the new faith can hardly be resisted'. Sometimes critics have pressed the parallels even without warrant. The similarity in the name of one of the books ascribed to him, *Mohamudgara* (moha-mudgara, Delusion's Hammer) and that of the Prophet of Arabia, has suggested to some scholars the quite untenable view of borrowing.

Śaṅkara's chief contribution to Hindu thought was his insistence on the oneness and unity of Brahma. He is uncompromisingly monistic (*advaita**). The Real is Brahma, and Brahma is absolutely homogeneous so that all differences and plurality are illusory, Brahma is impersonal, objectless thought, transcending all attributes, and thus without attributes. Brahma is neuter, above personality, beyond morals, transcending all desires and ends. Śaṅkara's creed is summed up in the Upanishadic doctrine of *ekam evādvitīyam* (one essence and no other). Brahma is the Ultimate Principle, the Final Reality, the Uncaused Cause.

The Supreme Spirit draws out from himself by a process of self-alienation first Īśvara the personal god as we know him, then the separate individual souls (*jīvātman*) who inhabit human and animal bodies, and also the varied manifestations of the phenomenal world. All these, including Īśvara, are unreal. The purpose of this creation, according to Śaṅkara, is mere sport (*līlā*). Brahma creates for his own amusement.

Since Brahma alone exists truly, all else, all phenomena, all nature, animate and inanimate, is *māyā**, illusion, caused by ignorance (*avidyā*) and sensed through the *upādhi* or 'limiting conditions' of the intellect, namely space, time, cause, and change. Māyā surrounds the Supreme Spirit, concealing it 'even as the smoke that rises from the fire hides the blaze for a time'. It is through māyā and avidyā, our heritage of ignorance and misrepresentation, that we see a multiplicity of things and witness change. As long as the cycle of life and death lasts, phenomena have the appearance of reality, for the same reason that things seen in a dream are real as long as the dream lasts. This *māyāvāda* (illusion-doctrine) of Śaṅkara was severly criticized by later philosophers, especially Vallabha, and dubbed not advaita, monism, but keval-advaita, 'mere monism', as distinct from pure monism, since it depended on māyā to explain the world.

The goal of Śaṅkara's philosophy is to be one with God, to rise above the illusive separateness of self and become part of the great ocean of being. When this absorption is complete the wheel of transmigration stops, because reincarnation can only continue in a separate self and a disparate personality. Emancipation therefore results in complete loss of individuality and identity, a doctrine which most of his successors, especially Rāmānuja, found extremely distasteful, and which they attacked with vigour.

According to Śaṅkara good works and morality are not sufficient for salvation, for virtue and vice have no validity or relevance except in the māyā-world of space and time. Moral distinctions have thus only a temporal validity and may be used as a means of getting to the path of true knowledge. But viewed from the standpoint of ultimate emancipation, virtue and vice are both equally neutral in the process of man's attaining to his highest destiny. The true self is totally indifferent to both virtue and vice.

The Vedas record the experiences of those who obtained knowledge by intuition and inspiration, hence Śaṅkara accepted the Vedas as divine revelation. He maintained that reason was of small use in philosophy. Although we do need intellect and logic (*tarka*) and knowledge of the scriptures (*śruti*), we need above all intuition and the desire to know. All our knowledge comes from the senses and reveals not reality, but only our sensory adaptation to it.

There are two kinds of knowledge which are to be clearly distinguished, since our whole destiny depends on it. One is *apara-vidyā*, a lower form of knowledge which deals with the illusory world of our senses and reason, and the other is *para-vidyā*, which is concerned with the only true reality, namely Brahma. Knowing Brahma, and knowing our identity with Brahma, is the only way to liberation.

Books

I. Aiyar, C. N. K. *Sri Sankaracharya*, Madras, 1934.
II. Bhashyacharya, N. *The Age of Sri Sankaracharya*, Madras, 1915.
III. Buch, M. *The Philosophy of Sankara*, Baroda, 1921.
IV. Dvivedi, M. N. *The Imitation of Sankara*, Bombay, 1895.
V. Raman, N. V. *Sankaracharya the Great*, Madras, 1923.
VI. Thibaut, G. *The Vedanta Sutra with Commentary of Sankaracharya*, London, 1904.

SANSKRIT (*saṁskṛita*, 'elaborated'), the principal of the post-Vedic languages of India, is regarded by Hindus as a sacred tongue, 'current among the gods' (I, p. 20). Actually Sanskrit is a comparatively late arrival among the ancient tongues, dating from about 300 BC, while its masterpieces were produced from some six centuries later. As its name implies, Sanskrit was an artificially 'put together' medium of communication, as opposed to the spontaneously and naturally evolved Prākṛit*. It constituted in effect an elaboration of a decadent form of Vedic, built upon rules mainly fixed by the grammarian Pāṇini* (*c.* 300 BC).

Four stages of Sanskrit are often distinguished, namely, (1) Pāṇinean Sanskrit, after Pāṇini who first codified the current rules governing the language, (2) Epic Sanskrit, the language of the *Mahābhārata* and the *Rāmāyaṇa*, (3) Classical Sanskrit, the language of the kathās, dramas, kāvyas, histories, and Purāṇas, and (4) Mediaeval Sanskrit, exemplified in the jargon of the monasteries, the 'dog Sanskrit' of craftsmen's handbooks, and other variants (*see* Literature).

A comparison between Vedic and Sanskrit shows that in phonology the two languages did not differ much; while in accidence it might be called not a development but a decadence from the Vedic system. Several Vedic grammatical forms are lost in Sanskrit, particularly in respect of mood; one form of the infinitive has survived in Sanskrit out of fifteen forms used in Vedic. A similar loss is found in tenses and prefixes.

Sanskrit however made up its losses by developing a technique of coining massive compound words, rare in Vedic, and in a complex grammatical and structural framework both in prose and verse. In addition to the seven Vedic metres a score of other metres came into vogue in Sanskrit, some of them hardly usable without verbal contortion.

The difference between Vedic and Sanskrit reflected the indigenous 'Hindu' milieu in which the latter language developed, as distinct from the Indo-Iranian background of early Vedic. The Indo-Iranian tribal communities gave place to new territorial kingdoms situated on great rivers and the jungle retreats of the ṛishis. The old Iranian gods faded in importance and were substituted by deities of new dimensions, Brahmā, Śiva, Vishṇu, Kṛishṇa, the Nāgas, the Liṅga. The supernatural, the demoniacal and the grotesque invaded Sanskrit almost from the beginning.

The development of Sanskrit was considerably modified by the infusion of a large number of foreign words. The philosopher Kumārila commented on how foreign words were picked up and transformed into Sanskrit by grammatical and phonetical alterations, often so cunningly that the original words were hardly recognizable.

Sanskrit thus had its roots in a decadent form of Vedic which gave it its structural core. The peculiarly Indian characteristics as distinct from the Iranian were due to the prevailing influence of the older dialectical forms of Prākṛit which itself had been modified by a diversity of aboriginal linguistic influences in India. The word borrowings give an indication of the areas in which these influences operated.

The indigenous Austric *ṅg* sounds are found in the name Gaṅgā (the river Ganges) and the word *liṅga*, both Austric words. Many place-name endings, like *gaṛh* (e.g. Rāmgaṛh) are aboriginal or Muṇḍa in origin. Tibeto-Burmese or north-eastern loan words include Bhullam-buthur, 'making a gurgling sound', which became Sanskritized into Brahmaputra, the name of India's largest river.

Similarly, Dravidian elements are strong in Sanskrit which derives much of its intonation from native speech. The phonetic system of Sanskrit is intermediate between Tamil and the Dravidian tongues on the one hand and the Indo-Iranian languages on the other. Certain sounds, unknown to the Aryan family of speech notably the cerebrals, found their way into Sanskrit from the Dravidian languages (VIII, p. 202), and it has been pointed out by some scholars that the syntax of Sanskrit, as of all other Aryan languages in India is fundamentally Dravidian rather than Aryan in character.

Words borrowed from the Dravidian tongues were sometimes arbitrarily changed and it is therefore not always easy to recognize the original. But in many cases, especially in the Sanskrit of the South, Dravidian words were taken over with scarcely any attempt at modification. The following are a few such words: *chaura*, 'thief'; *mālā*, 'garland'; *pāpa*, 'sin'; *pūjā*, 'worship'; *putra*, 'son'; *vaira*, 'hostile'. Name-endings such as *cheri*, 'place' (e.g. Pondicherry); *nād*, 'country' (e.g. Tamilnād); *nagar*, 'town' (e.g. Vijayanagar); *pur*, 'city' (e.g. Durgapur), are likewise Dravidian.

From Iran came a wide vocabulary of Indo-Iranian words that were part of the original inheritance of the Indo-Aryan period of history. In later times important words like *divira* (scribe), *kshatrapa* (satrap), *lipi* (writing), *mudrā* (seal), were adopted from Persian.

The evolution of Sanskrit received a further stimulus during the period of foreign (barbarian) domination of the north, starting from the Greeks who brought to bear on Indian life and culture fresh influences deriving from Alexandria and the Mediterranean Greek world. Evidence of the Greek heritage is found in the Sanskrit vocabulary of mathematics, astronomy, numismatics, warfare, the theatre and medicine, for example: *harija* (from Greek *horizon*); *hridroga* (Greek *hudrochoos*); *kendra* (*kentron*); *lipta* (*lepte*); *leya* (*leon*, lion); *parthona* (*Parthenos*); *trikona* (*trigonon*); *kona* (*gonia*, angle).

Inevitably further mutations of Sanskrit speech continued throughout the centuries of foreign domination and, as Kumārila observed, many loanwords from the Kushāns, Parthians and Śakas were picked up and assimilated (I, p. 274). Seed-beds of foreign influence enjoying great celebrity in academic matters were places like Taxila and Pushkalāvatī, and it was on this fertile soil that classical Sanskrit was first developed (VIII, p. 258). The use of Sanskrit for profane as opposed to sacred writing was to a great extent due to the initiative of the Mongolian Śaka and Kushān satraps of Western India during the second century AD, one of whom, Rudradāman, is responsible for the first official inscription in Sanskrit throughout.

Its so-called final and present form was fixed during the brāhminical revival whose vehicle was the Sanskrit language. This period saw the development of a characteristic feature, those strange linguistic monstrosities, the lumbering sesquipedalian compounds which reached their fulfilment in the *kāvya* and *gadya* forms of writing.

Sanskrit is capable of wonderful and varied sound effects because of the alternation of the softer sounds with the drumming effect of the aspirated consonants. There is therefore much scope for verbal melody of a rather harsh type. It is like the Indian elephant with a heavy plodding rhythm of alternating cadences. It permits the formation of long compounds where sounds are juxtaposed in extraordinary confusion that requires a precise knowledge of grammatical rules to sort out. To the ear unattuned to its heavy cadences it would appear harsh and lacking in sweetness.

Because of its extremely complicated grammar it is highly improbable that Sanskrit was ever a widely spoken language, current among the general populace, and some scholars are inclined to think that literary works in Sanskrit never had any real life at all, but were altogether scholastic productions. Much has been made of the incident recorded in Patañjali's *Mahābhāshya*, where a charioteer is represented as holding a discussion in Sanskrit with a grammarian on the derivation of an obscure word. Charioteers were frequently court bards and chroniclers and their familiarity with the priestly tongue does not necessarily indicate an acquaintance with it on the part of the general public.

The man in the street did not understand Sanskrit, and those who wished to reach the common people resorted to the Prākṛit vernaculars. When Buddha preached his doctrine he advocated the use of the dialects of the common folk. Aśoka used the language and scripts current in his domains to spread the Gospel of the Good Law. Tulsīdās, great scholar of Sanskrit though he was, preferred to write in the vernacular, defending his wise choice with the statement that his language was an earthen vessel containing ambrosia, while Sanskrit was a jewelled cup of extreme beauty which held poison. Kabīr, the great reformer, likened Sanskrit to the water of a well, and the language of the people to a running stream. Indeed, it is difficult to imagine that the artificial, stilted forms of Sanskrit grammar could ever have been used as a medium of popular expression in India. In his *Loom of Language* Frederick Bodmer discusses Sanskrit in a chapter entitled The Diseases of Language.

Modern Hindu reformers have frequently reiterated the same plaint, and have advocated the abandonment of Sanskrit as a vehicle of thought expression. As Rāmmohan Roy put it,

'The Sanskrit language, so difficult that almost a lifetime is necessary for its acquisition, is well known to have been for ages a lamentable check to the diffusion of knowledge, and the learning concealed under this almost impervious veil is far from sufficient to reward the labour of acquiring it'.

Contemporary scholarship has given a similar appraisal of Sanskrit and the Sanskrit classics. The Indian epics, the works of Kālidāsa, the aphorisms of Bhartṛihari, when they first became known to the West, aroused tremendous interest, for they represented a huge corpus of writings till then unknown to the Western world. These and other works even today, 'keep alive a certain superficial sympathy for Indian literature', as Max Müller expressed it; but the first flush of enthusiasm has passed, and scholars have considerably revised their opinion of its merits. Primarily the early writings retain their significance in the study of the history of mankind in the primitive stages of its development, but it were rash to go further in extolling their merits. That great advocate of Sanskrit studies, Max Müller, declared, 'I do not claim for the ancient Indian literature any more than I should willingly concede to the fables and traditions and songs of savage nations. I simply say that in the Veda we have a nearer approach to a beginning, and an intelligent beginning, than in the wild invocations of the Hottentots and Bushmen'. Serious students 'while gladly admitting their claim to be called pretty and attractive, could not think of allowing to Sanskrit literature a place by the side of Greek, Latin, Italian, French, English or German'. Harsh as this would appear to be, current scholarship would not greatly modify this opinion.

Books

I. Chakravarti, P. C. *The Linguistic Speculations of the Hindus*, 1933.

II. Chandrasekharan, K., and Sastri, B. H. S. *Sanskrit Literature*, 1951.

III. Frazer, R. W. *Literary History of India*, London, 1898.

IV. Keith, A. B. *Classical Sanskrit Literature*, 1924.

V. Keith, A. B. *History of Sanskrit Literature*, 1928.

VI. Krishnamachariar, M. *History of Classical Sanskrit Literature*, 1937.

VII. Macdonell, A. A. *History of Sanskrit Literature*, London, 1900.
VIII. Majumdar, R. C. (Ed.) *The Vedic Age*, London, 1951.
IX. Müller, F. Max. *History of Sanskrit Literature*, 1860.
X. Müller, F. Max. *The Heritage of India*, Ind. Ed., Calcutta, 1951.
XI. Sen, P. K. *Sanskrit Literature*, 1923.
XII. Weber, A. *History of Indian Literature: Vedic and Sanskrit*, 1878.

SĀRVABHAUMA (fl. AD 1480), 'whole-earth', the title given to the philosopher Vāsudeva, in tribute to the comprehensiveness and breadth of his learning. Sārvabhauma pursued his studies in logic at Mithilā, Bihār, at the Navya-Nyāya (New Nyāya) school of philosophy made famous by the twelfth-century logician Gaṅgeśa. His teacher Pakshadhara of Mithilā owned the only extant copy of Gaṅgeśa's famous treatise, *Tattva-chintāmaṇi*, and so jealous was the master of his possession that he imposed a condition on all his students that they would never write down what he taught, so that he might retain the monopoly of imparting the new logic. Before long Sārvabhauma had committed the work to memory, besides many valuable interpretations and commentaries. He then proceeded to the Sena capital of Navadvīpa, or Nadia, where he established a school which outrivalled his master's. Among Sārvabhauma's pupils were the saint Chaitanya*, the jurist Raghunandana writer on law*, Kṛishṇāndana (Āgama-vāgīśa), expounder of tantrik literature, and Raghunātha.

The latter, Raghunātha (1477–1547) (or Raghunātha Śiromaṇi), became the greatest of all authorities on Navya-Nyāya (the New Logic). He was born of poor parents and was five years old when he first came to the notice of Sārvabhauma. He had been asked by his mother to fetch fire for domestic purposes and when a piece of glowing charcoal was offered to him he immediately scooped up a handful of sand and received the burning coal. Sārvabhauma witnessed the incident and decided to train the resourceful boy. After completing his studies under Sārvabhauma, Raghunātha went to Mithilā to continue his education under the aged Pakshadhara. Once during a classroom debate he was treated contemptuously, and subjected to apparently deliberate insult by Pakshadhara his master. Burning with shame the young man went that evening to Pakshadhara's house armed with a knife, determined to kill the old man. As he was about to enter the house he overheard the teacher giving an account of the morning's debate to his wife and members of the household, in which he gave wholehearted praise to Raghunātha for his intelligence, shrewdness and self-control. Overcome with remorse the pupil made his way into the room, threw the knife on the floor, fell at his master's feet and confessed his intentions. The teacher pardoned him, and on the following day declared before the class that his pupil was in fact a greater logician than he.

At Nadia Raghunātha developed the academy of logic established by his erstwhile teacher Sārvabhauma, and wrote several works, including a commentary on Gaṅgeśa called the *Tattva-Chintāmaṇi-Dīdhiti*, 'The Essence of the Thought-Jewel's Splendour'.

Books

See under Philosophy.

SATĪ, 'true', a daughter of the sage Daksha*. When she came of age her father arranged a *svayaṁvara* so that she might choose her husband, and invited all the gods except Śiva whom Daksha hated. Satī however loved Śiva and at the svayaṁvara she went around the hall with the garland in her hand thinking devotedly of her Śiva. While thus lost in contemplation she threw the garland into the air mentally offering it to the god. At the same moment Śiva manifested himself and the garland fell around his neck, and Daksha was obliged to accept him as his son-in-law.

The great enmity between the two did not end there. Once when Daksha entered the hall where his son-in-law was seated with other deities, Śiva did not rise to greet him. Later when Daksha gave a sacrificial feast he did not invite Śiva, with disastrous consequences (*see* Daksha). Daksha's failure to invite her husband so mortified Satī that she created the sacrificial fire known as *Jvālā-mukhī*, 'fire-mouth', into which she threw herself and was consumed. The site is now said to be a small extinct volcano in the lower Himālayas north of the Panjāb, and is a place of pilgrimage. After this incident the term *satī* (anglicized suttee*) was applied to all widows and wives who immolated themselves.

According to one legend Satī was changed into a *kokila* (cuckoo); in another version she was reborn as the goddess Umā*. In yet another, Śiva restored her to life by picking up her charred body and dancing round the world with it seven times. But the popularly accepted story goes that Śiva recovered her corpse from the sacrificial fire and carried it on his head as a penance. Fearful lest by this means Śiva might obtain excessive power, Vishṇu with successive throws of his discus cut the body into bits. It fell to earth in 5, 51, 52, 72 or 108 pieces (the number varies in different versions), and each spot where it fell became a *pīṭha* (or *pīṭha-sthāna*, 'seat-place'), a sacred centre of pilgrimage. There is a great deal of confusion about these places, as also about which particular member of Satī's body fell there. More than a thousand places in India claim the honour of having received one or more of the pieces, most of them claiming the ears, breasts, and organ of generation.

The usually recognized pīṭhas are as follows: Arbudā (Mount Ābū) where the right breast of the goddess fell; its sanctity has been somewhat eclipsed by the numerous Jain shrines built in the area. Arāsana (or Arasur) near Mount Ābū; here the left breast of Satī fell and here she is worshipped in the form of the goddess Ambikā. Banāras where either the ear-rings or the left hand fell; the ear-rings give the name to the Maṇikarṇi pool at Banāras. Devīpātan, 'goddess-fall', where the right hand descended. The ancient temple was despoiled by one of Aurangzeb's officers to whom a dire punishment was meted out (*see* animal sacrifices). Faljur, in the Jaintiā Parganas, the left leg or the left knee-cap. Hinglāj in west Baluchistan, the forehead or the crown of the head. Hinglāj is sometimes identified with a place on the river Sarasvatī, not far from Siddhapur, in northern Gujarāt. Jālandhara in the Panjāb, the right breast or nipple, or stomach. Janasthāna in the Deccan, the cheeks, and three hairs from the pubes. Jvālamukhī (or Jvālapur) in East Panjāb, about four miles from Hardwār, the tongue, palate, scalp, foot or eye (see above). Kālīghāṭ (near Calcutta) also Ukule Ghāṭ, the fingers or great toe of the right foot. Kāmākhya, the organs of generation. This place is regarded as one of the most important of the Satī pīṭhas (*see* Kāmarūpa). Kashmīr (various places here claim the honour), the neck, ear, toe or knee. Labhpur, the lips, chin, palate, teeth, pubes. Madura the left eye or left breast, the left hand or rear portion. The temple of Mīnākshī* stands on the site. Mānasarovara at the foot of Mount Kailāsa where the right palm of the goddess fell. Muktināth in Nepāl, near the Gaṇḍakī river. Here the sex organs of Satī are said to have fallen. Paṭna (ancient Pāṭaliputra) where the *paṭ* or garment covering the genitals fell. Pūrṇagiri in Assam (some say near Poona), the buttocks, breasts or sex organs. Sugandha in southern Bengal, the nose, hair, right hand, the anus. Uḍḍiyāna (*see* strīrājya) identified with various places; the buttocks, the sex organs. Ujjain, the elbow, now the site of the Harsiddhi temple. Vindhyachal about five miles from Mirzāpur in Uttar Pradesh. It contains the temple of Vindhya-vāsanī (or Kauśikī) a form of the goddess Śakti*, once a famous rendezvous of the thugs. The toe of the left foot of Satī fell here.

Books

See under Mythology.

SATRĀJITA, the son of Nighna, whose story is told in the Purāṇas. Because he rendered homage and gave ardent praise to the sun, Satrājita was permitted to behold Sūrya the sun-god in his true form. From Sūrya he also received as a gift the wonderful *syamantaka* gem which yielded, but only to the virtuous, eight loads of gold every day, and magically repelled wild beasts, fire, robbers, famine and fear. But to the wicked it brought dread, disaster and death.

Satrājita, fearing the covetousness of Kṛishṇa, and dreading lest he take the gem away from him, gave it to his own brother *Prasena,* the second son of Nighna; but Prasena, being an evil man, was killed by a lion which carried off the jewel in his mouth. This lion was in turn met by Jāmbavat, a chaṇḍāla chieftain of a bear-totem clan, known as the 'king of the bears', who killed the lion and made off with the jewel. Jāmbavat was now pursued by Kṛishṇa*, subdued by stratagem and forced to surrender his daughter Jāmbavatī (through whom Kṛishṇa later became the father of Śāmba*) and to relinquish the jewel, which was then given back to Satrājita. In another legend Jāmbavat dies at the hands of Kṛishṇa in accordance with his own wish (*see* Rāma).

As a reward for restoring the jewel Kṛishṇa claimed Satrājita's beautiful daughter Satyabhāmā, 'true-light'. There had been many suitors for Satyabhāmā's hand, among them Śatadhanvan (or Śatadhanus), 'having a hundred bows', the son of the Yādava king Hṛidika, who in revenge for his loss slew Satrājita while he slept and obtained the gem. Once again the thief was pursued, and slain by Kṛishṇa, who this time appropriated the precious jewel himself and refused to give it up.

Balarāma the elder brother of Kṛishṇa, remonstrated with him over this unrighteous deed, 'worthy only of a low-born thief', and threatened to part company with him forever, whereupon Kṛishṇa reluctantly surrendered the jewel. It was finally agreed by Balarāma, Kṛishṇa and the princess Satyabhāmā that the jewel should be given to Akrūra, the son of Śvaphalka and uncle of Kṛishṇa. Akrūra received the gift joyously and he wore it ever after, 'moving about like the sun, adorned with a diadem of light'.

Satyabhāmā the daughter of Satrājita became one of the four principal wives of Kṛishṇa. She was so enamoured of Kṛishṇa that she agreed to give her husband in bondage to the sage Nārada in return for the assurance that she would be the wife of Kṛishṇa in all her future incarnations. Later she repented and was told by the sage that she could buy Kṛishṇa back for his weight in gold, but she soon discovered that no amount of gold could outweigh her husband. Then a *tulsī* leaf accidentally fell into the weighing-pan and immediately the scales moved and Kṛishṇa was outweighed, and thus restored to Satyabhāmā.

One day the mischief-making sage Nārada gave Kṛishṇa a flower from the wonderful Pārijāta tree of Indra's paradise, and Kṛishṇa presented it to another of his favourite wives, Rukmiṇī. This was duly reported to Satyabhāmā by Nārada. Filled with jealousy Satyabhāmā sulked and would not be appeased until Kṛishṇa promised to bring the whole tree for her. Together they visited Indra's paradise, partook of Indra's hospitality, and on their return Kṛishṇa carried away the sacred Pārijāta. Indra tried to recover the prize of his orchard but was defeated by Kṛishṇa who brought the tree down to earth and planted it in Dvārakā. After Kṛishṇa's death it was restored miraculously to Indra's heaven.

Satyabhāmā had ten sons by Kṛishṇa named, Bhānu, 'brightness', Su-bhānu, Svar-bhānu, Pra-bhānu, Bhānumat, Chandra-bhānu, Bṛihad-bhānu, Ati-bhānu, Śri-bhānu, and Prati-bhānu. These names are sometimes given to the Ādityas.

Books

See under Mahābhārata and Mythology.

SATYAKĀMA, 'truth-loving', a Vedic teacher of unknown origin whose adherence to truth is recorded in the *Chhāndogya Upanishad.* As a boy he desired to devote his life to the study of religion and the Vedas, and with this object in view approached a preceptor named Gautama (or Gautama Hāridrumata). As was required by tradition the latter asked the boy what *gotra* (family) he belonged to, since the Vedas could not be taught to a non-brāhmin. The lad replied that he did not know. He had asked his mother and she had told him, 'I do not know to what gotra you belong, my son. In my youth when I was moving about as a maid-servant I conceived you, so I cannot tell your gotra. My name is Jabālā, and you are Satyakāma. Say that you are Satyakāma Jābāla'.

Hearing this honest confession the preceptor was pleased and decided that the boy must be a brāhmin because he had spoken the truth. He told the boy, 'You who have not swerved from the truth, go and fetch fuel and I shall initiate you'.

Gautama gave him charge of his herds which under the boy's care grew from 400 lean to 1000 sturdy cattle. This training in industry was the foundation of Satyakāma's knowledge. After a few years in the forest the young man retraced his steps homeward with the herd, and on the way many truths were revealed to him one by one: the first was revealed to him by the bull of the herd, the second by the fire he made in his camp, the third by a swan, the fourth by a diver-bird, and so on. When he reached the *āśrama* (hermitage) of his teacher the latter looked at his pupil and remarked, 'My boy, you are shining like one who knows Brahma. Who has taught you?' He replied, 'Others than men'. But he desired to learn more from the lips of his own guru. Gautama thereupon taught him all he knew, 'leaving nothing out', and Satyakāma in turn became a famous guru.

It is interesting to note that Jābāla 'does not seem to be a word of Sanskrit origin and may be traced to a Hebrew word *yobel*, signifying ram's horn, whence jubilee'.

Books

See under Mythology.

SATYAVATĪ, daughter of Uparichara, a Vasu (demi-god) who according to the *Mahābhārata* later became king of Chedi by command of Indra. Uparichara was a Dāsa or non-Aryan, probably Dravidian, chieftain, whose people lived by fishing.

The story of the birth of Satyavatī tells how Uparichara out on a hunting expedition was away from his wife and five sons for several days. As he rested one day he began thinking about his lovely wife and his seed was voided. He placed it on a leaf and despatched it to his wife by a falcon. Another falcon thinking that the other bird was carrying a piece of meat swooped down and started a fight and the seed fell into the river Yamunā. In this sacred river there lived an *apsarā* named Adrikā who had been condemned by Brahmā's curse to live on earth in the form of a fish, and this apsarā swallowed the seed. Ten months later the fish was caught, its belly cut open and a boy and girl found inside.

The fisherman sent the boy to the reigning king, who adopted him and named him Matsya (fish), and when he grew up made him ruler of the fisher folk. The girl was adopted by the fisherman who called her Satyavatī. She was dark in colour and extremely beautiful, but had an odour of fish constantly clinging to her which could be smelled one *yojana* (nine miles) off. One day as she plied her adoptive father's ferry across the river Yamunā, the *ṛishi* Parāśara*, struck by her beauty, offered to remove the fishy odour from her body, provided she submitted to his embrace. He promised that she would become the mother of a famous son. The girl agreed to the proposition, and the ṛishi had union with her in the boat in broad daylight, but to spare the girl's modesty he put a screen of smoke around them. In due course a child was born on an island (*dvīpa*) of the same river, and he was called Dvaipāyana (island-born), later renowned as Vyāsa*, reputed author of the *Mahābhārata*.

After the birth of her child Satyavatī's virginity was miraculously restored to her, and she married king Śāntanu of the Lunar race of kings, and became the mother of Chitrāṅgada and Vichitravīrya (*see* Bhīshma). In some accounts she married Śāntanu first, and on his death married the ṛishi Parāśara.

Satyavatī is also known as Dāsa-nandinī (bringing joy to the Dāsa people), Dāseyī (of the tribe of the Dāsas), Gandha-kālī (smelly and black), Gandhavatī (smelling); Jhashodarī (fish bearing), Kālāṅganī (black-bodied), Matsya-gandhī (fish-smelling), Matsyodarī (coming from the belly of a fish), Yojana-gandhā (whose smell extends for a yojana, nine miles).

Books

See under Mahābhārata and Mythology.

SAVANA, originally used in the *soma** sacrifice to signify the three periods of the day when the soma juice was extracted. Later the term savana came to be applied to the three *lagna* or 'critical' periods of the day, namely, morning, noon and evening, when mantras are recited and ablutions performed by the twice-born.

These three critical periods are:
(1) *Saṁdhyā,* 'juncture', the morning twilight, or dawn, before sunrise. The term is also popularly used for the time of meeting between day and night, both in the morning and in the evening. The main observances of dawn include intoning the name of the deity when rising from bed; saying the morning prayers; answering the call of nature; ceremonial bathing, and the recitation of the gāyatrī mantra.
(2) *Madhyāhna,* 'midday', when the sun is at its zenith, also denoting any time after sunrise and before midday. Chips of wood are first offered to the domestic fire with appropriate mantras; the image of the household deity is worshipped with prayers, offerings of flowers, scents and food; then the five* daily sacrifices are made to the deities, sages, ancestors, guests and animals.
(3) *Saṁdhyāṁśa,* 'juncture-part', the period of dusk or evening twilight. Also called the evening *saṁdhyā*. Procedures include sipping of water, the gāyatrī mantra, Vedic ritual, offerings to images.

The savana or saṁdhyā ceremonies vary considerably from worshipper to worshipper, and are sometimes quite elaborate. A composite picture of the main items of observance would be more or less on the following lines: (*a*) on arising the worshipper invokes the name of the deity a certain number of times, sometimes cutting the procedure short by simply saying, for example, 'Name, one crore', i.e. 'I repeat the name of god ten million times'; (*b*) he performs the saṁkalpa (preparatory meditation) sitting on the bank of a stream or river. If he cannot go to the river he performs the service in the pūjā-room after investing the domestic shrine with 'river-like' qualities; (*c*) he says prayers to the Ganges to wash away his sins and deliver him from all evil. He then thinks of the seven sacred rivers, Gaṅgā, Yamunā, Godāvarī, Sarasvatī, Narmadā, Sindhu and Kāverī, and he invites these rivers to be present in the stream in which he happens to be, or in his brass water-pot if he is praying at home; (*d*) he has a bath (*snāna*), thinking of the water as that of the sacred Ganges; or he sprinkles a little water over himself from his pot; (*e*) he invokes the deity by *nyāsa* or touching of the limbs; (*f*) he turns to the sun, takes water in his hand and lets it run off the tips of his fingers, thus making a libation to the sun; this he does three times; (*g*) he performs the *āchamana* (mouth rinsing); this is done frequently throughout the ceremony; (*h*) he utters the gāyatrī mantra a fixed number of times, 10, 18, 28, 108 or 1008; (*i*) he pronounces the monosyllable *Oṁ*, cracks his fingers ten times in *tāla-traya* in all directions in order to drive off evil spirits; (*j*) he purifies himself with a sprinkling of water and also sprinkles water around him; (*k*) closing his right nostril with his finger he breathes out vigorously through his left nostril so that all his sins may depart from him; (*l*) he inhales water into his nose and then forcibly ejects it from his nostrils, another act for blowing away his sins; (*m*) if bathing in a stream he leaves the water and squats on the ground, facing east. He then rubs his forehead with the ashes of cowdung or sandalwood, makes his caste marks, thinks of his deity (in the evening he faces the setting sun for this part of the rite); (*n*) he sips water from his brass vessel and makes libations to the various deities, by pouring water on the ground, naming each deity in turn; (*o*) closing the right nostril with his thumb he invites Brahmā to come and reside in his navel, Vishṇu to stay in his chest, and Śiva to be seated in his forehead; (*p*) rising, he worships the sun, meditates on his deity and repeats the prescribed mantras and prayers; (*q*) he recites the names of the gods and goddesses such as Brahmā, Vishṇu, Śiva, Varuṇa, Rudra, Agni and others; then the heavens and hells; turning around the while 12, 24 or 48 times, and thus taking upon himself the spiritual potencies of the things he names; (*r*) he then adores the sacred fig-tree by walking around it 7, 14, 21, 28 or more times, by an increase of seven; (*s*) he dismisses the deity with a water offering and a wave of his hand; (*t*) he brings the whole ceremony to a close by a few more prayers and mantras.

Books

I. Dubois, Abbe. *Hindu Manners Customs & Ceremonies*, 3rd Ed., 1936.
II. Roy, N. K. *An Esasy on Hindu Domestic Rites*, 1901.
(*See also under* Worship.)

SĀVITRĪ, the beautiful and virtuous daughter of Aśvapati king of Madra, whose story is told in the *Mahābhārata*. Her splendour and beauty were such that none dared ask for her hand. When she reached the age of puberty her father sent her out with an escort to the neighbouring kingdoms to select her own husband. She found no one to her liking until on her homeward journey she stopped in a forest hermitage and there met and fell in love with the handsome Satyavān, 'the truthful', son of a king of Śālva wrongfully deprived of his throne, who was spending his life in the forest.

Sāvitrī was warned by a sage that Satyavān was not destined to live beyond a day fixed a few months hence, but that did not deter her and the young couple were married and lived a simple life in the forest. As the fatal time approached the wife took a vow of penance and fasting, and when the appointed day dawned she refused to leave her husband's side, but accompanied him to the forest to help in collecting fruit, herbs and fuel.

In the midst of his labours the husband fell down in a faint, and Sāvitrī took him in her arms and sat under a *nyagrodha* tree to await the coming of Yama, god of the dead. When the dread one appeared and carried off the soul of Satyavān, Sāvitrī followed him, and Yama soon divined her purpose. In vain did the god tell her of the hopelessness of her resolve and advise her to desist; in vain did he point out how futile were her appeals. He offered her gifts: sight for her blind father-in-law and the restoration of his usurped kingdom, and a 'century of sons' for herself. She accepted them all, but still following him said, 'Thou hast promised me what cannot be fulfilled unless my husband is restored to me, a century of sons'. Touched by her devotion, Yama relented at last: 'With cheerful heart I now unbind thy husband. He is free'. Satyavān was permitted to return to the land of the living, and sight and his kingdom were restored to her father-in-law.

A similar tale of devotion, also found in the *Mahābhārata*, is told of the beautiful Pramadvara, daughter of the nymph Menakā by the king of the celestial Gandharvas. When she was born her mother Menakā left her near the hermitage of a pious *ṛishi* who brought her up as his own daughter. She grew up to be a winsome and virtuous damsel and was in due course betrothed to a handsome young prince named Ruru. A few days before her marriage she accidentally trod on a serpent which bit her heel, whereupon she fell down in a swoon and in a short while died.

The inconsolable Ruru retired to the forest lamenting his fate when a celestial messenger informed him that the gods had been moved by his grief and had decreed that if he would cede half his own term of existence to the departed maiden he could have her restored to life. To this the youth gladly agreed and his beloved arose from the dead and returned to him. The couple were married and spent their days deeply devoted to each other and 'answered the call of Yama at the appointed time'.

Books

See under Mahābhārata and Mythology.

SAYINGS. India is very rich in proverbial lore, which abounds both in sacred and sectarian writings, in Sanskrit as well as in the vernaculars. It generally takes the form of what are called *vāchana* (from *vāch*, sound), a proposition or apothegm, pithily expressed and replete with hidden wisdom. The term *mahāvākya*, 'great saying' is applied to the gnomic sayings of supreme import found in the sacred texts, that have passed into proverbs and maxims (*kārikā*). Specifically a mahāvākya refers to the short maxims taken from the Vedas, mainly the Upanishads, which stress the identity of all things in Brahma.

From the *Bṛihadāraṇyaka Upanishad* we have the following: *aham brahmāsmi* (I am Brahma); *prajñānam brahman* (Brahma is knowledge); *aham eva idam* (I indeed am this); *ayam ātmā brahma* (this self is Brahma); *sarvosmi* (I am all); *neti, neti* (thou art 'not this, not this'); *āvir āvīr ma edhi, asato mā sad gamaya, tamaso mā jyotir gamaya, mṛityor mā amṛitam gamaya* (O Manifest, manifest to me; from the unreal to the real lead me, from darkness to light lead me, from death to deathlessness lead me); *paroksha-priyā iva hi devāḥ, pratyaksha-dvishaḥ* (obscure-loving verily the gods are, and clearness-hating).

From the *Chhāndogya Upanishad* we have: *tat tvam asi* (that thou art, i.e. that Supreme Soul, thou, the individual soul, art); *sarvam khalu idam brahma* (everything verily is Brahma); *ekam evādvitīyam* (one essence and no other).

From the *Īśa Upanishad: yas tvam asi so'ham asmi* (what thou art, that am

I); *tyaktena bhuñjītha* (enjoy by renunciation); *so'ham* (that am I; in reverse it is *haṁsa,* I am he).

From the *Māṇḍūkya Upanishad* we have: *śāntam śivam advaitam* (the tranquil, the blissful, the undivided). This was taken as the motto of Tagore's University; the motto was removed when it became a Union Government institution.

From the *Muṇḍaka Upanishad: brahma eva idam viśvam* (Brahma verily is this whole world); *brahmavid brahmaiva bhavati* (the Brahma-knowing, Brahma-indeed becomes); *satyam eva jayati* (truth* indeed prevails); *idam sarvam asi* (Thou art all this).

The following are a few sayings gleaned from other sources: *ekaṁ sad, viprā bahudā vadanti* (There is only One Real, but the wise speak of it variously); *ātmā vā are drashṭavyaḥ* (The Soul behold. This is the keynote of most schools of Hindu philosophy); *vidyayā amṛitam aśnute* (Through knowledge immortality is obtained); *brahma satyam; jagan mithya; jīvo brahmaiva nāparaḥ* (Brahma is truth, the world is false; the individual-soul is from Brahma non-different. This is said to summarize Vedānta philosophy); *sattaiva bodho, bodha eva cha satta* (The real is the rational, the rational the real. A saying of Śaṅkara's); *purusha evedam sarvam yad bhūtam yachchha bhāvyam* (Purusha is all this, all that was, all that shall be. This is from the *Ṛig-veda*); *sadāspadam sarvam sarvatra* (Everything everywhere is based on reality. A saying of Śaṅkara's); *yena na amṛitāsyām, kim tena kuryām* (What are these to me if I am not thereby to gain eternal life. Maitreyī to Yājñavalkya, in the *Śatapatha Brāhmaṇa*); *vaktuṁ sukaram, adhyavasātuṁ dushkaram* (to talk is easy, to do difficult).

Many sayings are expressed in figurative form called *upamā,* 'simile' and thousands of such upamās occur in Indian literature. They are extensively used in philosophical works to illustrate fundamental truths. A representative selection is given below.

A foolish man is an actor who is so engrossed in his artificial role that he even carries it into real life and loses touch with Reality.

To live merely to satiate the senses is like crossing a river on an alligator, thinking it is a log of wood.

To do one's allotted duty is to be like the wise artist who while devoted to his art, develops his higher powers through his role.

Putting faith in the things of this world is like crossing a turbulent stream in a clay boat.

The individual self is the dark cloud which obscures the sun which is the Higher Self.

Beware of the lure of the five senses by learning the lesson of the deer which is lured by soft music and caught in a mesh by a hunter; of the elephant which is caught while giving itself pleasure by rubbing itself against a tree trunk; of the moth singed by the light; of the fish hooked by the taste of the worm; of the bee lured by the smell of the flower.

To soothe lust by satisfaction is like tethering a raging elephant by the hair of a tortoise.

Depending on a *mantra* to save one is like expecting hidden treasure to rise out of the bowels of the earth by simply calling its name aloud.

The mind during meditation should be like a lamp in a windless place, where the flame does not flicker.

As salt dissolves in water and camphor in fire, so the self dissolves in the Eternal.

As the river flows into and vanishes in the ocean, so mind in Mind.

As the shape of a lump of earth must first disappear so that the pot might be formed, so man must disappear to form the divine.

Just as a snake in a dream, though unreal, can cause us to awaken, so the unreal objects of this world can make the wise man waken to Reality.

The wise man is like a blacksmith's anvil on which many experiences are hammered out without change in the anvil itself.

There is one moon (God) in the firmament, but it is reflected in numerous jars of water. (*Amṛitabindu Upanishad*).

As the spider pours forth its thread, as herbs grow on the earth and hairs from a man, so the universe grows from the Imperishable. (*Bṛihad-āraṇyaka Upanishad*).

Brahma abides even in our illusions. A man returning home at dusk and imagining that he sees a serpent (the phenomenal world) where there is actually a rope (Brahma), is not entirely in error. For the rope is there. If he can discern the truth he will see that what he believes to be a serpent is a rope. (*Śaṅkara.*)

As sparks shoot out of a blazing fire, so do all things proceed from the Imperishable. (*Muṇḍaka Upanishad*).

In religion a man should be like salt (the same within and without) like a fowl (able to pick out what is wholesome from the rubbish), and like a crane (watchful for his prey). (*Rāmānuja.*)

As by one clod of clay or by one nugget of gold all that is made of clay or gold may be known, since only the name and form now differ, so might all things be known by knowing Brahma. (*Chhāndogya Upanishad.*)

In shallow souls even the fish of small things can cause a commotion; in oceanic minds the largest fish makes hardly a ripple.

To look for reality by means of the senses is like searching for the son of a barren woman, or feeling for the horns of a hare, or looking for a bird's footprint in the sky.

Persons who perform rituals but are concerned with the world are like parrots taught to say God, God. When they are caught by a cat they shriek *Kaw, Kaw,* forgetting the divine lessons (*Kabīr*).

If asceticism can teach you after twenty years only to walk on water, better pay the boatman and save your time (*Rāmakṛishṇa*).

The almanacs contain predictions for rainfall, but squeeze the books and not a drop of water will you get. So also good sayings in books do not make one virtuous. (*Rāmakṛishṇa*).

Books

I. Champion, S. G. *The Eleven Religions & Their Proverbial Lore.* 1944.

II. Champion, S. G. *Racial Proverbs,* 1938.

III. Sen, S. K. *Hindu Proverbs,* 1901.

SCATOLOGY, although referring to matters pertaining to ordure (Greek, *skatos*, dung), covers the study of all things of anthropological interest relating to the ejestae, and the physiological processes associated with them. Students of the subject opine that scatology has occupied a more prominent position in Hinduism than in any other religion old or new.

The followers of certain tantrik cults proceed against all canons of personal cleanliness in the belief that part of the self resides in the things that are in constant contact with one's body, such as clothes, and that these should therefore not be changed. Perspiration is viewed as a form of oblation and the dirt that clings to the body as holy, since it is impregnated with the personal aura. For this reason they never change their clothes and when the clothes are beyond use they burn them. They do not bathe or wash themselves so that the holiness inherent in their persons might be conserved. The kāpālikas always rub their perspiration back into their bodies, believing that it is full of potent emanations and should not be dissipated or washed off.

With the orthodox Hindu the act of evacuation at times takes on the semblance of a ritual (*see* utsarga) and many taboos are associated with the function. A preoccupation with the anus is a feature of many occult* and yogic rites. Like the worshippers of Baal-Peor in ancient Canaan the votaries of certain left-hand sects of South India at some of their ceremonies used to make water and evacuate on the idol before sacrificing the animal victim to the deity (III, p. 110).

Certain Śaivite, especial śavavāda, sects, like the Aghorī, eat carrion and ordure and drink urine, both human (their own and others') and animal, at a ceremonial meal, holding that as excrement nourishes the soil so it can fertilize the sterile soul. They filter their excretions through a piece of cloth and drink the liquid, claiming that this renders them capable of great things and gives them knowledge of strange matters (II, p. 227) that other yogis acquire only after years of practice and penance. Vajrayāna and other tantrik cults teach that excreta are not to be distinguished from any good food. Even among the more orthodox sects the partaking of the excretions of the guru has been observed (I, p. 40).

The drinking of human urine once formed part of ancient fertility rites, and the significance of yellow-coloured water used in certain Hindu festivals such as Holi is believed to be a relic of this scatalogical practice. The claim that drinking human urine enhances the sexual powers has been substantiated, according to a recent writer, by Dr Butenandt's discovery in 1931 that the male sex hormone could be extracted from human urine.

Cow-dung and urine play a conspicuous part in the Hindu religion. Govardhana, the heaven of Kṛishṇa, takes its name from the word for cow-dung (*gobar*). The most potent of all purifying drinks, an obligatory beverage for those seeking readmission into their caste after excommunication, is the *pañchagavya*, which consists of the five products of the cow*, an emulsion of cow-dung, curds and ghee, dissolved in milk and cow's urine. Cow-dung is commonly used for dedaubing the hearth and walls of village houses and augments the sacrosanctity of places such as altars and sacrificial seats.

The sacred properties of *go-mūtra* or cow's urine are universally given credence in India. It can still be seen on occasion, although the practice is fast dying out, that the orthodox Hindu will cup his hands and drink direct from the flow of a urinating cow. Says Moore, writing in the last century, 'If the animal be retentive, a pious expectant will impatiently apply his finger, and by judicious tickling excite the grateful flow'.

Excessive concern with semen and morbid fear of its loss is another characteristic of Hindu occult practice. The techniques of conserving this liquid energy, of not allowing it to be expended, or by certain methods, of reabsorbing it after emission, are known to the practitioners of secret left-hand cults (*see* bindu).

Scatalogical substances are widely used in old wives' remedies and in magic. Menstrual blood is said to burst a boil; burning hair can cure asthma; the seminal fluid in an aphrodisiac; nail parings thrown into a mouse-hole can cure a cough; blood, both animal and human also has great magical virtue. The saliva of holy men is like the immortalizing *amṛita* or nectar of the gods. Scatomancy or divination by dung is practiced in certain parts of India (*see* sterility).

Derivative features of scatological interest in Hinduism are to be seen in various social customs. Observers have recorded that it is good manners to blow one's nose out with one's fingers and wipe them on the wall or the dress; it is utterly disgusting to the orthodox to use a handkerchief and then retain the soiled piece of linen for future use. 'The sight of a foreigner doing this,' says Abbe Dubois, 'is enough to make them feel sick'. Belching is not only permitted but is a sign that one has eaten well, and the louder the eructation the more appreciation is believed to be expressed. In times past it was not considered impolite to ease oneself of flatulence by loud crepitations.

Books

I. Bourke, J. G. *Scatalogic Rites of All Nations*, Washington, D.C., 1891.
II. Briggs, G. W. *Gorakhnath and the Kanphata Yogis*, Calcutta, 1938.
III. Dare, Paul. *Indian Underworld*, London, 1938.
IV. Moore, T. *The Hindu Pantheon*, London, 1810.

SCIENCE. The history of Hindu science goes back to the Indus Valley whose people were familiar with mining and the working of metals, who constructed well-planned buildings, some of them two and more stories high, manufactured a gypsum cement for joining stone and even metal, shared with many other ancient cultures the art of making lasting paints and dyes. Mohenjodaro had a public bath worked by an ingenious hydraulic system.

The scientific knowledge of the Vedic Aryans has been the subject of much contentious writing, but little can be said for certain about their achievements, unless the claims of certain Hindu scholars, mainly stemming from the writings of Dayānanda, are found acceptable. Vedic science certainly appears to have included the elements of mathematics, chemistry and biology, although some scholars would qualify even this with the observation that the mathematics was concerned mostly with the geometry of altar-building, that the chemistry dealt with the preparation of unguents, cosmetics, hair-oils and scents, and that the biology was merely a rough and ready catalogue of plants and animals from the point of view of their utility whose 'classification was as superficial as possible' (VII, p. 248).

It seems beyond doubt that much was contributed to ancient Indian science by the pre-Aryans. The indigenous peoples of India were familiar with the therapeutic and toxic properties of certain plants, they knew the art of cultivation and of seasonal and rotational sowing; they were skilled in many varied crafts, and possessed a good knowledge of navigation and meteorology. The Ājīvikas and Nāstikas were the first to speculate about the properties of matter and the 'five elements'. Their concept of a molecular and atomic world was taken over by the Āryans and incorporated into the Vaiśeshika system of philosophy. They also acquired much physiological knowledge by practical bodily experiments, including some extraordinary techniques of respiration and breath control, which again were embodied in the so-called Aryan science of Yoga.

Systematic expositions on scientific matters first began to be written some time after the Persian, Greek and 'barbarian' periods of Indian history in the early centuries of the present era. Astronomy and mathematics were strongly influenced by the Greeks, and by the speculations of the Alexandrian school. Surgery and medicine (āyurveda), navigation, architecture, biology, chemistry (alchemy), mechanics, and even horticulture, all bear the mark of foreign contributions. The long-accepted notion that Hindu mathematicians invented the zero and place-value in mathematics is now no longer regarded as tenable, or at best is open to dispute (*see* numerals).

All this knowledge was codified and systematized in numerous works in Sanskrit. But the part once believed to have been played by these works in the Muslim renaissance which reached its culmination in the reign of Ma'mun, is now regarded as exaggerated. It is held that the translations of Hindu works into Arabic during the time of the Baghdad Caliphate in the eighth and ninth centuries, is evidence not of the advanced progress of studies in India, but of the keen intellectual spirit prevailing in Baghdad at the time. For the Arabs ventured far afield in their pursuit of knowledge, and culled impartially wherever knowledge was to be found; they translated from Sanskrit with the same zeal as from Chinese, Greek, Latin, Pahlavi, Syriac and Coptic. Where Arab science borrowed in bulk it was not from the Hindus but from the Greeks.

Subsequent Hindu contributions to the advancement of science have been negligible, but since the time of Dayānanda (d. 1883) and under the inspiration of his *sanatva** teachings, a pseudo-scholastic attempt is sometimes made by Hindu paṇḍits to expound the mysteries of Vedic or Purāṇic aeronautics, Tantrik biochemistry, and so forth. This 'melancholy scholarship' tries to equate Mitra with oxygen, Varuṇa with hydrogen, and so on, and by reference to the Vedic or Sanskrit texts to turn out any chemical formula to order. Others find śāstrik evidence to prove that the ancient sages were acquainted with radioactivity, microbiology, radar and television. The Epic heroes, we are told by some zealots of this school of thought, flew the first aircraft, and devastated cities with atomic bombs.

It need hardly be added that most Hindu workers in the field of science today dismiss these theories, and have taken the path blazed by western science, and modern Indian scientists have done outstanding work in their respective fields. Sir C. V. Raman was awarded the Nobel Prize in 1930 for an important discovery on optical spectra relating to the diffusion of light, known after him as the Raman Effect. The brilliant researches both historical and in the laboratory of Sir P. C. Ray did much to restore faith in the scientific value of ancient Hindu chemistry. The work of Sir Jagdish Chandra Bose on the sensitive reactions and physiological processes of the living plant led him to invent the crescograph to measure the reaction of plants to stimuli, by means of which he was able to prove that plants have a sensitive nervous system and a rudimentary emotional life, and that they 'feel' pleasure and pain.

Books

I. Karpinski, L. C. 'Hindu Science'. *American Mathematical Monthly*, XXVI, 289, 1919.
II. Mehta, D. D. *Some Positive Sciences in the Vedas*, New Delhi, 1961.
III. Raj, Hans. *Science in the Vedas*, Ludhiana, 1956.
IV. Ray, P. *History of Chemistry in Ancient & Mediaeval India*, Calcutta, 1956.
V. Ray, P. C. *History of Hindu Chemistry*, 2 vols., 2nd Ed., Calcutta, 1902.
VI. Sarkar, B. K. *Hindu Achievements in Exact Science*, Allahabad, 1914.
VII. Seal, B. N. *The Positive Sciences of the Ancient Hindus*, London, 1915.
VIII. Winter, H. J. J. *Eastern Science*, London, 1952.

SCRIPTS. According to legend the alphabet was communicated to mankind in the secret symbolism engraved within the human body by five deities. Brahmā imprinted parts of the alphabet in the sutures of the skull; Vishṇu in the convolutions of the internal ducts and arteries; Śiva in the shape of the male organs; Pārvatī in the female breasts; Yama in the bony framework.

The characters of the still undeciphered Indus Valley seals represent the earliest known form of writing in India. They are probably not alphabetic, but composed of symbols, each of which is an ideogram. Some scholars, notably Friedrich Hrozný, have tried to trace similarities between the Indus Valley symbols and the Hittite script, but without success.

Vedic literature, extensive though it is, gives no indication of the existence of writing in early Aryan India. The Vedas imply that the 'texts' existed only in the memory of those who learnt them by heart. Writing is never mentioned. Reference to 'marks' in the early texts are vague, and authorities do not agree on their interpretation. Some scholars argue that the technicalities and complexities of Vedic literature, phonetics and grammar, could not have been conceived without the aid of some form of written symbols. But no specimen, or evidence of such a form has yet been discovered.

By the fourth century BC the sounds of the alphabet had already been arranged and classified phonetically, as we learn from the grammar of Pāṇini, which recognized a system of forty-six alphabetic sounds. But this and other works on grammar and phonetics never referred to written letters but only to voiced sounds. There is no record of when the transition from oral texts to written manuscripts took place in India, but it is established that the sacred texts were not reduced to writing till comparatively late, since the general prohibition against setting them down was very rigid. The *Mahābhārata* condemns the writers of the Vedas to hell.

Prior to that the 'text' itself was passed on by word of mouth from generation to generation. Such feats, remarkable though they are, were not unique, and were common to many ancient communities: the Greek, Druid, Polynesian, and the Moi of Indo-China, to name but a few.

Max Müller once pointed out that the oldest extant manuscript of the *Ṛig-veda* does not date from 1500 BC, the date generally assigned to its composition, but from AD 1500, three thousand years later. Earlier manuscripts there might have been, but if so they have perished. If, as some scholars maintain, writing was known in the Vedic Age, no trace of it survives. In any case it may be stated with certainty, that it was not Devanāgarī, which was evolved and perfected at least fifteen centuries after the Vedas were composed.

Some form of writing was supposed to have been brought to India from the West about the eighth century BC, but except for a few interpolated verses in the Buddhist texts referring to the 'sixty-four scripts' in use in Ancient India, we have no actual evidence of any one of them. Greek observers often referred to Indians as simple folk, ignorant of the art of writing, who conducted all matters by memory, and though this was by no means an accurate picture, it conveys the impression received by foreigners.

So far as our present knowledge goes, no Indian system of alphabetic writing was known prior to the 'barbarian' period, in the first few centuries BC, which saw the introduction of the earliest scripts. It is now generally agreed that writing was introduced from outside India, although subsequently elaborated in India itself. The very term *lipi* used for 'writing' is of foreign, Persian, origin, and Persian also is the word *divira,* meaning scribe.

These early scripts were *Kharoshṭhī**, used in the south-eastern provinces of the Persian empire and employed by Aśoka for some of his inscriptions, and *Brāhmī*, the precursor of the modern Indian alphabetic forms. The origin of Brāhmī was long in dispute. Jain writers preserve a tradition that it was bequeathed by the Jain patriarch Ṛishabha* to his daughter Brāhmī. Scholars like Edward Thomas held that it was of Dravidian origin. Others from James Prinsep to Émile Senart believed that it was derived from the Greek alphabet. Most scholars however, agree that Brāmhī originated from a Semitic source, and according to Diringer all historical and cultural evidence is best coordinated by the theory which suggests early Aramaic as the prototype of the Brāhmī script.

The ancestor of Brāhmī is thus believed to be of North Semitic provenance, and is ultimately traced back to forms of the Phoenician* and Moabitish alphabets with Aramaic modifications. About one third of the twenty-three letters of the North Semitic alphabet of the seventh century BC is identical with the oldest form of the corresponding Indian letters; another one third is somewhat similar; and the remaining third is dissimilar. Like Kharoshṭhī this early Brāhmī was most probably brought to India between 600 to 400 BC by traders coming by way of Mesopotamia, and the alphabet was gradually enlarged to suit the requirements of the Indian range of sounds. The original direction of the Brāhmī characters was from right to left, as seen in the inscription on a coin found in Eran in the Central Provinces, which would confirm its Semitic origin. The arrangement of Brāhmī in the later Nāgarī form as we know it was still some centuries away. Says Professor S. K.

Chatterji, 'The perfection of the Brāhmī alphabet as a worthy medium of Sanskrit, with its scientific and accurate orthography would appear to have taken place during the early centuries of the Christian era'. The script received its name about AD 300 after the brāhmin scribes who began to use it at that time. Subsequent to the evolution of Devanāgarī from Brāhmī the meaning of the latter script, the parent of Sanskrit writing, was lost to human remembrance for almost thirteen centuries until it was once again made intelligible when the English scholar James Prinsep deciphered it in 1837.

Before proceeding to the development of Brāhmī it may be useful to state that Jain and Buddhist writings list the following among the scripts current in India in the fourth century AD: (*a*) Hūna-lipi, the writing of the Huns (*b*) Yavanānī, the writing of the Yavanas or Greeks; (*c*) Chīna-lipi, Chinese writing; (*d*) Vaṅga-lipi, Bengali writing, probably a form of Kuṭila; (*e*) Damila, Dravidian writing; (*f*) Kharoshṭhī,* used in the north-west; (*g*) Brāhmī, now emerging as the dominant script.

The earliest written record in Brāhmī characters is the Piprāwā vase inscription (*c*. 400–200 BC) in a language which does not conform to any of the standard Prākṛits*. The inscription has been variously interpreted, and suggests a transitional phase of Brāhmī. Next in the order of antiquity is the Sohgaura copper-plate, (*c*. 250 BC) in the Brāmhī script of the Maurya period. Here again there is no certainty about the exact meaning of the engraving. Some of the Aśokan inscriptions (*c*. 230 BC) are written in Brāhmī, the language being not Sanskrit but Prākṛit vernaculars.

Students of the alphabet have tried to catalogue under separate heads the distinct type of writing that developed from the Brāhmī script, and the following are generally recognized as covering the main classes:

I. KUSHĀNA, of the first and second centuries AD, grew out of the crude scripts of the Mauryan and Śuṅgan forms of Brāhmī. So called because several varieties flourished in the extensive regions of the Kushān empire.

II. GUPTA script, which evolved from the basic Kushān characters, A lapidary and monumental style for inscriptions, as well as a cursive style for writing on strips of palm-leaf were evolved at the same time.

III. HARSHA script. During the time of Harsha Vardhana (d. AD 647) a script known as the siddha-mātrikā was evolved, simultaneously with 'nail-headed' and 'arrow-headed' types. The siddha-mātrikā was the form of writing in which Sanskrit works became known in China and Japan.

IV. NĀGARĪ*, also called Devanāgarī, is the script now used for the writing of Sanskrit.

V. SĀRADĀ, developed about AD 800 in the north-west, especially in Kashmīr. There are several variants of Śāradā, namely (*a*) Ṭakkarī or Ṭaṅkrī, the parent of Dogrī, Kuluī, Chameālī (Chamba district), (*b*) Sindhī, which evolved in Sind, (*c*) Laṇḍa (or Baniā) of the Panjāb, which shows Semitic, and probably Arab influences, as does Ṭakkarī. Multānī is a variety of Laṇḍa, (*d*) Gurmukhī, elaborated from Laṇḍa by the Sikh guru Aṅgad for the sacred writings of the Sikhs.

VI. KUṬILA, previously called Proto-Bengali, developed at the end of the eleventh century in eastern India, Uttar Pradesh, Bihār, Nepāl, Assam,

Bengal and Orissa, with triangular shaped letters and a little hook on the top left of each. From this evolved (*a*) Bāṅgālī of Bengal, and Maithili of Bihār, (*b*) Oṛiya of Orissa, written with curves instead of the horizontal line joining all the letters on the top, (*c*) Gujarāti, without the horizontal line on top, (*d*) Manipuri of Manipur, now extinct, (*e*) Kaithī, a cursive form of writing, used in Bihār and Uttar Pradesh, mainly by scribes, (*f*) Nepāli used in Nepāl and the lower foothills of the Himālayas.

VII. GRANTHA, an angular script of contentious origin, sometimes said to be derived from Brāhmī. It is the predecessor of Tamil, Telugu, Kanarese and Malayālam. It has been alternatively suggested that some form of 'Proto-Grantha' was brought by Semitic traders direct to the south coast of India, and that it was from this and not from Aramaic that the South Indian scripts were derived. In this case it may have been a pre-Brāhmī script which, early arranged in scientific order, could have served as a model for the Nāgarī alphabetic arrangement of the north. From Grantha local forms of writing such as *vaṭṭeḷuttu* (in popular use for Tamil) and *koleḷuttu* (for Malayālam) were evolved.

Books

I. Bühler, G. *On the Origin of the Indian Brahma Alphabet,* 2nd Rev. Ed., Strassburg, 1898.

II. Cust, R. N. 'On the Origin of the Indian Alphabet', *Journal of the Royal Asiatic Society,* Vol. XVI, n.s.

III. Diringer, D. *The Alphabet,* London, 1949.

IV. Lévi, S. 'Indian Writing', *Indian Antiquary,* Bombay, Vol. XXXIII.

V. Shamasastry, R. 'A Theory of the Origin of the Devanagari Alphabet,' *Indian Antiquary,* Bombay, Vol. XXXV.

VI. Sivamurti, C. *Indian Epigraphy and South Indian Scripts,* 1928.

VII. Upasak, C. S. *The History and Palaeography of Mauryan Brahmi Script,* Banaras, 1960.

SCRIPTURES. Traditionally the scriptures, that is, the sacred or canonical works of the Hindus, are considered in two great classes, namely śruti and smṛiti. The first, *śruti*, refers to that which was 'heard', i.e. divine knowledge directly inspired or revealed, and is restricted to the Vedas* only, as they were believed to have been divinely revealed to mankind through the ṛishis. That which appertains to the śruti is known as *śrauta*. In all matters pertaining to orthodox Hindus the śrutis are paramount in authority.

The term used in contradistinction to śruti is *smṛiti*, or that which was 'remembered'. Things appertaining to the smṛiti are called *smārta*, and include the kalpas or rules of ceremonial usage. The term smārta also has a sectarian significance. The authority of smārta works is valid provided it does not contradict the unimpeachable śrauta writings. Smṛiti is traditional knowledge and designates almost the entire body of post-Vedic classical Sanskrit literature. It is often referred to as *śāstra*, a term applied to any religious or philosophical treatise, or collectively to the codes and institutes of a whole department of knowledge, such as law (*dharma-śāstra*), or writings like the Purāṇas which are meant to inspire faith (*bhakti-śāstra*) or scientific treatises (e.g. *vāstu-śāstra*, architecture).

Smṛiti literature is generally taken to include the following, which are not mutually exclusive:

(1) The VEDĀṄGA, 'Veda-limb', the name of certain branches of post-Vedic studies regarded as auxiliary to the Vedas. The Vedāṅgas are conventionally divided into six headings, namely (*a*) *kalpa* or the ritual canon, including the dharma-śāstras or legal codes, (*b*) *jyotisha* or astronomy, (*c*) *śikshā* or phonetics, (*d*) *chhandas* or metre (*see* prosody), (*e*) *nirukta* or etymology, and (*f*) *vyākaraṇa* or grammar; these last four also formed part of the study of *bhāshikā* or philology.
(2) The SHAḌ-DARŚANA, 'six-viewpoints', the six orthodox schools of Hindu philosophy, namely, Nyāya, Vaiśeshika, Sāṁkhya, Yoga, Mīmāṁsā, and Vedānta.
(3) ITIHĀSA (*iti-ha-asa*, 'thus-indeed it was'), legendary or semi-legendary works, specifically the *Mahābhārata* and *Rāmāyaṇa* and often extended to the Purāṇas.
(4) PURĀṆA*, 'old', a fairly late redaction of ancient legends and themes rather heavily touched with superstition. The Purāṇas represent the most corrupt form of Hinduism.
(5) UPAVEDA, 'auxiliary Vedas', subsidiary treatises on medicine, music, architecture, erotics, alchemy and various arts and crafts. These were partly derived from original Vedic texts and traditionally associated with one or other of the Vedas. Thus āyurveda or medicine was an upaveda of the *Atharva-veda*; *dhanurveda* or archery was said to be part of the *Yajur-veda*; *gāndharva-veda*, the science of singing, was part of the *Sāma-veda*; *arthaveda* the science of *artha* or wealth, was part of the *Atharva-veda*.
(6) TANTRA, writings of the Śākta and Śaivite sects of the left hand, and also of certain antinomian Buddhist schools.
(7) ĀGAMA, scriptures of sectarian Hindus like the Vaishṇavites, Śaivites and Śāktas.
(8) UPĀṄGA, a generic name for any collection of treatises, although traditionally confined to the philosophical systems of Nyāya and Mīmāṁsā, the *dharma-sūtras*, the Purāṇas and the Tantras.

For the educated Hindu of today the scriptures consist of three *prasthāna* or 'supports' called the prasthāna-traya, comprising (*a*) the *Vedānta-sūtras* of Bādarāyaṇa, (*b*) the ten great Upanishads*, and (*c*) the *Bhagavadgītā**.

There are of course many other classes of scriptures which are regarded as authoritative by particular schools. The *chārvākas* and materialists do not regard even the Vedas as canonical, while others give reverence to the sacred writings of all religions and sects, if couched in Sanskrit. Lesser forms of sacred writings, sometimes classified with the scriptures are mentioned in Literary* Forms.

Books

See under Literature and Sanskrit.

SCULPTURE. The sculptor in stone, metal, wood or clay, was known as a *takshaṇā* (from *taksh*, carve, hew, fashion, create). Although his chief work was to make idols* for installation in temples, for taking out in processions, and for domestic worship, he also wrought profane works, and could carve in relief as well as create in the round.

There was an ancient belief that the most effective sculpture, like the most effective building, had to be an intrinsic part of the earth. So work was done on rocks *in situ*, growing naturally like a tree, and deriving its power from the soil. Early relief or incised work, as in the Indus Valley seals, is believed to have been based on this idea. Some background, however small, had to be given to the image to raise it from its isolated and powerless plane, to the background of an intrinsically related natural material. Later bas-reliefs were an extension of this idea. Many reliefs, unlike sculptures in the round, had colouring, They were first washed with a thin layer of plaster to which the colours were applied (XVI, p. 213).

The materials used by the sculptor, clay, stone, marble, metal or wood, were always carefully chosen, and sculptors specialized in different media. Each mineral*, metal*, or type of wood had its own virtues. Clay images were often thrown into the sea to dissolve and disappear after use. Images that were to be permanently installed in temples were made of stone. Those that had to be taken out in procession were wrought of wood or metal. Idols for domestic or private worship were made of clay, wood, or hollow metal. Strictly, hollow images in metal, being incomplete and deficient in substance, were considered a fraudulent facsimile of the deity, and their making was forbidden under penalty of curses for seven generations. But they were light and portable, and the prohibition was circumvented by placing a tiny scroll with an appropriate *mantra* inside the image with proper rites. These scrolls proved very useful to archaeologists in dating and identifying hollow metal images.

Indian sculpture shows a fine plastic sense and a natural genius for modelling, but in executing the work little account was taken of the aesthetic value of empty spaces and unadorned stone, since the Hindu sculptor had the *horror vacui* and could not bear to see a blank surface. The prodigality of his creativeness often outran judgment, and the final product was frequently heavily overburdened.

Some restraint was imposed by a high degree of stylization in the figures, which had to conform to certain fixed canons* of proportion. The more exalted figures were endowed with various stigmata* or bodily marks or physical characteristics such as long ear lobes, protuberances on the head and forehead, and a halo and nimbus. A multiplicity of arms symbolized the power of a deity, a device greatly admired by Indian critics, one of whom opines that the Indian artist 'not only understood the human body but was also capable of improving it' (XIV, p. 21).

Also to be taken into account by the sculptor were the stances and postures (*āsanas**), flexes and bends (*bhaṅga*) of the body (*see aṅgika*), hand gestures (*mudrā**), the consort of the deity, and the deity's weapon, vehicles (*vāhana**), and other symbols*, all of which were fixed by convention. Generally Buddhists concentrated on repose, e.g. the meditating Buddha, and Hindus on action, e.g. the Dancing Śiva, Vishṇu as Varāha (the boar) and Narsiṁha (the man-lion), and Durgā of the violent stance. The height of the plinth for a standing or sitting figure was likewise determined by set rules.

A belief in the magical virtues of the liṅga and yoni, and in the symbolism of *daṁpati* (husband-and-wife) pairs as indicative of the auspicious state of *saubhāgya* (married bliss) gave rise to another convention in Indian temple architecture, namely, erotic sculpture. This took many forms. The sculptures of Sānchī (*c.* 200 BC) show nude female figures, some with yoni exposed. Later, the liṅga figures were also freely rendered. The *liṅgodbhava* (liṅga theophany) was often a plain phallic emblem with the figure of Śiva or his spouse carved on it, the frenum forming a pointed arch over the head, as in the Gudimallam Śiva of the tenth century.

Buddhist shrines sometimes included *mithuna*, 'paired', groups, showing a man and a woman standing side by side. These were originally simple *daṁpati* pairs as seen in the stone railing of Budh Gaya. Similar couples in Buddhist cave temples are believed to be portraits of those who contributed towards the construction of the temple. The later *śilpa śāstras* (treatises on architecture) required the inclusion of erotic couples on the façades of Hindu temples (XI, p. 220) which in Khajurāho and the Black Pagoda go to extremes of licentiousness, depicting group union and even bestiality.

The technique of sculpture developed along four lines. First was relief work carved against the main body of the material which formed its background, abundantly exemplified in Buddhist and Hindu shrines throughout India. The second was work in the round as seen in temple idols and free-standing images of various kings. The third was modelling and moulding of plastic material with the hands, as in the making of clay images. The fourth was the highly skilled art of metal sculpture.

Indian metal sculpture is generally executed in bronze, worked by the *cire perdue* (French: 'lost wax') process. One of three methods may be used. In the first the model is first roughly done in plaster; this core is covered with a layer of wax on which the work is executed in all its detail. The wax is then covered with clay and when this outer clay is dry the whole is heated. The wax melts and runs out through previously made holes, so that there is a hollow space left by the 'lost wax' between the rough inner plaster core and the outer clay caste. Molten metal is then poured into this space. After it has solidified the clay covering is broken and the metal figure revealed. In the second method the figure is finely moulded in hard wax, then covered with clay and the whole dried and then heated. The wax runs out leaving a hollow mould into which the molten amalgam is poured. Later the clay shell is chipped away and the solid figure chased and polished to a fine finish. Both these methods result in a solid and heavy image, so that where a lighter image is required a third method is employed. Here a core of clay is moulded in detail. This is coated with a layer of wax which in turn is covered with clay. The whole is heated, the wax flows out and into the resulting mould between the two clays liquid metal is poured. When solidified the outer covering is broken and the innermost clay core chipped and washed out leaving a hollow statue which is sometimes as thin as tin foil and can be very difficult to handle.

The history of Indian sculpture may be briefly given. (The sculptural styles themselves are dealt with in greater detail under the relevant dynasties. For the chief periods of Indian art see the chronological table under 'Art'.) Indian sculpture begins with the specimens found in the Indus Valley*. The interest of the work uncovered at Mohenjodaro and Harappa lies not in its aesthetic excellence, or its influence but in its antiquity, since it dates from about the third millennium BC. Few of the sculptures have artistic merit, although they are relevant to the study of the continuity of Indian motifs and models through the ages. The bulk of the sculptural finds consists of steatite seals and figurines in terracotta and stone, such as the heavy-hipped Mother Goddess with elaborate headdress and ornaments, of Harappa; the male torso in red sandstone (this shows a masterly technique), and a little dancing figurine in grey stone, both of Harappa; a bronze dancing girl (made by the cire perdue process), and the bust of a bearded priest with a trefoil pattern shawl, of Mohenjodaro. There are other dancing figures, models of birds and animals, children's toys including a clay cart, and numerous seals with religious and ritual designs. Some of the work is executed with skill and vigour.

Some two thousand years were to elapse before the next phase of Indian sculpture was ushered in by the Mauryan period, in the third century BC. With the Mauryas we see the beginnings of Iranian and Hellenistic influence in the increasing use of stone and the distinctive high polish given to it, in the fine shaping of the stone, in the introduction of Achaemenian motifs such as the lion and the bull, in the floral and foliate designs. The Aśokan columns* and capitals represent the culmination of this period. The lions of the Sārnāth capital and the beautiful bull of the column of Rāmpūrva are among the outstanding examples of Mauryan art. The elephant carved out of a rock at Dhauli, bearing a rock-edict of Aśoka, belongs to the same period.

From this period also we see the beginnings of a lively religious art, springing from a widespread cult of tutelary deities of trees and forests personified in the *yakshas* and *yakshīs* and giant guardian figures which may have been set up at temple and palace entrances. These presuppose a long anterior development in wood, but no examples of the wooden figures have survived. The extant stone sculptures are heavy, fleshy, larger than life size, with both feet resting firmly on the ground; most of them are to be dated between 200 to 150 BC. The yaksha sandstone figure of Paṭna, the chaurī-bearer of Dīdārganj now in the Paṭna museum, the nude headless torso of a Jain *tīrthaṅkara* from Lohanpur near Paṭna, all bear the fine Mauryan polish. Similar works of the same period are the Pārkham statue in the Mathurā Museum, the Maṇibhadra yaksha of Pavaya, and the female yakshī of Besnagar now in the Calcutta Museum.

The finest examples of Indian sculpture between Aśoka and the Gupta period are found in the carvings on the columns, gateways and stone railings of Buddhist stūpas*, notably those of Bhārhut with their illustrations of the *Jātaka* stories and of Buddha's life; of Sānchī with its scenes of everyday activity and its animated yakshī figures; and of Budh Gaya whose reliefs provide a link with Mathurā and the Kushāns. Much of this work is akin to the art of the jeweller and in fact the sculpture on a column of the southern gate at Sānchī was executed by the ivory carvers of Bhīlsā. The medallion panels of the Amarāvati stūpa are among the finest in the whole of Indian art, even judged by the little that has survived. Amarāvatī art has been described as a synthesis of Bactrian art with that of Sānchī.

This early art is full of symbolism and its motifs have been traced back to

Mesopotamia, Persia, Greece and Central Asia. The Buddha image had not yet been evolved, and before the Gandhāra period the Buddhists had an almost semitic aversion to depicting the Blessed One in human form. They invariably represented him and the chief events of his life by symbols: for his birth the elephant or lotus; for his renunciation the horse; for his Enlightenment the Bo tree with the rail; for the first preaching the wheel or the deer; for the final *nirvāṇa* the stūpa. Buddha himself was represented by footprints, an empty throne, an umbrella or a lotus flower.

The sculpture of the Indian cave* temples is of considerable interest. The early caves such as those of Bhājā (75 BC), Bedsā (AD 100–200) and Kārle (AD 120) contain many unique reliefs, and sculptures of bulls, horses and elephants. The entrance to the Kārle caves is flanked by vigorous '*mithuna*' couples in high relief, who are thought to represent the donors and patrons of the temples. The tops of the columns in several caves are also decorated with animal and male and female figures. The caves of Khaṇḍagiri and Udaigiri have some extraordinary carvings, the most notable being a relief of Vishṇu in his boar incarnation, lifting the earth out of the abyss. Some of the finest sculpture in India is found at the cave temples of Aurungābād, Ellorā and Elephanta.

The Kushān period (second century BC to second century AD) saw the efflorescence of a Graeco-Buddhist form of art, especially in the province of Gandhāra* in Afghanistan. The influence of the Gandhāra school has been frequently belittled by Indian scholars, but there can be no doubt that it was of vital significance in the evolution of Indian art. Gandhāra art preserves evidence of a flourishing Hellenistic school in India from which many of the plastic masterpieces of later Indian art have been derived. Gandhāran sculpture captures the life of the times in very full detail, and we have passing before our view the whole rich panorama of that period in realistic scenes depicting all classes, 'from prince to pariah' (XIII, p. 54), their dress and customs, their domestic life in peacetime, their activities in war. Many Gandhāran reliefs have Greek subjects: Pallas Athene, bearded Atlantes, the Rape of Ganymede, Poseidon, Hercules, the hippocampus, tritons and centaurs.

During this time some nameless artist in Gandhāra took the Greek Apollo type and Indianized him in the first image of Buddha, giving him a Grecian profile, hyacinthine locks and Apollonian drapery, but seating him in the Indian fashion. Mahāyāna Buddhism which developed in this area spread this style throughout Asia. Buddhist sculpture reached perfection in the representation of Buddha. From the start Buddha's image was a masterpiece of supreme tranquillity, a perfect symbol of divine humanity.

It was only after Gandhāra that the school of Mathurā came into its own. The best work of Mathurā, produced between AD 150–300, is seen on railings and pillars in various sites, some of which consists of ornamental reliefs in foliate and medallion form. In them episodes of Buddha's life are carved on separate panels, and not within the framework of a single panel as at Bhārhut and Sānchī. It was at Mathurā that the Buddha image, conceived and perfected in Gandhāra was given its typically Indian features, and was turned out on a large scale. With it came scores of Bodhisattvas, Jainas, *tīrthaṅkaras*, and gods and goddesses of the Buddhist, Jain and Hindu pantheon. A feature of the Mathurā Buddhas is that most of them have a halo with an ornamental rim of semicircles, which some authorities believe is suggestive of a series of flattened snake hoods. This characteristic rim of semicircles is not found in Gandhāra nor in the later Gupta period, and when present in ancient Buddha images points unmistakably to Mathurā.

Among the Mathurā works of the Kushān period (second century BC to fourth century AD) are several that do not seem to have either Buddhist or Jain subjects, and were in fact given names by their discoverers drawn from alien themes. One such group is called Heracles and the Nemean Lion, another Silenus, and so on. Although Hellenistic influences are not excluded these works are now regarded as being Indian in character. The portrait sculpture of this period includes life-size images of Śaka and Kushān kings, including a now-headless figure of Kanishka believed to be the work of Central Asian craftsmen in India (XV, p. 86).

Many Mathurā sculptures depict scenes of revelry, dancing youths and girls, drinking and bacchanalian scenes; the natural and carefree female figures of the *yakshī* (lamia), the *vṛikshakā* (dryad) and the *apsarā* (nymph), richly jewelled, with prominent breasts, exaggeratedly broad hips, in sportive, graceful, or erotic attitudes, full of vigorous naturalism and frank sensuality, often lapsing into 'unabashed lewdness' (X, p. 525), all of which give evidence of the emergence of the full tide of Indian art.

The Mathurā workshops were commercialized and served as factories for the supply of images (mostly carved of the inferior mottled red sandstone from the local Sikri quarries), to Pāṭaliputra and Sārnāth in the east, Avanti and Ujjain in the west, and Taxila and even Central Asia in the north.

The work of the Mathurā school was taken in hand and perfected under the patronage of the Guptas (AD 320–490), whose sculpture represents the culmination of Mathurā art. Many of the Gupta shrines are adorned with stone sculptures of high quality and extraordinary vigour, portraying Hindu gods and goddesses. The masterpieces of the Gupta age are the sublime statues of Buddha, often shown standing, and robed in flowing drapery, with elaborately carved haloes. Such are the Buddhas of Sārnāth preaching his first sermon, or turning the wheel of the law. These superb Buddha figures express with matchless art the dignified serenity and majestic calm of the Blessed One. To the Gupta period belongs a wonderfully executed torso of a bodhisattva, now mutilated, found at Sānchī and at present in the Victoria and Albert Museum. The grace of the body is almost Grecian, and the neckband and waistband chastely carved, while the band across the shoulder with a deer-head decoration is a model of classical beauty. Contemporary with these works is a colossus of Buddha found at Sultāngunj and now in the Birmingham Museum, which is more than seven feet high, weighing over a ton, cast in pure copper by the *cire perdue* process. It is thought to have been fashioned in one of the Śaka satrapies about AD 450.

The sculptural art of the Pallavas (400–850) is seen at its best at Māmallapuram, particularly in the great carving on a perpendicular face of rock 88 feet long and 30 feet high, once called Arjuna's Penance, but renamed the Descent of the Ganges, a composition filled with a multitude of nāga kings and queens, flying beings, demons, men and animals. The Pallavas were also noteworthy as being the first to practice the kind of cire perdue bronze work that became famous under the Cholas. Although a few specimens of metal sculpture have been found before the Pallava period, there was no continuous tradition of metal sculpture in India and the art is believed to have reached the Pallava kingdom through traders from the West.

Chālukya (500–800) sculpture is found at the cave temples at Bādāmi and the structural temples there and at Aihole and Paṭṭadakal, and some of the work (especially the female figures) is said to be even superior to the Gupta in its dynamic force and freedom of movement. The contemporary Rāshṭrakūṭas (750–975) were responsible for some of India's finest carvings in the Elephanta Caves and in the Kailāsanātha temple at Ellorā.

The best examples of Orissan sculpture are found in the ninth and tenth century temples of Konārak and Bhuvaneśvar. The work is characterized by a profound sensuous appreciation of the living form. The figures of dancers and musicians in the Paraśurāmeśvara temple (750) are among the masterpieces of the Indian sculptor's art. Elsewhere, representations of animals such as the lion, elephant and horse are executed with power and sensitivity. A most extraordinary example of Orissan sculpture is found in the carvings of the Black Pagoda*.

Under the Pālas and Senas (730–1125) of Bengal Indian sculpture reached a high degree of excellence. The Pāla school was associated with Buddhist images in polished black stone, like the slender figures of Tārā and the bodhisattvas. But it was in metal casting that the best work was produced. The names of two master-craftsmen in stone work as well as painting have come down to us: Dhīmāna and Bhitpālo, both of the ninth century.

The finest Chandella (800–1204) sculptures are seen in the series of remarkable friezes on the temples of Khajurāho, depicting languorously posed females, and paring couples in passionate embrace. The work of the Solaṅkis (960–1240) is best represented at Girnār and Mount Ābū whose richly ornamental sculpture, stiff, formalized and lacking in naturalness, presents a fine display of conventional art.

Chola (900–1150) stone work is seen in the various Chola temples such as those built at Tanjore, but the Cholas are known particularly for their bronze sculpture executed by the cire perdue technique, an art acquired from the Pallavas. Excellent examples of this form are seen in the various figures of Śiva, of which Śiva Naṭarāja or Dancing Śiva is the most famous, and female lamp-bearers, statuettes of goddesses, and deified Śaivite saints.

The prodigal and richly ornamental style of Hoysaḷa (1100–1343) sculpture seen in Belūr and Halebīd is reminiscent of the work of the ivory carver, and in this respect is unequalled anywhere in India, and indeed in the world. It is said that among the models whose poses are immortalized in the temple carvings, was the beautiful queen Śantala of the Hoysaḷa dynasty. Also worthy of note are the wonderful animal friezes that decorate the temple walls.

Early in the fifteenth century the Chola and Chālukya schools merged and the best work of the South Indian sculptors was produced in the kingdom of Vijayanagar (1350–1565) whose influence lasted till the end of the sixteenth century. Most of the images are excessively embellished and lack the grace of the Chola period. The later Madura school of the Nāyyaka (1420–1736) was even more decorative and made little contribution to the development of the sculptural art of India.

Books

I. Anand, M. R. *Kama Kala: Notes on Hindu Erotic Sculpture*, Geneva, 1958.
II. Bachhofer, L. *Early Indian Sculpture*, 2 vols., Paris, 1929.
III. Boner, Alice. *Principles of Composition in Hindu Sculpture*, 1962.
IV. Bhattacharya, B. *Indian Buddhist Iconography*, Oxford, 1924.
V. Buchthal, H. *The Western Aspects of Gandhara Sculpture*, 1945.
VI. Codrington, K. de B. *Mediaeval Indian Sculpture*, 1929.
VII. Gangoly, O. C. *Indian Sculpture*, Calcutta, 1939.
VIII. Kar, C. *Classical Indian Sculpture*, London, 1950.
IX. Kramrisch, S. *Indian Sculpture*, 1933.
X. Majumdar, R. C. (Ed.) *The Age of Imperial Unity*, Bombay, 1951.
XI. Mitra, S. K. *The Early Rulers of Khajuraho*, Calcutta, 1958.
XII. Munshi, K. M. *The Saga of Indian Sculpture*, Bombay, 1957.
XIII. Smith, V. *History of Fine Art in India & Ceylon*, Ind. Ed. Bombay, n.d.
XIV. Thapar, D. R. *Icons in Bronze*, Bombay, 1961.
XV. Winstedt, R. (Ed.) *Indian Art*, London, 1947.
XVI. Zimmer, H. *The Art of Indian Asia*, New York, 2 vols., 1955.

SECRECY. The term *rahasya* is applied in Sanskirt texts to a mystery, a secret, a mystic doctrine or teaching, or generally to that which is hidden. Certain parts of the Vedas, and especially the Upanishads, are spoken of as rahasya. Many methods have been evolved for ensuring that esoteric doctrines are kept from being generally known. One such method is to use a form of language that is difficult to understand. A saying* of the *Bṛihad-āraṇyaka Upanishad* declares, 'The gods love the obscure and hate the obvious'. Sacred texts are frequently couched in a hermetic of symbolic manner called *saṁdhyā bhāshā*, 'twilight speech', employing an enigmatic, 'hidden' language, which has one meaning for the world and an entirely different meaning for the initiate. Ritual enigmas and riddles were in frequent use from Vedic times. *Mantras** and gnomic *ślokas* (verses) are such devices. These are not to be disclosed to the *paśu*, 'herd', i.e. the laity, but are reserved only for the *vīra*, 'heroes', or the initiated.

The purpose of *saṁdhyā* is usually to conceal secret doctrines from the masses, since the teachings can easily be misunderstood or misused and result in harm to the individual and danger to the community. Secrecy is also regarded as essential for preserving the potency of a doctrine, since its power is diffused if commonly known. Again, keeping a profound truth to oneself is to revere the truth and the guru who bestows it on one, and also to protect it from the influences of popular knowledge and the understanding of the vulgar. Speaking of their own teachings the tantras declare, 'The Vedas, Śāstras and Purāṇas are like harlots, accessible to all, but the tantrik science is well concealed like a woman of good family'. Finally, obscurity helps the pupil to rise, through the mystifications of ambiguity to a clear apprehension of the truth that breaks through all the distortions of communicated speech. Rahasya is therefore expressed through analogies, homologies, double-meanings, symbols, figures of speech, parables and legends.

Certain rahasya doctrines cannot even be put down in writing, however obscure, and may only be passed on by word of mouth. Teachings communicated verbally are sometimes spoken of as *karṇa-tantra*, 'ear-doctrines', so called because they are whispered into the initiate's ear. Many references to doctrines so delivered are found in the sacred writings. Thus in the *Bṛihad-āraṇyaka Upanishad* we are told that an enquirer named Artabhāga of the line of Jaratkāru questioned the sage Yājñavalkya about the destiny of the dead. Yājñvalkya replied, 'Artabhāga, take my hand. This is not for us to speak of in public. We two alone shall talk of this', and taking Artabhāga into a hidden place proceeded with the teaching. Rahasya methods include the imparting of the secret mantra*, which is only delivered by the guru when he is satisfied that his pupil will understand its import and will keep it as a great treasure, secret from all the world.

There are still other truths that are considered too profound even to be uttered, and an action is sometimes used to communicate them. Thus, in one of the profoundest messages delivered by the Buddha he said nothing but merely held up a flower. The significance of this act was understood by one of his disciples, who smiled, and the smile became the means of conveying the mystery to others. This smile of enlightenment was passed down through a succession of patriarchs until it reached Bodhidharma*, founder of Zen Buddhism.

The highest truth of all, the great 'truth of truths' (*satyasa satyam*) embodying the essence of divine wisdom is communicated in a state of complete silence and complete passivity. It reveals the mysteries of *śūnya** and other 'privatives', and is in effect the secret of secrets (*guhyād guhyam*).

Books

I. Crooke, W. 'Secret Messages & Symbols Used in India', *Journal of the Bihar & Orissa Research Society*, Bankipore, V., 1919, 461–2.
II. Woodroffe, J. (Arthur Avalon). *Principles of Tantra*, 2 vols., London, 1916.

SEDUCTION and its techniques was called *dūshaṇa*, a term meaning dishonouring or defiling, with particular reference to another man's wife or an unmarried girl. While condemned by the lawgivers the subject received frequent attention from writers on *kāmaśāstra*, and much of their advice was condensed in the form of aphorisms. Vātsyāyana and his successors give pointers regarding the types of women who are liable to succumb to male overtures without much resistance, the women who will resist such overtures, and the reasons for their resistance. Methods of seduction are also set forth. Sample *sūtras* on the subject are paraphrased below.

(1) The character of women* being what it is, most women may be seduced.
(2) Generally speaking it may be said that a woman desires every handsome man she sees, no less than a man desires every beautiful woman, although they do not or cannot for various reasons proceed further than mere wishing.
(3) The common notion that a man cares little for a woman who is easily won and desires one who is difficult is erroneous. Men welcome the easy gift, and do not always care for the trouble involved in obtaining the difficult.

(4) A woman refrains from intimacy for one or more of the following reasons: (*a*) because of her female nature, she shrinks even though she desires him; (*b*) love of her husband and family; (*c*) fear of discovery and scandal; (*d*) lack of opportunity; (*e*) fear that the man desires her only for her body and not because he loves her; (*f*) fear of being hurt and abandoned; (*g*) purely religious or moral considerations.
(5) Techniques of seduction vary according to circumstance; the character of the girl; the character of her father or husband; the nature of the community in which they dwell.
(6) Women's defences are weakened by (*a*) presents (*b*) praise (*c*) wine (*d*) music, and (*e*) persistence.
(7) Often if a woman remains unresponsive extreme methods are effective, for example, the man may threaten to force her to submit to his will and use physical violence to achieve his purpose. Or he may swear to commit suicide in some horrible manner.
(8) Sometimes an abject approach is successful, so that if all else fails he should fall at her feet and beg for her favours. Says Vātsyāyana 'However bashful, or angry, or cold she may be, she can never be completely indifferent to this gesture.'
(9) Bodily contact is useful. Thus, 'a man should cut out two figures on a leaf, representing himself and herself, and show them to her, touching her fingers or hands as he gives her the tracings'; or, 'he should sit near her and scratch his toes against her toes'; or, 'after washing his mouth he should spurt some water over her'; he should 'pretend to be ill so that she comes to his house and presses his head and feet'; he should 'touch her during games'.
(10) Suggestive tales are a means of softening her heart. He should tell her stories of great romances. He should relate his dreams with reference to other girls.
(11) Drugs, mantras and the casting of spells are not advisable. The technique of 'transferred love' commonly practised by the ignorant in the hope of securing the affections of the loved one should be avoided. In this the man or woman makes love to another while concentrating on the beloved. Such methods actually weaken the link that would otherwise draw the lover.
(12) In general the following can be made to succumb easily: the wife of an actor, dancer, jeweller, or one frequently absent on journeys; the young widow, maidservant, female ascetic, dancing girl, female artist or artisan, the working girl; a country girl on her first visit to a large town; a woman who keeps looking around at men as she walks; women who stand on the balcony and stare at passers-by; women who are fond of listening to tales of romance; women who have their own money and are not under anyone's control.
(13) A woman can be judged by the way she dresses. If she dresses to expose herself, she desires to be further exposed. If she wears a tight bodice which reveals the shape of her breast, she wants to be clasped tightly and longs for her bosom to be caressed.
(14) Women who are fond of drinking are of easy virtue. There is not much trouble in taking advantage of a woman who is even slightly tipsy, for 'a tipsy woman yearns for *gharshaṇa* (rubbing) above all else'.

(15) Women who love physical activity often yield during the lassitude that follows physical exertion, such as exercise, games or dancing.
(16) Women who delight in dressing up and showing off, present little difficulty, for the vain are weak by nature, and when flattered for their good looks feel the flattery incomplete unless it is followed up by more intimate activity where use is made of their charms.
(17) Excessive fondness for singing, and a tendency to garrulousness must be interpreted as a heightened sexual susceptibility. 'Excessive talkers have moist yonis'.
(18) Women who are fond of social activity, festivals, feeding the poor, visiting the sick, are restless, free from parental or husbandly control, and restless women succumb easily.
(19) Women married to men who are old, neglectful, unpleasant, miserly, jealous, dirty, ungainly, foul-smelling, sickly, deformed, uncouth and coarse, slovenly, superior or supercilious, can be easily had.
(20) But women are also perverse, and a woman married to an old man will seek the company of the young for a change, and one married to a young and dashing cavalier will look with longing on the mature and sedate man with grey hair. The handsome man will willingly be changed for a rough and ugly lover, and the tender lover for the cruel.
(21) A woman shows by these signs that she is losing interest in her husband, and it would be opportune when such signs are observed to prepare to seduce her: she speaks disparagingly of her husband before others; shows no signs of jealousy at his misdemeanours with other women; replies harshly or with indifference to his questions.
(22) Women can be won over by those in authority over their husbands, e.g. village women by village headmen, wives of shepherds by officers in charge of cattle, wives of traders by superintendents of trade, and any wives by the king.
(23) Women whose husbands, brothers, or sons are in trouble or in need, or seek employment; those who have transgressed the law and fear punishment, such women are easy prey.
(24) For those in authority in the kingdom seduction may be effected through bribery and threats; promises of advancement for the husband; guile, trickery or fraud by the intermediation of priests, mendicants, or beggar women. The king has little difficulty in getting the woman he wants, for finally, 'If a woman resist, her husband should be arrested as a traitor, and she should be made a slave in the royal harem'.
(25) As a last resort force is recommended for all. The *Bṛihadāraṇyaka Upanishad* says, 'A man should invite a woman to approach him. If she refuses he should bribe her. If she still does not grant him his desire he should hit her with a stick or with his hand and snatch her glory'.

Books

See under Kāmaśāstra.

SELEUCIDS. On the death of Alexander the Great in 323 BC his empire was partitioned among his generals, and Syria and Western Asia fell to the lot of his greatest commander, Seleucus Nicator (305–280 BC) one of whose first exploits was the attempt to recapture the Panjāb in 305 BC. Finding the conquest a more difficult task than he had imagined he was glad to come to terms with Chandragupta Maurya* the redoubtable śūdra who ruled Magadha and who now blocked his path.

Chandragupta who had received assistance from the Greeks in his struggle against the last ruler of the previous dynasty, Dhana Nanda, was also awake to the desirability of a treaty with so powerful an ally as Alexander's greatest general, and a treaty was accordingly arranged by which Chandragupta secured certain provinces in the north-west of India, while Seleucus was given six hundred elephants to assist him in his war against his rival Antigonus. The treaty was sealed by the marriage of Chandragupta with a Greek princess, probably a daughter of Seleucus. For his part Seleucus was presented with some potent aphrodisiacs, a commodity for which India was famous.

The Seleucid treaty ushered in a term of friendly relations between the Greeks and Indians. A policy of philhellenism was adopted by the Mauryan kings and the 'services of Greek philosophers and administrators were eagerly sought by the imperial government' (V, p. 273).

The ambassador of Seleucus to the court of Chandragupta was Megasthenes (306–298 BC) fragments of whose lost account of the Mauryan* empire are preserved in Strabo, Pliny, Arrian, Diodorus, Photius and others. Megasthenes was only the first of such envoys from the Hellenistic princes of the West, for Deimachus was the Greek emissary of Antiochus I, Soter (280–261 BC) to the Mauryan court of Bindusāra; and Dionysius was sent as ambassador to India by the Egyptian ruler Ptolemy Philadelphus (285–274 BC). The observations of these and other officials and travellers provide a rich legacy for the interpretation of life in India during one of the most important phases of her history.

In about 250 BC, while Aśoka* was reigning in Pāṭaliputra, Diodotus the governor of the Greek colonies in Bactria and Parthia threw off the Seleucid yoke and founded an independent kingdom. The succeeding Seleucid kings, Antiochus II (261–246 BC) and Seleucus III (226–223) were unable to suppress the rebellion. The reign of Antiochus III, the Great (223–187) marks the end both of the Seleucid suzerainty in the north-west and of the friendly relations between the Seleucids and India that had subsisted for so long. In 206 BC Antiochus led an expedition into the north-western provinces and forced the then Indian ruler to surrender a number of war elephants for his campaigns. He then tried to reconquer the lost Bactrian and Parthian provinces, but finding the task hopeless was forced to acknowledge their independence. Thereafter the Bactrians* were firmly established on the north-west frontiers of India.

Books

I. Bevan, E. R. *The House of Seleucus*, 2 vols, London, 1902.

II. Cunningham, A. *The Coins of Alexander's Successors in the East*, London, 1873.

III. Majumdar, R. C. (Ed.) *The Age of Imperial Unity*, Bombay, 1951.

IV. Puri, B. N. *India as Described by Early Greek Writers*, Allahabad, 1939.
V. Raychaudhuri, H. *Political History of Ancient India*, Calcutta, 6th Ed., 1953.

SEN, KESHAB CHANDRA (1838–1884), honoured by his compatriots with the title of *Brahmāṛishi*, was born in Calcutta, a kinsman of the Sena kings of Bengal. He was the son of wealthy and influential parents, and the grandson of the Secretary of the Asiatic Society of Bengal.

In 1857 he joined the Brahmo Samāj (Society of God) and collaborated with Devendranāth Tagore on a plan of action for the advancement of the Samāj. Keshab lectured in English and Devendranāth in the vernacular on the doctrines of theism and the philosophy of the Brahmo religion. While only twenty-two years of age he published his first tract and in partnership with Devendranāth launched the influential fortnightly, *Indian Mirror*, advocating social, religious, and political reform. He also founded a number of branch samājes in Bombay, Madrās and elsewhere.

Early in life Keshab began having mystical experiences. He felt deeply the inadequacy of human effort, and himself derived much strength from prayer, and contemplation of the Divine. He emphasized the need for repentance as a prerequisite to any attempt to reach godwards, and held that prayer was an essential discipline and indispensable adjunct to a godly life. He regarded prayer as a longing of the soul and laid much stress on its spontaneous outpouring. While praying he would wait for divine commands (*ādeśa*) and often claimed to have heard the voice of God. 'If this be madness', he said, 'I wish to be counted among the mad. It is the madness of faith. It is the lunacy of salvation.' He believed in 'intuition' which he defined as being above, anterior to and independent of reflection. Such intuitions were Cause, Substance, Power, Infinity, Duty. God was not a philosophical or historical divinity, but an ever-living and ever-present Reality. His outlook was deeply coloured by association with Christian missionaries for whom he had a profound regard. Through his influence many elements of Christianity were incorporated into the Brahmo dharma, such as the doctrine of the Trinity (which he identified with Sachchidānanda), Baptism and the Lord's Supper. Christ, he said, comes 'to fulfil and perfect that religion of communion for which Indians have been panting'.

As a reformer Keshab advocated widow-remarriage and the removal of the brāhminical thread. He rejected the entire Hindu philosophical system, including Vedānta. He sought to make social reform a plank for his Brahmo dharma, and for this and other reasons the disciple was finally obliged to break with his master, Devendranāth Tagore. In 1866 he appeared to be turning towards Christianity and his conversion seemed imminent. But he was unable to accept the uniqueness of Christ, believing that other men had also been 'above ordinary humanity'.

In the same year he founded the *Bhāratvarshīya Brahmo Samāj* (The Brahmo Samāj of India) to include peoples of all races and communities, based on the idea of the Fatherhood of God and the brotherhood of man. It had its own scriptures, the *Śloka-saṁgraha*, embodying theistic texts taken from Hindu, Buddhist, Jewish, Christian, Muhammadan, Zoroastrian and Confucian sources. In contradistinction, the older Brahmo Samāj of

Devendranāth Tagore was now called Ādi Samāj (First or Old Samāj) and became progressively more and more brāhminical in its creed.

The new Samāj of Keshab Chandra Sen taught that God's saving mercy adapts itself to the requirements of all times, places and peoples, according to the peculiarities of each race; that there was nothing specifically unique in the Hindu dharma and that its adaptation to the present age made a radical reform essential.

'The wide universe is the temple of God. Wisdom is the pure land of pilgrimage. Truth is the everlasting scripture. Love is the true spiritual culture. The destruction of selfishness is the true asceticism. So declare the Brahmos.'

Faith, he said, is the root of all religion, and prudence he termed 'the arithmetic of fools'.

In 1870 Keshab went to England where he was well received, among others by Queen Victoria. He gave over seventy lectures and talks in various public halls and chapels. He returned to India with fresh ideas of reform, especially with regard to the education and emancipation of women, and the dissemination of low-priced literature. He advocated temperance, organized poor relief, established an industrial school for boys, a working men's institute, an institute for young men, a society for promoting literacy and social intercourse among all classes. He formulated a new marriage ritual, discouraged child-marriage, gave his support to the remarriage of widows and inter-caste marriage. In 1872 he persuaded the Government to pass an Act legalizing Brahmo marriages, which was hailed as 'the crowning success of the prolonged efforts of reformers for the amelioration of the social life of India'. At about this time he met Dayānanda* who was soon to found the Ārya Samāj, and Rāmakṛishṇa* whom he introduced to the outside world.

Towards the end of his life Keshab's ideas grew increasingly vague and odd. For all his painstaking efforts to raise the ages for marriageable minors, he allowed his own daughter to marry the son of the Mahārāja of Cooch Bihār, although both were well under the age limits fixed by him. His appeal to *ādeśa* (divine command) fell on deaf ears and his followers began to lose faith in his 'guruism' and his ever-growing belief in his own divine commission. A schism in the Society resulted in a new samāj, called the *Sādhāraṇ Brahmo Samāj*, being founded in 1878, which made steady and solid progress in the field of education.

From this time on Keshab preached a new dispensation received, he claimed, through divine revelation, and taught mystical doctrines, which were a medley of Hinduism and Christianity, Yoga and the Cross. In 1881 he changed the name of his own samāj to *Nava Vidhāna* or New Dispensation, appointed twelve disciples to spread his teachings and flew a banner displaying the Cross, crescent and trident. He called God 'Mother', revived the old homa or Vedic sacrifices, and the āratī or fire-waving ceremony, introduced Chaitanya's religious dance, and the celebration of *Durgā Pūjā*, and expounded polytheism and idolatry as forms of theism. He suffered from periodic spells of profound nervous depression and his influence steadily waned, although he continued to be respected and even revered by all sections of society until his death in 1884.

Books

I. Farquhar, J. N. *Modern Religious Movements in India*, New York, 1915.
II. Mozoomdar, P. C. *Life and Teachings of Keshub Chunder Sen*, Calcutta, 1887.
III. Müller, Max. *Biographical Essays*, 1884.
IV. Parekh, M. C. *Rajarshi Keshab Chander Sen*, Rajkot, 1926.
V. Sastri, S. *History of the Brahmo Samaj*, 2 vols., Calcutta, 1911–12.
VI. Sen, Keshab Chandra. *Lectures in India*, 1890.
VII. Sen, P. K. *Keshab Chander Sen*, Calcutta, 1938.

SENSES. The term *indriya* is used for the organs of sense, by means of which we have direct perception* of the world about us and through which we are able to operate on the material substances* of this world. The *āśraya* or 'seat' of perception resides in the subtle body and operates over two groups of sensory and operative agents. These two groups of indriya or agents of perception and action are the *jñānendriya* and the *karmendriya.*

The *jñānendriya* are the 'knowing' agents, by means of which man apprehends the gross forms of manifested substance. The sphere or *vishaya* of the knowing agents is determined by the pure elements, and includes the fields of sound, touch, form, taste and smell, each agent being served in the physical body by an end organ or *golaka*, which is the actual physical medium of sense, namely, the ears, eyes, tongue, nose and skin. The names of the five jñānendriya are: (1) *Śrotra*, the power to hear, or to experience śabda (sound) through the agency of the karṇa (ear). (2) *Tvak* (or *tvach*), the power to experience sparśa (touch) i.e. to feel, by means of the charman (skin). (3) *Chakshus*, the power to experience *rūpa* (form) i.e. to see, by means of the *akshī* (eye). (4) *Rasana*, the power to experience *rasa* (taste), by means of the *jihvā* (tongue). (5) *Ghrāṇa*, the power to experience *gandha* (odour) i.e. to smell, by means of the *nāsikā* (nose).

The karmendriya are the 'action' agents, by means of which a man does things. They are: (1) *Vāk* (or *vāch*), the power to speak, through the agency of the larynx, throat and tongue. (2) *Upastha*, the power to procreate, through the organs of generation. (3) *Pāyu*, the power to excrete, through the excretory organs. (4) *Pāṇi*, the power to grasp, by means of the hand. (5) *Pāda*, the power of locomotion, by means of the feet.

Books

See under Philosophy.

SERPENT WORSHIP. The generic name for the various snake deities and serpent people of Hindu mythology is *Nāga*, frequently represented as gigantic snakes of the cobra species with expanded hood and many lesser heads, or with human head and serpent body. The spectacle marks on the cobra's head are supposed to be a half *svastika* (*svastikārdha*). Serpents are associated with Śiva and other 'dread' deities. They form the girdle of Śiva and adorn his person. His sacred thread is the serpent, his hair is knotted with one, he has serpents for bangles and anklets.

Snake deities are custodians of the treasures of land and sea, and are associated with hundreds of lakes, springs and wells throughout India. They also protect sacred precincts such as old abandoned temples (an avenue flanked by stone nāgas still traditionally forms the entrance to some temples), and ancient city boundary marks. Anthills are their favourite haunts, and many anthills are believed to be the abode of nāga treasure guardians. Departed spirits sometimes take snake forms and serpents are often regarded as representing one's deceased ancestors.

The Nāgas inhabit the chthonian kingdom of **Pātāla** (or Nāgaloka), the serpent region. It is the most beautiful realm of all the worlds of heaven, earth and hell. The sage Nārada once paid a visit to Pātāla and declared that it was far more beautiful than Indra's heaven, offering every imaginable luxury and sensuous delight. Hence it was also called Kāmaloka (love-kingdom). It was once conquered by the jealous Gandharvas, but was recaptured by the Nāgas with the help of Nārada. **Bhogavatī,** 'delightful', the capital of Pātāla is a jewel-walled (*maṇi-bhītti*) city of incalculable riches, where stands the fabulous *maṇi-maṇḍapa,* 'jewel-palace' of the Nāga king.

The Nāgas possess secrets little dreamt of by creatures living on the surface, and theirs is a realm of magic and magnificence. Here warriors who die in battle are made welcome by lovely nāga maidens who tend to them and satisfy their wants. The snake-people have great wisdom and are possessed of many wonderful powers. It was the touch of their king Vāsuki's jewel that restored the dead Arjuna to life; it was a draught of the Nāgas that restored the dead Bhīma and endowed him with immense strength. Female Nāgas were extremely beautiful and sometimes married mortals, e.g. Ulūpī, who married Arjuna.

Ophiolatria or snake worship was common in India from pre-Aryan times and is still widespread throughout the sub-continent. Temples are dedicated to snakes, special festivals (e.g. Nāgapañchamī) are held in their honour, and in several rites associated with their worship milk and sometimes blood is poured over the serpent images.

Mythologically, Nāgas are the progeny of **Kadrū,** daughter of the archṛishi Daksha and one of the thirteen who married the sage Kaśyapa. Her offspring accordingly bear the metronymic **Kādraveya.** The Kādraveya are the mortal enemies of their half-brother Garuḍa*, the eagle king. Kadrū, also called Surasā, appears in the *Rāmāyaṇa* trying to prevent Hanumān from giving chase to Rāvaṇa. She opens her mouth to swallow Hanumān but he distends his body to prevent her; she opens her mouth still wider, and he grows still bigger, and this goes on until her mouth is of cavernous dimensions. Then he suddenly shrinks to the size of a thumb and comes out of her right ear. She admits defeat and allows him to pass. Kadrū's chief descendants were the **Mahoraga** (*mahā-uraga,* 'great serpents') or **Nāgarāja** ('serpent kings'). In the Purāṇas several figure as guardians of the cardinal points (*see* direction). They are said to be nine, twelve, forty and sometimes eighty-eight hundred in number. The best known are named below.

ŚESHA, 'residue', so named because he was born from what remained after the creation of the three worlds and their inhabitants. Śesha's thousand heads are expanded into a mighty hood called *Maṇidvīpa* (*see* gems), and he forms the couch of the god Vishṇu who reclines on his coils and is shaded by the multiple hood which spreads like a canopy over his head. Śesha is depicted garbed in purple wearing a white necklace, and when shown with hands holds in one hand a plough and in the other a pestle. In cosmology* the earth is said to rest on the head of Śesha. At the end of each day of Brahmā (*see* aeon) all creation is destroyed by the fire that issues from the mouth of Śesha. He is frequently confused or identified with the other Great Nāgas, especially Ananta and Vāsuki. In some legends he became incarnate in Lakshmaṇa, Balarāma, and the grammarian Patañjali. Śesha is also known as Śeshanāga.

ANANTA, 'endless', is often identified with Śesha. He is dark blue in colour and guardian of the east. His great coils encircle the earth and Ananta therefore symbolizes eternity. He is sometimes regarded as a manifestation of Vishṇu. His wife is Ananta-śīrshā.

VĀSUKI, seven-headed Nāga king, is green in colour and guardian of the north. He served as the churning rope during the operations for obtaining amṛita, the divine nectar* or the elixir of life.

TAKSHAKA, nine-hooded son of Kadrū, is saffron coloured. He was the lord of the snake people against whom Janamejaya, great-grandson of Arjuna (*see* Abhimanyu) waged a war of extermination; his life was saved by Āstīka (see below) who persuaded Janamejaya to forgo his persecution of the serpent race. Uttering the name Āstīka is popularly believed to save a man from the effects of snake-bite. In many legends Takshakā is a female and the wife of Vāsuki.

KĀLIYA, a five-headed, fire-breathing demon serpent who dwelt in a deep pool of the river Kālindī (the Jamnā), devastating the countryside and menacing the herdsmen and other friends of the youthful Kṛishṇa. The boy-god plunged into the pool and was immediately wrapped in the deadly coils of the Nāga. Exercising his divine power he overcame the serpent and its brood, and placing his foot triumphantly on Kāliya's head was on the point of slaying him when he was entreated by Kāliya's wife to spare his life. Kṛishṇa agreed, but commanded him to leave the country and make his abode in the ocean. The *asura* Kālanemi was one of Kāliya's incarnations.

MĀNASĀ, sister of Vāsuki, is the queen of snakes, often represented with broken hips and blind of one eye. She was the wife of the sage Jaratkāru*, and this couple begat the sage Āstīka (see above). Mānasā has special power in counteracting the venom of snakes, and during the four months of the rainy season while Vishṇu sleeps she protects men from snake-bite. She is widely worshipped in rural Bengal, and is also known as Mānasādevī, Jagadgaurī, Nityā (eternal), Padmavatī, Vishaharā ('poison loss', because she has the power to counteract the venom of snakes).

Other important serpents are Varuṇa, white-skinned, seven-hooded guardian of the west; Padmaka (or Padmanābha), five-hooded, green-coloured, guardian of the south; Śaṅkhapāla, seven-hooded, yellowish guardian of the southwest; Kulika, thirty-hooded, brown guardian of the northwest; Mahāpadma, eleven-hooded, golden guardian of the northeast; Karkoṭaka, blue Nāga king, often depicted as a human being with a snake's tail. In mythology he was saved from fire by Nala*, and his people were defeated by the Haihaya* kings. Kambala, snake wizard, seldom seen; Dhṛitarāshṭra, a multi-hooded serpent of enormous size; Ābhoga, guardian of the southeast, who protects Varuṇa with his hood.

Books

I. Anonymous. *Ophiolatreia: An Account of Serpent Worship*, 1889.
II. Fergusson, J. *Tree & Serpent Worship*, 2nd Ed., London, 1873.
III. Oldham, C. F. 'The Nagas', *Journal of the Royal Asiatic Society*, 1901, pp. 461–73.
IV. Oldham, C. F. *The Sun and the Serpent*, 1910.
V. Rivett-Carnac, J. H. 'The Snake Symbol and the Worship of Siva', *Journal of the Royal Asiatic Society of Bengal*, Calcutta, xlviii, 17–30, 1829.
VI. Vogel, J. P. *Indian Serpent Lore*, London, 1926.

SEX MYSTICISM. Two forms of sexuality are distinguished in Hinduism. The first is sex for pleasure and procreation, the second is sex in its mystical and magical aspect. In the latter case power is achieved by control over sexual activity.

The first category forms the subject of erotics*, in which kāma or sexual love is treated as one of the purushārthas or ends of life (*see* ethics). The enjoyment of woman is extolled in numberless passages in Indian literature. It is held to be the most glorious thing in earth and heaven; as that which gives significance to living; as the true end of human existence. Even the ascetic sees before him as the goal of his austerities the possession of many women in a future incarnation, 'and this view breaks through,' says Meyer, 'even in grave, deeply ethical writings'. Kalayāṇamalla, sixteenth century writer on erotics, held that in this world of fleeting shadows, there is but one reality, the pleasure to be had from intercourse with woman; it is even superior to the bliss of union with the infinite.

Sex in its magical or mystical aspect is also prominent in Hinduism. Sex rites are practised in numerous cults, some of which have a long antecedent history. The earliest evidence of a sex cult is found in the Mohenjodaro seals, and the erect liṅga of the Śiva prototype of the Indus Valley, as well as the phallic and yoni stones found there.

The *Ṛig-veda* speaks of the indigenous phallus worshippers (*śiśna-devāḥ*) with disapproval, but in later Vedic writings eroticism and sex symbolism begin to gain ground. The White *Yajur-Veda* contains several passages relating to coition, one of which has been described as 'revoltingly obscene'; it comprises a series of dialogues between Vedic priests and their female partners, which go into lurid details of the sexual act. In the *Atharva-Veda* coition is conceived of in terms of a fire ritual and the rubbing together of two fire-sticks, the *aśvattha* and the *śamī*. 'The aśvattha (*ficus religiosa*) has mounted the śamī (*mimosa suma*); then a male child is produced. That do we bring to our wives.'

The Brāhmaṇas and Upanishads have several references to the act of union. The *Aitareya Brāhmaṇa* of the *Ṛig-veda* details the connection between coitus and the recitation of sacred verses in the Vājapeya* sacrifice. 'He separates the first two syllables, the woman separates her thighs; he utters the last two syllables the man activates his hips. This is pairing.' Another Brāhmaṇa compares oblations of ghee and rice to sexual union; 'Ghee is the milk of the woman and rice grains the essence of the man. Such is pairing and by this means does he propagate'. The *Śatapatha Brāhmaṇa* of the White *Yajur-veda* prescribes a certain *yoshā* (female) shape for the fire altar, and a *vṛishaṇa* (testicle) shape for the fire. The *Bṛihadāraṇyaka Upanishad* which is replete with phallic symbolism says, 'When Prajāpati created woman he revered her below, therefore should one revere woman below. He then drew out from himself the stone which projects (liṅga) and with that he impregnated her'. The *Garbhopanishad* purports to give information on sexual matters and explains how semen is produced.

Passages from the Brāhmaṇas and Upanishads speak of coition as a form of sacred rite and draw close parallels between the two. Thus, woman is equated with the sacred place; her hips and haunches with the sacrificial ground; the mons veneris to the altar, the pubic hairs to the *kuśa* grass, the moist labia to the soma press, the yellow vulva to prepared fuel, the red-tipped phallus to the ember, lust to smoke, penetration to the mystic chants, voluptuousness to sparks, movement to the burning heat, orgasm to the living flame and semen to the oblation.

Ritual sexuality is enjoined in the horse sacrifice, in the *mahāvrata* ceremonies, in the *vāmadevya* ritual (described in the *Chhāndogya Upanishad*), in the *vājapeya* and a host of others. Devotional literature both Śaivite and Vaishṇavite abounds in sexual analogies and many of the hymns have a strong erotic element in them.

Great temples have been built for sun, Saturn, and sex cults, and their walls depict all too plainly the purpose for which they were meant. Temple sculptures which portray coital postures and, in some instances, perversions, including animality, depicting the zoolatrous liasons of Hindu deities, are found at Konārak in the Black Pagoda; in the Bhuvaneśvar figures, the Mīnākshī temple pillars, Ellora sculptures, the Kauśāmbī terracotta figures of the Śuṅga period, and in Khajurāho. When Hiuen-Tsang the Chinese pilgrim visited India in the seventh century he described the still extant friezes of the notorious Sūrya temple at Multān as having the most licentious sculpture.

The philosophical basis of sex mysticism is comprehensively expounded in Hindu and Buddhist scriptures. All the streams of cult sexuality flow into the great river of Tantrism* for it is in Tantrism that one finds its full rationale, its completest expression, and its most extended philosophy. Sex is a natural activity, but like many other such natural activities has a transcendent and esoteric side which can be utilized in secret ways to reveal to man the hidden truths of the universe. The sexual act is a means of salvation, and one can obtain *mukti* (redemption) through *bhukti* (pleasure). Copulation brings siddhis and knowledge of Brahma. In gross sensual pleasure, as expounded in erotics, we have the lowest and most transient form of this revelation, which in any case cannot be clearly discerned because the participant's mind is clouded with the fumes of passion. To transcend this carnal state one must gain an understanding of the true meaning of sexual activity.

In the physical world the male and female genders* symbolize a dichotomy that exists in the Absolute as Śiva and Śakti, Kṛishṇa and Rādhā, Buddha and Tārā, and the bodhisattva Vajradhara and his śakti Lochanā. The power of lust sustains the cosmic order. There is an intimate connection between cosmic creation and the primal urge of men and women; and differences are resolved and harmony achieved between the macrocosm and the microcosm through sexual union.

The sex act is therefore regarded as the channel for the highest spiritual experience and a means of salvation. *Maithuna*, 'pairing', or coition, 'the origin of being, the root of the world, the foundation of pleasure', is elevated into a rite of spiritual enlightenment. Obligatory ritual practices among certain vāmachāra sects require regular sexual congress between monks and nuns, and *vīras* and *śaktis*, as in *chakrapūjā** and *strīpūja**. To realize the state of absoluteness the man conceives of himself as the male deity, then by *nyāsa* he transfigures his partner so that she becomes the śakti or his divine female counterpart and the consecrated field for his operations. The pair then unite, physically, mentally and spiritually.

These rites are preceded by periods of preparation, demanding prolonged concentration on matters pertaining to the sexual principle and the organs of generation. Meditation is prescribed on gods and goddesses joined in postures of maithuna. In certain forms of strīpūjā the devotees meditate on the exposed yoni of a living virgin or married woman; in chakrapūjā the rite commences with homage to a design on the ground symbolizing nine yonis. In one form of *trāṭaka* (*see* meditation) the ascetic fixes his eyes on the tip of his erected member and focuses his thoughts on Kāma god of lust. The phallus itself is frequently an object of worship. One of Śiva's names is Ūrdhva-liṅga or Ūrdhva-meḍhra, 'erect phallus', and one of the Indus Valley seals of a Śiva prototype portrays him thus. Among Śiva's symbols is the *jyā* or bowstring, and *sajjikā* is the name given to practitioners of a left-hand cult of sexuality and violence. Man in certain Śaivite cults was known as *śūlabhṛit*, i.e. endowed with a *śūla*, ' dart', or male member, which was used either autosexually (Śiva was known as Śūlapāṇi, ' penis holder') or in some unproductive form, e.g. by intercourse with a śūlā or prostitute.

It is frequently pointed out in the texts that union with a woman has its dangers, for coitus ends in emission, as a result of which man loses his vital energy and sustains a spiritual loss. Two methods are employed to obviate these hazards. One is the ascetic method of absolute continence, the other is the yogic technique of non-spilling (*askanda*). The first method is also used for occult purposes, based on the recognition of the powers resulting from the control of the sex urge. It implies the subjugation of the senses, and its symbol is the nude figure of the deity or saint with flaccid liṅga, spoken of as *nīcha-meḍhra*, ' down-penis'. Such a pendulous (*pralamba*) liṅga is shown in the famous statue of the Jain saint Gomaṭeśvara.

Jainism in fact greatly lessens the emphasis usually placed on sex in Hindu texts. Sex is a gateway which, when opened by sexual activity, releases and dissipates potent forces that could otherwise be utilized for self. But sexual indulgence is also a weakness and an evil to be overcome since it is the chief manifestation of lust. Besides, triumph over sex represents a conquest of the lower self by the higher, the desired goal of Jains and Buddhists. One of Śiva's weapons, the jyāhroḍa or unstrung bow, symbolizes his passive state as the ascetic Śiva.

The technique of askanda, 'non-spilling', is one of the great secrets of certain sex cults. It is used by adepts who seek to gain siddhis through the absorption of the potencies latent in unexpended semen. It entails the regulation of the sex act and the arrest of ejaculation by specific techniques, including breathing, a process spoken as of 'the immobility of the breath and semen', and in some cases as a 'return of the semen' (*see* bindu), even after it has been expended.

The restless agitation of gross sexual pleasure ending in emission (vega) must be controlled and transmuted into a motionless state characterized by the suspension of all ordinary processes of the mind, and the feeling of absolute homogeneity on the psychical plane, culminating in the non-dual state of supreme bliss which is the ultimate reality.

Maithuna thus becomes a type of *paramudrā**, a combined and unified concrete mudrā. There is no movement but a coming together in an archaic and symbolic pose that becomes the centre of a psychic whirlpool into which are drawn tremendous occult potencies that enter and operate through the united couple. There are many variations of this mudrā some of which are found in iconographic representations, in secret diagrams, drawings and paintings. While this pose is assumed many 'interior' acts take place, for which the *āsanas, mantras, prāṇayāmas* and other disciplines were merely a preparation. It is in fact the consummation of a long and difficult apprenticeship.

The pairing couple, during this act of esoteric maithuna, represent the union of the genders*, and embody a plane of being where thought is stilled, the breath immobilized, and semen arrested, and where man is able to contemplate the ultimate reality face to face. The supreme bliss that proceeds from ritual sexuality is believed to be the height of religious experience. In this state of non-duality all differences vanish, and everything, high and low, good and bad, ugly and beautiful is held to be the same. It is while in this pose that the couple apprehend the mystery of the whole cosmic process and taste the transcendent bliss of divine experience.

Many names are given to this state of esoteric maithuna of which the following are examples: *advaya*, 'non-duality'; *kāma-kalā*, 'love-time'; *aṅga-saṅga*, 'body-contact'; *gamana*, 'going'; *mahā-sukha*, 'great-bliss'; *mehanā*, the male organ; *rata*, 'gratification'; *rahas*, 'secret'; *rati-saṁgara*, 'love-battle'; *sama-rasa*, 'same-emotion'; *saṁ-prayoga*, 'together-yoked'; *saṁbhoga*, 'together enjoyment'; *saṁ-sarga*, 'together streaming'; *surata*, 'blessed joy'; *upashthya*, 'genitalation'; *vyavāya*, 'copulation'; *yāmala, yugala, yojana*, 'yoked'; *yuganaddha*, a state of union.

Books

I. Anand, M. R. *Kama Kala*, Geneva, 1958.
II. Campbell, R. A. *Phallic Worship*, 1888.
III. Dulaure, J. *The Gods of Generation*, N. Y., 1933.
IV. Gangoly, O. C. 'The Mithuna in Indian Art, *Rupam*, Calcutta, 22–23, 1925.
V. Goldberg, B. *The Sacred Fire: Sex in Religion*, London, 1931.
VI. Knight, R. P. *A Discourse on the Worship of Priapus*, London, 1865.
VII. Meyer, J. J. *Sexual Life in Ancient India*, London, 1930.
VIII. Phadke, N. S. *Sex Problems in India*, Bombay, 1929.

IX. Pusalker, A. D. 'Sisnadevah in Rigveda and Phallus Worship in Indus Valley', *Sarupa-Bharati*, Hoshiarpur, 1954.
X. Thomas, P. *Kama-Kalpa: The Hindu Ritual of Love*, Bombay, n.d.
XI. Wall, O. A. *Sex & Sex Worship*, London, 1919.

SIDDHI, 'attainment', or *vibhūti*, 'manifestation', are terms used for supernatural powers acquired by certain individuals. Patañjali declared that 'birth (i.e. heredity or natural endowment), drugs, mantras, austerities and *saṁyama* (concentration)' are means of gaining such powers, but they are generally believed to be acquired through training, especially in Haṭha Yoga.

Siddhis are also considered to be the direct or indirect result of a quest for enlightenment or knowledge. The pursuit of any method for attaining to such knowledge is termed *sādhanā*, 'gaining'; the person practicing sādhanā is called a *sādhaka* (fem. sādhikā), and the successful sādhaka is a *sādhu*. Since siddhis are magical in character the terms sādhana and sādhu* are also frequently used for sorcery and sorcerer respectively. It should be noted that the term *siddha*, although of identical origin, is applied to an adept of a special category (*see* nātha) and is not synonymous with sādhu.

There are supposed to be eight great siddhis, but scores of siddhis are actually enumerated, and no *āsana* (yogic posture), *prāṇayāma* (breathing exercise), or *mantra* (spell) is described in the textbooks but is followed by promises of the siddhis that accrue from its practice. The eight great siddhis are: (1) *aṇimā* or shrinking: the power of becoming infinitely small so that 'one can see things of the minutest size, even the inside of the *aṇu* or atom'; (2) *mahimā* or expanding: the power of becoming as vast as the cosmos and being able 'to watch the functioning of the galaxies as though all the worlds were laid out before one'; (3) *laghimā* or weightlessness: the power that enables one to levitate and move about at extraordinary speed; (4) *garimā* or weightfulness: the power of becoming 'even as heavy as a mountain, so that one cannot be moved'; (5) *prāpti* or the power of being transported anywhere so that 'one can touch distant objects like the moon'; (6) *prākāmya* or the power of an irresistible will: the power to obtain anything merely by desiring it. It is related to another siddhi often listed with it, namely, *kāma-avasāyitva*, the power of perfect contentment; (7) *vaśitva*, the power to 'control all creatures and elements, past, present and future'; and (8) *īśitva* or overlordship, by which 'one can rule over all things and enjoy unrivalled glory becoming like a god, and even create and destroy creatures, past, present and future'.

Among the lesser siddhis named many relate to those powers that 'give release from *saṁsāra*' i.e. from the cycle of transmigration. Certain āsanas (yogic postures) are said to 'unlock the gates of final liberation', others can 'give eternal salvation', or 'make as nothing the wheel of destiny'.

Some siddhis confer supernatural perception, such as knowledge of 'one's previous births and births to come'. The one who remembers his previous births, even to the things studied by him is known as a *jātismara*, 'life rememberer'. Other siddhis give knowledge of 'all hidden and subtle things'; knowledge of 'the heavenly worlds, of the planets, stars, universes and the whole cosmos'; understanding of 'the language of birds, beasts, reptiles, fishes and insects'; the foreknowledge of when and how one is going to die.

Among the superhuman faculties to be gained are the power of leaving the body at will, of flying through the air, in the body or out of the body; mastery over the elements; supernormal eyesight so that one can see 'even as far as the Pleiades'; supernormal hearing so that one can 'hear the grass as it grows'; the power of divination in all its forms; the power of turning baser metals into gold; control over gold and all precious metals and jewels; thought-reading, and 'power over all mortals, past present and future.'

Health and strength are among the more commonly named siddhis, especially those following yogic practices. These promise, 'perfection of body and strength, and bodily charm'; 'destruction of all ills'; 'the killing of all internal parasites'; 'cleansing the blood vessels of the heart'; the ability to 'withstand any degree of heat or cold'; and 'physical perfection so that one need have no fear of the god of death'.

Phallic siddhis are very numerous and there are many glowing descriptions of the wonderful sexual powers bestowed on one as a reward for devotion to certain practices. One can become 'irresistible to all women, past, present and future'; one can 'duplicate one's body so that one can enjoy thousands of women simultaneously' (*see* Saubari and gopī); or translate oneself into any form desired 'so as to enjoy the lust of any animal'. There is also the power called *parapūrakāyapraveśa* or 'the transcendently satisfying body-filling', which enables a man to enter into the body of another person in order to 'learn his mind, understand his experiences, and even enjoy his wives'. The 'all conquer-siddhis' appertaining to the dimensions and capacity of the male member are equally astounding.

In case anything has been overlooked in the long list of siddhis given, there is one all-inclusive siddhi known as the *para-siddhi*, 'transcendent power', in which all possibilities and impossibilities are comprehended.

Patañjali speaks of siddhis as 'impediments to the attainment of true perception', and other great thinkers of India also deprecate the pursuit of siddhis, since they are frequently rooted in desire and involve one in material things. The magician or wonder-worker is not regarded as a true adept and his performances are frowned upon by enlightened minds. But the truth is that the vast majority of yogic practitioners undergo their training with the sole object of acquiring these powers.

Psychologists who have studied the phenomena of Hindu occultism believe that although certain natural faculties can be developed to an extraordinary degree by resolute effort, most of the Hindu magical feats are the result of self-delusion, or the induced delusion of others. Speaking from first-hand experience Theos Bernard, who achieved remarkable success in Haṭha Yoga, which he followed for many years, declared, 'I have found that it holds no magic, performs no miracles, and reveals nothing supernatural' (I, p. 96).

Books

I. Bernard, Theos. *Hatha Yoga: The Report of a Personal Experience*, London, 1950.

11. Oman, J. C. *The Mystics, Ascetics and Saints of India: A Study of Sadhuism*, London, 1905.
See also under Occultism and Yoga.

SIKH, a sect of reformist Hindus founded by Nānak and further strengthened by a succession of nine other 'Gurus' or preceptors. These ten Sikh patriarchs were: (1) **Nānak*** (1469–1538) who was greatly influenced by the reformer Kabīr; (2) **Aṅgad** (b. 1538, proclaimed Guru in 1539, died 1552), the inventor of the Gurmukhī script in which some of the sacred writings of the Sikhs are enshrined; (3) **Amardās** (1469–1552–74) inaugurated the institution of the *laṅgar* (common kitchen) to abolish caste distinctions; (4) **Rāmdās** (1534–74–81) son-in-law of the last-named, to whom Akbar gave the site of the Golden Temple (the Har-mandir or Darbār Sāheb) at Amṛitsar. It was this guru who built the original lake temple there. Since then Amṛitsar (Immortal Pool) has been the headquarters of Sikhism; (5) **Arjan Dev** (1563–81–1606) son of Rāmdās, who in 1604 began the compilation of the *Adi-granth* (see below). He also wrote a lengthy epic poem, the *Sukhmaṇī*, and other mystical works. He was ordered by the emperor Jahāngīr to expunge from the Granth all passages at variance with orthodox Muslim belief and on his refusal was accused of collaborating with the rebel prince Khusrau and was tortured to death; (6) **Har-gobind** (1595–1606–45) Son of Arjan Dev first organized the Sikhs into a military brotherhood. He often came into conflict with the ruling powers, and was once imprisoned by Jahāngīr for ten years; (7) **Har-rāī** (1630–45–61) grandson of Har-gobind; and (8) **Har-kṛishaṇ** (1656–61–64) son of Har-rāī, were two lesser gurus. The latter was installed as guru at the age of five, and died of smallpox at the age of eight, but before death indicated a village where his successor would be found. This was (9) **Tegh Bahādur** (1622–64–75) son of Har-gobind. He was ordered by the emperor Aurungzeb to embrace Islam; he refused and was executed. It is said that during his imprisonment he was charged with looking in the direction of the emperor's harem, to which the guru replied, 'Emperor, I was not gazing at your queen's apartments. I was looking in the direction of the Europeans who are coming from beyond the western seas to tear down your purdah and destroy your empire'; (10) **Gobind Singh** (1666–75–1708) the tenth and last guru, the son of Tegh Bahādur, whom he succeeded as a lad, gave the present militaristic form and character to the originally pacificist Sikh religion.

Gobind Singh knew Sanskrit, Persian and Arabic, wrote inspiring poetry of great literary excellence in Panjābi, and was also the author of what is known as the *Dasam Granth* (Tenth Granth). He announced that he was the last of the gurus, and that there were to be no more gurus after him, because now there was an eternal guru—the *Granth Sāheb* (see below). But he is better known for having established the Sikhs on a powerful political and military basis. He is said to have introduced into Sikhism the worship of the terrible goddess, Durgā, and he founded the **Khālsa** (pure of faith) or Sikh Council, which, along with the Guru Granth or sacred book, did away with the need for further gurus. Gobind Singh once performed an impressive rite for a group of early converts. He called for a volunteer and then took him into a tent, from where he emerged a moment later with his naked sword dripping blood, and called for another volunteer, repeating the performance five times. He then brought out the five volunteers whom he had only tested and not actually slain. These five, known as the *pāñch-piāra* (five beloved ones) having passed through the ordeal were now made to baptise the guru. Says Sher Singh, 'Guru Gobind acquired so much attachment for the sword that sometimes his love for the weapon enters into a reverence which on occasions is indistinguishable from worship' (X, p. 35). There is no doubt that the violent philosophy he preached was far removed from the gentle pacifism of Guru Nānak. Gāndhi referred to him as 'a misguided patriot', but in the context of the political situation prevailing in his day the Sikhs found Gobind Singh a man after their own hearts, and fiery souls flocked to his banner. In a fateful encounter at Sirhind, near the city of Ambāla, all his sons were killed. Gobind Singh himself was slain by a Pathān in revenge for the killing of his father.

The history of the Sikhs from the time of Gobind Singh is full of strife. One result of the philosophy of violence is seen in the atrocities committed by Gobind Singh's agent *Bandā* who operated in the Deccan, destroyed mosques, sacked towns and massacred the population, until he was himself caught and horribly tortured to death. In a prolonged and inconclusive war with the Afghan chief Ahmad Shāh Durrāni, the Golden Temple was destroyed. The great one-eyed leader Ranjīt Singh (d. 1839) victoriously led the Sikh armies trained by veteran French generals, through many battles and established Sikh supremacy over the whole of the Panjāb. He had his capital at Lahore and rebuilt the Golden Temple at Amṛitsar. When he died four of his queens and seven slave women were burnt with him in accordance with the Hindu practice of suttee*. On the death of Ranjīt Singh there were two fierce wars with the British in the middle of the nineteenth century. Today the ruling Sikh chiefs include the mahārājas of Paṭiāla, Jind, Nābha, Kapūrthala and Farīdkoṭ.

Many tribes and castes make up the Sikh community. Half the Panjāb Sikhs are Jāt. Some have been drawn from the Arorā tribe of merchants; others from the Ramgaṛhia tribe whose men are now mainly mechanics. Some are *khattris* or warriors from whose stock Nānak sprang. There are also a number of Rājputs.

The Sikhs themselves have a number of what might almost be termed 'castes'. There are the *Nānakpanthi* (also called the Nānakshāhi) who are purely religious and non-political; they do not believe in all the teachings of Gobind Singh but follow the peaceful religion of prayer and meditation of Guru Nānak. Generally the Nānakpanthis do not wear the hair long, and are hardly distinguishable from other Hindus. The *Udāsi* are the followers of one of Guru Nānak's sons, Śrī Chand. Their claim to the big temples or gurudwāras led to a movement by the general body of Sikhs, who maintained that the offerings made to the temples 'went into their private pockets, which in some cases fed prostitutes' (X, p. 33). The *Sahajdāri* or 'easy-going', shave their heads like Hindus, and are often called *Mona* or shaven, in contradistinction from the *Keshdāri* who do not cut the hair (*see* head). The *Nirmala* are scholars of Hinduism. Gobind Singh first sent them to Banāras and many of them became deeply tinged with Hinduism. The *Gyāni* are the theologians of the Guru Granth.

Sikh nationalism today finds expression in the *Akāli*, 'deathless' movement. The many noble examples of non-resistance among Akāli followers in the face of ill-treatment by the government stand to their credit, but they have also frequently been criticized for their aggressiveness and violence.

SCRIPTURES. The Bible of the Sikhs is known as the *Guru Granth* (or *Granth Sāheb*). It is also called the *Ādi-Granth* or Original Granth to distinguish it from the later Granth of the Tenth Guru. The Guru Granth is written in Old Panjābi, Old Western Hindi, Marāṭhi, and in some parts in Persian (X, p. 110). It is composed of the writings and sayings of the gurus as well as of other saints and reformers who lived before Nānak, and thus preserves the earliest specimens of the poetry of the *bhakti* movement. It contains 3384 hymns and is about three times the size of the *Ṛig-Veda*. The chief authors were (*a*) the first five gurus; (*b*) the sixteen bhagats or saints, namely: Jaidev of Bengal; Nāmdev of Mahārāshṭra; Trilochana of Mahārāshṭra; Premānand of Gujerāt; Sadnā of Sind; Beni of the Panjāb; Rāmānanda; Dhannā of Rājputāna; Pīpā; Saiṅ; Kabīr; Ravidās; Mīrābāi; Farīd; Bhikhan; and Sūrdās; and (*c*) lesser hands such as Mardāna.

It is said that when the Granth was being compiled four bhagats asked for their hymns to be included, but these were rejected on the grounds that their compositions were pantheistical, quietist, pessimistic, and misogynistic respectively. The Granth does not quite escape polytheism as it practically assumes the Hindu pantheon, and it accepts the doctrine of *karma* and transmigration. It is usually divided into several parts, such as the *Japjī* ('jap', remembrance or praise) composed by Nānak; hymns of various kinds, *ślokas*, *gāthās*; the *Rāg*, consisting of musical measures; the *Bhog* containing verses by various authors, including Kabīr. Great reverence is paid to the holy book. It is placed on a special altar in Sikh temples, flowers are offered to it; it is fanned day and night; Sikhs bow in reverent homage before it. On certain occasions it is raised on a cushioned platform and taken out in procession to the chanting of sacred songs.

TEACHINGS. The teachings of Sikhism are mainly derived from Nānak who owes much to Kabīr, and were only added to by the later gurus. There is but one God; through hearing his name even the lowly become exalted; hearing his name is equal to a pilgrimage. He is the True Name. In the course of time the Granth suffered many doctrinal modifications and has yielded much to Hinduism. The teachings of Gobind Singh were again of a different character, being militant, in accordance with the needs of the age in which he lived.

Critics have frequently pointed out that while Sikhism ostensibly dropped many features of Hinduism, it has itself adopted similar features in a disguised form. Sikhism set aside the authority of the Vedas, but substituted for it the authority of the Guru Granth. It abolished sacrifice and hence did away with the priestly class. Nānak is regarded as an incarnation of God, possessing the sixteen *avatāra* signs of Rāma and Kṛishṇa. It is believed that Nānak performed miracles, cleansed lepers, and raised the dead. The other gurus are regarded as incarnations of Nānak, assuming his divinity upon their formal installation. Sanskrit lost its divine sanctity and Gurmukhī became the sacred script. Sikhism set its face against ceremonial and the meaningless repetition of the name of God, although Sikhs now lay great emphasis on the Name. It rejected the *ahiṁsā* doctrine of non-violence and dismissed all scruples about taking the life of animals for food as superstition, since all life lived on other life. Sikhs prohibit idolatry although they pay almost idolatrous homage to the Guru Granth; do not observe caste distinctions although they are greatly influenced by caste, many Sikhs still retaining their caste names and not intermarrying freely. Smoking, drug-taking, and the drinking of wine are also prohibited, though Sikhs are notoriously partial to liquor. Infanticide was stopped, the rights of women recognized (although four queens of Ranjīt Singh were burnt alive on his pyre); pilgrimage to holy places forbidden (but a visit to Amṛitsar is almost a religious duty with Sikhs).

A Sikh is not necessarily born a Sikh, but is initiated into the religion by a rite known as the *pahul*, 'gate', when he is of adult age. The baptism is performed by stirring some sweet water in an iron bowl with a two-edged dagger. With this water, known as *amṛit* (nectar) the initiate is anointed. After initiation he is entitled to use the honorific *Singh*, 'Lion' after his name. Most Sikhs are not baptized, but use the term Singh anyway. Orthodox Sikhs are distinguished by the five *kakka* (i.e. the five '*k*'s') namely: (1) *keśa* (top knot), the true Sikh's hair is never cut; (2) *kachhā* (short drawers); (3) *kaṛā* (iron bangle); (4) *kaṅgā* (comb); and (5) *kirpān* (short sword).

Although much is due to the reformers and bhagats, the influence of the jogis, including the Nāthas, on Sikhism is apparent. The jogis too do not recognize caste, revere the nātha (equivalent to the guru), have no scruples about eating meat, and have free kitchens. As Sher Singh observes, 'Most of the Sikh practices are found among them' (X, p. 103). No less important was the influence of the Persian mystics, the Muslims, Kabīr and the Vaishṇavas. Nānak's theism it is said was a synthesis of Islam and Rāmānuja.

Books

I. Banerjee, I. B. *Evolution of the Khalsa*, Calcutta, 1936.
II. Cunningham, J. D. *A History of the Sikhs*, London, 1918.
III. Gordon, J. H. *The Sikhs*, 1904.
IV. Macauliffe, M. A. *The Sikh Religion*, Oxford, 1909.
V. Macgregor, W. L. *The History of the Sikhs*, 1847.
VI. Malcolm, J. *Sketch of the Sikhs*, 1812.
VII. Scott, G. B. *Religion and Short History of the Sikhs*, 1930.
VIII. Singh, Khushwant. *The Sikhs*, London, 1953.
IX. Singh, Puran. *The Book of the Ten Masters*, Lahore, 1920.
X. Singh, Sher. *Philosophy of Sikhism*, Lahore, 1944.
XI. Singh, Teja. *Essays in Sikhism*, Lahore, 1944.
XII. Trumpp, E. (Tr.) *The Adi Granth*, London, 1877.

ŚIKHAṆḌIN, a reincarnation of Ambā daughter of the king of Kāśī who had been abducted by Bhīshma* to be given as wife to Vichitravīrya prince of Hastināpura. For this deed Bhīshma was cursed by the girl who swore that she would be born again and be responsible for his death. Accordingly, Ambā was reborn as a girl named Śikhaṇḍinī, daughter of Drupada king of Pañchāla.

Now Drupada had been told that this child was destined to become a man, so he brought her up and educated her as a man, and had her espoused to the daughter of Hiraṇya-varman ruler of the Daśarṇa tribe. The poor bride's discomfiture on her wedding night aroused the wrath of her father Hiraṇya-varman who threatened to destroy the kingdom of Drupada. Śikhaṇḍinī seeing her father's plight went into the forest resolving to kill herself. Here a kind-hearted *yaksha* (supernatural being) named *Sthūṇā-karṇa*, 'thick-ear', hearing of her fate agreed to exchange sexes with her temporarily. The delighted runaway (now a man named Śikhaṇḍin) returned home and performed his duties to the satisfaction of his newly wedded wife.

The obliging yaksha, however, was punished by Kubera, Lord of the yakshas, for changing his sex, and was condemned to retain the female sex he had assumed. When Śikhaṇḍin, true to his promise, came to the yaksha to return his borrowed male sex, Kubera was so pleased with his honesty that he allowed Śikhaṇḍin to remain a male as long as he lived. And because the yaksha had surrendered his sex in a worthy cause he was to get back his male sex as soon as Śikhaṇḍin died.

Śikhaṇḍin fought on the side of the Pāṇḍavas in the great battle of Kurukshetra, and on the ninth evening of that battle he became instrumental in the death of Bhīshma, as had been prophesied of yore.

Books

See under Mahābhārata and Mythology.

SIN, the taint resulting from the wilful or unknowing transgression of dharma*, the moral or spiritual law, is termed *dosha*, 'evil'. It is partly a consequence of birth for when soul is joined to body at birth we take over the results of all the actions (*karma**) of our past lives. This carry-over from our past, combined with the mental and physical characteristics inherited from our ancestors, along with our own ignorance (*avidyā*) results in sin. Sin is thus a form of pollution. Pollution or *sūtaka* (from sū, to be born, i.e. in impurity) is man's inheritance, his beginning, for he is conceived in pollution, engendered in lust, and created of semen and menstrual blood; and when his life is over he is polluted again, for death itself is pollution. Sin is conceived of as a morbid and sticky substance which fastens itself on every person from birth, and more of this viscid filth is added to him as a result of his living. Sin is transferable by physical contact, by speech, by thought. One should therefore avoid a sinner as one does a beggar with sores. Gods too are not exempt from sinning. Sin is remitted by purification, penance, sacrifice and knowledge.

Several facets of dosha are distinguished in Hindu ethics, namely:

(1) *Vighna*, an impediment to the attainment of perfection, although not necessarily sinful in itself. Among these impediments are,

'Women, soft couches, fashionable clothes, betel-chewing, gold and silver, jewels, perfumes, songs and music, dancing, theological discussion, mysticism, garrulousness, fame, wealth, ill-health (*vyādhi*), regularity, irregularity; sloth (*ālasya*, *mūḍha*, or *tandrā*), ambition, pride and passion'.

(2) *Aparāddhi*, a 'guilt'-bearing action or state of mind, causing one to take on the taint of sin. Many are mental attitudes and some are vices. Chief of these are: *dvesha* or 'aversion' emotions, e.g. *dvish* (hatred), *īrsha* (jealousy), *droha* (enmity), *mātsarya* (envy), *amarsha* (impatience), *manyu* (anger) and *krodha* (wrath); *durvachana*, 'bad words', including *asūyana* (grumbling, complaining); *parivāda* (censuring, slandering, back-biting); *mamatā*, 'mine' or possessive emotions, e.g. self-centredness, *asmitā* (egoism), *ichchhā* (desire), *lobha* (greed); *garva*, 'pride' emotions, e.g. haughtiness, *auddhatya* (self-righteousness, strongly condemned by Buddhists), *māna* (arrogance); *avirati*, sensuality, *kāmarāgo* (lust for women), *atyāhāra* (gluttony).

(3) *Pātaka*, 'downfall', specific immoral acts, crimes or sins. The lesser sins are referred to as *upa-pātaka*, and include marrying before one's elder brother or (in the case of girls) sister, the sale of wife or child, adultery, usury, lying, breaking an oath; teaching the Veda for money, or learning the Veda from a paid teacher; killing a man or woman of low caste; defiling a maiden of low caste. All these *upa-pātakas* are only morally degrading, and are to be distinguished from the five major sins known as the *mahā-pātaka*, 'great sins', or *pañcha-pātaka*, 'five sins', which are regarded as particularly heinous. They are: *brahma-hatyā*, 'brāhmin-cide', the murder of a brāhmin; *śiśu-hatyā*, 'foetus-murder', destruction of an unborn child, wilful abortion; *surāpāna*, 'surā-drinking', or drinking spirituous liquor; *svarṇa-steya*, 'gold-stealing'; *guru-talpa-gamana*, 'guru's-couch-intercourse', having sexual relations with the wife of one's preceptor. These five crimes cannot be wiped out by any means and those guilty of them will be tortured in hell and then suffer several incarnations as abjectly wretched villains.

The term *pāpa*, 'sin', is often used synonymously with dosha, and covers many aspects of dosha already considered above. Sin in its totality is personified in Hindu ritual and meditative practice as a hideous, black, demon-faced being called *pāpa-purusha*, 'sin-giant', who is a composite of all the sins: His head represents the killing of a brāhmin; his arms the killing of a cow; his eyes are woman-murder, his nose intoxication; his face is theft, his ears the dishonour of a guru, his shoulders association with outcastes; his chest adultery, his neck abortion, his belly injustice and oppression; his genitals violation of a virgin; his thighs slandering the righteous, and his feet associating with those who commit any of these crimes.

Books

See under Ethics.

SINGING is regarded as the highest manifestation of all voiced sounds*. Great, almost magical, value is attributed to words that are recited, intoned, chanted or sung.

Ordinary speech or *bhāshikā-svara*, 'speaking tone', has the narrowest compass of all voiced expression. Its usual progression is along a monotone, with occasional shifts to a tone or two above or below. It is generally voiced without variation of pitch and its accent is classed as *udātta* or middle in the language of prosody*. As the tone of ordinary conversation its inflections and ranges are spontaneous and unintentioned.

Purposive voiced sounds first came with the intoned mantras of the ṛishis and the chanted formulas of the priests during offerings, sacrifices and rituals. Here the efficacy of the voiced sound was ensured only by its precise utterance and correct intonation, keyed to the right variations of pitch and accent.

These intentioned formulas occur in the *Ṛig-veda,* are further exemplified in the *Yajur-veda,* and reach their full expression in the *Sāma-veda.* A specialist class of Vedic hierophants* was entirely devoted to the proper intoning of chants, which consisted partly of hymns of praise to the gods, but mainly of magical formulas to obtain material benefits like food, cattle, gold and sons.

The *Chhāndogya Upanishad,* one of the supplementary treatises of the *Sāma-veda* says, 'The essence of person is speech, the essence of speech is *ṛich* (hymn), the essence of ṛich is *sāman* (melody), and the essence of sāman is *udgītha* (the chant)'. The convenience of liturgical prosody was made the overriding factor in the arrangement of the intoned mantra. Syllables were therefore lengthened or shortened beyond recognition, words broken up and distorted so that often the period starts in the middle of a word, and the sound of the words ceases to have the ordinary meaning. The matter was further complicated by the fact that the manner of intoning chants was far from uniform. The methods varied considerably according to the śākhās or schools and show traces of environmental influences, those in the South differing from those of the North. Some of the later schools even bear traces of Muslim influence.

Out of the religious chant grew the secular song whose chief inspiration were the celestial Gandharvas*. From them comes the term *gāndharva* which means singing, song or singer. The art of secular singing was enshrined in the *Gāndharva-Veda* (*see* Music History).

Singing is generally called *gāyan,* derived from the root gā or gai, meaning song. Stemming from this are many related words such as *gāyatrī* (the name of a *mantra*), *gītā* (song), *gātha* (an ancient religious non-Vedic song), *saṁgītā* or *saṅgītā* (singing to the accompaniment of music), and the modern Hindi *gānā* (song).

In secular singing the words of a song are not of great importance. A verse, couplet, a single line, or even a string of meaningless syllables, may be suitable as a vehicle, and variations on these may be sufficient to invoke and sustain the mood intended. The accompaniment of a musical instrument is not necessary for a good singer, but sometimes a drum is used, so that the listeners may be better able to appreciate the rhythm, virtuosity and skill of the singer, particularly the patterns of sound, with the drum breaking the melody into staccato rhythms and creating the effect of a subtle incantation.

In singing a slight nasalization seems to be preferred in both men and women. In men the low, 'toad-like', throaty voice, and in women the high-pitched shrilling voice were considered the ideal. There are many styles of singing in Indian music In general they may be classified under the following broad categories:

ĀLĀPA (or ālāpaṇa), a classical form, often used in rāgas, but freely improvized on. Instead of words, meaningless syllables are frequently used, like *nā, tā, rī, adhi, tan.* It is free from set rhythms and structural timings and can therefore 'rise to metaphysical heights savouring of the cosmic rhythmic process of the Universe'. The term ālāpa is also used for the prelude to a rāga, in the sense of an overture.

BHAJAN, a song of devotional love, accompanied by drums and stringed instruments, based on traditional Hindu religious themes, usually associated with Kṛishṇa worship. It is extremely sentimental in expression. In Bengal it is called a *kīrtan* and was given its present character by the Vaishṇavite revivalist Chaitanya*. In the singing of kīrtans all the people of the village, young and old, rich and poor, once used to join. Each verse is sung by a soloist and then repeated by the congregation. Recitation and dancing are frequently part of the kīrtans.

PADA, an old form of song, generally based on some pithy saying, which is enlarged upon or repeated with variations. Often used in devotional singing, especially when related to some aspect of the Rādhā and Kṛishṇa love theme. Closely related to the pada, which is popular in Bengali and Hindi literature, is the *abhaṅga* of Mahārāshṭra used for short devotional lyrics.

DHRŪPAD, the most difficult of singing styles and one calculated to produce profound emotions. Used for deep devotional purposes, it may be said to correspond to Western church music. Originating in the fourteenth century the style was revived by Rāja Mānsingh (d. 1518) and Tansen* (d. 1610). It is sung in slow time, demanding a good command of breath and is therefore required to be sung by men 'with the strength of five buffaloes'. A lighter variety of the dhrūpad is the *dhamar* (or hori), which consists of variations on one theme, sung to different tunes.

KHYĀL (or khayāl), 'whim', reputedly invented by Sultān Hussain Shāh Sharqī of Jaunpur (fl. 1470), is characterized by an extremely variegated colourfulness made possible by introducing plenty of vocal ornamentation. It attained its perfection in Bengal. The theme is usually a love tale, sung by a woman. Another form considered suitable for a female voice is the *ṭappā* of north India, perfected by the songstress Shorī (*c.* 1700) who lived in the time of Mahmūd Shāh. It is supposed to have originated from a simple rural tune sung by camel drivers of the Panjāb.

ṬHUMRĪ, combines some of the features of the khyāl and ṭappā, is highly complex and plastic, but still leaves scope for plenty of ornamentation, and repeats words and lines in varied rhythms. It is extremely lively and frequently adapted to pantomime and dance. Further variations of this are seen in the *gat* (or gati), associated with the aṅgika* movement. The gat is a pattern of close-form music for instruments and the voice, leaving room for improvization. It was perfected by Feroz Khān (*c.* 1660), Masiyat Khān (*c.* 1680) and others. The polyrhythmic exchange between the soloist and tabla player that constitutes the chief feature of the gat gives the music its vitality.

Equally distinctive Muslim forms are found in the *ghazal* or lyrical ode of love and adoration to mistress or deity, derived from ultimately Persian sources, and sung as a light popular form of ṭhumrī; and the *qavāli*, a Muslim devotional song, invented by Amir Khusrau and often an elaboration of a verse from the Koran.

Books

See under Music.

ŚIŚUPĀLA (*śiśu-pāla*, 'youth's protector'), also called Sunītha, 'victorious', was the son of Damaghosha king of Chedi and Śrutadevā sister of Kṛishṇa's father Vasudeva. The kingdom of Chedi was situated between the Yamunā and the Vindhyas, with capital at Śuktimatī. The Chedi dynasty was an offshoot of the Yādavas and its most famous kings were Uparichara father of Satyavatī*, and the above named Śiśupāla.

Many legends are woven around the name of this terrible and mysterious figure, most of them telling of the fierce rivalry between the worshippers of Vishṇu and those of Śiva. According to the Purāṇas Śiśupāla in his former incarnation lived as the *daitya* king Hiraṇyakaśipu and then as Rāvaṇa. As Śiśupāla he was born with three eyes and four arms, but the extra members disappeared shortly after birth. He became a devotee of Śiva and was thus opposed to Kṛishṇa. Kṛishṇa however, promised Śiśupāla's mother that he would forgive her son even if the latter offended him a hundred times.

Although he was Kṛishṇa's cousin, Śiśupāla became his relentless enemy, especially after Kṛishṇa abducted his betrothed, Rukmiṇī*. At the rājasūya sacrifice of Yudhishṭhira he vehemently opposed Bhīshma's suggestion that the *arghya* (a customary gift of fruit and flowers) should go to Kṛishṇa as a token of his greatness. 'How can we honour an uncrowned chieftain,' he cried, 'with so many ruling kings of great valour present? If honour is due to age the offering should go to Vasudeva the father of Kṛishṇa; if it is due to the foremost monarch then Drupada should receive it; if wisdom is to be honoured Droṇa is certainly the most worthy; and if holiness is to get its reward then it should be given to Vyāsa. Least deserving of all is this cowherd of low birth, who has debased himself by eating the leavings of cowherds and has consorted with cowgirls; who as a child was a thief, and as a young man was a seducer and fornicator; and who, besides being a murderer was shameless enough to carry away by force the beautiful Rukmiṇī to whom I was betrothed.'

Great was the wrath of Kṛishṇa when he heard these words. This was the one hundred and first insult he had received from his cousin and he was now absolved from the promise he had given to Śiśupāla's mother. Bringing forth his discus he flung it at Śiśupāla whose head was severed from his body, which fell 'like a cliff struck by a thunderbolt'. His body was cremated with due solemnity and his son proclaimed king. This son, Dhṛishṭaketu, 'Audacious leader', fought on the side of the Pāṇḍavas at Kurukshetra.

Books

See under Mahābhārata and Mythology.

SĪTĀ, 'furrow', heroine of the *Rāmāyaṇa*, was so called because she appeared in a furrow ploughed up by her father Janaka* during a sacrificial rite for obtaining progeny. The 'native' (*Anārya*) birth of this princess has been suggested on the basis of this evidence of her 'mother-earth' origin. In the Vedas Sītā presides over agriculture. She was supposed to have lived in the Kṛita age as Vedavatī, and to be the incarnation of the goddess Lakshmī, reborn to encompass the destruction of the demon-king Rāvaṇa.

Sītā became the wife of Rāma, who won her in a contest by successfully bending the great bow of Śiva that her father Janaka possessed. She was Rāma's only wife, accompanied him in exile and was the personification of conjugal fidelity, purity and tenderness. When Rāma and his brother Lakshmaṇa were lured away from their hut and Sītā was left alone, Rāvaṇa approached her in the guise of a mendicant and was welcomed by her. He then revealed himself and asked her to be his wife. Sītā's eyes flashed fire as she replied, 'What madness prompts you to woo the wife of so mighty a warrior as Rāma, the sinless and saintly one, Rāma the strong-armed and valiant. I follow Rāma as a lioness follows a lion. Can you, a prowling jackal, hope to obtain a lioness?' Rāvaṇa thereupon transformed himself into a gigantic demon shape and carried Sītā off to his kindom of Laṅkā (Ceylon). As they passed over the mountains where the *vānara* (monkey) people dwelt she cast off her ornaments and a few garments to leave a trail for Rāma.

On reaching his palace Rāvaṇa left Sītā with his rākshasa handmaidens. She was confined in a secluded part of the palace grounds, in the beautiful aśoka grove, gorgeous as paradise, planned and laid out by Viśvakarman himself. Rāvaṇa tried by persuasion and cajolery to make her yield but she remained unmoved. During her captivity Sītā was shown great kindness by a friendly *rākshasī* (ogress) named Trijaṭā (or Dharmajñā), and also by Saramā, wife of Vibhīshaṇa, Rāvaṇa's younger brother, and their sympathy lessened the burden of her ordeal. It was while she sat in the *aśoka* grove that the monkey-chief Hanumān secretly visited her and promised to return with Rāma.

After necessary preparations Rāma invaded Laṅkā with his simian allies and defeated Rāvaṇa, restoring peace to Laṅkā. But Sītā was met coldly with the words,

'O princess of Videha, how could ever one like me keep even for a moment a woman who has fallen into the hands of another. I only undertook the effort of war to clear my name and that of my family. I am not able to stand your presence, even as a man with sensitive eyes cannot stand the light. Therefore go, I have no need for you. Be your way of life pure or not, you are like unto a sacrificial offering polluted by a dog.'

As she heard these words the young woman reeled with anguish and fell to the ground, 'like a banana tree that is hewn down'. When she recovered she told Rāma, 'I am not what you take me to be. Rāvaṇa's body touched mine as he carried me off, but am I to blame for that? In the excess of your anger you behave like a man of the street'. She then requested Lakshmaṇa to build a funeral pyre and when it was lit threw herself into the flames, but the gods rescued her and she emerged unscathed. In spite of this obvious proof of her innocence Rāma refused to be conciliated, although he permitted her to accompany him.

The party returned to Ayodhyā, where Rāma was solemnly crowned king. But he continued to be disturbed by jealous thoughts of Sītā. One day a washerman quarrelled with his wife whom he suspected of adultery. He refused to take her back saying he was not as stupid as Rāma to reinstate a wife who had lived with another man. When the story reached Rāma's ears the king was unable to endure the stinging reproach. He ordered his brother Lakshmaṇa to take Sītā to the jungle and put her to death. Sītā was far advanced in pregnancy at the time so Lakshmaṇa merely dipped his arrowhead in the sap of a certain tree which has a red juice, left Sītā to her fate in the forest, and returned to Rāma saying that his mission had been fulfilled.

Sītā in the meanwhile found refuge in the hermitage of the sage Vālmīki and here she became the mother of twin sons, LAVA and KUŚA. Another legend has it that she had only one son, Lava, but since he was without a playmate the sage Vālmīki shaped an image of a boy from a sheaf of *kuśa* grass and gave it life. This was the boy Kuśa. Sītā lived at the hermitage till her children reached the age of fifteen.

Now Rāma at this time inaugurated a horse sacrifice, and when the wandering horse came near the hermitage of Vālmīki the boys took possession of it. They defeated the royal army, wounding Lakshmaṇa, Śatrughna and Bharata, as well as Hanumān. Rāma himself went south to contend against the two strange boy-warriors, and was amazed to find that they resembled him in appearance. He then heard from the lips of Vālmīki that they were his own sons.

At Rāma's request Sītā returned to the capital where Rāma publicly declared her innocence before the assembled court. But the heart of Sītā was already too deeply scarred by the unjust treatment she had received at the hands of her husband. She called upon her mother to receive her, and the ground opened up and she was taken back into the bosom of the earth, the source from which she had sprung.

Her son Lava reigned over Northern Kośala with its capital at Śrāvastī (near modern Faizābād in Oudh), while Kuśa reigned at Southern Kośala with capital at Kuśāvatī (or Kuśasthalī) in the Vindhyas. Kuśa married Kumudvatī, a Nāga princess, the daughter of Kumuda, 'lotus' a Nāga king.

Sītā is also called A-yoni-jā, 'non-womb-born'; Bhūmi-jā, 'earth-born'; Pārthivī, 'earth-born'; and Jānakī, 'of Janaka'.

Books

See under Rāmāyaṇa and Mythology.

ŚIVA, one of the major gods of the later Hindu pantheon, forming with Brahmā and Vishṇu the great triad of Hindu deities. The word śiva occurs in the *Ṛig-veda,* not as the name of a god, but in a context where it only means auspicious. Śiva as the name of a god does not appear prominently before 200 BC.

The worship of a deity with the attributes of Śiva is, however, one of the most ancient in India, and may have been brought by the Maga or Vrātya peoples from outside India. Śiva's archetype is found in the Indus Valley, and in his evolution from his ancient conformation the Vedic Rudra represents a convenient and necessary phase. The name Śiva, the Red One, is related to the Tamil word for 'red', as is Śiva's other name, Śaṁbhu, which is cognate with the Tamil word for copper, the red metal. The name Rudra is also synonymous with red, and the metamorphosis from Rudra to Śiva was doubtless facilitated by this resemblance.

Like Rudra, Śiva assumed the direful features of a god who is the director of destinies. In the worship of Śiva was centred that element of dread and uncertainty that is associated with the unknown, and the unfathomable; the generative processes that precede birth; the powers and portents of death and destruction; the mystic forces of the human soul as well as the cosmic forces of nature. He assumed in his person every attribute of the natural mysticism welling up from the contemplation of nature in its malignant and mysterious aspects. In his final form he came to embody the character of fatality in the life epic of the universe, and as such he became Mahādeva (Great God) and Bhava (Being or Existence).

He is also the lord of the dance, *Naṭarāja*, 'dance-king', who executes the cosmic dances that typify the ordered movement of the universe. He performed one of his most wonderful dances to chastise ten thousand heretical hermits who lived in the forest of Taragam. Taking Vishṇu in the form of Mohinī with him as his wife he went to the forest dressed as a brāhmin, and blazed up in anger when the ṛishis, captivated by the woman, tried to slay Śiva. Another legend says that the wives of the ṛishis fell in love with Śiva, and this aroused the wrath of the ṛishis. They sent a fierce tiger against him but Śiva tore off its skin and used it for a shawl; a terrible serpent which was next sent out after him he slew and used as a neckband; a mighty elephant he ripped open and used its hide for a cloak. He cast down the asura Apasmāra, 'epilepsy' or 'insanity', also called Muyalaka (or Mauyalka) who tried to attack him, and placing him underfoot danced his wonderful Tāṇḍava dance* upon his prostrate body. The scene of this dance was said to have been Chidambaram*, the mythical centre of the universe. In another legend he danced this dance at Gaya on the prostrate body of the *asura* Gaya* in order to render him immobile. The ṛishis, the gods, and the celestial and infernal worlds assembled to see him dance, with the result that the ṛishis became his devotees. The serpent Śesha was so impressed with the dance that he left Vishṇu and practised austerities for many years to see the dance again.

Many facets of human activity and thought have been assimilated in the deification of Śiva. He is the god of destruction, the personification of the disintegrative forces of the cosmos, and many bloody rites are associated with his worship. He is also the god of regeneration and sexuality. The sacred Ganges which issues from Vishṇu's foot gets its fertilizing power as it descends to earth through Śiva's thick and luxuriant locks.

Some of Hinduism's most potent symbols are associated with Śiva in this aspect. His member is described as 'always stiff, always erect'. He is sexually alert at all times, his semen spills at the slightest provocation. The liṅga and yoni, male and female organs of generation, are basic Śaivite symbols. Pre-Aryan phallic or śiśna worship, medieval Śaivism* and tantrism*, all centre around the worship of Śiva and his consort, Śakti.

On the other hand Śiva is also the god of asceticism, and as such is called *Mahāyogi*, 'great yogi'. Legend says that he was condemned to perpetual asceticism for cutting off the fifth head of Brahmā* when that deity was disrespectful to him. The traditional representation of Śiva shows him naked, single-faced, with dishevelled or matted hair, ash besmeared, wearing a *muṇḍa-māla* ('skull-garland'), and huge pendent snake-earrings (*nāga-kuṇḍala*), sitting on a tiger skin under a tree or snake-hood canopy, absorbed in profound meditation.

Śiva is the god of the terrible, a flesh-eater, demanding animal, human and blood sacrifices; the lord of the cruel and evil side of things, haunting cemeteries, attended by hosts of *pramatha*, sprites and goblins; as well as *bhūta*, spirits, ghosts, and ghouls which live in trees and eat flesh; and the *vetāla*, or vampires which haunt cemeteries, animate dead bodies and feed on human blood. Among the most hideous members of his entourage is *Kīrti-mukha* (*kīrti-mukha*, 'renowned-face'), a terrible demon created by Śiva to fight Rāhu* who once opposed him. At the mere sight of Kīrtimukha the terrified Rāhu begged for mercy, and Śiva commanded the monster to desist. Since he had been created to swallow Rāhu, the demon demanded a meal and Śiva bade him eat his own feet. The monster ate his feet, his legs, belly, chest and arms till only the head remained. The grotesque face of Kīrti-mukha is used as a talisman among Śaivites, and is frequently found depicted in temple-sculpture, and works of art. Śiva is often accompanied by a voracious black dog which tears the flesh off living bodies and gulps without chewing.

Śiva is usually represented with either one or five faces, and four arms, the two upper hands holding the *ḍamaru* (a small hand-drum) and a flame of the consuming fire; the two lower hands are poised in *mudrās* of protection (*abhaya*) and action (*kriyā*). In some representations he holds a horn, trident, and drum, while with the fourth hand he makes a gesture symbolizing the bestowal of gifts. His whole body is encircled by the blazing *toraṇa*, an arch of flames.

Frequently, Śiva is shown with a third eye in the middle of his forehead. The eye was said to have burst forth to save the world from darkness when his wife Pārvatī once playfully stole behind him and covered his eyes with her hands. His third eye is an organ of destruction with which he reduced to ashes Kāma god of love for daring, while he was in penance, to arouse amorous desires in his wife Pārvatī.

He is also portrayed with a blue neck, caused as a result of his swallowing the poisonous scum at the Churning of the Ocean (*see* nectar). Śiva's vāhana or vehicle is the bull *Nandi*, son of Kaśyapa and Surabhī, also called Śālaṅkā-yana, Nādideha, and Tāṇḍava-tālika, the latter because he provides musical accompaniment when Śiva dances the Tāṇḍava. Among Śiva's weapons* are the *triśūla* or trident; the *pināka* or club; the *ājagava* or bow; the *khaṭvāṅga* or club with a skull at the end; and the *pāśa* or noose, for trapping and binding offenders. His celestial abode is Kailāsa, a mountain* in the Himā-layas. His wives are Pārvatī and other aspects of Śakti, and he is associated with various local female deities such as Mīnākshī*. His children are Gaṇeśa and Kārttikeya.

Śiva is said to have 1008 names or epithets, of which the best known are cited here: Ādinātha, 'first lord'; Ardhanārīśvara, 'Androgynous* lord'; Asitānga, 'black-limbed'; Babhrū, 'brown' (also used for Kṛishṇa); Bāleśvara, 'hair-lord'; Bhairava, 'terrible'; Bhairoṁ, modern variant of Bhairava; Bhava, 'existence'; Bhūteśvara, 'demon-lord'; Chandra-chūḍā, 'moon-crested'; Chandra-śekhara, 'moon-crested'; Dhūrjaṭi, 'mat-haired'; Ekambareśvara, 'one-garmented lord' i.e. nude; Gajasaṁhāra, 'elephant-destroyer', slayer of the elephant demon; Gaṅgādhara, 'Ganges-bearer'; Ghṛisheśvara, 'rubbing lord' i.e. lord of the coital act; Girīśa, 'mountian-lord'; Hara, 'seizer'; Hāṭakeśvara, ruler of the Hāṭaka people; Hiraṇya-retas, having 'golden semen'; Īśāna, 'ruler' of the north-east direction; Jambukeśvara, lord of Jambu i.e. India; Jaṭā-dhara, 'mat-haired'; Kāla, 'black' or 'time'; Kāla-saṁhāra, 'time-slayer'; Kapāla-mālin, 'skull-garlanded'; Kāpāleśvara, 'skull-lord'; Kapardin, wearing the kaparda, a braid or knot of hair; Kedār or Kedār-nāth, 'mountain-lord'; Kṛitti-vāsas, 'skin-clad'; Krodha, 'wrathful'; Mahādeva, 'great-lord'; Mahā-kāla, 'great-time' i.e. dissolver of Time; Mahāyogi, 'great-ascetic'; Maheśa, 'great-lord'; Maheśvara, 'great-lord'; Mṛityunjaya, 'death-destroyer'; Nandīśa (*see* Rāvaṇa); Naṭa-rāja, 'dance-king'; Naṭeśa, 'dance-lord'; Nīla-kaṇṭha (*see* poison); Pañch-ānana, 'five-faced'; Paśu-pati, 'animal-lord'; Prapitāmaheśvara, 'great-grandfather-god'; Sadā-śiva, 'eternal-Śiva'; Śaṁbhu, 'benign'; Saṁhāra, 'destruction'; Śaṁkara, 'beneficient'; Śarva, slaying with the śaru, 'arrow'; Śri-kaṇṭha, a respectful variation of Nīla-kaṇṭha; Sthāṇu, 'immoveable'; Śūla-bhṛit, 'śūla-endowed'; Śūla-pāṇi, 'śūla-holding'; Śvāśva, 'whose horse is a dog'; Tāmra-chūḍā, 'red-crested'; Tribhuvaneśvara, 'three-worlds lord'; Trilochana, 'three-eyed'; Tripurāntaka, 'triple-world ender' i.e. destroyer of earth, heaven and hell; Ugra-deva, 'fierce-god'; Vajreśvara, 'thunderbolt lord'; Viśva-nātha, 'universal-lord'; Viśveśvara, 'universal deity'; Vaidya-nātha, 'physician-lord'; Virūpāksha, having 'ill-formed eyes'; Viśālāksha, 'large-eyed'; Yogeśvara, 'lord of Yoga'.

Books

See under Mythology.

ŚIVĀJĪ (1627–1680) founder of the last of the great Hindu empires, that of the Marāṭhas*. He was Mahārāshṭra's greatest leader and the paragon of Indian patriots, for he wrenched from the clutches of the Moghul Emperor Aurungzeb a large mass of territory which became the nucleus of the greatest purely Hindu confederacy that ever existed. Śivājī inherited none of his loyalty from his father, *Shāhjī* (or Shāhjī Bhonsle), a military officer who served the Muslims and shifted his allegiance from Ahmadnagar to Bijāpur, from Delhi to Golkondā. It was Shāhjī's conquests for his Muslim masters that slowly deprived the last Vijayanagar emperor of his territorial possessions, and ultimately led to the downfall of that mighty Hindu state.

With an army made up largely of peasants, farmers and fishermen, Shāhjī's son Śivājī built up his empire. Marāṭha warriors had already acquired the arts of warfare under Muslim princes, and had grown in ability, wealth and power in the service of the Muhammadan kings of the Deccan. The strategy of guerilla warfare, in particular, they picked up from the greatest master of this art, Malik 'Ambar, the Abyssinian minister to the Sultān of Ahmadnagar.

For some time Śivājī's fortunes alternated between victories and reverses.

He once suffered a heavy defeat from Aurungzeb's army commanded by Rāja Jaisingh, and an agreement was signed by which Śivājī surrendered twenty of his forts, but was conceded the right of levying *chauth* (one fourth of the land revenue) and certain other taxes, including the *sardeśmukhī*; the latter was a tenth of the standard tax assessment which he levied only in the Deccan since he claimed to be the Sardeśmukh, or overlord, of the Deccan. In two years he started to recoup his losses, defeated the Moghul army and was crowned rāja.

His remarkable successes were largely due to the Spartan discipline of his troops, his genius for guerilla warfare, and his wise and tolerant administration. He was greatly beloved by his people for in a dark period of their history he pitted his cunning and bravery against the tyrant Aurungzeb. For the weak, for women, for the oppressed, he found a special place in his scheme of things. He was a chivalrous warrior and none dared in his camp to treat a captive woman with disrespect.

But in his subjection to orthodoxy he was a true child of his times, for he held the brāhmins in almost superstitious awe. He humbly submitted to the priests in all matters, faithfully performed all the religious rites required of him, generously endowed temples and brāhminical schools, and dutifully followed brāhmin guidance in social affairs. He had crowds of brāhmin office-seekers who followed him to obtain jobs in his administration, which the pious Marāṭha chieftain gave them, little dreaming that they were destined to disrupt his empire.

Despite his reverence for brāhmins, Śivājī, when the time came, was refused admittance to the kshattriya category by the priests, by his own Prime Minister, Moro Pant Piṅgle, and even his own Marāṭha Sardars, all of whom regarded him as a śūdra. The facile conversions of the past, by which śūdras and mlechchhas could become kshattriyas when their deeds merited the elevation, were no longer feasible under the critical eye of Muslim scrutiny. The brāhmins were prepared to perform his coronation rites, but only according to the non-Vedic or Purāṇic formula, as best befitting a śūdra, and Śivājī could get no priest to budge from the general resolve in this matter. Among these brāhmins was a renowned paṇḍit of Banāres named Gāgabhaṭ, who had long steadfastly maintained that the great warrior was a śūdra. But the lure of reward mitigated this rigid view and he later agreed, for a consideration, to crown in the orthodox manner, the man who had saved Hindu orthodoxy from Moghul oppression.

The beneficiaries of the coronation were, not unnaturally, the brāhmins, who received in full measure the largess of Śivājī. Eleven thousand priests, making a total of fifty thousand persons, with wives and children, crowded into his capital. The cost of the coronation is not known, but it is estimated at seven crore (seventy million) rupees. So seriously did it deplete his resources and so much money passed into the palms of the priests that Śivājī undertook an expedition to the Karṇāṭak for the sole purpose of squeezing the country of its accumulated wealth and returning home with the booty, to make up for what one writer calls his 'foolish feeding of worthless brāhmins'.

Śivājī died in 1680 at the age of fifty-three, leaving his empire to his dissolute son Śāmbhūjī.

Books

I. Kincaid, C. A. *The Grand Rebel, Sivaji*, London, 1939.
II. Kulkarni, V. B. *Sivaji: Portrait of a Patriot*, Bombay, 1963.
III. Rawlinson, H. G. *Sivaji the Maratha: His Life and Times*, Oxford, 1915.
IV. Sarkar, J. *Sivaji and His Times*, Calcutta, 1929.
V. Sen, S. *Sivaji Chhatrapati*, 1920.
VI. Temple, R. (*et al.*) *Sivaji and the Rise of the Marathas*, Calcutta, 1953.

ŚIVDAYĀL (1818–1878) or Shiv Dayāl Sāhib, also known as Tulsī Rām, born in Āgra, was the founder of the sect known as the Rādhasvāmi Satsaṅg. He began to proclaim his doctrine in 1861, and styling himself the Sant Satguru (Holy Preceptor) gathered an enthusiastic following from whom he selected a number of disciples. He taught a system of secret meditation which induced trance-like states. His successor was the ex-Postmaster General of the United Provinces, a great administrator who organized the sect and formulated its theology. Other successors were likewise intelligent and able men of advanced thought and liberal ideas.

The name Rādhasvāmi (spelled by the sect Rādhā Soāmi) signifies Lord of Rādhā, i.e. Kṛishṇa, and the gurus or spiritual leaders of the sect are regarded as incarnations of this deity. Soāmi represents the First Cause which manifests itself as the Word (Śabda), a divine emanation in the form of a mystical energy or sound-current. Rādhā personifies the Supreme Mother and Creative Principle. The Sant Satguru of the time is the incarnation of the invisible God, and his Supreme Son. This trinity of Father, Mother and Son constitutes the Godhead. The Sant Satguru is the source of deliverance and salvation. He is worshipped; his photograph is garlanded. Certain products of his body are consumed and the water in which he washes his feet is drunk. After his death his ashes are mixed with water and drunk by his followers.

Through the practice of a secret discipline called Surat-śabda-yoga, 'spirit-word-yoga', the human spirit is made to unite with the Word. The process entails concentration on the point between the eyes, repetition of the name of God, and meditation on the guru. Sundry other techniques based on yoga help to achieve various degrees of the trance state.

The human body, being regarded as a microcosm of the cosmos, is divided into heavenly regions, and the *nāḍis*, *chakras* and other parts of the subtle body are given the attributes of their divine prototypes. There is much talk of waves, forces, currents, supernormal glands and so on. Animal foods, intoxicating liquor, drugs, smoking, are forbidden; so are politics, gossip and idleness.

The religious meetings of the Rādhasvāmis are simple, and much stress is laid on social welfare. Their administrative centre at Dayālbāgh was established in 1914 near the tomb of the founder outside Āgra. The organization has set up a number of educational centres, academies, training institutions and small industries.

Books

I. Farquhar, J. N. *Modern Religious Movements in India*, New York, 1915.
II. Griswold, H. D. *Insights into Modern Hinduism*, New York, 1934.

III. Griswold, H. D. *The Radha Swami Sect*, Cawnpore, 1908.
IV. Phelps, M. H. (Ed.) *Discourses on Radha-Swami Faith*, New York, n.d.

SKILLS. A man of the world* was expected to be versed in the major sciences and skilled in various crafts in order that he might be competent to deal with the problems with which he would be likely to be confronted in the course of his life. The traditional list of these skills was first elaborated by fifth century writers on erotics who held that the *nāyaka* or city sophisticate, the man of culture and refinement, should be acquainted with the *chatuḥ-shashṭi*, the 'sixty-four' auxiliary arts as an aid to the supreme art of love. Later writers added to these essential accomplishments, a number of which also applied to women, naming as many as 528 subjects.

The names of the arts, crafts and sciences usually consist of the operative word affixed to one of the following terms: *jñāna*, 'knowledge' as in *ratha-jñāna*, 'chariot-knowledge' or charioteering; *karaṇa*, 'doing', as in *svarṇa-karaṇa*, 'gold-work', or the work of a goldsmith; *parīkshā*, 'examination', as in *ratna-parīkshā*, 'jewel-study'; *sādhanā*, 'guiding' as in *kāya-sādhanā* or physical culture; *śāstra*, 'scripture', as in *kāma-śāstra*, 'love-code'; *sūtra*, 'aphorism', as in *śulva-sūtra*, 'cord-mnemonics' or the art of measurement i.e. geometry; *tantra*, 'study', as in *strī-tantra*, the study of women; *vāda*, 'thesis', as in *kāya-vāda*, body knowledge; *veda*, 'knowledge' as in *dhanur-veda*, 'archery'; *vidhi*, 'rule' or 'law', as in *patrikā-vidhi*, 'letter-writing rules'; *vidyā*, knowledge, as in *sarpa-vidyā*, 'serpent-lore'; *yoga*, 'grasp', as in *mantra-yoga*, 'the yoga of spells'.

In recent years a large number of new compounds have been devised to include modern developments, for example, *aṇu-śāstra*, 'atomic science', and a number of these are referred back to ancient texts, so that it is not always easy to distinguish the traditional lists from the recent additions. Much of the theory of the traditional sciences, studies and skills was embodied in scriptures* such as the Vedāṅgas and Upavedas, and much in the *śilpa-śāstras* or manuals for handicraftsmen*, which were standard texts on architecture, painting, medicine, metallurgy, mechanics, cookery, horsemanship, and hundreds of manuals on the lesser crafts.

The sixty-four arts and accomplishments are listed under ten or twelve headings, ranging from the higher abstract sciences to the arts of the bed-chamber, and cover not only the genuine skills but many fanciful ones as well.

The GREATER RATS include a knowledge of drama (*nāṭya*), dancing (*nṛitta*), music*, the musical modes or *rāgas**, musical instruments; singing, sculpture (*takshaṇā*) in wood, stone, clay or metal; painting; architecture, including the designing and construction of temples, palaces, dwelling houses, tanks, dams, bridges and so forth. Also, a knowledge of mechanics*, āyurveda or the science of medicine and healing, and alchemy*.

PHILOSOPHY and related subjects include the six systems of philosophy*, knowledge of logic* and the construction of the syllogism*, an understanding of men and their motives; mnemonics or memory training; a knowledge of the Vedas, Upavedas, Vedāṅgas, Śāstras, Purāṇas and Tantras.

The SOCIAL SCIENCES demand an acquaintance with *nīti-śāstra*, 'welfare science', including economics (*vārtta*) and politics (*artha*); an understanding of agriculture, weather-lore, soil-lore, seasons, chronology, and all matters related to time (*kāla*), diurnal time, historical time and epochal time; weights and measures, astronomy and astrology, arithmetic (*gaṇita* or calculation), geometry (*śulva-sūtra, see* mathematics), shipbuilding and navigation (*nāvā-śāstra*); trade and shipping.

WARFARE calls for proficiency in archery (*dhanurveda*), charioteering (*ratha-jñāna*), and all those skills pertaining to *kshatra-vidyā*, 'knightly-lore', or military science.

The LITERARY ARTS include declamation and recitation from the Vedas, Epics and bardic chronicles, the art of story-telling; the writing and appreciation of poems and *kāvyas**; an understanding of etymology, exegetics (*nirukta*), grammar (*vyākaraṇa*), lexicography, the science of language, comprising dialects, prosody, rhetoric, verse-making, composition; familiarity with the 'eighteen scripts', although what these were is not known.

The HANDICRAFTS are treated of in handbooks called śilpa-śāstras. The heavenly architect Viśvakarman was the father of nine types of handicrafts, namely, those of the goldsmith, blacksmith, brazier, as well as shell-ornamentation, carpentry, gardening, pottery, weaving and painting.

The UNIVERSAL SCIENCES include metallurgy, the extracting, refining and alloying of metals*, the study of gems* and other elements of the mineral* world; horticulture (*udyāna-vidyā*), a knowledge of the medicinal value of herbs and other arcane subjects connected with the plant world; *paśu-vidyā* or animal lore; the training, breeding and care of animals, especially horses, elephants and cattle; *sarpa-vidyā* or serpent-lore; *paksha-vidyā* or bird-lore, the care and training of birds like the parrot and myna to speak and sing and memorise verses to carry to the loved one, also the sending of messages by carrier-pigeons.

The URBANE ARTS require a knowledge of etiquette; behaviour in visiting and receiving friends; knowledge of cock-fighting and ram-fighting, field and water sports, parlour games including chess, dice and gambling (*jūyam*); the ceremonial of festivals and *goshṭhī* or cultural gatherings. Since contingencies may arise when one may have to appropriate what does not belong to one, the art of purloining is not to be overlooked. A textbook on the subject called *Shaṇmukha-kalpa* is said to be extant.

The MAGICAL ARTS are also of importance to the man of the world and the lover. These include dexterity in juggling and legerdemain, and creating illusions; an understanding of mantras, charms and omens; knowing how to avert the evil eye, how to cast spells, how to make oneself invisible and acquire other siddhis*; mastery of disguise and impersonation to gain access to harems. Also argury and divination* as well as the interpretation of omens and portents.

The daily ritual of the man about town presupposes a thorough acquaintance with the arts of PERSONAL ADORNMENT. These include leaf-cutting for decorating the forehead; colouring and staining the teeth, hair and nails; hairdressing, hair styles and headdresses; cosmetics and ointments; facial makeup with sandalwood pastes, powder and paints; shampooing (the word comes from the Hindi word *chāmpana*) and massaging to soften and beautify the skin; the making of ornaments; the art of dressing; the making and trimming of clothes; dyeing textiles and weaving and designing fabrics. Needlework, perfumery, garland-making, and related crafts are also to be studied.

Lastly come the BEDCHAMBER ARTS including the tiling of floors; tracing designs on floors with rice-powder; caning of chairs and cots; arranging of beds and divans; arranging of pillows and bolsters; flower arrangement and the language of flowers; gesture language; the language of the betel-leaf (to offer a betel* sealed with two cloves means, 'I cannot see you'; garnishing the leaf spread out on the open palm, 'I am all yours', and so on), all leading up to the science of erotics (*kāmaśāstra*).

Books

See under Arts and under Handicrafts.

SLAVERY. Indian society, like that of Greece and Rome, was preeminently a slave society. Slaves formed one of the largest social classes of early times, and included such castes as the *Dāsas* (slaves) and certain sections of the śūdra caste. Hereditary slaves, both men and women, were attached to families, and formed part of the establishment of temples.

According to Aiyer, 'Abundant evidence of the existence of slavery is to be found in the most ancient Hindu literature' (I, p. 88). We find it in the Vedas, in the Epics and the Purāṇas. The legend of Hariśchandra reveals a society where people are freely bought and sold; the Pāṇḍavas become the slaves of the Kauravas at a throw of the dice; the hero Nala stakes his wife in a game of chance.

The Maurya king Bindusāra begged Antiochus Soter to *buy* and send him a philosopher, a fact suggesting that it was not unusual even for men of learning to be purchased in those days in India. Nothing was done by any of the ancient reformist sects, including Buddhism, to put an end to slavery. Slaves were maintained in Buddhist monasteries, and generally speaking the whole servile class fared well in a Buddhist dispensation; they were well cared for and were taught reading and handicrafts.

Slaves were classified according to the manner in which they were acquired and the functions they were expected to perform. Manu refers to seven kinds of slaves, and other lawgivers give their own categories. They included those who became slaves as a result of indebtedness; war captives; 'voluntary' slaves, who sold themselves in order to be fed; slaves by birth; slaves purchased in the market.

As a rule a slave had no property, and all that he possessed or earned belonged to his master. According to the *Arthaśāstra* of Kauṭilya it was possible for a slave to acquire property by his own labour performed without prejudice to his master; he could also acquire property by inheritance from his father, and could redeem himself and become free, but this type of slavery was only for the twice-born, excluding, of course, the brāhmin, who could never be enslaved. A female slave on whom a child was begotten by her master was entitled to her freedom along with the child, but this dubious benefit was seldom availed of since the woman was entirely dependent on her master.

Till recently, all the members of certain castes, like the *pañchama* Paraiyan were hereditary slaves. They were born slaves, remained serfs from father to son, and were part of the land on which they were born. The land-owner could sell them but only along with the land. Every landed proprietor had a community of Paraiyan to cultivate his fields.

The whole system of slavery was abolished by the British in the middle of the nineteenth century, but slavery continued to flourish for some decades after, and according to some, probably still exists clandestinely in certain parts of India.

Books

I. Aiyer, P. S. S. 'Slavery in India'. Ch. V. of *Evolution of Hindu Moral Ideals*, Calcutta, 1935.

II. Chanana, D. R. *Slavery in Ancient India as Depicted in Pali and Sanskrit Texts*, New Delhi, 1961.

III. Dange, S. A. *India from Primitive Communism to Slavery*, Bombay, 1949.

SOCIOLOGY. The sociological framework of the Hindus represents a unique system of its own, the elements of which are not found in the same measure anywhere else in the world. These features are dealt with separately and little more need be done here than give a brief directory of the main headings under which they are considered.

Fundamental to Hinduism is the system of castes, which forms the basis of law and the conventions regulating community life. It governs the institution of āśrama, education, the means of livelihood, and filters down to the smallest details of life such as the naming of children and modes of salutation.

The laws governing Hindu social life are found reflected in many observances relating to the joint family and marriage, and in such related matters as widowhood, polygamy, the matriarchy, and sonship. The conventions in regard to women* are manifold, and cover the subjects of childbirth, child-marriage, virginity, infanticide, incest, *niyoga*, *strītantra*, *strīrājya*, the harem, adultery and divorce. Closely linked with this is the field of erotics, and its connected subjects such as promiscuity, prostitution, androgyny, perversion and scatology.

Another area of Hindu mores and manners deals with music and the dance, games and gambling, diet and drinks, dress and travel, physical culture, evacuation, bathing, and personal cleanliness.

Politics, kingship, slavery, warfare, the army and related topics cover the political arena. At the end of the scale are matters pertaining to religion, ritual, worship, the sacraments, sacrifices, ending with death, suicide, suttee, the obsequies and *śrāddha* rites, and eschatology.

Books

I. Coomaraswamy, A. K. *Religious Basis of Indian Society*, New York, 1946.

II. Dubois, Abbe. *Hindu Manners, Customs & Ceremonies*, 3rd Ed., 1936.

III. Panikkar, K. M. *Hindu Society at the Crossroads*, Bombay, 1955.

IV. Prabhu, P. H. *Hindu Social Institutions*, London, 1939.

V. Rice, S. *Hindu Customs and Their Origin*, London, 1937.

VI. Sarkar, B. K. *Hindu Sociology*, Allahabad, 1920.

VII. Thomas, P. *Hindu Religion, Customs & Manners*, Bombay, n.d.
VIII. Valavalkar, P. H. *Hindu Social Institutions*, 2nd Ed., Baroda, 1942.

SOLAṄKI (961–1297) an early offshoot of the Chālukya* tribe of Gurjara barbarian stock. The Solaṅki branch settled in Gujarāt, Kāṭhiāwār and Cutch, and rose to prominence after some centuries. They are also referred to as the Chaulukya of Gujarāt and sometimes classed with the Rājputs.

The dynasty was founded by **Mūlarāja I** (*c.* AD 961) descended from a Gujar chief who fixed his capital at Aṇhilvāḍ (or Aṇahilavāḍa), modern Pātan, north-west of Ahmadābād, in the face of fierce opposition from the Chāhamānas, Paramāras and other neighbouring kings. Although generally Śaivite by religion the Solaṅki rulers were much under Jain influence.

Bhīma I (or Bhīmadeva I) (fl. 1030) is known to posterity chiefly on account of his minister and general *Vimala*, who was sent by him to Chandravatī, capital of the rebellious Dhaṇḍuka, a feudatory of Bhīmadeva. Chandravatī, lying at the foot of Mount Ābū, inspired the minister with its beauty and after he had completed his mission he devoted the remainder of his days to the construction there of the famous Jain temple named after him, the Vimala Temple, dedicated to the first tīrthaṅkara. It is one of the celebrated Dilwāra (or Dilāvārā) group of temples.

The most powerful ruler of the dynasty was **Siddharāja** (1094–1143) who ranks among the popular heroes of Gujarāt legend, at whose court the famous Jain scholar Hemachandra flourished. Siddharāja is also remembered for his capture of the fortress of Junagaḍh in Kāṭhiāwār in order to gain possession of the beautiful wife of the Junagaḍh prince. The fort was betrayed, but the wife burnt herself on a pyre rather than submit to the Solaṅki king.

At this time Jainism became the state religion. Legend relates that the next ruler **Kumārapāla** (1143–1172) who continued his predecessor's patronage of the great Jain scholar Hemachandra, inflicted heavy fines on the people even for killing fleas.

The next prominent ruler was **Vīrdhavala** (1210–1250) who did much to repel invaders, strengthen the state and embellish the capital. His ministers, the brothers *Vastupāla* and *Tejapāla*, built the second of the great Dilwāra temples on Mount Ābū, and also the magnificent Jain mountain* shrines at Śatruñjaya and Girnār. The Solaṅki dynasty survived till 1297 when the generals of Alā-ud-dīn annexed Gujarāt.

The rājas and merchant princes of Aṇhilvāḍ were great patrons of the arts, and are frequently referred to as the Indian Medicis. They were also sound politicians and bankers. The rulers acquired much wealth from sea-borne trade with the Arabs and Persians, and a substantial part of the wealth went into the construction of highly ornate and florid temples, mainly Jain, which are numbered in their hundreds. The capital of Aṇhilvāḍ alone contains over one hundred Jain temples. They crowned the tops of their hills with shrines, raising what are virtual temple cities on Mount Śatruñjaya in Kāṭhiāwār which has 860 temples; Mount Girnār also in Kāṭhiāwār with hundreds more; and Mount Ābū in Rājputāna which contains some of the finest examples of Jain architecture.

Particularly noteworthy examples of their work are the following three temples. The Sun Temple (1025) at Modera or Modhera, once the site of Maga* worship, stands on the edge of a large sacred pool, whose banks rise in terraces crowded with shrines large and small. It was dedicated to the sun-god and though not a Jain edifice its construction was nonetheless permitted by the liberal-minded Solaṅki rulers. One wall of the temple has a representation of the sun-god with Central Asian boots and a belt. The Vimala Temple (1050) on Mount Ābū is dedicated to Ādinātha the first *tīrthaṅkara*. It is built entirely of white marble and contains many elaborate sculptures, but its claim to uniqueness lies in the decorative treatment of the vaulted ceilings, which are quite extraordinary in their beauty. The carvings are of a 'lace-like delicacy' and were achieved not by chipping but by a laborious process of scraping, the craftsmen being rewarded according to the quantity of marble dust they could show. The Tejapāla Temple (1232) dedicated to Neminātha, the second of the famous Dilwāra temples, is also on Mount Ābū.

Books

I. Luard, C. E. *Dilwara Temples, with Antiquities of Mount Abu*, 1913.
II. Majumdar, A. K. *Chaulukyas of Gujerat*, Bombay, 1956.
(*See also under* History.)

SOMA, god of the moon and guardian of sacrifice and penance, lord of healing and herbs. In Purāṇic mythology Soma (who is also called *Chandra*) is said to be variously the son of Varuṇa, or Dharma, or of the ṛishi Atri by his wife Anasūyā, or of Prabhākara of the race of Atri. Other accounts say he was produced during the Churning of the Ocean.

Soma married twenty-seven of the daughters of the arch-mage Daksha, but because he treated ROHIṆĪ, the fourth wife, with partiality, Daksha cursed him with consumption, so that for fifteen days he grew smaller and smaller, until he repented and his strength was restored during the next fifteen days, a myth obviously referring to the waning and waxing of the moon. In one myth Soma abducted Tārā wife of Bṛihaspati* preceptor of the gods, and only surrendered her after a long struggle in which the gods and asuras also became involved. Disinherited by his father Varuṇa, Soma was refused entry to the abode of the gods and even the fact that Śiva wore his image on his forehead did not help his cause. Soma was therefore forced to remain in the sky. Soma is represented as copper-coloured, riding a car drawn by an antelope, or a three-wheeled chariot drawn by ten white horses, five on the right side of the shaft and five on the left.

Soma is also known as Bhagnātmā ('fractured being'), Indu ('drop' i.e. in the sky), Kumuda-pati ('lotus-lord'), Mṛigāṅka ('deer-marked'), Nakshatra-nātha ('constellation lord'), Niśākara ('night-maker'), Oshadhi-pati ('herb-lord'), Śaśin ('hare' of the sky); Sitāṁśu ('white-rayed'), Śiva-śekhara ('Śiva-crested'); Śveta-vāji (drawn by 'white horses').

The son of Soma and Tārā (or Rohiṇī) was *Budha*, the planet Mercury, who married Ilā (*see* Sudyumna), the Tiresias of Hindu mythology. Budha was also called Saumya (of Soma); Rauhiṇeya (from Rohiṇī); Śyāmāṅga ('black-bodied'). He was the author of a hymn in the *Ṛig-veda*. Budhvār (Wednesday) is named after him.

Books

See under Mythology.

SOMA, the name of a plant said to have been first cultivated in Indra's heaven. Indra performed all his heroic deeds while under the influence of the juice extracted from the leaves and stems of this divine herb. It was referred to as 'the King of Plants', and conferred vitality, immortality and inspiration. Originally grown only in the celestial kingdom it was brought down to earth by an eagle (*śyena*) and thereafter grew on Mount Mūjavat (Mūjavant or Maujavanta). The plant was also known to the ancient Persians and is related to the haoma of the Avesta.

Soma was raised to the position of a deity and sung of as 'everlasting, omnipotent, all-healing, the bestower of riches and giver of immortality'. In later mythology Soma became a deity of the moon. The whole of the Ninth Book of the *Ṛig-veda* is devoted to praise of Soma. 'Where there is eternal radiance, where life is free, where there is desire and delight, where joy and pleasure abide, there O Soma, make me immortal.'

The Soma rite was the basis of the Ṛig-vedic sacrificial system, and was chiefly concerned with the extracting and preparation of the sacred soma juice, followed by libations to the gods and the ritual drinking of the juice by the priests. The juice was described as sweet, delicious, pure and purifying, inspiring confidence, courage, faith and eloquence. Nothing shows more clearly how far the modern Hindus are removed from the ancient milieu than the fact that today the plant around which so much ritualism had grown up, is unidentifiable. Authorities variously hold that it is the milky climbing plant, *Asclepias acida*, or the Ephedra, or a type of uncultivated vine. The plant now used for soma rites is entirely different since its juice produces a nauseating effect quite unlike the exhiliration produced by the soma described in the *Ṛig-veda*.

The *soma-saṁsthā*, 'soma-establishment', takes the usual form of other *yajñas* (sacrifices*) but has a few special features of its own. It is generally celebrated at the end of the year, and the sacrificer is not to perform it more than three times in his life. On account of its great cost the sacrifice was usually reserved for kings and wealthy persons but was always attended by the general populace.

Preparations for the soma rites include its ritual purchase from a merchant. The merchant is supposed to offer only that variety of soma herb that had grown on Mount Mūjavant. Thrice he refuses to sell the plant, first for the price of a cow's foot, then for a quarter of a cow, and finally for a goat. He is then driven off with a stroke of an udumbara rod on the right shoulder, and three strokes with blades of kuśa grass on the left shoulder, and his merchandise is taken from him.

The soma cow, with which the soma was to have been purchased is borne on a cart to the sacrificial court or vedi. At the spot where the seventh footprint of the cow is imprinted on the soil from the point of its descent from the cart, an oblation is made; a plate of gold is placed on the footprint, and ghee and water poured around it in a magical protective circle. The sand of the footprint is put into a bucket, thus removing the cow (the footprint being the cow) from the earth. Later this sand is given to the sacrificer's chief wife who strews it on her hearth. The sacrificer steps into the seven footprints and then he and his wives and the priests sit around the golden plate while mantras are recited.

The ceremonial consecration of sacred utensils occupies an important part in the preparatory soma rites. Even if the sacrifice is of a single day's duration many kinds of utensils are used and over one hundred utensils and implements* are named. They include pots and pitchers, ladles, tongs, churning sticks, pestles and mortars, pounding stones, pressing stones, sieves and strainers, storing vessels and drinking vessels.

The introductory ceremony, the *pravargya*, commences with the pouring of fresh milk into a large earthenware vessel known as the *mahāvīra* pot, which is first made red-hot. This vessel receives worship and is regarded as the 'head of the sacrifice'. It is associated with the demon Makha the enemy of all sacrifice, who was beheaded by the deities. Originally an independent ceremony in honour of the sun, it was later incorporated in the soma ritual. At the close of the ceremony the sacrificial utensils are arranged to resemble a human figure, the mahāvīra pot standing for the head, with sacred kuśa grass for the hair, and so on.

Also part of the ceremony is the erection of the *sadas* or shed in the sacrificial enclosure where the soma is taken (*see* altar). The usual procedure is followed of addressing the spade used in digging, and of chanting mantras while pouring the water, while dislodging and shovelling out the earth. Draughts of sour milk or milk and water into which some blades of *kuśa* grass have been dipped are ladled out as oblations.

The soma herbs are rinsed and purified in a bath of water, and laid out on ox-hides preparatory to pressing. After further chants the *prasava* or pressing begins. The stalks of the plant are crushed between two stones, or sometimes pounded in a mortar. The pressing boards, the upper pressing stone (*adri*) and lower pressing stone (*grāvan*), or the mortar and pestle (*ulūkhala-musala*) are duly addressed in suitable verses during the entire proceedings. The noise of the pounding stones is described as the roaring of a bull, but this may only suggest the accompaniment of a bull-roarer, a ritual device of Austric origin.

The juice thus pounded or squeezed out flows down a board through a strainer or sheep's wool into large wooden vats known as *droṇa-kalaśa* or into earthen jars where it is stored. Cups of soma are then drawn off, mixed with milk, curds, ghee or honey, offered to the gods and then drunk by the participants. The number of rounds or cups drawn often characterizes the various soma sacrifices. In expiation for over-indulgence in the drinking of soma, leading to intoxication, misbehaviour, and forgetfulness of the ritual, the rite of *sautrāmaṇī* is performed. In this case a drink called *surā* was offered to Indra and other deities, instead of soma, along with a bull, sheep or goat.

The *savana* or extraction of soma juice takes place three times a day, morning, noon and evening, and different ceremonies attend these occasions. At the (a) *prātaḥ-savana*, 'dawn libation', a *stoma* (panegyric) or *stotra* (eulogium) of great praise, called the *bahish-pavamāna* ('outer hymns'), is sung outside the courtyard or beyond the altar area. The early morning extraction includes a serpentining procession or *prasarpaṇa* where the officiants proceed outside the vedi, bent forward in single file, each holding the shoulders of the man in front; they drag their feet and lick their lips, chanting the while. At the midday soma pressing they walk upright but with heads bowed; in the evening their heads are raised. At the (b) *mādhyaṁ-dina*, or 'mid-day' pressing, the grāvastut or hierophant addresses invocations to the pressing stones. The midday savana is dedicated exclusively to Indra, who also has a share in the morning and evening pressings. Accompanying the noonday ceremony is the *vāma-devya*, a chant or *sāman* mentioned in the *Chhāndogya Upanishad*. In later times the ceremony became transformed, like the *vājapeya**, into a rite involving sexual union. The stages of the act were entered upon in conjunction with the chanting of the sāman, so that the successive stages of coition coincided with the different verses of the Vedic text.

'He summons; he makes a request; together with the woman he lies down; he lies upon the woman; he comes to completion; he thus knows the *vāma-devya* as woven upon the act of copulation, and procreates himself from every copulation. One should never abstain from any woman: that is the rule.'

In the (c) *tṛitīya*, 'third' or evening pressing, the *agnishṭoma* sāman is sung. Such is the glow produced by this chant that the *yajamāna* (sacrificer) and the priest cover their heads and faces while chanting, while at the same time water is poured over the thighs of the yajamāna's wife. Other prayers are offered and chants sung. Finally the soma cups are cleaned and a purifying bath takes place.

Hundreds of variations of the soma ritual have been classified: some according to the deities invoked, or the number of officiating priests, the number of chants and invocations, the number of animals sacrificed, the type of praise (*shṭoma, shṭut, stoma, stotra*), the 'rounds' of soma drawn, offered to the deities, and drunk by the officiants. In the *shodaśin* (sixteen-fold) for example, there are sixteen officiating priests, sixteen chants and invocations, one to three animal victims. The scheme of classification given below covers the more important categories of the soma sacrifice.

The *ekāha*, 'one', are sacrifices completed within a single day, not counting the three or four preparatory days required for every soma sacrifice. The briefest of these is the *sādyaska*, 'immediate', in which the soma is bought, and the libations prepared and offered immediately. Others include the *vrātya-stoma* (*see* śodhana), the vājapeya*, the *agnishṭoma*, and the *jyotiḥ-shṭoma*. The *agnishṭoma* (or *angishṭut*) 'fire-praising', is the basic model of all soma sacrifices and is performed by those desirous of going to heaven. There are several variations of this prototype. Because it is devoted to Agni it is sometimes regarded as 'hateful to Indra' (*see* Bhaṅgāsvana). In the agnishṭoma sixteen priests officiate (hence one of its variants is called the shodaśin, from shodaśa, 'sixteen'), one to three animals are slain, twelve chants and invocations recited, and twelve 'rounds' of soma drunk. The hymns of praise (uktha) sung at the ekāha rites give the name to another type of agnishṭoma known as the *ukthya*, with fifteen chants. The *jyotiḥ-shṭoma*, 'light-praising' also has sixteen priests but thirty-three invocations, and is sometimes performed for warding off or causing bewitchment. In all of these sacrifices the usual three pressings take place, in the morning, noon and evening.

The *ahīna* class of soma sacrifices last from two to twelve days, such as the *garga*, a three-day soma rite; or the *pañcha-śāradiya* offered to the Maruts, lasting five days; the *dvādaśāha*, a twelve-day rite. The *ati-rātra* or 'overnight' sacrifice consists of twenty-nine chants and twenty-nine rounds of drinks, requires eighteen priests, calls for the sacrifice of four animals and takes three nightly recitations to complete. The *varuṇa-praghāsa*, so called because the participants eat barley in honour of Varuṇa, is performed at the full-moon of *Ashāḍha* (June–July), and its object is to obtain freedom from the snares of Varuṇa. In the course of the rite the wife of the sacrificer is questioned about any adulterous relations she may have had.

The *sattra*, 'session', class of soma rites, consisted of the greater ceremonies of more than twelve days duration, requiring the services of many officiants. Some sattras lasted thirty-three days, some for three months, others for six months, and a few for a year. The rarer sattras were supposed to last even longer, but were too complicated and expensive to be carried out in practice, and according to one authority were 'intended rather as intellectual exercises'. The sattras include the *rājasūya* (royal consecration*), *aśvamedha* (horse sacrifice), *gavāmayana**, and the *agni-chayana* (*see* altar).

Books

See under Sacrifice.

SOMADEVA (*c.* 1070), Kashmīri priest, author of a voluminous cycle of Sanskrit stories in verse, known as the *Kathā-sarit-sāgara*, or The Ocean of Rivers of Stories, one of the most notable of the Sanskrit kathā series. According to tradition the work was written by command and for the entertainment of Queen Sūryamatī, wife of the king of Kashmīr, and is a sort of *Arabian Nights*. It is divided into 124 chapters called *taraṅga*, 'waves', and contains many traces of its ultimately Buddhist origin, with even direct allusions to the Buddhist Jātakas; but the bulk of the material is derived from Guṇāḍhya. It contains several passages describing the blood-thirsty orgies performed in honour of the goddess Durgā.

Book XII of the *Kathā-sarit-sāgara* is often separately known as *Vetāla-pañcha-viṁśati*, or Twenty-five Tales of a Vampire, written by an unknown author of unknown date, but attributed to one Jambhala-datta. It relates how king Vikramasena of Ujjain is directed by an ascetic to remove a corpse hanging on a tree in a graveyard and convey it some distance away without uttering a word. To touch a corpse is defilement, and to visit a burial ground where magical Śākta rites take place is full of psychic danger, but the king is obliged to carry out the ascetic's behest. As he is carrying the corpse on his shoulder, a *vetāla*, a special kind of demon which attaches itself to dead bodies, begins to tell the king a story to while away the tedium of the long journey. The king is soon absorbed in the story and unthinkingly replies to a question put to him by the vampire, whereupon his burden disappears and he has to return to the graveyard to detach it from the tree and take it away once more, amid the ghoulish laughter of the other demons. This process is repeated till the vetāla has told the king twenty-five tales, which comprise the book.

Books

I. Penzer, N. M. (Ed.) *The Ocean of Story*, London, 1924–7.

SOMNĀTH, or more accurately Soma-nātha, 'Moon Lord', a title of Śiva, was the name of one of the most celebrated liṅgas*, around which was built a sea-washed Śiva temple famous in history. Situated near the present-day town of Pātan at the southern tip of the Kāṭhiāwār peninsula, Somnāth was a hallowed place of pilgrimage, closely associated with Kṛishṇa. It was to this liṅga that Kṛishṇa paid homage when the civil strife among the Yādava people warned him of his approaching end, and it was here too that he accidentally received his mortal wound from the hunter Jaras.

Although this would date the liṅga from the mythological age, there is another tradition to the effect that it was actually one of the monolithic idols of Mecca which was brought to India before Muhammad the Prophet began his campaign of destroying the idols of that city (V, p. 140).

The liṅga of Somnāth was of polished stone, and the visible portion of it, over seven feet in height, was adorned with a heavy jewel-encrusted chain of solid gold. Every day it was washed with holy water specially brought from the Ganges, and garlanded with flowers from Kashmīr. The inner shrine was built of wood and its fifty-six wooden pillars were covered with wonderfully-wrought silver inlaid with precious stones. Golden chandeliers were kept burning night and day.

The temple was endowed with the revenue of ten thousand villages for its support, and a troupe of five hundred dancing girls and two hundred musicians were in its service. A thousand brāhmins performed the daily ritual, and three hundred barbers were employed for shaving the heads and beards of the pilgrims. The temple's pyramidal roof rose in thirteen tiers and was surmounted by fourteen golden domes. The whole shrine area with the subsidiary buildings for its army of ministrants and devotees and rest-houses for pilgrims formed a town of its own which was surrounded by a series of massive fortifications.

In the winter of AD 1024 Mahmūd of Ghazni, having heard of the fabulous wealth of Somnāth, crossed the desert and appeared before its walls. The inhabitants, confident of the power of Śiva jeered at the invaders from the battlements. Mahmūd began his assault the next day. The Hindus defended themselves as best they could, calling upon Śiva to help them. Mahmūd made short work of storming the outer and inner defences of the citadel and broke into the temple amid a scene of terrible destruction typical of his barbarity. Over fifty thousand brāhmins were put to the sword, and thousands of others perished by drowning while trying to escape by sea.

The plunder was beyond Mahmūd's wildest expectations, and the priests who submitted offered him still more wealth if he would spare the sacred liṅga. But the Iconoclast retorting that he was the 'Scourge and not the Vendor of Idols' took up a heavy mace and with his own hand delivered the first shattering blow. His soldiers completed the work of destruction, sparing only a part of the liṅga on Mahmūd's orders. This part the conqueror carried to his capital of Ghazni where it was embedded in the threshold of a mosque so that the symbol, so detestable to Muslims, would forever be trodden underfoot by true believers.

Books

I. Burgess, J. *Temples of Somnath*, 1901.
II. Cousens, H. *Somnath and Other Mediaeval Temples in Kathiawar*, Calcutta, 1931.
III. Nazim, M. *The Life and Times of Sultan Mahmud of Ghazni*, Cambridge, 1931.
IV. Munshi, K. M. *Somanatha, the Shrine Eternal*, 1929.
V. Wilson, H. H. *Sketch of the Religious Sects of the Hindus*, Calcutta, 1846.

SONSHIP. The Sanskrit word for son, *putra*, is of Dravidian origin. In times past Hindus desired male progeny to carry on the family name, to defend the tribe against its enemies, to serve the clan in communal activities. And only sons could perform the all important funeral rites. The possession of a son was held to be absolutely essential to a man's salvation, and according to traditional derivation a *put-ra* is a 'hell-deliverer', since a man without a putra or son is consigned to the hell* called Put. This belief is still widely prevalent. When a young couple marry everyone awaits with great anxiety the birth of a son. And not only the living members of the family, for in the unseen world the ancestors also wait. More than one sacrifice was devised, and dozens of rites prescribed (e.g. *puṁsavana*), and hundreds of mantras and prayers composed, for the specific purpose of obtaining male progeny (*see* Jaratkāru).

Many kinds of sons (some texts list fourteen) were once recognized by Hindu law. The *aurasa* or son issuing from one's own body (lit., *uras*, chest) is the legitimate son, begotten by the father on his lawfully wedded wife of equal caste; the *sahoḍha* is the son who was conceived (but not born) before the marriage of his parents; the *paunarbhava*, the son of a twice-married woman, i.e. of a remarried woman by her second husband; the *pārāśara* (or pāraśava) the son by a concubine; the *kānīna*, 'bastard' the son of an unmarried girl (e.g. Vyāsa and Karṇa); the *kuṇḍa* the bastard of an adulterous wife; the *gūḍhaja* is the son whose father is not named or known and who is born in secret (*gūḍha*).

If a man was unable to have a son for any reason, he was permitted to adopt one legally. Sons so adopted could be taken from many categories of male children. One could adopt one's own child begotten illegitimately so that by adoption he would be entitled to all the rights of a legitimate heir. Sons could also be chosen from among those born by niyoga*. Such sons were called *kshetraja*, 'field-born' i.e. born on the *kshetra*, 'field' or property (wife) of the real husband, and hence the husband's property, whoever may have supplied the 'seed'. Sons were also picked from the *putrikā-putra*, 'daughter's son', that is, the son of a daughter who was married on the understanding that she would live in her father's house and that her son would be regarded as her father's son. This was done where the father had no sons but did have one or more daughters. Sons could also be taken from outside. Such is the *krītaka* or son 'bought' from his real parents, who may or may not be related to the adopting parents. As a rule only parents could give a child in adoption and therefore an orphan or a foundling could not be adopted. Exceptions were allowed in certain cases; thus the *apabiddha* (or *apaviddha*) was the child cast off by his parents and taken as a son by a stranger.

Adoption is called *poshpaka*, 'nourishing', and is the legal recognition of a child as one's son and heir; it is preceded by special procedures of affiliation of the adopted boy into the family, giving him the legal and spiritual status of a son.

Generally speaking, a man who has no male issue can adopt; so can a widower and even a bachelor. A woman as a rule cannot adopt for herself, the adoption can only be made for her husband and for his benefit. But the adoptive capacity of a woman (whether wife or widow) varied greatly in different localities. Daughters were sometimes adopted in Hindu society, but this is now very rare, and prevails chiefly among certain classes of prostitutes and temple dancing-girls.

The forms and terms of adoption also vary from place to place. As a rule the boy should be below five years of age, and the thread rite should not have been performed on him. If he already wears the thread this will have to be ceremonially broken and a new one substituted at the adoption ceremony. The rite of adoption includes the actual and formal giving up of the child by his real parents and the taking over of the child by his new parents. It has been described as a form of new birth. There is thus a complete severance of the child from his natural family; he stands in the same position as a natural-born son in the new family and has the right to perform the duties of a real son at his adoptive father's obsequies. He cannot inherit from his natural family except where by local custom he does not lose his rights in his natural family.

The chief forms of adoption are: (1) *Dattaka*, 'donated', the most common form, where the exchange is carried out between the two families with the appropriate ceremonies. Here the adopted boy must 'bear the reflection of a son', which is interpreted to mean that his mother, when a maiden, might have been married by the adoptive father. A man therefore cannot adopt his brother, uncle, daughter's son, sister's son and so on. (2) *Kṛitrima*, 'adopted', recognized only in Mithilā. Here the consent of the boy is necessary, and he must therefore have attained majority. No ceremonies are required. A kṛitrima son does not lose his right to property in his natural family and the child can be closely related to the adopter. (3) *Dvamushya*, 'twice-taken', obsolete except in parts of Bombay and Malabār. Here a person gives his son to another under an agreement that he should be considered as the son of both of them. The son inherits both in his natural and adoptive families. (4) *Illatum*, prevails among the Reddis and other castes in Madrās, especially in Bellary and Kurnool. A person who has no son but only daughters may adopt a son-in-law. This illatum son-in-law stands on the footing of a son with regard to succession, and in the case of a later-born natural son takes an equal share in the property.

Books

See under Law.

SOUL or Spirit, is termed *ātman* in Sanskrit, a word of uncertain origin, anciently used in the sense of wind or breath, as in *prāṇa*, and related to the Greek *atmos* and the German *Atem*, breath. It was later applied to mind, consciousness, ego and finally soul. The existence of the ātman in this last sense is not accepted by the *lokāyatas* (materialists) and by some Buddhist schools, but is held by most Hindu philosophical systems.

The *ātman* is often confused and identified with *jīva*, 'life', the principle of life, which is regarded as the vitalizing element in living things, affected by phenomena and subject to the experience of feeling and suffering. In a sense everything is said to have jīva, including gods, demons, plants and even so-called inanimate objects. In man the jīva is made up of the thinking apparatus, the indriyas or sense organs, and the vital winds*.

Sometimes the term jīva is used in place of ātman to mean the phenomenal self, also called *jīvātman*, the soul of an individual living being, as distinguished from the *Paramātman*, Supreme Soul, or Brahma (*see* God). The ātman is thus regarded as an *aṁśa* or fragment of the Supreme. 'Just as the space within a jar does not differ from the space without, so the individual soul is identical with the Universal.' Being an aṁśa or fragment it yearns to be united with the Whole (aṁśin). The identity of the individual soul and the Supreme Soul is the central teaching of the Upanishads and of Vedānta, where it is repeatedly stressed and explained by numerous examples and affirmed in countless maxims. A realization that the jīvātman is essentially one with the Paramātman constitutes true knowledge* and is a prerequisite condition of salvation.

Since the ātman is part of the eternal it has many attributes of the godhead; it is regarded as beginningless, unborn, etermal, transcendental, indestructible, without magnitude, beyond good and evil and so on (*see* God). It is diffused all over the world so that a man's soul is actually everywhere although he can only feel and act wherever his body happens to be and where his mind glows into localized consciousness (*see* psychology). The paradoxical relationship between the phenomena-bewildered man and his imperishable nucleus or ātman is expressed in numerous enigmatical stanzas such as the following from the *Taittirīya Āraṇyaka*, 'The blind one (i.e. one blind to the lure of phenomena) found the jewel (ātman), the one without fingers picked it up, the one without a neck put it on, and the one without a voice gave it praise'.

The ātman is the only permanent substratum in the individual. The body is perishable and disintegrates, and the mind evanescent and disperses, just as water when heated turns into steam. But the soul is gold. When gold is repeatedly treated by the method of *patta-pāka*, 'leaf-baking', and heated again and again, its purity becomes absolute; it reaches a state of *rakta-sāra*, 'red-throughout', i.e. pure gold, and the final result is indispersable by further heating. It is the permanent substance.

Being attached to the body and subject to earthly existence, the soul, although ubiquitous, is also atomic and disparate. It is the individual entity, the principle of life and sensation, and constitutes the cognitive, emotional or conative self. It is variously said to reside in the heart, head, the great toe or the left testicle; or to be outside the body like an aura, or around the head like a halo. Sometimes it is regarded as being as small as the thumb, stationed near the navel, and occasionally moving slowly all over the body. It is further bound by *māyā* (illusion), subject to pleasure-pain (*sukha-duḥkha*); acquires merit (*puṇya*) and demerit (*pāpa*), is guided by mind (*see* psychology) and acquires karma* and is thus enmeshed in the whirl of birth-death-rebirth (*saṁsāra*). The various ways (*marga*) of getting out of this recurrent cycle and attaining salvation is the chief preoccupation of Hindu and Buddhist philosophy.

Books

I. Narahari, H. G. *Atman in Pre-Upanishadic and Vedic Literature*, 1944.
II. Pillai, N. *Soul and Substance in Hinduism*, 1919.
See also under Philosophy.

SOUND in Sanskrit is called *śabda* a word of wide application and many meanings. In one sense it signifies verbal testimony or Vedic authority as a means to right knowledge*, and is so used in Nyāya philosophy. In Sāṁkhya philosophy it stands for the tanmātra or subtle element of sound. In the Mīmāṁsā* system it means, among other things, the Word, almost in the Gnostic sense of Logos. Here śabda is regarded as eternal, absolute, self-sufficient and authoritative.

Śabda is not mere verbal utterance, but is self-subsisting and potential, having existed before utterance otherwise it could not have been pronounced. The sound made in uttering a word is dissipated but the Word remains. The word or name precedes the object, and the proper intonation of the name can create the object it represents. Things are called or named before they can come into existence.

Sanskrit sounds in particular are considered to be real approximations to the eternal elements of ethereal sound, for Sanskrit is not regarded as a historical language based on rules of conventional speech but a manifestation of Being; and there is believed to be a vital connection between the sound of the Sanskrit word and the meaning it conveys.

The practical application of this theory is found in the belief in the magical power of the mantra* or spell. Often very cryptic and meaningless it can, if repeated often enough, penetrate the dense shell of the material world and derive potency from the occult spheres. Fine distinctions are made between the varieties of śabda, which are generally classed under four heads in decreasing order of subtlety:

(1) *Sphoṭa*, the eternal element of sound, is beyond perception. It is pure unmanifested sound and the creative principle of the universe. It is the world of Pure Being.

(2) *Nāda*, sometimes identified with sphoṭa, is defined as an unstruck and unstrikable sound, or as a state of continuous 'sounding'. Just as a man cannot see the colour of a flower on a dark night although it is there to be seen, so a person cannot hear the sound of the nāda although it is there to be heard. Most people are deaf to nāda but the hearing of it can be acquired through training (*see* kuṇḍalinī).

(3) *Anāhata,* 'unstruck', refers to sound potentially existing but not expressed, such as the ajapa mantra; it is the sound of thought on the verge of manifestation. It is not to be confused with pure unmanifested sound.
(4) *Āhata,* 'struck', i.e. sound produced by the physical action of one thing upon another. It includes the whole range of physical sound, whether audible to human ears or not.

The chief kinds of āhata or struck sounds are: (1) *svana,* the inanimate sounds of nature, like the crash of thunder, the roar of waterfalls, the rumble of earthquakes, the roll of chariots; (2) *dhvani,* the sounds of animate nature, such as the call of animals, the song of birds; it excludes the voiced sounds of men, but includes clapping, breaking wind and snoring; (3) *hrāda,* sounds produced by the action of animate things on inanimate, such as the noises made by the carpenter at work, the spinner, the blacksmith, the musician playing on his instrument, the sound of the galloping horse, the woodpecker, the bee in flight; (4) *anaka,* 'breath', the voiced sounds of the human being e.g. the murmur of crowds, the song of the vocalist. To this category belongs the most powerful of all āhata sounds, namely, *vāch,* the sound of the human voice; (5) *aśrāvya,* sounds 'inaudible' to human ears, like the 'speech' of tiny creatures such as ants.

All āhata sounds are produced by physical action, and are transmitted by reverberation. There are four stages in all struck sounds: (a) *spanda,* the pulsing or quivering that just precedes manifestation; (b) *paryanti,* the point from which the movement of sound commences; (c) *pashyanti,* the reverberation before impact is made; (d) *vaikharī,* the impact of the sound; the sound as actually heard.

Books

See under Philosophy and Yoga.

ŚRĀDDHA, a term covering a number of ceremonies performed at various times by all adult Hindus, except *sannyāsins* and women. Śrāddha rites are celebrated on many occasions such as pilgrimages, eclipses, births or marriages, and investiture with the sacred thread. Some lawgivers list ninety-six occasions in the year when śrāddha ceremonies are to be performed.

More particularly, śrāddha rites are associated with funeral and post-mortem observances. Unlike the obsequies* proper, the śrāddha rites are *maṅgala,* 'auspicious', although during their performance the sacred thread is shifted from its normal position over the left shoulder and under the right arm, to the right shoulder.

Fundamentally, śrāddhas are a form of homage to departed ancestors. Special texts elaborated from the domestic *gṛihasūtras,* relating to post-mortem rites, form the body of *śrāddha-kalpa* or funeral usage. Manu decreed that rites in honour of the *pitṛis* or deceased ancestors were more important than rites in honour of the gods.

The first śrāddha service for a dead kinsman is the *ekodishṭa,* which generally takes place on the eleventh day after death in the case of brāhmins, on the sixteenth day for kshattriyas, the twenty-first day for vaiśyas and the thirty-first day for śūdras. Thereafter, during the first year similar services are held after a fortnight, a month, two months, and three months, and are subsequently repeated on the anniversaries of the first śrāddha. Rites to the manes performed on the eighth day after the full moon, and hence called *ashṭaka*, 'eighth', are especially meritorious; in ancient times a cow used to be sacrificed at the ashṭaka ceremony. Special merit is likewise attached to such ceremonies if performed at holy places such as Gaya, Allāhābād, Kurukshetra, and Siddhapur on the Bindu Lake in Gujarāt, where they frequently take place in public sacred grounds and are believed to bring final emancipation to the ancestors.

For the śrāddha ceremonies invitations are sent to at least as many brāhmins as the number of the dead it is desired to commemorate, but more are often invited and are all regally fed and handsomely paid, since they represent the pitṛis, and whatever is given to them is magically translated to the departed ancestors. All near relatives, who are traditionally entitled to a share in the offerings made, are also invited. First the gods and then the hierarchy of pitṛis are invoked, the latter with the formula, 'May they ascend, the lowest, the highest, the midmost, the fathers'. This is followed by offerings of *tila* (sesamum), *udaka* (water) and finally the *piṇḍa* (rice-balls, *see* obsequies). As each offering is held up a pitṛi is named. The piṇḍa and udaka are then served to the guests (*see* community): a whole piṇḍa to very close relatives; a portion of the piṇḍa to near relatives; and the udaka to remoter relatives, who eat and drink in silence. What remains is thrown into the fire or given to a cow. The spirits and gods are then dismissed. The pitṛis or fully emancipated ancestors are sent away with the words, 'Depart ye fathers, on your deep ancient paths', while the preta, the spirit of the deceased, is told to 'abide in repose'.

It is to be noted that although the piṇḍa is the main item offered at śrāddha rites, other food is also served according to local custom, at times including meat such as pork, and fish, and also wine and arrack (country liquor). The meat of a rhinoceros, if available, was especially recommended for the śrāddha feast.

Relations who gather for such ceremonies are known as *sapiṇḍa* (co-sharers of the piṇḍa), *samānodaka* (sharers of the udaka) and so on, and their attendance at these functions is a matter of great importance in the Hindu community*, since sapiṇḍaship constitutes the principal evidence of kinship in the law of inheritance. The *gotra* or clan is in fact a corporate body bound together by this act of co-sharing the piṇḍa and udaka, by means of which a communion is established between the dead and living members of a family. These members vary according to custom but generally include a man's male (and sometimes female) relatives; paternal (sometimes maternal) kin, for three generations up and down, thus establishing the relationship of seven generations dead and living.

Some scholars tend to the view that if the śrāddha and other ancestor-worshipping rites do not have a direct shamanistic origin, there are none-theless strong indications of shamanistic influences. The officiating priest is held to be the embodiment of the manes, and to satisfy him is equivalent to appeasing the manes; in some places the priest is actually believed to be possessed by the spirit of the dead, and the things he says are supposed to be coming straight from the mouth of the deceased.

Books

See under Obsequies.

STERILITY. It has been said by the lawgivers that woman* is only fit for procreation. It is enough if she knows how to pound rice, cook, and produce children, but especially the last. To be the mother of one or more sons is indeed to be envied. On the other hand a barren wife is regarded as a blot on the family and the bane of the society in which she dwells. The gods are deaf to her prayers and what she offers them is rejected. Few things are more humiliating to a man than being the husband of an unfruitful woman, for she cuts off the vital line connecting him with the immemorial and unbroken past, and deprives him of continuity with the future. After his death there is no one to deliver him from the tortures of hell (*see* sonship).

In the past wives were sometimes stoned by the people of the community because of their inability to bear children, but more frequently they were returned to their parents. If, as often happened, they were rejected by their parents as well, they could only turn to prostitution to earn their livelihood. The ranks of public women were as frequently filled by childless women whose husbands were living, as by widows.

Curses and spells are frequently used for bringing about barrenness in rivals. The *Atharva-veda* records several such curses, which have come down from prehistoric times. Similarly cures for sterility are numerous, and at times drastic, including not only vows, prilgrimages, gifts to brahmins, and prayers to the gods, but the whole range of witchcraft and black magic as well. Cited below are a few of the more unusual remedies for sterility; needless to say, most of these are now obsolete.

Divine impregnation. The Vaishṇavite temple at Tirupati in the Carnatic had the reputation of making barren women fecund if they spent a night within its walls. It was said that Vishṇu would visit the temple in person and have congress with the supplicant. This belief provided opportunities for the resident priests which they were not slow to utilize. The following morning the women would have to describe the visitation of the deity to the priests, and having paid them the customary fee depart for home full of hope.

Priestly impregnation. Women desirous of having children often resorted to priests who were paid to perform the husband's functions. Such a system was a natural development from the custom of niyoga* which permitted mutual intercourse between a man and the wives of his brothers and cousins, and later admitted brāhmins and outsiders to the privilege.

Promiscuity. There were temples in India where a woman was promised a child if she granted her favours to a certain number of men at a special midnight ceremony. Others, like the women of Babylon, offered themselves after sunset to visitors at the temple gates, with the same end in view.

Phallic magic. Touching the liṅga of naked ascetics and sādhus is believed to be especially potent for stirring the roots of female fertility. Women desirous of having children often go to such men and kiss the member to render themselves magically receptive to their husband's seed (II, p. 88).

Solar impregnation. It was believed that strong sunlight could impregnate menstruating women; hence girls in their periods were kept in darkness, but sterile wives were exposed naked to the sun during menses (IV, p. 654).

Stone magic. At certain temples in South India barren women would sit astride stone slabs with stone projections conveniently placed in order to beget offspring, 'success depending upon the experience of an orgasm while in this position' (VI, p. 246).

Scatalogical rites. Many nauseous rites performed with bodily substances such as semen, menstrual fluid and human and animal ordure are recorded. A single instance will suffice. Till the end of the last century childless couples would frequent a famous temple near Seringapatam, whose deity was invoked for the blessed tokens of parenthood. After offering pūjā at the temple, the couple would repair to a public latrine and together collect a certain quantity of human faeces with their hands, carry it some distance off, shape it into a pyramid and mark it with a sign. They would then go to a neighbouring tank and mix some water with the filth adhering to their fingers and sip it, and follow this with sexual intercourse. After some days they would visit their pyramid and carefully examine it for maggots. If any were found it was a good omen because it signified that the woman would conceive. If none were found the experiment was repeated.

If every recourse failed it became necessary to adopt into the family a boy who would be formally accepted as a son of the childless man and who would perform the necessary sacrifices to the ancestors on the adoptive father's death.

Books

I. Bourke, J. G. *Scatalogic Rites of All Nations*, Washington, D.C. 1891.
II. Cutner, H. *A Short History of Sex Worship*, London, 1940.
III. Dare, Paul. *Indian Underworld*, London, 1938.
IV. Dingwall, E. J. *Woman: An Historical and Anthropological Compendium*, Vol. I, London, 1935.
V. Dubois, Abbe. *Hindu Manners, Customs and Ceremonies*, Oxford, 3rd Ed., 1936.
VI. Hutton, J. H. *Caste in India*, Bombay, 2nd Ed., 1951.
VII. Mace, D. & V. *Marriage, East and West*, London, 1960.

STIGMATA. According to a very ancient belief the great ones of the world bear on their bodies certain stigmata or marks which indicate their transcendent qualities and set them apart from lesser mortals. It used to be one of the duties of the midwife or astrologer to scrutinize the body of a new born child to see if he possessed such marks.

There are said to be 108 *lakshaṇa* or auspicious outward marks on the human body, called *vyañjana*, 'ornaments' or badges. Of these 76 are *anu-vyañjana* or minor ornaments, and 32 *mahā-vyañjana* or greater ornaments which are regarded as especially significant. It is believed that any person having on his body the 32 great signs will achieve world-wide fame. When Buddha was born wise men examined him and discovered that he possessed all 32 auspicious signs, betokening universal renown. The Buddhist, Hindu and Jain sects do not give the same particulars of these marks, but generally they include those mentioned below.

'Twelve are the permanent signs of the great ones': (1) curling hair, (2) long ears and long pendant earlobes, (3) long arms, (4) webbed hands (often shown in sculptures of the Buddha); (5) the *ushṇīsha*, 'heat', a slight protuberance on the top of the head, extremely hot to the touch; (6) the *ūrṇā*, 'wool', a twist of hair between the eyebrows, or a small curl on the forehead; (7) the *śrīvatsa*, a special mark, either circular, swastika-shaped, floral, or polygonal, formed by a curl of hair, or a mole, generally on the right side of the breast. It is often shown on statues of Buddha, Kṛishṇa and Vishṇu, and the Jain *tīrthaṅkaras*; (8) the sign of the wheel, lotus or swastika on the right breast; (9) the sign of the wheel and lotus on the palms and soles of the feet (for great saints); (10) the sign of the discus on the palms and soles of the feet (for great rulers); (11) the sign of a flag, iron goad, barley seed or swastika on the right side of the body; (12) the signs of the rainbow, triangle, water-pot, crescent, fish, cows's foot-print, on the left side of the body.

Books

See under Occultism and Sculpture.

STRĪPŪJĀ (*strī-pūjā*, 'woman-worship') one of the major rites in Śākta and Tantrik cults in which the nude female and the yoni* are objects of worship and meditation. By concentration on matters pertaining to the sexual principle the psychic centres of man are believed to be activated and stimulated till a high degree of enlightenment is attained. In Sanskrit literature woman is often referred to as a *latā*, 'creeper', because she is dependent on and clings to man, and the strīpūjā is therefore also called *latā-sādhana*, 'woman-magic', denoting the magical powers obtained by practising these rites. In variations of the rite, as in chakrapūjā*, several men and women are simultaneously engaged in its performance.

The woman concerned is specially selected, and receives instruction from the guru. By means of *nyāsa* (*see* worship) and other rituals she is consecrated for her role and transfigured into the incarnation of Śakti, the goddess herself. If there are several female participants, each one is regarded as the consecrated place where the sacrifice is to be performed. The men prepare themselves for this pūjā by partaking of highly seasoned foods and meats, as well as intoxicants, aphrodisiacs and erethitic drugs for five days in advance, refraining from sexual intercourse. Then they all meet together for a ceremonial meal.

The chosen woman is offered meat and wine; she is sprinkled with wine, and rendered sacred by various means, and then worshipped by the company in diverse ways. Describing one of these rites Wall says, 'The woman is seated on an altar with legs spread wide apart to display the sacred symbol, the yoni, which the priest kisses and to which he offers food and libations in sacred vessels called *argha*, which are shaped like the yoni. After these offerings have been consecrated by touching them to the living yoni, they are distributed among the worshippers and eaten' (I, p. 480).

Although the woman selected for this honour is sometimes chosen for her youth, beauty and virtue, she is frequently picked for her ugliness and evil repute. In fact a significant role is played in certain Tantrik rites by girls of depraved and debauched character, frequently prostitutes. The *ḍombī*, a washerwoman belonging to a caste once ranked amonst the lowest, was a favourite choice, being regarded as the living embodiment of the vulva in its absolute sense, free from all considerations of beauty, birth, social position or pleasure.

After all have participated, a sybaritic feast commences, the men being served by women wearing bells around their hips and ankles and nothing else. The metallic tintinnabulation serves to augment both the divine and erotic passions. The ritual feasting lasts for hours until the tantrik is in a state of great sexual tension which however he keeps perfectly controlled, diverting the bliss of the unexpended *bindu** from the physical to the psychic plane and by this means reaches a state of spiritual exaltation.

Great psychic potencies are believed to be released if this *pūjā* is performed with a nude virgin. The rite is then known as *kumārī-pūjā*, 'virgin-worship', or *kiśorī-bhāja*, 'girl-enjoying', the virgin selected being a girl just growing into womanhood. In some private forms of this rite, which may last for a week or more, the man waits upon the girl like a servant, bathes and dresses her, sleeps in the same room with her, later lies at her feet, then beside her, then embraces her, but at no time does he have intercourse with her.

Besides 'closed' strī-pūjā, i.e. without copulation, there are many rites involving the act of union, during which the 'interior' rites of esoteric *maithuna* are performed. The defloration of virgins in such cases falls into a special category, since the tremendous power believed to be released by the act is absorbed by the adept and used for magical purposes (*see* Virginity).

Books

I. Wall, O. A. *Sex & Sex Worship*, London, 1919.
II. Walters, M. *Sex Rites of Antiquity*, 1919.

STRĪRĀJYA (strī-rājya, 'female-realm') a semi-legendary state ruled entirely by women. Several such realms are mentioned in Sanskrit literature, variously said to be situated in Afghanistan, Orissa, Assam, Nepāl, Tibet, or on a distant island in the middle of the sea. One of these kingdoms was ruled by a queen named *Pramīlā* who fought against the epic hero Arjuna.

The seventh century Chinese pilgrim Hiuen-Tsang wrote of a kingdom of Amazons in the present Kumāon-Garhwāl region of the Himālayas. Only queens ruled there, the husband of the queen having no part in the government. Men only suppressed revolts and tended the fields. The same Chinese traveller refers to a second female realm in the present Baluchistan area.

Another strīrājya known as *Kadali* was located in Assam, and yet another, the mysterious state of *Uḍḍiyāna* was associated with the siddha adept Matsyendranāth* who lost himself in the toils of sensual pleasure with the enchantresses of Uḍḍiyāṇa, until his pupil Gorakhnāth turned 1600 of them into bats.

According to Indian legends the women of these places were possessed of extraordinary beauty and seductiveness. They were proficient in magic, were able to lure men, extract their seed with or without intercourse, and use it to impregnate themselves. They were credited with the ability to give birth to girls or boys as they chose; girls to keep the population of females stable, and boys for manual labour and a fresh supply of seeds. They were extremely passionate and could not be satisfied by normal intercourse with men. Their passions were gratified in a sort of communal orgy with a number of men and women devoting themselves to the orgasm of those females who were in oestrum at the time. The men indulged with the women one after the other or collectively. In the words of one Hindu manual, 'One holds her down, another unites with her, a third massages her hips, a fourth kisses her all over'. Sometimes the females had themselves thrashed till they bled, and favoured sapphism, the use of artificial aids, *coitus in ano*, and mutual *maukhya*.

It is quite likely that the existence of ancient matriarchal states formed the basis of some of the strīrājya legends, but the records of the orgies may either refer to tantrik or vāmachāra cult rites in isolated areas, or to the perverse devices employed by the hapless inmates of harems to satisfy their normal needs.

Books

See under Kāmaśāstra.

STRĪTANTRA (*strī-tantra*, 'female-lore)', comprises the study of woman as female with emphasis on her physical body. One of the words for woman in Sanskrit is *aṅganā*, 'having a body', which clearly expresses the underlying notion of this enquiry. Strītantra includes a consideration of the feminine types; of woman as partner in the sex act, the instrument of man's passion and the vessel for his seed; of female sex functions, menstruation, *ṛitu*, and conception.

In āyurveda it is specifically a study of women's diseases and gynaecology, particularly with reference to parturition (*prasūti*). Says Zimmer, 'Hindu medicine is concerned primarily with men. Women and female children, according to the prevalent Indian point of view, are of minor importance. Expectant mothers are excepted, because they bear male offspring.'

The female child becomes of increasing interest as she approaches the age of puberty, and a great many observations are made in the treatises concerning the ages of girls as they move towards the 'treasure period' of sexual utility. The truly mystical age of woman was considered to be the *vayaḥ-saṁdhi*, 'age-junction', generally translated 'puberty'. The term was sometimes used by the lawgivers for the period immediately preceding and following the onset of the first menses, and sometimes for the untouched virgin, between the ages of 15 and 17 years. It was also the time when the bloom was to be plucked.

Unmarried girls were classed under various age groups, many of the names being suggestive of the stage of their physical development. These groups were: (1) *nagnikā*, 'nude', any girl below five years; (2) *vāsū*, 'clothed', a girl of five years; (3) *gaurī*, 'white', a girl of six; (4) *vatsā*, 'calf', a girl of seven;

(5) *kanyā*, 'shining', a girl of eight; (6) *lagnikā*, 'clinging', a girl of nine. It was believed desirable for a girl to be married between nagnikā and lagnikā; (7) *bālikā*, 'with downy hair', a girl of ten; (8) *rajas-vala*, 'red-appearing', a girl beginning her menses; aged eleven; (9) *rohiṇī*, 'red', a girl of twelve; (10) *kumārī*, a 'girl' of thirteen; (11) *yuvatī*, 'juvenile', aged fourteen; (12) *duhitṛi*, one who could 'milk' the cows; a girl of fifteen; the term was also used for 'daughter'; (13) *yoshaṇā*, a 'young' girl of sixteen; (14) *kiśorī*, 'foal', an adolescent girl, aged seventeen; (15) *taruṇī* 'forested', a girl of eighteen; (16) *prauḍha*, 'mature' a fully developed girl of nineteen.

Medieval and later writers dwelt at length on the love-lorn woman, and vivid descriptions of women in varying moods of desire, expectation, and torment abound in Indian literature. One of the best known of such writers was **Keśavdās** (1555–1617) a Vaishṇavite Hindi poet of Orcha in Bundelkhand who lived under Jahāngīr and Shāh Jahān. He wrote many popular religious works and was the first great Hindi commentator on the art of poetry. He also wrote on erotics and his masterpiece on the subject is dedicated to a courtesan. In his *Rasika Priya* he classified the love-moods of women, and artists of the Rājput, Pahāṛi, Kāṅgṛā and other schools personified them in paintings*, while musicians composed rāgas to suit the theme. The hero or nāyaka is seldom depicted, but the heroine, *nāyikā*, is always delicately portrayed, in various postures, against varied backgrounds, and in different states of emotion.

Chie fof these personified moods are: (1) *nabodhā*, the shy maiden, frightened of meeting her lover alone; (2) *abhi-sārikā*, 'hastening-towards', a love-sick maiden who ventures out of her father's house at night to keep a tryst with her lover; (3) *vāsaka-sajjā*, 'dress-equipped'; the heroine, fully apparelled, waiting in her chamber or meeting place to receive her lover; (4) *mugdhā*, 'charming', a young woman, conscious of her charms, especially her physical attractions; (5) *smarāndhā*, 'love-blind', a woman blinded by her passion; (6) *saṁbhogā*, 'united joy', a woman looking forward to or actually in the process of enjoying the embrace of her lover; (7) *utkā*, 'longing', a woman waiting with deep longing for her lover, generally in a lonely place; (8) *svādhīna*, 'independent', a woman who is free from ties and in a position to indulge her passion as she wills; (9) *svādhīna-patikā*, one who is aware of having her patika, 'lord' i.e. husband or lover, in subjection and completely under her control; (10) *praushita-patikā*, the heroine pining for her lord, i.e. husband or lover, who is absent from home in some distant place e.g. the Yaksha's wife in Kālidāsa's *Meghadūta*; (11) *kalaha-āntaritā*, 'quarrel-separated', a heroine yearning for the company of her beloved but too proud to call him back after a quarrel; (12) *māninī*, a woman who is sulky towards her lover and rejects his advances; (13) *vipra-labdhā*, 'hurt-desire', a woman who has been deceived by her lover; a frustrated woman, e.g. an utkā (see above) whose lover has failed to turn up; (14) *khaṇḍitā*, 'immoral', a woman who is the victim of her faithless lover, who visits her with evidence of his deception e.g. he bears bite marks on his body, or is incapble of fulfilling his obligations because of sexual fatigue.

Writers on strītantra divide women into three or four types, laying special emphasis on their suitability as partners to different types of nāyaka (*see* man of the world). These types are: (1) *padminī*, 'lotus', the highest type of woman. She is beautiful, refined, spiritual, swan-like, with gently rounded hips and breasts, nose like the sesame flower, face like a moon nearing fulness, gentle in union, with a sweet, lotus-smelling pudenda; she prefers sentiment, gentleness and love to sexual intimacy, and submits to the latter only to please the male. She is a suitable mate for the *śaśa* (hare) or *mṛiga* (buck) type of man; examples of this type are Śakuntalā and Sītā; (2) *chitrinī*, 'painting' (also *hariṇī* or *mṛigī*, 'doe'), slender, beautiful, peacock-like, fond of lovely things; prefers courtship to the sexual act, and delights in the praise of her beauty; she sometimes tends to sensuality; her hips and breasts are well-rounded, and her pudenda has the odour of honey; makes an excellent mate for the *mṛiga* (buck), but is suitable for all types of men; example of this class, Draupadī; (3) *śaṅkhinī*, 'conch', with emphasis on the genital organ, is referred to as a *baḍavā*, 'mare'; she is voluptuous in appearance, average to tall in height, medium to heavy in build; with average to full breasts, large and deep vulva; well-developed *mons veneris* covered with luxuriant growth; she is the most concupiscent, difficult and selfish of all types and makes an excellent courtesan; she cares little for children, home, husband, family or name; cunning in disposition and violently aroused in intercourse, she finds pleasure only in having her 'conch' blown; it is difficult to find a suitable mate for her, the best being *vṛishabha* (bull); (4) *hastinī*, 'elephant'; of large physique, fond of food and with a huge sexual appetite; rather gross when aroused but is easily satisfied; makes an excellent wife and is very fond of children; has a flabby vulva, with scant pubic hair but with thick and very sensitive labia; the pudenda has a phosphoric odour; makes a suitable mate for any type of man.

Another aspect of strītantra frequently dealt with in texts on erotics, relates to sexual desire in women. This is said to depend on education (family tradition), experience, female type (see above), and stimuli. This last was said to be in man's power to control, provided he had a thorough knowledge of woman's erogenous zones. Certain parts of the female body were known to be particularly responsive to caress or stimulation. The term *madanāḍi* (*mada-nāḍi*, passion-pulse) was used for these erogenous zones which were regarded as crosspoints of the cosmos and as chakras* peculiar to the female body. They included the breasts, nipples, nape of the neck, folds of the buttocks, the labia and clitoris, although there were several other sensitive areas with some women, such as the lobe of the ear, the middle of the palm, the navel, the anus, the arch of the foot. Stimulation of these nāḍi, accompanied by the recitation of mantras, helped not only in assisting orgasm, but ensured the birth of a son.

In considering sexual desire in a female due account had to be taken of the phases of the moon. It was established by the ancients that *chandra-kalā*, 'moon-fraction', played an important part in the desire tides, since a woman had varying degrees of intensity on different days of the lunar month. In the ideal woman sensitivity was believed to be concentrated on the left side of the body during the full moon, starting from the forehead and, as the moon waned, working down the left side to the eyes, cheeks, lips and so on, till it reached the foot. On the new moon sensitivity began its ascent from the right foot, working up to the right side of the scalp. There might be a slight 'shift' of the starting point in different women, but the passage of the tender points was usually held to proceed as indicated.

Still another aspect of strītantra was *vakshaṇā*, 'invigoration', i.e. the female body considered as an area of voluptuousness, inspiring sensual passion in man. It is the demesne of carnal pleasure containing 'the hills of smoothness and cavities of delight'. Specifically vakshaṇā refers to the breasts, belly and buttocks, but frequently comprises all parts of the female form.

Sanskrit poets often detail the criteria by which a woman's beauty is judged. The hair is compared to a swarm of bees clinging to a tree; the forehead to the leaf of the *talkī*; the face is swan-like or like the full moon. She is lotus-eyed, or doe-eyed (*mṛigāksha*); her eyebrows are formed like a bow; her full lips are like the fruit of the bright red bimba tree; her cheeks are round and flushed with desire; her ears are like the *bhaki* fruit, the interior like the *guda* shell; her nose is like the sesame flower (*tilaphula*), or like the beak of a parrot (*śukanāsā*); long and curved noses are greatly admired, and one text has it that a woman's nose 'puts to shame the beak of Garuḍa, prince of birds'; her neck is curved like a serpent; her voice is husky and unclear like that of a peacock or swan; her arms are like ivory tusks; armpits like two 'haired mouths'; elbows like the joints of the murumbu branches. Her wrists are invisible and do not stand out; her fingers long and slender like a beanpod; her belly soft and rounded, girdled with three rings of fat. Her waist is narrow like that of a wasp, slender and inviting the male embrace; it is like the middle of a hand drum (*ḍamaru-madhya*). The navel is deep; the thighs are likened to banana trunks; the calves like the swelling abdomen of a spawning fish; the ankles, like the wrists, do not stand out; the feet rest flat on the ground like the pads of the lioness; the toes are spread out resembling the fruit of the tikka tree.

The *stanā* or breasts are pictured as 'shaped like lotus buds'; 'swelling like great pots'; 'full like ripe melons'; 'globular and so close together that there is hardly room between them for a lotus stalk'; 'upreared (sthiti) and protruding'. The lover derives much pleasure as he feels the impact of the 'rotund mammalia crowding against each other, with nipples like the berry of the *kāñjidruma*, inviting the lover's teeth'.

But the feature most frequently lauded in the Sanskrit writings are the *jaghana*, 'buttocks', or *bhasad*, 'devourer', the whole region from the buttocks to the pubes, including the *guda*, 'anus', termed 'an area of delight'. Graphic descriptions of the rear parts of Draupadī, Pārvatī, Rohiṇī, Rādhā and other legendary beauties are to be found in the classics and vernaculars. The hips are considered from two points of view. Firstly, the *śroṇi-bimba*, 'gluteal orb', provocatively projecting à tergo, is highly extolled, since an abundance of *sphich*, 'bottom', is the ideal of feminine beauty; its curve is compared to the *nitamba* or 'slope' of a hill, and a *nitambinī* or kallipygian woman with posterior undulating like the rolling mountainside is described with raptures. Secondly, the ideal woman should have *pṛithu-jaghana*, 'broad hips'; some even praise the 'elephant-hipped' female as promising exquisite pleasure and a 'century of sons'. The hero of the *Nāgānanda* wonders why his adored one burdens herself with heavy ornaments, since 'thy thighs are already wearied with bearing the weight of thy buttocks'. The clash between front and rear is another commonplace in descriptions of the female form, and a favourite hyperbole of the *kāvya* writers is that of a ravishing woman bending under the weight of her bulbous breasts, and only held upright by the counterpoise of her mountainous hips.

Finally, the main area of ecstasy, the *yoni**, 'sweet smelling like the wet perfume of night flowers', is considered in a category by itself.

Books

See under Kāmaśāstra.

STŪPA (Prākṛit, *thupa,* or *tope*), the earliest form of Indian architecture of which any considerable remains are extant. Originally a primitive burial mound, the stūpa was developed and elaborated by the Buddhists, and became their most characteristic architectural structure. At the height of Buddhist power the stūpa was the centre of a building complex constituting the Buddhist *vihāra* or monastery.

The stūpa consists of a large hemispherical solid dome of earth, brick and stone, called the *aṇḍa,* 'egg', the surface of which is finished off with a thick layer of plaster. On the dome of the stūpa is a small square structure called the *harmikā* or pedestal, which is further crowned by a *chhatra,* 'umbrella', symbol of royalty. Either within the harmikā or just beneath it was the casket known in Burmese as *hti* (simplified 'tee') which contained the relics, or *dhātu* of Buddha or of one of his close disciples. The enshrinement of a relic was originally the main purpose of the stūpa, although later stūpas were erected in commemoration of an important event, or simply as a place of Buddhist worship, and did not necessarily contain relics.

It sometimes became necessary to enlarge the stūpa owing to the deteriorating condition of the old one, or because of the growing importance of the site. In such cases another aṇḍa was built around the old, leaving the inner one intact. This outer facing was known as the *āchchhāda* or covering. In some cases stūpas were given as many as two or three āchchhādas, one over the other.

Through the ages the harmikā and umbrella over it took on many curious shapes, each Buddhist country evolving a style peculiar to its own genius. The variations may be seen in the stūpa of Nepāl, where large eyes are drawn on the four sides of the harmikā; in the typical *dāgoba* (from *dhātu-garbha,* 'relic-chamber') of Ceylon; in the elongated steeples of the Burmese shrines; in the immense storied terraces of Borobudur in Java; in the curved eaves and finials of Siam and Cambodia; and in the pagodas of China and Japan.

The dome of the Indian stūpa is surrounded by a *pradakshiṇa-patha,* 'processional path', along which pilgrims walk in performance of the rite of circumambulation. Sometimes there is a second processional path above ground level which is reached by a stairway. The whole area of the stūpa is fenced off by a stone railing called the *vṛiti,* 'enclosure', said to be derived from the pre-Aryan palisade that marked off the sacred arbours from the profane world. Originally of wood, it was later made of stone, and consisted of upright posts called *stambha* (Pāli, *thaba*), on which horizontal cross-beams called *sūchi* were placed, topped by an *ushṇīsha* or coping. On the four sides of the vṛiti were four *toraṇa* or ornamental gateways. The toraṇa was actually a type of symbolic archway covering the sacred threshold; it became the *torii* of Japanese and the *piu-lu* of Chinese Buddhist architecture. From this gateway the *gopuram* of the South Indian temple is also said to be derived. The manner of constructing the stone fences and gateways of the stūpa remained essentially like that of their wooden originals, the joints being the same as those employed by carpenters. Among the more famous stūpas are those at the places named below.

BHĀRHUT, in Central India, built by Aśoka in 250 BC and added to from 150 BC onwards during the Śuṅga and Kushān periods. It has now practically vanished, and its chief importance lies in the fragmentary sculptural work that still remains. The stone of the few existing columns, gateways and railings bears traces of early Persian workmanship, and is richly carved in bas-relief, with Buddhist symbols of the wheel, tree, lotus, griffin, and illustrations of Jātaka stories and scenes from Buddha's life. In the latter the method of 'continuous narrative' is employed, i.e. the various incidents in the same story are depicted in different parts of the same panel. The work is stiff, formal and archaic, and still uncertain in treatment. It contains many non-Aryan features.

SĀNCHĪ, near the ancient city of Vidisā or Bhīlsā in Bhopāl, Central India, about midway between the Mauryan capital of Pāṭaliputra and the western port of Barygaza. The 'Great Stūpa' of Sānchī was first built by Aśoka and later covered with an āchchhāda so that little of the original work is visible. In both the Bhārhut and Sānchī stūpas the influence of Persian masons is proved by the masons' marks in Kharoshṭhī letters engraved in the stone and also by the fluted bull capital of the Persepolitan order. Some of the motifs are of Mesopotamian or Persian inspiration. Much of the sculpture dates from Śuṅgan times, but the succeeding Āndhra rulers helped to preserve the original Sānchī shrines. The stone railings and four massive gateways of the main stūpa are elaborately carved with high technical skill, with a profusion of figures and reliefs, vividly depicting scenes of everyday activity and the life of the times. Women in graceful *tribhaṅga* poses often serve as brackets to the architraves. The Sānchī stūpa was discovered in 1818 by a party of British soldiers; they reported the discovery to the Calcutta headquarters of the East India Company who arranged for its excavation.

BUDH GAYA, built by Aśoka and added to during the Śuṅgan* and subsequent periods. The reliefs on the Budh Gaya balustrade predate those of Sānchī but are later than Bhārhut. The carvings are more fanciful and many animal grotesques are believed to be of early Persian origin. Sir John Marshall discerned in the Budh Gaya sculptures the presence of motifs of Hellenistic or West Asiatic origin such as winged and fish-tailed monsters, tritons, and the sun-god in his characteristic four-horse chariot. Historically the Budh Gaya reliefs provide a link between Bhārhut, and the Mathurā sculpture of the following Kushān period. As a result of constant restoration much of the original appearance of Budh Gaya was effaced. Early in the fourteenth century the Buddhists of Burma hearing that the scared shrine was in a state of ruin, sent Burmese masons to repair it. Among other things they used an arch in the restoration, a feature unusual in this type of architecture. Today the chief external mark of the Budh Gaya stūpa is a pyramidal tower, square in plan, rising to a height of 180 feet.

AMARĀVATĪ at the mouth of the Kistna in the Guntur district of Madrās, also the site of a great monastic university called Śri-dhanya-kaṭaka, was originally built about 200 BC, and reconstructed in AD 350. Almost two thousand square feet of surface on the stūpa railings and gates had once been covered with sculptured designs and carvings, but the stones were used for centuries by local Hindu rājas for private building and nothing now remains of it except an irregular trench marking its original position. The shape and size of the stūpa are deduced from carved representations in bas-reliefs on some of the surviving panels. The carvings on these panels and relief 'medallions' show extraordinary technical proficiency and delicacy of craftsmanship. They are among the greatest works of Indian art. Beautifully balanced in composition to fit the characteristic circular frames they portray excellently carved figures in vigorous though graceful action. The female figures with their tall, slender forms sensuously modelled, full busts and heavy hips led Coomaraswamy to describe Amarāvatī as 'the most voluptuous and most delicate flower of Indian sculpture'. It had great influence on the art of Ceylon and Southeast Asia.

SĀRNĀTH, near Banāras, the place where Buddha preached his first sermon. Once an imposing edifice and a famous educational centre containing buildings raised even before the Kushān period and added to in later centuries, the place was destroyed first by the Hindus and subsequently entirely demolished by Kutb-ud-dīn (AD 1195). In the eighteenth century the Rāja of Banāras looking for material to use as a breakwater in the construction of a bridge had over sixty cartloads of carved stone from Sārnāth thrown into the Ganges, including much of the stūpa of Aśoka along with the casket of relics. Material from Sārnāth was also used by the rāja to build a bazaar. Little more than the inner core now remains.

NĀGĀRJUNIKOṆḌA, on the Kistna, in the Āndhra region, was founded by Chāṁtamūla in the third century AD. It was called the Hill of Nāgārjuna in honour of the great Buddhist philosopher. The stūpa, two chaityas and twenty monasteries have now vanished and the site itself, which was discovered in 1925, is again destined to pass out of view as it will be submerged as a result of a near-by river-damming project. Nāgārjunikoṇḍa was situated not far from the important trading* centre known to the Romans as Maisolia. An artificial pool for aquatic sports and a stadium with ascending rows of stone galleries have been discovered at the site. A stadium is a Roman idea, suggesting it was borrowed by the Nāgārjunikoṇḍa builders from the Roman residents of Maisolia.

Other stūpas, mostly in ruins, are to be found in Mathurā, Taxila, Mānikyāla in the Panjāb, Nālandā once the site of the most famous Buddhist university in India, Peshāwar where a stūpa built by Kanishka* became famous throughout the Buddhist world, and several in the region between the deltas of the Kistna and Godāveri.

Books

I. Barua, B. M. *Bharhut*, 3 vols., Calcutta, 1934–37.
II. Burgess, J. *The Buddhist Stupas of Amaravati and Jaggayyapeta*, London, 1877.
III. Cunningham, A. *The Bhilsa Topes*, London, 1854.
IV. Cunningham, A. *Mahabodhi or the Great Buddhist Temple at Budhgaya*, London, 1892.
V. Marshall, J. *Guide to Sanchi*, 1936.
VI. Marshall, J. *The Monuments of Sanchi*, 3 vols., Calcutta, 1938.
VII. Mitra, R. L. *Budh Gaya*, Calcutta, 1879.
VIII. Sewell, R. *The Amravati Tope and Excavations on its Site*, 1877.

SUBANDHU (fl. AD 630) the author of a Sanskrit *gadya* (prose) romance called *Vāsavadattā*, about prince Udayana* of Vatsa and princess Vāsavadattā of Ujjain who fall in love with each other in a dream. Through the intermediation of two messenger-parrots they meet and decide to flee together on a magic steed to escape the decree of her father by which she is to marry another. After numerous adventures in which the princess is carried off by a rival suitor, she is finally turned to stone, but is restored to life again by the touch of her lover.

Apart from being involved and dry, the work has been condemned as in execrable taste, with its all too graphic descriptions of the heroine's physical attractions, its unredeemed sensuality, and its general tone of indelicacy. From the literary point of view it is burdened with stylistic accretions: incessant punning, heavy compounds strung together; overloading with alliteration. Hyperbole and vulgarity smother whatever beauty the work might have otherwise possessed.

Books

See under Sanskrit.

SUBSTANCE, or matter, called *dravya* in Sanskrit, is that by virtue of which all things are physically determined; it is the 'stuff' of which the world is made. In Vaiśeshika philosophy it is the first category* or predicable and is resolved into a number of eternal realities. Dravya may be regarded as a manifestation of Prakṛiti or Cosmic Substance.

Dravya is essentially a form of universal energy, which in the first stage of its manifestation is known as *tanmātra*, possessing the basic properties of experience or sensation. Only a very few schools of Hindu thought hold that matter is *achit* or 'without consciousness'; most thinkers, notably the Jains, hold that all matter is sentient and 'aware'. Tanmātra is defined as a fivefold extension of universal energy in its primary manifestation as the quintessence of matter. In effect it is potential matter, or matter in its most subtle form, which is without magnitude, although the five elements are implicit in it. The five forms of tanmātra are generally referred to as the Subtle or Potential Elements and listed as follows: (1) *śabda**, the essence of sound; (2) *sparśa*, the essence of touch; (3) *rūpa*, the essence of form; (4) *rasa*, the essence of taste; and (5) *gandha*, the essence of smell.

In Nyāya philosophy these forms of tanmātra are referred to as *artha*, or objects of the senses. The tanmātra then may be said to correspond to the matter apprehended in the sensation of sound, touch, shape, taste and smell. As the tanmātra integrate, disintegrate, and reintegrate, certain structures or atoms are formed. By a process of further 'materialization' these atoms become denser and give rise to molecules (*see* atom).

The subtle elements constituting the tanmātra cannot be apprehended by the senses at this tenuous early stage, but only after there is a further increase in accumulation of mass leading to the formation of *mahābhūta* (*mahā-bhūta*, 'great element') or pure elements, namely, ether, air, fire, water, and earth. Sometimes only four are given, ether being omitted from many lists. These pure elements are the 'materialized' forms of the tanmātra, and each mahābhūta represents the *vishaya* or sphere of action for the particular indriya* or organ of sense specialized in the perception of that mahābhūta. Each mahābhūta manifests one or more forms of tanmātra. The mahābhūta, along with their vishaya and tanmātra are:

(1) *Ākāśa,* or ether, which is the vishaya or sphere of action in which the ear functions. It is light, rarefied, elastic, all-pervasive, and is the essential medium for the operation of discrete things. Just as water is freer that earth, and air freer than water, so ether is freer than air. Ether manifests the tanmātra of sound.
(2) *Vāyu**, or air, the vishaya of the skin, for experiencing the world of tangibles. It is light, cold, dry, transparent, and rarefied. Air manifests sound and touch.
(3) *Tejas,* or fire, the vishaya of the eye, for experiencing the world of colour and form. It is hot, liquid, dry, luminous. Fire manifests sound, touch and form.
(4) *Āpas,* or water, the vishaya of the tongue, for gustatory experience. It is liquid, cold, and soft. Water manifests sound, touch, form and taste.
(5) *Pṛithivī* or earth, named after the goddess (*see* Dyaus) is the vishaya of the nose, for the world of smells and olfactory experience. It is heavy, rough, hard, inert, and opaque. Earth manifests sound, touch, form, taste and smell.

It is to be remembered that although advanced yogis and adepts can apprehend a mahābhūta or pure element, they do so by isolating it from the mixed constituents in which it is found. The mahābhūta rarely exist in the pure state, since all manifestations are combinations of mahābhūta, and form the gross elements or *bhūta* (adj. *bhautik*) of the world around us which the ordinary person knows and experiences through the senses* or *indriya.* Water for instance is never seen in the pure form of āpas, but combined with earth and air. The relationship of the gross and subtle elements may be expressed by saying that subtle matter (tanmātra) manifests in pure matter (mahābhūta) which in turn manifests in gross elements (bhūta).

Substances are classified in various ways. Firstly, according to the three aspects in which they exist, namely: (i) *Sthūla,* the gross or tangible form e.g. the material things around us; (ii) *Sūkshma,* subtle or intangible, such as the mahābhūta, which cannot be apprehended by the senses; and (iii) *Parama* or supreme, i.e. the divine aspect of things. Again, substances may be classified according to the *pañcha-bhautik* (five-bhūta) system, i.e. depending on whether they belong to the elements of ether, air, fire, water or earth. Again, they may be listed under one of the three *guṇa* or qualities* to which they belong. Finally they may be divided into the three kingdoms or worlds, namely: (a) *khānija*, 'pit-born', the inanimate things of the material world that come out of the earth, like minerals*, metals*, and other non-living substances; (b) *sthāvara*, 'stationary' things having life, including the whole Plant* World; (c) *jaṅgama*, 'moving' things, including the whole Animal* World.

Books

See under Philosophy.

ŚŪDRA, the fourth Hindu caste*. A tribe known as the Śūdra is mentioned in the *Mahābhārata* and Purāṇas, sometimes in association with the non-Aryan Ābhīras; they are referred to in Greek writings as *Sodrai*, who occupied parts of Sind and Rājputāna. One theory is that they were absorbed into the Aryan class structure as a fourth caste. On the other hand the śūdra caste may have evolved from a poor, uncultivated class of Aryans, who did menial work in the Aryan camps. According to the Vedas, śūdras were created from the feet of Purusha* in order to serve men.

In early times all those who were amenable to Aryan influence were freely admitted to the Aryan fold, and fitted into the Aryan social scheme in castes appropriate to their status. The śūdras therefore must have been strengthened by absorption of non-Aryan aboriginal peoples into their ranks. It is in fact still not easy to make a distinction between some classes of śūdras and the *pañchamas**.

There is considerable conflict of opinion regarding the original status and duties of the śūdras. Although the present-day class of cooks is mainly recruited from the ranks of brāhmins, in Vedic times it was the śūdra who cooked the food for the other castes, including the brāhmin householder. The prohibition of 'revived' brāhminism against eating food touched by a śūdra has no authority in holy writ. Furthermore, we learn from the *Chhāndogya Upanishad* that the Brāhmin Raikva taught the Vedas to a śūdra, which is not surprising when it is remembered that śūdras composed many of the sacred hymns included in the Vedas, and that the śūdra Vyāsa compiled, if he did not write, the *Mahābhārata*. From evidence provided by Jaimini, author of the *Pūrva-Mīmāṁsā*, as also from other texts, it is seen that a śūdra could perform Vedic sacrifices, and according to the *Saṁskāra Gaṇapati*, was eligible for the *upanayana* or thread ceremony, like other twice-born Hindus. In several other ancient rites we also find the śūdras taking an active part. In one ceremony the ritualistic milking of sacred cows was entrusted to them, and in yet another they had the task of selling the sacred soma juice, while the culmination of a third religious rite was marked by the ritual dancing of śūdra women.

In the post-Vedic period the presence of a śūdra was required at the ceremonial coronation of a king. After the ceremony the king paid a visit to various officials, including śūdras, and made them all an offering of gifts. According to one early text some of the king's ministers had to be śūdras.

In fact, several ancient dynasties of kings, notably the Mauryas, were of śūdra origin.

This state of affairs gradually gave way before the tide of the brāhminical revival. Already the approaching degradation of the śūdra was heralded in some of the early brāhminical texts. 'The śūdra is untruth itself', declared the *Śatapatha Brāhmaṇa,* and this ancient appraisal was taken up by the law-givers. After Manu and his legalists had disposed of the destinies of the śūdras, they were saddled with so many disabilities as to be virtually relegated to a condition where they lost their human status. The only prospect for a śūdra living under a brāhminical dispensation was to see his condition worsen like a galloping consumption.

The list of the disabilities of the śūdras and pañchamas (outcastes of still more abject status) is a catalogue of human folly that is unique in history. Many nations have at certain periods perpetuated atrocities against their fellows, but no nation can match the disgraceful record of brāhmin arrogance and bigotry against their co-religionists, which was maintained for centuries and buttressed up by every resource of religious force and social sanction.

The śūdra was barred from religious sacrifices. He could not partake of the sacred soma drink. He was no longer entitled to the initiation ceremony of rebirth. He dared not hear the sacred scriptures recited. If he listened to a recitation of the Vedas his ears were to be filled with molten lead; if he recited the sacred texts his tongue was to be torn out; and if he remembered them his body was to be split in twain. In effect he could not be taught the precepts of his own religion.

In the *Rāmāyaṇa* we have the not very edifying story in which the paragon of princely virtues, Rāma himself, is represented as slaying the śūdra Śambūka for practising religious austerities. A śūdra could not learn the occupations of the higher castes, especially those pertaining to the priestly or knightly professions. This is illustrated in the *Mahābhārata* story of Ekalavya, the Nishāda* youth, and his cruel treatment by Droṇa.

Since the brāhminical claim to superiority was based on purity of blood, any contamination from the lower castes was met with the gravest punishment. If a śūdra committed adultery with a woman of the first three castes, he was burnt alive, tied up in straw. The very presence of such a 'low-born fellow' was a source of defilement, and if by some mischance he tried to sit side by side with a high-born man, he was to be banished, 'after his backside had been cut off'. The touch of a śūdra was considered so polluting that it could even contaminate the Ganges.

Nothing was supposed to belong to a śūdra as his own, and whatever property he happened to possess could be appropriated by a brāhmin with perfect impunity. Indeed, a śūdra was not to accumulate wealth even if he were able to do so, for, says the *Manusmṛiti* pathetically, 'the sight of mere possession of wealth by a śūdra injures the brāhmin'.

From the śūdra was exacted in full measure the reverence and respect that brāhminical arrogance had engendered as a result of its own outpourings. The brāhmin could insult, beat and enslave a śūdra, but let the latter retaliate by an angry word of abuse and he would have a red hot iron, ten inches long, thrust into his mouth. According to the lawgivers the killing of a śūdra by a brāhmin was equivalent in magnitude to the killing of a cat, frog, lizard, owl, or crow.

Most of these disabilities are now things of the past. Muslim and European ideas from without and Hindu reform from within have greatly mitigated the plight of the lower castes in India, and things continue to improve. Miscegenation and clandestine crossing of the caste barriers sometimes makes the distinction between two adjacent castes very uncertain. On occasion in the past prominent śūdras married into vaiśya and kshattriya families and many śūdra females were taken as wives even by brāhmins. Certain pañchama tribes today claim śūdra status and many śūdras now move into the kshattriya class by simply appending the common kshattriya title 'Singh' to their names.

Some authorities classify the writing caste of *kāyasthas** as śūdras. The Gujars, descendants of the White Huns, are also put into the śūdra category. The grazier and cultivator castes are frequently śūdras, for example, the Kūrmi of Bihār and Oudh, and the Palli of South India (who often use the title of Mudaliar). Fishermen and manual labourers such as the Koli of coastal Bombay (from whom the English term *coolie* is derived) are śūdras. In 1931 a number of ancient cattle-keeping castes such as the Āhīr (*see* Ābhīra), Gopa, Goāla, and others, claiming descent from Kṛishṇa's clan, combined to form a caste known as the Yādava (*see* Yadu) and even claimed Rājput i.e. kshattriya, status. The influential Nāirs* of the South are also śūdas.

Books

I. Ambedkar, B. R. *Who Were the Sudras?* Bombay, 1946.
II. Ghosh, J. C. *Brahmin and Sudra*, Calcutta, 1902.
See also under Castes.

ŚŪDRAKA (fl. AD 580) author of a Sanskrit play called *Mṛichchhakaṭika* (*mṛid-śakaṭika* 'clay-cartlet') 'The Little Clay Cart', the title being derived from an unimportant episode in the sixth Act. The hero Chārudatta, is a brāhmin merchant of Ujjain who is beggared by his liberality. A rich courtesan, Vasantasenā, falls in love with him, but is herself courted and pursued by an evil-minded prince who ultimately strangles her and leaves her for dead. The brāhmin is accused of the murder, and is about to be executed when Vasantasenā, restored to life by a Buddhist mendicant, appears on the scene. Chārudatta is released, raised to high office and marries Vasantasenā.

This unusual play is full of life and action, has many comic situations and also a number of serious, near-tragic scenes. It is crowded with characters who, for a change, are not deities and demigods but ordinary men and women and who, besides Sanskrit, talk in seven varieties of Prākṛit vernaculars. It is conspicuously free from the religious element; its heroine is a dancing-girl; it breaks many of the hallowed conventions of Sanskrit dramatic art. Many similarities have been found between this drama and the plays of the New Attic Comedy.

Śūdraka was said to be familiar with the '*Ṛig-veda* and the *Sāma-veda*, the science of arithmetic, the art of the courtesan, and the management of the elephant', but the prologue of the play which elaborates his virtues and refers to him as twice-born is not authentic. The debased Sanskrit he uses and the fact that he is steeped in Buddhist ideas would indicate that he was not a brāhmin. His unusual name ('low-casteling') suggests to some authorities either a foreign or a śūdra origin. Little in fact is known about him. According to tradition he was a king, probably of Ābhīra stock, and his play, an adaptation from the dramatist Bhāsa, may have been touched up by Daṇḍin, a poet patronised by him. Śūdraka was said to have been blind from birth and recovered his eyesight through the favour of Śiva. At the age of 100 he installed his son as king and then committed suicide by self-immolation on a funeral pyre specially built for him. He remains, according to Dr M. A. Mehendale, 'a mere legendary figure' (II, p. 264).

Books

I. Karmarkar, R. D. 'The Authorship and Date of the Mrichchhakatika'. *New Indian Art,* 1939–40.
II. Majumdar, R. C. (Ed.) *The Age of Imperial Unity,* Bombay, 1951.
III. Pandey, C. B. *Sudraka,* Banaras, 1958.
IV. Ruben, W. *The Mrichchhakatika of Sudraka,* Leiden, 1948.
V. Ryder, A. (Tr.) *The Little Clay Cart,* Cambridge, Mass., 1905.
VI. Saletore, B. A. 'King Sudraka: An Historical Study.' *Journal of the University of Bombay,* July 1947–January, 1948.

SUDYUMNA, the Tiresias of Hindu mythology, was one of the sons of Manu Vaivasvata, and founder of the Lunar dynasty of kings. One day he accidentally wandered into a forest where he surprised Śiva and Pārvatī engaged in sexual congress. Śiva cursed him to become a woman and in this changed form Sudyumna became known as ILĀ (or Iḍā).

In the *Ṛig-veda* Ilā means variously, nourishment, a libation of milk, or a paean of praise. It is also a name given to a deity of speech or a goddess of earth. In one passage Ilā is represented as springing from a sacrifice performed by Manu for obtaining a son; Manu mispronounced the formula and a girl, Ilā, was born instead. She became the instructress of Manu and taught him new sacrificial rites. Upon her Manu begat the various races of mankind.

In later Purāṇic legends she was born as Sudyumna or Ila (or Iḍa) a man, and became Ilā, a woman, as a result of Śiva's curse. Ilā married Budha (or Mercury) son of Soma* the moon god, and became the mother of Purūravas*. Through the intercession of Śiva, or according to other versions, of Mitra, Varuṇa or Vishṇu, she was transformed into Sudyumna or Ila once more and fathered three sons. Still another story has it that she was made to change her sex every alternate month. There are many variations of this legend.

The story may be veiled reference to the tradition of a homosexual tribe known as the Saudyumna. According to one scholar it may have been the Aryan means of suggesting that this stock was not quite human.

Sudyumna was also known as Sadyumna. One of his sons was Utkala.

Books

See under Mythology.

SUFFERING, in Sanskrit, *duḥkha,* is one of the most important concepts in Hindu philosophy. The word is said to be derived from *du,* 'unpleasant', and *kha,* the axle-hole in a wheel, suggesting something that does not move well. It connotes all that is fraught with unpleasantness and pain. According to Hindu and Buddhist philosophy all man's activities lead to duḥkha, and even men who pursue the false goal of *sukha* (well-moving) or contentment, pleasure and happiness, find that they reap the consequences in trouble (*kleśa*), disappointment and pain.

Pleasure is only a fleeting interlude in a panorama of suffering. Birth, growth, living and dying, are all fraught with suffering. The immediate cause of suffering may be internal, like physical pain produced by intra-organic disorders; or it may be external, resulting from the actions of other men, as when one man strikes another; again it may be due to occult causes such as the influence of the planets; or to supernatural causes, such as the agency of demons. But the ultimate cause is believed to be lack of knowledge*, leading to preoccupation with self (*ahaṁkāra*), followed by action (*karma**), resulting in sin (*dosha*). Pain is the invariable concomitant of all action. The body is the abode of pain; the sensations the instruments of pain; the intellect the agent of pain; and ignorance leading to action the seed of pain. Pain being the manifestation of karma, it is laid down by Kapila that 'the complete cessation of pain is the complete goal of man'. The Four Noble Truths which embody the basic tenets of Buddhism relate entirely to the problem of suffering and pain.

This pessimism remained to plague Hindu and Buddhist thought till it was modified by the doctrine of *bhakti** and the saving grace of God.

Books

See under Philosophy.

SUICIDE was once very commonly practised in India by all classes of people, and those who took their own lives were not regarded as having committed a sin, but on the contrary as having performed a meritorious act, and the record of their deed was often preserved in stone or metal. *Satī* stones commemorating the virtuous wives who voluntarily died on the pyres of their husbands are extant in large numbers. In the Deccan there are numerous inscriptions which commemorate the pious souls who in fulfilment of a vow leapt from pillars, starved to death or drowned themselves.

Suicide is usually preceded by fasting and prayer; the means of suicide being selected beforehand, and the place decided accordingly. Some places are auspicious. Thus if a person goes to Amarakaṇṭaka, the source of the river Narmadā, and there, 'remaining pure, self-controlled, desisting from wrath, thinking good of all creatures', either starves to death, commits himself to the flames, or walks into the holy waters and drowns himself, he will stay one lakh of years in heaven and then be reborn as a king.

A widespread form of suicide for women was known as suttee*, in which a widow ascended the funeral pyre of her husband and was burned with him. In some parts of the Telugu speaking South, the wife was buried alive with her deceased husband. The rite of *jauhar,* once common among Rājputs, was an extension of suttee but on a much larger scale. Here the womenfolk of Rājput warriors, sometimes in their thousands, would immolate themselves *en masse* to preserve their honour in the face of defeat by an enemy.

Apart from suttee, suicide by burning was common among yogis and other ascetics from ancient times. The Indian *yogi* Kalyāṇa* who accompanied Alexander the Great to Susa burnt himself to death there. Strabo relates that an Indian king sent an embassy to Caesar Augustus and one of the members of the embassy burnt himself at Athens in 20 BC (*see* Romans).

In Malabār and other parts of south India in the Pāṇḍya, Chola, Tamil and Kannaḍa regions, when a king ascended the throne, a hundred or more of his close companions partook of a special meal with him and swore to burn themselves to the last man when he died. This terrible vow of suicide was known as *māmakham* (*mahā-makham,* 'great sacrifice') and was witnessed by the entire population of the city.

Suicide by drowning was also widely prevalent. At Prayāga the would-be suicide used to be conducted by priests in a boat to the holy confluence of the Ganges and Jamnā where with due ceremony he would be lowered into the water and was 'instantly swallowed amidst universal acclamation'. It is said that in olden days pilgrims would precipitate themselves head first from the *akshaya-vaṭa* or undying banyan tree at Prayāga whose branches overhung the river. The present tree is in an underground temple some distance from the stream. The ritual suicide of rulers was not unknown although comparatively rare. In some of the medieval principalities of Malabār and also Central and North India this occurred when the king was past his prime, and felt he was too old to govern, or when his rule was no longer effective. In AD 1020 the Chedi king Gāṅgeyadeva along with his 100 queens simultaneously drowned themselves at Prayāga. In 1068 the Chālukya king Someśvara I, when his powers began to wane, waded into the Tuṅgabhadra river and drowned himself to the sound of religious music, in full view of the courtiers who lined the beach. The Vaishṇavite mystic Chaitanya drowned himself in the sea near Purī. Both Rāma and Lakshmaṇa ended their lives by walking into the river Śarayū. The Marāṭhi poet Tukārām drowned himself in a river.

Suicide by starvation was regarded as particularly meritorious by both Hindus and Jains. Starving oneself to death is known as *prāyopaveśa* in Sanskrit, and *sallekanā* in Jain texts. Among the countless instances a notable example is that of Chandragupta Maurya who was said to have become a Jain towards the end of his reign and starved himself to death.

Another method of suicide was throwing oneself from an elevated place such as a precipitous rock or high tower. Near Girnār is a rock called Bhairava-jap, from which a leap to death on the rocks below was regarded as especially meritorious. Another method entailed going on an endless pilgrimage, being constantly on the move from one holy place to another till one died on the way from exhaustion. Journeys covering the whole of India are sometimes undertaken by pious persons wishing to end their days while on this holy mission. The Pāṇḍavas were said to have inaugurated this form of final sacrifice during their last journey to the Himālayas. Yet another form of suicide which achieved great notoriety was the rite performed at Purī during the processional of the chariot of the god Jagannātha*. As the car was being dragged along the route devout pilgrims would throw themselves under its giant wheels and be crushed to death. The general belief was that those who perished in this manner would ascend straight to the heavenly realms.

In former times sādhus belonging to certain sects performed a rite known as *trāga*. If they were subjected to oppression, if trouble threatened, or if they earnestly desired something that was being refused them, one of their sect dedicated himself to the cause in question, directed his thoughts towards the one responsible for the oppression or the person causing the obstacle, and then either committed suicide or was ceremonially sacrificed so that the guilt of killing a sādhu would fall upon that person's head.

Jogis, it is believed, can often tell the time of their own death. When malady overpowers them they are wont to focus their gaze towards the middle of their eyebrows until they descry the figure of a man. If he should appear without hands, feet or other member, they determine by the missing parts how much time they still have to live. If the figure is without a head they know that very little remains of their existence. They then either have themselves buried alive, or composing their minds assume the posture of meditation and pass away of their own will.

The reasons quoted in the texts for committing suicide were many. Some ended their lives because they were unable to perform their religious duties owing to old age, disease or incapacity, and were oppressed with the purposelessness of living. Those guilty of *mahāpātakas* or great sins (*see* dosha) were encouraged to commit suicide as a form of penance. Some, like the Jains, held that at certain stages of his progress towards *kaivalya* or spiritual enlightenment, a man may deliberately limit, by his suicide, the remaining activity of karma and further opportunities for sin, and so achieve the victory of the spirit over the blind will to live. Some committed suicide as a protest against some wrong, so that the sin of their death might fall on the oppressor's head this practice prevailed among certain bardic* clans of Rājputāna and among certain sādhus. Some ended their days because of disillusionment with the world; some in an excess of religious fervour. Widows generally committed *suttee** under pressure of public opinion. Finally, a man could offer his life to the deity in return for some favour, and then in fulfilment of his vow commit suicide.

Books

See under Sociology.

ŚUKRA, preceptor and physician of the *asuras* and *daityas,* was the son of the mage Bhṛigu (but sometimes referred to as the son of Kavi), and priest of the demon-king Bali. His wives were Śuśumā and Jayantī (see below).

The *Mahābhārata* credits him with the power of restoring the dead to life. In the war between the gods and asuras the honours of battle were for long evenly distributed. In order to gain ascendancy over the gods, Śukra underwent the onerous penance of inhaling the smoke of chaff with his head downwards for a thousand years. During his absence the gods attacked and slew a number of the asura hosts and their allies. In this attack Vishṇu killed Śukra's mother. Śukra thereupon cursed the god to be born several times in the world of men, and then restored his mother to life. The gods were now becoming alarmed lest the purpose of Śukra's penance be successfully accomplished, so Indra sent his daughter *Jayantī* to seduce him. But Śukra remained firm in his resolve, completed his penance, and only then married her.

After this he set about restoring the slain asuras to life. The disconcerted gods sent *Kacha,* a son of Bṛihaspati, to wrest his secret from him. Kacha frankly revealed his identity and his intention, and because of his honesty Śukra promised to teach him the secret in due time if found worthy. Now Śukra had a daughter, *Devayānī,* who fell in love with Kacha, and this greatly displeased the asuras who, finding a suitable opportunity, killed the youth and fed him to the jackals. When Śukra learnt of the deed through meditation, he called out to the digested bits of the youth, which flew out of the bowels of the animals, killing them in the process, and Kacha stood before the sage perfectly whole. The murder was done again and again by the asuras, but each time the youth was restored.

Finally the asuras burnt the body of the murdered youth, dissolved the ashes in wine and gave it to the unsuspecting sage to drink. Once again finding that Kacha was missing, and once more meditating on his whereabouts, Śukra discovered the awful truth, and realized that he could not restore Kacha without destroying his own frame. Now Kacha spoke up from within his belly saying, 'Master, teach me the mantra for restoring life, and I will come out of your body and restore you to life'. This was done and Kacha reassembled the sage's fragments and made him whole again. This incident allegedly prompted Śukra to prohibit the drinking of wine by the daityas, a prohibition later taken over by the Brāhmins.

In the end Kacha refused to make Devayānī his wife and she cursed him so that the life-restoring mantra lost its power, while he in turn condemned her to become the wife, not of a brāhmin, but of a kshattriya (*see* Yayāti).

Śukra is the name given to the 'white', 'sixteen-rayed' planet Venus and to its ruler. Other names for Śukra are UŚANAS (identified as the author of a lawbook) and Śukrāchārya (identified with the author of a treatise on Politics*). He is also known as Kāvya, son of Kavi, 'poet'; Daitya-guru, 'Daitya-teacher'; Maghā-bhava, son of Maghā. Jayantī is also called Jayanī, Devasenā, Tāvīshī.

Books

See under Mythology.

ŚUMBHA, son of Nisunda, a famous *daitya* (demon) chief who along with his brother Niśumbha became a devotee of Śiva and performed penances for one thousand years in order to become immortal. Śiva refused to grant them the privilege, and they continued their austerities for another eight centuries, this time to such effect that the gods trembled. To distract them from their purpose Indra sent two enchanting *apsarās**, Rambhā and Tilottamā who succeeded so well in their task of seduction that they kept the two daityas engaged in amorous combat for five thousand years, during which time the gods breathed freely again.

But their original purpose reasserted itself and dispatching the nymphs home, the demon pair resumed their mortifications, so that after one thousand years Śiva was forced to grant them power and strength exceeding that of the gods. Inflated with their newly acquired might the brothers stormed heaven and the gods appealed to Brahmā, Vishṇu and Śiva, but without success. Śiva could only suggest that they take their plea to the goddess Durgā. When the goddess appeared before Śumbha his passion was aroused and he expressed his desire to possess her. She agreed on condition that he defeat her in battle. Not knowing that the boon given him by Śiva was power over gods and not goddesses he was put to flight by Durgā who pursued and slew the presumptuous daitya and his brother, as well as their formidable generals, the 'bald-headed' Muṇḍa and Chaṇḍa. After the latter engagement Durgā was given the title of Chaṇḍā, Chaṇḍī, or Chāmuṇḍā.

This is the Purāṇic legend, but in the *Mahābhārata* the two daityas are known as Sunda and Upasunda, to encompass whose destruction Indra sent down the apsarā Tilottamā. Her beauty inflamed the passions of the brothers; they both claimed her, quarrelled over her and killed each other.

Books

See under Mythology.

ŚUNAḤŚEPHAS (*śunaḥ-śephas*, 'dog-testicles') a devout young brāhmin who became the protégé and adopted son of the celebrated sage Viśvāmitra. Accounts of his parentage differ in the Brāhmaṇas, *Rāmāyaṇa* and Purāṇas. In one version he lived in the forest with his father, a poor brāhmin ṛishi named Ajīgartta, and three brothers. In time of need his father sold him to Rohita the son of king Hariśchandra* for one hundred cows, and the king decided to use the boy as a sacrificial victim in place of his own son Rohita. Varuṇa to whom the sacrifice was to be offered accepted the substitution. For the price of another hundred cows the boy's father, Ajīgartta, agreed to tie his son to the sacrificial post, and for a third hundred he also agreed to slay him.

Another legend has it that Ambarīsha king of Ayodhyā, son of Māndhātṛi, was performing a sacrifice when Indra carried off the victim. The officiating priest, deprived of the prize at the critical moment, declared that only the sacrifice of a human victim could atone for the heinous interruption. After a long search Ambarīsha found a ṛishi named Ṛichīka who was willing to sell his son as a sacrifice. This son was Śunaḥśephas who was delivered to the king in exchange for a hundred thousand cows, ten million gold pieces and a fortune in jewels.

Śunaḥśephas was tied to the sacrificial post, and when about to be slain began reciting mantras in praise of the deities. Moved by his plight the gods rescued him, blessed him and gave him long life. Through Śunaḥśephas human sacrifices were thereafter abolished. The lad was received into the family of the sage Viśvāmitra* as his own son. Seven hymns in the Ṛig-veda are attributed to him. Śunaḥśephas is also known as Devarāta, 'God-gratifying'.

Books

I. Keith, A. B. 'The Rig-veda Brahmanas'. *Harvard Oriental Series,* New Haven, 23, pp. 299 ff.
II. Robinson, W. H. *The Golden Legend of India,* London, 1911.

ŚUṄGA (183–73 BC) a brāhminical dynasty of Magadha* that succeeded the Maurya* line of kings and ruled for a total period of 110 years. A brāhmin coterie desirous of ending the hated Buddhist régime of the Mauryas, found an instrument for their ambitions in the person of **Pushyamitra** (183–151 BC) the probably Iranian commander-in-chief of the Mauryan king Bṛihadratha.

Pushyamitra climaxed his careful preparations for the seizure of power by arranging for his royal master to review the army in the spring of 183 BC. In full view of the assembled host he suddenly raised his sword and severed the head of his sovereign, the last of the illustrious Maurya line. Pushyamitra was given brāhminical status, and he inaugurated the formal return of northern India to brāhminism by celebrating two magnificent horse sacrifices which were remembered in India for centuries after.

Under Bṛihadratha the Mauryans had already lost some of their territories in the north-west to the Bactrian* Greeks, and Pushyamitra's empire actually covered only western Bengal, Bihār, Āgra, Oudh and Mathurā. His capital remained the old Mauryan city of Pāṭaliputra. He lost Kaliṅga, and his territories south of the Narmadā were annexed by the Āndhras. The triumphal progress of Pushyamitra's sacrificial horse, which was escorted by his grandson Vasumitra, was checked by a Greek detachment in the Panjāb, probably led by Apollodotus, and the south-westward drive of the Śuṅgan prince was again halted in Rājputāna by another body of Greek troops. Pushyamitra later had to repulse a Greek invasion which was referred to both by Patañjali and Kālidāsa.

Under brāhmin pressure Pushyamitra began persecuting the Buddhists, burnt their monasteries, and killed their monks. He went so far as to issue a declaration that he would reward anyone who presented him with the head of a Buddhist.

Agnimitra (151–143 BC) son of Pushyamitra was the hero of Kālidāsa's* *Mālavikāgnimitra* which gives an account of his viceroyalty at the second Śuṅga capital at Vidisā.
Vasumitra (136–126 BC) son of Agnimitra, had already distinguished himself in his encounters with the Greeks while escorting his grandfather's sacrificial horse. He had further trouble with the raids of Bactrian* Greeks during his own reign. He was murdered in the course of a theatrical performance.
Bhāgabhadra (126–124 BC) or Bhadraka, the fifth Śuṅga king (a king is mentioned between Agnimitra and Vasumitra) is notable as being the ruler to whose court the Bactrian* Greek king Antialcidas sent his ambassador Heliodorus who raised a column* in honour of Vishṇu at Besnagar.

Greek incursions may have recommenced after Bhāgabhadra's death until the Greeks were recalled by troubles which broke out in Menander's own kingdom. But intermittent fighting with the Bactrians continued through the reigns of all Śuṅga rulers. The remaining five Śuṅgan kings were a succession of weaklings and bigots whose excesses aroused the censure of their subjects and alarmed even their brāhmin sponsors. The last of the Śuṅgas, **Devabhuti** (fl. 73 BC) was so worthless and dissolute that the brāhmins at length conspired to have him killed by a slave girl who visited him in the guise of a queen. His minister, a brāhmin priest, ascended the throne as the first of the Kaṇva kings of Magadha* in 73 BC.

Though few details are known about the Śuṅga dynasty they played an important part in the development of Indian art. Throughout their rule close contact with the Bactrian Greeks, both hostile and friendly, is clearly established. The founding of a second capital at Vidisā (or Bhīlsā, near modern Besnagar, in Eastern Mālwā or Gwālior) is of great significance in the history of Indian sculpture. The city was situated on the direct trade route from Pāṭaliputra to the seaport of Broach on the west coast and must have been influenced by various foreign factors. The Śuṅgan kings themselves, who were anti-Buddhist, made no contribution towards Buddhist works, but foreign merchants and local Buddhist guilds of that period were responsible for several notable examples of art and architecture. Near Bhīlsā stands the great stūpa* of Sānchi, one column of whose southern gate was the work of a guild of ivory carvers of Vidisā who made a gift of this column to the stūpa.

Śuṅgan art is also represented in the remains of the stūpa at Bhārhut. Today nothing is left of the stūpa itself except a portion of the railings surrounding it, and the columns and gateways. The stone-work is richly engraved with Buddhist reliefs, most of them being illustrations from the *Jātakas*, but several depicting domestic life. The work is crude in composition but nonetheless an important landmark in the development of Indian art.

Books

See under History and Magadha.

ŚŪNYA, 'void', or *śūnyatā*, 'voidness', a basic concept of Mahāyāna Buddhism and Hindu esoteric philosophy. The words signify privativeness, non-existence, or absence. In its hlgher interpretation it is not a negative concept but a dynamic one, implying vacuity or emptiness, but not lack. Nāgārjuna* (AD 150) starting with a series of denials gave śūnya the status of a major philosophical category, and after him śūnyatā became fundamental to Buddhist thought. Nāgārjuna showed that all relations, and the forms of existence produced by them, are dialectically negated, leaving only the Void. Subsequent Buddhist philosophy has ever since been associated with the doctrine of the Void which has been analysed under as many as eighteen categories.

The Void is beyond all specific character and above causal relationship, and is variously said to be Ultimate Reality, Thusness (*tathatā*), Nirvāṇa, the Middle Path, the Unconditioned, the Absolute. Śūnya-vāda, the void-doctrine, however, has been subject to much misinterpretation, which has led to strong criticism, and has been condemned as negative, pessimistic and nihilistic.

Śūnya in fact is the highest wisdom, according to Buddhism. Śūnya-vāda is the only way of communicating knowledge and understanding reality. In its absolute form it is an experience of final Non-Beingness flashing forth through the state of natural beingness which is our temporal human existence. It is not mere negation, but a Negation of negation that is an Existence-Being beyond existence and being. It is best defined by negatives since all positive expressions not only limit but pollute the pure concept of absolute śūnya.

In Hinduism the term śūnya has a less precise application, and facets of the notion of nothingness or privativeness are found in many important branches of Hindu life and thought. The idea of the Absolute or Brahma is best conveyed by negatives: *neti*, *neti*, 'not this, not this'. He is *nirguṇa*, without qualities; *amūrti*, without form; inexpressible, inconceivable, immeasurable, unfathomable, and so on. Define Him by positives and He becomes attenuated by those very attributes.

In the karma concept of Hinduism, the higher forces of this world are all *aḍrishṭa*, 'unseen', invisible, hidden from mortal understanding. All actions, even those outside one's knowledge and consciousness, exercise an irrevocable and irresistible impact on the invisible world. We reap the rewards and penalties of our good and bad deeds on that higher plane, even though they do not always produce visible results here. So the effects of a sacrifice are adṛishṭa, and even though not seen are very real, and have a profound significance in the unseen world. Adṛishṭa also refers to the hidden, unseen forces of phenomenal-empirical reality.

Similarly, silence is a dynamic concept, much more potent than sound. It is the best means of communicating rahasya or the profound secrets* of man and his destiny. The highest sound (*see* śabda) is a form of silence. The silent mantra has greater power than the intoned chant or whispered formula. The unstruck sound produced from ether, unheard by physical ears, delights the gods. Struck sounds give pleasure, unstruck sounds liberation. Yogis, by practice and meditation project their minds into the realm of the unstruck sound and are freed.

Absence is yet another conceptual fragment of the universal reality of śūnya. The things that matter are not there. At best they can only be apprehended and represented by symbols. The deepest devotion, the finest oblation (e.g. *prāṇāgnihotra*), the supreme sacrifices take place not outside but within oneself. Śūnya is an immutable pillar that supports the firmament, more stable than all of Indra's elephants. The absent liṅga of Chidambaram is revered as the most efficacious of all Śiva liṅgas. In the whole sphere of numerals* it is the empty zero that is most significant. Likewise, the blessings of the Ganges come from any stretch of water, correctly invoked, for the invisible Ganges is present in all. The highest enjoyment, the richest feasts are obtained through *tyāga* or renunciation.

In metaphysics the notion of voidness is also frequently met with. The term *abhāva*, 'non-existence', which in Mahāyāna implies a state devoid of identity or self-nature, was sometimes used to denote the progressively limiting conditions of the 'reality' of an empirical object. Vaiśeshika philosophy added a seventh category, abhāva, to the six of Kaṇāda, and subsequent refinements of its meaning were elaborated to clarify various nuances of the ontological, non-existence of things. Four kinds of abhāva are distinguished: (1) *Prāgabhāva*, antecedent non-existence, i.e. the non-existence of a thing before it actually comes into being, for example, before its production, as when fire is not there before it is lit. (2) *Pradhvaṁsābhāva*, the subsequent non-existence of a thing after it has had existence, for example, the non-existence of a flame after it has gone out. (3) *Anyonyābhāva*, or mutual non-existence, the non-existence of one thing as another thing, for example an elephant is nonexistent as a tree. (4) *Atyantābhāva*, 'absolute non-existence', as a pot is absolutely non-existent as a liquid pot. Other examples are a hare's horn, the child of a barren woman, a sky-flower, and, to quote Gauḍapāda's example, the footprints of a bird in the air.

Buddhist semantics held that words were not related to the objects they were supposed to denote, and Buddhist logicians, in a philological application of śūnyatā, expounded a doctrine of *apoha*, 'denying', by which they meant that every expression of a concept, for example, a cow, implied a total denial of itself, a non-cow. Accordingly, reality consists of a 'privative', and the existence of anything may be framed as the denial of its non-existence. Just as the world grew out of a state of non-worldness, so every concept is preceded by its own absence. To reach the cow, or any phenomenal object whatsoever, one must first pass through the whole logical, philosophical and empirical experience of the non-cow or whatever the object happens to be.

Books

See under Buddhism, Nāgārjuna and Philosophy.

ŚŪRA, a Yādava king who ruled over the Śūrasena people with capital at Mathurā on the Yamunā. He had four children, namely, Vasudeva, Kuntī, Samudravijaya and Śrutadevā. The last named married Damaghosha king of Chedi and became the mother of Śiśupāla*.

When Vasudeva, the eldest child of Śūra was born, the great drum called *Ānakadundu* was sounded in heaven because he was destined to become the father of the god Kṛishṇa*. Shortly after Kṛishṇa's death Vasudeva passed away and four of his wives burned themselves on his funeral pyre.

Samudravijaya became the father of NEMI (or Arishṭanemi) the twenty-second Jain *tīrthaṅkara**. Nemi was thus the cousin of Kṛishṇa. Jains claim that Nemi was far superior to Kṛishṇa both in physical prowess and intellectual and moral stature. He was gentle, unostentatious, chaste, and the exact opposite of Kṛishṇa.

Kuntī (also known as Pṛithā and Pārshṇī) was given by Śūra to his childless cousin Kuntibhoja king of the Kunti people and was brought up at his court. As a girl she showed such devotion to the sage Durvāsas that the latter rewarded her with a talisman by means of which she could summon any five gods to have congress with her. She called upon Sūrya the sun-god to test her power but when the god appeared he refused to leave without union, and as a result of his embrace she conceived and bore a son, Karṇa*. Ashamed of her lapse she exposed the child on the banks of the Yamunā where he was found and raised by a childless couple and grew up to become one of the great heroes of Hindu mythology. Subsequently Kuntī married Pāṇḍu king of Hastināpura whom she chose at a *svayaṁvara*. She bore three of the Pāṇḍava brothers by summoning three more gods, namely, Yudhishṭhira by Dharma, Bhīma by Vāyu, and Arjuna by Indra, making four gods in all by whom she had children. She transferred her power over the remaining fifth god to Mādrī, the second wife of Pāṇḍu, and Mādrī called upon the twin Aśvins; through them she bore Nakula and Sahadeva, the last two Pāṇḍava brothers. After the battle of Kurukshetra Kuntī retired to the forest where she lost her life in a forest conflagration.

Books

See under Mythology.

SURGERY, known in Sanskrit as *śalya,* was one of the branches of Āyurvedic study. The original meaning of the world śalya, 'arrow' or 'spear', indicates that it evolved from operations on the battlefield.

Charaka (2nd century AD) has little or nothing to say about surgery, and the subject is absent from the Bower Manuscript (AD 450), but the fourth century surgeon Suśruta refers to dissection of a kind. The corpse selected for the purpose, complete in all parts, had to be of a person, not too old, who had not died of poisoning or of any protracted disease. After removing all excrementitious matter from the entrails, the body was wrapped up in a rush mat and put into a large cage which was then placed in a fast-flowing stream and allowed to soften. After several days it was taken out and carefully rubbed with a hard whisk, and as the muscles and internal organs were exposed they were examined and studied. This procedure was recommended for surgeons. Physicians learnt the position of internal organs only by prodding the living body. According to the lawgiver Manu the very touch of a corpse brought defilement, a belief which established a general taboo on the handling of cadavers. Since surgery could best be learnt by dissection of the human body the profession was long held in abhorrence by the higher castes. When in modern times the first medical colleges were opened in the cities it was difficult to obtain students for training.

The ancients found a way around this difficulty by resorting to substitutes for the dead human flesh. Apprentice surgeons were taught by practising incisions on gourds; the puncturing and opening of tumours on the bladders of animals filled with mud and water; the piercing of hollow organs on thick lotus stalks; probing on dried cucumbers and worm-eaten wood; the application of caustics on pieces of meat; the giving of enemas on the ends of watermelons; bandaging was practised on a doll or lay figure. The stitching of wounds was perfected on bits of soft leather. On the living body suturing was effected by the use of horse-hair, plant fibres, animal gut and ants' heads, the latter by letting large ants nip the flesh and then cutting off their bodies.

Among the surgical concepts peculiar to Āyurveda was that of *marma* or vital junctions of muscle, bone, tissue, tendon. It was believed that injury to any of the one hundred and seven marmas was very serious. A knowledge of the marmas gave a rough descriptive idea of 'regional anatomy'*.

Anaesthetics were not generally used, but if it were considered necessary opium or some other drug was employed. Charaka and Suśruta mention the use of wine to induce insensibility before an operation.

On the whole the Hindus did not pay much attention to or make much progress in surgery, although they were familiar with contemporary methods of lithotomy, Caesarean section, amputation and bone-setting, operations for cataract and hernia, as well as such techniques as branding, cauterising, bleeding, incision, excision, scarification, puncturing, probing, drainage and suturing.

It would appear though that in one field at least Indian surgery did make considerable progress, and that was in rhinoplasty and otoplasty. In the words of one authority, 'probably the only valuable contribution to surgery to which India can lay claim is the art of forming artificial noses' (I, p. 266). The art of grafting noses and ears was perhaps unequalled in the ancient world. Suśruta describes these operations, but according to some scholars the text in question is a *réchauffé* of similar passages from Celsus, and consequently spurious. (II, p. 171).

Surgery and surgical instruments (yantra) are described in a number of Sanskrit medical works. There were twenty varieties of lancets and knives, twenty-five of forceps and pincers, twenty kinds of tubular instruments, thirty different probes (*śalākā*), as also spatulas, tongs, hooks and catheters, and twenty-six kinds of dressing, cloth and thread. But as they are all post-Greek it is believed that they were introduced by the Greeks or Romans, or by Buddhist monks who acquired these devices from foreign countries in the course of their extensive travels.

Surgery receded into the background once the Greek influence waned, and was almost completely neglected when the Buddhist ascendancy declined. It received its next impetus and experienced a brief revival by about the tenth century, some time after the advent of the Arabs.

Books

I. *Imperial Gazetteer of India*, Oxford, Vol. II, 1908.
II. Jolly, J. *Hindu Medicine*, Poona, 1951.
III. Mukhopadhyaya, G. N. *Surgical Instruments of the Ancient Hindus*, 2 vols., 1936.
IV. Sastri, M. N. *Surgery in Ancient India*, 1929.

ŚŪRPANAKHĀ, 'winnowing-fan nailed', a *rākshasī* or ogress, so named because of her huge splayed, claw-like nails (*nakha*), the daughter of Viśravas* and sister of the demon king Rāvaṇa.

During the exile of Rāma and Sītā in Pañchāvatī, in the great southern forest near the source of the Godāverī, Śūrpanakhā caught sight of the handsome Rāma and fell in love with him. She came to him with a proposal of marriage but was rebuffed by the hero, who sent her to Lakshmaṇa his brother. When Lakshmaṇa also rejected her she turned in a rage of jealousy on Sītā. Rāma called upon his brother to deal with her and Lakshmaṇa cut off her nose (*nāsika*) and ears. In commemoration of this incident the area of Pañchāvatī was thereafter known as Nāsik*.

Provoked and humiliated beyond endurance Śūrpanakhā appealed to her younger brother Khara for vengeance. Thirty man-eating rākshasas were immediately dispatched to deal with Rāma, but proved no match for the young hero who easily disposed of them. Khara sent for reinforcements to his warrior brother Dūshaṇa, and together they assembled an army of rākshasas to march against the presumptuous Rāma. In the ensuing brief combat both Dūshaṇa and Khara were slain and their army put to flight.

Foiled in her attempts to avenge herself by having Rāma killed, the ogress thought of another scheme. She went to Laṅkā, the kingdom of her eldest brother, the redoubtable Rāvaṇa, and reported the story to him. Knowing his weakness for the fair sex she dwelled at length on the charms of Sītā, whose lap she described as being like the lotus flower, and whose thighs like the trunks of slender banana trees. At the same time she warned Rāvaṇa that it was impossible to defeat Rāma in battle, and suggested that he use guile to seduce Sītā.

Thus began Rāvaṇa's* ill-starred adventure, around which the story of the *Rāmāyaṇa* revolves. Just before the last battle, when Rāvaṇa went forth to fight, Śūrpanakhā stood in his way, begging him not to venture against Rāma, but Rāvaṇa thrust her impatiently aside. For this insult she cursed her brother saying that he would never again see his beloved city of Laṅkā. It was in this final encounter that Rāma slew the great rākshasa monarch.

Books

See under Mythology and *Rāmāyaṇa.*

SŪRYA, the sun god. His name occurs as Shurias in the records of the Kassites and Mitanni, and according to some authorities 'appears to have been collected in Iran' (II, p. 84). Thus, 'although the worship of Sūrya has been a feature of Ṛig-vedic times, the sun cult as such was introduced into India later as a foreign form of worship' (III, p. 302). The *Bhavishya Purāṇa* preserves a tradition that the first sun-temple was built in Sindhu on the Chandrabhāga by Śāmba son of Kṛishṇa and Jāmbavatī, who brought the Śakadvīpa brāhmins (Maga* priests) to serve as priests of the new deity. Sūrya images of the Kushān period show him with a dagger, close-fitting coat, and high Central Asian boots (III, p. 320).

Along with Indra and Agni, Sūrya was one of the chief Vedic triad of deities, to whom a dozen hymns in the *Ṛig-veda* are addressed. He is referred to as 'the eye of Varuṇa', the god of the sun, and a manifestation of the divine energy of heaven. He is variously called the son of Dyaus, of Brahmā, or of Kaśyapa. In some versions he is the last son of Aditi, born as an imperfect lump which was shaped by his brother-Ādityas. A god of many aspects and as many names he is sometimes identified with Pūshan, and also spoken of as the husband of Ushas goddess of the dawn.

As VIVASVAT, 'brilliant' (the Vivahant of the Zoroastrian Avesta) he appears in his aspect of the Shining One of the firmament or the rising sun. His wife SARAṆYŪ daughter of the divine artisan Tvashṭṛi bore him the twins Yama and Yamī. Legend relates that she escaped from her husband in the form a of mare, leaving in her place Savarṇā, 'a woman of similar appearance'. From union with her Vivasvat became the father of Manu Vaivasvata*, the Manu of the present age. Discovering later how Saraṇyū had escaped him Vivasvat assumed the shape of a stallion and followed his wife. Seeing him thus the grazing Saraṇyū, now called Aśvinī (mare), desired her husband and the equine couple mated. 'In his haste his seed fell to the ground and she being desirous of offspring smelled it.' From this were born the Aśvins.*

In the Purāṇas the wife of Sūrya is SAṂJÑĀ, 'awakening', daughter of the celestial artificer Viśvakarman. Saṁjñā was unable to endure the effulgence of her husband, so her father placed the sun upon his lathe and cut away an eighth part of his radiance. From the blazing fragments that fell to earth Viśvakarman wrought the discus of Vishṇu, the trident of Śiva, the weapon of Kubera, the lance of Kārttikeya, the *āgneyāstra* or fire-weapon of Agniveśa, and the weapons* of many other gods.

But the fervour of Sūrya was still too great for Saṁjñā, and after bearing him a son Revanta (*see* Kubera), she gave her husband the nymph Chhāyā, 'shade', for a handmaid, and herself retired as an ascetic to the forest. Through union with Chhāyā, Sūrya begat Tapatī, goddess of the river Taptī, and Śani the personification of the planet Saturn (see below). Sūrya was also the father of Karṇa, the *Mahābhārata* hero, and Sugrīva the monkey king.

Sūrya was generous to his devotees, bestowing on them wealth and wisdom. In his equine aspect he communicated the *White Yajur-veda* to the sage Yājñavalkya. To Satrājita* who rendered him praise and homage he gave the wonderful jewel *syamantaka*. But to those who opposed him the sun-god was ruthless, destroying and blasting them with the flash of his anger. Once a group of *rākshasas* called Mandeha sought to overpower him, but he dispersed them with his blinding light.

Sūrya is described as dwarfish in stature, with a body of burnished copper and reddish eyes. His charriot is drawn by the ARUSHA, seven 'red' horses, or a seven-headed horse surrounded by a halo of rays. His charioteer is the legless ARUṆA, 'rosy', son of Kaśyapa and Kadrū, who represents the dawn and twilight. His paradise* is Vivasvatī or Bhāsvatī. Among his many titles are: Aṁśa, 'fragmented', i.e. by Viśvakarman; Arhapati, 'honoured Lord'; Bhāskara, 'light-maker'; Dinakara, 'day maker'; Dyumaṇi, 'sky-jewel'; Gabhastimat, 'possessing rays'; Graharāja, 'planet-king'; Karmasākshi, 'deed-witness'; Mārtāṇḍa, descended from Mṛitāṇḍa, 'lifeless egg' of the sky bird; Lokachakshuḥ, 'world-eye'; Ravi, 'conferring'; Sahasra-kiraṇa, 'thousand-rayed; Savitar or Savitṛi, 'stimulator' (a Vedic name sometimes applied to Tvashṭṛi); Vikartana, 'deprived' (i.e. of his beams by Viśvakarman).

The sect devoted exclusively to the worship of Sūrya as the supreme deity and the adoration of the solar orb is known as *Saura* (also Saurya, Saurapata), and its origin is traced to Zoroastrian influence. Strict Saura cultists do not eat until they have seen the sun, and do not eat after sunset. They brand their foreheads, arms and breasts with hot iron brands. The name Saura is also applied to the followers of the cult of *Śani* (Saturn), who is the son of Sūrya and Chhāyā (Shade) mentioned above (in some legends Śani is the son of Balarāma and Revatī). A great deal of malignant occultism is associated with his worship, and some authorities hold that all the left-hand sun cults are actually Saturn cults, perhaps originating with the Magas or Vrātyas.

Śani is usually depicted robed in black, riding on a vulture. Among his titles are Koṇa, 'angular', Krūra-lochana, 'evil eyed', Manda, 'slow', Paṅgu, 'lame', Asita, 'dark'. His cult is perverse and highly sexualized. Many of the temples ostensibly raised to the sun are dedicated to Saturn, and a number of them are adorned with licentious sculpture. Such was the temple of Konārak now in ruins (*see* Black Pagoda), as also the notorious sun temple at Multān which had hordes of temple prostitutes*. The *Padma-Purāṇa* recommends the dedication of prostitutes to a solar temple as the best means of attaining to paradise.

Books

I. Alexander, A. *The Worship of the Sun*, 1892.
II. Ghose, N. *The Aryan Trail in Iran and India*, Calcutta, 1937.
III. Upadhyaya, B. S. *India in Kalidasa*, Allahabad, 1947.

SUSPENDED ANIMATION is one of the most remarkable features of Indian occultism. Some yogis are credited with the ability to go into *samādhi*-like trances, with all the characteristic activities of the living organism such as movement, respiration and the beating of the heart, temporarily suspended, giving the appearance of death according to clinical diagnosis. After a period sometimes extending to several days they reanimate their bodies and resume normal life as before. Yogis occasionally demonstrate their power to do this by allowing themselves to be buried alive.

Such burial alive has often been recorded in the past. Contrary to popular belief it is not confined to India, and wonder-workers in Egypt, Arabia, Europe and Central America have sometimes demonstrated this feat. Drugs, auto-hypnosis, and many years training in scientific breath control have been variously put forward to explain such phenomena.

A celebrated case took place in Lahore in 1838 under the supervision and in the presence of the Mahārāja Ranjīt Singh of the Panjāb and his nobles, the British general Sir Claude Wade, and the Napoleonic veteran, General Reuben Ventura. The *yogi*, Haridās, was a professional magician, who made a living by allowing himself to be buried alive, and whose feats were recorded by European observers more than once.

On this occasion he took several days to prepare himself, for he intended to do something worthy of his distinguished audience. He changed his diet to whey, pulse-soup and soaked gram, of which he daily took less and less until he stopped eating altogether. Three days after this he declared himself ready, and the demonstration took place in the grounds of the mahārāja's palace. The yogi first stopped his ears and nostrils with wax, and sitting on a piece of white muslin assumed an easy cross-legged position (probably *siddhāsana*), then turned his tongue back into his gullet (the *paramudrā*, *khecharī*) and went into a trance. At a word from his assistant the cloth was drawn up over his head and made secure. He was lifted and placed in a box which was then sealed and locked. General Wade kept the keys himself and British soldiers stood guard over the box. Another account states that the box was buried in a shallow pit within a sealed pavilion. At the end of thirty days the box was opened in the presence of the Mahārāja, General Sir Claude Wade, Dr McGregor of the Horse Artillery, and many others.

The body was cold, stiff and emaciated, but did not quite have the appearance of death. There was no pulse or heart-beat, nor had the hair or nails grown, but the top of the head was considerably heated. The assistant removed the plugs from the ears and nostrils, forced open the jaws and with a finger drew the tongue forward again. Warm water was poured over the yogi and the limbs massaged, and in about two hours his colour returned and he was able to speak, but very weakly. He said that while in trance his thoughts and dreams were of a most delightful character, and that it was always painful for him to be awakened and forced to return.

Some authorities believe that in such cases although all physiological functions are suspended, a tiny ember in the form of a feeble rhythmic movement of the heart, so faint that it would certainly not be perceptible by the instruments available in India in the middle of the last century, had to be kept alive to ignite the flame of life again. Even in the case of burial in a pit, which is first covered with a board and then filled up with earth, the porosity of the raw earth would be sufficient to provide the small amount of oxygen necessary to keep the entranced yogi alive. Recent experiments have also proved that although a yogi is ostensibly in trance, the EEG (electro-encephalogram) curves which record the intensity and rhythm of electrical impulses in the brain, remain normal, showing that samādhi does not affect the electrical activity of the brain. But the psycho-galvanic reflex (used in lie-detectors) which reflects changes in the electrical properties of the body in response to emotional stimuli, remains consistently below normal.

There is no doubt that by long practice the yogi is able to control the functioning of his organism and voluntarily lower the basic metabolic rate, but although remarkable it is not supernatural and does not justify the claim that yogis buried alive cease from breathing altogether. Yogis of advanced degree are able to slow down the pulse and even stop the heart-beat for about the space of a minute. In this interval although the pulse cannot be felt by placing a finger on an artery, the sphygmograph (which measures blood pressure) continues to record feeble and irregular pulse waves. The weakening of the pulse is produced by contraction of the biceps, pectoralis and other muscles, thus compressing the brachial artery, and also by diminishing the blood flow by holding the breath. It is to be remembered that most normal persons can slow down their hearts by holding the breath and 'willing' the heart to beat more quietly. The degree of this 'Valsalva manoeuvring' (named after the sinuses of Valsalva which are bulges in the aortic walls) varies according to the individual.

Books

I. Honigberger, J. M. *Thirtyfive Years in the East*, London, 1858.
II. Koestler, A. *The Lotus and the Robot*, London, 1960.
III. Osborne, W. G. *The Court and Camp of Rungeet Singh*, London, 1838.
IV. Oswald, John. *Suspended Animal Life*, 1901.
V. Rao, H. V. G., *et al.* 'Some Experiments on a Yogi in Controlled States.' *Journal of The All Indian Institute of Mental Health*, Bangalore, July, 1958.

SUTTEE, anglicized orthography for the Sanskrit *satī,* the Hindu rite of suicide* of widows by self-immolation. The word is derived from Satī wife of Śiva who committed suicide because of an insult to which her husband had been subjected by Daksha her own father. The term was extended to mean the 'true' wife who remains faithful to the memory of her husband by not marrying again. Subsequently the term was applied to the rite in which a widow committed herself to the flames of the pyre on which the body of her husband was cremated.

Much speculation invests the origin of the custom. There is no evidence that it was ever current among the ancient Indo-Aryans who only used to bury a few of the chief possessions of the deceased along with him. Nor is there anything in the Vedas to show that it had Vedic sanction. One of the funeral hymns of the *Ṛig-veda* indicates that in the early *antyeshṭi* or obsequial* ceremonies the widow lay down beside the dead man after he had been placed on the unlit pyre; his bow was placed in her hand for a while, then the bow was taken and she was called to 'return to the land of the living'. She was allowed to marry the dead man's brother or continue to produce children by *niyoga**.

The first instances of suttee are recorded in the Indian Epics. Mādrī ascended the funeral pyre on the death of her husband Pāṇḍu, although some of the sages present tried to dissuade her from what they considered an unrighteous act. The four wives of Vasudeva father of Kṛishṇa namely Devakī, Bhadrā, Rohiṇī and Madirā, were voluntarily burned with him. When Kṛishṇa died five of his wives, Rukmiṇī, Gāndhārī, Sahyā, Haimavatī, and Jāmbavatī, immolated themselves on a pyre. When Sītā through Rāvaṇa's magic was made to believe that Rāma had been slain she wanted to be burned along with her husband.

The custom of suttee excited the curiosity and horror of the Greeks, who recorded several cases of widow burning and the self-immolation of Indian sages. The earliest actual historical instance of suttee is reported in the Greek chronicles which describe the burning of the wife of the Indian general Keteus who died in 316 BC while fighting Antigonus, with the observation that this custom prevailed among the Kathia tribe of the Panjāb.

By the first and second centuries AD the rite began to gain the support of the lawgivers, many of whom declared it to be a meritorious act on the part of the widow, upholding their contention by reference to verses from holy writ, some of which were corrupted or even forged* to serve their ends.

By the sixth and seventh centuries the life of a widow apart from her husband was unequivocally condemned as sinful by the *smṛiti* writers; it was declared preferable that she mount the funeral pyre. From that time onwards they began advocating it as a religious duty, by means of which a wife could secure salvation both for her husband and herself. The rite was at first restricted to the wives of princes and warriors, but in course of time the widows of weavers, masons, barbers, and others of lower caste adopted the practice. The advocacy of suttee was taken up in Purāṇic writings, and the *Padma-Purāṇa* (*c.* AD 1100) details the ceremonial procedure for the rite as it was then established.

Two kinds of suttee were distinguished, but neither offered any escape for the hapless widow. One was *saha-maraṇa*, 'co-dying', in which a widow burnt herself on the same fire as that on which her husband's corpse was cremated. The other was *anu-maraṇa*, 'after-dying', in which the widow died not on the funeral pyre of her husband, but later, on a pile lit with the embers preserved from the husband's pyre. This took place if the widow was in an 'impure' state, for example, menstruating (when a week was allowed to pass after the cessation of the flow), or pregnant (when two months were allowed to pass after the birth of the child).

The general pattern of suttee ceremonial ran as follows: After the husband's death the widow prepared to join him. She was given a ceremonial bath and dressed in her finery and ornaments; she bore all the distinguishing marks of a woman whose husband is living. She accompanied her husband's body to the cremation ground. Since she would soon have access to the spheres of heaven she was entrusted with messages to carry to deceased relations. Arrived at the pyre, she gave away her ornaments which were kept by the recipients as precious mementoes. She then mounted the pyre and sat beside the corpse, placing her husband's head on her lap. The pyre was then lighted.

How many women voluntarily ascended the pyre is of course impossible to determine, but the number of those sufficiently resolute to overcome the natural instinct to escape one of the most excruciating forms of death must have been small indeed. Reports of eyewitnesses do record the heroism of some women who sought this form of death of their own free will. Quoting a number of instances from accounts of foreign travellers Dr A. S. Altekar speaks of his own sister who as late as 1946 with indescribable fortitude carried out her resolve, committing herself to the flames within twenty-four hours of her husband's death in spite of the pressing entreaties of her relations.

But such isolated acts of heroism do not mitigate the general picture of brutality and sadism that is revealed in the lurid history of suttee. Altekar states. 'Even widows intensely anxious to follow their husbands were likely to recoil and jump out under the agony of the flames.' To avoid such eventualities special arrangements were made and precautions taken. For example, the pyre was laid in a pit to make escape impossible; or the widows were tied to the logs or chained to stakes; if they tried to escape they were hit on the head or pushed back with long bamboo poles; some were mercifully drugged with a decoction of dried saffron pistils, which kept them cheerful till the pyre was ignited.

Between AD 700 and 1000 the history of north India especially Kashmīr is filled with records of suttee. Kalhaṇa (*c.* 1150) mentions cases of Kashmīr queens bribing their ministers to make a pretence of dissuading them publicly from their apparently voluntary resolve to commit suttee, so that they might escape the ordeal without ignominy. He cites an instance where a wily brāhmin named Garga accepted the bribe of the queen Jayamatī but delayed going to the burning ground till after the queen had been burned.

Among the Rājputs and other warrior nations of northern India, the observance of suttee took on staggering proportions, since wives and concubines immolated themselves by the hundred. It became customary not only for wives but for mistresses, sisters, mothers, sisters-in-law and other near female relatives and retainers to burn themselves along with their deceased master. With Rājputs it evolved into the terrible rite of *jauhar* which took place in times of war or great peril in order to save the honour of the womenfolk of the clan. The earliest recorded instance of jauhar in Greek chronicles describes how after Alexander the Great captured one of the towns of the Agalassoi tribe, some twenty thousand citizens threw themselves into a huge pyre along with their wives and children. Similarly when the Rājputs were certain that they could not escape defeat or destruction by the enemy they would gather together their wives, women and children, heap firewood in plenty close about them and set it alight. When the holocaust was over the men would rush out to meet the enemy, fighting till they fell. A notable instance occurred when the Khilji Sultān, Alā-ud-dīn, attacked Chitor in 1303, reputedly to possess himself of the beautiful Rājput princess of Mewār, Padminī. When defeat was nigh the women of the fortress along with the princess Padminī were burnt to death, and the men met their end on the field of battle.

The custom of suttee was also adopted by the Sikhs, although the third Sikh guru, Amardās (d. 1574) condemned it. When the Sikhs were forced under Moghul tyranny to take to arms, they could not lag behind the other kshattriya clans, and Sikh mahārājas and princes were cremated along with their wives and slave girls. When the body of Ranjīt Singh (d. 1839) was burnt his four queens and seven concubines were burnt with him.

Suttee did not extend to South India until about the tenth century, but once it gained a hold there it reached terrible proportions, especially when the rulers of Vijayanagar or the Nāyyakas of Madura passed away. Says Thomson, 'Even Sikh and Rājput history contains nothing so horrible as the story of the Vijayanagar suttees; when a king died two or even three thousand of his wives were burnt with him'. The southern kingdoms also introduced some gruesome variations. One eyewitness records that when the last king of Tanjore died in 1801 his last two wives were burnt with him. A portion of the bones was reduced to powder, mixed with boiled rice and eaten by the twelve officiating brāhmin priests with the object of expiating the sins of the deceased.

Foreign observers have frequently recorded cases of suttee. Ibn Batuta (*c.* 1350) the African Muslim traveller confesses that he fainted when he witnessed the immolation of a Hindu woman on the pyre of her husband. Nicolo Conti (*c.* 1450), Venetian traveller in his account states that a woman was threatened with the loss of her right to property and possessions when she showed an unwillingness to burn herself. The *Akbarnāmāh* relates the case of one of Akbar's Hindu officers who in 1584 wanted forcibly to immolate his own mother on his father's funeral pyre, and was only prevented through the intervention of Akbar. François Bernier (*c.* 1660) French physician and traveller tells the case of a child widow of twelve being burnt at Lahore in spite of her desperate struggles and piteous cries. Niccolao Manucci (*c.* 1705) the Venetian relates that kshattriya women who were supposed to ascend the flames voluntarily were frequently burnt against their will. He himself rescued one such woman who eventually married a European friend. Job

Charnock the founder of Calcutta married a Hindu widow whom he had rescued from the pyre.

In a case reported in 1796 the wife was fastened on to the funeral pile of her husband, but as the night was dark and it was raining the woman managed to disengage herself and escape unseen. When it was discovered that there was only one body on the pyre a search was made and she was dragged from her hiding place. She pleaded to be spared but her own son insisted that she throw herself on the pile as he would lose caste and suffer everlasting humiliation. When she still refused the son with the help of some others present, bound her hands and feet and hurled her into the blaze.

The funerals of mahārājas and wealthy chieftains were like mammoth festivals, and many surviving accounts, written by Muslim and European observers tell of the wives and concubines being dragged resisting to the great pyre and forcibly consigned to the flames. All this was very far from the romantic picture of the faithful spouse voluntarily ascending the pyre.

Suttee was intermittently condemned by a few lawgivers, and occasionally by Sanskrit writers. The poet Bāṇa (fl. AD 650) wrote:

'The custom is a foolish mistake of stupendous magnitude, committed under the reckless impulse of despair and infatuation. It does not help the dead for he goes to heaven or hell according to his deserts. It does not ensure reunion since the wife who has uselessly sacrificed her life goes to the hell reserved for suicides. By living she can still do much good both to herself by pious works and to the departed by offering oblations for his happiness in the other world. By dying she only adds to her misery.'

But it was ultimately the Tantrik writers who unequivocally condemned suttee, branding it a barbaric custom contrary to the dictates of religion, humanity and common sense; they held that a woman who burnt herself, however noble her motives, would surely go to hell.

The Muslims tried to check suttee by instituting a permit system based on a declaration made by the widow that she wished of her own free will to become a satī, but the system was a mere formality for under pressure from their relations few women could resist making the declaration. The Portuguese strictly prohibited suttee in their territories by 1510, and took stern action against all relatives and bystanders and the custom soon died out in the areas under Portuguese control.

The British took no decisive action for years until the reports of missionaries and administrators showed it to be an evil whose extermination could brook no further delay. Between the years 1815 and 1828 there were 5100 recorded cases of suttee in Bengal (706 in 1817 near Calcutta alone), over 1150 in the Banāras area, over 700 in Paṭṇa, and hundreds more in scattered localities. Under pressure from the missionaries and Hindu reformers, notably Rāja Rāmmohan Roy*, Lord Bentinck's Regulation of 1829 made suttee a homicidal act. The orthodox party, in public assemblies and through their journals such as the *Chandrika*, violently opposed this interference with their sacred customs and fought their case in the Privy Council, but their petition was dismissed.

But though prohibited in British India the practice continued unchecked in Rājputāna, always the stronghold of suttee. When the mahārājas and nobles of Jodhpur, Jaipur, Udaipur, Mārwār and Bundi died their women had to ascend the pyre. Within thirty years of the British Regulation however, public opinion was ranged against it. So when the Mahārāna of Udaipur died in 1861 not a single one of his legal wives was prepared to be burnt with him in spite of every effort to induce them to 'preserve the honour of the Śiśodīyas'. They all flatly refused. Finally a slave girl was made to become a satī and was burnt along with the mahārāna's remains.

The following are some of the suggested reasons underlying the custom of suttee:

(1) The ancient belief that a man's possessions could be sent with him for use in the next world if they were burned or buried with him; his wife or wives being his chief possessions and the source of his greatest pleasure had to be dispatched to serve him in his next life.
(2) Male jealousy at the thought of leaving beautiful women behind after his death for others to enjoy.
(3) The hard-headed Greeks were not moved by what they regarded as a barbarous custom, and surmised that the real reason for suttee was to prevent a wife from poisoning her husband; the fact that she would have to die with him would serve to inhibit any such intentions.
(4) Fear of relations that the widow might misbehave and bring disgrace on the family (I, p. 357).
(5) Relatives did not wish to be burdened with the responsibility of having to support a widow; they coveted her wealth and wanted her out of the way; the son was relieved of the necessity of maintaining his mother; the male relatives took possession of the estate that the widow would otherwise have held for life.
(6) The compulsion of brāhmins, home, village, tradition. Recorded instances show that in the majority of cases the women who 'ascended the pyre' were forced to do so. They were drugged or carried forcibly to the scene, tied to the logs, held down by means of long poles to prevent escape.
(7) Cases of suttee freely undertaken were sometimes based on true affection, but in medieval times an important factor was the dread of facing the life of a widow*. To some even a painful death was preferable to the living hell of widowhood.
(8) The vanity and hope of enduring fame; in some Hindu houses the handmarks of women who underwent suttee were left imprinted on walls with turmeric paste; many of these women were honoured and almost deified and special 'satī stones' recording their virtue and fortitude were inscribed in their honour.
(9) The belief that a satī had great supernatural powers provided the motive for others to ensure that she burnt herself for their benefit. It was thought that a woman on her way to the pyre was capable of bestowing eternal bliss on anyone she cared to look upon; that by her act of devotion she earned for her husband and herself thirty-five million years of heavenly bliss; that she could descend to hell and force the powers of the pit to yield up her ancestors, relatives and friends and thus bring them salvation.

Books

I. Altekar, A. S. *The Position of Women in Hindu Civilisation*, 2nd Ed., Banaras, 1956.

II. Bentinck, Lord William. 'On the Suppression of Suttee.' In *Speeches and Documentation on Indian Polity, 1750–1921*, Vol. I, London, 1922.

III. Bushby, H. J. *Widow-burning*, 1855.

IV. Chaudhuri, J. B. *The Position of Women in Vedic Ritual*, 2nd Ed., Calcutta, 1956.

V. Mace, D. & V. *Marriage East & West*, London, 1960.

VI. Thompson, E. *Suttee: A Historical and Philosophical Enquiry into the Hindu Rite of Widow-Burning*, London, 1928.

SVABHĀVA, 'ownness' ,or intrinsicality, was one of the fundamental concepts of the nāstika* philosophical systems, especially as elaborated by the Chārvākas*. It implies that each individual and in fact each conscious being has his own intrinsic and innate disposition for which certain forms of living, livelihood, duties and ways of conduct and behaviour are appropriate.

Thus, each person has his own *svadarśana*, or 'own viewpoint', and each *darśana* is valid for that particular person at a particular place and time. Taking into account all men and all beings there are therefore an infinite number of darśanas not one of which has any universal validity. Svabhāva is also an 'own morality', distinctively suited to the individual according to his social, intellectual and spiritual status, and his strength and ability. Men differ and have different *adhikāra* or competency, and consequently different paths (*see* mārga) to their goals, and even different gods, or *ishṭa-devatā*, who provide for their particular needs.

Associated with this basic idea are numerous other concepts appropriate to the idea of 'ownness', which gives a man freedom only within his own sphere of being. Thus men have *svadharma*, or their 'own religion', and their own religious duties and obligations. From it comes the idea of *svakarma*, which lays on every man the obligation to do his duty in that state of life in which he has been born, i.e. to perform the duties of his own caste (*see Bhagavadgītā*). In the Gāndhian interpretation it implies clinging to one's own religion and a resistance to conversion to another creed, which is reprehensible and morally harmful.

In the political sphere two facets of svabhāva were brought to the fore by Gāndhi. One was *svarāj* or self-rule, the right of individuals to live their own lives and of nations to govern themselves. Flowing from this notion was another which Gāndhi also borrowed, namely, that of *svadeśi*, 'of one's own country', the duty of living as far as possible on the produce and manufactures of one's own land. It restricts a person to the use and service of his own immediate surroundings in preference to the more remote and especially the foreign. Thus, according to the svadeśi ideal it is better to use indigenously made clothes, even of poor quality, rather than foreign cloth, however good.

Books

See under Philosophy.

ŚVAPHALKA, 'dog-fruit', a *ṛishi* of great saintliness and moral strength mentioned in the *Mahābhārata* and Purāṇas whose presence wherever he dwelt ensured freedom from famine, plague, disease and untimely death. When the realm of the king of Kāśī was once afflicted with severe drought Śvaphalka was invited to visit the country and during his sojourn there rain fell in abundance.

The ruler of Kāśī, *Kāśīrāja*, had a beautiful daughter named GĀNDINĪ, 'cow-daily', who was born in the following manner. She remained in her mother's womb for twelve years and when her father commanded her to come forth she advised him first to make a present of a cow to the brāhmins every day until it was time for her birth. At the end of another three years she came forth from her mother's womb and continued the daily gift to the brāhmins as long as she lived, whence her name. Her father in due time gave her to Śvaphalka as a reward for his gift of rain, and through Śvaphalka Gāndinī became the mother of Akrūra, on whom was bestowed the wondrous *syamantaka* gem (*see* Satrājita).

Books

See under Mythology.

SVĀYAṀBHUVA, or Manu Svāyaṁbhuva, i.e. Manu the son of Svayaṁbhu, the 'self-existent' Brahmā. He was the first of the traditional Manus and the first ruler of the earth. In the beginning was Brahmā, the self-existent one, who divided himself into two parts, male and female, Purusha and Virāj, and from this duality of Brahmā came Manu Svāyaṁbhuva. It was from Brahmā manifested as Manu Svāyaṁbhuva that all the *prajāpatis*, *mahāṛishis*, and other mind-born sons of Brahmā were begotten.

Another version has it that Brahmā divided himself into Manu Svāyaṁbhuva, a male, and Śatarūpā, a 'hundred-aspected' female, and that Svāyaṁbhuva as male had intercourse with himself as Śatarūpā, and begot two sons and three daughters.

One son was PRIYAVRATA, the first of the kshattriyas (warrior princes) who, being dissatisfied that only half of the earth was illuminated at one time by the sun, followed the sun seven times around the earth in his chariot, resolved to turn night into day. The ruts of his chariot wheels formed the seven oceans and the seven continents. He married Kāmyā daughter of the *ṛishi** Kardama and begat ten sons and two daughters. Of the sons seven shared the seven continents, while three adopted the religious life, namely, Uttama, Tāmasa, and Raivata, and became respectively the third, fourth and fifth Manus*. Prasūtī, one of the daughters of Priyavrata married the sage Daksha.

The second son of Svāyaṁbhuva and Śatarūpā was UTTĀNAPĀDA (*see* Dhruva). Svāyaṁbhuva's daughter ĀKŪTI married the patriarch RUCHI and bore the twins Yajña, 'sacrifice', and Dakshiṇā, 'gift'. Another version has it that Ākūti was the mother of Svārochisha, the second Manu.

Books

See under Mythology.

SVAYAṀVARA, 'self-choice', a ceremony in which a girl chooses her own husband from a number of assembled suitors. It is not listed by Manu with the permissible forms of marriage, but is sometimes classed as a variant of the *gāndharva* form. Regarded as being Austric in origin the custom was also practised by many nomadic tribes of north-west India. In the Epics it is mentioned as common among kshattriyas, and in medieval India prevailed among high-ranking Rājputs.

When a girl reached marriageable age, her father invited all suitors duly qualified as to caste and rank to attend a svayaṁvara. Before the appointed day the bride would perform certain rites to enable her to make a good choice. She would pray, watch out for omens and go through various ritual acts. Some sort of ball game in honour of Lakshmī (as described in Daṇḍin's *Daśa-kumāra-charita*) was also played. The significance of these rites is now forgotten.

The suitors attended with their retinues, and each bard would give particulars of his patron's genealogy and deeds to a herald. On the day of the svayaṁvara the suitors would be allotted thrones in a separate pavilion and their names and accomplishments would be announced by the herald to the assembled guests and the bride's family. To the sound of trumpets and the blowing of conchs the maiden was carried into the assembly in a palanquin and took her seat in a special place between the galleries. In Epic time the girl offered herself as a prize in a contest of skill, such as archery, but this was not necessarily the decisive factor in her final choice, but was merely intended to give her a chance to observe the men more closely. When she had made up her mind she would place a garland over the neck of the man of her choice. The nuptials were often celebrated immediately by the priests in attendance.

Examples of svayaṁvara are seen in the stories of Sāvitrī and Satyavān, Damayantī and Nala, Sītā and Rāma, Draupadī and the Pāṇḍavas, Aja and Indumatī, Kuntī and Pāṇḍu.

Books

See under Marriage.

ŚVETADVĪPA (*śveta-dvīpa*, white island) in Hindu cosmology* represents the sixth island continent surrounding Jambu encircled by an ocean of milk. Frequently mentioned in Sanskrit literature, it clearly refers to a specific place, the exact location of which is not known. The *Mahābhārata* speaks of the white people of Śvetadvīpa on the northern shores of the Ocean of Milk as worshippers of Nārāyaṇa, a thousand-rayed god.

There has been much speculation about this place, which remains one of the mysteries of ancient Indian geography. It has been variously identified with Greece, with the Greek kingdoms of Parthia, and with Scythia, the country of the Śakas, because an alternative name for Śvetadvīpa was *Śakadvīpa*. An ancient brāhmin caste of India known as the śakadvīp are traced to the maga* priests of Persia. Others identify Śvetadvīpa with Tibet, China, Japan, Palestine, even with Britain, since the name of the island suggests white-skinned inhabitants.

Lassen supposed Śvetadvīpa to have been in Parthia where the brāhmins met with Christian missionaries, and some scholars believe the Epic references to be the account of a visit undertaken by Hindu travellers to the Christian* countries. Nicol McNicol thinks it refers to some Christian settlement in the north of India; Garbe identifies it with the shores of the Balkash Sea; Max Weber prefers Alexandria or some place in Asia Minor; and Dr Seal observes that the record contains decisive proof of an actual journey undertaken by some Indian Vaishṇavites to the coasts of Egypt or Asia Minor.

Books

I. Clarke, W. E. 'Sakadvipa and Svetadvipa.' *Journal of the American Oriental Society*, New Haven, xxxix, 1919, 209–42.

II. Maenchen-Helfen, Otto. 'Svetadvipa in Pre-Christian China.' *New Indian Antiquary*, Bombay, II, 1939, 166–68.

SWASTIKA (Sanskrit, Svastika), an auspicious symbol, an elaboration of the equal armed cross, but with the arms bent, hence also called the 'limbed cross'. Its name is said to be a combination of *su* (well) *asti* (is) *ka* (a noun ending) i.e. 'It is well'. The interjection *svasti* is used before and after pronouncing the sacred syllable *Oṁ*, and during sacrificial ceremonies (*see* mantra).

In Hinduism the swastika is supposedly derived either from the wheel*, symbolically reduced to four spokes and set at right angles to indicate the cardinal points, or from the two firesticks of the Vedic sacrificial fire which were always set down in the form of a cross. As a fire and sun symbol it was also called the fire cross or solar cross. In general the simple equal armed cross did not have any particular significance in Hinduism, but the swastika was very important indeed.

The symbol was well known among the ancients. Proof of its widespread use has been substantiated by archaeological discoveries in Egypt; in Hissarlik, site of Homer's Troy; in China, Greece, Scandinavia, Scythia, Mexico and Peru. The swastika is supposed to be marked on the hood of the cobra, and is in fact often found in association with the heliolithic culture of snake-worshipping peoples such as the Nāgas.

In India two kinds of swastika are distinguished. The right hand or male, representing the vernal sun, where the right end of the horizontal bar has an arm bending downwards, with the ends of the other three arms moving in the same direction, so that the cross moves clockwise. It is so called because if one goes around the figure with one's right side towards the centre of the cross, one will move in the direction indicated by the bent arms. The left hand or female cross, representing the autumnal sun, goes in the opposite, anti-clockwise direction, and is considered inauspicious.

The auspicious swastika, a symbol of good luck, is often found stamped on various objects. A series of small swastikas are a very popular motif for border designs on textiles. The rainy season is especially devoted to its honour in Mahārāshṭra, when women draw swastikas on floors and worship them.

A 'good luck' *āsana* (yogic sitting posture) named *svastikāsana* is sometimes assumed in meditation in the form of an 'inclosed' as distinct from an outstretched cross. Here two crosses are formed by squatting with crossed legs and with arms crossed over the breast.

Books

I. Greg, R. P. *On the Meaning and Origin of the Fylfot and Swastika,* London, 1884.

II. Haslam, R. *The Cross and the Serpent,* 1849.

III. Loewenstein, P. J. 'Swastika and Yin-Yang.' *China Society Occasional Papers,* London, 1942.

IV. Wilson, T. *Swastika: The Earliest Known Symbol and Its Migration,* Washington, 1894.

SWING. The swing (*dola* or *hindola*), either to and fro or in circular motion has a peculiar prominence in Hinduism. It is a common feature in descriptions of Hindu paradise, and gods and goddesses are frequently depicted disporting themselves on swings.

Its movement symbolizes bliss and the cessation of care; a flying motion away from things mundane. The gentle dizziness it causes has a soporific effect and helps to induce ecstatic and trance-like moods. There is also the obvious coital significance in the to and fro movement, and the 'circumambulatory' or worshipful symbolism in the wheel swing. In other contexts the swing signifies doubt or the wavering of the mind and uncertainty, and in a yet deeper sense the cycle of *saṁsāra,* the coming and going of man on the earthly plane, the formation and dissolution of the universe.

One mode of worshipping a deity is to swing his image in a swing. The guru is also thus swung as an act of homage. Special swing fesitvals such as the *Hindola, Jhūlana-yātrā, Pushpadola,* are held in honour of certain deities in many parts of India, and the swing figures in a number of other Hindu festivals, particularly *Holi.* Swinging platforms are made, decorated with flowers and hangings, and the gods are placed on them and swung. Songs are sung in a special metre known as hindola, and the devotees dance before the swinging deity. Sometimes women are placed on the swing along with an image of Kṛishṇa to symbolize their surrender to him in the act of intimacy.

Another form of the *dola-yātrā* or swing festival, also called *chakra-pūjā* (but not to be confused with the Tantrik rite), was performed by men in honour of Gaurī or Māriyammā or some other goddess. This was best done when the sun entered Aries and probably had a solar origin. The priest first beat the fleshy upper part of the back of the man who was to undergo the swinging, until it was quite numb, and then inserted iron hooks under the muscles. The man was then raised off the ground and whirled around at the end of a horizontal pole mounted on a high vertical bearing. Throughout this 'hook-swinging' process the man was to show no signs of pain but had to laugh and jest and gesticulate in order to arouse the good humour of the spectators. After being swung for a prescribed time he was lowered to the ground and had his wounds dressed. Hook-swinging was once widely practised in Bengal and South India till its practice was forbidden, and sheep and other animals were swung around instead. The British authorities put a stop to both these customs.

The purpose of swinging festivals is not known but it is said to be variously an act of worship to please the deity; a mimetic representation of the motion inaugurating the season of love; or a symbolic representation to augment the power of the sun.

Books

See under Festivals.

SYLLOGISM. Indian logic does not make verbal distinctions between subject, predicate and copula, nor does it employ the accidental 'moods' of the Aristotelean syllogism. It claims to have a natural lay-out of the processes of thinking itself, independent of artifice and form.

The complete syllogistic expression is known as the *nyāya-prayoga*, 'logical linking'. Each stage or link of the syllogism is known as the *avayava*, 'member', and various such stages have been laid down. The original syllogism had ten links, and revolved around two terms and a reason, for example, in establishing whether 'the hill has fire because it smokes', the terms 'hill' and 'fire' are the two terms involved. The subject under discussion that is known to both parties i.e. the given substantive, is known as the *paksha*. In the course of the syllogistic process it roughly corresponds to the minor term which is the subject of the conclusion in the Aristotelean syllogism. Here the term 'hill' is the paksha.

The term indicating the fact proposed to be established, inferred or inferentially predicated, is known as the *sādhya*, 'concludable', e.g. 'fire'. In the discussion it roughly corresponds to the major term, which is the predicate of the conclusion in the Western syllogism. The *hetu* (see below) or 'reason', roughly corresponds to the middle term, e.g. 'because it smokes'. There is said to be a *vyāpti* or invariable concomitance between 'fire' and 'smoke', which assists in the *parāmarśa* (or subsumptive reflection) subsuming the smoke in the hill being caused by fire.

The ten avayava of the original syllogism are as follows: (i) *jijñāsā*, the desire to know a fact e.g. whether the hill has fire, since it smokes; (ii) *saṁśaya* (*see* knowledge), 'doubt' concerning the fact, e.g. Perhaps the hill does not have fire; perhaps what looks like smoke is dust; (iii) *śakya-prāpti*, 'capable of attainment', or belief in the probability of the fact e.g. It is likely that the hill has fire; (iv) *prayojana*, 'first meeting', the object or motive of discussion, e.g. Now to show that the hill has fire; (v) *saṁśaya-vyudāsa*, 'doubt-discarding', the removal of doubt, usually by showing that the opposite is not true, e.g. The hill is not without fire; (vi) *pratijñā*, the declaration, proposition, or thesis to be established e.g. The hill has fire; (vii) *hetu*, 'reason', the ground for the inference e.g. Because the hill is smoking; (viii) *udāharaṇa* or example. This is formed of a universal observation and an example e.g. Whatever smokes has fire, for instance the hearth. The example, in this case 'hearth', is called *sapaksha*; (ix) *upanaya*, or 'application', or the co-relation between the universal observation and the present instance e.g. And so is this hill smoking; (x) *nigamana*, or conclusion, implying what is known as *anumiti* or inferential cognition, leading to the result, e.g. Therefore the hill has fire.

These ten avayava (members) of the Hindu syllogism were listed in theory, having first been laid out or suggested by Gautama the founder of the Nyāya* system; or by a Jain logician; they were reduced to five members (the last five in the list) by Vātsyāyana. It is these last five members that constitute the main propositions of the classical Hindu syllogism, and according to the commentators they represent the full circuit of human reasoning, thus: (vi) pratijñā stands for *śabda* or testimony; (vii) hetu represents anumāna or inference (*see* logic); (viii) udāharaṇa represents pratyaksha or perception*; (ix) upanaya represents upamāna or analogy (*see* knowledge); and (x) nigamana represents the culminating stage of proof.

These five members were delcared to be still too cumbersome, and the Mīmāṁsakas* reduced them to three, using either the first three or the last three of Vātsyāyana's list. It will be noted that the last three form the Aristotelean syllogism in the Barbara mood. The Buddhists still further reduced these members to two only, namely udāharaṇa and upanaya, declaring that no person endowed with a minimum capacity for reasoning required the rest of the clumsy scaffolding to erect the structure of his thought.

Books

See under Logic.

SYMBOLS. The representation of an object or being by a symbol or emblem (*chihna*) related to it in some way is very common in Hinduism. Fundamentally all things are one since they are only fragments of a Supreme Unity, and things as they appear to us are therefore to be regarded as transmutations of a higher reality. Belief in the notion of the microcosm*, in the esoteric relationships between things, in the doctrine of signatures, all lend strength and variety to Hindu symbolism.

Some things are more intimately linked on the phenomenal plane because of similarity in origin or appearance, or because they are related by association, tradition or mystical ties, and these occult affinities are the basis of a complex of symbolism which finds expression on a profuse variety of forms. It permeates Hindu and Buddhist mythology, ritual, art, architecture, literature and religion.

The animal*, plant* and mineral* worlds provide symbols of deep esoteric significance. The body, head, hands, sex organs (liṅga and yoni); animals and birds, like the bull, elephant, swan, eagle, snake, fish; plants like the lotus and the *tulsī*; hills, rocks, stones like the *śālagrāma*; shapes, colours, designs, such as the wheel*, saffron, the *maṇḍala** are all regarded as tokens of hidden truth or physical manifestations of divine or mundane mysteries. A king is symbolized by the throne, umbrella or footstool, which are believed to take on the aura of regal authority and power; the sādhu* by his rosary, the *kamaṇḍalu* (water-pot), or *daṇḍa* (staff); the brāhmin or the monk by the *pustaka* or book or his bundle of scrolls.

Most of the important symbols are to be found in legends connected with the deities. In iconographic and pictorial representations, the gods are invariably shown with at least a few of their traditional insignia and bearings. Meditation on the deity is often chanelled through one of these transcripts.

In mythology the deities are described in association with their symbols, such as weapons, animal vehicles and so forth. Every god has his appointed (*a*) consort or *śakti*, (*b*) offspring (*c*) sacred sites, cardinal directions, jurisdiction, (*d*) names and titles, (*e*) modes of manifestation (*avatāra*, *vyūha*), (*f*) animal mounts or *vāhana**, (*g*) companions, (*h*) auspicious bodily marks, (*i*) stances and gestures (*āsanas*, *mudrās*), (*j*) weapons*, (*k*) musical instruments, (*l*) colours, numbers, flowers, dress, jewels and ornaments, (*m*) maṇḍalas or magical patterns, and (*n*) magical sounds (*mantras*).

Books

I. Crooke, W. 'Secret Messages and Symbols used in India.' *Journal of the Bihar & Orissa Research Society*, Bankipore, V, 1919, 451–62.
II. Westropp, H. M. & Wake, C. S. *Ancient Symbol Worship*, New York, 1875.
III. Yule, M. *Ancient Hindu Symbolism*, 1891.

TAGORE, anglicized form of the Bengali Ṭhakur (originally, the Kolarian word for God), the name of an illustrious family of modern Bengal. Of brāhmin origin, their latitudinarian outlook and intimate relationship with non-brāhmins and non-Hindus earned for them the censure of their co-religionists. They were regarded as degraded, and classed with the Pirāli brāhmins (so named after a Muslim *pīr* or saint, Khān Jahān Ali, with whom they were associated). The Tagores discontinued the performance of Hindu rites, had no reverence for paṇḍits and took to Western ways, some of them even going to the length of eating beef. These 'Europeanized Bengalees' were held to be reprobates and outcastes and no strictly religious family of Hindus would eat or intermarry with them. Says Thomson, 'They have no real place in the orthodox system' (IV, p. 12).

Among the more prominent members of this family was Prasannakumār Tagore (1801–1868) who gained a reputation for public spirit and liberality; before he died he disinherited his son on the latter's conversion to Christianity. His nephew Jotindramohan Tagore (1831–1907) made liberal endowments to religious, charitable and educational institutions. Jotindramohan's brother, Sourindromohan Tagore (1840–1919) founded the Bengal Academy of Music and received titles of honour from many learned associations throughout the world.

Another outstanding member of the family was 'Prince' Dwarkanāth Tagore (1795–1846), a friend of Rāmmohan Roy*, who used his ample means in active philanthropy and the reform of Hinduism, especially working for the abolition of suttee, the freedom of the Press, and Hindu education. He visited England twice, on the first occasion being entertained by Queen Victoria. On his return to India he refused to undergo the purificatory ceremony of *prāyaśchitta*, regarding it as so much nonsense. He died and was buried in London.

Dwarkanāth's son was the well-known religious and social reformer Devendranāth Tagore (1818–1905). Brought up on John Locke, David Hume, and other Western philosophers, he came to reject the Vedas, except for a few fragments from the Upanishads, and found no satisfaction in Vedānta. He joined the Bramho Samāj of Rāmmohan Roy in the belief that it was the end of his search for a true *dharma* or religion, but was soon disillusioned to find that the doctrine of Rāma's incarnation was being preached from the pulpits of the Samāj, that non-brāhmins were excluded when the Vedas were recited, and that most of the Samājists were themselves idolators at home. His eloquence and fervour against these practices contributed greatly to their termination, and to the revival of a higher religion. Devendranāth became the leader of a new Hindu theistic movement, and laid the foundations of a reformed Society called the Sādharaṇ ('Universal') Brahmo Samāj. He turned away disappointed from the precepts of the Upanishads, declaring, 'These Upanishads could not meet all our needs nor fill our hearts'. Subsequently he left the Brahmo Samāj altogether and retired to a retreat known as Śāntiniketan, 'the Abode of Peace', which later became the seat of a famous university, started by his son Rabindranāth Tagore*.

Here the 'Mahāṛishi', as Devendranāth was now known, preached to a few disciples a more mystical form of the Brahmo Dharma. He supported a pristine form of Hinduism, shed of all the superfluities of caste, scriptures, observances, and so forth, and himself discarded the sacred thread. He claimed to receive illuminating experiences intuitively; in such states he would get messages (*ādeśa*) from the Almighty, which he then disclosed to his disciples. Convinced now that social reforms would flow spontaneously from a reformed religion he devoted his remaining days entirely to mystical communion and meditation. He died in 1905.

Notable among the later Tagores were the painter Abanindranāth Tagore, whose 'voluptuous mysticism' set a new trend in modern Indian painting; and his uncle the famous poet Rabindranāth Tagore*.

Books

I. Furrell, J. W. *The Tagore Family*, 1892.
II. Mitra, K. C. *Dwarkanath Tagore*, 1870.
III. Tagore, Devendranath. *Autobiography*, 2nd Ed., London, 1944.
IV. Thompson, E. *Rabindranath Tagore*, 2nd Ed., London, 1948.

TAGORE, RABINDRANĀTH (1861–1941), Bengali poet and humanist, born in Calcutta, was the son of Devendranāth Tagore* and one of the youngest of his mother's fourteen children. He received his education partly at home and partly in two schools in Calcutta. In 1878 at the age of sixteen he went to London, where he stayed for about two years. On his return he wrote a number of poems that gained him the acclaim of his contemporaries. He felt deeply the death of his wife, his father, his daughter, and his son, all within a few years of each other at the beginning of the present century. In 1913 he was awarded the Nobel Prize for Literature, and in 1915 received a knighthood. He travelled widely, wrote a massive quantity of verse and prose and died in 1941 greatly mourned by his countrymen.

From his family background Tagore acquired a rich cultural inheritance which he further enlarged by observation and study. Steeped in the Upanishadic teaching of which his father Devendranāth was so fitting an exponent, the poet himself in later years seemed to be the incarnation of one of India's ancient *ṛishis*. He was deeply imbued with the ancient writings, particularly the Upanishads and the Buddhist texts, and profoundly acquainted with mediaeval Bengali literature, the works of Vidyāpati and Chaṇḍidās and of the bhakti cult; his soul was nurtured on Vaishṇavism and the Baul* songs of rural Bengal. From these sources he drew his sustenance. He has not inaptly been described as a modern Baul.

Tagore started writing poetry at the age of thirteen, and before he was fifteen resolved to imitate the old romantic poetry of Bengal. He had heard the story of the English boy-poet Thomas Chatterton and said, 'Leaving aside the suicide part I girded up my loins to emulate Chatterton'. He published his own poems as the original work of a medieval Vaishṇava poet named Bhānu Siṁha, a synonymous transcription of his own name. The measure of his success may be gauged from the fact that a Bengali scholar, then in Germany, wrote a thesis on the lyric poetry of medieval Bengal in which he gave the place of honour to Bhānu Siṁha and got his Ph.D degree on the strength of it!

Tagore was subject to mystical experiences from the age of seventeen, and has frequently described them:

'I suddenly felt as if some ancient mist had in a moment lifted from my sight and the ultimate significance of all things was laid bare . . . I found that facts that had been detached and dim had a great unity of meaning, as if a man groping through a fog suddenly discovers that he stands before his own house . . . An unexpected train of thought ran across my mind like a strange caravan carrying the wealth of an unknown kingdom . . . Immediately I found the world bathed in a wonderful radiance with waves of beauty and joy swelling on every side, and no person or thing in the world seemed to me trivial or unpleasing.'

His philosophy was based upon broad issues and generalized themes, a synthesis of Brahmo Samāj (he had joined the Brahmo fold but later left), Upanishadic philosophy and Buddhism. Reality is one, he believed, call it Brahma, the Absolute, the Real or the Infinite, and man is but a fragment of the Real. He remained a theist all his life, a firm believer in the personal and abiding relationship between the Infinite and the finite, which he described as an eternal drama between Deity and devotee. The Absolute needs the finite since the finite contributes its share to the Ultimate Reality. In *Gītāñjali* he cries, 'O thou Lord of all the heavens, where would be thy love if I were not?' The *Jīvan-devatā* (Life-Lord i.e. the Absolute) to him represented *Satyam* (truth), *Śivam* (goodness) and *Sundaram* (Beauty).

From this monotheistic standpoint he worked out a philosophy of Man. The Absolute can be perceived only through the human personality. Man can know Him and please Him only through himself. 'I make God man, and man God.' The Infinite one is love; love is the highest truth and the most perfect relationship. The end of love is harmony among men. He felt this synthesis within himself and declared, 'I seem to experience in the wholeness of my vision the rhythm of all humanity'.

His social philosophy naturally echoed these feelings, and his novels, dramas and poems are all touched with a mystical light which penetrates the dark recesses of social injustice, the folly of caste and untouchability, the cruelty of brāhmin exploitation, the stupidity of superstition. He advocated purity, self-discipline, love, forgiveness and equality. His *Gītāñjali* 'Song Offering', (1910) is a book of prayer-songs and pleas for social justice. 'Lord', he cries, 'I want to be a gardener in your garden.' In the same book he says,

'Leave this chanting and singing and telling of beads. Whom dost thou worship in this lonely dark corner of a temple with all doors shut? Open thine eyes and see thy God is not before thee. He is there where the tiller is tilling the hard ground and where the path-maker is breaking stones.'

His *Rakta-karavīr*, 'Red Oleanders', a social drama touched with the same mysticism, is an impassioned protest against the machine age and a plea for human dignity.

The cosmopolitan outlook of Rabindranāth Tagore is well conveyed in an early novel of his entitled *Gorā*, which also poignantly portrays the confusion of emergent brāhmin Bengal. It tells the story of a young man of brāhmin family, a fanatical believer in Hinduism, bent on strengthening and reviving the ancient Vedic rites and the strict observance of caste, who discovers in the end that he is not an Indian, still less a high caste brāhmin, but the foundling child of an English-Irish couple killed in the Indian Mutiny and reared by sympathetic Hindus.

Tagore travelled extensively throughout his life. He toured the length and breadth of India, lecturing in most of the famous Indian universities. He visited at various times, frequently more than once, Ceylon, Burma, Singapore, the Dutch East Indies, Siam, Indochina, and China (1924), Hong Kong and Japan—he was greatly impressed with the cleanliness, industry and politeness of the Japanese people. He also lectured in Iran, Iraq, Greece, and the Balkans, Italy, France, Holland, Belgium, Switzerland, Germany, Sweden, Norway, Denmark, Canada, South America and the Soviet Union (1930), and paid frequent visits to England and the U.S.A.

Wherever he went he preached humanism and internationalism, and the more he travelled the more deeply he realized the need for new dimensions in thinking, and how men's efforts in this direction were constantly being cramped by politicians, patriots and chauvinists. All the great nations had made important contributions to the common fund of human achievement. He held that 'the civilizations evolved in India, China, Persia, Judea, Greece or Rome, are like several mountain peaks having different altitudes, temperature, flora and fauna and yet belonging to the same chain of hills'.

In 1912 Tagore composed the song that is now India's national anthem, *Jana Gana Mana*, but he despised narrow patriotism. As a humanist he could find beauty in all lands and was happy with the people of all nations. He declared, 'Politics had debased morality and given rise to a perpetual contest of lies, deception, cruelty, and hypocricy, and has increased inordinately the national habits of vainglory'. For Gāndhi he had some regard, referring to him as 'the first real politician that this country has produced'. But his cosmopolitanism and anti-nationalism alienated him from his own people and even brought him into conflict with Gāndhi whose philosophy he later came to denounce as 'a doctrine of narrowness, negation and despair'.

To the end of his life he opposed chauvinism and the 'collective selfishness' which is lauded in the guise of nationalism. But he had a deep love for India and his works frequently touched on the political situation around him. He was knighted in 1915 but surrendered his title four years later in protest at the suppression of the Panjāb riots, stating in a letter to the Viceroy that under the circumstances badges of honour were out of place and incongruous and that, 'I for my part wish to be shorn of all special distinctions'. Subsequently he permitted the use of the title again.

Tagore did not have much formal education and never acquired a degree. He disliked tutors and schools. In a classroom he felt like a 'caged rabbit', and a 'museum specimen'. In his view children in school are inert and unresponsive, 'while lessons are pelted at them like hailstones on flowers'. He was impressed with the educational experiments taking place in the West, especially the 'playway' or education-through-play being used in Germany, England and Italy.

In December 1921 he converted his father's Śāntiniketan retreat into the nucleus of a World University known as the Viśva-bhāratī. The university embodies several ancient Indian ideals, but is modelled in many respects on European lines. It has been described as 'a happy blending of East and West'. Tagore believed that 'the fittest place for such an endeavour was India, the heart of Asia, into which had flowed currents from Vedic, Buddhist, Semitic, Zoroastrian and other streams originating from Judea to Japan'. His aim was to develop in his students a 'feeling of intimacy with nature'. Classes were held outdoors in natural surroundings. The school was to be a meeting-place of East and West, with stress on Man. Today scholars and artists of international fame study in unpretentious thatched cottages and teach their pupils in the open under the shade of trees.

Tagore's admiration for the West was expressed through most of his writings, and although he never failed to keep in mind the ancient and all but forgotten glories of his own country, he had stern words for those of his compatriots who were ready to break away completely from 'the new and now assimilated Western heritage'. He said, 'Our anxiety to alienate our hearts and minds from the West is spiritual suicide. If in a spirit of vainglory we shout from the housetops that the West has produced nothing that has an infinite value, then we can only doubt the value of any product of the East.' In another typical passage he says,

'The foreigner writes our history, we translate it; the foreigner discovers our grammar, we cram it! If we want to know what there is next door, we have to look into William Hunter. And yet with such crass indifference on our own part we are not ashamed to prate about the duties of others towards our country.'

His creative fertility was immense. He composed over two thousand songs and lyrics in a wide variety of styles. Some of his early verses were inspired by Thomas Moore, and some by Shelley and Wordsworth, but in later years he ranged over a wide field for his inspiration. He wrote hundreds of longer poems and ballads, eight novels, some books of travel and memoirs, eleven volumes of short stories, two dozen plays and a large mass of miscellaneous essays on literary criticism, and social, religious, philosophical, historical, political and other topics.

He revolutionized the Indian theatre by introducing new modes of stage production. After first experimenting with Western melodies he began composing his own music, mostly in the *dhrūpad* and *kīrtan* styles, for many of his lyrics, and thus laid the foundations for a new development in Indian popular music. He wrote boat songs, folk songs, love, festive and funeral songs. Towards the end of his life he turned to painting and produced more than one thousand five hundred paintings and sketches of fantastic and at times surrealist character which seemed to reflect his mystical temperament.

Strange as it seems it required the nod of recognition from Europe for India to awaken to his greatness. 'India', says Professor G. Venkatachalam, 'recognized the greatness of Tagore as a poet, only after Europe had put the seal of approval on his genius.' And a Bengali scholar and critic confesses, 'He was born in Bengal, but in a Europeanized atmosphere, in which there was hardly any indigenous element', and he goes on to say, 'Bengal has not given Rabindranāth to Europe—rather, Europe has given him to the Bengalis. By praising him, European scholars praise their own gift' (V, p. 316).

Judgment on Tagore's written work is difficult because the bulk of it is vague and diffuse both in thought and expression. What he has to say has been better said by other forgotten humanists and internationalists in the three or four decades preceding his birth. His poems are wistful, sentimental, mystical and verbose; they often appear to be a mere stringing together of words as if written because the writer had nothing better to do. Much of it is saccharine and effeminate, replete with affectations and mannerisms, full of monotonous yearnings after the Infinite and nebulous stirrings for the brotherhood of all mankind. It often descends to banality. His own translations into English of his works have not improved the mushy and often obscure symbolism. His plays lack constructive power and appear to be a cross between the medieval mystery play of Europe and the drama of rustic Bengal. His characters are often inadequately motivated, and the whole action takes place in an unrealistic and sentimentalized world.

But most of what he wrote, essays, drama, and above all poems, was new to his countrymen, and was expressed in simple and sometimes moving form, springing from the depths of his being. It was the reflection of a great soul, of immense stature, and did much to bring to his people an awareness of their part in a common human destiny.

Books

I. Aronson, A. *Rabindranath Tagore Through Western Eyes*, Allahabad, 1942.
II. Bhattacharya, V. *Tagore, Citizen of the World*, Delhi, 1961.
III. Radhakrishnan, S. (Ed.) *Rabindranath Tagore, A Centenary Volume*, New Delhi, 1961.
IV. Tagore, R. *The Religion of Man*, New York, 1931.
V. Thompson, E. *Rabindranath Tagore*, 2nd Ed., London, 1948.

TAMIL, the most highly cultivated of the Dravidian tongues, spoken by about fifteen million people in south-east India and southern Ceylon. The name is derived from the ancient Damila, a non-Aryan warlike people of South India who figure in early Buddhist and Jain records.

Tamil is an extremely refined medium of communication, and there is no ground for supposing, as the early Sanskrit writers did, that it was spoken by a primitive people. The language has a rich and varied vocabulary and is extraordinary in its subtlety and sense of logic, and the refinements of its grammar bear comparison with the most precise for expressing nuances of thought and meaning. It is remarkably rich in honorifics, a characteristic of a decadent rather than a primitive culture, which suggests a highly mature stage of civilization. The manner in which the negative form of the verb is obtained is both ingenious and logical, while 'the system of interrogatives is as perfect as could be formed by the human mind' (IV, p. 202).

The prodigious literary output of Tamil has to a certain extent been reduced to order by its systematic arrangement into anthologies in which much of the best material has been preserved. Some of the writings, according to Tamil tradition, go back many thousands of years. Tamil legend speaks of three great literary academies called *śaṅgam*, which met at or near Madura, and early Tamil writing is referred to as śaṅgam literature. All the three śaṅgams most probably flourished between the first and fifth centuries AD, under the patronage of Pāṇḍyan kings, but they have been ascribed a hoary origin, and the chronology allotted to the poets of these śaṅgams is extremely confused.

The first śaṅgam was supposed to have met about 10,000 BC, convened by the *ṛishi* Agastya, the mythical Apostle of the Deccan, and even the gods participated in its deliberations. It was held on Mount Mahendra in the Kumārī Nādu and lasted for four thousand four hundred and forty years. But a great flood swept over the country and nearly all the writings perished, although fragments of a work known as the *Agattiyam* were saved. This was a treatise on Tamil grammar attributed to Agastya himself. According to Tamil Śaivites another important work also survived the Flood, namely, the *Nānmarai*, or 'Four Scriptures', dealing respectively with virtue, wealth, pleasure and bliss. The present version, said to be a redaction of the original, is one of the basic scriptures of the Śaivites.

The second śaṅgam traditionally lasted three thousand seven hundred years, and only one example of this period survives, namely, the *Tolkāppiyam*, the earliest extant Tamil work, a grammar of the language by a Jain author, known after it as Tolkāppiyar (*c* AD ?200–450?). Believed to have been written long before the sage Vyāsa compiled the Vedas, it nonetheless shows an acquaintance with Pāṇini and Manu. It deals with phonetic rules, word construction, syntax, literary convention, rhetoric and prosody.

The third śaṅgam is said to have lasted one thousand eight hundred and fifty years, and the work of its poets was collected into the *Eṭṭuttogai*, 'Eight Anthologies', and the *Pattup-pāṭṭu*, 'Ten Idylls', comprising a total of 2,500 hymns, ballads, erotic verses, and lyrics in praise of the country, of gods and of kings, by about three hundred authors. Some poems by Kapilar* are included in the *Pattup-pāṭṭu*. Most of these poems were sung by minstrels at the princely courts, and are as archaic sounding to the modern Tamil student as *Beowulf* and *Piers Plowman* are to the student of modern English.

These great collections were all but forgotten by the Tamils themselves till the end of the last century, and have yet to be fully and critically edited. The writings contain references to the Yavanas (Greeks) as brave seafarers, as bodyguards to the kings, and as palace guards. The possibility of Greek influence on śaṅgam literature has sometimes been mooted.

The first truly great poetical composition in Tamil is a work by Tiruvaḷḷuvar* (*c.* AD 400) known as the *Kuṛaḷ*, the most venerated book south of the Godāverī. A sister of Tiruvaḷḷuvar, named Avvaiyār, is a highly revered poetess in her own right, who has a splendid martial ode to her credit. Also worthy of note by an unknown but probably contemporary author is the romantic epic *Chintāmaṇi*. It is full of grandeur and beauty, with exquisite descriptions of natural scenery, and shows a delicate and masterly handling of its story.

Jain influence is once more discerned in the *Nālaḍiyār* (?400–800?), originally consisting of 8,000 verses written, one each, by as many Jains. To test their worth the verses were cast into a stream by order of a king, and only 400 floated, while the rest disapperaed beneath the waters. These 400 poems constitute the present Nālaḍiyār. There is no mention of god in the collection, but a burning sense of morality pervades the whole work, which is written in a terse and vigorous style.

The middle of the seventh century saw the birth of another Tamil masterpiece, the subject of much critical commentary. Written by the poet Ilaṅgō* it tells of the awe-inspiring wrath of a woman whose husband was unjustly slain by a king. To the same period belongs a sequel to this classic written by Śāttaṇ, with a Buddhist bias.

In the ninth century the poet Kambaṇ wrote a *Rāmāyaṇa*, a highly finished and popular work, based in part on an earlier Jain epic, also in Tamil. The character of Rāvaṇa is drawn in heroic proportions before whom Rāma is an unimpressive little figure. It is said by Tamil scholars to challenge comparison with the *Rāmāyaṇa* of Vālmīki.

The period between the seventh and ninth centuries saw the rise of two powerful religious currents which found expression in Tamil poetry and constitute the chief glory of Tamil literature. These were the works of the Śaivite saints and Vaishṇavite hymn writers. The Śaivite material was put together in the *Tirumuṛai*, an anthology of hymns by sixty-three devotees, including Tirumūlar, Appar, Saṁbandar, and Sundarar, Nambi and Śekkiḷār, and a masterpiece by Māṇikkavāśagar*. Together they constitute the canon of the Śaiva-Siddhānta* school. The Vaishṇavite hymns were composed by a group of poets known as the Āḷvārs*, who flourished in the same period. Their hymns collected into a volume of 4,000 verses are known as the *Prabandham*, and constitute the prayer and hymn book of the South Indian Vaishṇavas.

What is sometimes called the Golden Age of Tamil literature was at its height between the tenth and thirteenth centuries. Sanskrit influences predominated along with the writings in Tamil, and there appeared a debased form of composition called *maṇi-pravālam*, made up of a mixture of Sanskrit and Tamil, Sanskrit phrases and grammatical forms being intermingled with Tamil. This artificiality led to a deterioration of style and language from which

Tamil writing did not recover until it came under the influence of English literature five centuries later.

In the seventeenth century a reaction against the Sanskrit trend set in, best exemplified in the anti-brāhminical writings of the Sittar (or Siddha) school (*see* Nāthas). The Sittars were a Tamil sect who, while retaining Śiva as the name of the one God, rejected everything in Śiva worship inconsistent with pure theism. They have been described as quietists in religion and alchemists in science. Their mystical poems, especially the *Śiva-vākyam*, are held in high regard. They are strong against idolatry, and according to some critics their works bear traces of Christian influence.

A literary curiosity indicative of the influences operating on South Indian writing at this period was the work of Vīramāmuṇivar (1680–1747), the Tamil name of Father Constanzio Beschi, an Italian Jesuit, whose *Tembāvaṇi* written in irreproachable Tamil contains stories from the Old and New Testaments. It is regarded as a Tamil classic and has been the subject of commentary by Hindu and Tamil scholars.

The work of Christian missionaries in the revival of Tamil letters is universally acknowledged in the South today. 'They simplified the script, introduced punctuation, gave an impetus to prose works; wrote the first Tamil treatises on science, introduced the printing press, produced Tamil tracts, books and magazines, and set up societies for promoting Tamil writing' (V, p. 9).

Of recent writers in Tamil two are particularly worthy of notice. The first is Subramaṇya BHARATI (d. 1921), whose poems, written in terse simple style are tempered and restrained, albeit full of patriotic fervour. He was a great lover of Shelley and in his own verse tried to combine the best of the old and the new, introducing forms and expressing sentiments reminiscent of the Romantic Revival. The second is Rāmaliṅga PILLAI (b. 1888) who started his career as a painter and with Gāndhi's encouragement turned to writing poetry. His work earned for him in 1949 the title of Poet Laureate in Tamil.

Books

I. Aiyangar, M. S. *Tamil Studies*, Mandras, 1914.
II. Dikshitar, V. R. R. *Studies in Tamil Literature and History*, London, 1930.
III. Kingsbury, F. and Philips, G. E. *Hymns of the Tamil Saivite Saints*, Calcutta, 1921.
IV. Majumdar, R. C. (Ed.) *The Vedic Age*, London, 1951.
V. Paranjoti, V. *Saiva Siddhanta*, 2nd Ed., London, 1954.
VI. Pillai, M. S. P. *Tamil Literature*, Tinnevelly, 1929.
VII. Pillai, S. V. *History of Tamil Language and Literature*, Madras, 1956.

TĀNSEN (1550–1610) one of the greatest musicians and singers of northern India. Neglected and then abandoned by his Hindu parents in childhood, he was adopted by a Muslim couple and brought up as a Muhammadan. Among his teachers was the saint Sūrdās. After serving at the court of two other kings he was summoned by Akbar in 1563 to appear before him. His performance so captivated the emperor that he gave the singer two lakhs of rupees and installed him at his court.

Many fantastic anecdotes are told about the power of Tānsen's music. A solemn *dhrūpad* played by him produced rain out of season; the heat-producing *dīpaka* once lit up all the candles in Akbar's court; on another occasion its burning heat set fire to the Jamnā river. Another melody caused unattended musical instruments near him to play spontaneously.

Among Hindus he is held chiefly responsible for the deterioration of Hindu music. He is said to have corrupted the classic *rāgas*, introducing new and unconventional variations of old rhythms, and invented several new musical forms. The Persianizing of Hindu music with its softening of the scholastic modes is attributed to him. To him is also due the element of sweetness and harmony in northern music, an element to which much of the older doctrinaire theories of musical structure were sacrificed.

Tānsen became a sort of patron saint of dancing-girls. It was believed, and still is, that chewing the leaves of the tamarind three growing about his grave at Gwālior gives wonderful richness to the voice, and girls make a pilgrimage there for the purpose.

Books

See under Music.

TANTRISM, the teachings followed by certain left-hand sects of Hindus and Buddhists. The word *tantra* is of obscure origin, for which a number of derivations have been suggested, among them: the word *tan*, 'stretch', or that which extends the faculties of man; *tanu*, 'body', because of its stress on the bodily functions; *tanti*, 'rope', for securing the devotee; *tantri*, 'harp', for the music and beauty of its philosophy; *tadantara*, 'interiorness', from its secret teachings; *tantu*, 'thread', suggesting the 'loom' of the tantras whereon is revealed the warp and woof (male and female principles) of which the vast magical fabric of the cosmos is composed.

The origin of tantrism is unknown. Some hold it to be the most ancient of all Indian cults, the original religion of the pre-Aryan inhabitants of India, and the prototype of yoga and other magical techniques. Some incline to the view that it was brought to India by the Vrātyas*, who are thought to have come by way of the north-west and settled in eastern India, and adduce as evidence the fact that tantrism is more deeply rooted in the border regions along the line of their presumed migration, from Afghanistan and Kashmīr along the north-west borders of Uttar Pradesh (such as Garhwāl) to Bengal and Assam in the East.

It is particularly in eastern India that tantrism reached its culmination, and most major works of this philosophy are of eastern origin. Indeed scholars believe that 'the whole of the culture history of the eastern part of India from AD 700 to 1200 is locked up in the tantras' (III, p. 275).

A pronounced 'Mongolian' influence can be traced in tantrism. One mode of tantrik *sādhanā* or practice is called *chīnāchāra*, 'Chinese Way', which was brought to India by the Taoist adept Bogar* and another tantrik master, Vasishṭha*. It stresses the drinking of wine, blood and urine, meditation on the organs of generation, worship of the nude female, sexual indulgence including incest, and various other antinomian* practices. The region of

Mahāchīna (Greater China) where this doctrine originated is identified with China or Tibet, and to this region sixty-four out of the one hundred and ninety-two canonical tantras are assigned. Much of the later development of Mahāyāna tantrism stems from Nepāl, Bhutān and Sikkim.

It is to be borne in mind that the form taken by Buddhist tantrism of chīnāchāra is quite alien to Buddhism proper. Tantrism has for many centuries been a pan-Indian phenomenon and has left its mark on most of the major sects. It is found among Buddhists (followers of Asaṅga and Nāgārjuna), Śaivites (sects like the Śāktas, Siddhas, Nāthas, Kāpālikas, Rasavādas), Saurapatas (sun-worshippers, actually Saturn-worshippers, akin to the Maga people), Soma-Siddhāntins (moon-cultists), and Vaishṇavites (Sahajīyās, Pañcharātras).

Chief among the extreme left-hand tantrik cults are those grouped under the heading of *Kaula*, whose votaries are known as *kaulika*. The term is of undetermined origin, variously held to be derived from: the name of the goddess Kālī; the *kaulina*, 'nobility', as its heroes (*vīra*) are called; the *kula* or family of the chosen; the *kulaṭā* or unchaste woman with whom their rites are associated; the *kaulika* or weaver on the tantra or loom of the sectarian beliefs; the goddess Kaulinī, associated with the *kuṇḍalinī* and its arousal; the followers of the *Kaulopanishad* which contains the seeds of many Kaula doctrines, further amplified in the Kulārṇava and other tantras.

The canon of tantrism, called the *Tantra*, is believed by the *tāntrika* (follower of tantrism) to have been revealed by Śiva as the specific scripture for the present *Kali-yuga*, and is regarded by the adherent as superior to the Vedas. Its pantheistic philosophy is somewhat akin to Vedānta tinged with the Sāṁkhya doctrine of Prakṛiti. A large part of the tantrik scriptures is written in the form of dialogues between Śiva and his wife Pārvatī in the course of which the tantrik doctrines are expounded. Conventionally the topics treated by the Tantras are (1) the creation of the universe (*sṛishṭi*), (2) its dissolution (*pralaya*), (3) worship of the deities, (4) spiritual exercises (*sādhanā*), (5) rituals, (6) magical powers, and (7) meditation (*dhyāna*).

The extant Tantras are all relatively late writings, the earliest dating from the seventh or eighth centuries AD, and the most important being composed between the twelfth and seventeenth centuries. The literature is very abundant and most of it is still untranslated. Some of the Tantras are extremely recondite since the basic teachings were communicated by word of mouth and only part was written down in hermetic form (*see* secrecy). Again, much of the literature has not been considered worthy of translation as it is couched in a crude form of Sanskrit, is repetitious, puerile or meaningless, being more often than not, the lucubrations of barely literate scribes. Apart from the obscurity of the subject matter and the vulgarity of expression, the baseness of its teachings resulted in thousands of volumes of tantrik writings being destroyed by orthodox Hindus and by the Muslims.

Among the chief extant classics of tantrism is the *Guhya-samāja* (*c.* AD 650), one of the oldest Buddhist tantras, supposedly composed by Asaṅga, and so named because it was the product of the 'secret conclaves' which emerged from the ruins of dissolved Buddhist monastic orders. Another famous text is the *Mañjuśrī-mūlakalpa* (AD 750) also of Buddhist origin. The *Rudra-*

yāmala (*c.* AD 1000) and the *Brahma-yāmala* (*c.* AD 1100) are both Hindu. The *Kulārṇava Tantra* (1150) is sometimes attributed to the ninth century but actually belongs to the twelfth.

Tantrism contains the loftiest philosophical speculation, side by side with the grossest obscenities; the most rarified metaphysics with the wildest superstition. Some of its moral precepts are high, but its ritual is debased by the most reprehensible practices, and it has been condemned by a Hindu critic as 'at once the most revolting and horrible that human depravity could think of' (IV, p. 65).

Although not ostensibly hostile to the Vedas it is non-Vedic and in tacit opposition to them and to Hindu orthodoxy. In general the Tantras may be said to breathe a spirit of revolt against the conventional schools. Its doctrines cut across all caste stratifications, and open the way to all classes, and some of its rites even give pre-eminence to the pariah and the untouchable. The sexes are treated with equality in Tantrism, quite unlike the degraded position assigned to women in orthodox Hinduism. In many forms in fact greater honour is accorded to women than to men. Some of the greatest tantrik adepts have been women of the lower castes.

In its generally understood form tantrism is associated with occultism* in its worst forms, including diabolism and black magic; the employment of *mantras* (magical spells), *yantras* and *maṇḍalas* (magical diagrams), bells, incense, flowers, candles and rosaries in various sorcerous ceremonies; the practice of special stances (*āsanas*) and gestures (*mudrās*) for acquiring occult powers and siddhis*; mystical alchemy*; body culture including esoteric *prāṇayāma* or breathing exercises; a belief in the subtle body and the *chakras**; the practice of cultic nudity*; the worship of the female principle (*see* strīpūjā) and the yoni; perverse sexuality; self-indulgence and debauchery and doing what one desires; antinomianism* in everyday life, including the eating of meat and the drinking of wine; preoccupation with ordure and other scatalogical* substances, with cadavers, graveyards and cremation grounds (*see* necrophilia).

An important feature in tantrism is the element of the direful and the awe-inspiring, to which the term *bhairav*, 'terror' is applied. Its source is Śiva in his aspect of Bhairava and his consort Śakti in her aspect of Bhairavī (Kālī, Durgā, Chaṇḍī, etc.) who body forth the elements of universal dread. In the eight 'terror' shapes of Śiva he is described as black-limbed, destructive, wrathful, red-crested and so on, and these forms manifest the awesome mysteries of the cosmos, including all life's uncomprehended forces, from the pain of birth and the panic of living to the fearful uncertainties of death. Bhairava was born from a drop of malignant blood that fell from Śiva's left temple when he was insulted at Daksha's feast and became the personification of his hate and rage. His companions are ghouls, demons and ogresses, and his *vāhana* or vehicle a misshapen dog with evil fangs and slavering jaws, who is as terrible to behold as the god himself. The bhairav or terror aspects of the deity are invoked in ceremonial maledictions, and form the subject of meditation of tantrik devotees at graveyards during necrophilic* rites.

Tantrik Mahāyāna touches extremes of obscenity in its teachings. Its texts extol perverse aspects of the Ādi, Dhyāni, and Pratyeka Buddhas, called

Demoniacal Buddhas, whose names are Heruka, Achala, Vajra-bhairava, and Hevajra. Another such Buddha is called *Kālachakra*, 'black-wheel', i.e. the Wheel of Time or Death, and followers of Kālachakrayāna (Death-Way) are taught techniques for eluding the hazards of time and death. All these Buddha beings have female counterparts. In the sexual mysticism of *Vajrayāna* or Kāmavajrayāna, 'lust-thunderbolt-way', the thunderbolt is synonymous with the male organ. It represents an elaboration of the Yogāchāra school founded by the Buddhist philosopher Asaṅga and is utterly antinomian, with a 'sexual' interpretation applied to all precepts and legends.

In the *Guhya-samāja Tantra*, Buddha is represented in acts of continuous debauchery with female beings. In other texts the *vajra*, 'thunderbolt', Buddha is conceived of as everlastingly embracing the body of Tārā or some other Śakti*, and Mahāyāna concepts are given a tantrik interpretation, for example, the Tathāgata is the male organ, the five vital airs represent the semen; Sukhāvatī or paradise is the yoni*. The truth, as discovered by Śākyamuni is that 'Buddhahood abides in the female organ'. In order to experience some of Buddha's divine nature the adept must similarly unite with woman.

In tantrik and other left-hand sects, the highest stages of sexuality are regarded as being of magical character. The antinomian vaijātya relationships with another's wife, with a virgin, and even one's own sister, daughter or mother, fall short of the ultimate requirement. The final stages in the tantrik's progress involve union with the females of the Pit, demonesses, *ḍākinīs* (fiendesses) and other dread beings. Having achieved these distinctions in hell he turns his final assault heavenwards and takes his pleasure of the wives of the gods in the highest spheres. This form of phallic sorcery is known only to a few great adepts, and little is committed to writing lest its practice break the continuum of creation. But its potency is felt even when the first step is taken in *vaijātya* and promiscuous relations with another's wife or an unmarried girl. Hence did the sage Śvetaketu advise that promiscuity be everlastingly unthinkable.

In order to achieve his objective the tantrik does not necessarily have to move from his own sphere. By dint of meditation and magic mantras he draws these divine beings down to him. By means of his extraordinary imagination he draws psychic maṇḍalas and creates an *axis mundi* or cosmic crosspoint which becomes the meeting ground where he can contact them. The Tantras describe how the *apsarās* or celestial nymphs crowd around him but he quickly disposes of this simple fare. The wives of the gods are forced by the irresistible power of the tantrik ritual to offer themselves to the adept, 'oppressed by the enormity of their desire for him'. In tantrik cults gods and demons with exaggerated members are frequently represented in statues and pictures in the state of maithuna with heavenly beings, in postures natural and unnatural, with other gods witnessing the act and consumed with desire for a similar experience. The tantrik adept claims to bring this experience to concrete form in his own rite.

In a final orgy of lust and power he multiplies his body like Kṛishṇa and Saubhari, enlarges his member in conformity with the enormous demonian or divine capacity, and girding himself with commensurate powers satisfies all the beings from heaven and hell who crowd around him seeking to be assuaged. His 'worship' takes the form of sexual activity of tremendous proportions and the whole purpose of it all is to achieve supernatural powers. In spite of these cosmic feats the tantrik adept rarely reaps a greater reward on the earthly plane than such *siddhis* as the ability to live on snowy mountain summits without clothes, or draw up water through the anus.

Books

I. Bagchi, P. C. *Studies in the Tantras*, Calcutta, 1939.
II. Bhattacharya, B., ed., *Guhya-Samaja-Tantra*, Baroda, 1931.
III. Briggs, G. W. *Gorakhnath and the Kanphata Yogis*, Calcutta, 1938.
IV. Chattopadhyaya, D. *Lokayata, or Ancient Indian Materialism*, New Delhi, 1959.
V. Dasgupta, S. B. *An Introduction to Tantrik Buddhism*, Calcutta, 1950.
VI. Kiernander, M. *Rites of the Left Hand*, 1923.
VII. Marquès-Rivière, J. *Tantrik Yoga, Hindu and Tibetan*, London, n.d.
VIII. Woodroffe, John. *Principles of Tantra*, 2 vols, London, 1914.
IX. Woodroffe, John, (Ed.) *Kularnava Tantra*, 1917.
X. Wright, S. R. *Hidden Doctrines of the Tantrik Masters*, 1921.

TĀRAKĀ, female *daitya* (demon) who was changed into a *rākshasa* (ogre) by the sage Agastya. She lived in a forest named after her, on the banks of the Ganges, and carried on fearful depredations in the surrounding countryside. The sage Viśvāmitra asked Rāma to slay her, but the hero only cut off her two arms as he was reluctant to kill a female. His brother Lakshmaṇa also cut off her nose and ears. In revenge she brought down by the power of her magic, a hail of stones which assailed Rāma and Lakshmaṇa and decimated all the nearby villages. Viśvāmitra again appealed to Rāma to destroy her and put an end to her evil activities, and gave Rāma a magic bow and arrow for the purpose. With this weapon Rāma went forth and killed her.

Tārakā's son by the demon Savahu was the redoubtable *Mārīcha*. The *Rāmāyaṇa* relates how he once came with a band of rākshasas to interfere with the sacrificial ceremony of Viśvāmitra, whereupon Rāma slew the rākshasas and threw a weapon at Mārīcha which drove him a hundred *yojanas* (one yojana is about nine miles) out to sea.

Mārīcha afterwards became the minister of Rāvaṇa and accompanied him to the hermitage of Rāma and Sītā to work out a prearranged plan. In order to lure Rāma away from Sītā's side Mārīcha assumed the shape of a golden deer which Rāma pursued and finally overtook and slew. As he lay dying Mārīcha called out in the voice of Rāma for help, then re-assumed his own rākshasa form and derided Rāma. In the meantime Lakshmaṇa heard the voice of Rāma calling for help and plunged into the forest, although Sītā tried to assure him that it was not the voice of Rāma at all. It was while Sītā was left alone and unprotected that Rāvaṇa appeared and carried her away.

Books

See under Rāmāyaṇa and Mythology.

TAXATION. The ancient Hindu writers on politics declared that the treasury, or *kośa*, which was one of the constituent elements of the state, was fed by the 'stream of taxation'. According to the lawgivers a king's duty was to protect the state. In exchange for his protection the people undertook to pay him a wage of one cow for every fifty bought and sold; one fiftieth part of gold; one tenth of the crops; as well as provide him with women and a warrior retinue. The lawbooks say that a king should tax the people like the bee gathers honey and a leech draws blood; mildly but surely; slowly but with unremitting intent.

According to the ancient records almost every trade, activity and commodity was liable to taxation. All wage-earners, employers, artisans, were subject to tax. Taxes were levied for water, property, income, gambling, prostitution, excise, liquor, external trade, internal trade, imports and exports.

Kauṭilya and other writers on politics advocate the exaction of taxes by fair means or foul. Devices such as opening a 'subscription' to obtain funds for the state, and forcible demands on pain of imprisonment and torture, were all to be taken into account when the state needed money. People not donating were reviled; they lost the king's favour and at the first opportunity a means was found of discovering some 'criminal' acts against them so that they could be imprisoned, their property confiscated and their families scattered. Government agents posing as sorcerers, priests, magicians, astrologers and so on, devised fraudulent ways of relieving men of their wealth: by playing on their superstitious nature, or inducing them to part with their money because it might bring them bad luck, was unsafe or unpropitious; or persuading them that money given on such and such occasion would earn a million times more merit than at any other time. They would point out dread omens and demand large sums to avert the impending calamities; or declare the locality haunted by evil spirits and collect money to propitiate them; or arrange a fraudulent spectacle like a miraculous serpent with many heads, and charge fees for viewing it. Prostitutes could lure the rich and cause their property to be seized. In extreme cases it was even permissible for a state agent to poison one man and accuse another of the crime to have him deprived of his property (I, p. 105).

Books

I. Bhambhri, C. P. *Substance of Hindu Polity*, Meerut, 1960.
II. Sen, P. *The History of Taxation in India*, 1902.
(*See also under* Politics.)

TELUGU, the language of the Āndhras, is a Dravidian tongue, its name derived from *tene*, honey, to indicate its mellifluence. Telugu has a script of its own allied to Sanskrit, but being originally written on palm-leaves it developed, like Oṛiya, a cursive outline.

There is no available information on Telugu literature before the eleventh century AD, although the Āndhras themselves had been in existence for centuries before, being mentioned in the Purāṇas. All pre-eleventh century inscriptions or *śāsanas* are in Prākṛit or Sanskrit. Such writings as may have been in existence prior to that time were probably rough and crude in character, of the type referred to as *deśi*, 'rural', in contrast to the ornate artificiality of courtly literature called *margi*. Early margi poetry was mainly religious in character, and consisted largely of translations from Sanskrit.

Nanniah (fl. 1022–1063) was the purohita (family priest) of one of the kings of the Second Chālukya dynasty. His translation into Telugu of the first three cantos of the *Mahābhārata* is regarded as a classic. Written in the champū (prose and verse) style, it set the fashion for Telugu writing. Nanniah was the earliest of the Great Three who translated the Sanskrit epic, the other two being Tikkanna and Errāpragada.

Tikkanna (1220–1300), a brāhmin, came from a family of poets and ministers. Legend relates that the king of the country desired a poet to complete the work of Nanniah, and circulated one of his stanzas asking the poets of the realm for a similar stanza. No entries were satisfactory, but Tikkanna simply re-wrote the stanza, which was declared by the court paṇḍits to be even better than Nanniah's. The king appointed him court poet and entrusted him with the task of completing the *Mahābhārata*. Tikkanna is said to have dictated his translation of it to a potter, who was the only amanuensis capable of taking down his fast dictation, and who, in fact, helped him when he was at a loss for words.

Errāpragada (1280–1350) the last of the Great Three to translate the *Mahābhārata*, did not belong to the priestly caste, and was a staunch Śaivite. His rather severe rendering is a model of technical excellence.

Atharvana (1240–1310) traditionally regarded as a contemporary of Nanniah's who had allegedly burned down the house where Atharvana lived in order to destroy his superior version of the *Mahābhārata*. He is the only notable Jain writer in Telugu literature, and the author of an early Telugu grammar.

Śrīnātha (1375–1450) regarded by some as the supreme poet of Telugu literature, was born of humble parents and began writing while still in his teens. He lived like Byron and wrote much erotic verse, most of which is still extant. In his majestic and ornate style he sang of Śiva's exploits and of the glory of the Āndhras.

Potana (fl. 1460) a Śaivite devotee who avoided kings and courts as a hindrance to true living, preferring poverty instead. In one of his works it was necessary to have a *rākshasa* (ogre) address abusive words to Śiva; to atone for this blasphemy Potana wrote another ode wholly in praise of the deity. He was also a devotee of Kṛishṇa, and his poems on that deity are used in Āndhra as standard devotional hymns.

Pinavīra (1430–80) or Pinavīra-bhadriah, at the age of ten was a prodigy of learning as well as a poet. Legend has it that Śrīnātha himself came to him while he was playing with other boys in the street, to ask for his opinion on one of his own works. The opinion was given without the boy even deigning to look up. He is said to have wasted his substance in riotous living and on women. On one occasion having promised the king to compose a work within a certain time, he postponed it till the last day, then locked himself up in a room. When his brother peeped in he was surprised to see a woman writing furiously. Confronted with this later the poet declared that it was the goddess Sarasvatī in person who had come to compose for him.

Āndhra literature received great encouragement from the Vijayanagar kings, chief of them being Kṛishṇadeva Raya (1509–29) who sponsored a movement for breaking away from translations and religious themes. Among his protégés the principal were eight in number, known as the *ashṭa-diggajā*, or 'eight elephants'.

Peddana (fl. 1520) or Allasani Peddana, poet laureate and personal friend of the above Kṛishṇadeva Raya. His *Manucharita* with its exquisite descriptions of nature and remarkable character studies changed the course of Telugu literature. It so pleased the king his patron that he insisted on being one of the pole-bearers of the poet's palanquin. Peddana is spoken of as the 'grandsire of Telugu poetry'.

Tenali (fl. 1520) or Tenali Rāmakṛishṇa, another of the *ashṭa-diggajās* attached to the Vijayanagar court, was a Śaivite by birth and became a convert to Vaishṇavism. A court jester and humourist, he made the life of the orthodox miserable with his scathing satire. Tenali's best poetical work is the *Pāṇḍuraṅga-mahātmya*, about a brāhmin who lives a life of dissipation and debauchery and dies in a town sacred to Vishṇu. He is claimed by Yama who wishes to take him to hell for his wickedness, and by the servants of Vishṇu since he died in Vishṇu's sacred city. Vishṇu eventually gets his man.

Kumārī **Molla** (1509–30), a potter woman whose *Rāmāyaṇa*, a tender and sentimental narration, is the most widely read and popular epic in Telugu literature. She ranks with the best Telugu poets.

Vemana (fl. 1550), considered the most important of all Telugu writers. Little is known of his personal life. He was a poet of the people and his satires were chiefly directed against caste distinctions and the fair sex. There is hardly a Telugu proverb or pithy saying not attributed to Vemana. Of the brāhmins he says that 'they imitate the solitude of the dog, the meditations of the crane, the chanting of the ass, and the bathing of the frog'. Of the scriptures: 'The Vedas are like courtesans, deluding men.' Of certain funeral customs, 'O you asses, why do you make balls of food (*piṇḍa*) and give them to the crows in the name of your ancestors? Is a dung eating-crow an ancestor of yours?' Again, 'Why do you bow down to a bull made of stone, and lambaste the trotting bullock?'

The downfall of the Vijayanagar empire in the latter half of the sixteenth century saw the rapid decline of Telugu letters, and such writings as were produced in exile in the Tamil country were mostly insignificant works not even remotely reflecting the great works of the past. The seventeenth century was virtually a blank, and the eighteenth and early nineteenth centuries constitute a literary Dark Age. The mellifluous lilt of Telugu seemed now to be inimical to the higher flights of literary achievement. The influence of the West resulted in poor imitations of Wordsworth and the poets of the Romantic Revival, without their depth or finesse of feeling.

Today the outlook is hardly any better. In the words of one critic, 'It must be confessed that the novel has not made much headway in Telugu. Literary criticism as understood in the West has not yet developed. There are few biographies of outstanding merit' (II, p. 260). The charge could be reiterated all down the line. The 'literary renaissance' sweeping the country is not even on the horizon, unless a revival of the age-old religious and mythological themes, with stereotyped strophes is to be regarded as the sign of an awakening.

Books

I. Chenchiah, P., & Bhujanga, M. *A History of Telugu Literature*, Calcutta, n.d.
II. Gokak, V. K. *Literature in Modern Indian Languages*, New Delhi, 1957.
III. Raja, M. B. R. *A History of Telugu Literature*, Oxford, 1928.
IV. Raju, P. T. *Telugu Literature*, Bombay, 1944.
V. Rao, T. R. *A Historical Sketch of Telugu Literature*, 1931.
VI. Sitaramaiya, K. *Handbook of Telugu Literature*, 1931.

TEMPLE. The Hindu temple, *mandira*, 'gladdening', is chiefly meant to be a dwelling place for the god. There is therefore only one essential element in the Hindu temple, namely, the *vimāna* or shrine, containing a little cell, usually dark, called the *garbha-gṛiha*, 'womb-house', where the god in the form of an idol or emblem, duly consecrated, is installed. Sometimes there is a second chamber behind the first, to house the consort of the deity. All other parts of the temple are additions and elaborations around this simple sanctuary.

The term vimāna actually refers to the celestial chariots of the deities and also to the tall, many-storied palaces of their heavenly abodes. In accordance with this there is built over the vimāna, as a symbol of its sanctity, a tapering tower called the *śikhara*, 'summit', and many theories have been put forward to explain its origin and shape. Some say it originated from the peaked huts in which the pre-Aryans housed their idols. The deities of South Indian temples are still taken out in large processional carriages with tapering top that suggest a pre-Aryan model. Others trace the śikhara to the elevated Buddhist stūpas*, while still others think that it is a direct descendant of the Indo-Aryan portable altar, built to imitate the celestial *ratha* or chariot.

Devotees who came to worship the deity stood on a little cleared space before the vimāna or shrine. This was later raised to form a platform, and then a pavilion protected by a roof supported on pillars, finally evolving into the *maṇḍapa* or pillared hall. Its roof was flat but lesser śikharas were sometimes built over the maṇḍapa as well. Outside, and to the left of the maṇḍapa stood a *dhvaja* or flagstaff, supposed to be a relic of the Vedic *yupa** or sacrificial post.

The maṇḍapa was first built detached from the vimāna so that there were two separate buildings, the small shrine with a steeple housing the god, and a large covered pavilion for the worshippers. Further additions were sometimes worked on the maṇḍapa. To the front portion of the maṇḍapa was attached a small pillared porch or entrance hall called the *ardha-maṇḍapa*, 'half maṇḍapa', and between the maṇḍapa and the shrine there was an ancillary chamber known as the *antarāla*, 'intermediate'. Sometimes all these parts had separate śikharas or steeples, the one over the vimāna always being the tallest.

The worshipper entering the temple from the outside would walk up a short flight of steps passing a flagstaff on his left, outside the temple. He would then go through a small pillared hall (the *ardha-maṇḍapa*), then through the large pillared hall (the *maṇḍapa*), continue through an intermediate passage (*antarāla*) and find himself before the shrine (*vimāna*) containing the holy of holies (*garbha-gṛiha*) where the idol stood.

Parts of the temple are set apart for the preparation of sacrificial food, the recitation of mantras, the sacred fire, the storing of the consecrated utensils and implements. Within the temple enclosure are several subsidiary buildings comprising the assembly hall; the *nāṭ mandir* or dancing hall (for the female temple dancers); the *bhog mandir* or hall of offerings; shrines dedicated to the consort of the patron deity, to Hanumān the monkey-god, to Nandi the bull vehicle of Śiva, and other minor deities, and sometimes pillared halls called *chaultrī*, like the Halls of the Thousand Pillars, so characteristic of South Indian temples. Some South Indian temples, such as those of Vijayanagar, had a *kalyāṇa-maṇḍapa*, "beautiful chamber', consisting of an open pavilion with raised platform for the reception of the deity and his consort at the annual celebration of his marriage.

Worshippers pay their devotions by various rites and salutations (*see* worship), by gifts to the gods and brāhmins, and also by circumambulation of the shrine or temple enclosure. Many temples have special ambulatory passages called *pradakshiṇa-patha*, 'processional paths', probably of Buddhist origin.

While this style of architecture prevailed in northern India, the Dravidian or South Indian temple had a few distinguishing features, because the South Indian temple ceremonials were much more elaborate and included many 'social' activities of the deity, such as his outing on festive occasions, and his marriage once a year.

The temple in South India is often a self-contained organic unit and some are like miniature towns. The temple, maṇḍapa and subsidiary structures have a broad open courtyard, known as the *prākāram* going around them on all four sides. It is an outgrowth of the processional path. Outside the prākāram and enclosing the whole area rises a high wall in the shape of a quadrilateral. In the middle of one or more of the sides of this enclosing wall rises a very high and richly sculptured gateway known as the *gopuram*, which probably derives its name from the 'cow-gate' of the Vedic village. It is to be noted that while in the North Indian temple the main tower is built over the vimāna or shrine of the god, which is in the centre of the temple complex, in South India it is raised over the entrance gateways and is the most conspicuous feature of the temple seen from the outside. The typical gopuram (e.g. the Pāṇḍya) is oblong in plan and tapers as it rises, often to a height of 150 feet. The summit is flat and surmounted by a long barrel-vaulted, gable-ended roof, a relic of the keel-roof of the Buddhist chaitya hall.

Outside the walled area is yet another prākāram or open courtyard, with shrines, pillared maṇḍapas, tanks (*teppakulam*) for ablutions, and subsidiary buildings, the whole of this area being enclosed within four walls having one or more gopurams. Sometimes there are as many as four or five such concentric walls, each with its gopurams, and each enclosing an open courtyard with miscellaneous shrines.

Books

See under Architecture.

TEXTILES. Fabrics were made in ancient India out of vegetable fibres, woven hair, animal wools, and cotton. Indian cotton growing and weaving are believed to owe their origin to the Austric aboriginals of the country. A fragment of cotton cloth, dyed with the red extract of the madder root found in Mohenjodaro along with some bobbins, indicates that by the second millennium BC India had a knowledge not only of cotton weaving, but of the process of mordant dyeing* as well. The Greek seaman Nearchus (fourth century BC) spoke of Indians wearing 'tree linen', i.e. cotton, probably of the cotton-tree, and this material was apparently widely used at that time. A Greek word for an Indian cotton fabric, from which the English name for a type of muslin is derived, is *sindon*, which is etymologically related to Sind in India.

In the Vedas, Epics and Purāṇas, and in the early Buddhist and Jain writings we find many references to the textile arts of India. Fabrics are named and the apparel worn by monarchs and rich noblemen is sometimes described, but it is impossible to glean any satisfactory clue as to the nature of the materials used. Patterns of gold seem to have been woven into some of the clothing, and the outer garments were often studded with jewels which 'dazzled the beholder and made the gods envious'. One prince wore a robe that 'made him shine like the sun'. The Purāṇas mention the *agni-śuchi-vāsa* (fire-purified apparel) made of incombustible material, which was used during religious ceremonies of great potency, although exactly what this fabric was is not known. Some authorities believe it may have been a light fibrous variety of asbestos, probably imported from Egypt, where the priests used to wear asbestos cloth (IX, p. 136).

From the days of classical Greece and Rome, Indian textiles were prized in Europe as luxuries, but these also included Chinese silks some of which reached the Mediterranean shores by way of India. Among the silk fabrics mentioned in the ancient texts are *kausheya*, made from the *kośa* or cocoon; *patrorṇa*, made from varieties of wild silk; and *chīna-paṭṭa*, 'Chinese cloth', a very fine material highly valued in all parts of the civilized world. The name of the silk fabric today known as *tussore* (or tusser), comes from the Sanskrit word *tasara* (or *trasara*), the weaver's shuttle, so called from the ancient method of its manufacture. Today the best pure silk of India comes from Āgra, Banāras, Hyderābād, and Tanjore; the finest printed silks from Surāt; and the best damasked silks from Bahāwalpur.

Many elements of textile design and techniques were introduced by the barbarian peoples who invaded and settled in India during the early centuries of the present era. The precise extent of their contributions cannot be gauged with any certainty, but the comparison of age-old methods used by the peoples of Central Asia with those used in India have helped to reveal that a substantial legacy was received from them. The costumes of the women of Gurjara ancestry in Gujarāt and Kāṭhiāwār, and beautiful fabrics such as the patola (*see* dyeing) still reflect the bright hues and exquisite patterns of their Central Asian prototypes. By the tenth century Gurjara textiles were being exported by Arab traders westwards to Egypt and eastwards as far as Bali, Java and South China.

With the coming of the Muslims a whole new range of fabrics was introduced. Traditional patterns and techniques used in India today have been traced to the tent-dwelling bedouin of Arabia, the Berbers of North Africa, the Saracens of Syria, the Fatimites of Egypt; to the Persian cities of Balkh, Bokhara, Yezd and Kashan, and the Afghan cities of Kabul and Herat.

The art of embroidery is known to have come with the Muhammadans, and many embroidery styles are of Central Asian origin. A fine example is the *phūlkāri*, 'flower-craft' of the Panjāb worked on lengths of homespun cloth or cotton material. The art is now dying out but continues to be done on a small scale by Jāt women who use patterns handed down for centuries. European tourists and museums now boast the finest pieces. The design called *bāgh*, 'garden' covers every inch of the cloth so that not a thread of the original fabric is visible. One tiny corner of the phūlkāri is always left unfinished, or is completed in black thread to avoid the guilt of perfection and ward off the evil eye. The embroidery is worked with soft silk floss of many colours, special attention being paid to the borders, which are often more beautiful than the centre. Phūlkāri work is done on shawls, bed-spreads, head coverings and cushion covers.

In Bengal the *kānthā* or 'rag' embroidery was introduced not more than two centuries ago. Here designs are embroidered mostly on discarded sāṛīs which are first folded to the required thickness, the edges tucked in and varied designs in white or coloured thread embroidered in. Kānthās are used as wraps, bed-spreads, book-coverings, cushion covers, comb and mirror sachets, and so on.

Since strict Muslims never wore pure silk, many varieties of mixed silk fabrics came into vogue. Such were the *mashru*, a tie-dye cloth of mixed silk and cotton; the *himru*, a brocaded variety of the same; the *jamaivar* (English: jamewar) a brocaded length of coloured silk, wool or cotton, used as a shawl. Resplendent hangings of brocaded silk, cotton and wool, illustrating scenes from the Epics were hung on the walls of inner shrines in Hindu temples, an idea said to be taken from the tapestry cloth used for covering the Caaba in Mecca.

In the north, especially in Kashmīr and the Himāchal Pradesh, wraps and head shawls are made from *pashmina* (or pashima), the soft underfur of hairy animals, particularly the mountain goat. The manufacture of the famous Cashmere shawls was begun only about the middle of the last century. The fabric made from the coarser and longer hair of animals is known as *patu* (or *puttoo*) and is used for coverings and blankets.

The superb Indian brocades of the Moghul period acquired an even greater renown than the earlier fabrics. One was made of heavy silk with a design of very fine gold and silver wire running through it. The wire used for this purpose was drawn out with great skill, it being estimated that two shillings worth of silver was drawn out to 800 yards of wire. The best known example of this class was the kimkhāb, (from Chines kin, 'gold', and Persian khwāb, 'dream') anglicized *kincob*. Kāñchi, Banāras, Ahmadābād and Surāt are still famous for their kincobs, and their imaginative names serve to reflect their beauty: peacock's neck (*murgala*), nightingale's eyes (*bulbul-chashm*), and sunlight-and-moonbeams (*dhūp-chānd*). Moghul emperors gave a further impetus to the textile arts, and gold and silver brocades studded with gems and pearls, fine figured muslins, and printed fabrics of fabled excellence were produced under royal patronage and, on a smaller scale, on the estates of the lesser nobility.

The English names of several varieties of textiles are derived from the terminology of India and the neighbouring countries, attesting their oriental lineage. Such are: *calico,* a cotton, usually printed, named after the town of Calicut in South India; *baft,* a kind of calico, from the Persian word meaning 'woven'; *chintz,* a cotton cloth, slightly glazed, from the Sanskrit *chihna,* 'speckled', because of the early hand-painted designs on them; *cashmere,* a shawl of very fine wool, from the state of Kashmīr; *kerseymere,* a fine twilled woollen cloth, also from Kashmīr; *damask,* a patterned linen, named from Damascus; *gingham,* a striped or checked plain, close-weave cotton, from the Malay word *giṅgan,* 'striped'; *gurrah,* the name of a coarse kind of muslin, comes from the Hindi *gāṛhā,* 'thick'; *dungaree,* a heavy calico, from the Hindi *duṅgrī*; *jaconet,* a cotton fabric, the name of which comes from Jagannāth, near Purī; *madras,* a light-weight cotton used for shirting, etc., from the town of the same name; *nainsook,* a kind of muslin, derived from the Sanskrit *nayana-sukha,* 'eye-delighting'; *seersucker,* a light, crinkly-weave cotton, from the Persian *shīrushakar,* 'milk and sugar'; *satara,* woollen cloth, from Sātārā; *surat* a coarse undyed cotton, from Surāt, a place north of Bombay; *surah,* twilled silk, also from Surāt; *palampore,* a flowered chintz, from *palaṅg-push,* 'bed-cover'; *taffeta,* a silk stuff, from Persian *tāftah,* 'woven'.

Many of these, as their names indicate, were introduced to Europe, but many new fabrics, dyes, patterns and techniques were received from the West at the same time. Portuguese commodities from Goa into the interior included damasks and satins, with the latest European designs. With the British, French, Dutch and others, came the fine white cambric, the silk challis, the gauzy chiffon, the crinkled crêpe, cretonne, gaberdine, lacework and nettings, fine organdie, the light transparent voiles, mattress and pillow tickings, the silk-worsted poplin, and velvets and plushes.

Perhaps the most famous of the Indian textiles was the extremely fine cotton or cotton mixture called *muslin.* The local name for this material was *mal* (English mull, or mullmull), a name believed to be derived from the ancient Mālava tribe who made a plain variety of this fabric. The weaving of fine muslins was brought to perfection by the Muhammadans, and the term muslin is in fact derived from the town of Mosul, in Iraq. The art was brought to India by the Moghuls, and top quality fabrics of this type began to be made in Dacca under the patronage of the Muslim rulers of Bengal. The finest muslins in India, and therefore the finest in the world, were the *jāmdānī* or figured muslins of Dacca. An interesting point is that the best muslins were made only during the rainy season, since the weaving of the fine thread was helped by the moisture in the air.

The names given to these muslins are suggestive of their excellence and their unbelievable fineness. Such are *ābrawan,* which means 'running water'; *baft-havā,* 'woven-air'; *shabna,* 'evening dew'. Gossamer stuffs of like quality made in the Muslim centres of South India were known as 'sloughs of serpents' and 'vapour of milk'. A standard test for the excellence of muslin fabrics was to see if a length could easily be drawn through a finger-ring. It had to be barely perceptible to the touch, and if laid just below the surface of a clear stream was invisible. Tavernier speaks of a jewelled coconut presented to a Persian king which contained a muslin turban-piece thirty yards long. The story goes that the emperor Aurangzeb once rebuked his daughter for appearing in a public place with nothing on. On the contrary, she is said to have replied, not only was she fully dressed, but her muslin garment was wrapped seven times around her body. Dr James Taylor who made a study of textiles in the middle of the last century recorded, 'A skein which a native weaver measured in my presence in 1846 and which was afterwards carefully weighed, proved to be in the proportion of upwards of 250 miles to the pound'.

At the beginning of the seventeenth century, during the reign of Jahāngīr, a new method of printing on calico and chintz was introduced. This was done by means of wooden blocks, a technique ultimately Chinese in origin. It was, in effect, a first step towards the modification of the ancient art of painting on fabrics and of creating designs by various means of differential dyeing. Modern designs*, often taken from Portuguese and other European sources, were introduced to suit the new method of production. The blocks once made could print an almost limitless quantity of material, so that a few stereotyped patterns served the needs of the average manufacturer. Except for the limited patronage of a few nobles there was little incentive for the large class of specialist craftsmen to continue in the ancient techniques with the traditional finesse and care.

The final blow to the indigenous textile industry was delivered with the introduction of machinery for the manufacture and printing of textiles. By the beginning of the nineteenth century tens of thousands of Indian weavers and designers were thrown out of employment by competition from the power-loom, and many starved to death, prompting Lord Bentinck's famous Minute which began, 'The bones of the cotton-weavers are bleaching the plains of India'.

But progress in this direction was inevitable. Merely to clothe the people of India had become a major problem, and the mills turned out cloth as fast as they could to keep up with the growing demand. M. K. Gāndhi tried to meet the situation by popularising *khaddar*, a rough home-spun material, hand woven in the villages, but this like much else had a political end. The great mill owners gave him their allegiance but their factories went ahead with large-scale machine production.

Today the traditional fabrics are made on hand-looms as part of a small village industry which caters mainly to the tourist trade, and their products are frequently adapted to suit the demands of European taste. Indigenous dyes are being replaced by anilines; the vivid colours, considered too gaudy to suit the Western markets, are being subdued, and the designs made in conformity with modern requirements. In spite of every effort it would seem that the traditional art of making textiles in the old way can no longer be kept alive.

Books

I. Baker, G. P. *Calico Painting and Printing in the East Indies*, 1920.
II. Bhushan, J. B. *The Costumes & Textiles of India*, 1959.

III. Dongerkery, K. *The Romance of Indian Embroidery*, Bombay, 1951.
IV. Gulati, A. N. *The Patolu of Gujerat*, Bombay, 1951.
V. Irwin, J. *Indian Embroidery*, London, 1951.
VI. Irwin, J. *Shawls: A study in Indo-European Exchange*, London, 1955.
VII. Kramrisch, Stella. 'Kantha.' *Journal of the Indian Society of Oriental Art*, Calcutta, Vol. 7, 1939.
VIII. Mehta, R. J. *The Handicrafts and Industrial Arts of India*, Bombay, 1960.
IX. Ray, J. C. *Ancient Indian Life*, Calcutta, 1948.
X. Rieftsthal, R. M. *Persian & Indian Textiles*, New York, 1923.
XI. Steel, F. A. 'Phulkari Work in the Punjab.' *Journal of Indian Art*, London, Vol. 2, No. 24, 1888.
XII. Taylor, James. *Descriptive and Historical Account of the Cotton Manufactures of Dacca*, 1851.
XIII. Watson, J. F. *The Textile Manufactures of India*, 1866.
XIV. Wheeler, M. (Ed.) *Textiles and Ornaments of India*, New York, 1956.

THEATRE. The Sanskrit term for all forms of representation on the stage is *nāṭya*, 'movement'. In classical theory it is often confined to drama alone, but more frequently is used to include dancing, acting, mime and allied arts pertaining to the theatre. The study of aṅgika* or bodily postures is closely connected with nāṭya.

Broadly, nāṭya falls into three chief categories, namely: (1) *nāṭaka*, or drama proper, specifically the heroic play; (2) *nṛitya*, the mimetic arts, mime, pantomime and also ballet. In classical theory nṛitya is concerned with the emotions (*bhāva*); (3) *nṛitta*, the dance, based on time and rhythm, accompanied by music. It may be said to be a form of 'pure dance'.

In a related scheme of classification the arts of the stage are divided into two categories, namely, *rūpaka* or drama proper, and *uparūpaka*, the minor forms of drama, mime and dance. As this scheme is the basis of most classical discussions on art theory it may be given here for reference. It should be noted that the terms nāṭya, nṛitya, nṛitta, rūpaka and others have been variously defined and there is much overlapping in meaning, and confusion among the theorists about their precise content. The significance of these terms as given here is traditional and commonly accepted.

Rūpaka ('form, appearance, or image') applies to drama proper. Ten forms of rūpaka are generally distinguished, of which the first systematic account was given in the *Daśarūpaka* of Dhanañjaya (fl. AD 950). These ten forms are: (1) *nāṭaka* (or nāṭya), drama in its highest form, in five to ten acts. It is the heroic play; the subject is not invented by the poet but is drawn from mythology or history; the hero is a god or king, and the language of the play lofty; the classical unities and proprieties are observed, and it is conventionally said to be based on sentiment (*rasa*); (2) *prakaraṇa*, is like the nāṭaka, save in the social status of the hero or heroine, who is of a rank below royalty, such as a brāhmin, minister, or wealthy merchant. It is sometimes a comedy of manners. An example of the prakaraṇa is Bhavabhūti's *Mālatī-mādhava*; (3) *bhāṇa*, or monologue, generally comical and often extremely coarse. It is usually the imaginary conversation of one man, e.g. the *viṭa* or man of the world, with others who are not present. He asks questions, as himself, and replies as someone else, pretends to listen, then questions him again, and so on. It includes mime. Four bhāṇas, known as the *Chatur-bhāṇī*, ascribed to such authors as Śūdraka, Vararuchi and others were discovered and published in 1922; (4) *prahasana*, or farce, generally a short play of one act, portraying the tricks and quarrels of low characters. It is usually a very coarse, comical and absurd satire, and often makes religious sects the butt of its ridicule; (5) *ḍima*, a legendary play in four acts, dealing with gods and demons, characterized by power, malignancy and fury, and excluding all elements of love, comedy and grace. There is magic, sorcery and occult combat, with plenty of celestial phenomena; (6) *vyāyoga*, a variation of the nāṭaka or heroic play. A military spectacle, with raids, battles, and sieges, often in one act. Its theme is legendary and knightly, with love, comedy and grace excluded; (7) *samavakāra*, the supernatural drama, as a rule in three acts, concerned with heroic emotions, and with gods and demons as the only characters. A popular theme is the Churning of the Ocean; (8) *vīthī*, a one-act play, like the bhāṇa, but with two or three actors instead of one. There is an outline plot and the love sentiment prevails; (9) *aṅka*, a simple one-act play, usually in the form of a play within a play as in *Hamlet*. It is often called the *garbhāṅka*, 'embryo-act'. Examples are found in Harsha's *Priyadarśikā*, and Bhavabhūti's *Uttara Rāma-charita*. A variety of aṅka is the *utsṛishṭāṅka*, which introduces many young women sorrowing and weeping and, contrary to accepted practice, has a tragic ending; (10) *īhā-mṛiga*, the term applied to a fanciful or mythical animal, e.g. half elephant and half fish. On the stage the name is said to be derived from the fact that in this type of drama, which is usually in four acts, a girl, as hard to attain as a gazelle (*mṛiga*), is sought after and pursued (*īhā*). There is always a conflict of wills between the hero and his rivals for the possession of the girl. For example, in one īhā-mṛiga, Kṛishṇa deprives Śiśupāla of Chedi of his promised bride, Rukmiṇī.

Minor forms of drama are termed *uparūpaka*. As the rūpaka is based on the nāṭaka or nāṭya, the uparūpaka is based on the nṛitya, and provides opportunities for dance, music and mime, although the dramatic element predominates. The uparūpaka forms include: (1) *bhāṇikā*, a little bhāṇa or monologue play, with dance and mime (2) *chhāya-nāṭaka*, 'shadow-play', originally a village show. When introduced on the regular stage it was used as an *entr'acte*. In this the shadows of wooden cut-outs of the characters, which include men, women, animals, and semi-animal grotesques, are cast on a screen, their loose limbs manipulated by strings. The accompanying legend is recited in song or verse; (3) *nāṭika*, a little drama (nāṭaka); a play with fewer acts and a less exalted theme. A lesser heroic play, with the amorous element predominating; (4) *goshṭhī*, pantomime, with music, drama, dance and mime; (5) *hallīśa*, a glorified dance-drama. In this form the dance element was predominant; (6) *nāṭya-rāsaka*, a ballet and pantomime; (7) *prakaraṇika*, a prakaraṇa (see above), with hero and heroine of the merchant class; (8) *prasthāna*, based on a mimetic dance; the hero and heroine are slaves; (9) *saṭṭaka*, a nāṭika, but in Prākṛit throughout, with no Sanskrit at all. It has a dance or two; (10) *troṭaka*, a drama usually depicting the love of a mortal for a goddess, in which the distracted lover utters confused speech; (11) *pāñchālī-nāṭaka*, a puppet play of the marionette theatre, a form of village entertainment, especially popular in the Pañchāla country, hence its name.

Puppets are frequently mentioned in Sanskrit litertaure and a talking puppet made to impersonate Sītā is found in one of the plays of Rājaśekhara. From those who manipulated the *putrikā*, or puppets, came terms like *sūtradhāra* (thread-holder) and *sthāpaka* (arranger) of the classic drama*; (12) *yātrā*, 'procession', a form of drama that evolved from the religious and festive processions, based on the popular folk traditions of antiquity. In Bengal such plays, always performed without a stage, have an ancient history. They were originally musical, with accessories of miming, dancing and bits of dialogue added, all around the nucleus of a plot. Music and song always predominated, the whole generally being Vaishṇavite in content. There was a loose narration of some mythological stories, plentifully sprinkled with love-songs, many of them vulgar, and irrelevant in sequence. Briefly, a pious-prurient village dramatic festival.

Books

See under Dramaturgy.

THREAD CEREMONIES. Various kinds of thread or cord made from cotton, grass, fibre, or similar material, of varying length and with a varying number of knots, are used as rings, wristlets, necklets and bands in Hindu rites and ceremonies. Generally white thread is used for orthodox occasions, brightly coloured threads for fesivals, and dark blue for witchcraft. The use of thread for religious purposes has been explained as due to the belief that it forms a magical barrier; when used as a ring or necklet, a magical circle keeping off evil influences and preventing the dissipation of good forces. It is also a symbol of 'binding' one to another, or to a mode of life. Measured against one's person and consecrated, the thread can take on aspects of the individual's life.

In a festival associated with the goddess Gaurī women take lengths of cotton thread sixteen times their own height, fold them into skeins and put them into earthen pots along with pieces of coconut and new grain, and lay them before the image of the goddess. On the third day the skeins are worshipped and worn by the women around the neck and after a few days removed and thrown into the water or buried. In Mahārāshṭra thread is wound around a sacred tree during certain festivals and the tree worshipped with *mantras* and circumambulation. Elsewhere a red or saffron silk strand of fourteen threads tied with fourteen knots is worshipped and fastened around the right wrist on special occasions.

The *Śrāvaṇa* full-moon in July–August, seems to be particularly associated with thread rites, and at least three festivals occur during this time when knotted threads are the object of worship. In one such ceremony held on *Śrāvaṇī-pūrṇimā* and called *pavitrāropaṇa*, rings, wristlets, and necklets, made from knotted twists of cotton are sprinkled with *pañchagavya* (the five products of a cow) and worshipped. They are then placed around the neck of an image of Kṛishṇa, wound around a Śiva liṅga or laid at the feet of Vishṇu.

Another custom, observed on Śrāvaṇa full moon is the *raksha-bandhan* 'protective-tying', when rākhī or bracelets of coloured thread and tinsel are tied by women on the wrists of their menfolk, thus binding them to protect and guard them during the year. Many legends are told of the origin of this custom. Vishṇu's wife tied such a bracelet around the wrist of her husband as a charm when he took on the Vāmana (dwarf) incarnation to slay the demon Bali. After her rescue Sītā tied it around the wrist of her brother-in-law Lakshmaṇa as a symbol that he should protect her against future dangers. In commemoration of this event all brothers are pledged to protect their sisters when this token is tied to their wrist.

The most celebrated of the thread rites, and one of the most important of the Hindu sacraments, is the initiation ceremony of *upanayana*, in which a boy is helped to cross the threshold from childhood to adolescence. Before the ceremony the boy is regarded as 'once-born' and a śūdra, and an orthodox brāhmin will not allow his son to eat with him before he has undergone this rite. After the ceremony he becomes a *dvija*, 'twice-born', and is admitted to the privileges of his caste and has access to the sacred books. The ceremony is of very ancient origin, dating back to Indo-Iranian times. It is still practised by the Parsees of India who call it *naujat* or new birth. Parsee children, both boys and girls, receive this religious initiation after they have attained the age of six.

In Ancient India girls were admitted to the upanayana ceremony at the age of eight, and were entitled thereafter to the privileges of Vedic education, but later this right was revoked and only boys were eligible for initiation. Some authorities maintain that the rite was reserved for brāhmin boys only, but there is abundant evidence to show that it was open to the first three castes. Brāhmin boys were initiated at the age of eight, kshattriyas at the age of eleven, and vaiśyas at the age of fourteen.

Fundamentally the upanayana was a sacrament symbolizing the boy's readiness for receiving sacred knowledge, and was thus a rite of formal admission to a school of Vedic studies. Several related observances were incorporated into the regular ceremony, of which not all were necessarily performed nor the order of their performance consistently maintained. Fifteen steps marked the complete ceremony the details of which are given below.

(1) The boy, wearing only a *kaupīna* or loin-cloth was 'brought before' the guru or preceptor, thus giving the name *upanayana*, to the whole ceremony; (2) in the *paridāna*, 'giving', the father requests the guru to accept the boy as a brahmachāri student under his care, and then formally gives him into the custody of the guru; (3) the guru in turn hands the boy over to the care of the gods Savitṛi, Pūshan, the Aśvins, Soma, Agni and Prajāpati; (4) the *nāma-pṛichchha*, 'name-asking', the teacher asks the boy's name and other particulars; (5) in the *svīkaraṇa*, 'accepting', the teacher extends his hand and touches the boy's thumb, hand, breast, or shoulder, as a token of acceptance; (6) the teacher then offers the boy a *vaikaksha* (mantle or upper garment), which in ancient times was made of *ajina* (deerskin) but later of cloth, and also a vāsa or lower garment; (7) the guru ties around the boy's waist the *mekhalā* (girdle) made of a triple cord. It was from the mantle and girdle that the sacred thread (see below) of the twice-born evolved. In earlier days the student appeared before the guru for the first time already dressed thus;

(8) the guru gives the neophyte a *daṇḍa* or staff, symbolizing the beginning of his long journey to perfection; (9) in the *añjali-pūraṇa*, 'palm-filling', the guru fills his cupped hands with water and empties them into the cupped hands of his pupil, and thereafter touches the boy's breast over his heart, intoning mantras throughout; (10) the *aśmārohaṇa* or 'stone-mounting' now follows; the guru commands the student to mount a stone and enjoins him, 'Like this stone be steadfast and firm'; (11) this is followed by the rite of *dadhi-prāśana*, 'curd-eating', in which the pupil is given some curds to eat, as a sign that he should clear his mind and ingest what is going to be taught to him; (12) in the *āditya-darśana*, 'sun-showing', the pupil is shown the sun and it is explained to him that the light of the sun should be his ideal in his quest for knowledge; (13) then comes the *sāvitrī-vrata*, or the rules governing the Sāvitrī (i.e. Gāyatrī) mantra, which is the climax of the upanayana ceremony. Only after this is the student formally taken in charge and accepted as a member of the twice-born. The mantra is first recited by the guru *pāda* by *pāda*, and the chela repeats it after him in like manner hemistich by hemistich, and finally the whole verse is recited and repeated. In mediaeval times the mantra was recited in different metres for different castes; (14) the *samidh-ādāna*, 'firewood receiving', consists of the placing of a piece of sacrificial wood by the pupil into the fire with the mantra, 'May fire put intelligence into me, progeny into me, and lustre into me'. This part of the ceremony symbolized the student's right to tend the sacrificial fire and take an active part in religious rites from now on; (15) the ceremony concludes with the rite of *agni-pradakshiṇa* 'fire-circumambulation' when the student walks around the sacred fire. He then goes to the assembled guests asking for alms, indicating that he is now a student and that his religious education has begun.

Today the most important part of the upanayana is the *yajñopavīta*, 'ceremony of the thread', i.e. the donning of the sacred thread for the first time, and the idea of religious instruction is now almost completely divorced from the ceremony. The thread is a relic of the upper garment and the girdle that used to be given to the pupil by his master in ancient days; it was unknown to the early writers on ritual. The thread is spun by a virgin girl and is made up of not less than three strands; it has as many knots as there are *pravara* (exalted ones) among the pupil's ancestors. The three strands are variously interpreted as standing for the three Vedas, for purity in thought, word and deed, and so on. The type of thread used depends on the caste* of the pupil. Sometimes it is made of *muñja* grass and is referred to as *mauñji*, but it is more commonly made of cotton, and called *upavīta* or *tantu*.

Immediately after the sacred thread is worn the student enacts a mimic performance symbolizing his journey to Banāras or Kashmīr for religious education, and his return or *samāvartana* (which in the past was actually another ceremony taking place many years later) all on the same day. In other words, in its present development the educational sense of the upanayana has altogether ceased and it has now become, in the words of one Hindu authority, 'a ceremonial farce which is performed some time before the marriage of a twice-born'. In this case it is called *janeo*, and is commonly performed by many sādhus and sectarian Hindus as part of a ceremony of initiation into their order.

The sacred thread is usually worn over the left shoulder, going diagonally across the breast, and under the right arm to the right hip. It is worn as a garland around the neck when making the water offering to saints; and during the performance of the *śrāddha* rites it is shifted to the right shoulder. The thread is often taken off completely when an action prohibited by caste rules is performed, for example, when liquor is being drunk.

Those who have received the sacred thread renew it after performing certain ceremonies on the Śrāvaṇa full moon. The old cord is cast into the sacrificial fire, and a new cord put on.

Books

See under Sacraments.

THUG (Hindi, *ṭhag*, from Sanskrit *sthag*, 'conceal'), a member of a secret fraternity of assassins whose origin and rites have been the subject of much fanciful speculation. They were worshippers of Bhavānī, a form of the goddess Kālī*, and they offered human sacrifices to her by strangling victims in her honour.

The thugs are first mentioned in the twelfth century, but they certainly had a much earlier origin. The seventh-century Chinese traveller Hiuen-Tsang gives a contemporary account of hereditary bandits who robbed their victims and murdered them as a religious duty, and it seems that even in his day the caste was many centuries old.

According to their traditions the goddess Bhavānī herself instituted the cult in ancient times by assembling her votaries and teaching them on a clay dummy the secret art of throttling with a cord. Some authorities have stated that strangulation was the only method used by the thugs, in order to avoid the spilling of blood, but evidence shows that poisoning (the toxin of the *dhatūrā* or thorn apple being favoured), drowning, or burning alive, were sometimes resorted to. Women were not acceptable to the goddess, and the thugs attributed their later downfall to the fact that some of the members angered her by offering her female victims.

The thugs flourished in Uttar Pradesh and Central India, their chief place of pilgrimage being the ancient Kālī temple of Mirzāpur near Banāras. To a lesser extent they also operated in the Deccan where they had many secret tabernacles. A thug confessed to Meadows Taylor, who studied their cult, that the mysteries of his order, the marking down of the victim, the methods of strangling, and the rite of burying the body in a hidden grave, were all depicted on the walls of the Ellorā* caves for those who had eyes to see.

There were several degrees in the society. A period of fasting and worship and the taking of sacred vows, was followed by the ceremonial presentation of a pickaxe as a token of initiation. This implement was regarded with great veneration. On it the thugs took their most solemn oaths, and by means of it they practised divination, reading the omens of life or death, failure or success, before an enterprise, and many curious legends are related about the sacred pickaxe of the thugs. The probationary period was devoted to acquiring the art of making a wise selection of victims, of luring them to a convenient spot where they might be safely dispatched by the thug assassin, and the digging of graves for the murdered men. Having successfully accomplished these assignments the thug was admitted to the last grade, and given a noose washed in holy water and anointed with oil.

The intended victim was always taken unawares from behind. He was garrotted by a quick jerk of the noose or scarf and then released, and the goddess invited in a quick invocatory whisper to witness the scene; another jerk and another invocation to the goddess; and finally the slow strangulation till death. This was supposed to give the goddess time to come and relish the agony of the sufferer. The thugs never lacked victims in India, for every festival, fair or pilgrimage provided them with material in plenty for their cruel devotions.

Although a Hindu goddess, Bhavānī later had many devotees among the Muhammadans, especially around Delhi, who formed organizations of their own. Often thugs, both Hindu and Muhammadan, held responsible posts in villages and towns, and were in a splendid position to mark down prospective candidates for the noose, and let their fellow members know by a nod or sign which victim was endowed with money, for robbery was one of the more practical objectives of thuggee.

The English authorities first took notice of the thugs in 1799, and later Lord Bentinck set up a special department to deal with them. Extremely drastic measures, amounting almost to war were started in 1831. The large gangs were suppressed in about four years and the lesser gangs by 1861, although stray desperadoes continued to operate for some time thereafter. The last known thug was hanged in a Panjāb jail in 1882.

Books

I. Pike, D. W. *Secret Societies*, London, 1939.
II. Sleeman, W. *Rambles and Recollections of an Indian Official*, 1836.
III. Sleeman, W. *Diaries in Oudh*, 1839.
IV. Somerville, A. *Crime and Religious Belief in India*, Calcutta, 1931.
V. Taylor, Meadows, *Confessions of a Thug*, 1870.
VI. Wightman, A. J. *No Friend of Travellers: the Origin of the Thugs*, London, 1959.

TIME, or *kāla* in Hindu philosophy is the power that limits the existence of eternal elements in matter. In the mundane world it is the category* that distinguishes 'then' form 'now', and gives the appearance of succession to all events. Very early in the history of Buddhist speculation the concept of time came to be regarded as inherent in *māyā*, and the perception of change and the idea of past, present, and future, were held to be illusions which could only be resolved in *nirvāṇa*.

To the adherents of the belief in illusive time, no less than to those to whom time was an integrative category inherent in all being, every activity and movement had a time relationship. As popularly comprehended time was the lengthening of a metaphysical 'timeless moment' in which both the devoid-of-time state of nirvāṇa as well as the full revolution of Brahmā's time could be resolved. All things are conditioned by time and in esoteric practice the observance of the calendar, in relation to the doing of things, and the expectation of their being duly done at times appointed, was a precondition of their efficacy. Timeliness was all.

Time is considered in three ranges. The first is cosmic or epochal time determined in terms of the life span of Brahmā. The Hindu notion of this range of time (*see* aeon), as well as the idea of recurrent cataclysms, seems to have come from the Chaldeans and was probably borrowed from them. The second range is calendar* time, measured in units of days and months used in determining the seasons, historical eras and dynasties. The last is horological time for measuring the duration of the day and is determined by lesser units.

Each unit of time in all three ranges is believed to have two wings and to be made up of a 'day-and-night' separated by twilight periods. A unit is therefore made up of dawn (*saṁdhyā*), day, twilight (*saṁdhyāṁśa*), and night. Even the infinitesimally fractional truṭi (see below) is made up of these intervals.

It is to be remembered that there was no fixed standard of time measurement, since the criterion of the 'motion' of time, as it were, was believed to differ with the seasons, and with individuals, depending on circumstances. A moment experienced by one person was not necessarily as long as the moment of another. In the case of instrumental measurement, this presented no uniformity either, as the instruments were not standardized till comparatively late. Present-day equivalents of ancient Hindu time units given below are rationalized and approximate.

The *truṭi*, 'particle' or atom of time, was the smallest unit of duration; it is a theoretical unit found in astronomical treatises; in modern terms it ranges anywhere between one ten thousand millionth of a second, to one kshaṇa; some computations extend it to over a second. The *kshaṇa*, 'moment', loosely ranging from 2/45ths of a second to about 4 seconds. It is the unit of physical change and represents the time occupied by any single antecedent step in a causal series before the subsequent step begins. It is the smallest unit of time taken for any 'leap' of nature, for the rearrangement of particles, for change in direction or speed, or for a shift from one phase to the next in a natural event. The *nimesha* (or *nimisha*), 'blink' or the twinkling of an eye; strictly the time taken for the upward or downward movement of the eyelid in the act of blinking. It is equal to four kshaṇas. The *lava*, 'fraction', is the duration of a completed blink i.e. the time taken to shut and open the eyes in the act of blinking; it equals 8 kshaṇas. The *vipala*, 'fleeting', is the duration of four and a half nimeshas or about $2\frac{1}{2}$ complete blinks.

The *tāla*, 'handclap', is the time taken to bring the hands together in the act of clapping. It ranges from $\frac{1}{4}$ second to $\frac{3}{4}$ second. It is an extremely elastic unit and Bharata, the writer on music and drama, recognized no less than 22 tālas or musical beats. The *aṇu-druta*, 'fractional druta' (see below), is equal to $1\frac{1}{4}$ vipalas, or $\frac{1}{2}$ second; it is sometimes identified with the tāla. The *druta*, 'swift' is the duration of two aṇu-drutas. It is described as the time taken for a hand clap followed by a sideward movement of the right hand; it lasts one second. The *kāshṭhā*, 'piece' is the duration of a pulse-beat, said to equal one and three-fifths of a druta, 4 vipalas, or 18 nimeshas. The *laghu*, 'light', is the duration of a handclap and two or more finger counts. (A finger count consists of the thumb touching the tips of the fingers in turn.) It equals 2 drutas, 1¼ kāshṭhās, or about 2 seconds.

The *mātrā*, 'measure', an elastic unit very commonly used, ranges between the time taken to pronounce a short vowel (*see* prosody), to the time taken to stroke the knee three times with a circular motion and then snap the fingers once. The mātrā is equal to 2 laghus and may last about four seconds. It is sometimes called a *guru*, 'great'. Besides being a time measure in music, the mātrā is also used in prāṇayāma and other occult exercises. The *pala* is equal to 15 kāshṭhās, 60 vipalas, or roughly about 24 seconds; while the *kalā* is equal to about 2 palas or 30 kāshṭhās i.e. about 48 seconds. In another reckoning it ranges from 8 seconds to 2 minutes. The *ghaṭikā*, so named from the ghaṭa or water-bowl, a sort of clepsydra which had a hole pierced in it and was placed in water; the time it took to sink was a ghaṭīkā. It was also called a *nālika*. The ghaṭīkā equals 30 kalās or 60 palas i.e. 1,440 seconds or 24 minutes. The *muhūrta* (or muhurtta) is equal to 2 ghaṭīkās or 2,880 seconds or 48 minutes, i.e. 1/30th of a day. The influence of any given planet is said to be at its highest for one muhūrta.

The *saṁgava* ranges from 3 muhūrtas (about 2½ hours) to 10 nālikas (4 hours). It is so named from one of the Vedic divisions of the day; it was the time when the cows were rounded up for milking. The *prahara*, 'striking' of a gong, also called the *yāma*. Watches were generally kept for the length of a yāma; it is equal to 3¾ muhūrta or 3 hours. The *kāla*, used in the sense of appointed time or due season, also applied to the meal-time, of which there are two a day. It is between 6 to 8 hours. The *divasa* (solar day) or *nakta* (night) is equal to 4 praharas, 15 muhūrtas, 30 ghaṭīkās, or 12 hours (*see* calendar). The *ahorātra*, 'day-and-night' is equal to 8 praharas, 30 muhūrtas, 60 ghaṭīkās, or 24 hours. Fifteen ahorātras make a *paksha* or 15 days.

Books

I. Callahan, J. F. *Four Views of Time in Ancient Philosophy*, Cambridge, Mass., 1948.
II. Schayer, S. *Contributions to the Problem of Time in Indian Philosophy*, Cracow, 1938.
III. Wallace, K. *Time in Hindu Philosophy*, 1931.
IV. Zimmer, H. 'Some Aspects of Time in Indian Art'. *Journal of the Indian Society of Oriental Art*, I, 1933.

TĪRATH, RĀM (1873–1906). Tīrath Rām, Swāmi Rām, or Rām Tīrath as he was variously known, was a precocious poet-saint of poor Panjābi parentage, who married when quite young and had one child. At the age of twenty he was appointed Professor of Mathematics at the Forman Christian College where he had earlier received his own education. In 1898 he started an Urdu journal and wrote numerous poems and articles for the press. Two years later he decided to become a *fakir* or mendicant and retired for three years to the Himālayas where he was greatly affected by the beauty of his environment, feeling in all things the presence of God. 'The clouds dissolve but leave a permanent message. They are only postmen. Miss not the Lord's love letter they have brought you'. Later he travelled to Japan and America and lectured extensively on 'Practical Vedānta', and the means of finding in the things around a mirror in which to see God.

An attractive and cheerful personality, he had an unbounded sympathy for all religions with which he came into contact. He was deeply interested in the Bible and claimed to have been baptized with the Holy Ghost (I, p. 73). He showed an appreciation of Islam and Sikhism, and his ideas took on a progressively mystical content. He felt a growing consciousness of himself and others as divine. He used to address his audience in such ways as, 'The Infinite One in the form of Ladies and Gentlemen'. In answer to religious queries he would often 'just laugh and laugh for minutes together' and say nothing at all.

His increasing generosity towards other faiths, and his refusal to accept the pretentions of Hindu superiority aroused the animosity of many of his brethren. They taunted him with his ignorance of Sanskrit and lack of comprehension of the deeper meanings underlying Hindu philosophy. His interpretation of Vedānta continued to be personal and poetic rather than philosophical. Of any good thing, beautiful scene, virtuous action, he would exclaim, 'Ah, this is Vedānta'. But he was getting more and more depressed by the relentless antagonism of his opponents, the 'slaves and knaves, the hypocrites and humbugs' as he called them, who wore the ochre robe and the sacred thread. At the age of thirty-three he died by drowning, and no one knows whether by accident or indifference, or with intent.

Books

I. Griswold, H. D. *Insights into Modern Hinduism*, New York, 1934.
II. Singh, Pritam. *Saints and Sages of India*, New Delhi, 1948.
III. Singh, Puran. *The Story of Swami Ram Tirath, the Poet-Monk of the Panjab*, Madras, 1924.
IV. Tirath, Swami Ram. *In the Woods of God Realisation*, 3 vols, Lucknow, 1930–31.

TĪRTHAṄKARA, 'ford-finder', the title of Jain patriarchs of the highest order, so called because they show men the passage through the dark waters of life. They are also known as *jina*, 'conqueror', because they have overcome evil, solved the problems of this world, and attained perfect knowledge, comprehending all things, unlimited by time, space and object. The Jain* religion is named after this appellation of the victorious tīrthaṅkaras.

There are said to be twenty-four tīrthaṅkaras of the present cycle, all of them kshattriyas. Each had a slightly shorter life than his predecessor; each was shorter in stature than the last. The mother of each tīrthaṅkara had a series of fourteen dreams at the beginning of her pregnancy, and every child was born with portents and celestial signs. Most of the tīrthaṅkaras, through long penances, became mere collections of bones and sinews, and underwent during their spiritual travail all the experiences of the three worlds.

Practically nothing is known for certain about the early tīrthaṅkaras, and only glimpses of truth are discernible in the stories of the twenty-second and twenty-third, while the last is a historical personage. Most of them are known only by their names and symbols. They are: (1) Ṛishabha* and his symbol, the bull; (2) Ajita, and the elephant; (3) Śambhava and the horse; (4) Abhinandana, the ape; (5) Sumati, heron; (6) Padmaprabha, red lotus; (7) Supārśva, swastika; (8) Chandraprahba, moon; (9) Suvidhi, dolphin; (10) Śītala, the śrīvatsa sign on the breast; (11) Śreyāṁsa, rhinoceros; (12) Vāsupūjya, buffalo; (13) Vimala, hog; (14) Ananta, hawk or porcupine; (15) Dharma, thunderbolt; (16) Śānti, antelope. Śānti was the king of Hastināpura, and reputedly ruled over the whole of India; (17) Kunthu, goat; (18) Ara, the *nandyāvarta* diagram, or a fish; (19) Malli, jar, or the colour blue. In some accounts Mallī is a beautiful princess, the daughter of the ruler of Mithilā who refused to marry and devoted her life to meditation; (20) Suvrata, tortoise; colour, black; (21) Nami, blue lotus; colour, golden; (22) Arishṭanemi or Nemi, the conch, or battle-trumpet. He was the cousin of Kṛishṇa (*see* Śūra); (23) Pārśva*, hooded serpent; colour, blue; (24) *Mahāvīra**, lion; colour, golden. A historical figure, mentioned in Buddhist records.

Books

I. Jacobi, Hermann. 'On Mahavira and His Predecessors'. *Indian Antiquary*, Bombay, IX, 1880, 158–83.
II. Jain, C. *The Tirthankaras of the Jain Religion*, 1928.

TIRUVAḶḶUVAR (*c.* AD 300–400) author of the first great poetical work in the Tamil language, was probably an outcaste, being either a pariah or a *vellāla* cultivator of the fifth caste. In some accounts he is referred to as a low-caste weaver, while in others, the brāhmins, in order to claim some share in his work, say he was the child of a brāhmin father and a pariah woman. Little more is known of him except that he was a man of wide sympathies, whose intimate friends included a sea-captain, an expatriate prince, a brāhmin mendicant, and several outcaste men and women.

Tiruvaḷḷuvar was the author of the *Kuṛaḷ*, consisting of 1330 short (*kuṛu*) couplets treating of virtue, wealth and pleasure. Its high ethical content, the nobility of its thought, the universality of its doctrines, and the fact that it is entirely unfettered by caste prejudices or sectarian bias, has earned for it a universal acclaim. The *Kuṛaḷ* has been translated into all the major languages of India, and all sects, Vaishṇavite, Śaivite and Jain, claim it as their own. Parts of the work are Jain in tone, but most of it is an eclectic exposition of bhakti or devotional faith. Its great strength lies in its moral precepts, which are remarkably Christian in spirit and which, it has been said, 'bear a striking resemblance to the Sermon on the Mount'. European critics have drawn attention to the fact that Tiruvaḷḷuvar lived at St Thomé or Mylāpur (now a suburb of Madrās), where a Christian community had existed from the early centuries of the Christian era, and where Christian influences had long been at work. Says Dr G. U. Pope, 'I cannot feel any hesitation in saying that the Christian scriptures were among the sources from which the poet derived his inspiration'.

The *Kuṛaḷ* is the object of almost divine veneration in the Tamil country; its precepts are as binding as the Ten Commandments on the Jews, and oaths are taken on it in courts of law in some parts of South India. It is called 'the Veda of the Tamils', revered as the greatest of their literary treasures, and its language is held up as a criterion of literary excellence. The *Kuṛaḷ* may be said to have left as important an impress on the language and thought of the Tamil people as Dante's great work on Italy.

Books

I. Chakravarti, A. *Introduction to Tirukural*, Madras, 1953.
II. Dikshitar, V. R. R. (Ed. & Tr.) *Tirukural*, Adyar, 1949.
III. Ellis, F. W. (Ed.) *The Sacred Kural*, 1818.
IV. Popley, H. A. (Tr. & Ed.) *The Sacred Kural*, Calcutta, 1931.
V. Rajagopalachari, C. *Kural—The Great Book of Tiruvalluvar*, Madras, 1956.

TODA, a polyandrous tribe, now numbering about one thousand herdsmen of the Nilgiri Hills in South India. They live in hive-like mud and wicker huts, sometimes half buried in the earth, the only entrance being through a very low door near the ground. The ribs forming the walls and roof of the hut meet from either side and thus produce a series of arches.

The Todas have very abundant hair and physically resemble the Nambūdri brāhmins. They may represent the remnant of an ancient Aryan migration pre-dating the one that finally settled the Aryans in northern India. They later came to be listed with the outcaste Pañchamas, and the language now spoken by them is classed as an 'uncultivated' Dravidian tongue.

The Todas are a purely pastoral people. Their economy revolves around the buffalo, of which there are two kinds, both belonging to the same breed. The ordinary buffaloes are tended by the common tribes-people, while the sacred buffaloes are kept in a separate enclosure and tended by a special patriarchal class of priests, whose chief prayers are supplications to the gods to protect the sacred animals committed to their charge. The function of the priest is almost that of a dairyman; there are elaborate rituals connected with the care and milking of the sacred beasts, and many taboos surround both priests and buffaloes. Buffalo flesh is only eaten during a sacramental meal when a bull is ritually slain. The Toda deities are distinctly anthropomorphic and live lives very much like the Todas themselves and have their own dairies and buffaloes.

The Todas practice polyandry. Besides her husband a Toda woman may have permanent relations with other men with the permission of her husband. In addition to this she may on certain occasions entertain yet others, without incurring the displeasure of society. Among the candidates for the Toda hell are those 'jealous and grudging people' who disapprove of their wives consorting with others at such times (I, p. 426).

Books

I. Bhattacharya, H. (Ed.) *The Cultural Heritage of India*, Vol. IV, Calcutta, 1956.
II. Rivers, W. H. R. *The Todas*, London, 1906.

TOWNS. Archaeological discoveries in Mohenjodaro, Harappā and other sites, indicate that the people of the **Indus Valley** were acquainted with the amenities of an urban existence from at least 2000 BC. There is evidence of well-planned cities, with broad roads, and many-storied buildings of burnt brick. Their civilization was comparable to that of other contemporary civilizations in Mesopotamia.

That this highly organized society was not confined to the north is borne out by evidence from the *Ṛig-veda,* which gives the names of the ancient Anārya* kingdoms, their chief towns and their rulers. The pre-Aryans, we learn, had strongly fortified foundations, cities 'with a hundred gates', and armed forces with a thousand chariots. Legends about Rāvaṇa and his wonderful capital at Laṅkā (Ceylon), and about Hiraṇyāksha and his successors, reveal the awe in which the essentially pastoral Aryans held them and their sophisticated civilization.

The early **Vedic** Aryans do not appear to have had any idea of town-building, and seemingly acquired the art from their native predecessors. By the early Epic period a number of important towns had sprung into existence. Some are described in the Epics themselves, of which traditions are also preserved in the Purāṇas, and a number are mentioned in Buddhist and Jain records.

Descriptions of **Epic** towns as given in the *Mahābhārata* and *Rāmāyaṇa* are lavish with eulogistic accounts of prosperity, pleasure and piety. Here is a summary of an account of Ayodhyā, capital of Kośala, taken mainly from the *Rāmāyaṇa.*

'Of unequalled splendour is the sacred city, embellished with marble palaces, whose domes resemble the tops of mountains, adorned with banners and high arched porticoes, beautified with stone temples and sacred tanks, graced with charming buildings and spacious gardens. It is guarded by brave heroes who ride on elephants, chariots and horses. The halls are filled with dancing girls and musicians who intoxicate the air with their notes. The bazaars are crowded with merchants from all corners of the kingdom. The city is laid out in several quarters, the large houses with gardens for the three castes, small squalid huts for the śūdras in keeping with their servile birth, while outside the town, like the dens of unclean animals, are the dwellings of the outcastes.

'The precious city is sanctified by the presence of thousands of brāhmins and sages, in power equal to the gods, whom it is an honour to feed with śāli rice, whose presence is perfumed with natural incense, and around whose sacred necks are garlands of scented flowers. Thus the holy city of Kośala echoes to the twang of the bow, the thunder of war-chariots, the music of the flute, tabor and harp, and the songs of the moon-bosomed dancers, while from the *agrahāras* (the quarters reserved for brāhmins) proceed the sounds of the holy ones reading and teaching the Vedas, śāstras, logic, poetry, stories, rules for sacrifice, precepts for kings, and the holy science of yoga which makes them immortal'.

It has been suggested, although with little justification, that much of this account is post-Mauryan and may be a reminiscence of the cities of Achaemenian Iran, or the poleis of the Hellenistic empires of Asia. The scanty archaeological remains that survive of the Epic cities would indicate that they were much more modest foundations than the descriptions suggest. The typical town of those days was encircled by a wall and moat. Its central feature was the *basadi* or shrine of the patron deity, which was surrounded by a collection of mud huts. Here the hierophants dwelt, here the vendors sold their flowers and foodstuffs, here the temple girls plied their trade. The whole area was virtually a slum. The modern word *basti* or slum is in fact derived from the old word for the shrine precincts.

It is noteworthy that many towns were built upon more ancient foundations established by the fire-worshipping and sun-worshipping Magas or other immigrant foreign tribes. A brief list of some of the Epic towns is given here. Ahichhatra, in the Bareilly District, originally Ahikshetra, or the field or place of the Ābhīra* tribe, later the capital of the Northern Pañchālas. Ayodhyā*, capital of Kośala and of the Solar kings of whom the most eminent was Rāma. It was a few miles from modern Fyzābād, near Lucknow. Champā, capital of Aṅga one of the ancient Bāleya* kingdoms north-west of Bengal. Hastināpura, near an old bed of the Ganges about sixty miles north-east of Delhi, was founded by a descendant of Bharata*; it later became the Kaurava capital. Indraprastha, on the Jamnā, the capital of Yudhishṭhira and the Pāṇḍavas. Kāmpilya, capital of Drupada* the South Pañchāla king. Kanyākubja (or Kanauj*) founded by Amāvasu son of Purūravas. Kapilavastu, capital of the Śākya state, and birthplace of Buddha*. Karṇāl, named after its founder Karṇa* of *Mahābhārata* fame. Kāśī (Banāras*), one of the most sacred cities of the Hindus. The king of Kāśī joined the Pāṇḍava side in their war against the Kauravas. Kauśāmbī, near Allāhābād; in Buddha's time ruled by the Vatsa king Udayana*. Its ruins were described by Hiuen-Tsang. Kusinagara, in the district of modern Gorakhpur, where Buddha*died. Mithilā, capital of Videha, the kingdom of the philosopher king Janaka*. Prayāga, modern Allāhābād*, situated at the confluence of the Ganges, Jamnā and the subterranean Sarasvatī. Pushkalāvatī, near present-day Peshāwar, was the capital of the ancient country of Gandhāra*. Rājagṛiha, capital of ancient Magadha* before Pāṭaliputra. Sānchī, site of a famous stūpa*, was situated on the great trade route midway between Pāṭaliputra and Barygaza. Śākala, capital of the ancient Madra* tribe and later of Menander the Bactrian Greek king. Sāketa, near Ayodhyā, was the capital of Kośala after Ayodhyā had been abandoned. It was beseiged by the Bactrian* Greeks. Śrāvastī, modern Saheth Maheth near Fyzābād in Oudh, founded by a descendant of Purañjaya* and ruled in the Epic period by Lava son of Rāma. It was the site of the Jetavana grove (*see* Buddha). Śuktimatī, capital of the Chedi kingdom of Śiśupāla*. Taxila, capital of Gandhāra* and one of the most renowned cities of ancient north-west India. Viraṭā*, capital of the Matsya kingdom, a probably Scythian foundation. Vaisālī, capital of the Lichchhavi* kingdom, founded by Manu Vaivasvata.

The **Maga** foundations are of particular interest for their history goes back many centuries before they became sacred cities of the Hindus. Very frequently Maga sites were taken over by the Buddhists before they became sacred to the Hindus. An inscription dating from the twelfth century A D found near Gaya refers to Magian or Persian priests who constructed sun temples in India, and the tradition of Magian building activity in India is indeed very old. The chief Maga centres are given below in alphabetical order.

Avanti, first called Māghas, then Māhishmatī, later Ujjain*. Dvārakā (or Dvārāvatī), originally Dizh-i-Kaiwan, 'Saturn's Fort', an ancient place of Maga worship which became Kṛishṇa's capital. The Dvārakā of the *Mahābhārata* was submerged beneath the sea and the present Dvārakā is named after it. In Śaṅkara's time it was the site of one of his monasteries. Gaya*, originally Gah-i-Kaiwan, 'Saturn's Residence', remained for many centuries a seat of Magian worship, and is still referred to by its inhabitants as Maga. Hardwār*, originally named Maya, an ancient seat of Zoroastrian worship. It is the place where the Ganges descending from the Himālayas first enters the plains. Konārak, another Maga centre of sun-worship, originally the arak, 'area' or Fortress of Saturn, now the site of the Black Pagoda* built in the form of a chariot of the sun. Mathurā*, originally Mayatar or Mahetar, one of the earliest Maga foundations, later intimately associated with Kṛishṇa's life. Modera (or Modhera) in Kāṭhiāwār, eighteen miles south of Pātan, an early Maga stronghold and site of a medieval sun-temple (*c.* 1025) built by the Solaṅkis. Multān, an old seat of the Persian solar cult, and site of a Sūrya* temple of great antiquity. Nāsik*, a place of prehistoric sanctity and meeting-place of many ancient cultures. Pāṭaliputra, first a Maga town, later the capital of the Maurya dynasty. Purī, centre of sun-worship, and the site of the famous temple of Jagannātha. Surāt, another old Maga foundation, was the capital of the Asuras or Suras. Its older name, Sūryapura, or sun-city, indicates its Zoroastrian associations. It is mentioned in the *Mahābhārata* and the Periplus. It was renamed by the Muslims after the Koranic 'sura' or chapter. When the tide of Islam dislodged the Zoroastrians of Persia, those who fled by sea took refuge in the same region bringing their sacred fires with them. Sanjān where the persecuted Parsees, as they became known, landed from Persia; Udvada, which contains the oldest Parsee sacred fire in India; Navsari where the Parsee priests receive their initiation and confirmation, are all in the land of the ancient Suras.

Places also became sacred through legendary association of long ago with the deeds of gods and heroes. From before the Epic period the *tri-sthalī*, 'three-places' or the three holiest towns of the Hindus were Prayāga, Kāśī and Gaya. The **Seven Sacred Cities** are variously given. The following names are most frequently cited: (1) Ayodhyā, birthplace of Rāma; (2) Mathurā, birthplace of Kṛishṇa; (3) Hardwār, the place where the Ganges descends to the plains; (4) Gaya, sacred to Vishṇu; (5) Kāśī or Banāras, city of Śiva; (6) Prayāga, where the three sacred rivers meet; and (7) Dvārakā, the capital of Kṛishṇa. To these certain South Indian towns were sometimes added, such as Kāñchi, Madura, and Rāmeśvaram. The number of sacred cities slowly grew until it came to include the twelve places where the liṅgas* of Śiva were to be found, and the fifty-two places or *pīṭhas* where the limbs of the goddess Satī* had fallen to earth.

The Persians, Greeks, Parthians, Kushāns, Śakas and other foreign invaders of the early historical periods made considerable contributions to Indian architecture, the construction of roads, and the establishing of cities. They were responsible for many civic innovations in the Mauryan empire. The town of Pāṭaliputra was built in part with the help of Perisan architects and indeed throughout the Mauryan period the Persian element predominated.

With the coming of the **Greeks** and the establishment of the Seleucid and Indo-Bactrian kingdoms, Greek influence was brought to bear on Indian town-planning, civic engineering and the construction of public buildings. It is known that small Greek colonies such as the hill state of Nysa* between the Kābul and Indus rivers, existed in India long before the invasion of Alexander the Great. A Greek colony frequently started as a garrison and grew into a full-fledged *polis*, with Greek administration and civic forms, and many Greek cities in Asia Minor and in India grew up in the same way. Several *poleis* of great importance belonging to this period were founded by the Greeks. Alexander himself founded more than one town in the north-west, and numerous others, if not actually founded by him were named in his honour.

Alexandria sub-Caucasum, near modern Charikar, thirty miles north of Kabul, was the northernmost of these cities. A little further south was *Alexandria of the Arachosians*, which survives as Kandahār, itself a corruption of Sikandar (Alexander). There was an *Alexandria Bucephala* on the Jhelum, and several Alexandrias in Sind and the Panjāb which are often confused. *Alexandria on the Indus* was established at the spot where the Akesines (the Chenāb) joins the Indus. After the overthrow of the Macedonian power in the Panjāb this town became famous as a great Graeco-Buddhist centre, and as 'Alasanda of the Yonas' is mentioned in the *Mahāvaṁsa*, the chronicle history of Ceylon. *Alexandria of the Sogdians* was situated in northern Sind, and yet another Alexandria on the Indus survived as *Iomousa*, capital of southern Panjāb in Menander's time. Alexander also founded Cartana (Begram), Cadrusi (Koratas) and Nicaea on the Jhelum.

The Bactrian Greeks founded several towns of some importance in the history of India. The capital of Demetrius (190 BC) was *Euthydemia*, a new name he gave to the old Śaka* capital of Śākala in memory of his father. He also built *Demetria* in Sind, and another Demetria in Arachosia.

Among the conquests of Apollodotus (175 BC) was the seaport of *Barygaza* at the mouth of the Narmadā. The original name of the place is unknown but its Sanskritized form was Bhṛigukachchha (Bhṛigu's marsh), associated in legend with Paraśurāma, and today shortened to Broach. During the Greek and barbarian period it was one of the foremost trading* ports of India, linked by sea routes to the Western world: with Alexandria via the Red Sea and with Babylon via the Persian Gulf. Overland eastwards Barygaza was linked with the Gangetic trading centres, being the terminus of the main caravan road from Pāṭaliputra through Bhārhut, Sānchī, and Ujjain*. To the inland city of Ujjain the port was what Piraeus was to Athens. Barygaza thus linked Pāṭaliputra with the world of Greece. In the middle of the first century AD there was a large settlement of Greek traders in Barygaza which continued to prosper till well into the Śaka period. The merchant author of Periplus (AD 80) speaks of the country inland from Barygaza as full of mementoes of Greek occupation—Hellenic shrines, barracks, and great wells dug by them. Through Barygaza the current of foreign ideas reached Ujjain and this cultural contact was to a great extent responsible for the new trends in the development of Indian literature, drama and science in Ujjain.

Menander's cities in India included Peucela (Pushkalāvatī) and Dionysopolis in Gandhāra; Bucephala, Nicaea and Iomousa in the Panjāb; and Demetria and Theophilia in Sind. At least two towns were occupied by Greek garrisons, namely, Daedala, a military colony of Cretan mercenaries, which Stephanus calls an Indo-Cretan city, and Salagissa, east of the Sutlej, which was a colony of Pisidian mercenaries.

How many other foundations have been obliterated by subsequent invasions of Śaka and Parthian nomads, and their successors, one cannot say. Names were changed and in the course of time many an ancient Greek colony became Indianized and its origins forgotten. From records left by Greek Buddhists we know of the existence of Greek towns now unidentifiable. One Greek donor of a Buddhist cave near Karle proclaims himself a citizen of Dattamiti, which may have been Demetria in Patalene (or Pattala) on the Indus delta; we know that this trading depot was a centre of Greek commerce for centuries before the rise of Barygaza. Five other Greek donors to the Karle caves came from an unidentified town on the Indian coast called Dhenukaka.

It has been suggested that *Junagaḍh* in Saurāshṭra was originally Yonagarh (Greek town); if this be so, we have here an illustration of how old names underwent a process of corruption, often past all recognition.

The influx of Greek traders to the seaports of western India was facilitated by the discovery made about AD 50 by a Greek captain named Hippalus, of the existence of the monsoon wind blowing regularly across the Indian ocean. Greek traders also came from various other not too distant settlements, the best known being the island of Dioscorides (now Socotra) in the Indian Ocean (*see* Trade). This was colonized by Greek seamen and remained a Greek outpost for over seven centuries, with Greek as the only language spoken there till it fell to the Arabs in the eighth century AD.

Nor did South India escape the attention of Greek mariners and merchants. The site of Yavanapura or 'Greek Town' in South India mentioned in the *Mahābhārata* has not been satisfactorily established, but some identify it with the trading* town of Nelcynda on the Malabār coast.

Following the Greeks, the **Barbarians*** also built new cities or reclaimed the more ancient foundations that had fallen into decay. Most of the towns established by the Kushāns, Śakas and Huns were situated in the northwest, where their line of garrisons reached into India. One relic of their town-building activity survives in the affix *khand*, a Śaka or Kushān word meaning 'city', which occurs in Pāṇini as *kantha* in a geographical context. Examples are seen in such names as Samarqand, Tashkent, Khokhand, Yarkand in Central Asia, and in India in Bundelkhand, Baghelkhand, Kandesh, Khandagiri and others. Other important towns founded or revived by the barbarians were Taxila, Kandahār, Kanishkapura, Peshāwar, and Siālkoṭ. The influence of their cultures also left its mark on the city of Mathurā and the wide area between the Chambal and Sutlej.

Besides these regions, which lay in the direct path of the invaders, the ports and towns of the west coast like Broach, Dvārakā and Ujjain had always been cosmopolitan in character. Gujerāt in particular was the melting-pot of innumerable races. Says Dr Sankalia, 'The position and structure of Gujerāt are mainly responsible for its complex culture. Its seafront was the gateway from earliest times through which ideas, influences and cultures passed to and fro as a result of commercial and other intercourse' (VII, p. 4).

The **Muhammadan** period ushered in a radical change in the disposition of the important urban centres of India. The kingdoms of the Muslim rulers were spread throughout the country; they re-named ancient towns of great Hindu sanctity, and set up hundreds of new Islamic foundations, creating a new geographical nomenclature so prolific and ubiquitous today as hardly to require listing.

With the **Europeans** came another spate of new townships, scattered throughout the country. Most of these saw their beginnings as trading factories, and many nations contributed to their growth. The Portuguese with Goa in the west and San Thomé in the east; the Dutch with Pulicat, Surāt and Chinsura; the Danes with Serampore, the French with Pondicherry and Chandernagore, to name but a few. In 1640 the English set themselves up in Madrās, at that time a collection of mud huts. In 1661 Charles II received Bombay from the Portuguese as part of the dowry of Catherine of Braganza; seven years later Charles transferred it to the East India Company at an annual rental of ten pounds; it was a fishing village, infested with mosquitoes, with a feverish unhealthy climate, its wealth consisting of coconuts and salt pans. In 1690 the foundations of Calcutta on the river Hugli were laid. The founder of this city, Job Charnock is also remembered for having married a Hindu widow he had rescued from committing suicide on the funeral pyre of her husband.

The English as a rule made no attempt to change place-names, and when they founded a new site they usually named it after the nearest village, although their transliterations often disguised the original name. Their contributions to the Indian gazeteer are therefore meagre, and even where English-appearing are often not necessarily English. Abbottabad was named after Major James Abbott, the first Deputy Commissioner of the Hazara District, but Campbellpur is not to be traced to anyone named Campbell, but is the English pronunciation of the local village of Kāmilpur i.e. Perfect Place.

Books

I. Altekar, A. S. *Towns and Cities in Gujerat & Kathiawar*, 1926.
II. Briggs, H. G. *Cities of Gujarashtra*, 1849.
III. Dave, J. H. *Immortal India*, Bombay, 4 vols., 1961.
IV. Forrest, G. W. *Cities of India*, 1903.
V. Franklin, G. *The Holy Cities of India*, 1890.
VI. Lal, Kanwar. *Holy Cities of India*, Delhi, 1961.
VII. Sankalia, H. D. *The Archaeology of Gujerat*, Bombay, 1941.
VIII. Toy, S. *The Strongholds of India*, London, 1957.
IX. Tripathi, R. *The Great Towns of India*, 1910.

TRADE & SHIPPING. Information on the nature and extent of ancient Indian trade and shipping from Indian writings is scanty, and most of the data now available has been culled from research into outside sources such as the clay tablets of the Middle East, the Bible, and Greek and Roman chronicles. Buddhist and Jain records in Pāli and Sanskrit, and early Tamil works, provide some supplementary material.

The Austrics, probably the earliest seafaring aboriginals, introduced the outrigger canoe, and may have had commerce with neighbouring countries, but no definite facts are extant. Engravings on the Mohenjodaro seals indicate that vessels used by the Indus Valley people were similar to the Arab dhow of the Persian Gulf today. Artifacts found on the Indus Valley sites point to mercantile contact with Sumeria, Egypt, Crete and the adjacent countries. The reference in the *Ṛig-veda* to vessels with a hundred oars and to storm-proof boats provided with wings, is clearly to a foreign people and not to the ancient Indians. The Aśvins who possess these boats had their home in a far-off island and were ruled by a king named Tugra. The fact that the rudder, anchor, and sail are not mentioned in the Vedas has led some authorities to believe that the Vedic Indians took no part in ocean shipping.

Evidence from other sources confirms early trade between India and Egypt, Mesopotamia and Judea, this trade being carried on chiefly with ports on the west coast. It was from one of these ports that the ships of Tarshish brought Solomon his ivory, apes and peacocks. The oft-quoted *Bāveru Jātaka* referring to a period some centuries later narrates that Indian merchants exported peacocks to Bāveru (Bābiru or Babylon). The library of Assurbanipal contains ideographs for Indian cotton, and the obelisk of Shalmaneser III bears engravings of Indian monkeys and elephants.

From the *Arthaśāstra* we learn that in Mauryan times (third century BC) one of the six government Departments which was concerned with war had an official known as the Master of the Fleet, and on the mercantile side there was a Superintendent of Ships. By this time the Greeks of Alexandria were trading regularly with India. The Romans* followed immediately in the wake of the Greeks, and both have left copious records of their contacts with India. Ports are frequently named and merchandise listed.

Trade with Persia and Arabia was also extensive during the first centuries before and after the present era. The Arabs had a large share of the trade across the desert routes through Arabia, although Arab notices of India do not start till after the Islamic period. Navigation by the monsoon winds remained an Arab monopoly until the secret was discovered by the Greek navigator Hippalus in about AD 50. Thereafter, sped on by the winds mariners ventured from Arabia Eudaemon (Aden) across the heavy seas, stopping over at the island of Dioscorides (Socotra), and then proceeding straight on to Muziris in Malabār.

Chief among the Greek and Roman records is Pliny's *Natural History* (*c.* AD 75), which sheds much light on Indian mercantile activity. In about AD 80 an unknown author who had settled in Egypt made a voyage to the Indian coast and compiled a work known as the *Periplus of the Erythrean Sea* (Circumnavigation of the Indian Ocean). Written in Greek, it is a seaman's guide to the Indian Ocean with descriptions of river-mouths, ports, merchandise and trade. The astronomer Ptolemy of Alexandria in his *Geography* (*c.* AD 160) also gives much useful information about India. Dr Caldwell, the great authority on the Dravidian languages, declared that the three works, namely, Pliny's Natural History, the Periplus, and Ptolemy's Geography, contain the largest stock of aboriginal Indian words preserved in any written documents of ancient times. Some of these words, along with a small number of Sanskrit and indigenous terms for Indian commodities have passed into the vocabulary of Western commerce.

From India were exported in King Solomon's time, such merchandise as ivory (Hebrew, *shen habbin*, from Sanskrit *ibha danta*, 'elephant teeth'); apes (Heb. *qoph*, from Sk. *kapi*), and peacocks (Heb. *tukiim*, from Tamil *tokei*). To other parts of the world went rich cargoes of rice, gems and spices. Rice comes from the Greek *oryza*, ultimately from the Tamil *arisi*; cinnamon (Greek *karpios*, from Tamil *karppu*); ginger (Gk. *zingerberis*, Tam. *inchiver*); aloes (Heb. *ahalim*, Tamil *aghil*) also reached the West through Indian trade. Camphor (Latin *camphora*, from Sanskrit *karpūra*) was an important commodity, till mediaeval times purchased by Indian merchants from the eastern archipelago and exported to the West. Many strange stories are told of the mysterious Land of Camphor or the Camphor Islands in legends of the east. Pepper, 'the passion of the Yavanas' (Greek *peperi* from Tamil *pippali*) was exported from Malabār and was prized throughout Europe. When Alaric spared Rome in AD 408 he demanded and obtained as part of the ransom, three thousands pounds of pepper. Indian jewellery was in great demand, as well as perfume, dyes, tortoise-shell, sandalwood, corals and pearls and other gems. The beryl (Greek *beryllos*, Sanskrit *vaidūrya*), especially the beryl of Padiyur in Coimbatore and of Vaniyambadin in the Salem district were in special demand. Muslins and textiles* were also popular, as well as silks, much of the latter coming by way of China. Tiberius issued an order forbidding the use of transparent silk as indecent.

For her part India imported tin, lead, wine and slave girls, but this far from balanced the huge exports. Pliny complained of the annual drain of gold to India and the East to pay for all these oriental luxuries.

The major Indian ports during this period were mainly on the west coast, with a few on the east coast, and several figured in Greek and Roman records. *Barbarike*, near modern Karāchi, the city of the Barbara. *Pattala* (or Patalene), further inland, at the apex of the Indus delta. *Barygaza* (or Broach), at the mouth of the Narmadā, the principal distribution centre for western India, from where goods were carried inland; from here commodities were transported to the town of Paiṭhān, twenty days journey south of Barygaza, and from there to Tagara (?Devagiri), ten days east of Paiṭhān, to the Śaka town of Ujjain, the western marts of Sind, and the Gangetic trading areas as far east as Pāṭaliputra. *Sopāra* (or Surparaka), a little north of Bombay, sometimes identified with the Biblical Ophir (Sophir of the Septuagint), where Hiram of Tyre sent his ships for the materials required for the building of Solomon's Temple; it remained an important seaport till Roman times. Not far from it is Kānheri whose famous cave-temples may have received Western inspiration. Ophir is said to have been a town of the Ābhīra tribe. *Calliena* (or Kalyāṇa), near Bombay; many of the donors whose names are inscribed in the caves of Kānheri and Junnar were merchants of Kalyāṇa. *Musiris* (or Muziris) in the Chera country in Malabār. The route from Arabia Eudaemon (Aden) to Musiris across the Indian Ocean passed the Dioscorida Islands (Socotra) which had a considerable Graecized Indian colony. *Nelcynda*, also in Malabār, a little south of Musiris. Near by was another port called *Carura*. Nelcynda may have been the 'Yavanapura'

(Greek-town) mentioned in the *Mahābhārata*. *Kāveripaṭṭanam* (or Puhar, or Kakandi), on the east coast, at the mouth of the northern branch of the Kāverī. Yavana (Greek or Roman) carpenters helped to build the palace of the Chola king of Kāveripaṭṭanam. The city had a large foreign, Yavana, colony. *Arikamedu*, on the east coast, a Chola port, and a prosperous trading depot situated near *Pondicherry* (the Podonke of Ptolemy). In recent excavations Arikamedu proved to be a treasure trove of Roman goods such as glassware, amphorae, and red-glazed Arretine pottery. *Masalia* (or Maisolia), modern Masulipatam, on the east coast, on the estuary of the Kistna, whose muslins were so highly prized by the ladies of Rome that, as the story has it, an ounce of muslin used to sell in Rome for an ounce of gold. Roman gold coins have been found on the site.

Information on trade during the period immediately following the Romans is obtained from several Christian writers who visited the country and left descriptions of the coastal ports and inland towns in which their co-religionists lived. Most notable among them was Cosmas Indicopleustes (*c.* 522). Much important information on the subject is likewise contained in the writings of Chinese* travellers, notably the great trio: Fa-hien (*c.* 410), Hiuen-Tsang (630), and I-tsing (*c.* 675).

This too was the period of the great overland caravan routes, intermittently used from time immemorial, which were now flourishing arteries of merchantile activity. From the trading centres of Smyrna in Asia Minor, Antioch in the Levant, and Petra at the apex of the Gulf of Aqaba, the merchandise of the western world flowed overland across Mesopotamia and Persia through the north-western regions into the heart of India, to centres like Mathurā, Ujjain and Pāṭaliputra.

Conversely, from China the westward borne trade moved along the great 'silk routes', skirting the southern wastes of the Gobi across Nan Shan and the Taklamakan desert east of the Palmirs to Tashkurgan, and then followed one of several routes into India. This international highway was closed when the Arabs defeated the Chinese in the middle of the eighth century and assumed supremacy in Central Asia. For centuries thereafter the sea routes remained the principal channels of commerce between India and the Far East.

Arab notices of India start about the ninth century. During the Baghdad Caliphate the port of Basra at the head of the Persian Gulf was founded mainly for trade with India, and we hear of the fabulous Sea of Lār which washes the coasts of India from Gujarāt to Malabār, and of the exotic merchandise from Hindustān being carried to Iraq, Syria, Rum and Egypt. The Voyages of Sindbad the Sailor belong to this epoch, and relate his adventures in the mysterious continent.

Trade with the regions of Hinterindia*, namely Burma, Siam, Cambodia, Malaya, Java, Sumatra and Borneo, resulted in a prolific cultural intercourse which lasted for several centuries, from about the second to the twelfth centuries AD, and left a permanent impress of the Hindu and Buddhist religions on these areas.

Much of the early merchandise shipped to these countries was transported in foreign bottoms, but there is no doubt that the Indian nations possessed ships of their own, although very few details can be gleaned concerning them and Indian nautical techniques in general. Hindu and Buddhist works refer to sea voyages in vessels of one hundred oars, carrying a thousand persons, but this is taken to be an exaggeration. Pliny, who obtained accurate measurements, left no record of an Indian ship of over seventy-five tons. Fa-hien travelled from Ceylon to Java in a vessel carrying only two hundred passengers.

The Chinese travellers who visited India between the fifth and seventh centuries spoke of cargo-bearing junks or tall unsteady vessels of two to three tiers, into which one clambered by means of long ladders. All the boats had outriggers and up to three masts. They were steered by large oars, the rudder being unknown. Pliny in his account of Taprobane (Ceylon) describes the mariners of that country employing a device that must have been used by Indians as well, and to which a reference is also found in the Sutta Piṭaka. They would take birds out to sea with them, which they would let loose from time to time, and follow the direction of their flight as the birds made for land. Medieval writers speak of another device, an ancient Chinese invention, known in India as the *machchha-yantra*, 'fish-instrument', a primitive mariner's compass, consisting of a magnetized flat iron fish floating in a vessel of oil.

Except for the Cholas, who established great overseas colonies, no Indian kings possessed a navy, or had any conception of the importance of the sea for defence. Vijayanagar had a number of ports, but the fleet was used for coastal trade, and all foreign goods were brought in foreign ships. A few texts were written on the subject of shipping, but they were generally fanciful and shed little light on the subject. Treatises of this period mention the different kinds of wood used in ship-building. Four main kinds are distinguished, named after the four castes, and there are details as to the length, breadth, and height of ships, the type and number of masts; the decorative carvings and the colours to be used for them; the auspicious diagrams to be drawn on the prow; the construction of the prow itself with the carved head of a lion, buffalo, snake, elephant, bird, garuḍa, or man.

The first European notices speak in high terms of Indian vessels and of the men who man them. Speaking of the Indian ships seen by him, Nicolo Conti (*c.* 1440) says, 'The natives of India build some ships larger than ours, with five sails and as many masts. Some are so built in compartments that should one part be shattered, the other portion remaining entire may accomplish the voyage.'

It is quite likely that Vasco da Gama in 1498 used Indian sailors to help him complete his journey from East Africa, for in East Africa he found Indian seamen who could navigate by the stars and had nautical instruments of their own. A sixteenth century miscellany called the *Yukti Kalpataru*, 'Magical Wishing-Tree', compiled by one Bhoja, treating of the subject of elephants, horses, swords, jewels, ornaments, flags, and other assorted themes, also treats fancifully and didactically of ships and their utility, but little useful information can be gained from it.

The Moghul fleets were small and used largely for coastal defence. Those of the Marāṭhas were efficient but used primarily for piracy on the Koṅkaṇ coast. No overseas trade by their vessels is recorded. By the seventeenth century European ships were bringing and taking commodities across the world, and whatever impetus might have been given at the time to indigenous effort in this direction was largely stifled. In the sphere of ship-building, which was carried out on a limited scale, two names stand out: the Parsee shipbuilder Lowjee Nassaranji of Surāt, whose work received both European and Indian patronage, and the Eurasian James Kyd (after whom the Kidderpore docks of Calcutta are named), who for nearly thirty years constructed and repaired the East India Company's vessels.

Books

I. Basham, A. L. 'Notes on Seafaring in Ancient India.' *Art and Letters*, London, XXIII, pp. 60 ff., 1949.

II. McCrindle, J. W. *The Commerce and Navigation of the Erythrean Sea*, Calcutta, 1879.

III. Mookerjee, R. K. *History of Indian Shipping and Maritime Activity*, London, 1912.

IV. Phipps, J. *Papers Relating to Shipping in India*, Calcutta, 1840.

V. Rawlinson, H. G. *Intercourse Between India and the Western World*, Cambridge, 1916.

VI. Rogers, S. *The Indian Ocean*, 1932.

VII. Schoff, W. H. (Tr.) *The Periplus of the Erythrean Sea*, London, 1912.

VIII. Vincent, D. *The Commerce of the Ancients in the Indian Ocean*, London, 1807, 2 vols.

IX. Warmington, E. H. *Commerce Between the Roman Empire and India*, Cambridge, 1928.

X. Wheeler, R. E. M. 'Arikamedu: an Indo-Roman Trading Station.' *Ancient India*, Delhi, II, 1946.

TRANCE STATES. The nearest Sanskrit equivalent for the term trance is *śamana*, 'pacification', a state of mental quietude in which the agitations of the spirit are stilled, the stresses of existence neutralized, and equanimity attained. It is regarded as the 'highest step' (*parama-pada*) in one's development, and is the experience of final beatitude and bliss in which one is 'free from death' (*vimṛityu*). The term has a wide connotation and embraces all mental, psychical and spiritual states achieved by purposive effort to bring to an end the feverish condition of *mohana*, 'infatuation', resulting from involvement with things material (*see* māyā).

In śamana the yogi becomes one with the spirit of the universe, when all trace of mental activity and of self is destroyed, and only the object of one's contemplation remains. This 'extinction' of the ego-illusion, this release from the fetters of ignorance, and allaying of life's bewilderment, may come during one's lifetime as a result of meditation, leading to one of the trance-like states of *samādhi*; it may be experienced while in a condition of induced bodilessness as in *videha*; it may come to the emancipated soul only after death and final release as in *mukti*; or again, it may be a state of final absorption in God as in *sāyujya*. The chief varieties of śamana are listed below.

The state of *samādhi*, 'conjoining' is the climax of all intellectual and spiritual activity, and the last stage of yoga, and has been variously defined and named, union, absorption, conjunction, enstasis, stasis. It is said to be a state of profound, passive and absorptive contemplation of and participation in the bliss of the Absolute. It is a condition of superconsciousness and unqualified beatitude. Two broad categories of samādhi are sometimes distinguished: (i) *Savikalpa*, 'differentiated', samādhi, or the experience of the absolute in which the distinction between worshipper and worshipped is recognized and maintained; it is also spoken of as saṁprajñāta samādhi; (ii) *Nirvikalpa*, 'undifferentiated' samādhi, in which the soul merges with God and there is no distinction between devotee and deity; it is also spoken of as asaṁprajñāta samādhi.

Many other facets of samādhi are found reflected in other terms closely related in meaning. Among them are: *kaivalya*, from kevala, 'one's own', a term common to Jainism; the realization of one's own self as being identical with the highest; complete absorption in the Unity; the one who attains this state is a *kaivalin*; *apavarga*, 'turning away' or completion; the absolute deliverance which, according to Nyāya* philosophy comes from a realization that all things associated with the world and our individual selves are vehicles of pain and obstacles to the knowledge of the true reality of Brahma; apavarga is the release that follows realization; *nirvāṇa* (Pāli, nibbāna), 'extinction', a Buddhist term referring to the blowing out of the flame of self, resulting in emancipation from matter; the concept of 'extinction' has been the subject of much criticism from opponents of this idea, but Buddhists hold that the term does not imply annihilation; *śūnyatā*, 'voidness' (*see* śūnya), another Buddhist term, is the state of *nairātma*, 'non-selfness' or essencelessness or contentlessness, often confused with nirvāṇa; it is an experience of the purest truth; *turīya*, the 'fourth' of the dream* states of the soul; a condition of supernormal awareness; *nirodha*, 'restraint', a condition of ecstacy, resulting from the arrest or cessation of all states of consciousness; it is the total repression of mentation, so that the mind is without sensory or intellectual content, having no longer experience, but only revelation; Patañjali described yoga as *chitta-vṛitti-nirodha*, mental-action-control (*see* psychology); *videha*, 'bodilessness' or exteriorization*, when the soul quits the bodily frame for short or long periods.

Several trance states are achieved by means of sex-magical techniques described in tantrik and other left-hand cult books. Among them are: *unmani*, the state of abstraction from the body, achieved by practice of certain mudrās, especially the *khecharī-mudrā*; it is referred to as yoga sleep; related to it is the experience of *jyoti* or 'radiance', resulting from the awakening of the kuṇḍalinī; *yugala*, 'yoked', a form of tantrik śamana achieved during *maithuna* performed as a technique of sex* mysticism; *bindu*, 'drop', the metaphysical point, out of space and time, is the 'area' in which samādhi is experienced; the term also has a reference to semen and relates to magical practices, either auto-sexual, or hetero-sexual, and the control of certain plexuses to bring about 'eroto-comatose' samādhi; it is sometimes confused with śoshaṇa; *śoshaṇa*, 'exhaustion' as a means of spiritual lucidity is very old, very secret, and said to be extremely dangerous, resulting even in death; exhaustion may be brought about by torture, flagellation, asceticism, starvation, but particularly through sexual activity; in this case it utilizes the moment of 'exhaustive orgasm' which temporarily frees the soul, enabling it to wander about and experience visions on other occult planes; it is essential to perfect the technique lest the body in its attenuated state be unable to survive the experience.

One of the four chief ends of life, according to Hindu ethics* is *moksha*, 'deliverance', actually the final emancipation from the bondage of existence and in this sense not strictly a form of trance. Moksha is the state of deliverance after death, so that the soul returns no more to earth, having been released from the cosmic circuit of birth-death-rebirth. It is the final liberation of the soul from the body and must be distinguished from the temporary śamanas such as samādhi. The term *mukti*, 'freedom' is sometimes used as a synonym for moksha. In fact, mukti refers mainly to what is called *jīvan-mukti*, 'living release' i.e. salvation while one is alive and still here on earth. The *mukta* or one who attains jīvan-mukti does not have to wait for death to attain salvation, but has it immediately here and now. Sometimes those who attain samādhi are called muktas.

Certain states of intimate union with God are spoken of as *sāyujya*, 'co-union', or absorption in God, union with the deity or conjunction with Him, a state generally reserved for saints of the highest order. Five grades of this state are recognized: (1) *sālokya*, 'co-placed', being on the same plane with God i.e. in the heavenly abode of the deity; (2) *sāmīpya*, 'nearness' to the deity, i.e. in a place in paradise near to God; (3) *sārūpya*, 'likeness' to God, or in appearance and form like unto God; (4) *sārshṭi*, 'co-ranking' with and equalling the glory of God; (5) *sāyujya*, absorption in God, with complete loss of identity in Him.

Books

I. Bussy, A. *Trances and Ecstacies*, 1932.
II. Poussin, L. de La Vallée. *The Way to Nirvana*, Cambridge, 1917.
III. Stcherbatsky, S. T. *The Conception of Buddhist Nirvana*, Leningrad, 1927.
IV. Wilson, H. *The Way Across*, 1919.

TRAVEL. Till comparatively recent times orthodox Hindus were forbidden to travel, a prohibition that applied not only to travel beyond the borders of India, but to travel ouside their particular state or province. Thus the brāhmins of Pañchāla could not visit Vaṅga and those of Chedi could not journey to the land of Vidarbha. If they did so they were regarded as unclean until they had undergone the *prāyaśchitta* ceremony of purification.

In actual fact the social mobility of the Indian was far less restrictive than would appear from the interdictions of the lawgivers, and there is hardly anything in Indian history to warrant the belief that the Hindu remained bound to the soil of his native land. Says the *Aitareya Brāhmaṇa*, 'There is no happiness for him who does not travel. Living with the same people the best of men becomes a sinner. Indra is the friend of travellers. Therefore wander.' The ancient Indians seem to have been great travellers, although they preserved no record of their wanderings, and information is to be gleaned only from outside sources, or by inference.

The heterogeneous peoples of the Indus Valley were in touch with the ancient contemporary civilizations of Egypt and the Far East. Dravidian merchants brought home from their travels, the prehistoric legend of the

Great Deluge. To the Hebrew Kings they sold ivory, apes and peacocks; to the priests of Assyria the teak for the roofs of the temple of the Moon at Mugheir in Ur; and to Nebuchadnezzar II of Babylon, the timber for his palace at Birs Nimrud.

Indian mercenaries fought in the contingents of Darius the Great, formed the light division of the army of Xerxes, shared the defeat of Darius III at Gaugamela, and gave assistance to Alexander the Great in his fight with his enemies on the Indus. This information we obtain from Greek sources.

Berosus records that crowds of strangers, Indians among them, lived in Babylon, and according to Athenaeus, Indians took part in the processions of Ptolemy Philadelphus in Alexandria in the third century BC. From the period of the Ptolemies we have the unique inscription on the ruins of a shrine at Redeṣiye between Edfu and the ancient Berenike, recording the visit of an Indian with a name that survives as Sophon (probably Subhānu), who crossed the desert from the Red Sea to the Nile on his way to Alexandria. We have also the record of Cornelius Nepos saying that Metellus Celer received from the king of the Sueri some Indians who had been driven ashore by a storm in Germany in the course of a voyage of commerce.

Virgil tells us that Indian soldiers fought under Antony and Cleopatra at Actium, and in Pliny we find proof of India's long-established overseas trade with Rome. Dion Chrysostom who lived in the reign of Trajan mentions Indians among the cosmopolitan crowds he found in the bazaars of Alexandria, and adds that they came 'by way of trade'. A colony of Indian merchants was exterminated along with others in Alexandria during the massacre of Caracalla. Rome too, we know, had its share of Indian fortune-tellers, conjurers and prostitutes.

Eusebius preserves the story of a party of Indian philosophers who visited Athens and conversed with Socrates, for the tradition of itinerant sophists and wandering teachers was as well established in India as in Greece. It would appear that certain sects of yogis in particular have been great travellers down to recent times. As late as the eighteenth century the record of one such yogi showed that he had travelled all over India, visiting important shrines in Central, Western and Southern India; then proceeded to Ceylon and Malaya and returned to India. From India he went to Kābul, Khorāsān, Herāt, Astrakhān and Moscow. Then on his return journey via Persia he visited Hamadān, Shirāz, Basra, Bahrain, Karāchi, and went on to Nepāl and Tibet. He is known to have visited several of these places more than once (I, p. 3).

Travellers to China and Southeast Asia were also to be found in all periods, starting from the second century AD. Hundreds of Indian scholars preceded the Hindu and Buddhist colonists who set up flourishing empires in Further India. South China had large communities of Indian settlers. From Chinese sources we learn that three thousand Indians resided in the kingdom of Wei in northern China in the early part of the sixth century. Indian scholars were employed on the Chinese Astronomical Board in the seventh century AD, bringing back to India much astronomical and mathematical knowledge, painstakingly copied into Sanskrit from the original Chinese works, even down to the mistakes made in them.

It is significant that although many of the Chinese pilgrims who came to India left copious records of their travels, 'not one of the numerous Indian monks who went to China and settled there has left a scrap of record about his journey to and experiences in China' (II, p. 298).

This consistent silence on the part of the Hindus does not indicate any lack of social mobility, but, according to one scholar, reveals a conspicuous feature of the orthodox Hindu character, namely, an exaggerated sense of *sanatva** or the 'ancientness' of their own history and civilization and the uniqueness of their own heritage, which makes them reluctant to set down the achievements of other races lest it betray an indebtedness to them.

The tendency to travel received a considerable set back under the Brāhminical dispensation, particularly after the Revival. The prohibition was inspired by the dangers of spiritual contamination through contact with the outside world. Only the heretical Buddhists continued to travel, exposing their persons to the unwholesome auras of alien peoples and places, drinking impure waters, eating foods grown in unrighteous lands. Roads, according to medieval writers, were particularly dangerous, since along the highways went men of all classes, bearing with them the uncertainties, fears, discomforts, engendered by their feelings of homelessness and insecurity, and polluting the roads with their passions. Inns, where wayfarers rested, were specific areas of occult danger, breeding the same fears and uncertainties of the road. Here again peoples of different castes and countries met and lived together, creating, as it were, a blanket of poisonous vapours.

Indeed, so great were the dangers of foreign travel believed to be, and so sedulously did the lawgivers attempt to guard righteous men from them that travel was made an offence. This was particularly applicable to travel overseas. The *Baudhāyana Dharmaśāstra* forbids sea voyages to brāhmins and prescribes a severe penance for any transgression of the prohibition. Manu declared that a brāhmin who had gone to sea was unworthy of being entertained at a śrāddha ceremony.

To the present day many orthodox Hindus will not journey across the *kālapāni*, 'black waters', as the seas are called, to avoid exposing themselves to the spiritual corruptions of travel.

Books

I. Briggs, G. W. *Gorakhnath and the Kanphata Yogis*, Calcutta, 1938.
II. Dutt, S. *Buddhist Monks and Monasteries of India*, London, 1962.
III. Eling, S. *Travel and Pilgrimage among the Hindus*, 1923.

TRIŚAṄKU, first called Satyavrata, was a descendant of Ikshvāku and the father of Hariśchandra of the Solar race. For the crime of seducing the wife of a citizen of the realm, his father's court priest Vasishṭha condemned him to become a *chaṇḍāla* (a man of degraded caste) and had him banished for twelve years. During the prince's exile a terrible famine ravaged the land. Learning that the family of the sage Viśvāmitra, the rival of Vasishṭha, were on the verge of starvation and Viśvāmitra himself absent in a far off country, Triśaṅku hung deer's flesh on a tree on the banks of the Ganges and thus provided for them without exposing them to the infamy of eating food offered by a chaṇḍāla. When at length even deer's flesh was not available Triśaṅku killed Vasishṭha's miraculous cow Kāmadhenu, and gave some of the flesh to Viśvāmitra's sons and ate some himself. Because he had impaled his reputation with the 'three arrows' of adultery, cow-killing and beef-eating, Vasishṭha branded him with the accursed name of Triśaṅku.

Distressed and humiliated the prince desired to perform a great sacrifice which would help him to ascend bodily to heaven. Vasishṭha declared that for him it would be impossible and refused even to make the attempt, so Triśaṅku appealed to Vasishṭha's sons, who likewise refused to undertake the office. The prince then appealed to Viśvāmitra, who, remembering the assistance that Triśaṅku had rendered to his family, promised to perform the sacrifice that would raise him to heaven.

He first reinstated Triśaṅku in his father's kingdom; then in a prodigious effort of concentrated will, the ṛishi bore down all other opposition and helped Triśaṅku ascend to heaven. But in heaven his entry was barred by Indra and the other gods, and Triśaṅku was hurled down from the celestial abodes, head foremost. Viśvāmitra in a fearsome rage, thundered that he would create another heaven and make new creatures. He began by forming several constellations in the sky, and on earth called into being the coconut tree, a new species of fish, certain plants, the fat-tailed sheep, and new varieties of rice and vetch. In great trepidation Brahmā and the other deities went to the sage and begged him to desist and agreed to make Triśaṅku immortal. His flight earthwards was arrested and he was allowed to remain suspended in the empyrean with his head downwards, where he still shines among the constellations created by Viśvāmitra as the Southern Cross.

Books

See under Mythology.

TRUTH, in Sanskrit, *satya,* is one of the basic virtues of Hindu ethics and the chief pillar of the Hindu dharma. Truth is inclusive of all other virtues and represents good in its entirety. The earliest of all the *yugas* or aeons was known as *satya-yuga.* Those who express truth in their lives without faltering are entitled to their reward in *Satya-loka,* the abode of truth, which is Brahma's heaven.

From the *Māṇḍukya Upanishad* aphorism, *satyam eva jayati,* 'Truth indeed triumphs', comes the motto on the Government of India official crest, and it is in this absolute sense that M. K. Gāndhi named his autobiography, 'My Experiments with Truth'.

In everyday life truth is a powerful weapon against all evil forces, whatever temporary set-backs may be experienced. This truth is not the transcendent truth of satya, but a personal honesty and rectitude called *ārjavam.* He who always speaks and thinks the truth acquires a force that is irresistible. It is said, 'That man in whom truth is fully rooted, his words must bear fruit'. A person who has always and invariably spoken the truth can by the power called *satya-kriyā,* 'truth-action', make anything come to pass by simply saying it.

Manu counselled, 'One should speak the truth and speak it pleasantly and not harshly. Nor should one speak untruth because it is pleasing.' This ancient precept has generally been honoured by Hindus, whose practise of this virtue has been remarked on by outsiders from ancient times. Exceptions are first found in the works of Muslim writers of the medieval period, who could see no merit in anything done by the kafirs, and who vilified the Hindus as perfidious and untrustworthy. Europeans at times shared this prejudice. The extreme view is taken by the splenetic Abbé Dubois who exhausts his vocabulary in describing their shortcoming in this respect. 'It is impossible', he concludes, 'to fathom their minds and discover what they really mean' (I, p. 306).

But the emphasis on satya in Indian religion and tradition is undeniable, and witnesses to the Hindu adherence to truth far outweigh the hostile evidence. Megasthenes (*c.* 302 BC) declared after close contact with the people that no Indian had ever been convicted of lying and that in the signing of contracts witnesses and seals were regarded as superfluous. The honesty of Hindus and their love of truth was confirmed by Hiuen-Tsang (AD 630). Marco Polo (1293) declared that Hindus were famed for their honesty and would not tell a lie 'for anything on earth'. A British officer, Sir William Sleeman, who during the last century spent his life among Hindu peasants said, 'I have had before me hundreds of cases in which a man's property, liberty and life depended upon his telling a lie, and he has refused to tell it' (II, Vol. II, p. 68).

Books

I. Dubois, Abbé. *Hindu Manners, Customs and Ceremonies,* London, 3rd Ed., 1936.
II. Sleeman, W. E. *A Journey Through the Kingdom of Oudh,* 1858.
III. Yule, Henry. *Book of Ser Marco Polo,* 1871.

TUKĀRĀM (1607–1649), Marāṭhi religious writer, born near Poona. The son of a struggling śūdra grocer, he was left an orphan at an early age. He became a devotee of Viṭṭhobā, the god of Paṇḍharpur, and grievously neglected his domestic affairs. Of his two wives one died of hunger at the age of eighteen, and the other made his life very unhappy as she was, not without provocation, very bitter-tongued.

His generosity was boundless, and he gave away his money, his possessions, his own and even his wife's clothes, to beggars and medicants. Unsuccessful in both business and family relations he abandoned the world and became a wandering devotee. Throughout his life he suffered harassment at the hands of brāhmins.

He received his mystic initiation from a saint in a dream. Most of his *abhaṅga* or hymns are devoted to Kṛishṇa and are touching in their simple faith. 'My enemies are not in the world outside. It is the passions within me that bring dangers. Who but thou canst save us Lord?' 'Like a beggar I have taken my stand at thy door. O God, send me an alms of some sweetmeat of thy love.' His poems do not rise to very great heights but he is popular in Mahārāshṭra. He was a great favourite of Śivājī, but refused the latter's request to visit his court. It is said that when he felt his end approaching he walked into a river and drowned himself.

Books
I. Fraser, J. N., and Edwards, J. F. *Life and Teachings of Tukaram*, Madras, 1913.
II. Ranade, K. *The Poems of Tukaram*, 1918.
See also under Marāthi.

TULSĪDĀS (?1527–1623?), 'slave of Tulsī', Hindi poet, a native of Oudh, was seventh in descent from the philosopher Rāmānanda* in the succession of master and pupil. In some accounts he is referred to as a Kanauji brāhmin, but it is more likely that he belonged to a low caste. Tradition says that he was abandoned by his superstitious parents at birth because he was born with teeth, and was found and brought up by a wandering ascetic.

He was happily married, but his only son died before reaching maturity. One day when his wife Ratnāvalī was away visiting her father, Tulsīdās swam the Jamnā while the river was in spate, in order to meet her. His wife rebuked him for this saying that if he had as much devotion for Rāma the earth would become gold. These chance words were like a revelation to him and he forthwith left home to become a *sannyāsin*, or mendicant.

He was said to have had a vision of the monkey-god Hanumān who bestowed on him the power of working miracles. According to one apocryphal legend, when he was imprisoned by the emperor Shāh Jahān a myriad monkeys appeared and started pulling the prison apart. He was freed by the emperor, and in return advised him to quit Delhi since it was the abode of Rāma, and this the emperor is said to have done. Actually Shāh Jahān did not come to the throne till five years after the poet's death.

Tulsīdās wrote more than a dozen works, but is chiefly renowned for his Eastern Hindi version of the *Rāmāyaṇa*, called the *Rāma-charita-mānasa*, 'The Lake of Rāma's Deeds', which maintains a consistently pure and lofty moral tone, and is as well known in northern India as the Bible is in Europe.

The poet never wearied of voicing the theme that there is only one Supreme Being; that sin is hateful; that man is infinitely sinful and unworthy of salvation; that the Supreme Being, in his infinite mercy became incarnate in the person of Rāma to relieve the world of sin. In Tulsīdās Rāma becomes Absolute Knowledge and Absolute Love, a Hindi version of the Logos and Everlasting I Am. Throughout the work emphasis is laid on duty to one's neighbour, and the doctrine of universal brotherhood. Many critics hold that there can be no doubt that the poet was influenced by Christian ideas, derived from the Nestorian Christians.

Books
I. Grierson, G. A. 'Tulsidas, Poet and Religious Reformer'. *Journal of the Royal Asiatic Society*, 1903.
II. Jindal, K. B. *A History of Hindi Literature*, Allahabad, 1955.
III. Macfie, J. M. *The Ramayana of Tulsidas: or the Bible of Northern India*, Edinburgh, 1930.
IV. Wadhwa, K. L. *Tulsidas and the Ramayana*, 1912.

UDAYANA, the name of several kings of the Vatsa dynasty ruling at Kauśāmbī. In Buddha's day one Udayana (*c.* 500 BC) was famous as the king of the Vatsya *mahājanapada*.

Another legendary Udayana is celebrated in Sanskrit literature. He was the son of Sahasrānīka, a king of the Lunar dynasty ruling at Kauśāmbī, capital of the Vatsya kingdom, and was hence also known as Vatsarāja. Udayana is the beau ideal of Sanskrit literature, a Hindu Don Juan, who appears as the hero of many Sanskrit masterpieces.

In one legend, which is the subject of a romance by Subandhu*, Vāsavadattā, daughter of one of the Pradyota kings of Ujjain, sees Udayana in a dream and begins to pine away for love of him. Her father Chaṇḍasena, who disapproves of Udayana, lures the young man to the capital and makes him a prisoner. But Udayana is set free by the king's minister, and elopes with the princess. In another legend the princess Anasūyā is stricken with love at the sight of him; then a certain princess Padmāvatī falls in love with his portrait; yet another, Sāgarikā, becomes enamoured after hearing his name; and sundry other beauties are similarly affected with an undying passion for him. In addition to satisfying their inclinations Udayana dallies with their handmaidens and female friends. The story of his love for Ratnāvalī, his queen's attendant, actually a princess of Ceylon, forms the subject of a play by Harsha.

Udayana is described as tender, passionate, amorous, devoted to the arts, to dancing and music. He is tall, moon-faced and large-eyed. Sanskrit treatises on the art of love add further physical details.

Udayana's son, Naravāhanadatta, is also devoted to the service of the fair sex, but he is more stern and violent, and not as engaging as his celebrated father.

Books

See under Mythology and Literature.

UDDĀLAKA, *ṛishi* authority on Vedic ritual and philosophy, was the son of one Aruṇa of Pañchāla and was hence also known as Āruṇi. His guru or preceptor was the sage *Dhaumya*, a mysterious personage whose descendants served as the family priests of the Pāṇḍavas, and one of whom anointed Yudhishṭhira* at Hastināpura. Dhaumya had two great pupils, Uddālaka and *Uttaṅka*, both of whom were taught many secrets of profound import relating to sexual mysticism while at his hermitage. Uttaṅka was said to have received much spiritual knowledge from Kṛishṇa. His meditations generated so much heat that it gave birth to a fire-breathing demon later slain by a descendant of Purañjaya*. According to one legend Dhaumya once absented himself from his hermitage when his wife was expected to be in *ṛitu* (*see* menstruation) and Uttaṅka was told to cohabit with her to teach him that the ṛitu was on no account to be wasted.

Dhaumya's other pupil, Uddālaka, was also given a number of practical demonstrations on erotic lore. It is related that when his guru once ordered Uddālaka to stop a breach in a watercourse in a field, he threw himself into the breach in the absence of any other object to stop the flow. The association of Uddālaka with certain aspects of sex worship, the adoration of the yoni, and semen retention, suggests that the story may have another allegorical significance. His master gave him the title of Vājaśravasa (*vāja-śravasa*, 'swift-flowing').

Uddālaka was responsible for composing several formulas of sacrificial ceremonial. Says Oldenberg,

'When the time shall have come for the enquiries which will have to create order out of the chaotic names of teachers and other celebrities of the Brāhmaṇa period, it may turn out that the most important centre for the formation and diffusion of the Brāhmaṇa doctrine will have to be looked for in Āruṇi and in the circles which surrounded him.'

Uddālaka's son, the ṛishi *Śvetaketu*, 'white light', figures prominently in the *Śatapatha Brāhmaṇa* and the Upanishads. It was to Śvetaketu that Uddālaka taught his famous practical lessons on the true self recorded in the Upanishads.* Śvetaketu was the author of a treatise on a *kāmaśāstra**, and his name, like his father's is linked with certain sexual techniques. According to the *Mahābhārata*, Śvetaketu put a stop to the custom of women consorting freely with other men. His anger was aroused when he saw a brāhmin take his mother's hand and lead her away before his father's eyes. The father explained that this practice had prevailed from time immemorial and there was no ground for offence, 'since female beings of all kinds are unhindered'. But Śvetaketu refused to accept this convention and introduced the rule of wifely fidelity to a single man.

Another of Uddālaka's sons was *Nachiketas*, of whom the following story is told in the *Kaṭha Upinashad* and the Brāhmaṇas. One day Āruṇi (i.e. Uddālaka) in an effort to attain heaven by means of a sacrifice of cows and gifts to brāhmins, was interrupted during the ritual by his son Nachiketas who said, 'You have not given enough. To whom shall I your son be given as a gift?' The father did not reply at first, but on the question being repeated retorted hotly, 'To Yama'. So Nachiketas journeyed to the underworld and met Yama, ruler of the dead, who asked him his business. The young man said, 'I want true knowledge of the destiny of the soul. Every man must die some day. Today he is here and tomorrow he is no longer here. Where is he? What is the truth?'

Yama tried to dissuade him from proceeding with his enquiries, but the youth persisted and Yama finally revealed to him the secret of the immortality of the *ātman* (soul). 'There are two paths in life', the King of the Dead explained,

'One is the path of material satisfaction and sensual pleasure, which can only lead to ensnarement in the phenomenal world and slavery to the senses. Its fruits are temporary and unsatisfying. The other path is that of righteousness, through which we realize the highest, noblest and best in our nature. Because our longing for the good becomes progressively fulfilled we can find satisfaction only along this path, for it leads to a richer and fuller existence.'

Among Uddālaka's pupils were Yājñavalkya*, Śaunaka (grandson of Gṛitsamada*) and Kahoḍa. *Kahoḍa* married Uddālaka's daughter Sujātā, but was so devoted to study that he neglected his wife. His unborn son while still in the mother's womb rebuked his father and Kahoḍa incensed at the child's impertinence cursed him to be born with eight (*ashṭa*) crooked limbs (*vakra*). The child when born was found to be deformed in the arms, legs, neck, chest, hips and male organ, and was named *Ashṭāvakra*. Kahoḍa along with several other learned brāhmins was once defeated in argument at the court of Janaka by a Buddhist sage. For this he and his companions were thrown into a river to drown. When Ashṭāvakra reached the age of twelve he set out and recovered his father from the depths of the river and was restored to grace. As the lad was unable to obtain a bride because he was deformed his father made him bathe in a sacred stream and straightened him out again.

Books

See under mythology.

UJJAIN (Pāli for the Sanskrit *vijayani*, 'victorious'), known to ancient Greek geographers as Ozene, is situated on the Sipra river in Central India. According to mythology the city had been in existence under many names from the dawn of the first *yuga*. As Māghas it was a sacred city of the Maga people.

Throughout its long history Ujjain was a meeting ground of nations, associated from remote antiquity with foreign races. It lay in the direct line of the great trade* routes leading from the seaport of Broach (Barygaza) to the western markets of Sind and the Gangetic trading centres as far as Pāṭaliputra. Foreign commodities and exotic luxuries flowed through the town, but above all it was the channel for the ingress of new ideas and inspirations. It remained for centuries one of the most prolific centres of Indian culture.

In the epic and early historical period the city and the surrounding country were known as Avanti or Māhishmatī. As Māhishmatī (from Māghas) it was the home of the heterogeneous Haihaya tribes, who were notorious, among other things, for their sexual laxity (*see* adultery). Subsequently it passed to the Bhoja tribe, who were classed as mlechchhas, descended from Druhyu son of Yayāti. Avanti was famous in Buddha's day and figures prominently in Buddhist chronicles as one of the *mahājanapadas**, ruled over by the Pradyota dynasty. Under Chandragupta it was absorbed by the Mauryan empire and became Aśoka's capital when he was viceroy (275 BC) during his father's reign. It once contained a celebrated *stūpa*.

In later times the country around Avanti was called Mālwā. This name is said to be derived from a republican tribe of Scythian origin known to the Greeks as Malloi, and to later chroniclers as Malli, Malla, or Mālava, who originally lived between the Rāvi and Chenāb and offered stout resistance to Alexander. They eventually surrendered sending the conqueror presents of chariots, battle armour, bales of cotton, and also 'white iron'. In the succeeding centuries, under pressure from tribes of the north-west, they moved slowly into Rājputāna, settling in the district known after them as Mālavanagara (now Nagar) in Jaipur. Ujjain fell to the Mālavas in the first century BC, and here they founded the Mālava dynasty. The Mālavas were the first to employ the Vikrama Saṁvat, the era commencing 58 BC (*see* era), reputedly established by the semi-legendary king Vikramāditya, whose capital was Ujjain. But the era is also called Kṛita, possibly after one of their leaders who may have commemorated a victory over some Śaka rival by inaugurating the new era. The name of the Mālavas is preserved in the area known today as Mālwā; in the town of Mālwā in Madhya Bhārat; in a musical *rāga* called malla; in the name of the cloth, *malla*, which became *mal-mal*, a kind of muslin.

Following a brief struggle the Mālavas succumbed to the Śaka dynasty of the Kardamakas who under Chashṭana made Ujjain their capital in AD 77. The Śakas ruled Ujjain till AD 398, during which time, says Professor P. T. S. Ayyangar, 'the trade of India with Europe was much developed and Ujjain became the entrepôt of India's foreign commerce' (I, p. 13), mainly through the port of Barygaza.

Under the Kardamakas the city of Ujjain developed into one of the foremost seats of learning in all India (III, p. 185). From Alexandria Greek astronomy reached Ujjain which became an important centre for astronomical studies; indeed, Indian scientific astronomy may be said to have been born there. The city became the central longitude from which all astronomical calculations were made, and for centuries thereafter remained the first meridian of Indian geographers. Many centuries later Jaisingh II (fl. 1700) of Jaipur built one of his famous observatories there. Similar influences from Ujjain radiated over the spheres of mathematics, science, art and drama. The scene of Śūdraka's *Mṛichchhakaṭika* or Little Clay Cart was laid in Ujjain and its neighbourhood, as was also the scene of a play by Bhāsa.

In the fourth century AD both the Mālavas and the Śakas submitted to the Guptas, and in the sixth century to the Huns. One branch of the Mālavas, known as the Aulikara continued to flourish in semi-independence at Daśapura (or Mandasor). They earned renown when one of their kings named Yaśodharma (or Vishṇuvardhana Yaśodharmadeva) headed a confederacy of Śaka and Indian princes and delivered a crushing blow to the Hun conqueror Mihirakula in AD 528, compelling him to retire to Kashmīr, where he died. For this feat Yaśodharma earned the title of Vikramāditya.

A dynasty of Mālava chiefs continued to rule intermittently in Ujjain through all the vicissitudes of dynastic struggles elsewhere; their names, preserved on Mālava coins, present further proof of their foreign origin. In the beginning of the seventh century eastern Mālwā was under a minor branch of the imperial Guptas who became involved in the wars that finally raised Harsha* to the throne of Kanauj and gave him sovereignty over the Mālwā area. After the death of Harsha the history of Ujjain is linked with that of the newly formed Rājput dynasties of Hunnish origin, notably the Pratihāra* (eighth century) and Paramāra (tenth and eleventh centuries). Up to this time Ujjain had been associated for a longer period of its history with foreign rule than with indigenous.

In 1235 Ujjain was captured by Iltutmish, Sultān of Delhi, who destroyed, among other fine buildings, a famous old temple dedicated to Mahākāla (Śiva). The city was once again taken and destroyed by the Khiljis who became Sultāns of Mālwā in 1305, and from them passed to the Ghoris and then to the Moghuls. In 1792 the city was partly burned by the Marāṭhas.

Ujjain is one of the seven sacred cities of the Hindus. It is the site of the great Amareśvara liṅga, and the spot where the elbow of the goddess Satī* fell to earth. A great *Kumbha-mela* is held at Ujjain every three years.

Books

I. Ayyangar, P. T. S. *Bhoja Raja*, Madras, 1931.
II. Lal, Kanwar. *Holy Cities of India*, Delhi, 1961.
III. Majumdar, R. C. (Ed.) *The Age of Imperial Unity*, Bombay, 1951.

UMĀ, wife of Śiva, was the daughter of Himavat who personified the Himālayas, and of Menā (or Menakā) a beautiful being with whom even the god Indra fell in love. Among the children of Himavat and Menā were two daughters, Umā, and Gaṅgā goddess of the Ganges, and a son named Maināka, personification of a high mountain. When Indra clipped the wings of the great mountain peaks, Maināka escaped by hiding under the sea, and reappeared when it was safe again. He still stands, and has been identified with various lofty peaks, in the Himālayas, in Central India, or in the extreme south of India.

In another version Himavat and Menā had three daughters, who gave themselves up to the most rigorous austerities. One sister lived upon a single leaf of the *parṇā* tree, and was called Ekaparṇā; the other sister lived on one leaf of the *pāṭalā* tree and was known as Ekapāṭalā. How the third and eldest daughter surpassed her two sisters is related in the *Harivaṁśa*. She was exceedingly beautiful and was believed to be a reincarnation of the self-immolated Satī*, Śiva's previous wife. As such she approached Śiva as his spouse, but the god was now averse to sexual pleasure and spurned her. Hurt and humiliated she decided to outdo her sisters in austerities. She subsisted on nothing, not even a single leaf of the parṇā, so that she was called Aparṇā. This extraordinary abstinence so alarmed her mother that she cried out, 'U-ma', meaning, 'O, don't', and by this name the daughter became known throughout the three worlds. Her devotion to Śiva pleased the deity and he consented to make her his wife. Many stories are related about the domestic differences of this loving pair.

Apart from the mythological derivation there are other meanings given to her name. Umā is said to signify light, speech, or peacemaker. The name is first mentioned in the *Kena Upanishad* as that of a goddess, and she is often identified with Pārvatī and Durgā. It seems that she was a deity of pre-Aryan origin and her name is related to the word *ammā,* meaning mother, a suffix of several South Indian village godlings*. As the daughter of Himavat, Umā is also called Haimavatī.

Books

See under Mythology.

UPANISHAD (*upa-nishad*, 'near-sitting'), a class of works embodying the mystical and esoteric doctrines of ancient Hindu philosophy, and believed to be so named because they were discourses delivered to chosen pupils who were permitted to 'sit near' their gurus (preceptors) to receive the sacred teaching.

Although now regarded as the philosophical and meditative portions of the Vedas, the Upanishads were not originally recognized as part of the Vedic canon at all, and had their origins outside Vedic Hinduism. A comparative study of Upanishadic philosophy has led some scholars to think that some of its basic concepts were Austric* in origin, notably its pantheism, its eschatology, and its doctrine of transmigration. The *Chhāndogya Upanishad* relates that the Vedic god Indra came as a student to acquaint himself with the knowledge of Brahma, and was able to grasp the sophisticated doctrines only with considerable difficulty.

The Upanishads were composed in their present form between 400–200 BC. They are later in date than the older *saṁhitās* and Brāhmaṇas, although they constitute part of the Brāhmaṇas or are embodied in the Āraṇyakas. They are characterized by a total absence of any brāhmin exclusiveness in their teachings. Where the Brāhmaṇas* have to do with 'works', the Upanishads deal with 'knowledge', and constitute in effect the philosophical foundation of Vedānta.

The Upanishads represent a reaction from the sacrificial and priestly ritualism of the Brāhmaṇas. In them we have the first consistent expression of a philosophical doctrine in Hinduism. But this expression is characterized by intuitive understanding rather than by logical systematization into any scheme of philosophy as such. It is extremely subtle, sublime and profound, and has had an overwhelming influence on Indian thought. Every school of Hindu philosophy is indebted to the Upanishads, as their teachings are the fountainhead and source of them all. Although containing traces of the old mythology and sacerdotalism, the Upanishads transcend them and soar to the highest realms of metaphysical speculation. Sāṁkhya owes to the Upanishads the doctrine of Prakṛiti and the theory of the three guṇas; Yoga is rooted in the *Śvetāśvatara Upanishad*; Mīmāṁsā develops from the *Kaṭhopanishad*; and Vedānta is based on several of these treatises.

In spite of its great importance Upanishadic philosophy has not been 'popular' in any sense of the term. Its doctrines are too recondite to satisfy the average person, and it remains a teaching which few can appreciate. Its rarefied flights have a fascination for the metaphysically minded, as is found expressed in the extravagant and oft-quoted tribute paid to it by Schopenhauer, 'It has been the solace of my life; it will be the solace of my death'.

The Upanishads present not one but several doctrines. The lesser Upanishads cover many systems of thought and reflect a wide variety of beliefs and superstitions. But the major Upanishads deal with some of the great problems which have vexed man from time immemorial: the nature of God and the soul, of man and the world, and the relation between them; the nature and purpose of existence; the ultimate reality and its nature; the attainment of salvation by man.

The fundamental doctrine of the Upanishads is the identity of the individual soul with the Universal Soul or Brahma, and is essentially an enquiry into the nature of Brahma. This is the chief object of Upanishadic speculation, which lays special and repeated emphasis on the great truth regarding the identity of the individual soul with the Universal Soul. This concept is expressed in a number of famous *kārikās* or sayings* found in these writings.

Brahma is eternal and without attributes. He is the infinite, immutable and unlimited Reality, and cannot be fixed, defined or known. In the words of Yājñavalkya in his explanation to Gārgī, a female interlocutor, 'That which is above the heaven, and that which is beneath the earth, that which men call past, present and future, all that is woven within and without and throughout space, O Gārgī, is Brahma'.

All phenomenal existence is illusion (*māyā*), arising from *avidyā* or lack of knowledge*, which results in action (*karma*), thus keeping the cycle of birth-death-rebirth endlessly revolving. True understanding of the nature of Brahma, and of our identity with it, will bring to a stop this cycle of *saṁsāra* and lead to liberation. The path leading to the realization of Brahma is not easy, but, in the words of the *Kaṭhopanishad*, 'like the razor's edge, is difficult to cross and hard to tread'.

Individual ātmans or souls, like all other individual phenomena, are mutable and inconstant. They are perpetually changing their form, their identity and their individuality. This transcience leads to frustration that only contact with the permanent can resolve. The *Muṇḍaka Upanishad* expresses this in the parable of the two birds. These birds are bound one to another in friendship and have made their homes in the same tree. One bird (the transcendental or impersonal self) just looks on, while the other bird (the empirical or personal self) pecks at the sweet fruit. The eating bird weary of pecking here and there becomes dejected, but when through meditation, it becomes aware that the other—the impersonal self—is indeed spirit, dejection vanishes.

In this universe of changing things, in this pageant of *nāmarūpa* (name-form) which is the phenomenal world, what is there that can be regarded as permanent or fixed? Neither matter nor mind, neither breath nor fire, neither movement nor death. Nothing except Brahma. All things exist in him. 'That from which beings are born, that in which when born they live, and that into which they enter at death, that is Brahma.' It is the one changeless truth. Only paramātman (Brahma) has actual existence. Brahma is 'one only without a second' (*ekam evādvitīyam*).

The truth of the oneness of things is brought out in a famous dialogue between Uddālaka and his son Śvetaketu in the *Chhāndogya Upanishad*. The sage tells the son to break first the fruit and then the seed within the fruit of the *nyagrodha* or fig-tree. Breaking the seed the son finds nothing, and the father explains, 'My son, from that finest essence which you do not perceive, this great tree exists. In that subtle essence all exists. It is the True. It is the self. And thou, O Śvetaketu, art that.' Then making the son dissolve salt in water he bids him taste the water from the surface, from the middle and from the bottom, to show him how all the water has become salt. 'So also the subtle essence is universally diffused in all things wherever found. It is the true self, and thou Śvetaketu, art it.' Similarly we learn from the *Kaṭha Upanishad* that like Brahma the self is never born and never dies. 'If the slayer thinks he can slay, or if the slain thinks he is slain, they both do not know the truth, for the self neither slays nor is slain.'

In the course of expounding these fundamental doctrines the Upanishads treat of various other matters of philosophical import such as the nature of the embodied soul, the relationship between the body, mind and senses. It outlines various means of salvation, worship, and meditation, and explains the eschatological principles of its teachings.

There are about 150 'major' Upanishads, but 108 is the traditional recognized number of the texts. They vary greatly in length; the *Īśa* would occupy a single printed page, the *Bṛihadāraṇyaka Upinashad* at least fifty pages. The five, seven, ten or thirteen 'principal' Upanishads are generally chosen from those named here.

The ṚIG-VEDIC Upanishads are: (*a*) *Aitareya* (i.e. the *Aitareya Upinashad*), so called from its inclusion in the *Aitareyā Brāhmaṇa*. An Upanishad written in prose, expressing Vedāntic ideas, and discussing the question of the self and Brahma; (*b*) *Kauśītaki,* forms part of the *Kauśītaki Āraṇyaka,* which itself is included in the *Kauśītaki Brāhmaṇa* of the *Ṛig-veda.* It represents one of the early Upanishads.

The SĀMA-VEDIC Upanishads are: (*a*) *Chhāndogya,* early and fairly long, composed in prose with a few verses interspersed; it comprises eight chapters of the *Chhāndogya Brāhmaṇa.* So named after the chhandoga or priest of the *Sāma-veda.* It is notable for presenting the development of brāhminical theology, and contains expositions on the sacred syllable Oṁ. One of the sages associated with the *Chhāndogya Upanishad* was Śāṇḍilya, a descendant of Śāṇḍila, and expounder of the famous aphorism 'tat tvam asi' which was also used by Uddālaka; (*b*) *Kena* (or *Kenopanishad*), an early, very brief, mixed prose and verse Upanishad, forming the tenth chapter of the *Jaiminīya Brāhmaṇa.* So named because of the first word of its opening verse, *kena,* 'by whom?' It is devoted to the glorification of Umā (Devī) who explains to the gods Agni, Vāyu and Indra, the mystery of Brahma, the unfathomable central power of the universe.

The YAJUR-VEDIC Upanishads are (*a*) *Bṛihadāraṇyaka,* 'great forest'; an early, lengthy, prose Upanishad intermixed with verse. It forms part of the *Śatapatha Brāhmaṇa* included in the White *Yajur-veda,* the last section of which represents this Upanishad. It is ascribed to the sage Yājñavalkya. A considerable portion of the sixth chapter of this Upanishad deals in a detailed manner with sexual subjects; (*b*) *Īśa,* a very short prose (except for two verses) Upanishad, forming the last (fortieth) chapter of the *Vājasaneyī Saṁhitā* of the White *Yajur-veda.* So named because its first word is *īśa,* Lord. It is also called the *Saṁhitopanishad*; (*c*) *Taittirīya,* an early prose Upanishad, included in the *Taittirīya Brāhmaṇa* of the Black *Yajur-veda*; (*d*) *Śvetāśvatara,* 'white steed', comparatively late and wholly in verse. So called because it is related to the Śvetāśvatara school of the Black *Yajur-veda,* founded by a teacher of that name. It represents a theistic treatise with Śiva as the deity of deities, and probably influenced the Vaishṇavite *Bhagavadgītā.* It is one of the basic texts of Śaivism; (*e*) *Maitrāyaṇi* (or Maitri—a second text exists which is known by the latter name), included in the Maitrāyaṇi branch of the Black *Yajur-veda.* It is in prose with occasional verse; (*f*) *Kaṭha,* or the *Kaṭhopanishad,* written in verse. It is connected with the Kaṭha of the Black *Yajur-veda.* This Upanishad covers the subject of Vedānta, the nature of the Ultimate Being, and the path of Yoga.

The ATHARVA-VEDIC Upanishads are (*a*) *Muṇḍaka,* in mixed prose and verse.

Why it is so named is not clear, but possibly from a reference to the Śirovrata (*śiras, 'head'*) or 'head-vow', a rite in which one had to hold fire over one's shaven head, in order to become the recipient of the knowledge of Brahma taught in it. It is traditionally linked with the *Atharva-veda*; (*b*) *Māṇḍūkya*, so called because it was revealed by the sage Maṇḍūka. It consists of only twelve verses, but is believed to contain the essence of the 108 Upanishads. Its theme is the syllable *Oṁ*; (*c*) *Praśna*, in mixed prose and verse. It is so called because of the six 'questions' discussed and solved in it. It is traditionally linked with the *Atharva-veda*. The questions in the Praśna are solved by the ṛishi Pippalāda, the founder of the Paippalāda school of the *Atharva-veda*.

Besides these major writings there are hundreds of lesser Upanishads. A number were composed along with the major works and are as old as they are; some were produced during the Epic period, many others of varied character followed at still later periods. These lesser Upanishads are for the most part devoid of literary merit, being repetitive and generally poorly written, with many grammatical inaccuracies. Several are merely incoherent sentences joined together. They range from writings which expound the teachings of one or other of the 'schools' of philosophy, or propagate the virtues of a particular sect or deity, to treatises dealing in tawdry fashion with the old themes of Brahma, *Oṁ*, the āśramas, asceticism, the *siddhis*, and sex. Some Upanishads advance the notion that matter is eternal, that God 'created' the universe, that the universe is the actual substance of Brahma. Many are not connected with the Vedas and some are even anti-Vedic, revealing a contempt for caste, and obviously written under Buddhist influence. A complete critical bibliography of all the Upanishads has yet to be compiled

The following are a few of the better known minor Upanishads. *Jābāla*, an early Upanishad, advocates extreme ascetisicm and the subjugation of all desire; it gives esoteric information about the mode of life of the *paramahaṁsas* or religious mendicants. The *Svasanved* holds that there is no god, no heaven, no hell, no reincarnation, no world. That the Vedas and Upanishads are the work of presumptuous fools; that ideas are illusions and words untrue; that deluded people cling to gods and temples and 'holy men', though in reality there is no difference between Vishṇu and a dog. The *Garbha* gives secret details on sexual matters, describes how semen is produced and in parts reads like a treatise on embryology; it advocates meditation on the embryo as a means of preventing rebirth in a new womb. The *Prāṇāgnihotra* in prose, discourses on the relation of the parts and functions of the body to those of the agnihotra* sacrifice, and implies that sacrifice is unnecessary. Those who read this Upanishad are promised the same reward as those who die in Banāras, i.e. deliverance from transmigration. The *Vajrasūchika*, attributed to Aśvaghosha*, is concerned with refuting the caste system and the brāhminical doctrine of inequality; it appears to be Buddhist in origin. The *Allopanishad*, i.e. the 'Allah Upanishad', might be mentioned as a type of this class of writing, that was being produced not only by sectarians of the early Hindu period, but by non-Hindus in recent times. This Upanishad was written in the seventeenth century at the instance of Dārāh Shikoh, the son of the Moghul emperor Shāh Jahān, in praise of Islam.

Books

I. Aiyar, N. K. *Thirty Minor Upanishads*, Madras, 1914.
II. Deussen, Paul. *Philosophy of the Upanishads*, Edinburgh, 1906.
III. Gough, A. *Philosophy of the Upanishads*, London, 1882–4.
IV. Hume, R. E. *The Thirteen Principal Upanishads*, London, 1921.
V. Keith, A. B. *The Religion and Philosophy of the Veda and Upanishads*, Cambridge, Mass., 1925.
VI. Milburn, R. G. *The Religious Mysticism of the Upanishads*, 1924.
VII. Müller, Max. *The Upanishads*, 2 vols., Oxford, 1879–82.
VIII. Nikhilananda, Swami. *The Upanishads*, 2 vols, New York, 1938.
IX. Radhakrishnan, S. (Ed.) *The Principal Upanishads*, 1953.
X. Radhakrishnan, S. *The Philosophy of the Upanishads*, London, 1924.
XI. Ranade, R. D. *Constructive Survey of Upanishadic Philosophy*, Poona, 1926.

URVAŚĪ, an apsarā or celestial courtesan, mentioned in the *Ṛig-veda*, the *Śatapatha Brāhmaṇa*, and the Purāṇas. In one legend she was painted into existence by the sage Nārāyaṇa*; the later Purāṇas make this celebrated *apsarā* a prostitute. She was so ravishing that at the very sight of her the gods Mitra and Varuṇa while engaged in performing a sacrifice, emitted their seed. This seed was gathered and put into a jar. What still remained on the ground became the sage Vasishṭha, and what was in the vessel became the sage Agastya. She later seduced Vibhāṇḍaka father of Ṛishyaśṛiṅga*.

The incident with Mitra and Varuṇa aroused the wrath of the two frustrated deities, and they cursed their temptress to live upon earth. On earth she met the renowned king Purūravas*, and it is with him that her story is chiefly associated. Purūravas having beheld the beautiful apparition immediately fell in love with her. She agreed to marry him on condition that her two pet rams be allowed to sleep at her bedside, and provided the king never showed himself naked before her.

The gods, who were now impatient for the return of their favourite apsarā to *svarga* (heaven), ordered the *gandharvas* (celestial servitors) to steal the two rams from her at night. Urvaśī cried out for help and Purūravas jumped up, undressed as he was, in order to give chase to the thieves, whereupon the gods sent a vivid flash of lightning and revealed the naked king to his wife. The promise having been broken, Urvaśī disappeared, and Purūravas went in search of her, wandering for many months as one demented. When he found her at last at Kurukshetra, bathing with her nymphs, she declared that she was pregnant and asked him to return after a year, at which time she would deliver to him a son, and allow him to lie with her for one night annually.

In vain Purūravas pleaded with Urvaśī not to be cruel; in vain he urged her to return home. The nymph did not relent, but she returned to him as promised, once every year. At these meetings she delivered first his son Āyu, and thereafter successively five (or eight) sons in as many years.

Owing to his great devotion the gandharvas decided to grant the king any boon he desired, and he asked for the privilege of remaining eternally with Urvaśī. He was made to perform a special fire-sacrifice, after which he 'obtained a seat in the heavenly sphere and was never more separated from his beloved'. Some authorities see a solar symbolism in this legend, Purūravas being the sun, and Urvaśī the morning mist or dew.

The story of Purūravas and Urvaśī forms the subject of a drama by Kālidāsa called *Vikramorvaśī,* in which Purūravas appears as king Vikrama.

Books

See under Mythology.

USHAS, goddess of the dawn, was the guardian of daybreak even before the Aryan dichotomy in western Asia. She corresponds to the Greek Eos and the Roman Aurora. In the Vedas she is one of the Ādityas, the daughter of Dyaus or Vivasvat and the sister of Rātri (Night). In another myth she is referred to as the daughter of Prajāpati who himself desired her. Ushas, horrified at the idea, ran away, taking on many animal forms to escape her father. Prajāpati likewise changed forms to embrace her, and in this manner the incestuous pair brought into existence all the species of living things.

The twenty-one Ṛig-vedic hymns addressed to Ushas are the most beautiful in the whole of Vedic literature. She is the friend of mankind, visiting every dwelling place, despising not the poor or insignificant; she is the ever-young, ever-beautiful, immortal goddess. 'Long departed are those men who first saw Ushas arise, daughter of the sky, young maid in white robes. We gaze on her now, as others will, down the long avenues of time. O dawn, auspicious one, shine afar'.

Books

See under Mythology.

UŚĪNARA, the ruler of an ancient kingdom named after him, situated to the north-west, near Gandhāra. He later led his tribe, the Uśīnara, into the plains of India and occupied the Panjāb and the Middle Country.

He was the hero of an originally Buddhist legend later embodied in the *Mahābhārata.* In the latter version a pigeon pursued by a falcon sought refuge in Uśīnara's bosom. The falcon would not accept the king's plea for mercy on the pigeon's behalf, and claimed that the pigeon was his legitimate prey and his food, but he finally agreed to spare the bird's life provided he received an equal weight of Uśīnara's own flesh. Uśīnara cut off a piece of flesh from his thigh and placed it on the scales, but the pigeon proved to be heavier; he cut again and again but still the pigeon outweighed the flesh. Finally the King placed his whole body on the balance and this outweighed the pigeon. The falcon, who was in reality Vishṇu in disguise, flew away after restoring Uśīnara's lost flesh, and the pigeon, who was actually Agni, thanked the king and departed after bestowing wealth and blessings upon him.

Yet another test was put to Uśīnara by Vishṇu. This time the god appeared to the king in the guise of a brāhmin who demanded that Uśīnara's own son, Vṛihadgarbha, be cooked and served him for a meal. The king slew and cooked his son and placed the dish before the brāhmin who then ordered him to partake of the dish first. Uśīnara took up a morsel of his son's flesh and was about to put it into his mouth when the brāhmin stopped him, praised his devotion, restored Vṛihadgarbha to life and vanished.

Uśīnara had five sons, of whom three founded dynasties and ruled tribes named after them. They were Yaudheya, Ambashṭha and Śivi.

Yaudheya, 'warrior', was the leader of a republican tribe of the Panjāb, with capital near Multān. They were referred to by Pāṇini, and were sometimes spoken of in association with the tribe of Trigartta. The *Mahābhārata* gives a description of their defeat by Arjuna. In historical times they were instrumental in ending Kushān power in India.

Ambashṭha was the founder of a democratic kshattriya-śūdra Scythian tribe of eastern Panjāb, who were known as warriors and later as farmers. Their priests were also physicians renowned for their medical lore. A legend makes them descendants of Dhanvantari. References to them are found in the *Aitareya Brāhmaṇa*, in Manu and in Arrian and Ptolemy. Like other tribes of the north-west (*see* Maga) they found their way across the Gangetic plain to Bengal, and a present-day Bengali caste claims descent from them (II, p. 97).

Śivi (or Śibi), famous in myth, is often confused with his father as the hero of the tale of the falcon and pigeon mentioned above. He was the founder of a republican tribe whose defeat by Sudāsa is referred to in the *Ṛig-veda*. In popular legend Śivi, like his father, was celebrated for his piety and spirit of self-sacrifice. The tribe of Śivi probably occupied the present Swāt valley. They were known to the Greeks as Sibai, and are mentioned as having come into contact with Alexander's invading army. An industrious, enterprising and warlike people, they wore skins for clothing and carried cudgels. According to Arrian they claimed descent from those members of the expedition of Hercules who had been left behind in India (*see* Nysa). Another theory is that they were of pre-Aryan, probably Sumerian stock (II, p. 82). At Kurukshetra they fought on the side of Duryodhana. In historical times they settled first in Rājputāna and then further east, and some authorities hold that they even ventured as far as the Chola country.

Books

I. Ghurye, G. S. *Caste and Race in India*, London, 1932.
II. Law, B. C. *Tribes in Ancient India*, Poona, 1943.

UTATHYA, an Aṅgiras ṛishi, who married Bhadrā, daughter of Soma, a woman of extraordinary beauty. The god Varuṇa beheld her and, overcome with desire, abducted her from the sage's hermitage. In a holy rage Utathya cursed the 'world-destroyer Varuṇa who poses as the guardian of the universe', and then drank up all the rivers, lakes, seas and oceans, including the lake of Varuṇa and the river Sarasvatī, leaving the whole world without moisture. Only after Varuṇa had restored Bhadrā did the ṛishi's anger subside, and he gave back the waters to the parched earth.

Another of Utathya's wives was *Mamatā* who while pregnant was importuned by the holy sacrificial priest Bṛihaspati for the sexual embrace. She cried, 'I am with child. Desist from this deed, for the offspring of Utathya in my womb has already studied the Vedas and Vedāṅgas. Thy seed has irresistible power, and two cannot find room within me'. Even the babe within the womb cried out, 'Do not give way to your lust. This place is much too small for two. And I was here first. I pray you do not crowd me'. In spite of these entreaties Bṛihaspati had his will, and impregnated Mamatā.

But he that occupied the womb still resisted Bṛihaspati's seed, and when the seed was not yet fully mature, kicked it out (I, p. 114). This ejected embryo was later to become the great sage Bharadvāja*. Bṛihaspati cursed the first seed that it might be plunged into profound darkness. The child thus cursed was born blind and was named *Dīrghatamas* (*dirgha-tamas*, 'long darkness'). He was also known as Dīrghatapas ('long penance') for his later austerities, and was said to have regained his sight through worshipping the god Agni. In some legends (in the *Mahābhārata*) Dīrghatamas is called the son of Kāśirāja, and in others (in the *Ṛig-veda*) he is the son of Uchāthya. Among his sons were Dhanvantari and Dīrghaśravas.

Dīrghatamas sought instruction with the sages of the Saurabheya (descendants of the divine cow Surabhī*), and from the followers of this cow-cult he acquired their ways, which among other things included promiscuity. He introduced his young wife Pradveshī to the cult and lived on her earnings, a proceeding which was repugnant to the hermits among whom he dwelt, and he was excommunicated. His wife now demanded that he keep her, since it was the duty of the husband to support the wife and not the other way about, and the sage in anger agreed to support her if she would remain faithful to him, even after death, and threatened to introduce certain changes in the marriage laws.

Thereupon, with the help of her sons, Pradveshī threw her husband into the Ganges, but he saved himself from drowning by clinging to a raft, and was finally rescued by Bali, king of the Anavas. After this bitter experience Dīrghatamas ordained that every woman was to be subject to her husband, abide by his will, and should have only one husband, dead or alive. The remarriage of widows was absolutely forbidden. At Bali's own request Dīrghatamas begat five sons on Sudeshṇā the king's wife, after whom the five Bāleya* kingdoms of the east were named.

By the śūdra (low-caste) maidservant of Bali, named Uśij, Dīrghatamas became the father of *Kakshīvat*, a famous *ṛishi*. Kakshīvat was also called Kakshīvān, or Kakshīvant; he is also known as Pajriya, because he was of the race of Pajra. He was connected with the healing work of the Aśvins; composed several hymns, and has been called 'one of the most important authors of the *Ṛig-veda*' (II, p. 73). He was magnanimously treated by king Svanaya who gave him his daughter in marriage and made him valuable gifts in gold, cattle, horses and chariots. In one of his hymns Kakshīvat extols the bounty of the king.

Books

I. Meyer, J. J. *Sexual Life in Ancient India*, 2 vols., London, 1930.
II. Upadhya, B. S. *Women in the Rigveda*, 2nd Ed., Banaras, 1941.

UTSARGA, 'evacuation', constitutes a major class of Hindu *śodhanas* or purificatory rites. The term is used for any process leading to the emission from the body of waste or excess matter, such as semen, urine or faeces. It implies an abandonment of impurities, and the liberation of the body and the spirit from their evil influences.

It is often confined in its meaning to the act of excretion alone, which plays an essential part in Hindu occult and meditative practice. Critics have frequently condemned yoga for its 'preoccupation with bowel functions', and its importance is shown by the constant stress laid on it. Among the many sayings in Sanskrit and the vernaculars which relate to this aspect of existence, a common one is that a man who evacuates once a day is a *yogi* (ascetic), he who does so twice a day is a *bhogi* (worldling), and he who evacuates thrice a day is a *rogi* (sick man).

The 'ritual' of evacuation has rarely been described, and the classic on the subject still remains the twenty-three paragraphs of the Abbé Dubois, which he wrote over a century and a half ago, after much hesitation and apology, having obtained the particulars from a Hindu book on ritual. These 'Rules to be observed by Brāhmins when answering the calls of nature', set forth in some detail the procedure to be observed during the function. Since his time scatalogical data are part of the picture sought by anthropologists in the study of human races and their customs, and no apology need be made today for giving attention to such matters.

Ecological factors have been shown to account for many customs prevalent in different parts of the world. The Europeans use of paper, and the Arabs application of sand and stones are doubtless due to the exigencies of the climate and the general environment. In a different milieu such practices can arouse feelings of disgust in others. The Abbé Dubois writes, 'Hindus look upon the European habit of using paper as an utter abomination, and never speak of it without disgust. Some even refuse to believe that anyone can have such loathsome habits, and think it is a libel invented out of hatred for Europeans'.

The Indian environment and the demands of hygiene and cleanliness can therefore account for many of the purificatory rites practised by the Hindus. In evacuation the procedure was, and in the villages may still be said to be, as follows. The place set aside for the purpose is always some distance, 'at least a bowshot', away from the house, so that a wind, however strong, will not carry any odour into the dwelling place. The site should not be in the vicinity of sages, brāhmins, cows, another's excreta; nor near a temple, river's edge, pond, well, public roadway or other public place; nor near a sacred tree or anthill; nor a ploughed field. The person must walk to the selected spot without treading on ash, bones, worms or refuse. He should squat low (this position is also taken for urination, even by men), taking care not to face the sun, moon, or any fire, nor a temple, shrine, image or sacred tree. While relieving himself he should remain silent, holding no thought in his mind. He should complete his business with all possible speed. He should never commit the offence of looking behind, for that is the habit of an animal, and the sight is a great pollution.

Now, taking his brass waterpot in his right hand and holding his privates with his left hand he must arise and make for a nearby stream. Here he should pick up a handful of earth, being careful that this earth is not taken from the roadsise, temple, cemetery, a nest of ants, or thrown up from a rat-hole. He should moisten it with water and rub the dirty part three times to five times, the left hand invariably being used for the purpose. The whole area is then washed and rinsed with water. Finally the face is washed and the mouth rinsed eight times (four times after urination). The orthodox follow this with a bath.

The operation of cleansing oneself after evacuation is regarded as very offensive, and till the beginning of the last century there were certain places in southern India, such as the interior of Mysore, where the function was carried out by a woman. Women went out with men to perform the duty after they had answered the call of nature, much as the court pages performed these unpleasant offices for many European monarchs till the eighteenth century.

Books

I. Bourke, J. G. *Scatalogic Rites of All Nations*, Washington, D.C., 1891.
II. Dubois, Abbé. *Hindu Manners, Customs and Ceremonies*, Oxford, 3rd Ed., 1936.

VĀHANA, 'carrier' or 'bearer', generally translated 'vehicle', is the bird or animal associated with the major Hindu deities. The vāhana is nowhere found in company with the old Vedic gods; it seems to have been introduced as part of the *Vrātya* ritual, and figures prominently in Purāṇic Hinduism. In this popular form of the religion each of the deities of the Hindu pantheon is represented as accompanied by, riding on the back of, or being drawn in a chariot by a specific animal or bird. Such an animal or bird is known as the vāhana of that deity.

The following is a brief list of some of the gods, along with their vāhanas: Agni, god of fire, has the ram for a vāhana; Bhairava, the fierce aspect of Śiva, the dog; Brahmā, the Creator, the *haṁsa*, i.e. the goose or swan; Durgā, wife of Śiva, the tiger or lion, sometimes the parrot; Gaṇeśa, elephant-headed god of good fortune, the rat; Indra king of the gods, the elephant Airāvata; Kārttikeya god of war, the peacock Paravāṇi (Kārttikeya as Subrahmaṇya, carries a cock); Kāma god of love, a parrot (but his banner bears the *makara* or sea-monster); Lakshmī, goddess of wealth, the owl; Nirṛiti, one of the godlings, has a man for a vehicle; Pārvatī, wife of Śiva, a lion; Śani or Saturn, the vulture; Sarasvatī goddess of wisdom, the peacock or swan, sometimes a parrot; Śītalā goddess of smallpox rides on an ass; Śiva, the Destroyer, the white bull Nandi; in sculpture Śiva is often depicted having Vāsuki the cosmic serpent as a girdle, and having a *mṛiga* (deer) springing from his finger; Varuṇa, god of the seas, the sea-monster or *makara*; Vāyu god of the winds, the antelope; Vishṇu, the Preserver, has Garuḍa the eagle and Ananta the serpent; Yama, god of the dead, the buffalo.

Books

See under Mythology.

VAIŚESHIKA, one of the six orthodox systems of Hindu philosophy. Its founder, the author of the *Vaiśeshika-sūtra*, was *Kaṇāda* (?*c*. 250 BC–AD 100), whose name signifies 'eater of atoms', because he resolved reality into its smallest possible 'atomic divisions'. He may therefore be called the Democritus of Hindu philosophy. From his habit of meditating all day and seeking food at night, he was given the cognomen of *Aulūka* (from *ulūka*, 'owl'); he was also known as Kaṇabhuj or Kaṇabhuksha. It is believed that all these names were merely descriptive, and that his real name is forgotten, though some think he may have been the sage Kāśyapa.

Vaiśeshika philosophy forms a sort of supplement to the Nyāya system, although it was probably in existence before Nyāya. Where the latter stresses logic, Vaiśeshika analyses physical notions such as space, time, cause, matter and so forth, and deals with the nature of the world. Like the Nyāya system the Vaiśeshika in its earliest form is atheistical, although a Supreme Soul or God (Paramātman) was introduced later. Paramātman fashioned the world from the substances which have existed from all time. God is the creator of the world but not of its constituent elements.

In Vaiśeshika, enquiry is arranged under six predicables or categories* called *padārtha*, namely: (1) *Dravya*, 'substance'*, regarded as the foundation of the universe and believed to be composed of nine eternal realities, subdivided into two groups, one group called *paramāṇu*, consisting of earth (*pṛithivī*), water (*āpas*), fire (*tejas*), and air (*vāyu*); and the other group consisting of ether (*ākāśa*), time (*kāla*), space (*dik*), soul (*ātman*), and mind (*manas*). (2) *Guṇa** or attribute; twenty-four basic guṇas are distinguished. (3) *Karma**, action, or motion. (4) *Sāmānya*, 'generality', or that which characterizes all the members of a given class. It relates to the principle by which the understanding, in a selective process, reassembles into one group a number of similar objects belonging to that group. (5) *Viśesha* or particularity, distinguishing one member from another of the same class. It is by means of viśesha that the atoms of the paramāṇus (earth, air, fire and water) are distinguished from one another. Everything has its viśesha, its unique essence or particular feature, and it is this that marks one individual from another, and group from group. It is this category which gives its name to the Vaiśeshika system of philosophy. (6) *Samavāya*, 'relation' or combination, i.e. the relationship that exists between a substance and its qualities, or between a whole and its parts. To these original six predicables a seventh was added: (7) *Abhāva*, 'non-existence', not mentioned as a separate category, but added by the later commentators and given considerable importance by them (*see* śūnya).

Books

I. Faddegon, B. *The Vaiseshika System*, Amsterdam, 1918.
II. Gough, A. E. (Tr.) *Vaiseshika-sutra, with Commentaries*, Banaras, 1873.
III. Keith, A. B. *Indian Logic and Atomism: Nyaya & Vaiseshika*, Oxford, 1921.
IV. Sinha, N. *The Vaiseshika Sutras*, Allahabad, 1923.
V. Thomas, F. W. (Ed.) *Vaiseshika Philosophy*, Banaras Ed., 1962.

VAISHṆAVISM, the religion devoted to the worship of Vishṇu and his two chief incarnations, Rāma and Kṛishṇa, with their consorts. Vaishṇavism has an obscure origin and an uncertain history, but its development from the medieval period on has been rapid and remarkable.

Its chief tenet is that of *bhakti*, or devotion to a personal god of grace, which some scholars trace back to Varuṇa in the Vedas and to certain passages in the Upanishads. But the Vedic origin is tenuous and has only recently been invoked to prove its priority, while in the Upanishads the worship of the godhead is only permitted as a concession to human weakness.

The Bhakti cult probably had a non-Vedic genesis. Fragments of such a cult are scrappily discernible in the first and second centuries BC in the creeds of certain non-Aryan tribes like the Sātvata. These early faiths seem to have become blended in the doctrines of the Pañcharātra* sect, which embodied many of the ancient primitive features later associated with Vaishṇavism. Another tribe intimately connected with Vaishṇavism were the Ābhīra, who made significant contributions to the mythology of Kṛishṇa's early life. The doctrine of the saving grace of god appears to have emerged under Christian influence.

Among the principal features of Vaishṇavism were: its strongly anti-brāhminical and anti-priestly attitude, well exemplified in the works of the Marāṭha saints; its use of the vernaculars, like Hindi, Tamil and Marāṭhi, in place of Sanskrit; its emphasis on absolute faith, and complete and total self-surrender to god, as in Lokāchārya's *mārjāra* (cat-hold) theory; its stress on devotion through image-worship and simple ritual rather than through knowledge or the intermediary of priests; and finally, its development of its own form of ritualism, including caste marks, etc.

The chief landmarks in the history of Vaishṇava literature are: the *Pañcharātra Āgamas* of Śāṇḍilya and his successors (*c.* AD 100); the composition of the *Nārāyaṇīya*, the *Anugītā* and the *Harivaṁśa* (completed *c.* AD 500), all now embodied in the *Mahābhārata*; the hymns of the early Āḷvārs* (*c.* AD 650), Tamil poet-saints; the *Bhagavadgītā* (*c.* AD 750); the composition of the *Vishṇu Purāṇa* (*c.* AD 800) and the *Bhāgavata Purāṇa* (*c.* AD 900). With Śaṅkara Vaishṇavism received a temporary setback, although he himself is supposed to have edited and perfected the *Bhagavadgītā*, ridding it of its anti-brāhminical elements. The sect was reinstated by Rāmānuja, 'who brought the soul back to Hindu philosophy', and its progress thereafter was unimpeded.

A catalogue of the great Vaishṇavite personalities in religion and letters would include, in rough chronological order, the following: Rāmānuja (?1017–1137?); Nimbārka (?1130–1200); Jayadeva (fl. 1100); Lokāchārya (1130–1210); Madhva (1197–1280); Deśika (fl. 1230); Nāmdev (1270–1350); Umāpati (fl. 1320); Vidyāpati (1368–1475); Chaṇḍidās (1350–1430); Narasiṁha Mehto (1414–80); Sadnā (fl. 1420); Rāmānanda (?1360–1470?); Raidās (fl. 1430); Kabīr (1440–1518); Chaitanya (1485–1534); Vallabha (1489–1531); Mīrābāi (?1450–1547?); Sūrdās (1483–1563); Dādū (1544–1603); Haridās (fl. 1580); Keśavdās (1555–1617); Tulsīdās (1532–1623); Malukdās (1574–1682); Nābhādās (*c.* 1625); Tukārām (1607–49); Bihārilāl (1603–63); Lāldās (d. 1648); Rāmdās (1608–81); Charandās (1703–82); Jagjīvandās (1682–1720).

Among the lesser Vaishṇavite sub-sects are: the Haridāsa (or Dāsa) sect whose devotional songs were written by the saints of Karṇāṭaka; its creed is based on the dvaita system of Madhva; the Śrīvaishṇava of the Tamil country, the most inclusive, who recognize all the *avatāras* of Vishṇu; the Sahajīyā who stress the Rādhā-Kṛishṇa aspect and often tend to antinomianism; the Kiśorī-bhāja who practice a form of religious sexualism and virgin-worship; and the Sakhībhāva who indulge in homosexuality. The itinerant bards of Bengal known as the Bauls are also Vaishṇavite.

Books

I. Aiyangar, S. K. *Early History of Vaishnavism in South India*, Madras, 1920.

II. Bhandarkar, R. G. *Vaishnavism, Saivism and Minor Religious Systems*, Strassburg, 1913.

III. De, S. K. *Early History of the Vaishnava Faith and Movement in Bengal from Sanskrit and Bengali Sources*, Calcutta, 1942.

IV. Deming, W. S. *Ramdas and the Ramdasis*, Calcutta, 1928.

V. Gonda, J. *Early Aspects of Vaishnavism*, Utrecht, 1957.

VI. Karmarkar, A. P. *Mystic Teachings of the Haridasas of Karnataka*, Dharwar, 1939.

VII. Mallik, G. N. *The Philosophy of the Vaishnava Religion*, 1927.

VIII. Rajagopalachariar, T. *Vaishnavite Reformers of India*, Madras, 1909.

IX. Rao, T. A. G. *History of Sri-Vaishnavas*, Madras, 1923.

X. Raychaudhuri, H. C. *Materials for the Study of the Early History of the Vaishnava Sect*, Calcutta, 1936.

VAIŚYA, the third of the four Hindu castes. Although traditionally regarded as one of the 'twice-born', and entitled to some of the privileges accorded to the two upper castes, the vaiśya was generally held in low esteem. He was the trader, grocer, money-lender and merchant, and as such he had some claim to consideration since he was in a position to pay the brāhmin liberally for his services, and his usefulness to the community as a whole has never been in doubt.

According to the lawgivers, the vaiśya was usually classed with the śūdra*, and the occupations open to these two classes were almost identical. Out of the eight forms of marriage, the two prescribed for the vaiśyas are the same as those recommended for śūdras. When a brāhmin marries beneath his caste, his sons by a vaiśya or a śūdra inherit equal shares. There is a common formula of salutation and welcome for a vaiśya and a śūdra guest, and both of them are to be given food together with one's servants.

The caste was sweepingly condemned by many lawgivers as dishonest, avaricious, miserly, unscrupulous, and mammonistic. They acquired their wealth by fraudulence and cheating. Manu spoke of goldsmiths and their ilk as 'deceivers in open daylight', evading taxes and shirking their responsibility to the state. The vaiśya has made and still makes a substantial contribution to the welfare of the state, and some of the greatest philanthropists of India have come from this class. But tradition dies hard, and all too frequently the term *bania* (from Sanskrit *vaṇij*, 'trader') has been synonymous with the black-marketeer, the exploiter of his employees, the shady dealer, adulterating the commodities he sells, guilty of every sharp practice, and willing to barter his soul for profit.

Some of the vaiśya sub-castes are listed here. Often they belong to the Jain persuasion. Many have passed into the kshattriya fold, claiming the higher status by virtue of their earlier origin. From the north and north-west come the *Arorā* of the Panjāb, many of whom arrogate to themselves the rank of kshattriyas; and the *Ahār* (or Āhīr), of north and central India, sometimes equated with the Āhīras, who are graziers and hersdmen; from Rājputāna are the *Jaisvāl* and the *Osvāl,* the latter predominating in Mewār and mainly Jain by religion. In western India we have the *Modaka* or Modh banias, descendants of the Gurjaras; also from western India are the *Rastogi* and the *Bañjārā,* the latter extending to Central India, and the *Bhāṭia,* prominent in Bombay. The *Agarvāla* of upper India are said to be of aboriginal origin and some trace their descent from a nāga ancestress; they too are mostly Jain by religion. In Bihār the *Bhār* are prominent; they were at one time a ruling caste in Bihār to whom many forts and reservoirs are attributed; today they are mainly labourers and small cultivators. The flourishing *Cheṭṭiār* of south India are often classed with the *kayashthas.*

Books

I. Ghurye, G. S. *Caste and Class in India,* Bombay, 1950.
II. Morya, N. N. *The Castes of India,* 1913.

VAIVASVATA, or Manu Vaivasvata, i.e. Manu the son of Vivasvat the sun-god, also known as Satyavrata, was the Noah of Hindu mythology. He was the seventh of the traditional Manus, and the Manu of the present age, the *Kali-yuga.* He is the central figure in the Hindu legend of the Flood, different versions of which are found in the *Śatapatha Brāhmaṇa,* the *Mahābhārata* and the Purāṇas.

According to legend, at the end of one of the *kalpas* or 'days' of Brahmā, the giant demon *Hayagrīva* (*haya-grīva,* 'horse-neck') stole the Veda as it slipped out of the mouth of the sleeping Brahmā. There was consternation in the seven celestial worlds, and the god Vishṇu decided to assume the form of a fish in order to recover the stolen scripture, and at the same time to save Manu from the coming flood, and instruct him in the wisdom of the Veda.

One day as Manu was engaged in his devotions on the banks of a river he scooped up a handful of water for the purpose of *āchamana* (ablutionary rinsing of the mouth) and found that he had caught a tiny fish. The fish appealed to him not to throw it back into the river, but to protect it from the larger fish. 'Take care of me, and I will take care of you', the little fish promised. Manu put the fish in a small earthen vessel and as it grew rapidly larger day by day he had to find larger and larger vessels for it; then he moved it to a pond, then a lake, then the sea, and finally only the ocean was big enough to contain his charge. Manu now realized the divinity of the fish which was indeed none other than Vishṇu in his *Matsya,* 'fish', incarnation. The god warned him that there would shortly be a flood which would destroy all living things, and advised Manu to build a boat and embark on it with the seeds of all created things, and also, according to some versions, the seven great ṛishis or sages. This Manu did, and when the flood came he fastened his ship to the mighty horn of the divine fish, using the cosmic serpent Śesha as a rope, and was thus saved from destruction. Vishṇu then slew the demon Hayagrīva and recovered the Veda; because of this incident Vishṇu himself is often called by the name of the daitya, Hayagrīva.

When the flood subsided Manu's ship rested on the Naubandhana (or the Trikūṭa) mountain in the Himālayas. Here Manu disembarked and inaugurated sacrificial rites to the gods, a practice followed by mankind thereafter. From his sacrifice a woman was created, named Ilā (*see* Sudyumna) who declared herself to be his daughter. With her he cohabited and produced offspring, and thus became the progenitor of the whole human race. All the Solar and Lunar dynasties mentioned in the Purāṇas are said to have sprung from him, and are sometimes referred to as the Mānava, a loose term of contentious application, According to the traditional account Manu had nine sons, but this number varies and so do their names and the dynastic lines or races they established. The chain of descent of the various dynasties is discrepantly given in the Vedas, Epics and Purāṇas, and the dynastic confusion still remains to be sorted out.

The nine sons of Manu were: (1) **Ikshvāku**,* founder of the *Sūrya vaṁśa*, 'Solar race'. The elder branch formed the Kośala dynasty with capital at Ayodhyā and included such kings as Māndhātṛi, Hariśchandra, Raghu Rāma, and Agnivarṇa. The younger branch of Videha had its capital at Mithilā and its chief king was Janaka. (2) **Nābhāga** or Nābhāna of the Vaiśālī line. (3) **Dhṛishṭa** of the Dhārshṭaka line. (4) **Śaryāti**, who ruled in Ānarta, ancient name of Gujerāt. Among his descendants was Haihaya. (5) **Narishyanta**, ancestor of the Śakas. (6) **Karūsha** of the Karūsha line. (7) **Pṛishadhra** was excluded from a share of the earth because of the non-observance of rituals. He was the progenitor of the nomadic peoples of Central Asia. (8) **Prāṁśu**, ancestor of certain aboriginal tribes. (9) **Sudyumna**, founder of the Lunar line.

The Lunar race, called the *Chandra vaṁśa* or *Soma vaṁśa*, begins with Chandra (or Soma) the son of the sage Atri. Soma's son was Budha who married Ilā (i.e. Sudyumna in his female form). Ilā's son was Purūravas (or Aila), hence the Lunar dynasty is also named *Aila vaṁśa.*

Purūravas's younger son Amāvasu founded the Kanyākubja line, while another son, called Āyu became the father of Kshatravṛiddha founder of the Kāśī line. Yet another of Purūravas's sons was Nahusha who became the father of Yayāti.

Yayāti's children were Druhyu, founder of the Druhyus of Gandhāra; Turvaśu, founder of the Turvaśus; and Anu, Yadu and Puru.

Anu became the progenitor of the Ānava, Uśīnara, Yaudheya, Ambashṭha, Sauvīra, Kekeya, and Madra dynasties of north-west India; and of the Aṅga, Vaṅga, Kaliṅga, Puṇḍra, and Suhma lines of eastern India.

Yadu was the ancestor of the Haihaya, Yādava, Vidarbha, Bhoja, Chedi, Vṛishṇi, and Avanti dynasties.

Puru was the ancestor of the Paurava, Bharata, Pañchāla, Kaurava, Pāṇḍava and another Chedi lines.

Books

I. Datta, S. *The Flood Legend in Hindu Literature*, 1916.
II. Frazer, J. G. *Ancient Stories of a Great Flood*, 1916.
(*See also under* Mythology.)

VĀJAPEYA, (*vāja-peya*, 'vigour draught'), an ancient one-day soma ritual in which animals, including the cow, were sacrificed to the Maruts or storm-gods and other deities. It was performed by kings and by priests aspiring to the highest positions. The number seventeen figured prominently in this ceremony. Sixteen priests and the *yajamāna* or sacrificer, making seventeen persons in all, officiated; there were seventeen chants, seventeen invocations, and altogether seventeen animals were sacrificed. Although technically lasting for one day, its preparation and consummation stretched over seventeen days. Each guest was given seventeen small cups of *soma* wine.

The *hoṭri*-priest recited the formula while the *adhvaryu*-priest performed the active side of the sacrifice. A rite of sexual union was an important part of the celebrations. The participating woman was first ritually transfigured to become the consecrated place for the performance of the rite. Says the *Bṛihadāraṇyaka Upanishad*:

'Her lap is a sacrificial altar; her hairs the sacrificial grass; her skin the press of the soma plant; the two lips of the vulva are the central fire. Verily, great is the world to him who practices sexual intercourse knowing the vājapeya sacrifice.'

The adhvaryu-priest acted in accordance with the text as recited. When the hotṛi split up the two parts of a *śloka* or verse, the woman was made to part her thighs; when he recited two verses together the adhvaryu effected penetration; when the verses were repeated the action was performed; when the hotṛi's recitation became inaudible the adhvaryu emitted his semen. The texts seem to indicate that different verses were used for different postures of sexual union. In some versions the acting couple (who may be the sacrificer and his wife) climbed the *yūpa** or sacrificial post, which was surmounted by a solar wheel, and were turned slowly round three times.

One of the culminating moments of the vājapeya sacrifice was a chariot race of seventeen vehicles, in which the chariot of the yajamāna was allowed to reach the finishing line first to symbolize the success of his sacrifice.

Books

See under Sacrifice.

VĀKĀṬAKA (AD 250–520), a line of kings who ruled the northern Deccan between the decline of the Sātavāhanas in the third century, and the rise of the Chālukyas in the sixth century AD. Their capital was first at Purikā then Nāsik, and later at Pravarapura.

The antecedents and career of this dynasty are obscured by their frequent matrimonial alliances with the Nāgas, Āndhras, Guptas and other indigenous lines, but they appear in many ways to have been a product of

Graeco-Indian liaison. The antiquarian Bhau Daji held that 'the Vākāṭakas were a dynasty of Yavanas or Greeks'.

The dynasty was founded by **Vindhyaśakti** (*c.* AD 249), and the Vākāṭakas are often referred to by this alternative title. Although little can be said definitely about the ancestry of this king, it is known that he belonged to a line of the Kilakilā, 'leprous', i.e. white, kings, who according to the *Vishṇu Purāṇa* were Yavanas, i.e. Greeks or Kushāns (*see* Kaiṅkilā). At first Vindhya-śakti remained a feudatory of the Sātavāhanas of Vidarbha and a subordinate ally of the Bhāraśiva Nāgas, but he later grew in strength, became independent, extended his sway over a large part of Central India, and in Yavana fashion founded the era of AD 248–49. Because of his power and influence he was accorded orthodox status as a high-born Hindu, and granted the right to perform Vedic sacrifices.

Pravarasena I (*c.* 340) or Pravīra, his son and successor was influential enough to get his own son, Gautamīputra (who died in 344 but did not rule), married to a daughter of the Bhāraśiva king, Bhavanāga. Pravarasena, described in some records as a *saṁrāṭ* or universal monarch, was reputed to have performed as many as four horse sacrifices. His kingdom extended from Bundelkhand in the north to Berār in the south.

Rudrasena II (385), son of Gautamīputra by the Bhāraśiva princess, married Prabhāvatī, a daughter of Chandra-gupta II of the Gupta line. Rudrasena died young and his widow reigned until her sons came of age. The court was consequently much under Gupta influence, and the later rulers became Buddhists. They were noted for their many works for the glory of Buddhism, the last of which was the excavation of cave temple No. XVI at Ajantā, which lay under their direct government, and its presentation to a Buddhist religious order about AD 490. The decline of the Vākāṭakas coincided with the decline of the Guptas in the sixth century.

The Vākāṭakas gave their patronage to sculpture and the graphic arts, and endowed with equal liberality Hindu and Buddhist shrines. They are to be counted among the most glorious of the contemporary dynasties of the Deccan, and deserve a high place of honour among them. Indeed, Jouveau-Dubreuil says, it was 'the dynasty that excelled all others and the one that had the greatest civilization of the whole of the Deccan.'

Books

I. Ghosh, N. N. *Early History of India*, Allahabad, 1948.
II. Jouveau- Dubreuil, G. *Ancient History of the Deccan*, 1919.
III. Majumdar, R. C. (Ed.) *The Gupta-Vakataka Age*, Lahore, 1946.

VALLABHA (1479–1531), also known as Vallabhāchārya, the son of a Telugu brāhmin of South India, acquired early renown as a child of prodigious intellect, having mastered at the age of seven the four Vedas, the six systems of philosophy, and the eighteen Purāṇas. He journeyed north to study in Banāras, and lived for a time in Vṛindāvana. While on a visit to Mathurā, the god Kṛishṇa manifested himself to Vallabha and commanded him to promulgate a new and joyous way of worshipping him, to select disciples, male and female, so that the god might sport with his devotees as in times past. Vallabha travelled all over India propagating his teaching among the people, finally settling down in Banāras where he wrote many works, mainly in Sanskrit. It is said that one day he went to the Ganges, stepped into the water and disappeared in a flash of light.

He founded an important sect that flourishes among merchants and traders in Bombay, Cutch, Gujerāt, Rājputāna and Central India, and he himself is regarded by his followers as an incarnation of Kṛishṇa. His disciples and the disciples of his son *Viṭṭhalnāth*, eight in number, were known as the *ashṭa chhāp*, 'eight seals', because their poems in Hindi are regarded as the criteria of excellence. Vallabha is referred to as the Āchārya, 'leader', and Viṭṭhalnāth as Gosvāmin (or Gosāīṁ).

Vallabha held that Śaṅkara's philosophy was not true advaita (monism) but a mere form of it, which Vallabha dubbed *keval-advaita*, 'mere monism', since it had to depend on māyā or illusion. Vallabha called his own type of monism *śuddh-advaita* or pure monism. According to Vallabha, in the beginning Brahma was not joyful, since he was all alone. Desiring to be many he created the universe and its inhabitants, which sprang from him like sparks from a burning fire. Brahma and the purified soul are one, although the soul is to be regarded as individual, as a part of, but not identical with God. The phenomenal world of *māyā* is not illusion since it is separated from Brahma by his own will.

The Supreme Deity is personified as Kṛishṇa. He creates the world by the force of his will. Not only is he the *kartṛi* or creator, he is also the *bhoktṛi* or enjoyer, of the world. The material universe is divine, and to renounce well-being and mortify the flesh, to fast and do penance, to restrain passion and show indifference to the pleasures of this world are not virtues. They constitute an affront to the deity, since he has provided man with the bounty (*pushṭi*) of this world so that he might enjoy it. Vallabha himself was married and held that marriage was not a hindrance to the devout life. His system is sometimes called *pushṭi-mārga*, 'abundance way', since it calls upon its followers to enjoy to the full the good things of nature which god has provided for man's delight.

Kṛishṇa appeared in many forms in times past to please his devotees, his favourite forms being those of a child (Bāla-gopāla), or of a youth at the height of his physical powers. The love of Kṛishṇa for the *gopīs* (milkmaids) was interpreted literally by the followers of Vallabha; it was taken to be a means of experiencing intimately the presence of the deity. In their *rāsa-maṇḍala*, 'joy circle', worshippers enacted the love scenes of Kṛishṇa and the cow-girls in the belief that they thus provided an opportunity for Kṛishṇa's mystic participation in their pleasure. All ceremonies and festive observances were marked by a spirit of 'sportive enjoyment'. In re-enacting the scenes of Kṛishṇa's childhood and manhood, in singing and dancing, in praising and talking of Kṛishṇa, the god is seen everywhere, and everything becomes an object of love and devotion. Observing this, Kṛishṇa uplifts the spirits of his devotees to his celestial paradise in Vṛindāvana to enable them to partake of the divine joys there. The final reward of their devotion when they die, is admission to the eternal sports (līlā) of Kṛishṇa's paradise.

The ritual of worship includes eight daily ceremonies connected with the idol of Kṛishṇa. This idol is gently awakened every morning, washed and dressed, offered pān (betel-leaves), taken out to tend the cattle, escorted home, fed, entertained with music and dancing, and in the evening put to sleep.

The present gurus or leaders of the Vallabha sect are referred to as *mahārāja*, 'great king', and are descendants of the seven sons of Gosvāmin. Today there are over one hundred mahārājas, their chief being the one who presides over the temple of Naṭdvāra in Rājputāna, which is said to contain the idol from the main temple of Mathurā smuggled out of that city during the Muslim persecution. The idol is believed to be the actual abode of Kṛishṇa.

Extraordinary reverence used to be paid to the mahārājas; his words were treated with absolute obedience; his look (*darśan*) was believed to bestow benediction and grace; the water in which his feet were washed was held to have purifying and medicinal properties and was drunk by disciples, as was the water with which he rinsed his mouth. To the mahārāja the devotees were expected to surrender, in theory at least, all their material possessions. By the formality of *saṁ-arpaṇa*, 'con-ferring', the mind, body, property (*man, tan, dhan*) were made over to the mahārāja. The initiation ceremony included the taking of the following oath: 'Oṁ. Kṛishṇa is my refuge and to him I consecrate my body, senses, life, heart, faculties, my wife, house, family, property, and my own self'.

There were no public places of worship and devotees had to resort to the private temples of the mahārājas, which gave scope for widespread abuses. Women of the sect, the wives and daughters of the devotees, were encouraged to submit to caresses and, if required, to surrender themselves to the mahārājas. The mahārājas claimed a first share in every pleasure of their followers, including, according to the general scandal, the *jus primae noctis*.

The cult came into notoriety and was exposed in a famous court case in 1862, when the then mahārāja was accused in the Bombay High Court of gross profligacy. It was found by the court that 'all the songs connected with the worship of Kṛishṇa which were produced before us were of an amorous character, and of a corrupting and licentious tendency, and these were sung by young females to the mahārājas upon festive occasions in which they are identified with the god in his most licentious aspect. In these songs as well as stories, the subject of sexual intercourse is prominent. Adultery is made familiar to the minds of all, and is nowhere denounced but on the contrary is commended' (IV, p. 137).

The sect has since recovered from these unpleasant deviations and flourishes today in Western India.

Books

I. Anonymous, *History of the Sect of Maharajas or Vallabhacharyas in Western India*, London, 1865.

II. Bhandarkar, R. G. *Vaishnavism, Saivism and Minor Religious Systems*, Strassburg, 1913.

III. Ghoshal, S. *The Krishna Cult of Western India*, 1901.

IV. Thomas, P. *Kama-Kalpa: The Hindu Ritual of Love*, Bombay, n.d.

V. Wilson, H. H. *Sketch of the Religious Sects of the Hindus*, Calcutta, 1846.

VĀLMĪKI, 'anthill', the patronymic of a *bhārgava* sage (i.e. a descendant of Bhṛigu), of probably pre-Aryan or Nāga origin, who was the reputed author of the *Rāmāyaṇa*. He was brought up by the outlandish Kirātas and for many years lived by robbery and plunder. The ṛishi Nārada saw in him all the marks of a future 'emperor of poets', and advised him to change his mode of life. Vālmīki abandoned his old ways and took to study, but refused to compose anything until he had a worthy subject and a worthy measure in which to enshrine it. Nārada foretold that he would meet the hero of his future work, and at the proper time would find the right verse form.

Vālmīki's hermitage was situated at Chitrakūṭa, on the river Piśuni (or Mandākinī) in the modern district of Banda in Bundelkhand. To this hermitage came Rāma and Sītā more than once for rest and refuge during their exile, and from them the sage learned about their many adventures. It was here too that Sītā came when she was banished by the suspicious Rāma, and here that she gave birth to her two sons Lava and Kuśa. The sage undertook the education of the two boys, and taught them the story of their father's exploits.

Vālmīki had found his subject but he was still without a suitable metre for his noble theme. One day as he walked along the banks of the Piśuni wrapt in thought, he saw a female heron grieving for her mate who had been killed by a hunter. So stricken was the poet at the sight that his emotions burst forth into a stream of metrical speech, which was the *śloka*. Brahmā then conveyed to him through the *ṛishi* Nārada that it was in this measure that he should compose the epic now known as the *Rāmāyaṇa*.

Books

I. Aurobindo, Sri. *Vyasa and Valmiki*, Bombay, 1956.
II. Das, J. G. *India's Epic Poets*, 1919.
See also under Mythology.

VĀMADEVA, Vedic ṛishi, author of several hymns, including the entire fourth *maṇḍala* of the *Ṛig-veda*. His mother was a woman of very low caste but he was endowed with divine wisdom from the time he was conceived. In order to avoid the disgrace of being born in the usual way from the lowly womb of an outcaste woman, the future ṛishi prayed that he might come out 'laterally, from the side'. This method of birth was regarded as being particularly auspicious, and according to a later legend it was in this manner too that Buddha was born, issuing from his mother's side.

The gods were alarmed at the request of the unborn babe, and Indra himself descended from heaven to reason with him, and tried to persuade him to be born in the usual manner, but in vain. When the time of his birth arrived he assumed the form of a hawk and emerged with all haste from his mother's riven side.

Vāmadeva grew up in extreme poverty; he confesses in one of his Vedic verses that in his extremity he had cooked and eaten the entrails of a dog, a diet resorted to only by outcastes of utter degradation. Manu explains the matter by saying that this is proof that man does not become impure merely by eating impure things.

Books

See under Mythology.

VĀNARA, an animal belonging to the vana, 'forest', specifically the monkey. Vānara was the name given to the monkey people who inhabited the region of the Ṛishyamūka mountain near lake Pampā in the Nilgiris, and who helped Rāma in his search for Sītā and his campaign against Rāvaṇa. It is believed that the term Vānara refers to the *anasya,* 'noseless' i.e. platyrhine, peoples of South India, or to some totemic tribes who bore a monkey emblem on their banner or worshipped the monkey.

The Vānara were ruled by Sugrīva* whose army was commanded by the famous monkey chieftain Hanumān*. The Vānara artisan Nala*, son of Viśvakarman the divine artisan, had the power of making stones float on water, and helped to build a bridge over the eternally 'unfordable straits' between India and Laṅkā, that enabled Rāma and his allies to cross to Ceylon. This bridge is known to this day as Rāma-setu, or Rāma's Bridge, and is still to be seen as a series of little islands. It is now also popularly known as Adam's Bridge.

The Vānara physician Sushena, son of Varuṇa, was able by his surgical skill and knowledge of herbs to heal the wounds of Rāma and his warriors and to restore to life Rāma's dead brother Lakshmaṇa.

The half-brother of king Sugrīva, Bālin*, was also a monkey chieftain of considerable power. He usurped Sugrīva's kingdom and reigned in Kishkindhyā until he was slain by Rāma.

Books

See under Mythology and Rāmāyaṇa.

VARĀHAMIHIRA (505–587), Indian astronomer, mathematician and philosopher, born near Ujjain. His father's name, Ādityadāsa, 'sun-slave', and the suffix of his own name, 'mihira', from Mithra the Persian sun-god, suggest Persian affinities. He is regarded as one of the Nine Gems at the court of Vikramāditya.

In his *Pañcha-siddhāntikā,* 'five treatises', Varāhamihira summarized the sum total of Indian astronomical knowledge of his day. These siddhāntas, sometimes written in the *kāvya* style were:

(1) *Paitāmaha,* 'grandfather', or ancient, which discusses Vedāṅga astronomy, though some authorities find in its name a suggestive pointer to the Greek mathematician and philosopher Pythagoras. It incorporates information going back to AD 80.
(2) *Vāsishṭha,* named after the *ṛishi,* represents a transitional phase between the old Indian astronomy and the Western system.
(3) *Sūrya,* named after the sun god and attributed to one Lāṭa. The *Sūrya-siddhānta* was first revealed by Sūrya to Asura Magha, or Asura Maya, both

parts of whose name suggest probable Maga influence on the work. In one of its stanzas the sun god tells Asura Magha, 'Owing to the curse of Brahmā you will undergo reincarnation as a barbarian. Go therefore to the Romaka city and I will impart to you this science'. This is an allusion to the foreign source from which the book was derived, since the city of Romaka is either Rome or Alexandria. In this treatise Indian astronomy for the first time appears in its fully developed classical form. It includes material dating back to AD 400, although the present text dates from about AD 1000.
(4) *Romaka*, i.e. Roman or Alexandrian, is derived from Ptolemy. The Romaka adopts not the Indian yuga system of millions of years, but a new one of 2,850 years, thus departing entirely from Indian tradition, and makes calculations for the meridian of Yavanapura, 'Greek city'. The year of 365 days, 5 hours, 55 minutes and 12 seconds, corresponds exactly to the tropical year of Hipparchus (fl. 160 BC).
(5) *Paulīśa*, based on the astronomical works of Paulus of Alexandria (*c.* AD 378). It gives a table of sines and two trigonometrical rules.

Varāhamihira's own writings include the *Bṛihat-saṁhitā*, an encyclopaedic work dealing with the study of omens from natural, especially celestial occurrences, and containing much of interest for the student of religion. He lays great stress on the need for astrology, and adds, 'As a night without a lamp; as a sky without the sun; so is a king without astrologers'. It is essential to consult astrologers before building a new house, digging wells, laying out gardens and tanks, searching for underground waters, or fashioning idols. Eleven chapters are devoted to *śākuna*, 'augury'. He also wrote a treatise on auspicious seasons for weddings, and another on the proper time for kings to go to war or undertake an expedition. Two other works on horoscopes, the *Horā-śāstra* (from Gk. horā), also called the *Bṛihad-jātaka*, 'great nativity'; and a shorter *Laghu-jātaka*, 'brief nativity', are well known and still studied; the latter contains several words which are of Greek origin.

Books

I. Gangooly, P., & Sengupta, P. *Surya Siddhanta*, Calcutta, 1935.
II. Thibaut, G., and Dvivedi, S. *The Pancha-siddhantika of Varahamihira*, Banaras, 1889.

VARUṆA, a deity of Indo-European origin, personification of the all-enveloping heaven, known to the ancient Greeks as Uranus, and believed to correspond to the Ahura Mazda of the Iranians. His name appears in a Mitanni inscription of Asia Minor (see below).

At first Varuṇa was the sustainer of the universe, the presiding deity of *ṛita*, or the moral order of the cosmos and the rightness underlying all things. In general his character far surpassed that of any other Vedic deity. Nothing was hidden from him; his *pāśa*, 'noose', caught the wicked; as a judge he rewarded righteousness and punished iniquity, but was ever forgiving to those that were penitent. 'It is he who makes the sun to shine in the heavens, and the winds that blow are his breath. He has hollowed out the channels of the rivers which flow at his command, and he has made the depths of the sea'.

But in the new environment of India there was a need scarcely less important than the regulation of metaphysical law, and that was the prosaic need for seasonal rain. Varuṇa therefore underwent a slow etiolation of his powers, until he was finally dethroned by Indra. He became 'prince of oceans', commanding innumerable white horses, and as the Indian Neptune he received the worship of fishermen.

According to legend he once ran off with Bhadrā wife of Utathya, but later he restored her. He is paid little homage in India today, and the only existing temple dedicated to him is on the island of Bali. Varuṇa's paradise is *Vasudhā-nagara*, 'wealth-yielding town'; his palace is *Sukha*, 'pleasant', situated on *Pushpa-giri*, 'flower-mountain'. Over his throne, protecting him from the waters is the hood of the great serpent Ābhoga. Varuṇa is regent of the west; his *vāhana* or vehicle is the *makara*, or sea-monster.

Varuṇa was regarded as the chief of the Ādityas, and as such was associated with the god **Mitra** who was his constant companion. But the connection of these two deities is even older than the Indo-Iranian period, for the names of Varuṇa (Uru-w-na) and Mitra (Mi-it-ra) appear along with those of Indra and Nāsatya i.e. the Aśvins, in a Mitanni inscription at Boghaz Koi in Asia Minor dated about 1400 BC. In the Vedic period the name Mitra was a variant of the Old Persian Mithra. But whereas Varuṇa represented the night heavens, Mitra was a god of daylight and of the sun. The Middle Persian form of the name was Mihr or Mihira, from which several prominent Persian and Hindu proper names were derived, including Buzurgmihir and Varāhamihira. Mitra appears with Varuṇa in the mishap with the nymph Urvaśī that resulted in the birth of the sages Vasishṭha and Agastya.

Varuṇa is also called Prachetas, 'intelligent'; Ambu-rāja, 'water-king'; Jala-pati, 'water-lord'; Ad-dāma, 'surrounder'; Pāśin or Pāśa-bhṛit, 'noose-carrier'; Vāri-loma, 'moist-haired'; Yādaḥ-pati, 'king of aquatic creatures'; Yādo-nātha, 'lord of sea monsters'. Makara, the vāhana of Varuṇa, is also called Kaṇṭaka, 'thorny'; Asita-danta, 'black-toothed'; Jala-rūpa, 'water-formed'.

Books

See under Mythology.

VASISHṬHA, not to be confused with Vasishṭha* the tantrik adept, was a celebrated *ṛishi* (sage) of the Tṛitsu tribe, who appears in the *Ṛig-veda*, the *Mahābhārata*, the *Rāmāyaṇa* and the Purāṇas. He was first born as the son of Brahmā, but for cursing Nimi, son of Ikshvāku, he had to leave his earthly body. His next incarnation came when the gods Mitra and Varuṇa emitted their seed at the sight of the lovely nymph Urvaśī and caused him to be born from it.

Vasishṭha is the writer of the seventh *maṇḍala* of the *Ṛig-veda*, and of several other hymns in the same *saṁhitā* (collection). One of these was composed when, after a long fast, he came to the dwelling of the god Varuṇa in search of food, but the house-dog barked at him and tried to keep him out. On the spur of the moment the sage improvised a hymn beginning, 'protector of the dwelling', and so appeased the animal which allowed him to enter the house.

In Indian tradition Vasishṭha stands for the perfect orthodox brāhmin ideal, although he served the non-Aryan king Sudāsa and the barbarian Śakas (Scythians) and Yavanas (Greeks). In the Ṛig-veda he is condemned for 'worshipping false gods'. He also officiated as the family priest of Ikshvāku* and his descendants down to the 60th generation, a clear indication, it would seem, that the name Vasishṭha, like many others in ancient Hindu mythology is a dynastic or family name.

Vasishṭha was the lifelong rival of the sage Viśvāmitra*. Their rivalry was intensified all the more after he defeated Viśvāmitra in a fierce struggle over the possession of his miraculous wish-granting cow Kāmadhenu* which Viśvāmitra had long coveted. But the honours of the struggle were on the whole evenly distributed.

In the course of another encounter connected with the cannibalistic Kalmāshapāda*, Vasishṭha lost one hundred of his sons. His grief at this loss was boundless and he tried in various ways to end his life. He threw himself down from Mount Meru but the rocks he fell upon turned as soft as cotton; he passed without harm through a blazing jungle; he plunged into the depths of the sea and into the turbulent Śatadru (Sutlej), but the river split into a hundred shallow streams and he was saved. He tied a noose around his neck and threw himself into another river, but the river untied the noose and deposited him on the shore. Hence the river was known as Vipāśa, 'un-noosed', now called the Beas.

Coming to hear that his rival Viśvāmitra had ordered the river Sarasvatī to bring Vasishṭha to him so that he might slay him, Vasishṭha directed the river to carry him to his rival, but on seeing the great Viśvāmitra on the banks, all ready armed to slay him, Vasishṭha hastily commanded the river to bear him away in another direction. For this act of disobedience to him Viśvāmitra punished the Sarasvatī by turning her waters into blood.

Further conflict between the two sages arose over king Triśaṅku's* attempt to ascend to heaven; and again during the persecution of Hariśchandra*. Vasishṭha was finally obliged to recognize the brāhminhood of Viśvāmitra, wrested from heaven by 'learning, great works, and penance inconceivable'.

Vasishṭha's favourite wives were Ūrjā, daughter of Daksha, by whom he had seven sons; and the beautiful and devoted Arundhatī, a paragon of conjugal excellence, a model housewife and a perfect cook, who personified the morning star. The eldest son of Vasishṭha by a *chaṇḍālī* (low-caste) woman was Śaktri (or Śakti), who became the father of Parāśara*. The descendants of the sage were called Vāsishṭha and Vāshkala.

Books

See under Mythology.

VASISHṬHA, legendary Tantrik adept, not to be confused with Vasishṭha* the *ṛishi*. He was an indefatigable seeker after truth, and meditated and practised austerities for six thousand years in a lonely wilderness, in order to learn a secret hidden even from the gods. His efforts were unsuccessful, and Brahmā suggested that since what he sought was so extraordinary, he might continue his meditations for another ten centuries. Vasishṭha accepted the divine counsel and went into a long trance, but this too failed to give him the the knowledge he desired. Exasperated by the futility of all his pains he cursed aloud, and suddenly the beautiful Buddhist goddess Tārā appeared before him. With a smile she counselled him to go to Mahāchīna (i.e. either China or Tibet) and follow the teachings of Buddha 'in the Chinese fashion' (*chīnāchāra*).

Vasishṭha repaired immediately to Mahāchīna where Buddha was residing. To his great astonishment and abhorrence he found Buddha in a deeply drunken state, with a foul smell emanating from his mouth, and surrounded by thousands of women. These women were young and handsome, adorned with dazzling jewels, but otherwise naked, and quite devoid of shame. Like Buddha they were drunk and elated, and filled with desire.

The horrified saint appealed to Buddha for an explanation and was told that the ritual requirements for the attainment of 'universal *siddhis*' (powers), and knowledge beyond that which Brahmā could impart, included the drinking of wine, blood and urine, the worship of the naked female, and sexual union. Overcoming his repugnance Vasishṭha performed the ritual of the *pañchatattva* (*see* Chakrapūjā), partaking of meat, fish, cereals, wine and sexual intercourse, and became an adept with extraordinary occult powers and a clear understanding of all truths.

He then returned to India and taught his disciples the esoteric disciplines of chīnāchāra. One of the first temples dedicated to his patron goddess was built at Kāmākhyā, where she was worshipped under that name, or as Tārā. Chīnāchāra is a variant of tantrism* and a very remote and perverse form of Buddhism.

Books

I. Bhattacharya, B. *Introduction of Buddhist Esoterism*, Oxford, 1932.
II. Chatterji, S. K. *India and China: Ancient Contacts*, Calcutta, 1961.
III. Dasgupta, S. B. *Obscure Religious Cults*, Calcutta, 1946.

VASUGUPTA (770–830) of Kashmīr, an early Śaivite philosopher, whose system of 'idealistic monism' was cast in orthodox mould. He accepted the Śaivāgamas and the Siddhānta works, but was influenced by Advaita. He expounded his doctrines in a book entitled *Śiva-sūtra*. His philosophy deals with the threefold principle of God, Soul and Matter, and hence is called *Trika*, 'triad'. The evolution of the world is explained in terms of emanations from Śiva. It recognizes a single reality with two aspects, one immanent and one transcendent, in addition to thirty-six *tattvas* or categories, among them the eternal and changeless Śiva (the static aspect of consciousness), and Śakti (the active aspect of consciousness), the Universal Will, Knowledge, Action, and Māyā the limiting or obscuring principle.

What is needed for salvation is *pratyabhijñā* (prati-abhijñā, 'back-remembrance') or recognition, that the Universal and individual spirits are one, and the realization that the divine reality is within the individual self, just as a love-sick woman is not consoled by the mere presence of her lover; she must recognize him to be consoled. The bondage of our ignorance is overcome by our apprehension of this reality. The soul must recognize itself as God, and as a result there will ensue a progressive dissolution of the 'manifest many', and a realization through the threefold (trika) reality, of the eternal and never-changing One (Śiva).

Since this form of Śaivism* was founded and developed in Kashmīr, it is known as Kashmīr Śaivism, or the Śaivism of the Northern School, and because it deals with the threefold principle of God, Soul and Matter, it is also called Trika-śāsana or Trika-śāstra, or simply Trika.

Books

I. Carpenter, J. E. *Theism in Mediaeval India,* London, 1921.
II. Chatterji, J. C. *Kashmir Saivism,* Srinagar, 1914.
III. Leidecker, K. F. *The Secret of Self-Recognition,* Madras, 1938.
IV. Murti, G. S. (Ed.) *The Secret of Recognition,* Adyar, Madras, 1938.
(*See also under* Śaivism.)

VĀYU, Indo-Iranian and Vedic god of wind*, who holds a prominent place in the Vedas. He is said to have sprung forth from the breath of Purusha, and his chariot, pulled by a thousand horses, is driven by Indra, who acts as his charioteer. In later times his importance diminished, and he became regent of the north-west quarter.

In the Purāṇas and Epics he is the king of the heavenly singers and servitors, the *gandharvas,* and the father of the Pāṇḍava prince, Bhīma, and of the monkey chief Hanumān. Legend has it that Vāyu was invited by the sage Nārada to break the summit of Mount Meru. The wind-god blew for a year with all his terrible might, but failed in his efforts because the eagle Garuḍa shielded the mountain with his wings, His chance came when Garuḍa was absent one day; he attacked the mountain and broke off the summit, hurling it into the sea, where it became the island of Laṅkā (Ceylon).

A licentious and cruel god, Vāyu was said to have made the hundred daughters of king Kuśanabha hump-backed, because they did not submit to his embraces. This gave the name Kanyā-kubja, 'maidens-crooked', to the king's capital city of Kanauj.

Vāyu is often used to symbolize strength, persistence, ruthlessness, omnipresence and other qualities. He has a prominent position in the philosophy of Madhva.

Vāyu is also called Vāta; Pavana (in which form he is a god of physical strength); Anila (with whom are associated the forty-nine godlings of the wind); Gandha-vaha, 'perfume-bearer'; Jala-kāntāra, 'whose forest is water'; Sadā-gati or Satata-ga, 'ever-moving'.

Books

See under Mythology.

VEDA. The primary scriptures of Hinduism, the Vedas (from the root *vid,* 'know') are revered as *apaurusheya,* 'not of human origin', and are honoured by epithets usually reserved for the gods, such as eternal, imperishable, infallible, indestructible. They are in fact greater than the gods, for when the gods perish the Vedas still remain. The *āmnāya*, or sacred text of the Vedas, enshrines the knowledge believed to have been revealed by the self-existent, all-knowing Brahma, to certain inspired *ṛishis* of old. These ṛishis 'heard' the Vedas, which are therefore referred to as *śruti*.

According to Hindu tradition, the Vedas existed in their eternal and perfect form from the beginning of time. At the end of each *kalpa* or aeon, Īśvara (God) uttered the original Veda as he remembered it. Since God himself shared with all other beings in the universal disintegration concomitant with the descending kalpas, he remembered less and less. At the beginning of the *dvāpara-yuga* (the age preceding our own) the Veda consisted of 100,000 verses and had four divisions. By the beginning of the *kali-yuga* (our present age) these had become confused. Much was lost and much perverted. From this disordered mass the sage Vyāsa salvaged as much as he could, arranged the material in its present form under four headings, and passed them on to his four principal disciples: the *Ṛig-veda** to Paila; the *Yajur-veda** to Vaiśampāyana; the *Sāma-veda** to Jaimini; the *Atharva-veda** to Sumantu (or Aṅgiras).

The Vedas consist primarily of four collections or recensions of hymns, detached verses and sacrificial formulas. They are named according to the traditional purpose of their poetical portions which are called *saṁhitā*, 'put together', a term that is often used as a synonym for the Vedas themselves, more specifically for the mantra portions (see below). Originally only the first three Vedas, namely, the *Ṛig*, *Yajur* and *Sāma*, were recognized as canonical, and designated by Manu as the '*trayī*' (triad), 'milked out from the fire, air and sun'. Actually the *Ṛig-veda* was regarded as *the* Veda, the *Yajur* and *Sāma* as supplementary, while the *Atharva-veda* was not included among the śruti. Certain specialized priests (*see* hierophant) were associated with the Vedas, and during the sacrifices and ceremonies each chanted hymns from the Veda known to him.

Strictly the term Veda stands for the parts known as the *Mantras* and *Brāhmaṇas*. The appendages to the Brāhmaṇas are known as the *Āraṇyakas*, and the concluding portions of the Āraṇyakas are called *Upanishads*. These four divisions of the scriptures are generally classified separately thus:

(1) *Mantra**, those portions of the Vedas comprising the metrical psalms of praise, as distinct from the liturgical prose portions of the Brāhmaṇas. The mantras constitute the main body of the saṁhitā compilations, and are the most ancient part of the Vedas.
(2) *Brāhmaṇa**, manuals of ritual and prayer for priestly guidance, giving details of sacrificial ceremonial; they belong to a later date than the mantras.
(3) *Āraṇyaka,** 'forest' treatises for hermits and saints, which form appendages to the Brāhmaṇas.
(4) *Upanishad**, philosophical treatises which often formed part of the Brāhmaṇa or were embedded in the Āraṇyaka. They consist of secret and mystical doctrines and metaphysical discourses. Broadly speaking the Mantras and the Brāhmaṇas are known as *karma-kāṇḍa*, or parts dealing with sacrificial actions; and the Āraṇyakas and Upanishads are called the *jñāna-kāṇḍa* or the portions dealing with knowledge.

The Vedas were composed in an archaic form of Sanskrit called Vedic*. They were handed down orally through a succession of teachers, being progressively expanded, and suffering changes and variations as the canon grew. Parts of the text bear traces of their original Iranian environment, as well as of the change of milieu when the Aryans migrated to India. Some are dated about 1000 BC., and the earliest form of others probably dates from about 800 BC. Large masses of pre-Aryan indigenous material were also absorbed, notably in the *Atharva-veda*, and some interpolated compositions are of comparatively recent date. The accepted texts of the present canon were probably closed about 200 BC.

The Vedic saṁhitās once existed in 1131 recensions, as follows: 21 of the *Ṛig-veda*, 1000 of the *Sāma-veda*, 9 of the *Atharva-veda*, and 101 of the *Yajur-veda*. The teachings of the Vedas and their variants produced a number of schools called *śākhā*, 'branches', and Vedic teachers became famous for their particular version of the text. Each śākhā had its own rules of interpretation called the *prāti-śākhya*. The present versions of the Vedas have therefore been spoken of as 'hymn books in a revised edition', the original edition being lost, unrecognizable, or distorted in the course of about two millenniums.

Even after the introduction of the alphabet, the preservation of the Veda in written form was not encouraged; it was in fact strongly prohibited. The Vedas themselves proscribed such methods; the *Mahābhārata* condemned to hell those who wrote it down, and Kumārila-bhaṭṭa (*c.* AD 730) denounced the writing down of the Vedas as a sacrilege; he held that memorizing the Vedas from written texts was pointless since it brought no merit. The Vedas were meant to be 'heard' in the literal sense. It is no wonder then that with the passage of time Vedic learning became an exercise in mnemonics, and quite removed from reality. In spite of attempts at the restoration of Vedic values, such as was done by reformers like Dayānanda and others, it must be said that the Vedas still continue to be venerated only from a distance. The Vedic gods have been largely abandoned, and the Vedic sacrifices are now virtually obsolete.

An important aspect of the myth of brāhminism relates to the origin of the sacred scriptures. Although the transmission of the Vedas was always regarded as having been entrusted exclusively to divinely inspired brāhmin remembrancers, and was finally set down by brāhmin amanuenses, many non-Aryan ṛishis, and sages of mixed antecedents, have contributed to these great works. To quote Pargiter, 'Tradition ascribes the earliest Ṛig-vedic hymns to non-Aryan kings and ṛishis'. The *Mahābhārata* relates how, in keeping with the best Indian traditions, and in contrast to the brāhminical pretentions of later days, religious teachings were often received from people belonging to the lowest classes of the social order. Bhandarkar suggests that those Vedic hymns where the deities are given the appellation of Asura were composed by seers of Asura stock who had embraced the Aryan religion.

Authors of the Vedas include not only brāhmins and kshattriyas, but also numerous śūdras and half-castes, such as Dīrghatamas, Jamadagni, Kakshīvat, Kaṇva, Kavasha, Mahīdāsa, Sārisṛikta, Stambamitra, Trasadasyu Vāmadeva, and Viśvāmitra. Among the female Vedic teachers and composers of hymns and verses preserved in the Vedas the following are prominent. Āpalā of the Atri family, who married, contracted a skin disease and was cured through intimacy with the god Indra; Ghoshā, daughter of Kakshīvat and grand-daughter of Dīrghatamas, who composed two entire hymns in the tenth book of the *Ṛig-veda* and was cured by the Aśvins of a skin disease; Romaśā who having reached puberty composed an erotic hymn: Śāśvatī who composed a joyous phallic verse at the recovery of her husband's lost virility; Viśvavārā of the Atri family, who composed a sacrificial hymn. Gārgī the Vedic philosopher, Āsaṅga (who, however, may have been a eunuch), Lopāmudrā, wife of Agastya, Maitreyī, wife of Yājñavalkya; Mamatā, wife of Utathya; Nivāvarī, and Prātitheyi, were all celebrated women scholars mentioned in the Vedas. Sikatā, Sulabhā, Vāchaknavī, and Vaḍavā were composers of Vedic hymns and also Vedic teachers.

Books

See under Vedism.

VEDĀNTA, 'acme of the Vedas', one of the six orthodox systems of Hindu philosophy, founded on the Upanishads, and technically classified as *uttara* (later) Mīmāṁsā, to distinguish it from the *pūrva* (earlier) Mīmāṁsā* of Jaimini. Vedānta was first formulated by the philosopher **Bādarāyaṇa** (?250 BC to AD 450?), whose extremely pithy and almost unintelligible *Vedānta-sūtra* (also called the Brahma-sūtra) has been the subject of numberless commentaries. Some scholars identify him with Vyāsa, compiler of the Vedas and *Mahābhārata*. Others hold that he was the guru of Jaimini, founder of Mīmāṁsā, but too little is known of him to justify either hypothesis. There is yet another tradition, as old as the Epics, that Vedānta, that crowning triumph of the Indian philosophical intellect, crystallized not in India but in Mahāchīna, or Tibet.

Vedānta claims to be an exposition of the deepest truths of the Vedas, which record the experiences of those who gained knowledge of the highest order through intuition and inspiration. According to Vedānta the object of existence is not release but realization. Man is one with the Real, and it is meaningless to speak of freeing oneself from the Real. Knowledge alone brings realization and dispels the darkness that conceals one's true nature from one's comprehension. This realization is not obtained through *tarka* (logic) as stated by Nyāya philosophy, for the laws governing logical enquiry by the limited human intellect can never hope to fathom the nature of the Ultimate. Knowledge of the Ultimate can only be gained by the direct intuition of inspired sages, and has been so received and recorded in the Upanishads. Just as the Mīmāṁsā is founded on the Brāhmaṇas, so the Vedānta bases its teachings on the Upanishads.

Vedānta is uncompromisingly monistic and pantheistic, and its creed is summed up in the *mahāvākyas*, or great sayings* of the Upanishads, such as *evam evādvitīyam*, 'one essence and no other', of the Chhāndogya Upanishad. Only Brahma has existence: He is the Ultimate Principle, the Final Reality and the Indivisible One. References in the sacred writings to more than one principle are merely allegorical and descriptive. Thus the Purusha (Spirit) and Prakṛiti (Matter) of Sāṁkhya are not separate and independent principles but only seeming modifications of a single Reality.

The whole phenomenal world around us, of nature and of man, has merely a phantom existence. It is in fact the result of *māyā**, 'illusion', and lacks reality. Māyā is not only a net holding us in thrall, but also a veil concealing from our vision the nature of the True Reality. Ignorance of this leads to the great heresy of *avachchheda*, 'sectionism', or separatedness, a belief that things exist apart from the Absolute. Ignorance is responsible for *saṁsāra*, the continuous cycle of birth-death-rebirth, which lasts as long as we remain in the toils of the great illusion. The only way to rend the bonds is by realizing the transcendently supreme fact that Brahma is all, and that we too are Brahma. *Paramātman* (the Supreme Soul) and *jīvātman* (the individual soul) are identical.

Three schools of philosophy have developed from interpretations of the opening verse of the *Vedānta-sūtra* of Bādarāyaṇa, 'Now, therefore, enquiry should be made into Brahma', and this *Brahma-jijñāsa*, 'Brahma knowledge', is the whole of Vedānta in a nutshell. The three schools referred to are *Advaita* (non-dualism) founded by Śaṅkara*; *Viśishṭādvaita* (qualified non-dualism), founded by Rāmānuja*, and *Dvaita* (dualism) founded by Madhva*. Śaṅkara is generally held to have given the correct interpretation, and his exposition is regarded as the culmination of the Vedānta system. He turned the Vedānta into the strictest form of monism.

Books

I. Abhedananda, Swami. *Attitude of Vedanta Towards Religion*, Calcutta, 1947.
II. Belvalkar, S. K. *Vedanta Philosophy*, Poona, 1929.
III. Deussen, Paul. *The System of Vedanta*, Chicago, 1912.
IV. Guénon, René. *Man & His Becoming According to Vedanta*, London, 1945.
V. Müller, Max. *Three Lectures on Vedanta Philosophy*, London, 1894.
VI. Radhakrishnan, S. *The Brahma-Sutra*, London, 1960.
VII. Thibaut, George. *The Vedanta-Sutras*, Oxford, 1904.

VEDIC, the language in which the Vedas, the sacred scriptures of the Aryan Indians, were composed. Its origins are still not clear, but it is generally believed to be derived from a language called, for convenience, Proto-Aryan*, an early Prākṛit which may have been the common ancestor of Avestic (the language of the Zoroastrian Avesta), Vedic, and other ancient tongues. Vedic is also called Old Indo-Aryan, and is classed with the Primary Prākṛits.

Vedic is thus a close relation of Avestic, but the Avestic inflections are more ancient than the Vedic, and it is thus a younger relation of the Zoroastrian sacred tongue. It has been said that the language of the Avesta is closer to the Vedas than the Vedas are to epic Sanskrit, and almost any Vedic word, and sometimes phrases and even whole stanzas can be changed into their Avestan equivalents, without verbal or syntactical alteration, by merely applying certain phonetic rules.

Vedic is the predecessor of classical Sanskrit*, from which it differs as much as the Greek of Homer differs from classical Greek. It also differs from

Sanskrit in grammar, vocabulary, metre, style, and spirit. The four Vedas and Brāhmaṇas are marked with accents (*udātta*, *anudātta*, and *svarita*), but in classical Sanskrit accent plays no part (III, p. 16). Again, whereas Vedic literature is mainly religious, Sanskrit has a large 'profane' element. Then, the spontaneous nature-worship of the Vedas is to be contrasted with the Sanskrit worship of Vishṇu, Śiva, Brahmā, and various zoomorphic and phallic deities. The Vedas are marked by a robust optimism and describe a period of tribal organization, while Sanskrit writers depict a different milieu, a time of established kingdoms, sophisticated life and meditative philosophy.

Vedic literature is generally divided into five periods: (1) Ṛig-vedic, named after certain hymns of the Ṛig-veda, written in the earliest form of Vedic, most akin to Avestic; (2) Vedic of the Tenth Book of the *Ṛig-veda*, which is slightly later in date and form than the rest of the *Ṛig-veda*. Vedic from this period onwards is spoken of as Later Vedic; (3) the Brāhmaṇa period, largely prose, written in pedantic style with ritualistic purpose, indicative of the growing influence of caste; (4) the Āraṇyaka period, when the forest treatises, and the post-Brāhmaṇa philosophical Upanishads were composed; (5) the Sūtra period (*c.* 500 BC to AD 100), written in verses characterized by gnomic style of great brevity. The *sūtras* were the inspiration of a large literature later copied from this style. The Vedāṅgas are sometimes included in this period.

The work of the grammarian Pāṇinī marks the transition between Vedic and Classical Sanskrit.

Books

I. Jackson, A. V. W. *Avesta Grammar in Comparison with Sanskrit*, 1892.
II. Rapson, E. J. (Ed.) *Cambridge History of India*, Vol. I, 1922.
III. Sastri, G. *A Concise History of Classical Sanskrit Literature*, 2nd Ed., Calcutta, 1960.

VEDISM, a term covering the beliefs and practices of the Aryans, about the period 1000 BC, some time after they had begun to settle in India. These beliefs and practices were distinct enough from those of later Hinduism to merit the distinctive appellation of Vedism. The term is derived from the sacred books of the Aryans called the Vedas* (Books of 'Knowledge'), and the Vedic Age refers to the period when the way of life depicted in the Vedas, particularly the *Ṛig-veda*, had become established in India.

From evidence gleaned from a wide field of enquiry, including scattered accounts in the Vedas and *Mahābhārata*, the history of the Aryan invasion of India has been pieced together. From about 1500 BC a number of related Aryan tribes moved into India in successive waves by way of the valleys of the Swāt, Kābul, Kurram and Gomal rivers. Sometimes peacefully, but more often by violence and conquest, they occupied the Indus and Gangetic plains, and slowly forged eastwards towards Bengal and Assam. Penetration of the south took place many centuries after the conquest of most of the north had been achieved, and the tale of its progress is unfolded in part in the *Rāmāyaṇa*.

There can be no doubt that the Vedic Aryans were of 'an aggressively proselytizing character' (I, p. 20), who extended their sway through conquest and ruthless colonization. The native tribes were stigmatized variously as demons, ogres, monkeys, black-skinned, dwarfish, noseless, speakers of crude languages, men without worship. Says Bhandarkar, 'The Aryans, with all the arrogance and narrowness of fanatics, never thought that there could be any other rites except their own' (I, p. 20). So the natives were further vilified as riteless, priestless, non-sacrificers, without prayer, without Indra, and worshippers of mad gods.

The true aspect of the evidence bears a very different complexion. The Aryans, although better armed, were in many ways inferior to their Anārya victims. According to Piggot, 'The Aryan advent in India was, in fact, the arrival of barbarians into a region already highly organized into an empire based on a long-established tradition of literate, urban culture' (VIII, p. 257). This should be borne in mind along with the statement of a learned German Sanskritist, that the highly admired Vedic mantras are the hymns of barbarians to barbarian gods.

The early Vedic poems are full of a childlike wonder concerning the problems of life, particularly in relation to natural phenomena. How does the sun remain unsupported in the skies? How do the sparkling waters of the river flow into the sea without filling it? How does the rough red cow, give soft white milk? Nature in all her glory is the theme of many early hymns of great beauty. There is a keen delight in the splendour of the hills and the murmur of brooks, the glorious beauty of daybreak, and a deep joy in life, described with spontaneity and depth of feeling.

Of speculation on the metaphysical level, and morose brooding over the mysteries of life and death, there is scant evidence in these early hymns, although some scholars find in certain questions, and in such replies as '*ko veda*', who knows? the seeds of incipient scepticism that germinated in the enquiry and discussion of Upanishadic philosophy.

The early Vedic religion was a form of simple nature-worship. So far as evidence goes there were neither temples nor idols. The *yāgaśālā* or place of sacrifice could be laid out almost anywhere. The gods attended the sacrifices through invocations contained in the hymns, and their invisible presence was assumed during the rites. Tribal history, legends and hymns were preserved by the priests, who handed down the tradition by word of mouth. But no priestly mediation was necessary in the early Vedic period, and priests merely assisted the chieftain or the householder in performing the rites. A more personal relationship existed between the Vedic Aryan and the gods he worshipped. Some of the hymns are frankly *suvṛikti*, or 'good charms', designed to win the favour of the gods by flattery.

Numerous deities are lauded in the Vedas, suggesting polytheism, although some scholars discern a strong sense of underlying unity. Several hymns appear to be definitely monotheistic in tone, while others are distinctly pantheistic. Chief among the Ṛig-vedic deities were Aditi, a Mother Goddess, and her children the Ādityas; Agni, god of fire; Aryaman, god of the manes; the Aśvins, twin gods of the heavens; Dyaus the sky god; the Maruts, gods of the storm; Mitra god of light; Parjanya a rain deity; Pṛithivī, earth goddess; Rudra, chief of the storm deities; Saraṇyū mother of the Aśvins;

Sūrya the sun god; Ushas goddess of the dawn; Varuṇa deity of the water; Vāyu god of wind; Vivasvat, one aspect of the sun-god; Yama god of death.

The evolution of religious thought in the Vedas was typified by the predominant deity of each succesisve period as follows: Dyaus, symbolizing the unsophisticated animism and nature worship of the early Aryans; Varuṇa, introducing the moral and ethical concept, especially the notion of Ṛita or the law of cosmic order; Indra, god of conquest and domination; Prajāpati, the notion of ritual worship. Brahmā represents the hybrid concept of Aryan and indigenous ideas around which the new mythology and sacerdotalism grew up.

In the early hymns native phallic worship was regarded with abhorrence. Sorcery and witchcraft were denounced; whereas in the later sections of the Vedas, particularly in the *Atharva-veda*, witchcraft, spells and magical rites were recommended and prescribed for many varied purposes.

An important place in Vedic ethics is given to the concept of *ṛita*, the sum total of moral law, justice, order and truth. The ideal life was one of virtuous deeds, especially liberality, self-restraint, duty, and heroism in battle, and the reward of this life was a place in heaven. Those who failed to follow the path of virtue were consigned to the dark abyss. The dead were either buried or burned. The Ṛig-vedic hymns do not allude to the transmigration of souls.

Fasting and asceticism are mentioned as a means of obtaining superior powers, but these means and objectives were not generally advocated. The Vedic Aryans had a pagan love for the good things of life. They had no food restrictions and ate flesh freely, and although the cow was regarded as worthy of every care because of its utility, it was slaughtered and eaten on occasion. They drank intoxicating drinks and loved hunting, gambling, dancing and music.

Vedic society was organized on a tribal basis, and, whatever the racial purity of the original invaders may have been, it is evident that by the Vedic period, native had been largely merged with Aryan, despite numerous hymns expressing the antagonism of the Vedic Aryans towards the dark-skinned aboriginals. The chief tribes of the Vedic period, such as the Yadu, Turvaśu, Druhyu, Anu, Puru, Kuru, Pañchāla, Bhārata, Tṛitsu and others, were mixed with aboriginal dynastic lines to an almost indistinguishable degree.

Each tribe, headed by a chieftain, consisted of a number of related families of which the father was the head. The tribes-people were organized into functional and occupational units, which subsequently degenerated into an elaborate caste system. The *Ṛig-veda* in a doubtful hymn, the *Purusha-sūkta*, does refer to the four castes, but the caste system as understood in later Hinduism, with its concept of untouchability, unseeability, and so forth, was quite unknown. Vedism offers no sanction for the iron rule of caste.

Monogamy was the rule in Ṛig-vedic India, and women in general and wives in particular received great honour, shared with their husbands in the performance of the sacrifices, and had a considerable say in domestic matters. The *Ṛig-veda* contains no reference to child-marriage, nor does it prohibit the remarriage of widows.

Books
I. Bhandarkar, D. R. *Some Aspects of Ancient Indian Culture*, Madras, 1940.
II. Bhargava, P. L. *India in Vedic Times*, Lucknow, 1956.
III. Bloomfield, M. *The Religion of the Veda*, New York, 1908.
IV. Das, A. C. *Rigvedic India*, Calcutta, 1921.
V. Deshmukh, P. S. *Religion in Vedic Literature*, Bombay, 1933.
VI. Giri, M. *Vedic Culture*, Calcutta, 1947.
VII. Majumdar, R. C. (Ed.) *The Vedic Age*, London, 1951.
VIII. Piggott, S. *Prehistoric India*, Penguin Books, 1950.
IX. Pillai, G. K. *Vedic History*, Allahabad, 1959.
X. Prabhavananda, Swami. *Vedic Religion and Philosophy*, Mylapore, 1920.
XI. Ragozin, Z. A. *Vedic India*, 2nd Ed., Delhi, 1961.
XII. Wheeler, Talboys, *India Vedic and Post Vedic*, Indian Ed., Calcutta, 1950.

VEGA, 'jerk' or ejaculation. The mere physical impact of a consummated sexual act was often regarded in legend as sufficient to cause procreation, and Hindu mythology is filled with instances of gods and mortals inadvertently creating progeny through the impact or shock of the vega. In the case of *ṛishis*, especially those renowned for their celibacy, the impulse of ejaculation was itself potentially creative, irrespective of where the semen was deposited. One of the most familiar stratagems used by the gods was to cause the ṛishis, whose continence was disrupting the peace of the cosmos, to shed their seed, and thus cool their ardour. The sight of a beautiful nymph at a time when they were bursting with the fulness of their power was often sufficient to precipitate the vega.

A typical instance is the story of the ṛishi *Mankanaka*, whose chastity and prolonged austerities greatly perturbed the gods. One day while he was innocently performing his ablutions on the banks of the Sarasvatī, a nymph was hastily despatched by the gods to effect his vega. She walked seductively before him in transparent robes, and at the sight of her his seed fell into the waves. From this there arose seven ṛishis who were in some way connected with the wind gods.

Hindu legend tells of many similar incidents. Vyāsa, intent on a sacrificial rite, beholds an *apsara*; his seed falls on a firestick and from it a son is created. Ṛishyaśṛinga is born when a gazelle picks up the seed of his father's vega which came forth when he beheld the nymph Urvaśī. Vasishṭha and Agastya are born of the seed of the gods Mitra and Varuṇa emitted into a pot at the sight of the nymph Urvaśī. Satyavatī is born from the seed shed by the king of Chedi who while on a hunting expedition is carried away by thoughts of his wife. Bharadvāja's seed in voided into a bucket at the sight of a nymph, and gives rise to the hero named Droṇa, 'bucket'. Agni's six emissions are gathered by Svāhā in a golden urn and grow to become the six-headed war god Kārttikeya. Drupada is born after his father tried in vain to stamp out his seed expended at the sight of Menakā. Śaradvant son of Gotama lets his seed fall into a canebrake and thus becomes the father of twins. Kaṇḍu's vital essence so permeates the body of the apsarā who breaks his resistance, that it comes forth from her body in the form of perspiration and finally becomes a lovely child. Dadhīcha son of Atharvan ejects his seed into a river at the sight of an apsarā and from it a son is born.

In the more practical treatises of the *kāmaśāstra* the mere vega is not sufficient for procreation, and the *kshetra* or 'field' of the female womb is as necessary as the male seed. Much space is devoted in some of these texts to the analysis of the conditions leading up to vega both in man and woman—the relationship between the physical peculiarities of the genital organs, the duration of the act, and the intensity of the consummation. Specific instructions are given for the choice of a partner of the right type, and various combinations are worked out to ensure a satisfactory vega for both sides.

The question of the woman's vega is also discussed at length. It is said that just as a eunuch who has never experienced gratification can never understand by description alone the feelings accompanying vega, so a man is utterly incapable of understanding the female vega, or vice versa. That the woman's experience is of a different kind is generally agreed, and that it is of a more intense nature is shown by several legends in Hindu mythology, for example the story of Bhaṅgāsvana.

Man's pleasure is held to lie in the physical sensation of union and in the act of emission, while a woman's pleasure is derived from the knowledge that the man desires her, and the fact that she is capable of giving him pleasure.

The love act, in so far as a woman is concerned, is compared to luring a pet snake out of a hole by offering it milk. From the physical point of view this is wherein woman finds her gratification. Woman's vega is said to start from the moment of union, like a snake putting its head out of a hole; is continued throughout the union, like the snake moving out, and is completed in the final voluptuous throe like the snake completely freed from the hole. An incomplete vega, even with the snake half-way out gives satisfaction to a woman, just as the snake can enjoy the milk even with its body half-way out of the hole. This 'protracted' consummation which may be hardly perceptible to the woman herself differs from the immediate and final consummation of the man.

A woman may enjoy her union without ever experiencing the snake completely out of the hole. The dangers to the family and ultimately to the state of permitting woman's consummation to become 'manlike' as a matter of course, is frequently pointed out. The snake should normally be firmly tethered to its hole, and allowed only rare opportunities for complete emancipation.

Books

See under Kāmaśāstra.

VEṆA, a sixth in descent from Manu Svāyaṁbhuva whose legend is found in the *Mahābhārata,* the Purāṇas and *Harivaṁśa.* He was the patriarchal ruler of many tribes and peoples in the eastern regions of India, whose interests he served with great zeal and wisdom at first, but he gradually broke away from the original dharma and began to exert a corrupting influence on the pure faith. He prohibited all worship and sacrifice except to himself and brought class-confusion and disorder to society by permitting inter-caste marriage. A later addition to the story says that he fell into Jain and Buddhist heresies.

His ṛishi advisers remonstrated with him in vain, and at last, their patience exhausted, attacked him with blades of holy *kusa* grass which miraculously turned to spears in their hands, and ended his existence. In the absence of a ruler to govern the country, anarchy arose and the sages decided to appoint a successor. As Veṇa was childless the ṛishis rubbed his thigh and there emerged a dwarfish man, 'like a charred log', with a flat, black face, representing the evil, sinful and hoglike (*kola*) nature of Veṇa. The dwarf was made to sit down (*nishīda*), and from this incident the dwarf's descendant's became known as the Nishāda* and the Kol (Kolarian*) people.

Freed from the incubus of his unregenerate nature, the soul of Veṇa was reconciled to Vishṇu and his corpse began to glow. The ṛishis thereupon 'churned' the right hand of the cadaver and from the churning there arose the majestic form of *Pṛithu*, Veṇa's issue made manifest. As soon as he emerged the *ājagava* or 'primordial bow' of Śiva fell from heaven for his use, and he was invested with universal dominion, thus becoming the first consecrated king in the world. In the *Ṛig-veda* he is mentioned as the author of a hymn.

Since the misrule of Veṇa the Earth had withheld her bounty and men suffered from a great famine. Pṛithu seized his mighty bow to force the Earth to yield her fruits. Hastening to escape from him she assumed the form of a cow and when finally caught she promised to surrender her treasures if a calf were given to her. Pṛithu made Manu Vaivasvata her calf and then began to milk the Earth who proceeded to bestow upon mankind the blessings of her fruits. Because the Earth received fresh life from Pṛithu she was called Pṛithivī. The 'milking' of the Earth in this legend has been the subject of a considerable interpretation and symbolism.

Pṛithu is also known as Pṛithī, or Pṛithī-vaiṇya. There are several other Pṛithus, one being a descendant of Ikshvāku of the Solar line of kings.

Books

See under Mythology.

VIJAYANAGAR (1336–1565–1646), a Hindu kingdom of the Deccan embracing roughly the area of the modern state of Madrās. The city of Vijayanagar was originally the capital of the Hoysala* dynasty, after whose decline it was taken over as the capital of the new realm. The kingdom was founded, on the advice of the Hoysala king, by two brothers of unknown and disputed origin, named Hakka and Bukka (also called Vīrabukka), who claimed descent from the epic hero Yadu. It grew through political and matrimonial alliance with one or other of the neighbouring states, including, on one occasion, the marriage of a Hindu Vijayanagar princess with a Muslim Bahmanī prince, and through wars against the Muslim powers of the south.

The ruler of the kingdom was a prince known as the *rāya*, and under the leadership of a series of remarkable rāyas and still more remarkable ministers, the state of Vijayanagar became the cynosure of the East, and one of the most wealthy kingdoms of Asia. Travellers were unanimous in extolling its grandeur, its magnificent temples, the opulence of its sovereigns. The Portuguese traveller Domingo Paes (*c.* 1520) estimated that the city was as large as Rome, with a population countless in number, 'so much so that I do not wish to write it down for fear it should be thought fabulous'. Its overflowing markets displayed wares from Lisbon to Peking; cinnabar, camphor, musk, and pepper came from Malabār; silk from China; ivory from Alexandria; rubies from Pegu; Ormuz horses were imported by the Portuguese who also supplied velvets, damasks, satins and taffetas. Much of its wealth was in fact due to trade with the Portuguese. It was described as the most opulent and best provided kingdom in the world, and in the words of the Muslim envoy Abdur Razzāq, 'such that the pupil of the eye hath never seen a place like it'.

The rāyas, notably *Kṛishṇa Rāya* (1509–29), also known as Kṛishṇadeva Rāya, were great builders and patrons of the arts. They ushered in the Augustan Age of Tamil literature through their patronage of Tamil poets; they were responsible for the efflorescence of Telugu and Kanarese poetry, and donated large sums for Sanskrit studies. They encouraged scholars, musicians, philosophers, religious teachers and saints.

But they also encouraged the priests. An epigraphic inscription of 1652 preserves the legend that the empire had been founded 'for the protection of gods, cows and brāhmins'. Vijayanagar became the centre of orthodoxy and was thus implanted with the seeds of its own decay. Ritualists were given full scope for their endless ceremonial. On religious festivals there was a mass slaughter of animals, and sometimes even human sacrifices, such as when sixty men were slain to ensure the security of a dam near Hospet. Enormous gifts were conferred on brāhmins whose mantras were believed to protect the realm. Both inside and outside Vijayanagar the Deccan's religious life was being guided by paṇḍits whose prescriptions were strangling the free exercise of the religious spirit.

Vijayanagar's splendour was the type of barbaric magnificence that Rome knew in the days of her decline. While the rāyas and nobles revelled in luxury and maintained armies of women in their harems; while the priests battened on the unparalleled feast of power bestowed on them by the kings and made a mockery of religion at their sybaritic festivities with hordes of dancing girls, the people suffered terrible hardships, and the serfs and labourers lived in abject squalor. The wonderful monuments that were built 'rose out of the sweat of slaves and prisoners of war'. Taxes were exorbitant, and methods of collecting them ruthless in the extreme. Punishments included mutilation of hands and feet, beheading, impaling alive, hanging by a hook, and casting to elephants to be trampled and torn.

Women were expendable and prostitution was regarded as an honourable profession, the revenues from which were used to pay for the twelve thousand police agents who protected the state by a system of spying, intimidation and torture. Some of the kings and nobles had a thousand wives and concubines apiece. The rite of suttee was common, and widows and female slaves were both burned and buried alive with their husbands and masters. On the death of a king as many as two or three thousand of his wives were burned alive with him (VI, p. 29).

During the stewardship of *Rāmrāja,* the Minister and *de facto* ruler of Vijayanagar, the decline of the kingdom was accelerated. He made no attempt to conceal his contempt for the neighbouring Muslim princes and treated their ambassadors with open discourtesy. In one of his wars with Ahmadnagar he laid the countryside waste, dishonoured Muslim women, and permitted Hindu rites to be performed in Muslim holy places. His arrogance, intolerance and ambition reached such heights that the Muslim Sultans were finally incensed beyond endurance, and for once they decided to set aside their private feuds and unite to crush the empire.

The Vijayanagar army that lumbered out to meet the mobile Muslim forces at Tālikoṭa on the river Kistna in January 1565, consisted of 703,000 infantry, 32,600 horses, 551 elephants, and 100,000 merchants, prostitutes and other camp followers. It was commanded in person by the aged minister, Rāmrāja, who sat in a golden litter, wearing a brocaded cap, and accompanied by the inevitable female betel-bearers. When his counsellors, aware of the seriousness of the situation, advised him to get off his perch and ride a horse he ignored their advice. 'Fie upon it!' he is reported to have said, 'the war is unworthy of my notice. There is absolutely no cause for apprehension'. As the battle waxed furious he decided upon caution, descended and took a golden chair, canopied with a gold embroidered umbrella, embellished with pearls and gold chains.

The battle of Tālikoṭa, one of the most tragic in Indian annals, was decided by the Muslim artillery. The Muslims had several hundred cannon which had been cast in the foundries of Ahmadābād. These they loaded with copper coins and fired into the closely-packed ranks of their opponents, with devastating effect. The rout that followed was completed by a cavalry charge. The Vijayanagar army in confusion retreated towards the capital whose gates were undefended. They were pursued by the Muslims who captured the fabulous city three days later. In the meantime the Muslims were able to decimate at leisure the remnant enemy forces and divide the spoils. The plunder was so great that every private soldier became rich in gold, jewels, tents, arms, horses and slaves. Rāmrāja himself had already been captured and beheaded on the battlefield.

The conquerors entered Vijayanagar and went to work with axe and crowbar and fire, to complete the work of destruction, which lasted for several months. Around the city to a distance of twelve leagues, everything was burned and reduced to ashes. A traveller who visited the site of Vijayanagar a few years later found it a mere shell, the haunt of the tiger and the elephant. Today this once proud city is known as the Hampi ruins, from a village near by.

The remnants of the ruling family escaped to Penukoṇḍā, 120 miles to the south, and later, in 1600 to Chandragiri, and from there they carried on the dynastic tradition on an attenuated scale, but could do nothing to prevent the continuous encroachments on their domains. We find the last 'Karṇāṭaka Emperor', Raṇga III, appealing to the Moghul emperor Shāh Jahān for protection against the dismemberment of his state, and promising to turn Muslim if necessary. The plea went unheeded.

The final act of the last Vijayanagar ruler was to grant to Francis Day, the English factor in 1639, the site for Fort St. George, around which the city of Madrās was to develop into one of the strongholds of European ascendancy in South India.

Books

I. Heras, Henry. *The Aravidu Dynasty of Vijayanagar*, Madras, 1927.
II. Karmarkar, D. P. (Ed.) *Vijayanagar Sexcentenary Commemoration Volume*, Dharwar, 1936.
III. Majumdar, R. C. (Ed.) *An Advanced History of India*, London, 1948.
IV. Saletore, B. *Social and Political Life in the Vijayanagar Empire*, 2 vols., Madras, 1934.
V. Sewell, R. A. *A Forgotten Empire: Vijayanagar*, London, 1900.
VI. Thompson, Edward. *A History of India*, London, 1927.

VIKRAMĀDITYA (?95 BC–AD 78?) the name or title of an unidentified king of Ujjain celebrated in Indian tradition. No definite facts are known about him, and it is impossible to separate the historical from the legendary in the story of his career. According to the least controversial account his father was Gardabhilla of Ujjain, who ravished the sister of the court astrologer to the Śaka ruler of Sindhu. On the persuasion of the aggrieved brother of the girl the Śaka chieftain invaded Ujjain, expelled Gardabhilla and established his suzerainty over the kingdom.

Seventeen years later Gardabhilla's son, Vikramāditya, overthrew the Śakas and recaptured Ujjain. He then reputedly went on to conquer the whole of India, bringing peace and prosperity to the country. His reign marked the beginning of a new era known as the Vikrama Saṁvat (*see* era), the most important of India's many systems of dating, commencing from 58 BC, and first used by the Mālava kings of Ujjain. Vikramāditya fell in battle against his rival, Śālivāhana, king of the Deccan, who is also credited with having established an era called the Śaka era, dating from AD 78.

Vikramāditya had a reputation for great virtue, justice and valour, besides being a patron of literature and the arts. Among his protégés were nine men of outstanding merit known as the Nine Gems (*nava-ratna*), namely: (1) Dhanvantari, a physician; (2) Kshapaṇaka, (3) Śaṅku and (4) Vetālabhaṭṭa, poets; (5) Amarasiṁha (*c.* AD 680) lexicographer; (6) Kālidāsa (*c.* AD 450) poet and dramatist; (7) Varāhamihira (*c.* AD 550) astronomer; (8) Ghaṭakarpara, author of a kāvya (short epic) describing how a young wife sends a cloud messenger to her absent husband during the rainy season, and (9) Vararuchi (*c.* AD 579) author of a *kāvya*, a monologue-play, a romance, a work on poetics, a Prākṛit grammar, a collection of folk-tales and a treatise on astronomy. He is sometimes identified with the grammarian Kātyāyana, but is believed to be none other than Barzuchihar, or Burzuya (fl. AD 579), court physician of Khusrau I, Nushirwan, who visited India and lived there for some time.

It would appear that the tradition of Vikramāditya enshrines the memory of more than one king, since the numerous legends about him extend over several centuries; in any case the Nine Gems could not possibly have been contemporaries. Many historians regard his existence as altogether fictitious. The name Vikramāditya was used as a title by the Chālukya kings, and was applied to several other monarchs, among them: Kanishka (*c.* AD 120) the Kushān emperor; Samudra-gupta (*d.* AD 379) and Chandra-gupta II (*d.* AD 415) of the Gupta dynasty; Harsha (*d.* AD 648); Yaśodharma of Mālava who broke the power of the Huns under Mihirakula in AD 528; and Bhoja of Dhārā (*d.* 1060).

Books

I. Altekar, A. S. 'Who Founded the Vikrama Era?'. *Proceedings of the All-India Oriental Conference*, XII, Vol. II, pp. 501–2.

II. Edgerton, F. *Vikrama's Adventures*, 1901.

III. Mookerji, R. K. (Ed.) *Vikrama Volume*, Ujjain, 1948.

IV. Pandey, R. B. *Vikramaditya of Ujjayini*, Banaras, 1951.

V. Vyas, K. B., 'The Vikrama Problem'. *Annals of the Bhandarkar Oriental Research Institute*, Poona, XXVII, 209 ff.

VIRĀṬA, the name of the king of the Virāṭa country, who ruled over the Matsya people and had his capital at Matsya (near modern Jaipur). From the evidence of traditions concerning him, some scholars believe that Virāṭa was the chieftain of a Scythian tribe settled in India.

During the thirteenth year of their exile, the five Pāṇḍava brothers and their wife, Draupadī, living in disguise in order to fulfil the conditions of their exile, came to the kingdom of Virāṭa and took service with the king. Yudhishṭhira became the king's private companion and taught him to play dice, an art in which he had perfected himself during his exile; Bhīma became the king's head cook, but soon exhibited his physical prowess by overcoming and killing the wrestler Jīmūta; Arjuna, attired as a eunuch taught the ladies of the court the art of dance; Nakula was given care of the horses; and Sahadeva became the royal cowherd. Draupadī served as the queen's waiting-maid, with the stipulation that she should not be required to wash feet, or to eat the food left by others.

It happened that Kīchaka, the queen's brother, and commander of the royal army, was smitten with love for Draupadī and sought to possess her. Her husbands Yudhishṭhira and Arjuna did not seem disposed to help her so she appealed to Bhīma, and together they planned retribution. She made an assignation with Kīchaka and while he was on his way Bhīma waylaid and slew him. Bhīma then rolled his bones and flesh into a large ball so that no one might distinguish that he had ever been a man.

Draupadī was judged by the other Virāṭa princes to have been responsible for Kīchaka's disappearance and was condemned to be burnt alive, whereupon Bhīma, drawing his hair over his face as a disguise, and tearing up a tree for a club, put the princes to flight and rescued her. The king, terror-stricken at these new developments, asked Draupadī to leave his domain, but she begged to remain a little while longer, predicting that the kingdom would shortly be protected by the king's servitors.

Now, among Virāṭa's enemies were the predatory *Trigartta*, a tribe figuring in the later Kurukshetra battle on the side of the Kaurava, Duryodhana. This tribe originally occupied a region near Kashmīr, then migrated to Kāṅgṛā, and later settled in the region between the Rāvi, Beas and

Sutlej, the 'three rivers' from which comes their name, with their capital at Jālandhara (modern Jullunder).

Sure enough, shortly after Draupadī's prediction, *Suśarman* the rāja of Trigartta, hearing that the commander-in-chief Kīchaka was dead, allied himself with the Kauravas and attacked the Matsya capital, taking the king captive. But the Pāṇḍava brothers repulsed their combined forces and won a victory, rescued the royal prisoner and made Suśarman captive. For bravery in battle Virāṭa offered Arjuna his daughter *Uttarā* for a bride, but Arjuna requested that she be given to his son Abhimanyu. This was done, amid great rejoicing.

In the Mahābhārata war, Virāṭa fought on the side of the Pāṇḍavas, and was slain by Droṇa, while his son Uttara was slain in the battle by Śalya.

Books

See under Mythology, and Mahābhārata.

VIRGINITY was not especially esteemed in the Hindu social system. On the contrary, it was believed that a virgin could never attain spiritual enlightenment in this world, or reach the abodes of bliss in the next, since she still bore the token of her unfruitful state. A menstruating* virgin presented an even more dire figure of peril.

The *Mahābhārata* tells of Subhrū, daughter of the sage Kuṇi, who refused to marry since she had dedicated herself to severe austerities. At the time of her death she learnt that she could not go to heaven because her body had not been enlivened by the sacrament of marriage. She was able to persuade the sage Śriṅgavat to marry her, stayed with him for one night, and was thus enabled to gain entry into heaven. The *Baudhāyana Sūmārta Sūtra* declares that the corpse of an unwed maiden can be burnt only after a formal marriage is performed after death (II, p. 33). This led to some strange practices, such as were once current among the Nambūdris, where post-mortem defloration was said to have been customary.

Virginity in Hindu erotics and marriage rites did not necessarily have reference to the hymenal intactness of the girl, but rather to the fact that no male had been allowed access to her. Women like the much-married Mādhavi whose maidenhead was restored after the birth of each of her children could only be regarded as virgins in theory. It was necessary for the girl to be *akshatā*, 'uninjured', but this meant that she be free from the injury of pollution and sexual experience. Dr Aiyer says, 'No pre-eminence was attached to virginity as distinguished from chastity in the scale of virtues' (I, p. 66).

There seems to have been an almost universal belief in ancient and medieval India in the perils attending the condition of virginity, and particularly in the dangers of initiatory intercourse with a girl. Hymenal blood was considered extremely potent and its touch brought contamination. The shedding of blood, reprehensible at all times, became more so in the case of virgin blood. A man is particularly prone to its injury because the excitement of the sexual act finds him defenceless against the psychic dangers inherent in all contact with virgins. It was believed that a woman untouched by the 'male rod' was liable on defloration to flash forth a devastating aura that could bring ruin to a man, blight to his cattle, and desolation to his home. If he were spared these calamities he would receive his deserts in more terrible forms in the next world. The ruler who did not avenge by dire penalties the dishonouring of a virgin would invite misfortune to the realm.

The legitimate groom of the newly wedded virgin was to some extent protected by the magical ritual of marriage, and the 'besprinkling' of the wife with the juice of some herb e.g. the *dūrvā* plant, was believed to sanctify and neutralize her virulence. This was confirmed by the sprinkling of ejaculation (*see* abhisheka). Indeed, the dangers of the initial act were regarded as so great that in many parts of India special precautions were taken to ensure that the husband did not have to face them.

Hence the need arose for defloration to be performed by those over whom the power was innocuous, such as a mother, aunt, or close female relative. This was common in the eastern regions, according to Vātsyāyana, and modern authorities confirm that it is still practised. Dr C. Chakraberty points out that 'the hymen of Hindu girls is generally torn in their early girlhood by the forefinger of their mother in daily washing the vulva with water' (III p. 325). The procedure of 'deep cleaning' appears to be fairly widespread in Bengal and the South.

There were other classes of people who were regarded as being naturally endowed with the power to withstand the dangers attendant on the act. Kings, symbolizing the majesty and power of the realm, were natural agents for neutralizing the scathing shock while plucking the flower of the virgin. Indian historians have recorded how virgins were deflowered by rulers in various parts of India. This *droit du seigneur* sometimes included the *jus primae noctis*. Among the Andhras the bride used to be deflowered by the king and then allowed to return to her husband (V, p. 189); the rulers of various other regions were entitled to enjoy the prettiest marriageable maidens; among some sects (*see* Vallabha) young girls were said to be presented to the guru for ritual defloration.

By the sacred nature of their calling priests were also immune to the contaminating flash. The kings of Calicut used to pay priests to deflower their wives. Where in any place priests were unable to cope with the demand, temple defloration was performed by means of a small stone liṅga set in a stone saddle especially erected for the purpose on the temple premises, on which virgin brides were made to sit. Hence also the divine Gandharvas, patrons of the nuptial couch, especially Viśvāvasu, to whom the bridegroom ceremonially offered his wife's virginity on the wedding night (*see* marriage).

Since tremendous psychic potencies were believed to be engendered by intercourse with a virgin, the defloration rite was often performed in tantrik ceremonies (*see* strīpūjā) to utilize the powers thus released. The rite was considered extremely perilous if ignorantly or lustfully performed. But adepts who knew the art were said to put in great stores of psychic energy by such means. Medieval tantrik retreats were hotbeds of this form of sex magic. One Hindu writer referring to this period says, 'Even innocent maidens visiting the monasteries were seduced to surrender their chastity to the monks to help the latter to attain Realization' (IV, p. 33).

Books

I. Aiyer, P. S. S. *Evolution of Hindu Moral Ideals*, Calcutta, 1935.
II. Altekar, A. S. *The Position of Women in Hindu Civilization*, 2nd Ed., Banaras, 1956.
III. Chakraberty, C. *The Cultural History of the Hindus*, Calcutta n.d. ?1945.
IV. Jindal, K. B. *A History of Hindi Literature*, Allahabad, 1955.
V. Upadhyaya, S. C. (Ed.) *Kamasutra of Vatsyayana*, Bombay, 1961.

VIRILITY. The branch of Āyurveda dealing with the restoration of the flagging virile powers of man by aphrodisiacs and other means, to endow him with 'stallion-like' qualities, so that he can 'enjoy and satisfy a hundred women a day', is known as *vājīkaraṇa* (*vājī-karaṇa*, 'stallion-making').

Although Vātsyāyana, the fifth century writer on erotics, held that a small and thin male member was the sign of a good lover, he and his successors prescribed many formulas for improving the dimensions of that organ. Vājīkaraṇa had a wide variety of aims, namely: to enlarge, strengthen and roughen the male member; to increase a man's power of erection; to augment the secretion of semen (*śukra-janana*); to purify the semen (*śukra-śodhana*); to delay the onset of ejaculation.

Text-books on erotics, and Sanskrit classics too, are filled with a miscellaneous assortment of observations on the subject. Much had come down from the aboriginal tribal tradition, and much was added to the lore by the various invading races. India had specialized in this matter from ancient times. It is recorded that aphrodisiacs were included among the presents given by Chandragupta to Seleucus Nicator.

A selection of the methods used by the ancients may be briefly listed. It was generally appreciated that the telling of stories could be used to arouse sexual desire, and special stories were composed for the purpose, on the principle that 'even those who hear of the love encounter feel the urge for performance gathering within them'. The contemplation of paintings and sculptural representations of gods and goddesses, and men and women, in various erotic poses was also known to help inflame the spark of love. Love-inspiring diets included certain herbs and fruit (e.g. the āmalaka), and foods like honey, yolk of egg, fish, onion, garlic, meat and meat broths; alcohol was a common aphrodisiac; boiled testicles of sheep and goats were also known for their stimulating properties. Various drugs were compounded, to be taken either internally or used for local application; alchemical potions with mercury and gold were also used. Various scatalogical substances were believed to have rejuvenative properties and were extremely popular and generally taken in small quantities internally. These included animal and human seminal secretions, the urine of the cow or bull, cow-dung mixed with goat-dung and ghee. Also very popular was local massage with invigorating herbal ointments. Sometimes insects with stings were dropped on the member, and other hairy insects were ground, mixed with oil and rubbed on, causing a permanent swelling of the skin. Vātsyāyana recommended pendulation, believing that the member should not always be tied up, but periodically allowed to remain freely pendant; occasionally one should lie face downwards and let the organ hang through a hole in the cot.

The recitation of secret *mantras* can arouse the twenty-four *nāḍis* (pulses) that cause sexual desire. Similarly certain *mudrās* or fixed positions of the fingers of the man can excite the woman. Certain forms of *yoga*, including breathing techniques and physical culture have an aphrodisiac effect on both men and women. An important part is played in *vājīkaraṇa* by perfumes, which include not only the pleasantly aromatic scents made from flowers, but offensive animal smells used in combination, that have a powerfully stimulating effect on the sexual centres. Apart from these there are many secret recipes employed as aids to stimulation and erethism, such as anointing the body with a salve of certain herbs, the application of collyrium, especially prepared in a human skull, to the rims of the eyelids. The use of amulets is widespread although their confection can often be a difficult process e.g. the eye of a peacock sealed at an auspicious moment in a golden armband worn on the right arm or wrist; or the stone of a certain fruit gathered in certain circumstances and eaten on the thirteenth day of the dark half of a particular month; spices and herbs gathered from distant places, mixed with honey and applied to the phallus before union helps to satisfy the partner.

Vātsyāyana gives several fanciful nostrums. If a person takes the garlands from a corpse, mixes them with the powdered bones of a certain bird and applies the concoction to the girl's forehead and his own feet, she will desire him immoderately. The man should smear his body with the powdered bones of a she-vulture which has died a natural death, not in captivity. The man should sprinkle over his head certain powered ingredients mixed with the excreta of a red-faced monkey.

In the absence of results from these methods one could always have recourse to *apadravya* or artificial aids (*see* olisboi).

Books

See under Kāmaśāstra.

VISHṆU, one of the major gods of the Hindu pantheon. In the Ṛig-vedic period Vishṇu was a deity of secondary importance, associated with Indra in his struggle against the powers of evil. The derivation of his name from the root *vish*, to pervade, is comparatively late. He is partly Dravidian in origin, and Przyluski expresses the view that his name is Dravidian and that he bears many marks of indigenousness. Iṇ the Brāhmaṇas, Vishṇu is spoken of as the luckiest (*śreshṭha*) of the gods. One legend, also in the Brāhmaṇas, relates that the gods grew so jealous of his good fortune that they sent ants to gnaw the bowstring as he leaned upon his bended bow; the string snapped, the bow sprang back and severed his head from his body. His head was later restored.

Vishṇu gradually grew in importance, and by the time of the *Mahābhārata* he emerges as a god of paramount importance and the second god of the Hindu triad, being regarded as the Preserver, just as Brahmā is the Creator, and Śiva the Destroyer. To the Vaishṇavites he is the greatest of all the gods. In the Purāṇas he is frequently referred to as *Nārāyaṇa*, the ever-present and all-pervading spirit, associated with the primeval waters, who is represented as reclining on a lotus or upon the coils of the serpent Śesha, floating on the waters. From Vishṇu's toe flows the sacred Ganges, and from his navel sprouts a lotus, bearing upon its petals the god Brahmā. A legend in the *Mahābhārata* adds that Śiva sprang from Vishṇu's forehead, Vishṇu is the most humble of the great deities of the Hindu pantheon, as the story of the test conducted by the sage Bhṛigu* demonstrated.

An important legend linked from earliest times with Vishṇu concerns the 'three great strides' with which he is said to have stepped over the universe. First mentioned in the *Ṛig-veda* these three strides were the subject of much speculation among the early commentators. Some held that Vishṇu, the all-pervading, covered the earth, atmosphere and sky; or that the three steps were the spheres of fire, lightning and the sun; others opined that they were the positions of the sun at rising, zenith and setting. This myth was embodied in the famous *avatāra* legend in which Vishṇu appears as Vāmana the dwarf, to dispossess the daitya (aboriginal) king Bali.

Vishṇu was later assigned the function of redeemer, and all the indigenous saviour-myths were absorbed into a cycle of legend surrounding his name. In most of these myths he appears in order to vanquish evil, which is usually embodied in the person of a godless king or a demon of formidable power, such as Hiraṇyāksha or the asuras Madhu, Kaiṭabha, and others. A probable reason underlying this common theme is that it gave the policy of Aryan aggrandizement the semblance of a crusade, and mitigated the ruthless subjugation of 'native' heroes.

Vishṇu appeared on earth in several forms, each time as a saviour of mankind or as a destroyer of some evil. These incarnation on the earthly scene are known as his *avatāra*, 'descents', and the best known and usually accepted avatāras are ten in number, as follows:

(1) *Matsya* or fish, in which form he appeared in order to save Vaivasvata, the seventh Manu, from the Deluge.
(2) *Kūrma*, or tortoise, the form assumed by him during the Churning of the Ocean to obtain the elixir of immortality.
(3) *Varāha*, or boar, the guise assumed during his struggle with the demon Hiraṇyāksha.
(4) *Narasiṁha*, or the man-lion, in which form he overcame the tyrant Hiraṇyakaśipu.
(5) *Vāmana*, the dwarf, who overcame the daitya (demon) king Bali.
(6) *Paraśurāma*, or Rāma of the Axe, who delivered the brāhmins from the tyranny of the kshattriyas.
(7) *Rāma*, the incarnation in which he slew Rāvaṇa, a powerful native king. Such was the extent of this enterprise that one of the world's great epics, the *Rāmāyaṇa*, was written around the theme. In his crusade Rāma received all his assistance from indigenous peoples.
(8) *Kṛishṇa*, the most important of all the avatāras of Vishṇu.
(9) *Buddha*, a perverse incarnation of the god, who assumed this form to found the false religion of Buddhism in order to lead wicked men and demons to reject the Vedas, deny the gods, and abjure caste, and so effect their own damnation.
(10) *Kalki*, the last incarnation of Vishṇu that is yet to come at the end of

the present *Kali yuga* or Age of Darkness, when Vishṇu will appear riding on a white horse.

These are the ten traditional avatāras, but the devout *Bhāgavata Purāṇa* enumerates twenty-two, and other legends add to them still more, since 'his incarnations are innumerable like the rivulets flowing from an inexhaustible lake'. The *ṛishis, manus,* gods, *prajāpatis,* were all fragments of Vishṇu, among them Nārada, Kapila, Dattātreya, Vyāsa, Dhanvantari, and kings like Ṛishabha father of Bharata, and Pṛithu.

Vishṇu is represented with a dark complexion; his four hands hold a padma (lotus), a gadā (mace), a śaṅkha (conch), and a chakra (discus) which, when he destroys the enemy returns to his grasp. He also has a bow called the *śārṅga,* a conch called the *pāñchajanya,* a sword called the *nandaka.* He is frequently depicted wearing the holy *kaustubha* jewel around his neck. On his breast is a peculiar star-shaped mark, the sign of his immortality, called *śrīvatsa,* 'transcending the years', and from this mark grows a tuft of curly hairs. Vishṇu's *vāhana* or vehicle is the eagle Garuḍa. His celestial dwelling is the glorious city of Vaikunṭha where he rules with his wife Lakshmī.

Like the other great gods of Hindu mythology, Vishṇu was given many titles of which the chief are as follows: Ananta-śayana, 'reposing on Ananta'; Bhakta-dāsa, 'his devotee's slave'; Chatur-bhuja, 'four-armed'; Gadādhar, 'club-bearer'; Hari, 'tawny'; Hṛishīkeśa, 'erect-haired' (a town near Hardwār is dedicated to him); Jala-śāyin, 'water-reposing'; Janārdana, 'men-afflicting'; Kaiṭabha-jit, 'Kaiṭabha-vanquisher'; Keśava, 'the hairy'; or 'the radiant'; Kirīṭin, 'diadem-wearing' (also applied to Indra); Madhu-sūdana, 'destroyer of Madhu'; Mukunda, 'deliverer'; Nārāyaṇa* 'moving on the waters'; Padma-nābha, 'lotus-navelled'; Pañchāyudha, 'five-weaponed'; Pāṇḍu-raṅga, 'white-coloured' (although Vishṇu is frequently depicted dark); Perumāḷ, known as such in parts of south India; Pītāmbara, clothed in yellow garments'; Puṇḍarīkāksha, 'lotus-eyed'; Raṅga-nātha, 'Lord of Hues' or 'Lord of Arenas'; Śārṅgin, 'carrying the bow *śārṅga*'; Śrīdhara, 'prosperity-bearer'; Śrīnivāsa, 'splendour-raimented'; Tri-vikrama, 'three-striding'; Uru-gāya, 'wide-going'; Uru-krama, 'wide-strider'; Varada-rāja, 'boon-granting king'; Vasudeva, 'Beneficent Lord'; Veṅkaṭachala, 'moving upon the hills'; Veṅkaṭanātha, 'Hill Lord'; Veṅkaṭeśvara, 'Hill God'; Viṭhobā (or Viṭṭhobā), the title under which Vishṇu is worshipped in Paṇḍharpur on the Bhīma river, especially by Marāṭhas; Viṭṭhal, the Kanarese form of Viṭhobā; Viśvaksena, 'general who is turned in all directions'; Viśvarūpa, 'of many forms; omnipresent'.

Books

I. Gupta, S. K. *The Legends of Vishnu,* 1931.
II. Rodriguez, E. A. *Religion of Vishnoo: The Ten Avatars,* 1849.

(*See also under* Vaishṇavism.)

VIŚVAKARMAN (*viśva-karman,* 'all-accomplishing'), is referred to in the *Ṛig-veda* as the personification of the all-creative power, and the architect of the universe, sometimes identified with Prajāpati. Some hymns describe him as offering up the whole universe in a sacrifice and finally sacrificing himself.

He is represented as the artisan of the gods and artificer of their weapons. He brought to perfection the science of *sthāpatya*, or architecture, and was the master of all the arts, of handicrafts, of carpentry, the maker of celestial chariots and fashioner of divine ornaments. He was the one who moulded the image of Jagannātha and shaped the island of Laṅkā (Ceylon). His son, the monkey architect Nala, constructed Rāma's bridge to enable Rāma to cross from India to Ceylon.

According to the Purāṇas, Viśvakarman, through union with the divine nymph Ghṛitāchī became the progenitor of many mixed castes. He was the father of Saṁjñā, wife of the sun-god Sūrya*, and in order to protect her from being consumed by the fiery effulgence of her husband, he trimmed the sun's orb and made various weapons from the portions cut off.

The name of Viśvakarman is in many myths linked with that of **Tvashṭṛi,** a deity of ancient Aryan origin, once worshipped in north-east Persia and Khorasan. Tvashṭṛi is likewise the divine artisan, the ideal artist, and 'shaper' of things, all form being made by him, celestial and terrestrial, human and divine, animals, plants and inanimate things. It is Tvashṭṛi who shapes man and woman, even from the seminal germ in the mother's womb. He is the Hindu Vulcan; at his forge he sharpens the axe of the priest-god Bṛihaspati, and moulds the vajra or thunderbolt of Indra and the weapons of the other celestial rulers. He it was who made the infernal assembly hall of Yama and the heaven of Varuṇa. He had a three-headed son named *Viśvarūpa* ('all-forms') who was slain by Indra. For this Tvashṭṛi cursed Indra, but he pronounced the curse wrongly and the dread words hurtled back to him and struck him down instead. His daughter Saraṇyū married Vivasvat (*see* Sūrya). The name Tvashṭṛi is also borne by one of the divine Ādityas, by one of the Rudras, and by a prince descended from Bharata.

Both Viśvakarman and Tvashṭṛi are associated with **Ṛibhu,** 'skilful', a name once also applied to Indra, Agni, the Ādityas and other gods. In the Purāṇas Ṛibhu is the son of Brahmā, and one of the Kumāras. The *Vishṇu Purāṇa,* composed by the sage Nārāyaṇa, was first communicated by Brahmā to Ṛibhu. Ṛibhu had a famous pupil, *Nidāgha,* son of the sage Pulastya, to whom he gave 'deep instruction in the true and immortal wisdom'. Ṛibhu had three sons, known as the Ṛibhava, namely, Ṛibhukshan, Vibhu and Vāja. In some myths they are the sons of Viśvakarman, in others of Tvashṭṛi and Saraṇyū. Originally mortals, the Ṛibhus obtained the boon of immortality and were given a dwelling in the solar sphere, where they help to support the sky. In the *Ṛig-veda* they are referred to as skilled workmen and are often described as elf-like. They fashioned the steeds of Indra and the chariots of the Aśvins, and made their parents young again.

Viśvakarman (and also Brahmā) is known as Vidhātṛi, 'Creator'; Kāru, 'workman'; Takshaka, 'carver'; Sudhanvan, 'having a good bow'. Viśvarūpa is also known as Triśiras, 'three-headed'.

Books

(*See under* Mythology.)

VIŚVĀMITRA, one of the greatest *ṛishis* of Hindu mythology. According to the Vedas he was the son of king Gādhi of Kanyākubja (hence he is also known as Gādhija, 'born of Gādhi', who was himself a scion of the Kuśika* family of the Bharatas). The *Harivaṁśa* states that Viśvāmitra was 'a Paurava and a Kauśika' by heritage, but he may well have been a śūdra (I, p. 166), a member of a low caste, for he is closely associated with the slave-like *dasyu* peoples, and he and his descendants ministered to the servile tribes.

According to the generally prevalent legend though, he was a kshattriya by birth, conceived by a woman of 'brāhmin-like qualities' (*see* Aurva) and by the end of his life had raised himself to brāhminhood through austerities and inflexible determination. He figures in several incidents in the *Mahābhārata*, while in the *Rāmāyaṇa* he is the adviser of Rāma's father, and Rāma's own guru.

The most noteworthy feature of Viśvāmitra's career was his life-long struggle against his brāhmin rival Vasishṭha*, a struggle believed to typify the contest for supremacy between brāhmins and kshattriyas in early India. Both these great ṛishis occupy a prominent place in the *Ṛig-veda*. Viśvāmitra was the author of the hymns of the third *maṇḍala*, which contains the *gāyatrī mantra*, and Vasishṭha of the seventh maṇḍala. Both ṛishis appear in legends about Hariśchandra*, a patient and devoted king whom Viśvāmitra harried. Both men at different times acted as family priests to king Sudāsa*, and both were involved in a contest with Sudāsa's son Kalmāshapāda in the course of which one hundred of Vasishṭha's sons were devoured by Kalmāshapāda. Both sages had control over the elements and the rivers; in one of their fights Viśvāmitra turned the waters of the Sarasvatī into blood because it had obeyed the orders of Vasishṭha.

Viśvāmitra, who coveted Kāmadhenu* the miraculous cow of his rival Vasishṭha, suffered a humiliating defeat in his efforts to obtain her. He therefore resolved to become a brāhmin through ascetic practices. The story goes that the sons of Vasishṭha mocked and reviled him for attempting the impossible task of obtaining brāhmin status, and this so incensed Viśvāmitra that with a flash of his wrath he reduced the hundred impertinent sons of Vasishṭha to ashes, cursing them to be reborn as degraded outcastes for seven hundred births.

Viśvāmitra himself had a hundred and one sons, but after the fidelity and endurance displayed by his pupil Śunaḥsephas* he adopted the lad as his own and proposed to make him the eldest of his sons. Fifty of his sons agreed to this and Viśvāmitra blessed them; the middle son, named Madhuchhandas, remained indifferent as he was dedicated to a life of worship and was in the throes of composing a hymn, now embodied in the *Ṛig-veda*; but the remaining fifty sons objected and incurred their father's wrath. He pronounced a curse upon them so that they and their descendants inherited only the outer fringes of his domains and became the ancestors of the border tribes, and of outcaste peoples like the Āndhras, Puṇḍras and Śabaras.

Viśvāmitra grew in might, and in the course of one of his adventures he set about creating new worlds. He helped king Triśaṅku* to ascend to heaven, and in other ways was in danger of disrupting the order of the cosmos. The *Mahābhārata* and *Rāmāyaṇa* relate that the powers he acquired through his austerities so alarmed the gods that Indra sent the apsara Menakā* to tempt him to concupiscence. This ravishing beauty was the mother of the nymph Pramadvara and was indirectly responsible for the creation of Drupada*. Clad in diaphanous veils she danced before the sage during his spiritual exercises, and succeeded in seducing him. She became through him the mother of Śakuntalā. Ashamed of his infatuation Viśvāmitra dismissed the heavenly damsel 'with accents not unkind', and returned once more to his meditations. Another attempt was made to seduce him, but Rambhā* the *apsara* sent this time was cursed by the sage to become a stone and remained petrified for a thousand years.

After his manifold adventures the great sage, now full of years and bowed down with the weight of his superhuman powers, was accepted without reserve as a brāhmin, not only by the assembled deities but by his quondam rival, Vasishṭha. He was given all the dignities and privileges of brāhmin-hood and in this status of equality paid all honour to Vasishṭha.

Among the pupils of Viśvāmitra was Gālava, and among his sons Ashṭaka.

Books

I. Ambedkar, B. R. *Who Were the Shudras?*, Bombay, 1946.
II. Das, R. V. *Vishvamitra, Rishi of Rishis*. 1911.
(*See also under* Mythology.)

VIVEKĀNANDA (1863–1902) sectarian name of Narendranāth Dutt, born in Calcutta, a member of the kāyastha or clerical caste. A graduate of a Christian missionary college, he was well acquainted with Western philosophy and from his youth was steeped in the agnosticism of Herbert Spencer and J. S. Mill.

At an early age he met Keshab Chandra Sen*, and joined the Brahmo Samāj ('Society of God'), convinced of the perfectability of man by his own efforts, a conviction that stayed with him throughout his life. In 1882 he met Rāmakṛishṇa*, and although not impressed with him at first, soon came under his spell, eventually becoming his most famous disciple—a Plato to his Socrates. He was given the new name of Vivekānanda and the title of 'svāmi', and it was as Swāmi Vivekānanda that he rose to international fame. He spent six years in retirement and contemplation in the Himālayas, and subsequently undertook an extensive tour of western and southern India. After the death of Rāmakṛishṇa he had visions and raptures, and on one occasion exhorted his disciples to 'become like Christ and aid in the redemption of the world'. He became the best known exponent of modern Vedānta and the most zealous of Hindu missionaries.

In 1893 he was sent by the Rāja of Rāmnād to the Parliament of Religions in Chicago as the representative of Hinduism. He travelled by way of Colombo, Singapore, Hong Kong, Canton, Nagasaki and Tokyo, crossing the Pacific to Vancouver and Chicago, lecturing all along the way. At the Parliament of Religions he proved a brilliant advocate of his cause. He gave the Americans an extremely idealized version of Hinduism, judiciously adjusting his exposition to their sentiments. Most of his American public had never seen an Indian before and they were carried away by the commanding presence of this robed and turbaned stranger, who was like their dreams of a wise man from the East. His enthusiasm and eloquence made his mission a complete success, and he was described in an American paper as 'an orator by divine right and undoubtedly the greatest figure in the Parliament of Religions.'

Vivekānanda went on to England and lectured on Vedānta, making some notable converts, among them an Englishwoman, Miss Margaret Noble (Sister Nivedita), famous for her book, *The Web of Indian Life*. On a second trip to America Vivekānanda founded the Vedānta Society of San Franscisco, and lectured extensively in several foreign countries, establishing Rāmakṛishṇa Missions, named after his beloved guru. He returned to India in 1897 and founded a *maṭha* (monastery) near Calcutta, and travelled throughout the country spreading the gospel of reformed Hinduism. An indefatigable worker in his cause, he laboured ceaselessly and without thought for himself, and died in 1902 'burned to the socket'.

Vivekānanda stood for the Vedāntic religion in its universal aspect. He held Śaṅkara's doctrine of *māyā*, 'illusion', describing creation as the play or sport of God, an act done for His own amusement, and like Śaṅkara paid homage to the Mother of the Universe in her various aspects. He accepted all faiths as true, but challengingly declared that Hinduism was 'the mother of all religions'. He felt that all forms of doubt, disbelief, scepticism, agnosticism and even atheism, had a place within the Hindu fold, along with Vedānta, deism and bhakti (faith). He defended idolatry and at the same time maintained that there was no polytheism in India, since there was a universal acceptance of the one divine power behind all manifestation.

In his social philosophy he opposed child-marriage, brāhmin oppression of the lower castes, and the backwardness of women. He stressed the need for service to the poor, the illiterate and the sick; believed that no law or religion was higher than 'Service to Mankind'. As practical Vedāntists, he said, 'the Americans are better than we are' (VII, Vol. III, p. 428), for without its practical application Vedāntism as preached in India, 'however fine and wonderful it may be, is absolutely valueless'. He felt the need for more of that vigour in Hindu society that he found among the Muhammadans and proposed a combination of Islam and Vedānta. 'Vedāntic brain and Islamic body is our only hope', he concluded with characteristic courage (VII, Vol. VI, p. 376).

While admitting that renunciation and the monastic life were paths to salvation, he nevertheless held that it was a mistake completely to eschew the material side of life, and stood for a sort of 'muscular Hinduism'. 'You will understand the *Gītā* all the better if you have strong biceps', he asserted, 'the ātman cannot be known by the weak'. He deplored the pacifism in the life and thought of Hindu India; for him Vedānta breathed one message, 'Strength'. Non-violence, moral and intellectual, was suicide, and was responsible for the downfall of Buddhism. He stressed the divine in man. 'You are divinities on earth! Sinners? It is a sin to call man so. We are the greatest God that ever was or will be. Bow down to nothing but your own higher self.'

According to Vivekānanda, Kṛishṇa, Buddha, Christ, Rāmakṛishṇa were all incarnations of God. They were the great 'bubbles' produced by the cosmic sea. 'Every worm', he said, 'is brother of the Nazarene', and he foresaw a time when 'Christs will be in number like bunches of grapes upon a vine' (III, p. 69).

Strenuously opposing Christian claims he resented the work of missionaries, but himself promoted his reforms along Christian missionary lines and borrowed much from their methods. He declared that he wanted to 'make a European society with India's religion' (V, p. 110). The Rāmakṛishṇa Mission now has over one hundred centres in all parts of the world, and carries out an extensive programme of cultural, educational, social, as well as spiritual activities.

Books

I. Barrows, J. H. (Ed.) *The World's Parliament of Religions*, 2 vols, 1893.
II. Farquhar, J. N. *Modern Religious Movements in India*, New York, 1915.
III. Griswold, H. D. *Insights into Modern Hinduism*, New York, 1934.
IV. Rolland, Romain, *The Life of Vivekananda and the Universal Gospel*, Calcutta, 1953.
V. Sen, K. M. *Hinduism*, Harmondsworth, Middlesex, 1961.
VI. Virajananda, Swami (Ed.,) *Life of Swami Vivekananda*, Almora, 1924–28.
VII. Vivekananda, Swami, *Complete Works*, Almora, 7 vols., 1919–22.
VIII. Wendell, Thomas, *Hinduism Invades America*, New York, 1930.

VOWS are taken by Hindus for a multitude of reasons, and the term *vrata*, 'vowed' is used for a religious observance undertaken as a result of a vow. It is a means of drawing the attention of the deity to what one desires, and is a promise to the deity of some sacrifice in return for the desired object. Thus, in times past, in exchange for the recovery of her sick child a mother might dedicate her daughter as a temple prostitute, or for the birth of a son throw her next born into the Ganges, or again, for the death of an enemy a man might starve to death or immolate himself on a pyre.

Today the obligations of a vow are generally confined to such holy disciplines as fasting, continence, pilgrimages, reading of sacred books, the performance of some domestic rite, the feeding of brāhmins, or a regimen of self-denial, such as permanently or for a time abstaining from sweet things or from a favourite item of food. Many of the vratas have now been reduced to simple forms of observance a few of which are cited below.

Very popular is the *akhaṇḍ-dīp*, 'uninterrupted light', where on the first day of a month a lamp made of gold, silver, bronze or brass is lighted and fed with pure ghee (clarified butter); the lamp remains lighted for thirty days till the next new moon; this votive observance is made to ensure all-round prosperity. The *Ananta-vrata* is a fourteen-year vow, begun on the fourteenth day of the bright half of *Śrāvaṇa* (July–August) with fasting and worship; a sacred thread is tied by the husband to the wife's left arm, and by the wife to the husband's right arm. A fast is observed on the fourteenth day of every month thereafter for fourteen years. Once tied the thread is only untied on the next anniversary of that day; this is repeated for fourteen years. The vow is made to the serpent Ananta who in return bestows blessings. The *pradosha*, 'evening' is a vrata of special worship offered to Śiva, particularly on the *trayodaśa* or 'thirteenth' day of each *paksha* or fortnight of the month. It must be performed during the evening twilight.

In the *chāndrāyaṇa*, 'moon's course', a vow is taken to observe a special fast in which the number of morsels eaten per day is gradually reduced by one, starting from fifteen at the full moon to nothing during the night of no moon; after that it is increased at the same rate until the next full moon, when normal diet is resumed. The *kṛichchhra*, 'severe' is a kind of minor penance undertaken as a vow, where the person lives on *pañchagavya* (a compound of milk, curds, ghee, cow-urine and cowdung) on one day and fasts on the next day. There are many forms of *nirjala*, 'without water', vows, in which no water is taken. The chief of these is the nirjala observed on the *ekādaśī* (eleventh day) of the bright fortnight of the month of *Jyeshṭha* (May–June) which falls in the hot season. The observance of this vow confers great spiritual benefits. In the *prabodhini*, 'waking', an all-night vigil is kept; the chief of these is observed on the eleventh day of the bright fortnight of *Kārttika* (October–November).

Books

(*See under* Sacrifices.)

VRĀTYA, an obscure non-Vedic ethnic group or sect mentioned in the Vedas, about whom there is much unsettled speculation. Scholars have sometimes identified the Vrātyas with the Maga* people who came to India by way of the Indus Valley from south-west Iran, and eventually settled in eastern India, in Magadha. In the Indus Valley they left many traces of their culture, some aspects of their religion in the proto-Śiva cult, as well as a fragment of their name in the term *vrāti* which was used to designate the large settlements where they lived (I, p. 47).

In their progress eastwards from the Indus Valley they left further traces of their presence among the heterogeneous tribes of the Himālayan foothills, the Lichchhavis, the Mallas and others, who are referred to by Manu as the children of the Vrātya kings (IV, pp. 123, 127). They finally settled in Magadha which became the focus of Vrātya culture. The earliest cultural centres of ancient India were located in the Indus Valley and the lower Gangetic plain, and in both the areas the religious and cultural evolution seems to have run on similar lines.

There are several hypotheses concerning the Vrātyas. They have sometimes been identified with a non-Aryan people who may have brought with them from outside India some features of the cults of ancient Elam or Babylonia. They have been called the precursors of the yogis and are classed among the earliest of India's ascetics and mystics, of proto-Śaivite affiliation. Some find evidence to support the view that they were bacchantes, the followers of a fertility cult which included ritual dancing and flagellation. Others again regard them as an advance guard of the Aryan invaders. By Manu's time they were classed as brāhmins who had neglected to perform the prescribed rites and were expelled from their caste.

The term vrātya is variously interpreted as meaning (*a*) 'fallen', i.e. from the status of Aryan peoples, (*b*) one who is 'uninitiated' in Aryan ways, (*c*) one who undertakes a *vrata* or vow and (*d*) a pious vagrant. The *Mahābhārata* brands the Vrātyas as the scourings of society, classing them with poisoners, pimps, abortionists, drug-addicts, drunkards, illegitimates, mixed castes and half-castes. They were credited with magical powers, and were believed to practice the more malignant forms of sorcery.

Their deity, leader or king, *Ekavrātya*, is mentioned in an obscure hymn of the *Artharva-veda*, which also devotes an entire book to the Vrātyas. Little is known about this deity who is equated with a manifestation of the cosmic principle or supreme power of the universe, and whose identity with the prototypal Śiva of the Indus Valley has frequently been suggested. Says Bhandarkar, 'It seems that the Vrātya cult which was afterwards developed into Śaivism, originally came to the Indus Valley with the migration of the Magadhas from outside India' (I, p. 48).

Among the rites and practices associated with the Vrātyas the following are the most conspicuous. They held what appears to have been an early form of Sāṁkhya–Yoga philosophy, and advocated the doctrine of *tapas* or asceticism, which they practised in many extreme forms, e.g. they would remain standing for a year at a time. They were familiar with the notion of the seven vital airs and the disciplines of breath-control, and named more than ten kinds of breathing, with their concomitant powers. They were acquainted with the techniques of concentration, of 'soul-expansion', and the enhancement of personality and consciousness by disciplines, with experiences of trance and *samādhi*. They regarded the body as a microcosm*, of which the universe was the macrocosm. They experimented with secret recipes for the elixir of life, which earned them the reputation of being 'swallowers of poison' (III, p. 25).

Associated with them was the *gavām-ayana** sacrifice ending with the *mahāvrata*, a great solstitial rite of archaic origin. A cart drawn by a horse or mule served the nomadic Vrātyas as a place of sacrifice and worship; the Vrātya priest was accompanied by a *māgadha*, a cantor or minstrel, and a harlot known as a *puṁśchalī* (or śūlā), or a naked female who represented what later came to be known as *śakti*.

The ceremonial dress of the Vrātya priesthood was distinctive. They wore black, or white robes with black figures on them. A ceremonial turban and two ram-skin shawls, one white one black, thrown over the shoulders completed the costume. On ritual occasions their feet were shod with sandals. As a weapon they carried a sharp-pointed wooden lance (prototype of Śiva's *śūla*), an unstrung bow (*jyāhroḍa*) and a magical bowl. They also wore an ornament around the neck (the *nishka*), and had ceremonial ear-rings which played an important part in their rites, their ears having been bored on initiation. Many of these items, it will be observed, are now the stock-in-trade of yogis, Kānphaṭas, Aghorīs, and other wonder-workers commonly known as sādhus.

Research is slowly strengthening the tenuous links that bind the ancient religious systems of the Middle East with the cults of prehistoric India. Little more is needed to establish a plausible connection between Chaldean and Elamite magic, the religion of pre-Zoroastrian Persia, the cults of the

Indus Valley, the magic rites of the Vrātyas of the Middle Gangetic plain, and the arcane teachings of the heterodox Jain and Buddhist cults. Who the Vrātyas were and whence they came can only be indicated in outline in the absence of positive knowledge; more than this were mere conjecture. Whatever their origin and the extent of their influence, the Vrātyas disappeared from history. The strong arm of the main Aryan advance laid them low long before the Epic period. Those who accepted the Aryan way of life were reluctantly admitted into the fold of the twice born. The ceremony of their conversion, or their restoration to brāhminical society, known as the *vrātya-stoma*, having served its purpose, has metamorphosed into a rite for sanctifying errant Hindus who have strayed from the observances of their caste. It is the only positive relic in Hinduism today of one of the most mysterious of all the peoples who found their way to the Indian peninsula.

Books

I. Bhandarkar, D. R. *Some Aspects of Ancient Indian Culture*, Madras, 1940.
II. Choudhary, R. K. *The Vratyas in Ancient India*, Banaras, 1964.
III. Karmarkar, A. P. *The Religions of India: The Vratya or Dravidian Systems*, Lonavla, 1950.
IV. Raychaudhuri, H. *Political History of Ancient India*, 6th Ed., Calcutta, 1953.
V. Sastri, H. P. *Absorption of the Vratyas*, 1926.

VṚINDĀ, the beautiful and saintly wife of a low-caste man named *Jaladhara*. Her virtue was so great that it endowed her husband with divine power, so that even Śiva could not gain mastery over him. On Śiva's persuasion Vishṇu assumed the form of Jaladhara and seduced the faithful woman. Having lost something of his perfection through the infidelity of his wife Jaladhara was now easily slain by Śiva. When the unfortunate widow discovered the deception she threw herself into the flames of her husband's funeral pyre. Vishṇu, wishing that her charms might be preserved transformed her body into the Gaṇḍakī river and her lovely hair into the *tulasī* plant.

The Gaṇḍakī river in Nepāl is revered as the occasional resting place of Vishṇu who visits it from time to time and lies in the riverbed embracing Vṛindā. In this river a black stone is found, called the *śālagrāma*, which is believed to be the sperm of Vishṇu. The stone occurs in different sizes, from a small pebble to one large enough to cover the whole hand. It is a sort of fossilized shell or ammonite with peculiar markings and colours to which all kinds of interpretations are given: black stones give fame, white ones destroy sin, blues give peace, yellows confer sons. According to the *Atharva-veda* the house without a śālagrāma is as impure as a cemetery. The stone is kept wrapped in a perfumed cloth and is highly esteemed. To touch or drink water in which this stone has been washed is to receive absolution from all sins, and to be assured of a place in heaven. Dying Hindus hold it in their hands as the key to a blissful future life.

The sacred *tulasī* (or *tulsī*) plant, the Indian basil (*ocymum sanctum*) represents the hair of Vṛindā and is believed to be occupied by the spirit of the beautiful woman every evening. In the morning she leaves the plant. Hindus grow the tulasī in the courtyard of their houses, sometimes in a special brick enclosure called Vṛindāvana. It is tenderly cared for, watered and worshipped with the waving of lamps and circumambulation. The leaves are not plucked at night when Vṛindā dwells in the plant. The goddess Śakti was once enraged at Vṛindā so the tulasī leaf is never offered to her in rites associated with her worship.

On the bright eleventh day of the month of *Kārttika* (October–November) the tulasī is ceremonially married to Vishṇu, who is represented either by an image or by the śālagrāma stone. The plant and the stone are washed and offered turmeric and red lead; then, to the chant of mantras the marriage neck-thread is placed over the plant and rice showered on the pair. The stone is then made to touch the plant. This ceremony marks the opening of the Hindu marriage season.

In some legends Vṛindā is identified with Rādhā, and thus associated with Kṛishṇa.

Books

I. Underhill, M. M. *The Hindu Religious Year*, Calcutta, 1921.
II. Kincaid, C. A. *Tale of the Tulsi Plant*, 1916.

(*See also under* Mythology.)

VYĀSA, 'arranger', was the title given to several old authors and compilers of ancient works. The Purāṇas mention nearly thirty Vyāsas. Specifically the name refers to the ṛishi who supposedly arranged the Vedas and compiled the *Mahābhārata*. It is also the alias of the philosopher Bādarāyaṇa who founded the Vedānta philosophy. Some authorities have tried to identify the poet and the philosopher, but it is impossible that their respective tasks could have been the work of one man, since they are separated by many centuries.

The semi-legendary Vyāsa of *Mahābhārata* fame was born on an island (*dvīpa*) on the Yamunā, not far from the modern town of Kalpi, the illegitimate and half-caste (II, p. 8) son of the *ṛishi* Parāśara* by the non-Aryan Dāsa princess Satyavatī. In accordance with the custom of niyoga he raised issue on the daughters of the indigenous king of Kāśī, becoming the father of Pāṇḍu and Dhṛitarāshṭra, and thus the grandsire of the main protagonists of the Mahābhārata war. He had yet another son named Śuka. According to the legend Vyāsa was busy getting fire from two rubbing sticks when the beautiful *apsarā Ghṛitāchī* suddenly appeared before him in diaphanous robes. A violent storm arose in his soul 'which surged all through his limbs and caused his seed to fall' (III, p. 263). It fell on the lower fire-stick and the sage thus sparked his son Śuka into being.

Vyasa is also known as Kānīna, 'bastard'; Kṛishṇa-Dvaipāyana, 'dark-skinned island-born'; Śāśvatas, 'immortal'; and Vedavyāsa, 'Veda-arranger'. Besides the Vyāsa, called Bādarāyaṇa, who founded the Vedānta philosophy, another Vyāsa (*c.* AD 600) wrote a commentary on Patañjali's *Yoga-sūtra*.

Books

I. Aurobindo, Sri. *Vyasa and Valmiki*, Bombay, 1956.
II. Chatterji, S. K. *Kirata-Jana-Krti: The Indo-Mongoloids*, Calcutta, 1951.
III. Meyer, J. J. *Sexual Life in Ancient India*, 2 vols., London, 1930.

WARFARE. In Hindu polity war, or *vigraha*, was one of the six conditions of international relations, and the army* or *bala* one of the seven constituents of the state. Much of the art of warfare was overburdened with pedantic theory. After attempts at appeasement, bribery, internal dissension, and threat had been resorted to and failed, the whole force of the state was to be pitted against the enemy. This was war.

Two kinds of war were distinguished. The *dharma-yuddha*, 'righteous war', was fought according to the chivalric code of kings and warriors. It was a struggle of good against evil; a crusade or jihad for the establishment of right. Blatant acts of aggression were frequently put into this category. Their justification was expressed in the *Mahābhārata* by Kaṇika of the line of Bharadvāja, who advocated the usurpation of degenerate dynasties as a righteous act. The tactics of *dharma-yuddha* were open (*prakāśa*), and it was without secrecy or stratagem, although recourse to magical means and *mantras* (spells) was permissible. Hence it was also called *mantra-yuddha*, war by spells. The *kūṭa-yuddha*, 'false war', was actuated by greed (*lobha*) for territory or spoils, or lust for conquest and massacre. This type of warfare employed the methods of the *asura* (godless), hence was also called *asura-yuddha*, and included subversion, secret agents, treachery, poisoning of drinking wells, killing of cattle, and sorcerous means. Among the latter was illusion (*māyā*), of which only two examples need be given: 'The king is dressed up like a god or disguised as a pillar, and when the enemy comes to worship him, slays him'; 'The king visits the enemy dressed as a woman, or as a devil or evil spirit, and kills him at close quarters' (III, p. 333).

Once a king decided to make war he had to get himself and his country in readiness to carry it through. He put the affairs of the state in order; despatched his spies to ascertain the strength and disposition of the enemy forces; and collected his army and material resources. The formation of the army on the march, the methods of setting up camp, and the order of battle were all of vital importance.

Roads had to be cleared by specialists trained in the job. The three types of roads were those that led through forests, those that traversed hills, and the narrow defiles between hills. The troops on the march had to be specially deployed: like a column, if the ground was level; in the likeness of a wedge or a waggon, when approaching a valley; in the shape of a rhombus or a boar, when crossing a river; like two triangles, or like a *makara* or shark in hilly country; in a long, pointed line like a thorn, when going through a mountain pass; with extended wings like Garuḍa, when the terrain was mixed.

The camp should invariably be disposed in the shape of a lotus, and pitched on high ground, near a supply of flowing water like a river or large stream, with sentries posted all around. The site of the battlefield should be in full view of the king, and care should be taken to see that it is strategically situated in relation to the sun, wind, water, elevation and forest. There should be no risk of sudden enemy attack from the rear, or from a hidden position. Spies and reconnaissance parties should be kept busy bringing in intelligence of the strength and position of the enemy army. Pitfalls were commonly dug outside the camp area by both sides, and a cow was therefore released near the enemy camp to find out whether the track was dangerous.

The king, commander-in-chief and subordinate generals, each had a spacious area cleared for their tents, all richly adorned; and each had special apartments reserved for women. In the order of establishing camp precedence was given first to the king, and his harem and spies; then the commander-in-chief and his harem and spies; then the subordinate commanders and their harems in descending order of rank. The harems were frequently sizeable encampments and the king and commanders were accompanied till the medieval period by their retinue of betel-servers and nautch women even while the battle was in progress.

Debauchery and moral laxity was rife among the soldiers, and prostitutes and catamites formed a regular part of the camp following. The duty of the women was to provide entertainment, to prepare food, and to stand behind the men during the engagement and 'utter encouraging words' (V, p. 164). Among the non-combatant camp-followers were conjurers, soothsayers, astrologers, fakirs, physicians, quacks, grooms, mechanics, civil officers of state, carpenters, sappers and surveyors. Professional panegyrists frequently followed the troops to sing their valour and inspire them with confidence. There was a huge commissariat for the provision of food and supplies, provender for cattle, spare weapons, chariot spare parts, pots of poisonous snakes, and inflammable materials.

The morale of the troops, often to a large extent composed of mercenaries, was poor, and they were not to be depended on unless sustained by the courage of numbers. Hindus believed implicitly in the strength of numbers, which they frequently put pell-mell into the field in a disorderly mass against the enemy without concerted plan. This vast mass, which fully mobilised and including auxiliaries and non-combatants sometimes numbered half a million men, was slow, cumbersome and unwieldy. The commanders and subordinate commanders could not co-ordinate their movements, and a shrewd enemy general with quick moving units often had the advantage over such a closely packed field. Many were the easy victories of a handful of Greek, Kushān, Hun, Afghan and European troops against what a Muslim chronicler gleefully referred to as 'kafir rabble'. The king himself was not expected to fight but encouraged his army from the rear (III, p. 247). The complete dependence of Hindu military operations on a single man, the king or commander-in-chief, added a further element of weakness, for the enemy had only to pick out the leader and slay him for the whole army to give up the fight and turn and flee.

Siege warfare was employed from early times, but the theory was riddled with primitive notions. The king was advised to attack that part of the citadel over which he saw a crow or crows flying frequently. The sight of a lizard or chameleon should give him pause for these were creatures from whom omens were read with difficulty and whose interpretations were ambiguous. As a rule scientific methods of fortifying, besieging and defending strongholds were neglected. Towns were invested until famine forced surrender, or until the patience of the besiegers was exhausted and they simply raised the siege and departed. To take a place by assault was too troublesome and hazardous. Many improved siege techniques were learnt from the Greeks and other invaders, of which one relic survives in the Sanskrit word *suruṅgā*, meaning a mine or underground tunnel, which is derived from the Greek syrinx. Vestiges of other aspects of war borrowed from the Greeks are found in such words as *khalīna*, meaning a horse-bit, which comes from the Greek *kalinos*; and *kramela* from the Greek *kamelos* meaning camel.

A considerable time would be spent in religious functions before the battle. Prayers were addressed to the deities, to the guardians of the quarters (*lokapālas*), to the Aśvins, and to the godlings of rivers, mountains, trees and plants. The whole war was regarded as a sacrifice, and the *Mahābhārata* speaks of Kurukshetra in such a manner. The battlefield was the altar, the warriors the sacrificial victims, the blood of the slain oblations of clarified butter. Killing and being killed were not acts of unrighteousness but forms of sacrament.

Astrologers and soothsayers studied the stars and observed omens and finally announced the auspicious day and time for battle. The night before the battle representative weapons and musical instruments were sprinkled with fragrant water, anointed with ghee and moved before the sacred fire to the recitation of mantras. At midnight the *purohita*, or king's priest, made a special offering and threw the sacrificial ladle high into the air completing a magical mantra before it touched the ground. An amulet made from the skin of an antelope was tied to the king's arm. Mantras were pronounced over the king, the commanders, and three elephants, chariots and war-horses. The assembled army was purified for the sacrifice, and the warriors slept that night with their weapons beside them.

Surprise tactics and night manoeuvres were not generally favoured, as commanders had no wish to be deprived of their sleep or suffer the discomforts of expeditious movement. Thus in later times night raids by a handful of Europeans time and again threw Indian troops into disorder and routed a whole army. Indian military science entered a new phase when Moghul and Sikh rulers enlisted in their services European generals and military adventurers. Only when they came into fighting contact with Europeans did they begin to appreciate the value of discipline, drilling, the orderly disposition of men during the march and in camp, and effective strategy in the field.

The early writers on the art of warfare mentioned certain established rules that were observed by all those who fought a 'righteous' war. Thus, all fighting was to be done during the daytime; blood spilt after sunset was believed to be consumed by demons and ogres who haunted battlefields; after sunset therefore the warrior desisted from the fray and returned to his camp. Again, only men of equal rank or equally matched could fight one another. A king could fight only a king and not anyone of inferior status. Combatants armed with the same kind of weapon could fight one another: a chariot-fighter could fight only another chariot-fighter; foot-soldiers only foot-soldiers; a warrior in armour with another in armour, and so on. Thus, a dismounted horseman could not be touched except by another dismounted horseman. In the case of personal combat, every fight was to be preceded by a challenge from one party and acceptance by the other. A warrior engaged in personal combat with another could not be attacked or hit by a third party. Fighting had to stop when the opponent was grievously disabled, or was disarmed or had his weapon broken or bowstring cut, or who was dismounted, or had lost his armour or chariot, or who abandoned the fight and ran away. A brāhmin could not be killed unless he assumed the role of a warrior i.e. dressed like a warrior, armed himself as such and participated in the fighting. If he was present as a priest or adviser he could not be slain.

Non-combatants like charioteers, attendants carrying weapons, drum-beaters, conch-blowers, camp-followers and musicians, could not be struck. Women, eunuchs, the aged, infirm, insane, children, outcastes, those who were in terror, or intoxicated or asleep, those who were naked, those engaged in eating and drinking or answering the call of nature, those walking peacefully along the road, could not be attacked. Peasants and cultivators were never to be touched. Megasthenes observed that during a battle between two armies the peasants unconcernedly continued their ploughing, or watched the fray, secure in the knowledge that they would not be molested. Fruit orchards and flower gardens and fields ready for harvesting, temples and places of worship, could not be touched. It was prohibited to use poisoned weapons, hidden weapons like the sword-stick, blazing or fire-throwing weapons, or barbed weapons such as drew out the entrails.

The panic-stricken and scattered foe were not to be followed in hot pursuit but left to escape if they could. Surrender was betokened by laying down one's arms and 'asking for mercy with loose hair and folded hands'; by eating grass like a cow, or holding a straw in the mouth, or by crying out, 'I am yours'; or by asking for refuge.

There were also chivalric rules governing the aftermath of battle. One was advised never to lament a hero killed in battle for he brings glory to his king, honour to his family, and becomes the lord of a thousand beautiful nymphs. The slain warriors on the victorious side were cremated with due ceremony, their wives ascending the pyre if they desired. Prisoners of war were banished to the outskirts of the kingdom for one year, after which they became free. The able-bodied among them were sometimes offered the choice of serving as slaves to their captors for one year, and were promised freedom thereafter. Maidens were married to warriors, after the king and commanders had had their pick. Hiuen-Tsang (*c.* 630) records that a defeated general was not slain or tortured, but was made to change his dress for that of a woman. Most of them killed themselves rather than face the disgrace of this situation.

Victors permitted the obsequies of slain enemy leaders and warriors to be performed after the battle. The king was laid out in state and a train of princes, merchants, agriculturists and śūdras came to pay their last respects. Bards sang songs in praise of the heroic warrior. The body was then laid on the funeral pyre and the bodies of other warriors laid on lesser pyres around him according to rank. Those women among the war captives who had not been selected by the victorious side were permitted to ascend the pyre if they desired.

Those on the victorious side who deserted the field to save their skins were stoned to death, or rolled up in grass mats and burnt. The main buildings of the enemy capital, such as palaces and even temples were destroyed and the sites sown with castor-oil seeds, cotton, or cereals.

Much of the ancient chivalric code was modified after contact with the Kushāns, Śakas and Huns, fierce warriors who fought by their own ruthless standards. But on the whole a general understanding of the need for a law of warfare prevailed, and some of the Hindu ideals were accepted by them in course of time. Relics of the epic ideal are discernible in the medieval Rājput code, and survived in the standards set by Śivājī, which were remarkable for their humanity considering the age in which he lived. But Śivājī's successors were ruthless and barbaric; their objectives aggrandizement and plunder; their code not a whit better than that of the vandal armies of the Afghans and Turks. It was the brutal encounters with these latter invaders that finally put an end to the ancient rules of Hindu warfare.

Books

I. Chakravarty, P. C. *The Art of War in Ancient India*, 1932.

II. Date, G. T. *The Art of War in Ancient India*, London, 1929.

III. Dikshitar, V. R. R. *War in Ancient India*, 2nd Ed., Madras, 1948.

IV. Ray, H. C. 'Notes on War in Ancient India', *Journal of the Department of Letters*, 1927.

V. Upadhyaya, B. S. *India in Kalidasa*, Allahabad, 1947.

WEAPONS. The tools of war were called *āyudha* in Sanskrit, and were often given a supernatural significance, much of Indian symbolism being built around the weapons of the gods. In Hindu and Buddhist iconography several deities are represented as carrying a weapon of some kind, with which they are traditionally associated, e.g. Śiva and the trident, Vishṇu and the discus, the Maruts and their bows and arrows, Agni and the spear, Varuṇa and the noose, Indra and the thunderbolt, Yama and the *pāśa* (rope), Kāla and the sword and shield, Viśvakarman and the battle-axe.

Most of the divine weapons were fashioned by the celestial artisan Viśvakarman, from the blazing fragments of Sūrya's orb, which he cut off with his own magical weapon, and these are usually described as dazzling and resplendent. Others were made from the bones of Dadhīcha by Tvashṭṛi and were possessed of great power. The Vedic texts indicate that the more dangerous and devastating weapons were known as *āsura*, so called because they were believed to have been invented by the asuras or demons in their war with the gods. In like manner the Aryan warriors were often discomfited by the terrible weapons used by their Anārya enemies. Even in later times, after the introduction of guns and cannon, Śukra in his treatise on politics, classed the more lethal weapons as āsura.

The warrior in the field was protected against enemy weapons by the *varma* or armour worn by him, consisting of a coat of leather with wooden boards or pieces of horn or metal to guard the breast. There are references in the *Ṛig-veda* to the coat of mail and the helmet. There were also different pieces for protecting the head, neck, shoulders, chest, hands, privates, thighs, knees and feet. In addition he carried a shield made of metal, wood, beaten pulp and leaves, or tree-bark.

More than four hundred weapons are mentioned in the texts, the majority now unidentifiable. They were often fancifully named, depending on whether they were 'hurled' or 'not-hurled', 'upward-going', 'straight-going', 'directioned', 'undirectioned'. Some were named according to their properties, as 'drying', 'drenching', 'flaming', 'spitting', 'pulverising', 'biting', 'noisome', 'darkness-causing', 'thunder-creating'. Some were named after their shape, such as that of a horse, heron, club, serpent, eagle, carriage-shaft, ploughshare, leaf, navel, ewe, garland, crocodile, pestle, skull-bracelet. They may be named to indicate that they were one, two, or even hundred-headed; some had a single opening; others two, three or a hundred openings; some had one, two or more points or edges, or were round, blunt, pointed, and so forth. Some did not slay, but 'produced illusions', 'caused deep sleep', 'produced a soothing effect', 'caused righteousness', or 'resulted in bewitchment'. These four hundred-odd weapons were first classed under one hundred and eight heads, which were reduced to thirty-two types, and this number further decreased to five chief categories.

The **mukta,** 'thrown', weapons are projected by hand. These include primitive devices used by aboriginal tribes, and rākshasas, such as stones and wooden weapons. The *valaitaḍi,* a bent stick or boomerang was first used by the Austrics; it later took the shape of a shortened club-like weapon with a knob at one end which was hurled at the enemy. Indra in the *Mahābhārata* wields the boomerang. The spear and the arrow shot from the bow (*see* archery) also belong to the 'thrown' class. The prototype of the *parañja* or *gośiras,* a lance or short spear, was presented by Indra to Manu the first king on earth. Other types include the *tomara,* a light throwing spear; the *kunta* or lance with a barbed head; the *paṭṭiśa* or spear with a metal head having three razor-sharp teeth; the *śakti,* a special spear associated with Kārttikeya. Then there was the long spear, the *śūla,* and the śūla with three prongs called the *triśūla* or trident, the personal weapon of Śiva, fashioned for him by Viśvakarman. In tantrik texts the śūla is often used metaphorically to denote the erect member of Śiva.

The **amukta,** 'not-thrown', were the weapons held in the hand while fighting. This class includes clubs (*daṇḍa*), swords and daggers. The ***paraśu,*** battle-axe or hatchet, probably of Semitic origin, was the weapon of Paraśurāma, received by him from Śiva. Another common weapon under this head was the *aṅkuśa,* a hook with a handle, used for hooking the enemy's neck and drawing him down during the fight. Later the aṅkuśa developed into a goad, such as are used for elephants. It was the weapon of Śiva. Indra also used a hook, along with a net called *Indra-jāla,* which was thrown over the enemy to render him helpless. It was once loaned to Arjuna. In philosophy the net of Indra is used as a synonym for the world's illusions, or for the snare of phenomena. Sometimes it is said that each of its interstices has a mirror and that in this net one sees the whole universe reflected and becomes aware of the interdependence of all things.

The general term for 'unthrown' hand weapons used in close combat is *asi,* loosely translated 'dagger'. The *maushṭika,* a 'fist' weapon with sharp edges was used for in-fighting. One variety was the *vaitastika* (from vitasti, 'span') a small weapon gripped in the hand, with claw-like iron hooks attached to it. A similar type, the *vāg-nāg* (or *bāgh-nakh*), 'tiger's claw' was a favourite weapon of Śivājī. Some authorities hold that the ancient vaitastika was 'a pistol or small hand-gun the size of a span' (I, p. 137). The term *asi* was also frequently used for the sword. It is described as cruel, fearful, fiery, powerful, unassailable, victorious. The whole sword class of weapons was devised by Brahmā for the benefit of the gods to enable them to overcome the demons. The asi was worn on the left side and used with thirty-two classical movements. The principal asi weapons are the *asidhenu* or dagger; the *kartṛikā* or hunter's knife, which, as the weapon of Śiva is often described as having a serrated edge; the *kṛipāṇa* or short sword, carried by warriors and now forming part of the traditional dress of Sikhs as the kirpān; the *khaḍga*, a broad-bladed dagger; the *pṛithu-parśu* or broadsword, of which Megasthenes said, 'All Indian warriors wear swords of great breadth, and when they engage in close fighting they grasp these with both hands so that the blow may be the stronger'; the *nandakī*, a long slender-bladed sword, usually equipped with a hand-guard, originally the weapon of Vishṇu. The asi weapons were generally used in conjunction with a *kheṭa* or shield, also called *phalaka* if made of the bark of trees or of fibre, and *charman* if made of leather.

The heaviest of 'unthrown' arms were the clubs, which required great physical strength to wield. The *musala* or mace was the chief weapon of the *rākshasas*. It was also adopted by the great hero Balarāma. The sixteenth book of the *Mahābhārata* is named after this weapon. Agni gave a magical mace, the *kaumodakī* to Kṛishṇa to help him in overcoming Indra during the burning of the Khāṇḍava forest. A smaller variety, the *drughaṇa* was a short club with a spiked head. The *gadā* or lesser mace was like the 'Indian club', but with a spiked head. The original gadā was made from the bones of an asura named Gadā, and became the favourite weapon of Vishṇu, one of whose titles is Gadādhara, 'club-bearer'. It remained hidden in the primeval waters until it appeared during the Churning of the Ocean. The *mudgara* or hammer, was a stout hammer-headed weapon; the *mayūkhi*, similar to the quarter-staff, was a long, heavy wooden staff gripped at one end with one hand, and a little lower down with the other hand; the *parigha* was a long wooden beam or tree trunk used by ogres and demons in their wars. The word later came to mean the battering-ram. The *sīra* or plough served as a weapon to king Janaka, and, known as *lāṅgala*, was the weapon of Balarāma. Balarāma also used the *hala* or ploughshare which is described as a large piece of metal with another crooked piece across one end of it. The *laguḍa*, a short heavy staff, and the *daṇḍa*, a long staff, were often carried by ascetics known as *daṇḍins*. Two weapons of Śiva belonged to this class: the *pināka*, club (sometimes bow), and the *khaṭvāṅga*, a club surmounted by a skull or a piece of human bone; the khaṭvāṅga is carried by some classes of sādhus who employ it for magical purposes.

The **muktāmukta** (*mukta-amukta*, 'released, not-released') class of weapons, of which the best example is the *pāśa* (from paśī, to bind), a rope noose like a lasso, the chosen weapon of Varuṇa and Yama. The pāśa was often fixed on a triangular, square or circular frame with a suspended ball of lead. When flung it fell over the head of the victim and settled around his neck, the lead ball stunning him. Śiva presented a pāśa to Arjuna after the Kirāta incident.

The **yantra-mukta** 'machine propelled', weapons included the catapult and other heavy long-range arms frequently used in siege warfare. The catapult or *prayukta* was usually on wheels and used for hurling stones or fire-balls to set fire to enemy forts. There were also water machines for letting down water, boiling oil and unpleasant liquids in torrents on the heads of those attempting to scale walls. The *jāmadagnya* was a contrivance for discharging several arrows at once; the *yānaka* a machine for discharging pointed shafts. The *ratha-musala*, 'chariot-clubbing' was a chariot equipped with a horizontal wheel over the driver's head; to this wheel were attached a number of clubs which were whirled around by the movement of the wheel and then released, causing great damage. The chariot is sometimes described as being self-propelled, moving without horse or driver.

The **mantra-mukta,** 'spell-discharged', were magical weapons also called *māntrika,* since it was necessary to recite a mantra before and during use. Such were the *kāmarūpaka,* a weapon which took shape at the will of the user; and the *satyavān* which acted as directed.

A number of fire-missiles of various kinds are also mentioned in ancient Indian texts, although their precise mode of operation is not clear, as a result of which much fanciful conjecture has been ventured concerning their nature. The chief fire-missiles were as follows. The *āgneyāstra,* 'fire-missile' was one, of which the prototype was fashioned by Viśvakarman out of a fragment of Sūrya's orb. It was given by Bharadvāja the sage to Agniveśa the son of Agni; Agniveśa gave it to Droṇa from whom it passed to several kings, including Sagara. It may have been a fire-ball released from a catapult, although some authorities think differently. 'Fire-arms sounding like the latest atomic bombs vaguely called the *āgneyāstra* in the Mahābhārata were also used; they were obviously fired from some kind of field gun or artillery' (I, p. 137).

The *brahmāstra,* was a dread missile devised by Brahmā and given to Indra who presented it to Rāma. It had sharp edges surrounded by tongues of searing flame and was described as absolutely irresistible. With it Rāma killed Rāvaṇa. The *agnigula* (or agniguḍa) was a fireball. These were made of animal dung mixed with wood shavings, metal fragments and powdered metal, resinous leaves, lac and oils. They were ignited and projected from a sling or catapult, or used on arrow-heads or spears. The *śataghnī,* 'hundred-slaying', another fiery weapon, was described as a large, round or cylindrical projectile filled with inflammable substances and hurled at the enemy. It came from the aerial city of Saubha and was used by Kṛishṇa. In later times the term was applied to cannon.

Among the war material collected from the battlefield of Kurukshetra after the great encounter were various resinous substances and charcoal, which suggest the use of fire-projectiles. Some Hindu authorities believe that the original home of gunpowder was India. The Turkish word *top,* and the Persian word *tufang* are said to be derived from the Sanskrit *dhūpa,* vapour or smoke.

Two types of weapons of a magical character are classified, sometimes with the 'thrown', with the 'thrown-not-thrown', the 'machine-propelled', and also the 'spell-discharged', since they share the qualities of all these. One is the *chakra* and the other the *vajra*. The chakra or discus was a flat sharp-edged missile, with four, six, eight, sixteen, thirty-two or more spokes. When flung it whirled outward, severed the head or body of the opponent, and returned to the hand of the thrower. The discus of Vishṇu, called the *sudarśana*, 'beautiful to behold', was forged by Viśvakarman. The vajra or thunderbolt is shown in representations as two trident heads joined at the base to point in opposite directions. The vajra was fashioned for the gods out of the bones of the sage Dadhīcha on the model of a prototype made of adamant. Its qualities were irresistible power and absolute immutability. The vajra is an important symbol in tantrism, representing the liṅga as well as the reality of the Absolute (*vajra-sattva*, 'adamantine existence'). It is deified in the image of Vajreśvara, 'Thunderbolt Lord'. The *vajranābha* was the thunderbolt given by Agni to Kṛishṇa to help him defeat Indra and burn the Khāṇḍava forest.

Books

I. Acharya, P. K. *Glories of India*. Allahabad, n.d.
II. Aziz, Abdul, *Arms and Ornaments*, 1936.
III. Chakravarti, P. C. *The Art of War in Ancient India*, Dacca, 1930.
IV. Date, G. T. *The Art of War in Ancient India*, 1933.
V. Dikshitar, V. R. R. *War in Ancient India*, Madras, 1948.
VI. Egerton, W. *An Illustrated Handbook of Indian Arms*, 1880.
VII. Oppert, G. *On the Weapons of the Hindus*, 1917.
VIII. Ray, J. C. 'Firearms in Ancient India'; *Chapter V* of *Ancient Indian Life*, Calcutta, 1948.

WEIGHTS & MEASURES. The 'measure' or *tulāmāna* is one of the philosophical categories subsumed under quantity, mass, number (*rāśi*), size, and weight. It pertains to gross elements in aggregate and conglomerate mass. Elements in their pure form are not regarded as material, and hence are beyond the scope of the tulāmāna (weights-and-measures) concept.

A system of weights and measures was quite probably brought to India by the Phoenicians, but indigenous systems were devised in India from ancient times, although these varied considerably from period to period and from one part of the country to another. We know from the *Arthaśāstra* and from Pāṇini that attempts were made from time to time to ensure a standard of uniformity for weights and measures in certain states. A Nanda king tried to introduce uniform standards in the fourth century BC, and another attempt was made by Samudra-gupta more than five centuries later.

Items were weighed in a *tulā* or balance, against commonplace objects like seeds, grains of barley, berries, shells, and so on, and a system of weights, often hypothetical, worked out. Many of the weights were descriptively named after the seed, shell or berry in question. Weights were also closely linked with coinage, and several coins were named after the weights used (*see* numismatics). Measures of capacity, including liquid measures, were gauged by the cupped hands, by jars, buckets and baskets, and used interchangeably with weights. Measures of capacity were also related to measures of area, e.g. the *droṇa*, 'bucketful', a measure of dry and liquid capacity, was also a square measure, the latter determined by the acreage that could be sown with one bucketful of corn.

A similar flexibility existed in the systems of linear measures. The result was that a given system of weights and measures was only valid in a particular period and a particular area. A *kākiṇī* or a *kishku* in fifth-century Ujjain differed appreciably from the same weight and measure in Pāṭaliputra. The details below give a very rough scale covering the most important of all these systems.

Theoretically all weights and measures start from the *aṇu* or atom. The 'measure' of two atoms is a *dvyaṇuka*, and of three atoms a *tryaṇuka*. Then follows the *paramāṇu*, ranging, in modern parlance, from one millionth to 1/349525ths of an inch. It represents the first of the 'material' weights or measures. The *trasareṇu* is made up of not less than thirty atoms and is visible as a mote in a sunbeam. Five trasareṇu make one *reṇu*, which is sometimes described as a settled speck of dust. The weight of one grain of dust stirred up by a passing chariot is called *ratha-dhūli*, 'chariot-dust', and is equal to 8 trasareṇu. The *bālāgra*, 'hair-tip', is equal to 8 ratha-dhūli. The nit, or egg of a louse, called *likṛitā* (also likshā or likhyā) is the weight, or the length of 8 bālāgra. The mustard seed, or *sarshapa* is equal to 3 likṛitā or 24 trasareṇu, and the *yūkā*, 'louse' is equal to between 4 to 8 likṛitā. The *gaura* or 'white' mustard seed is equal to 3 sarshapa or 72 trasareṇu, and the *yava*, or barley grain is equal to 3 gaura, 6 to 12 sarshapa, or 34 to 45 likṛitā.

The *guñjā*, a kind of berry, is the smallest of the jeweller's weights. It is equal to 2 yavas or barley grains. The *kṛishṇala*, a 'black' berry, is about 1½ guñjās. The *rattī* (rattikā, rati, or raktika), a kind of red berry, is between 1½ to 3 guñjās; between 5 to 8 grains of rice; between 3 to 15 yavas. The *nishpāva* is a weight of considerable variation. It is used for weighing gold and silver and is generally regarded as being a little less than 2 guñjās. The *mashaka*, a silver weight, is equal to about 2 rattīs. The *kākiṇī*, 'cowrie', used for gold, is between 2 to 6 guñjās. The *māna* is between 1 to 2 kākiṇīs. The *māshi*, 'bean', is a jeweller's weight, about 17 grains troy; or 4 kākiṇī, 7 to 8 guñjās, 5 kṛishṇala, 2 to 10 rattīs, 3 to 4 mānas. It is also equal to ¼ sāṇa and the māsha is therefore also called a *śāṇapāda*. The *śāṇārdha* is a 'half-śāṇa', or 2 māshas. The *dharaṇa* of 3 to 16 māshas, is also the name of a silver coin. The *śāṇa* is equal to 4 māshas or 2 śānārdhas; the *tolā* to 2 śāṇas or 8 to 12 māshas, approximately 210 grains. The *karsha*, also called thse *uvarṇa* is 2 tolās, 10 to 24 māshas, or 80 rattīs. The suvarṇa is also the name of a gold coin, and kārshāpaṇa the name of a copper coin weighing one karsha. The *purāṇa* (or pūraṇa) 'old' or 'full', used for weighing silver is equal to about 20 māshas; it is also the name of a coin. The *śatamāna*, 'hundred-māna', equal to 4 karshas, 8 śāṇas, 10 dharaṇas, 32 māshas, 100 mānas, 160 mashakas, 320 rattīs, is used for weighing gold and silver. The *pala* (or *nishka*), originally a neck ornament of gold, then the name of a coin, and finally the name of a weight equal to 4 karshas or 64 māshas.

The following are some of the chief measures of capacity. The *śukti*, oyster shell, about one ounce; the *mushṭi*, 'fist' i.e. what can be contained in one closed handful; the *pala*, which is equal to 3 śukti or 2 to 5 mushṭi; the *paṇa* (or *prasṛita*), an open handful, equal to 2 to 3 palas; the *añjali* or what can be contained in two cupped hands, equal to 2 to 3 paṇas, or approximately 16 suvarṇas. The *kuñchi*, equal to 8 paṇas or handfuls; the *nikuñchaka*, from half a kuñchi to 3 kuñchis, or one-fourth of a kuḍava; the *kuḍava*, a vessel 4 fingers wide and 8 fingers long, containing 12 handfuls. The *pātra*, 'bowl', containing 16 suvarṇas, or 8 to 20 palas; the *śera* (or sera), equal to 10 to 25 palas, or, in the modern system, 2 lbs.; the *sarāva*, 'dish', equal to 2 kuḍavas; the *prastha*, or 2 sarāvas, 4 kuḍavas, 32 palas, 48 handfuls; the *pushkala*, 'drum', or 20 to 50 palas, or 2 to 4 śeras. The *tulā*, 'balance', so called because the quantity could conveniently be measured in a tulā or scales; it is equal to 5 śeras, 145 ounces troy, or 100 palas. The *āḍhaka* equals 4 prasthas, or approximately 7 lbs 10 ozs.; the *kaṁsa*, 'jar', is equal to 2 āḍhakas; the *kalaśa*, 'pitcher' is equal to 4 kaṁsas. The *droṇa*, 'bucket' is a measure of capacity and also of area i.e. as much as could be sown with a droṇa full of corn. A droṇa is equal to 1 to 3 kalaśas, 2 to 4 kaṁsas, 4 āḍhakas, 6 shashṭhaka (a 'sixth' part of a droṇa, so called because one sixth of the wheat harvest was taken as a tax by the king), or 16 pushkalas, 32 to 64 śeras, 128 kuñchis, 200 palas, and 1,024 mushṭis or fistfuls. The *śūrpa* (or sūrpa), 'winnowing-basket', equals 2 droṇas; the *goṇī* (or goṇā), 'sack' equals 4 droṇas; the *khāri*, 4 to 16 droṇas, or 3 bushels; the *ghaṭa*, 'pitcher', 1 to 20 droṇas; the *kumbha*, 'jar', 20 droṇas, or 8 to 30 gallons; the *bhāra*, 'load', is 20 tulās, 2,000 palas, or 2½ maunds; the *āchita*, 'loaded', a barrow load, equal to 2 to 10 bhāras; and the *vāha*, 'vehicle', a cartload, or 10 to 20 bhāras.

Like weights, measures are also extremely unsystematized, vary from region to region and from period to period. The *māna*, or measure of length, is sometimes used for square measure, and sometimes as a measure of capacity. In measuring a man (for sculpture), house (for building), or other, object, special measures and canons of proportion* are used. Like weights, measures of length also start from the hypothetical aṇu or atom, and proceed to the *dvyaṇuka*, the *paramāṇu*, the *yava*, etc., and are said to be equal to the length of an atom, two atoms, a grain of barley and so on.

The *aṅgula*, 'finger's' breadth, or the breadth of the thumb, is one of the basic units of measurement. It varies from the breadth of a child's little finger, to the breadth of an adult's thumb, and is said to be 3 to 12 yavas in length; usually regarded as ¾ of an inch. The *pāda*, 'foot' of a man, is equal to 8 to 12 aṅgulas or 2/7ths of a prakrama; the *gopāda*, 'cow's foot', was also used for the same measure. The *prādeśa* or the spread of thumb and forefinger, or the distance between the wrist and tip of the middle finger, is between 8 to 15 aṅgulas, or 6 to 10 inches. The *vitasti*, 'span', is called by Pāṇini the *dishṭi*, 'direction', from the Kharoshṭhī diṭhi, meaning 'span'. It is also called *gokarṇa*, 'cow's ear'. It is between 12 to 19 aṅgulas, or about 9 inches. Often identified with the vitasti is the *hasta*, 'hand', which is the length of the extended hand, or the distance between the tips of the fully stretched thumb and middle finger, or the length of the *tala* or palm of the hand, this latter being used in the canons of proportion; it is also said to be the length of the forearm, and is spoken of as a cubit. There are 7 kinds of hasta ranging from 16 to 32 aṅgulas but the average is often fixed at 18 inches. The *aratni*, 'elbow', or *ratni*, is the measurement from the elbow to the tip of the finger, and is about 18 to 28 aṅgulas or approximately 2 feet.

The *pada*, 'step' consists of 30 aṅgulas; the *prakrama*, 'stride', of 35 aṅgulas; the *kishku*, 'handle' of an axe, of 42 aṅgulas, or about 2½ feet. The *khāta paurusha* or 'trench mansize', is used for measuring the depth of moats; it is about 84 aṅgulas or 5′ 3″; the *vyāma*, 'outstretched', the distance of the outstretched arms, is equal to 88 aṅgulas or about 5′ 5″; the *dhanus*, 'bow', equal to 4 hastas or 96 aṅgulas; the *aksha*, 'axle', equal to 104 aṅgulas; the *kāṇḍa*, 'section', or 108 aṅgulas; the *daṇḍa*, 'pole', a widely used measure, between 100 to 300 aṅgulas, or 3 to 5 cubits, or 5 to 12 feet; the *hastī*, 'elephant', from 196 to 224 aṅgulas, 7 to 9 aratni, 8 to 15 feet.

The *rajju*, 'cord' is from 1,500 aṅgulas to 1,930 aṅgulas, from 7 to 12 daṇḍas, from 25 to 40 yards; the *paridesa*, 'circuit', from 2 to 5 rajjus, often used as a measure of area; the *krośa*, 'shout', or the distance of an earshot i.e. ½ mile to 2¼ miles; the *gohambhā* 'cow-moo', the distance at which the lowing of a cow can be heard in quiet dusk; the *gavyūti*, 'pasturage', a measure of area is equal to 7 to 15 rajjus, and as a measure of distance to between 700 to 3,500 daṇḍas, or 2 krośas, or approximately 5 miles; the *yojana*, 'yoke', is the distance a cart driven at one yoking of the bullocks can travel, it is equal to 4 krośas, or 7 to 9 miles.

Longer distances were reckoned by the space a man could walk or ride in one day, or, as stated in the *Pañchaviṁśa Brāhmaṇa*, by placing 1,000 cows on the top of one another, or by a thousand days' journey of a horse, or by the distance between the two outstretched wings of the sun-bird, or from the point of sunrise to sunset.

Books

I. Malik, S. K. *Weights and Measures in Ancient India*, 1902.
II. Schneider, R. *Hindu Weights and Measures*, 1928.

WHEEL. The wheel or *chakra*, an archaic symbol of the sun, was used in the religious rites of many ancient peoples the world over. It may have been brought to India by the sun-worshipping Maga immigrants from Susa, south-west Persia, and its use may have received a further impetus with the coming of the Zoroastrian Persians.

The wheel has varying significance, depending on which of its several facets is being considered: the wheel as a sphere (the sun), as a circle (the *maṇḍala*), as the spokes (the points of the compass), as the centre (the *axis mundi*), as a rotating hoop (the power of the whirlwind) and as a concentration of energy (the *chakra** of the subtle body). It is the shape of Vishṇu's discus, the symbol of Buddhism (the *dharma-chakra* or Wheel of the Law), the recurrent cycle of time (*kāla-chakra*), the spheres of heaven and hell, and the all-pervading power of force (*daṇḍa-chakra*).

In the more prosaic everyday world it is the ubiquitous tool of the potter, the oil-presser and the miller. The spokes of the wheel, symbolically reduced to four and set at right angles to indicate the cardinal directions, are said to be the origin of the cross and of the swatsika. The chakra is an auspicious sign, and according to Buddhist belief the mark of a wheel on a person's palms, the soles of his feet or on his forehead gives promise of success in all undertakings. Variations of the wheel design play a major part in religious symbolism. The Buddhist Wheel of the Law is usually represented with thirty-two spokes, but it may have a much greater number so as to cover as many directions as possible.

Ceremonial wheel movements in a 'right' direction are always considered lucky, and varieties of such movements have found many religious applications. Some Mahāyāna monks carry little cylindrical cases containing mantras which they revolve by turning a handle, and in this way derive the benefit both for the mechanical repetition of mantras, as well as for the circumambulatory movement which is regarded as so auspicious. The rite of *dola-yātrā*, in which a man is suspended on a pole and swung around on hooks, is best done when the sun enters Aries, an indication of the wheel's solar origin. During the festival of *Jagannātha* (who may have been a solar deity), it was the custom of those devotees who aspired to paradise to immolate themselves under the wheels of the giant carriage. The climax of the ceremonial ascent to the top of the *yūpa* or sacrificial post in ancient times, was reached when the Vedic priest squatted on top of the wheel which was horizontally placed on its summit, and was turned in a sun-wise direction. The victor after battle mounted a chariot and drove around in a small circle, and was thereafter known by the title of *chakravartin*, 'wheel-turner', or conqueror. The most important of the tantrik rites, that of *chakrapūjā*, derives its name from the fact that the devotees sit in a circle.

The movement of the wheel is best exemplified in devotional circumambulation during a pilgrimage*. Circumambulation is also performed around holy persons, and even holy books. In the *rāsa-līlā* dance, Kṛishṇa stands in the centre while the *gopīs* or milkmaids dance in a circle around him. The circumambulation of the altar is part of many solemn rites including the Hindu marriage ceremony where the bridegroom leads the bride three times around the sacred fire. The circumambulation of the corpse by the mourners, although in a 'contrary' direction is part of the funeral ceremony.

In all circular movements, whether of the wheel, or of the dancers, or the pilgrims, the direction followed is of the utmost importance. The auspicious movement is always deasil or rightwards, and is ultimately determined from the direction one is facing. One must face east to get one's true bearings or 'orientation', so the auspicious side is on one's right, or *dakshiṇa*, which is also the south side. In the *pradakshiṇa* or circumambulation rite, the right hand must be on the side of the sacred object. The left-hand movement gives a 'withershins' turning, which is unlucky, being associated with evil, sickness and death, and used in all diabolical worship. Buddhists turn their prayer-wheels clockwise, while the Bon (demonist) priests turn theirs anti-clockwise. The movement of the auspicious male swastika is clockwise and of the female or inauspicious one is anti-clockwise.

So powerful is the effect of the contrary movement that when performed with ritual intent it is even believed to influence external events. Sorcerers in Malabār and Gujarāt employ this knowledge. There was the droll case of a bania who was reputed to be able to control the weather by applying this magic force. For this purpose he used a special spinning wheel made out of dead men's bones. Whenever the rain-clouds were gathering the merchant would set his virgin daughter to turning the wheel in a reverse way to unweave the clouds and so prevent rainfall in order to raise the price of the corn he had to sell. The villagers were convinced that because of this the rain was prevented from falling in spite of other ceremonies being performed to bring it on.

M. K. Gāndhi's use of the spinning wheel, which was supposed to have broken the back of the Manchester cotton trade, has now become almost a ritual in India, and 'mass spinning' takes place throughout the country on his birth and death anniversaries as a tribute to his memory. His spinning wheel has merged with the Buddhist Wheel of the Law to form the circular emblem on India's national flag.

Books

I. Duckworth, S. *The Spinning Orb*, 1890.
II. Kiernander, M. *Rites of the Left Hand*, 1923.
III. Oman, J. C. *Indian Life, Religious and Social*, London, 1907.
IV. Simpson, W. *The Buddhist Praying Wheel: The Symbolism of the Wheel and Circular Movements in Religious Ritual*, London, 1896.

WIDOW. It has been said that there is no more unfortunate character in the whole range of Hinduism than the *vidhavā* or widow. The treatment meted out by Hindu society to women who had the misfortune of losing their husbands was so merciless that it has been affirmed that the rite of suttee, in which a woman burnt herself on the funeral pyre of her husband, was often willingly undergone by the widow just to escape from the degradation of widowhood.

This deplorable attitude was not found in ancient India, either among the pre-Aryans or the Vedic Indians. In Vedic times the widow married the younger brother or other suitable relative of the deceased husband, as is substantiated by a Ṛig-vedic verse that formed part of the funeral rites of the deceased. The widow lies beside her husband on the unlit funeral pyre, and after a short interval the brother or other relative of the deceased holds her hand and addresses her thus: 'Rise O woman, return to the world of the living. Thou liest by the side of one whose life is departed. Be thou now the full-fledged wife of this thy husband who now grasps thy hand and woos thee.'

This contentious stanza has been the subject of endless commentary and debate. Some commentators held that it merely meant that the widow, after going through the formality of showing willingness to join her husband in the next world, was brought back to live among men, but as a widow. Others held that it was employed in certain ceremonies by the living husband and wife who went through a symbolic death-rite. Medieval authorities employed the verse as the prescribed mantra for widow-burning.

The fact that widow remarriage was permitted by the Vedic Indians is attested by the Epics, and several instances are recorded in the historical period. The common practice of *niyoga*, almost universally sanctioned, is virtually a form of widow remarriage. The *Atharva-veda* approves the remarriage of widows, and gives assurance that the performance of the marriage ritual between a woman and her second husband will ensure a legitimate union both in this world and the next, and in another context even refers to the 'eleventh husband' of a woman (II, p. 161). Although the sage Dīrghatamas is said to have decreed that a woman should not marry a second time, the *Mahābhārata* expressly states that a woman marries her husband's brother after the death of her husband, and records numerous instances where widows remarry or are sought after as wives. Ugrāyudha asked for the hand of Satyavatī, widow of Śāntanu; she did not accept his offer but instead married Parāśara through whom she bore the renowned sage Vyāsa. Arjuna had a son by the widowed daughter of Airāvata, the Nāga king.

In the *Jātakas* we read that the king of Kośala made the widowed queen of Kāśī his chief queen. The *Arthaśāstra* of Kauṭilya recognizes the remarriage of a widow, but makes a proviso that she return to the family of her former husband the property which she had received from him. From historical records we learn that Chandra-gupta II married Dhruvadevī, the widow of his elder brother Rāma-gupta. Chandrāpīḍa and Tārāpīḍa, both Kashmīr kings of the eighth century AD, were the sons of King Durlabhaka by a merchant's beautiful widow. Vastupāla exponent of Jainism was the son of a remarried widow. Hammīra king of Chitor married a widow, daughter of Maldeo, and their son ruled Udaipur.

A few lawgivers also conceded remarriage under certain circumstances. According to Parāśara a woman may remarry if her husband dies, disappears for a certain number of years, renounces the world, is impotent, or is expelled from his caste. Nārada and Baudhāyana define the *punarbhū* as a widow, or a woman who has left a husband whom she does not love, or who is impotent, expelled from his caste, or mad, and has married another man. The son of such a woman is called a *paunarbhava*. Other commentators speak of the punarbhū (remarried state) as a woman who has remarried on the death of her husband. Vasishṭha recognizes widow-remarriage, not necessarily with the brother-in-law, but with outsiders as well.

By the sixth and seventh centuries most other lawgivers unconditionally opposed remarriage, on the plea that a woman belonged to her husband both in this world and the next; that she was bound to him for all time and could never be given to another without incurring the heinous sin of adultery. The remarried widow was deemed worse than a harlot, not only bringing shame on her family and on her caste, but causing her husband untold misery in the other world.

To the orthodox family of the medieval period a widow was ill-luck incarnate. If young and childless as well, she was all the more calamitous, as a husbandless, barren, menstruating female. Her presence brought contamination, the sound of her voice was a curse, her glance was poisonous, her very existence was perilous and brought ill-luck and woe to all her relations. She was treated as a thing apart for she was already half dead. Her fate has been frequently described. A few days after her husband's death the female relatives invade the widow's house. They push her violently about, make her sit on a stool, cut the thread of her *tāli* (neck ornament), and have a barber shave her head. She is then called by the opprobrious term *muṇḍa*, 'baldie'. This tonsure is repeated as soon as the hair grows a little, since it is believed that a long braid of hair would put the husband in bondage in the next world (I, p. 160).

From now on she must wear only white clothes. Never again can she wear the *sindūra* mark on the forehead, or jewellery, ornaments or other indications of *saubhāgya* or married bliss. She is forbidden to use a cot, and must sleep on the ground. She cannot cook or help in cooking the family's food; she must eat only once a day and only enough to keep her alive. She is denied even the simple pleasure of chewing pān. She is debarred from all religious affairs and cannot participate in wedding ceremonies or any joyous festivities. Even her son cannot be invited for a *śrāddha*.

Shunned by all, even the servants of the household, left in isolation and subjected to scorn and abuse, her possessions, if she had any, coveted by her relations who want her out of the way, it is no wonder that she sometimes chose to end her existence by suttee. The pitiable lot of the widow in Hindu society became the subject of much criticism when it was first put before the public conscience by Christian missionaries. Says A. S. Altekar, 'It was only with the advent of Western ideas during the second quarter of the last century that some leaders of thought began to realize the iniquity of compelling widows to lead a life of enforced celibacy' (I, p. 158). Rāmmohan Roy and Īshvarachandra Vidyāsāgar were among the great reformers who attempted to legalize widow remarriage in Hindu society. But the prejudice is still very strong, and the number of Hindus willing to marry widows is almost negligible.

Betrothed girls were also regarded as married, even though they did not necessarily live with their husbands. If he died before union and she was still *akshatā*, 'uninjured', i.e. an untouched virgin, she was permitted to remarry under certain rules, but few cared to marry her. In most cases a girl betrothed even verbally was regarded as a widow if her betrothed died. Differences in age between husbands and wives are still very great, accounting for the high proportion of young widows. A survey conducted as recently as 1948 showed that the age of widows ranged between 8 and 54, the average age being 20. 16 per cent of widows had had no married life at all, and 14 per cent had lived with their husbands for only one year. The average period of married life was seven years (III, p. 236).

Since remarriage is practically out of the question, those widows who have no means of support, and whose parents will not take them back, are destined for the streets or for the rescue homes. Such rescue homes were not always what they purported to be, and the inmates were at the mercy of their benefactors. In a rescue home in Bombay 70 out of 188 widows had been seduced (III, p. 238). The strenuous efforts of reformist societies, of women social workers and leaders, and the outspoken criticism of the press have done much to end these scandals.

Books

I. Altekar, A. S. *The Position of Women in Hindu Civilisation,* 2nd Ed., Banaras, 1956.

II. Chaudhuri, J. B. *The Position of Women in Vedic Ritual,* 2nd Ed., Calcutta, 1956.

III. Mace, D. and V. *Marriage, East and West,* London, 1960.

IV. Malabari, B. M. *Infant Marriage and Enforced Widowhood,* Bombay, 1887.

V. Pandit, R. *Essay on the Plight of Hindu Widows,* 1907.

WIND in Hindu mythology is personified as the god Vāyu* (or Vāta). In Vaiśeshika it is one of the subtle elements; in Āyurveda it is one of the three bodily humours; in Yoga and Hindu philosophy it is the term for the vital energies or airs of the body. In the latter sense the alternative term *prāṇa* (see below) is generally used for the vital airs, and is also employed as a synonym for wind, breath, life, life-force and soul. The control of this vital breath through the practice of prāṇayāma is one of the fundamental techniques of yoga. Traditionally ten *vāyus* or vital airs are listed, divided into two groups of five each, which are named below.

PRĀṆĀDI are the winds of the inner body. They include (1) the *prāṇa,* a term universally adopted for all the vital airs, but specifically applied to the wind that has its seat in the heart, and is also called *asu,* 'breath'. It is blood-red or yellow in colour and controls respiration. It is a forward wind, related to the east, and linked with the sun; (2) the *apāna* has its seat in the rectum, is purple and orange in colour, and controls ejection i.e. excretion and ejaculation. It is a down wind, of the west, linked with fire; (3) *samāna,* has its seat in the navel, is white or green in colour, and controls digestion. A consummating wind, of the north, and of the clouds; (4) *udāna,* has its seat in the throat, is pale blue, and controls speech and coughing. An upward wind, of the zenith, and of the sky; (5) *vyāna,* moves all over the body, or according to some authorities, has its seat in the genitals; is flame-coloured and controls the circulation. A reciprocal wind, of the south, and of the moon.

NĀGĀDI are the five vāyu belonging to the outer body. They are (1) *nāga,* 'snake', which controls eructation and retching; (2) *kūrma,* 'tortoise', controls blinking, and the dropping of the eyelids in sleep; (3) *kṛikara,* 'partridge', controls sneezing, hunger and thirst; (4) *devadatta,* 'god-given', controls yawning and dozing; and (5) *dhanañ-jāya,* 'treasure-winning', controls hiccuping. It is also the air that remains in the body during coma, swoon or trance, and after death.

Books

I. Brown, G. W. 'Prana and Apana'. *Journal of the American Oriental Society,* New Haven, XXXIX, 1919, 104-12.

II. Ewing, A. H. 'The Hindu Conception of the Functions of Breath'. *Journal of the American Oriental Society,* New Haven, XXII, 1901, 249–308.

III. Sharma, R. S. *The Vital Winds in Yoga,* 1929.

WOMEN. The notorious subordination of the Hindu woman is believed by many authorities to be entirely due to the lawgivers. To some scholars it is inconceivable that the healthy-minded Aryans who entered the Indian peninsula would have subjected their women to the fate they later suffered under the legalistic dispensation, or indeed that Aryan women would have allowed themselves to suffer the general contumely in which they came to be held. It was inevitable that the patriarchal social system of the Vedic age should place certain restrictions upon the female sex, but these were nothing compared to the terrible degradation of their later estate. In spite of certain passages of rhetorical praise the lot of women in the lawbooks was abject.

In the Vedic period most religious rites and ceremonies were open to women, who had equal privileges of participation and observance with their menfolk. They took an active part in the sacrifices, sang the *sāman* chants and executed ritual acts. Certain sacrifices could be performed only by women. Such were the *sītā* harvest sacrifice, the *rudrabali* sacrifice to ensure the fecundity of cattle, and the *rudrayāga* to secure good husbands for daughters. Some of the texts in which these and other rites were detailed spoke as if referring to men only, but it was recognized that by the use of what was technically known as *uha*, 'modification', the gender could be altered and other necessary changes made in the sacred formula to render it applicable, if necessary, to women also. It was not long before this rule was ignored, and the texts read as though applying to males only, and so it has remained.

The Vedic Age produced a score of eminent female scholars, poets and teachers; in fact a number of the hymns of the *Ṛig-veda* were composed by women. But by the time of the lawgivers the literate woman had become anathema. Manu decreed that women had no right to study the Vedas. Not only did literacy become a rare quality in women, but it was even regarded as disreputable, and learning was considered a qualification of women of ill fame. The belief prevailed that disaster would befall the family if a woman held book or pen in her hand. Says A. S. Altekar, 'It is within the memory of us that orthodox Hindu society regarded it not only unbecoming, but also inauspicious for a woman to be able to read and write.'

Girls were once given the same kind of basic education as boys, and those who belonged to the upper castes were entitled to the *upanayana* or sacred thread ceremony. But the lawgivers declared women to be inherently impure and hence unfit to receive this sacrament. In the *Bhagavadgītā* women are lumped together with sinners, slaves and outcastes. Medieval writers like Mitramiśra held that women were quite ineligible not only for the upanayana but for most other religious rites as well. Says D. P. Mukerji, 'The Hindu woman, religiously is a śūdra, and is not entitled to the gāyatrī mantra'. (X, p. 17). A man could not eat with his wife since she had śūdra status even if born of brāhmin parents; it was especially meritorious if she ate his leavings. A Hindu woman is not supposed to walk side by side with her husband, but must remain a few paces behind him. If she touches a consecrated image its divinity is destroyed and it is rendered useless. Orthodox Hindus, like the Digambara Jains, hold that women can never attain salvation except by being reborn as men.

Already by the Epic period women, in the orthodox Hindu view, had come to be regarded as intrinsically evil, spiritually contaminate, poisoning by their very presence, and obstacles to salvation. They were considered incapable of controlling themselves, ritually impure at all times, avid for illicit affairs, hard of mind, small in judgment, eager to exhibit their persons. The Creator had implanted in women a love for trinkets, dishonesty, untruth, malice, wickedness, cruelty and impure desires. Women, according to the texts, are the root of all evil and suffering. Behind even the most innocent exterior there is a raging passion of lust, since they are beings of insatiable sexual appetite. So great is their desire for the pleasures of the bed that they will give themselves to the meanest of men if they get the opportunity; they have no qualms about being faithless to their husbands and disloyal to their families. A virtuous woman is only one who has lacked the opportunity, or is afraid of discovery. Fickle in their affections they can change lovers as easily as they can shed their garments. Their tears and protestations are of no account for they are falsehood incarnate. Special apartments should be built to keep them sequestered and precautions taken to guard them.

The *Taittirīya Saṁhitā* declares that a good woman is worse than a bad man. The *Maitrāyaṇa Saṁhitā* describes woman as Untruth. The *Mahābhārata* says, 'Woman is an all-devouring curse. In her body the evil cycle of life begins afresh, born out of lust engendered by blood and semen. Man emerges mixed with excrement and water, fouled with the impurities of woman. A wise man will avoid the contaminating society of women as he would the touch of bodies infested with vermin.' The Lawbook of Manu states that killing a woman, like the drinking of liquor, is only a minor offence. It was equated with the killing of a śūdra. The Lawgiver even advises a man not to sit in a lonely place with his own sister, daughter or mother. (II, p. 147). Manu, according to one writer, 'depicts the licentiousness and grossly sensuous character of women in general in such terms as cannot be reproduced without violating decency and modesty' (VIII, p. 19). 'There are three kinds of wine,' declare the Purāṇas, 'but the most intoxicating is woman; there are seven kinds of poison, but the most venemous is woman.' The *Mahābhārata* concludes, 'A man with a hundred tongues who lived for a century would still not be able to complete the task of describing the vices and defects of a woman' (I, p. 321).

In common with all early patriarchal societies the Vedic tribal society preferred sons to daughters. Females were an encumbrance and a burden from birth. They were an impediment in war; they had to be protected in time of peace; they were unclean and dangerous during menses, pregnancy and childbirth; they had to be provided with a dowry when married; they were of no use to anyone as widows. No desire is ever expressed in the *Ṛig-veda* for the birth of daughters, and in the *Atharva-veda* their birth is deprecated.

It was commonly believed that being born a girl was the penalty for some sin committed in a previous incarnation. Till recently in Rājputāna the birth of a girl was not announced, or it was merely said that 'nothing' had been born. The expectant friends then went away 'grave and quiet' (VII, p. 271). Female infanticide was therefore practised on a wide scale from earliest times. The casting away of the children of unmarried mothers, of unwanted girl babies, and the destruction of the foetus are mentioned in the Vedic texts. The *Yajur-veda* speaks of girls being exposed when born, a custom that continued through the centuries unchecked. In Bengal a woman might drown her child in fulfilment of a vow; in western India female infants were strangled or smothered; among the Rājputs parents used to kill their children 'by refusing proper nourishment or sometimes even poisoning the nipples of the mother's breast' (IX, p. 822).

The practice of infanticide was declared illegal by the Regulation of 1802 promulgated by Lord Wellesley, but it has been pointed out that it is still practised by neglect (VII, p. 271). It is known that many girls are allowed to die unattended in cases where medical aid would be summoned if a son were sick.

The cumulative effect of such ignominious practices laid a heavy burden of guilt on the Hindu woman. She expiated her sins by abject submission to the dictates of orthodoxy. Manu declared, 'Day and night woman must be kept in subordination to the males of the family: in childhood to the father, in youth to her husband, in old age to her sons'. It was with particular reference to her attitude towards her husband that the Hindu woman's position was believed to be best expressed. The virtuous woman (*sādhvī*) is the slave and devotee of her husband, and treats him as a divinity. She is described as *pati-vratā*, 'husband-obeying', and *pati-devatā*, 'husband-deifying'. Complete devotion, absolute fidelity and submissiveness to him was the least that any wife owed to her husband, and these virtues were greatly extolled in the Hindu scriptures. Manu says, 'Even though the husband be destitute of virtue, and seeks pleasure elsewhere, he must be worshipped as a god.' The law ordained that if the wife showed disrespect to her husband because of his evil passions, she would be deprived of her ornaments and furniture. If she was quarrelsome and questioned his actions she could be superseded. The *Padma Purāṇa* declares, 'Be a husband aged, infirm, deformed, debauched, offensive, a drunkard, a gambler, a frequenter of places of ill repute, living in open sin with other women, and destitute of honour, still a wife should regard him as a god.'

Hindu myth and legend have idealized the docile, patient, uncomplaining wife. Such for instance was Sītā, wife of Rāma, who followed her husband through all the vicissitudes of his career, and in the end accepted disgrace, public abuse and banishment at his hands. As the fruit of such devotion great powers were said to accrue to the Hindu wife. By means of this power Anasūyā made the sun stand still and changed Brahmā and Vishṇu into babes; through it Sāvitrī brought her dead husband back to life; with its scorching power Damayantī once burnt a hunter who approached her in the forest with evil intent; by its power Sītā kept off Rāvaṇa from fulfilling his wicked designs.

But the generally demoralizing effect of such excessive subordination both on the husband and the wife was felt by many Hindu reformers, who held that far from elevating the marriage partnership it served to debase it. Said M. K. Gāndhi, 'Hindu culture has erred on the side of excessive subordination of the wife to the husband. This has resulted in the husband usurping and exercising authority that reduces him to the level of the brute.'

Woman was believed to have been created for certain fixed functions.

According to Manu the ideal wife had to be clever and economical in managing the household and careful in cleaning the utensils. Another authority has it that a woman's main business is to pound rice, cook, and produce children, especially male children. Sterility in woman was the supreme curse. Lastly, she had to serve as the vessel of her husband's pleasure. A woman's mind, says a modern Hindu writer, 'is saturated with the idea that nature designed her for the enjoyment of man, and that she has no other function than to serve him.' (IX, p. 296.)

The ownership of property was also conditioned by the general attitude. In early times husband and wife were joint owners (*daṁpati*) of the household assets. But by the decree of the lawgivers a woman became the property of her husband and all her stock of wealth was his. She was indeed allowed some personal possessions, which were known as *strīdhana*, 'female property', over which she had complete control. It included such things as jewellery, ornaments, clothing, *śulka* (the money given to the bride at the time of her marriage), gifts of her husband, friends, relatives, and a woman's own earnings by spinning and other virtuous means.

Apart from this Hindu women were and continue to be subject to many proprietary disabilities. If a woman inherits property (e.g. on the death of her husband) her power of alienation over her estate is limited in various ways. Thus when a man dies issueless and his widow succeeds him she is only a limited owner, the male heirs next in order to the deceased having a contingent right to the estate as 'reversioners', who will inherit on the death of the widow. Although meant to safeguard the welfare of the Hindu widow, it frequently made her life a hell on earth, and according to some authorities, became one of the chief factors in the perpetuation of the rite of suttee. Reversioners were interested that the main obstacle in the way to their inheritance should be removed as soon as possible after the death of their relative.

Books

I. Altekar, A. S. *The Position of Women in Hindu Civilisation*, 2nd Ed. Banaras, 1956.
II. Ambedkar, B. R. 'The Rise and Fall of the Hindu Woman'. *The Mahabodhi*, Calcutta, Vol. 59, Nos. 5-6, pp. 137–151.
III. Bader, C. *Women in Ancient India*, London, 1930.
IV. Chaudhuri, J. B. *The Position of Women in the Vedic Ritual*, 2nd Ed., Calcutta, 1956.
V. Cormack, Margaret, *The Hindu Woman*, London, 1961.
VI. Das, R. M. *Women in Manu and his Seven Commentators*, Banaras, 1962.
VII. Mace, D. and V. *Marriage East and West*, London, 1960.
VIII. Madhavananda, Swami. *Great Women of India*, Almora, 1953.
IX. Majumdar, R. C. (Ed.) *An Advanced History of India*, London, 1948.
X. Mukerji, D. P. *Modern Indian Culture*, 2nd Ed., Bombay, 1948.
XI. Phadke, N. S. *Sex Problems in India*, Bombay, 1929.
XII. Pinkham, Mildreth, *Women in the Sacred Scriptures of Hinduism*, London, 1961.

WORSHIP in Hinduism takes countless forms. The term *upāsana* is of general connotation, covering all types of devotional service to the deity, and in the Upanishads it is often used for contemplative and meditative rather than ritual worship.

The highest form of devotion is the worship of Brahma in his purest form, Brahma without attributes (*nirguṇa*), based on the realization of the identity of the self with Brahma. The second is the worship of Brahma with attributes (*saguṇa*) i.e. Brahma or Brahmā, as creator, ruler, provider, Lord of Life and Death. The third and most popular form is the worship of a *pratīka* or symbol of the deity. This form is for those who are incapable of higher meditative worship. The symbol may be a picture, an idol*, or the sun or any natural phenomenon, and all Hindus, even those who perform the higher forms, worship God in the pratīka form as well.

Ritual is essential in all Hindu worship, and generally two kinds are recognized. One is Vedic, based on the Vedas, as explained in the *Pūrva-mīmāṁsā* and elaborated in the kalpa-sūtras; the second is *āgamic*, mainly concerned with the adoration of idols, which varies with the individual sects. There are different āgamas for different parts of India, giving details about the construction of temples, the installation of idols, the modes of devotion, and so on. In all rites and ceremonies a distinction is made between those that are *nitya* or obligatory, and those that are *kāmya* or optional.

Devotions may be performed privately in simple religious services, like *saṁdhyā* or the daily rituals; they may be performed by tending the *aupāsana* or sacred household fire, which is likewise attended by simple rites. The recitation of texts (*pāṭha*), the repetition of *mantras* (*japa*), meditation (*dhyāna*), are also modes of worship. Worship in some of the 'joy' cults (e.g. Vallabha) include *hāsya*, 'laughter', and *lāsya*, 'artistic gestures', and movements such as dancing, while the left-hand cults include collective drinking and sexual practices. Communal worship may follow the model of a Christian church service with singing of *bhajans* and *kīrtans* (hymns). The modern *satsaṅg* or 'assembly of the virtuous' represents communal worship of this kind, with hymns, prayers and a sermon.

In private worship several preparatory forms may be observed prior to the actual meditation on the deity. The *sādhaka* or worshipper sits in the *padmāsana* or cross-legged posture and cleanses himself and his surroundings by purificatory mantras, then proceeds to protect himself from the undesirable distractions of demons, by means of three passes, namely (1) *tāla-traya*, 'clap-trio', where he claps three times with the fingers of the right hand on the left palm, raising his hands a little higher after each clap; (2) *dig-bandha*, 'quarter-binding', in which he performs the ritual *chhoṭikā* ('snapping' of the right-hand thumb and middle finger) ten times in the direction of the ten quarters, namely, the eight points of the compass, and above and below; (3) *agni-prākāra*, 'fire-wall', where he erects an imaginary fire-screen around himself by drawing three circles in the air about him with the right index finger.

Sometimes the worshipper proceeds to the rite of *nyāsa*, 'applying', consisting of the placing of the hand or other limb on something with the intention of transferring power. In the commonest form of nyāsa the worshipper places the tips of his fingers or the palm of his right hand on various parts of his own body, accompanying this action by a mantra, imagining at the same time that the corresponding part of the deity is thereby being placed in him, and in this manner filling his own body with the divine power. The rite is terminated by a movement that 'spreads' the deity all over the body. In certain types of tantrism the parts concentrated on are the genitals and the organs of excretion to endow them with vital energy for the performance of the paramudrās.

The various attentions paid to an installed deity or idol, whether in a household shrine or in a public temple, are collectively referred to as the *upachāra*. The order and method of the service are not uniform and there is no fixed number of items constituting the service. Vaishṇavas generally list sixteen upachāras, Śāktas have more, but the number in all cases varies considerably and there are in fact literally hundreds of variations on the generally prescribed forms. Some of the services offered to the idol are also offered to one's guru (preceptor) or a distinguished guest, since they are regarded as representative of the deity. The following are the chief upachāras:

(1) *Prabodha*, 'awakening': at dawn the doors of the chamber in which the deity is housed are ceremonially opened by the priests and attendants. The flowers used on the previous day are thrown away and the chamber swept. The god is gently roused from sleep. Apart from the nightly sleep there may be a midday sleep, while some of the major deities have long periods of slumber particularly during certain months. Special 'arousal' ceremonies take place after such divine hibernations.

(2) *Snāna*, 'bathing': after being awakened the god may get his teeth washed and his mouth rinsed, after which he may be given a ceremonial bath and anointed with sandal-wood paste (a small pebble, śālagrāma or bāṇaliṅga is sometimes used as a substitute for the god), then dressed in fresh robes and decked in ornaments. Most of these sacred rites take place behind a curtain between the worshipper and the idol, but at each stage of the procedure the priest tinkles a little bell (ghaṇṭā) which he holds in his left hand to mark the phases of worship.

(3) *Āvāhana*, 'inviting', also called *havana*, 'invocation'; the calling upon the deity by his name or appellative. Sacrificial offerings are placed before a fire, the bell (ghaṇṭā) is rung and a conch-shell (śaṅkha) blown to summon him. In the daily worship in a temple the invocation and dismissal of the god are often dispensed with as the deity is permanently in residence.

(4) *Archaka*, the 'adoration' of the deity on his presumed arrival. This includes *svāgata* or the 'welcoming' of the deity; *namaskāra*, 'obeisance-making', or the formal salutation; and *praṇāma*, 'reverent salutation'. The deity may be presented with garlands (*mālya*), proffered a seat (*āsana*), given water (*pādya*) for washing his feet, and for ablutionary sipping (*āchamana*). Such services are as a rule also offered to the guru or preceptor and to distinguished guests.

(5) *Pradakshiṇa*, 'circumambulation', the rite in which the worshipper walks around the image or the shrine where the god is housed. In many temples special ambulatories are provided to enable the worshipper or pilgrim* to perform this act of homage.

(6) *Balidāna*, 'gift-offering'; this consists of various offerings collectively termed *bali*, generally rice, grain and ghee. The term bali is extended to apply to the feeding of birds, and sometimes even to the sacrificial killing of animals in the name of the deity. Other offerings include flowers (*pushpa*), which are placed at the feet of the god; water (*arghya*), mixed with perfume (*gandha*) and mustard seed, saffron and other spices; incense (*dhūpa*), camphor and aromatic vapours; betel (*tāmbūla*); sandal-wood paste (*chandana*) which is smeared on the forehead.
(7) *Āratī*, 'waving' the ceremony of waving a lighted lamp (*dīpa*) before the image, generally in a clockwise direction, accompanied by the chanting of mantras. Sometimes a vessel filled with saffron or vermilion-coloured water is waved instead. The object of the āratī rite is to please the deity with bright lights and colours and also to counteract the evil eye.
(8) *Prasāda*, 'favouring' or seeking the favour of the deity by offerings of food; the term is also applied to the food so offered, such as the rice, fruit, sweetmeats and other delicacies placed before the idol. Uncooked food (and lighted lamps) are always placed on the image's left, and cooked food on the image's right. Food is generally offered in the morning, afternoon and evening, but at the larger temples more frequently. At Purī the god is given refreshments fifty-two times during the day. In Śiva worship no cooked food is ever offered (III, p. 187). Food which is offered to the guru is also called prasāda, and what remains is afterwards distributed among and eagerly received by the *chelas* and disciples. All things touched by the idol or guru are believed to be endowed with a wonderful potency and when used their aura benefits the user.
(9) *Prārthana*, 'supplication' to the deity; making one's request known to the deity; petitioning god for personal favours, and help in private matters.
(10) *Visarjana*, 'dismissal'; the last part of ceremonial and domestic worship when the deity is bidden farewell and takes his departure. In private worship this is accompanied by an appropriate mantra and a gesture indicating that the service is over; in temple worship by the cessation of ceremonial actions and chants and the closing of the shrine door. Where the deity is enshrined on a portable altar he is carried into his bed-chamber where he joins his wife or wives. Sometimes he is put to sleep.

In the larger temples the services are on a royal scale. The deity has a small army of priests and attendants who dress, feed and work for him. He is entertained by dancing girls, fanned by a retinue of hereditary fanners, bathed, garlanded and robed. He holds court and hears petitions. Certain important occasions, such as the changing of the golden sacred thread, are attended by very elaborate ceremonial.

On big festival days the deity is taken in procession around the town in a special car (*see* Jagannātha); his marriage is celebrated annually when he and his consort are carried through the streets to accompaniment of loud music; and on their return to the temple may be taken for a ride on the bridal raft, the *teppam*, around the sacred tank. This festival, known as the *teppotsavam*, is a very popular one in South Indian shrines.

Books

I. Farquhar, J. N. 'Temple and Image Worship in Hinduism.' *Journal of the Royal Asiatic Society*, London, 1928, 15–23.

II. Keith, A. B. *The Religion and Philosophy of the Veda*, 2 vols., Cambridge, Mass., 1925.

III. Morgan, K. W. (Ed.) *The Religion of the Hindus*, New York, 1953.

IV. Parrinder, G. *Worship in the World's Religions*, London, 1961.

WRITING. The earliest writings in India are those found engraved on permanent material. The Indus Valley seals, still undeciphered, and the Aśokan edicts on pillars and rocks represent two widely separated areas of this phase. Entire Sanskrit dramas have been found inscribed on rocks, and lesser compositions on small stone tablets, but as a rule stone was rarely used for literary texts. Metal objects also furnish some evidence of early writing, copper plates being used for the purpose from about AD 100.

Except for such inscriptions practically all ancient writing that may have been contemporaneous with the permanent engravings on stone or metal, is lost. The Indian climate was not conducive to the preservation of manuscripts, and the earliest examples of Indian writing on perishable material are to be found outside the country. In Chinese Turkestan wooden tablets with Sanskrit writing dating from AD 300 have been dug out of the desert sands; from Central Asia come a few MSS. of the fifth century AD; from Japan material dating from the sixth century; and tenth century records from Nepāl. In India itself there is one MS. of the eleventh century, and a very few of the twelfth and thirteenth centuries.

Early writing was done on leaves, birch-bark being used in the north, and palm-leaves in South India. The oldest Sanskrit manuscripts of this type are found in Turfan and other parts of Central Asia. The leaves were manufactured by a special process. In the north the inner bark of the birch was smoothly cut away and fastened together in convenient layers. Writing on birch-bark continued till about two hundred years ago whenever the material was readily available. In the South, palm-leaves were dried, boiled, dried again, flattened and smoothed with stones and shells. Well-beaten cotton cloth, dried and processed, was also used in most parts of India.

The letters were written on the material in black ink with a reed pen. The early Sanskrit term for pen, *melā*, is derived from the Greek melan, black; and the Sanskrit term for pen, *kalama*, from the Greek kalamos, suggesting that the use of these was acquired from the Greeks, probably from the north-west of India. In some parts of India, especially the south, the leaf was scratched with a pointed stylus or iron pencil. The usual procedure was to hold the leaf on the left palm with the stylus poised stationary over it, and the hand holding the leaf moved beneath it. Soot, charcoal, lamp-black, or cow-dung was then rubbed into the inscribed grooves. The other end of the stylus was a blade which was used to trim the leaves and make them of uniform size. A sheaf of such birch-bark or palm-leaf manuscripts was placed between wooden boards and held in position by a cord drawn through two holes and tied together with a knot. This explains how the Sanskrit word *grantha*, 'knot', came to mean a book, text or treatise.

Writing was also done on leather or skin. The word for book, *pustaka*, is derived from the Persian *post*, meaning skin, since some of the earliest books in the north-west of India were written in areas under Persian influence, and on the skins of animals. J. Przyluski believes that the term Kharoshṭhī (the name of one of the scripts) meant 'writing on the skin of an ass'. Paper, used in China from the second century BC, was introduced into India by the Muslims, and its advent in about AD 800 marked a new era in the art of writing and communication, although it was not in popular use till comparatively modern times.

Books

I. Bannerjee, J. P. *The Origin and Development of Hindu Writing*, 1916.
II. Poonawala, T. *The Art of Writing in Ancient India*, 1922.
III. Macdonell, A. A. *India's Past*, Oxford, 1927.

YADU, a king of the Lunar line, son of Yayāti* and Devayānī. He was of non-Aryan origin and is referred to in the *Ṛig-veda* as a *dāsa* or 'slave'. Because he had refused to take on his father's decrepitude he was cursed to the effect that his posterity would not hold dominion for long. From his father he received the southern portion of the kingdom and for a time his descendants prospered. They took part in the famous Battle of the Ten Kings.

A legend relates that Yadu while sailing on the sea fell into the hands of Dhūmavarna, 'smoke-coloured', a serpent king, and that he was given the five daughters of the king in marriage. From this union of Yadu with the serpent princesses sprang seven families, known after him as the YĀDAVA, all classed as daityas (aboriginals). A Yādava prince founded the Chedi line of Central India, and another became the progenitor of the family in which Kṛishṇa was born. It was during Kṛishṇa's time that the curse placed upon the descendants of Yadu came to fulfilment and the whole race perished; some slain in a feud and the rest submerged by the sea.

According to certain accounts a few Yādavas escaped the general calamity and survived to found noble dynastic lines, among them the Yādavas of Deogiri (*see* Chālukya), the *rājas* of Vijayanagar, and dozens of petty royal houses in South India, all claiming kshattriya status, although their claims have never been accepted. As recently as 1927, the Madrās High Court ruled that the Yādava community were of śūdra caste.

Books

See under Mythology.

YĀJÑAVALKYA, a celebrated, semi-legendary teacher, sage and lawgiver, to whom are attributed the White *Yajur-veda*, the *Śatapatha Brāhmaṇa*, the *Bṛihadāraṇyaka*, the *Yājñavalkya Smṛiti* (a code of law), and the doctrine of yoga which was reputedly imparted by him to Janaka king of Videha. In all probability the name is that of a school called after the sage, of whose life some fragments have been pieced together. In the *Mahābhārata* he attends the *rājasūya* (royal consecration) ceremony of Yudhishṭhira, and in the *Śatapatha Brāhmaṇa* is the spiritual adviser to Janaka father of Sītā.

The Upanishads relate that when he was about to renounce the life of the householder for that of a hermit, he wished to divide his property between his two wives, *Maitreyī* and *Kātyāyanī*. 'My Lord', Maitreyī enquired, 'if this whole earth, full of wealth, belonged to me, should I by means of it become immortal?', and when he replied in the negative she said, 'What should I do with that through which I do not become immortal!' She refused her share and instead received from her husband instruction in the great esoteric truths.

Among the teachers of Yājñavalkya were Uddālaka*, Vaiśampāyana (see below), and Vāshkala. The latter, *Vāshkala* (or Bāshkala) bears a *daitya* (aboriginal) name and was probably non-Aryan; an important recension of the *Ṛig-veda* is named after him. From the incidents of Yājña-valkya's life it would appear that he himself was, if not non-Aryan, at least strongly anti-brāhminical. He ate beef and was a dissenter from the religious teachings and practices of his time, and his opinions were 'in contradiction with the *Ṛig-veda*' (II, p. 128). He supported Janaka in his long contention with the brāhmins and often silenced them with his crushing arguments and scathing comments on their practices.

At a great philosophical congress of sages and scholars from all over India which had been summoned by Janaka, he proved his superiority in the knowledge of sacred writ and ceremonial, defeating such theologians as his own teacher Uddālaka, the great Śākalya (who was confounded so effectively that 'his head fell off'), Aśvala the pupil of Śaunaka, as well as *Gārgī*, one of the most learned female philosophers in the history of Hinduism who had never been defeated by anyone before this; she is mentioned in the *Bṛihadāraṇyaka Upanishad*. She appeared nude in the learned assembly and put several shrewd questions to the savants, and one of them warned her that her head too would fly off, not because she was nude, but because she was excessively garrulous.

Yājñavalkya denounced brāhminical avarice, declaring that sacrifices offered by the brāhmins were not for the benefit of the sacrificer who paid the expenses, but for the priest who claimed both fee and blessings. He urged that the brāhmin's prayer, 'Give me gold!' or 'Give me cows!' should be changed to 'Give me light!' The brāhmins declared that what was said to be predetermined could be altered by sacrifice, but he maintained that there were two wheels on the chariot of every man's life: *daiva* or destiny, and *purusha-kāra* or man's efforts, i.e. free will. Yājñavalkya is traditionally regarded as having prepared the way for Buddha.

The story of how the White *Yajur-veda* was revealed to him also has a strong anti-brāhminical touch. It is said that his guru, *Vaiśampāyana*, a mighty sage who assisted Vyāsa in arranging the Vedas and the *Mahābhā-rata*, accidentally kicked to death his sister's child, and called upon his disciples to join him in the performance of an expiatory sacrifice. Yājña-valkya refused to be associated with the 'wretched and inefficient brāhmins', and a quarrel took place. Guru therefore called on chela to return the wisdom imparted to him, and Yājñavalkya thereupon spewed up his acquired learning which fell to the ground stained with blood. The other pupils were transformed into partridges (tittiri) who picked up the disgorged texts. These texts now constitute the *Taittirīya* saṁhitā of the *Yajur-veda*, also called the Black *Yajur-veda* because it is so obscure, formless and ill-digested. The name is alternatively derived from the sage Tittiri.

Determined to acquire wisdom by his own merit Yājñavalkya retired to the solitudes and for a long time underwent severe penances, until the god Sūrya in the form of a horse (vājin) revealed the true texts to him. From this episode the sage was named *Vājasaneya*, and the text of the *Yajur-veda* revealed to him is called the *Vājasaneyī Saṁhitā*, also spoken of as the White *Yajur-veda*, because it is clear and bright.

Books

I. Jayaswal, K. P. *Manu and Yajnavalkya*, Calcutta, 1930.
II. Mookerji, R. K. *Education in Ancient India*, London, 1947.
III. Mookerji, R. K. 'Yajnavalkya.' Ch. I of *Men and Thought in Ancient India*, 2nd Ed., Bombay, 1957.

YAJUR-VEDA (?700–?300 BC), the second Veda, compiled mainly from Ṛig-vedic hymns, but showing considerable deviation from the original Ṛig-vedic text. It also has prose passages of a later date. The *Yajur-veda*, like the *Sāma-veda saṁhitā* (collection), introduces a geographical milieu different from that of the *Ṛig-veda*. It is not so much the Indus and its tributaries any more, but the areas of the Sutlej, Jamnā and Ganges rivers. Along with this we find new development of religious and social life, an age when the Epic tribes contended for supremacy in the Indo-Gangetic plain, and the castes were already clearly divided. The *Yajur-veda* represents a transition between the spontaneous, free-worshipping period of the *Ṛig-veda* and the later brāhmanical period when ritualism had become firmly established.

The *Yajur-veda* is a priestly handbook, arranged in liturgical form for the performance of sacrifices (*yaja*), as its name implies. It embodies the sacrificial formulas in their entirety, prescribes rules for the construction of altars, for the new and full-moon sacrifices, the *rājāsūya*, the *aśvamedha*, and the *soma* sacrifices. Strict observance of the ceremonial in every detail was insisted upon, and deviations led to the formation of new schools, there being over one hundred Yajur-vedic schools at the time of Patañjali (200 BC). Much of the *śākhā* literature grew up out of variants of the Yajur-vedic texts.

In the Y*ajur-veda* the sacrifice becomes so important that even the gods are compelled to do the will of the brāhmins. Religion becomes a mechanical ritual in which crowds of priests conduct vast and complicated ceremonies whose effects are believed to be felt in the farthermost heavens. Its underlying principles were so ridden with superstition and belief in the power of the priests to do and undo the cosmic order itself that critics have likened their formulas to the ravings of mental delirium. The priest especially associated with the Yajur-vedic ceremonial was the *adhvaryu*.

The *Yajur-veda* now consists of two *saṁhitās*, which once existed in one hundred and one recensions. Both the saṁhitās contain almost the same subject matter but differently arranged. The *Taittirīya Saṁhitā*, commonly called the Black *Yajur-veda* for its obscurity of meaning, was known in the third century BC, and is the older of the two. It has been described as an 'undigested jumble of different pieces', and as having 'a motley character'. In this saṁhitā the distinction between the *Mantra* and the *Brāhmaṇa* portions is not as clear as in the other Vedas. The *Vājasaneyī Saṁhitā*, or the White *Yajur-veda*, was communicated to the sage Yājñavalkya* by the sun-god in his equine form. It has a much more methodical arrangement and brings order and light, as opposed to the confusion and darkness of the Black *Yajur-veda*.

Books

I. Griffiths, R. T. H. *The Texts of the White Yajur-veda*, 1899.
See also under Vedism.

YAMA, god of departed spirits, judge and punisher of the dead, a Ṛig-vedic deity, was the son of the sun-god Vivasvat, and regent of the south quarter. In the *Mahābhārata* he is the divine father of Yudhishṭhira. Originally a mortal, he was the first to find his way into the celestial spheres by the 'Path of the Fathers', and was deified as a result.

He is described as green in colour, apparelled in red and with a defective leg. The story goes that he was punished by having his foot covered with maggoty sores for trying to kick Chhāyā, his father's handmaid. On his plea for forgiveness his father gave him a cock which picked off the maggots and saved the leg, but his foot remained shrivelled thereafter. Yama's *vāhana* or vehicle is the buffalo, his messengers the pigeon and the owl, his weapon a mace, and he carries a noose called *kāla-sūtra*, 'black thread' to secure his victims.

Two grim four-eyed hounds called the Sārameya, sons of Indra's watch-dog Saramā, guard the approach to his dread kingdom. In his city *Yamapuri* there is a long procession of souls wending their way to his palace of *Kālīchī*, which is guarded by the doorkeeper *Vaidhyata*. The souls are conducted by the messenger *Yamadūta* to the presence of Yama who sits on his judgment-throne called *Vichāra-bhū*, 'examination place', waited upon by two attendants, Mahāchanda and Kālapurusha. His record keeper *Chitragupta* reads out the balance-sheet of each person's deeds, which are recorded in his great register *Agra-sandhānī*. The good and evil deeds are reckoned and judgment passed by Yama, with the god Varuṇa assisting. The good are then sent to one of the higher lokas or worlds, and the sinful are sent to hell to receive their deserts. The festival of *Chitra Pūrṇimā*, on the full-moon day of the month of Chaitra, is dedicated to Chitragupta.

Yamī is the twin sister of Yama, and these two are often spoken of as the first human pair. There is a hymn in the *Ṛig-veda* describing Yamī's attempt to entice her brother into having sexual relations with her. 'Let us unite in intimate embrace', she urges him, 'be a husband and go with zeal into the body of your wife.' But Yama rejects her advances. In some legends Yamī is described as the wife of Yama. Among his other wives are *Hemamālā*,

Suśīlā, and *Vijayā*. It is said that the latter could not resist peeping into the forbidden southern regions of hell, and there saw her mother in torment. On her pleading with her husband and performing austerities she obtained her mother's release.

A legend relates that when Yama died, Yamī mourned the death of her lover and spouse, and to console her the gods created Night, which covered her sorrow, as all else, with a veil. When she awoke in the morning her grief was gone.

Yama's titles are: Mṛityu, 'death'; Kāla, 'time'; Antaka, 'ender'; Kṛitānta, 'maker of the end'; Śamana, 'calming'; Daṇḍa-dhara, 'rod-bearer'; Bhīma-śāsana, 'terrible chastiser'; Pitṛi-pati, 'lord of the manes'; Preta-rāja, 'ghost king'; Śrāddha-deva, 'śrāddha deity'; Dharma-rāja, 'justice king'; Śīrṇa-pāda, 'rotten foot'.

Books

See under Mythology.

YAYĀTI, son of Nahusha a king of the Solar Line, of whom several legends are told in the *Mahābhārata* and the Purāṇas. He was once invited to heaven by Indra who sent his chariot to enable him to make the journey. On the way he was treated to a philosophical discourse by Mātali, Indra's charioteer, and was so impressed by what he heard that he resolved to put into practice the lessons he had learnt. On his return to his own kingdom he applied the precepts of Mātali and ruled his people with such wisdom that he rendered the whole realm free from passion and decay. Yama, god of death, complained to Indra that men no longer came to his domain, so Indra sent the god of love to Yayāti's kingdom, accompanied by the beautiful nymph Aśruvindu-matī, 'tear-drop', to excite the king's passion. In this she succeeded only too well for he now began to devote himself overmuch to sensual delights.

One day while Yayāti was riding through the forest he heard cries proceeding from a deep pit. Looking within he saw a beautiful girl and helped her out. She was Devayānī, daughter of the priest Śukra*. It transpired that she had come to a forest stream with her friend and companion, the beautiful Sarmishṭhā, daughter of Vṛishaparvan an *asura* king. While they were bathing the wind-god Vāyu exchanged their clothes and a quarrel ensued between the girls regarding the ownership of their apparel. Devayānī scowled at Sarmishṭhā and the latter slapped her and pushed her into the pit, from whence she had been rescued.

Yayāti took the distressed maiden home and her father on hearing the story demanded satisfaction from Vṛishaparvan who in justice decreed that on her marriage Devayānī should be given Sarmishṭhā for a servant. Devayānī had earlier been put under a curse which decreed that although a brāhmin herself she would marry a kshattriya, and thus it came about that she became the wife of Yayāti, and had as her servant girl, her erstwhile friend Sarmishṭhā. By this reprehensible *pratiloma* marriage Yayāti and Devayānī became the parents of two sons, namely, Yadu*, ancestor of the Yādavas, and Turvaśa (or Turvaśu). According to the *Harivaṁśa* the mother of Yadu was not Devayanī but Madhumatī, daughter of a demon (i.e. aboriginal) king of Mathurā. The *Ṛig-veda* designates both Yadu and Turvaśu as *dāsas* or slaves.

Yayāti succumbed to the charms of his wife's handmaiden Sarmishṭhā, whose importunities he could not resist, and through her he became the father of Puru, ancestor of the Pauravas; Druhyu, whose line ruled in Gandhāra; and Anu, ancestor of the Ānavas, Aṅgas, Vaṅgas, and Kaliṅgas. Incensed by her husband's infidelity Devayānī returned to the house of her father Śukra, who uttered a curse against Yayātī, condemning him to premature old age. But on the plea of his daughter, Śukra agreed to transfer the curse to any of Yayāti's children who would be willing to bear it. All refused except his youngest son Puru, who assumed his father's old age so that his father might assume his youth.

Yayāti cursed all his children, except Puru, and proceeded to give himself over to carnal pleasures in real earnest, indulging in sensuality in all its forms. After a thousand years of this life he came to the conclusion that *kāma* (lust) is never quenched by kāma, and renounced his borrowed vigour to Puru and made him his successor at Pratishṭhāna. The now aged Yayāti retired to the forest with his wife and devoted himself to mortifications. He died of voluntary starvation and ascended to heaven.

The faithful Puru was succeeded by his son Janamejaya; and so on the succession went from father to son. In a direct line from Puru came the Bhāratas, Pañchālas, Kauravas, Pāṇḍavas, Chedis and other famous kings of the Paurava branch of the Lunar Line.

Books

See under Mythology.

YOGA, one of the six orthodox systems of Hindu philosophy, believed to have been founded by the sage Yājñavalkya, and later codified by Patañjali in his *Yoga-sūtra*. Yoga has been defined as a form of mental and physical discipline, a code of ascetic practices, mainly pre-Aryan in origin, containing relics of many primitive conceptions and observances. There is evidence to show that some of the yoga disciplines were in existence at the time of the Indus Valley civilization. It may have been an early system of magical ritualism, and yoga still retains in its meaning an overtone of occultism and sorcery.

Yoga is often regarded as the practical and dynamic expression of the system of thought and life for which the Sāṁkhya school provides the theoretical and metaphysical basis. It is a feature of most forms of Hindu contemplation, and great stress is laid on it. 'Even a deity cannot obtain liberation without yoga.' Yoga accepts the twenty-five principles of the Sāṁkhya teaching, and some schools add a twenty-sixth, namely, Īśvara or God, who however is not a creator, preserver or destroyer, but merely one of several objects on which the soul may meditate. God was not an integral part of the early yoga system, and the passages in Patañjali's *Yoga-sūtra* treating of God, 'are unconnected with the other parts of the book, nay, even contradict the foundations of the system' (VIII, p. 189).

The term yoga has, in some opinion, been derived from the root *yuj*, 'yoke or join', its aim being to teach the means by which the human soul (*jīvātman*) might attain complete union with the universal soul (*Paramātman*). One who practises yoga is called a yogi of *yogin* (fem. *yoginī*), and the term *yogārūdha* (*yoga-ārūdha*, 'mounted on yoga') applies to one who is well advanced in yogic techniques.

There are several forms of yoga, depending on whether emancipation, *samādhi*, mental energy, *siddhis* or physical powers are sought, and also on the paths or *mārga* followed to attain these. Each form of yoga has a certain number of *bhūmi*, 'stages', which the aspirant has to traverse in his journey to liberation or knowledge. Thus there are fifteen stages in *rāja-yoga*, sixteen in *mantra-yoga*, nine in *bhakti yoga*, ten in *laya-yoga*, and so on. Generally the eight stages of *haṭha-yoga* (below) are regarded as the prototype, and the stages of the other yogas, whether greater or fewer than this in number, are variations of these eight basic stages of haṭha-yoga.

The chief forms of yoga are *karma-yoga*, salvation through works; *bhakti-yoga*, salvation through faith; *jñāna-yoga*, through knowledge; *mantra-yoga*, through the use of mantras or spells; *laya-yoga*, through the activation of the *chakras** or subtle centres of the body; *haṭha-yoga*, through physical culture; and *rāja-yoga* through spiritual culture.

HAṬHA-YOGA deals chiefly with the body and its powers and functions, and is best considered as a part of physical culture*. The syllable *ha* is said to represent the sun, and *ṭha* the moon, and these symbolise the polarity found in each human being, e.g. the two genders* in each man, the two breaths in the two nostrils, the two main channels* of the subtle body, and so on. The union of the sun and moon in the body is interpreted in various ways.

It is haṭha yoga, with its various exercises and postures, and its strong leaning towards occultism, that is associated in the popular mind with yoga in general. Haṭha yoga prescribes eight stages for the attainment of its objective. They are: (1) *Yama*, restraint, especially external control, like non-injury and continence, (2) *niyama*, or internal control, like equanimity, and meditation; (3) *āsana** or bodily postures; (4) *prāṇayāma* or breath* control; (5) *pratyāhāra*, control of the senses; (6) *dhāraṇa* or meditation; (7) *dhyāna* or contemplation; and (8) *samādhi*, a form of super-consciousness.

Apart from Patañjali's *Yoga-sūtra*, the most authoritative accounts of yoga teachings are found in: *Goraksha-śataka* by Gorakhnāth*; *Haṭha-yoga Pradīpikā* by Svātmārāma Svāmin (fl. 1430), strongly Buddhist; *Śiva-saṁhitā*, a tantrik text; and *Gheraṇḍa-saṁhitā*, by Gheraṇḍa, a Vaishṇavite of Bengal (*c.* 1350).

The form of yoga followed by genuine aspirants is known as RĀJA-YOGA, 'king-yoga', which lays stress on mental and spiritual, rather than physical culture. Its purpose is to make man a ruler over all his mental and spiritual equipment. In theory it comprises the eight stages of haṭha-yoga (in some cases subdivided into fifteen stages), carried out 'on a higher plane', but in fact it is confined to the last four stages of haṭha-yoga. The highest form of yoga is what is referred to as *rāja-adhirāja-yoga*, 'king of kings yoga', or *mahā-yoga*, which is the yoga without any external forms and techniques. 'All other yogas taken together do not amount to a tiny fraction of this yoga.' It is the pure, one-pointed contemplation of the Supreme Principle by means of which the mind is freed from anger, lust, fear, greed, jealousy and melancholy.

Books

I. Behanan, K. T. *Yoga: A Scientific Evaluation*, London, 1938.
II. Bernard, Theos. *Hatha Yoga*, London, 1950.
III. Coster, G. *Yoga and Western Psychology*, London, 1935.
IV. Danielou, A. *Yoga: Method of Reintegration*, London, 1949.
V. Dasgupta, S. N. *Yoga Philosophy*, Calcutta, 1930.
VI. Dasgupta, S. N. *Yoga as Philosophy and Religion*, London, 1924.
VII. Eliade, M. *Yoga, Immortality and Freedom*, New York, 1958.
VIII. Garbe, R. *Philosophy of Ancient India*, Chicago, 1897.
IX. Wood, Ernest, *Great Systems of Yoga*, New York, 1954.
X. Woods, J. H. *The Yoga System of Patanjali*, Cambridge, 1914.

YONI, 'holder', the vulva, also used to mean origin, nest, lap or womb. It refers specifically to the female organ, as a symbol of sexual pleasure and the matrix of generation. It includes (1) the *bhaga*, 'dispenser' of delight, which refers especially to the pubes, (2) the *vedha*, 'breach', opening or cleft, the labia, (3) the *yoni* or vagina, often compared to the interior of a mollusc or conch-shell and believed to possess a life of its own; of the twenty extra muscles which the female body is supposed to have, five each are in the two breasts and the remaining ten are in the yoni, (4) the *garbha*, 'womb', shaped like the *rohit*, a kind of fish, narrow at the opening, expanded at the upper end.

In Sanskrit literature and in vernacular religious writings the yoni is treated as a sacred area, a soft pad of pleasure, a zone of felicity, an occult region, an *axis mundi* worthy of reverence, a symbol of cosmic mysteries. It is described as the abode of pleasure, the source of great bliss (*mahāsukha*), the vessel holding the 'delight of delights'. The female organ has been created as honey to attract the male organ; it is the second mouth of the Creator which sends out a silent command to men to come and sip. It is the chief ruler of the universe and brings under its subjection men in all walks of life.

In its profound, esoteric sense, it is the sacred field in which the seed of all creatures is planted and nourished. All men have their birth from here; all lie in the womb, receiving sustenance and spirit from the vital pulsations of the ultimate that are concentrated here; and in due time all things emerge from here. The yoni is the emblem of the Ultimate, the keeper of the great mysteries, symbolizing in its shape the mystical *śūnya*, 'zero', or emptiness in which all things are inherent.

The Brāhmaṇas and Upanishads compare the female sexual parts to the sacred area of the sacrificial ceremony: the hips and haunches to the sacrificial ground, the mons veneris to the altar, the pubic hairs to the *kusā* grass, and sexual intercourse to a higher form of worship. Temples were sometimes dedicated to the worship of the yoni (*see* Kāmarūpa), and in tantrik ceremonial the yoni receives adoration, either in the form of a representation in stone or drawing, or by the worship of the yoni of a nude woman who sits before the worshippers with legs apart. Such rituals centring on the female genitalia are called *bhaga yaja*, 'vulva rites'. Some tantrik sects believe that a man can attain the highest bliss 'by concentrating his mind on the soul seated in the female organ' (II, p. 458), an idea derived from a belief common in many parts of the world that exposure of the female organ of generation enhances the fertility of fields, cattle and mankind, brings down rain and ensures prosperity. In the tantrik sects of Buddhism, paradise or Sukhāvatī is likened to the yoni, and Buddha is described as 'dwelling in the vagina of the female in the name of semen' (I, p. 157).

Representations of the yoni are found in *yantras* and *maṇḍalas*, and in dozens of other symbols on objects used in daily life. An ancient yoni symbol was the shell; another was the ring-stone or female-stone, called *piṇḍikā*, *pīṭha* or *strīśilā*, examples of which are found in the Indus Valley. These may be small stones with natural perforations through them; they are especially lucky if they fit the organ of the finder for he then consecrates the stone and wears it thus, secured by a piece of string. Such stones are believed to have magical properties and to be imbued with the divine spirit.

Large rock formations with holes in them are also regarded as sacred, and children, old people, the sterile, the pregnant, the sick, are made to crawl through the hole, and are regarded as born again, purified, or absolved from sin after this procedure. The Marāṭha chieftain Śivājī crawled through the Śrigundi stone near Bombay to purify himself for the sin of having treacherously killed his enemy Afzal Khān.

Books

I. Dasgupta, S. B. *An Introduction to Tantrik Buddhism*, Calcutta, 1950.
II. Majumdar, R. C. (Ed.) *The Struggle for Empire*, Bombay, 1957.
See also under Sex, *and* Sociology.

YUDHISHṬHIRA, eldest of the Pāṇḍavas*, was the son of Dharma god of justice and Pāṇḍu's wife Kuntī. He was the ideal of justice, integrity and truthfulness. Brought up at the Kaurava court of his uncle Dhṛitarāshṭra, he acquired great proficiency in the use of the spear under the training of the mighty Droṇa.

When the time came to name the *yuvarāja* or heir apparent to the throne of Hastināpura, the blind king Dhṛitarāshṭra selected his just and upright nephew in preference to his own son Duryodhana, thus causing the long-standing feud between the Kauravas and Pāṇḍavas to break forth openly. Filled with bitterness Duryodhana refused to be placated, and Yudhishṭhira and his four brothers were compelled to go into exile to the city of Vāraṇāvata (modern Allāhābād or Banāras), rich in jewels and gold. Duryodhana schemed for their further chastisement and humiliation, but his plot to destroy them in a fire with the connivance of his agent, Purochana* came to naught.

During this exile the Pāṇḍavas contracted many important alliances, among others with Kṛishṇa king of Dvārakā and with the king of the Pañchālas. When Arjuna won the beautiful Draupadī*, Yudhishṭhira became one of her husbands too. He also married Devikā by whom he had a son named Yaudheya (or Devaka).

After the return of the Pāṇḍavas from their first exile Dhṛitarāshṭra divided his kingdom, giving the Pāṇḍavas the south-western country of Khāṇḍava-prastha, including the Khāṇḍava forest. In this area the Pāṇḍavas built their capital, Indraprastha, on the banks of the Jamnā near modern Delhi, and here Yudhishṭhira ruled with justice, bringing peace and prosperity to the realm. The palace of Indraprastha was constructed by the asura architect Maya and had such wonderful flooring and ceilings that visitors could not distinguish between crystal floors and pools of water. Duryodhana on a visit once fell into a pool thinking it was the floor.

On the return of Arjuna from his own exile Yudhishṭhira performed the *rājasūya* (royal consecration) sacrifice, which led to the slaying of Jarāsandha* king of Magadha by Bhīma, and the slaying of Śiśupāla by Kṛishṇa. The success of the sacrifice further incensed the Kauravas. Duryodhana contrived with the help of Śakuni* to inveigle Yudhishṭhira into a gambling match, as a result of which Yudhishṭhira lost his kingdom, himself, his brothers, and Draupadī. A last throw of the dice condemned the Pāṇḍavas to their second exile, which was to last for thirteen years.

Throughout the period of their second exile it was Yudhishṭhira who counselled restraint and charity. Even when Jayadratha* abducted Draupadī it was he who pleaded clemency on his behalf and saved him from the wrath of Bhīma. Yudhishṭhira seemed to be completely devoid of anger and bitterness. Anger, he said, was the cause of self-destruction. None but the ignorant regard anger as equivalent to energy and power, for the wise understand that forgiveness is the greater triumph.

For twelve long years the Pāṇḍavas lived in the forest of *Kāmyaka* on the banks of the Sarasvatī, where they had many adventures, including an encounter with the ogre Vaka. Here they were visited by wise men and gods, among them Dharma, Hanumān, Kubera, Kṛishṇa, and Mārkaṇḍeya, who showed them many wonders, taught them diverse arts and skills, and bestowed upon them many precious gifts, including the power to remain unrecognized for one year, so as to fulfil the final condition of their exile.

The wanderers then journeyed to Virāṭa* where they entered the service of the king, Yudhishṭhira instructing the king in the art of playing dice. Once again he advised his brothers to act with caution and even dissuaded them from defending Draupadī against insult in case their identity should be revealed. At the end of their exile Yudhishṭhira tried to effect a reconciliation with the Kauravas, but failed, and when Kṛishṇa was sent as an emissary to Duryodhana the latter threatened to whip him. In the inevitable war that followed (*see* Kurukshetra) Yudhishṭhira did not distinguish himself as a warrior, at times behaving like a coward and running from the fray. At this critical time even his regard for truth deserted him and it was his duplicity that led to the death of the heroic Droṇa.

After the great battle Kṛishṇa saluted him as king of Hastināpura and he reluctantly accepted the honour. He was greatly afflicted by the horrors of the war and full of sorrow for the brave knights who had fallen in combat, and did what he could to console the bereaved Dhṛitarāshṭra and Gāndhārī for the tragic loss of all their hundred sons. The Pāṇḍava family priest Dhaumya anointed Yudhishṭhira king of Hastināpura and after some time his sovereignty was confirmed by an *aśvamedha* sacrifice. A snow-white horse was selected and Arjuna was appointed to follow it, and many adventures befell him on the way.

A series of disasters now followed, as though a curse was come upon the Pāṇḍavas. The blind Dhṛitarāshṭra with his queen Gāndhārī, and Kuntī the mother of the three elder Pāṇḍavas, who had retired to a hermitage, were burnt to death in a forest fire. Then came the news of the extermination of the Yādavas and the slaying of their divine king Kṛishṇa. Arjuna, bringing back the last remnants of the Yādavas was defeated and almost killed by the Ābhīra tribe.

Growing remorse at the folly of the recent war embittered the last days of the Pāṇḍavas, and burdened with grief they resolved to withdraw from the world. Yudhishṭhira divided the kingdom into two parts, giving Parīkshit, grandson of Arjuna, the city of Hastināpura, and Yuyutsu son of Dhṛitarāshṭra by a handmaid the kingdom of Indraprastha. Having abdicated his throne Yudhishṭhira then cast off his royal garments and assumed the beggar's garb, his brothers and Draupadī doing likewise, and with them departed for the Himālayas on their way to Mount Meru, followed by a lean hound. This *mahā-prasthānika*, 'great departure', episode forms the 17th Book of the *Mahābhārata*.

One by one the brothers and Draupadī fell by the way until only Yudhishṭhira and his hound were left. At Mount Meru he was invited to enter the celestial realms but refused because his dog was denied entry. As he turned his back on the golden gates he was recalled by Indra who commended him on his fidelity to the animal. The dog was in fact none other than Dharma god of justice.

Finding that the Kauravas are installed in high places in heaven and seeing no signs of his brothers Yudhishṭhira leaves heaven and proceeds to the nether world, and here he stays, trying to assuage the anguish and tortures of Draupadī and his brothers. All this proves to be only a trial and the whole scene in hell an illusion to test him. It suddenly vanishes and Indra appears and invites him to svarga or heaven, where he sees ensconced on thrones of gold not only Draupadī and his brothers, but also Dhṛitarāshṭra (now king of the *gandharvas* or celestial musicians), Karṇa, Abhimanyu, Pāṇḍu, Kuntī, Droṇa, and all the other peerless warriors. Yudhishṭhira himself ascends the jewel-studded throne reserved for him and settles down to enjoy his life of everlasting bliss. In the words of the *Mahābhārata*,

'So may all mortals rise to everlasting felicity, casting off their bodily remains and entering the shining portals of the celestial city, by doing kindly deeds, by uttering gentle words, and enduring all suffering with patience. The holy life of bliss is prepared for all the virtuous sons of men.'

Books

See under Mahābhārata, and Mythology.

YŪPA, the sacrificial post of Vedic times. In ancient sacrificial rites the *yūpa* stood at the side of the *vedi* or altar, and in the larger ceremonies just before the *yāgaśālā* or hall of sacrifice. All sacrificial victims had to be tied to the *yūpa* preparatory to sacrifice.

The yūpa was usually made of the coniferous *dāru* (deodar) tree, in accordance with detailed instructions regarding its shape and size given in Vedic texts. Its height was seventeen cubits for the greater sacrifices, but shorter for the less important ones. The top of the post had a slight protuberance called the *chashāla*, 'knob', representing the glans penis, affixed to which was a *kaṭaka*, 'ring', or wheel. The *Śatapatha Brāhmaṇa* tells how to set the wheel up with its hub fitted horizontally on the top of the post. The yūpa appears to have been a relic of liṅga worship and some law-books categorically prohibited the setting up of yūpas, declaring that the touch of a yūpa was as polluting as that of a funeral pyre or a menstruating woman.

Associated with the yūpa was an ancient rite known as the *dūrohaṇa*, 'difficult climb'. This was meant to raise the participant from the sphere of the profane to that of the sacred, and to free him from worldly shackles during the ceremony. It was performed by the priest or the *yajamāna* (generally the king) climbing the yūpa by means of seventeen steps. At the summit he squatted on top of the wheel which was turned thrice in a sunwise motion; he then announced with arms outstretched like the wings of a bird, 'We have reached the gods in heaven'. The rite was associated with the yoking of horses and the mounting of a chariot on the eve of a race or before a battle, and from it there survives the title of *chakravartin* given in days of yore to a great emperor. At the end of the ceremony the reverse process, or descent from the sacred sphere took place. Some authorities discern here the origin of the legendary Rope Trick*. After the sacrifice was over a chip of the yūpa called the *svaru*, 'splinter', was offered as a substitute for the yūpa itself, since it was believed that the yūpa had become charged with malignant power and was capable of causing spiritual contamination, and therefore had to be consumed by fire.

In later temple architecture the yūpa was often represented by the *dhvaja* or flagstaff set up before the temple, which subsequently developed into a free-standing column*. The *āmalaśilā* that crowned the early columns may have been a relic of the wheel on top of the yūpa.

Books

I. Fern, V. (Ed.) *Ancient Religions*, New York, 1950.
II. Sen, S. N. *The Hindu Sacrificial Place*, 1919.
III. Simpson, W. *The Buddhist Praying-Wheel: the Symbolism of the Wheel and Circular Movements*, London, 1896.

ZOROASTRIANISM. There is more than one Zoroaster known to tradition. Francis Barrett, in his biography of Zoroaster writes, 'we find no less than five Zoroasters mentioned in history'. The period in which Zoroaster is supposed to have flourished is therefore of considerable elasticity. Aristotle, Eudoxus and others gave him an antiquity of 5000 years before the Trojan War; Berosus places him at 2000 years BC; Pahlavi inscriptions speak of him as living 300 years before Alexander the Great. Assurbanipal of Assyria mentioned Assara Mazas (Ahura Mazda) in an inscription of about 700 BC, thus indicating an acquaintance with the reformed Zoroastrian pantheon. One of these Zoroasters is known to the history of goety as the patriarch of the magical arts. The date of the Zoroaster of religious history is probably to be fixed, according to certain modern scholars, including Eduard Meyer, at about 1000 BC. He was mainly a reformer who declared war against the debased magian cults of his time but accepted many of the existing deities and adapted many of the existing hymns, centring his ritual around a temple where the sun was worshipped in its aspect of fire. The name by which he is known was probably not his real name, but an ancient magian title meaning 'golden disk' (*zer-tasht*) in reference to the sun which was the chief object of Zoroastrian adoration.

The religion of Zoroaster has had a profound influence on the religious and cultural history of the Hindus. The Vrātyas* may have represented a pre-Zoroastrian wave of immigrants from Iran, but the Māgas* bore specific elements of the Zoroastrian religion which they introduced into India. According to the *Bhavishya Purāṇa* the Magas sprang from Jarasasta (Zoroaster) and wore girdles around their waist. They were priests of the sun and of Saturn, and the connection between them and the later maga brāhmins and Śakadvīp brāhmins has been pointed out. Pārśva* the Jain *tīrthaṅkara* was probably of Persian descent, and the influence of Zoroastrianism on the Jains, as on the Indian gymnosophists or naked sādhus suggested by some authorities may have some basis in truth.

The influence of the Zoroastrian kings of Achaemenian Iran* on the culture of Mauryan* India has long been established. The ancient Magian foundations such as Multān, Mathurā, Dvārakā, Gaya and Konārak, to name but a few of India's most sacred towns, bespeaks the wide Zoroastrian activity in India. The Parsees who sought refuge in India from Islamic oppression belonged to Sasanian Iran.

There is an interesting though highly contentious theory that Buddhism itself was an offshoot of Zoroastrianism. It is admitted in many quarters that very little is actually known about Buddha. Dr Nalinaksha Dutt, Professor of Pāli in the University of Calcutta says,

'We possess no authentic accounts of the life of Gautama, the founder of Buddhism. Two poems in the *Sutta Nipāta* and a few earlier suttas supply us with some data, but we have to rely for details upon comparatively later works, which appear to have preserved older traditions handed down in some form of ballad poetry' (III, p. 365).

According to some scholars many indications point to an early Zoroastrian influence on Buddha's life and works. Dr Spooner believed that Buddha received Zoroastrian inspiration. Buddha selected as his headquarters the town of Gaya, for many centuries a centre of magian worship (IV, p. 6). His father's clan, the Śākyas of Kapilavastu were related to the Mongol-Persian Śakas of Śakadvīpa, long associated with the Magas Like the Zoroastrians the Śakas married their own sisters (I, p. 126). Buddha's mother belonged to the clan of the Lichchhavis who were related to the Indian Magas, and her name Māyā, is said to be a variant of Maga.

Other scholars go so far as to maintain that Buddha did not exist at all. They point to the striking parallels in the lives of Zoroaster and Buddha down to details of their parentage, birth, careers, teachings and death, and suggest that Buddha was an altogether mythical* personage whose life and works were modelled on Zoroaster's. To those who accept the traditional account of Buddha's life they point out that nothing of this is historical, and that the earliest records of him have been preserved in hymns and poetry like the exploits of Beowulf and King Arthur.

This theory, along with much other fanciful speculation about the Magians has generally been dismissed out of hand, but whatever its obvious limitations it does point to strong influences operating from Persia on native thought and religion in India from earliest times.

Books

I. Hodivala, S. K. *Parsis of Ancient India*, Bombay, 1920.
II. Majumdar, R. C. (Ed.) *The Vedic Age*. London, 1951.
III. Majumdar, R. C. (Ed.) *The Age of Imperial Unity*. Bombay, 1951.
IV. Samaddar, J. N. *The Glories of Magadha*, Patna, 1925.
V. Summers, M. *Witchcraft & Black Magic*, London, 1945.

INDEX

Items in full capitals indicate article headings. The entry after an item indicates the article in which it is to be found.

Advaitānanda – Chaitanya
AEON
aerial city – gandharva, Hariśchandra
Aesculapius – Āyurveda history
AESTHETICS
Afzal Khān – yoni
agada – poison
Adalassoi – suttee
ĀGAMA
āgamic worship – worship
Agarkar – Marāṭhi
Agarvāla – vaiśya
AGASTYA
Agattiyam – Tamil
Agesilaus – Kanishka
Aghāsura – Kṛishṇa
Aghata – Guhila
aghnyā – cow
Aghorī – Kāpālika
Agnāyī – Agni
Āgneya – Agni
āgneyāstra – weapons
Āgneyī – Aṅgiras
agni – fire
AGNI
agni-chyana – altar
agnidagdha – fire
āgnīdhra – hierophant
agniguḍa – weapons
agnigula – weapons
AGNIHOTRA
AGNIHOTRI, S. N.
agnikula or agnikuṇḍa – Rājputs
Agnimitra – Śuṅga
agni-pradakshiṇa – marriage, thread ceremonies
agni-prākāra – worship
agniśālā – architecture
agnisāra – purification
agnishṭoma – soma
agnishṭut – Bhaṅgāsvana, soma
agnishvātta – ancestors
agni-śuchi-vāsa – textiles
AGNIVARṆA
Agniveśa – Agni, Āyurveda history
agnosticism – nāstika
agnyādheya – fire
agnyupasthāna – agnihotra
agochari – meditation
Āgra – textiles
Agradās – Hindi
agrahāra – sacrifice
Āgrahāyaṇī – sacrifice
Agra-sandhānī – Yama
āgrayaṇa – sacrifice
agriculture – Austric
Ahalyā – Gotama, Nyāya
aham brahmāsmi – sayings
ahaṁkāra – psychology
ahaṁ-pratyaya – perception
Ahar – Guhila
Ahār – vaiśya
āhata – sound
āhavanīya – fire
Ahi – asura
Ahichhatra or Ahikshetra – Ābhīra
Āhika – Pāṇini
AHIṀSĀ
ahīna – soma
Āhīr – Ābhīra
Ahirbudhnya – Rudra
Ahirkshetra – Ābhīra
āhitāgni – fire
Ahmadābād – Vijayanagar
Ahmadnagar – Vijayanagar
Ahmad Shāh Durrānī – Marāṭha, Sikh
Āhom – Assamese
ahorātra – calendar, time
Āhuka – Kṛishṇa
Ahura Mazda – asura
āhuta – sacrifice
Aihole – Chālukya
Aila – Purūravas
Aila-vaṁśa – Vaivasvata
Ailūsha – Mahīdāsa
Aindra – grammar
Aindrī – Indra, Śakti
Airāvata – elephant
Aitareya – Āraṇyaka, Brāhmaṇa, Mahīdāsa, Upanishad
aitihya – knowledge
Aiyaṇar – androgyny
Aja – God, Raghu
Aja (tribe) – Divodāsa
Aja-ekapād – cosmology
ājagava – archery
ajahala – poetics
Ajaikapāda – Rudra
Ajamīḍha – Bharata
Ajāmila – mantra
Ajātaśatru – Magadha
AJANTĀ (or Ajaṇṭā)
ajapa – mantra
ajātivāda – Gauḍapāda
ajeyatā – brāhmin
Ajīgartta – Śunaḥśephas
ajina – thread ceremonies
Ajiśaka – Hinterindia
Ajita – tīrthaṅkara
AJITA (Keśakambalin)
ajīva – Jainism
ĀJĪVIKA
Ajmere – Chāhamāna
ājñā – chakra
ajñāna – knowledge
ājya – sacrifice
Akāli – Sikh
Akanishṭha – bodhisattva

ākāśa – Jainism, substance
ākāśa-vidyā – meteorology
Akbar – Dādū, Mīrābāī, Muslim, Tānsen
Akbarnāmāh – suttee
Akesines (same as Chenāb)
akhaṇḍ-dīp – vows
akhāṛā – education
Akho – Gujarāti
akhrā – Kolarian
Ākhu-ratha – Gaṇeśa
ākhyāna – literary forms
ākhyāyikā – literary forms
akriyā – mārga
akriyā-vāda – Ājīvika
akrodh – equanimity
Akrūra – Kṛishṇa, Satrājita
aksha – dice, weights and measures
Akshapāda – Nyāya
akshara – literary forms
akshatā – virginity
akshauhiṇī – army
Akshaya Navamī – festivals
akshaya vaṭa – fig-tree
akshī – eye
Akshobhya – bodhisattva
akshya baṭ (same as akshaya vaṭa)
Akūpāra – cosmology
Ākūti – Svāyaṁbhuva
alaka – head
Alakā – paradise
alaṁbushā – channels of the subtle body
Alaṁbusha – Ṛishyaśṛiṅga
Alaṁbushā – Atharvan, Pulastya
alaṁkāra – poetics
Alāndī – Jñānadeva
ālāpa – rāga, singing
ālāpaṇa – singing
Ālāra – Buddha
alaripu – bharata-nāṭyam
ālasya – sin
alāta – Gauḍapāda
alāta-chakra – knowledge
alātaśānti – Gauḍapāda
Alā-ud-dīn (see under Khilji)
Āḷavandār – Āḷvār
ālaya-vijñāna – Mahāyāna
al-Bīrūnī – historiography, mathematics
ALCHEMY
alcohol – drinks
ALEXANDER (the Great)
Alexander of Epirus – Aśoka
Alexandria – alchemy, Varāhamihira
Alexandria (in India) – towns
Alfred (King) – Christianity
al-Gurgān – Muslim
Ālhā – Chandella
Aliṇa – Divodāsa
āliṅgana – erotics
ālipāna – designs
Alkor – consummation
ALLĀHĀBĀD
Allāhābād Pillar – epigraphy, Guptas
Allasani Peddana – Telugu
Allopanishad – Upanishad
al-Masūdī – Pratihāra
Almora – paradise
alobha – ethics
ālpanā – designs
alphabet – scripts
ALTAR
ĀLVĀR (or Āḷvār)
Alwār – Harsha
āmalaka – column, minerals, plants
āmalaśilā – column
amānta – calendar
Amara – etymology
Amarakaṇṭaka – rivers (under Narmadā)
amaraśilā – column
Amarasiṁha – etymology
Amarāvatī – paradise
Amarāvatī (town) – Āndhra, Hinter-
india, stūpa
Amardās – Sikh
Amareśvara – liṅga
Amarnāth – liṅga
amaroli – paramudrā
amarsha – sin
AMARU
amātya – politics
Amāvasu – Purūravas
amāvāsya – calendar
Amazons – strīrājya
Ambā – Bhīshma, godlings
Ambālikā – Bhīshma
Ambapālī – Buddha, prostitution
ambara – chakra
Ambarīsha – hell, Māndhātṛi
amaroli – paramudrā
ambashṭha – physician
Ambashṭha – Uśīnara
Amber – Rājputs (under Kachhwāha)
Ambhi – Alexander
Ambhiya – Gandhāra
Ambikā – Bhīshma, Gaṇeśa, godlings,
Satī
Amīr Khusrau – music history
Amitābha – bodhisattva, China
Amitagati – Kanarese
amlikā – Gorakhnāth
ammā – Umā
Ammā – godlings
Ammā – pūrṇā – godlings
āmnāya – historiography, Veda
Amoghasiddhi – bodhisattva
Amoghavarsha I – Rāshṭrakūṭa
Āmrakārdava – Chandragupta II
amṛita – nectar
Amṛitsar – Sikh

aṁśa – music, rāga, soul
Aṁśa – Sūrya
aṁśin – soul
amukta – weapons
amūrti – śūnya
amusements – games
anāhata – chakra, sound
Aṇahilavāḍa (same as Aṇhilvāḍ)
Anahita – godlings
anaka – sound
Ānaka-dundu – Śūra
Anala – Agni
ānanda – God, hierophant
Ānanda – Buddha
Ānandagiri – philosophy
Ānanda-loka – paradise
ānandamaya-kośa – body
Ānanda-tīrtha – Madhva
ānandātman – body
Ānanda-vardhana – poetics
Anaṅga – Kāma
Anaṅgabhīm – Orissa
Anaṅga-raṅga – kāmaśāstra
Ananta – serpent worship, tīrthaṅkara
Anantānanda – Rāmānanda
Ananta-śīrshā – serpent worship
Anantavarman – Orissa
anantavijaya – animals
Ananta-vrata – vows
Anaraṇya – Rāvaṇa
Anargha-rāghava – drama history
Ānarta – Bhṛigu, Balarāma
ANĀRYA
Anasūyā – Atri, Śakuntalā
Anāthapiṇḍika – Buddha
anātmavāda – nāstika
ANATOMY
anatta – Buddhism
Ānava – Kekaya, Utathya, Yayāti
ANCESTORS
aṇḍa – stūpa
aṇḍaja – animals
Āṇḍāl – Āḷvār
Andamanese – Kolarian, pañchama
Āṇḍār Nambi – Śaiva Siddhānta
andāzah – numerals
Andhaka – asura, Kurukshetra
ĀNDHRA
ANDROGYNY
anekatva – Jainism
aṅga – anatomy, Jainism, literary forms
Aṅga – Bāleya, Karṇa, mahājanapada
Ṛishyaśṛiṅga
aṅga-bhāva – aṅgika
Aṅgad – Sikh
Aṅgada – Bālin
Aṅgada – Lakshmaṇa
Āṅgadi – Lakshmaṇa
aṅgahāra – dance
Aṅgami – eye, pañchama
aṅganā – strītantra
Aṅgāra – Kārttikeya
Aṅga-sthala – Liṅgāyat
AṄGIKA
AṄGIRAS
Āṅgirasa – Aṅgiras
aṅgula – weights and measures
aṅguli – hand
aṅgushṭha – hand
Aṅguttara-nikāya – Buddhist scriptures
Aṇhilvāḍ – Solaṅki
Anila – Vāyu
Ānili – Hanumān
aṇimā – siddhi
ANIMALS
ANIMAL SACRIFICE
Aniruddha – Pradyumna
añjali – mudrā, weights and measures
añjali-pūraṇa – thread ceremony
añjana – eye
Añjanā – Hanumān
aṅka – theatre
aṅkuśa – weapons
annamaya-kośa – body
Annaṁbhaṭṭa – philosophy
Anna Perenna – godlings
anna-prāśana – sacraments
Anna-pūrṇā – godlings
anointing – aspersion
Aṇojjā – Mahāvīra
Anomā (river) – Buddha
anṛita – dharma
Anśumān (or Anśumat) – Sagara
antaḥ-karaṇa – psychology
antaḥpura – harem
Antaka – Yama
antarā – rāga
antarāla – temple
Antarīksha – paradise
antar-yāmin – psychology
anthills – serpent worship
anthropolatry – microcosm, occultism
Antialcidas – Bactrians
Antigone – drama history
Antigonus – Seleucids
Antigonus Gonatas – Aśoka
ANTINOMIANISM
Antiochus I (Soter) – Seleucids
Antiochus II – Seleucids
Antiochus III (the Great) – Seleucids
Antony – Bengali
Antony, Mark – travel
antyaja – pañchama
antyeshṭi – obsequies
aṇu – atom
Anu – Bali, Divodāsa, Yayāti
anuāhārya-pachana – fire
anubhāva – empathy

anudātta – prosody
aṇu-druta – time
Anugītā – Mahābhārata
anukaraṇa – poetics
anu-kramaṇi – etymology
anukṛiti – Bharata
anuloma – eligibility
anumāna – logic
Anumati – calendar
anumiti – syllogism
Anūpa – Haihaya
anupallavi – rāga
anuprāsa – poetics
Anurādhapura – Buddhist history, Pāṇḍya
anurāga – love
anurakta – love
anus – chakra
anushṭubh – prosody
anustaraṇī – cow
anusvāra – mystic syllables
anuvāda – education
anuvādī – music
anuvāka – literary forms
ānvīkshikī – syllogism
anyonyābhāva – śūnya
Aornus – Nysa
Apabhraṁśa – Prākṛit
apabiddha – sonship
āpad-dharma – ethics
apadravya – olisboi
Āpalā – Veda
apāna – wind
apara – direction
aparāddhi – sin
Aparānta – geography
apara-vidyā – Śaṅkara
aparigraha – asceticism
Aparṇā – Umā
āpas – substance
Āpas – Gaṅgā
Apasamāra – Śiva
Āpastamba – ritual canon
apaurusheya – Veda
Āpava – Brahmā
apavarga – trance
apaviddha – sonship
aphrodisiacs – virility
Āpiśali – grammar
apoha – śūnya
Apollodotus – Bactrians
Apollonius of Tyana – occultism
Appar – Śaiva Siddhānta
aprāpyakāri – perception
apsarā – nymph
āptopadeśa – knowledge
Āptya – Agni
Ara – tīrthaṅkara
Arabian Nights – kathā, Somadeva
Arachosia – Parthians
Ārāḍa (same as Ālāra)
Ārādhya – Liṅgāyats
ārāma – education
Aramaic – Kharoshṭhī, nāgarī
araṇī – fire
araṇya – Āraṇyaka
ĀRAṆYAKA
Arāsana (or Arāsur) – Satī
Ārasiṁha – kāmaśāstra
āratī – worship
aratni – chakra, weights and measures
Aratta – miscegenation
aravinda – plants
Arbudā – mountains, Satī
archā – idolatry
archaka – worship
ARCHERY
Archilochus – Greeks
architects, cosmic (see artificers)
ARCHITECTURE
Archytas – mechanics
Ardashir I – Iran
Ardha-māgadhī – Prākṛit
ardha-maṇḍapa – temple
ardhanārī – androgyny
Ardhanārīśvara – androgyny
areca nut – betel
Ares – Kārttikeya
argha – strīpūjā
arghya – baths, marriage, Śiśupāla, worship
arhat (or arhant) – hierophant
Arikamedu – Chola, trade
arishṭa – Charaka, physician
Arishṭa – Kṛishṇa
Arishṭā – gandharva
Arishṭanemi – Śūra
Aristotle – Bharata, syllogism, Zoroastrianism
Arjan Dev – Sikh
ārjavam – truth
Ārjīkīyā (same as Beas)
ARJUNA
Arjuna-kārtavīrya – Haihaya
Arjuna's Penance – Pallava
ark or arka – Black Pagoda
armed ascetics – sādhu
armour – weapons
ARMY
Arnold, Sir Edwin – Gāndhi
ārogya – āyurveda
ārohī – music
āropa – poetics
Arorā – vaiśya
Arrian – archery, Uśīnara
arrow – archery
Arsaces – Parthians
ārsha – community, marriage

ārsha-jñāna – perception
ārsheya – community
ART
Artabhāga – secrecy
Artaxerxes Mnemon – Greeks
artha – category, ethics, politics, substance
arthakrama – poetics
arthāpatti – knowledge
Arthaśāstra – Kauṭilya
arthavāda – law
arthaveda – scriptures
artificers (cosmic) – Prajāpati, Viśvakarman
artificial sexual aids – olisboi
Aruḷnandi – Śaiva Siddhānta
Aruṇa – Sūrya
Aruṇa of Pañchāla – Uddālaka
Aruṇāchalam – liṅga
Aruṇāśva – Kanauj
Arundhatī – Vasishṭha, consummation
Arundhatī-darśana-nyāya – consummation
Āruṇi – Uddālaka
Arusha – Sūrya
Ārushī – Chyavana
Arvān – asura
Arvarīvat – ṛishi
Arvāvasu – Raibhya
āryā – prosody
Ārya – Aryans
Āryabhaṭa – mathematics
Aryaman – Aditi
ARYAN
Aryan language – Proto-Aryan
Ārya Samāj – Dayānanda
Āryāvarta – geography
asafoetida – diet
Asamanjas – Sagara
asaṁprajñāta – trance
asaṁyukta – mudrā
ĀSANA
ASAṄGA
Āsaṅga – Kaṇva
āsanna – politics
Āsapūri – Śakti
asat – God
aśaucha – menstruation
ASCETICISM
Āshāḍha – calendar
ASHES
ashṭa-chhāp – Vallabha
ashṭa-diggajā – Telugu
Ashṭādhyāyī – Pāṇini
ashṭaka – literature, sacrifice, śrāddha
Ashṭaka – Chaitanya, Gālava
ashṭāṅga – āyurveda
Ashṭāṅga-hṛidaya-saṁhitā – Āyurveda history
Ashṭāṅga-saṁgraha – Āyurveda history
Ashṭāvakra – Uddālaka
Ashur – Mesopotamia
asi – weapons
Asi – Banāras
Asidhenu – weapons
Asiknī (same as Chenāb)
asipattra-vana – hell
Asita – Buddha
askanda – rudrāksha, sex mysticism
Aśmaka – Kalmāshapāda, Mahājanapada
aśmārohaṇa – marriage, thread ceremonies
asmitā – sin
aśoka – plants
AŚOKA
asparsha – asceticism
ASPERSION
ĀŚRAMA – education, ṛishi
aśrāvya – sound
āśraya – senses
aśru – sacrifice
Aśruvindumatī – Yayāti
Assaji – Buddha
Assakenoi – Alexander
Assam – Kāmarūpa, rivers (under Brahmaputra)
ASSAMESE
Assurbanipal – Mesopotamia, Trade, Zoroastrianism
asteya – ethics
asthāi – rāga
asthi – bodily substances
āstika – nāstika
Āstīka – serpent worship
astra – mantra, weapons
astrology – astronomy, divination
ASTRONOMY
asu – wind
Asur – asura, Kolarian
ASURA
āsura – marriage, weapons
Asura Magha (or Maya) – Varāhamihira
asūyana – sin
aśva – man of the world
AŚVAGHOSHA – drama history
Aśvala – Gṛitsamada
Āśvalāyana – Brāhmaṇa, Gṛitsamada
aśvamedha – horse sacrifice
Aśvapati – Kekaya, Sāvitrī
Aśvasena – Pārśva
aśvattha – fig-tree
Aśvatthāman – Droṇa, longevity
Āsvayuji – sacrifice
AŚVIN
aśvinī – bandha
Āśvini – calendar
Aśvinī – Sūrya
asyavāmīya – Ṛig-veda

Atala – cosmology
ATHARVAN
Atharvana – Telugu
Atharvāṅgiras – Atharvan
ATHARVA-VEDA
atheism – nāstika
Athenaeus – travel
ati-bhaṅga – bhaṅga
atidhṛiti – prosody
atirātra – soma
Atīsa (Dīpaṅkara) – education, Pāla
atiśakvarī – prosody
atiśayokti – poetics
ātitheya – compassion
Atithigva – Divodāsa
atka – dress
ātma-liṅga – Rāvaṇa
ātman – soul
Ātmīya Sabhā – Roy, R.
ATOM
Ātreya – Atri
ATRI
Atri-smṛiti – salutation
atta – Buddhism
aṭṭha-kathā – Malayālam
Attic Comedy – Bhāsa, drama history
Attock – Gandhāra
atyāhāra – sin
atyashṭi – prosody
atyukti – poetics
audārya – poetics
auddhatya – sin
audumbara retirement – āśrama
augury – divination
Augustus – Greeks, Romans
Aulikara – Ujjain
Aulūka – Vaiśeshika
aum – mystic syllables
aupāsana – fire
Aurangābād – cave temples
Aurangzeb – Banāras, Mathurā, Music history, Muslim, Nimbārka, painting, Sikh
aurasa – sonship
aureole – body, Iran
AUROBINDO
AURVA
aushadha – medicine
Auśija – miscegenation
AUSTRIC
Auttami – Manu
Auttānapādi – Dhruva
avabhṛitha – baths
avachchheda – Vedānta
Avadaiyar Kovil – Pāṇḍya
avadāna – literary forms
Avadāna-śataka – literary forms
Avadhi – language
avadhūta – hierophant
avadhūtikā – channels of the subtle body
avadhyatā – brāhmin
avagraha – perception
āvāhana – worship
avaidika – nāstika
avakshepa – logic
Avalokiteśvara – bodhisattva
Avanti – Haihaya, Ujjain, Vaivasvata
Avantipura – Kashmīr
Avantivarman – Kashmīr
avarṇa – pañchama
avarodha – harem
avarohī – music
avarta – music
āvāsa – education
avasarpiṇī – Jainism
āvasathya – fire
avasthā – dreams
Avataṁsaka – Buddhist scriptures
avatāra – God
avāya – perception
avayava – syllogism
āveśa – exteriorisation
Avestic – Vedic
Avicenna – Āyurveda history, hot and cold
Avīchi – hell
avidyā – knowledge
avirati – sin
avrohī (same as avarohī)
Avvaiyār – Tamil
Avyakta – Purusha
axis mundi – wheel
aya – canons of proportion
āya – canons of proportion
ayam ātmā brahma – sayings
ayana – Nārāyaṇa
Ayanaghosha – gopī
āyatana – altar
AYODHYĀ – towns
Āyogava – pañchama
ayonija – animals
Āyu (or Āyus) – Purūravas
āyudha – weapons
ĀYURVEDA
ĀYURVEDA HISTORY
āyus – āyurveda
Āyushmān – Dhruva
āyush-yāṇi – pregnancy
ayya – Āndhra
Ayyaṇar (same as Aiyaṇar)
Ayyar – brāhmin
Azilises – Śaka
Azes – Śaka

Bābhan – kshattriya
Bābhravya – kāmaśāstra

Babhrū – Śiva
Babhrū-vāhana – Arjuna
Bābur – Guhila, karuṇa, Rājput, sanatva
Babylonians – Maga, Mesopotamia, numerals, Vrātya
Bactra (Bactria) – Bactrians
BACTRIANS
bāḍā (same as bāṛā)
Baḍaga – pañchama
Bādāmi – cave temples, Chālukya
Bādarāyaṇa – Vedānta
Badarināth – Ganges, Śaṅkara
baḍavā – strītantra
Baḍavā – Aśvin
badī – calendar
Badīsa – pregnancy
bael (same as bilva)
BĀGH
Bāghela – Rājputs
Bāghelkhaṇḍ – Rājputs
Bāgh-gumpha – cave temples
Bāghiṇi (river) – Bāgh
Bahādur Shāh – Guhila
bahish-kṛita – purification
bahish-pavamāna – soma
Bāhlīka – Bactrians, Parthians
Bahmanī – Vijayanagar
Bahram Yasht – Aryan
Bāhu (or Bāhuka) – Sagara
Bāhubali – Ṛishabha
bahūdaka – asceticism
Bāhu-dantiputra – Kauṭilya
Bāhuka – Nala, Sagara
bahulāvāsya – calendar
bahvṛicha – hierophant
Baiga – pañchama
bairāgi (and bairāgiṇī) – equanimity
baka – birds
Bakadalbhya – dog
Bakāsura – Kṛishṇa
bakhar – Marāṭhi
Bakhshāli manuscript – mathematics
Bakhtiār Khilji (see Khilji)
bakula – plants
bala – antinomianism, army
Bala (asura) – same as Vala
Balabhadra – Balarāma
Bāla-charita – Bhāsa
Baladeva – Balarāma
Bāla-gopāla – Vallabha
bālāgra – weights and measures
Balāhi – bard, pañchama
Bālaji – Vishṇu
Bālāki – Gārgya
Balandharā – Bhīma
BALARĀMA
Balarāmdās – Oriya
Balaśrī – Āndhra, Greeks
Balbodh – nāgarī
Balbutha – miscegenation
BĀLEYA
Bāleśvara – Śiva
Bālhi (or Bālhīka) – Bactrians
bali – worship
Bali (Ānava king) – Utathya
Bali (daitya king) – Hiraṇyāksha
Bālī (monkey king) – Bālin
bālikā – strītantra
BĀLIN
Balkh – Bactrians
Ballāla (poet) – literary forms
Ballāla (king) – Hoysala
ballet – theatre
Bammoja – architecture
Bāmyān – Gandhāra
bāṇa – archery
Bāṇa (asura) – Pradyumna
BĀṆA (writer)
Bāṇabhaṭṭa – Bāṇa (writer)
bāṇaliṅga – liṅga
Banaphari – barbarians, Śaka
BANĀRAS
Bāṇāsura – Pradyumna
Banavāsi – Āndhra
Bandā – Sikh
bandana – dyeing
Bande Mātaram – Bengali
BANDHA
bandhana – erotics
bandhu – community
Baṅgadarśan – Bengali
Bāṅgālī – Bengali
Baṅgaru – language
Bānī – Dādū
bania – vaiśya
Baniā – scripts
banian – fig-tree
Bañjārā – vaiśya
banner festival – pole ceremonies
banyan (same as banian)
Bappa (or Bappasvāmi) – Pallava
Bappa Rāwal – Guhila
baptism – aspersion
bāṛā (or bāḍā) – betel
Barābar hill – cave temple
Barahin-devī – godlings
Barbara – barbarians
BARBARIANS
Barbarike – trade
BARD
bargīt – Assamese
Bārhadratha – Magadha
Bārhaspatya – Bṛihaspati
Bārhaspatya Arthaśāstra – politics
barhiḥ – grasses
Barhishad – ancestors
Baroḍā inscriptions – numerals
barrenness – sterility

Barrett, Francis – Zoroastrianism
Bartholomew, St. – Christianity
Barygaza – trade, towns
Barzuchihar – Vikramāditya
basadi – towns
Basava – Liṅgāyat
basavi – prostitution
basilica – cave temples
Bāshkala (same as Vāshkala)
basivi – prostitution
bastard – sonship
basti – āyurveda, purification
basti (slum) – see towns
BATH
Battle of the Ten Kings – Divodāsa
Batuta, Ibn (see Ibn Batuta)
Baudhāyana – ritual canon
Baudhāyana Sūmārta Sūtra – virginity
Baul – bard
Bāveru Jātaka – trade
bayadère – prostitution
bear totem – Satrājita
Beas – rivers
beau ideal – man of the world
beauty – aesthetics
bed of nails – asceticism
Bedsā – cave temples
beef – cow, diet
begging – hierophant (under bhikshu), sādhu
Behat (same as Jhelum)
bel (same as bilva)
Belātthiputta – Sañjaya
Belāvala – rāga
Beḷgoḷā – Ṛishabha
Belūr – Hoysaḷa
Belva – Buddhism
Benfrey, Theodor – Greeks
Bengal – Bāleya, Pāla
BENGALI (or Bāṅgālī)
Beni – Sikh
Bentham, Jeremy – Roy
Bentinck, Lord – thug, suttee
Beowulf – Tamil
Berār (same as Vidarbha)
Bernier, François – suttee
Berosus – travel, Zoroastrianism
Beschi, Constanzio – Tamil
Besnagar – Śuṅga
besprinkling – aspersion
BESTIALITY
BETEL
Betwa – rivers (under Jamnā)
Bezbarua – Assamese
Bezwāda – Āndhra
Bhadrā – Utathya, levirate, Kṛishṇa
Bhadrabāhu – Jainism
Bhadraka – Śuṅga
Bhadrakāpya – pregnancy
bhadra-log – Bengali
Bhadrāśva – Atri, geography
bhaga – yoni
Bhaga – bhakti, Rudra
Bhāgabhadra – Śuṅga
Bhāgadatta – Bactrians, Kāmarūpa
bhagāsana – paramudrā
bhagat – bhakti
BHAGAVADGĪTĀ
Bhagavān – bhakti
Bhagavat – bhakti
Bhāgavata (sect) – bhakti, Pañcharātra
Bhāgavata Purāṇa – Purāṇa
bhaga yaja – yoni
Bhagīratha – Sagara
Bhāgīrathī – Ganges
Bhāguri – nāstika
Bhaimī – Nala
bhairav – tantrism
Bhairava – rāga, Śiva, tantrism
Bhairavī – Śakti, tantrism
Bhairoṁ – Śiva
Bhājā – cave temples
bhajan – singing
bhakta – bhakti
Bhaktacharan – Oriya
Bhakta-mālā – Hindi
BHAKTI
bhakti-mārga – bhakti
Bhalānasa – Divodāsa
Bhāmaha – poetics
bhāṇa – theatre
bhaṇḍārā – sacrifice
Bhandārkar, R. G. – Prārthanā Samāj
bhāṅg – drugs
BHAṄGA
BHAṄGĀSVANA
Bhaṅgi – pañchama
bhāṇikā – theatre
bhanitā – literary forms
Bhañja – Orissa
Bhānu – Satrājita
Bhānu Siṁha – Tagore (R.)
Bhār – vaiśya
bhāra – weights and measures
BHARADVĀJA
Bhāraśiva – Kushān, Vākāṭaka
BHARATA (king)
BHARATA (writer)
Bharata (Jain) – Ṛishabha
Bharata (bhakta) – bhakti
Bharata (brother of Rāma) – Kekaya
Bhārata (India) – Bharata (king)
Bhārata (tribe) – Bharata (king)
BHARATA-NĀṬYAM
Bhārata-varsha – Bharata (king)
Bharati – Tamil
Bhāratī – Śaṅkara
Bharatināth – Nātha

Bharatpur – kshattriya
Bhāratvarshīya Brahmo Samāj – Sen
BHĀRAVI
Bhārgava – Bhṛigu
Bhārhut – stūpa
BHARTṚIHARI
bhāryādhikārika – kāmaśāstra
BHĀSA
bhasad – yoni
bhāshā – language
bhāshya – literary forms
bhāshikā – philology
bhāshikā-svara – singing
Bhāskara (mathematician) – mathematics
Bhāskara (philosopher) – philosophy
Bhāskara (the sun) – Sūrya
bhasman – ashes
bhastrākā – prāṇayāma
Bhāsvatī – paradise
bhaṭ – bard
Bhaṭārka – Maitraka
Bhāṭia – vaiśya
Bhaṭkhaṇḍe – music history
bhaṭṭa – bard, hierophant
Bhaṭṭāchārya – hierophant
Bhaṭṭa-nārāyaṇa – drama history
Bhaṭṭanāyaka – poetics
Bhatti (or Bhattil) – Rājputs
Bhaṭṭi – Bhartṛihari
Bhaṭṭi-kāvya – Bhartṛihari
Bhaṭṭopala – astronomy
Bhau Daji – Vākāṭaka
bhautik – substance
Bhautya – Manu
bhāva – bhakti, empathy
Bhava – Śiva
BHAVABHŪTI
bhava-chakra – Buddhism, eschatology
bhāva-liṅga – Liṅgāyat
Bhavanāga – horse sacrifice, Vākāṭaka
Bhavānanda – Rāmānanda
Bhavānī – thug
Bhāvaviveka – philosophy
Bhavishya Purāṇa – Purāṇa, Zoroastrianism
bhaya – empathy
bhayānaka – empathy
bheda – advaita, politics
bhedābheda – advaita
bhedana – prāṇayāma
Bhela – Āyurveda history
bheshaj – Āyurveda history
bheshajāni – Atharva-veda
Bhikhan – Sikh
bhikku – hierophant
bhikshu – hierophant
Bhil (or Bhīl) – Guhila, Kolarian
Bhīlsā (same as Vidisā)
BHĪMA – Rudra
Bhīma (father of Damayantī) – Nala
Bhīma (river) – rivers (under Kistna)
Bhīma I – Solaṅki
Bhīma-bhoi – Oriya
Bhīmaratha – Divodāsa, Nala
Bhīma-śaṅkara – liṅga
Bhīma-śāsana – Yama
Bhimeśvara – liṅga
bhinna – ear
bhishaj – physician
BHĪSHMA
Bhīshmaka – Rukmiṇī
Bhīshmāshṭamī – Bhīshma
bhīta – Orissa
Bhīta (or Bhītargāoṅ) – architecture
Bhitpālo – painting
Bhog – Sikh
bhoga – mārga
Bhogar – Bogar
Bhogavatī – serpent worship
bhogī – kāmarūpa
bhog mandir – temple
Bhoi – Orissa
Bhoja – Rukmiṇī, Vaivasvata
Bhoja – mechanics
Bhoja of Dhārā – Paramāra
Bhoja I – Pratihāra
Bhojakaṭa – Rukmiṇī
Bhojpuri – language
bhoktri – dreams
Bhonsle – Śivājī
Bhoṭia – Kirāta
bhrama – logic, knowledge
bhramara – animals, mantra
bhramari – prāṇayāma
Bhramarī – Śakti
bhrānti – knowledge
BHṚIGU
Bhṛigukachchha – towns
Bhṛiṅgi – dance
bhṛita – army
bhrū-madhya – chakra
Bhubaneśvar (same as Bhuvaneśvar)
Bhūkaśyapa (Vasudeva) – Kṛishṇa
bhukti – antinomianism
Bhumaka – Śaka
bhūmi – bodhisattva, Yoga
Bhūmi – Dyaus
bhūmikā – asceticism
bhūmikā – mārga
Bhūpālī – rāga
bhūr bhuvaḥ svaḥ – mantra
bhūr loka – cosmology
bhūta (element) – substance
bhūta (spirit) – obsequies, Śiva
Bhūtam – Āḷvār
Bhūtanāth – Nātha
bhūtātman – body
bhūta-vidyā – occultism

Bhūteśvara – Śiva
Bhūti – ṛishi
Bhuvaneśvar – Orissa
bhuvar-loka – cosmology
bībhatsa – empathy
Bidpai – Pañchatantra
bīdrī – handicrafts
Bihār – Pāla
Bihāri – language
Bihārilāl – Hindi
bīja (sperm) – pregnancy
bīja (syllable) – mystic syllables
Bīja-gaṇita – mathematics
Bījak – Kabīr
bījākshara – mystic syllables
Bijāpur – Śivājī
Bijjala – Ābhīra
Bikaner – Rājputs (under Rāthor)
bile – humours
BILHAṆA
bilva – plants
bimba – perception
Bimbā – godlings
Bimbisāra – Magadha
BINDU
Bindu (lake) – pilgrimage
Bindumatī – Māndhātṛi
Bindusāra – Maurya
birch-bark – writing
BIRDS
Birhor – Kolarian
Bithūr – Brahmā
black magic – occultism
BLACK PAGODA
Black Yajur-veda – Yajur-veda
blinking – Ikshvāku
BLOOD
blood-drinking – blood
blood-letting – Āyurveda
blowing-gun – Austric
Bo (tree) – fig-tree
Boccaccio – Pañchatantra
Bodh Gaya (same as Budh Gaya)
bodhi – Buddha
bodhi tree – fig-tree
BODHIDHARMA
BODHISATTVA
bodily marks – stigmata
BODILY SUBSTANCES
BODY
BOGAR
Boghaz koi – Aśvin, Indra, Varuṇa
bol – dance
Bombay – godlings, towns
bone – dhātu
boomerang – cow, weapons
Bopadeva (same as Vopadeva)
Bopp, Franz – Proto-Aryan language
Bose, J. C. – science
boustrophedon – kāvya
bow – archery
Bower Manuscript – Āyurveda history
brāhma – marriage
BRAHMĀ
Brahma (or Brahman) – God
brahmachakra – chakra
brahmachāri (or -chārin) – āśrama
brahmacharya – continence, āśrama
brahmadaṇḍa – chakra
Brahmadatta – asura
Brahmagupta – mathematics
brahma-hatyā – sin
Brahma-jijñāsa – Vedānta
Brahma-loka – paradise
brāhmaṇ – brāhmin
BRĀHMAṆA
Brahmaṇaspati – Bṛihaspati
brahmāṇḍa – cosmology
Brahmaṇī – Śakti
Brahmaputra – river
brahma-randhra – chakra
brahmaṛishi – ṛishi
Brahma-saṁpradāya – Dādū
Brahma-siddhānta – mathematics
brahmāstra – weapons
Brahma-sūtra – Vedānta
Brahmāvarta – geography
Brahma-veda – Atharva-veda
Brahma-yāmala – tantrism
brahma-yuga – aeon
Brāhmī – script
BRĀHMIN
brāhminism – brāhmin
brāhminical revival – brāhmin
Brāhmo Samāj – Roy
brāhmya – alchemy, marriage
Brāhui – language
Brāj – Kṛishṇa
Brāj-bhāsha – Hindi, language
Brājnāth Bādajena – Oriya
Branchidae – Nysa
breasts – strītantra
BREATH CONTROL
Bṛihadāraṇyaka – Āraṇyaka, Upanishad
Bṛihadaśva – Mahābhārata
Bṛihadbala – Agnivarṇa
Bṛihaddeśī – music history
Bṛihad-jātaka – Varāhamihira
Bṛihadratha – Jarasandha, Maurya
Bṛihan-manas – Jayadratha
BṚIHASPATI (priest of the gods)
BṚIHASPATI (nihilist)
Bṛihaspati (legalist) – ritual canon
bṛihat – literary forms
bṛihatī – prosody
Bṛihat-kathā – Guṇāḍhya
Bṛihat-kathā-mañjarī – kathā
Bṛihat-saṁhitā – Varāhamihira

Brindāban (same as Vṛindāvana)
Brinjari – human sacrifice
Broach (same as Barygaza)
Bruges – Bhṛigu
Bucephala – towns
buch – coconut
Buchanan, Dr. – Āndhra
budbuda – knowledge
BUDDHA
Buddha-charita – Aśvaghosha
Buddhaghosha – Buddhist history
Buddhata – Mahāyāna
Buddha-vaṁsa – Buddhist scriptures
buddhi – psychology
Buddhī – Gaṇeśa
BUDDHISM
BUDDHIST SCRIPTURES
BUDDHIST HISTORY
Budha – Soma
Budhasvāmin – Guṇāḍhya
Budh Gaya – stūpa
buffalo – Toda
Bukka – Vijayanagar
bull – cow
bull-roarer – soma
Bundelā – Rājputs
Bundelkhaṇḍ – Rājputs (under Bundelā)
Bundi – Muslim
bungalow – architecture
Burañji – Assamese
burial alive – suspended animation
Burzuya – Vikramāditya
but (image) – idolatry
butea frondosa – plants (under palāśa)
buttocks – strītantra
Buzurgmihir – Varuṇa

Cabral, Pedro – Kerala
Calcutta – Kālī, towns
CALENDAR
Calicut – Kerala, politics
Calliena (same as Kalyān)
Camdodia – Hinterindia, numerals
camel – warfare
camphor – betel
Canarese – Kanarese
cannibalism – human sacrifice
canoe – Austric
CANONS OF PROPORTION
Canopus – Agastya
Caracalla – travel
cardinal points – wheel, direction
Carey, William – Bengali
Carura – trade
caryatid – columns
cash – numismatics
CASTE
CASTE MARKS
cat-hold – Lokāchārya
catapult – weapons
catechu – betel
CATEGORY
Cathaei – Alexander
Cauvery – same as Kāverī
CAVE TEMPLES
Celsus – surgery
ceremony – ritualism
chāchari – meditation, paramudrā
CHĀHAMĀNA
Chaikitaneya – livelihood
chaitanya – psychology
CHAITANYA
Chaitanya Charitāmṛita – Chaitanya
chaitra – calendar
chaitra-ratha – paradise
Chaitrī – sacrifices
chaitya – cave temples
chakora – birds
CHAKRA (plexus)
chakra (discus) – weapons
chakra (wheel) – wheel
Chakradatta – Āyurveda history
Chakrapāṇi – Āyurveda history, bodhisattva, Pāla
CHAKRAPŪJĀ – swing
chakravāka – birds
chakravartin – kingship, wheel, yūpa
Chakrāyudha – Kanauj
chakshudāna – paṭṭa
chakshus – senses
Chākshusha – Dhruva
CHĀLUKYA
Chālukya (Later) – Hoysala
Chamār – pañchama
chāmara – kingship
Chamariyā – godlings
chamatkāra – aesthetics
Chambal – river
Chameālī – scripts
Champā – Bāleya
Champādhipa – Karṇa
champū – literary forms
Chāṁtamūla – stūpa
chamū – army
chamū-nātha – army
Chāmuṇḍā – Śakti
Ch'an – Bodhidharma
chanaka – bindu
Chāṇakhya – Kauṭilya
Chañchalā – Lakshmī
Chanda – Buddha
Chaṇḍa – liṅga, Śumbha
chaṇḍāla – pañchama
Chāṇḍālī – prākṛit
chandana – plants, worship
Chaṇḍasena – Udayana
Chand-bardai – Chāhamāna

CHANDELLA
Chaṇḍeśvara – law
Chaṇḍī – Purāṇa
CHAṆḌIDĀS
Chaṇḍikā – human sacrifice
Chaṇḍipāṭha – Purāṇa
Chandra – Soma
Chāndra (yogis) – human sacrifice
Chandrabhāga (same as Chenāb)
Chandra-chūḍā – Śiva
Chandragiri – Vijayanagar
Chandragupta Maurya – Maurya
Chandragupta I – Gupta
CHANDRAGUPTA II
chandra-kalā – strītantra
chandra-kānta – gems
Chandra-ketu – Lakshmaṇa
Chandrāpīḍa – widow
Chandraprabha – tīrthaṅkara
Chandra-śekhara – Śiva
Chandrātreya – Chandella
Chandra-vaṁśa – Vaivasvata
Chandravarma – Śaka
Chandravarman – Chandella
Chandravatī – Solaṅki
Chandra-yajña – sacrifice
chāndrāyaṇa – asceticism, vows
Chandwār – Kanauj
Channabasava – Liṅgāyat
CHANNELS OF THE SUBTLE BODY
Chāṇūra – Kṛishṇa
chāpa – archery
chāra – espionage
character – karma
charaka – education
Charaka – Āyurveda history
chāraṇ – bard
charaṇa – śākhā
charaṇam – rāga
charaṇa-pūjā – guru
Charaṇa-vyūha – Ṛig-veda
Charandās – Hindi
charas – drugs
Chārāyaṇa – kāmaśāstra
chāri – dance
chariot – army
charita – literary forms
charita-kāvya – bard
charity – karuṇā
charkhā – Gāndhi
charman – anatomy, weapons
Charmanvatī (same as Chambal)
Charnock, Job – suttee, towns
Charpaṭi – Nātha
Charsaddā – Gandhāra
charu – sacrifice
Chāru – Rukmiṇī
Chārudatta – Bhāsa
chārutā – aesthetics
CHĀRVĀKA
charyā – Bengali
charyā-pada – Nātha
chashāla – yūpa
Chashṭana – Śaka
chātaka – birds
Chatterji, Bankim Chandra – Bengali
Chatterji, Sarat Chandra – Bengali
Chatterton, Thomas – Tagore (R.)
chatuḥ-shashṭi – skills
chatur-aṅga – army, gambling
Chatur-bhāṇi – theatre
chatur-bhuja – Vishṇu
chaturdaśa-ratnam – nectar
chatur-māsa – calendar
chātur-māsya – sacrifice
chaturthī-karma – consummation
Chaturvarga-chintāmaṇi – Hemādri
chātur-varṇa – caste
chaturvedi – hierophant
chātvāla – altar
Chaube – hierophant
Chaucer, Geoffrey – Bactrians
Chauhān – Chāhamāna
chaula – head
chaultrī – temple
Chauna – Buddha
Chaulukya – Solaṅki
Chauraṅgīnāth – Nātha
Chaura-pañchāśika – Bilhaṇa
chaurī – kingship
chauth – Śivājī
Chedi – mahājanapada, Nala, Satyavatī, Śiśupāla, Vaivasvata
chela – guru
chemistry – alchemy, minerals
Chenāb – rivers
chenda – musical instruments
Chera – Kerala
Cheraman – Kerala
Chero – Kolarian
cheroot – drugs
Chersonese – Hinterindia
Cheruman – pañchama
Cherusseri – Malayālam
chess – gambling
cheshṭā – karma
chetanā – psychology
chetas – psychology
Cheṭṭiār – kāyastha, vaiśya
Chhāgalāṇḍa – chakra
chhala – logic
Chhandaḥ-śāstra – prosody
chhandas – prosody
chhandoga – hierophant, Upanishad
Chhāndogya – Brāhmaṇas, Upanishad
chhāp – caste marks
chhapa (stanza) – Gujarāti
Chhatarkhai – caste

chhatra – kingship, stūpa
chhatrapati – Śaka
Chhāyā – Sūrya
chhāya-nāṭaka – theatre
chhaya-vāda – Hindi
chhidra – ear, orifices
chhinna – ear
chhinnakā – asceticism
chhoṭikā – worship
Chidambara (poet) – kāvya
CHIDAMBARAM
chihna – symbols
chikitsā – āyurveda
chikitsaka – physician
Chiklīta – godling
childbirth – pregnancy
CHILD MARRIAGE
chiṁṭa – sādhu
CHINA
chīnāchāra – tantrism
chīna-paṭṭa – textiles
chin-mudrā – mudrā
chintā – psychology
chintāmaṇi – gems
Chintāmaṇi – Tamil
Chiplunkar – Marāṭhi
chirajīva – longevity
Chirakāri – Gotama
chirañjīva – longevity
chit – psychology
chitā – necrophilia
chitāsana – necrophilia
Chitor (or Chitorgaṛh) – Guhila
Chitpāvan – Marāṭha
Chitragupta – Yama
Chitrakūṭa – Atri, Kekaya, Vālmīki
Chitrakūṭa – Guhila
Chitralekhā – Pradyumna
Chitrāṅgada – Bhīshma
Chitrāṅgadā – Arjuna
Chitraratha – paradise
chitra-śikhaṇḍin – ṛishi
Chitra-vāhana – Arjuna
chitrinī – channels of the subtle body, strītantra
chitta – psychology
Chittagong – Bāleya
Chittagutta – aesthetics
chitta-vṛitti – karma, mind
Choḍagaṅga – Orissa
Chokhā – Nāmdev
CHOLA (or Choḷa)
Chola-maṇḍala – Chola
cholī – dress
Chota Nāgpur – Orissa
Chou – breath control, numerals
CHRISTIANITY
Chrysostom, St. – Christianity
chūḍā – head
chūḍā-karaṇa – head
Chūhra – pañchama
Chulik – Chālukya
chulikā – dramaturgy
Chullavagga – Buddhist scriptures
chumbana – erotics
Chunār – architecture
Chuṅganur – menstruation
chūrṇa – alchemy
Churning of the Ocean – nectar
chūshaṇa – erotics
Chutia – human sacrifice
chuṭiya (or chuṭia) – head
Chuṭukula – Āndhra
chyāvana – alchemy
CHYAVANA
chyle – bodily substances
cigar – drugs
cinnabar – alchemy
circumambulation – pilgrimage, wheel
cire perdue – sculpture
cleansing – purification
Clearchus of Soli – Maga
Clement of Alexandria – Christianity
Cleopatra – travel
Cleophis – Alexander
Cochin – Kerala
COCONUT
coins – numismatics
cold – hot and cold
collyrium – eye
COLUMN
commerce – trade
COMMUNITY
Comorin, Cape – Paraśurāma
compass, points – direction
COMPASSION
concentration – meditation
conception – pregnancy
conch – animals
confession – Jains, Mahāvīra
Conjeeveram – Pallava
consciousness – psychology
Constantine the Great – Romans
CONSUMMATION
Conti, Nicolo – suttee, trade
CONTINENCE
Cooch Bihār – Sen
cookery – diet
coolie – śūdra
Coromandel – Chola
Cosmas Indicopleustes – Christianity, numismatics
cosmetics – caste marks
COSMOLOGY
cotton – textiles
courtesan – prostitution
COW
cowrie – animals, numismatics

crafts – handicrafts, skills
Cranganore – Christianity
creation – cosmology
cremation – obsequies
crime – sin
Criminal Tribes – pañchama
crocodile – animals
cross – swastika
crow – bird
Ctesias of Cnidos – Āyurveda history, Greeks, Mesopotamia, occultism
cummerbund – caste
cummin – diet
cunnilingus – perversions
Curzon, Lord – Europeans
Cuttack (Kaṭak) – Orissa
cynicism – nāstika

Dabistan – sādhu
dacoits – sādhu
Dadhi – cosmology
Dadhīcha (or Dadhyanch) – Atharvan
dadhi-prāśana – thread ceremonies
DĀDŪ
Daedala – towns
da Gama, Vasco – Europeans, Kerala, trade
dāgoba – stūpa
Dahae – Anārya, Phoenicians
Dahana – Rudra
dahanopala – gems
daitya – asura
daiva – hand, karma, marriage
Ḍāk – Assamese
Dakash – Daksha
ḍākinī – godlings
DAKSHA (ṛishi)
Daksha (place) – Pāṇini
Dāksheya – Pāṇini
Dākshi – Pāṇini
dakshiṇa – direction, Hinduism
dakshiṇā – sacrifice
dakshiṇāchāra – Hinduism
dakshiṇāgni – fire
Dakshiṇāpatha – miscegenation
dakshiṇāyana – calendar, divination
Dakshineśvar – Rāmakṛishṇa
Dakshiṇi-Rāi – godlings
Dalbhya – livelihood
Dalpatrām – Gujarāti
dama – equanimity
Dama – Marutta
Damaghosha – Śiśupāla
Dāmajada – Śaka
ḍamaru – musical instruments
Damayantī – Nala
damḍī – numismatics
Damila – Tamil
damn – numismatics
Dāmodara – Kṛishṇa
Dāmodaragupta – kāmaśāstra
daṁpati – women
daṁśana – erotics
dāna – compassion, politics
dānastuti – Ṛig-veda
dānava – asura
DANCE
DAṆḌA – weapons, weights and measures
Daṇḍa – Ikshvāku
Daṇḍa-dhāra – Yama
Daṇḍaka – Ikshvāku
Daṇḍanāth – Nātha
daṇḍa-nīti – politics
Daṇḍapāṇi – Buddha
daṇḍin – hierophant
DAṆḌIN
Dantapura – Jagannātha, Kaliṅga
Danteśvarī – human sacrifice
Dantidurga – Rāshṭrakūṭa
Danu – asura, rākshasa
Dārā Shikoh – Upanishad
darbha – grasses
darbha-ashṭamī – grasses
Dardic – language
Darius – Greeks, metals, travel
darpaṇa – Kāma
darśana – eye, perception, philosophy
darśa-vāsya – calendar
darśa-yajña – sacrifice
daru – dance
dāru – plants
Dāruka – Kṛishṇa
Dāruvana – liṅga
dāsa – Anārya, name
Daśa-kumāra-charita – Daṇḍin
Dasam Granth – Sikh
daśanāmi – sādhu
Daśānana – Rāvaṇa
Daśapura – Ujjain
Dāśa-rājña – Divodāsa
Daśaratha – Raghu
Daśaratha Jātaka – Rāmāyaṇa
Dāśārha – Kṛishṇa
Daśārṇa – Śikhaṇḍin
Daśa-rūpaka – theatre
Daśāśvamedha – horse sacrifice
Dāsbodh – Marāṭhi
dāsī – eligibility
Dasma – Pūshan
Dasra – Aśvin
Dasyu – Anārya
datta – ethics
dattaka – sonship
Dattaka – kāmaśāstra
Dattamitra – Bactrians
Dattātreya – Atri

Dattila – music history
daughters – women
daughter-in-law – joint family
Daulatābād – Chālukya
Davids, Rhys – Dravidian
Day, Francis – Vijayanagar
daya – compassion
dāya – joint family
Dāyabhāga – law
Dayāl, Shiv (same as Śivdayāl)
Dayālbāgh – Śivdayāl
DAYĀNANDA
Dayānāth – Nātha
Dayarām – Gujarāti
deasil – pilgrimage
death – eschatology, necrophilia, obsequies
death-rites – obsequies
decimal system – numerals
defecation – utsarga
deflowering – ahiṁsā, consummation, prostitution, virginity
deha – body
dehātmavāda – nāstika
dehavāda – physical culture
dehavṛitti – anatomy
dehin – body
Deimachus – Seleucids
Delhi – Chāhamāna
delivery – pregnancy
Deluge – Vaivasvata
Demetria – towns
Demetrius – Bactrians
Demetrius of Alexandria – Christianity
Democritus – Vaiśeshika
demonology – occultism
Demotic – numerals
deodār (same as dāru)
Deogaṛh – architecture
Deogiri – Chālukya
Deori – human sacrifice
Depressed Castes – pañchama
destiny – karma
Derozio, Henry – Dutt (M.)
deśa – category
Descent of the Ganges – Pallava, sculpture
deśī – Prākṛit
DESIGNS
DEŚIKA
deśya – Prākṛit
determinism – nāstika
deul – Orissa
deva – God
Devabhūti – Śuṅga
devadāsī – prostitution
devadatta – wind
Devadatta – Buddha
Devagiri – Chālukya
Devahutī – Sāṁkhya
Devaka – Kaṁsa, Yudhishṭhira
Devakī – Kṛishṇa, Śiva
Devala – Pāṇini
Devamātṛi – Aditi
Devanāgarī – nāgarī
Devarāja – kāmaśāstra
Devarāta – Śunaḥśephas
devaṛishi – ṛishi
Deva-samāj – Agnihotri
Devaśarma – exteriorisation
Devasenā – Kārttikeya, Śukra
devatā – godling
deva-yāna – eschatology
Devayānī – Yayāti
Devī – Śakti
Devikā – Yudhishṭhira
Devī Māhātmya – Purāṇas
Devīpātan – animal sacrifice, Satī
Devī-sūkta – Brahmā
dhairya – asceticism
dhaivata – music
dhāman – paradise
dhamanī – anatomy
dhamar – singing
Dhammapada – Buddhist scriptures
dhammilla – head
Dhanadeva – nāgarī
Dhanaka – Haihaya
Dhana Nanda – Nanda
Dhanañjaya – festivals, theatre
dhanañjāya – wind
Dhaṇḍuka – Solaṅki
Dhaṅga – Chandella
ḍhāngar – Marāṭha
Dhannā – Rāmānanda
dhanurveda – archery
dhanus – archery, weights and measures
Dhanushkoṭi – Rāma
DHANVANTARI
Dhanyakaḍa – Āndhra
Dhanyakaṭaka – Āndhra
Dhār (or Dhārā) – Paramāra
Dharamnāth – Nātha
dharamśāla – Dravidian, Jainism
dharaṇa – weights and measures
dhāraṇā – meditation, perception
dhāraṇī – mantra
Dharaṇī – Paraśurāma
Dharanikoṭa – Āndhra
DHARMA
Dharma – tīrthaṅkara
Dharma – Nātha
dharma (space) – Jainism
Dharma-chakra-pravartana – Buddha
dharma-chakrāsana – āsana
Dharmajñā – Sītā
dharma-kāya – Mahāyāna
Dharmakīrtti – philosophy

dharma-megha – bodhisattva
Dharmapāla – Pāla
Dharma-parīksha – Kanarese
Dharmarāja – Yama
Dharma-ratna – law
dharma-śāstra – ritual canon
dharma-sūtra – ritual canon
Dharma-vyādha – lifelihood
Dharmottara – philosophy
Dhārshṭaka – Vaivasvata
dhataki – plant world
Dhātṛi – Aditi
dhātu – bodily substances
dhātu – metals
dhātu (relics) – stūpa
dhatūrā – thug
dhātvāgni – bodily substances
Dhauli – Orissa
Dhaumya – Uddālaka
dhauti – purification
Dhava – Gaṅgā
dhāvana – baths
Dheḍ – pañchama
Dhenuka – Balarāma
Dhenukaka – towns
Dhenukakati – Gandhāra
Ḍhillikā – Chāhamāna
Dhīmāna – Pāla, painting
Dhinodhar – Nātha
dhishṇya – altar
dhotī – dress
Dhoyī – Pāla
Dhṛishṭa – Vaivasvata
Dhṛishṭadyumna – Drupada
Dhṛishṭaketu – Śiśupāla
Dhṛitarāshṭra – Kaurava
Dhṛitarāshṭra – serpent worship
dhṛiti – asceticism
dhrūpad – singing
dhruvā – implements, music
DHRUVA
Dhruva – Rāshṭrakūṭa
Dhruvabhaṭa – Maitraka
Dhruvadevī – Chandragupta II
dhūma – āyurveda
Dhūmavarṇa – Yadu
dhūma-varti – drugs
dhūmkuria – Kolarian
Ḍhunḍhā – Hiraṇyāksha
Dhundhu – Purañjaya
dhūni – sādhu
dhūpa – weapons, worship
Dhūrjaṭi – Śiva
dhūrta – gambling
dhvaja – drama history, flags, temple, yūpa
dhvajamaha – pole ceremonies
dhvajāropaṇa – pole ceremonies
dhvaja-stambha – column
dhvani – sound, poetics
Dhvanyāloka – poetics
dhyāna – meditation
Dhyāna (sect) – Bodhidharma
dhyāna-mudrā – āsana
dhyānāsana – āsana
Dhyāni-Buddha – Mahāyāna
DIAGNOSIS
diamond – gems
dice – gambling
Dīdārganj – sculpture
Diddā – Kashmīr, kingship
didhishū – eligibility
DIET
Digambara – Jainism
dig-bandha – worship
Dig-darśan – Bengali
dig-gaja – direction
Dīghanikāya – Buddhist scriptures
Dignāga – philosophy
digvijaya – kingship
dik – category
dik-pāla – direction
dīkshā – initiation
Dīkshitar – music history
Dilāvārā – same as Dilwāra
Dilīpa – Raghu, Sagara
Dilwāra – Solaṅki
ḍima – theatre
Dimbhaka – Jarāsandha
dina-kārya – man of the world
dinār – numismatics
Ḍiṅgala – language
Diṅnāga – philosophy
Diodorus – Alexander
Diodorus Siculus – Mesopotamia
Diodotus – Bactrians
Diogenes – Kalyāṇa
Dion Chrysostom – Greeks, travel
Dionysius – Seleucids
Dionysopolis – towns
Dionysus – Nysa, Greeks, Music History
Dioscorides – towns
Dioscuri – Aśvin
dīpa – worship
dīpaka – rāga
Dipaṅkara – Jātaka
Dīpāvalī – Dīvālī
Dīpavaṁsa – Buddhist scriptures
DIRECTION
Dīrghaśravas – livelihood
Dīrghatamas – Utathya
Dīrghatapas – Utathya, Nyāya
Dīrghāyus – Mārkaṇḍeya
diseases – āyurveda
dishṭi – weights and measures
dishṭika – nāstika
DITI
div – God

Dīvālī – festivals
divasa – calendar, time
DIVINATION
divira – scripts
DIVODĀSA
DIVORCE
divya – aspersion, quality
divya-ratna – gems
Divyāvadāna – Aśoka, literary forms
Doāb – Purūravas
Dobe – hierophant
DOG
Dogrā – kshattriya
Dogrī – scripts
doha – Greek
dohā – Bengali, Hindi
dohada – plants
dohana – paramudrā
dola – swing
dola-yātrā – swing
ḍom – pañchama
ḍombī – strīpūjā
Don Juan – Udayana
Dorasamudra – Hoysala
Dorotheus, bishop – Christianity
dosha – humours
dosha – sin
doshabhogya – Lokāchārya
DOWRY
drama – theatre
DRAMA HISTORY
DRAMATURGY
dramma – numismatics
Drangiana – Parthians
DRAUPADĪ
Drāviḍa – brāhmin
DRAVIDIAN – language
dravya – substance
dravya-vidyā – medicine
DREAMS
DRESS
Dṛiḍhabala – Āyurveda history
DRINKS
dṛishṭānta – logic, Nyāya
dṛiśya – Bharata
droha – sin
droit du seigneur – polygamy, virginity
droṇa – weights and measures
DROṆA
droṇa-kalaśa – soma
Droṇasakha-Jātaka – human sacrifice
drowning – suicide
drughaṇa – weapons
DRUGS
Druhyu – Divodāsa, Yayāti
Druids – scripts
Drumālika – Kaṁsa
DRUPADA
druta – time
dryness – hot and cold
duāri-paṭuā – paṭṭa
dualism – advaita
Dubois, Abbé – compassion, prostitution, utsarga
Duḍḍā – Maitraka
Dugdha – cosmology
duhitṛi – strītantra
duḥkha – suffering
duḥkhānta – Pāśupata
Duḥsaha – rivers (under Narmadā)
Duḥśala – Kaurava
Duḥśalā – Jayadratha
Duḥśāsana – Śakuni
Dundu (Vasudeva) – Kṛishṇa
durgā – politics
Durgā – Kālī
Durgā Māhātmya – Purāṇa
Durlabhaka – widow
Durmukha – Kaurava
dūrohaṇa – yūpa
dūrvā – grasses
durvachana – sin
DURVĀSAS
DURYODHANA
dūshaṇa – seduction
Dūshaṇa – Śūrpanakhā
Dushyanta – Śakuntalā
DUTT (Madhusudan)
Dutt (Narendranāth) – Vivekānanda
dvādaśāha – soma
dvaidhībhāva – kingship
Dvaipāyana – Vyāsa
dvaita – advaita
dvaitādvaita – Nimbārka
dvamushya – sonship
dvāpara-yuga – aeon
Dvāpara – Nala
Dvārakā – Kṛishṇa, towns
Dvārakānāth – Kṛishṇa
dvārapāla – godlings
Dvārasamudra (same as Dorasamudra)
Dvārāvatī – Dvārakā
dvesha – sin
dvija – caste
dvija-ṛishi – ṛishi
dvish – bhakti, sin, antinomianism
Dvivedi – hierophant, Hindi
Dvivida – Balarāma
dvyaṇuka – atom
DYAUS
DYEING
dyūta – gambling

EAR
east – direction
Echidna – Nāga
eclipse – Rāhu

economics – politics
Edessa – Christianity
EDUCATION
egg, cosmic – Brahmā
EGYPT
ejaculation – vega
Ekachakra – Bhīma
ekāgratā – meditation
ekāha – soma
Ekalavya – Nishāda
Ekaliṅga – liṅga
Ekambara – Orissa
Ekambareśvara – Śiva
Ekambareśvara temple – Pallava
ekam evādvitīyam – sayings
EKANĀTHA
Ekāntika – Pañcharātra
eka-pada – aṅgika
Ekaparṇā – Umā
Ekapāṭalā – Umā
Ekuttara-nikāya – Buddhist scriptures
Ekavrātya – Vrātya
ekodishṭa – śrāddha
ektāra – sādhu
Elala (or Eḷara) – Chola
Elam – Maga, Vrātya
Elammā – godlings
Eleanor of Aquitaine – Matsyendra
elements – substance
ELEPHANT
Elephanta – cave temples
ELIGIBILITY
elixir vitae – alchemy
Ellamā – godling
Ellichpur (same as Achalapura)
ELLORĀ
Elutaccan – Malayālam
embalming – Ikshvāku
embryology – pregnancy
EMPATHY
Emūsha – Hiraṇyāksha
endogamy – elligibility
endurance – asceticism
Eos – Ushas
Ephthalite – Marāṭha
epicureanism – Chārvāka
EPIGRAPHY
EQUANIMITY
ERA
Eran – Huns, scripts
Eratosthenes – Alexander
Ernādan – pañchama
erogenous zones – strītantra
EROTICS
Errāpragada – Telugu
ESCHATOLOGY
ESPIONAGE
eternal – God
etheric double – body
ETHICS
Ethiopians – Greeks
Etruscans – Maga
Eṭṭuttogai – Tamil
ETYMOLOGY
Eucratides – Bactrians
Eudamus – Alexander
Eudoxus – Zoroastrianism
eunuch – androgyny
Euripides – drama history
EUROPEANS
Eusebius – perception
Euthydemia – Śaka, towns
Euthydemus I – Bactrians
evacuation – utsarga
evil – sin
evil eye – eye
excretion – utsarga
exegesis – etymology
exogamy – elligibility
EXTERIORISATION
EYE
Ezhuttachan – Malayālam

fable – kathā
fabrics – textiles
Fa-hien – Guptas, Mathurā, Pāṭaliputra
Faizābād (same as Fyzābād)
fakir – asceticism
Fakirmohan – Oriya
Faljur – Satī
fallacy – logic
family – community
Farīd – Sikh
Farīdkoṭ – Sikh
fasting – festivals, vows
fat – bodily substances
fatalism – nāstika
Feast of Tabernacles – architecture
feet (metrical) – prosody
feet (body) – foot
fellatio – perversions
Fergusson, James – Indology
feringhee – āyurveda
Ferishta – Iran
Feroz Khān – singing
FESTIVALS
ficus bengalensis – fig-tree
ficus glomerata – fig-tree
ficus indica – fig-tree
ficus religiosa – fig-tree
FIG TREE
fighting ascetics – sādhu
figures of speech – poetics
Firdausi – Iran
FIRE
Fire Sermon – Buddhism
fire-walking – pañchama (under Baḍaga)

Fitch, Ralph – ahiṁsā
fish-smelling woman – Satyavatī
FIVE DAILY SACRIFICES
'fixing' the eyes – meditation
FLAGS
Flavians – Romans
flesh – bodily substances
Flood – Vaivasvata
flying machines – mechanics
flying through the air – necrophilia
food – diet
FOOT
FORGERIES
Fort St. George – Vijayanagar
Fort William College – Bengali
Frazer, Sir James – kingship
free will – Yājñavalkya
friendship – compassion
funeral rites – obsequies
furniture – handicrafts
Fyzābād – towns

Gā – incest
Gabhastala – cosmology
Gabhastimat – Sūrya
gadā – weapons
Gadādhar – Vishṇu
Gādhi – Kuśika
Gādhī – Pāṭaliputra
Gādhija – Viśvāmitra
gadya – literary forms
Gāgabhaṭ – Śivājī
Gagrā (same as Gogrā)
Gāhaḍavāla – Kanauj
Gāhaṛwāra – Kanauj
Gahininīth – Nātha
gai – drama history
gairika – rivers
gajakaraṇi – purification
Gajasāhvāya – Śakuntalā
Gajasaṁhāra – Śiva
GĀLAVA
Galenic school – humours
gall – humours
Gama (same as da Gama)
gamadvāra – architecture
gamak – rāga
GAMBLING
GAMES
gāna – Bharata
gaṇa – community
Gaṇa – godlings
Gaṇadevatā – godlings
Gaṇadhara – Mahāvīra
gaṇakatā – divination
gāna-mārga – music history
Gaṇaparvata – godlings
Gaṇapati – Gaṇeśa
Gāṇapatya – Gaṇeśa
Gaṇḍa – Chandella
Gaṇḍakī – Ganges, Vṛindā
gandha – substance
gandha (perfume) – worship
Gandhamādana – mountains
gāndhāra – music
GANDHĀRA
gāndhārī – channels of the subtle body
Gāndhārī – Kaurava
GANDHARVA
gāndharva – marriage, singing
Gāndharva-veda – music history
Gandharvī – Lakshmaṇa
Gandha-vyūha – Buddhist scriptures
GĀNDHI, M.K.
Gāndinī – Śvaphalka
gāṇḍīva – archery
GAṆEŚA
Gaṇeśvara – Gaṇeśa
GAṄGĀ (goddess)
Gaṅgā – Ganges
Gaṅga (dynasty) – Orissa
Gaṅgādhara – Śiva
Gaṅgādvāra – Hardwār
Gaṅgaikoṇḍa – Chola
Gaṅgaikoṇḍa-cholapuram – Chola
Gaṅgā-pātra – brāhmin
Gaṅgāsāgara – pilgrimage
GANGES
Gaṅgeśa – philosophy
Gāṅgeya – Bhīshma
Gāṅgeyadeva – suicide
Gaṅgotri – Ganges
gaṇika – prostitution
gaṇita – crafts
gāñja – drugs
Gañjām – Hinterindia
gaṇyamāna – canons of proportion
garbha – dramaturgy
garbha – Gujarāti
garbhā-dhāna – pregnancy
garbha-dhāraṇa – pregnancy
garbha-gṛiha – temple
garbhāṅka – theatre
Garbhopanishad – pregnancy, Upanishad
Garbha Upanishad (same as Garbhopanishad)
Gardabhilla – Vikramāditya
gardens – horticulture
garga – soma
Garga (or Gārga) – Gārgya
Gārgī – Upanishads, Yājñavalkya
Gārgī-saṁhitā – astronomy, Greeks
GĀRGYA
gārhapatya – fire
garimā – siddhi
Garmukhteśvar – Gaṅgā (goddess)
GARUḌA

garva – sin
gat (same as gati)
gātha – dance, Malayālam
Gāthā – Prākṛit
Gāthin – Kuśika
gati – dance, singing
gātra-haridrā – marriage
gauḍa – poetics
Gauḍa – Bāleya, brāhmin
GAUḌAPĀDA
Gauḍavaho – Kanauj
Gaugamela – travel
Gauhāṭi – Kāmarūpa
Gaur – Pāla
gaura – weights and measures
Gauṛa – Bāleya
Gaurāṅga – Chaitanya
gaurī – strītantra
Gaurī – Śakti
Gaurīya – law
Gaurjarī – Prākṛit
Gautama (philosopher) – Nyāya
Gautama (ṛishi) – Gotama
Gautama (legalist) – ritual canon
Gautama (see also Gotama)
Gautama Buddha – Buddha
Gautama Hāridrumata – Satyakāma
Gautameśa – liṅga
Gautamī – matriarchy
Gautamī Balaśrī – Āndhra
Gautamīputra – Vākāṭaka, Āndhra
Gautamīputra Sātakarṇi – Āndhra
Gavalgaṇa – Kaurava
GAVĀMAYANA
gavyūti – weights and measures
GAYA (town)
Gaya (asura) – Śiva
gāyan – singing
gāyatrī – prosody
GĀYATRĪ
Gāyatrī-mantra – Gāyatrī
Gaya-wāl – brāhmin
Gebir – Muslims
gehapati – kingship
Gehlot – Guhila
gejjai – dance
GEMS
GENDER
GEOGRAPHY
geometry – mathematics
gesture – aṅgika
Ghālib – Hindi
ghana-pāṭha – reciting
ghaṇṭika – chakra
Ghaṇṭiku – godlings
Ghārpuri – cave temple
gharshaṇa – breath control
ghāṭ – baths
ghaṭa – time, weights and measures
Ghaṭakarpara – Vikramāditya
ghaṭīkā – time
Ghaṭotkacha – Bhīma
ghaṭṭa – baths
ghazal – singing
ghee (same as ghṛita)
Gheraṇḍa – yoga
Gheraṇḍa-saṁhitā – yoga
Ghīasuddin Taghlaq – kāmaśāstra
Ghora Āṅgirasa – Aṅgirasa
Ghori dynasty – Ujjain
Ghoshā – Veda
Ghosuṇḍi – nāgarī
Ghoṭakamukha – kāmaśāstra
ghrāṇa – senses
Ghṛisheśa (or Ghṛisheśvara) – liṅga, Śiva
ghṛita – sacrifice
Ghṛitāchī – apsarā
Ghushmeśvar – liṅga
Gibbon, Edward – barbarian, Muslim
Gilchrist, John – Hindi
Giridhāri – Mīrābāī
Girijā – Śakti
Girīśa – Śiva
Girivraja – Kekaya, Magadha
girls – strītantra
Girnār – epigraphy, mountains
gītā – singing
Gītā – Bhagavadgītā
Gītāgovinda – Jayadeva
Gītāñjali – Tagore (R.)
gladiator – games
glass – handicrafts
goala – śūdra
Gobind Singh – Sikh
GOD
Godā (same as Godāvarī)
Godā – Āḷvār
godāna – education
Godāvarī – rivers
GODLINGS
Gods and demons, struggle between – Agastya, Durvāsas, Śukra
goghna – diet
gohambhā – weights and measures
Gogrā – rivers
gokarṇa – weights and measures
Gokarṇa – liṅga
Gokhale, Gopāl Kṛishṇa – Marāṭhi, Prārthanā Samāj
Gokula – Kṛishṇa
golaka – senses
Golden Bough – politics
Golden Chersonese – Hinterindia
Golkondā – Chālukya
Goloka – paradise
Gomaṭa – Ṛishabha
Gomaṭeśvara – Ṛishabha
Gomatī (same as Gūmtī)

gomeda – gem
Gomedaka – cosmology
Gommaṭa – Ṛishabha
go-mūtra – cow
Gonada (same as Gonanda)
Gonanda (Kashmīr)
Gonardīya – Kāmaśāstra, Patañjali
Gond (or Goṇḍ) – Kolarian, language
Goṇḍā – Patañjali
Gondophernes – Christianity, Parthians
goṇī – weights and measures
Goṇikā – Patañjali
Goṇikāputra – kāmaśāstra, Patañjali
gopā – espionage, politics
Gopa – śūdra
Gopachandra – Bāleya
gopada – cow
gopāda – weights and measures
Gopāla – Kṛishṇa
Gopālkṛishṇa – Oriya
Gopatha – Brāhmaṇa
GOPĪ
Gopīchand – Nātha
gopikā – gopī
go-prachāra – cow
gopuram – temple
Gorā – Nāmdev, Tagore (R.)
GORAKHNĀTH
Goraksha-śataka – Gorakhnāth
gorochanā – cow
gosāīṁ – Vallabha
Gośāla – Ājīvika
gośālā – Ājīvika
gosava – incest
goshṭhī – theatre
gośiras – weapons
gosvāmi (or gosvāmin) – Chaitanya, hierophant, Vallabha
GOTAMA
Gotama (philosopher) – (same as Gautama)
Gotamī – Buddha
Gothic – Ādibhāsha
gotra – community
gotra-kāra – community
Govardhana – Kṛishṇa
Govardhanadhara – Kṛishṇa
Govardhanrām – Gujarāti
Govinda – Kṛishṇa
Govindapāda – Śaṅkara
graha – calendar, rāga, occultism
Graharāja – Sūrya
Grāharipu – Ābhīra
grāma – community, music
grāmadevatā – godlings
grāmaṇī – community, royal consecration
GRAMMAR
grantha – writing
Grantha – scripts
granthi – kuṇḍalinī
GRASSES
grāvan – soma
grāvastut – hierophant
Great Bear – Atri, consummation
Great Mother – godlings, Śakti
GREEKS
Greenwich – Ujjain
greetings – salutation
Gregory of Tours – Christianity
gṛiha – community
Gṛihakūṭa (mountains) – Buddhist scriptures
gṛihapati – community
gṛihastha, gṛihasthya – āśrama
gṛihin – ritual canon
gṛihya – community, ritual canon
gṛihya-sūtra – ritual canon
grīshma – calendar
GṚITSAMADA
guda – chakra
Gudguddāpur – Khaṇḍoba
gūḍha – espionage
gūḍhaja – sonship
Gudnaphar – Christianity
Gūgā – Nātha
guhā – education
Guha – Kārttikeya, Nishāda
GUHILA
Guhilot – Guhila
guhyād-guhyam – secrecy
Guhyaka – Kubera
Guhya-samāja – tantrism
Gujar – Hun
Gujarāt – Hun, towns
GUJARĀTI – scripts
gulma – army
gulpha – chakra
gumphā – cave temples
Gūmtī – Ganges
guṇa – quality
GUṆĀḌHYA
guṇāguṇa – ethics
guñjā – numismatics, weights and measures
Guntupalle – cave temples
GUPTA
Gupta era – era
Gupta script – script
Gurjara – Hun, Pratihāra
Gurmukhī – scripts
GURU
guru – time
Guru Granth – Sikh
guru-kula – education
guru-talpa-gamana – sin
guvāka – betel
Gwālior – Marāṭha

Gyāni – Sikh
gymnosophists – nudity
gynaecology – strītantra

Hadda – Gandhāra
Hāḍī – Nātha
HAIHAYA
Haimavatī – Umā
hair – head
Hakka – Vijayanagar
hala – weapons
HĀLA
halāhala – poison
Hālāhalā – Ājīvika
Halebīd – Hoysala
Hāli – Hindi
hallīśa – theatre
hallucination – knowledge
Halmidi stone – Kanarese
Hamlet – theatre
Hammīra – Chāhamāna, rāga
halo – head
Hampi – Vijayanagar
Haṁsa (king) – Jarāsandha
Haṁsa (caste) – caste
haṁsa – birds, hierophant (under parama-haṁsa)
HAND
HANDICRAFTS
HANUMĀN
haoma – soma
Hara – Śiva
Harappā – Indus Valley
Harasiddhī – Śakti
hārda – love
HARDWĀR
HAREM
Har-gobind – Sikh
Hari – Vishṇu
Haridās – Hindi, Vaishṇavism
Haridās – suspended animation
Harigovind – Jayadeva
Harihara – androgyny
harijan – pañchama
Harikela – Bāleya
hariṇī – strītantra
HARIŚCHANDRA
Hariśchandra – Hindi
Harisheṇa – epigraphy
Harisiṁha – law
Hārīta – Āyurveda History
harītaka – plants
Hāritī – godlings
Harivaṁśa – Mahābhārata
Harkṛishaṇ – Sikh
harmikā – stūpa
Har-rāī – Sikh
HARSHA
Harsha of Kashmīr – Kalhaṇa
Harsha script – nāgarī, script
Harsha-charita – Bāṇa
Harsiddhi – Satī
hartāl – Gāndhi
Haryaṅka – Magadha
Haryaśva – Gālava, Purañjaya
hāsa – empathy
hashish – drugs
hasta – hand, weights and measures
hasta-mudrā – mudrā
hastī – weights and measures
hasti-jihvā – channels of the subtle body
Hastin – Bharata
Hastināpura – Bharata, Kauravas
hastinī – strītantra
Hastyāyurveda – elephant
hāsya – empathy, worship
Hāṭaka – cosmology
Hāṭakeśvara – Śiva
haṭha-yoga – yoga
Haṭha-yoga – Gorakhnāth
Haṭha-yoga Pradīpikā – yoga
Hāthigumphā – cave temples, Kaliṅga
Hathor – cow
hatred – antinomianism
havana – worship
havir-dhāna – altar
havir-yajña – sacrifice
havis – sacrifice
Havishmat – ancestors
Haya – asura
Haya-grīva – godlings, Vaivasvata
Haya-śiras – Aurva
Haya-śīrsha – Aurva
HEAD
head-hunting – Austric
heat – hot and cold
heaven – paradise
Hecateus of Miletus – Greeks, occultism
hedonism – antinomianism, nāstika
Helen of Troy – Rāmāyaṇa
Heliodorus – column
Heliogabalus – Romans
heliolithic – Nāga
HELL
HEMACHANDRA
Hemāḍa-pantī – Hemādri
Hemādri – paradise
HEMĀDRI
Hemakūṭa – mountains
Hemamālā – Yama
hemanta – calendar
hemp – drugs
henotheism – God
Hephaestion – Alexander
Heracles (same as Hercules)
Hercules – Greeks, Mathurā, Nāga, Nysa, Pāṇḍya

heredity – pregnancy
heresy – Hinduism, nāstika
Hermaeus – Bactrian, Kushān
hermaphrodite – androgyny
Hero of Alexandria – mechanics
Herodotus – Greeks, Nāga
Heruka – tantrism
Hesydrus – rivers (under Sutlej)
hetu – logic, syllogism
hetvābhāsa – logic
Hevajra – tantrism
Hezekiah – Jews
Hiḍimba – Bhīma
Hiḍimbā – Bhīma
Hieratic – numerals
HIEROPHANT
Hillola – rāga
Hill Tribes – Pañchama
Himālaya – mountains
Himavat – Umā
hiṁsā – ahiṁsā
hīnaka – prāṇayāma
Hīnayāna – Buddhist history
hindāsa – numerals
HINDI
Hindki – language (under Lahndā)
Hindola – rāga, swing
HINDUISM
Hindvi – language (under Western Hindi)
hiṅg – āyurveda history
Hinglāj – Satī
HINTERINDIA
Hippalus – trade
Hipparchus – Varāhamihira
Hippocratic oath – Āyurveda history, physician
Hīrā – Lakshmī
Hiram of Tyre – trade
Hiraṇya-garbha – cosmology
Hiraṇya-kaśipu – Hiraṇyāksha
HIRAṆYĀKSHA
Hiraṇyapura – Arjuna
Hiraṇyaretas – Śiva
Hiraṇyavaha – rivers (under Son)
Hiraṇya-varman – Śikhaṇḍin
Hissarlik – wheel
HISTORIOGRAPHY
HISTORY
Hitopadeśa – kathā
Hittites – Proto-Aryan
Hiuen-Tsang – Ajantā, Ayodhyā, Chālukya, education, Harsha, human-sacrifice, Orissa, Pallava, Pāṇḍya, strīrājya, thug, warfare
hlādinī – Chaitanya
Ho – Kolarian
Hoernle, Rudolf – Āyurveda history
Holeya – caste
Holi – festivals
holidays – festivals
Holikā – Hiraṇyāksha
Holkar – Marāṭha
Holtzmann – Pāṇḍavas
homa – pūjā
Homer – Greeks, wheel, Vedic
homosexuality – perversions
hookāh – drugs
hook-swinging – swing
horā – divination
Horā-śāstra – Varāhamihira, divination
hori – singing
horror vacui – aesthetics
HORSE
HORSE SACRIFICE
HORTICULTURE
Hōryūji – Ajantā
hospitals – ahiṁsā
HOT AND COLD
hotṛi – hierophant
howdah – elephant
HOYSALA (or Hoyśāḷa)
hrāda – sound
hṛidaya – chakra
Hṛidika – Satrājita
Hṛishīkeśa – Hardwār, Vishṇu
Hsuan-Tsang (same as Hiuen-Tsang)
hti – stūpa
Huligammā – godlings
Hultzsch, Dr. – Kanarese
HUMAN SACRIFICE
Humāyūn – history
HUMOURS
Hūna – Huns
HUNS
Hunter, Sir William – Āndhra, rivers (under Mahānadi), Tagore (R.)
Hussain Shāh Sharqī – singing
huta – sacrifice
hutāśani – festivals
Huvishka – Kushān
Hydaspes (same as Jhelum)
Hyderābād – Ellorā
Hydraotes or Hyarotes – rivers (under Rāvi)
Hyphasis (same as Beas)

Iamboulos – philosophy
Ibn Batuta – Kerala, rope-trick, suttee
Ibn Sīnā (same as Avicenna)
Ibrāhīm Lodī – geography
ichchhā – sin
iḍā – channels of the subtle body
iḍā – sacrifice
Iḍa (or Iḍā) – Sudyumna
Iḍāviḍā – Pulastya

IDOLATRY
īhā – perception
īhāmṛiga – animals, theatre
ikat – dyeing
Ikhtiār Khilji – Muslims, Pāla
Ikshu – cosmology, Ikshvāku
IKSHVĀKU
Ila (or Ilā) – Sudyumna
ILAṄGŌ (or Ilaṅgō-aḍigaḷ)
Ilavan – coconut
Ilāviḍā – Pulastya
Ilāvṛita – paradise
Iliad – Rāmāyaṇa
illatum – sonship
illusion – knowledge
Iltutmish – liṅga, Ujjain
Ilūsha – Mahīdāsa
Ilvala – Agastya
image – idolatry
imitation – art
immortality – dreams, physical culture
IMPLEMENTS
impregnation – pregnancy
inauguration – aspersion
INCEST
Indian Mirror – Sen
Indirā – Lakshmī
Indo-Aryan – language
Indo-Bactrian – Kharoshṭhī
Indo-Chinese – language
Indo-European – Proto-Aryan
Indo-Germanic – Proto-Aryan
INDOLOGY
Indore – Marāṭha
INDRA
Indrabhūti – Matsyendra
Indra-dhvaja-pūjā – pole ceremonies
Indradyumna – Jagannātha
Indra-jāla – weapons
Indrajit – Rāvaṇa
Indra-mahotsava – pole ceremonies
Indrāṇī – Indra
Indraprastha – Yudhishṭhira
Indrasena – Nala
indriya – senses
Indumatī – Raghu
Indus – rivers
INDUS VALLEY
infanticide – promiscuity, women
INITIATION
ink – writing
inns – travel
inscriptions – epigraphy
interdining – caste
intermarriage – caste
invisibility – harem
Iomousa – towns
Iqbāl – Hindi
irā – rivers (under Rāvi)
IRAN – Ajantā, numismatics, cave temples, stūpa
irāvat – elephant
Irāvat – Arjuna
Irāvatī – rivers (under Rāvi)
Iron Pillar – metals
īrsha – sin
Īśa – God, Upanishads
Īśāna – Śiva
ish – sacrifice
ishṭa-devatā – God
ishṭa-liṅga – Liṅgāyat
ishṭi – sacrifice
ishu – archery
īśitva – siddhi
Islam – Vivekānanda, Muslim
Īśvara – God
Īśvarakṛishṇa – philosophy
Īśvara-pratyaksha – perception
Itarā – Mahīdāsa
itihāsa – historiography, scriptures
I-tsing – Nālandā
Izhavan – coconut

Jabālā (or Jābāla) – Satyakāma, Jews
Jābāla – Upanishads
Jābāli – Javāli
jādu-paṭuā – paṭṭa
Jagaddala – education
Jagaddeva – divination
Jagaddhātṛi – Śakti
Jagadgaurī – serpent worship
Jaganmātā (or Jaganmātṛi) – Śakti
jaganmohan – Black Pagoda
JAGANNĀTHA
Jagannāth-dās – Oriya
jāgaraṇa – festivals
jagatī – Hoysala, prosody
jaghana – strītantra
Jagjīvandās – Hindi
jāgrat – dreams
Jahāngīr – art, Guhila, Sikh
Jahnu – Sagara
Jaichand – Kanauj
Jaidev (same as Jayadeva)
Jaimini – Mīmāṁsā
Jaimini Bhārata – Kanarese
Jaiminīya – Sāma-veda
Jaiminīya Brāhmaṇa – Upanishad
JAINISM
Jaipur – Rājputs (under Kachhwāha), Virāṭa
Jaisal – Rājputs (under Bhatti)
Jaisalmer – Rājputs (under Bhatti)
Jaisingh, Rāja – Śivājī
Jaisingh II – astronomy, Muslim, Ujjain

Jaisvāl – vaiśya
Jaitrapāl – Marāṭhi
Jājali – caste
Jajāti – Orissa
Jājnagar (or Jājpur) – Orissa
Jakanāchārya – Hoysala
Jala – cosmology
Jaladhara – Vṛindā
Jalālābād – Gandhāra
Jālandhar – Nātha
jālandhara – bandha
Jālandhara (or Jullunder) – Virāṭa, Satī
Jalandhijā – Lakshmī
jalāśayi – asceticism
jalpa – logic
JAMADAGNI
jāmadagnya – weapons
Jāmbavat – Satrājita
Jāmbavatī – Satrājita
Jambha – Kṛishṇa
Jambhala-datta – Somadeva
Jambu (Jambu-dvīpa) – paradise
Jambukeśvara – Pāṇḍya
jāmdānī – textiles
jamna – rivers
jana – body, community
Janābāī – Nāmdev
Jana Gana Mana – Tagore (R.)
JANAKA
Janakapura – Janaka
Jānakī-haraṇa – kāvya
Janamejaya – Arjuna, Yayāti
janāntikā – mantra
janapada – community
Jānapadī – Gotama
janapati – community
Janārdana – God, Vishṇu
janar-loka – paradise
Janasthāna – Satī
Jandial – Gandhāra
jaṅgama – animals, Liṅgāyat
janeo – thread ceremonies
jānu – chakra
japa – repetition
Japjī – Sikh
jāra – adultery
Jarā – Jarāsandha
Jaras – Śāmba
JARĀSANDHA
Jarasasta – Zoroastrianism
JARATKĀRU – rahasya
jarāyuja – animals
Jaritā – Jaratkāru
Jaritāri – Jaratkāru
jāt – caste
Jāt – kshattriya
Jāta – Haihaya
jaṭā – head
jātaka – divination
JĀTAKA
jātakarman – pregnancy
jāṭa-pāṭha – reciting
Jatavarman – Pāṇḍya
Jaṭāyu – Garuḍa
jāti – logic, music
Jaṭilā – matriarchy
jātismara – siddhi
jāti-svaram – Bharata nāṭyam
jauhar – suttee
JAVĀLI
Jaya – asura
Jayachandra – Kanauj
JAYADEVA
Jayadeva – Kāmaśāstra
JAYADRATHA
jāyājīva – livelihood
Jaya-maṅgalā – kāmaśāstra
Jayanī – Śukra
Jayanta and Jayantī – Indra
Jayantī – Śukra
Jayāpīḍa – kāmaśāstra, Kashmīr
JAYARĀŚI
Jayasi – Hindi
Jejāka – Chandella
Jerome, St. – Christianity
Jetavana – Buddha
jewels – gems
JEWS
Jhālī – Mīrābāī
jhasha (fish) – Pradyumna
Jhelum (or Jhelam) – rivers
Jhūlana-yātrā – swing
jihvā – implements, senses
jihvāgra – chakra
jihvamūla – chakra
jijñāsā – logic, syllogism
Jīmūta – Virāṭa
Jīmūta-vāhana – law
jina – tīrthaṅkara
Jind – Sikh
jīva – soul, Jainism
Jīvaka – Āyurveda history
jīvan-mukti – trance
jīvātman – body, soul
jīvikā – livelihood
jñāna – knowledge
JÑĀNADEVA
jñāna-kāṇḍa – Veda
jñāna-mārga – mārga
Jñāna-siddhi – Matsyendra
jñānendriya – senses
Jñāneśvarī – Jñānadeva
Jñātṛika – Mahāvīra
Jodhpur – Rājputs (under Rāthor)
Jogā – Nāmdev
jogi – hierophant, sādhu
johar (same as jauhar)
Johiyā – Kushān

John, Metropolitan of India – Christianity
JOINT FAMILY
Jones, Sir William – Indology
Jouveau-Dubreuil, Gabriel – architecture
jubilee – Jew
juggernaut – Jagannātha
jugupsā – empathy
juhū – implements
Jujhoti – Chandella
Julian – Romans
Jullunder – Jālandhara
Jumnā (same as Jamnā)
Junagaḍh – towns, Solaṅki
Jungle Tribes – Pañchama
Junnar – cave temples
jus primae noctis – virginity
Justin (Greek writer) – Bactrians
Justinian – diet
Jvālāmukhī (or Jvālāpur) – Satī
jyā – archery
jyāhroḍa – archery, sex, Vrātya
jyeshṭha – hand
Jyeshṭhā – godlings
jyoti – kuṇḍalinī
jyotiḥ-shṭoma – soma
Jyotirīśa – kāmaśāstra
jyotir-liṅga – liṅga
jyotisha – astronomy

Ka – Prajāpati
Kabandha – rākshasa
kabarī – head
KABĪR
Kacha – Śukra
Kachāri – human sacrifice
kachha (or kachhā) – dress, Sikh
kachchhapa – mudrā
Kachchhapagāta – same as Kachhwāha
Kachhwāha – Rājputs
Kadali – strīrājya
Kadamba – Āndhra
Kādambarī – Bāṇa
Kādar – pañchama
Kadavā – child marriage
Kadphises I & II – Kushān
Kādraveya – serpent worship
Kadrū – serpent worship
Kadvat – Prajāpati
kafni – sādhu
Kahoḍa – Uddālaka
Kaikasī – Pulastya
Kaikeya – Kekaya
Kaikeyī – Kekaya
Kailāsa – mountains
Kailāsanātha – Ellorā, Pallava
Kaiṅkilā – Āndhra
Kait – Kāyastha
Kaiṭabha – asura
Kaithī – scripts
kaivalin – trance
kaivalya – trance
Kakandi – trade
Kākatīya – Chālukya
Kākavarṇa – Magadha
kākiṇī – numismatics, weights and measures
kakka – Sikh
kākola – hell
kaksha – chakra
Kakshīvat – Utathya
Kakudmatī – Pradyumna
Kakutstha – Purañjaya
kalā – bodily substances, handicrafts, time
kāla – time
Kāla – Yama, Śiva
kāla-chakra – microcosm, tantrism, China
Kālachakrayāna – tantrism
Kalachuri – Ābhīra, Chālukya
Kalachuri era – era
Kālaḍī – Śaṅkara
Kālahasti – liṅga
Kālakā – asura, Kaśyapa
Kālakañja (or Kālakeya) – asura, Kaśyapa
kalama – writing
Kālāma (same as Ālāra)
Kālamukha – Pāśupata
Kālanemi – asura
Kālañjar – Chandella
Kalanos – Kalyāṇa
Kalāpa – Agnivarṇa
kālapāni – travel
Kālapurusha – Yama
kalaśa – columns, weights and measures
kalāsam – Kathākali
Kālāśoka – Magadha
kāla-sūtra – Yama
Kālayavana – Gārgya
KALHAṆA
Kali (spirit of Kali yuga) – Nala
KĀLĪ
Kālīchī – Yama
KĀLIDĀSA – Māgha
Kālīghāṭ – Kālī, Satī
Kālika – Buddha
Kālikā-Purāṇa – human sacrifice
Kalīlah va Dimnah – Pañchatantra
Kāliñjar (same as Kālañjar)
Kalinda – rivers (under Jamnā)
Kālindī (same as Jamnā)
KALIṄGA
kalinos – warfare
Kāliya – serpent worship

kali-yuga – aeon
KALKI
Kalla – Pallava
Kāllan (or Kāllar) – cow
Kallaṭabhaṭṭa – philosophy
KALMĀSHAPĀDA
kalpa – aeon
kalpa – ritual canon
kalpaṇā – psychology
kalpa-vṛiksha (or kalpa-druma, kalpa-taru, kalpa-vallī) – plants
Kalpi – Vyāsa
Kalvār – Pallava
KALYĀṆA
Kalyāṇa – Bilhaṇa, Chālukya, trade
Kalyāṇamalla – kāmaśāstra
kalyāṇa-maṇḍapa – temple
Kalyāṇī – Chālukya, trade, Bilhaṇa
kāma – ethics, love
KĀMA
kāma-avasāyitva – siddhi
KĀMADHENU
Kāmagiri – Kāmarūpa
Kāmākshī – Śakti
Kāmākshī temple – Pallava
Kāmākshyā – Kāmarūpa
Kāmākhyā – Kāmarūpa
kamala – plants
Kāmaloka – serpent worship
Kāmamañjarī – Marīchi
Kāmandaka – politics
kamaṇḍalu – sādhu
kāmāṅka – erotics
kāmarāgo – sin
KĀMARŪPA
kāmarūpaka – weapons
KĀMAŚĀSTRA
Kāmasūtra – kāmaśāstra
Kāmavajrayāna – tantrism
Kambala – serpent worship
Kambaṇ – Tamil
KĀMBOJA – mahājanapada
kambustha – animals
Kameśvari – Śakti
Kammālan – caste
Kāmpilya – Drupada
Kāmrūp (same as Kāmarūpa)
kaṁsa – weights and measures
KAṀSA
kāmya – worship
Kaṁyā – Svāyaṁbhuva
Kāmyaka – Yudhishṭhira
kāmyeshṭi – sacrifice
Kaṇabhaksha (or Kaṇabhuj) – Vaiśeshika
Kaṇāda – Vaiśeshika
Kanara – Āndhra
KANARESE
KANAUJ
Kāñchi (or Kāñchipuram) – Pallava
kañchuka – māyā
kañchuki – dress
kañchukin – dramaturgy
kāṇḍa – literary forms, archery, weights and measures
Kandahār – Gandhāra
kāṇḍaṛishi – hierophant
kandarpa – love
kandaśāka – plants
kandasāra – paradise
kandayoni – chakra
Kandh – Kolarian
kāṇḍikā – literary forms
KAṆḌU
kaṅgā – Sikh
Kāṅgṛā – painting
Kanhaiya – Kṛishṇa
Kānheri – cave temples, trade
kanikā – hand
Kaṇika – politics, warfare
Kānīna – sonship
Kānipā – Kāpālika
KANISHKA
Kāṅkāyana – āyurveda history
Kannaḍa – Kanarese
Kaṇṇagi – Ilaṅgō
Kānphaṭa yogi – Gorakhnāth
kantha – towns
kānthā – textiles
kaṇṭha – chakra
kaṇṭhaḍ – sādhu
Kaṇṭhaka – Buddha
kaṇṭhi-badala – marriage
kaṇṭhika – mantra
kānti – poetics
Kāntipura – Nāga
Kanuri – Austric
KAṆVA (ṛishi)
Kāṇva (ṛishi line) – Brāhmaṇa, Kaṇva
Kāṇva (dynasty) – Magadha
kanyā – strītantra
kanyā-dāna – marriage
Kanyākubja – brāhmin, Kanauj, Kuśika, Vaivasvata
Kanyā-kumāri – Śakti, liṅga (under Suchīndram)
kanyā-saṁprayuktaka – kāmaśāstra
kapāla-bhāti – breath control, purification
Kāpāleśvar – Nāsik
KĀPĀLIKA
Kapālin – Rudra
kaparda – head
Kapardin – Pūshan
kapha – humours
Kapila – Sāṁkhya
Kapila – Sagara
KAPILAR

Kapilavastu
Kapilendra – Orissa
Kāpiśa – Śaka
Kapiśā – Piśācha
Kāpiśeya – Piśācha
Kapishṭhala – Yajur-veda
kapittha – plants
Kāpu – nudity
Kapūrthala – Sikh
Kara – Orissa
kaṛā – Sikh, sādhu
Karālī – Śakti
Kaṛā-liṅga – sādhu
Karambhād – Pūshan
karaṇa – calendar, dance
kāraṇa – Pāśupata
kāraṇa-śarīra – body
kāranavan – Nāir
karaṇḍa – head
Kāraskara – miscegenation
Karaṭaka and Damanaka – kathā
Kardama – godlings, Svāyaṁbhuva
Kardamaka – Śaka
Kareṇumatī – Pāṇḍava
Karhāḍa – human sacrifices
kārikā – literary forms, sayings
Karīshiṇī – godlings
Kārkala – Ṛishabha
Karkoṭa – Kashmīr
Karkoṭaka – serpent worship
Kārle (or Kārlī) – cave temple
KARMA
karma-gṛiha – alchemy
karma-kāṇḍa – Veda
karma-śraya – body
karma-yoga – mārga, yoga
karmendriya – senses
karṇa – ear
KARṆA
Karṇāl – Karṇa
Karṇasundarī – Bilhaṇa
Karṇāṭa – Brāhmin
Karṇāṭaka – Kanarese
Karṇāṭaka emperor – Vijayanagar
karṇa-tantra – secrecy
karṇa-vedha – ear
Karṇī – Kaṁsa
karṇika – mantra
Karpūra-mañjarī – drama history
karsha – numismatics, weights and measures
kārshapāṇa – numismatics
Kārtavīrya – Haihaya
kartṛi – God, joint family
kartṛikā – weapons
KĀRTTIKEYA
karuṇā – compassion
Karūsha – Vaivasvata
kārya – Pāśupata
Kāsha – Kashmīr
KASHMĪR
Kashmīri – language
Kashmīr Śaivism – philosophy, Vasugupta
kāshṭhā – time
Kāśī – Banāras
Kaśipu – Kaśyapa, Haihayas
Kāśīrāja – Śvaphalka, Utathya
Kāśīrām – Bengali
Kassapa (disciple of Buddha) – same as Kāśyapa
Kassites – Aryans, Daksha, Diti, Mesopotamia, Sūrya
kaśu (berry) – numismatics
KAŚYAPA (ṛishi)
Kāśyapa (disciple of Buddha) – Bodhidharma, Buddha
Kāśyapa (physician) – Āyurveda history
Kaṭachuri – Ābhīra
kaṭaka – yūpa
KATHĀ
Kaṭha – Upanishad
KATHAK
KATHĀKALI
Kathā-sarit-sāgara – Somadeva
Kathia – suttee
Kāṭhiāwār – Maitraka
KĀTYĀYANA
Kātyāyanī – Yājñavalkya
Kaula – tantrism
kaulika – tantrism
Kaulopanishad – tantrism
Kaumāra – Kārttikeya
kaumāra-bhṛitya – āyurveda
Kaumodakī – weapons
Kaumudī-mahotsava – Guptas
Kauṇḍinya – grammar, Hinterindia, Pāṭaliputra
kaupīna – thread ceremonies
KAURAVA
Kauravya – Arjuna
Kaurusha – Pāśupata
Kausalyā – Raghu
Kauśāmba – Kuśika
Kauśāmbī – mahājanapada, Udayana
kausheya – textiles
Kaushītaki (same as Kauśītaki)
Kauśika – rāga
Kauśika – Kuśika, hell
kauśikī – channels of the subtle body
Kauśikī – Satī, Śakti
Kauśītaka – Kuśika
Kauśītaki – Agastya, Kuśika
Kauśītaki – Āraṇyaka, Brāhmaṇa, Upanishad
kaustubha – gems
Kauthuma – Sāma-veda
KAUṬILYA

Kautsa – Raghu, etymology
kautuka – marriage
Kauverī – Kubera
kavacha – sādhu, mantra
kāvaḍi – Kārttikeya
kāvanmaram – plants
Kavasha – Mahīdāsa
Kāverī – rivers
Kāveripaṭṭanam – Chola, trade
kavi – poetics
Kavi – Śukra
Kavirāja-mārga – Kanarese
Kaviśekhara – kāmaśāstra
KĀVYA
Kāvyādarśa – Daṇḍin
Kāvyālaṁkāra – poetics
Kāvya-prakāśa – poetics
kāvya-śāstra – poetics
kāya – hand
kāya-sādhanā – physical culture
KĀYASTHA
Kāyavya – caste
kāyotsarga – āsana
Kedār (or Kedārnāth or Kedāreśa) – liṅga
Kedāra – rāga
KEKAYA
Ken – rivers (under Jamnā)
Kena – Upanishad
Kenopanishad – Upanishad
KERALA (or Keraḷa)
keśa – Sikh
Keśakambalin – Ajita
keśānta – education
Kesari – Hanumān
Keśāri – Orissa
Keśava – Vishṇu
Keśavdās – Hindi, strītantra
keśdāri – Sikh
Keśidhvaja – mārga
keśin – hierophant
Keśin (or Keśī) – asura, Mesopotamia
Keśinī – Pulastya, Sagara
Keteus – suttee
ketu – flags
Ketu – Rāghu
Ketumāla – geography
Ketumatī – Pulastya
kevala – Jainism, trance
keval advaita – Vallabha
kha – orifices of the body
khaḍāśrī – asceticism
khāḍava – music
khaddar (or khādi) – Gāndhi
khaḍga – weapons
khadira – plant world
Khajurāho – Chandella
khāki – dyeing
khalīna – warfare
Khālsa – Sikh
khaṇḍa – literary forms
Khaṇḍagiri – cave temple
Khaṇḍāriya Mahādeo – Chandella
Khāṇḍava (forest) – Agni, Jaratkāru, Yudhishṭhira
Khāṇḍava-prastha – Yudhishṭhira
Khaṇḍerao – Khaṇḍobā
Khāṇḍikya – mārga
KHAṆḌOBĀ
Khaṇḍojī – Kārttikeya
khānija – minerals
Khān Jahān Ali – Tagore (R.)
khappar – sādhu
Khara – Śūrpanakhā
Khāravela – Kaliṅga
khāri – weights and measures
Khaṛī-boli – Hindi
KHAROSHṬHĪ
kharpara – sādhu
Kharva – Kratu
Kharvar – Rājputs
Khaśā – Kaśyapa
Khāsi – language, matriarchy
khāṭā – Nāsik
khāta-paurusha – weights and measures
khattri – kāyastha
khaṭvāṅga – weapons
Khaṭvāṅga – Raghu
khayāl – singing
khecharī-mudrā – paramudrā
kheda – elephant
Khedbrahmā – Brahmā
khejṛa – Dādū
Kherwāri – language
kheṭa – weapons
Khijiṅga – Orissa
khila – Ṛig-veda
Khilji – Ujjain
Khilji (Alā-ud-dīn) – Chāhamāna, Chālukya, Guhila, Muslim, Paramāra, Solaṅki
Khilji (Bakhtiār) – Muslims
Khilji (Ikhtiār) – (same as Ikhtiār)
khilya – Kratu
Khond (or Khoṇḍ) – animal sacrifice, human sacrifice, Kolarian
Khuddaka-nikāya – Buddhist scriptures
Khusrau I – Vikramāditya
Khusrau II – Ajantā
khyāl – singing
Khyāti – Bhṛigu
khyāti – knowledge
Kīchaka – Virāṭa
Kīchaka (country) – Bhīma
Kīkata – Magadha
Kilakilā – Vākāṭaka
kili-pāṭṭu – Malayālam
kiṁnara – Kubera

kiṁpurusha – Kubera
Kindavila – Jayadeva
Kingsley, Charles – Gāndhi
KINGSHIP
kinnara (same as kiṁnara)
KIRĀTA
Kirāt-ārjunīya – Bhāravi
kirīṭa – hand
kirīṭin – Vishṇu
Kirmīra – Bhīma
kirpān – weapons
kīrtan – singing
Kīrtavarman – Chandella
Kīrtimān (or Kīrtivat) – Dhruva
Kīrtimukha – Śiva
Kishkindhyā – Bālin
kishku – weights and measures
kiśorī – strītantra
kiśorī-bhāja – strīpūjā, virginity
Kiśorikā – Gupta
Kiśorilāl – Kṛishṇa
kiss – erotics
Kistna – rivers
kitava – gambling
kitten hold – Lokāchārya
kleśa – suffering
KNOWLEDGE
Koch – antinomianism
Kodaga – kshattriya
Kodagu – language
koftgāri – handicrafts
Kohala – music history
Kohinoor – gem, Jagannātha
kohola – drinks
Koka (or Koka-paṇḍita) – kāmaśāstra
Kokila – Satī
KOL (or Kolarian) – language
kolam – designs
Kolami – language
Kolarian (same as Kol)
Koleḷuttu – scripts
Koli – śūdra
komala – music
Koṇa – Sūrya
Konārak – Black Pagoda
Kondāne – cave temples
Koṅgoda – Orissa
Koṅkaṇ – Kerala
Kophen – Nysa
Koraga – pañchama
Koran – Roy
Korava – pañchama
kordax – music history
Koṛkai (or Koḷkai) – Pāṇḍya
Koṛṛavai – Kārttikeya
kośa – body
kośa (treasury) – taxation
Kosala (or Kośala) – mahājanapada
Kośali – language
Kosha – etymology
koshṭha – anatomy
Kosi – Ganges
Koṭarī – Śakti
Koṭṭavi (or Koṭori) – godling
Kōvalaṇ – Ilaṅgō
kramaka – reciting
krama-pāṭha – reciting
kramela – warfare
KRATU
Krauncha – cosmology, Kārttikeya
Kravyād – Agni
kṛichchhra – vows
kṛikara – wind
kṛipā – compassion
Kṛipa – Gotama, longevity
kṛipāṇa – weapons
Kṛipī – Gotama
Kṛiśānu – Aryans
KṚISHṆA
Kṛishṇa (same as Kistna)
Kṛishṇa I – Rāshṭrakūṭa
Kṛishṇadās – Chaitanya
Kṛishṇadeva Rāya – Vijayanagar
Kṛishṇa-Dvaipāyana – Vyāsa
kṛishṇala – weights and measures
Kṛishṇa-miśra – drama history, Chandella
Kṛishṇānanda – Sārvabhauma
Kṛishṇa-paksha – calendar
Kṛishṇa-Rāya – Vijayanagar
Kṛishṇa-śarma – festivals
Kṛishṭa Purāṇa – Marāṭhi
kṛita – era, Ujjain
krītaka – sonship
Kṛitānta – Yama
Kṛitavarman – Kṛishṇa, Kurukshetra
Kṛitavīrya – Haihaya
kṛita-yuga – aeon
kṛitrima – sonship
kṛitrima-liṅga – olisboi
Kṛittikā – Kārttikeya
Kṛittivāsa – Bengali
Kṛityakā – godlings
kriyā – mārga, ritualism
krodha – sin
Krodha – Daksha
Krodhā (same as Krodhavaśā)
Krodhavaśā – Piśācha
krośa – weights and measures
Kshaharāta (or Ksharāta) – Śaka
kshāla – baths
kshamā – equanimity
Kshamā – ṛishi
kshaṇa – time
kshaṇika-liṅga – liṅga
kshānti – equanimity
Kshapaṇaka – Vikramāditya
Ksharāta – Śaka

kshātra – marriage
Kshatrapa – Śaka
kshatra-vidyā – kingship
kshatra-vṛiddha – Purūravas
kshattri – kāyastha
Kshattri – Bhīshma
KSHATTRIYA
Kshemendra – Kalhaṇa, kathā, kāmaśāstra
Kshemiśvara – Pratihāra
kshetra – pregnancy
kshetraja – sonship
kshetrapāla – godlings
Kshiprā – rivers (under Siprā)
Kshīra – cosmology
Kshīrābdhi – Lakshmī
Kshīrapāṇi – āyurveda history
Ktesias (same as Ctesias)
KUBERA
Kuberanāgā – Nāga
Kubjā – Kṛishṇa
Kuchnī – antinomianism
Kuchumāra – kāmaśāstra
kuḍava – weights and measures
Kuḍmala – hell
kudṛishṭi – eye
kuhū – channels of the subtle body
Kui – Kolarian
Kukkola (same as Koka)
Kukkura – dog
kukkuṭa – birds
Kukudmatī – Pradyumna
kula – community
kulapati – community
Kulārṇava Tantra – tantrism
Kulaśekhara – Āḷvār, Kerala, Mīnākshī
Kulika – serpent worship
Kulīn – polygamy
Kullar – cow
Kulottuṅga I – Chola
Kuluī – scripts
Kumāon – geography
Kumāra – Brahmā, Kārttikeya
Kumāradāsa – kāvya
Kumāra-devī – Guptas
Kumāragupta – Guptas
KUMĀRAJĪVA
Kumārapāla – Solaṅki
Kumāra-saṁbhava – Kālidāsa
Kumārasīra – pregnancy
kumārī – strītantra
KUMĀRILA (or Kumārila-bhaṭṭa)
kumārī-pūjā – strīpūjā
kumbha – nectar
kumbha – weights and measures
kumbhaka – breath control
KUMBHAKARṆA
Kumbhakonam – Art
KUMBHA-MELA
Kumbhāṇḍa – cosmology
Kumbhīnaśī – asura
Kumbi – caste, child-marriage
kumuda – plants
Kumuda – Sītā
Kumudvatī – Sītā
Kunchan-nambiār – Malayālam
kuñchi – weights and measures
kuṇḍa – sonship, altar
Kundalavana – Buddhist history
KUṆḌALINĪ
Kuṇi – virginity
Kuñjara – Agastya
Kunju Kurup – Kathākali
kunta – weapons
kuntala – head
Kunthu – tīrthaṅkara
Kuntī – Pāṇḍava, Śūra
Kuntibhoja – Śūra
Kūr – Nāga
Kuṛaḷ – Tiruvaḷḷuvar
Kurichchhan – caste
Kūrkū – Kolarian
Kūrma – nectar
kūrma – wind
Kūrmi – śūdra
Kuru – Bharata, mahājanapada
Kurukh – language
KURUKSHETRA
Kurumba – Pallava
Kurup – Nāir
Kuru-Pañchāla – Bharata
kuruvañji – Bharata-nāṭyam
kuruvinda – gems
kuśa – grasses
Kuśa – Sītā, Kuśika, cosmology
Kuśadhvaja – Janaka, Rāvaṇa
Kuśāmba – Kuśika
Kuśanabha – Vāyu
Kuśasthalī – Balarāma, Sītā
Kuśāvatī – Sītā
KUSHĀN
Kushāna (script) – scripts
Kushmāṇḍa – godling
KUŚIKA
Kusinagara (same as Kusināra)
Kusināra (or Kusinagara) – Buddha
Kusumadhvaja – Pāṭaliputra
Kusumapura – Pāṭaliputra
kūṭāgra – architecture
kūṭatā – logic
Kutb Minār – columns
Kutb-ud-dīn – Kanauj, stūpa
kuṭila – aṅgika
Kuṭila – scripts
kuṭilakā – asceticism
kuṭīra – architecture
Kuṭṭanīmata – kāmaśāstra

Kutti – Nāir
Kuttu – dance
Kuvalāśva – Purañjaya
kuvalaya – plants
Kuvalayāpīḍa – Kṛishṇa
Kuvera (same as Kubera)

Labhpur – Satī
laboratory – alchemy
Lāḍha – Bāleya
Lād Khān – Chālukya
laghimā – siddhi
laghu – dance, literary forms, time
Laghu-arthanīti – Hemachandra
Laghu-jātaka – Varāhamihira
lagna – savana
lagnikā – strītantra
laguḍa – weapons
Lahndā – language, Prākṛit
lahrā – musical instruments
Lahuli – Austric
Lājpat Rāi – Dayānanda
lakes – pilgrimage
Lakhnautī – Pāla
lakshaṇa – stigmata
LAKSHMAṆA
Lakshmaṇa – Duryodhana
Lakshmaṇa – Pāla, Jayadeva
Lakshmaṇavati – Pāla
LAKSHMĪ
Lakshmīṅkarā – Matsyendra
Lakshmī-pūjā – festivals (under Dīvālī)
Lakshmīśa – Kanarese
lakshya – meditation
lakula – Pāśupata
Lakulīśa – Pāśupata
Lāl – Kṛishṇa
lālā – saliva
lalanā – chakra
lālasā – love
lalāṭa – chakra
Lāldās – Hindi
Lalitā – festivals, rāga, Śakti
Lalitāditya – Kanauj, Kashmīr
Lalitavistara – Buddhist scriptures, Prākṛit
Lalla – mathematics
Lallā – language
Lallūjīlāl – Hindi
Lambaḍi – pañchama, human sacrifice
lamba-māna – canons of proportion
lambha – kathā
Laṇḍa – script
lāṅgala – weapons
laṅgar – Sikh
laṅgoṭī – dress
LANGUAGE – philology
Laṅkā – Kubera
Laṅkāvatāra – Asaṅga, Buddhist scriptures
Lār, Sea of – trade
laśuna – plants
Lassen, Christian – Indology
lāsya – dance, worship
lāṭ – column
latā – plants, strīpūjā
Lāṭa – geography, Varāhamihira
latā-sādhana – strī-pūjā
Later Chālukya – Hoysala
Lāṭyāyana – Śākhā
Lauhitya (same as Brahmaputra)
laukika – Prākṛit
Lauṛiyā – column
lava – time
Lava – Sītā
lavaṇa – alchemy
Lavaṇa – cosmology
Lavaṇa – Rāma, asura
Lavaṇi – Marāṭhi
LAW
Lawrence, D. H. – Marāṭhi
laya – rāga, chakra, music
laya – aeon
laya-yoga – chakra
leeches – āyurveda
left side – antinomianism
Lelatindra – Orissa
leṇa – education
lepa – minerals
lepaka – architecture
lesbianism – perversions
Levā – child marriage
LEVIRATE
LICHCHHAVI
Life Divine – Aurobindo
Likhita – ritual canon
likhyā (also likṛitā or likshā) – weights and measures
līlā – Chaitanya, māyā
Līlāvatī – mathematics
Limbu – Austric
LIṄGA
liṅga (symptoms) – Āyurveda history
Liṅgarāja temple – Orissa
liṅga-śarīra – body
Liṅga-sthala – Liṅgāyat
LIṄGĀYAT
liṅgodbhava – sculpture
linguistics – philology
lipi – scripts
liquids – aspersion
liquor – drinks
LITERARY FORMS
LITERATURE
litholatria – minerals, architecture
LIVELIHOOD
lobha – sin

Lochanā – bodhisattva
Lodhā – kshattriya
Lodī, Sikandar – Kabīr
LOGIC
Logos – Mahāyāna, sound
Lohabāhu – Orissa
Lohara – Kalhaṇa
loha-śaṅku – hell
loha-śāstra – metals
Lohit – rivers (under Brahmaputra)
lohitoda – hell
loka – cosmology
LOKĀCHĀRYA
lokāloka – cosmology
Lokamātā – Lakshmī
loka-pāla – direction
lokāyata – nāstika
Lolā – Lakshmī
Lollatā – poetics
loma – breath control
Loma-harshaṇa – Mahābhārata, Purāṇa
Lomapāda – Ṛishyaśṛinga
Lomaśa Ṛishi cave – cave temples
LONGEVITY
Lopāmudrā – Agastya
lotus – plants
LOVE
Loyang Chia-lan Chi – Bodhidharma
Loyang monastery – Buddhist history
Luipā – Matsyendra
Lumbini – Buddha
Lunar Race or Line – Vaivasvata
luṅgī – dress

Mā – godlings, Śakti
Macaulay, Lord – cosmology, law, Marāṭha
Machiavelli, Niccola – Kauṭilya
mada – elephant
Mada – Chyavana
Madā – nectar
madana – love
Madana – Chandella, Kāma
madanāḍi – strītantra
Madanotsava – Kāma
Madayantī – Kalmāshapāda
maddalam (same as muddalam)
Mādhava – Vishṇu
Mādhava – āyurveda history
Mādhavī – Gālava, Lakshmī
Madhu – asura
Madhuchhandas – Viśvāmitra
madhuparka – marriage
mādhurya – poetics, love
Madhumatī – Yayāti
Madhusudhan Rao – Oriya
MADHVA
Madhyadeśa – Kurukshetra
madhyāhna – savana
Mādhyamika – Nāgārjuna
mādhyaṁ-dina – soma
Mādhyaṁ-dina – Brāhmaṇa
Madirā – Kṛishṇa
MADRA (or Madraka) – mahājanapada
Madrās – Vijayanagar, towns
Mādrī – Pāṇḍavas
Madura – Pāṇḍya
madya – chakrapūjā
MAGA
māgadha – bard, Vrātya
MAGADHA – Kurukshetra
Māgadhī – Prākṛit
Magahi – language
Magas of Cyrene – Aśoka
MĀGHA
Maghā – Śukra
Māgha-mela – Allāhābād
Maghar – Kabīr
Māghas – Ujjain
magi – Maga
magic – occultism, mango trick, rope trick, suspended animation
Mahā-ammā – godlings
Mahābaleśvar – rivers (under Kistna), liṅga
Mahābali – Hiraṇyāksha
Mahābalipuram – Hiraṇyāksha, Pallava
mahābandha – paramudrā
MAHĀBHĀRATA
Mahābhāshya – Patañjali
Mahābhinishkramaṇa – Buddha
mahābhūta – substance
Mahāchanda – Yama
Mahāchīna – Mongolian, tantrism, Vasishṭha, Vedānta
Mahādeva – Śiva
Mahādevī – Śakti
Mahāgovinda – architecture
MAHĀJANAPADA
Mahājanī – nāgarī
Mahākāla (or Mahākāleśvara) – liṅga, Śiva
Mahākālī – Śakti
mahā-karuṇā – compassion
mahākāvya – kāvya
Mahāmalla (or Mahāmallapuram) – Pallava
mahā-maṇḍaleśvar – sādhu
mahāmantrin – kingship
Mahāmāyā – Śakti
mahāmudrā – paramudrā
Mahāmbā – godlings
Mahānadi – rivers
Mahānāma – Buddhist scriptures
mahānirvāṇa – Buddha
mahant – hierophant

Mahānu-bhāva – Marāṭhi
Mahāpadma – Nanda
Mahāpadma – serpent worship
Mahā-pari-nirvāṇa – Buddhist scriptures
mahā-pātaka – sin
Mahā-pātra – brāhmin
Mahāprabhū – Chaitanya
Mahāprajāpatī – Buddha
mahāpralaya – aeon
mahāprasāda – antinomianism
mahā-prasthānika – Yudhishṭhira
Mahār – pañchama, Marāṭha
mahārāja – politics, Śaka
mahārāja (cult leader) – Vallabha
mahārājādhirāja – Śaka, kingship
Mahārājika – godlings
Mahārāshṭra – Marāṭha
Mahārāshṭri – Prākṛit
mahāṛishi – ṛishi
mahar-loka – paradise
mahāsaṁmata – kingship
Mahāsaṅghika – Buddhist history
mahā-senāpati – army
Mahāsthāma – bodhisattva
mahā-sukha – sex mysticism
Mahāsurī – Śakti
mahat – psychology
Mahātala – cosmology
mahātattva – psychology
mahātma – hierophant
māhātmya – literary forms
Mahāvagga – Buddhist scriptures
mahāvākya – sayings
Mahāvaṁsa – Prākṛit, Buddhist scriptures
Mahāvastu – Buddhist scriptures
mahāvedha – paramudrā
mahāvīra – soma
MAHĀVĪRA
Mahāvīra – mathematics
Mahāvīra-charita – Bhavabhūti
mahāvrata – gavāmayana
mahāyajña – Five Daily Sacrifices
MAHĀYĀNA
mahāyoga – yoga
Mahāyogi – Śiva
mahāyuddha – Kurukshetra
mahāyuga – aeon
Mahendra – Aśoka
Mahendra – mountains
Mahendrapāla – Pratihāra
Mahendravarman I – Pallava
Maheśa (or Maheśvara) – Śiva
Māheśvarī – Śakti
Mahī – Mahīdāsa
Mahī – rivers
MAHĪDĀSA
mahimā – siddhi
Mahinda – Aśoka
Mahisha – asura
Mahishāsuranāśinī – Śakti
mahishī – aśvamedha, kingship
Māhishmatī – Ujjain, promiscuity
Mahishya – pañchama
Mahmūd of Ghazni – Chandella, Mathurā, Muslim, Paramāra, Pratihāra, Somnāth
Mahmūd Shāh – singing
Mahobā – Chandella
Mahoraga – serpent worship
mahout – elephant
Maināka – Umā
Maisolia (same as Masalia)
Maithili – language, scripts
maithuna – sex
maithuna-jvara – love
MAITRAKA
Maitrāvaruṇa – hierophant
Maitrāyaṇa Saṁhitā – women
Maitrāyaṇi – Upanishads
Maitrāyaṇīya – Yajur-veda
Maitreya – bodhisattva, Pāśupata
Maitreyī – Yājñavalkya
maitrī – compassion
Maitri – Upanishad
maitrya – compassion
Mahāpahit – Hinterindia
majjā – bodily substances
majjana – baths
Majjhima Nikāya – Buddhist scriptures, Greeks
makara – animals
makāra – chakrapūjā
Makha – soma
Makkhali Gośāla – Ājīvika
Makrān – Indus Valley
mala – anatomy
mālā – repetition
Malabār – Kerala
Mālādhav-vasu – Bengali
Mālatī-mādhava – Bhavabhūti
Mālava – Ujjain, rāga
Mālavikāgnimitra – Kālidāsa
Malaya – mountains
MALAYĀLAM
Malayodhvaja – Mīnākshī
Malik ‘Ambar – Marāṭha
Malik Kāfūr – Chālukya, Hoysala, Pāṇḍya, Rāmeśvaram
Mālinī – Bāleya
Mālinī – Pulastya
Mālinī (river) – Śakuntalā
Malitamma – Hoysala
Mālkhed – Rāshṭrakūṭa
Mālkos (or Mālkush) – rāga
Malla – rāga, Ujjain, Vrātya
Malla – Khaṇḍoba
Mallāri – Khaṇḍoba

Malli – tīrthaṅkara
Malli – Alexander, Ujjain
Mallikā – bestiality
Mallikārjuna – liṅga
Mallinātha – kāvya
Malloi – Ujjain
Malto – language
Malukdās – Hindi
Mālwā – Ujjain
mālya – worship
māmakham – suicide
Māmakī – bodhisattva
Māmallapuram – Pallava
mamatā – sin
Mamatā – Utathya
Mammaṭa – poetics
māṁsa – bodily substance, chakrapūjā
MAN OF THE WORLD
māna – sin, weights and measures, canons of proportion
Māna – Agastya, Orissa
manana – education
manas – chakra, psychology
mānasa – mantra
Mānasa (or Mānasarovara) – mountains, pilgrimage
Mānasā – serpent worship
mānasā putra – Prajāpati
MĀNASĀRA
manaskāra – meditation
Mānava – Manu, Vaivasvata
Mānava-dharmaśāstra – Manu
Mānbhāv – Marāṭhi
Mandākinī – Vālmīki
MAṆḌALA
maṇḍala – literary forms, politics
maṇḍala-nṛitya – dance
Maṇḍana (or Maṇḍana Miśra) – Śaṅkara
maṇḍapa – temple
Mandapāla – Jaratkāru
mandāra – plants
Mandara – paradise
Mandasor – epigraphy, Ujjain
Māṇḍavī – Janaka, Kekaya
Mandeha – Sūrya
MĀNDHĀTṚI
Maṇḍi – painting
mandira – temple
Mandodarī – Rāvaṇa
mandra – music
Māṇḍu – Paramāra
Maṇḍūka – Upanishad
Māṇḍūkeya – Ṛig-veda
Māṇḍūkya – Upanishad
manes – ancestors
Manetho – astronomy
maṅgala – literary forms, Bengali
Maṅgala – Kārttikeya
maṅgalāshṭa – marriage
Maṅgaleśa – Chālukya
Mangalore – Kerala
MANGO TRICK
maṇi – gem
Maṇi – Khaṇḍoba
Maṇibhadra – Kubera
Maṇi-bhītti – serpent worship
maṇidvīpa – gems
Maṇigrīva – Kubera
Maṇi-karṇikā – Banāras
Manikchandra – Nātha
MĀṆIKKAVĀŚAGAR
Mānikyāla – stūpa
Maṇimalla – Khaṇḍoba
maṇi-maṇḍapa – serpent worship
Maṇimegalai – Ilaṅgō
maṇi-pravālam – Tamil, Malayālam
Maṇipura – Arjuna
maṇipūra – chakra
Manipuri – dance, scripts
Manīyā – Chandella
mañjishṭhā – dyeing
Mañjula – mathematics
Mañjuśrī – bodhisattva, Buddhist scriptures, China
Mañjuśrī-mūlakalpa – tantrism
maṅkha – hierophant
Mankanaka – vega
manmatha – love
manomaya-kośa – body
Mānsingh – singing
Mantharā – Kekaya
MANTRA – kingship, Veda
mantra-kṛit – community
mantra-mukta – weapons
mantra-yoga – yoga
māntrika – weapons
mantriparishad – kingship
MANU (patriarch)
MANU (lawgiver)
Manu-charita – Telugu
Manu-saṁhitā – Manu (lawgiver)
Manucci, Niccolao – suttee
manusha – body
manushya – compassion
Manu-smṛiti – Manu (lawgiver)
Manu Vaivasvata – Vaivasvata
manvantara – aeon, Manu (lawgiver)
Mānyakheṭa – Rāshṭrakūṭa
manyu – sin
Māra – Buddha
marakata – gems
Marakī – godlings
MARĀṬHA
MARĀṬHI
Marava – Pallava
Maravar – cow
Mardāna – Nānak
MĀRGA

Mārgaśīrsha – calendar
margosa – fig-tree, plants (under nīm)
Mārīcha – Tārakā
Mārīchī – bodhisattva
MARĪCHI
marīchikā – kuṇḍalinī, knowledge
mariner's compass – trade
Mārishā – Kaṇḍu
Māriyammā – godlings
mārjana – baths
mārjāra – Lokāchārya
mark (bodily) – caste marks
Mārkaṇḍeya – longevity
Mārkaṇḍeya-purāṇa – Purāṇa
markaṭa – Deśika
marma – anatomy
MARRIAGE
marrow – bodily substances
Mars – Kārttikeya
Marshall, John – Indus Valley
Marshman, John – Bengali
Mārtāṇḍa – Kashmīr, Sūrya
Maru – Agnivarṇa
Marud-vṛiddhā – rivers (under Rāvi)
Marut – Diti
Māruta – Diti, paradise
MARUTTA
Mārwār – Rājputs (under Rāthor)
Mārwāṛī – Hindi, Jainism, nāgarī
māsa – calendar
Masalia – trade
māsha – numismatics, weights and measures
mashaka – numismatics, weights and measures
Maskarīn – hierophant
masochism – perversions
masturbation – perversions
Mas'ūd – language
Mas'ūdi (same as al-Masūdī)
Masulipatam (same as Masalia)
Mātā – godlings
Mātali – Indra
Mataṅga – music history
MATAṄGA
Mātaṅga-līlā – elephant
Mātaṅgī – godlings
Matarām – Hinterindia
Mātariśvan – Agni, dog
materialism – nāstika
materia medica – medicine
maṭh (or maṭha) – education
Māṭhara – Kanishka
MATHEMATICS
MATHURĀ
mati – knowledge
Matinara – names
Matipura – Harsha
mātrā – nāgarī, time
mātṛi – Śakti
MATRIARCHY
mātṛikā – mantra, music
Mātṛikā – Śakti
mātṛi-yoni – antinomianism
Matsa – Virāṭa
mātsarya – sin
matsya – chakrapūjā
Matsya – mahājanapada, Satyavatī, Vaivasvata, Vishṇu
matsya-nyāya – kingship
MATSYENDRA (or Matsyendranāth)
matter – substance
Mattrā – same as Mathurā
Mau – Greeks
Maudgalya – equanimity
Maues – Śaka
Maujavanta – Soma
Maukhari – Kanauj
maukhyā – perversions
maula – army
mauna – asceticism
Mauneya – Māndhātṛi
mauñji – thread ceremonies
MAURYA
maushṭika – weapons
Mauyalka – Śiva
maxims – sayings
MĀYĀ
Māyā (or Māyādevī) – Buddha
Maya – Hardwār
Maya – asura
Mayas, the – numerals
Māyādevī – Pradyumna
Māyāpur – Hardwār
Mayatār – Mathurā
Māyāvatī – Pradyumna
Maynāmatī – Nātha
Maypole – pole ceremonies
Māyu (or Kiṁnara) – Kubera
mayūkhi – weapons
Mayūra – Bāṇa, dance, Maurya
Mayūrāshṭaka – Bāṇa
Mazhabi – caste
measures – weights and measures
meat-eating – diet
Mecca – Somnāth
MECHANICS
meda – bodily substances
Medapāṭa – Guhila
Medhātithi – Kaṇva
meḍhra – purification
meḍhra-bandha – bandha
meḍhrati – purification
MEDICINE
Medicis, the – Solaṅki
medinī – asura
MEDITATION
megalithic culture – Nāga

Megasthenes – Mathurā, Pāṇḍya, Seleucids, weapons
Megha – rāga
Meghadūta – Kālidāsa
Meghanāda – Rāvaṇa
Meghavāhana – Kashmīr
Megha-vijaya-gani – kāvya
Meharaulī – metals
Mekalā – rivers (under Narmadā)
mekhalā – thread ceremonies
Mekhapanthī – Śakti
mela – festivals
mela (or melakartā) – music
melā – writing
meṁdī – plants
Menā (or Menakā) – Gangā, Umā
Menakā – Viśvāmitra
Menander (ruler) – Bactrians
Menander (dramatist) – drama history
Menon – Nāir
MENSTRUATION
mercury – alchemy
meriah – human sacrifice
Meros – Nysa
Meru – paradise, Ṛishabha
merudaṇḍa – chakra
MESOPOTAMIA
METALS
Metellus Celer – travel
metempsychosis – eschatology
METEOROLOGY
metre – prosody
Mewār – Guhila
Meyer, Eduard – Zoroastrianism
Meykaṇḍa – Śaiva Siddhānta
mica – alchemy
MICROCOSM
Mihira – Maitraka, Varuṇa
Mihira Bhoja – Pratihāra
Mihirakula – Huns
Milinda (same as Menander)
MILINDAPAÑHO
Milton, John – Dutt (M.)
MĪMĀṀSĀ
mīmāṁsaka – Mīmāṁsā
mime – theatre
MĪNĀKSHĪ
Mīnanāth – Matsyendra
mind – psychology
MINERALS
MĪRĀBAI
Mīr-taqi – Hindi
Mirzāpur – thug, Satī
MISCEGENATION
Miśra – brāhmin
mitāhāra – ethics
Mitāksharā – law
Mitanni – Daksha, Diti, Rāma, Sūrya
Mithi – Janaka
Mithilā – Janaka, education, brāhmin, philosophy
Mithra – Varuṇa
Mithradates I – Parthians
mithuna – sculpture
mithyā – logic
mithyā-dṛishṭi – Hinduism
Mitra – Varuṇa
Mitramiśra – women
Mitrasaha – Kalmāshapāda
Mittra, Dīnabandhu – Bengali
mlechchha – pañchama, barbarians
Moabitish – script
mochi – pañchama
modaka – Gaṇeśa
Modaka – Hun
Modera (or Modhera) – towns, Solaṅki
Modh – Hun
Moḍi – nāgarī
Moggaliputta Tissa – Buddhist history, Buddhist scriptures
Moggallāna – Buddha, Nālandā
Mogul (or Moghul) – Muslim
moha (or mohana) – māyā
Mohamudgara – Śaṅkara
Mohan – Kṛishṇa
mohana – māyā
Mohenjodaro – Indus Valley
Mohinī – androgyny
Moi of Indochina – scripts
moistness – hot and cold
moksha – trance
Molla – Telugu
Mombā – godlings
Mona – Sikh
Monghyr – Pāla
MONGOLIANS
monism – advaita
monkeys – animals
monkey-hold – Deśika
Mon-Khmer – language
monologue – theatre
moon, waxing and waning – Soma, vows
Moore, Thomas – Tagore (R.)
Mophis – rivers (under Mahī)
Moplah – Kerala
moral philosophy – ethics
Morasu – human sacrifice
Moropant – Marāṭhi
Moses – Jews
Moses (Nestorian prelate) – Christianity
Mother Goddess – godlings, Śakti
mother-in-law – joint family
MOUNTAINS
Mouru – Maurya, paradise
mouth (in sex) – perversions
Mrammas – Hinterindia
Mṛichchhakaṭika – Śūdraka

mṛiga – animals, man of the world
Mṛigaśiras – sacrifice
Mṛigavyādha – Rudra
mṛigī – strītantra
Mṛigī – Ṛishyaśṛinga
Mṛikaṇḍa – Mārkaṇḍeya
Mṛitāṇḍa – Sūrya
mṛittikā – minerals
Mṛityu – Yama
Muchukunda – Māndhātṛi
mucus – humours
Mudaliar – śūdra
muddalam – musical instruments
Mudgala – equanimity
mudgara – weapons
mūḍha – sin
muditā – equanimity
MUDRĀ
Mudrā-rākshasa – drama history
mudrikā – mudrā
Mugdhabodha – Hemādri
muggu – designs
Muhammad, the Prophet – Somnāth
Muhammad ibn-Kāsim – Muslim
Muhammad of Ghor – Chāhamāna, Chandella, Kanauj, Pratihāra
Muhammad Khilji – Muslim
Muhammadan – Muslim
muhūrta – time, divination
Mūjavant – Soma
Mūjavat – Soma
mukha – dramaturgy
mukha-liṅga – liṅga
mukta – trance, weapons
muktā – gems
Muktābāi – Jñānadeva
muktaka – literary forms
muktāmukta – weapons
Mukteśvar – Marāṭhi
Mukteśvara temple – Orissa
mukti – trance
Muktināth – Satī
Mukunda – Orissa, Vishṇu
Mukundrāj – Marāṭhi
mukuṭa – head
mūla-bandha – bandha
Mūladeva – kāmaśāstra
mūlādhāra – chakra
Mūlaka – Kalmāshapāda, geography
Mulār – Śaiva Siddhānta
Mūlarāja I – Solaṅki
mūlasirā – anatomy
Müller, Max – Aryans, Brāhmaṇa, Sanskrit, Ṛig-veda, Indology
Multān – towns, Sūrya
Multānī – scripts
Mumbā – godlings
muṇḍa – widow
Muṇḍa – Kolarian
Muṇḍa – Śumbha
Muṇḍaka – Upanishad
muṇḍa-mālā – Śiva
muṇḍāsana – necrophilia
muni – asceticism, hierophant
Munī – gandharva
muñja – grasses
Muñja – Paramāra
Mura (same as Muru)
Muraḷī – Khaṇḍoba
Murali – Kṛishṇa
Murāri – drama history, Kṛishṇa
mūrchhana – breath control
mūrchhanā – music
murder – necrophilia
mūrti – idolatry
Muru – Kāmarūpa
Murugaṇ – Kārttikeya
Murukināḍu – brāhmin
Murukuṇḍa – Kolarian
musala – weapons, soma
Musalli – caste
mushka – chakra
mushṭi – weights & measures
Mushṭika – Kṛishṇa
MUSIC
MUSIC HISTORY
MUSICAL INSTRUMENTS
Musiris – Kerala, Christianity, Romans, trade
MUSLIMS
Musuṛi (same as Musiris)
Mūtiba – Kolarian
mutilation – asceticism
Muttra (same as Mathurā)
Muyalaka (same as Mauyalka)
Muziris (same as Musiris)
Mycenae – cow
Mylapore – Christianity
myrtle (same as meṁdī)
Mysore – Hoysala, asura (under Mahisha)
MYSTIC SYLLABLES
MYTHOLOGY

Nābha – Sikh
Nābhā (or Nābhāji or Nābhādās) – Hindi
Nābhāga (or Nābhāna) – Vaivasvata
Nābhāgarishṭa – caste
Nabhānedishṭha – Aryans
nābhi – chakra
Nābhi – Ṛishabha
Nachiketas – Uddālaka
nāda – sound, kuṇḍalinī
Nadanta – dance
nāḍi – channels of the subtle body, diagnosis

Narasiṁha I – Black Pagoda
Narasiṁhavarman I & II – Pallava
Naravāhana-datta – Udayana
NĀRĀYAṆA
Nārāyaṇa – kathā
Nārāyaṇa (lake) – pilgrimage
Nārāyaṇīya – Pañcharātra
Nārī-kavacha – Kalmāshapāda
nārikela (or nārikera) – coconut
Narishyanta – Vaivasvata
Narmadā – rivers
Narmadā – Māndhātṛi
Narmadā-śaṅkar – Gujarāti
narmadeśvara – minerals
nāsāgra – chakra
Nāsatya – Aśvin
NĀSIK
Nāsik inscription – epigraphy
nāsikā – breath control
nāsikāgra – meditation
Nāsir-ud-dīn of Tūs – Muslim
NĀSTIKA
Naṭa – rāga
nāṭaka – theatre
Naṭarāja – Śiva
Naṭ-dvāra – Vallabha
NĀTHA
Nātha-muni – Āḷvār
nāṭika – theatre
nāṭ mandir – temple
nāṭuvan – Bharata-nāṭyam
nāṭya – theatre
nāṭya-rāsaka – theatre
Nāṭya-śāstra – Bharata
Naubandhana (mountain) – Vaivasvata
nauli – bandha
nautch – dance
Navadvīpa (or Nadia) – education, Pāla, Sārvabhauma
Navanītaka – Āyurveda history
nava-ratna – gems, Vikramāditya
Navasāhasāṅka – Paramāra
Nava Vidhāna – Sen (K.C.)
Navsari – towns
Navya-Nyāya – Sārvabhauma, philosophy
navy blue – dyeing
naya – Jainism
Nayachandra-suri – Chāhamāna
Nāyaka – Śakti
nāyaka – man of the world
Nāyaṇār – Śaiva Siddhānta
nayanonmīlana – eye
nayika – kāmaśāstra
nāyikā – dramaturgy, strītantra
Nāyyaka – Pāṇḍya
Nāyyar (same as Nāir)
Nearchus – Alexander, promiscuity, textiles
Nebuchadnessar – Jews, travel, Mesopotamia
necrolatria – architecture
NECROPHILIA – Nāir
NECTAR
Nedumarān – Pāṇḍya
NEGRITO
Nehushtan – Jews
Nelcynda – trade
Nemi – Śūra
Nemichandra – Kanarese
Nepāli – scripts
nepathya – dramaturgy
Nerbuddā – rivers (under Narmadā)
Nero – Romans
neshṭṛi – hierophant
neti – purification
neti, neti – God
neṭṛi – dramaturgy
New Attic Comedy – Śūdraka
ṅga – Bāleya
Nhāvi – Nāga
nibandha – ritual canon, law
nibbāna – trance
Nicaea, Council of – Christianity
Nicaea (on the Jhelum) – towns
nīcha-meḍhra – sex
nicha-śirasi – asceticism
Nidāgha – Viśvakarman
nidāna – diagnosis, Buddhism
Nidāna-sūtra – prosody
nidhi – Kubera
nididhyāsana – education
nidrā – dreams
nigama – āgama
nigamana – syllogism
nighaṇṭu – etymology
Nighna – Satrājita
nigraha-sthāna – logic
nihilism – nāstika
Nikashā – Pulastya
Nikāya – Buddhist scriptures
Nikumbha – asura
nikuñchaka – weights and measures
nīla – gems
Nīla – levirate
Nīlagiri – cave temples
Nīlakaṇṭha – astronomy, elephant, poison
Nīlanāga – Nāga
nīla-sādhana – necrophilia
nīl-darpaṇ – Bengali
nilotpala – plants
nīm – plants
Nimandi – Nimbārka
NIMBĀRKA
nimbus – Iran
nimesha – time
Nimi – Ikshvāku

nimisha – time
Nimisha (same as Naimisha)
nimitta – Buddha, kuṇḍalinī
Nīmnāth – Nātha
nine bodily apertures – orifices
Nine Gems – Vikramāditya
Niramitra – Pāṇḍava
Nirañjana – Dādū
nirdharma – antinomianism
nirgrantha – nudity
nirguṇa – God
nirhetu – Lokāchārya
nirīśvara – nāstika
nirjala – vows
Nirmala – Sikh
nirmāṇa – chakra
nirmāṇa-kaya – Mahāyāna
nirṇaya – logic, law
nirṇeka – baths
nirodha – psychology, trance
Nirṛiti – godlings
nirukta – etymology
nirvachana – law
nirvahaṇa – dramaturgy
nirvāṇa – trance, Buddhism
nirvikalpa – trance
nirvishaya – logic
Niśaṭha – Balarāma
Niśchaya – meditation
Nishada – Nishāda
NISHĀDA
nish-chalin – asceticism
nishedha – law
nishka – numismatics, weights and measures, Vrātya
nish-kāma-karma – Bhagavatgītā
nish-kramaṇa – sacraments
nishpāva – weights and measures
nishprabha – logic
Niśumbha – Śumbha
Nisunda – Śumbha
Nitala – cosmology
nitamba – strītantra
nitambinī – strītantra
nīti – politics
Nītisāra – politics
Nītiśāstra – politics
Nīti-śataka – Bhartṛihari
Nītivākyāmṛita – politics
nitya – Veda, worship
Nityā – serpent worship
Nityānanda – Chaitanya
Nivāta-kavacha – Hiraṇyāksha
Nivāvarī – Veda
Nivedita, Sister – Vivekānanda
nīvi – dress
nivṛitti – karma
Nivṛittināth – Jñānadeva
niyama – ethics
niyati – Ājīvika, karma, māyā
niyoga – levirate
Niyogi – brāhmin
Noah – Vaivasvata
Nobel Prize – Tagore (R.)
Noble, Margaret – Vivekānanda
non-dualism – advaita
non-injury – ahiṁsā
non-violence – ahiṁsā
north – direction
nose, tip of – trāṭaka, chakra
Nṛipat (or Nrup) – Orissa
Nṛipatuṅga – Kanarese
Nṛi-siṁha – Hiraṇyāksha
nṛitta – dance, theatre
nṛitya – theatre
NUDITY
NUMERALS
NUMBERS
NUMISMATICS
nyagrodha – fig-tree
nyāsa – rāga, worship
NYĀYA
nyāya-prayoga – syllogism
Nyāya-sūtra – Nyāya
NYMPH
NYSA (or Nysaea)
Nysaeus – Nysa

obscenity – antinomianism
OBSEQUIES
OCCULTISM
ochre robe – sādhu
Odantapura – education
oḍava – music
Oḍiyan – occultism, sādhu
Oḍra – Prākṛit, Orissa
Oḍradeśa – Orissa
Oghavatī – levirate
ojaḥ sahaḥ saha ojaḥ – mantra
ojas – bodily substances
ojhā – occultism
Okkāta – Śākya
Olābībī – godlings
oli – paramudrā
OLISBOI
Olympus – paradise
oṁ – mystic syllables
omen – Charaka
Oṁkāra (or Oṁkareśvara) – liṅga
oṁ maṇi padme huṁ – mantra
oṁ tat sat – mantra
Onam – Hiraṇyāksha
Onesikritus – Kalyāṇa
Ophir – trade
opium – drugs
Orakkal – Chālukya
Oraon – Kolarian

ordeal – law
Oresme, Nicolas – rope-trick
Oretes – Orissa
orgasm – vega
ORIFICES OF THE BODY
ORISSA
OṚIYA
ORNAMENTS
Ortona – Christianity
oshadhī – plants
Osvāl – vaiśya
outcaste – pañchama
outrigger canoe – Austric
Oxus (Ikshu or Vaṅkshu) – Ikshvāku
Oxydracae – Alexander
Oxyrhynchus papyrus – Kanarese
Ozene – Ujjain

pada – literary forms, mārga, singing, weights and measures
pāda – foot, prosody, senses, weights and measures
padaka – reciting
padam – Bharata-nāṭyam
pāda-mudrā – foot
pādāṅgushṭha – foot
pada-pāṭha – reciting
pādapīṭha – kingship
padārtha – category
padāti – army
paddhati – literary forms
padma – plants, chakra
Padmagupta – Paramāra
Padmaka – serpent worship
Padmanābha – serpent worship, Vishṇu
Padmañji – Marāṭhi
Padmapāṇi – bodhisattva
Padmaprabha – tīrthaṅkara
padma-rāga – gems
Padmasambhava – Nālandā
Padmaśri – kāmaśāstra
Padmavatī – serpent worship
Padmāvatī – Chāhamāna, Rāmānanda, Jayadeva
Padmāvatī (dynasty) – Nāga
padminī – strītantra
Padminī – Guhila
Padoja – architecture
pādukā – kingship
padya – literary forms
pādya – baths, worship
Paes, Domingo – Vijayanagar
paga – Orissa
pagoda (coin) – numismatics
pagoda – stūpa
Pahāṛi – language
Pahlava – Parthian
pahul – Sikh
Pai (Govinda) – Kanarese
Paijavana – Divodāsa
Paikuli inscription – Iran
Paila – Mahābhārata
pain – suffering
PAINTING
Paippalāda – Upanishad
Paiśācha – marriage
Paiśāchi – Prākṛit
Paitāmaha – Varāhamihira
Paiṭhān – Āndhra, trade
Pajra – Utathya
pāka – sacrifice
Pāka – Arjuna, Indra
paksha – calendar, community, syllogism, time
Pakshadhara – Sārvabhauma
paksha – vidyā – birds, skills
Paktha – Divodāsa
Pakudha – Ājīvika
pala – time, weights and measures
PĀLA
Pālakāpya – āyurveda history, elephant
palāśa – plants
Pāli – Prākṛit
Palibotra – Pāṭaliputra
Paliyan – pañchama
PALLAVA
pallavi – rāga
Palli – śūdra
Palni – mountains
Palurā – Hinterindia
Pampa – Kanarese
Pampā – rivers (under Kistna)
Pampāsati – architecture
pān (pān-supāri) – betel
paṇa – numismatics, weights and measures
panacea – alchemy
Pānan – caste
pañcha-bhauta – substance
pañcha-bhūta-liṅga – liṅga
pañcha-drāviḍa – brāhmin
pañcha-gauḍa – brāhmin
pañchagavya – cow
Pañchajana – Sagara, Kṛishṇa
Pañcha-janāḥ – Divodāsa
pāñcha-janya – animals
pañchākshara – mantra
pāñchala – poetics, kāmaśāstra
Pañchāla – mahājanapada
pāñchālī-nāṭaka – theatre
PAÑCHAMA
Pañchama – rāga
pañcha-mahā-yajña – Five Daily Sacrifices
Pañchama-sāra – music history
pañchāṅga – calendar

pañcha-pātaka – sin
pañcharātra – calendar
PAÑCHARĀTRA
pañcha-śāradiya – soma
Pañcha-śāyaka – kāmaśāstra
Pañcha-siddhāntikā – Varāhamihira
pañcha-śīla – Buddhism
PAÑCHATANTRA
pañcha-tapas – asceticism
pañcha-tattva – chakrapūjā
Pañchāvatī – Nāsik
Pañchaviṁśa – Brāhmaṇa
pañcha-vṛiksha – plants
pañchāyat – law, politics
pañchāyatana – God
Pañchāyudha – Vishṇu
pāñch-piara – Sikh
pāṇḍa – bard, hierophant
Pandaia – Pāṇḍya
paṇḍāl – architecture
paṇḍanallur – Bharata-nāṭyam
Pāṇḍarā – bodhisattva
PĀṆḌAVA
Paṇḍharpur – Nāmdev, Tukārām, Vishṇu
Pandion – Pāṇḍya
paṇḍit – hierophant
Pāṇḍu – Pāṇḍavas
Pāṇḍuraṅga – Vishṇu
Pāṇḍuraṅga-mahātmya – Telugu
PĀṆḌYA
pāṇi – senses
Paṇi – dog, Phoenicians
pāṇi-grahaṇa – marriage
Panikkar – Nāir
Paṇin – Pāṇini
PĀṆINI
Pāṇinīyam – Pāṇini
Pānipat – geography
Pānipat (First Battle) – Chāhamāna
Pānipat (Third Battle) – Marāṭha
Panjābi – language
paṅka – minerals
Pantaenus of Alexandria – Christianity
pantomime – theatre
pāpa – sin
pāpa-purusha – sin
paper – writing
para – direction
parable – secrecy
Pārada – Sagara
pārada – alchemy
pāradārika – kāmaśāstra
paradharma – Bhagavadgītā
PARADISE
Paraiyan – caste, pañchama
parakīya – antinomianism
parama – substance
parama-haṁsa – birds, hierophant
Paramahaṁsa Samāj – Prārthanā Samāj
Paramāṇu – atom
parama-pada – trance
PARAMĀRA
paramaṛishi – ṛishi
paramārśa – syllogism
paramārtha – ethics
Paramātman – God
Parameshṭhin – God, nāstika
Parameśvara – God
Paraṁjaya – Purañjaya
paraṁparā – śākhā
PARAMUDRĀ
paraṇa – dance
parañja – weapons
Parañjaya (same as Purañjaya)
Parāntaka I – Chola
Paraprakṛitī – Śakti
parapūrakāyapraveśa – siddhi
Parāsaṁvid – God
pārāśara – sonship
PARĀŚARA
para-śarīra – body
pāraśava – sonship
para-siddhi – siddhi
Parasīka – Mauryas
Pārasnāth – Nātha, mountains
paraśu – weapons
PARAŚURĀMA
Paraśurāmeśvara temple – Orissa
Paravāṇi – Kārttikeya
Parāvasu – Raibhya
para-vidyā – Śaṅkara
parāvṛitti – bindu
pardhan – bard
Pargiter, F. Eden – brāhmin, Indology
Pāri – Kapilar
pariah – pañchama
pari-chālana – paramudrā
paridāna – thread ceremonies
parideśa – weights and measures
paridhī – fire
parigha – weapons
Parihāra – Pratihāra
Parihaspura – Kalhaṇa
Pārijāta – paradise, plants
parikramā – pilgrimage, wheel
Parīkshit – Arjuna
parimāṇa – canons of proportion
pariṇamana – Buddhist scriptures
Parinirvāṇa – Buddha
Pāripātra (same as Pāriyātra)
paripūrṇatā – poetics
parisaṁkhyā – law
parishad – law, politics
pariśishṭa – literary forms
parivāda – sin
parivīta – archery
parivrājaka – hierophant

Pāriyātra – Harsha, mountains
Parjanya – Aditi
Parjanya-vāta – Vāyu
Parkham statue – sculpture
Parli – liṅga
Parliament of Religions – Vivekānanda
parṇā – Umā
Parnian – Phoenician
paroksha – knowledge
Parsee – horticulture, Zoroastrianism
pārshada – law, literature, politics
pāshaṇḍa – nāstika
pārshṇi – foot
Pārshṇī (same as Kuntī)
PĀRŚVA (Jain)
Pārśva (Buddhist) – Kanishka
Pārśvika (same as Pārśva)
Pārtha – Arjuna
Parthava – Parthians
PARTHIANS
Pārthivī – Sītā
Parushṇī – Rāvi
pārushya – logic, paradise
parva – literary forms
pārvaṇa – sacrifice
PĀRVATĪ
paryagni – fire
paryanti – sound
paryudāsa – law
pāśa – Śaivism, weapons
Paśchimāchala – mountains
pāshaṇḍa – nāstika
pashyanti – sound
Pāśī – Yama
Pāśin – Varuṇa
paśu – animals, initiation, quality, Śaivism
paśu-bandha – animal sacrifice
paśu-karma – pūjā
PĀŚUPATA
Paśupati – Śiva
paśu-vidyā – animals
paṭa – Pāṭaliputra, paṭṭa, dress
pātaka – sin
patākā – flags
patākā – mudrā
pāṭalā – Umā
Pātāla – serpent worship
Patalene – trade
PĀṬALIPUTRA – Satī
Pātan – Solaṅki, Somnāth
PATAÑJALI
pātar – prostitution
patari – bard
paterfamilias – sacrifice
pāṭha – reciting
Pāṭhak – names
pāṭhaśāla – education
pāṭhya – Bharata
pati – Śaivism
paṭi – paṭṭa
Paṭiāla – Sikh, Rājput (under Bhatti)
pati-devatā – women
patigaṇita – numerals
Pātimokkha – Buddhist scriptures
pati-vratā – women
Paṭna – Pāṭaliputra
patnī-śālā – altar
patola – dyeing
pātra – weights and measures, sādhu, canons of proportion
patrorṇa – textiles
PAṬṬA
Paṭṭadakal – Chālukya
Pattala – trade
patta-pāka – soul
patti – army
paṭṭikā – paṭṭa
paṭṭiśa – weapons
pattra – paṭṭa
Pattup-pāṭṭu – Tamil
paṭuā – paṭṭa
Paulīśa – Varāhamihira
Pauloma – Kaśyapa
Paulomī – Indra
Paulus of Alexandria – Varāhamihira
paunarbhava – sonship
Pauṇḍra – games
Pauṇḍraka – Kṛishṇa
paurāṇika – hierophant
Paurava – Yayāti
Pavana – Vāyu
Pavanarekhā – Kaṁsa
Pāvaka – Agni
Pavamāna – Agni
Pāvapuri – Mahāvīra
pavitra – grasses
pavitrāropaṇa – thread ceremonies
pavitrī – sādhu
payār – Bengali
pāyu – senses, perversions, chakra
peacock – Jews
Peddana – Telugu
pederasty – perversions
pediatrics – āyurveda
Peithon – Alexander
pen – writing
Penukoṇḍā – Vijayanagar
Peoples of India – races
PERCEPTION
Perdiccas – Alexander
Periapurāṇam – Śaiva Siddhānta
Periplus of the Erythrean Sea – Trade
Persians – Iran
Perumāḷ – Kerala, Vishṇu
PERVERSIONS
Peshāwar – Gandhāra, Kushān
Peshwār (or Peshwā) – Marāṭha

peśī – bodily substances
Peucela – towns
Peutingerian Tables – Romans
Pey – Āḷvār
phagu – Gujarāti
phala – karma
phāla – Balarāma
phalaka – weapons
phala-tṛishṇā – psychology
phaṭ – mantra
phena – knowledge
PHILOLOGY
philosopher's stone – alchemy
PHILOSOPHY
Philostratus – drama history, Greeks
phlegm – humours
PHOENICIANS
PHONETICS
phūlkāri – textiles
PHYSICAL CULTURE
PHYSICIAN
physiology – āyurveda
pickaxe – thug
Pieng-tsu – Bogar
Piers Plowman – Tamil
Pījavana – Divodāsa
PILGRIMAGE
Pillai Lokāchārya – Lokāchārya
Pillai (Rāmaliṅgam) – Tamil
Pillayar – Gaṇeśa
Pillu – rāga
Pilpay – Pañchatantra
pināka – weapons
Pinākin – Rudra
Pinavīra-bhadriah – Telugu
piṇḍa – obsequies, sacrifice
Pindāri – sādhu
piṇḍi – dance
piṇḍikā – yoni
Piṅgā – Śakti
piṅgalā – channels of the subtle body
Piṅgala – prosody, language
piñjrapol – ahiṁsā, Jainism
Pīpā – Rāmānanda
pīpal – fig-tree
Pīpāvati – Rāmānanda
pippala – fig-tree
Pippalāda – Atharva-veda, Upanishad
Piprāwā inscription – script
pippalī – plants
Pirāli – caste
PIŚĀCHA
pishṭa-pañchāṅgula – hand
Piśitāśana – Pulastya
Piśuni – Vālmīki
piṭaka – Buddhist scriptures
Piṭaka Romaka – Romans
Pitalkhorā – cave temple
Pitāmaha – Brahmā, ancestors
Pītāmbara – Vishṇu
pīṭha – Satī, yoni
Pīṭha – Kṛishṇa
pīṭha-marda – dramaturgy
pīṭha-sthāna – Satī
pitṛi – ancestors
pitṛi-paksha – ancestors
Pitṛi-pati – Yama
pitṛi-yāna – eschatology
pitta – humours
Pīvarī – incest
place-value – numerals
Plaksha – cosmology
PLANTS
Plato – Milindapañho
Plautus – drama history
plāvini – breath control
Playoga – Kaṇva
Pleiades – Kārttikeya
plexus – chakra
Pliny – trade, travel
plot – dramaturgy
Plutarch – Greeks, Romans
Podiyil – Agastya
Podonke (same as Pondicherry)
POETICS
POISON
poison-maiden – poison
Pokarna – Śaka
Pokhar-sevaka – caste
Pokunātivaru – caste
POLE CEREMONIES
Pole Star – consummation, Dhruva
Polerammā – godlings
police – Vijayanagar, espionage
polis – towns
POLITICS
polo – games
Polo (Marco) – Chola
polyandry – matriarchy
POLYGAMY
polygyny – polygamy
polytheism – God
Pompeii – Ajantā
Pondicherry – Chola, trade, Aurobindo
Poṅgal – festivals
Ponna – Kanarese
Ponwār – Paramāra
Poppaea – Romans
portents – divination
ports – shipping
Portuguese – Vijayanagar, suttee
Porus – Alexander
poshpaka – sonship
possession – exteriorisation, Gaṇeśa
posta – drugs
postures of sex – erotics
Potana – mahājanapada

Potana – Telugu
potṛi – hierophant
Powaḍa – Marāṭhi
Powār – Paramāra
Poygai (or Poykai) – Āḷvār
prabandha – literary forms
Prabandham – Tamil, Āḷvārs
prabhā – body
Prabhā – Purūravas
Prabhākara – Atri, philosophy
Prabhāsa – Gaṅgā, Kṛishṇa
PRABHĀVA
Prabhāvatī – Pradyumna, Pārśva, Vākāṭaka
Prabhu – kshattriya
prabodha – worship
Prabodha-chandrodaya – drama history
prabodhini – vows
Prachetas – Kaṇḍu, Varuṇa
Prāchinabarhis – Kaṇḍu
Prāchīna-garbha – Dhruva
Prāchyā – Prākṛit
Prāchyā Māgadhi – Assamese
pradakshiṇa – pilgrimage, wheel
pradakshiṇa-patha – pilgrimage
prādeśa – weights and measures
pradeśinī – hand
Pradhāna – Purusha
pradhvaṁsābhāva – śūnya
pradosha – vows
Praveshī – Utathya
prāḍvivāka – kingship
Pradyota – Udayana, Ujjain
PRADYUMNA
prāgabhāva – śūnya
Prāgjyotisha – kāmarūpa
Prāgudya – geography
prahaṇana – erotics
prahara – time
prahasana – theatre
Prahlāda – Hiraṇyāksha
prahuta – sacrifice
PRAJĀPATI
prājāpatya – marriage
prajñā – knowledge
Prajñāparamitā – Buddhist scriptures
prākāmya – siddhi
prākāram – temple
prakaraṇa – logic, theatre
prakaraṇika – theatre
prakāsha – kuṇḍalinī
prakrama – weights and measures
prākṛit – music
PRĀKṚIT
prakṛiti – politics, prosody
Prakṛiti – Purusha
prakṛitilaya – exteriorisation
pralamba – sex
Pralamba – Balarāma
pralaya – aeon
Pramadvara – Sāvitrī
pramāṇa – knowledge, canons of proportion
pramantha – fire, fig-tree
pramatha – Śiva
prameya – category
Pramīlā – strīrājya
Pramlochā – Kaṇḍu
Prāṁśu – Vaivasvata
prāṇa – wind
prāṇādi – wind
prāṇāgnihotra – agnihotra
prāṇa-liṅga – Liṅgāyat
praṇāma – worship
prāṇamaya-kośa – body
prāṇa-pratishṭhā – idolatry
praṇaya – love
prāṇayāma – breath control
praṇayana – politics
praṇidhi – espionage
Praṇūna – miscegenation
prapāṭhaka – literary forms
prapatti – Lokāchārya
prāpti – siddhi
prāpyakāri – perception
prārthana – worship
PRĀRTHANĀ SAMĀJ
prasāda – bhakti, poetics, worship
prāsāda – architecture
prasarpaṇa – soma
Praśastapāda – philosophy
praśasti – literary forms
praśāstṛi – hierophant
prasava – soma
Prasena – Satrājita
Prasenajit – mahājanapada, Magadha, bestiality
prāśitra – prabhāva, sacrifice
praśna – literary forms
Praśna – Upanishad
prasṛishṭi – aeon
prasṛita – weights and measures
prastara – grasses
prastha – weights and measures
prasthāna – theatre
prasthāna-traya – scriptures
prasthiti – aeon
prastotṛi – hierophant
prasūti – strītantra
Prasūti – Daksha
prātaḥ-savana – soma
Pratāparudradeva – Chālukya
Pratardana – Divodāsa
pratibhā – divination, poetics
prati-bimba – perception
pratigarjana – physical culture
PRATIHĀRA
pratihartṛi – hierophant

Y**

pratijñā – syllogism
pratīka – worship
prati-kramaṇa – Jainism
pratikṛiti – idolatry
pratiloma – eligibility
pratimā – idolatry
Pratimā-nāṭaka – Bhāsa
pratimukha – dramaturgy
prati-nāyaka – dramaturgy
Pratīpa – Gaṅgā
prātiśākhya – śākhā
pratishṭhā – idolatry
Pratishṭhāna (on the Godāvarī) – Āndhra
Pratishṭhāna (near Allāhābād) – Allāhābād
pratishṭhātṛi – hierophant
Prātitheyi – Veda
Prativindhya – Draupadī
pratyabhijñā – Vasugupta
pratyāhāra – meditation
pratyaksha – perception
pratyarpaṇa – physical culture
Pratyeka-Buddha – Mahāyāna
Pratyūsha – Gaṅgā
Prauḍa – Brāhmaṇa
prauḍha – strītantra
pravara – community
Pravarapura – Harsha, Vākāṭaka
Pravarasena – Prākṛit
Pravarasena I – Vākāṭaka
Pravarasena II – Kashmīr
pravargya – soma
praveśaka – dramaturgy
Pravīra – Vākāṭaka
pravṛitti – karma
Prayāga – Allāhābād
prāyaśchitta – purification
prayatna – psychology
prayer-wheel – wheel
prayojana – syllogism
prāyopaveśa – suicide
prayukta – weapons
predicables – category
PREGNANCY
prema – love
Premānand – Gujarāti
Premchand – Hindi
Premsāgar – Hindi
preta – obsequies
Preta-rāja – Yama
pretya-bhāva – eschatology, karma
priest – hierophant
Prinsep, James – Indology, scripts
Pṛishadhra – Vaivasvata
Pṛishata – Draupada
pṛishṭha – sacrifice
Pṛiśnī – Diti
Pṛithā – (same as Kuntī)
Pṛithī (or Pṛithī-vaiṇya) – Veṇa
Pṛithivī – Dyaus
pṛithivī – substance
Pṛithu – Veṇa
pṛithu-jaghana – strītantra
pṛithu-parśu – weapons
Pṛithvirāj III – Chāhamāna
prīti – love
Priyadarśikā – Harsha
Priyadās – Hindi
Prīyaṁvadā – Śakuntalā
Priyavrata – Svāyaṁbhuva
professions – livelihood
Prometheus – Agni
PROMISCUITY
pronominalisation – Austric
pronunciation – phonetics
proportion – canons of proportion
PROSODY
PROSTITUTION
PROTO-ARYAN LANGUAGE
Proto-Australoid – Austric
Proto-Prākṛit – Proto-Aryan language
proverbs – sayings
Przyluski, J. – Austric, quality, writing
Pseudo-Callisthenes – Christianity
PSYCHOLOGY
Ptolemy – trade, Varāhamihira
Ptolemy Philadelphus – Aśoka, travel, Seleucids
puberty – strītantra
pud – hell
Pūdam – Āḷvār
pudgala – Jainism
Pudukottai – Chola
pūga – caste
pugree – head
Puhar – trade
PŪJĀ
pūjaka – hierophant
pūjārī – brāhmin
Pukkaśa – pañchama
Pulaha – ṛishi
Pulai – Pulayan
Pulakeśin II – Chālukya
Pulamāyi – Śaka
PULASTYA
Pulayan – pañchama
Puliah (same as Pulayan)
Pulinda – Kolarian
Pulipāṇi – Bogar
Pulkasa – pañchama
Pulomā – asura, Chyavana
Pulomā – Āndhra
Puloman – Chyavana
pulse – diagnosis
Pulumāvi (or Pulumāyi) – Āndhra
puṁsavana – pregnancy
puṁśchalī – Vrātya

punar-ādheya – fire
punarbhū – widow
punar-mṛityu – eschatology
Punarvasu – āyurveda history
punch – drinks
punch-marked coins – numismatics
puṇḍarīka – plants
Puṇḍarīka – elephant
Puṇḍarīka-viṭṭhal – music history
puṇḍra – caste marks
Puṇḍra – Bāleya
Puñjī-kāshṭhalā – Rāvaṇa
puṇya – ethics
puṇya-śālā – ahiṁsā
puppet-play – theatre
pur – Dravidian
pūraka – prāṇayāma
Puraṁdara – Anārya
Puraṁdaradāsa – music history
purāṇa (or pūraṇa) – weights and measures
PURĀṆA
Pūraṇa – Ājīvika
Puranbhagat – Nātha
PURAÑJAYA
Purātana – Śaivism
purdah – harem
Pūrī (or Puri) – Jagannatha, Śaṅkara
PURIFICATION
Purikā – Vākāṭaka
Pūrṇagiri – Satī
pūrṇamāsa-yajña – sacrifice
pūrṇimānta – calendar
pūrṇimāvāsya – calendar
PUROCHANA
purohita – hierophant, kingship
Puru – Yayāti, Divodāsa
Purukutsa – Māndhātṛi, Divodāsa
Purukutsanī – levirate
PURŪRAVAS
Purus – Alexander
PURUSHA
Purusha-charita – Hemachandra
purusha-kāra – Yājñavalkya
purusha-medha – human sacrifice
Purushapura – Kushān
purushārtha – ethics
Purusha-sūkta – caste, forgeries, human sacrifice, Ṛig-veda
Purushottama – God
pūrva – Jainism
Pūrvagaṅgā – rivers (under Narmadā)
Pūrva-mīmāṁsā – Mīmāṁsā
pūrva-nivāsa – Jātaka
pūrva-vāda – law
Pūrvi – rāga
pūshā – channels of the subtle body
PŪSHAN
pushkala – weights and measures
Pushkala – Gandhāra
Pushkalāvatī – Gandhāra
Pushkar – Brahmā
Pushkara – Gandhāra, cosmology, Nala
pushpa – worship
Pushpadanta – Kātyāyana
Pushpadola – swing
Pushpagiri – paradise
Pushpaka – Haihaya, Kubera, Rāvaṇa
Pushpapura – Pāṭaliputra
pushpa-rāga – gems
Pushpotkaṭā – Indra, Pulastya
pushṭi – mārga, Vallabha
Pushṭī – Gaṇeśa
Pushyamitra – Mauryas, Śuṅgas
pustaka – writing
put – hell
Pūtanā – Kṛishṇa
pūti-mṛittika – hell
putra – sonship
putra-kāmyā – sacrifice
putrikā – theatre
putrikā-putra – sonship
Pyrrhonism – Chārvāka
Pythagoras – Varāhamihira

qavāli – singing
quadriga – Greeks
QUALITY
quintessence – alchemy, bodily substances
Qutb-ud-dīn (same as Kutb-ud-dīn)

RACE
Rādhā – gopī, Karṇa
Rāḍha – Bāleya, brāhmin
Rādhānāth – Oriya
Rādhasvāmi – Śivdayāl
Radheya – Karṇa
rāḍ-yajña – sacrifice
RĀGA
rāga – love
Rāghava – Rāma
Rāghava-pāṇḍavīya-yādavīya – kāvya
RAGHU
Raghu-nandana – law
Raghunātha Śiromaṇi – Sārvabhauma
Raghupati – Rāma
Raghuvaṁśa – Kālidāsa
rāgiṇi – rāga
rāgmālā – rāga, strītantra
rahasya – secrecy
RĀHU
Rāhula – Buddha
RAIBHYA
RAIDĀS

Raikva – śūdra
rain – meteorology
Raivata – Balarāma, Manu
rāja – kingship
rājadaṇḍa – kingship
Rājagṛiha – Magadha
rāja-kanyā – prostitution
Rājamalla – Ṛishabha
Rājamundry – Chālukya, liṅga
rāja-nīti – politics
rājanya – khsattriya
Rājarāja – Chola
Rājarānī temple – Orissa
rājaṛishi – ṛishi
rajas – quality, menstruation
Rājaśekhara – drama history
Rājaśekhara – Kanarese
Rājasthānī – Nāgarī, language
rājasūya – royal consecration
rajas-vala – strītantra
Rajatādri – mountains
Rājataraṁgiṇī – Kalhaṇa
rāja-yoga – yoga
Rājbansi – nudity, dance
Rājendra I & II – Chola
Raji – Purūravas
rajju – weights and measures
Rājkoṭ – Gāndhi
Rājmahal – language
RĀJPUT – bard
Rājputāna – Rājput
Rājya – Kanauj
Rājyapāla – Pratihāra
Rājyaśrī – Kanauj
Rājyavardhana – Kanauj
Rākā – Pulastya
Rakhamābāī (or Rakhamāī) – Rukmiṇī
rākhī – thread
rakshā-bandhan – thread ceremonies
Rākshas – rākshasa
RĀKSHASA
rākshasa – marriage
rakta – blood, bindu
Rakta-karavīr – Tagore (R.)
rakta-sāra – soul
Raktavījā – Kālī
raktika – weights and measures
rama – love
RĀMA
Ramābāi, Paṇḍitā – Prārthanā Samāj
Rāmachandra – Rāma
Rāmachandradeva – Chālukya
Rāma-charita-mānasa – Tulsīdās
Rāmagupta – Gupta, Chandragupta II
Ramaini – Kabīr
RĀMAKṚISHṆA
Rāma-kṛishṇa-viloma – kāvya
Rāma-līlā – dance
RĀMĀNANDA
RĀMĀNUJA
Rāmaputta (same as Uddaka)
Rāma-rājya – Rāma
Rāma-setu – vānara
Rāmatāpanīyopanishad – Rāma
RĀMĀYAṆA
Rambhā – apsarā
Rāmdās – music history, Marāṭhi, Sikh
RĀMEŚVARAM
Ramgaṛhia – Sikh
Rāmī – Chaṇḍidās
Rāmjośi – Marāṭhi
Rāmnād – Pāṇḍya
Rāmopākhyāna – Mahābhārata
Rāmprasād – Bengali
Rāmpūrva – column
Rāmrāja – Vijayanagar
rānā – Guhila
Rānaḍe, Mahādeo Govind – Marāṭhi, Prārthanā Samāj
Raṇasthambhapura – Chāhamāna
Rāṇāyanīya – Sāma-veda
raṅga – dramaturgy
Raṅga III – Vijayanagar
Raṅgalāl – Bengali
Raṅganātha – Vishṇu
raṅgoli – designs
Rānī gumphā – cave temples
Ranjīt Singh – Jagannātha, Sikh, suspended animation
Ranna – Kanarese
Ranthambhor – Chāhamāna
Rantideva – Bharata
Rāṛhi – brāhmin
rasa (chyle) – bodily substances
rasa (liquid or mercury) – alchemy
rasa (narrative poem) – Gujarāti
rasa (sentiment) – empathy
rasa (subtle substance) – substance
rasa (taste) – medicines
rasābhāsa – empathy
rasak – Gujarāti
rāsa-līlā (same as rās-līlā)
Rasālu – Nātha)
rāsa-maṇḍala – dance, Kṛishṇa, Vallabha
rasana – senses
Rasa-ratnakāra – Nāgārjuna
rasa-śāstra – poetics
Rasātala – cosmology
rasavāda – alchemy
rasāyana – alchemy
rasha – logic
rāshṭra – Marāṭha, politics
RĀSHṬRAKŪṬA
Rāshṭrika – Marāṭha
rāśi – calendar, weights and measures
rasika – poetics
Rasika Priya – strītantra

rās-līlā – dance, wheel
Rāso – Hindi
Rastogi – vaiśya
Ratannāth – Nātha
ratha – army, altar, Dravidian
ratha-dhūli – weights and measures
ratha-kāra – army
ratha-musala – weapons
Rathītara – Aṅgiras
Rāthor – Rājputs
rati – numismatics, weights and measures
rati – love
Ratī – Kāma
Rati-mañjarī – kāmaśāstra
Rati-rahasya – kāmaśāstra
Rati-ratna-pradīpikā – kāmaśāstra
ratna – gems
Ratnakāra – law
Ratnapāṇi – bodhisattva
Ratna-saṁbhava – bodhisattva
Ratnāvalī – Harsha
ratni – weights and measures
ratnin – royal consecration
rātri – calendar
Rātri – Ushas
rātriṁdivam – calendar
rattī (or rattikā) – weights and measures
Rauchya – Manu
raudra – empathy
Raudrāśva – apsarā, Atri
Raurava – hell
Rāval – sādhu
RĀVAṆA
Rāvaṇa-vadha – Bhartṛihari
Ravi – Sūrya
Rāvi – river
Ravidās – Raidās
rāya – Vijayanagar
rechaka – dance, prāṇayāma
rechita – dance
RECITING
recognition – Vasugupta
recreation – games
Reḍḍi – kshattriya
reincarnation – eschatology
remedies – āyurveda
reṇu – weights and measures
Reṇu – Jamadagni
Reṇukā – Paraśurāma
REPETITION
retas – bindu
retas-bandha – bandha
Revā – rivers (under Narmadā)
Revanta – Kubera
Revata – Balarāma
Revatī – Balarāma
reverberation – physical culture
Revival, brāhminical – brāhmin
Rhazes – hot and cold, Muslim
rhetoric – poetics
rhinoceros – animals
rhythm – prosody
Ṛibhava – Viśvakarman
Ṛibhu – Viśvakarman
Ṛibhukshan – Viśvakarman
rice – plants
ṛich (or ṛicha) – literary forms
Ṛichīka – Aurva
Ṛiddhi – Kubera
riddles – secrecy
ṚIG-VEDA
Ṛig-vidhāna – Gṛitsamada
ṛijīsha – hell
Ṛijupālika – Mahāvīra
ṛiksha – ṛishi
Ṛiksha – mountains
Ripuñjaya – Magadha
ṛishabha – music
ṚISHABHA
ṚISHI
Ṛishikesh – Hardwār
Ṛishyamūka – vānara, Mataṅga
ṚISHYAŚṚIṄGA
ṛita – dharma
rīti – poetics
Rīti-kal – Hindi
ṛitu – menstruation, calendar
RITUAL CANON
RITUALISM
Ṛituparṇa – Nala
Ṛitu-saṁhāra – Kālidāsa
ṛitvij – hierophant
RIVERS
roads – travel
rock-cut architecture – cave temple
roga – diagnosis
Rohidās – Raidās
Rohilkhaṇḍ – Harsha
rohiṇī – strītantra
Rohiṇī – Kṛishṇa, Kaśyapa, Soma
Rohita – Hariśchandra
Rohitāśva – Hariśchandra
Rohtās – Hariśchandra
Roma-harshaṇa – Purāṇa
romaka – alchemy
Romaka – Varāhamihira
Romaka – Romans
Romaka Jātaka – Romans
romāñcha – erotics
ROMANS
Romapāda – Ṛishyaśṛiṅga
Romaśā – Veda
ROPE TRICK
rosary – japa
Roth, Rudolph von – etymology, Indology
ROY (Rāmmohan)

ROYAL CONSECRATION
ruchi – love
Ruchi – Svāyaṁbhuva, sacrifice
Ruchī – exteriorisation
RUDRA
rudrabali – woman
Rudradāman – Śaka
Rudraka (same as Uddaka)
rudrāksha – plants
Rudrammā – Chālukya
Rudrāṇī – Śakti
Rudrasena II – Vākāṭaka
rudrayāga – woman
Rudra-yāmala – tantrism
Rukmin – Rukmiṇī
RUKMIṆĪ
Rūmā – Bālin
Rumaṇvat – Jamadagni
rūpa – substance
rūpaka – theatre, poetics
rūpaka (coin) – numismatics
rupee – numismatics
Ruru – hell, Sāvitrī
Ruskin, John – Gāndhi

Śabara – dance, Kolarian
Śābara – philosophy
Sabari – Kolarian
Sabarmatī – Gāndhi
Sābarmatī – rivers
śabda – sound
śabdam – Bharata-nāṭyam
sabhā – politics
sabhya – fire
sabhyatā – community
sachchidānanda – God
Śachī – Indra
SACRAMANTS
SACRIFICE
sadas – altar
Sadāśiva – kingship
sadasya – hierophant
Saddharma-puṇḍarīka – Kumārajīva, Buddhist scriptures
sādhaka – siddhi
sādhanā – siddhi
Sādharaṇ Brahmo Samāj – Sen (K.C.), Tagore
sādhāraṇa – kāmaśāstra
SĀDHU
sādhvī – women
sādhya – syllogism
Sādhya – godlings
sadism – asceticism, erotics
Sadnā – Hindi
sādyaska – soma
Sadyumna – Sudyumna
saffron robe – sādhu
Sagala – Śaka
Sāgar Island – pilgrimage, Sāṁkhya
SAGARA
sāgara – Sagara
sagotra – community
saguṇa – God
Sahadeva – Pāṇḍava, Jarāsandha
sahaja – antinomianism
sahajdāri – Sikh
sahajīyā – antinomianism
sahajoli – paramudrā
Sāhasāṅkha – Paramāra
Sahasrānīka – Udayana
sahasrāra – chakra
Sahasrārjuna – Haihaya
Saheth Maheth (same as Śrāvastī)
sahetu – Deśika
Sahishṇu – ṛishi
sāhitya – poetics
Sāhitya-darpaṇa – poetics
sahoḍha – sonship
Sahya (or Sahyadri) – mountains
sahyā – Kṛishṇa
Śaibyā – Hariśchandra, bhakti
Śailendra – Hinterindia
Śailodbhava – Orissa
Saiṅ – Sikh
Saindhava – Arjuna, Jayadratha
Śaineya – Kṛishṇa
sainya – army
Śainya – gārgya
Śaiśunāga – Magadha
śaiva – marriage
Śaivāgama – Śaivism
ŚAIVA SIDDHĀNTA
ŚAIVISM
Sajjikā – sādhu
ŚAKA
Śaka era – era
Śakābda – era
Śakadvīpa – Śvetadvīpa
Śākala – Ṛig-veda
Śākala (Siālkoṭ) – Śaka
Śākalya – grammar
Śākapūṇi – etymology
Sakara – Śaka
śakāra – dramaturgy
Śākārī – Prākṛit
Śakasena – Āndhra
Śākaṭāyana – grammar
Sāketa – Bactrians
ŚĀKHĀ
sākhī – Kabīr
sakhī – gopī
Sakhībhāva – androgyny
śākhin – hierophant
Śakra – Indra
śakra-dhanus – archery
sākshin – dreams

Śākta – Śakti
Śaktāgama – āgama, Śakti
Śaktāsura – Kṛishṇa
śakti – chakrapūjā, kingship, weapons
ŚAKTI
śakti-chālana – paramudrā
Śaktri (or Śakti) – Kalmāshapāda, Parāśara
sakulya – community
śākuna – divination
ŚAKUNI
ŚAKUNTALĀ
Śakuntalā – Kālidāsa
śakvarī – prosody
ŚĀKYA
Śākyamuni – Buddha
śakya-prāpti – syllogism
sāl – plants
sāla – dowry
Śāḷa – Hoysala
śāla (or sāla) – (same as sāl)
śālā – Dravidian
salaam – salutation
śālabhañjaka – āsana
Salagissa – towns
śālagrāma – Vṛindā
śalākā – surgery
Śālaṅkāyana (or Nandi) – Śiva
Śalātura – Pāṇini
śāli – towns
Śālihotra – horse
SALIVA
Śālivāhana – Āndhra, Vikramāditya
sallekanā – suicide
Śālmala – cosmology
Śālmali – hell
sālokya – trance
Śālottarīya – Pāṇini
Salsette – cave temples
salts – alchemy
SALUTATION – worship
Śālva – Bhīshma, Sāvitrī
śalya – surgery
Śalya – Madra
sam – music
śama – equanimity
sāma – politics
sama-bhaṅga – bhaṅga
samādh – Gorakhnāth
samādhāna – meditation
samādhi – trance
samādhi-mudrā – āsana
sāmaga – hierophant
sāma-hasta – mudrā
samāhvaya – gambling
sāman – Sāma-veda
śamana – trance
Śamana – Yama
samāna – wind
samāna – promiscuity
samānodaka – community
Samanta-bhadra – bodhisattva
Samanta-pañchaka – Paraśurāma
sāmānya – Vaiśeshika
sama-pada – aṅgika
samāpana – consummation
sama-rasa – sex mysticism
saṁarpaṇa – Vallabha
Samataṭa – Bāleya
samavakāra – theatre
samāvartana – education
samavāya – perception, politics, Vaiśeshika
SĀMA-VEDA
Sāma-vidhānā – Brāhmaṇa
Sāmayāchārika-sūtra – ritual canon
Samaya-mātṛikā – kāmaśāstra
ŚĀMBA
Śāmbalī – Śāmba
Saṁbandar – Śaiva Siddhānta
saṁbandham – Nāir
Śambara – asura, Pradyumna
Sambhar – Dādū
saṁbhava – knowledge
Śambhava – tīrthaṅkara
śāṁbhavī-mudrā – meditation
saṁbhoga – chakra
saṁbhoga-kāya – Mahāyāna
Śaṁbhu – Śiva
Śambhūjī – Marāṭha
Śambhuyaśa – Orissa
Saṁbodhi – Buddha
Śambūka – Rāma
saṁdaṁśa – sacrifice
saṁdeśa – Malayālam
saṁdhi – dramaturgy, Pāṇini, politics
saṁdhyā – aeon, calendar, dance, savana
saṁdhyā bhāshā – secrecy
Saṁdhyākara – Pāla
saṁdhyāṁśa – aeon, calendar, savana
saṁgati – logic, poetics
saṁgava – time
saṁgha – politics
saṁgītā – singing
Saṁgītā-Makaranda – music history
Saṁgītā-ratnākara – music history
Saṁgītā-sudhā – music history
Saṁgraha-śāstra – Asaṅga
saṁgrahītṛi – royal consecration
saṁhāta – hell
saṁhitā – literary forms
saṁhitā-pāṭha – reciting
Saṁhitopanishad – Upanishad
śamī – plants
samidh-ādāna – thread ceremonies
sāmidhenī – fire
sāmīpya – trance

samiti – politics
śamitṛi – hierophant
saṁ-jīvana – hell
saṁjīvanī – Hanumān
saṁjñā – knowledge
Saṁjñā – Sūrya
saṁkalpa – meditation
Śaṁkara (same as Śaṅkara)
Śaṁkarāchārya – Śaṅkara
Śaṁkaradeva – Assamese
Saṁkarshana – Balarāma
SĀṀKHYA
saṁkhyā (number) – quality
saṁkīrtan – Chaitanya
saṁkrānti – calendar, divination
Saṁnatī – Kratu
sāṁnāyya – sacrifice
saṁnidhātṛi – kingship
saṁnyāsin (same as sannyāsin)
saṁpat – ethics
Saṁpāti – Garuḍa
saṁpradāya – Hinduism
saṁprajñāta – trance
sāṁprayogika – kāmaśāstra
saṁpūrṇa – music
samrāj (or saṁrāṭ) – politics
śaṁsa – drama history
saṁsāra – eschatology, karma
saṁśaya – knowledge
saṁśaya-vyudāsa – syllogism
saṁskāra – sacraments
Saṁskāra Gaṇapati – śūdra
Saṁskṛita (same as Sanskrit)
saṁsthā – sacrifice
saṁtānaka – plants
saṁtosha – equanimity
Samudra-gupta – Gupta
samudra-mathana – nectar
samudrāru – animals
Samudravijaya – Śūra
saṁvāda – Ṛig-veda
saṁvādī – music
Saṁvaraṇa – Bharata
Saṁvarta – Marutta
Sāṁvatā (bhagat) – Nāmdev
saṁyama – meditation
saṁyoga – perception, diagnosis, quality
Saṁyogitā – Chāhamāna
śaṁ yoḥ – mantra
saṁyukta – mudrā
Saṁyutta-nikāya – Buddhist scriptures
śāṇa – numismatics, weights and measures
Sanaka – Brahmā
Sananda – Brahmā
śāṇapāda – weights and measures
śānārdha – weights and measures
Sanat – Brahmā
Sanātana – Brahmā
sanātana – Hinduism
sanātana dharma – ethics, sanatva
SANATVA
sañcharī – rāga
Sānchī – Āndhra, stūpa
sandalwood (same as chandana)
saṅdhi (same as saṁdhi)
saṅdhyā (same as saṁdhyā)
Saṅdhyākara-nanda – literary forms
Śāṇḍila – Upanishad
Śāṇḍilī – Agni
Śāṇḍilya – Upanishad, Pañcharātra
Sāndīpani – Kṛishṇa
Sandracottus – Maurya
śaṅgam – Tamil
saṅgha (same as saṁgha)
Saṅgha – Buddha
Saṅghamitrā – Aśoka
saṅgītā (same as saṁgītā)
Śani – Sūrya
Sanjān – towns
Sañjaya – Bengali, Hinterindia, Kaurava
SAÑJAYA
Saṅjñā (same as Saṁjñā)
ŚAṄKARA (or Śaṅkarāchārya)
Sānkāśyā – Janaka
śaṅkha – animals
Śaṅkha – ritual canon
Śaṅkha (same as Śāṅkhāyana)
Śaṅkhapāla – serpent-worship
śaṅkha-pashāli – purification
Śaṅkhāsura – Kṛishṇa
Śāṅkhāyana – Brahmaṇa, kāmaśāstra, Ṛig-veda, śākhā
śaṅkhinī – channels of the subtle body, strītantra
Saṅkīsa – column
śaṅku – archery
Śaṅku – Vikramāditya
śaṅkuśī – asceticism
sannikarsha – perception
sannyāsa – āśrama
sannyāsi (or -nyāsin) – āśrama
saṅsāra (same as saṁsāra)
Sānsiya – pañchama
SANSKRIT
śānta – empathy
Śāntā – Ṛishyaśṛiṅga
Santāl – Kolarian
saṅtānaka (same as saṁtānaka)
Śāntanava – Bhīshma
Śāntanu – Gaṅgā
Śānti – tīrthaṅkara
śānti – equanimity
Śāntiniketan – Tagore (R.)
Śānti-parvan – politics
Śantushita – Jātaka
sapaksha – syllogism

sapiṇḍa – community
sapiṇḍī-karaṇa – obsequies
saptāha – calendar
saptak – music
saptaka – literature
sapta-padī – marriage
saptaṛishi – ṛishi
Sapta-sandhāna – kāvya
Saptaśatī – Purāṇa
sapta-sindhava – rivers
śara – archery
sāra – poetics
Śarabha – Hiraṇyāksha, animals
Sarabos (same as Gogrā)
śarad – calendar
Śāradā – scripts, numerals
Śāradā-devī – Rāmakṛishṇa
Śāradaṇḍayanī – levirate
Śaradvant – Gotama
Śaradvat – Gotama
Saraikala – Parthians
sārakaraṇa – purification
Sarala-dās – Oriya
Saramā – dog, Pulastya
Sārameya – dog
śaraṇāgati – bhakti
saraṅgi – musical instruments
Saraṇyū – Sūrya
sārasa – birds
Sārasvata – Brahmā
sarasvatī – phonetics, prabhāva
Sarasvatī – rivers
Sarasvatī – Brahmā
sarāva – weights and measures
Śarayū – rivers
sardeśmukhī – Śivājī
Sardis – Maurya
śārdūla – animals
sargam – music
sāṛī – dress
sārikā – birds
Sāriputta – Buddha, Nālandā
Śāriputra-prakaraṇa – Aśvaghosha
śarīra – body
śārīra-sthāna – anatomy
śarīrin – body
Sārisṛikta – Jaratkāru
Sarju (same as Gogrā)
Sarkar, Sir Jadunath – Marāṭha
Śarma – brāhmin
Sarmanokhegas – Romans
Sarmishṭhā – Yayāti
Sārnāth – columns, stūpa
śārṅga – archery
Śārṅgadeva – music history
Śārṅgī – Jaratkāru
Śārṅgikā – Jaratkāru
Sarojin – Brahmā
sarovara – pilgrimage
Sarpa – Rudra
Sarpa-nāma – altar
sarpa-sattrin – Arjuna
sarpa-vidyā – animals
Sarpis – cosmology
sarshapa – weights and measures
sārshṭi – trance
Sarsutī (same as Sarasvatī, river)
sārūpya – trance
Śarva – Rudra
SĀRVABHAUMA
Sarvakāma – Nala
sarva-maṅgala – alchemy
sarva-medha – sacrifice
Śarvarī – caste
Sarvāstivāda – Buddhist history
sarvaushada – alchemy
Śaryāta – Chyavana
Śaryāti – Haihaya
śaśa – man of the world
Śaśabindu – Māndhātṛi
Śaśāda – Ikshvāku
śāsana – epigraphy, literary forms, law
Śaśāṅka – Bāleya, Kanauj
sāshṭāṅga – salutation
Śaśin – Soma
śāstra – scriptures
śāstri – hierophant
Śāśvatas – Vyāsa
Śāśvatī – Veda
sat – God
Śatadhanu – bhakti
Śatadhanvan (or Śatadhanus) – Satrājita
Śatadru – rivers (under Sutlej)
śataghnī – weapons
śataka – literary forms
Sātakarṇi – Āndhra
śatamāna – numismatics, weights and measures
Śatānīka – Draupadī
Śatapatha – Brāhmaṇa
Sātārā – Marāṭha
Śatarūpā – Brahmā
Sātavāhana – Āndhra
sat-chit-ānanda (same as sachchidānanda)
satī – suttee
SATĪ
sat-kārya-vāda – sāṁkhya
Satlaj (same as Sutlej)
Satnāmi – Hindi
Śāttaṇ – Ilaṅgō
SATRĀJITA
satrap – kshattriya
Satraps – Śaka
Śatrughna – Lakshmaṇa
Śatruñjaya – mountains
Satsai – Hindi
satsaṅg – worship

saṭṭaka – theatre
Sattasai – Hāla
sattra – soma
Sattva – God
sattva – quality
Saturn – Sūrya
Sātvata – Pañcharātra
satya – truth
Satyabhāmā – Satrājita
Satyadhṛiti – Gotama
satyāgraha – Gāndhi
SATYAKĀMA
Sātyaki – Kṛishṇa
satya-kriyā – truth
satya-loka – paradise
Satyā-Nārāyaṇa – Nārāyaṇa
Satyapīr – Bengali, Nārayāṇa
Satyārtha Prakāśa – Dayānanda
satyasa satyam – secrecy
Satyasiddhi Śāstra – Kumārajīva
satyavān – weapons
Satyavān – Sāvitrī
SATYAVATĪ (daughter of Uparichara)
Satyavatī (daughter of Gādhi) – Aurva
Satyavrata – Vaivasvata, Gālava, Triśaṅku
satya-yuga – aeon
satyr – gandharva, music history
Saubala – Śakuni
Saubaleyī (or Saubalī) – Kaurava
Saubha – Hariśchandra
saubhāgya – widow, menstruation
Saubhari – Māndhātṛi
śaucha – purification, ethics
Sauda – Hindi
Saudāsa – Kalmāshapāda
Saudyumna – Sudyumna
śaulka – marriage
Saumya – Soma
Śaunaka – Gṛitsamada, pregnancy
saunanda – Balarāma
Saundar-ānanda – Aśvaghosha
Saura – Sūrya
Saurabheya – Utathya
Saurapata – Sūrya
Śaurasenī – Prākṛit
Saurāshṭra – Śaka
Saurāshṭri – Prākṛit
Saurya – Sūrya
sautrāmaṇī – soma
Sautrāntika – Buddhist history
Sauvīra – Jayadratha
śava – necrophilia
Savahu – Tārakā
SAVANA
savana – soma
Śavara – Kolarian
Sāvarṇa (or Sāvarṇi) – Manu
Savarṇā – Sūrya
śavāsana – necrophilia
Sāvatthi (same as Śrāvastī)
śavavāda – necrophilia
savikalpa – trance
Savitar – Sūrya
sāvitra-chayana – altar
Savitṛi – Sūrya
SĀVITRĪ (wife of Satyavān)
Sāvitrī (wife of Brahmā) – Gāyatrī
Sāvitrī (or Savitṛi) mantra – Gāyatrī
sāvitrī-vrata – thread ceremonies
śayana – aṅgika
Sāyaṇa – etymology
śayanāsana – āsana
SAYINGS
sāyujya – trance
SCATOLOGY
scepticism – nāstika
Scheduled Castes – pañchama
Schopenhauer, Arthur – Upanishads
Schroeder, Leopold von – Pāṇḍavas
Schweitzer, Albert – ahiṁsā, karuṇā
SCIENCE
SCRIPTS
SCRIPTURE
SCULPTURE
Scylax – Greeks, Iran
Scythes – Nāga
Scythian – Nāga, Śaka
seasons – calendar
SECRECY
secret society – thug, tantrism
sects – Hinduism
SEDUCTION
Śekkiḷār – Śaiva Siddhānta
SELEUCIDS
Seleucus III – Seleucids
Seleucus Nicator – Seleucids
semen – bindu, bodily substances, vega
Semiramis – Mesopotamia
SEN (K.C.)
Senā (bhagat) – Rāmānanda
Sena – Pāla
senā (or senānī) – army
senāpati – army
Senart, Émile – script
sensationalism – nāstika
SENSES
Sepala – Kāpālika
sera (or śera) – weights and measures
Serampore (same as Śrirāmpur)
serfdom – slavery
Seringapatam (or Śriraṅgapatan) – godlings, sterility
SERPENT WORSHIP
Śesha (or Śeshanāga) – serpent worship
Śeśodīya (same as Śiśodīya)
Setubandham – Prākṛit
Sevadāsī – equanimity

Seven Pagodas – Pallava
SEX MYSTICISM
sex, change of – androgyny
sexual freedom – promiscuity
shaḍakshara – mantra
Shaḍaksharadeva – Kanarese
shaḍāṅga – painting
shaḍ-darśana – philosophy
shaḍguṇa – politics
shaḍja – music
shadow – occultism
shadow-play – theatre
shaḍ-varga – canons of proportion
Shaḍ-viṁśa – Brāhmaṇa
Shāh Jahān – Vijayanagar
Shāhjī – Marāṭha
Shāhū – Marāṭha
Shahnameh – Iran
Shaikh Muhammad – Marāṭhi
Shalmaneser – trade, Mesopotamia
shaman – ṛishi
shamanism – śrāddha
shampoo – skills
Shān – Assamese
Shānān – pañchama
shaṇmukhāsana – āsana
shaṇmukhi – orifices
Sharqī – Hussain Shāh
shashṭhaka – weights and measures
Shashṭhī – godlings
shaṭ-chakra-bheda – kuṇḍalinī
shaṭ-karma – purification
Shaṭpura – asura
shaṭsampat – ethics
shell – animals
Shelley, Percy Bysshe – Tagore (R.)
shipping – trade
Shīrāla – Gorakhnāth
shodaśin – soma
Shore temple – Pallava
Shorī – singing
shṭhīvana – saliva
shṭoma – soma
shṭut – soma
Siālkoṭ (same as Śākala)
Sibai – Uśīnara
Śibi – Uśīnara
siddha – alchemy, Nātha, siddhi
siddha-mātṛikā – script
Siddhānta – astronomy, mathematics
siddhānta – logic
Siddhānta-śiromaṇi – mathematics
Siddhapur – śrāddha
Siddharāja – Solaṅki
Siddhārtha – Buddha, Mahāvīra
SIDDHI
Siddhī – Gaṇeśa
sieve – pregnancy
Sighelm – Christianity
Śigru – Divodāsa
Sikatā – Veda
Sikeloi – Divodāsa
SIKH
śikhā – head
ŚIKHAṆḌIN
śikhara – temple
Sikkandar Lodi – Kabīr
Sikri quarry – sculpture
śikshā – phonetics
śīla – Buddhism
śilā – minerals
Śilappadigāram – Ilaṅgō
silence – śūnya
śilpa – art
śilpa-śāstra – handicrafts, painting, skills
sīmanta – pregnancy
sīmantonnayana – pregnancy
siṁhāsana – kingship, āsana
Siṁhāsana-dvātriṁśikā – kathā
Siṁhikā – Rāhu
simile – poetics, sayings
Simonides – Greeks
Sīmuka – Āndhra
SIN
Śina – Gārgya
Sindbad the Sailor – Black Pagoda, trade
Sindhī – language, scripts
Sindhia – Marāṭha
Sindhu – rivers (under Indus), Jayadratha
Sindhurāja – Paramāra
sindūra – caste marks, China
Siṅg-Boṅgā – Kolarian
Singh – Sikh
SINGING
siṅgnād – sādhu
Śini – Gārgya, Kṛishṇa
Sinīvālī – godling
Siprā – rivers
sīra – weapons
sirā – anatomy
Śīra-dhvaja – Janaka
śiras – head
śiras-chakra – head
śirastra – head
Siri Puḷumāyi – epigraphy
Sirkap – Gandhāra, Parthians
Śīrṇa-pāda – Yama
Śirovrata – Upanishad
śīrsha – head
Sirsukh – Parthians
śishya – guru
śiśira – calendar
śiśiratā – maṇḍala
śiśna – liṅga, Śiva
śiśna-devāḥ – sex mysticism
śiśna-devatā – liṅga
Śiśodīya – Guhila

śiśu-hatyā – sin
Śiśunāga – Magadha
ŚIŚUPĀLA
Śiśupāla-vadha – Māgha
śīta – hot and cold
sītā – woman
SĪTĀ
Sītābeṅgā cave – drama history
śītakāri – breath control
Śītala – tīrthaṅkara
Śītalā – godlings
śītāli – breath control
śītkṛita – erotics
Sittar – Tamil, Nātha
ŚIVA
Śiva (tribe) – Divodāsa, Uśīnara
Śivā – Aṅgiras
Śivagītā – Śaivism
ŚIVĀJĪ – yoni
Śivājī II – Marāṭha
Śiva-jñāna-bodham – Śaiva Siddhānta
Śiva-saṁhitā – yoga
Śiva-śarman – Hiraṇyāksha
Śiva-sūtra – Vasugupta
Śiva-vākyam – Tamil
ŚIVDAYĀL
Śivi – Uśīnara
skambha – God
Skanda – Kārttikeya, Alexander
Skanda-gupta – Gupta
skandha – Buddhism
Skiapodes – Greeks
SKILLS
SLAVERY
sleep – dreams
ślesha – poetics
śleshmā – humours
śloka – prosody
Śloka-saṁgraha – Guṇādhya, Sen (K.C.)
smara – love
smara-daśā – love
smaraṇī – repetition
smārta – ritual canon, scriptures
Smārta Bhaṭṭāchārya – law
Smārta-sūtra – ritual canon
śmaśāna – necrophilia
śmaśru – sādhu
smile – Bodhidharma, secrecy
smoking – drugs
smṛiti – scriptures
Smṛiti – Aṅgiras
snake-charmers – Kāpālika, sādhu
snāna – baths
snātaka – education
sneha – love
snehana – āyurveda
Soa – rivers (under Son)
śobhā – poetics
SOCIOLOGY
Socotra – trade, towns
Socrates – perception
Socratic dialogue – Milindapañho
śodhana – purification
Sodrai – śūdra
so-ham – sayings
Sohgaura copper plate – script
śoka – empathy
SOLAṄKI
Solar Race or Line – Vaivasvata
sollukattu – Bharata-nāṭyam
Solomon – Jews, trade
SOMA (moon)
SOMA (ritual)
soma – chakra
Somadā – Lakshmaṇa
SOMADEVA (writer of tales)
Somadeva – politics
Soma-loka – paradise
Somānanda – philosophy
Somapura – education
Somapurī – education
soma-saṁsthā – soma (ritual)
Soma-śarman – Hiraṇyāksha
Somasiddhāntin – tantrism
Soma-vaṁśa – Vaivasvata
Someśvara I – suicide
SOMNĀTH
Somnāthpur – Hoysala
son – sonship
Son (or Sona) – rivers, Ganges
song – singing
śoṇita – menstruation
SONSHIP
Sopāka – pañchama
Sopāndeva – Jñānadeva
Sopāra – trade
Sophir – trade
Sophocles – drama history
śoshaṇa – trance
soteriology – eschatology
SOUL
SOUND
south – direction
space – category
Spalirises – Parthians
spanda – sound
Spanda-sūtra – philosophy
sparśa – substance
sparśa-maṇi – alchemy
spells – Atharva-veda
sphaṭika – gems
sphich – strītantra
sphoṭa – sound
Sphoṭāyana – grammar
spies – espionage
spinning wheel – wheel
spittle – saliva
sports – games

spying – espionage
ŚRĀDDHA
śraddhā – ethics
Śraddhā – Aṅgiras
Śrāddha-deva – Yama
śrāddha – kalpa – ritual canon, Hemādri
Śraddhotpāda – Aśvaghosha
śramaṇa – Buddha, hierophant
Śramanāchārya – Romans
Srashṭṛi – Brahmā
śrauta – scriptures
Śrauta-sūtra – ritual canon
śrāvaka – Buddha, Buddhist history, Jainism
śravaṇa – education
Śrāvaṇa – calendar
Śravaṇa-beḷgoḷā – Ṛishabha
Śrāvaṇi – sacrifice
Śrāvaṇī-pūrṇimā – thread ceremonies
Śrāvasta – Purañjaya
Śrāvastī – Buddha, Purañjaya, Sītā
śravya – Bharata
śreṇi – caste, politics
śreshṭha – Vishṇu
Śreyāṁsa – tīrthaṅkara
Śrī – Lakshmī
Śrībhāshya – Rāmānuja
Śrī-dhanya-kaṭaka – Āndhra, stūpa
Śrīdhara – mathematics, philosophy
Śrigundi – yoni
Śrīharsha – philosophy, Harsha
Śrīkakulam – Āndhra
Śrīkālahasti – liṅga
Śrīkanṭha – Bhavabhūti
Śrīmad Bhāgavatam – Purāṇa
Srinagar – Kashmīr
Śrīnātha – Telugu
Śṛiṅga-giri – Śṛiṅgeri
śṛiṅgāra – love
Śṛiṅgāra-śataka – Bhartṛihari
Śriṅgavat – virginity
Śṛiṅgeri – Śaṅkara, Rishyaśṛiṅga
Śrīnivāsa – Vishṇu
śriṅkhala – sādhu
Śrī-Pulumāvi – Āndhra
Śrīrāga – rāga
Śrirāmpur – Bengali
Śriraṅgam – Pāṇḍya
Śriraṅgapatam (same as Seringapatam)
Śrīśaila – liṅga
sṛishṭi – aeon
Śrī-vaishṇava – Vaishṇavism
Śrīvatśa – philosophy
śrīvatsa – stigmata
śrī-vidyā – chakra
Śrīvijaya – Hinterindia
śrīyantra – maṇḍala
śroṇi-bimba – strītantra
srotas – anatomy
śrotra – senses
śrotriya – reciting, hierophant
sruch – implements
Śrutadevā – Śūra, Śiśupāla
Śrutakarman – Draupadī
Śrutakīrtti – Draupadī
Śrutakīrttī – Lakshmaṇa
śrutaṛishi – ṛishi
Śrutasenā – levirate
Śrutasoma – Draupadī
Śrutāvatī – Bharadvāja
śruti – music, scriptures
sruva – implements
stage – theatre
Stambamitra – Jaratkāru
stambha – column
stanā – strītantra
stars – ṛishi
stealing – crafts
stegosaurus – animals
Stephanus – towns
Stephens, Thomas – Marāṭhi
STERILITY
sthala – Liṅgāyat
sthāna (pitch) – music
sthāna (stand) – aṅgika, āsana
sthāna (topic) – āyurveda history
sthaṇḍila – altar
Sthāṇu – Rudra
Sthāṇvīśvara – Kanauj
sthāpaka – dramaturgy
sthāpanā – dramaturgy
sthapati – architecture
sthāpatya – architecture, Viśvakarman
sthāvara – plants
Sthavira – Buddhist history
sthāyi – raga
sthiti – aeon
sthūla – substance
sthūla-bhūtaṇi – atom
sthūla-śarīra – body
Sthūṇā-karṇa – Śikhaṇḍin
STIGMATA
stoma – soma
stones, precious – gems
stone women – Gautama, Viśvāmitra
stone worship – architecture, minerals
story – kathā
stotra – literary forms
Strabo – Pāṇḍya, promiscuity
strīdhāna – women
STRĪPŪJĀ
STRĪRĀJYA
strīratna – kingship
strīśilā – yoni
STRĪTANTRA
Strzygowski – Iran
stukā – head

stūpa (tuft of hair) – head
STŪPA (tumulus)
styāna – meditation
style – poetics
Suari – Kolarian
Subāhu – Nala, Kaurava
Subalu – Kaurava
SUBANDHU
śubhā – channels of the subtle body
Subhadra – Buddha
Subhadrā, Arjuna, Pradyumna
Subhrū – virginity
subrahmaṇya – hierophant
Subrahmaṇya – Kārttikeya
SUBSTANCE
subtle body – body
sucharita – ethics
sūchi – stūpa
Śuchi – Agni
Suchīndram – liṅga
Sudakshiṇa – Kāmboja
Sudakshiṇā – Sagara
sudarśana – weapons
Sudarśana – Śaka, Maurya
Sudāsa (or Sudās) – Divodāsa
śuddh – music
śuddha – purification
śuddh-ādvaita – Vallabha
Śuddhi – purification
Śuddhodana – Buddha
Sudeshṇā – Utathya, drinks
śudh – purification
sudhā – drinks
sudharmā – paradise
śudi – calendar
Sudkavān – Bāleya
ŚŪDRA
Śūdra (tribe) – Ābhīra
ŚŪDRAKA – Bāṇa
SUDYUMNA
SUFFERING
Sugandha – Satī
Sugaṅgeya – Pāṭaliputra
Sugrīva – Bālin
Suhma – Bāleya
Suhotra – Pāṇḍava
SUICIDE
Sujāta – Haihaya
Sujātā – Buddha, Uddālaka
Śuka – Vyāsa
Sukala – human sacrifice
Sukanyā – Chyavana
Śuka-saptati – kathā
sukha – suffering
Sukha – Rāmānanda, Varuṇa
Sukhāvatī – bodhisattva, yoni
Sukhāvatī Vyūha – bodhisattva, Buddhist scriptures
Sukhmaṇī – Sikh
śukla-paksha – calendar
śukra – bindu, bodily substances
ŚUKRA (or Śukrāchārya)
sukṛita – ethics
sūkshma – substance
sūkshma-jagat – microcosm
sūkshma-śarīra – body
sūkta – Ṛig-veda
śukti – weights and measures
Śuktimān – mountains
Śuktimatī (river) – rivers (under Jamnā)
Śuktimatī (town) – Śiśupāla
sukumāratā – poetics
śūla – sex, Vrātya, weapons
śūlā – Vrātya
Sulabhā – Veda
śūlabhṛit – sex
śūlagava – animal sacrifice
Sulaimān – Pratihāra
Śūlapāṇi – sex mysticism
śulka – dowry, marriage, women
Śūlki – Orissa
sulphur – alchemy
Sultānganj – sculpture
Śulva-sūtra – mathematics
Sumālī – Pulastya
Suman – Aśoka
Sumanā – Marutta
Sumantra – Raghu
Sumantu – Atharva-veda, ritual canon
Sumatī – Sagara
Sumati – Manu (lawgiver), tīrthaṅkara
Sumatra – numerals
ŚUMBHA
Sumedha – Jātaka
Sumeru – paradise
Sumitrā – Raghu
summum bonum – ethics
sumud-ātmajā – apsarā
sun – Sūrya, wheel
sun (or moon) standing still – Atri, Hanumān
Śuna-hotra – Gṛitsamada
Śunaḥ-puchchha – dogs
ŚUNAḤŚEPHAS
Śunaka – Atharva-veda, dogs, Hanumān, Gṛitsamada
Śunaka-kapeya – dog
Sunāman – Kaṁsa
Sunandā – Nala
Sunda – Śumbha
Sundarar – Śaiva Siddhānta
Sundareśvar – Mīnākshī, Pāṇḍya
sundarī – dance
ŚUṄGA
Sunītā – incest
Śunītha – Śiśupāla
Sunīti – Dhruva
Śuno-lāṅgūla – dogs

sūnṛita – Pārśva
Sūnṛitā – Dhruva
ŚŪNYA
śūnyatā – trance, śūnya
śūnya-vāda – Nāgārjuna
Supārśva – paradise, tīrthaṅkara
Supermind – Aurobindo
supti – dreams
sura – asura
surā (or sūra) – drinks
Surā – cosmology
ŚŪRA (father of Vasudeva)
Śūra (tribe) – Ābhīra
Śūra (family of Bengal) – Pāla
Surabhī – Kāmadhenu
Śūrābhīra – Ābhīra
Suraṅgama – Buddhist scriptures
surāṅganā – apsarā
surāpāna – sin
Surasā – snake worship
Śūrasena – Mathurā
Surāshṭra – geography
Surāt – towns
Surati – rāga
Sūrāvalī – Hindi
Sūrdās – Hindi
Sureśvara (same as Maṇḍana)
SURGERY
sūri – hierophant
sūrmi – politics
śūrpa (or sūrpa) – weights and measures
ŚŪRPANAKHĀ
Surparaka – trade
Sūrsāgar – Hindi
Sursura – Rāmānanda
Suruchi – Dhruva
suruṅgā – warfare
SŪRYA
Sūrya – Varāhamihira
Sūryā – Pūshan
sūrya-darśana – sacraments
sūrya-kānta – gems
Sūryakavi – kāvya
Sūryamatī – Somadeva
Sūryapura – (same as Surāt)
Sūrya-śataka – Bāṇa
Sūrya-siddhānta – sanatva, Varāhamihira
Sūrya-vaṁśa – Vaivasvata
Susa – Maga,Maurya, wheel
Susanāga – Magadha
Suśarman – Virāṭa
Sushena – Jamadagni, vānara
Sushṇa – Dravidian
sushumṇā – channels of the subtle body
sushupti – dreams
Suśīlā – Yama
Suśobhanā – Arjuna
SUSPENDED ANIMATION
Suśruta – āyurveda history
Śuśumā – Śukra
sūta – bard
Sūta – Karṇa
sūtaka – sin
Sutala – cosmology
Sutlej – rivers
sūtra – literary forms
sūtra-dhāra – dramaturgy, architecture
sūtra-grāhin – architecture
Sūtrālaṅkāra – Asaṅga
Sutta (or Sutta-piṭaka) – Buddhist scriptures
SUTTEE
Śutudrī – rivers (under Sutlej)
suvarṇa – numismatics, weights measures
Suvarṇa-bhūmi – Hinterindia
Suvarṇa-dvīpa – Hinterindia
Suvarṇanābha – Kāmaśāstra
Suvidhi – tīrthaṅkara
suvrata – tīrthaṅkara
Suvrata – Kalhaṇa
suvṛikti – Vedism
SVABHĀVA
svadarśana – svabhāva
svadeśi – Gāndhi, svabhāva
svadhā – mantra
Svadhā – Aṅgiras, ancestors
svadharma – svabhāva
svādhyāya – education
svādishṭhāna – chakra
svāgata – worship
svāhā – mantra
Svāhā – Agni
svakarma – svabhāva
svakīya – antinomianism
svāmi – hierophant
svāmin – kingship, Śaka
Svāminātha – Kārttikeya
svana – sound
Svanaya – Utathya
Śvapāka (or Śvapach) – pañchama
ŚVAPHALKA
svapna – dreams
Svapna-chintāmaṇi – divination
Svapna-vāsava-datta – Bhāsa
svara – music
svarāj – svabhāva
Svabhānu – Purūravas
Svarga – paradise
svarita – prosody
svar-loka – paradise
svarṇa-bhadra – minerals
svarṇa-rekhā – minerals
svarṇa-steya – sin
Svārochisha – Manu
svaru – yūpa
Svasanved – Upanishad

svasti – mantra
svastika – swastika
svastikārdha – serpent worship
Svatantra-yogāchāra – philosophy
Svātmārāma – Yoga
svatrāṇa – kingship
Svayaṁbhu – Svāyaṁbhuva
SVĀYAṀBHUVA
SVAYAṀVARA
svechchhāchāra – antinomianism
ŚVETADVĪPA
Śvetaketu – Uddālaka
Śvetāmbara – Jainism
Śvetāśvatara – Upanishad
svīkaraṇa – thread ceremonies
swadeshi (same as svadeśi)
swāmi (same as svāmi)
swarāj (same as svarāj)
SWASTIKA
swearing-in – aspersion
sweating – āyurveda
SWING
syād (or syād-vāda) – Jainism
Śyām – Kṛishṇa
Śyāmā – Śakti
syamantaka – Satrājita
śyena – sacrifice, soma
Śyenī – Garuḍa
syllable – mystic syllables, prosody
SYLLOGISM
SYMBOLS
syncretism – Hinduism
Syrian Christians – Christianity
syrinx – warfare

taboo – Austric
tabuva – Austric
tadbhava – Prākṛit
tadsama – Prākṛit
Tagara – trade
TAGORE (family)
TAGORE, RABINDRANĀTH
Taila II – Chālukya
Tailaṅga – Telugu
tairthikīya – Hinduism
Taittirīya – Āraṇyaka, Brāhmaṇa, Upanishad
Taittirīya Saṁhitā – Yajur-veda
Tajik – Iran
Tājikā – astronomy
tajjalān – God
Tāj Mahal – Marāṭha
Takht-i-Bahai – Gandhāra
Ṭakkarī – scripts
Taksha – Gandhāra
Takshaka – serpent worship, Gandhāra
takshaṇā – sculpture
Takshaśilā – Gandhāra
tala – hand, weights and measures
tāla – time
Tala – cosmology
Tāla-jaṅgha – Haihaya
talam – dance
talamāna – canons of proportion
talātala – hell
tāla-traya – worship
tāli – marriage, prostitution
tālikettu – prostitution
Tālikoṭa – Vijayanagar
Talkāḍ – Kanarese
tālu – chakra
Talwaṇḍi – Nānak
tamarind – Gorakhnāth
tamas – quality
Tāmasa – Manu
Tamasā (river) – Rāma
tāmbūla – betel
TAMIL
Tāmisra – hell
Tāmralipti – Bāleya, Hinterindia
Tāmraparṇi – rivers
tāna (or tānam) – music
Tāṇḍaka – Brāhmaṇa
Tāṇḍava – dance
Tāṇḍava-tālika – dance
tandrā – sin
Tāṇḍya – Brāhmaṇa
T'ang – Ajantā, Kanauj
taṅgka (same as thaṅ-ka)
Tanjore – Chola
ṭaṅka – numismatics
Ṭaṅkrī – scripts
tanmātra – substance
TĀNSEN
Tantra – tantrism
Tantrākhyāyika – kathā
tāntrika – tantrism
TANTRISM
tantu – thread
tapana – hell
tapar-loka – paradise
tapas – asceticism
tapasvin – asceticism
Tapatī (same as Taptī)
tapo-loka – paradise
tapovana – asceticism
ṭappā – singing
Taprobane – rivers (under Tāmraparṇi)
Taptī – rivers, Bharata
Taqqi, Shaikh – Kabīr
tāra – music
Tārā (Buddhist goddess) – China, bodhisattva, Vasishṭha
Tārā – Bālin, Bṛihaspati
Tāra – Bālin

Tārā-bāī – Marāṭha
Taragam – Śiva
Tarāin – Chāhamāna
tāraka – Kuṇḍalinī
Tāraka – Kārttikeya
TĀRAKĀ – Bṛihaspati
Tārakā-maya – Bṛihaspati
Tārakeśvara – liṅga
tarana – Bharata-nāṭyam
Tāranātha – painting
taraṅga – Somadeva
Tārāpīḍa – widow
Tāripennu – human sacrifice
tarka – logic
Tarkaratna – Bengali
Tarka-saṁgraha – philosophy
tarka-vidyā – Nyāya
tarpaṇa – sacrifice, worship
Tarumā – Hinterindia
taruṇī – strītantra
tat – musical instruments, dance
Tathāgata – Mahāyāna
tathatā – Mahāyāna
Taṭīka – Rāma
tatkar – Kathak
Tatti – Hindi
tattva – category
Tattva-chintāmaṇi – Sārvabhauma
tat tvam asi – sayings
Tattvopaplavasiṁha – Jayarāśi
Tāvatiṁsa – Buddha
Tavernier, Jean Baptiste – mango trick
Tāvīshī – Śukra
TAXATION
Taxila – Gandhāra
Tegh Bahādur – Sikh
Tejapāla – Solaṅki
tejas – substance
tejo-vardhana – alchemy
Teliṅga – brāhmin
TELUGU
Tembāvaṇi – Tamil
TEMPLE
Tenali – Telugu
Teṅgalai – Lokāchārya
teppakulam – temple
teppam – worship
teppotsavam – worship
terānā – music
Terence – drama history
Tevāram – Śaiva Siddhānta
textbooks – handicrafts
TEXTILES
thaba – stūpa
ṭhakūr-bāṛi – architecture, temple
thāmba – Dādū
Thānesar – Kanauj
thaṅ-ka (temple banner) – Ajantā
tharvad – Nāir
that – dance
thāṭ (or thāṭa) – music
THEATRE
Theophila – towns
Theravāda – Buddhist history
third eye – eye
thirmanam – Bharata-nāṭyam
Thomas, St. – Christianity
Thomas of Cana – Christianity
Thomas, Edward – scripts
Thoreau, Henry – Gāndhi
THREAD CEREMONIES
THUG
ṭhumrī – singing
thupa – stūpa
Tigāwa – architecture
ṭīkā – caste marks
Tikkanna – Telugu
ṭikki – head
tila – śrāddha
Tilak, Bāl Gaṅgādhar – Marāṭhi, Ṛig-veda, Prārthanā Samāj
tilaka – caste marks
Tillai – Chidambaram
tillana – Bharata-nāṭyam
Tilottamā – apsarā
TIME
Timi – animals
Timiṁgila – animals
Tīmūr – geography
Tinnevelly – Pāṇḍya
tintiḍī – Gorakhnāth
Tipammā – godlings
Tipu Sultān – occultism
tiranokku – kathākali
TĪRATH, RĀM
Tiresias – Sudyumna
Tirhut – Janaka
tirmanam – dance
tīrtha – pilgrimage
TĪRTHAṄKARA
tīrthika – Nālandā
Tīrthrāj – Allāhābād
Tirumaḷai – Pāṇḍya, mountain
Tirumaḷiśai – Āḷvār
Tirumandiram – Śaiva Siddhānta
Tirumaṅgai – Āḷvār
Tirumūlar – Śaiva Siddhānta
Tirumuṛai – Śaiva Siddhānta
Tirupati – Hinduism, mountain, prostitution
Tiruppāṇ – Āḷvār
Tiruvāimoḷi – Āḷvār
TIRUVAḶḶUVAR
Tiruvaṇṇāmalai – liṅga
Tiruvarur – liṅga
Tiruvāśagam – Māṇikkavāśagar
tithi – calendar
titikshā – equanimity

Tittiri – Yājñavalkya
tiveri – hierophant
tīvra – music
Tiyan – coconut
Tod, James – Hindi, Rājput
TODA – cave temples
toddy – drinks
Toḍī – rāga
toilet – man of the world
Tokhāri – Kushān
ṭol – education
tolā – weights and measures
Tolkāppiyam – Tamil
Tolstoy, Leo – Gāndhi
tomara – weapons
Tomara – Chāhamāna
Toṇḍai – Pallava
tonsure – head
tope – stūpa
topee – head
toṛah – dance
Toramāna – Huns
toraṇa – stūpa, Śiva
torreh – head, dress
torture – Kauṭilya, politics, law
Tosalaka – Kṛishṇa
Totāpuri – Rāmakṛishṇa
totemism – names
TOWNS
toys – Maga, Vrātya
TRADE AND SHIPPING
trāga – suicide
Trajan – Romans, travel
TRANCE STATES
transmigration of the soul – eschatology
transmission of the Vedas – śākha
transvestism – androgyny
trapā – erotics
Trasadasyu – Māndhātṛi
trasareṇu – weights and measures
trāṭaka – meditation
Travancore – Kerala
TRAVEL
trayī – Atharva-veda
trees – plants
tree, hanging carcass on – human sacrifice, Gorakhnāth
treta-yuga – aeon
tribes – pañchama, races
tribhaṅga – aṅgika
Trichinopoly – Chola
Tridaśa – God
tridosha – humours
Trigartta – Uśīnara, Virāṭa
Trijaṭā – Sītā
Trika – Vasugupta
trikāya – Mahāyāna
Trikūṭa – Vaivasvata
Trilochan – Sikh
Trimūrti – cave temples, God
tṛiṇa – grasses
Tṛiṇabindu – Pulastya
Tṛiṇāvartta – Kṛishṇa
trinity – God
Tripiṭaka – Buddhist scriptures
tripuṇḍra – caste marks
Tripura – Kālī
Tripura-sundarī – Śakti
Tripurāsura – Kālī
Tripurī – Ābhīra
triratna – Buddhism, Jainism
Triśalā – Mahāvīra
TRIŚAṄKU
tṛishā – love
Tṛishā – Pradyumna
trishṭubh – prosody
Triśiras – Viśvakarman
tri-sthalī – towns
triśūla – weapons, hierophant
Trita – Agni
tṛitīya – hand, soma
Tṛitsu – Divodāsa, Bharata, Vasishṭha
Trivandrum – Kerala
Trivandrum Plays – Bhāsa
Trivedi – hierophant
triveṇi – channels of the subtle body
Triveṇī – Allāhābād
Triyāmā – (same as Jamnā)
Trojan War – Rāmāyaṇa
troṭaka – theatre
Troy – swastika, brāhmin
TRUTH
truṭi – time
Tryaksha – liṅga
Tryambaka (or Tryambakeśvara) – liṅga, Rudra
tryaṇuka – atom
Tughlugs – miscegenation
TUKĀRĀM
tukṛa – dance
tulā – weights and measures
Tulādhāra – caste
tulāmāna – weights and measures
tulasī – Vṛindā
tullal – Malayālam
tulsī – Vṛindā
TULSĪDĀS
Tuḷu – language
Tuluva – Āndhra
Tumbura – gandharva, rākshasa
Tuṇḍa – Kālī
Tuṇḍikera – Haihaya
Tuṅga – Orissa
Tuṅgabhadra – rivers (under Kistna)
turaṁga – army
Turanian – language

turīya – dreams
turmeric – plants
Turushka – Kushān
Turvaśa (or Turvaśu) – Divodāsa, Yayāti
turyāga – dreams
turyātīta – dreams
Tushita – bodhisattva, godling, Jātaka
Tuticorin – Pāṇḍya
tvach – senses
tvak – senses
Tvashṭṛi – Viśvakarman
twins – purification, occultism
tyāga – asceticism
Tyāgarāja – music history
tyāgī – asceticism
Tyre – Phoenicians

Uchāthya – Utathya
Uchchhaiḥ-śravas – horse
uchchhishṭa – sacrifice
uchchhvāsa – literary forms
udāharaṇa – syllogism
Udaigiri – cave temples
Udaipur – Guhila
udaka – śrāddha
udāna – wind
Udāna – Buddhist scriptures
Udaṇḍapura – Pāla, education
udāratva – poetics
Udāsi – Sikh
udāsīna – politics
udātta – prosody
UDAYANA
Udayana (philosopher) – philosophy
Udāyi – Magadha
Udbhaṭa – poetics
Uddaka – Buddha
UDDĀLAKA
uḍḍīyana – bandha
Uḍḍiyāna – Matsyendra, strīrājya
Uddyotakara – philosophy
Udenāth – Nātha
udgātṛi – hierophant
udgītha – singing
Uḍho – Kṛishṇa
Uḍipi – Madhva
Uḍra – Orissa
udumbara – fig-tree
Udvada – towns
udyāna – horticulture
Ugra – Mīnākshī, pañchama, Rudra
Ugrasena – Kaṁsa, Nanda
Ugraśravas – Mahābhārata
Ugrāsura – Kṛishṇa
Ugrāyudha – widow
ūha – knowledge, woman
UJJAIN
ujjāyi – breath control
ukha – altar
uktha – soma
ukthya – soma
Ulfilas – Proto-Aryan
Ulladah – pañchama
Ulmuka – Balarāma
Ulugh Beg – astronomy, Muslim
ulūkhala-musala – soma
Ulūpī – Arjuna
UMĀ
Umāpati – language
Umāpati – Śaiva Siddhānta
unapproachable – pañchama
uñchhavṛitti – asceticism
unicorn – cow
Universal Christian Topography – Christianity
unmāna – canons of proportion
unmani – trance
Unnatī – Garuḍa
unnetṛi – hierophant
unseeable – pañchama
untouchable – pañchama
upabhṛit – implements
upachāra – logic, poetics, worship
upādhi – names, Śaṅkara
upādhyāya – hierophant
upāgama – āgama
upakurvāṇa – education
Upāli – Buddha
upamā – poetics, sayings
upamāna – canons of proportion, knowledge
upāṁśu – mantra
upanāgarikā – poetics
upanaya – syllogism
upanayana – thread ceremonies
Upāṅga – scriptures
UPANISHAD
upa-pātaka – sin
upapatti – law
Upaplavya – Kurukshetra
Upa-purāṇa – Purāṇa
Uparichara – Satyavatī
uparūpaka – theatre
upāsaka – Buddha
upa-saṁhāra – dramaturgy
upāsana – worship
upastha – senses
upasthya – sex mysticism
Upasunda – Śumbha
upavāsa – festivals
upavasatha – sacrifice
upaveda – scriptures
upavīta – thread ceremonies
upāya – mārga, Buddhist scriptures
upekshā – equanimity

Upendra-bhañja – Oriya
Urāli – menstruation
Uraon (same as Oraon)
ūrdhva-bāhu – asceticism
ūrdhva-liṅga – sex mysticism
ūrdhva-meḍhra – sex mysticism
ūrdhva-mukhi – asceticism
ūrdhvāṅga – āyurveda
ūrdhva-retas – bindu
Urdu – Hindi
Ūrjā – Vasishṭha
Ūrmilā – Lakshmaṇa
ūrṇā – stigmata
Uru – Aṅgiras
Uruvelā – Buddha
Ūrva – Aurva
URVAŚĪ
Urvī – Dyaus
Uśanas – Kauṭilya, Śukra
Ūshā – Pradyumna
USHAS
ushman – hot and cold
ushṇa – hot and cold
ushṇih – prosody
ushṇīsha – dress, stigmata, stūpa
Uśij – Utathya
UŚĪNARA
UTATHYA
utensils – implements
Utkala – Sudyumna
Utkala – Orissa, brāhmin
Utkaliṅga – Orissa
Utopia – Milindapañho
utpala – plants
Utpala – philosophy
utplavana – dance
utprekshā – poetics
utsāha – kingship
UTSARGA
utsarpiṇī – Jainism
utsava – festivals
utsṛishṭānka – theatre
Uttama – Dhruva, Manu
Uttānapāda – Dhruva
Uttaṅka – Uddālaka
uttara – law
Uttara – Virāṭa
Uttarā – Virāṭa
Uttara-kuru – promiscuity
Uttara-Mīmāṁsā – Mīmāṁsā
Uttara Rāma-charita – Bhavabhūti
uttarāyaṇa – calendar, divination

vaccination – āyurveda history
vāch – senses, sound
Vāch – Brahmā
Vāchaknavī – Veda
vāchana – sayings, Liṅgāyat
Vāchaspati (legalist) – law
Vāchaspati (or Vāchaspati Miśra) – philosophy
vāchika – mantra
vāda – logic, mārga
Vaḍagalai – Deśika
Vaḍama – brāhmin
vādana – musical instruments
Vaḍavā – Veda
Vāda-vidyā – Nyāya
Vadhryaśva – Divodāsa
vādī – music
vādin – hierophant
vāditra – musical instruments
vādya (same as vāditra)
Vagai – Pāṇḍya
Vāgbhaṭa – Āyurveda history
Vāgeśvarī – Śakti
vagga – Buddhist scriptures
Vāghela (same as Bāghela
vāghya – Khaṇḍoba
vāg-nāg – weapons
vāha – weights and measures
VĀHANA
vahi – bard
vāhin (or vāhinpati) – army
Vāhlīka – Bactrians
Vahni – Agni
Vāhuka – Nala
Vaibhāshika – Buddhist history
Vaibhrāja – paradise
Vaidarbha (same as Vidarbha)
vaidarbha – poetics
Vaidhyata – Yama
vaidika – hierophant
vaidya – physician
Vaidya, C. V. – barbarian
Vaidyanātha – liṅga
vaijātya – antinomianism
vaijayanta – paradise
Vaijayanti – Āndhra
vaikaksha – thread ceremonies
Vaikarttana – Karṇa
vaikhānasa – hierophant
Vaikhānasa – Pañcharātra
Vaikharī – sound
Vaikuṇṭha – paradise
Vaikuṇṭha Perumāḷ – Pallava
vairāgī – hierophant
vairāgya – equanimity
Vairāgya-śataka – Bhartṛihari
Vairāja – ancestors, paradise
Vairochana – bodhisattva
Vairochi – Pradyumna
Vaiśākha – calendar
Vaiśālī – Lichchhavi, Mahāvīra
Vaiśampāyana – Abhimanyu, Yājñavalkya

VAIŚESHIKA
Vaishṇavī – Śakti
Vaishṇavi-mudrā – meditation
VAISHṆAVISM
vaiśika – kāmaśāstra
Vaiśravaṇa – Kubera
vaiśvadeva – sacrifice
Vaiśvānara – asura, Agni
VAIŚYA
Vaitāl Deul – Orissa
Vaitaraṇī – hell
vaitastika – weapons
VAIVASVATA
Vāja – Viśvakarman
VĀJAPEYA
Vājasaneya – Yājñavalkya
Vājasaneyī Saṁhitā – Yajur-veda
vājī-karaṇa – virility
vājin – Yājñavalkya
Vajjī – Lichchhavi
vajra – gems, liṅga, weapons
vajra – sacrifice
Vajra – Pradyumna
Vajra-bhairava – tantrism
Vajra-datta – Arjuna
Vajradhara – bodhisattva
Vajradhātveśvarī – bodhisattva
Vajra-nābha – weapons, Pradyumna
vajra-nābha – weapons, Kṛishṇa
Vajrānaka – Kārttikeya
Vajrapāṇi – bodhisattva
vajra-sattva – weapons, liṅga
Vajrasattva – Nāgārjuna
Vajra-sūchika – Aśvaghosha
Vajrayāna – tantrism
Vajreśvara – God, Śiva, weapons
vajrinī – channels of the subtle body
vajroli – paramudrā
vajroni – paramudrā
vāk – senses
Vaka – Bhīma
VĀKĀṬAKA
vākovākya – drama history
Vākpati – Kanauj
vakra – logic
vakroti – poetics
vakshaṇā – strītantra
Vākya-padīya – Bhartṛihari
vāla – Kratu
Vala – asura
Valabhī – Maitraka
valaitaḍi – weapons
Vālakhilya – Kratu
Vālika – Kalmāshapāda
Vālhīka – Bactrians
Vālin – Bālin
VALLABHA (or Vallabhāchārya)
Vallabhī (same as Valabhī)
vallī – literary forms, plants
Vālmīkeśvara – liṅga
VĀLMĪKI
vāma – antinomianism, direction, Hinduism
vāmā (woman) – antinomianism, Hinduism
vāmāchāra – antinomianism, Hinduism
VĀMADEVA
Vāmādevī – Pārśva
vāma-devya – soma
Vāmana – Hiraṇyāksha, poetics
Vāmeśvara – liṅga
vaṁśa – community, literary forms
vānaprastha (or vānaprasthya) – āśrama
VĀNARA
Vanashpara – barbarian
vanaspati – plants
vānaspatya – plants
vañchana – logic
Vaṅga – Bāleya
Vañji – Kerala
vaṅkshaṇa – chakra
Vaṅkshu – Ikshvāku
Vannān – pañchama
Vapushmat – Marutta
vāra – calendar
Varadā – Śakti
Varadarājasvāmi – Pallava
Varāha – Hiraṇyāksha
VARĀHAMIHIRA
Vārali – rāga
varaṇa – marriage
Varaṇā – Banāras
Vārāṇasī – Banāras
Vāraṇāvata – Yudhishṭhira
Vararuchi – Vikramāditya
varāṭa – numismatics
Vardhamāna – Mahāvīra, philosophy
Vardhana – Kanauj
Vārendra – brāhmin
varga – community, canons of proportion, literary forms
vārisāra – purification
vāri-vihāra – kingship
Vārkarī – Jñānadeva
varsha – calendar
Vārkshī – matriarchy
varma – weapons
varṇa – caste
varṇam – Bharata-nāṭyam
varṇāśrama-dharma – Hinduism
varti – drugs
vārtta – politics
Vārttika – Kātyāyana
Varuṇa – serpent worship
VARUṆA
varuṇa-praghāsa – adultery
Varuṇī – Śakti

vasā – animal sacrifice
vāsa – thread ceremonies, dress
vāsana – psychology
vasanta – calendar
Vasanta – rāga
Vasava – Liṅgāyat
Vāsavadattā – Udayana, Subandhu
Vasco da Gama (same as da Gama)
vashaṭ – mantra
Vāshkala – Vasishṭha, Yājñavalkya
Vasishka – Kushān
VASISHṬHA (ṛishi) – ritual canon
VASISHṬHA (Tantrik adept)
Vāsishṭha – Varāhamihira
Vāsishṭhīputra – Āndhra
vaśitva – siddhi
vasti – āyurveda, purification
vastra – dress
vastu – dramaturgy
vāstu-jñāna – architecture
Vastupāla – Solaṅki
vāsū – strītantra
Vasu – Dhruva, Jamadagni, Gaṅgā
Vasubandhu – Asaṅga, Gupta
Vasudeva – Vishṇu
Vasudeva, father of Kṛishṇa – Kṛishṇa, Śūra
Vasudeva (King) – Magadha
Vāsudeva – Kṛishṇa
Vāsudeva (Kushān king) – Kushān
Vāsudeva (philosopher) – Sārvabhauma
Vasudhā-nagara – paradise
Vasudharā – Buddha
VASUGUPTA
Vāsuki – serpent worship
Vasumitra – Śuṅga, Kanishka
Vāsusena – Karṇa
Vāsupūjya – tīrthaṅkara
vaṭa – fig-tree
Vāta – Vāyu
Vātāpti – Agastya, Chālukya
vātasāra – purification
vatsā – strītantra
Vatsa – mahājanapada, Udayana
Vatsabhaṭṭi – epigraphy
vatsalatā – love
vatsara – calendar
Vatsarāja – Udayana, Pratihāra
Vatsāsura – Kṛishṇa
Vātsyāyana – kāmaśāstra, philosophy
vaṭṭeḷuttu – scripts
vayaḥ-saṁdhi – strītantra
vayasa-vidyā – birds
Vāyavī – Śakti
vāyu – wind
VĀYU
VEDA
Veda-mātṛi – Gāyatrī
vedanā – Buddhism
Vedāṅga – scriptures
VEDĀNTA
Vedānta-deśika – Deśika
Vedānta-sūtra – Vedānta
vedārambha – education
Vedārtha-prakāśa – etymology
Vedavatī – Rāvaṇa
vedha – yoni
vedhas – hierophant
vedi – altar
VEDIC
VEDISM
VEGA
vegetable kingdom – plants
vegetarianism – diet
vehicle – vāhana
veiling of women – harem
Velanāḍu – brāhmin
Velāvalī – rāga
Vellāla – pañchama
Vellore (or Velur) – art
Vemāna – Telugu
VEṆA
Vena (Venna or Venya) – rivers (under Kistna)
Veṅgi – Chālukya, Pallava
Veṇī-saṁhāra – drama history
Veṅkaṭamakhin – music history
Veṅkaṭanātha – Deśika
Veṅkaṭeśvara – Vishṇu
Ventura, General Reuben – suspended animation
veṇu – musical instruments
Venur – Ṛishabha
Venus – Śukra
vepu – fig-tree
vermilion – blood
versification – prosody
Veśara – architecture
veśyā – prostitution
vetāla – Śiva
Vetālabhaṭṭa – Vikramāditya
Vetāla-pañcha-viṁśati – Somadeva
veterinary science – animals
Vetravatī – Betwa
vettila – betel
vibhāga – quality
Vibhāṇḍaka – Ṛishyaśṛiṅga
Vibhāsa – rāga
Vibhāshā – Prākṛit, Buddhist history
vibhāva – God
Vibhīshaṇa – Pulastya, Rāvaṇa
vibhītaka – gambling
Vibhu – Viśvakarman
vibhūti – siddhi
vichāra – knowledge, meditation, law
Vichāra-bhū – Yama
vichchhitti – poetics
Vichitravīrya – Bhīshma

Victoria, Queen – Sen, Tagore
vidagdha – kāvya
Vidarbha (or Vaidarbha) – Agastya, Nala, Raghu, Vaivasvata, Sagara
Videha – Janaka
videha – exteriorisation
Vidhātṛi – Viśvakarman
vidhavā – widow
vidhi – law
Vidisā – Śuṅga
vidruma – gem
Vidura – Bhīshma
vidūshaka – dramaturgy
vidyā – knowledge
Vidyādhar – godling
Vidyāpati – language, law, Pañchatantra
Vidyārambha – education
Vidyāraṇya – āyurveda history
Vidyāsāgar, I. C. – Bengali
vidyut – mantra
vighna – sin
Vighneśa – Gaṇeśa
vigils – festivals
vigraha – idolatry, war
vihāra – cave temples, education
vijaya – Bengali
Vijaya – asura
Vijayā – Pāṇḍava, Śakti, Yama
VIJAYANAGAR
Vijayapura – Pāla
vijigīshu – politics
vijña – māyā
vijñāna – Asaṅga, Mahāyāna
Vijñānabhikshu – philosophy
vijñānamaya-kośa – body
vijñānavāda – Asaṅga
Vijñāneśvara – law
vikalpa – knowledge, law
vikāra – sāṁkhya
Vikarṇa – ear
Vikartana (or Vikarttana) – Sūrya
Vikhanas – Pañcharātra
Vikrama-charita – kathā
VIKRAMĀDITYA
Vikramāditya VI – Chālukya, law
Vikramapurī – education
Vikrama Saṁvat – era
Vikramasena – Somadeva
Vikramaśilā – education
Vikramorvaśī – Kālidāsa
vikṛit – music
Vikṛita – Daksha
Vikukshi – Ikshvāku
vilambita – music
vilana – Śakti
vilāsa – māyā
vilāsinī – prostitution
vilva – bilva
Vimala – tīrthaṅkara, Solaṅki
Vimala-kirti – bodhisattva
vimāna – Indra, temple, mechanics, Chola
vimarśa – dramaturgy
vimṛityu – trance states
vimukha – dramaturgy
vīna – musical instruments
Vināsana – rivers (under Sarasvatī)
Vinatā – Garuḍa
Vinateya – matriarchy
vinaya – ethics
Vinaya – Buddhist scriptures
Vināyaka – Gaṇeśa, Garuḍa
Vināyakā – Garuḍa
Vindhya – mountains
Vindhyachal – Satī
Vindhyaśakti – Vākāṭaka
Vindhyāvalī – Hiraṇyāksha
Vindhya-vāsanī – Satī, Śakti
vipala – time
viparita-karaṇī – paramudrā
viparyaya – gender, knowledge
Vipāśa – rivers (under Beas)
vipra – hierophant
Viprachitti – Agastya, asura, Daksha, Rāhu
Vipula – exteriorisation
vīra – initiation, quality
Vīra Ballāla III – Hoysala
Vīrabhadra – Daksha
Vīrabhadrā – Dhanvantari
Vīra-bukka (same as Bukka)
Virādha – rākshasa
virāj – prosody
Virāj – Brahmā
Virāja – paradise, incest
Virājānanda – Dayānanda
vīrakka – minerals
virāma – Nāgarī
Vīramāmuṇivar – Tamil
Vīrasena – Nāga
Vīraśaiva – Liṅgāyat
VIRĀṬA
Vīrdhavala – Solaṅki
Virgil – travel
VIRGINITY
VIRILITY
Virochana – Hiraṇyāksha
Vīr-singh – language
virtues – ethics
viruda – names
vīrūdh – plants
vīrya – asceticism
viś – community
Viśākhadatta – drama history
Viśāla – Lichchhavi, Mahīdāsa
Viśālāksha – politics
visarjana – worship
viśesha – Vaiśeshika

visha – poison
Vishaharā – serpent worship
Vishāṇin – Divodāsa
vishaya – substance
vishkambhaka – dramaturgy
VISHṆU – ritual canon
Vishṇugupta – Kauṭilya, grammar
Vishṇupad – Gaya
Vishṇuśarma – Pañchatantra
Vishṇu-svāmi – gopī
Vishṇuvardhana – Chālukya, Hoysala, Ujjain
viśishṭādvaita – Rāmānuja
Vismāpana – gandharva
vismaya – empathy
viśpati – community
Viśravas – Pulastya
viśuddha – chakra
Viśuddhi-magga – Buddhist scriptures
Viśva-bhāratī – Tagore (R.)
Viśvadeva (or Viśvedevāḥ) – godlings
Viśvaka – Kṛishṇa
VIŚVAKARMAN
VIŚVĀMITRA
Viśvanātha – liṅga, Śiva
Viśvanātha – Pāṇḍya
Viśvanātha temple – prostitution
Viśvapāṇi – bodhisattva
Viśvarūpa – Viśvakarman
Viśvarūpa (same as Maṇḍana)
Viśvavārā – Veda
Viśvāvasu – gandharva, Jamadagni
Viśvedeva – godlings
Viśveśvara – liṅga
Viśveśvara temple – Banāras
viṭa – dramaturgy
Vītahavya – Haihaya
Vīta-hotra – Haihaya
Vitala – cosmology
vitaṇḍā – logic
Vītapāla – Pāla
Vitastā – rivers (under Jhelum)
vitasti – weights and measures, weapons
Vitatha – Gārgya
vīthī – theatre
Vitruvius – mechanics, Mānasāra
Viṭṭhal – Vishṇu
Viṭṭhala temple – architecture
Viṭṭhalnāth – Vallabha
Viṭṭhobā – Nāmdev, Tukārām, Vishṇu
Vituṇḍa – Kālī
vivādī – music
vivāha – marriage
Vivasvat – Sūrya
Vivasvatī – paradise
viveka – meditation
VIVEKĀNANDA
Vivekasindhu – Marāṭhi
viyoni – olisboi
Voltaire – kāmaśāstra (under Kshemendra), Indology
Vonones – Parthians
Vopadeva – Hemādri
VOWS
Vrāchaḍi – Prākṛit
vrata – ethics, vows
vrata-chārin – education
vrāti – Vrātya
VRĀTYA
vrātya-stoma – purification, Brāhmaṇas
vṛiddhi – literary forms
Vṛiddhagaṅgā (same as Godāverī)
vṛiddha-trayī – āyurveda history
Vṛihad-garbha – Uśīnara
Vṛijji (same as Vajji)
vṛiksha – plants
vṛiksha-devatā – plants
vṛikshakā – sculpture
Vṛinda – āyurveda history
VṚINDĀ
Vṛindāvana – Kṛishṇa, Vṛinda
vṛishabha – man of the world
Vṛishabha – Liṅgāyat
vṛishala – Āndhra
vṛishaṇa – sex mysticism
Vṛishaparvan – Yayāti
Vṛishṇi – Kurukshetra, Vaivasvata
vṛishotsarga – cow
vṛiti – stūpa
vṛitta – prosody
Vṛitta-vilāsa – Kanarese
Vṛitra – asura
Vṛitraghna – asura
vṛitti – karma, psychology
vyādhi – āyurveda
Vyāḍi – grammar
vyā hṛiti – mantra
vyāja-stuti – poetics
vyākaraṇa – grammar
vyākhyāna – āsana
vyāla – animals
vyāma – weights and measures
Vyāmāsura – Kṛishṇa
vyāna – wind
vyañjana – poetics, stigmata
vyāpti – syllogism
VYĀSA
Vyāsokta – caste
vyavahāra – law
vyavapāda – law
vyāyoga – theatre
vyoma-ga – mechanics
vyoman – paradise
Vyomaśiva – philosophy
vyūha – God
Vyushitāśva – levirate
vyut – purification

Wade, Sir Claude – suspended animation
Wakhan – Śaka
Warangal – Chālukya
WARFARE
WEAPONS
weather – meteorology
Wei – travel
WEIGHTS AND MEASURES
Wellesley, Lord – women
Wells, H. G. – Aśoka
Wema – Kushān
west – direction
Western Satraps – Śaka
wet elements – alchemy, orifices
wheat – plants
WHEEL
White Yajur-veda – Yajur-veda
WIDOW
Wilkins, Charles – Bengali, Indology
Williams, Tennessee – Marāṭhi
WIND
wind, breaking – Agastya, Kumbhakarṇa, sound
witches – necrophilia, occultism
withershins – wheel
WOMEN
women, types of – strītantra
word numerals – numerals
Wordsworth, William – Tagore (R.)
WORSHIP
WRITING – scripts

Xenocrates – Gandhāra
Xerxes – travel, Nysa, Iran

yab-yum – Asaṅga, Matsyendra
Yādava – Yadu, Chālukya
Yādava-prakāśa – philosophy, Rāmānuja
YADU
yāgaśālā – altar
Yāja – Drupada
yajamāna – sacrifice
yajña – sacrifice
yajñānta – sacrifice
YĀJÑAVALKYA – secrecy, ritual canon
Yājñavalkya kāṇḍa – Āraṇyaka
yājnika – hierophant
yajñopavīta – thread ceremonies
YAJUR-VEDA
yaksha – Kubera
yakshī – Kubera
Yakshu – Divodāsa
yāli – animals
YAMA – Sāvitrī, Uddālaka
yāma – time
yama – ethics
Yamadūta – Yama
yamaka – poetics
yāmala – sex mysticism
Yamani – rāga
yama-paṭa – Paṭṭa
Yamapuri – Yama
Yamī – Yama
Yamunā – rivers (under Jamnā)
Yāmunāchārya – Rāmānuja
yāna – Buddhist scriptures, mārga, politics
yānaka – weapons
yantra – maṇḍala, mechanics
yantra-mukta – weapons
Yasa – Buddha
yaśasvinī – channels of the subtle body
Yāska – etymology
Yaśodā – Kṛishṇa, Mahāvīra
Yaśodhara – kāmaśastra
Yaśodharā – Buddha
Yaśodharma – Ujjain
Yaśovarman – Kanauj
yati – Jain, hierophant
Yati – Bhṛigu
yātrā – theatre, pilgrimage
Yātu (or Yātu-dhāna) – rākshasa
Yaudheya – Uśīnara, Yudhishṭhira
Yaudheya (tribe) – Kushān, Śaka
yautaka – dowry
yava – weights and measures
Yavakrīta – Bharadvāja
Yavana – Greeks
Yavana-jātaka – astronomy
yāvanāla – plants
Yavanānī – scripts
Yavanapura – trade, towns
yavanikā – drama history, dramaturgy
yavasa – grasses
YAYĀTI
Yima – Yama
Yimeh – Yama
Yimi – Yama
yobel – Jews
yo evam veda – knowledge
YOGA
Yogāchāra – Asaṅga
yoga-hasta – āsana
yoga-rochanā – alchemy
yogārūdha – yoga
yoga-sāra – alchemy
Yoga-sūtra – Patañjali
Yogeśvara – Śiva
yogi – hierophant, yoga
yoginī – Kālī, yoga
yogi-pratyaksha – perception
yogyatā – eligibility
yojana – weights and measures
Yona – Milindapañho, Greeks
Yonaka – Milindapañho, Greeks
YONI